lonely planet

Greek Islands

**David Willett Kate Daly
Carolyn Bain Rosemary Hall
Brigitte Barta Paul Hellander**

LONELY PLANET PUBLICATIONS
Melbourne • Oakland • London • Paris

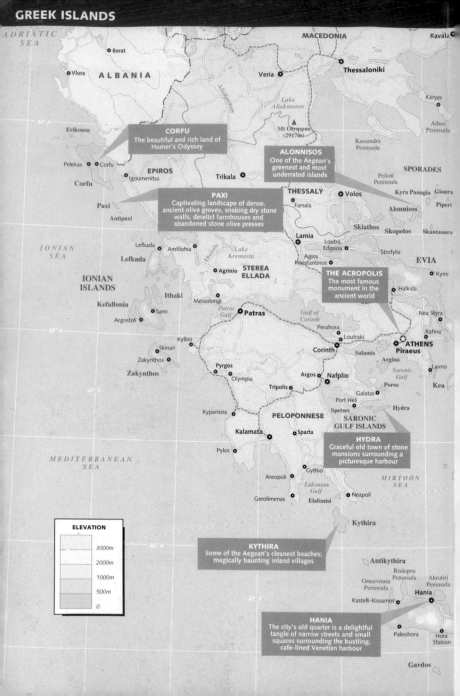

GREEK ISLANDS

ADRIATIC SEA

MACEDONIA

Kavala

Berat

Vlora

ALBANIA

Veria

Thessaloniki

Karyes

Athos Peninsula

Erikousa

Mt Olympus (2917m)

Kassandra Peninsula

SPORADES

CORFU
The beautiful and rich land of Homer's Odyssey

Pelekas • Corfu

EPIROS

Igoumenitsa

Trikala

ALONNISOS
One of the Aegean's greenest and most underrated islands

Pelion Peninsula

Kyra Panagia · Gioura

Corfu

PAXI
Captivating landscape of dense, ancient olive groves, snaking dry stone walls, derelict farmhouses and abandoned stone olive presses

THESSALY

Farsala

Volos

Alonnisos

Piperi

Paxi

Antipaxi

Lamia

Skiathos

Skopelos

Skantzoura

Lefkada

Amfilohia

Lake Kremasta

STEREA ELLADA

Loutra Edipsou

Strofylia

EVIA

IONIAN SEA

Lefkada

Agios Konstantinos

Kymi

IONIAN ISLANDS

Agrinio

THE ACROPOLIS
The most famous monument in the ancient world

Halkida

Ithaki

Messolongi

Patras Gulf

Nea Styra

Kefallonia

Sami

Argostoli

Gulf of Corinth

Perahora

Rafina

Patras

Loutraki

ATHENS

Piraeus

Skinari

Kyllini

Corinth

Salamis

Aegina

Lavrio

Zakynthos

Pyrgos

Argos · Nafplio

Saronic Gulf

Poros

Kea

Zakynthos

Olympia

Tripolis

Galatas

Kyparissia

Port Heli

Hydra

Spetses

SARONIC GULF ISLANDS

PELOPONNESE

Kalamata

Sparta

HYDRA
Graceful old town of stone mansions surrounding a picturesque harbour

Pylos

Areopoli · Gythio

MIRTOÖN SEA

MEDITERRANEAN SEA

Lakonian Gulf

Gerolimenas

Elafonisi

Neapoli

Kythira

ELEVATION

3000m

2000m

1000m

500m

0

KYTHIRA
Some of the Aegean's cleanest beaches; magically haunting inland villages

Antikythira

Rodopos Peninsula

Gramvousa Peninsula

Akrotiri Peninsula

Kastelli-Kissamos

Hania

HANIA
The city's old quarter is a delightful tangle of narrow streets and small squares surrounding the bustling, cafe-lined Venetian harbour

Paleohora

Hora Sfakion

Gavdos

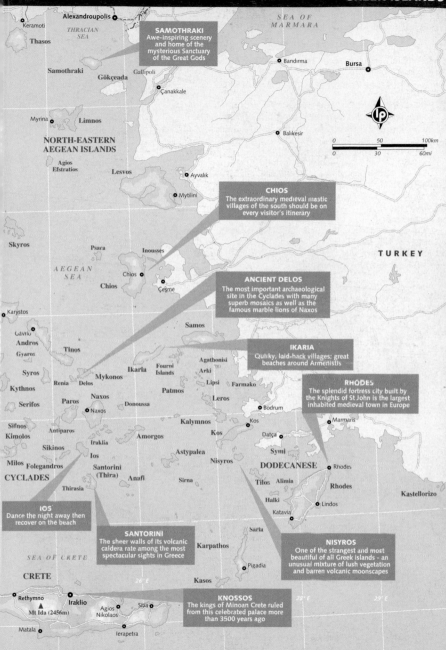

Alexandroupolis

Keramoti

THRACIAN SEA

Thasos

SEA OF MARMARA

Bandırma

Bursa

SAMOTHRAKI
Awe-inspiring scenery and home of the mysterious Sanctuary of the Great Gods

Samothraki

Gökçeada

Gallipoli

Çanakkale

Myrina

Limnos

Balıkesir

NORTH-EASTERN AEGEAN ISLANDS

0   50   100km

0   30   60mi

Agios
Efstratios

Lesvos

Ayvalık

Skyros

Mytilini

CHIOS
The extraordinary medieval mastic villages of the south should be on every visitor's itinerary

Psara

Inousses

AEGEAN SEA

Chios

Chios

Çeşme

TURKEY

Karystos

ANCIENT DELOS
The most important archaeological site in the Cyclades with many superb mosaics as well as the famous marble lions of Naxos

Gávrio

Andros

Samos

Gyaros

Tinos

IKARIA
Quirky, laid-back villages; great beaches around Armenistis

Syros

Ikaria

Fourni
Islands

Agathonisi

Arki

Kythnos

Renia

Delos

Mykonos

Lipsi

Farmako

RHODES
The splendid fortress city built by the Knights of St John is the largest inhabited medieval town in Europe

Serifos

Paros

Naxos

Patmos

Leros

Bodrum

Sifnos

Naxos

Donoussa

Kalymnos

Kos

Marmaris

Kimolos

Antiparos

Amorgos

Kos

Datça

Sikinos

Iraklia

Astypalea

Symi

Milos

Folegandros

Ios

Santorini
(Thira)

Anafi

Nisyros

DODECANESE

Rhodes

CYCLADES

Sirna

Tilos

Alimia

Rhodes

Thirasia

IOS
Dance the night away then recover on the beach

NISYROS
One of the strangest and most beautiful of all Greek islands - an unusual mixture of lush vegetation and barren volcanic moonscapes

Halki

Lindos

Kastellorizo

SANTORINI
The sheer walls of its volcanic caldera rate among the most spectacular sights in Greece

Katavia

Saria

SEA OF CRETE

Karpathos

CRETE

Pigadia

Kasos

Rethymno

Iraklio

Sitia

KNOSSOS
The kings of Minoan Crete ruled from this celebrated palace more than 3500 years ago

Mt Ida (2456m)

Agios
Nikolaos

Matala

Ierapetra

Greek Islands
2nd edition – March 2002
First published – February 2000

Six-monthly upgrades of this title available free on
www.lonelyplanet.com/upgrades

Published by
Lonely Planet Publications Pty Ltd ABN 36 005 607 983
90 Maribyrnong St, Footscray, Victoria 3011, Australia

Lonely Planet offices
Australia Locked Bag 1, Footscray, Victoria 3011
USA 150 Linden St, Oakland, CA 94607
UK 10a Spring Place, London NW5 3BH
France 1 rue du Dahomey, 75011 Paris

Photographs
Many of the images in this guide are available for licensing from
Lonely Planet Images.
email: lpi@lonelyplanet.com.au
Web site: www.lonelyplanetimages.com

Front cover photograph
Quintessentially Greek church on the Island of Ios, Cyclades,
(David Ian Hall)

ISBN 1 74059 050 3

text & maps © Lonely Planet Publications Pty Ltd 2002
photos © photographers as indicated 2002

Printed by SNP SPrint Pte Ltd
Printed in Singapore

Although the authors and Lonely Planet try to make the information as accurate as possible, we accept no responsibility for any loss, injury or inconvenience sustained by anyone using this book.

Contents – Text

DODECANESE 313

NORTH-EASTERN AEGEAN ISLANDS 389

EVIA & THE SPORADES 454

MAP LEGEND   back page

METRIC CONVERSION   inside back cover

Contents – Maps

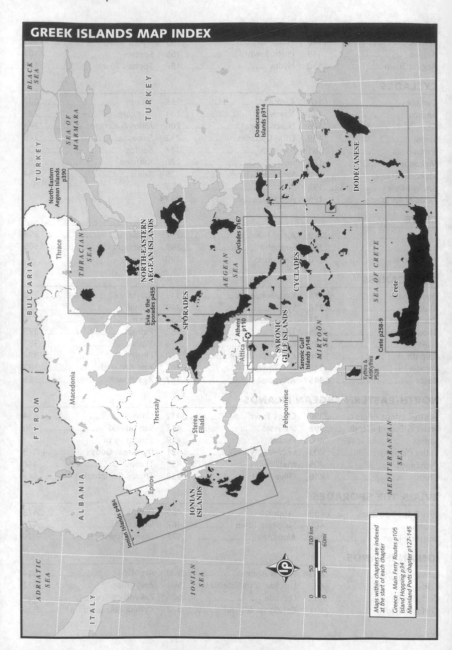

GREEK ISLANDS MAP INDEX

Maps within chapters are indexed
at the start of each chapter

Greece – Main Ferry Routes p105
Island Hopping p34
Mainland Ports chapter p127–145

The Authors

David Willett

David is a freelance journalist based near Bellingen on the mid-north coast of New South Wales, Australia. He grew up in Hampshire, England, and wound up in Australia in 1980 after stints working on newspapers in Iran (1975–78) and Bahrain. He spent two years working as a sub-editor on the Melbourne *Sun* before trading a steady job for a warmer climate. Between jobs, David has travelled extensively in Europe, the Middle East and Asia.

He is a regular visitor to Athens as coordinator of Lonely Planet's guide to Greece and co-author of the *Athens* city guide. He is also the author of Lonely Planet's guide to Tunisia, and has contributed to various other guides, including *Africa, Australia, Indonesia, South-East Asia, Mediterranean Europe* and *Western Europe*.

Paul Hellander

Paul has never really stopped travelling since he first looked at a map in his native England. He graduated from Birmingham University with a degree in Greek before heading for Australia. He taught Modern Greek and trained interpreters and translators before donning the hat of a travel writer. Paul has contributed to some 24 LP titles including *Greek Islands, Rhodes & the Dodecanese, Crete, Cyprus, France, Israel & the Palestinian Territories, Europe, Singapore, Central America* and *South America*. When not travelling with his Mac and Nikons, he lives in Adelaide, South Australia where he studies the history of political intelligence, listens to the BBC World Service, cooks Thai food and grows hot chillies. He was last seen plotting yet more forays to Europe's Mediterranean basin.

Rosemary Hall

Rosemary was born in Sunderland, England. She graduated in fine art, but fame and fortune as an artist eluded her, so she spent a few months bumming around Europe and India. After teaching in northern England, she decided to find something more exotic, finally landing a job in Iraq. When, after two years, the Iraqi government refused to renew her work permit, she settled in London, tried to make it again as a painter, did supply teaching, and then travelled in India, South-East Asia and Africa.

Rosemary researched Iraq for Lonely Planet's *Middle East on a Shoestring* and wrote the 1st edition of *Greece*. She is the co-author of four walking guides to London.

Brigitte Barta

Brigitte was born in Wellington, New Zealand. At the age of six months her parents took her to live in Berlin, via Naples, and she first visited Greece when she was three. She grew up mostly in Melbourne, Australia, and has also lived in England, Germany, Spain, Switzerland, the US and Greece, where she spent a year on the island of Santorini. She currently resides in San Francisco and works in the New Media department at Lonely Planet's Oakland office. One of these days, she'll stop day-dreaming about moving back to Greece and just do it.

Carolyn Bain

Carolyn was born in Melbourne, Australia (the third-largest Greek city in the world) and first visited Greece as a teenager (on a package tour from Scandinavia, no less). She was therefore eminently qualified to island-hop around the Ionians in search of the perfect beach, best kalamari and any unattached shipping magnates. Due to an unfortunate shortage of shipping magnates, she continues her job as an author for Lonely Planet and is based in Melbourne.

Kate Daly

Born in Sydney, Kate spent several formative childhood years in the remote country town of Wee Waa, in north-western NSW. She dropped out of an arts/law degree in 1985, and turned to travel instead – hitchhiking up Australia's east coast and through the Northern Territory. Returning to uni she studied writing and has a BA (Communications) from the University of Technology, Sydney. Kate has travelled widely in North- and South-East Asia and Europe. Her first experience of the extraordinary islands of the Aegean was via Turkey. On the work front, she's done it all, from copywriter in Tokyo, to editor in Melbourne. She has written for Lonely Planet's *Out to Eat Melbourne 2000*, and contributed to Lonely Planet's *Queensland* and *Australia* guides.

FROM THE AUTHORS
David Willett

I'd like to thank all the friends who have contributed so much to my understanding of Athens over the years, especially Maria Economou from the Greek National Tourism Office; the Kanakis family; Ana Kamais; Matt Barrett; Tolis Houtzoumis; and Alex and Pavlo.

Thanks also to my friends around the Peloponnese: Petros and Dimitris in Nafplio; Yiannis in Sparti; the irrepressible Voula in Gythio; the Dimitreas family from Kardamyli; and Andreas the magician from Patras.

Special thanks to my partner, Rowan, and our son Tom for holding the fort at home during my frequent trips away.

Paul Hellander

Updating a travel guide invariably involves the input of many people. I would like to mention some who helped in ways big and small to make my work just that little bit easier: Byron & Marcus Hellander (Ioannina), Maria Haristou and Andonis Konstandinidis (Thessaloniki), Giannis Mourehidis (Konitsa), Alekos and Valentini Papadopoulos (Thessaloniki), Angeliki Kanelli (Athens), Nikos and Anna Hristodoulou (Lipsi), Raphael Delstanche (Rhodes), Alex & Christine Sakellaridis (Halki), Minas Gializis (Karpathos), Emmanouil Manousos (Kasos), Nikos Perakis (Kato Zakros), Vasilis Skoulas (Anogia), Tony Fennymore (Hania), Vangelis Skoulakis (Kissamos), Mihalis Manousakis (Hania). Professional thanks also to Geoff Harvey, DriveAway Holidays (Sydney), Peugeot-Sodexa (Paris), Kostas Lambrianos, Dodekanisos Naftiliaki (Rhodes), Tonia Marangou, Minoan Lines (Piraeus) and finally the adept editors and designers at LP who put this book together. Stella Hellander – wife, companion and photographer – this time, this one is just for you!

Rosemary Hall

I am grateful to George (Vrachos Camping) and George Papadimitrio (Kalambaka) for getting my laptop into action again when I couldn't; the staff at the EOT and Municipal Tourist offices in Arahova, Volos and Larisa; the staff at Planet Internet Café (Larisa); the staff at Thalpos Leisure & Services (Skopelos); Pakis Athanasiou at Ikos Travel and Maria at Liadromia Hotel (Alonnisos) and Poppi at South Evia Tours, Karistos (Evia) for invaluable assistance.

Thanks to Kristina Brooks-Tsalapatani and Nikkos Sikkes for filling me in on all the changes that have taken place on Skyros in the last two years; Bridget Johnson and Dave Dix for keeping an eye on my flat while I was away and, as usual, to David Willett for support and good humour in his emails and our telephone conversations.

Finally, and most importantly, thank you to all the people who offered sympathy and practical help when, halfway through my trip, I received a telephone call telling me of my mother's death. These include my father, staff at First Choice Tours on Skiathos, David Hall and Janet Wright whose assistance at this difficult time enabled me to get back to the UK faster than I believed possible, and to everyone at Lonely Planet involved in the production of this book.

I dedicate my contribution to this book to my mother who always encouraged me in my travels.

Brigitte Barta

Many people were extremely generous with their time and insights during the course of my research. Thanks go to Margarita and Kostas Moukas, whose energy and devotion to conservation and restoration on Lesvos is an inspiration. Aristides Sifneos, also on Lesvos, provided background on history and special places. Christos Karagiannidis, clown king of Thasos, gave me a crash course on the best of his island, and Tatiana and Iordanis Iordanidis intensified my fondness for Samothraki. Anna Dakoutros (Santorini) and Theodore and Güher Spordilis (Chios) took hospitality too far, despite my protests – thank you. I would also like to thank Maria Kollerou at Myrina Tourist & Travel Agency (Limnos), Samiotis Tours (Lesvos), Smaragda at the Chios tourist office, and ITSA Travel (Samos). Dimitris Tsavdaridis, on Santorini, put me in touch with all the right people and kept my sangria cup filled – D, you are the secret ingredient in this cocktail. In Athens, Maria and Sophia Brakoulia gave me a soft landing and showed me a good time, and in London their brother, Andreas, did the same. I hope you will let me reciprocate sometime soon. Back at home my nonstop gratitude goes to Rob Guerin for patience, understanding and courage at the crossroads and beyond. And thanks to Dermot Burgess for taking my photo.

Carolyn Bain

The Greeks once again showed that while they're not too flash at adhering to advertised opening hours or providing easily decipherable ferry schedules, they more than compensate for this with their kindness and warmth. I met countless friendly, helpful Greeks who made my job a lot more pleasurable, and my heartfelt thanks go out to all of them. I must particularly thank Christina Avloniti in Corfu Town, who helped me make sense of the ferries; Noula Mouzakiti in Agios Stefanos, and her staff, who made sure I got to the Diapondia islands and also showed me a great time in their town; Dora in Nydri on Lefkada who gave me valuable help and information; and the Makis family of Poros on Kefallonia, who so kindly came to my rescue during the car debacle.

Others I must thank are Sarah Vermoolen for her excellent company and assistance on Corfu, and all the great people I met on Paxi who made it so damn hard to leave their wonderful island. Thanks to Ann Buckley, my neighbour on Ithaki, and especially to my sister, Jules Bain, for her great company and support on Kefallonia. Thanks also to Jules and John for their hospitality in London post-research. And finally, thanks to Cameron Lloyd, the Most Cultured Man in Brisbane, for sharing good lobster, bad wine and many fine ouzo-commercial moments on lovely Kythira.

Kate Daly

Thank you to all those overworked travel agents and visitor information offices (official or otherwise) who were generous with their time under hectic peak season conditions, and to all the kind souls along the way who offered information, ouzo, coffee, cake (and best of all cake & ice cream), sweets and trademark Greek wide smiles. A huge thank you to Brigitte Barta for advice along the way, and to Paul Hellander, Carolyn Bain and David Willett for advice and assistance. Thanks also to Kieran Grogan for making it happen in the first place. Lastly, an inadequate thank you to Mikey for coping with Typhoon Katie.

This Book

This is the 2nd edition of LP's *Greek Islands* guide. David Willett was the coordinating author for this edition and updated the introductory, Athens and Saronic Gulf Islands chapters. Paul Hellander updated the Crete and Dodecanese chapters. Rosemary Hall updated Evia and the Sporades, Carolyn Bain was responsible for the Ionian Islands chapter, Brigitte Barta for the North-East Aegean Island chapter and Kate Daly for the Cyclades chapter.

FROM THE PUBLISHER

The 2nd edition of *Greek Islands* was produced in Lonely Planet's Melbourne office. Production was coordinated by Darren O'Connell (editorial) and Yvonne Bischofberger (mapping and design). The editing and proofing team included Melanie Dankel, Lara Morcombe, Janine Eberle, Shelley Muir, Helen Yeates, Susannah Farfor, Bethune Carmichael, Bridget Blair and Yvonne Byron. Mapping prowess was lent by Agustín Poó y Balbontin, Sally Morgan, Csanad Csutoros, Joelene Kowalski and Yvonne Bischofberger. General credits to Kieran Grogan, Tony Davidson, Adrian Persoglia, Mark Griffiths, Mark Germanchis, as well as the GIS unit for providing the data for Athens maps, LPI for the pics, Maria Vallianos for the front cover and Matt King for the illustrations, which were drawn by Clint Curé (Q-ray), Kelli Hamblett (KH), Martin Harris (MH), Kate Nolan (KN) and Tamsin Wilson (TW).

Thanks to Emma Koch for the language chapter, to Helen Papadimitriou, Chris Tsismetzis and Anastasia Safioleas for additional Greek language pointers and to Emma Sangster for watching brief assistance.

THANKS

Many thanks to the travellers who used the last edition and wrote to us with helpful hints, advice and interesting anecdotes. Your names appear in the back of this book.

ACKNOWLEDGMENTS
Maps

Portions of the maps in this book include intellectual property of EPSILON and are used by permission. Copyright © 2000 Epsilon International SA. All Rights Reserved.

Foreword

ABOUT LONELY PLANET GUIDEBOOKS

The story begins with a classic travel adventure: Tony and Maureen Wheeler's 1972 journey across Europe and Asia to Australia. Useful information about the overland trail did not exist at that time, so Tony and Maureen published the first Lonely Planet guidebook to meet a growing need.

From a kitchen table, then from a tiny office in Melbourne (Australia), Lonely Planet has become the largest independent travel publisher in the world, an international company with offices in Melbourne, Oakland (USA), London (UK) and Paris (France).

Today Lonely Planet guidebooks cover the globe. There is an ever-growing list of books and there's information in a variety of forms and media. Some things haven't changed. The main aim is still to help make it possible for adventurous travellers to get out there – to explore and better understand the world.

At Lonely Planet we believe travellers can make a positive contribution to the countries they visit – if they respect their host communities and spend their money wisely. Since 1986 a percentage of the income from each book has been donated to aid projects and human rights campaigns.

Updates Lonely Planet thoroughly updates each guidebook as often as possible. This usually means there are around two years between editions, although for more unusual or more stable destinations the gap can be longer. Check the imprint page (following the colour map at the beginning of the book) for publication dates.

Between editions up-to-date information is available in two free newsletters – the paper *Planet Talk* and email *Comet* (to subscribe, contact any Lonely Planet office) – and on our Web site at www.lonelyplanet.com. The *Upgrades* section of the Web site covers a number of important and volatile destinations and is regularly updated by Lonely Planet authors. *Scoop* covers news and current affairs relevant to travellers. And, lastly, the *Thorn Tree* bulletin board and *Postcards* section of the site carry unverified, but fascinating, reports from travellers.

Correspondence The process of creating new editions begins with the letters, postcards and emails received from travellers. This correspondence often includes suggestions, criticisms and comments about the current editions. Interesting excerpts are immediately passed on via newsletters and the Web site, and everything goes to our authors to be verified when they're researching on the road. We're keen to get more feedback from organisations or individuals who represent communities visited by travellers.

Lonely Planet gathers information for everyone who's curious about the planet – and especially for those who explore it first-hand. Through guidebooks, phrasebooks, activity guides, maps, literature, newsletters, image library, TV series and Web site we act as an information exchange for a worldwide community of travellers.

Research Authors aim to gather sufficient practical information to enable travellers to make informed choices and to make the mechanics of a journey run smoothly. They also research historical and cultural background to help enrich the travel experience and allow travellers to understand and respond appropriately to cultural and environmental issues.

Authors don't stay in every hotel because that would mean spending a couple of months in each medium-sized city and, no, they don't eat at every restaurant because that would mean stretching belts beyond capacity. They do visit hotels and restaurants to check standards and prices, but feedback based on readers' direct experiences can be very helpful.

Many of our authors work undercover, others aren't so secretive. None of them accept freebies in exchange for positive write-ups. And none of our guidebooks contain any advertising.

Production Authors submit their manuscripts and maps to offices in Australia, USA, UK or France. Editors and cartographers – all experienced travellers themselves – then begin the process of assembling the pieces. When the book finally hits the shops, some things are already out of date, we start getting feedback from readers and the process begins again ...

WARNING & REQUEST

Things change – prices go up, schedules change, good places go bad and bad places go bankrupt – nothing stays the same. So, if you find things better or worse, recently opened or long since closed, please tell us and help make the next edition even more accurate and useful. We genuinely value all the feedback we receive. A well-travelled team reads and acknowledges every letter, postcard and email and ensures that every morsel of information finds its way to the appropriate authors, editors and cartographers for verification.

Everyone who writes to us will find their name listed in the next edition of the appropriate guidebook. They will also receive the latest issue of *Planet Talk*, our quarterly printed newsletter, or *Comet*, our monthly email newsletter. Subscriptions to both newsletters are free. The very best contributions will be rewarded with a free guidebook.

We may edit, reproduce and incorporate your comments in all Lonely Planet products, such as guidebooks, Web sites and digital products, so let us know if you don't want your comments reproduced or your name acknowledged.

Send all correspondence to the Lonely Planet office closest to you:

Australia: Locked Bag 1, Footscray, Victoria 3011
USA: 150 Linden St, Oakland, CA 94607
UK: 10a Spring Place, London NW5 3BH

Or email us at: talk2us@lonelyplanet.com.au

For news, views and updates see our Web site: www.lonelyplanet.com

HOW TO USE A LONELY PLANET GUIDEBOOK

The best way to use a Lonely Planet guidebook is any way you choose. At Lonely Planet we believe the most memorable travel experiences are often those that are unexpected, and the finest discoveries are those you make yourself. Guidebooks are not intended to be used as if they provide a detailed set of infallible instructions!

Contents All Lonely Planet guidebooks follow roughly the same format. The Facts about the Destination chapters or sections give background information ranging from history to weather. Facts for the Visitor gives practical information on issues like visas and health. Getting There & Away gives a brief starting point for researching travel to and from the destination. Getting Around gives an overview of the transport options when you arrive.

The peculiar demands of each destination determine how subsequent chapters are broken up, but some things remain constant. We always start with background, then proceed to sights, places to stay, places to eat, entertainment, getting there and away, and getting around information – in that order.

Heading Hierarchy Lonely Planet headings are used in a strict hierarchical structure that can be visualised as a set of Russian dolls. Each heading (and its following text) is encompassed by any preceding heading that is higher on the hierarchical ladder.

Entry Points We do not assume guidebooks will be read from beginning to end, but that people will dip into them. The traditional entry points are the list of contents and the index. In addition, however, some books have a complete list of maps and an index map illustrating map coverage.

There may also be a colour map that shows highlights. These highlights are dealt with in greater detail in the Facts for the Visitor chapter, along with planning questions and suggested itineraries. Each chapter covering a geographical region usually begins with a locator map and another list of highlights. Once you find something of interest in a list of highlights, turn to the index.

Maps Maps play a crucial role in Lonely Planet guidebooks and include a huge amount of information. A legend is printed on the back page. We seek to have complete consistency between maps and text, and to have every important place in the text captured on a map. Map key numbers usually start in the top left corner.

Although inclusion in a guidebook usually implies a recommendation we cannot list every good place. Exclusion does not necessarily imply criticism. In fact there are a number of reasons why we might exclude a place – sometimes it is simply inappropriate to encourage an influx of travellers.

Introduction

The Greek Islands have long been one of Europe's favourite holiday destinations. It's hardly surprising: with more than 1400 islands scattered around the blue waters of the Aegean and Ionion Seas, there's something for everyone. For some it's the opportunity to escape to the far-flung island paradise of their dreams, for others it's the opportunity to explore the remains of some of Europe's oldest civilisations. For most people though, the greatest attraction is the lure of sand, sea – and more than 300 days of guaranteed sunshine a year.

Until recent times, the islands were little more than remote outposts of Greece, left behind by the 20th century. Populations and economies were in serious decline as people headed to the mainland – and overseas – in search of work and opportunity.

Tourism was all but unheard of. Only the idle rich had the time or money for such exploits. All that has changed with the advent of modern transport and communications. Cheap airfares have put the islands within everyone's reach.

Tourism has boomed, breathing new life into island economies. Today, islands such as Kos, Paros and Rhodes are the prime target for millions of package-holidaymakers who come to Greece every year in search of two weeks of sunshine by the sea.

Every island is different. There are party islands, quiet romantic islands, islands for walkers, islands for windsurfers, islands for history buffs, islands for gays and islands for lesbians. There's even an island for the chronically sick (who come seeking a cure).

There's an island for everyone – the challenge is to find it. That means island-hopping, using Europe's largest ferry network. Every inhabited island has a ferry service of some sort, even if it is only a weekly supply boat.

Island-hopping is part of the fun. Like the islands themselves, the boats come in all shapes and sizes. The giant modern superferries that work the major routes have all the facilities of a luxury hotel, while the small open ferries that chug around the back blocks are more reminiscent of WWII landing craft.

Facilities these days are decidedly modern but reminders of the past are everywhere: the Minoan palaces of Crete were built by one of Europe's oldest civilisations. Mycenaean and classical Greek sites are overlooked by towering Venetian, Frankish and Turkish castles, while elaborate Byzantine churches stand alongside crumbling, forgotten mosques.

Despite tourism, islanders have retained a strong sense of tradition. Tradition and religion were the factors that kept the notion of Greek nationhood alive during hundreds of years of foreign occupation, and Greeks have clung to their traditions more tenaciously than in most European countries; even hip young people participate with enthusiasm.

The traditions manifest themselves in a variety of ways, including regional costumes – such as the embroidered dresses and floral headscarves worn by the women

THE GREEK ISLANDS

AUSTRIA, HUNGARY, MOLDOVA, UKRAINE, SLOVENIA, CROATIA, ROMANIA, BOSNIA-HERCEGOVINA, BLACK SEA, YUGOSLAVIA, BULGARIA, FYROM, ITALY, ALBANIA, GREECE, AEGEAN SEA, TURKEY, IONIAN SEA, ATHENS, MALTA, MEDITERRANEAN SEA, LIBYA, EGYPT

of Olymbos, on Karpathos, and the baggy pantaloons and high boots worn by elderly Cretan men. Young Cretans have adopted the traditional black, fringed kerchief as a fashion accessory.

Other traditions take the form of festivals, where people express their *joie de vivre* through dancing, singing and feasting.

Whether it is festival time or not, the Greek capacity for enjoyment of life is immediately evident.

Food and wine are cheap by European standards, and Greeks love to eat out with family and friends. All this adds up to the islands being one of Europe's most friendly and relaxed destinations.

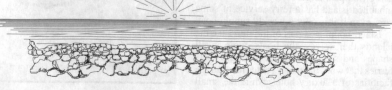

Facts about the Greek Islands

HISTORY

The Greek Islands were the birthplace of two of Europe's earliest civilisations, the Cycladic and the Minoan.

Both can be traced to the introduction of Bronze Age smelting techniques in about 3000 BC by settlers from Phoenicia (on the coast of modern Lebanon). The Cyclades were the first to blossom. The most impressive legacy of this civilisation is the statuettes carved from Parian marble – the famous Cycladic figurines, which depicted images of the Great Mother (the earth goddess). The finest examples were produced during the Early Cycladic period, which lasted from 3000 to 2100 BC.

The people of the Cycladic civilisation were also accomplished sailors who developed prosperous maritime trade links. They exported their wares to Asia Minor (the west of present-day Turkey), Europe and north Africa, as well as to Crete and continental Greece. The Cycladic civilisation lasted until about 1100 BC, but its later stages were increasingly dominated by the Minoan civilisation that evolved on nearby Crete.

The Minoans, named after the mythical King Minos, drew their inspiration from two great Middle Eastern civilisations: the Mesopotamian and the Egyptian. The civilisation reached its peak in the period between 2100 and 1500 BC, producing pottery and metalwork of remarkable beauty and a high degree of imagination and skill.

The famous Minoan palaces at Knossos, Phaestos, Malia and Zakros on Crete were built at this time. They were destroyed by a violent earthquake in about 1700 BC, but were rebuilt to a more complex, almost labyrinthine design with multiple storeys, sumptuous royal apartments, reception halls, storerooms, workshops, living quarters for staff and an advanced drainage system. The interiors were decorated with the celebrated Minoan frescoes, now on display in the Archaeological Museum at Iraklio.

After 1500 BC, the civilisation began to slip into decline, both commercially and militarily, against Mycenaean competition from the mainland – then reached an abrupt end around 1100 BC, when Dorian invaders and natural disasters ravaged Crete.

Some historians have suggested that the Minoan civilisation's demise was accelerated by the effects of the massive volcanic explosion on the Cycladic island of Santorini (Thira) in 1450 BC, an eruption vulcanologists believe was more cataclysmic than any on record. They theorise that the fallout of volcanic ash from the blast caused a succession of crop failures, with resulting social upheaval.

The Dorian period from 1200 to 800 BC is generally referred to as Greece's 'age of darkness', which sounds a bit unfair for a period that saw the arrival of the Iron Age and emergence of geometric pottery. The Dorians were responsible for founding the city of Lindos, on Rhodes, around 1000 BC.

By 800 BC, when Homer's *Odyssey* and *Iliad* were first written down, Greece was undergoing a cultural and military revival with the evolution of the city-states, the most powerful of which were Athens and Sparta. Greater Greece – Magna Graecia – was created, with south Italy as an important component. The unified Greeks repelled the Persians twice, at Marathon (490 BC) and Salamis (480 BC). The period that followed was an unparalleled time of growth and prosperity, resulting in what is called the classical (or golden) age.

The Golden Age

In this period, the Parthenon was commissioned by Pericles, Sophocles wrote *Oedipus the King,* and Socrates taught young Athenians to think. At the same time, the Spartans were creating a military state. The golden age ended with the Peloponnesian War (431–404 BC) in which the militaristic Spartans defeated the Athenians. So embroiled were they in this war that they failed to notice the expansion of Macedonia to the north under King Philip II, who easily conquered the war-weary city-states.

Philip's ambitions were surpassed by those of his son Alexander the Great, who marched triumphantly into Asia Minor, Egypt, Persia and what are now parts of Afghanistan and India. After Alexander's untimely death in 323 BC at the age of 33, his generals divided his empire between themselves. The Dodecanese became part of the kingdom of Ptolemy I of Egypt.

Roman Rule & the Byzantine Empire

Roman incursions into Greece began in 205 BC. By 146 BC the mainland had become the Roman provinces of Greece and Macedonia. Crete fell in 67 BC, and the southern city of Gortyn became the capital of the Roman province of Cyrenaica, which included a large chunk of north Africa. Rhodes held out until AD 70.

In AD 330 Emperor Constantine chose Byzantium as the new capital of the Roman Empire and renamed the city Constantinople. After the subdivision of the Roman Empire into Eastern and Western Empires in AD 395, Greece became part of the Eastern Roman Empire, leading to the illustrious Byzantine age.

In the centuries that followed Venetians, Franks, Normans, Slavs, Persians, Arabs and, finally, Turks all took their turn to chip away at the Byzantine Empire. The Persians captured Rhodes in 620, but were replaced by the Saracens (Arabs) in 653. The Arabs also captured Crete in 824.

Other islands in the Aegean remained under Byzantine control until the sack of Constantinople in 1204 by renegade Frankish crusaders in cahoots with Venice. The Venetians were rewarded with the Cyclades, and they added Crete to their possessions in 1210.

The Ottoman Empire & Independence

The Byzantine Empire finally came to an end in 1453 when Constantinople fell to the Turks. Once more Greece became a battleground, this time fought over by the Turks and Venetians. Eventually, with the exception of Corfu, Greece became part of the Ottoman Empire.

Much has been made of the horrors of the Turkish occupation in Greece. However, in the early years at any rate, people probably marginally preferred Ottoman to Venetian or Frankish rule. The Venetians in particular treated their subjects little better than slaves. But life was not easy under the Turks, not least because of the high taxation they imposed. One of their most hated practices was the taking of one out of every five male children to become janissaries, personal bodyguards of the sultan. Many janissaries became infantrymen in the Ottoman army, but the cleverest could rise to high office – including grand *vizier* (chief minister).

Ottoman power reached its zenith under Sultan Süleyman the Magnificent (ruled 1520–66), who expanded the empire to the gates of Vienna. His successor added Cyprus to their dominions in 1570, but his death in 1574 marked the end of serious territorial expansion.

Although they captured Crete in 1669 after a 25-year campaign and briefly threatened Vienna once more in 1683, the ineffectual sultans of the late 16th and 17th centuries saw the empire go into steady decline. They suffered a series of reversals on the battlefield, and Venice succeeded in recapturing the Peloponnese in 1685–7 in a campaign that saw them advance as far as Athens. The Parthenon was destroyed in the fighting by a shell that struck a store of Turkish gunpowder.

Chaos and rebellion spread across Greece. Pirates terrorised coastal dwellers and islanders, while gangs of *klephts* (anti-Ottoman fugitives and brigands) roamed the mountains. There was an upsurge of opposition to Turkish rule by freedom fighters – who fought each other when they weren't fighting the Turks.

The long-heralded War of Independence finally began on 25 March 1821, when Bishop Germanos of Patras hoisted the Greek flag at the monastery of Agias Lavras in the Peloponnese. Fighting broke out almost simultaneously across most of Greece and the occupied islands, with the Greeks making big early gains. The fighting was savage, with atrocities committed on both sides. The islands weren't spared the horrors of war. In 1822, Turkish forces massacred 25,000 people on the island of Chios, while another 7000 died on Kassos in 1824.

Eventually, the Great Powers – Britain, France and Russia – intervened on the side of the Greeks, defeating the Turkish-Egyptian fleet at the Battle of Navarino in 1827. The island of Aegina was proclaimed the temporary capital of an independent Greek state, and Ioannis Kapodistrias was elected the first president. The capital was soon moved to Nafplio in the Peloponnese, where Kapodistrias was assassinated in 1831.

Amid anarchy, the European powers stepped in again and declared that Greece should become a monarchy. In January 1833, 17-year-old Prince Otto of Bavaria was installed as king of a nation (established by the London Convention of 1832) that consisted of the Peloponnese, Sterea Ellada (Central Greece), the Cyclades and the Sporades.

King Otho (as his name became) displeased the Greek people from the start, arriving with a bunch of upper-class Bavarian cronies to whom he gave the most prestigious official posts. He moved the capital to Athens in 1834.

Patience with his rule ran out in 1843 when demonstrations in the capital, led by the War of Independence leaders, called for a constitution. Otho mustered a National Assembly that drafted a constitution calling for parliamentary government consisting of a lower house and a senate. Otho's cronies were whisked out of power and replaced by War of Independence freedom fighters, who bullied and bribed the populace into voting for them.

By the end of the 1850s, most of the stalwarts from the War of Independence had been replaced by a new breed of university graduates (Athens University had been founded in 1837). In 1862 they staged a bloodless revolution and deposed the king. But they weren't quite able to set their own agenda, because in 1863 Britain returned the Ionian Islands (a British protectorate since 1815) to Greece. Amid the general euphoria that followed, the British were able to push forward young Prince William of Denmark, who became King George I.

His 50-year reign brought stability to the troubled country, beginning with a new constitution in 1864, which established the power of democratically elected representatives and pushed the king further towards a ceremonial role. An uprising in Crete against Turkish rule was suppressed by the sultan in 1866–68, but in 1881 Greece acquired Thessaly and part of Epiros as the result of another Russo-Turkish war.

In 1897 there was another uprising in Crete, and the hot-headed prime minister Theodoros Deligiannis responded by declaring war on Turkey and sending help to Crete. A Greek attempt to invade Turkey in the north proved disastrous – it was only through the intervention of the Great Powers that the Turkish army was prevented from taking Athens.

Crete was made a British protectorate in 1898, and the day-to-day government of the island was gradually handed over to the Greeks. In 1905 the president of the Cretan assembly, Eleftherios Venizelos, announced Crete's union *(enosis)* with Greece, although this was not recognised by international law until 1913. Venizelos went on to become prime minister of Greece in 1910 and was the country's leading politician until his republican sympathies brought about his downfall in 1935.

Although the Ottoman Empire was in its death throes at the beginning of the 20th century, it was still clinging onto Macedonia. It was a prize sought by the newly formed Balkan countries of Serbia and Bulgaria, as well as by Greece, leading to the Balkan wars. The first, in 1912, pitted all three against the Turks; the second, in 1913, pitted Serbia and Greece against Bulgaria. The outcome was the Treaty of Bucharest (August 1913), which greatly expanded Greek territory by adding the southern part of Macedonia, part of Thrace, another chunk of Epiros, and the North-Eastern Aegean Islands, as well as recognising the union with Crete.

In March 1913, King George was assassinated by a lunatic and his son Constantine became king.

WWI & Smyrna

King Constantine, who was married to the sister of the German emperor, insisted that Greece remain neutral when WWI broke out in August 1914. As the war dragged on, the Allies (Britain, France and Russia) put increasing pressure on Greece to join forces with them against Germany and Turkey. They made promises that they couldn't hope to fulfil, including land in Asia Minor. Venizelos favoured the Allied cause, placing him at loggerheads with the king. Tensions between the two came to a head in 1916, and Venizelos set up a rebel government, first in Crete and then in Thessaloniki, while the pressure from the Allies eventually persuaded Constantine to leave Greece in June 1917. He was replaced by his more amenable second son, Alexander.

Greek troops served with distinction on the Allied side, but when the war ended in 1918 the promised land in Asia Minor was not forthcoming. Venizelos took matters into his own hands and, with Allied acquiescence, landed troops in Smyrna in May 1919 under the guise of protecting the half a million Greeks living in that city (just under half its population). With a firm foothold in Asia Minor, Venizelos now planned to push home his advantage against a war-depleted Ottoman Empire. He ordered his troops to attack in October 1920 (just weeks before he was voted out of office). By September 1921, the Greeks had advanced as far as Ankara.

The Turkish forces were commanded by Mustafa Kemal (later to become Atatürk), a young general who also belonged to the Young Turks, a group of army officers pressing for Western-style political reforms. Kemal first halted the Greek advance outside Ankara in September 1921 and then routed them with a massive offensive the following spring. The Greeks were driven out of Smyrna and many of the Greek inhabitants were massacred. Mustafa Kemal was now a national hero, the sultanate was abolished and Turkey became a republic.

The outcome of the failed Greek invasion and the revolution in Turkey was the Treaty of Lausanne of July 1923. This gave eastern Thrace and the islands of Imvros and Tenedos to Turkey, while the Italians kept the Dodecanese (which they had temporarily acquired in 1912 and would hold until 1947).

The treaty also called for a population exchange between Greece and Turkey to prevent any future disputes. Almost 1.5 million Greeks left Turkey and almost 400,000 Turks left Greece. The exchange put a tremendous strain on the Greek economy and caused great hardship for the individuals concerned. Many Greeks abandoned a privileged life in Asia Minor for one of extreme poverty in shantytowns in Greece.

King Constantine, restored to the throne in 1920, identified himself too closely with the war against Turkey, and abdicated after the fall of Smyrna.

WWII & the Civil War

George II, Constantine's son, became king in 1930 and appointed the dictator General Metaxas as prime minister. Metaxas' grandiose ambition was to take the best from Greece's ancient and Byzantine past to create a Third Greek Civilisation, though what he actually created was a Greek version of the Third Reich. His chief claim to fame was his celebrated *okhi* (no) to Mussolini's request to allow Italian troops to traverse Greece in 1940. Despite Allied help, Greece fell to Germany in 1941, which was followed by carnage and mass starvation. Resistance movements sprang up, eventually polarising into royalist and communist factions.

A bloody civil war resulted, lasting until 1949 and leaving the country in chaos. More people were killed in the civil war than in WWII and 250,000 people were left homeless. The sense of despair that followed became the trigger for a mass exodus. Almost a million Greeks headed off in search of a better life elsewhere, primarily to Australia, Canada and the USA. Villages – whole islands even – were abandoned as people gambled on a new start in cities like Melbourne, Chicago and New York. While some have drifted back, the majority have stayed away.

The Colonels

Continuing political instability led to the colonels' coup d'etat in 1967, led by Georgos Papadopolous and Stylianos Patakos. King Constantine (son of King Paul, who succeeded George II) staged an unsuccessful counter coup, then fled the country. The colonels' junta distinguished itself by inflicting appalling brutality, repression and political incompetence upon the people.

In 1974 they attempted to assassinate Cyprus' leader, Archbishop Makarios. When Makarios escaped, the junta replaced him with the extremist Nikos Samson, a convicted murderer. The Turks, who comprised 20% of the population, were alarmed at having Samson as leader. Consequently, mainland Turkey sent in troops and occupied North Cyprus, the continued occupation of which is one of the most contentious issues in Greek politics today. The junta, by now in a shambles, had little choice but to hand power back to the civilians.

In November 1974 a plebiscite voted 69% against restoration of the monarchy, and Greece became a republic. An election brought the right-wing New Democracy (ND) party into power.

The Socialist 1980s

In 1981 Greece entered the EC (European Community, now the EU). Andreas Papandreou's Panhellenic Socialist Movement (PASOK) won the next election, giving Greece its first socialist government. PASOK promised removal of US air bases and withdrawal from NATO, which Greece had joined in 1951.

Six years into government these promises remained unfulfilled, unemployment was high and reforms in education and welfare had been limited. Women's issues had fared better, however – the dowry system was abolished, abortion legalised, and civil marriage and divorce were implemented. The crunch for the government came in 1988 when Papandreou's affair with air stewardess Dimitra Liana (whom he subsequently married) was widely publicised and PASOK became embroiled in a financial scandal involving the Bank of Crete.

In July 1989 an unprecedented conservative and communist coalition took over to implement a *katharsis* (campaign of purification) to investigate the scandals. It ruled that Papandreou and four ministers should stand trial for embezzlement, telephone tapping and illegal grain sales. It then stepped down in October 1990, stating that the catharsis was complete.

The 1990s

An election in 1990 brought the ND back to power with a majority of only two seats. The tough economic reforms that Prime Minister Konstantinos Mitsotakis was forced to introduce to counter a spiralling foreign debt soon made his government deeply unpopular. By late 1992, allegations began to emerge about the same sort of government corruption and dirty tricks that had brought Papandreou unstuck. Mitsotakis himself was accused of having a secret hoard of Minoan art. He was forced to call an election in October 1993.

Greeks again turned to PASOK and the ageing, ailing Papandreou, who had been cleared of all the charges levelled in 1990. He marked his last brief period in power with a conspicuous display of the cronyism that had become his trademark. He was finally forced to hand over the reins in January 1996 after a lengthy spell in hospital.

Papandreou's departure produced a dramatic change of direction for PASOK, with the party abandoning his left-leaning politics and electing experienced economist and lawyer Costas Simitis as the new prime minister. Cashing in on his reputation as the Mr Clean of Greek politics, Simitis romped to a comfortable majority at a snap poll called in October 1996.

Simitis belongs to much the same school of politics as Britain's Tony Blair. Since he took power, PASOK policy has shifted right to the extent that it now agrees with the opposition New Democracy on all major policy issues. His government has focused almost exclusively on the push for further integration with Europe, which has meant more tax reform and more austere measures – as dictated by the EU in Brussels. His success in the face of constant protest, and the skill with which his government handled the difficult diplomatic challenge presented by the 1999 NATO conflict with Serbia, has earned him the grudging respect of the Greek electorate, who handed him a mandate for another four years in April 2000.

The goal of admission to the euro club was achieved at the beginning of 2001, and Greece is scheduled to adopt the euro as its currency in 2002.

Foreign Policy

Greece's foreign policy is dominated by its extremely sensitive relationship with Turkey, its giant Muslim neighbour to the east.

After decades of constant antagonism, these two uneasy NATO allies were jolted to their senses (literally) by the massive earthquake that devastated the İzmir area of western Turkey in August 1999. Dramatic television coverage of the disaster prompted a popular call for Greece to join the rescue effort. Greek teams were among the first on the scene, where they were greeted as heroes. The Turks were quick to return the favour after the Athens quake, which followed on 7 September 1999. The relationship has continued to blossom, despite the occasional hiccup, and at the time of research the two countries were contemplating mounting a joint bid to stage the 2008 European Cup.

It's an extraordinary turn-around. It wasn't that long ago that the merest incident – trivial to the outsider – would bring the two to the brink of war.

While Turkey remains the top priority, Greece has also had its hands full in recent years coping with events to the north precipitated by the break-up of former Yugoslavia and the collapse of the communist regimes in Albania and Romania.

GEOGRAPHY

Greece lies at the southern tip of the rugged Balkan Peninsula. Most of the mainland is mountainous, dominated by the Pindos Ranges. There are land borders to the north with Albania, the Former Yugoslav Republic of Macedonia, and Bulgaria; and to the east with Turkey.

The mainland, however, is but a small part of Greece. It also has some 1400 islands, of which 169 are inhabited. They contribute only a small percentage of the nation's total land mass of 131,900 sq km, but are responsible for extending Greek territorial waters over more than 400,000 sq km.

The majority of islands are spread across the shallow waters of the Aegean Sea between Greece and Turkey. These are divided into four main groups: the Cyclades, the Dodecanese, the islands of the North-Eastern Aegean, and the Sporades. The two largest Aegean islands, Crete and Evia, do not belong to any group.

The other island groups are the Saronic Gulf Islands, which lie south of Athens and the Peloponnese, and the Ionians, in the Ionian Sea between Greece and southern Italy.

Like the mainland, most of the terrain is extremely rugged. Crete has half a dozen peaks over 2000m, the highest of which is Mt Ida at 2456m. Evia, Karpathos, Kefallonia and Samothraki all boast peaks of more than 1500m.

Like the mainland, most of the ground is too arid, too poor and too steep for agriculture. There are several exceptions, like Naxos and Crete, both of which are famous for the quality of their produce.

GEOLOGY

The earthquake that struck Athens on 7 September 1999, leaving 139 dead and 100,000 homeless, served as a savage reminder that Greece lies in one of most seismically active regions in the world.

The quake was just one of more than 20,000 quakes recorded in Greece in the last 40 years. Fortunately, most of them are very minor – detectable only by sensitive seismic monitoring equipment. The reason for all this activity is that the Eastern Mediterranean lies at the meeting point of three continental plates: the Eurasian, African and Arabian. The three grind away at each other constantly, generating countless earthquakes as the land surface reacts to the intense activity beneath the earth's crust.

The system has two main fault lines. The most active is the North Aegean Fault, which starts as a volcano-dotted rift between Greece and Turkey, snakes under Greece and then runs north up the Ionian and Adriatic coasts. Less active but more dramatic is the North Anatolian Fault that runs across Turkey, which is renowned for major tremors like the 7.4 monster that struck western Turkey on 17 August 1999, leaving more than 40,000 dead. Seismologists maintain that activity along the two fault lines is not related.

CLIMATE

Most of the islands enjoy a climate that is typically Mediterranean with hot, dry summers and mild winters.

There are plenty of variations. Snow is very rare in the Cyclades and the Dodecanese, but the mountains of Crete are covered in snow from November until April. Snow is also common on the mountains of Evia.

In July and August, the mercury can soar to 40°C (over 100°F) in the shade just about anywhere. July and August are also the months of the *meltemi*, a strong northerly wind that sweeps the Aegean. The wind is caused by air pressure differences between north Africa and the Balkans. The wind is a mixed blessing: it reduces humidity, but plays havoc with ferry schedules and sends everything flying – from beach umbrellas to washing hanging out to dry.

The Ionian Islands escape the meltemi and have less severe winters than northern Greece, but are the areas with the highest rainfall. Crete stays warm the longest – you can swim off its southern coast from mid-April to November.

November is when the rains are supposed to start in most areas.

ECOLOGY & ENVIRONMENT

Greece is belatedly becoming environmentally conscious; regrettably, it is often a case of closing the gate long after the horse has bolted. Deforestation and soil erosion are problems that go back thousands of years. Olive cultivation and goats have been the main culprits, but firewood gathering, shipbuilding, housing and industry have all taken their toll.

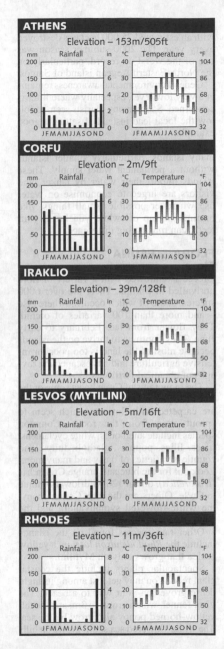

Forest fires are also a major problem, with an estimated 25,000 hectares destroyed every year. The 2000 summer season was one of the worst on record, particularly on the North-Eastern Aegean island of Samos.

General environmental awareness remains at a very low level, especially where litter is concerned. Sadly, many tourists seem to follow the local lead instead of setting a good example.

Water shortages are a major problem on many islands, particularly smaller islands without a permanent water supply. These islands import their water by tanker, and visitors are urged to economise on water use wherever possible: small things, like turning the tap off while you brush your teeth, can make a big difference.

FLORA & FAUNA
Flora
Greece is endowed with a variety of flora unrivalled in Europe. There are over 6000 species, some of which occur nowhere else – and more than 100 varieties of orchid. They flower from late February to early June. They continue to thrive on the islands because most of the land is too poor for intensive agriculture and has escaped the ravages of chemical fertilisers.

The mountains of Crete boast some of the finest displays. During spring the hillsides are carpeted with flowers, which seem to sprout even from the rocks. Common species include anemones, white cyclamens, irises, lilies, poppies, gladioli, tulips, and countless varieties of daisy and many more. Look out for the blue and orange Cretan Iris (*Iris cretica*), one of 120 wildflowers unique to Crete. Others are the pink Cretan ebony, the white-flowered symphyandra and the white-flowered *Cyclamen cretica*.

Other rare species found on the islands include the *Rhododendron luteum*, a yellow azalea that grows only on Mytilini.

Spectacular plants include the coastal giant reed. You may get lost among its high, dense groves on your way to a beach. The giant fennel, which grows to 3m, and the tall yellow-horned poppy also grow by the sea. The white-flowered sea squill grows on hills above the coast. The beautifully perfumed sea daffodil grows along southern coasts, particularly on Crete and Corfu. The conspicuous snake's-head fritillary (*Fritillaria graeca*) has pink flowers shaped like snakes' heads, and the markings on the petals resemble a chequer board – the Latin word *fritillu* means dice box.

Autumn brings flowers too, especially crocuses.

Fauna
Greece also has a large range of fauna, but you won't encounter much of interest unless you venture out into the prime habitat areas of northern Greece.

You're unlikely to encounter much in the way of wildlife on most of the islands. The exception is on larger islands like Crete and Evia, where squirrels, rabbits, hares, foxes and weasels are all fairly common. Reptiles are well-represented too. The snakes include several viper species, which are poisonous. For more information on snakes in Greece, see the Health section in the Facts for the Visitor chapter. You're more likely to see lizards, all of which are harmless.

Bird-watchers have more chance of coming across something unusual than animal spotters do. Greece has all the usual Mediterranean small birds – larks, thrushes, wagtails, tits, warblers, bee-eaters, swallows, flycatchers and chats – as well as some more distinctive local species such as the hoopoe.

A large number of migratory birds, most of which are merely passing by on their way from

MH

The hoopoe, part of the kingfisher family

winter feeding sites in north Africa to summer nesting grounds in Eastern Europe, can also be seen. Out of a total of 408 species of migratory birds in Europe, 240 have been sighted in Greece. About 350 pairs (60% of the world's population) of the rare Eleonora falcon nest on the remote island of Piperi in the Sporades.

One of the pleasures of island-hopping in Greece is watching the dolphins as they follow the boats. Although there are many dolphins in the Aegean, the striped dolphin has recently been the victim of murbilivirus – a sickness that affects the immune system. Research into the virus is being carried out in the Netherlands. You can get more information about dolphins from the Greek Society for the Protection & Study of Dolphins & Cetaceans (☎/fax 21 0422 3305, e delphis@hol.gr), Pylis 75–79, Piraeus 18 533.

Endangered Species

Europe's rarest mammal, the monk seal, was once very common in the Mediterranean, but is now on the brink of extinction in Europe – it survives in slightly larger numbers in the Hawaiian islands.

There are only about 400 left in Europe, half of which live in Greece. There are about 40 in the Ionian Sea and the rest are found in the Aegean. These sensitive creatures are particularly susceptible to human disturbance, and now live only in isolated coastal caves. The majority of reported seal deaths are the result of accidental trapping, but the main threat to their survival is the continuing destruction of habitat. Tourist boats are major culprits. The Hellenic Society for the Study & Protection of the Monk Seal (☎ 21 0522 2888, fax 21 0522 2450, Solomou 18, Athens 106 82, has a seal rescue centre on Alonnisos, and the WWF funds a seal watch project on Zakynthos.

The waters around Zakynthos are also home to the last large sea turtle colony in Europe, that of the loggerhead turtle (*Careta careta*). The loggerhead also nests in smaller numbers on the Peloponnese and on Crete. The Sea Turtle Protection Society

of Greece (☎/fax 21 0523 1342, e stps@compulink.gr), Solomou 57, Athens 104 32, runs monitoring programs and is always looking for volunteers.

The Mediterranean Monk Seal

National Parks

Visitors who expect Greek national parks to provide facilities on a par with those in countries like Australia and the US will be very disappointed. Although all have refuges and some have marked hiking trails, Greek national parks provide little else in the way of facilities.

The majority of Greece's national parks are on the mainland with the exception of Samaria Gorge National Park on Crete. There are marine parks off the coast of Alonnisos in the Sporades, and at Lagonas Bay on Zakynthos in the Ionians. See the respective island chapters for information about these parks.

GOVERNMENT & POLITICS

Since 1975, democratic Greece has been a parliamentary republic with a president as head of state. The president and parliament, which has 300 deputies, have joint legislative power.

The PASOK party of Prime Minister Simitis holds 163 seats in the current parliament.

Greece is divided into regions and island groups. The regions of the mainland are Attica (which includes Athens), the Peloponnese, Central Greece (officially called Sterea Ellada), Epiros, Thessaly, Macedonia and Thrace. The island groups are the Cyclades, Dodecanese, North-Eastern Aegean, Sporades and Saronic Gulf, all in the Aegean Sea, and the Ionian, which is in the Ionian Sea. The large islands of Evia and Crete do not belong to any group. For administrative purposes these regions and groups are divided into prefectures (*nomoi* in Greek).

ECONOMY

Although Greece has the second-lowest income per capita of all the EU countries (after Portugal), its long-term economic future looks brighter now than for some time. Tough measures imposed by successive governments have cut inflation to less than 3%, the Greek stock market has been booming since 1997 and investor confidence appears high.

Tourism is Greece's biggest earner, contributing an estimated US$9 billion a year in foreign exchange. It accounts for a large part of the 50% of the workforce employed in service industries (contributing 59% of GDP). The importance of agriculture has declined rapidly since WWII, with 22% of the workforce now engaged in the agricultural sector (contributing 15%).

POPULATION

A census is taken every 10 years in Greece. The census taken in 2001 was the first since the 1991 census recorded a population of 10,264,156 – an increase of 5.4% on the 1981 figure. Women outnumbered men by more than 200,000. Greece is now a largely urban society, with 68% of the population living in cities. By far the largest is Athens, with more than 3.5 million people living in the greater Athens area. Less than 15% of people live on the islands, the most populous of which are Crete (537,000), Evia (209,100) and Corfu (105,000).

PEOPLE

Contemporary Greeks are a mixture of all of the invaders who have occupied the country since ancient times. Additionally, there are a number of distinct ethnic minorities living in the country.

The country's small Roman Catholic population is of Genoese or Frankish origin. They live mostly in the Cyclades, especially on the island of Syros, where they make up 40% of the population. The Franks dominated the island from AD 1207 to Ottoman times.

About 300,000 ethnic Turks who were exempt from the population exchange of 1923 live in Thrace. There are also small numbers of Turks on Kos and Rhodes which, along with the rest of the Dodecanese, did not become part of Greece until 1947.

The small Jewish communities on the islands of Evia (at Halkida) and Rhodes date back to the Roman era. There are also Jewish communities in several mainland cities, including Athens, Kavala and Thessaloniki. Thessaloniki had a large Jewish community before WWII, mostly descendants of 15th-century exiles from Spain and Portugal. In 1941, the Germans entered Thessaloniki and herded 46,000 Jews off to Auschwitz; most never returned. They comprised 90% of Thessaloniki's Jews and more than half the total number in Greece. Today there are only about 5000 Jews living in Greece.

You will come across Roma (Gypsies) everywhere in Greece, but especially in Macedonia, Thrace and Thessaly. There are large communities of Roma in the Thracian towns of Alexandroupolis and Didymotiho.

The collapse of the communist regimes in Albania and Romania produced a wave of economic refugees across Greece's poorly guarded northern borders, with an estimated 300,000 arriving from Albania alone. These refugees have been a vital source of cheap labour for the agricultural sector; fruit and vegetable prices have actually gone down as a result of their contribution. Albanians also have a reputation as fine stone masons, and their influence can be seen everywhere.

The latest arrivals have been the Kurds, fleeing from Turkey and northern Iraq. Athens, Thessaloniki and Patras all have growing Kurdish communities. Athens also has a substantial Bangladeshi community.

EDUCATION

Education in Greece is free at all levels of the state system, from kindergarten to tertiary. Primary schooling begins at the age of six, but most children attend a state-run kindergarten from the age of five. Private kindergartens are popular with those who can afford them. Primary school classes tend to be larger than those in most European countries – usually 30 to 35 children. Primary school hours are short (8am to 1pm), but children get a lot of homework.

At 12, children enter the *gymnasio,* and at 15 they may leave school, or enter the *lykeio,* from where they take university-entrance examinations. Although there is a high percentage of literacy, many parents and pupils are dissatisfied with the education system, especially beyond primary level. The private sector therefore flourishes, and even relatively poor parents struggle to send their children to one of the country's 5000 *frontistiria* (intensive coaching colleges) to prepare them for the very competitive university-entrance exams.

ARTS

Walk around any capital city in Europe, America or Australasia and the influence of ancient Greek art and architecture is plain to see. It's there in the civic buildings, in the monumental public sculptures, in the plan of the city streets themselves. The product of a truly extraordinary civilisation, the humanism and purity of form of Greek art has inspired artists and architects throughout history.

Ironically, the influence of Greek art has spread throughout the world due to a reality that many travellers (and indeed the Greeks themselves) find unpalatable. This is the fact that many of the greatest works of ancient Greek art haven't had a home in Greece itself for hundreds, sometimes thousands, of years. From the Parthenon frieze taken by Lord Elgin and now displayed in the British Museum to the famous *Nike (Winged Victory of Samothrace)* in Paris' Louvre museum, the work of the Greek masters is held in the collections of the great museums of the world. Many of the great ancient Greek buildings, too, are found in countries other than Greece as they date from the time of the expansive ancient Greek world, which encompassed parts or all of countries such as Italy, Iran, Turkey, Syria and Libya.

Travellers to Greece itself shouldn't despair, however. There's plenty left to see! The buildings, paintings, pots, sculptures and decorative arts of ancient Greece can be found in the country's streets, cities and islands, as well as in its wonderful museums. They may not be in their original form – it takes a stretch of the imagination to envisage the *Hermes of Praxiteles* with arms, and the magnificent and austere form of buildings such as the Parthenon overlaid with gaudily coloured paintings and sculptures – but they manage to evoke the early history of the Greek nation more powerfully than a library of history books ever could.

Architecture

Of all the ancient Greek arts, architecture has perhaps had the greatest influence. Greek temples, seen throughout history as symbols of democracy, have been the inspiration for architectural movements such as the Italian Renaissance and the British Greek Revival.

One of the earliest known architectural sites of ancient Greece is the huge palace and residential complex at Knossos on Crete, built in the Minoan period. Its excavation and reconstruction was begun by Sir Arthur Evans in 1900. Visitors today can see the ruins of the second residential palace built on this site (the first was destroyed by an earthquake in 1700 BC), with its spacious courtyards and grandiose stairways. They can also marvel at the many living rooms, storerooms and bathrooms that give us an idea of day-to-day Minoan life. Similar palaces on Crete, usually of two storeys and built around a large courtyard, have since been excavated at Phaestos, Agia Triada, Malia, Gournia and Zakros.

The Minoan period was followed by the Mycenaean. Instead of the open, labyrinthine palaces of the Minoans, the Mycenaeans used their advanced skills in engineering to build citadels on a compact, orderly plan, fortified by strong walls.

The next great advance in ancient Greek architecture came with the building of the first monumental stone temples in the Archaic and classical periods. From this time, temples were characterised by the famous orders of columns, particularly the Doric, Ionic and Corinthian These orders were applied to the exteriors of temples, which retained their traditional simple plan of porch and hall but were now regularly surrounded by a colonnade or at least a columnar facade.

Theatre design was also a hallmark of the classical period. The tragedies of Aeschylus, Sophocles and Euripides and the comedies of Aristophanes were written and first performed in the Theatre of Dionysos, built into the slope of Athens' Acropolis in the 5th century BC. Other theatres dating from this period can be found throughout Greece.

During the Hellenistic period, private houses and palaces, rather than temples and public buildings, were the main focus of building. The houses at Delos, built around peristyled (surrounded by columns) courtyards and featuring striking mosaics, are perhaps the best examples in existence.

Sculpture

Taking pride of place in the collections of the great museums of the world, the sculptures of ancient Greece have extraordinary visual power and beauty.

The prehistoric art of Greece has been discovered only recently, notably in the Cyclades and on Crete. The pared-down sculptures of this period, with their smooth and flattish appearance, were carved from the high-quality marble of Paros and Naxos in the middle of the 3rd millennium BC. Their primitive and powerful forms have inspired many artists since, particularly those of the 20th century.

In the Mycenaean period, small terracottas of women with a circular body or with arms upraised were widely produced. These are known to modern scholars as phi (ϕ) and psi (ψ) figurines from their resemblance to these letters of the Greek alphabet.

Displaying an obvious debt to Egyptian sculpture, the marble sculptures of the Archaic period are the true precursors of the famed Greek sculpture of the classical period. The artists of this period moved away from the examples of their Oriental predecessors and began to represent figures that were true to nature, rather than flat and stylised. Seeking to master the depiction of both the naked body and of drapery, sculptors of the period focused on figures of naked youths *(kouroi),* with their set symmetrical stance and enigmatic smiles. At first the classical style was

rather severe; later, as sculptors sought ideal proportions for the human figure, it became more animated.

Unfortunately, little original work of the classical period survives. Most freestanding classical sculpture described by ancient writers was made of bronze and survives only as marble copies made by the Romans. Looking at these copies is a bittersweet experience. On the one hand, they are marvellous works of art in their own right. On the other, they make us aware of what an extraordinary body of work has been lost. Fortunately, a few classical bronzes, lost when they were being shipped abroad in antiquity, were recovered from the sea in the 20th century and are now in the collection of the National Archaeological Museum, Athens.

The sculpture of the Hellenistic period continued the Greeks' quest to attain total naturalism in their work. Works of this period were animated, almost theatrical, in contrast to their serene Archaic and classical predecessors. The focus was on realism. Just how successful the artists of this period were is shown in the way later artists, such as Michelangelo, revered them. Michelangelo, in fact, was at the forefront of the rediscovery and appreciation of Greek works in the Renaissance. He is said to have been at the site in Rome in 1506 when the famous Roman copy of the *Laocoön* group, one of the iconic sculptural works of the Hellenistic period, was unearthed.

Pottery

Say the words 'Greek art' and many people immediately visualise a painted terracotta pot. Represented in museums and art galleries throughout the world, the pots of ancient Greece have such a high profile for a number of reasons, chief among these being that there are lots of them around!

Practised from the Stone Age, pottery is one of the most ancient arts. At first, vases were built with coils and wads of clay but the art of throwing on the wheel was introduced in about 2000 BC and was then practised with great skill by Minoan and Mycenaean artists.

Minoan pottery is often characterised by a high centre of gravity and beak-like spouts. Painted decoration was applied as a white clay slip (a thin paste of clay and water) or one which fired to a greyish black or dull red. Flowing designs with spiral or marine and plant motifs were used. The Archaeological Museum in Iraklio, on Crete, has a wealth of Minoan pots.

Mycenaean pottery shapes include a long-stemmed goblet and a globular vase with handles resembling a pair of stirrups. Decorative motifs are similar to those on Minoan pottery but are less fluid.

The 10th century BC saw the introduction of the Protogeometric style, with its substantial pots decorated with blackish-brown horizontal lines around the circumference, hatched triangles, and compass-drawn concentric circles. This was followed by the new vase shape and more crowded decoration of the pots of the Geometric period. By the early 8th century, figures were introduced, marking the introduction of the most fundamental element in the later tradition of classical art – the representation of gods, men and animals.

Painting

The lack of any comprehensive archaeological record of ancient Greek painting has forced art historians to largely rely on the painted decoration of terracotta pots as evidence of the development of this Greek art form. There are a few exceptions, such as the Cycladic frescoes in houses on Santorini, excavated in the mid-to-late 20th century. Some of these frescoes are now in the collection of the National Archaeological Museum in Athens.

These works were painted in fresco technique using yellow, blue, red and black pigments, with some details added after the plaster had dried. Plants and animals are depicted, as well as men and women. Figures are usually shown in profile or in a combination of profile and frontal views. Stylistically, the frescoes are similar to the paintings of Minoan Crete, which are less well-preserved. Reconstructed examples of frescoes from the Minoan period can be seen at the Palace of Knossos, on Crete.

Music & Dance

The folk dances of today derive from the ritual dances performed in ancient Greek temples. One of these dances, the *sirtos,* is depicted on ancient Greek vases, and there are references to dances in Homer's works. Many Greek folk dances, including the sirtos, are performed in a circular formation; in ancient times, dancers formed a circle in order to seal themselves off from evil influences.

Each region of Greece has its own dances, but one dance you'll see performed everywhere is the *kalamatianos,* originally from Kalamata in the Peloponnese. It's the dance in which dancers stand in a row with their hands on one another's shoulders.

Singing and the playing of musical instruments have also been an integral part of life in Greece since ancient times. Cycladic figurines holding instruments resembling harps and flutes date back to 2000 BC. Musical instruments of ancient Greece included the lyre, lute, *piktis* (pipes), *kroupeza* (a percussion instrument), *kithara* (a stringed instrument), *aulos* (a wind instrument), *barbitos* (similar to a violin cello) and the *magadio* (similar to a harp).

If ancient Greeks did not have a musical instrument to accompany their songs, they imitated the sound of one. It is believed that unaccompanied Byzantine choral singing derived from this custom.

The *bouzouki,* which you will hear everywhere in Greece, is a mandolin-like instrument similar to the Turkish *saz* and *baglama.* It is one of the main instruments of *rembetika* music – the Greek equivalent of the American Blues. The name rembetika may come from the Turkish word *rembet,* which means outlaw. Opinions differ as to the origins of rembetika, but it is probably a hybrid of several different types of music. One source was the music that emerged in the 1870s in the 'low life' cafes, called *tekedes* (hashish dens), in urban areas and especially around ports. Another source was the Arabo-Persian music played in sophisticated Middle Eastern music cafes *(amanedes)* in the 19th century. Rembetika was popularised in Greece by the refugees from Asia Minor.

The songs that emerged from the tekedes had themes concerning hashish, prison life, gambling, knife fights etc, whereas cafe aman music had themes that centred on erotic love. These all came together in the music of the refugees, from which a subculture of rebels, called *manges,* emerged. The manges wore showy clothes even though they lived in extreme poverty. They worked long hours in menial jobs, and spent their evenings in the tekedes, smoking hashish and singing and dancing. Although hashish was illegal, the law was rarely enforced until Metaxas did his clean-up job in 1936. It was in a tekes in Piraeus that Markos Vamvakaris, now acknowledged as the greatest *rembetis,* was discovered by a recording company in the 1930s.

Metaxas' censorship meant that themes of hashish, prison, gambling and the like disappeared from recordings of rembetika in the late 1930s, but continued clandestinely in some tekedes. This polarised the music, and the recordings, stripped of their 'meaty' themes and language, became insipid and bourgeois. Recorded rembetika even adopted another name – *Laïko tragoudi* – to disassociate it from its illegal roots. Although WWII brought a halt to recording, a number of composers emerged at this time. They included Apostolos Kaldaras, Yiannis Papaïoanou, Georgos Mitsakis and Manolis Hiotis. One of the greatest female rembetika singers, Sotiria Bellou, also appeared at this time.

During the 1950s and 1960s rembetika became increasingly popular, but less and less authentic. Much of the music was glitzy and commercialised, although the period also produced two outstanding composers of popular music (including rembetika) in Mikis Theodorakis and Manos Hatzidakis. The best of Theodorakis' work is the music that he set to the poetry of Seferis, Elytis and Ritsos.

During the junta years, many rembetika clubs were closed down, but interest in genuine rembetika revived in the 1980s – particularly among students and intellectuals. There are now a number of rembetika clubs in Athens.

Since independence, Greece has followed mainstream developments in classical music. The Athens Concert Hall has performances by both national and international musicians.

Comparatively few Greek performers have hit it big on the international scene. The best-known is Nana Mouskouri, one of the largest-selling female artists in the world. Others include Demis Roussos, the larger than life singer who spent the 1980s strutting the world stage clad in his caftan, and the US-based techno wizard Yanni.

You'll also find all the main forms of Western popular music. Rock, particularly heavy metal, seems to have struck a chord with young urban Greeks, and Athens has a lively local scene as well as playing host to big international names. The biggest local bands are *Xylina Spathia* (Wooden Swords) and *Tripes* (Holes).

Literature

The first known, and greatest, ancient Greek writer was Homer, author of the *Iliad* and *Odyssey.* Nothing is known of Homer's life; where or when he lived, or whether, as it is alleged, he was blind. The historian Herodotus thought Homer lived in the 9th century BC, and no scholar since has proved nor disproved this.

Herodotus (5th century BC) was the author of the first historical work about

The bouzouki can be heard wherever Greek music is played

Western civilisation. His highly subjective account of the Persian Wars has, however, led him to be regarded as the 'father of lies' as well as the 'father of history'. The historian Thucydides (5th century BC) was more objective in his approach, but took a high moral stance. He wrote an account of the Peloponnesian Wars, and also the famous *Melian Dialogue,* which chronicles the talks between the Athenians and Melians prior to the Athenian siege of Melos.

Pindar (c.518–438 BC) is regarded as the pre-eminent lyric poet of ancient Greece. He was commissioned to recite his odes at the Olympic Games. The greatest writers of love poetry were Sappho (6th century BC) and Alcaeus (5th century BC), both of whom lived on Lesvos. Sappho's poetic descriptions of her affections for other women gave rise to the term 'lesbian'.

Dionysios Solomos (1798–1857) and Andreas Kalvos (1796–1869), who were both born on Zakynthos, are regarded as the first modern Greek poets. Solomos' work was heavily nationalistic and his *Hymn to Freedom* became the Greek national anthem.

The best-known poets of the 20th-century are George Seferis (1900–71), who won the Nobel Prize for literature in 1963, and Odysseus Elytis (1911–96), who won the same prize in 1979. Seferis drew his inspiration from mythology, whereas Elytis' work is surreal.

The highly acclaimed poet Constantine Cavafy (1863–1933) was a resident of Alexandria in Egypt; his themes ranged from the erotic to the philosophical.

The most important novelist of the 20th century is Nikos Kazantzakis (1883–1957), whose unorthodox religious views created such a stir in the 1920s. See the boxed text 'Nikos Kazantzakis – Crete's Prodigal Son' in the Crete chapter.

Nikos Dimou is a modern writer who has created a similar stir with his controversial observations on Greek society. His book *I Dystihia tou na Eisai Ellinas* (The Misery of Being Greek) has sold more than 100,000 copies. None of his works are available in English, but that may change. He has a Web site in English (W www.ndimou.gr).

Apostolis Doxiadis achieved international fame in 2000 with his unusual novel *Uncle Petros and Goldbach's Conjecture.* He's better known at home as a film director. He also has a Web site (W www.apostolosdoxiadis .com).

See the Books section in the Facts for the Visitor chapter for more information.

Drama

Drama in Greece can be dated back to the contests staged at the Ancient Theatre of Dionysos in Athens during the 6th century BC for the annual Dionysia festival. During one of these competitions, Thespis left the ensemble and took centre stage for a solo performance regarded as the first true dramatic performance. The term 'thespian' for actor derives from this event.

Aeschylus (c.525–456 BC) is the so-called 'father of tragedy'; his best-known work is the *Oresteia* trilogy. Sophocles (c.496–406 BC) is regarded as the greatest tragedian. He is thought to have written over 100 plays, of which only seven major works survive. These include *Ajax, Antigone, Electra, Trachiniae* and his most famous play, *Oedipus Rex.* His plays dealt mainly with tales from mythology and had complex plots. Sophocles won first prize 18 times at the Dionysia festival, beating Aeschylus in 468 BC, whereupon Aeschylus went off to Sicily in a huff.

Euripides (c.485–406 BC), another famous tragedian, was more popular than either Aeschylus or Sophocles because his plots were considered more exciting. He wrote 80 plays of which 19 are extant (although one, *Rhesus,* is disputed). His most famous works are *Medea, Andromache, Orestias* and *Bacchae.* Aristophanes (c.427–387 BC) wrote comedies – often ribald – which dealt with topical issues. His play *The Wasp* ridicules Athenians who resorted to litigation over trivialities; *The Birds* pokes fun at Athenian gullibility; and *Plutus* deals with the unfair distribution of wealth.

Drama continues to feature prominently on the domestic arts scene, although activity is largely confined to Athens and Thessaloniki. The first couple of the modern Greek theatre are playwrights Thanasis

Reppas and Mihailis Papathanasiou, also noted writers of screenplays and movie directors. Unfortunately, performances of their work are only in Greek.

Film
Greeks are avid cinema goers, although most of the films they watch are North American or British.

The Greek film industry has long been in the doldrums, largely due to inadequate funding. The problem is compounded by the type of films the Greeks produce, which are famously slow moving, loaded with symbolism and generally too avant-garde to have mass appeal.

The leader of this school is Theodoros Angelopoulos, winner of the Golden Palm award at the 1998 Cannes Film Festival for *An Eternity and One Day*. It tells the story of a terminally ill writer who spends his last day revisiting his youth in the company of a 10-year-old boy. His other films include *The Beekeeper* and *Alexander the Great*.

Although it produces no action films, the Greek cinema has shown in recent years that it does have a lighter side. *Orgasmos tis Ageladas* (The Cow's Orgasm), a comedy by Olga Malea, certainly takes the prize for the most intriguing title. It relates the adventures of two girls from Larissa who are frustrated by the restrictions of small-town society. The big hit at the time of research was *Safe Sex,* a light-hearted look at sexuality directed by Thanasis Reppas and Mihailis Papathanasiou.

SOCIETY & CONDUCT
Traditional Culture
Greece is steeped in traditional customs. Name days, weddings and funerals all have great significance. Name days are celebrated instead of birthdays. A person's name day is the feast day of the saint after whom the person is named; on someone's name day an open-house policy is adopted and refreshments are served to well-wishers who stop by to give gifts. Birthdays hardly warrant a mention. Weddings are highly festive occasions, with dancing, feasting and drinking sometimes continuing for days.

Greeks tend to be more superstitious than other Europeans. Tuesday is considered unlucky because it's the day on which Constantinople fell to the Ottoman Turks. Many Greeks will not sign an important transaction, get married or begin a trip on a Tuesday.

Greeks also believe in the 'evil eye', a superstition prevalent in many Middle Eastern countries. If someone is the victim of the evil eye, then bad luck will befall them. The bad luck is the result of someone's envy, so one should avoid being too complimentary about things of beauty, especially newborn babies. To ward off the evil eye, Greeks often wear a piece of blue glass, resembling an eye, on a chain around their necks.

Dos & Don'ts
The Greeks' reputation for hospitality is not a myth, although it's a bit harder to find these days. Greece is probably the only country in Europe where you may be invited into a stranger's home for coffee, or even a meal. This can often lead to a feeling of uneasiness in the recipient if the host is poor, but to offer money is considered offensive. The most acceptable way of saying thank you is through a gift, perhaps to a child in the family.

When drinking wine, it is the custom to half fill the glass. It is also bad manners to empty the glass, so it must be constantly replenished – requiring the constant toasts that are a feature of a Greek night out.

Personal questions are not considered rude in Greece, and if you react as if they are you will be the one causing offence. You will be inundated with queries about your age, salary, marital status etc.

If you go into a *kafeneio,* taverna, or shop, it is the custom to greet the waiters and assistants with *'kalimera'* (good day) or *'kalispera'* (good evening) – likewise if you meet someone in the street.

You may have come to Greece for sun, sand and sea, but if you want to bare all, other than on a designated nude beach, remember that Greece is a traditional country, so take care not to offend the locals.

[continued on page 42]

Island Hopping

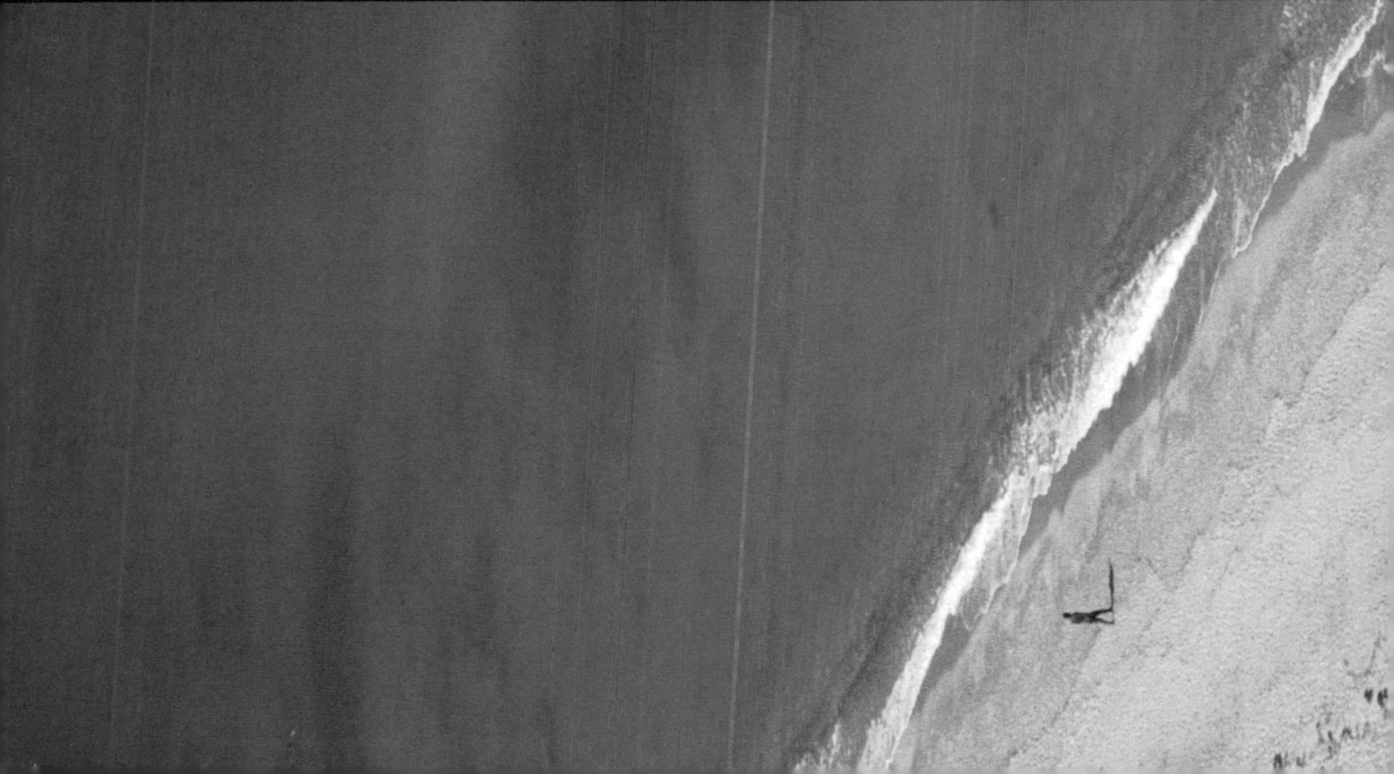

The following grand tour of the islands takes in all the major island groups except the Sporades.

The tour should take about four weeks, allowing a couple of days for each island and at least five days for Crete. Ferry details have been supplied to help you along the way.

Athens

The tour begins in Athens. It's not the greatest place to be in the middle of summer, but it's worth setting aside a day to visit the Acropolis and to explore the Plaka district – and to confirm ferry schedules. Save the wild times until later in your trip, because you'll need to be up early to catch the morning ferry to the Cyclades. There are also six hydrofoils weekly (4 hours, €34)

Piraeus (Athens) to Santorini		
Duration 9 *hours*	Cost €18	Frequency 4 *daily*

Cyclades

The Cyclades are the archetypal Greek islands as seen in the travel brochures: whitewashed villages clinging to barren hillsides, geraniums in brightly painted pots, golden beaches and blue seas.

Santorini Start by heading out to Santorini, the most southern and the most spectacular of these islands. The first glimpse of Santorini is simply unforgettable, its capital of Fira perched precariously atop the

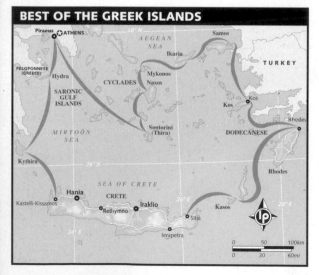

BEST OF THE GREEK ISLANDS

Title page: Alone in paradise. Pefkoulia beach, north-west coast of Lefkada, Ionian Islands (Photographer: George Tsafos)

sheer walls of a volcanic caldera – created by a massive eruption in around 1650 BC. Several companies offer diving trips out to view the new underwater volcano that has been slowly reforming.

Santorini's major site, ancient Akrotiri, is another legacy of the eruption. Excavations at this former Minoan outpost, which was buried in volcanic ash, uncovered the fabulous frescoes of the Thira collection. They are now in the National Archaeological Museum in Athens.

Santorini has good connections south to Crete, but this tour heads north to Naxos. As well as the ferries there are two daily hydrofoils (1½ hours, €19.20)

Santorini to Naxos		
Duration *3 hours*	Cost *€9.30*	Frequency *4 daily*

Naxos Naxos is the largest and greenest of the Cyclades, famous for its wine, cheese and fresh produce. Hora, the bustling capital, is a maze of small alleyways surrounding the historic Kastro, built by renegade Frankish Crusaders in the 13th century. The mountainous interior offers some wonderful trekking, while the beach at Agios Giorgios is perfect for windsurfing and sailing.

Naxos's central position means it has excellent ferry connections, both to other islands within the group and to the North-Eastern Aegean islands of Ikaria and Samos.

Naxos to Mykonos		
Duration *3 hours*	Cost *€6*	Frequency *4 daily*

Best Ancient Sites

- Knossos, Crete
- Delos, Cyclades
- Acropolis of Lindos, Rhodes, Dodecanese
- Sanctuary of the Great Gods, Samothraki, North-Eastern Aegean
- Temple of Aphaia, Aegina, Saronic Gulf Islands

Right: The Lions of Delos keep watch over the ancient city, Delos Island, Cyclades (Photographer: Chris Christo)

Mykonos Some people might opt to skip this leg, a short hop north and head direct from Naxos to Ikaria. Accommodation prices may be beyond the budget of many travellers in summer, but it's not for nothing that Mykonos is one of Greece's most popular destinations.

As well as great nightlife – not all of it gay, it has some fine beaches (if your abs are up to it) and water sports of every conceivable description. Mykonos is also the departure point for excursions to the sacred island of Delos, the most important archaeological site in the Cyclades. Delos was one of the great religious centres of ancient Greece; it boasts an astonishing array of temples and sanctuaries as well as the much photographed Lions of Naxos. Mykonos has good connections to Crete, and five boats a week to the next stop, Ikaria in the North-Eastern Aegean.

Mykonos to Ikaria
Duration *3 hours*   Cost €10   Frequency *5 weekly*

North-Eastern Aegean

These islands are the perfect spot for people who want to escape and unwind.

Ikaria Ikaria is the opposite to Mykonos: a place so laid back that virtually nothing happens. The beaches at Livadi and Mesahti on the north coast are among the best in the Aegean – perfect for recovering from the excesses of Mykonos. Ikaria has regular connections to several of main islands in the Cyclades, and five boats a week south-east to Samos.

Best Beaches

- Pori Beach, Koufonisia, Cyclades
- Milopotas Beach, Ios, Cyclades
- Around Lefkos, southern Karpathos, Dodecanese
- Livadia and Mesahti Beach, Ikaria, North-Eastern Aegean
- West Coast of Lefkada, Ionians

Left: The inviting beach of Nas, near Armenistis on the island of Ikaria, North-Eastern Aegean (Photographer: Brigitte Barta)

Ikaria to Samos		
Duration *3 hours*	Cost €7	Frequency *5 weekly*

Samos It's a case of back to reality when you hit Samos, which gets a lot of summer visitors. Samos suffered badly in the forest fires of 2000, but it remains one of the prettiest islands in the Aegean. The mountains and unspoiled villages of the interior are ideal for trekking. The north coast is popular with windsurfers. Samos is only 3km from Turkey, and many companies offer day trips to nearby Ephesus.

Samos is also the main transport hub of the North-Eastern Aegean, and services include two hydrofoils daily (3½ hours, €19.50) south to Kos in the Dodecanese.

Samos to Kos		
Duration *5½ hours*	Cost €11.50	Frequency *1 weekly*

Dodecanese

If would be easy to spend the entire month in the Dodecanese, such is the variety of attractions.

Kos Kos can get too busy for some, but it's worth sticking around long to check out the sites. Kos Town is dominated by the massive Castle of the Knights, one of the great fortresses built by the Knights of St John in the 14th century to guard against the Ottomans. Kos also boasts a wealth of archaeological sites dating back to Hellenistic times. When you feel that you've absorbed enough culture for one day, it's time to start checking out some of the many bars in town.

Kos has daily ferry and hydrofoil (two hours, €20.60, two daily) connections to Rhodes.

Kos to Rhodes		
Duration *3½ hours*	Cost €10.30	Frequency *1 daily*

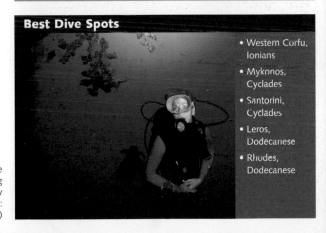

Best Dive Spots

- Western Corfu, Ionians
- Mykonos, Cyclades
- Santorini, Cyclades
- Leros, Dodecanese
- Rhodes, Dodecanese

Right: The islands provide a great venue for diving of all levels of proficiency (Photographer: Gavin Anderson)

ISLAND HOPPING

Rhodes Rhodes has the lot! The old walled city of Rhodes, built by the Knights of St John at the beginning of the 14th century, is Europe's finest example of medieval defensive architecture. A stroll along the splendid Avenue of the Knights (now Ippoton) should be at the top of any itinerary. The Acropolis of Lindos, in the south-east, overlooks a postcard perfect village of pretty whitewashed houses.

Rhodes is also popular with walkers. Most tourists stick to the beach, leaving the interior surprisingly unspoiled. Water sports enthusiasts will find everything from diving to windsurfing.

Rhodes is the hub of the Dodecanese ferry network, and services include three boats a week to Crete via Kasos.

Rhodes to Kasos		
Duration *5 hours*	Cost €16	Frequency *3 weekly*

Kasos After the bright lights of Kos and Rhodes, you'll feel like you're stepping back in time when you reach Kasos. Its picturesque old port of Fry is set against a backdrop of barren, rocky, hills. It's the perfect place to get a glimpse of traditional island life for a couple of days before continuing to the port of Sitia on Crete.

Best Water sports

- Mykonos, Cyclades
- Paros, Cyclades
- Ios, Cyclades
- Skiathos, Sporades
- Lefkada, Ionians

Left: Windsurfing at Makrygialos beach, Karpathos Island, in the Dodecanese (Photographer: Paul Hellander)

Kasos to Sitia
Duration 2½ hours   Cost €7.70   Frequency 3 weekly

Crete

Crete is Greece's largest and most southerly island, and a place with a wealth of attractions for all seasons.

Most people head west from Sitia, but it's worth staying around long enough to visit Zakros. This small village is the starting point for a walk through the Valley of the Dead to the remote Minoan palace site of Kato Zakros.

Most of the north coast between Sitia and Iraklio has become a monument to package tourism and is best seen from the bus. Culture buffs will want to spend a couple of days in Iraklio, taking in the archaeological museum and making a day trip to see the famous Minoan palace of Knossos.

Iraklio also has some notable reminders of its Venetian past, including the wonderful Bembo and Morosini fountains, while the massive fortifications remain impressive.

From Iraklio, head west and use either Hania or Rethymno as a base to walk the Samaria Gorge – just one of many excellent treks in the area. Paleohora, on the south coast, is a popular place to hang. The waters around here stay warm longer than anywhere else in Greece, and there are some good coastal walks.

The departure point from Crete is the small port of Kastelli-Kissamos, in the north-west. It has ferries to Kythira three times a week – phone ahead to check which days.

Kastelli-Kissamos to Kythira
Duration 4 hours   Cost €12.90   Frequency 3 weekly

Best Trekking

- Western Crete
- Andros, Cyclades
- Naxos, Cyclades
- Samos, Cyclades
- Lesvos, North-Eastern Aegean

Right: Crete provides a multitude of trekking possibilities, including the Lefka Ori mountain ranges with the village of Lakki in the foreground (Photographer: Neil Setchfield)

Ionians

Kythira Remote Kythira belongs more properly to the Peloponnese than to the Ionians, the island group with which it has been associated since the days of the British Ionian Protectorate. It matters not when you get there; it's just part of the island's mystery.

Kythira is an unusual place with no outstanding attractions, but it possesses a strange allure that makes it curiously hard to leave.

When the time comes, there are four hydrofoils weekly to Piraeus via the Saronic Gulf islands – but none from Tuesday to Thursday.

Kythira to Hydra		
Duration *4 hours*	Cost €17	Frequency *4 weekly*

Saronic Gulf Islands

Hydra Hydra is the Saronic Gulf island with the most style and the perfect final port of call. Try to arrive on a Monday, when the weekend visitors from Athens have left. Its perfect horseshoe harbour is one of the prettiest around, surrounded by hillsides of graceful old stone mansions. There are some good walks around the island, as well as the opportunity for divers to take the plunge one more time.

There are frequent hydrofoils to Piraeus (1¼ hours, €13.80, seven daily) as well as ferries.

Hydra to Piraeus		
Duration *3½ hours*	Cost €7.35	Frequency *2 daily*

Athens

Try to plan your itinerary so that you return to Athens a day or two before you fly out – both to guard against possible ferry cancellations and to ensure enough time to check out those fabulous Minoan frescoes from Santorini at the National Archaeological Museum.

Best Kept Secrets

Ah, we could tell you but then they wouldn't be secrets, would they?

Left: Inaccessibility provides the small Cretan village of Loutro with a chance to remain one of Greece's best-kept secrets (Photographer: Diana Mayfield)

Ancient Greek Mythology

Mythology was an integral part of life in ancient times. The myths of ancient Greece are the most familiar to us, for they are deeply entrenched in the consciousness of Western civilisation. They are accounts of the lives of the deities whom the Greeks worshipped and of the heroes they idolised.

The myths are all things to all people – a ripping good yarn, expressions of deep psychological insights, words of spine-tingling poetic beauty and food for the imagination. They have inspired great literature, art and music – as well as the odd TV show.

The myths we know are thought to be a blend of Dorian and Mycenaean mythology. Most accounts derive from the works of the poets Hesiod and Homer, produced in about 900 BC. The original myths have been chopped and changed countless times – dramatised, moralised and even adapted for ancient political propaganda, so numerous versions exist.

The Greek Myths by Robert Graves is regarded as being the ultimate book on the subject. It can be heavy going, though. *An Iconoclast's Guide to the Greek Gods* by Maureen O'Sullivan makes more entertaining reading.

Bad weather was often blamed on Poseidon's temper

The Twelve Deities

The main characters of the myths are the 12 deities, who lived on Mt Olympus.

The supreme deity was **Zeus**, who was also god of the heavens. His job was to make laws and keep his unruly family in order by brandishing his thunderbolt. He was also the possessor of an astonishing libido and vented his lust on just about everyone he came across, including his own mother. Mythology is littered with his offspring.

Zeus was married to his sister **Hera**, the protector of women and the family. Hera was able to renew her virginity each year by bathing in a spring. She was the mother of Ares, Hebe and Hephaestus.

Ares, god of war, was the embodiment of everything warlike. Strong and brave, he was definitely someone to have on your side in a fight – but he was also hot-tempered and violent, liking nothing better than a good massacre. Athenians, who fought only for such noble ideals as liberty, thought that Ares must be a Thracian – whom they regarded as bloodthirsty barbarians.

Hephaestus was worshipped for his matchless skills as a craftsman. When Zeus decided to punish man, he asked Hephaestus to make a woman. So Hephaestus created Pandora from clay and water, and, as everyone knows, she had a box, from which sprang all the evils afflicting humankind.

The next time you have a bowl of corn flakes, give thanks to **Demeter**, the goddess of earth and fertility. The English word 'cereal', for products of corn or edible grain, derives from the goddess' Roman name, Ceres. The Greek word for such products is demetriaka.

The goddess of love (and lust) was the beautiful **Aphrodite**. Her tour de force was her magic girdle, which made everyone fall in love with its wearer. The girdle meant she was constantly pursued by both gods and goddesses – the gods because they wanted to make love to her, the goddesses because they wanted to borrow the girdle. Zeus became so fed up with her promiscuity that he married her off to Hephaestus, the ugliest of the gods.

Ancient Greek Mythology

Athena, the powerful goddess of wisdom and guardian of Athens, is said to have been born (complete with helmet, armour and spear) from Zeus' head, with Hephaestus acting as midwife. Unlike Ares, she derived no pleasure from fighting, preferring to use her wisdom to settle disputes peacefully. If need be, however, she went valiantly into battle.

Poseidon, the brother of Zeus, was god of the sea and preferred his sumptuous palace in the depths of the Aegean to Mt Olympus. When he was angry (which was often) he would use his trident to create massive waves and floods. His moods could also trigger earthquakes and volcanic eruptions. He was always on the lookout for some real estate on dry land and challenged Dionysos for Naxos, Hera for Argos and Athena for Athens.

Apollo, god of light, was the son of Zeus by the nymph Leto. He was the sort of person everybody wanted to have around. The ancients Greeks associated sunshine with spiritual and intellectual illumination. Apollo was also worshipped as the god of music and song, which the ancients believed were heard only where there was light and security.

Apollo's twin sister, **Artemis**, seems to have been a bit confused by her portfolio. She was worshipped as the goddess of childbirth, yet she asked Zeus to grant her eternal virginity; she was also the protector of suckling animals, but loved hunting!

Hermes, messenger of the gods, was another son of Zeus – this time by Maia, daughter of Atlas. He was a colourful character who smooth-talked his way into the top ranks of the Greek pantheon. Convicted of rustling Apollo's cattle while still in his cradle, he emerged from the case as the guardian of all divine property.

Zeus then made Hermes his messenger, and fitted him out with a pair of winged golden sandals to speed him on his way. His job included responsibility for commerce, treaties and the safety of travellers. He remained, however, the patron of thieves.

Hermes completes the first XI – the gods whose position in the pantheon is agreed by everyone. The final berth is normally reserved for **Hestia**, goddess of the hearth. She was as pure as driven snow, a symbol of security, happiness and hospitality. She spurned disputes and wars, and swore to be a virgin forever.

She was a bit too virtuous for some, who relegated her to the ranks of the Lesser Gods and promoted the fun-loving **Dionysos**, god of wine, in her place. Dionysos was a son of Zeus by another of the supreme deity's dalliances. He had the job of touring the world with an entourage of fellow revellers spreading the word about the vine and wine.

[continued from page 32]

Treatment of Animals

The Greek attitude to animals depends on whether the animal is a cat or not. It's definitely cool to be a cat. Even the mangiest-looking stray can be assured of a warm welcome and a choice titbit on approaching the restaurant table of a Greek. Most other domestic animals are greeted with a certain indifference. You don't see many pet dogs, or pets of any sort for that matter.

The main threat to animal welfare is hunting. Greek hunters are notorious for blasting anything that moves, and millions of animals are killed during the long 'open' season, from 20 August to 10 March, which encompasses the bird migratory period. The Hellenic Wildlife Rehabilitation Centre (☎ 0297 028 367, e ekpaz@x-treme, W www.ekpaz.gr), on the island of Aegina, reports that 80% of the animals it treats have been shot.

RELIGION

About 98% of Greeks belong to the Greek Orthodox Church. Most of the remainder are either Roman Catholic, Jewish or Muslim.

The Greek Orthodox Church is closely related to the Russian Orthodox Church and

Ancient Greek Mythology

Lesser Gods

After his brothers Zeus and Poseidon had taken the heavens and seas, **Hades** was left with the underworld (the earth was common ground). This vast and mysterious region was thought by the Greeks to be as far beneath the earth as the sky was above it. The underworld was divided into three regions: the Elysian Fields for the virtuous, Tartarus for sinners and the Asphodel Meadows for those who fitted neither category. Hades was also the god of wealth, in the form of the precious stones and metals found deep in the earth.

Pan, the son of Hermes, was the god of the shepherds. Born with horns, beard, tail and goat legs, his ugliness so amused the other gods that eventually he fled to Arcadia where he danced, played his famous pipes and watched over the pastures, shepherds and herds.

Other gods included **Asclepius**, the god of healing; **Eros**, the god of love; **Hypnos**, the god of sleep; **Helios**, god of the sun; and **Selene**, goddess of the moon.

Q-ray

Zeus produced Athena from his forehead – spear and all!

Mythical Heroes

Heroes such as **Heracles** and **Theseus** were elevated almost to the ranks of the gods. Heracles, yet another of Zeus' offspring, was performing astonishing feats of strength before he had left the cradle. His 12 labours were performed to atone for the murder of his wife and children in a bout of madness. The deeds of Theseus included the slaying of the Minotaur at Knossos.

Other heroes include **Odysseus**, whose wanderings after the fall of Troy are recorded in Homer's *Odyssey*, and **Jason**, who led his Argonauts to recover the golden fleece from Colchis (in modern Georgia). **Xena**, regrettably, does not feature anywhere. The strapping 'warrior princess' of TV fame is a scriptwriter's invention – not a myth!

---

together with it forms the third-largest branch of Christianity. Orthodox, meaning 'right belief', became the official religion in the 4th century in the time of Constantine the Great, who was converted to Christianity by a vision of the Cross.

During Ottoman times membership of the Orthodox Church was one of the most important criteria in defining a Greek, regardless of where he or she lived. The church was the principal upholder of Greek culture and traditions.

Religion is still integral to life in Greece, and the Greek year is centred on the festivals of the church calendar. Most Greeks, when they have a problem, will go into a church and light a candle to the saint they feel is most likely to help them.

Throughout the islands you will see hundreds of tiny churches dotted around the countryside. Most have been built by individual families in the name of their selected patron saint as thanksgiving for God's protection.

If you wish to look around a church, you should dress appropriately. Women should wear skirts that reach below the knees, and men should wear long trousers and have their arms covered. Regrettably, many churches are kept locked nowadays, but it's usually easy enough to locate caretakers, who will be happy to open them up for you.

LANGUAGE

See the Language chapter at the back of this book for pronunciation details and useful phrases. For a more comprehensive guide to language, see Lonely Planet's *Greek phrasebook*. The boxed text 'Transliteration & Variant Spellings: An Explanation' takes a look at the vagaries of turning Greek into English.

The Glossary chapter at the back of the book contains some common Greek words.

Transliteration & Variant Spellings: An Explanation

The issue of correctly transliterating Greek into the Latin alphabet is a vexed one, fraught with inconsistencies and pitfalls. The Greeks themselves are not very consistent in this respect, though things are gradually improving. The word 'Piraeus', for example, has been variously represented by the following transliterations: Pireas, Piraievs and Pireefs; and when appearing as a street name (eg, Piraeus Street) you will also find Pireos!

This has been compounded by the linguistic minefield of diglossy, or the two forms of the Greek language. The purist form is called Katharevousa and the popular form is Dimotiki (Demotic). The Katharevousa form was never more than an artificiality and Dimotiki has always been spoken as the mainstream language, but this linguistic schizophrenia means there are often two Greek words for each English word. Thus, the word for 'baker' in everyday language is *fournos*, but the shop sign will more often than not say *artopoieion*. The baker's product will be known in the street as *psomi*, but in church as *artos*.

A further complication is the issue of anglicised versus hellenised forms of place names: Athina versus Athens, Patra versus Patras, Thiva versus Thebes, Evia versus Euboia – the list goes on and on! Toponymic diglossy (the existence of both an official and everyday name for a place) is responsible for Kerkyra/Corfu, Zante/Zakynthos and Santorini/Thira. In this guide we usually provide modern Greek equivalents for town names, with one or two well-known exceptions, eg, Athens and Patras. For ancient sites, settlements or people from antiquity, we have tried to stick to the more familiar classical names; so we have Thucydides instead of Thoukididis, Mycenae instead of Mykines.

Problems in transliteration have particular implications for vowels, especially given that Greek has six ways of rendering the vowel sound ee, two ways of rendering the o sound and two ways of rendering the e sound. In most instances in this book, *y* has been used for the ee sound when a Greek *upsilon* (υ, Υ) has been used, and *i* for Greek *ita* (η, Η) and *iota* (ι, Ι). In the case of the Greek vowel combinations that make the ee sound, ie, οι, ει and υι, an *i* has been used. For the two Greek e sounds αι and ε, an e has been employed.

As far as consonants are concerned, the Greek letter *gamma* (γ, Γ) appears as g rather than y throughout this book. This means that *agios* (Greek for male saint) is used rather than *ayios*, and *agia* (female saint) rather than *ayia*. The letter *delta* (δ, Δ) appears as d rather than dh throughout this book, so *domatia* (rooms), rather than *dhomatia*, is used. The letter *fi* (φ, Φ) can be transliterated as either f or ph. Here, a general rule of thumb is that classical names are spelt with a ph and modern names with an f. So Phaistos is used rather than Festos, and Folegandros is used rather than Pholegandros. The Greek *chi* (ξ, Ξ) has usually been represented as h in order to approximate the Greek pronunciation as closely as possible. Thus, we have 'Haralambos' instead of 'Charalambos' and 'Polytehniou' instead of 'Polytechniou'. Bear in mind that the *h* is to be pronounced as an aspirated *h*, much like the *ch* in loch. The letter *kapa* (κ, Κ) has been used to represent that sound, except where well-known names from antiquity have adopted by convention the letter c, eg, Polycrates, Acropolis.

Wherever reference to a street name is made, we have omitted the Greek word 'odos', but words for avenue (*leoforos*) and square (*plateia*) have been included.

Facts for the Visitor

PLANNING
When to Go
The best times to visit are in late spring/early summer and in autumn. The islands emerge from tourist hibernation in time for Easter, when the first visitors start to arrive. Conditions are perfect between Easter and the end of June. The weather is pleasantly warm in most places, but not too hot; beaches and ancient sites are relatively uncrowded; public transport operates on close to full schedules; and accommodation is cheaper and easy to find.

The most popular time to visit is during July and August. It's party time on the islands and everything is in full swing. It's also very hot – in July and August the mercury can soar to 40°C (100°F) in the shade, the beaches are crowded, the ancient sites are swarming with tour groups, and in many places accommodation is booked solid.

The season starts to wind down in September, and conditions are ideal once more until the end of October.

By the beginning of November most of the tourists have disappeared. Life on some of the smaller islands comes to a virtual standstill - but life does go on. You'll always be able to find a place to stay and a place to eat. Winter can be a great time to visit some of the more popular islands – places like Crete, Mykonos, Rhodes and Syros. These places are completely different without the crowds.

Maps
Mapping is an important feature of this guide. Unless you are going to trek or drive, you probably won't need to buy additional maps.

Most tourist offices hand out free maps, but they are often out of date and not particularly accurate. The same applies to the cheap 'tourist maps' sold on every island.

The best maps are published by the Greek company Road Editions. There is a wide range of maps to suit various needs, starting with a 1:500,000 map of Greece.

Crete is covered by the company's 1:250,000 maroon-cover mainland series. Other islands are covered by its blue-cover island series. At the time of writing, the series featured Corfu, Kea (Tzia), Kefallonia and Ithaki, Kos, Lefkada, Milos, Paxi & Antipaxi, Rhodes, Santorini, Syros and Zakynthos. Maps of Andros, Kythira, Mykonos, Naxos, Paros and Samos should be available by the time you read this. The scale of these maps ranges from 1:100,000 for larger islands like Corfu and Rhodes to 1:30,000 for Syros.

Even the smallest towns and villages are clearly marked, and the distance indicators are spot-on – important when negotiating your way around the backblocks. Useful features include symbols to indicate the location of petrol stations and tyre shops.

Freytag & Berndt's 15-map Greece series has good coverage of the islands.

What to Bring
Sturdy shoes are essential for clambering around ancient sites and wandering around historic towns and villages, which tend to have lots of steps and cobbled streets. Footwear with ankle support is preferable for trekking, although many visitors get by with trainers.

A day-pack is useful for the beach, and for sightseeing or trekking. A compass is essential if you are going to trek in remote areas, as is a whistle, which you can use should you become lost or disorientated. A torch (flashlight) is not only needed if you intend to explore caves, but comes in handy during occasional power cuts. If you like to fill a washbasin or bathtub (a rarity in Greece), bring a universal plug as Greek bathrooms rarely have plugs.

Many island camping grounds have covered areas where tourists without tents can sleep in summer, so you can get by with a lightweight sleeping bag and foam bedroll.

You will need only light clothing – preferably cotton – during the summer months.

During spring and autumn you'll need a light sweater or jacket in the evening.

In summer, a broad-rimmed sun hat and sunglasses are essential (see the Health section later in this chapter). Sunscreen creams are expensive, as are moisturising and cleansing creams.

If you read a lot, it's a good idea to bring along a few disposable paperbacks to read and swap.

RESPONSIBLE TOURISM

Ideally, being a responsible tourist entails an effort to minimise the detrimental effects of tourism – and maximise the benefits. This starts with such fundamental things as being polite and respectful.

The most irresponsible thing that a tourist can do is to 'souvenir' stones or small pieces of pottery from ancient sites. If every visitor picked up a stone from the Acropolis, there would soon be nothing left.

An easy way to be a responsible tourist is to economise on water use. Fresh water is a precious commodity on most islands, many of which have to bring in water by tanker. You can help by taking such simple measures as turning off the tap off while you're brushing your teeth, and having short showers. Litter disposal is another area where tourists can help by setting a good example.

TOURIST OFFICES

Tourist information is handled by the Greek National Tourist Organization, known by the initials GNTO abroad and EOT (Ellinikos Organismos Tourismou) in Greece.

Local Tourist Offices

The EOT's head office (☎ 21-0331 0561/0562, fax 21 0325 2895, ⓔ gnto@ eexi.gr, ⓦ www.gnto.gr) is at Amerikis 2, Athens 105 64. There are about 25 EOT offices throughout Greece. Most EOT staff speak English, but they vary in their enthusiasm and helpfulness. Some offices, like that in Athens, have loads of useful local information, but most have nothing more than glossy brochures, usually about other parts of the country. Some have absolutely nothing to offer except an apology.

In addition to EOT offices, there are also municipal tourist offices. They are often more helpful.

Tourist Offices Abroad

GNTO offices abroad include:

Australia
(☎ 02-9241 1663/1664/1665) 51–57 Pitt St, Sydney NSW 2000
Austria
(☎ 1-512 5317) Opernring 8, Vienna A-1015
Belgium
(☎ 2-647 5770) 172 Ave Louise Louizalaan, B1050 Brussels
Canada
Montreal: (☎ 514-871 1535) 1170 Place Du Frere Andre, Quebec H3B 3C6
Toronto: (☎ 416-968 2220) 91 Scollard St, Ontario M5R 1G4
Denmark
(☎ 332 5332) Vester Farimagsgade 1, 1606 Copenhagen
France
(☎ 01 42 60 65 75) 3 Ave de l'Opéra, Paris 75001
Germany
Berlin: (☎ 30-217 6262) Wittenbergplatz 3A, 10789 Berlin 30
Frankfurt: (☎ 69-236 561) Neue Mainzerstrasse 22, 60311
Hamburg: (☎ 40-454 498) Neurer Wall 18, 20254
Munich: (☎ 89-222 035/036) Pacellistrasse 5, 2W 80333
Israel
(☎ 3-517 0501) 5 Shalom Aleichem St, Tel Aviv 61262
Italy
Milan: (☎ 02-860 470) Piazza Diaz 1, 20123
Rome: (☎ 06-474 4249) Via L Bissolati 78–80, 00187
Japan
(☎ 03-350 55 917) Fukuda Bldg West, 5F 2-11-3 Akasaka, Minato-Ku, Tokyo 107
Netherlands
(☎ 20-625 4212) Kerkstraat 61, Amsterdam GC 1017
Sweden
(☎ 8-679 6480) Birger Jarlsgatan 30, Box 5298 S, 10246 Stockholm
Switzerland
(☎ 01-221 0105) Loewenstrasse 25, 8001 Zürich
UK
(☎ 020-7734 5997) 4 Conduit St, London W1R ODJ

USA
  Chicago: (☎ 312-782 1084) Suite 600, 168
  North Michigan Ave, Chicago, Illinois 60601
  Los Angeles: (☎ 213-626 6696) Suite 2198, 611
  West 6th St, Los Angeles, California 92668
  New York: (☎ 212-421 5777) Olympic Tower,
  645 5th Ave, New York, NY 10022

Tourist Police

The tourist police work in cooperation with the regular Greek police and EOT. Each tourist police office has at least one member of staff who speaks English. Hotels, restaurants, travel agencies, tourist shops, tourist guides, waiters, taxi drivers and bus drivers all come under the jurisdiction of the tourist police. If you think that you have been ripped off by any of these, report it to the tourist police and they will investigate.

If you need to report a theft or loss of passport, the tourist police will act as interpreters between you and the regular police. The tourist police also fulfil the same functions as the EOT and municipal tourist offices, dispensing maps and brochures, and giving information on transport.

VISAS & DOCUMENTS
Passport

To enter Greece you need a valid passport or, for European Union (EU) nationals, travel documents (ID cards). You must produce your passport or EU travel documents when you register in a hotel or pension in Greece. You will find that many accommodation proprietors will want to keep your passport during your stay. This is not a compulsory requirement: they need it only long enough to take down the details.

Visas

The list of countries whose nationals can stay in Greece for up to three months without a visa includes Australia, Canada, all EU countries, Iceland, Israel, Japan, New Zealand, Norway, Switzerland and the USA. Other countries included are Cyprus, Malta, the European principalities of Monaco and San Marino, and most South American countries. The list changes, so contact Greek embassies for the full list. Those not on the list can expect to pay about US$20 for a three-month visa.

North Cyprus Greece will refuse entry to people whose passport indicates that they have visited Turkish-occupied North Cyprus since November 1983. This can be overcome if, upon entering North Cyprus, you ask the immigration officials to stamp a piece of paper (loose-leaf visa) rather than your passport. If you enter North Cyprus from the Greek Republic of Cyprus (only possible for a day visit) an exit stamp is not put into your passport.

Visa Extensions If you want to stay in Greece for longer than three months, apply at a consulate abroad or at least 20 days in advance to the Aliens Bureau (☎ 21 0770 5711), Leoforos Alexandras 173, Athens. Take your passport and four passport photographs along. You may be asked for proof that you can support yourself financially, so keep all your bank exchange slips (or the equivalent from a post office). These slips are not always automatically given – you may have to ask for them. The Aliens Bureau is open 8am to 1pm Monday to Friday. Elsewhere in Greece apply to the local police authority. You will be given a permit, which will authorise you to stay in the country for a period of up to six months.

Most travellers get around this by visiting Bulgaria or Turkey briefly and then re-entering Greece.

Travel Insurance

A travel insurance policy to cover theft, loss and medical problems is a good idea. The policies handled by STA Travel and other student travel organisations are usually good value.

There is a wide variety of policies available; check the small print. Some policies specifically exclude 'dangerous activities', which can include scuba diving, motorcycling, even trekking. A locally acquired motorcycle licence is not valid under some policies.

You may prefer a policy that pays doctors or hospitals direct rather than you having to pay on the spot and claim later. If you have to claim later make sure you keep all documentation. Some policies ask you to call back (reverse charges) to a centre in your home country where an immediate assessment of your problem is made.

Check that the policy covers ambulances or an emergency flight home.

Driving Licence & Permits
Greece recognises all national driving licences, provided the licence has been held for at least one year. It also recognises an International Driving Permit, which should be obtained before you leave home.

Hostel Cards
A Hostelling International (HI) card is of limited use in Greece. The only place you will be able to use it is at the Athens International Youth Hostel.

Student & Youth Cards
The most widely recognised (and thus the most useful) form of student ID is the International Student Identity Card (ISIC). Holders qualify for half-price admission to museums and ancient sites and for discounts at some budget hotels and hostels. Several travel agencies in Athens are licensed to issue cards. They are listed in the Information section of the Athens chapter. You will need to show documents proving you are a student, provide a passport photo and cough up €35.

Aegean Airlines offers student discounts on domestic flights, but there are no discounts on buses, ferries or trains.

Seniors Cards
See the Senior Travellers section later in this chapter.

Copies
All important documents (passport data page and visa page, credit cards, travel insurance policy, air/bus/train tickets, driving licence etc) should be photocopied before you leave home. Leave one copy with someone at home and keep another with you, separate from the originals.

It's also a good idea to store details of your vital travel documents in Lonely Planet's free online Travel Vault in case you lose the photocopies or can't be bothered with them. Your password-protected Travel Vault is accessible online anywhere in the world – create it at W www.ekno .lonelyplanet.com.

EMBASSIES & CONSULATES
Greek Embassies & Consulates
The following is a selection of Greek diplomatic missions abroad:

Albania (☎ 42-34 290/291) Ruga Frederik Shiroka, Tirane
Australia (☎ 02-6273 3011) 9 Turrana St, Yarralumla, Canberra ACT 2600
Bulgaria (☎ 92-946 1027) San Stefano 33, Sofia 1504
Canada (☎ 613-238 6271) 76–80 Maclaren St, Ottawa, Ontario K2P OK6
Cyprus (☎ 02-680 670/671) Byron Boulevard 8–10, Nicosia
France (☎ 01 47 23 72 28) 17 Rue Auguste Vacquerie, 75116 Paris
Germany (☎ 30-236 0990) Kurfürstenstrasse 130, D-10785 Berlin
Ireland (☎ 01-676 7254) 1 Upper Pembroke St, Dublin 2
Israel (☎ 03-605 5461) 47 Bodenheimer St, Tel Aviv 62008
Italy (☎ 06-854 9630) Via S Mercadante 36, Rome 3906
Japan (☎ 03-340 0871/0872) 3-16-30 Nishi Azabu, Minato-ku, Tokyo 106
Netherlands (☎ 070-363 87 00) Amaliastraat 1 37, 2514 JC, The Hague
New Zealand (☎ 04-473 7775) 5–7 Willeston St, Wellington
South Africa (☎ 12-437 351/352) 1003 Church St, Hatfield, Pretoria 0028
Sweden (☎ 08-663 7577) Riddargatan 60, 11457 Stockholm
Turkey (☎ 312-436 8860) Ziya-ul-Rahman Caddesi 911, Gaziosmanpasa 06700, Ankara
UK (☎ 020-7229 3850) 1A Holland Park, London W11 3TP
USA (☎ 202-939 5818) 2221 Massachusetts Ave NW, Washington DC 20008

Embassies & Consulates in Greece

All foreign embassies in Greece are in Athens and its suburbs, while there are additional consulates of various countries in Thessaloniki, Patras, Corfu, Rhodes and Iraklio. They include:

Albania
Embassy: (☎ 21 0723 4412) Karahristou 1, Athens 115 21
Consulate: (☎ 231 054 7435, fax 231 054 6656) Odysseos 6, Thessaloniki

Australia
Embassy: (☎ 21 0645 0404) Dimitrou Soutsou 37, Ambelokipi, Athens 115 21
Consulate: (☎ 231 024 0706, fax 231 026 0237) Ionos Dragoumi 20, Thessaloniki (also represents New Zealand)

Bulgaria
Embassy: (☎ 21 0647 8105) Stratigou Kalari 33A, Psyhiko, Athens 154 52
Consulate: (☎ 231 082 9210, fax 231 085 4004) N Manou 12, Thessaloniki

Canada
Embassy: (☎ 21 0727 3400) Genadiou 4, Athens 115 21
Consulate: (☎ 231 025 6350, fax 231 025 6351) Tsimiski 17, Thessaloniki

Cyprus
Embassy: (☎ 21 0723 7883) Irodotou 16, Athens 106 75
Consulate: (☎ 231 026 0611) Nikis 37, Thessaloniki

France
Embassy: (☎ 21 0361 1663) Leoforos Vasilissis Sofias 7, Athens 106 71
Consulate: (☎ 2661 033 788) Polyla 22, Corfu
Consulate: (☎ 231 024 4030, fax 231 024 4032) McKenzie King 8, Thessaloniki

Germany
Embassy: (☎ 21 0728 5111) Dimitriou 3 & Karaoli, Kolonaki, Athens 106 75
Consulate: (☎ 2661 031 453) Guilford 57, Corfu
Consulate: (☎ 281 0226 288) Zografou 7, Iraklio
Consulate: (☎ 2241 063 730) Parodos Isiodou 12, Rhodes
Consulate: (☎ 231 023 6315, fax 231 024 0393) Karolou Dil 4a, Thessaloniki

Hungary
Embassy: (☎ 21 0672 5337) Kalvou 16, Athens 154 52
Consulate: (☎ 231 0547 397) Danaïdou 4, Thessaloniki

Ireland
Embassy: (☎ 21 0723 2771) Leoforos Vasileos Konstantinou 7, Athens 106 74

Consulate: (☎ 2661 032 469) Kapodistria 20a, Corfu

Israel
Embassy: (☎ 21 0671 9530) Marathonodromou 1, Athens 154 52

Italy
Embassy: (☎ 21 0361 7260) Sekeri 2, Athens 106 74
Consulate: (☎ 231 093 4000) Papanastasiou 90, Thessaloniki

Japan
Embassy: (☎ 21 0775 8101) Athens Tower, Leoforos Messogion 2–4, Athens 115 27

Netherlands
Embassy: (☎ 21 0723 9701) Vasileos Konstantinou 5–7, Athens 106 74
Consulate: (☎ 281 034 6202) Avgoustou 23, Iraklio
Consulate: (☎ 2241 031 571) Alexandrou Diakou 27, Rhodes
Consulate: (☎ 231 028 4065) Komninon 26, Thessaloniki

New Zealand
Consulate: (☎ 21 0687 4701) Kifissias 268, Halandri

South Africa
Embassy: (☎ 21 0680 6645) Kifissias 60, Maroussi, Athens 151 25
Consulate: (☎ 231 072 2519) Tsimiski 51, Thessaloniki

Sweden
Consulate: (☎ 231 028 4065) Komninon 26, Thessaloniki

Turkey
Embassy: (☎ 21 0724 5915) Vasilissis Georgiou 8, Athens 106 74
Consulate: (☎ 2241 023 362) Iroon Politechniou 12, Rhodes
Consulate: (☎ 231 024 8452) Ag Dimitriou 151, Thessaloniki

UK
Embassy: (☎ 21 0723 6211) Ploutarhou 1, Athens 106 75
Consulate: (☎ 2661 030 055) Menekratou 1, Corfu
Consulate: (☎ 281 022 4012) Apalexandrou 16, Iraklio
Consulate: (☎ 2241 027 247) Pavlou Mela 3, Rhodes
Consulate: (☎ 231 027 8006) El Venizelou 8, Thessaloniki

USA
Embassy: (☎ 21 0721 2951) Leoforos Vasilissis Sofias 91, Athens 115 21
Consulate: (☎ 231 024 2905) Tsimiski 3, Thessaloniki

Phone numbers listed incorporate changes due in Oct 2002; see p55

Generally speaking, your own country's embassy won't be much help in emergencies if the trouble you're in is remotely your own fault. Remember that you are bound by Greek laws. Your embassy will not be sympathetic if you end up in jail after committing a crime locally, even if such actions are legal in your own country.

In genuine emergencies you might get some assistance, but only if other channels have been exhausted. For example, if you need to get home urgently, a free ticket home is exceedingly unlikely – the embassy would expect you to have insurance. If you have all your money and documents stolen, it might assist with getting a new passport, but a loan for onward travel is out of the question.

CUSTOMS

There are no longer duty-free restrictions within the EU. This does not mean, however, that customs checks have been dispensed with – random searches are still made for drugs. Upon entering the country from outside the EU, customs inspection is usually cursory for foreign tourists. There may be spot checks, but you probably won't have to open your bags. A verbal declaration is usually all that is required.

You may bring the following into Greece duty-free: 200 cigarettes or 50 cigars; 1L of spirits or 2L of wine; 50g of perfume; 250ml of eau de Cologne; one camera (still or video) and film; a pair of binoculars; a portable musical instrument; a portable radio or tape recorder; a typewriter; sports equipment; and dogs and cats (with a veterinary certificate).

Importation of works of art and antiquities is free, but they must be declared on entry, so that they can be re-exported. Import regulations for medicines are strict; if you are taking medication, make sure you get a statement from your doctor before you leave home. It is illegal, for instance, to take codeine into Greece without an accompanying doctor's certificate.

An unlimited amount of foreign currency and travellers cheques may be brought into Greece. If, however, you intend to leave the country with foreign banknotes in excess of US$1000, you must declare the sum upon entry. Restrictions apply to the importation of sailboards into Greece.

It is strictly forbidden to export antiquities (anything over 100 years old) without an export permit. This crime is second only to drug smuggling in the penalties imposed. It is an offence to remove even the smallest article from an archaeological site.

The place to apply for an export permit is the Antique Dealers & Private Collections Section, Archaeological Service, Polygnotou 13, Athens.

Vehicles

Cars can be brought into Greece for four months without a carnet; only a green card (international third party insurance) is required. Your vehicle will be registered in your passport when you enter Greece to prevent you from leaving the country without it.

MONEY
Currency

Greece was gearing up for the transition to the euro at the time of writing, scheduled for January 2002. Its national currency, the drachma (dr), became part of the basket of euro currencies at the beginning of 2001, fixed at a rate of 340.75 dr to €1. Already it is compulsory to display prices and issue receipts in euro as well as drachma. Prices for this book have been calculated by dividing the 2001 drachma prices by 340.75, and then rounding up to the nearest five cents.

The new euro banknotes and coins were due to be introduced on 1 January 2002, ushering in a two-month period of dual use of euros and drachma. By 1 March 2002, the drachma will be withdrawn. Only euro notes and coins will remain in circulation and prices will be displayed in euros only. There will be seven euro notes in different colours and sizes; they come in denominations of 500, 200, 100, 50, 20, 10 and five euros. These notes will be the same everywhere: the €5 note in France will be the same €5 note in Italy and Portugal.

There are eight euro coins, in denominations of two and one euros, then 50, 20, 10, five, two and one cents. Each state will be able to decorate the reverse side of the coins with its own designs, but all euro coins can be used anywhere that accepts euros.

At the time of writing, people appeared surprisingly unemotional about the impending disappearance of the drachma, which has been the country's currency since independence. For the record, a collector's set of the last days of the drachma should include coins in denominations of five, 10, 20, 50, 100 and 500 dr, and banknotes of 100, 200, 500, 1000, 5000 and 10,000 dr.

Exchange Rates

country	unit		euro
Albania	100 lekē	=	0.77
Australia	A$1	=	0.57
Bulgaria	1 leva	=	0.52
Canada	C$1	=	0.71
Japan	¥100	=	0.92
New Zealand	NZ$1	=	0.48
United Kingdom	UK£1	=	1.62
United States	US1	=	1.11

Warning It's all but impossible to exchange Turkish lira in Greece. The only place you can change them is at the head office of the National Bank of Greece, Pancpistimiou 36, Athens – and it'll give only about 75% of the going international rate.

Exchanging Money

Banks will exchange all major currencies in either cash, travellers cheques or Eurocheques. The best-known travellers cheques in Greece are Thomas Cook and American Express. A passport is required to change travellers cheques, but not cash.

Commission charged on the exchange of banknotes and travellers cheques varies not only from bank to bank but from branch to branch. It's less for cash than for travellers cheques. For travellers cheques, the commission can be as much as €4.40 for amounts under €100, and €5.90 for amounts over €100.

Post offices can exchange banknotes – but not travellers cheques – and charge less commission than banks. Many travel agencies and hotels will also change money and travellers cheques at bank rates, but their commission charges are higher.

If there is a chance that you may apply for a visa extension, make sure you receive, and keep hold of, a bank exchange slip after each transaction.

Cash Nothing beats cash for convenience – or for risk. If you lose it, it's gone for good and very few travel insurers will come to your rescue. Those that will, normally limit the amount to about US$300. It's best to carry no more cash than you need for the next few days, which means working out your likely needs when you change travellers cheques or withdraw cash from an ATM.

It's also a good idea to set aside a small amount of cash, say US$50, as an emergency stash.

Travellers Cheques The main reason to carry travellers cheques rather than cash is the protection they offer against theft. They are, however, losing popularity as more and more travellers opt to put their money in a bank at home and withdraw it at ATMs as they go along.

American Express, Visa and Thomas Cook cheques are all widely accepted and have efficient replacement policies. Maintaining a record of the cheque numbers and recording when you use them is vital when it comes to replacing lost cheques. Keep this record separate from the cheques themselves. US dollars are a good currency to use.

ATMs ATMs (automatic teller machines) are to be found in almost every town large enough to support a bank – and certainly in all the tourist areas. If you've got MasterCard or Visa/Access, there are plenty of places to withdraw money.

Cirrus and Maestro users can make withdrawals in all major towns and tourist areas.

AFEMs (Automatic Foreign Exchange Machines) are common in major tourist areas. They take all the major European currencies, Australian and US dollars and Japanese yen, and are useful in an emergency.

Credit Cards The great advantage of credit cards is that they allow you to pay for major items without carrying around great wads of cash. Credit cards are now an accepted part of the commercial scene just about everywhere in Greece. They can be used to pay for a wide range of goods and services such as upmarket meals and accommodation, car hire and souvenir shopping.

If you are not familiar with the card options, ask your bank to explain the workings and relative merits of the various schemes: cash cards, charge cards and credit cards. Ask whether the card can be replaced in Greece if it is lost or stolen.

The main credit cards are MasterCard, Visa (Access in the UK) and Eurocard, all of which are widely accepted in Greece. They can also be used as cash cards to draw euros from the ATMs of affiliated Greek banks in the same way as at home. Daily withdrawal limits are set by the issuing bank. Cash advances are given in local currency only. Credit cards can be used to pay for accommodation in all the smarter hotels. Some C-class hotels will accept credit cards, but D- and E-class hotels rarely do. Most upmarket shops and restaurants accept credit cards.

The main charge cards are American Express and Diner's Club Card, which are widely accepted in tourist areas but unheard of elsewhere.

International Transfers If you run out of money or need more for whatever reason, you can instruct your bank back home to send you a draft. Specify the city and the bank as well as the branch that you want the money sent to. If you have the choice, select a large bank and ask for the international division. Money sent by electronic transfer should reach you within 24 hours.

Security
The safest way of carrying cash and valuables (passport, travellers cheques, credit cards etc) is a favourite topic of travel conversation. The simple answer is that there is no foolproof method. The general principle is to keep things out of sight. The front pouch belt, for example, presents an obvious target for a would-be thief – only marginally less inviting than a fat wallet bulging from your back pocket.

The best place is under your clothes in contact with your skin where, hopefully, you will be aware of an alien hand before it's too late. Most people opt for a money belt, while others prefer a leather pouch hung around the neck. Whichever method you choose, put your valuables in a plastic bag first – otherwise they will get soaked in sweat as you wander around in the heat.

Costs
Greece is still a cheap country by northern European standards, but it is no longer dirt-cheap. A rock-bottom daily budget would be €25. This would mean hitching, staying in youth hostels or camping, staying away from bars, and only occasionally eating in restaurants or taking ferries. Allow at least €50 per day if you want your own room and plan to eat out regularly as well as travelling about and seeing the sights. You will still need to do a fair bit of self-catering. If you really want a holiday – comfortable rooms and restaurants all the way – you will need closer to €100 per day. These budgets are for individuals travelling in high season (July/August). Couples sharing a double room can get by on less.

Your money will go a lot further if you travel in the quieter months. Accommodation, which eats up a large part of the daily budget, is generally about 25% cheaper outside high season. There are fewer tourists around and more opportunities to negotiate even better deals. All prices quoted in this book are for the high season.

Prices vary quite a lot between islands, particularly for accommodation. Hydra and Mykonos are the most expensive; the cheapest tend to be the most remote islands.

Tipping & Bargaining
In restaurants the service charge is included in the bill but it is the custom to leave a small tip. The practice is often just to round off the bill. Likewise for taxis – a small amount is appreciated.

Bargaining is not as widespread in Greece as it is further east. Prices in most shops are clearly marked and non-negotiable. The same applies to restaurants and public transport. It is always worth bargaining over the price of hotel rooms or *domatia* (the Greek equivalent of the British B&B, minus the breakfast), especially if you are intending to stay a few days. You may get short shrift in high season, but prices can drop dramatically in the low season. Souvenir shops and market stalls are other places where your negotiating skills will come in handy. If you feel uncomfortable about haggling, walking away can be just as effective – you can always go back.

Taxes & Refunds
The value-added tax (VAT) varies from 15% to 18%. A tax-rebate scheme applies at a restricted number of shops and stores; look for a Tax Free sign in the window. You must fill in a form at the shop and present it with the receipt at the airport on departure. A cheque will (hopefully) be sent to your home address.

POST & COMMUNICATIONS
Post
Post offices *(tahydromio)* are easily identifiable by means of the yellow signs outside. Regular postboxes are also yellow. The red boxes are for express mail only.

Postal Rates The postal rate for postcards and airmail letters to destinations within the EU is €0.55 for up to 20g and €0.85 for up to 50g. To other destinations the rate is €0.60 for up to 20g and €0.90 for up to 150g. Post within Europe takes five to eight days and to the USA, Australia and New Zealand, nine to 11 days. Some tourist shops also sell stamps, but with a 10% surcharge.

Express mail costs an extra €1.85 and should ensure delivery in three days within the EU – use the special red postboxes. Valuables should be sent registered post, which costs an extra €2.35.

Sending Mail Do not wrap a parcel until it has been inspected at a post office. In Athens, take your parcel to the Parcel Post Office (☎ 21 0322 8940) in the arcade at Stadiou 4, and elsewhere to the parcel counter of a regular post office.

Receiving Mail You can receive mail at poste restante (general delivery) at any main post office. The service is free of charge, but you are required to show your passport. Ask senders to write your family name in capital letters on the envelope and underline it, and to mark the envelope 'poste restante'. It is a good idea to ask the post office clerk to check under your first name as well if letters you are expecting cannot be located. After one month, uncollected mail is returned to the sender. If you are about to leave a town and expected mail hasn't arrived, ask at the post office to have it forwarded to your next destination, c/o poste restante.

See the Post section in the Athens chapter for addresses of post offices that hold poste restante mail.

Parcels are not delivered in Greece, they must be collected from the parcel counter of a post office – or, in Athens, from the Parcel Post Office.

Telephone
The Greek telephone service is maintained by the public corporation known as Organismos Tilepikoinonion Ellados, which is always referred to by the acronym OTE (pronounced O-tay).

The system is modern and reasonably well maintained. There are public telephones just about everywhere, including some unbelievably isolated spots. The phones are easy to operate and can be used for local, long distance and international calls. The 'i' at the top left of the push-button dialling panel brings up the operating instructions in English.

All public phones use OTE phonecards, known as *telekarta*, not coins. The cards cost €2.95 for 1000 units, €5.60 for 2000 units, €12.35 for 5000 units, and €24.10 for 10,000 units. The 1000-unit cards are widely available at *periptera* (street kiosks), corner shops and tourist shops; the others can be bought at OTE offices. A local call uses 10 units for one minute.

It's also possible to use these phones using a growing range of discount card schemes, such as *Kronokarta* and *Teledome*, which involve dialling an access code and then punching in your card number. The cards come with instructions in

Phone numbers listed incorporate changes due in Oct 2002; see p55

Greek and English. They are easy to use and buy double the time.

It is no longer possible to use public phones to access other national card schemes, such as Telstra Australia's Telecard, for international calls. These calls can be made from private digital phones, but the time you spend on the phone is also charged at local call rates. It's better to use Kronokarta or Teledome.

International calls can also be made from OTE offices. A counter clerk directs you to a cubicle equipped with a metered phone, and payment is made afterwards. Villages and remote islands without OTE offices almost always have at least one metered phone for international and long distance calls – usually in a shop, *kafeneio* (cafe) or taverna.

Reverse charge (collect) calls can be made from an OTE office. If you are using a private phone to make a reverse charge call, dial the operator (domestic ☎ 151, international ☎ 161). To call internationally direct from Greece, dial the Greek international access code (☎ 00), followed by the country code for the country you are calling, then the local area code (dropping the leading zero if there is one) and then the number. The table below lists some country codes and per-minute charges:

country	code	cost per minute
Australia	61	€0.29
France	33	€0.29
Germany	49	€0.29
Ireland	353	€0.29
Italy	39	€0.29
Japan	81	€0.41
Netherlands	31	€0.29
New Zealand	64	€0.67
Turkey	90	€0.35
UK	44	€0.29
USA & Canada	1	€0.29

Off-peak rates are 25% cheaper. They are available to Africa, Europe, the Middle East and India between 10pm and 6am; to the Americas between 11pm and 8am; and to Asia and Oceania between 8pm and 5am.

To call Greece the international access code is ☎ 30.

Ekno Communication Service Lonely Planet's eKno global communication service provides low-cost international calls – for local calls you're usually better off with a local phonecard. eKno also offers free messaging services, email, travel information and an online travel vault, where you can securely store all your important documents. You can join online at Ⓦ www.ekno.lonelyplanet .com, where you will find the local-access numbers for the 24-hour customer-service centre. Once you have joined, always check the eKno Web site for the latest access numbers for each country and updates on new features.

Mobile Phones

Few countries in the world have embraced the mobile phone with such enthusiasm as Greece. It has become the essential Greek accessory; everyone seems to have one.

If you have a compatible GSM mobile phone from a country with an overseas global roaming arrangement with Greece, you will be able to use your phone in Greece. You must inform your mobile phone service provider before you depart in order to have global roaming activated.

Greece has three mobile service providers – Panafon, CosmOTE and Telestet. Of the three CosmOTE tends to have the best coverage in more remote areas like some of the remoter villages, so you could try re-tuning your phone to CosmOTE if you find mobile coverage is patchy. All three companies offer pay-as-you-talk services by which you can buy a rechargeable SIM card and have your own Greek mobile number: a good idea if you plan to spend some time in Greece. The Panafon system is called '· la Carte', the Telestet system 'B-free' and CosmOTE's 'COSMO KARTA'.

USA and Canadian mobile phone users will not be able to use their mobile phones in Greece, unless they are dual system equipped.

Fax & Telegraph

Most post offices in Greece have fax machines; telegrams can be sent from any OTE office.

Warning: Phone Number Changes

Greece is implementing a new national numbering plan to alleviate a shortage of numbers in the telephone system and to allow users to better understand call charges. As a result dialling numbers in Greece could be a little problematic during 2002.

The new plan means that all numbers now have 10 digits. The key features of the scheme are:

The area code now has to be dialled for every number, even when calling from within the same geographical area. So, for instance, to call an Athens number from within Athens, you need to include the area code 01.

Also, all numbers now have a 0 added at the start of the local number (which follows the area code). For example, if you want to dial the old Athens number 01-123 4567 it now becomes 01 0123 4567.

To further complicate things, from **20 October 2002**, the area code's leading 0 will be replaced with a 2 for fixed phones and with a 6 for mobile phones. So the Athens number 01 0123 4567 will change to 21 0123 4567. The numbers listed in this book incorporate this change, so **if you dial any number in this book before 20 October 2002 remember to dial 0 instead of the first digit.**

The old numbers will work until 20 January 2002; from then until 20 October 2002 callers to old numbers will get a recorded message.

Email & Internet Access

Greece was slow to embrace the wonders of the Internet, but is now striving to make up for lost time. Internet cafes are springing up everywhere, and are listed under the Information section for cities and islands where available.

There has also been a huge increase in the number of hotels and businesses using email, and these addresses have been listed where available. Some hotels catering for travellers offer Internet access.

DIGITAL RESOURCES

A good place to start is the *500 Links to Greece* site at Ⓦ www.corfu1.com. It has links to a huge range of sites on everything from accommodation to Zeus.

The address Ⓦ www.greektravel.com takes you to an assortment of interesting and informative sites on Greece by Matt Barrett. The Greek Ministry of Culture has put together an excellent site, Ⓦ www.culture.gr, with loads of information about museums and ancient sites. Other sites include Ⓦ www .gogreece.com/travel and Ⓦ www.aegean .ch. You'll find more specialist Web sites listed through the book.

The Lonely Planet Web site (Ⓦ www .lonelyplanet.com) gives a succinct summary on travelling to Greece, postcards from other travellers and the Thorn Tree bulletin board, where you can ask questions before you go or dispense advice when you get back. The subWWWay section links you to other useful travel resources on the Web.

You'll find addresses of more specialist Web sites listed throughout the book.

BOOKS

Most books are published in different editions by different publishers in different countries. As a result, a book might be a hardcover rarity in one country while it's readily available in paperback in another. Fortunately, bookshops and libraries search by title or author, so your local bookshop or library is best placed to advise you on the availability of the following recommendations.

Lonely Planet

The 5th edition of Lonely Planet's guide to *Greece* has comprehensive coverage of mainland Greece as well as the islands, while The Lonely Planet guides to *Mediterranean Europe* and *Western Europe* also include coverage of Greece, as does *Europe on a shoestring*. Regional titles include *Corfu & the Ionians*, *Rhodes & the Dodecanese* and *Crete*. *Crete Condensed* is part of the popular pocket guide series. The handy *Greek phrasebook* will help enrich your visit.

Katherine Kizilos vividly evokes Greece's landscapes, people and politics in her book *The Olive Grove: Travels in Greece*. She explores the islands and borderlands of her father's homeland, and life in her family's village in the Peloponnese mountains. The book is part of the Journeys travel literature series. These titles are available at major English-language bookshops in Athens, Thessaloniki, Rhodes and Iraklio. See the Bookshop entries in these sections for more details.

Guidebooks

For archaeology buffs, the *Blue Guides* are hard to beat. They go into tremendous detail about all the major sites, and many of the lesser known ones. They have a separate guide for Crete.

Travel

English writer Lawrence Durrell, who spent an idyllic childhood on Corfu, is the best known of the 20th-century philhellenes who helped in Greece's struggle for self-determination. His evocative books *Prospero's Cell* and *Reflections on a Marine Venus* are about Corfu and Rhodes respectively. His coffee-table book *The Greek Islands* is one of the most popular books of its kind. Even if you disagree with Durrell's opinions, you will probably concede that the photographs are superb. *My Family and Other Animals* by his brother Gerald Durrell is a hilarious account of the Durrell family's chaotic and wonderful life on Corfu.

Under Mount Ida: A Journey into Crete by Oliver Burch is a compelling portrayal of this diverse and beautiful island – full of insights into its landscape, history and people.

The Colossus of Maroussi by Henry Miller is now regarded as a classic. Miller relates his travels in Greece at the outbreak of WWII with feverish enthusiasm.

People & Society

Of the numerous festivals held in Greece, one of the most bizarre and overtly pagan is the carnival held on the island of Skyros, described in *The Goat Dancers of Skyros* by Joy Coulentianou.

The Cyclades, or Life Amongst the Insular Greeks by James Theodore Bent (first published 1885) is still the greatest English-language book about the Greek Islands. It relates the experiences of the author and his wife while travelling around the Cyclades in the late 19th century. The book is now out of print but the Hellenic Book Service may have a second-hand copy; see the Bookshops section later in this chapter.

Time, Religion & Social Experience in Rural Greece by Laurie Kain Hart is a fascinating account of village traditions – many of which are alive and well beneath the tourist veneer.

History & Mythology

A Traveller's History of Greece by Timothy Boatswain & Colin Nicholson gives the layperson a good general reference on the historical background of Greece, from Neolithic times to the present day.

Modern Greece: A Short History by CM Woodhouse is in a similar vein, although it has a right-wing bent. It covers the period from Constantine the Great to 1990.

Mythology was an intrinsic part of life in ancient Greece, and some knowledge of it will enhance your visit. *The Greek Myths* by Robert Graves is regarded as the definitive book on the subject. Maureen O'Sullivan's *An Iconoclast's Guide to the Greek Gods* presents entertaining and accessible versions of the myths. There are many translations of Homer's *Iliad* and *Odyssey*, which tell the story of the Trojan War and the subsequent adventures of Odysseus. The translations by EV Rien are among the best.

The Argonautica Expedition by Theodor Troev encompasses Greek mythology, archaeology, travel and adventure. It relates the voyage undertaken by the author and his crew in the 1980s following in the footsteps of Jason and the Argonauts.

Mary Renault's novels provide an excellent feel for ancient Greece. *The King Must Die* and *The Bull from the Sea* are vivid tales of Minoan times.

Poetry

Sappho: A New Translation by Mary Bernard is the best translation of this great ancient poet's works.

Collected Poems by George Seferis, *Selected Poems* by Odysseus Elytis and *Collected Poems* by Constantine Cavafy are all excellent translations of Greece's greatest modern poets.

Novels

The most well known and widely read Greek author is the Cretan writer Nikos Kazantzakis, whose novels are full of drama and larger-than-life characters. His most famous works are *The Last Temptation*, *Zorba the Greek*, *Christ Recrucified* and *Freedom or Death*.

English writer Louis de Berni'res has become almost a cult figure following the success of *Captain Corelli's Mandolin*, which tells the emotional story of a young Italian army officer sent to the island of Kefallonia during WWII.

Australian journalists George Johnston and Charmian Clift wrote several books with Greek themes during their 19 years as expatriates, including Johnston's novel *The Sponge Divers*, set on Kalymnos, and Clift's autobiographical *A Mermaid Singing*, which is about their experiences on Hydra.

The Mermaid Madonna and *The Schoolmistress with the Golden Eyes* are two passionate novels by Stratis Myrivilis, set in two villages on the island of Lesvos.

Athenian writer Apostolos Doxiadis has charmed critics the world over with his latest novel, *Uncle Petros and Goldbach's Conjecture*. It's an unlikely blend of family drama and mathematical theory, although you don't need to be a mathematical genius to enjoy the book. If you are and you can prove the conjecture – that every even number greater than two can be written as the sum of two prime numbers – you could be in line to collect a prize of US$1 million offered by the publishers.

Botanical Field Guides

The Flowers of Greece & the Aegean by William Taylor & Anthony Huxley is the most comprehensive field guide to Greece. The Greek writer, naturalist and mountaineer George Sfikas has written many books on wildlife in Greece. Among them are *Wildflowers of Greece*, *Trees & Shrubs of Greece* and *Medicinal Plants of Greece*.

Children's Books

The Greek publisher Malliaris-Paedia puts out a good series of books on the myths, retold in English for young readers by Aristides Kesopoulos. The titles are *The Gods of Olympus and the Lesser Gods*, *The Labours of Hercules*, *Theseus and the Voyage of the Argonauts*, *The Trojan War and the Wanderings of Odysseus* and *Heroes and Mythical Creatures*.

Robin Lister's retelling of *The Odyssey* is aimed at slightly older readers (ages 10 to 12), but makes compelling listening for younger children.

Bookshops

There are several specialist English-language bookshops in Athens, and shops selling books in French, German and Italian. There are also good foreign-language bookshops in Iraklio, Rhodes, Patras and Thessaloniki (see those sections for details).

All other major towns and tourist resorts have bookshops that sell some foreign-language books. Imported books are expensive – normally two to three times the recommended retail price in the UK and the USA. Many hotels have second-hand books to read or swap.

Abroad, the best bookshop for new and second-hand books about Greece, written in both English and Greek, is the Hellenic Book Service (☎ 020-7267 9499, fax 7267 9498, ⓔ hellenicbooks@btinternet.com), 91 Fortress Rd, Kentish Town, London NW5 1AG. It stocks almost all of the books recommended here. Its Web site is Ⓦ www.hellenicbookservice.com.

FILMS

Greece is nothing if not photogenic, and countless films have made the most of the country's range of superb locations. The islands do, of course, figure prominently.

Kefallonia has also featured as the setting for the big budget movie version of *Captain Corelli's Mandolin*, starring Nicholas Cage in the title role.

Mykonos was the setting for the smash hit *Shirley Valentine*, featuring Pauline Collins in the title role and Tom Conti as her Greek toy boy. *Mediterraneo* (1991) is an Italian movie that achieved cult status worldwide. It was set on Kastellorizo.

NEWSPAPERS & MAGAZINES

Greeks are great newspaper readers. There are 15 daily newspapers, of which the most widely read are *Ta Nea*, *Kathimerini* and *Eleftheros Typos*.

After almost 50 years as a daily newspaper, the *Athens News* (€1.50) has become a weekly. It appears on Friday with an assortment of news, local features and entertainment listings. The prime source of daily news is now the Athens edition of the *International Herald Tribune* (€1.35), which includes an eight page English-language edition of the Greek daily *Kathimerini*. Both are widely available in Athens and at major resorts. You'll find *Kathimerini* at W www.ekathimerini.com.

Foreign newspapers are also widely available, although only between April and October on smaller islands. You'll find all the British and other major European dailies, as well as international magazines such as *Time*, *Newsweek* and the *Economist*. The papers reach Athens (Syntagma) at 3pm on the day of publication on weekdays, and at 7pm on weekends. They are not available until the following day in other areas.

RADIO & TV

Greece has two state-owned radio channels, ET 1 and ET 2. ET 1 runs three programs; two are devoted to popular music and news, while the third plays mostly classical music. It has a news update in English at 7.30am Monday to Saturday, and at 9pm Monday to Friday. It can be heard on 91.6 MHz and 105.8 MHz on the FM band, and 729 KHz on the am band. ET 2 broadcasts mainly popular music.

Commercial radio stations tend to confine their broadcasts to major urban areas. The hills around Athens are bristling with radio transmitters, but the choice is very limited on the islands.

The best short-wave frequencies for picking up the BBC World Service are:

GMT	frequency
3am to 7.30am	9.41 MHz (31m band)
	6.18 MHz (49m band)
	15.07 MHz (19m band)
7.30am to 6pm	12.09 MHz (25m band)
	15.07 MHz (19m band)
6.30pm to 11.15pm	12.09 MHz (25m band)
	9.41 MHz (31m band)
	6.18 MHz (49m band)

As far as Greek TV is concerned, it's a case of quantity rather than quality. There are nine TV channels and various pay-TV channels. All the channels show English and US films and soapies with Greek subtitles. A bit of channel-swapping will normally turn up something in English.

VIDEO SYSTEMS

If you want to record or buy video tapes to play back home, you won't get a picture unless the image registration systems are the same. Greece uses PAL, which is incompatible with the North American and Japanese NTSC system. Australia and most of Europe use PAL.

PHOTOGRAPHY & VIDEO
Film & Equipment

Major brands of film are widely available, although they can be expensive in smaller towns. In Athens, expect to pay about €4.40 for a 36-exposure roll of Kodak Gold ASA 100; less for other brands.

You'll pay more on the islands, particularly in remoter areas, when old stock can also be a problem.

Video cartridges are readily available in large towns and cities, but make sure you buy the correct format. It is usually worth buying at least a few cartridges duty-free to start off your trip. Because of the brilliant sunlight in summer, you'll get better results using a polarising lens filter.

Restrictions

Never photograph a military installation or anything else that has a sign forbidding photography. Flash photography is not allowed inside churches, and it's considered taboo to photograph the main altar.

Greeks usually love having their photos taken, but always ask permission first. The same goes for video cameras.

TIME

Greece is two hours ahead of GMT/UTC and three hours ahead on daylight-saving time, which begins on the last Sunday in March, when clocks are put forward one hour. Daylight saving ends on the last Sunday in September.

So, when it is noon in Greece it is also noon in İstanbul, 10am in London, 11am in Rome, 2am in San Francisco, 5am in New York and Toronto, 8pm in Sydney and 10pm in Auckland.

ELECTRICITY

Electricity is 220V, 50 cycles. Plugs are the standard continental type with two round pins. All hotel rooms have power points and most camping grounds have supply points.

WEIGHTS & MEASURES

Greece uses the metric system. Liquids – especially barrel wine – are sold by weight rather than volume: 959g of wine, for example, is equivalent to 1000mL.

Remember that, like other continental Europeans, Greeks indicate decimals with commas and thousands with points.

LAUNDRY

Large towns and some islands have laundrettes. They charge from €5.30 to €10 to wash and dry a load. Hotel and room owners will usually provide you with a washtub if requested.

TOILETS

Most places in Greece have Western-style toilets, especially hotels and restaurants that cater for tourists. You'll occasionally come across Asian-style squat toilets in older houses, *kafeneia* and public toilets.

Public toilets are rare, except at airports and bus and train stations. Cafes are the best option if you get caught short, but you'll be expected to buy something for the privilege.

One peculiarity of the Greek plumbing system is that it can't handle toilet paper, apparently the pipes are too narrow. Whatever the reason, anything larger than a postage stamp seems to cause a problem – flushing away tampons and sanitary napkins is guaranteed to block the system. Toilet paper etc should be placed in the small bin provided in every toilet.

HEALTH

Travel health depends on your predeparture preparations, your day-to-day health care while travelling and how you handle any medical problem or emergency that does develop. While the list of potential dangers can seem quite frightening, few travellers experience more than upset stomachs.

Predeparture Planning

Health Insurance Refer to Travel Insurance under Visas & Documents earlier in this chapter for information.

Warning Codeine, which is commonly found in headache preparations, is banned in Greece; check labels carefully, or risk prosecution. There are strict regulations applying to the importation of medicines into Greece, so obtain a certificate from your doctor that outlines any medication you may have to carry into the country with you.

Health Preparations Make sure you're healthy before you start travelling. If you are embarking on a long trip make sure your teeth are OK.

If you wear glasses take a spare pair and your prescription.

If you require a particular medication take an adequate supply, as it may not be available locally. Take the prescription or, better still, part of the packaging showing the generic rather than the brand name (which may not be locally available), as it will make getting replacements easier.

Phone numbers listed incorporate changes due in Oct 2002; see p55

Medical Kit Check List

Following is a list of items you should consider including in your medical kit – consult your pharmacist for brands available in your country.

☐ **Aspirin or paracetamol (acetaminophen in the USA)** – for pain or fever

☐ **Antihistamine** – for allergies, eg, hay fever; to ease the itch from insect bites or stings; and to prevent motion sickness

☐ **Cold and flu tablets, throat lozenges and nasal decongestant**

☐ **Multivitamins** – consider for long trips, when dietary vitamin intake may be inadequate

☐ **Antibiotics** – consider including these if you're travelling well off the beaten track; see your doctor, as they must be prescribed, and carry the prescription with you

☐ **Loperamide or diphenoxylate** – 'blockers' for diarrhoea

☐ **Prochlorperazine or metaclopramide** – for nausea and vomiting

☐ **Rehydration mixture** – to prevent dehydration, which may occur, for example, during bouts of diarrhoea; particularly important when travelling with children

☐ **Insect repellent, sunscreen, lip balm and eye drops**

☐ **Calamine lotion, sting relief spray or aloe vera** – to ease irritation from sunburn and insect bites or stings

☐ **Antifungal cream or powder** – for fungal skin infections and thrush

☐ **Antiseptic (such as povidone-iodine)** – for cuts and grazes

☐ **Bandages, Band-Aids (plasters) and other wound dressings**

☐ **Water purification tablets or iodine**

☐ **Scissors, tweezers and a thermometer** – note that mercury thermometers are prohibited by airlines

Immunisations No jabs are required for travel to Greece but a yellow fever vaccination certificate is required if you are coming from an infected area. There are, however, a few routine vaccinations that are recommended. These should be recorded on an international health certificate, available from your doctor or government health department. Don't leave your vaccinations until the last minute as some require more than one injection. Recommended vaccinations include:

Tetanus & Diphtheria Boosters are needed every 10 years and protection is highly recommended.

Polio A booster of either the oral or injected vaccine is required every 10 years to maintain immunity after childhood vaccination. Polio is still prevalent in many developing countries.

Hepatitis A The most common travel-acquired illness that can be prevented by vaccination. Protection can be provided in two ways – either with the antibody gamma globulin or with the vaccine Havrix 1440. Havrix 1440 provides long-term immunity (possibly more than 10 years) after an initial injection and a booster at six to 12 months. Gamma globulin is a ready-made antibody, which should be given as close as possible to departure because it is at its most effective in the first few weeks after administration; the effectiveness tapers off gradually between three and six months.

Rabies Pretravel rabies vaccination involves having three injections over 21 to 28 days and should be considered by those who will spend a month or longer in a country where rabies is common, especially if they are cycling, handling animals, caving, travelling to remote areas, or for children (who may not report a bite). If someone who has been vaccinated is bitten or scratched by an animal they will require two booster injections of vaccine; those not vaccinated will require more.

Basic Rules

Care in what you eat and drink is the most important health rule; stomach upsets are the most likely travel health problem (between 30% and 50% of travellers in a two-week stay experience this) but the majority of these upsets will be relatively minor. Don't become paranoid; trying the local food is part of the experience of travel, after all.

Avoid climatic extremes: keep out of the sun when it's hot, dress warmly when it's cold. You can avoid insect bites by covering bare skin when insects are around, by screening windows or beds and by using insect repellents.

Seek local advice: if you're told the water is unsafe due to jellyfish, crocodiles or bilharzia, don't go in. In situations where there is no information, discretion is the better part of valour.

Food & Water Tap water is safe to drink in Greece, but mineral water is widely available if you prefer it. You might experience mild intestinal problems if you're not used to copious amounts of olive oil, however, you'll get used to it and current research says it's good for you.

If you don't vary your diet, are travelling hard and fast and missing meals, or simply lose your appetite, you can soon start to lose weight and place your health at risk. Fruit and vegetables are good sources of vitamins and Greece produces a greater variety of these than almost any other European country. Eat plenty of grains (including rice) and bread. If your diet isn't well balanced or if your food intake is insufficient, it's a good idea to take vitamin and iron pills.

In hot weather make sure you drink enough – don't rely on feeling thirsty to indicate when you should drink. Not needing to urinate or very dark yellow urine is a danger sign. Always carry a water bottle with you on long trips. Excessive sweating can lead to loss of salt and therefore muscle cramping. Salt tablets are not a good idea as a preventative, but in places where salt is not used much, adding salt to food can help.

Everyday Health

Normal body temperature is up to 37°C (98.6°F); more than 2°C (4°F) higher indicates a high fever. The normal adult pulse rate is 60 to 100 per minute (children 80 to 100, babies 100 to 140). As a general rule the pulse increases about 20 beats per minute for each 1°C (2°F) rise in fever.

Respiration (breathing) rate is also an indicator of illness. Count the number of breaths per minute: Between 12 and 20 is normal for adults and older children (up to 30 for younger children, 40 for babies). People with a high fever or serious respiratory illness breathe more quickly than normal. More than 40 shallow breaths a minute may indicate pneumonia.

Environmental Hazards

Sunburn By far the biggest health risk in Greece comes from the intensity of the sun. You can get sunburnt surprisingly quickly, even through cloud. Use a sunscreen and take extra care to cover areas that don't normally see sun. A hat helps, as does zinc cream or some other barrier cream for your nose and lips. Calamine lotion is good for mild sunburn. Greeks claim that yogurt applied to sunburn is soothing. Protect your eyes with good-quality sunglasses.

Prickly Heat Prickly heat is an itchy rash caused by excessive perspiration trapped under the skin. Keeping cool, bathing often, drying the skin and using a mild talcum powder, or resorting to air-conditioning even, may help until you acclimatise.

Heat Exhaustion Dehydration or salt deficiency can cause heat exhaustion. Take time to acclimatise to high temperatures, and drink sufficient liquids. Wear loose clothing and a broad-brimmed hat. Do not do anything too physically demanding.

Salt deficiency is characterised by fatigue, lethargy, headaches, giddiness and muscle cramps and in this case salt tablets may help. Vomiting or diarrhoea can deplete your liquid and salt levels.

Heat Stroke This serious, sometimes fatal, condition can occur if the body's heat-regulating mechanism breaks down and the body temperature rises to dangerous levels. Long, continuous periods of exposure to high temperatures can leave you vulnerable to heat stroke. You should avoid excessive alcohol consumption or strenuous activity when you first arrive in a hot climate.

The symptoms are feeling unwell, not sweating very much or at all and a high body temperature (39° to 41°C or 102° to 106°F). Where sweating has ceased the skin becomes flushed and red. Severe, throbbing headaches and lack of coordination will also occur, and the sufferer may be confused or aggressive. Eventually the victim will become delirious or convulse. Hospitalisation is essential, but in the interim get victims out of the sun, remove their clothing, cover them with a wet sheet or towel and then fan continually. Give fluids, if they are conscious.

Fungal Infections Fungal infections, which are more frequent in hot weather, are most likely to occur on the scalp, between the toes (athlete's foot) or fingers, in the groin and on the body (ringworm). You get ringworm (a fungal infection, not a worm) from infected animals or by walking on damp areas like shower floors.

To prevent fungal infections wear loose, comfortable clothes, avoid artificial fibres, wash frequently and dry carefully. If you do get an infection, wash the infected area daily with a disinfectant or medicated soap and water, and dry well. Apply an antifungal cream or powder (tolnaftate). Expose the infected area to air or sunlight as much as possible and wash all towels and underwear in hot water as well as changing them often.

Hypothermia Too much cold is just as dangerous as too much heat, particularly if it leads to hypothermia. Although everyone associates Greece with heat and sunshine, the mountain regions of Crete and Evia can be cool, even in summer. There is snow on the Lefka Ori (White Mountains) of Western Crete from November to April.

Hypothermia occurs when the body loses heat faster than it can produce it and the core temperature of the body falls. It is surprisingly easy to progress from very cold to dangerously cold due to a combination of wind, wet clothing, fatigue and hunger, even if the air temperature is above freezing. It is best to dress in layers; silk, wool and some of the newer artificial fibres all insulate well. A hat is important, as a lot of heat is lost through the head. A strong, waterproof outer layer is essential, as keeping dry is vital. Carry basic supplies, including food containing simple sugars to generate heat quickly and lots of fluid to drink. A space blanket should always be carried in cold environments.

Symptoms of hypothermia are exhaustion, numb skin (particularly toes and fingers), shivering, slurred speech, irrational or violent behaviour, lethargy, stumbling, dizzy spells, muscle cramps and violent bursts of energy. Irrationality may take the form of sufferers claiming they are warm and trying to take off their clothes.

To treat mild hypothermia, first get the person out of the wind and/or rain, remove their clothing if it's wet and replace it with dry, warm clothing. Give them hot liquids – not alcohol – and some high-kilojoule, easily digestible food. Do not rub victims; instead allow them to slowly warm themselves. This should be enough to treat the early stages of hypothermia. The early recognition and treatment of mild hypothermia is the only way to prevent severe hypothermia, which is a critical condition.

Motion Sickness Sea sickness can be a problem. The Aegean is very unpredictable and gets very rough when the *meltemi* wind blows. If you are prone to motion sickness, eat lightly before and during a trip, and try to find a place that minimises disturbance – near the wing on aircraft, close to midships on boats, near the centre on buses. Fresh air usually helps; reading and cigarette smoke don't. Commercial motion-sickness preparations, which can cause drowsiness, have to be taken before the trip commences; when you're feeling sick it's too late. Ginger (available in capsule form) and peppermint (including mint-flavoured sweets) are natural preventatives.

Infectious Diseases

Diarrhoea Simple things like a change of water, food or climate can all cause a mild bout of diarrhoea, but a few rushed toilet trips with no other symptoms is not indicative of a major problem.

Dehydration is the main danger with any diarrhoea, particularly in children or the elderly as dehydration can occur quite quickly. Under all circumstances *fluid replacement* (at least equal to the volume being lost) is the most important thing to remember. Weak black tea with a little sugar, soda water, or soft drinks allowed to go flat and diluted 50% with clean water are all good.

Hepatitis Hepatitis is a general term for inflammation of the liver. It is a common disease worldwide. The symptoms are fever, chills, headache, fatigue, feelings of weakness and aches and pains, followed by loss of appetite, nausea, vomiting, abdominal pain, dark urine, light-coloured faeces, jaundiced (yellow) skin and the whites of the eyes may turn yellow. **Hepatitis A** is transmitted by contaminated food and drinking water. The disease poses a real threat to the Western traveller. You should seek medical advice, but there is not much you can do apart from resting, drinking lots of fluids, eating lightly and avoiding fatty foods. People who have had hepatitis should avoid alcohol for some time after the illness, as the liver needs time to recover.

Hepatitis E is transmitted in the same way, and can be very serious in pregnant women. There are almost 300 million chronic carriers of **Hepatitis B** in the world. It is spread through contact with infected blood, blood products or body fluids; for example, through sexual contact, unsterilised needles and blood transfusions, or contact with blood via small breaks in the skin. Other risk situations include having a shave, tattoo, or having your body pierced with contaminated equipment. The symptoms of type B may be more severe and may lead to long-term problems. **Hepatitis D** is spread in the same way, but the risk is mainly in shared needles.

Hepatitis C can lead to chronic liver disease. The virus is spread by contact with blood – usually via contaminated transfusions or shared needles.

Tetanus This potentially fatal disease is found worldwide. It is difficult to treat but is preventable with immunisation.

Rabies Rabies is a fatal viral infection and is caused by a bite or scratch by an infected animal. It's rare, but it's found in Greece. Dogs are noted carriers as are cats. Any bite, scratch or even lick from a warm-blooded, furry animal should be cleaned immediately and thoroughly. Scrub with soap and running water, and then clean with an alcohol or iodine solution. If there is any possibility that the animal is infected medical help should be sought immediately. Even if the animal is not rabid, all bites should be treated seriously as they can become infected or can result in tetanus. A rabies vaccination is now available and should be considered if you are in a high risk category, eg, if you intend to explore caves (bat bites can be dangerous), work with animals, or travel so far off the beaten track that medical help is more than two days away.

Sexually Transmitted Diseases Sexual contact with an infected sexual partner spreads these diseases. While abstinence is the only 100% preventative, using condoms is also effective. Gonorrhoea, herpes and syphilis are among these diseases; sores, blisters or rashes around the genitals, discharges or pain when urinating are common symptoms. In some STDs, such as wart virus or chlamydia, symptoms may be less marked or not observed at all in women. Syphilis symptoms eventually disappear completely but the disease continues and can cause severe problems in later years. The treatment of gonorrhoea and syphilis is with antibiotics.

There are numerous other sexually transmitted diseases, for most of which effective treatment is available. There is currently no cure for herpes.

HIV/AIDS Infection with the human immunodeficiency virus (HIV) may lead to acquired immune deficiency syndrome (AIDS), which is a fatal disease. Any exposure to blood, blood products or body fluids may put the individual at risk. The disease is often transmitted through sexual contact or dirty needles – vaccinations, acupuncture, tattooing and body piercing can be potentially as dangerous as intravenous drug use.

If you do need an injection, ask to see the syringe unwrapped in front of you, or take a needle and syringe pack with you.

Fear of HIV infection should never preclude treatment for serious medical conditions.

Insect-Borne Diseases

Typhus Tick typhus is a problem from April to September in rural areas, particularly areas where animals congregate. Typhus begins with a fever, chills, headache and muscle pains, followed a few days later by a body rash. There is often a large painful sore at the site of the bite and nearby lymph nodes are swollen and painful. There is no vaccine available. The best protection is to check your skin carefully after walking in danger areas such as long grass and scrub. A strong insect repellent can help, and serious walkers in tick areas should consider having their boots and trousers impregnated with benzyl benzoate and dibutylphthalate. (See the Cuts, Bites & Stings section following for information about ticks.)

Lyme Disease Lyme disease is a tick-transmitted infection, which may be acquired throughout Europe. The illness usually begins with a spreading rash at the site of the bite and is accompanied by fever, headache, extreme fatigue, aching joints and muscles, and mild neck stiffness. If untreated, these symptoms usually resolve over several weeks but over subsequent weeks or months disorders of the nervous system, heart and joints may develop. The response to treatment is best early in the illness. The longer the delay, the longer the recovery period.

Cuts, Bites & Stings

Skin punctures can easily become infected in hot climates and may be difficult to heal. Treat any cut with an antiseptic such as povidone-iodine. Where possible avoid bandages and Band-Aids, which can keep wounds wet.

Although there are a lot of bees and wasps in Greece, their stings are usually painful rather than dangerous. Calamine lotion or sting relief spray will give relief and ice packs will reduce the pain and swelling.

Snakes Always wear boots, socks and long trousers when walking through undergrowth where snakes may be present. Don't put your hands into holes and crevices, and be careful when collecting firewood.

Snake bites do not cause instantaneous death and antivenenes are usually available. Keep the victim calm and still, wrap the bitten limb tightly, as you would for a sprained ankle, and then attach a splint to immobilise it. Then seek medical help, if possible with the dead snake for identification. Don't attempt to catch the snake if there is even a remote possibility of being bitten again. Tourniquets and sucking out the poison are now comprehensively discredited.

Jelly Fish, Sea Urchins & Weever Fish Watch out for sea urchins around rocky beaches; if you get some of their needles embedded in your skin, olive oil will help to loosen them. If they are not removed they will become infected. Be wary also of jelly fish, particularly during the months of September and October. Although they are not lethal in Greece, their stings can be painful. Dousing in vinegar will deactivate any stingers that have not 'fired'. Calamine lotion, antihistamines and analgesics may reduce the reaction and relieve the pain. Much more painful than either of these, but thankfully much rarer, is an encounter with the weever fish. It buries itself in the sand of the tidal zone with only its spines protruding, and injects a painful and powerful toxin if trodden on. Soaking your foot in very hot water (which breaks down the poison) should solve the problem. It can cause permanent local paralysis in the worst instance.

Bedbugs & Lice Bedbugs live in various places, but particularly in dirty mattresses and bedding. Spots of blood on bedclothes or on the wall around the bed can be read as a suggestion to find another hotel. Bedbugs leave itchy bites in neat rows. Calamine lotion or sting relief spray may help.

All lice cause itching and discomfort. They make themselves at home in your hair, your clothing or in your pubic hair. You catch lice through direct contact with infected people or by sharing combs, clothing and the like. Powder or shampoo treatment will kill the lice and infected clothing should then be washed in very hot water.

Leeches & Ticks Leeches may be present in damp conditions. They attach themselves to your skin to suck your blood. Trekkers often get them on their legs or in their boots. Salt or a lighted cigarette end will make them fall off. Do not pull them off, as the bite is then more likely to become infected. An insect repellent may keep them away.

You should always check your body if you have been walking through a potentially tick-infested area as ticks can cause skin infections and other more serious diseases. If a tick is found attached, press down around the tick's head with tweezers, grab the head and gently pull upwards. Avoid pulling the rear of the body as this may squeeze the tick's gut contents through the attached mouth parts into the skin, increasing the risk of infection and disease. Smearing chemicals on the tick will not make it let go and is not recommended.

Scorpions Scorpions are found in dry, rocky country. They are seldom seen because they hunt at night, but it's sensible to wear good footwear and to take care when lifting rocks.

Sheepdogs These dogs are trained to guard penned sheep. They are often underfed and sometimes ill-treated by their owners. They are almost always all bark and no bite, but if you are going to trek into remote areas, you should consider having rabies injections (see Rabies). You are most likely to encounter these dogs in the mountain regions of Crete. Wandering through a flock of sheep that one of these dogs is guarding (possibly discreetly) is asking for trouble.

Women's Health
Antibiotic use, synthetic underwear, sweating and contraceptive pills can lead to fungal vaginal infections, especially when travelling in hot climates. Fungal infections are characterised by a rash, itch and discharge and can be treated with a vinegar or lemon-juice douche, or with yogurt. Nystatin, miconazole or clotrimazole pessaries or vaginal cream are the usual treatment. Maintaining good personal hygiene and wearing loose-fitting clothes and cotton underwear may help prevent these infections.

Sexually transmitted diseases are a major cause of vaginal problems. Symptoms include a smelly discharge, painful intercourse and sometimes a burning sensation when urinating. Medical attention should be sought and male sexual partners must also be treated. For more details see the earlier section on Sexually Transmitted Diseases. Besides abstinence, the best thing is to practise safer sex using condoms.

Hospital Treatment
Citizens of EU countries are covered for free treatment in public hospitals within Greece on presentation of an E111 form. Inquire at your national health service or travel agent in advance. Emergency treatment is free to all nationalities in public hospitals. In an emergency, dial ☎ 166. There is at least one doctor on every island in Greece and larger islands have hospitals. Pharmacies can dispense medicines that are available only on prescription in most European countries, so you can consult a pharmacist for minor ailments.

All this sounds fine, but although medical training is of a high standard in Greece, the health service is badly underfunded and one of the worst in Europe. Hospitals are overcrowded, hygiene is not always what it should be and relatives are expected to bring in food for the patient – which could be a problem for a tourist. Conditions and treatment are better in private hospitals, which are expensive. All this means that a good health-insurance policy is essential.

Phone numbers listed incorporate changes due in Oct 2002; see p55

WOMEN TRAVELLERS

Many women travel alone in Greece. The crime rate remains relatively low, and solo travel is probably safer than in most European countries. This does not mean that you should be lulled into complacency; bag snatching and rapes do occur, although violent offences are rare.

The biggest nuisance to foreign women travelling alone are the guys the Greeks have nicknamed *kamaki*. The word means 'fishing trident' and refers to the kamaki's favourite pastime, 'fishing' for foreign women. You'll find them everywhere there are lots of tourists; young (for the most part), smooth-talking guys who aren't in the least bashful about sidling up to foreign women in the street. They can be very persistent, but they are a hassle rather than a threat.

The majority of Greek men treat foreign women with respect, and are genuinely helpful.

GAY & LESBIAN TRAVELLERS

In a country where the church still plays a prominent role in shaping society's views on issues such as sexuality, it should come as no surprise that homosexuality is generally frowned upon. While there is no legislation against homosexual activity, it pays to be discreet and to avoid public displays of togetherness.

This has not prevented the Greek Islands from becoming an extremely popular destination for gay travellers. Mykonos has long been famous for its bars, beaches and general hedonism, while Kos, Paros (and Antiparos), Rhodes, Santorini and Skiathos all have their share of gay hang-outs.

The town of Eressos on the island of Lesvos (Mytilini), birthplace of the lesbian poet Sappho, has become something of a place of pilgrimage for lesbians.

Athens also has a busy gay scene, as does Thessaloniki.

Information The *Spartacus International Gay Guide,* published by Bruno Gmünder (Berlin), is widely regarded as the leading authority on the gay travel scene, with a wealth of information on gay venues around the islands.

There's also stacks of information on the Internet. *Roz Mov* at W www.geocities.com/ WestHollywood/2225/index.html is a good place to start. It has pages on travel info, gay health, the gay press, organisations, events and legal issues – and links to lots more sites.

Gayscape has a useful site at W www .gayscape.com/gayscape/menugreece.html with lots of links.

DISABLED TRAVELLERS

If mobility is a problem, visiting the Greek Islands presents some serious challenges – particularly the smaller islands without airports. The hard fact is that most hotels, ferries, museums and ancient sites are not wheelchair accessible.

If you are determined, then take heart in the knowledge that disabled people do come to the islands for holidays. But the trip needs careful planning, so get as much information as you can before you go. The British-based Royal Association for Disability and Rehabilitation (RADAR) publishes a useful guide called *Holidays & Travel Abroad: A Guide for Disabled People,* which gives a good overview of facilities available to disabled travellers in Europe. Contact RADAR (☎ 020-7250 3222, fax 020-7250 0212, e radar@radar.org.uk) at 12 City Forum, 250 City Road, London EC1V 8AF.

SENIOR TRAVELLERS

Card-carrying EU pensioners can claim a range of benefits such as reduced admission charges at museums and ancient sites and discounts on trains.

TRAVEL WITH CHILDREN

The Greek Islands are a perfect playground for children, and it's especially easy if you're staying by the beach or at a resort hotel where there are lots of other children.

Don't be afraid to take children to ancient sites. Many parents are surprised by how much their children enjoy them. Young imaginations go into overdrive when let loose somewhere like the 'labyrinth' at Knossos.

Hotels and restaurants are usually very accommodating when it comes to meeting the needs of children, although highchairs are a rarity outside resorts. The service in restaurants is normally very quick, which is great when you've got hungry children on your hands.

Fresh milk is readily available in large towns and tourist areas, but hard to find on the smaller islands. Supermarkets are the best place to look. Formula is available everywhere, as is condensed and heat-treated milk.

Mobility is an issue for parents with very small children. Strollers (pushchairs) aren't much use on the islands unless you're going to spend all your time in one of the few flat spots. They are hopeless on rough stone paths and up steps, and a curse when getting on/off ferries. Backpacks or front pouches are best.

Children under four travel for free on ferries, and pay half fare up to the age of 10. Most large ferries have play areas for small children, and electronic games for older kids. On domestic flights, you'll pay 10% of the fare to have a child under two sitting on your knee. Kids aged two to 12 pay half fare.

Matt Barrett's Web site has lots of useful tips for parents (W www.greecetravel.com/kids/index.html), while daughter Amarandi has put together some tips for kids (W www.greece4kids.com).

USEFUL ORGANISATIONS
Automobile Associations
ELPA (☎ 21 0779 1615), the Greek automobile club, has its headquarters on the ground floor of Athens Tower, Messogion 2–4, Athens 115 27. ELPA offers reciprocal services to members of national automobile associations on production of a valid membership card. If your vehicle breaks down, dial ☎ 104.

DANGERS & ANNOYANCES
Theft
Crime, especially theft, is low in Greece, but unfortunately it is on the increase. The worst area is around Omonia in central Athens – keep track of your valuables here, on the metro and at the Sunday flea market. The vast majority of thefts from tourists are still committed by other tourists; the biggest danger of theft is probably in dormitory rooms in hostels and at camp sites. So make sure you do not leave valuables unattended in such places. If you are staying in a hotel room, and the windows and door do not lock securely, ask for your valuables to be locked in the hotel safe – hotel proprietors are happy to do this.

Bar Scams
Bar scams continue to be an unfortunate fact of life in Athens, particularly in the Syntagma area. The basic scam is always some variation on the following theme: solo male traveller is lured into bar on some pretext (not always sex); strikes up conversation with friendly locals; charming girls appear and ask for what turn out to be ludicrously overpriced drinks; traveller is eventually handed an enormous bill.

Fortunately, this practice appears confined to Athens. See under Information in the Athens chapter for the full run-down on this scam and other problems.

LEGAL MATTERS
Consumer Advice
The Tourist Assistance Programme exists to help people who are having trouble with any tourism-related service. Free legal advice is available in English, French and German from July 1 to September 30. The main office (☎ 21 0330 0673, fax 21 0330 0591) is at Valtetsiou 43–45 in Athens. It's open 10am to 2pm Monday to Friday. Free advice is also available from the following regional offices:

Iraklio Consumers' Association of Crete
  (☎ 281 024 0666) Milatou 1 and Agiou Titou
Patras Consumers' Association of Patras
  (☎ 261 027 2481) Korinthou 213B
Volos Consumers' Association of Volos
  (☎ 2421 039 266) Haziagari 51

Drugs
Greek drug laws are the strictest in Europe. Greek courts make no distinction between possession and pushing. Possession of even a small amount of marijuana is likely to land you in jail.

BUSINESS HOURS
Banks are open 8am to 2pm Monday to Thursday, and 8am to 1.30pm Friday. Some

banks in large towns and cities open between 3.30pm and 6.30pm, and Saturday morning.

Post offices are open 7.30am to 2pm Monday to Friday. In the major cities they stay open until 8pm, and open 7.30am to 2pm Saturday. The opening hours of OTE offices (for long distance and overseas telephone calls) vary according to the size of the town. In smaller towns they are usually open 7.30am to 3pm daily; 6am to 11pm in larger towns; and 24 hours in major cities like Athens and Thessaloniki.

In summer, shops are open 8am to 1.30pm and 5.30pm to 8.30pm Tuesday, Thursday and Friday, and 8am to 2.30pm Monday, Wednesday and Saturday. They open 30 minutes later in winter. These times are not always strictly adhered to. Many shops in tourist areas are open seven days a week. Periptera are open from early morning until late night. They sell everything from bus tickets and cigarettes to hard-core pornography. Opening times of museums and archaeological sites vary, but most are closed Monday.

PUBLIC HOLIDAYS

All banks and shops and most museums and ancient sites close public holidays. National public holidays in Greece are:

New Year's Day 1 January
Epiphany 6 January
First Sunday in Lent February
Greek Independence Day 25 March
Good Friday March/April
(Orthodox) Easter Sunday March/April
Spring Festival/Labour Day 1 May
Feast of the Assumption 15 August
Ohi Day 28 October
Christmas Day 25 December
St Stephen's Day 26 December

SPECIAL EVENTS

The Greek year is a succession of festivals and events, some of which are religious, some cultural, others an excuse for a good knees-up, and some a combination of all three. The following is by no means an exhaustive list, but it covers the most important events, both national and regional. If you're in the right place at the right time, you'll certainly be invited to join the revelry.

January

Feast of Agios Vasilios (St Basil) The year kicks off with this festival on 1 January. A church ceremony is followed by the exchanging of gifts, singing, dancing and feasting; the New Year pie (*vasilopitta*) is sliced and the person who gets the slice containing a coin will supposedly have a lucky year.

Epiphany (the Blessing of the Waters) On 6 January, Christ's baptism by St John is celebrated throughout Greece. Seas, lakes and rivers are blessed and crosses immersed in them. The largest ceremony takes place at Piraeus.

February-March

Shrove Monday (Clean Monday) On the Monday before Ash Wednesday (the first day of Lent), people take to the hills throughout Greece to have picnics and fly kites.

Carnival The Greek carnival season is the three weeks before the beginning of Lent (the 40-day period before Easter, which is traditionally a period of fasting). The carnivals are ostensibly Christian pre-Lenten celebrations, but many derive from pagan festivals. There are many regional variations, but fancy dress, feasting, traditional dancing and general merrymaking prevail. The Patras carnival is the largest and most exuberant, with elaborately decorated chariots parading through the streets. The most bizarre carnival takes place on the island of Skyros where the men transform themselves into grotesque 'half man, half beast' creatures by donning goat-skin masks and hairy jackets. Other carnivals worth catching are those on Zakynthos and Kefallonia.

Carnival season brings out the beast in the Skyrotians

March

Independence Day The anniversary of the hoisting of the Greek flag by Bishop Germanos at Moni Agias Lavras is celebrated on 25 March with parades and dancing. Germanos' act of revolt marked the start of the War of Independence. Independence Day coincides with the Feast of the Annunciation, so it is also a religious festival.

March-April

Easter Easter is the most important festival in the Greek Orthodox religion. Emphasis is placed on the Resurrection rather than on the Crucifixion, so it is a joyous occasion. The festival commences on the evening of Good Friday with the *perifora epitavios,* when a shrouded bier (representing Christ's funeral bier) is carried through the streets to the local church. This moving candle lit procession can be seen throughout the country. From a spectator's viewpoint, the most impressive of these processions climbs Lykavittos Hill in Athens to the Chapel of Agios Georgos. The Resurrection Mass starts at 11pm on Saturday night. At midnight, packed churches are plunged into darkness to symbolise Christ's passing through the underworld. The ceremony of the lighting of candles that follows is the most significant moment in the Orthodox year, for it symbolises the Resurrection. Its poignancy and beauty are spellbinding. If you are in Greece at Easter you should endeavour to attend this ceremony, which ends with fireworks and a candle lit processions through the streets. The Lenten fast ends on Easter Sunday with the cracking of red-dyed Easter eggs and an outdoor feast of roast lamb followed by Greek dancing. The day's greeting is *Hristos anesti* ('Christ is risen'), to which the reply is *Alithos anesti* ('Truly He is risen'). On both Palm Sunday (the Sunday before Easter) and Easter Sunday, St Spyridon (the mummified patron saint of Corfu) is taken out for an airing and joyously paraded through the town. He is paraded again in Corfu town on 11 August.

Feast of Agios Georgos (St George) The feast day of St George, patron saint of Greece and shepherds, takes place on 23 April or the Tuesday following Easter (whichever comes first).

May

May Day On the first day of May there is a mass exodus from towns to the country. During picnics, wildflowers are gathered and made into wreaths to decorate houses.

June

Navy Week This festival celebrates the long relationship between the Greek and the sea with events in fishing villages and ports throughout the country. Volos and Hydra have unique versions of these celebrations. Volos re-enacts the departure of the *Argo,* legend has it that Iolkos (from where Jason and the Argonauts set off in search of the Golden Fleece) was near the city. Hydra commemorates Admiral Andreas Miaoulis, who was born on the island and was a hero of the War of Independence, with a re-enactment of one of his naval victories, accompanied by feasting and fireworks.

Feast of St John the Baptist This feast day on 24 June is widely celebrated. Wreaths made on May Day are kept until this day, when they are burned on bonfires.

July

Feast of Agia Marina (St Marina) This feast day is celebrated on 17 July in many parts of Greece, and is a particularly important event on the Dodecanese island of Kassos.

Feast of Profitis Ilias This feast day is celebrated on 20 July at hill-top churches and monasteries dedicated to the prophet, especially in the Cyclades.

August

Assumption Greeks celebrate Assumption Day (15 August) with family reunions. The whole population seems to be on the move either side of the big day, so it's a good time to avoid public transport. The island of Tinos gets particularly busy because of its miracle-working icon of Panagia Evangelistria. It becomes a place of pilgrimage for thousands, who come to be blessed, healed or baptised, or just for the excitement of being there. Many are unable to find hotels and sleep out on the streets.

September

Genesis tis Panagias (the Virgin's Birthday) This day is celebrated on 8 September throughout Greece with religious services and feasting.

Exaltation of the Cross This is celebrated on 14 September throughout Greece with processions and hymns.

October

Feast of Agios Dimitrios (St Dimitri) This feast day is celebrated in Thessaloniki on 26 October with wine drinking and revelry.

Ohi (No) Day Metaxas' refusal to allow Mussolini's troops free passage through Greece in WWII is commemorated on 28 October with remembrance services, military parades, folk dancing and feasting.

Phone numbers listed incorporate changes due in Oct 2002; see p55

December
Christmas Day Although not as important as Easter, Christmas is still celebrated with religious services and feasting. Nowadays much 'Western' influence is apparent, including Christmas trees, decorations and presents.

Summer Festivals & Performances

There are cultural festivals throughout Greece in summer. The most important is the Athens Festival (June-August), with performances in the Theatre of Herodes Atticus. Others include the Thasos Festival (July and August); the Renaissance Festival in Rethymno (July and August); the Hippocratia Festival on Kos (August); and the Patras Arts Festival (August and September).

Thessaloniki hosts a string of festivals and events during September and October, including the International Trade Fair and the Feast of Agios Dimitrios (details on the latter in the preceding list).

The nightly *son et lumi're* (sound and light show) in Athens and Rhodes runs from April to October. Greek folk dances are performed in Athens from mid-May to September and in Rhodes from May to October.

ACTIVITIES

See the Activities special section.

COURSES
Language

If you are serious about learning the language, an intensive course at the start of your stay is a good way to go about it. Most of the courses are in Athens, but there are also special courses on the islands in summer.

The Hellenic Culture Centre (☎/fax 21 0360 3379, 2275 031 978, e hcc@hcc.gr, w www.hcc.gr) runs courses on the island of Ikaria from June to October. Two-week intensive courses for beginners cost €470 and involve 40 classroom hours. The centre can also arrange accommodation.

The Athens Centre (☎ 21 0701 2268, fax 21 0701 8603, e athenscr@compulink.gr, w www.athenscentre.gr), Arhimidous 48 in the suburb of Mets, runs courses on the island of Spetses in June and July.

Corfu's Ionian University runs courses in Modern Greek and Greek Civilisation in July and August. Details are available at Deligiorgi 55–59 (☎ 21 0522 9770) in Athens, or from the Secretariat of the Ionian University (☎ 2661 022 993/994) at Megaron Kapodistria 49, Corfu Town.

Other Courses

The Dora Stratou Dance Company (☎ 21 0324 4395, fax 21 0323 6921, e grdance@hol.gr, w http://users.hol.gr/~grdance), Sholiou 8, Athens 105 58 runs workshops at its headquarters in Plaka during July and August.

The Skyros Centre, on Skyros, runs courses on a whole range of subjects, from yoga and dancing, to massage and windsurfing. The emphasis is on developing a holistic approach to life. There is a branch in Skyros Town, but the main 'outdoor' complex is at Atsitsa Beach, on the west coast. For detailed information on its fortnightly programs contact the Skyros Centre (☎ 020-7267 4424, fax 7284 3063, e skyros@easynet.co.uk), 92 Prince of Wales Rd, London NW5 3NE, UK.

WORK
Permits

EU nationals don't need a work permit, but they need a residency permit if they intend to stay longer than three months. Nationals of other countries are supposed to have a work permit. Most people prefer to leave Greece every three months rather than become involved in all the red tape.

Bar & Hostel Work

The bars of the Greek Islands could not survive without foreign workers and there are thousands of summer jobs up for grabs every year. The pay is not fantastic, but you get to spend a summer in the islands. April/May is the time to go looking. Hostels and travellers' hotels are other places that regularly employ foreign workers.

Harvest

Seasonal harvest work seems to be monopolised by migrant workers from Albania, and is no longer a viable option for travellers.

Volunteer Work

The Hellenic Society for the Study & Protection of the Monk Seal (☎ 21 0522 2888, fax 21 0522 2450), Solomou 18, Athens 106 82; the Sea Turtle Protection Society of Greece (☎/fax 21 0523 1342, ⓔ stps@compulink.gr), Solomou 57, Athens 104 32; and Hellenic Wildlife Rehabilitation Centre (☎ 2297 028 367, ⓔ ekpaz@x-treme) on Aegina all employ volunteers.

Street Performers

The richest pickings are to be found on Mykonos, Paros and Santorini. Plaka is the place to go in Athens.

Other Work

There are often jobs advertised in the classifieds of the English-language newspapers, or you can place an advertisement yourself. EU nationals can also make use of the OAED (Organismos Apasholiseos Ergatikou Dynamikou), the Greek National Employment Service, in their search for a job.

ACCOMMODATION

There is a range of accommodation available in Greece to suit every taste and pocket. All places to stay are subject to strict price controls set by the tourist police. By law, a notice must be displayed in every room, which states the category of the room and the price charged in each season.

Accommodation owners may add a 10% surcharge for a stay of less than three nights, but this is not mandatory. A mandatory charge of 20% is levied if an extra bed is put into a room. During July and August, accommodation owners will charge the maximum price, but in spring and autumn, prices will drop by up to 20%, and perhaps by even more in winter. These are the times to bring your bargaining skills into action.

Rip-offs rarely occur, but if you suspect you have been exploited by an accommodation owner, report it to either the tourist police or regular police and they will act swiftly.

Mountain Refuges

You're unlikely to have much need of Greece's network of mountain refuges –

unless you're going trekking in the mountains of Crete. See the Crete chapter for details of the refuges at Mt Ida and in the Lefka Ori.

Camping

There are almost 200 camping grounds dotted around the islands. A few are operated by the EOT, but most are privately run. Very few are open outside the high season (April-October). The Panhellenic Camping Association (☎/fax 21 0362 1560), Solonos 102, Athens 106 80, publishes an annual booklet listing all the camp sites and their facilities.

Camping fees are highest from 15 June to the end of August. Most camping grounds charge from €3.55 to €4.40 per adult and €2.35 to €2.95 for children aged four to 12. There's no charge for children aged under four. Tent sites cost from €2.95 per night for small tents, and from €3.55 per night for large tents. Caravan sites start at around €5.90.

Between May and mid-September it is warm enough to sleep out under the stars, although you will still need a lightweight sleeping bag to counter the pre-dawn chill. It's a good idea to have a foam pad to lie on and a waterproof cover for your sleeping bag.

Freelance (wild) camping is illegal, but the law is seldom enforced – to the irritation of camping ground owners. It's more likely to be tolerated on islands that don't have camp sites, but it's wise to ask around before freelance camping anywhere in Greece.

Apartments

Self-contained family apartments are available in some hotels and domatia for either long- or short-term rental. Prices vary considerably according to the amenities offered.

Domatia

Domatia are the Greek equivalent of the British bed and breakfast, minus the breakfast. Once upon a time domatia comprised little more than spare rooms in the family home, which could be rented out to travellers in summer; nowadays, many are purpose-built appendages to the family house. Some come complete with fully equipped kitchens. Standards of cleanliness are generally high. The decor runs the gamut from cool grey marble floors, coordinated pine furniture, pretty lace curtains and tasteful pictures on the walls, to so much kitsch, you are almost afraid to move in case you break an ornament.

Domatia remain a popular option for budget travellers. They are classified A, B or C. Expect to pay from €17.60 to €29.35, and €23.50 to €47 for a double, depending on the class, whether bathrooms are shared or private, the season and how long you plan to stay. Domatia are found throughout the mainland (except in large cities) and on almost every island that has a permanent population. Many are open only between April and October.

From June to September domatia owners are out in force, touting for customers. They meet buses and boats, shouting 'Room, room!' and often carrying photographs of their rooms. In peak season, it can prove a mistake not to take up an offer – but be wary of owners who are vague about the location of their accommodation. 'Close to town' can turn out to be way out in the sticks. If you are at all dubious, insist they show you the location on a map.

Hostels

There is only one youth hostel in Greece affiliated to the International Youth Hostel Federation (IYHF), the excellent Athens International Youth Hostel (☎ 21-0523 4170). You don't need a membership card to stay there; temporary membership costs €1.80 per day.

Most other youth hostels in Greece are run by the Greek Youth Hostel Organisation (☎ 21 0751 9530, fax 21 0751 0616, ℮ y-hostels@ otenet.gr), Damareos 75, 116 33 Athens. There are affiliated hostels in Athens, Olympia, Patras and Thessaloniki on the mainland, and on the islands of Crete and Santorini.

Hostel rates vary from €4.70 to €5.90 and you don't have to be a member to stay in any of them. Few have curfews.

There is a XEN (YWCA) hostel for women in Athens.

Traditional Settlements

Traditional settlements are old buildings of architectural merit that have been renovated and converted into tourist accommodation. You'll find them on many of the islands; Hania (Crete) and Rhodes Town are two places with a good range of possibilities. Most are equivalent in price to an A- or B-class hotel.

Pensions

Pensions in Greece are virtually indistinguishable from hotels. They are classed A, B or C. An A-class pension is equivalent in amenities and price to a B-class hotel, a B-class pension is equivalent to a C-class hotel, and a C-class pension is equivalent to a D- or E-class hotel.

Hotels

Hotels in Greece are divided into six categories: deluxe, A, B, C, D and E. Hotels are categorised according to the size of the room, whether or not they have a bar, and the ratio of bathrooms to beds, rather than standards of cleanliness, comfort of the beds and friendliness of staff – all elements that may be of greater relevance to guests.

As one would expect, deluxe, A- and B-class hotels have many amenities, private bathrooms and constant hot water. C-class hotels have a snack bar, rooms have private bathrooms, but hot water may only be available at certain times of the day. D-class hotels may or may not have snack bars, most rooms will share bathrooms, but there may be some with private bathrooms, and they may have solar heated water, which means hot water is not guaranteed. E-classes do not have a snack bar, bathrooms are shared and you may have to pay extra for hot water – if it exists at all.

Prices are controlled by the tourist police and the maximum rate that can be charged for a room must be displayed on a board behind the door of each room. The classification is not often much of a guide to price. Rates in D- and E-class hotels are generally comparable with domatia. You can pay from €35 to €60 for a single in high season in C-class and €45 to €80 for a double.

Prices in B-class range from €50 to €80 for singles, and from €90 to €120 for doubles. Prices in A-class are not much higher.

FOOD

Greek food does not enjoy a reputation as one of the world's great cuisines. Maybe that's because many travellers have experienced Greek cooking only in tourist resorts. The old joke about the Greek woman who, on summer days, shouted to her husband 'Come and eat your lunch before it gets hot' is based on truth.

Until recently, food was invariably served lukewarm – which is how Greeks prefer it. Most restaurants that cater to tourists have now cottoned on to the fact that foreigners expect cooked dishes to be served hot, and improved methods of warming meals (including the dreaded microwave) have made this easier. If your meal is not hot, ask that it be served *zesto,* or order grills, which have to be cooked to order. Greeks are fussy about fresh ingredients, and frozen food is rare.

Greeks eat out regularly, regardless of socioeconomic status. Enjoying life is paramount to Greeks and a large part of this enjoyment comes from eating and drinking with friends.

By law, every eating establishment must display a written menu including prices. Bread will automatically be put on your table and usually costs between €0.30 and €1.20 per person, depending on the restaurant's category.

Where to Eat

Tavernas Traditionally, the taverna is a basic eating place with a rough-and-ready ambience, although some are more upmarket, particularly in Athens, and resorts and big towns. All tavernas have a menu, often displayed in the window or on the door, but it's usually not a good guide as to what's actually available on the day. You'll be told about the daily specials – or ushered into the kitchen to peer into the pots and point to what you want. This is not merely a privilege for tourists; Greeks also do it because they want to see the taverna's version of the dishes on offer. Some tavernas don't open

until 8pm, and then stay open until the early hours. Some are closed on Sunday.

Greek men are football (soccer) and basketball mad, both as spectators and participants. If you happen to be eating in a taverna on a night when a big match is being televised, expect indifferent service.

Psistaria These places specialise in spit roasts and charcoal-grilled food – usually lamb, pork or chicken.

Restaurants A restaurant *(estiatorio)* is normally more sophisticated than a taverna or psistaria – damask tablecloths, smartly attired waiters and printed menus at each table with an English translation. Ready-made food is usually displayed in a *bain-marie* and there may also be a charcoal grill.

Ouzeria An *ouzeri* serves ouzo. Greeks believe it is essential to eat when drinking alcohol so, in traditional establishments, your drink will come with a small plate of titbits or *mezedes* (appetisers) – perhaps olives, a slice of feta and some pickled octopus. Ouzeria are becoming trendy and many now offer menus with both appetisers and main courses.

Galaktopoleia A *galaktopoleio* (literally 'milk shop') sells dairy produce including milk, butter, yogurt, rice pudding, cornflour pudding, custard, eggs, honey and bread. It may also sell home-made ice cream. Look for the sign *'pagoto politiko'* displayed outside. Most have seating and serve coffee and tea. They are inexpensive for breakfast and usually open from very early in the morning until evening.

Zaharoplasteia A *zaharoplasteio* (patisserie) sells cakes (both traditional and Western), chocolates, biscuits, sweets, coffee, soft drinks and, possibly, bottled alcoholic drinks. They usually have some seating.

Kafeneia Kafeneia are often regarded by foreigners as the last bastion of male chauvinism in Europe. With bare light bulbs, nicotine-stained walls, smoke-laden air, rickety wooden tables and raffia chairs, they are frequented by middle-aged and elderly Greek men in cloth caps who while away their time fiddling with worry beads, playing cards or backgammon, or engaged in heated political discussion.

It was once unheard of for women to enter a kafeneia but in large cities this situation is changing.

In rural areas, Greek women are rarely seen inside kafeneia. When a female traveller enters one, she is inevitably treated courteously and with friendship if she manages a few Greek words of greeting. If you feel inhibited about going into a kafeneio, opt for outside seating. You'll feel less intrusive.

Kafeneia originally only served Greek coffee, but most also serve soft drinks, Nescafé and beer. Most kafeneia are open all day every day, but some close during siesta time (roughly from 3pm to 5pm).

Meals

Breakfast Greeks are not big morning eaters; most have coffee and perhaps a cake or pastry for breakfast. Budget hotels and pensions offering breakfast generally provide it continental-style (rolls or bread with jam, and tea or coffee), while more upmarket hotels serve breakfast buffets (Western and continental-style). Otherwise, restaurants and galaktopoleia serve bread with butter, jam or honey; eggs; and the budget travellers' favourite, yogurt *(yiaourti)* with honey. In tourist areas, many menus offer an 'English' breakfast – which means bacon and eggs.

Lunch This is eaten late – between 1pm and 3pm – and may be either a snack or a complete meal. The main meal can be lunch or dinner – or both. Greeks enjoy eating and often have two large meals a day.

Dinner Greeks also eat dinner late. Many people don't start to think about food until about 9pm, which is why some restaurants don't bother to open their doors until after 8pm. In tourist areas dinner is often served earlier.

A full dinner in Greece begins with appetisers and/or soup, followed by a main course of either ready-made food, grilled meat, or fish. Only very posh restaurants or those pandering to tourists include Western-style desserts on the menu. Greeks usually eat cakes separately in a galaktopoleio or zaharoplasteio.

Greek Specialities

Snacks Favourite Greek snacks include pretzel rings sold by street vendors, *tyropitta* (cheese pie), *bougatsa* (custard-filled pastry), *spanakopitta* (spinach pie) and *sandouits* (sandwiches). Street vendors sell various nuts and dried seeds such as pumpkin for €0.60 to €1.50 a bag.

Mezedes In a simple taverna, possibly only three or four mezedes (appetisers) will be offered – perhaps *taramasalata* (fish-roe dip), *tzatziki* (yogurt, cucumber and garlic dip), olives and feta (sheep or goat cheese). Ouzeria and restaurants usually offer wider selections.

Mezedes include *ohtapodi* (octopus), *garides* (shrimps), *kalamaria* (squid), dolmades (stuffed vine leaves), *melitzanosalata* (aubergine or eggplant dip) and *mavromatika* (black-eyed beans). Hot mezedes include *keftedes* (meatballs), *fasolia* (white haricot beans), *gigantes* (lima beans), *loukanika* (little sausages), tyropitta, spanakopitta, *bourekaki* (tiny meat pie), *kolokythakia* (deep-fried zucchini), *melitzana* (deep-fried aubergine) and *saganaki* (fried cheese).

It is quite acceptable to make a full meal of these instead of a main course. Three plates of mezedes are about equivalent in price and quantity to one main course. You can also order a *pikilia* (mixed plate).

Soups Soup is normally eaten as a starter, but can be an economical meal in itself with bread and a salad. *Psarosoupa* is a filling fish soup with vegetables, while *kakavia* (Greek bouillabaisse) is laden with seafood and more expensive. *Fasolada* (bean soup) is also a meal in itself. *Avgolemano soupa* (egg and lemon soup) is usually prepared from a chicken stock. If you're into offal, don't miss the traditional Easter soup *mayiritsa* at this festive time.

Salads The ubiquitous (and no longer inexpensive) Greek or village salad, *horiatiki salata*, is a side dish for Greeks, but many drachma-conscious tourists make it a main dish. It consists of peppers, onions, olives, tomatoes and feta cheese, sprinkled with oregano and dressed with olive oil and lemon juice. A tomato salad often comes with onions, cucumber and olives, and, with bread, makes a satisfying lunch. In spring, try *radikia salata* (dandelion salad).

Main Dishes The most common main courses are *moussaka* (layers of eggplant or zucchini, minced meat and potatoes topped with cheese sauce and baked), *pastitsio* (baked cheese-topped macaroni and bechamel, with or without minced meat), dolmades and *yemista* (stuffed tomatoes or green peppers). Other main courses include *giouvetsi* (casserole of lamb or veal and pasta), *stifado* (meat stewed with onions), *soutzoukakia* (spicy meatballs in tomato sauce) and *salingaria* (snails in oil with herbs). *Melizanes papoutsakia* is baked eggplant stuffed with meat and tomatoes and topped with cheese, which looks, as its Greek name suggests, like a little shoe. Spicy *loukanika* (sausage) is a good budget choice and comes with potatoes or rice. Lamb fricassee, cooked with lettuce, *arni fricassée me maroulia*, is usually filling enough for two to share.

Fish is usually sold by weight in restaurants, but is not as cheap nor as widely available as it used to be. Calamari (squid), deep-fried in batter, remains a tasty option for the budget traveller at €3.55 to €4.70 for a generous serve. Other reasonably priced fish (about €3.55 a portion) are *marides* (whitebait), sometimes cloaked in onion, pepper and tomato sauce, and *gopes*, which are similar to sardines. More expensive are *ohtapodi* (octopus), *bakaliaros* (cod), *xifias* (swordfish) and *glossa* (sole). Ascending the price scale further are *synagrida* (snapper) and *barbounia* (red mullet). *Astakos* (lobster) and *karabida* (crayfish) are top of the range at about €44 per kilo.

Fish is mostly grilled or fried. More imaginative fish dishes include shrimp casserole and mussel or octopus saganaki (fried with tomato and cheese).

Desserts Greek cakes and puddings include baklava, *loukoumades* (puffs or fritters with honey or syrup), *kataïfi* (chopped nuts inside shredded wheat pastry or filo soaked in honey), *rizogalo* (rice pudding), *loukoumi* (Turkish delight), *halva* (made from semolina or sesame seeds) and *pagoto* (ice cream). Tavernas and restaurants usually only have a few of these on the menu. The best places to go for these delights are galaktopoleia or zaharoplasteia.

Island Specialities

Greek food is not all moussaka and souvlaki. Every region has its own specialities and it need not be an expensive culinary adventure to discover some of these. Corfu, for example, which was never occupied by the Turks, retains traditional recipes of Italian, Spanish and ancient Greek derivations. Corfiot food is served in several restaurants and includes *sofrito* (lamb or veal with garlic, vinegar and parsley), *pastitsada,* (beef with macaroni, cloves, garlic, tomatoes and cheese) and *burdeto* (fish with paprika and cayenne).

Santorini's baby tomatoes flavour distinctive dishes, not least a rich soup as thick and dark as blood. The *myzithra* (soft ewe's-milk cheese) of Ios is unique, and the lamb pies of Kefallonia and Crete are worth searching for. Andros' speciality is *froutalia,* a spearmint-flavoured potato and sausage omelette, while a Rhodes omelette is loaded with meat and zucchini.

Vegetarian Food

Greece has few vegetarian restaurants. Unfortunately, many vegetable soups and stews are based on meat stocks. Fried vegetables are safe bets as olive oil is always used – never lard. The Greeks do wonderful things with artichokes *(aginares)*. They can be served stuffed, as a salad, as a meze (particularly with *raki* in Crete) or used as the basis of a vegetarian stew.

Vegetarians who eat eggs can rest assured that an economical omelette can be whipped up anywhere. Salads are cheap, fresh, substantial and nourishing. Other options are yogurt, rice pudding, cheese and spinach pies, and nuts.

Lent, incidentally, is a good time for vegetarians because the meat is missing from many dishes.

Fast Food

Western-style fast food has arrived in Greece in a big way – creperies, hamburger joints and pizza places are to be found in all the major towns and resort areas.

It's hard, though, to beat eat-on-the-street Greek offerings. Foremost among them are the *gyros* and the souvlaki. The gyros is a giant skewer laden with slabs of seasoned meat, which grills slowly as it rotates and the meat is trimmed steadily from the outside; souvlaki are small individual kebab sticks. Both are served wrapped in pitta bread, with salad and lashings of tzatziki.

Another favourite is *tost,* which is a bread roll cut in half, stuffed with the filling(s) of your choice, buttered on the outside and then flattened in a heavy griddle iron. It's the speciality of the Everest fast-food chain, which has outlets nationwide.

Fruit

Greece grows many varieties of fruit. Most visitors will be familiar with *syka* (figs), *rodakina* (peaches), *stafylia* (grapes), *karpouzi* (watermelon), *milo* (apples), *portokalia* (oranges) and *kerasia* (cherries).

Many will not, however, have encountered the *frangosyko* (prickly pear). Also known as the Barbary fig, it is the fruit of the opuntia cactus, recognisable by the thick green spiny pads that form its trunk. The fruit are borne around the edge of the pads in late summer and autumn and vary in colour from pale orange to deep red. They are delicious but need to be approached with extreme caution because of the thousands of tiny prickles (invisible to the naked eye) that cover their skin. Never pick one up with your bare hands. They must be peeled before you can eat them. The simplest way to do this is to trim the

ends off with a knife and then slit the skin from end to end.

Another fruit that will be new to many people is the *mousmoula* (loquat). These small orange fruit are among the first of summer, reaching the market in mid-May. The flesh is juicy and pleasantly acidic.

Self-Catering

Eating out in Greece is as much an entertainment as a gastronomic experience, so to self-cater is to sacrifice a lot. But if you are on a low budget you will need to make the sacrifice – for breakfast and lunch at any rate. All towns and villages of any size have supermarkets, fruit and vegetable stalls and bakeries.

Only in isolated villages and on remote islands is food choice limited. There may only be one all-purpose shop – a *pantopoleio,* which will stock meat, vegetables, fruit, bread and tinned foods.

Markets Most larger towns have huge indoor *agora* (food markets), which feature fruit and vegetable stalls, butchers, dairies and delicatessens, all under one roof. They are lively places that are worth visiting for the atmosphere as much as for the shopping. The markets at Hania (Crete) are a good example.

Smaller towns have a weekly *laïki agora* (street market) with stalls selling local produce.

DRINKS
Nonalcoholic Drinks

Coffee & Tea Greek coffee is the national drink. It is a legacy of Ottoman rule and, until the Turkish invasion of Cyprus in 1974, the Greeks called it Turkish coffee. It is served with the grounds, without milk, in a small cup. Connoisseurs claim there are at least 30 variations of Greek coffee, but most people know only three – *glyko* (sweet), *metrio* (medium) and *sketo* (without sugar).

After Greek coffee, the next most popular coffee is instant, called Nescafé (which it usually is). Ask for Nescafé *me ghala* (me-**ga**-la) if you want it with milk. In summer, Greeks drink Nescafé chilled, with or without milk and sugar – this version is called *frappé.*

Espresso and filtered coffee, once sold only in trendy cafes, are now also widely available.

Tea is inevitably made with a tea bag.

Fruit Juice & Soft Drinks Packaged fruit juices are available everywhere. Fresh orange juice is also widely available, but doesn't come cheap.

The products of all the major soft-drink multinationals are available everywhere in cans and bottles, along with local brands.

Milk Fresh milk can be hard to find on the islands and in remote areas. Elsewhere, you'll have no problem. A litre costs about €1.20. UHT milk is available almost everywhere, as is condensed milk.

Water Tap water is safe to drink in Greece, although sometimes it doesn't taste too good – particularly on some of the islands. Many tourists prefer to drink bottled spring water, sold widely in 500mL and 1.5L plastic bottles. If you're happy with tap water, fill a container with it before embarking on ferries or you'll wind up paying through the nose for bottled water. Sparkling mineral water is rare.

Alcoholic Drinks

Beer Greek beers are making a strong comeback in a fast-growing market long dominated by the major northern European breweries. The most popular beers are still Amstel and Heineken, both brewed locally under licence and available everywhere, but many consumers are switching to local beers like Mythos, Alpha and Vergina. Mythos has claimed a healthy share of the market since it was launched in 1997 and is the most widely available. It has proved popular with drinkers who find the northern European beers a bit sweet.

Imported lagers, stouts and beers are found in tourist spots such as music bars and discos. You might even spot Newcastle Brown, Carlsberg, Castlemaine XXXX and Guinness.

Supermarkets are the cheapest place to buy beer, and bottles are cheaper than cans.

Wine According to mythology, the Greeks invented or discovered wine and have produced it in Greece on a large scale for more than 3000 years.

The modern wine industry, though, is still very much in its infancy. Until the 1950s, most Greek wines were sold in bulk and were seldom distributed any farther afield than the nearest town. It wasn't until industrialisation (and the resulting rapid urban growth) that there was much call for bottled wine. Quality control was unheard of until 1969, when appellation laws were introduced as a precursor to applying for membership of the European Community. Wines have improved significantly since then.

Don't expect Greek wines to taste like French wines. The grape varieties grown in Greece are quite different. Some of the most popular and reasonably priced labels include Rotonda, Kambas, Boutari, Calliga and Lac des Roches.

The most expensive wines are the Kefallonian Robola de Cephalonie, a superb dry white, and those produced by the Porto Carras estate in Halkidiki. Good wines are produced on Rhodes (famous in Greece for its champagne) and Crete. Other island wines worth sampling are those from Samos (immortalised by Lord Byron), Santorini, Kefallonia and Paros. *Aspro* is white, *mavro* is red and *kokkinelli* is rosé.

Spirits Ouzo is the most popular aperitif in Greece. Distilled from grape stems and flavoured with anise, it is similar to the Middle Eastern *arak*, Turkish *raki* and French Pernod. Clear and colourless, it turns white when water is added. A 700mL bottle of a popular brand like Ouzo 12, Olympic or Sans Rival costs about €4.40 in supermarkets. In an ouzeri, a glass costs from €0.90 to €1.50. It will be served neat, with a separate glass of water to be used for dilution. Connoisseurs insist that the best ouzo comes from Lesvos. Plomariou is one of the better brands.

The second-most popular spirit is Greek brandy, which is dominated by the Metaxa label. Metaxa comes in a wide choice of grades, starting with three star – a high-octane product without much finesse. You can pick up a bottle in a supermarket for about €4.40. The quality improves as you go through the grades: five star, seven star, VSOP, Golden Age and finally the top-shelf Grand Olympian Reserve (€18). Other reputable brands include Cambas and Votrys. The Cretan speciality is raki, a fiery clear spirit that is served as a greeting (regardless of the time of day).

Retsina

A holiday in Greece would not be the same without a jar or three of retsina, the famous – some might say notorious – resinated wine that is the speciality of Attica and neighbouring areas of central Greece.

Your first taste of retsina may well leave you wondering whether the waiter has mixed up the wine and the paint stripper, but stick with it – it's a taste that's worth acquiring. Soon you will be savouring the delicate pine aroma, and the initial astringency mellows to become very moreish. Retsina is very refreshing consumed chilled at the end of a hot day, when it goes particularly well with tzatziki.

Greeks have been resinating wine, both white and rosé, for millennia. The ancient Greeks dedicated the pine tree to Dionysos, also the god of wine, and held that land that grew good pine would also grow good wine.

No-one seems quite sure how wine and pine first got together. The consensus is that it was an inevitable accident in a country with so much wine and so much pine. The theory that resin entered the wine-making process because the wine was stored in pine barrels does not hold water, since the ancients used clay amphora rather than barrels. It's more likely that it was through pine implements and vessels used elsewhere in the process. Producers discovered that wine treated with resin kept for longer, and consumers discovered that they liked it.

Resination was once a fairly haphazard process, achieved by various methods such as adding crushed pine cones to the brew and coating the insides of storage vessels. The amount of resin also varied enormously. One 19th-century traveller wrote that he had tasted a wine 'so impregnated with resin that it almost took the skin from my lips'. His reaction was hardly surprising; he was probably drinking a wine with a resin content as high as 7.5%, common at the time. A more sophisticated product awaits the modern traveller, with a resin content no higher than 1% – as specified by good old EU regulations. That's still enough to give the wine its trademark astringency and pine aroma.

Hic, it takes a while, but it's a taste worth..hic... acquiring.

The bulk of retsina is made from two grape varieties, the white savatiano and the red roditis. These two constitute the vast majority of vine plantings in Attica, central Greece and Evia. Not just any old resin will do; the main source is the Aleppo pine (Pinus halepensis), which produces a resin known for its delicate fragrance.

Retsina is generally cheap and it's available everywhere. Supermarkets stock retsina in a variety of containers ranging from 500mL bottles to 5L casks and flagons. Kourtaki and Cambas are both very good, but the best (and worst) still flows from the barrel in traditional tavernas. Ask for heema, which means 'loose'.

If you're travelling off the beaten track, you may come across *chipura,* a moonshine version of ouzo that packs a formidable punch. You'll most likely encounter chipura in village kafeneia or private homes.

ENTERTAINMENT
Cinemas
Greeks are keen movie-goers and almost every town of consequence has a cinema. English-language films are shown in English with Greek subtitles. Admission ranges from €4.10 to €5.90.

Discos & Music Bars
Discos can be found in big cities and resort areas, though not in the numbers of a decade ago. Most young Greeks prefer to head for the music bars that have proliferated to fill the void. These bars normally specialise in a particular style of music – Greek, modern rock, 1960s rock, techno and, very occasionally, jazz.

Ballet, Classical Music & Opera
Unless you're going to be spending a bit of time in Athens or Thessaloniki, you're best off forgetting about ballet, classical music and opera while in Greece. See the Entertainment section of the Athens chapter for information on venues.

Theatre
The highlight of the Greek dramatic year is the staging of ancient Greek dramas at the Theatre of Herodes Atticus in Athens during the Hellenic Festival from mid-June to early September. See the Special Events section of the Athens chapter for more information.

Rock
Western rock music continues to grow in popularity, but live music remains a rarity outside Athens and Thessaloniki.

Traditional Music
Most of the live music you hear around the resorts is tame stuff laid on for the tourists. If you want to hear music played with a bit of passion, the *rembetika* clubs in Athens are recommended.

Folk Dancing
The pre-eminent folk dancers in Greece are the ones who perform at the Dora Stratou Theatre on Filopappos Hill in Athens, where performances take place nightly in summer. Another highly commendable place is the Old City Theatre, Rhodes City, where the Nelly Dimoglou Dance Company performs from May to October. Folk dancing is an integral part of all festival celebrations and there is often impromptu folk dancing in tavernas.

SPECTATOR SPORTS
Soccer (football) remains the most popular spectator sport, although basketball is catching up fast following the successes of Greek sides in European club competition in recent years.

Greek soccer teams, in contrast, have seldom had much impact on European club competition, and the national team is the source of constant hair-wrenching. The side's only appearance in the World Cup finals, in the USA in 1994, brought a string of heavy defeats. The two glamour clubs of Greek soccer are Olympiakos of Piraeus and Panathinaikos of Athens. The capital supplies a third of the clubs in the first division (see Spectator Sports in the Athens chapter for more information). OFI, from Iraklio on Crete, is the only island team in the first division.

The season lasts from September to mid-May; cup matches are played on Wednesday night and first division games on Sunday afternoon. Games are often televised. Entry to a match costs around €5.90 for the cheapest terrace tickets, or €15 for a decent seat.

Olympiakos and Panathinaikos are also the glamour clubs of Greek basketball. Panathinaikos was European champion in 1996, and Olympiakos followed suit in 1997. Both were upstaged in 2001 by Maroussi (from northern Athens), which reached the final of the European club championships.

Basketball receives no pre-match publicity in the English-language papers, so you'll need to ask a local for information about fixtures. There are no island teams in the national competition.

Phone numbers listed incorporate changes due in Oct 2002; see p55

SHOPPING

Greece produces a vast array of handicrafts.

Antiques

It is illegal to buy, sell, possess or export any antiquity in Greece (see Customs earlier in this chapter). However, there are antiques and 'antiques'; a lot of items only a century or two old are regarded as junk, rather than part of the national heritage. These items include handmade furniture and odds and ends from rural areas in Greece, ecclesiastical ornaments from churches and items brought back from far-flung lands. Good hunting grounds for this 'junk' are Monastiraki and the flea market in Athens, and the Piraeus market held on Sunday morning.

Ceramics

You will see ceramic objects of every shape and size – functional and ornamental – for sale in Greece. The best places for high-quality handmade ceramics are Athens, Rhodes and the islands of Sifnos and Skyros.There are a lot of places selling plaster copies of statues, busts, grave stelae and so on.

Leather Work

There are leather goods for sale throughout Greece; most are made from leather imported from Spain.

The best place for buying leather goods is Hania on Crete. Bear in mind that the goods are not as high quality nor as good value as those available in Turkey.

Jewellery

You could join the wealthy North Americans who spill off the cruise ships onto Mykonos to indulge themselves in the high-class gold jewellery shops there.

But although gold is good value in Greece, and designs are of a high quality, it is priced beyond the capacity of most tourists' pockets.

If you prefer something more reasonably priced, go for filigree silver jewellery – a speciality of the town of Ioannina in Epiros.

Bags

Tagari bags are woven wool bags – often brightly coloured – which hang from the shoulder by a rope. Minus the rope, they make attractive cushion covers.

JEAN-BERNARD CARILLET

JOHN ELK III

Title Page: Yachting around the Greek Islands enables travellers to experience some of the area's more remote havens, such as Fourni Beach on Rhodes' west coast
(Photographer: Judi Willoughby)

Top: Snorkelling is enjoyable just about anywhere in the Greek Islands

Bottom: Crete's Samaria Gorge is one of Europe's premier treks.

The Greek Islands have plenty of possibilities for people who want to do more with their time than laze around on the beach waiting for the evening's partying to begin.

Water sports of all descriptions are a speciality throughout the islands, but nowhere more so than in the Cyclades. There's no finer way to blow way the cobwebs than an hour's windsurfing. Trekking opportunities also abound. Indeed, on some islands walking is the only way to get around!

TREKKING

The islands are a veritable paradise for trekkers – at the right time of the year. Trekking is no fun at all in July and August, when the temperatures are constantly up around 40°C. Spring (April-May) and autumn (September-October) are the best times.

Some of the most popular treks, such as the Samaria Gorge on Crete, are detailed in this book, but there are possibilities just about everywhere. Lesvos, Naxos and Samos are other favourite destinations for trekkers.

On small islands it's fun to discover pathways for yourself. You are unlikely to get into danger as settlements or roads are never far away. You will encounter a variety of paths: *kalderimi* are cobbled or flagstone

Right: Valleys on Lesvos, in the North-Eastern Aegean, such as Potamia Valley, are prime trekking destinations.

DAVID TIPLING

paths which link settlements and date back to Byzantine times. Sadly, many have been bulldozed to make way for roads.

If you're going to be venturing off the beaten track, a good map is essential. Unfortunately, most of the island maps are pitifully inadequate. The best maps are produced by Athens company Road Editions (see Maps in the Planning section of the Facts for the Visitor chapter for details).

Organised Treks

There are a number of companies running organised treks. One of the biggest is **Trekking Hellas** (☎ 21 0323 4548, fax 21 0325 1474, ⓔ trekking@compulink.gr, ⓦ www.trekking.gr; Filellinon 7, Athens 105 57).

Its program includes a nine-day island-hopping trek through the Cyclades visiting Andros, Mykonos, Delos, Paros, Naxos and Santorini, and an eight-day trek in Western Crete that takes in the Samaria Gorge. The treks cost about €90 per day, including full board and an English-speaking guide. Trekking Hellas also runs half-day weekend treks in the Lake Korision area of southern Corfu for €49.90, including transfers from Corfu Town. You'll find more information about organised treks in the Hania and Rethymno sections of the Crete chapter, and in the Hydra section of the Saronic Gulf Islands chapter.

DIVING & SNORKELLING

There are some excellent dive sites around the Greek Islands. Unfortunately, diving is subject to strict regulations in order to protect the many antiquities in the depths of the Aegean.

For starters, any kind of underwater activity using breathing apparatus is strictly forbidden other than under the supervision of a diving school. Diving is permitted only between sunrise and sunset, and only in specified locations. There are also strict controls on what you can do while you are diving. Underwater photography of archeological finds is prohibited, as is spear fishing with diving equipment.

Don't be put off by all the red tape. Diving is rapidly growing in popularity, and there are diving schools on the islands of Corfu, Crete (at Rethymno), Evia, Hydra,

MICHAEL AW

Left: Taking the plunge

Leros, Milos, Mykonos, Paros and Antiparos, Rhodes, Santorini and Skiathos. See the respective island chapters for details. Most charge around €50 for a dive, and from €250 for courses; prices include all equipment.

Check out the Internet Scuba Diving Club's Web site at W www.isdc.gr for more information about diving.

Snorkelling is enjoyable just about anywhere in the islands, and has the great advantage of being totally unencumbered by regulations. All the equipment you need – mask, fins and snorkel – are cheaply available everywhere. Especially good places are Monastiri on Paros; Paleokastritsa on Corfu; Telendos Islet (near Kalymnos); Ammoöpi in southern Karpathos; Xirokambos Bay on Leros; and anywhere off the coast of Kastellorizo. Many dive schools (see above) also use their boats to take groups of snorkellers to prime spots.

Organised Dives

Trekking Hellas (see the Trekking section earlier) offers eight day diving holidays in Corfu, and seven day dive tours through the Cyclades which include dives off Mykonos and Santorini.

Right: Travellers taking their first diving lesson at Kalithea Thermi, Rhodes

YACHTING

Despite the disparaging remarks among backpackers, yachting is *the* way to see the Greek Islands. Nothing beats the peace and serenity of sailing the open sea, and the freedom of being able to visit remote and uninhabited islands.

The free EOT booklet *Sailing the Greek Seas*, although long overdue for an update, contains lots of information about weather conditions, weather bulletins, entry and exit regulations, entry and exit ports and guidebooks for yachties. You can pick up the booklet at any GNTO/EOT office either abroad or in Greece. The Internet is the place to look for the latest information. The Hellenic Yachting Server site, ⓦ www.yachting.gr, has general information on sailing around the islands and lots of links.

The sailing season lasts from April until October. The best time to go depends on where you are going. The most popular time is between July and September, which ties in with the high season for tourism in general. Unfortunately, it also happens to be the time of year when the *meltemi* is at its strongest. The meltemi is a northerly wind that affects the Aegean throughout the summer. It starts off as a mild wind in May and June, and strengthens as the weather hots up – often blowing from a clear blue sky. In August and September, it can blow at gale force for days on end.

The meltemi is not an issue in the Ionian Sea, where the main summer wind is the *maistros*, a light to moderate north-westerly that rises in the afternoon. It usually dies away at sunset.

In winter, the Ionians are effected by the *gregali*, a north-east wind created by depressions moving east in the central Mediterranean. It can blow up to Force 8 on the 12-point Beaufort Scale used by Greek meteorologists.

If your budget won't cover buying a yacht there are several other options open to you. You can hire a bare boat (a yacht without a crew)

JOHN BORTHWICK

Left: Yachting isn't all hard work

if two crew members have a sailing certificate. Prices start at US$1300 per week for a 28-footer that will sleep six. It's an option only if two crew members have a sailing certificate; otherwise you can hire a skipper for an extra US$100 per day.

Most of big hire companies are based in and around Athens. They include:

Aegean Tourism (☎ 21 0346 6229, fax 21 0342 2121) Kadmias 8, Athens
Alpha Yachting (☎ 21 0968 0486, fax 21 0968 0488, e mano@ otenet.gr) Poseidonos 67, Glyfada
Ghiolman Yachts & Travel (☎ 21 0323 3696, fax 21 0322 3251, e ghiol man@travelling.gr) Filellinon 7, Athens
Hellenic Charters (☎/fax 21 0988 5592, e hctsa@ath.forth net.gr) Poseidonos 66, Alimos
Vernicos Yachts (☎ 21 0985 0122, fax 21 0985 0120, w www.verni cos.gr) Poseidonos 11, Alimos

You'll find details about yacht charter companies on the islands of Milos, Paros and Syros in the Cyclades chapter.

Yachting Tours

Trekking Hellas (see the previous Trekking section for details) also offers a range of yachting and sailing holidays around the Cyclades and the Ionians. The possibilities include eight-day tours through the Cyclades by caique or by yacht.

WINDSURFING

Windsurfing is the most popular water sport in Greece.

Many people reckon that Vasiliki on Lefkada is one of the best places in the world to learn the sport. Hrysi Akti on Paros is another favourite.

There are numerous other prime locations around the islands, including Ormos Korthiou on Andros; Kalafatis Beach on Mykonos; Agios Giorgios Beach on Naxos; Mylopotas Beach on Ios; Prasonisi in the south of Rhodes; around Tingaki on Kos; Kokkari on Samos; around Skala Sotira on Thasos; Koukounaries Beach on Skiathos; and Skyros.

You'll find sailboards for hire almost everywhere. Hire charges range from €10 to €17, depending on the gear and the location. If you are a novice, most places that rent equipment also give lessons. Plan on spending about €150 for a 10-hour beginners' course.

Sailboards can be imported freely from other EU countries, but the import of boards from other destinations, such as Australia and the US, is subject to some quaint regulations. Theoretically, importers need a Greek national residing in Greece to guarantee that the board will be taken out again. Contact the **Hellenic Windsurfing Association** (☎ 21 0323 0330, fax 21 0322 3251, e ghiolman@ghiolman.com; Filellinon 7, Athens) for more information.

SAILING

Sailing facilities are harder to find, although the same locations recommended previously for windsurfing are all also ideal for sailing.

Hrysi Akti on Paros and Mylopotas Beach on Ios are two of the best locations. Hire charges for Hobie cats (catamarans) range from €20 to €25, depending on the gear and the location.

The best season (for experienced sailors) is during July and August, when the *meltemi* guarantees a solid northerly wind up to 30 knots. Beginners will prefer the lighter winds found in June and September.

The country's main racing club is the **Hellenic Offshore Racing Club** (☎ 21 0412 2357, fax 21 0422 7038, e horc@otenet.gr, w www .horc.gr; Akti Dilaveri 3, Mikrolimano, Piraeus 185 33). Most events are contested in the waters of the surrounding Saronic Gulf, but the club also organises the annual Aegean Rally in mid-July. The 2001 event visited the islands of Leros, Ios and Milos. Check the club's Web site for details – and links to other sailing sites.

OTHER WATER SPORTS

You'll find a host of other water sports, such as jetskiing, parasailing and waterskiing, around the islands, mainly in the resort areas of islands like Corfu, Crete, Kos, Mykonos, Paros, Skiathos and Rhodes.

GOLFING

Golf has yet to take off in Greece, and the country's few courses are located with expatriates and tourists in mind rather than locals.

The only courses on the islands are **Xenia Golf Club** (☎ 2241 051 255; Paralia Afandou, Rhodes), **Corfu Golf Glub** (☎/fax 2661 094 220; near Paleokastritsa, western Corfu) and **Elounda Golf Club** (☎ 2841 041 903, fax 2841 041 889; near Agios Nikolaos, Crete).

Golfers travelling via Athens can get a game at **Glyfada Golf Club** (☎ 21 0894 6820, fax 21 0894 3721), by the coast 9km south-east of the city centre.

GEERT COLE

Left: There are many ideal sailing locations throughout the Greek Islands.

Getting There & Away

AIR

Most travellers arrive in Greece by air, the cheapest and quickest way to get there.

Airports & Airlines

Greece has 16 international airports, but only those in Athens, Thessaloniki and Iraklio (Crete) take scheduled flights.

Athens handles the vast majority of flights, including all intercontinental traffic. Thessaloniki has direct flights to Amsterdam, Belgrade, Berlin, Brussels, Dusseldorf, Frankfurt, İstanbul, Cyprus, London, Milan, Moscow, Munich, Paris, Stuttgart, Tirana, Vienna and Zürich. Most of these flights are with Greece's national airline, Olympic Airways, or the flag carrier of the country concerned. Iraklio's sole scheduled connection is to Amsterdam with Transavia.

Greece's other international airports are at Mykonos, Santorini (Thira), Hania (Crete), Kos, Karpathos, Samos, Skiathos, Hrysoupolis (for Kavala), Aktion (for Lefkada), Kefallonia and Zakynthos. These airports are used exclusively for charter flights, mostly from the UK, Germany and Scandinavia. Charter flights also fly to all of Greece's other international airports.

Olympic Airways is no longer Greece's only international airline. Cronus Airlines flies direct from Athens to London, Paris and Rome, and via Thessaloniki to Cologne, Dusseldorf, Frankfurt, Munich and Stuttgart.

Buying Tickets

If you are flying to Greece from outside Europe, the plane ticket will probably be the most expensive item in your travel budget, and buying it can be an intimidating business. There will be a multitude of airlines and travel agencies hoping to separate you from your money, so take time to research the options. Start early – some of the cheapest tickets must be bought months in advance, and popular flights tend to sell out early.

Discounted tickets fall into two categories – official and unofficial. Official discount schemes include advance-purchase tickets, budget fares, Apex, Super-Apex and a few other variations on the theme. These tickets can be bought from travel agencies or direct from the airline. They often have restrictions – advance purchase being the usual one. There might also be restrictions on the period you must be away, such as a minimum of 14 days and a maximum of one year.

Unofficial tickets are simply discounted tickets the airlines release through selected travel agencies.

Return tickets can often be cheaper than a one-way ticket. Generally, you can find discounted tickets at prices as low as, or even lower than, Apex or budget tickets. Phone around travel agencies for bargains.

If you are buying a ticket to fly out of Greece, Athens is one of the major centres in Europe for budget air fares.

In Greece, as everywhere else, always remember to reconfirm your onward or return

Air Travel Glossary

Alliances Many of the world's leading airlines are now intimately involved with each other, sharing everything from reservations systems and check-in to aircraft and frequent-flyer schemes. Opponents say that alliances restrict competition. Whatever the arguments, there is no doubt that big alliances are the way of the future.

Courier Fares Businesses often need to send urgent documents or freight securely and quickly. Courier companies hire people to accompany the package through customs and, in return, offer a discount ticket which is sometimes a bargain. However, you may have to surrender all your baggage allowance and take only carry-on luggage.

Fares Airlines traditionally offer 1st-class (coded F), business class (coded J) and economy class (coded Y) tickets. These days there are so many promotional and discounted fares available that few passengers pay full fare.

Lost Tickets If you lose your airline ticket, an airline will usually treat it like a travellers cheque and, after inquiries, issue you with another one. Legally, however, an airline is entitled to treat it like cash and if you lose it then it's gone forever. Take very good care of your tickets.

Onward Tickets An entry requirement for many countries is that you have a ticket out of the country. If you're unsure of your next move, the easiest solution is to buy the cheapest onward ticket to a neighbouring country or a ticket from a reliable airline which can later be refunded if you do not use it.

Open-Jaw Tickets These are return tickets where you fly out to one place but return from another. If available, this can save you backtracking to your arrival point.

Overbooking Since every flight has some passengers who fail to show up, airlines often book more passengers than they have seats. Usually excess passengers make up for the no-shows, but occasionally somebody gets 'bumped' onto the next available flight. Guess who it is most likely to be? The passengers who check in late. If you do get 'bumped', you are normally offered some form of compensation.

Reconfirmation Some airlines require you to reconfirm your flight at least 72 hours prior to departure. Check your travel documents to see if this is the case

Restrictions Discounted tickets often have various restrictions on them – such as needing to be paid for in advance and incurring a penalty to be altered or cancelled. Others are restrictions on the minimum and maximum period you must be away.

Round-the-World Tickets RTW tickets give you a limited period (usually a year) in which to circumnavigate the globe. You can go anywhere the carrying airlines go, as long as you don't backtrack. The number of stopovers or total number of separate flights is decided before you set off and they usually cost a bit more than a basic return flight.

Ticketless Travel Airlines are gradually waking up to the realisation that paper tickets are unnecessary encumbrances. On simple one-way or return trips, reservations details can be held on computer and the passenger merely shows ID to claim their seat.

Transferred Tickets Airline tickets cannot be transferred from one person to another. Travellers sometimes try to sell the return half of their ticket, but officials can ask you to prove that you are the person named on the ticket. On an international flight, tickets are compared with passports.

bookings by the specified time – usually 72 hours before departure on international flights. If you don't, there's a risk you'll turn up at the airport only to find you've missed your flight because it was rescheduled, or that the airline has given the seat to someone else.

Charter Flights

Charter flight tickets are for seats left vacant on flights that have been block-booked by package companies. Tickets are cheap but conditions apply on charter flights to Greece. A ticket must be accompanied by an accommodation booking. This is normally circumvented by travel agencies issuing accommodation vouchers that are not meant to be used – even if the hotel named on the voucher actually exists. The law requiring accommodation bookings was introduced in the 1980s to prevent budget travellers flying to Greece on cheap charter flights and sleeping rough on beaches or in parks. It hasn't worked.

Charter flight tickets are valid for up to four weeks, and usually have a minimum-stay requirement of at least three days. Sometimes it's worth buying a charter return even if you think you want to stay for longer than four weeks. The tickets can be so cheap that you can afford to throw away the return portion.

The travel section of major newspapers is the place to look for cheap charter deals. More information on charter flights is given later in this chapter under specific point-of-origin headings.

Courier Flights

Another budget option (sometimes even cheaper than a charter flight) is a courier flight. This deal entails accompanying freight or a parcel that will be collected at the destination. The drawbacks are that your time away may be limited to one or two weeks, your luggage is usually restricted to hand luggage (the parcel or freight you carry comes out of your luggage allowance), and you may have to be a resident of the country that operates the courier service and apply for an interview before they'll take you on.

Travel Agencies

Many of the larger travel agencies use the travel pages of national newspapers and magazines to promote their special deals. Before you make a decision, there are a number of questions you need to ask about the ticket. Find out the airline, the route, the duration of the journey, the stopovers allowed, any restrictions on the ticket and – above all – the price. Ask whether the fare quoted includes all taxes and other possible inclusions.

You may discover when you start ringing around that those impossibly cheap flights, charter or otherwise, are not available, but the agency just happens to know of another one that 'costs a bit more'. Or the agent may claim to have the last two seats available for Greece for the whole of July, which they will hold for a maximum of two hours only. Don't panic – keep ringing around.

If you are flying to Greece from the USA, South-East Asia or the UK, you will probably find the cheapest flights are being advertised by obscure agencies whose names haven't yet reached the telephone directory – the proverbial bucket shops. Many such firms are honest and solvent, but there are a few rogues who will take your money and disappear, only to reopen elsewhere a month or two later under a new name. If you feel suspicious about a firm, don't give them all the money at once – leave a small deposit and pay the balance when you get the ticket. If they insist on cash in advance, go somewhere else or be prepared to take a big risk. Once you have booked the flight with the agency, ring the airline to check you have a confirmed booking.

It can be easier on the nerves to pay a bit more for the security of a better-known travel agency. Firms such as STA Travel, with offices worldwide, Council Travel in the USA or Travel CUTS in Canada offer good prices to Europe (including Greece), and are unlikely to disappear overnight.

The fares quoted in this book are intended as a guide only. They are approximate and are based on the rates advertised by travel agencies at the time of writing.

Phone numbers listed incorporate changes due in Oct 2002; see p55

Travel Insurance

The kind of cover you get depends on your insurance and type of ticket, so ask both your insurer and your ticket-issuing agency to explain where you stand. Ticket loss is usually covered. Buy travel insurance as early as possible. If you buy it just before you fly, you may find you're not covered for such problems as delays caused by industrial action. Make sure you have a separate record of all your ticket details – preferably a photocopy.

Paying for your ticket with a credit card sometimes provides limited travel insurance, and you may be able to reclaim the payment if the operator doesn't deliver. In the UK, for instance, credit card providers are required by law to reimburse consumers if a company goes into liquidation and the amount in contention is more than UK£100.

Travellers with Special Needs

If you've broken a leg, require a special diet, are travelling in a wheelchair, are taking a baby, or whatever, let the airline staff know as soon as possible – preferably when booking your ticket. Check that your request has been registered when you reconfirm your booking (at least 72 hours before departure) and again when you check in at the airport.

Children under two years of age travel for 10% of the standard fare (or free on some airlines) as long as they don't occupy a seat. But they do not get a baggage allowance. 'Skycots' should be provided by the airline if requested in advance. These will take a child weighing up to about 10kg. Olympic Airways charges half-fare for accompanied children aged between two and 12 years, while most other airlines charge two-thirds.

Departure Tax

The airport tax is €12 for passengers travelling to destinations within the EU, and €22 for other destinations. It applies to travellers aged over 5, and is paid when you buy your ticket, not at the airport.

Passengers aged over two departing from Athens are liable for a further €10.30 as a contribution to facilities at the new airport, and a security charge of €1.29. These charges also are paid when you buy your ticket.

The USA

Discount travel agencies in the USA are known as consolidators (although you won't see a sign on the door saying Consolidator). San Francisco is the ticket consolidator capital of America, although some good deals can be found in Los Angeles, New York and other big cities. Consolidators can be found through the Yellow Pages or the major daily newspapers. The *New York Times,* the *Los Angeles Times,* the *Chicago Tribune* and the *San Francisco Examiner* all produce weekly travel sections in which you will find a number of travel agency ads.

Council Travel, America's largest student travel organisation, has around 60 offices in the USA; its head office (☎ 800-226-8624) is at 205 E 42 St, New York, NY 10017. Call it for the office nearest you or visit its Web site at Ⓦ www.ciee.org. STA Travel (☎ 800-777-0112) has offices in Boston, Chicago, Miami, New York, Philadelphia, San Francisco and other major cities. Call the toll-free 800 number for office locations or visit its Web site at Ⓦ www.statravel.com.

New York has the widest range of options to Athens. The route to Europe is very competitive and there are new deals almost every day. At the time of writing, Virgin Atlantic led the way, offering Athens for US$944 return in high season via London, falling to US$740 at other times. Olympic Airways flies direct at least once a day, and Delta Airlines flies direct three times a week. Apex fares with Olympic range from US$730 to US$1015, depending on the season. These fares don't include taxes.

Boston is the only other east coast city with direct flights to Athens – on Saturday with Olympic Airways. Fares are the same as for flights from New York.

There are no direct flights to Athens from the west coast. There are, however, connecting flights to Athens from many US cities, either linking with Olympic Airways in New York or flying with one of the European national airlines to their home country, and then on to Athens. At the time of writing,

Virgin Atlantic was offering Los Angeles–Athens for US$982 return in high season, falling to US$879 at other times.

Courier flights to Athens are occasionally advertised in the newspapers, or you could contact air freight companies listed in the phone book. You may even have to go to the air freight company to get an answer – the companies aren't always keen to give out information over the phone. *Travel Unlimited* (PO Box 1058, Allston, MA 02134, USA) is a monthly travel newsletter from the USA that publishes many courier flight deals from destinations worldwide. A 12-month subscription to the newsletter costs US$25, or US$35 for residents outside the US. Another possibility (at least for US residents) is to join the International Association of Air Travel Couriers (IAATC). The membership fee of US$45 gets members a bimonthly update of air courier offerings, access to a fax-on-demand service with daily updates of last minute specials and the bimonthly newsletter the Shoestring Traveler. For more information, contact IAATC (☎ 561-582-8320) or visit its Web site, ☒ www .courier.org. However, be aware that joining this organisation does not guarantee that you'll get a courier flight.

If you're travelling from Athens to the USA, the travel agencies around Syntagma offer the following one-way fares (prices do not include airport tax): Atlanta €340, Chicago €340, Los Angeles €380 and New York €265.

Canada

Canadian discount air ticket sellers are also known as consolidators and their air fares tend to be about 10% higher than those sold in the USA. The *Globe & Mail*, the *Toronto Star*, the *Montreal Gazette* and the *Vancouver Sun* carry travel agencies' ads and are a good place to look for cheap fares.

Travel CUTS (☎ 1800-667 2887) is Canada's national student travel agency and has offices in all major cities. Its Web address is ☒ www.travelcuts.com.

Olympic Airways has two flights weekly from Toronto to Athens via Montreal.

There are no direct flights from Vancouver, but there are connecting flights via Toronto, Amsterdam, Frankfurt and London on Canadian Airlines, KLM, Lufthansa and British Airways. You should be able to get to Athens from Toronto and Montreal for about C$1150/950 in high/low season or from Vancouver for C$1500/1300.

For courier flights originating in Canada, contact FB On Board Courier Services in Montreal (☎ 514-631 7929). It can get you to London for C$760 return.

At the time of writing, budget travel agencies in Athens were advertising flights to both Toronto and Montreal for €330, plus airport tax.

Australia

Two well-known agencies for cheap fares are STA Travel and Flight Centre. STA Travel (☎ 03-9349 2411) has its main office at 224 Faraday St, Carlton, VIC 3053, and offices in all major cities and on many university campuses. Call ☎ 131 776 Australia-wide for the location of your nearest branch or visit its Web site at ☒ www.statravel .com.au. Flight Centre (☎ 131 600 Australia-wide) has a central office at 82 Elizabeth St, Sydney, and there are dozens of offices throughout Australia. Its Web address is ☒ www.flightcentre.com.au.

Olympic Airways has two flights weekly from Sydney and Melbourne to Athens. Return fares normally cost from about A$1799 in low season to A$2199 in high season.

Thai International and Singapore Airlines also have convenient connections to Athens, as well as a reputation for good service. If you're planning on doing a bit of flying around Europe, it's worth checking around for special deals from the major European airlines. Alitalia, KLM and Lufthansa are three likely candidates with good European networks.

If you're travelling from Athens to Australia, a one-way ticket to Sydney or Melbourne costs about €550, plus airport tax.

New Zealand

Round-the-World (RTW) and Circle Pacific fares are usually the best value, often cheaper than a return ticket. Depending on which airline you choose, you may fly across Asia, with possible stopovers in India, Bangkok or Singapore, or across the USA, with possible stopovers in Honolulu, Australia or one of the Pacific Islands.

The *New Zealand Herald* has a travel section in which travel agents advertise fares. Flight Centre (☎ 09-309 6171) has a large central office in Auckland at National Bank Towers (corner Queen and Darby Sts) and many branches throughout the country. STA Travel (☎ 09-309 0458) has its main office at 10 High St, Auckland, and has other offices in Auckland as well as in Hamilton, Palmerston North, Wellington, Christchurch and Dunedin. The Web address is Ⓦ www.sta.travel.com.au.

The UK

Airline ticket discounters are known as bucket shops in the UK. Despite the somewhat disreputable name, there is nothing under-the-counter about them. Discount air travel is big business in London. Advertisements for many travel agencies appear in the travel pages of the weekend broadsheets, such as the *Independent on Saturday* and the *Sunday Times*. Look out for the free magazines, such as *TNT*, which are widely available in London – start by looking outside the main railway and underground stations.

For students or travellers under 26, popular travel agencies in the UK include STA Travel (☎ 020-7361 6161), which has an office at 86 Old Brompton Rd, London SW7 3LQ, and other offices in London and Manchester. Visit its Web site at Ⓦ www.statravel .co.uk. USIT Campus Travel (☎ 020-7730 3402), 52 Grosvenor Gardens, London SW1WOAG, has branches throughout the UK. The Web address is Ⓦ www.usitcam pus.com. Both of these agencies sell tickets to all travellers but cater especially to young people and students. Charter flights can work out as a cheaper alternative to scheduled flights, especially if you do not qualify for the under-26 and student discounts.

Other recommended bucket shops include: Trailfinders (☎ 020-7937 1234), 194 Kensington High St, London W8 7RG;

Bridge the World (☎ 020-7734 7447), 4 Regent Place, London W1R 5FB; and Flightbookers (☎ 020-7757 2000), 177–178 Tottenham Court Rd, London W1P 9LF.

British Airways, Olympic Airways and Virgin Atlantic operate daily flights between London and Athens. Pricing is very competitive, with all three offering return tickets for around UK£220 in high season, plus tax. At other times, prices fall as low at UK£104, plus tax. British Airways has flights from Edinburgh, Glasgow and Manchester.

Cronus Airlines (☎ 020-7580 3500) flies the London-Athens route five times weekly for UK£210, and offers connections to Thessaloniki on the same fare. Most scheduled flights from London leave from Heathrow.

The cheapest scheduled flights are with EasyJet (☎ 0870 6 000 000), the no-frills specialist, which has two Luton-Athens flights daily. One-way fares range from UK£52 to UK£112 in high season, and from a bargain UK£17 to UK£42 at other times. Its Web site is Ⓦ www.easyjet.com.

There are numerous charter flights between the UK and Greece. Typical London-Athens charter fares are UK£99/149 one way/return in the low season and UK£119/ 209 in the high season. These prices are for advance bookings, but even in high season it's possible to pick up last-minute deals for as little as UK£69/109. There are also charter flights from Birmingham, Cardiff, Glasgow, Luton, Manchester and Newcastle.

If you're flying from Athens to the UK, budget fares start at €75 to London or €90 to Manchester, plus airport tax.

Continental Europe

Athens is linked to every major city in Europe by either Olympic Airways or the flag carrier of each country.

London is the discount capital of Europe, but Amsterdam, Frankfurt, Berlin and Paris are also major centres for cheap air fares.

Across Europe many travel agencies have ties with STA Travel, where cheap tickets can be purchased and STA-issued tickets can be altered (usually for a US$25 fee). Outlets in major cities include: Voyages

Wasteels (☎ 08 03 88 70 04, fax 01 43 25 46 25), 11 rue Dupuytren, 756006 Paris; STA Travel (☎ 030-311 0950, fax 313 0948), Goethestrasse 73, 10625 Berlin; and Passaggi (☎ 06-474 0923, fax 482 7436), Stazione Termini FS, Gelleria Di Tesla, Rome.

France has a network of student travel agencies, which can supply discount tickets to travellers of all ages. OTU Voyages (☎ 01 44 41 38 50) has a central Paris office at 39 Ave Georges Bernanos (5e) and another 42 offices around the country. The Web address is Ⓦ www.otu.fr. Acceuil des Jeunes en France (☎ 01 42 77 87 80), 119 rue Saint Martin (4e), is another popular discount travel agency.

General travel agencies in Paris include Nouvelles Frontières (☎ 08 03 33 33 33), 5 Ave de l'Opéra (1er), Ⓦ www.nouvelles -frontieres.com, and Voyageurs du Monde (☎ 01 42 86 16 00) at 55 rue Sainte Anne (2e).

Belgium, Switzerland, the Netherlands and Greece are also good places for buying discount air tickets. In Belgium Acotra Student Travel Agency (☎ 02-512 86 07) at rue de la Madeline, Brussels, and WATS Reizen (☎ 03-226 16 26) at de Keyserlei 44, Antwerp, are both well known agencies. In Switzerland SSR Voyages (☎ 01-297 11 11) specialises in student, youth and budget fares. In Zurich there is a branch at Leonhardstrasse 10 and there are branches in most major cities. The Web address is Ⓦ www.ssr.ch.

In the Netherlands NBBS Reizen is the official student travel agency. You can find it in Amsterdam (☎ 020-624 09 89) at Rokin 66 and there are several other agencies around the city. Another recommended travel agency in Amsterdam is Malibu Travel (☎ 020-626 32 30) at Prinsengracht 230.

If you're travelling from Athens to Europe, budget fares to a host of European cities are widely advertised by the travel agents around Syntagma. Following are some typical one-way fares (not including airport tax):

destination	one-way
Amsterdam	€170
Copenhagen	€175
Frankfurt	€165
Madrid	€220

destination	one-way
Milan	€145
Munich	€165
Paris	€165
Rome	€125

Turkey

Olympic Airways and Turkish Airlines share the İstanbul-Athens route, with at least one flight a day each. The full fare is US$330 one way. Students qualify for a 50% discount on both airlines.

There are no direct flights from Ankara to Athens; all flights go via İstanbul.

Cyprus

Olympic Airways and Cyprus Airways share the Cyprus-Greece routes. Both airlines have three flights daily from Larnaca to Athens, and there are five flights weekly to Thessaloniki. Cyprus Airways also flies from Paphos to Athens once a week in winter, and twice a week in summer.

LAND
Turkey

Bus The Hellenic Railways Organisation (OSE) operates Athens-İstanbul buses (22 hours, €67.50) daily except Wednesday, leaving the Peloponnese train station in Athens at 7pm and travelling via Thessaloniki and Alexandroupolis. Students qualify for a 20% discount and children under 12 travel half price. See the Getting There & Away sections for each city for information on where to buy tickets. Buses from İstanbul to Athens leave the Anadolu Terminal (Anatolia Terminal) at the Topkapı *otogar* (bus station) at 10am daily except Sunday.

Train There are daily trains between Athens and İstanbul (€58.70) via Thessaloniki (€39) and Alexandroupolis (€19.50). There are often delays at the border and the journey can take much longer than the supposed 22 hours. You'd be well advised to take the bus.

Car & Motorcycle The crossing points are at Kipi, 43km north-east of Alexandroupolis, and at Kastanies, 139km north-east of Alexandroupolis.

Bulgaria
Bus The OSE operates two Athens-Sofia buses (15 hours, €45.50) daily except Monday, leaving at 7am and 5pm. It also operates Thessaloniki-Sofia buses (7½ hours, €19, four daily).

Train There is a daily Athens-Sofia train (18 hours, €30.65) via Thessaloniki (nine hours, €15.60). From Sofia, there are daily connections to Budapest (€48.10) and connections to Bucharest (€81) on Wednesday and Sunday.

Car & Motorcycle The Bulgarian border crossing is at Promahonas, 145km northeast of Thessaloniki and 50km from Serres.

Albania
Bus There is a daily OSE bus between Athens and Tirana (€35.20) via Ioannina and Gjirokaster. The bus departs Athens (Peloponnese train station) at 7pm arriving in Tirana the following day at 5pm. There are buses from Thessaloniki to Korça (Korytsa in Greek) daily at 8am and noon. The fare is €19.

Car & Motorcycle If travelling by car or motorcycle, there are two crossing points between Greece and Albania.

The main border crossing is 60km northwest of Ioannina. Take the main Ioannina-Konitsa road and turn left at Kalpaki. This road leads to the border town of Kakavia. The other border crossing is at the town of Krystallopigi, 14km west of Kotas on the Florina-Kastoria road.

Former Yugoslav Republic of Macedonia
Train There is a daily train from Thessaloniki to Skopje (three hours, €12.50) at 6.15am. It continues to the Serbian capital of Belgrade (12 hours, €28.50).

Car & Motorcycle The main crossing between Greece and FYROM is at Evzoni, 68km north of Thessaloniki. This is the main highway to Skopje, which continues to Belgrade.

Western Europe
Overland travel between Western Europe and Greece is almost a thing of the past. Air fares are so cheap that land transport cannot compete. Travelling from the UK to Greece through Europe means crossing various borders, so check whether any visas are required before setting out.

Bus There are no bus services to mainland Greece from the UK, nor from anywhere else in northern Europe. Bus companies can no longer compete with cheap air fares.

Train Unless you have a Eurail pass or are aged under 26 and eligible for a discounted fare, travelling to Greece by train is prohibitively expensive. Indeed, the chances of anyone wanting to travel from London to Athens by train are considered so remote that it's no longer possible to buy a single ticket for this journey. The trip involves travelling from London to Paris on the Eurostar (UK£105 to UK£165 one way), followed by Paris-Brindisi (UK£102.50 one way), then a ferry from Brindisi to Patras – and finally a train from Patras to Athens.

Greece is part of the Eurail network. Eurail passes can only be bought by residents of non-European countries and are supposed to be purchased before arriving in Europe. They can, however, be bought in Europe as long as your passport proves that you've been there for less than six months. In London, head for the Rail Europe Travel Centre (☎ 08705 848 848), 179 Piccadilly, W1. Sample fares include US$420 for an adult Eurail Selectpass, which permits eight days' 1st-class travel in two months, and US$294 for the equivalent youth pass for 2nd-class travel. Check the Eurail Web site (**W** www.eurail.com) for full details of passes and prices.

If you are starting your European travels in Greece, you can buy your Eurail pass from the Hellenic Railways Organisation offices at Karolou 1 and Filellinon 17 in Athens, and at the station in Patras and Thessaloniki.

Greece is also part of the Inter-Rail Pass system. A one-month Global Pass (all zones) costs UK£319 for travellers over 26, and UK£229 for under 26. See the Inter Rail Web site (**W** www.interrailnet.com) for details.

Car & Motorcycle Before the troubles in the former Yugoslavia began, most motorists driving from the UK to Greece opted for the direct route: Ostend, Brussels, Salzburg and then down the Yugoslav highway through Zagreb, Belgrade and Skopje and crossing the border to Evzoni.

These days most people drive to an Italian port and get a ferry to Greece. Coming from the UK, this means driving through France, where petrol costs and road tolls are exorbitant.

SEA
Turkey

There are five regular ferry services between Turkey's Aegean coast and the Greek islands. Tickets for all ferries to Turkey must be bought a day in advance. You will almost certainly be asked to turn in your passport the night before the trip but don't worry, you'll get it back the next day before you board the boat. Port tax for departures to Turkey is €8.80.

See the relevant sections under individual island entries for more information about the following services.

Rhodes to Marmaris There are daily ferries from Rhodes to Marmaris (€47 one way) between April and October and less frequent services in winter. Prices vary, so shop around.

The hydrofoils on this route are cheaper. There are also daily services to Marmaris (weather permitting) from April to October for €32.30/39.70 one way/return, plus port tax.

Chios to Çeşme There are daily Chios-Çeşme boats from July to September, dropping steadily back to one boat a week in winter. Tickets cost €38.50/50 one way/return, plus port taxes.

Kos to Bodrum There are daily ferries in summer from Kos to Bodrum (ancient

Halicarnassus) in Turkey. Boats leave at 8.30am and return at 4pm. The one-hour journey costs €30-38 return, including port taxes.

Lesvos to Ayvalık There are up to four boats weekly on this route in high season. Tickets cost €38/47 one way/return.

Samos to Kuşadası There are two boats daily to Kuşadası (for Ephesus) from Samos in summer, dropping to one or two boats weekly in winter. Tickets cost around €41 return, plus taxes.

Italy

There are ferries to Greece from the Italian ports of Ancona, Bari, Brindisi, Trieste and Venice. For more information about these services, see the Patras, Igoumenitsa, Corfu and Kefallonia sections.

The ferries can get very crowded in summer. If you want to take a vehicle across it's a good idea to make a reservation. In the UK, reservations can be made on almost all of these ferries at Viamare Travel Ltd (**☎** 020-7431 4560, fax 7431 5456, **e** ferries@viamare.com), 2 Sumatra Rd, London NW6 IPU.

You'll find all the latest information about ferry routes, schedules and services on the Internet. For a good overview try **W** www.ferries.gr. Most of the ferry companies have their own Web sites, including:

ANEK Lines
  www.anek.gr
Fragline
  www.fragline.gr
Hellenic Mediterranean Lines
  www.hml.it
Italian Ferries
  www.italianferries.it
Marlines
  www.marlines.com
Minoan Lines
  www.minoan.gr
Blue Star Ferries
  www.bluestarferries.com
Superfast
  www.superfast.com
Ventouris
  www.ventouris.gr

Ferries from Italy at a Glance

origin	destination	company	duration (hours)	price (€)	frequency
Ancona	Corfu	ANEK	14½	63.40	1 weekly
Ancona	Igoumenitsa	ANEK	15	63.40	1 daily
Ancona	Igoumenitsa	Blue Star	15	61.35	1 daily
Ancona	Igoumenitsa	Minoan	15-19	71.60	6 weekly
Ancona	Igoumenitsa	Superfast	15	78.10	1 daily
Ancona	Patras	ANEK	21	63.40	1 daily
Ancona	Patras	Blue Star	21	61.35	1 daily
Ancona	Patras	Minoan	20-25	71.60	6 weekly
Ancona	Patras	Superfast	19-21½	78.10	2 daily
Bari	Corfu	Marlines	10½	39.65	1 weekly
Bari	Corfu	Ventouris	10	45.50	6 weekly
Bari	Igoumenitsa	Marlines	12	39.65	4 weekly
Bari	Igoumenitsa	Ventouris	11½	45.50	1 daily
Bari	Igoumenitsa	Superfast	9½	51.40	1 daily
Bari	Patras	Superfast	15½	51.40	1 daily
Bari	Patras	Ventouris	17½	45.50	3 weekly
*Brindisi	Corfu	Italian Ferries	3¼	65.00	1 daily
*Brindisi	Corfu	Ventouris H/S	3¼	65.00	6 weekly
*Brindisi	Igoumenitsa	Ventouris H/S	4	65.00	6 weekly
Brindisi	Corfu	Blue Star	7	48.15	1 daily
Brindisi	Corfu	Ventouris	7	44.60	6 weekly
Brindisi	Corfu	Fragline	7	43.80	6 weekly
Brindisi	Igoumenitsa	Blue Star	8½	48.15	1 daily
Brindisi	Igoumenitsa	Five Star Lines	8½	42.00	3 weekly
Brindisi	Igoumenitsa	Fragline	8	43.80	1 daily
Brindisi	Igoumenitsa	Medlink	8½	44.00	3 weekly
Brindisi	Igoumenitsa	Ventouris	8	44.60	6 weekly
Brindisi	Kefallonia	Medlink	11	44.00	4 weekly
Brindisi	Patras	Blue Star	13	48.15	1 daily
Brindisi	Patras	Five Star Lines	15½	42.00	3 weekly
Brindisi	Patras	Hellenic Mediterranean	15	47.00	3 weekly
Brindisi	Patras	Medlink	14	44.00	3 weekly
*Brindisi	Paxi	Ventouris H/S	4¾	82.20	3 weekly
*Brindisi	Paxi	Italian Ferries	4½	82.20	1 daily
Trieste	Corfu	ANEK	21	71.35	2 weekly
Trieste	Igoumenitsa	ANEK	22-24	71.30	1 daily
Trieste	Patras	ANEK	29-31	71.30	1 daily
Venice	Corfu	Minoan	19-27	71.60	1 daily
Venice	Igoumenitsa	Blue Star	26	61.35	4 weekly
Venice	Igoumenitsa	Minoan	20½-25½	71.60	1 daily
Venice	Patras	Minoan	26-35	71.60	1 daily
Venice	Igoumenitsa	Blue Star	35	61.35	4 weekly

(*high-speed catamaran)

Doric Temple of Aphaia, Aegina

Hydra's hungry cats line up to sample the morning's catch

Local produce at the Glyfada market, south of Athens

Hydra Town's busy port with its pastel mansions stacked up the hillside

The sun sets over the island of Santorini

Crates of small fish, Naxos

Village of Apollonas, Naxos

The ferry services table in this chapter is for high season (July and August), and prices are for one-way deck class. Deck class on these services means exactly that. If you want a reclining, aircraft-type seat, you'll be up for another 10% to 15% on top of the listed fares. Most companies offer discounts for return travel. Prices are about 30% less in the low season.

Ancona to Patras This route has become increasingly popular in recent years. There can be up to three boats daily in summer, and at least one a day year-round. All ferry operators in Ancona have booths at the *stazione marittima* (ferry terminal) off Piazza Candy, where you can pick up timetables and price lists and make bookings.

Superfast Ferries (☎ 071-207 0218) provides the fastest and most convenient service. It has also accepts Eurail passes. Pass users must pay port taxes and a high season loading of €8.80 in July and August. ANEK Lines (☎ 071-207 2275) and Blue Star Ferries (☎ 071-207 1068) are about 20% cheaper.

Bari to Corfu, Igoumenitsa & Patras Superfast Ferries (☎ 080-52 11 416) also accept Eurail passes on its Bari-Patras route. Ventouris (☎ 080-521 7609) and Marlines (☎ 080-52 31 824) operate to Corfu and Igoumenitsa. Ventouris sails on to Patras three times weekly.

Brindisi to Corfu, Igoumenitsa, Patras & Paxi The route from Brindisi to Patras is the cheapest and most popular of the various Adriatic crossings. There can be up to five boats daily in high season. Most travel via Corfu and Igoumenitsa.

Companies operating ferries from Brindisi to Greece are: Blue Star Ferries (☎ 0831-548 115), Costa Morena; Five Star Lines (☎ 0831-524 869), represented by Angela Gioia Agenzia Marittima, Via F Consiglio 55; Fragline (☎ 0831-548 540), Via Spalato 31; Hellenic Mediterranean Lines (☎ 0831-528 531), Corso Garibaldi 8; Med Link Lines (☎ 0831-548 116/7), represented by Discovery Shipping, Costa Morena; and Ventouris (☎ 0831-521 614), Corso Garibaldi 56.

Blue Star Ferries and Hellenic Mediterranean accept Eurail passes, although you will still have to pay the port tax of €6.45 and a high-season loading of €8.80 in July and August. Hellenic Mediterranean issues vouchers for travel with Med Link on days when there is no Hellenic Mediterranean service. Ventouris Ferries (see earlier) and Italian Ferries (☎ 0831-590 305), Corso Garibaldi 96, operate high-speed catamarans to Corfu and Paxi.

Brindisi to Kefallonia Med Link stops at Sami (€44, 11 hours) on its Brindisi-Patras run during August and early September.

Trieste to Patras ANEK Lines (☎ 040-322 0561), Stazione Marittima di Trieste, has daily boats to Patras via Igoumenitsa.

Venice to Patras Minoan Lines (☎ 041-240 7101), Stazione Marittima 123, has boats to Patras via Corfu and Igoumenitsa. Blue Star Ferries (☎ 041-277 0559), Stazione Marittima 123, sails via Igoumenitsa four times weekly.

Cyprus & Israel

Two companies ply the route between Piraeus and the Israeli port of Haifa, via the port of Lemesos (Limassol) on Cyprus. These boats also stop at Rhodes and various other Greek islands.

Salamis Lines leaves Haifa at 7pm Sunday and Lemesos at 4pm Tuesday, reaching Rhodes at 11am Wednesday and Piraeus at 9.30am Thursday. The return service departs Piraeus at 7pm on Thursday, and stops at Patmos on the way to Rhodes, Lemesos and Haifa. Bookings in Haifa are handled by Rosenfeld Shipping (☎ 04-861 3670), 104 Ha'Atzmaut St, and in Lemesos by Salamis Tours (☎ 05-355 555), Salamis House, 28 October Ave.

Poseidon Lines has two services. The *Sea Serenade* sails from Haifa at 8pm Friday and Lemesos at 2pm Saturday, reaching Rhodes at 8am Sunday and Piraeus at 6.30am Monday. It leaves Piraeus at 7pm on Monday, stopping Patmos on the way to Rhodes, Lemesos and Haifa. It switches to a different timetable in late July and August, leaving Haifa at 8pm Thursday and making additional stops at Iraklio (Crete) and Santorini on the way to Piraeus. On the way back, it skips Patmos but calls at Mykonos, Santorini and Iraklio.

Poseidon's *FB Olympia* leaves Haifa at 8pm Monday and Lemesos at 2pm Tuesday, reaching Rhodes at 6.30am Wednesday and Piraeus at 7am Thursday. It departs Piraeus at 7pm Thursday, and stops at Patmos on the way to Rhodes, Lemesos and Haifa. Bookings in Haifa are handled by Caspi Travel (☎ 04-867 4444), 76 Ha'Atzmaut St, and in Lemesos by Poseidon Lines Cyprus (☎ 05-745 666), 124 Franklin Roosevelt St.

Salamis and Poseidon charge the same fares. Deck class from Haifa costs €97 to Rhodes, Iraklio and Santorini, and €106 to Piraeus. Fares from Lemesos are €62 to Rhodes, Iraklio and Santorini, and €70.50

to Piraeus. Aircraft-type seats cost about 10% more, while a berth in the cheapest cabin costs about 50% more.

You'll find the latest information on these services on the Internet: **W** www .ferries.gr for Poseidon Lines, and **W** www .viamare.com/Salamis for Salamis Lines.

ORGANISED TOURS

If a package holiday of sun, sand and sea doesn't appeal to you, but you would like to holiday with a group, there are several companies that organise special-interest holidays.

There are lots of UK companies specialising in package holidays to unspoilt areas of Greece, including Laskarina (☎ 01629-824 881) – Web site **W** www.laskarina.co.uk; Greek Islands Club (☎ 020-8232 9780); Greek Options (☎ 020-7233 5233); and Simply Ionian (☎ 020-8995 9323).

Island Holidays (☎ 0176-477 0107) specialises in cultural holidays on Crete.

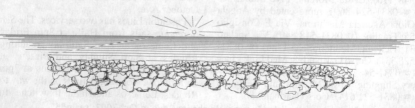

Greece is an easy place to travel around thanks to a comprehensive public transport system.

Buses are the mainstay of land transport, with a network that reaches out to the smallest villages. Trains are a good alternative, where available. To most visitors, though, travelling in Greece means island hopping on the multitude of ferries that crisscross the Adriatic and the Aegean. If you're in a hurry, Greece also has an extensive domestic air network.

The information in this chapter was for the 2001 high season. You'll find lots of travel information on the Internet also. The Web site W www.ellada.com is a useful general site with lots of links, including airline timetables.

AIR
Domestic Air Services
Olympic Airways The vast majority of domestic flights are handled by the country's much-maligned national carrier, Olympic Airways, together with its offshoot, Olympic Aviation.

Olympic has offices wherever there are flights (see the tables following), as well as in other major towns. The head office (☎ 21 0966 6666) is at Leoforos Syngrou 96 in Athens. The toll-free number for reservations is ☎ 0801 44444.

The prices listed in this book are for full-fare economy, and include domestic taxes and charges (see the following Departure Tax section for details). Olympic also offers cheaper options between Athens and some of the more popular destinations such as Corfu, Iraklio, Lesvos, Rhodes and Thessaloniki. There are discounts for return tickets for travel between Monday and Thursday, and bigger discounts for trips that include a Saturday night away. You'll find full details on the Internet at W www.olympic-airways.gr, as well as information on timetables.

The baggage allowance on domestic flights is 15kg, or 20kg if the domestic flight is part of an international journey. Olympic offers a 25% student discount on domestic flights, but only if the flight is part of an international journey.

Other Airlines Crete-based Aegean Airlines is the sole survivor of the many new airlines that emerged to challenge Olympic following the 1993 decision to end Olympic's monopoly on domestic flights.

While other airlines have come and gone, Aegean appears to have settled in for the long run following its merger with international operator Cronus Airlines in June 2001. It offers flights from Athens to Alexandroupolis, Corfu, Hania, Ioannina, Iraklio, Kavala, Lesvos, Rhodes, Santorini and Thessaloniki; from Thessaloniki to Iraklio, Lesvos, Rhodes and Santorini, and from Iraklio to Rhodes.

Full-fare economy costs slightly more than Olympic, but Aegean often has special deals. It offers a 20% youth discount for travellers under 26, and a similar discount for the over 60s.

You'll find details of prices and timetables on the Internet at W www.aegeanair.com. Aegean's toll-free number for reservations is ☎ 0801 20000.

Mainland Flights
Olympic and Aegean offer at least 15 flights a day between them to Thessaloniki (€92.50, 55 minutes). Both airlines also have two flights a day to Alexandroupolis (€87.75, 65 minutes) and Kavala (€85.15, one hour). Olympic also has five flights a week to Prevezaa (€60.45, one hour).

Mainland to Island Flights
Olympic Airways operates a busy schedule to the islands, particularly in summer. Athens has flights to 22 islands, with services to all the island groups as well as to three destinations on Crete – Hania, Iraklio and Sitia. Thessaloniki also has flights to all the island groups except the Sporades. See

the tables of summer flights (between 14 June and 26 September) from Athens and Thessaloniki to the Greek islands for details (fares given are one way). Aegean often has special fares on some of the more popular routes, so check around.

In spite of the number of flights, it can be hard to find a seat during July and August. Early bookings are recommended.

Flight schedules are greatly reduced in winter, especially to Mykonos, Paros, Skiathos and Santorini.

Inter-Island Flights

Olympic and Aegean both fly the Iraklio-Rhodes route; all other flights are operated by Olympic. See the accompanying table for details.

Air Services Within Greece

Flights from Athens to the Greek Islands (High Season)

destination	duration (min)	price (€)	freq. (weekly)	destination	duration (min)	price (€)	freq. (weekly)
Astypalea	65	74.55	5	Limnos	60	64.00	21
Chios	50	67.50	35	Milos	45	61.30	7
Corfu	50	92.45	26	Mykonos	45	78.65	43
Hania (Crete)	50	85.10	25	Naxos	45	75.45	7
Iraklio (Crete)	60	78.95	42	Paros	45	74.00	21
Sitia (Crete)	85	83.95	3	Rhodes	60	92.45	38
Ikaria	50	70.30	6	Samos	60	71.60	35
Karpathos	120	96.85	3	Santorini	50	83.35	56
Kefallonia	60	74.10	10	Skiathos	40	65.45	8
Kos	55	85.10	21	Skyros	50	55.50	2
Kythira	45	61.00	6	Syros	35	62.80	9
Leros	65	77.50	7	Zakynthos	35	72.20	7
Lesvos	50	80.15	29				

Flights from Thessaloniki to the Greek Islands (High Season)

destination	duration (min)	price (€)	freq. (weekly)	destination	duration (min)	price (€)	freq. (weekly)
Chios	50	76.30	3	Limnos	50	56.00	6
Corfu	50	73.40	3	Mykonos	75	91.30	2
Hania (Crete)	75	103.30	2	Rhodes	115	105.40	2
Iraklio (Crete)	110	97.00	3	Samos	80	88.00	3
Lesvos	60	76.30	6				

Inter-Island Flights (High Season)

origin	destination	duration (min)	price (€)	freq. (weekly)	origin	destination	duration (min)	price (€)	freq. (weekly)
Chios	Lesvos	60	41.40	1	Kastellorizo	Rhodes	45	35.80	7
Iraklio	Rhodes	45	79.50	4	Lesvos	Limnos	35	48.50	4
Iraklio	Santorini	40	56.05	2	Mykonos	Rhodes	60	78.10	2
Karpathos	Rhodes	40	44.30	14	Mykonos	Santorini	30	54.00	6
Karpathos	Kasos	15	23.50	3	Rhodes	Santorini	60	76.90	6
Kasos	Rhodes	40	44.30	3					

Domestic Departure Tax

The airport tax for domestic flights is €12, paid as part of the ticket. It applies to all passengers aged over five. Passengers aged over two departing from Athens must pay an additional €7.21 for the privilege of using the facilities at the new Eleftherios Venizelos International Airport, plus a security charge of €1.29. These charges also are paid as part of the ticket.

All prices quoted in this book include these taxes and charges where applicable.

BUS

All long-distance buses, on both the mainland and the islands, are operated by regional collectives known as KTEL (Koino Tamio Eispraxeon Leoforion). Every prefecture on the mainland has its own KTEL, which operates local services within the prefecture and services to the main towns of other prefectures. Most can be found on the Internet at W www.ktel.org. Fares are fixed by the government.

Mainland Services

The network is comprehensive. With the exception of towns in Thrace, which are serviced by Thessaloniki, all the major towns have frequent connections to Athens. The islands of Corfu, Kefallonia and Zakynthos can also be reached directly from Athens by bus – the fares include the price of the ferry ticket.

Larger towns usually have a central, covered bus station with seating, waiting rooms, toilets, and a snack bar selling pies, cakes and coffee. Big cities like Athens, Patras and Thessaloniki have several bus stations, each serving different regions.

Most booking offices have timetables in both Greek and Roman script. They show both the departure and return times – useful if you are making a day trip. Times are listed using the 24-hour-clock system.

When you buy a ticket you will be allotted a seat number, noted on the ticket. The seat number is indicated on the back of each seat of the bus, not on the back of the seat in front; this causes confusion among Greeks and tourists alike. You can board a bus without a ticket and pay on board, but on a popular route, or during the high season, this may mean having to stand. Keep your ticket for the duration of the journey; it will be checked several times en route.

Buses do not have toilets on board and they don't have refreshments available, so make sure you are prepared on both counts. Buses stop about every three hours on long journeys. Smoking is prohibited on all buses in Greece; only the chain-smoking drivers dare to ignore the no-smoking signs.

Fares and journey times on some of the major routes are: Athens-Thessaloniki (7½ hours, €26.40); Athens-Patras (three hours, €11.75); Athens-Volos (five hours, €17); and Athens-Corfu (11 hours, including ferry, €26.70).

Island Buses

Island bus services are less simple to summarise! There's an enormous difference in the level of services. Crete (which is split into three prefectures) is organised in the same way as the mainland – each prefecture has its own KTEL providing local services and services to the main towns of other prefectures. Most islands have just one bus company, operating out of the main town; some have just one bus.

As on the mainland, larger towns usually have a central, covered bus station with seating, waiting rooms, toilets, and a snack bar selling pies, cakes and coffee. In small towns and villages the 'bus station' may be no more than a bus stop outside a *kafeneio* or taverna that doubles as a booking office.

On islands where the capital is inland rather than a port, buses normally meet the boats. Some of the more remote islands have not yet acquired a bus, but most have some sort of motorised transport – even if it is only a bone-shaking, three-wheeled truck.

TRAIN

Most Greeks regard train travel as a poor alternative to road travel.

For starters, the rail network is limited. There are two main services: a standard-gauge line north from Athens to Thessaloniki and Alexandroupolis, and a narrow-gauge line from Athens to the Peloponnese.

There are also two very distinct levels of service: slow, stopping-all-stations services that crawl around the countryside, and express intercity trains that link the major cities.

The slow trains represent the country's cheapest form of public transport. The fares have hardly changed for years; 2nd-class fares are absurdly cheap, and even 1st class is much cheaper than bus travel. The downside is that the trains are painfully slow, uncomfortable and unreliable. There seems to be no effort to upgrade the dilapidated rolling stock. Unless you are travelling on a very tight budget, they are best left alone. Sample journey times and fares on these trains include Athens-Thessaloniki (7½ hours, 1st/2nd class €21/14), Athens-Patras (five hours, €7.95/5.30), and Thessaloniki-Alexandroupolis (seven hours, €14.60/9.70).

The intercity trains that link the major cities are a much better way to travel. The services are not necessarily express – the Greek terrain is too mountainous for that – but the trains are modern and comfortable. There are 1st- and 2nd-class smoking/non-smoking seats and there is a cafe-bar on board. On some services, meals can be ordered and delivered to your seat.

Ticket prices for intercity services are subject to a distance loading on top of the normal fares. Seat reservations should be made as far in advance as possible, especially in summer. Sample journey times and fares include Athens-Thessaloniki (six hours, 1st/2nd class €37.30/27.60), Athens-Patras (3½ hours, €13.80/10) and Thessaloniki-Alexandroupolis (5½ hours, €21.90/16.20).

A comfortable night service runs between Athens and Thessaloniki, with a choice of couchettes (from €5.90), two-bed compartments (€19) and single compartments (€29.35).

Eurail and Inter-Rail cards are valid in Greece, but it's not worth buying one if Greece is the only place you plan to use it. The passes can be used for 2nd-class travel on intercity services without paying the loading.

Tickets can be bought from OSE booking offices in a few major towns, otherwise from train stations. There is a 30% discount on return tickets. You'll find information on fares and schedules on the Hellenic Railways Organisation Web site at Ⓦ www.ose.gr.

CAR & MOTORCYCLE

Many of the islands are plenty big enough to warrant having your own vehicle. Roads have improved enormously in recent years, particularly on the larger, more visited islands like Crete. Few people bother to bring their own vehicle from Europe; there are plenty of places to hire cars.

There are also plenty of places to hire motorcycles, although the islands are not the best place to initiate yourself into motorcycling. There are still a lot of gravel roads – particularly on the islands. Novices should be particularly careful; dozens of tourists have accidents every year.

Almost all islands are served by car ferries, but they are expensive. Sample prices for small vehicles include Piraeus-Mykonos for €57.25; Piraeus-Crete (Hania and Iraklio) for €61.65; and Piraeus-Rhodes for €76.30. The charge for a large motorcycle is about the same as the price of a 3rd-class passenger ticket.

Petrol in Greece is expensive, and the farther you get from a major city the more it costs. Prices vary from petrol station to petrol station. Super can be found as cheaply as €0.70 per litre at big city discount places, but €0.75 to €0.85 is the normal range. You may pay closer to €0.90 per litre on many islands. The price range for unleaded – available everywhere – is from €0.75 to €0.85 per litre. Diesel costs about €0.60 per litre.

See the Documents section in the Facts for the Visitor chapter for information on licence requirements, and the Useful Organisations section for information about the Greek automobile club (ELPA).

Warning If you are planning to use a motorcycle or moped, check that your travel insurance covers you for injury resulting from a motorcycle accident. Many insurance companies don't offer this cover, so check the fine print!

Road Rules

In Greece, as throughout Continental Europe, you drive on the right and overtake on the left. Outside built-up areas, traffic on a main road has right of way at intersections. In towns, vehicles coming from the right have right of way. Seat belts must be worn in front seats, and in back seats if the car is fitted with them. Children under 12 years of age are not allowed in the front seat. It is compulsory to carry a first-aid kit, fire extinguisher and warning triangle, and it is forbidden to carry cans of petrol. Helmets are compulsory for motorcyclists if the motorcycle is 50cc or more.

Outside residential areas the speed limit is 120km/h on highways, 90km/h on other roads and 50km/h in built-up areas. The speed limit for motorcycles up to 100cc is 70km/h and for larger motorcycles, 90km/h.

Drivers exceeding the speed limit by 20% are liable for a fine of €58.70; and by 40%, €147. In practice, most tourists escape with a warning. Other offences and fines include: illegal overtaking (€293.50); going through a red light (€293.50); driving without a seat belt (€147.75); motorcyclist not wearing a helmet (€147.75); wrong way down one-way street (€147.75); and illegal parking (€29.35).

The police have also cracked down on drink-driving laws – at last. A blood-alcohol content of 0.05% is liable to incur a fine of €147.75, and over 0.08% is a criminal offence.

The police can issue traffic fines, but payment cannot be made on the spot – you will be told where to pay.

If you are involved in an accident and no-one is hurt, the police will not be required to write a report, but it is advisable to go to a nearby police station and explain what happened. A police report may be required for insurance purposes. If an accident involves injury, a driver who does not stop and does not inform the police may face a prison sentence.

Rental

Car Most of the big multinational car hire companies are represented in Athens and on the major tourist islands. High-season weekly rates with unlimited mileage start at about €380 for the smallest models, such as a Fiat Seicento. The rate drops to about €300 per week in winter. To these prices must be added VAT of 18%, or 13% on the islands of the Dodecanese, the North-Eastern Aegean and the Sporades. Then there are the optional extras, such as a collision damage waiver of €10.30 per day (more for larger models), without which you will be liable for the first €4400 of the repair bill (much more for larger models). Other costs include a theft waiver of at least €4.40 per day and personal accident insurance. It all adds up to an expensive exercise. The major companies offer much cheaper prebooked and prepaid rates.

You can find much better deals at some of the local companies. Their advertised rates can be up to 50% cheaper, and they are normally more open to negotiation, especially if business is slow. If you want to take a hire car to another country or onto a ferry, you will need advance written authorisation from the hire company. Unless you pay with a credit card, most hire companies will require a minimum deposit of €120 per day. See the Getting Around sections of cities and islands for details of places to rent cars.

The minimum driving age in Greece is 18 years, but most car hire firms require you to be at least 21 (23 for larger vehicles).

Motorcycle Mopeds and motorcycles are available for hire wherever there are tourists to rent them. In many cases their maintenance has been minimal, so check the machine thoroughly before you hire it – especially the brakes: you'll need them!

Motorcycles are a cheap way to travel around. Rates range from €10 to €15 per day for a moped or 50cc motorcycle to €25 per day for a 250cc motorcycle. Out of season these prices drop considerably, so use your bargaining skills. By October it is sometimes possible to hire a moped for as little as €5 per day. Most motorcycle hirers include third-party insurance in the price, but it's wise to check this. This insurance will not include medical expenses.

BICYCLE

Cycling has not caught on in Greece, which isn't surprising considering the hilly terrain. Tourists are beginning to cycle in Greece, but you'll need strong leg muscles. You can hire bicycles in most tourist places, but they are not as widely available as cars and motorcycles. Prices range from €5.90 to €12 per day, depending on the type and age of the bike. Bicycles are carried free on ferries.

HITCHING

Hitching is never entirely safe in any country in the world, and we don't recommend it. Travellers who decide to hitch should understand that they are taking a small but potentially serious risk. People who do choose to hitch will be safer if they travel in pairs and should let someone know where they are planning to go. Greece has a reputation for being a relatively safe place for women to hitch, but it is still unwise to do it alone. It's better for a woman to hitch with a companion, preferably a male one.

Some parts of Greece are much better for hitching than others. Getting out of major cities tends to be hard work, and Athens is notoriously difficult. Hitching is much easier in remote areas and on islands with poor public transport. On country roads, it is not unknown for someone to stop and ask if you want a lift even if you haven't stuck a thumb out. You can't afford to be fussy about the mode of transport – it may be a tractor or a spluttering old truck.

WALKING

Unless you have come to Greece just to lie on a beach, the chances are you will do quite a bit of walking. You don't have to be a trekker to start clocking up the kilometres. The narrow, stepped streets of many towns and villages can only be explored on foot, and visiting the archaeological sites involves a fair amount of legwork. See the What to Bring, Health and Trekking sections in the Facts for the Visitor chapter for more information about walking.

BOAT
Ferry

For most people, travel in Greece means island hopping. Every island has a ferry service of some sort, although in winter services to some of the smaller islands are fairly skeletal. Services start to pick up again from April onwards, and by July and August there are countless services crisscrossing the Aegean. Ferries come in all shapes and sizes, from the giant 'superferries' that work the major routes to the small, ageing open ferries that chug around the backwaters.

Routes The hub of Greece's ferry network is Piraeus, the port of Athens. Ferries leave here for the Cyclades, Dodecanese, the North-Eastern Aegean Islands, Saronic Gulf Islands and Crete. Athens' second port is Rafina, 70km east of the city and connected by an hourly bus service. It has ferries to the northern Cyclades, Evia, Lesvos and Limnos. The port of Lavrio, in southern Attica, is the main port for ferries to the Cycladic island of Kea. There are regular buses from Athens to Lavrio.

Ferries for the Ionian Islands leave from the Peloponnese ports of Patras (for Kefallonia, Ithaki, Paxi and Corfu) and Kyllini (for Kefallonia and Zakynthos); from Astakos (for Ithaki and Kefallonia) and Mytikas (for Lefkada and Meganisi), both in Sterea Ellada; and from Igoumenitsa in Epiros (for Corfu).

Ferries for the Sporades leave from Volos, Thessaloniki, Agios Konstantinos, and Kymi on Evia. The latter two ports are easily reached by bus from Athens.

Some of the North-Eastern Aegean Islands have connections with Thessaloniki as well as Piraeus. The odd ones out are Thasos, which is reached from Kavala, and Samothraki, which can be reached from Alexandroupolis year-round and also from Kavala in summer.

See the Ferry Departures table in the Mainland Ports chapter for a full list of sailings, journey times and prices from mainland ports, and the individual island chapters for inter-island ferries.

Schedules Ferry timetables change from year to year and season to season, and ferries are subject to delays and cancellations at short notice due to bad weather, strikes or boats simply conking out. No timetable is infallible, but the comprehensive weekly list of departures from Piraeus put out by the EOT in Athens is as accurate as humanly possible. The people to go to for the most up-to-date ferry information are the local port police *(limenarheio),* whose offices are usually on or near the quay side.

There's lots of information about ferry services on the Internet. Try Ⓦ www.ferries.gr, which has a useful search program and links. Many of the larger ferry companies now have their own sites, see the Getting There & Away chapter for details.

Throughout the year there is at least one ferry a day from a mainland port to the major island in each group, and during the high season (from June to mid-September) there are considerably more. Ferries sailing from one island group to another are not so frequent, and if you're going to travel in this way you'll need to plan carefully, otherwise you may end up having to backtrack to Piraeus.

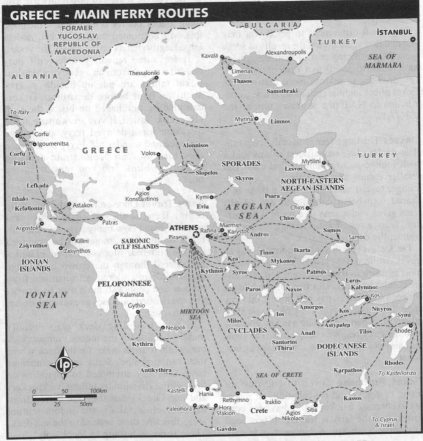

GREECE - MAIN FERRY ROUTES

Phone numbers listed incorporate changes due in Oct 2002; see p55

Travelling time can vary considerably from one ferry to another, depending on how many islands are called in at on the way to your destination. For example, the Piraeus-Rhodes trip can take between 15 and 18 hours depending on the route. Before buying your ticket, check how many stops the boat is going to make, and its estimated arrival time.

Costs Prices are fixed by the government, and are determined by the distance travelled rather than by the facilities of a particular boat. There can be big differences in the size, comfort and facilities of boats offering rival services on a given route, but the fares will be the same.

The small differences in price you may find at ticket agencies are the results of some agencies sacrificing part of their designated commission to qualify as a 'discount service'. The discount is seldom more than €0.30. Ticket prices include embarkation tax, a contribution to NAT (the seaman's union) and 8% VAT.

Classes The large ferries usually have four classes: 1st class has air-con cabins and a posh lounge and restaurant; 2nd class has smaller cabins and sometimes a separate lounge; tourist class gives you a berth in a shared four-berth cabin; and 3rd (deck) class gives you access to a room with 'airline' seats, a restaurant, a lounge/bar and, of course, the deck.

Deck class remains an economical way to travel, while a 1st-class ticket can cost almost as much as flying on some routes. Children under four travel for free, while children between four and 10 pay half price. Full fares apply for children over 10. Unless you state otherwise, when purchasing a ticket, you will automatically be given deck class. Throughout this book, prces quoted are for deck class tickets.

Ticket Purchase Given that ferries are prone to delays and cancellations, it's best not to purchase a ticket until it has been confirmed that the ferry is leaving. If you need to reserve a car space, however, you may

need to pay in advance. If the service is then cancelled you can transfer your ticket to the next available service with that company.

Agencies selling tickets line the waterfront of most ports, but rarely is there one that sells tickets for every boat, and often an agency is reluctant to give you information about a boat for which they do not sell tickets. This means you have to check the timetables displayed outside each agency to find out which ferry is next to depart – or ask the port police.

In high season, a number of boats may be due at a port at around the same time, so it is not beyond the realms of possibility that you might get on the wrong boat. The crucial thing to look out for is the name of the boat; this will be printed on your ticket, and in large English letters on the side of the vessel.

If for some reason you haven't purchased a ticket from an agency, makeshift ticket tables are put up beside a ferry about an hour before departure. Tickets can also be purchased on board the ship after it has sailed. If you are waiting at the quayside for a delayed ferry, don't lose patience and wander off. Ferry boats, once they turn up, can demonstrate amazing alacrity – blink and you may miss the boat.

Ferry Travel Once on board, the fun really begins. It can be absolute chaos in high season. No matter how many passengers are already on the ferry, more will be crammed on. Bewildered, black-shrouded grannies are steered through the crowd by teenage grandchildren, children get separated from parents and people stumble over backpacks and overloaded suitcases as everyone rushes to grab a seat.

Greeks travelling deck class usually make a beeline for the indoor lounge/snack bar, while tourists make for the deck where they can sunbathe. Some ferry companies have allegedly attempted to capitalise on this natural division by telling backpackers and non-Greeks that they are barred from the deck-class saloon and indoor-seating area, directing them instead to the sun deck. There is no such thing as 'deck only' class

The joys of ferry travel

on domestic ferries, although there is on international ferries.

All ferries now provide non-smoking areas, although they are often right next to smoking areas – or right in the middle of them.

On overnight trips, backpackers usually sleep on deck in their sleeping bags – you can also roll out your bag between the 'airline' seats. If you don't have a sleeping bag, claim an 'airline' seat as soon as you board. Leave your luggage on it – as long as you don't leave any valuables in it. The noise on board usually dies down around midnight so you should be able to snatch a few hours of sleep.

The food sold at ferry snack bars ranges from mediocre to inedible, and the choice is limited to packets of biscuits, sandwiches, very greasy pizzas and cheese pies. Most large ferries also have a self-service restaurant where the food is OK and reasonably priced, with main courses starting at around €5. However, if you are budgeting, have special dietary requirements, or are at all fussy about what you eat, take your own food with you.

Inter-Island Boat

In addition to the large ferries that ply between the large mainland ports and island groups, there are smaller boats that link islands within a group, and occasionally, an island in one group with an island in another.

In the past these boats were always sturdy old fishing boats – known as caïques – but gradually these are being replaced by new purpose-built boats, which are usually called express or excursion boats. Tickets tend to cost more than tickets for the large ferries, but the boats are very useful if you're island hopping.

Hydrofoil

Hydrofoils offer a faster alternative to ferries on some routes, particularly to islands close to the mainland. They take half the time, but cost twice as much. They do not take cars or motorcycles. Most routes operate only during high season, and according to demand, and all are prone to cancellations if the sea is rough. The ride can be bumpy at the best of times.

The biggest operator is Minoan Flying Dolphin, which runs the busy Argosaronic network linking Piraeus with the Saronic Gulf Islands and the ports of the eastern Peloponnese (plus occasional services south to the Ionian island of Kythira). Minoan also operates hydrofoils from Piraeus and Rafina to the eastern Cyclades, and from Agios Konstantinos, Thessaloniki and Volos to Evia and the Sporades.

Hydrofoil services in the eastern and south Cyclades are operated by Speed Lines out of Santorini. These Santorini Dolphins operate daily between Santorini, Ios, Naxos, Paros, Tinos and Syros, with services to Folegandros, Sikinos and Milos once or twice weekly – and occasional services to Iraklio on Crete.

The Dodecanese has its own network, centred on Rhodes, and connections to the North-Eastern Aegean islands of Ikaria and Samos. Other routes are between Kavala and Thasos in the North-Eastern Aegean, and from Alexandroupolis to Samothraki and Limnos.

Tickets cannot be bought on board hydrofoils – you must buy them in advance from an agency. You will be allocated a seat number.

Catamaran

High-speed catamarans have rapidly become an important part of the island travel scene. They are just as fast as the hydrofoils – if not faster – and much more comfortable.

Phone numbers listed incorporate changes due in Oct 2002; see p55

They are also much less prone to cancellation in rough weather.

Minoan again is the major player. It operates giant, vehicle-carrying, high-speed cats from Piraeus and Rafina to the Cyclades, and smaller Flying Cats from Rafina to the central and northern Cyclades and on many of the routes around the Saronic Gulf.

Blue Star Ferries uses its Seajet catamarans on the run from Rafina to Syros, Paros, Naxos, Ios and Santorini. It also operates a service to Tinos and Mykonos, stopping once a week at Andros, Syros, Paros, Naxos and Amorgos.

These services are very popular; book as far in advance as possible, especially if you want to travel on weekends.

Taxi Boat

Most islands have taxi boats – small speedboats that operate like taxis, transporting people to places that are difficult to get to by land.

Some owners charge a set price for each person, others charge a flat rate for the boat, and this cost is divided by the number of passengers. Either way, prices are usually quite reasonable.

Yacht

See the Island Hopping special section for information about yachting.

LOCAL TRANSPORT
To/From Airports

Local buses operate to a few airports (see individual entries in the appropriate chapters), but on many islands the only way to get to the airport is by taxi. Check-in is an hour before departure for domestic flights.

Bus

Most island towns are small enough to get around on foot. The only places where you may need to use local buses are in Iraklio and Rhodes. The procedure for buying tickets is covered in the Getting Around section for each city.

Metro

Athens is the only city in Greece large enough to warrant an underground system. See the Athens chapter for details.

Taxi

Taxis are widely available in Greece except on very small or remote islands. They are reasonably priced by European standards, especially if three or four people share costs.

Yellow city cabs are metered. Flagfall is €0.74, followed by €0.24 per kilometre (€0.44 per kilometre outside town). These rates double between midnight and 5am. Costs additional to the per-kilometre rate are €1.18 from an airport, €0.59 from a bus, port or train station and €0.30 for each piece of luggage over 10kg. Grey rural taxis do not have meters, so you should always settle on a price before you get in.

The taxi drivers of Athens are legendary for their ability to part locals and tourists alike from their money – see the Dangers & Annoyances section in the Athens chapter. If you have a complaint about a taxi driver, take the cab number and report your complaint to the tourist police. Taxi drivers in other towns in Greece are, on the whole, friendly, helpful and honest.

ORGANISED TOURS

Tours are worth considering only if your time is very limited, in which case there are countless companies vying for your money. See island chapters for more information.

Organised Treks

Trekking Hellas (☎ 21 0331 0323/24/25/26, fax 21 0324 5548, ℰ info@trekking.gr, ☼ www.trekking.gr), at Filellinon 7, Athens 105 57, is a well-established company which specialises in treks and other adventure activities for small groups. It offers treks on the islands of Andros, Corfu and Crete, as well as a range of diving and sailing holidays. See the Island Hopping special section for more information about Trekking Hellas activities.

Athens Αθήνα

Ancient Athens ranks alongside Rome and Jerusalem for its glorious past and its influence on Western civilisation, but the modern city is a place with which few people fall in love.

However inspiring the Acropolis might be, most visitors have trouble coming to terms with the surrounding urban sprawl, the appalling traffic congestion and the pollution.

The city is not, however, without its redeeming features. The Acropolis is but one of many important ancient sites, and the National Archaeological Museum has the world's finest collection of Greek antiquities.

Culturally, Athens is a fascinating blend of East and West. King Otho and the middle class that emerged after independence were intent on making Athens a European city, but the influence of Asia Minor is everywhere – the coffee, the kebabs, the raucous street vendors and the colourful markets.

HISTORY

The early history of Athens is so interwoven with mythology that it's hard to disentangle fact from fiction.

The Acropolis has been occupied since Neolithic times. It was an excellent vantage point, and the steep slopes formed natural defences on three sides. By 1400 BC the Acropolis was a powerful Mycenaean city.

Its power peaked during the so-called golden age of Athens in the 5th century BC, following the defeat of the Persians at the Battle of Salamis. It fell into decline after its defeat by Sparta in the long-running Peloponnesian War, but rallied again in Roman times when it became a seat of learning. The Roman emperors, particularly Hadrian, graced Athens with many grand buildings.

After the Roman Empire split into east and west, power shifted to Byzantium and the city fell into obscurity. By the end of Ottoman rule, Athens was little more than a dilapidated village (the area now known as Plaka).

Then, in 1834, Athens became the capital of independent Greece. The newly crowned

Highlights

- The inspirational Acropolis (and outdoor dining below it)
- The treasures of the National Archaeological Museum
- Panoramic views from Lykavittos Hill
- The lively rembetika clubs
- Sunset over the sea at Cape Sounion

Athens p110
Plaka p114
Acropolis p117

King Otho, freshly arrived from Bavaria, began rebuilding the city along neoclassical lines, featuring large squares and tree-lined boulevards with imposing public buildings. The city grew steadily and enjoyed a brief heyday as the 'Paris of the Mediterranean' in the late 19th and early 20th centuries.

This came to an abrupt end with the forced population exchange between Greece and Turkey that followed the Treaty of Lausanne in 1923. The huge influx of refugees from Asia Minor virtually doubled the population overnight, forcing the hasty erection of the first of the concrete apartment blocks that dominate the city today. The belated advent of Greece's industrial age in the 1950s brought another wave of migration, this time of rural folk looking for jobs.

ATHENS

ATHENS

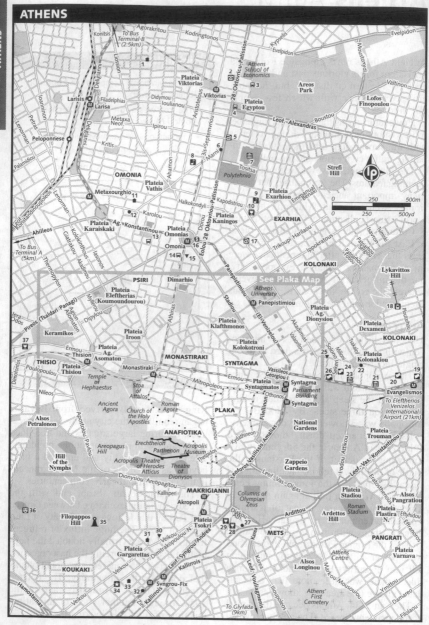

Konitsis
Agorakritou
Kodringtonos
To Bus Terminal B (2.5km)
Ioasson
Delgianni
1

Plateia Viktorias
Aristotelous
Viktorias
2
Athens School of Economics
28 Oktovriou-Patission
Kypselis
Evelpidon
Evelpidon
Moustoxydi
Valtinon

Larisis
Filadelfias
Larisa
Didymou Ioulianou
Aristotelous
3
Plateia Egyptou
Areos Park
Lofos Finopoulou

Peloponnese
Ioanninon
Petras
Lenorman
Metaxa Neof
Ipirou
Leof. Alexandras
Boustou

Palamidiou
Kritis
5
Marni
6
Tositsa
Strefi Hill

OMONIA
Acharnon
Plateia Vathis
8
31is-Septemvriou
7
Polytehnio
9
Plateia Exarhion
10
Emmanuel Benaki

Metaxourghio
11
Karolou
Halkokondyli
Kapodistriou
Plateia Kaningos
EXARHIA

Konstantinoupoleos
12
Ag. Konstantinou
13
Dirou
Plateia Omonias
17
Trikoupi Harilaou
Ippokratous
KOLONAKI

Ahilleos
Plateia Karaiskaki
14
16
15
Omonia
Panepistimiou
Lykavittos Hill

To Bus Terminal A (5km)
Iasonos
PSIRI
Dimarhio
Athens University
18
Plateia Dexameni

Keramikos
Plateia Eleftherias (Koumoundourou)
Athinas
Panepistimiou
Plateia Ag. Dionisiou
KOLONAKI

37
Ermou Thision
Plateia Iroon
Plateia Klafthmonos
Stadiou
25
Plateia Kolonakiou
19

THISIO
Plateia Thisiou
Plateia Ag. Asomaton
MONASTIRAKI
Plateia Kolokotroni
SYNTAGMA
26
24
23
21
20

Temple of Hephaestus
Monastiraki
Mitropoleos
Ermou
Vassileos Georgiou
22
Evangelismos

Ancient Agora
Stoa of Attalos
Roman Agora
PLAKA
Plateia Syntagmatos
Othonos
Syntagma Parliament Building
Syntagma
To Eleftherios Venizelos International Airport (21km)

Alsos Petralonon
Church of the Holy Apostles
ANAFIOTIKA
Filellinon
National Gardens
Plateia Trouman

Hill of the Nymphs
Areopagus Hill
Erechtheion
Parthenon
Acropolis Museum
Zappeio Gardens

Acropolis
Theatre of Herodes Atticus
Theatre of Dionysos
Leoforos Vassilissis Amalias
Plateia Stadiou
Alsos Pangratiou

36
Dionisiou-Areopagitou
MAKRIGIANNI
Columns of Olympian Zeus
Roman Stadium
Plateia Plastira N.
PANGRATI

Filopappos Hill
35
Akropoli
Ardittou
Ardettos Hill
Plateia Varnava

31
30
Plateia Tsokri
29
28
27
METS

Plateia Gargarettas
Veikou
KOUKAKI
Kallirrois
Alsos Longinou
Athens Centre
Plateia Varnava

34
33
32
Svngrou-Fix
Kallirrois
Athens' First Cemetery

To Glyfada (9km)

The city's infrastructure, particularly road and transport, could not keep pace with such rapid and unplanned growth, and by the end of the 1980s the city had developed a sorry reputation as one of the most traffic-clogged and polluted in Europe.

The 1990s appear to have been a turning point in the city's development. Jolted into action by the failed bid to stage the 1996 Olympics, authorities embarked on an ambitious program to prepare the city for the 21st century. Two key elements in this program have been an extension of the metro network, and the construction of a new international airport at Spata, east of Athens.

These projects played an important role in the city's successful bid to stage the 2004 Olympics. The Olympics have now created a momentum of their own; confidence is riding high and billions are being poured into city centre redevelopment.

ORIENTATION

Although Athens is a huge, sprawling city, nearly everything of interest to travellers is located within a small area bounded by Plateia Omonias (Omonia Square) to the north, Plateia Monastirakiou (Monastiraki Square) to the west, Plateia Syntagmatos (Syntagma Square) to the east and the Plaka district to the south. The city's two major landmarks, the Acropolis and Lykavittos Hill, can be seen from just about everywhere in this area.

Syntagma is the heart of modern Athens; it's flanked by luxury hotels, banks and expensive coffee shops and dominated by the old royal palace – home of the Greek parliament since 1935.

Omonia has developed a sorry reputation for sleaze in recent years, but this is set to change with the announcement of a plan to transform Plateia Omonias from a traffic hub into an expanse of formal gardens. This is guaranteed to create traffic chaos, since all the major streets of central Athens meet here. Panepistimiou (El Venizelou) and Stadiou run parallel south-east to Syntagma, while Athinas leads south to the market district of Monastiraki. Monastiraki is in turn linked to Syntagma by Ermou – home to some of the city's smartest shops – and Mitropoleos.

Mitropoleos skirts the northern edge of Plaka, the delightful old Turkish quarter that was virtually all that existed when Athens was declared the capital of independent Greece. Its labyrinthine streets are nestled on the north-eastern slope of the Acropolis, and most of the city's ancient sites are close by. It may be touristy, but it's the most attractive and interesting part of Athens and the majority of visitors make it their base.

Streets are clearly signposted in Greek and English. If you do get lost, it's very easy to find help. A glance at a map is often enough to draw an offer of assistance. Anyone you ask will be able to direct you to Syntagma (**syn**-tag-ma).

ATHENS

PLACES TO STAY			
1	Hostel Aphrodite	4	Mavromateon Bus Terminal (Southern Attica)
11	Athens International Youth Hostel	5	Museum Internet Cafe
31	Art Gallery Hotel	6	USIT-ETOS Travel
33	Marble House Pension	7	National Archaeological Museum
		8	Rodon Club
PLACES TO EAT		9	AN Club
15	Marinopoulos Supermarket	10	Fairytale
25	Marinopoulos Supermarket	12	OSE Office
30	Veropoulos Supermarket	13	Bus No 051 to Bus Terminal A
		14	Bus No 049 to Piraeus
OTHER		16	National Bank of Greece
2	OTE main office	17	Bits & Bytes Internet Cafe
3	Mavromateon Bus Terminal (Marathon & Rafina)	18	Funicular

19	British Embassy
20	German Embassy
21	Goulandris Museum of Cycladic & Ancient Greek Art
22	British Council
23	Benaki Museum
24	Italian Embassy
26	Danish Embassy
27	Key Tours Office & Terminal
28	Granazi Bar
29	Lamda Club
32	Olympic Airways
34	Tourist Police
35	Monument of Filoppapos
36	Dora Stratou Theatre
37	Plus Soda (winter)

INFORMATION
Tourist Offices
Athens' main EOT tourist office (☎ 21 0331 0561/0562, fax 21 0325 2895, ℮ info@ gnto.gr) is close to Syntagma at Amerikis 2. It has a useful timetable of the week's ferry departures from Piraeus, and information about public transport prices and schedules from Athens. It also has a useful free map of Athens, which has most of the places of interest, and the main trolleybus routes, clearly marked. The office is open 9am to 4pm Monday to Friday.

The EOT office at the airport (☎ 21 0353 0445) is open 9am to 9pm daily.

The tourist police (☎ 21 0924 2700) are open 24 hours a day at Dimitrakopoulou 77, Koukaki. Take trolleybus No 1, 5 or 9 from Syntagma. It also has a 24-hour information service (☎ 171).

Money
Most of the major banks have branches around Syntagma, which are open 8am to 2pm Monday to Thursday and until 1.30pm Friday. The National Bank of Greece, at the corner of Karageorgi Servias and Stadiou, is open extended hours for foreign exchange dealings only: 3.30pm to 6.30pm Monday to Thursday; 3pm to 6.30pm Friday; 9am to 3pm Saturday; and 9am to 1pm Sunday.

American Express (AmEx; ☎ 21 0322 3380), Ermou 7, Syntagma, is open 8.30am to 4pm Monday to Friday and 8.30am to 1.30pm Saturday.

Eurochange (☎ 21 0322 0155), Karageorgi Servias 4, Syntagma, is open 8am to 8pm Monday to Friday and 10am to 6pm weekends. It changes Thomas Cook travellers cheques without commission.

The banks at the airport are open 7am to 9pm.

Post & Communications
The main post office is at Eolou 100, Omonia (postcode 102 00), which is where mail addressed to poste restante will be sent unless specified otherwise. If you're staying in Plaka, it's best to get mail sent to the Syntagma post office (postcode 103 00). Both are open 7.30am to 8pm Monday to Friday,

until 2pm Saturday and 9am to 1.30pm Sunday. Parcels over 2kg going abroad must be posted from the parcels office at Stadiou 4 (in the arcade). They should not be wrapped until they've been inspected.

The main OTE telephone office, at 28 Oktovriou-Patission 85, is open 24 hours a day. There is another office at Athinas 50, south of Omonia, next to Klaoudatos department store, open 7.30am to 2pm. Some useful telephone numbers include:

general telephone information	☎ 134
numbers in Athens and Attica	☎ 131
numbers elsewhere in Greece	☎ 132
international telephone	☎ 161
international telephone (info)	☎ 162
international telegrams	☎ 165
domestic operator	☎ 151/152
domestic telegrams	☎ 155
wake-up service	☎ 182

Email & Internet Access
Internet cafes are popping up like mushrooms all over Athens. Most charge from €4.40 to €5.90 per hour of computer time, whether you're on the Net or not. The following is a list of places around the city centre:

Bits & Bytes Internet Cafe Akadimias 78, Exarhia; open 9am to midnight daily
Museum Internet Cafe 28 Oktovriou-Patission 46, Omonia, next to National Archaeological Museum; open 9am to 3am daily
Plaka Internet World Pandrosou 29, Monastiraki; open 11am to 11pm daily
Skynet Internet Centre Corner Voulis & Apollonos, Plaka; open 9am to 11pm Monday to Saturday
Sofokleous.com Internet Café Stadiou 5, Syntagma, behind Flocafé; open 10am to 10pm Monday to Saturday, 1pm to 9pm Sunday

Travel Agencies
The bulk of the city's travel agencies are around Plateia Syntagmatos, particularly just south of it on Filellinon, Nikis and Voulis. Many of these agencies employ touts to roam the area looking for custom. Give them a miss – these places are responsible for most of the rip-offs described under Travel Agencies in the

Dangers and Annoyances section later in this chapter.

Reputable agencies include STA Travel (☎ 21 0321 1188, 21 0321 1194, ℮ sta travel@robissa.gr), Voulis 43, and USIT-ETOS Travel (☎ 21 0324 0483, fax 21 0322 8447, ℮ usit@usitetos.gr), Filellinon 7. USIT-ETOS has another branch (☎ 21 0522 2228, ℮ etosath@usitetos.gr) opposite the National Archaeological Museum at 28 Oktovriou-Patission 53A and Marni.

Both STA Travel and USIT-ETOS also issue International Student Identity Cards (ISIC).

Bookshops
Athens has four good English-language bookshops. The biggest is Eleftheroudakis, which has branches at Panepistimiou 17, Syntagma, and at Nikis 4, Plaka.

The others are Pantelides Books, Amerikis 11, Syntagma; Compendium Books, Nikis 28, Plaka; and Booknest, on the mezzanine level of the arcade at Panepistimiou 25–29, Syntagma. Compendium also has a second-hand books section. All these shops stock Lonely Planet guides.

Cultural Centres
The British Council (☎ 0369 2314), Plateia Kolonakiou 17, and the Hellenic-American Union (☎ 21 0362 9886), Massalias 22, hold frequent concerts, film shows, exhibitions etc. Both also have libraries.

Laundry
Plaka has a convenient laundry at Angelou Geronta 10, just off Kydathineon near the outdoor restaurants.

Medical & Emergency Services
For emergency medical treatment, ring the tourist police (☎ 171) and they'll tell you where the nearest hospital is. Don't wait for an ambulance – get a taxi. Hospitals give free emergency treatment to tourists. For hospitals with outpatient departments on duty, ring ☎ 106. For first-aid advice, ring ☎ 166. You can get free dental treatment at the Evangelismos Hospital, Ipsilandou 45.

Dangers & Annoyances
Pickpockets Pickpockets have become a major problem in Athens. Their favourite hunting grounds are the metro system and the crowded streets around Omonia, particularly Athinas. The Sunday market on Ermou is another place where it pays to take extra good care of your valuables.

Travel Agencies Several travel agents in the Plaka/Syntagma area employ touts to patrol the streets promoting 'cheap' packages to the islands. These touts like to hang out at the bus stops on Amalias, hoping to find naive new arrivals who have no idea of prices in Greece.

Potential customers are then taken back to the agency, where slick salespeople then pressure them into buying outrageously overpriced packages. Lonely Planet regularly hears complaints from victims of this scam. There is no need to buy a package; you will always be able to negotiate a better deal yourself when you get to the island of your choice. If you are worried that everywhere will be full, select a place from the pages of this guide and make a booking.

Taxi Touts Taxi drivers working in league with some overpriced C-class hotels around Omonia are a problem. The scam involves taxi drivers picking up late-night arrivals, particularly at the airport and Bus Terminal A, and persuading them that the hotel they want to go to is full. The taxi driver will pretend to phone the hotel of choice, announce that it's full and suggest an alternative. You can ask to speak to your chosen hotel yourself, or insist on going where you want.

Q-ray

Make sure the taxi driver doesn't take you for a ride

PLAKA

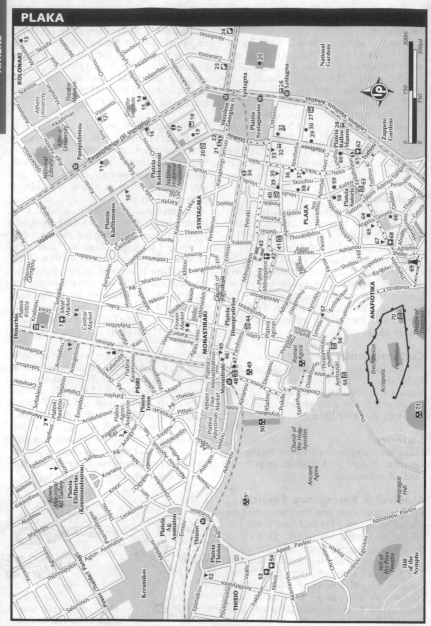

Taxi drivers frequently attempt to claim commissions from hotel owners even if they have just gone where they were told. If the taxi driver comes into the hotel, make it clear to hotel staff that the driver is there on his own accord.

Bar Scams Lonely Planet receives a steady flow of letters warning about bar scams, particularly around Syntagma. The most popular version runs something like this: friendly Greek approaches solo male traveller and discovers that the traveller knows little about Athens; friendly Greek then reveals that he, too, is from out of town. Why don't they go to this great little bar that he's just discovered and have a beer? They order a drink, and the equally friendly owner then offers another drink. Women appear, more drinks are provided and the visitor relaxes as he concludes that the women are not prostitutes, just friendly Greeks. The crunch comes at the end of the evening when the traveller is presented with an exorbitant bill and the smiles disappear. The conmen who cruise the streets playing the role of the friendly Greek can be very convincing: some people have been taken in more than once.

THINGS TO SEE
Walking Tour

The following walk starts and finishes at Syntagma Square and takes in most of Plaka's best-known sites. Without detours, it will take about 45 minutes. The route is marked with a dotted line on the Plaka map.

From Syntagma, walk along Mitropoleos and take the first turning left onto Nikis. Continue along here to the junction with Kydathineon, Plaka's main thoroughfare, and turn right. Opposite the church is the **Museum of Greek Folk Art** (☎ 21 0322 9031, Kydathineon 17, Plaka; admission €1.50; open 10am-2pm Tues-Sun), which houses an excellent collection of embroidery, weaving and jewellery. After passing the square with the outdoor tavernas, take the second turning left onto Adrianou. A right turn at end of Adrianou leads to the small square with the **Choregic Monument**

PLAKA

PLACES TO STAY		OTHER		• 38	STA Travel
4	Hotel Cecil	6	OTE	39	Acropolis Rugs; Greek Travel
9	Hotel Tempi	7	Rembetiki Stoa Athinaton		Phones
14	XEN (YWCA)	11	Booknest	40	Skynet Internet Centre
58	Acropolis House Pension	12	OSE Office	41	National Welfare Organisation
59	Hotel Adonis	13	Hellenic-American Union	42	Church of Agios Eleftherios
60	Festos Youth & Student	15	Pantelides Books	43	Athens Cathedral
	Guesthouse	16	Eleftheroudakis Books	44	Plaka Internet World
64	Student & Travellers' Inn	17	EOT Tourist Office	47	Stavros Melissinos
		18	Parcel Post Office	48	Museum of Traditional Greek
PLACES TO EAT		19	Athens Festival Box Office		Ceramics
1	Bengal Garden	20	Sofokleous.com Internet Café	49	Library of Hadrian
2	Pak Bangla	21	Eurochange	50	Stoa of Attalos
3	Embros	22	National Bank of Greece	51	Temple of Hephaestus
5	Fruit & Vegetable Market	23	Egyptian Embassy	53	Stavlos
8	Meat Market	24	French Embassy	54	Berlin Club
10	Vasilopoulou	25	Parliament Building	55	Paul & Alexandra
33	Neon Cafe	26	Bus E95 to Airport		Kanellopoulos Museum
35	Furin Kazan Japanese	27	CHAT Terminal	56	Old Athens University
	Fast-Food Restaurant	28	GO Tours Pick-Up Point	61	Eurochange
45	Savas	29	Olympic Airways	62	Lava Bore
46	Thanasis	30	CHAT Office	63	Museum of Greek Folk Art
52	To Steki tou Elia	31	USIT-ETOS Travel	66	Plaka Laundrette
57	Eden Vegetarian	32	Bus No 040 to Piraeus	68	Brettos
	Restaurant	34	American Express	69	Choregic Monument of
65	Taverna Vizantino	36	Eleftheroudakis Books		Lysicrates
67	Plaka Psistaria	37	Compendium Books	70	Acropolis Museum
				71	Theatre of Herodes Atticus

Phone numbers listed incorporate changes due in Oct 2002; see p55

of Lysicrates, erected in 334 BC to commemorate victory in a choral festival.

Turn left and then right onto Epimenidou; at the top, turn right onto Thrasilou, which skirts the Acropolis. Where the road forks, veer left into the district of **Anafiotika**. Here the little white cubic houses resemble those of the Cyclades, and olive-oil cans brimming with flowers bedeck the walls of their tiny gardens. The houses were built by the people of Anafi, who were used as cheap labour in the rebuilding of Athens after independence.

The path winds between the houses and comes to some steps on the right, at the bottom of which is a curving pathway leading downhill to Pratiniou. Turn left onto Pratiniou and veer right after 50m onto Tholou. The yellow-ochre Venetian building with brown shutters at No 5 is the old university.

At the end of Tholou, turn left onto Panos. At the top of the steps on the left is a restored 19th-century mansion which is now the **Paul & Alexandra Kanellopoulos Museum** (☎ *21 0321 2313, Panos 2; admission €1.50; open 8am-2.30pm Tues-Sun)*. Retracing your steps, go down Panos to the ruins of the **Roman Agora**, then turn left onto Polygnotou and walk to the crossroads. Opposite, Polygnotou continues to the **Ancient Agora**. At the crossroads, turn right and then left onto Poikilis, then immediately right onto Areos. On the right hand side are the remains of the **Library of Hadrian** and next to the library is the **Museum of Traditional Greek Ceramics** (☎ *21 0324 2066, Areos 1; admission €1.50;*

open 10am-2pm Wed-Mon). The museum is housed in the **Mosque of Tzistarakis**, built in 1759. After independence it lost its minaret and was used as a prison.

Ahead is Plateia Monastiraki (Monastiraki Square), named after its small church. To the left is the metro station and the **flea market**. Monastiraki is Athens at its noisiest, most colourful and chaotic; it's teeming with street vendors.

Turn right just beyond the mosque onto Pandrossou, a relic of the old Turkish bazaar. At No 89 is Stavros Melissinos, the 'poet sandalmaker' of Athens who names the Beatles, Rudolph Nureyev and Jackie Onassis among his customers. Fame and fortune have not gone to his head – he still makes the best sandals in Athens, priced from €11.

Pandrossou leads to Plateia Mitropoleos and the **Athens Cathedral**. The cathedral was constructed from the masonry of over 50 razed churches and from the designs of several architects. Next to it stands the much smaller, and far more appealing, old **Church of Agios Eleftherios**. Turn left after the cathedral, and then right onto Mitropoleos and back to Syntagma.

Acropolis

Most of the buildings now gracing the Acropolis (☎ *21 0321 0291; site & museum adult/student €5.90/2.95; site open 8am-6.30pm daily; museum open 8am-6.30pm Tues-Sun, noon-6.30pm Mon Apr-Oct; site & museum open 8am-4.30pm daily Nov-Mar)* were commissioned by Pericles during

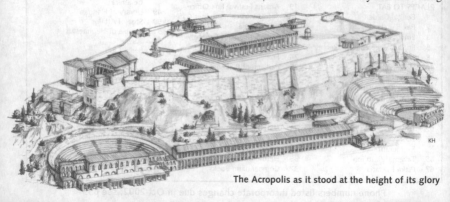

The Acropolis as it stood at the height of its glory

ACROPOLIS (ANCIENT)

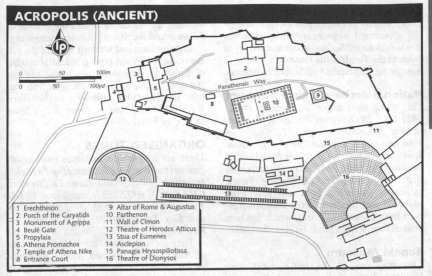

Panathenaic Way

1 Erechtheion	9 Altar of Rome & Augustus
2 Porch of the Caryatids	10 Parthenon
3 Monument of Agrippa	11 Wall of Cimon
4 Beulé Gate	12 Theatre of Herodes Atticus
5 Propylaia	13 Stoa of Eumenes
6 Athena Promachos	14 Asclepion
7 Temple of Athena Nike	15 Panagia Hrysospiliotissa
8 Entrance Court	16 Theatre of Dionysos

the golden age of Athens in the 5th century BC. The site had been cleared for him by the Persians, who destroyed an earlier temple complex on the eve of the Battle of Salamis.

The entrance to the Acropolis is through the **Beule Gate**, a Roman arch that was added in the 3rd century AD. Beyond this is the **Propylaia**, the monumental gate that was the entrance in ancient times. It was damaged by Venetian bombing in the 17th century, but it has since been restored. To the south of the Propylaia is the small, graceful **Temple of Athena Nike**, which is not accessible to visitors.

Standing supreme over the Acropolis is the monument that more than any other epitomises the glory of ancient Greece: the **Parthenon**. Completed in 438 BC, this building is unsurpassed in grace and harmony. To achieve perfect form, its lines were ingeniously curved to counteract unharmonious optical illusions. The base curves upwards slightly towards the ends, and the columns become slightly narrower towards the top, with the overall effect of making them both look straight.

Above the columns are the remains of a Doric frieze, which was partly destroyed by Venetian shelling in 1687. The best surviving pieces are the controversial Parthenon Marbles, carted off to Britain by Lord Elgin in 1801.

The Parthenon, dedicated to Athena, contained an 11m-tall gold-and-ivory statue of the goddess completed in 438 BC by Phidias of Athens (only the statue's foundations exist today).

To the north is the **Erechtheion** with its much-photographed Caryatids, the six maidens who support its southern portico. These are plaster casts – the originals (except for the one taken by Lord Elgin) are in the site's museum.

Ancient Agora

The Agora *(market; ☎ 21 0321 0185, western end of Adrianou; admission €3.55; open 8.30am-3pm Tues-Sun)* was the marketplace of ancient Athens and the focal point of civic and social life. Socrates spent much time here expounding his philosophy. The main monuments are the well-preserved **Temple of Hephaestus**, the 11th-century **Church of the Holy Apostles** and the reconstructed **Stoa of Attalos**, which houses the site's museum.

ATHENS

Changing of the Guard
Every Sunday at 11am a platoon of tradition-ally costumed *evzones* (guards) marches down Vasilissis Sofias, accompanied by a band, to the Tomb of the Unknown Soldier in front of the parliament building on Syntagma.

National Archaeological Museum
This is the most important museum (☎ 21 0821 7717, 28 Oktovriou-Patission 44; adult/student €5.90/2.95; open 12.30pm-7pm Mon, 8am-7pm Tues-Sun Apr-Oct; 10.30am-5pm Mon, 8am-5pm Tues-Sun Nov-Mar) in the country, with finds from all the major sites. The crowd-pullers are the magnificent, exquisitely detailed gold artefacts from Mycenae and the spectacular **Minoan frescoes** from Santorini (Thira), which are here until a suitable museum is built on the island.

Benaki Museum
This museum (☎ 21 0367 1000, Cnr Vasilissis Sofias & Koumbari 1, Kolonaki; adult/student €5.90/2.95, open 9am-5pm Mon, Wed, Fri & Sat, 9am-midnight Thurs, 9am-3pm Sun) houses the collection of Antoine Benaki, the son of an Alexandrian cotton magnate named Emmanual Benaki. The collection includes ancient sculpture, Persian, Byzantine and Coptic objects, Chinese ceramics, icons, two El Greco paintings and a superb collection of traditional costumes.

Goulandris Museum of Cycladic & Ancient Greek Art
This private museum (☎ 21 0801 5870, Cnr Vasilissis Sofias & Neofytou Douka 4, Kolonaki; adult/student €2.95/1.50; open 10am-4pm Mon & Wed-Fri, 10am-3pm Sat) was custom-built to display a fabulous collection of Cycladic art, with an emphasis on the early Bronze Age. Particularly impressive are the beautiful marble figurines. These simple, elegant forms, mostly of naked women with arms folded under their breasts, inspired 20th-century artists such as Brancusi, Epstein, Modigliani and Picasso.

Lykavittos Hill
Pine-covered Lykavittos is the highest of the eight hills dotted around Athens. From the summit there are all-embracing views of the city, the Attica basin and the islands of Salamis and Aegina – pollution permitting.

The southern and western sides of the hill are occupied by the posh residential suburb of Kolonaki. The main path to the summit starts at the top of Loukianou, or you can take the **funicular railway** (single/return €1.50/2.95, 9.15am-11.45pm daily) from the top of Ploutarhou.

ORGANISED TOURS
There are four main companies running organised tours around Athens: **Hop In Sightseeing** (☎ 21 0428 5500, Zanni 29, Piraeus); **CHAT** (☎ 21 0322 3137, Xenofontos 9); **GO Tours** (☎ 21 0921 9555, Athanassiou 20); and **Key Tours** (☎ 21 0923 3166/3266, Kaliroïs 4).

They include a half-day sightseeing tour of Athens (€29.35), and Athens by Night (€40), which takes in the *son et lumière* (sound-and-light show) before a taverna dinner with folk dancing.

You will find brochures for the tour companies everywhere; all the hotels listed in the following Places to Stay chapter act as a booking agent for at least one tour company. The hotels often offer substantial discounts on the official tour prices as a service to their customers – discounts that aren't available if you book directly.

SPECIAL EVENTS
The annual Hellenic Festival is the city's most important cultural event, running from mid-June to late September. It features a line-up of international music, dance and theatre at the Theatre of Herodes Atticus. The setting is superb, backed by the floodlit Acropolis.

Tickets sell out quickly, so try to buy yours as soon as possible. They can be bought at the festival box office (☎ 21 0322 1459, fax 21 0323 5172) in the arcade at Stadiou 4, Syntagma. The box office opens three weeks before the start of the festival, from 8.30am to 4pm Monday to Friday and 9am to 2.30pm weekends. There are student discounts for most performances on production of an ISIC.

PLACES TO STAY
Camping
Athens Camping (☎ 21 0581 4114, fax 21 0582 0353, *Leoforos Athinon 198*) Adult/tent €4.70/3.55. Open year-round. This place is 7km west of the city centre on the road to Corinth, making it the nearest camp site to the city centre. It has reasonable facilities but nothing else going for it.

There are other camping grounds southeast of Athens near Cape Sounion and north-east of Athens at Shinias Beach.

Hostels
Athens International Youth Hostel (☎ 21 0523 4170, fax 21 0523 4015, *Victor Hugo 16*) Bed in 2–4-bed dorm for member €8.40. Situated in Omonia, the location isn't overly salubrious, but otherwise this excellent HI-affiliated place is almost too good to be true. It occupies the former C-class Hotel Victor Ougo, which has been completely renovated – it even has double-glazed windows. The rooms are spotless and include bathroom, sheets and pillowcases. Facilities include a guest kitchen, laundry and free safety deposit boxes. There is no curfew.

XEN (YWCA; ☎ 21 0362 4291, fax 21 0362 2400, e xene7@hol.gr, *Amerikis 11*) Singles/doubles with bathroom €29.35/ 35.20, €26.40/32.30 per night for stays over 2 nights. The XEN is an option for women only. There are laundry facilities and a snack bar, which charges €2.35 for continental breakfast. Annual membership costs €2.95.

Hotels
Athens is a noisy city and Athenians keep late hours, so an effort has been made to select hotels in quiet areas. Plaka is the most popular place to stay, and it has a good choice of accommodation right across the price spectrum. Rooms fill up quickly in July and August, so it's wise to make a reservation.

Plaka Student & Travellers' Inn (☎ 21 0324 4808, fax 21 0321 0065, e *students-inn@ ath.forthnet.gr, Kydathineon 16*) Dorm beds €11.75-17.60, singles/doubles with shared bathroom €30.85/39.65, singles/ doubles with bathroom €35.25/49.90. The

Student Inn occupies a converted nursing home, and is veritable maze of rooms large and small – some with fine old timber floors. The dorms here are good value, especially in the quieter months. All dorms share communal bathrooms. Rooms are heated in winter. Facilities include a courtyard with big-screen TV, Internet access and a travel service.

Festos Youth & Student Guesthouse (☎ 21 0323 2455, fax 21 0321 0907, e con solas@hol.gr, *Filellinon 18*) Dorm beds €11.75, doubles/triples with shared bathroom €26.40/38.15. This place has long been popular with travellers despite being on one of the noisiest streets in Athens. It tends to cram beds into the rooms in summer. A popular feature is the bar on the 1st floor, which also serves meals, including several vegetarian items.

Plaka also has some good mid-range accommodation. *Acropolis House Pension* (☎ 21 0322 2344, fax 21 0324 4143, *Kodrou 6–8*) Singles/doubles from €47.70/57.25. This is a beautifully preserved 19th-century house, which retains many original features. Another feature of the Acropolis House is that it boasts undoubtedly the most complex pricing structure in Athens, with discounts for stays of three days or more, supplements for air-conditioning etc. All the rooms are heated in winter. Breakfast costs €4.95 per person.

Hotel Adonis (☎ 21 0324 9737, fax 21 0323 1602, *Kodrou 3*) Singles/doubles €33.75/60.20. Opposite the Acropolis House Pension, this comfortable modern hotel represents one of the best deals around. All the rooms come with air-con and TV. There are good views of the Acropolis from the 4th-floor rooms, and from the rooftop bar. Prices include breakfast.

Monastiraki *Hotel Tempi* (☎ 21 0321 3175, fax 21 0325 4179, e *tempihotel@ travelling.gr, Eolou 29*) Singles with shared bathroom €22, singles/doubles/triples with bathroom €27.90/37/44. This friendly family-run place was named one of the world's top 50 budget hotels by Britain's *Independent* newspaper. Yiannis and Katerina keep the place spotless, and the rooms at the front have balconies overlooking pretty Plateia Agia Irini with its flower market and church – not to mention views to the Acropolis. There is also a communal kitchen with a refrigerator and facilities for preparing hot drinks and snacks. Credit cards are accepted, which is unusual for a budget hotel.

Hotel Cecil (☎ *21 0321 7909, fax 21 0321 8005,* e *cecil@netsmart.gr, Athinas 39)* Singles/doubles/triples €39.65/52.85/69. If there were a prize for the best restoration job, it should go to the owners of the Hotel Cecil. They have done a magnificent job in reviving this fine old hotel, with its beautiful high, moulded ceilings and polished timber floors. The rooms are tastefully furnished and equipped with air-con and TV. Prices include breakfast.

Koukaki *Marble House Pension* (☎ *21 0923 4058, fax 21 0922 6461, Zini 35a)* Singles/doubles/triples with shared bathroom €23.50/41.10/44, with bathroom €29.35/47/49.90. This isn't exactly backpacker territory, but this pension, on a quiet cul-de-sac off Zini, is one of Athens' better budget hotels. All rooms have a bar fridge, ceiling fans and safety boxes for valuables, and air-con is available for an extra €8.80.

Art Gallery Hotel (☎ *21 0923 8376, fax 21 0923 3025,* e *ecotec@otenet.gr, Erehthiou 5)* Singles/doubles/triples €44/52.25/62.50. This is a small, friendly place that's full of personal touches – like fresh flowers. It's run by the brother-and-sister team of Ada and Yannis Assimakopoulos, who are full of information about the city. The rooms are heated in winter, when cheaper long-term rates are available. A generous breakfast costs €5.

Omonia & Surrounds *Hostel Aphrodite* (☎ *21 0881 0589, fax 21 0881 6574,* e *hostel-aphrodite@ath.forthnet.gr, Einardou 12)* Dorm beds €11.75, singles/doubles/triples with shared bathroom €27.90/35.20/39.70, with bathroom €30.80/38.15/42.55. The Aphrodite is 10 minutes' walk from the train stations, and has very clean, good-sized rooms – many with balconies. It seems to be party time every night at the downstairs bar.

In the morning, the bar becomes the breakfast room. Facilities include Internet access. The hostel is five minutes' walk from Victorias metro station.

PLACES TO EAT
Plaka For most people, Plaka is the place to be. It's hard to beat the atmosphere of dining out beneath the floodlit Acropolis.

Taverna Vizantino (☎ *21 0322 7368, Kydathineon 18)* Mains €3.25-11.30. This place is the best of the outdoor restaurants around the square on Kydathineon. It prices its menu realistically and is popular with locals year-round. The daily specials are good value, with dishes like stuffed tomatoes (€4.25), pastitsio (€2.95) and baked fish (€5.60).

Plaka Psistaria (☎ *21 0324 6229, Kydathineon 28)* Plaka Psistaria has a range of gyros and souvlaki to eat here or take away. The dash of paprika and extra-garlic tzatziki gives this place the edge over dozens of similar places around town. Try its chicken souvlaki wrapped in pitta bread (€1.35) or pork gyros (€1.20), and ask for *apola* – with the lot!

Eden Vegetarian Restaurant (☎ *21 0324 8858, Lyssiou 12)* Mains €5.60-8.50. Closed Tues. The Eden is unchallenged as the best vegetarian restaurant in Athens. It has been around for years, substituting soya products for meat in tasty vegetarian versions of mousakas (€4.70), and other Greek favourites. You'll also find vegie burgers (€5.30), mushroom stifado (€8.50), as well as organically produced beer and wine.

Syntagma Fast food is the order of the day around busy Syntagma with an assortment of Greek and international offerings.

Neon Café (☎ *21 0324 6873, Mitropoleos 3)* Mains €3.40-5.75. Neon Café is stylish modern cafeteria, near the south-west corner of Plateia Syntagmatos, with a good selection of meals, as well as coffee and cakes. You'll find spaghetti or fettucine napolitana for €3.40, and Bolognese or carbonara for €4.40. Main dishes include mousakas (€4.25), roast beef with potatoes (€4.70) and pork kebab (€5.75).

Furin Kazan Japanese Fast-Food Restaurant (☎ *21 0322 9170, Apollonos 2*) Mains €4.70-15.25. Open 11am-11pm Mon-Sat. Anyone suffering from a surfeit of Greek salad and souvlakis should head for the Furin Kazan. It's reassuring to see that it is always full of Japanese visitors, obviously enjoying the food at the cheapest and best Japanese restaurant in town. There's a selection of rice and noodle dishes as well as old favourites like chicken yakitori, but it's the sashimi and sushi trays that steal the show.

Makrigianni *To 24 Hours* (☎ *21 0922 2749, Syngrou 44*) Mains €4.10-5.90. Open 24 hours. This is something of an institution among Athenian night owls. It closes only on Easter Sunday, and seems to be at its busiest in the wee small hours. The customers are as much of an attraction as the food: you'll be rubbing shoulders with an assortment of hungry cabbies, middle-aged couples dressed for the opera, and leather-clad gays from the area's many bars – all tucking into steaming bowls of the house speciality, *patsas* (tripe soup). It also has a constantly changing choice of other popular taverna dishes.

Monastiraki There are some excellent cheap places to eat around Monastiraki, particularly for gyros and souvlaki fans. *Thanasis* and *Savas*, opposite each other at the bottom end of Mitropoleos, are the places to go.

Thisio *To Steki tou Elia* (☎ *21 0345 8052, Epahalkou 5*) Mains €4.40-5.90. To Steki tou Elia specialises in lamb chops, which are sold by the kilogram (€11.75). Locals swear that they are the best in Athens, and the place has achieved some sort of celebrity status. Eat here with Greek friends, and they will constantly be pointing out famous personalities rolling up their sleeves to tuck into great piles of chops and a few jars of retsina. There are pork chops (€5.90) and steaks (€4.40) for those who don't eat lamb, as well as dips, chips and salads.

Psiri There are loads of possibilities in Psiri, just north-west of Monastiraki. The narrow streets are dotted with numerous trendy ouzeris, tavernas and music bars, particularly the central area between Plateia Agion Anargyron and Plateia Iroön.

Embros (☎ *21 0321 3285, Plateia Agion Anargyron 4*) Meze €4.10-11.15. Embros is a popular spot with seating in the square, and a choice of about 20 mezedes. They include delicious cheese croquettes (€3.40) and chicken livers wrapped in bacon (€4.70).

The renovators have yet to reach the streets just north of Psiri, around Plateia Koumoundourou, but the area has been adopted by the city's Bangladeshi community and it's the place to head for a good cheap curry and a cold beer. Try the *Pak Bangla* (*Menandrou 13*) or the tiny *Bengal Garden* (*Korinis 12*).

Self-Catering The following are supermarkets in central Athens: *Marinopoulos* (*Kanari 9, Kolonaki*); *Vasilopoulou* (*Stadiou 19, Syntagma*); *Marinopoulos* (*Athinas 60, Omonia*); and *Veropoulos* (*Parthenos 6, Koukaki*). For the best range of fresh fruit and vegetables, head for the markets on Athinas.

ENTERTAINMENT
The best source of entertainment information is the weekly listings magazine *Athenorama*, but you'll need to be able to read some Greek to make much sense of it. English-language listings appear daily in the Kathimerini supplement that accompanies the *International Herald Tribune*, while the *Athens News* carries a 16-page weekly entertainment guide.

Bars
Most bars around Plaka and Syntagma are places to avoid, especially if there are guys outside touting for customers.

Brettos (☎ *21 0323 2110, Kydathineon 41*) A delightful little place right in the heart of Plaka. Very little has changed here in years, except that being old-fashioned has suddenly become very fashionable. It's a family-run business, which acts as a shopfront for the family distillery and winery in Kalithea. Huge old barrels line one wall, and the shelves are stocked with a colourful collection of bottles that is backlit at night. Shots of Brettos brand spirits (ouzo, brandy and many more) cost €1.80, as does a glass of wine.

Most bars in Athens have music as a main feature. Thisio is a good place to look, particularly on Iraklidon.

Stavlos (☎ 21 0345 2502, *Iraklidon 10*) This venue has a rock bar playing mainly alternative British music, and more mellow sounds in the cafe/brasserie outside.

Berlin Club (☎ 21 0671 5455, *Iraklidon 8*) This club, next door to Stavlos, is known for its special theme nights, which you'll see advertised around town.

Discos

Discos operate in central Athens only between October and April. In summer, the action moves to the coastal suburbs of Glyfada and Ellinikon.

Lava Bore (☎ 21 0324 5335, *Filellinon 25*) Admission €6. Open 10pm-5pm daily. The Lava Bore is one city centre disco that stays open all year, although Filellinon 25 is its third address in five years. The formula remains much the same: a mixture of mainstream rock and techno, and large beers for €2.95. Entry includes free drink.

Plus Soda (winter ☎ 21 0345 6187, *Ermou 161, Thisio; summer* ☎ 21 0894 0205, *Eurualis 2, Glyfada*) Plus Soda is more glamorous with a cast of DJs turning out a diet of techno, trance and psychedelia for an energetic crowd of under 25s.

Gay Bars

The greatest concentration of gay bars is to be found around Makrigianni, south of the Temple of Olympian Zeus.

Granazi Bar (☎ 21 0924 4185, *Lembesi 20, Makrigianni*) Open 11pm-4am. The Granazi has long been at the forefront of the gay scene. These days, the ambience is Pet Shop Boys – played at a volume that permits only body language. It's popular with the under 35 crowd, who come to party.

Lamda Club (☎ 21 0922 4202, *Lembesi 15, Makrigianni*) Open 11pm-5am. The Lamda is the most risque of Makrigianni's bars, with chunky chains adorning the

walls and murals of well-muscled guys strutting their stuff. There's a dance floor upstairs, playing a mixture of Greek and mainstream Western rock, and various other rooms.

Fairytale (☎ 21 0330 1763, *Kolleti 25, Exarhia*) Open 10pm-3am. This intimate hole-in-the-wall bar is a favourite haunt of young lesbians.

Rock & Jazz Concerts

The *Rodon Club* (*Marni 24*), north of Omonia, hosts touring international rock bands, while local bands play at the *AN Club* (*Solomou 20, Exarhia*).

Rembetika Clubs

Rembetiki Stoa Athanaton (☎ 21 0321 4362, *Sofokleous 19*) Open 3pm-6pm, midnight-6am Mon-Sat Oct-May. The best-known club is the almost legendary Stoa Athanatonis, which occupies a hall above the central meat market. Despite its strange location, it features some of the biggest names on the local rembetika scene. Access is by a lift in the arcade at Sofokleous 19.

Greek Folk Dances

Dora Stratou Dance Company (☎ 21 0921 6650, *Dora Stratou Theatre, Filopappos Hill*) Adult/student €11.75/5.90. Performances 10.15pm daily May-Oct, also 8.15pm Wed & Sun. The Dora Stratou group has earned an international reputation for authenticity and professionalism, performing a wide selection of dances from around the country. The theatre is signposted from the western end of Dionysiou Areopagitou. Tickets can be bought at the door.

Sound-and-Light Show

Hill of the Pnyx Theatre (☎ 21 0322 1459, *Hill of the Pnyx*) Adult/child €8.80/4.40. English-language shows 9pm nightly Apr-Oct; French-language 10pm Wed, Thur, Sat-Mon; German-language 10pm Tues & Fri. This 'sound and light' spectacle here is not one of the world's best, but it is an enduring and integral part of the Athens tourist scene. The Hill of the Pnyx is west of the Acropolis off Dionysiou Areopagitou.

Spectator Sport

Almost half of the 18 teams in the Greek soccer first division are based in Athens or Piraeus. The most popular are Olympiakos (Piraeus) and Panathinaikos (Athens), who play at the Olympic Stadium on the alternate Sunday.

Shopping

The National Welfare Organisation shop, on the corner of Apollonos and Ipatias, Plaka, is a good place to go shopping for handicrafts. It has top-quality goods and the money goes to a good cause – the organisation was formed to preserve and promote traditional Greek handicrafts.

GETTING THERE & AWAY
Air

Athens is served by Eleftherios Venizelos International Airport at Spata, 21km east of Athens.

Facilities at the new airport, named in honour of the country's leading 20th-century politician, are immeasurably better than at the city's former airport at Ellnikon. Where Ellnikon was shabby and outdated, the new airport gleams. Built by a German consortium, everything is absolutely state of the art. In addition to standard facilities like cafes, restaurants, shops and banks, the new airport also has a hotel for transit passengers – although the Sofitel was still unfinished at the time of writing.

For Olympic Airways flight information ring ☎ 21 0936 3363, and for all other airlines ring ☎ 21 0969 4466/4467. The head office of Olympic Airways (☎ 21 0926 7251/52/53/54) is at Leoforos Syngrou 96. The most central Olympic Airways branch office (☎ 21 0926 7444, international ☎ 21 0926 7489) is at Filellinon 13, just off Plateia Syntagmatos.

See the Getting Around chapter for information on flights to/from the islands.

Bus

Athens has two main intercity bus stations. The EOT gives out schedules for both with departure times, journey times and fares.

Terminal A is north-west of Omonia at Kifissou 100 and has departures to the Peloponnese, the Ionian islands and western Greece. To get there, take bus No 051 from the junction of Zinonos and Menandrou, near Omonia. Buses run every 15 minutes from 5am to midnight.

Terminal B is north of Omonia off Liossion and has departures to central and northern Greece as well as to Evia. To get there take bus No 024 from outside the main gate of the National Gardens on Amalias. EOT misleadingly gives the terminal's address as Liossion 260, which turns out to be a small workshop. Liossion 260 is where you should get off the bus. Turn right onto Gousiou and you'll see the terminal at the end of the road.

Buses for Attica leave from the Mavromateon terminal at the junction of Alexandras and 28 Oktovriou-Patission.

Train

Athens has two train stations, located about 200m apart on Deligianni, which is about 1km north-west of Omonia. Trains to the Peloponnese leave from the Peloponnese station, while trains to the north leave from Larisis station – as do all the international trains.

Services to the Peloponnese include eight trains to Patras, four of which are intercity express (€10, 3½ hours), while services north include 10 trains a day to Thessaloniki, five of which are intercity express (€27.60, six hours). The 7am service from Athens is express right through to Alexandroupolis, arriving at 7pm. There are also trains to Volos and Halkida, Evia.

The easiest way to get to the stations is on metro Line 2 to Larisa, outside Larisis station. The Peloponnese station is across the footbridge at the southern end of Larisis station. Tickets can be bought at the stations or at the OSE offices at Sina 6 and Karolou 1.

Car & Motorcycle

National Rd 1 is the main route north from Athens. It starts at Nea Kifissia. To get there from central Athens, take Vasilissis Sofias from Syntagma and follow the signs. National Rd 8, which begins beyond Dafni,

The Rocky Road to 2004

The eyes of the world will be upon Athens for 17 days in August 2004 when athletes from some 200 countries descend on the city for the 29th Olympiad.

It will be the end of a dramatic seven years of what is turning into an emotional roller-coaster ride for the people of Athens. Back in 1997, when the city won the right to host the games, there was jubilation that the games were coming home to Greece after 108 years. Slowly but surely, the magnitude of the task ahead began to sink in – and jubilation gave way to anxiety. Anxiety was replaced by alarm after Sydney raised the organisational standard to new heights in 2000. It quickly developed into despondency amid a series of dire warnings from the International Olympic Committee (IOC) about the lack of progress.

At the time of writing, the IOC appeared sufficiently satisfied with recent developments to issue an assurance that Athens would not be stripped of the games, leading to a huge sense of relief. Doubtless there will be many more ups and downs before the ride comes to an end.

Many people have questioned the sanity of staging the games in August in one of Europe's hottest and most polluted capitals. The environmental watchdog, Greenpeace, has expressed concerns over the possible effects of traffic fumes on the health of athletes. Organisers argue that August is normally a quiet traffic month, because most Athenians have enough sense to abandon the city for the coast and the islands. It remains to be seen if this exodus is repeated in Olympic year.

The Olympics seem sure to be a source of constant anxiety right up until the opening ceremony, but Greece is deeply committed – both emotionally and financially – to making them work.

Olympic Venues

The centrepiece is the 80,000-seat Olympic Stadium, in the northern suburb of Maroussi, which will stage the athletic events as well as the opening and closing ceremonies. The stadium has doubled as the city's number one soccer venue since it was completed in 1996.

The stadium is part of the Athens Olympic Sports Complex, next to Irini metro station, which also includes an indoor sports hall for gymnastics and basketball, a swimming complex with diving pool, a velodrome and a tennis centre. The rhythmic gymnastics, table tennis and water polo will take place 4km south of the stadium at the Galatsi Olympic Indoor Hall.

---

is the road to the Peloponnese. Take Agiou Konstantinou from Omonia.

The northern reaches of Syngrou, just south of the Temple of Olympian Zeus, are packed solid with car-rental firms.

Ferry

See the Piraeus section of the Mainland Ports chapter for information on ferries to/from the islands.

GETTING AROUND
To/From the Airport

There are two special express bus services operating between the airport and the city as well as a service between the airport and Piraeus.

Service E94 operates between the airport and the eastern terminus of Metro line 3 at Ethniki Amyna. There are departures every 16 minutes, according to the official timetable, between 6am and midnight. The journey takes about 25 minutes.

Service E95 operates between the airport and Plateia Syntagmatos. This line operates 24 hours with services approximately every 30 minutes. The bus stop is outside the National Gardens on Amalias on the eastern side of Plateia Syntagmatos. The journey takes between an hour and 90 minutes, depending on traffic conditions.

Service E96 operates between the airport and Plateia Karaïskaki in Piraeus. This line

The Rocky Road to 2004

The other main area of Olympic activity is in the costal suburb of Faliro. Karaïskaki Stadium, home ground for the Olympiakos soccer club, will host the preliminary rounds of – what else – soccer (the semi-finals and finals will take place at the Nea Philadelphia Stadium, 3km west of the Olympic Stadium), while the nearby Peace and Friendship Stadium will be used for handball and basketball. The yachting will be held in Faliro Bay, and the beach volleyball at Faliro Beach.

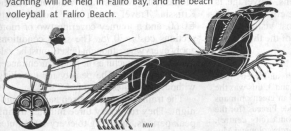

The Faliro Ippodromo, Athens' premier horse-racing track, will host the judo, boxing and tae kwon do. Naturally enough, the marathon will start from Marathon – the town which gave the race its name. It will finish at the Panathenaic Stadium – the home of the first modern Olympic Games. The stadium will also host the archery.

Other venues include the Markopoulo Olympic Shooting and Equestrian Centre, 10km south of Peania; the Ano Liossia Olympic Indoor Hall, in northern Athens, which will stage the wrestling; the Nikea Olympic Hall, in western Athens, where the weightlifting will take place; a new Olympic Centre at Ellnikon, the old international airport, will hold the baseball, softball, hockey and badminton events; the Vouliagmeni Olympic Triathlon Centre, 8km south of Glyfada; and the Goudi Olympic Modern Pentathlon Centre, west of central Athens. The cycling road race will be raced through Athens' historical centre and the mountain-biking event will be staged at Mt Parnitha. The rowing and kayaking events look certain to be held at a new Olympic Rowing Centre at Shinias, near Marathon, despite continuing controversy about the destruction of coastal wetlands.

Soccer is the only event that will be staged outside Attica, with Iraklio, Patras, Thessaloniki and Volos to host group and quarterfinal matches.

For updated details on Olympic venues and news log on to the official Athens 2004 Web site at Ⓦ www.athens.olympic.org.

also operates 24 hours, with services approximately every 40 minutes.

Tickets for all these services cost €2.95. The tickets are valid for 24 hours, and can be used on all forms of public transport in Athens – buses, trolleybuses and the metro.

Taxi fares vary according to the time of day and level of traffic, but you should expect to pay €14.70-20.55 from the airport to the city centre, and €17.60-23.50 to Piraeus, depending on traffic conditions. Both trips should take no longer than an hour.

Bus & Trolleybus

Blue-and-white suburban buses operate from 5am to midnight. Route numbers and destinations, but not the actual routes, are listed on the free EOT map. The map does, however, mark the routes of the yellow trolleybuses, making them easy to use. They also run from 5am to midnight.

There are special buses that operate 24 hours a day to Piraeus. Bus No 040 leaves from the corner of Syntagma and Filellinon, and No 049 leaves from the Omonia end of Athinas. They run every 20 minutes from 6am to midnight, and then hourly.

Tickets for all these services cost €0.45, and must be purchased before you board – either from a ticket booth or from a *periptero* (kiosk). The same tickets can be used on either buses or trolleybuses and must be validated as soon as you board. The

Phone numbers listed incorporate changes due in Oct 2002; see p55

penalty for travelling without a validated ticket is €17.60.

Metro

The opening of the first phase of the long-awaited new metro system has transformed travel around central Athens. Coverage is still largely confined to the city centre, but that's good enough for most visitors. The following is a brief outline of the three lines that make up the network:

Line 1 Line 1 is the old Kifissia-Piraeus line. Until the opening of Lines 2 and 3, this was the metro system. It is indicated in green on maps and signs. Useful stops include Piraeus (for the port), Monastiraki and Omonia (city centre), Plateia Viktorias (National Archaeological Museum) and Irini (Olympic Stadium). Omonia and Attiki are transfer stations with connections to Line 2; Monastiraki will eventually become a transfer station with connections to Line 3.

Line 2 Line 2 runs from Sepolia in the north-west to Dafni in the south-east. It is indicated in red on maps and signs. Useful stops include Larisa (for the train stations), Omonia, Panepistimiou and Syntagma (city centre) and Akropoli (Makrigianni). Attiki and Omonia are transfer stations for Line 1, while Syntagma is the transfer station for Line 3.

Line 3 Line 3 runs north-east from Syntagma to Ethniki Amyna. It is indicated in blue on maps and signs. Useful stops are Evangelismos (for the museums on Vasilissis Sofias) and Ethnik Amyna (buses to the airport). Syntagma is the transfer station for Line 2.

Travel on Lines 2 and 3 costs €0.75, while Line 1 is split into three sections: Piraeus-Monastiraki, Monastiraki-Attiki and Attiki-Kifissia. Travel within one section costs €0.60, and a journey covering two or more sections costs €0.75. The same conditions apply everywhere though: tickets must be validated at the machines at platform entrances before travelling. The penalty for travelling without a validated ticket is €23.50.

The trains operate between 5am and midnight. They run every three minutes during peak periods, dropping to every 10 minutes at other times.

Taxi

Athenian taxis are yellow. The flag fall is €0.75, with a €0.60 surcharge from ports, and train and bus stations, and a €0.90 surcharge from the airport. After the day rate (tariff 1 on the meter) is €0.23/km. The rate doubles between midnight and 5am (tariff 2 on the meter).

Baggage is charged at the rate of €0.30 per item over 10kg. The minimum fare is €1.50, which covers most journeys in central Athens.

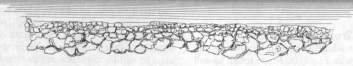

Mainland Ports

This chapter is designed to provide all the information a traveller needs to get from the mainland to the islands. It begins with the ports that serve more than one island group: Piraeus, Rafina, Thessaloniki and Gythio. The remaining ports are grouped according to the island groups they serve as designated in the following list:

Saronic Gulf Islands
  Piraeus
Cyclades
  Piraeus, Rafina, Thessaloniki, Lavrio
Crete
  Piraeus, Gythio, Kalamata, Thessaloniki
Dodecanese
  Piraeus, Thessaloniki
North-Eastern Aegean Islands
  Piraeus, Rafina, Thessaloniki,
  Alexandroupolis, Kavala, Keramoti,
Ionian Islands
  Patras, Astakos, Gythio, Igoumenitsa, Kyllini,
  Neapoli, Sagiada
Evia & the Sporades
  Thessaloniki, Agios Konstantinos, Volos

Piraeus Πειραιάς

postcode 185 01 • pop 171,000

Piraeus (pir-ay-**ahs**) is the port of Athens, the main port of Greece and one of the major ports of the Mediterranean.

Piraeus has been the port of Athens since classical times, when the two were linked by defensive walls. Nowadays, Athens has expanded sufficiently to meld imperceptibly into Piraeus. The road linking the two passes through a grey, urban sprawl of factories, warehouses and concrete apartment blocks. The streets are every bit as traffic-clogged as Athens, and behind the veneer of banks and shipping offices most of Piraeus is pretty seedy. The only reason to come here is to catch a ferry or hydrofoil.

Orientation

Piraeus is 10km south-west of central Athens. The largest of its three harbours is

MAINLAND PORTS

the Great Harbour (Megas Limin) on the western side of the Piraeus Peninsula. All ferries leave from here, as well as hydrofoil and catamaran services to Aegina and the Cyclades. There are dozens of shipping agents around the harbour, as well as banks and a post office. Zea Marina (Limin Zeas), on the other side of the peninsula, is the main port for hydrofoils to the Saronic Gulf Islands (except Aegina). East of here is the picturesque, small harbour Mikrolimano.

The metro line from Athens terminates at the north-eastern corner of the Great Harbour on Akti Kalimassioti. Most ferry departure points are a short walk from here. A left turn out of the metro station leads after 250m to Plateia Karaïskaki, which is the terminus for buses to the airport.

South-east of Plateia Karaïskaki, the waterfront becomes Akti Poseidonos, which leads into Vasileos Georgiou beyond Plateia Themistokleous. Vasileos Georgiou is one of the two main streets of Piraeus, running south-east across the peninsula; the other main street is Iroön Polytehniou, which runs south-west along the ridge of the peninsula, meeting Vasileos Georgiou by the main square, Plateia Korai.

Information

EOT has a fairly useless office (☎ 21 0452 2586/2591) overlooking the harbour at Zea Marina. For the record, it's open 8am to 3pm Monday to Friday. The telephone number of Piraeus' port police is ☎ 21 0412 2501.

Money There are lots of places to change money at the Great Harbour, including virtually all the ticket and travel agencies. The Emporiki Bank, just north of Plateia Themistokleous on the corner of Antistaseos and Makras Stoas, has a 24-hour automatic exchange machine. The National Bank of Greece has a Great Harbour branch at the corner of Antistaseos and Tsamadou, and another branch above the maritime museum at Zea Marina.

Post & Communications The main post office is on the corner of Tsamadou and Filonos, just north of Plateia Themistokleous. It's open 7.30am to 8pm Monday to Friday and until 2pm Saturday. The OTE is just north of here at Karaoli 19 and is open 24 hours.

You can check email at the Surf Internet Café, Platonos 3, just off Iroön Polytehniou. It's open 8am to 9pm Monday to Friday and 8am to 3pm Saturday.

Archaeological Museum

If you have time to spare in Piraeus, the archaeological museum (☎ 21 0452 1598, Harilaou Trikoupi 31; admission €1.50; open 8.30am-3pm Tues-Sun) is a good place to spend it. The star attraction is a magnificent statue of Apollo, the Piraeus Kouros. It is the oldest larger-than-life, hollow bronze statue yet found. It dates from about 520 BC and was discovered, buried in rubble, in 1959.

Hellenic Maritime Museum

The maritime museum (☎ 21 0451 6822, Akti Themistokleous; admission €1.20; open 9am-2pm Tues-Sat) has a collection spanning the history of the Greek navy from ancient times to the present day, with drawings and plans of battles, models of ships, battle scenes, uniforms and war memorabilia.

Places to Stay

There's no reason to stay at any of the shabby hotels around Great Harbour when Athens is so close. The cheap hotels are geared more towards accommodating sailors than tourists. Whatever happens, don't attempt to sleep out – Piraeus is the most dangerous place in Greece to do so.

Hotel Delfini (☎ 21 0412 9779, fax 21 0417 3110, Leoharous 7) Singles/doubles with bathroom €26.40/35.20. The Delfini is an uninspiring C-class hotel, but OK in an emergency. Make sure you don't get taken there by one of the touts who hang around the port or you will wind up paying over the odds.

Places to Eat

Great Harbour There are dozens of cafes, restaurants and fast-food places along the waterfront.

Restaurant I Folia (☎ 21 0421 0781, Akti Poseidonos 30) Mains €2.45-4.20. This tiny restaurant, opposite Plateia Karaïskaki, is perfect for a quick bite before you board a ferry.

You'll find fresh fruit and vegetables at the *markets* on Demosthenous. Opposite the markets is *Pairaikon supermarket* (☎ 21 0411 7177; open 8am-8pm Mon-Fri, 8am-4pm Sat).

Zea Marina The choice is more limited over at Zea Marina.

La Tradizione (☎ 21 0451 7519, Akti Moutsoupoulou 12) Mains €4.10-6.75. You'll find pasta dishes and pizzas at this Italian restaurant next to the Flying Dolphin office.

Getting There & Away

Bus There are two 24-hour bus services between central Athens and Piraeus. Bus No 049 runs from Omonia to the Great Harbour, and bus No 040 runs from Syntagma to the tip of the Piraeus peninsula. This is the

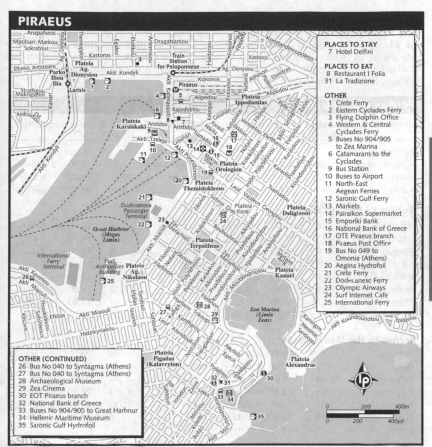

PIRAEUS

PLACES TO STAY
7 Hotel Delfini

PLACES TO EAT
8 Restaurant I Folia
31 La Tradizione

OTHER
1 Crete Ferry
2 Eastern Cyclades Ferry
3 Flying Dolphin Office
4 Western & Central
  Cyclades Ferry
5 Buses No 904/905
  to Zea Marina
6 Catamarans to the
  Cyclades
9 Bus Station
10 Buses to Airport
11 North-East
   Aegean Ferries
12 Saronic Gulf Ferry
13 Markets
14 Pairaikon Supermarket
15 Emporiki Bank
16 National Bank of Greece
17 OTE Piraeus branch
18 Piraeus Post Office
19 Bus No 049 to
   Omonia (Athens)
20 Aegina Hydrofoil
21 Crete Ferry
22 Dodecanese Ferry
23 Olympic Airways
24 Surf Internet Cafe
25 International Ferry

OTHER (CONTINUED)
26 Bus No 040 to Syntagma (Athens)
27 Bus No 040 to Syntagma (Athens)
28 Archaeological Museum
29 Zea Cinema
30 EOT Piraeus branch
32 National Bank of Greece
33 Buses No 904/905 to Great Harbour
34 Hellenic Maritime Museum
35 Saronic Gulf Hydrofoil

MAINLAND PORTS

service to catch for Zea Marina – get off at the Hotel Savoy on Iroön Polytehniou – and leave plenty of time as the trip can take over an hour in bad traffic. The fare is €0.45 on each service. There are no intercity buses to or from Piraeus.

E96 buses to the airport leave from the southern side of Plateia Karaïskaki.

Metro The metro is the fastest and easiest way of getting from the Great Harbour to central Athens (see the Getting Around section of the Athens chapter). The station is at the northern end of Akti Kalimassioti.

Train Railway services to the Peloponnese actually start and terminate at Piraeus, although most schedules don't mention this fact. The train station is a block north of the metro station. See the Getting There & Away section of the Athens chapter for more information about trains.

Getting Around

Local bus bus Nos 904 and 905 run between the Great Harbour and Zea Marina. They leave from the bus stop beside the metro at Great Harbour, and drop you by the maritime museum at Zea Marina.

Phone numbers listed incorporate changes due in Oct 2002; see p55

Getting to the Islands

Ferry Piraeus is the busiest port in Greece with a bewildering array of departures and destinations, including daily services to all the island groups except the Ionians and the Sporades. See the Ferries from Piraeus table in this section for a complete list of destinations.

For the latest departure information, pick up a weekly ferry schedule from the tourist office in central Athens and at the airport.

MAINLAND PORTS

Ferries from Piraeus

destination	duration (hours)	price (€)	frequency	destination	duration (hours)	price (€)	frequency
Ferries to Crete							
Agios Nikolaos	12	22.60	3 weekly	Kastelli-Kissamou	12	17.10	2 weekly
Hania	10	19.90	1 daily	Rethymno	10-12	21.40	1 daily
Iraklio	10	21.10	2 daily	Sitia	14½	23.40	3 weekly
Ferries to the Cyclades							
Amorgos	10	15.00	2 daily	Naxos	6	14.70	6 daily
Anafi	11	19.70	4 weekly	Paros	5	14.70	6 daily
Folegandros	6-9	14.70	4 weekly	Santorini	9	18.00	4 daily
Ios	7½	15.80	4 daily	Serifos	4½	11.45	1 daily
Kimolos	6	13.20	2 weekly	Sifnos	5	12.60	1 daily
Kythnos	2½	9.10	3 daily	Sikinos	8-10	17.00	9 weekly
Milos	7	14.70	2 daily	Syros	4	12.90	3 daily
Mykonos	5½	15.10	3 daily	Tinos	4½	13.80	1 daily
Ferries to the Dodecanese							
Astpalea	12	21.40	3 weekly	Lipsi	16	28.00	1 weekly
Halki	22	29.50	2 weekly	Nisyros	13-15	23.20	2 weekly
Kalymnos	10-13	21.80	1 daily	Patmos	9½	21.00	1 daily
Karpathos	18½	24.40	4 weekly	Rhodes	15-18	26.70	2 daily
Kasos	17	24.00	4 weekly	Symi	15-17	21.20	2 weekly
Kos	12-15	23.20	2 daily	Tilos	15	21.80	2 weekly
Leros	11	19.70	1 daily				
Ferries to the Ionians							
Agia Pelagia (Kythira)	6½	16.50	2 weekly				
Ferries to the North-Eastern Aegean							
Chios	8	17.00	1 daily	Lesvos (Mytilini)	12	22.50	1 daily
Fournoi	10	17.60	3 weekly	Limnos	13	21.00	4 weekly
Ikaria	9	17.00	1 daily	Samos	13	20.50	2 daily
Ferries to the Saronic Gulf Islands							
Aegina	1¼	4.40	1 hourly	Poros	2½	6.45	4 daily
Hydra	3½	7.35	2 daily	Spetses	4½	10.00	1 daily

The departure points for the various ferry destinations are shown on the map of Piraeus. Note that there are two departure points for Crete. Ferries for Iraklio leave from the western end of Akti Kondyli, but ferries for other Cretan ports occasionally dock there as well. It's a long way to the other departure point for Crete on Akti Miaouli, so check where to find your boat when you buy your ticket.

Hydrofoil & Catamaran Minoan Lines operates Flying Dolphins (hydrofoils) and high-speed catamarans to the Cyclades and the Saronic Gulf from early April to the end of October. It also has occasional services to the Ionian island of Kythira.

Services to Aegina leave from Great Harbour, near Plateia Themistokleous. Some services to Poros, Hydra and Spetses also leave from here, but most leave from Zea Marina. Services to the Cyclades leave from the northern side of Plateia Karaïskaki.

See the table in this section for a complete list of destinations. For the latest departure information, pick up a timetable from the Flying Dolphin offices quayside at Great Harbour and Zea Marina.

Tickets to Aegina can be bought quayside; tickets to other destinations should be bought in advance from Flying Dolphin offices. Phone ☎ 21 0428 0001 for reservations; you can make credit card payments by phone.

Rafina Ραφήνα

postcode 190 09 • pop 10,000
Rafina, on Attica's east coast, is Athens' main fishing port and second port for passenger ferries. The port is much smaller than Piraeus and less confusing – and fares are about 20% cheaper, but you have to spend an hour on the bus and €1.80 to get there.

The port police (☎ 22 9402 2888) occupy a kiosk near the quay, which is lined with fish restaurants and ticket agencies. The main square, Plateia Plastira, is at the top of the ramp leading to the port.

MAINLAND PORTS

Hydrofoils from Piraeus

destination	duration (hours)	price (€)	frequency	destination	duration (hours)	price (€)	frequency
Cyclades (*from Zea Marina)							
Kythnos	1¾	17.60	5 weekly	Serifos	2¾	22.30	daily
Milos	4½	28.80	daily	Sifnos	3½	24.95	daily
Mykonos	3½	29.65	2 daily	Syros	2½	25.25	2 daily
Naxos	3¼	27.30	2 daily	Tinos	3	27	daily
Paros	2½	28.80	2 daily				
Peloponnese (*most from Zea Marina)							
Ermioni*	2	15.85	4 daily	Leonidio*	2½	21.15	daily
Gerakas*	3½	23.80	daily	Monemvasia*	2½	26.15	daily
Kyparissi*	3	22.30	daily	Porto Heli*	2	17	6 daily
Saronic Gulf Islands (*most from Zea Marina)							
Aegina	½	8.50	hourly	Poros*	1	12.35	6 daily
Hydra*	1¼	13.80	7 daily	Spetses*	2	19.10	7 daily
Ionian Islands (from Zea Marina)							
Kythira	5	30.80	daily				

Phone numbers listed incorporate changes due in Oct 2002; see p55

Getting There & Away

Bus There are frequent buses from the Mavromateon terminal in Athens to Rafina (one hour, €1.50) between 5.45am and 10.30pm. The first bus leaves Rafina for the Athens bus terminal at 5.50am and the last at 10.15pm.

Getting to the Islands

Ferry Blue Star Ferries operates a daily service at 8am to Andros (two hours, €7.35), Tinos (3½ hours, €11.15) and Mykonos (4½ hours, €12.65). The company also has a daily evening ferry to Andros, continuing to Tinos and Mykonos on Friday.

The Maritime Company of Lesvos has four boats weekly to Limnos (10 hours, €17).

There are also ferries to the ports of Karystos (1¾ hours, €5.60, two daily) and Marmari (1¼ hours, €3.80, four daily) on the island of Evia.

Catamaran Blue Star Ferries and Minoan Lines operate high-speed catamarans to the Cyclades.

Blue Star has three services daily to Tinos (1¾ hours, €22.30) and Mykonos (2¼ hours, €25.25), departing at 7.40am, noon and 5.30pm. The 7.40am service continues to Paros (three hours, €25.55); on Tuesday it goes all the way to Amorgos (five hours, €29.05).

Minoan operates giant vehicle-carrying catamarans on a daily run to Syros (1¾ hours, €21.15), Mykonos (two hours, €25.25), and Paros (three hours, €25.55). They continue to Santorini (4¾ hours, €29.35) six times weekly, stopping at Ios (four hours, €25.55) four times weekly.

Minoan operates smaller catamarans on the daily 7.55am route to Tinos (1½ hours, €22.30), Mykonos (two hours, €25.25) and Paros (2¾ hours, €25.55).

The Wednesday morning service also calls at Andros (one hour, €14.70), and continues from Paros to Amorgos (4½ hours, €29.05) and Ios (5½ hours, €25.55). Minoan operates an additional 3pm service to Tinos and Mykonos five times weekly.

Thessaloniki
Θεσσαλονίκη

postcode 541 00 • pop 750,000

Thessaloniki, also known as Salonica, is Greece's second-largest city. It's a bustling, sophisticated place with good restaurants and a busy nightlife. It was once the second city of Byzantium, and there are some magnificent Byzantine churches, as well as a scattering of Roman ruins.

Orientation

Thessaloniki is laid out on a grid system. The main thoroughfares – Tsimiski, Egnatia and Agiou Dimitriou – run parallel to Nikis, which runs along the waterfront. Plateias Eleftherias and Aristotelous, both on Nikis, are the main squares. The city's most famous landmark is the White Tower (no longer white) at the eastern end of Nikis. The train station is on Monastiriou, the westerly continuation of Egnatia beyond Plateia Dimokratias, and the airport is 16km to the south-east. The old Turkish quarter is north of Athinas.

Information

Tourist Office The EOT (☎ 23 1022 2935), Plateia Aristotelous 8, is open 8.30am to 8pm Monday to Friday and until 2pm Saturday.

Money Most banks around town are equipped with credit card-friendly ATMs. You will find most banks along central Tsimiski. The National Bank of Greece at Tsimiski 11 opens on weekends for foreign exchange only.

Midas Exchange, at the western end of Tsimiski close to the Ladadika district, is handy for people using the ferry terminal. It's open 8.30am to 8.30pm Monday to Friday, until 2pm Saturday and 9am to 1.30pm Sunday.

Post & Communications The main post office is at Aristotelous 26 and is open 7.30am to 8pm Monday to Friday, until 2.15pm Saturday and 9am to 1.30pm

THESSALONIKI

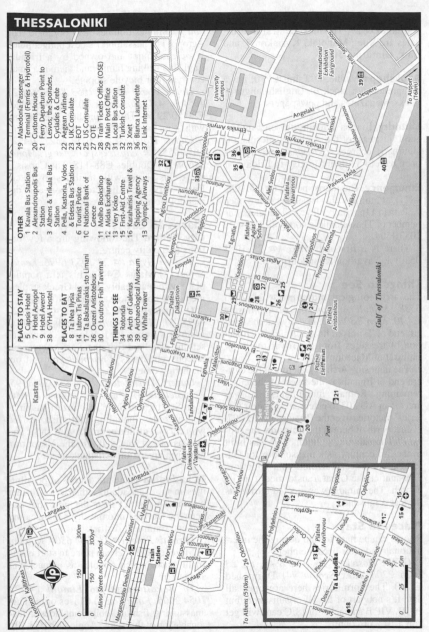

PLACES TO STAY
5 Capsis Hotel
7 Hotel Acropol
9 Hotel Averof
38 CYHA Hostel

PLACES TO EAT
8 Ta Nea Ilysia
14 Iatros Tis Pinas
17 Ta Bakaliarakia sto Limani
26 Ouzeri Aristotelous
30 O Loutros Fish Taverna

THINGS TO SEE
34 Rotonda
35 Arch of Galerius
39 Archaeological Museum
40 White Tower

OTHER
1 Kavala Bus Station
2 Alexandroupolis Bus Station
3 Athens & Trikala Bus Station
4 Pella, Kastoria, Volos & Edessa Bus Station
6 Tourist Police
10 National Bank of Greece
11 Molho Bookshop
12 Midas Exchange
13 Very Koko
15 First-Aid Centre
16 Karaharisis Travel & Shipping Agency
13 Olympic Airways
19 Makedonia Passenger Terminal (Ferries & Hydrofoil)
20 Customs House
21 Ferry Departure Point to Lesvos, the Sporades, Cyclades & Crete
22 Aegean Airlines
23 UK Consulate
24 EOT
25 US Consulate
27 OTE
28 Train Tickets Office (OSE)
29 Main Post Office
31 Local Bus Station
32 Turkish Consulate
33 Xnet
36 Bianca Laundrette
37 Link Internet

Sunday. The OTE, open 24 hours, is at Karolou Dil 27. The most central Internet cafes are Xnet, Manolaki Kyriakou 5, and Link, Dimitriou 50.

Bookshops Molho, at Tsimiski 10, has a comprehensive stock of English-language books, magazines and newspapers.

Laundry Bianca Laundrette, on Antoniadou (just east of the Arch of Galerius, off Gournari), charges €5 to wash and dry. It's open 8am to 8.30pm Monday to Friday.

Emergency The tourist police (☎ 23 1055 4871), at 5th floor, Dodekanisou 4, are open 7.30am to 11pm daily all year. The telephone number of Thessaloniki's port police is ☎ 23 1053 1504.

There is a first aid centre (☎ 23 1053 0530) at Navarhou Koundourioti 6.

Things to See
The **archaeological museum** (☎ 23 1083 0538, Manoli Andronikou 6; admission €4.40; open 8.30am-3pm daily), at the eastern end of Tsimiski, houses a superb collection of treasures from the royal tombs of Philip II of Macedon.

The imposing **Arch of Galerius** at the eastern end of Egnatia is the finest of the city's remaining Roman monuments. It was erected in AD 303 to celebrate Emperor Galerius' victories over the Persians in AD 297.

Just north of here is the **Rotonda**, the oldest of Thessaloniki's churches. It was built in the 3rd century as a mausoleum for Galerius, but never fulfilled this function. Constantine the Great transformed it into a church. The minaret was erected during its days as a mosque.

Places to Stay
Rooms can be hard to find during the international trade fair in September.

GYHA Hostel (☎ 23 1022 5946, fax 23 1026 2208, Alex Svolou 44) Dorm bed €7.40. The dormitories here are open all day. It's not part of the HI organisation, but an HI, VIP Backpacker or ISIC card will get you a 10% discount.

Hotel Acropol (☎ 23 1053 6170, Tandalidou 4) Singles/doubles €17.60/26.50 The Acropol is Thessaloniki's best budget hotel. It's clean, quiet and owned by a friendly English-speaking family and there is a small courtyard for bicycle storage.

Hotel Averof (☎ 23 1053 8498, fax 23 1054 3194, Leotos Sofou 24) Singles/doubles €20.50/29.50. This is another quiet option, with attractive pine-furnished rooms.

Capsis Hotel (☎ 23 1052 1321, fax 23 1051 0555, ℮ capsis@spark.net.gr, Monastiriou 18) Doubles €88-118. The Capsis is an A-class hotel with facilities to match. Rates vary according to season and demand. Prices include breakfast.

Places to Eat
City Centre The following are a few options in the city centre.

Ta Nea Ilysia (☎ 23 1053 6996, Leotos Sofou 17) Mains €4-5. This is a popular place with reasonably priced Greek staples, including good mousakas (€4.40).

O Loutros Fish Taverna (☎ 23 1022 8895, M. Koundoura 5) Meals €6-9. O Loutros is a must for fish lovers. As well as serving excellent fish, there are often spontaneous renderings of *rembetika* music from the happy diners.

Ouzeri Aristotelous (☎ 23 1023 3195, Aristotelous 8) Mains €7. Open to late Mon-Sat, to 6pm Sun. This ouzeri has first-rate mezedes including cuttlefish stuffed with cheese, grilled eggplant with garlic and prawns in red sauce. It's in the Vosporion Megaron arcade off Aristotelous.

Ta Ladadika There are dozens of possibilities in the Ta Ladadika district, a former warehouse district near the port that has been transformed into the city's main eating and entertainment district.

Iatros tis Pinas (☎ 23 1054 6304, Katouni 7) Mezedes €3. A cheap place to start is this small place, which doubles as a snack bar and ouzeri.

Ta Bakaliarakia sto Limani (☎ 23 1054 2906, Fasianou 4) Closes 6pm. This unassuming fish-and-chip joint does a reasonable job of this staple Anglo dish (€3.50).

Entertainment

Music bars abound in **Ta Ladadika**. The best advice is to wander around until you find a sound that you like. *Very Koko* (☎ 23 1054 4554, Plateia Morihovou) is a good place to start if you want Greek music.

Getting There & Away

Air Olympic shares the route to Athens with Aegean Airlines. Both charge €84, although discounts are often available. See the Getting There & Away chapter at the start of this book for information on international flights, and the following Getting to the Islands section for flights to the islands from Thessaloniki.

The Olympic Airways office (☎ 23 1036 8666) is at Navarhou Koundourioti 1–3. Aegean Airlines (☎ 23 1028 0050) is at El Venizelou 2

Bus There are numerous bus terminals, most of them near the train station. Frequent buses for Athens and Trikala leave from Monastiriou 65 and 67, opposite the train station; buses for Alexandroupolis leave from Koloniari 17 behind the train station; buses for Volos leave from Anagenniseos 22. Kavala buses leave from Langada 59, on the main road north out of Thessaloniki.

Train There are eight trains a day to Athens and five to Alexandroupolis. All international trains from Athens stop at Thessaloniki. You can get more information from the OSE office at Aristotelous 18 or from the train station.

Getting Around

To/From the Airport The airport (☎ 23 1047 3212) is 16km south-east of the city. You can get there on public bus No 78, which stops outside the train station and near the ferry terminal; the fare is €0.50. A taxi costs about €7.50.

Bus There is a flat fare of €0.30 within the city on city buses, paid either to a conductor at the rear door or to coin-operated machines on driver-only buses.

Getting to the Islands

Air Olympic has flights to Limnos (€56, one daily), Mytilini (€76.30, six weekly), Corfu (€73.40, three weekly), Iraklio (€96.85, three weekly), Mykonos (€91.30, three weekly), Rhodes (€105.40, three weekly), Hania (€103.30, two weekly), Chios (€76.30, two weekly) and Samos (€88, two weekly).

Aegean has two flights daily to Iraklio (€98.60) and a daily flight to Rhodes (€104.50).

Ferry There is a weekly ferry, on Sunday, to Chios (18 hours, €31.40) via Limnos (seven hours, €16.50) and Lesvos (13 hours, €25.50) throughout the year.

There are three boats weekly to Iraklio on Crete (23 hours, €37.90) via the Cyclades ports of Mykonos (13½ hours, €29.05) and Santorini (19 hours, €31.15), stopping twice a week at Tinos (12½ hours, €28.50) and Paros (15¼ hours, €29.05), and once a week at Skiathos (5¾ hours, €13.20), Syros (11¼ hours, €26.40) and Naxos (15¼ hours, €27.30).

There are also additional boats just to Skiathos (seven hours, €13.20, three weekly) in July and August, and to Rhodes (21 hours, €45, weekly) via Samos and Kos throughout the year.

Ferry tickets are available from Karaharisis Travel & Shipping Agency (☎ 23 1052 4544, fax 23 1053 2289), Navarhou Koundourioti 8.

Hydrofoil & Catamaran In summer there are six hydrofoils weekly to the Sporades islands of Skiathos (3¼ hours, €26), Skopelos (four hours, €25.50) and Alonnisos (4½ hours, €25.50). Tickets can be purchased from Karaharisis Travel & Shipping Agency (see Ferry earlier).

Gythio Γύθειο

postcode 232 00 • pop 4900
Gythio (yee-thih-o), once the port of ancient Sparta, is an attractive fishing town at the head of the Lakonian Gulf. It is the most convenient port of departure for the Ionian

island of Kythira, and also has services to Kastelli-Kissamos on Crete.

Orientation

Most things of importance to travellers are along the seafront on Akti Vasileos Pavlou. The bus station is at the northern end, next to the small triangular park known as the Perivolaki. Vasileos Georgiou runs inland from here past the main square Plateia Panagiotou Venetzanaki, and becomes the road to Sparta.

The square at the southern end of Akti Vasileos Pavlou is Plateia Mavromihali, hub of the old quarter of Marathonisi. The ferry quay is opposite this square. Beyond it, the waterfront road becomes Kranais. A causeway leads out to Marathonisi Islet at the southern edge of town.

Information

The EOT (☎/fax 2733 024 484) is about 500m north of the waterfront at Vasileos Georgiou 20, open 11am to 3pm Monday to Friday.

The post office is on Ermou, in the newer part of the town two blocks north of the bus station, and the OTE office is between the two at the corner of Herakles and Kapsali. Travellers can access email at Electron Computers, Kapsali 5, opposite OTE.

The tourist police (☎ 2733 022 271) share lodgings with the regular police (☎ 2733 022 100) on the waterfront between the bus station and Plateia Mavromihali.

Things to Do

According to mythology, the island of **Marathonisi** is ancient Cranae, where Paris (a prince of Troy) and Helen (the wife of Menelaus of Sparta) consummated the love affair that sparked the Trojan War.

An 18th-century **tower** at the centre of the island has been restored and converted into a **museum** (☎ 2733 024 484, Marathonisi; admission €1.50; open 9am-7pm).

Gythio's small **ancient theatre** is next to an army camp on the northern edge of town. Most of ancient Gythio lies beneath the nearby Lakonian Gulf.

Places to Stay & Eat

Xenia Karlaftis Rooms to Rent (☎ 2733 022 719, Kranais) Singles/doubles/triples with bathroom €20.55/26.40/29.35. This is the best budget option in town, located opposite Marathonisi Islet. There's a communal kitchen area upstairs with a fridge and small stove for making tea and coffee.

Saga Pension (☎ 2733 023 220, fax 2733 024 370, Kranais) Singles/doubles with bathroom €20.55/29.35. The French-run Saga, 150m from the port, is also good value for comfortable rooms with air-con and TV.

Oinomagereion O Potis (☎ 2733 024 253, Moretti 5) Mains €2.95-8.25. This cheerful place has an interesting menu with a good selection of salads. It's just uphill from Plateia Mavromihali, at the corner of Tzannibi Gregoraki and Moretti.

General Store & Wine Bar (☎ 2733 024 113, Vasileos Georgiou 67) Mains €5.30-10.30. For something completely different, head inland to this tiny restaurant run by the Greek-Canadian Thomakos family.

You'll find an unusually varied and imaginative menu featuring dishes like orange and pumpkin soup (€2.95) and fillet of pork with black pepper and ouzo (€10.30).

Getting There & Away

There are five buses a day to Athens (4¼ hours, €14.10) via Sparta (one hour, €2.50).

Getting to the Islands

ANEN Lines operates services from Gythio to Kastelli-Kissamos on Crete (seven hours, €15.60) via Kythira (2½ hours, €7.10) three times weekly between June and September.

The schedule is always subject to constant change, so check with Rozakis Travel (☎ 2733 022 207, fax 2733 022 229, e ro sakigy@otenet.gr), on the waterfront near Plateia Mavromihali, before coming here to catch a boat.

These services travel via Kalamata once a week in high season.

Mainland Ports to the Saronic Gulf Islands

There are hydrofoil connections to the Saronic Gulf Islands from many minor ports on the eastern coast of the Peloponnese.

Many of these ports are hard to get to by land, and cannot be considered as options for getting to the islands. Others represent a viable alternative, but only for travellers who want to travel via **Nafplio** – main town and transport hub of the Argolis Peninsula. There are hourly buses to Nafplio (2½ hours, €8.25) from Terminal A in Athens.

Porto Heli, at the south-western tip of the Argolis, has at least five hydrofoils a day to Spetses (15 minutes, €4.40) and Hydra (one hour, €7.95). There are three buses a day to Porto Heli (two hours, €4.85) from Nafplio. These buses continue to the tiny village of **Costa**, right opposite Spetses. There are caïques and water taxis across the intervening straits.

Galatas, on the eastern side of the Argolis, is just across the water from the island of Poros. There are three buses a day from Nafplio (two hours, €5.15), travelling via the site of ancient Epidaurus. Ports like **Gerakas**, **Kyparissi**, **Leonidio** and **Monemvasia** are best considered as day trips from the islands.

Mainland Ports to the Cyclades

LAVRIO λαύριο
postcode 195 00 • pop 2500
Lavrio is an unattractive industrial town on the east coast of Attica, 10km north of Sounion. It is worth a mention only because it is the departure point for ferries to the islands of Kea and Kythnos.

Getting There & Away
Bus There are buses every 30 minutes to Lavrio from the Mavromateon terminal in Athens (1½ hours, €2.95).

Getting to the Islands
Goutos Lines runs the F/B *Myrina Express* from Lavrio to Kea (1¼ hours, €5.15) and Kythnos (3½ hours, €7.50). From mid-June, there are ferries to Kea every morning and evening from Monday to Friday, and up to six daily at weekends. Three ferries weekly continue to Kythnos. In winter there are ferries to Kea every day except Monday, returning every day except Wednesday. One service a week continues to Kythnos. The EOT in Athens gives out a timetable for this route. The ticket office at Lavrio is opposite the quay.

Mainland Ports to the Ionians

PATRAS Πάτρα
postcode 260 01 • pop 153,000
Patras is Greece's third-largest city and the principal port for ferries to the Ionian Islands, as well as for international services to Italy. It's not particularly exciting and most travellers hang around only long enough for transport connections.

Orientation
The city is easy to negotiate and is laid out on a grid stretching uphill from the port to the old *kastro* (castle). Most services of importance to travellers are along the waterfront, known as Othonos Amalias, in the middle of town and Iroön Polytehniou to the north. The various shipping offices are to be found along here. The main thoroughfares of Agiou Dionysiou, Riga Fereou, Mezones, Korinthou and Kanakari run parallel to the waterfront. The train station is in the middle of town on Othonos Amalias, and the main bus station is close by.

Information
Tourist Offices The EOT (☎ 261 062 0353) is outside the international arrivals terminal at the port. In theory, it's open 8am to 10pm Monday to Friday; in practice, it's often closed. The most useful piece of information is an arrow pointing to the helpful

MAINLAND PORTS

tourist police (☎ 261 045 1833), upstairs in the embarkation hall, who are open 7.30am to 11pm daily.

Money The National Bank of Greece on Plateia Trion Symahon has a 24-hour automatic exchange machine.

Post & Communications The post office, on the corner of Zaïmi and Mezonos, is open 7.30am to 8pm Monday to Friday and until 2pm Saturday. The main OTE office, on the corner of Dimitriou Gounari and Kanakari, is open 24 hours. There is

also an OTE office at the port, near the EOT office.

For Internet access, head inland. There are several places around the upper reaches of Gerokostopoulou. Netp@rk, Gerokostopoulou 37, and the co-managed Netrino Internet Café, Karaiskaki 133, are both open 10am to 2am daily and charge €2.35 per hour.

Laundry The laundrette on Zaïmi, a little way uphill from Korinthou, charges €6.75 to wash and dry a load and is open from 9am to 3pm and 5.30pm to 9pm Monday

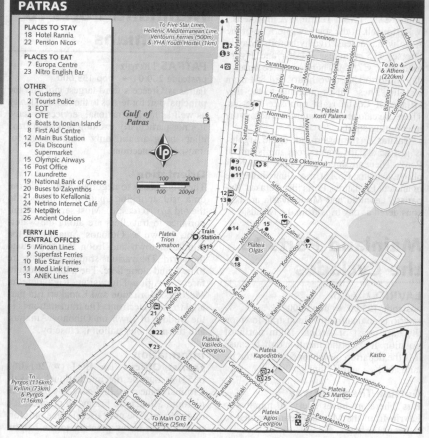

PATRAS

PLACES TO STAY
18 Hotel Rannia
22 Pension Nicos

PLACES TO EAT
7 Europa Centre
23 Nitro English Bar

OTHER
1 Customs
2 Tourist Police
3 EOT
4 OTE
6 Boats to Ionian Islands
8 First Aid Centre
12 Main Bus Station
14 Dia Discount Supermarket
15 Olympic Airways
16 Post Office
17 Laundrette
19 National Bank of Greece
20 Buses to Zakynthos
21 Buses to Kefallonia
24 Netrino Internet Café
25 Netp@rk
26 Ancient Odeion

FERRY LINE
CENTRAL OFFICES
5 Minoan Lines
9 Superfast Ferries
10 Blue Star Ferries
11 Med Link Lines
13 ANEK Lines

To Five Star Lines,
Hellenic Mediterranean Line,
Ventouris Ferries (500m)
& YHA Youth Hostel (1km)

Gulf of Patras

Plateia Trion Symahon

Train Station

Plateia Olgas

Plateia Vasileos Georgiou

Plateia Kapodistrio

Plateia Agios Georgiou

Plateia 25 Martiou

Kastro

To Rio & & Athens (220km)

To Pyrgos (116km), Kyllini (73km) & Pyrgos (116km)

To Main OTE Office (25m)

to Friday, 9am to 3pm on Saturday and closed Sunday.

Left Luggage There's a left-luggage office at the train station. It charges €3.25 per item per day, or €1.65 if you have a train ticket – so buy your ticket before you drop off your bags.

Emergency There is a first-aid centre (☎ 261 027 7386) on the corner of Karolou (28 Octavriou) and Agiou Dionysiou.

Things to See & Do

There are great views of the Ionian islands of Zakynthos and Kefallonia from the Venetian **kastro**, which is reached by the steps at the top of Agiou Nikolaou.

Places to Stay & Eat

Pension Nicos (☎ 261 0623 757, Cnr Patreos & Agiou Andreou) Singles/doubles/triples with bathroom €14.70/23.50/41.10. Nicos is easily the best budget choice in town. The sheets are clean, the water is hot and it's close to the waterfront. There are also cheaper rooms with shared bathroom.

Hotel Rannia (☎ 261 022 0114, fax 261 022 0537, Riga Fereou 53) Singles/doubles with bathroom €29.35/44. This C-class hotel, facing Plateia Olgas, has comfortable air-con rooms with TV.

Europa Centre (☎ 261 043 7006, Othonos Amalias 10) Mains €3-5.30. This convenient cafeteria-style place is close to the international ferry dock. It has taverna dishes, spaghetti and a choice of vegetarian meals.

Nitro English Bar (☎/fax 261 027 9357, Pantanasis 9) Mains €7.35-8.80. This is the perfect spot for Brits pining for a taste of the Old Dart. You'll find daily specials like steak and kidney pie or shepherd's pie, Sunday roasts and a choice of English beers. It's also well set up for travellers with a shower room and Internet access.

Dia Discount Supermarket (Agiou Andreou 29) is not the largest supermarket in town, but it's ideally located for travellers planning to buy a few provisions and keep moving.

Getting There & Away

Bus There are buses to Athens (three hours, €11.75) every 30 minutes from the main bus station on Othonos Amalias. The last service leaves at 9.45pm. These buses terminate a long way from the centre of Athens at Terminal A on Kifissou. This can be a real hassle if you're arriving in Athens after midnight – when there are no connecting buses to the city centre, leaving newcomers at the mercy of the notorious Terminal A taxi drivers. It's best to leave before 8.30pm.

There are also services to three daily to Thessaloniki (9½ hours, €27.80, three daily) and Kalamata (four hours, €13.35, two daily)

Train The train is the best way to travel to Athens. The station is conveniently central on Othonos Amalias, and the trains take you to the centre of Athens, within easy walking distance of the metro network.

There are at least eight services daily. Half of them are slow trains, which take five hours and cost €5.30. The intercity trains to Athens take 3½ hours and cost €10. The last intercity train leaves Patras at 6.30pm. If you want to skip Athens and head straight to the islands, all trains continue to the port of Piraeus. Holders of Eurail passes can travel free, but will need a reservation.

There are also trains to Kalamata (six hours, €5.30, two daily).

Getting to the Islands

Bus Buses to the Ionian islands of Lefkada (€9.70, two daily) and Kefallonia leave from the Ktel Kefallonia bus station (☎ 261 027 7854) at the corner of Othonos Amalias and Gerokostopoulou. Services to Kefallonia travel by ferry to Poros (€7.95) and continue by road to Argostoli (€10).

Buses to Zakynthos (3½ hours, €8.80) leave from the Ktel Zakynthos bus station (☎ 261 022 0219) at Othonos Amalias 58. They also travel via the port of Kyllini.

Ferry There are two ferries daily to the Ionian islands of Kefallonia (2½ hours, €10) and Ithaki (3¾ hours, €10.90) and at least one a day to Corfu (seven hours, €17.90).

Phone numbers listed incorporate changes due in Oct 2002; see p55

MAINLAND PORTS

Services to Italy are covered in the Getting There & Away chapter at the start of this book. Ticket agencies line the waterfront:

ANEK Lines (☎ 261 022 6053) Othonos Amalias 25: Ancona and Trieste via Corfu and Igoumenitsa
Blue Star Ferries (☎ 261 063 4000) Othonos Amalias 12–14: Brindisi direct; Ancona and Venice via Igoumenitsa and Corfu
Five Star Lines (☎ 261 042 2102) cnr Iroon Polytehniou and Naum Ellas: Brindisi via Igoumenitsa
Hellenic Mediterranean (☎ 261 045 2521) cnr Iroon Polytehniou and Pente Pigadion: Brindisi via Kefallonia and Corfu
Med Link Lines (☎ 261 062 3011) Giannatos Travel, Othonos Amalias 15: to Brindisi direct or via Kefallonia and Igoumenitsa
Minoan (☎ 261 042 1500) cnr Norman 1 and Athinon: Ancona via Igoumenitsa; Venice via Igoumenitsa and Corfu
Superfast Ferries (☎ 261 062 2500) Othonos Amalias 12: Ancona direct or via Igoumenitsa; Bari via Igoumenitsa
Ventouris Ferries (☎ 261 045 4873/4) Iroon Polytehniou 44–46: Bari direct

KYLLINI Κυλλήνη

The tiny port of Kyllini (kih-**lee**-nih), 78km south-west of Patras, warrants a mention only as the jumping-off point for ferries to Kefallonia and Zakynthos. Most people pass through Kyllini on buses from Patras that board the ferries. If you get stuck, the port police (☎ 2623 092 211) at the quay can suggest accommodation.

Getting There & Away

There are buses to Kyllini (1¼ hours, €4.40) from the Zakynthos bus station in Patras.

Getting to the Islands

There are boats to Zakynthos (1½ hours, €4.40, up to seven daily) and to Poros (1¼ hours, €6.20, three daily) and Argostoli (2¼ hours, €8.80, two daily) on Kefallonia.

NEAPOLI Νεάπολη
postcode 230 70 • pop 2500
Neapoli (nih-**ah**-po-lih), close to the southern tip of the eastern prong of the Peloponnese, is the 'other' port serving Kythira – which is clearly visible to the south.

Few travellers come this way; the ferries from Gythio are much more convenient – see the Gythio section earlier in this chapter. Neapoli is popular enough with local holiday-makers to have three seafront *hotels* and several *domatia*.

Getting There & Away

There are 11 buses a day from Athens to Sparta (3¼ hours, €12.05), and four buses a day from Sparta to Neapoli (three hours, €8.25).

Getting to the Islands

There are daily ferries from Neapoli to Agia Pelagia on Kythira (one hour, €4.70). Alexandrakis Shipping (☎ 2734 022 940, fax 2734 023 590), Akti Voiou 160, opposite the ferry quay, handles tickets.

IGOUMENITSA Ηγουμενίτσα
postcode 461 00 • pop 6800
Igoumenitsa, opposite the island of Corfu, is the main port of north-western Greece. Few people stay any longer than it takes to buy a ticket out. The bus station is on Kyprou. To get there from the ferries, follow the waterfront (Ethnikis Antistasis) north for 500m and turn right up 23 Fevrouariou. After two blocks turn left onto Kyprou and the bus station is on the left.

Places to Stay & Eat

If you get stuck for the night, you'll find signs for *domatia* around the port.

Hotel Egnatia (☎ 2665 023 648, fax 2665 023 633, Eleftherias 2) Singles/doubles with bathroom €29.40/38.15. The Egnatia is clean, comfortable and conveniently central, 100m from the bus station.

Alekos (☎ 2665 023 708, Ethnikis Andistasis 84) Mains €3.50-5.50. Alekos serves excellent Greek food, such as mousakas (€3.80) and veal with aubergines (€5.20). It is very popular with locals.

Getting There & Away

Bus Destinations include Athens (eight hours, €27.15, four daily), Preveza (2½ hours, €6.75, two daily) and Thessaloniki (eight hours, €25.25, one daily).

Getting to the Islands

Ferry There are ferries to Corfu Town hourly between 5am and 10pm (1¾ hours, €4.10). Ferries also go to Lefkimmi in southern Corfu (one hour, €2.50, six daily), and Paxi (1¾ hours, €5, one daily). Agency booths opposite the quay sell tickets. Boats are a mixture of closed hull ferries and smaller landing craft type ferries.

There are also weekly passenger and car ferries to Kerkyra from Sagiada (45 minutes, €3.80), 20km north of Igoumenitsa.

Hydrofoil & Catamaran There are four hydrofoil services weekly to Corfu (35 minutes, €8.80) and Paxi (one hour, €10.30). Call Milano Travel 2665 026 670 for details.

Mainland Ports to the Sporades

VOLOS Βόλος
postcode 380 01 • pop 112,000

Volos is a bustling city on the northern shores of the Pagasitic Gulf, and the principal port for ferry and hydrofoil services to the Sporades.

According to mythology, Volos was ancient Iolkos – from where Jason and the Argonauts set sail on their quest for the Golden Fleece.

Orientation & Information

Volos is laid out on an easy grid system stretching inland parallel to the waterfront (called Argonafton), which is where most things of importance to travellers are to be found. The main square, Plateia Riga Fereou, is at the north-western end of Argonafton.

The EOT (☎ 2421 023 500, fax 2421 024 750) is on the northern side of the square. It has maps and hotel information as well as bus, ferry and hydrofoil schedules. In summer, the office is open 7.30am to 2.30pm and 6pm to 8.30pm Monday to Friday, and 9.30am to 1.30pm weekends and holidays. The tourist police (☎ 2421 072 421) are in the same building as the regular police at 28 Oktovriou 179.

The National Bank of Greece on Argonafton has an ATM. Magic Net Café, Iasonos 141, is Volos' largest Internet cafe. It is open 9am to 4am daily.

Places to Stay

Hotel Avra (☎ 2421 025 370, fax 2421 028 980, e avra@internet.gr, Solonos 3) Singles/doubles €29.40/47.5. The rooms are comfortable and have a TV and bathroom.

Hotel Kypseli (☎ 2421 024 420, fax 2421 026 020, Agiou Nikolaou 1) Singles/doubles €29.40/47.05, singles without bathroom €23.55. This place has a prime location on the waterfront and rooms with TV, fridge and balcony.

Places to Eat

Volos is famous for its food, particularly for the range and quality of the mezedes (literally 'tastes') found at its many ouzeria. You'll find *ohtapodi* (octopus) prepared a dozen different ways, *htypiti* (a mixed feta cheese and hot pepper dip); *spetsofaï* (chopped sausages and peppers in a rich sauce); and many more.

Nautilia (☎ 2421 025 340, Borel 4) Mezedes €1.80-6.50. Excellent mezedes at this old style ouzeri include squid (€3.80), shrimp saganaki (€6.50) and spetsofaï (€4.70). If you can't stand the traffic fumes, or the fishy pong from the harbour opposite, then join the weather beaten old fishers in the cavernous interior, with its bare walls and ancient TV.

O Kuklus Tsipoiradiko (☎ 2421 020 872, Mikrasiaton 85) Mezedes €0.90-5.90. This place is a favourite student hangout. The speciality is potatoes (€0.90) baked in a traditional wood-fired oven.

Harama Restaurant (☎ 2421 038 402, Dimitriados 49) Mains €1.90-4.10. This rough-and-ready looking place serves excellent, low priced ready-made food.

Getting There & Away

Bus Destinations include Athens (five hours, €17, nine daily) and Thessaloniki (three hours, €11.80, five daily).

Train Most services to Volos involve changing trains at Larisa, on the main

MAINLAND PORTS

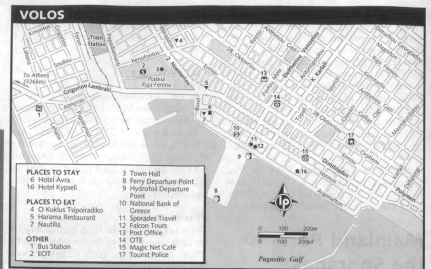

VOLOS

PLACES TO STAY
6 Hotel Avra
16 Hotel Kypseli

PLACES TO EAT
4 O Kuklus Tsipoiradiko
5 Harama Restaurant
7 Nautilia

OTHER
1 Bus Station
2 EOT

3 Town Hall
8 Ferry Departure Point
9 Hydrofoil Departure Point
10 National Bank of Greece
11 Sporades Travel
12 Falcon Tours
13 Post Office
14 OTE
15 Magic Net Café
17 Tourist Police

Pagasitic Gulf

Athens-Thessaloniki line. However, there are two direct intercity trains a day to Athens (five hours, €19.40).

Getting to the Islands
Ferry There are ferries daily to Skiathos (3½ hours, €8, four daily), Glossa (Skopelos, 3½ hours, €9.70), Skopelos Town (4½ hours, €10, four daily) and Alonnisos (five hours, €11.50, three daily). Buy tickets from Sporades Travel (☎/fax 2421 035 846), Argonafton 33.

Hydrofoil In summer, there are daily hydrofoils to Skiathos (1¼ hours, €16.80, four daily), Glossa (1¾ hours, €19.10), Skopelos Town (2¼ hours, €20 60, five daily) and Alonnisos (2½ hours, €22.60, four daily). Tickets are available from Falcon Tours (☎ 2421 025 688), on Argonafton.

AGIOS KONSTANTINOS
Άγιος Κωνσταντίνος
postcode 350 06 • pop 2360
Agios Konstantinos, 175km north-west of Athens, is the closest and most convenient of the ports serving the Sporades for travellers setting out from Athens.

Places to Stay
With judicious use of buses from Athens, you probably won't need to stay overnight before catching a Sporades-bound ferry or hydrofoil.

Hotel Olga (☎ 0235 31 766, fax 0235 33 266, Eivoilou 6) Singles/doubles €22/31.40. The Olga is a good option if you get stuck. Like most of the town's hotels, it's right on the seafront. The spacious rooms are equipped with TV and air-con.

Getting There & Away
Bus There are hourly buses to Agios Konstantinos from Athens Terminal B (2½ hours, €9.85).

Getting to the Islands
Ferry There are ferries daily from Agios Konstantinos to Skiathos (3½ hours, €9.40, two daily), Skopelos Town (4½ hours, €9.40, four daily) and Alonnisos (5½ hours, €13.30, one daily).

Hydrofoil There are three hydrofoils daily to Skopelos Town (2¼ hours, €23.60), Alonnisos (2½ hours, €26.40); most services also stop at Skiathos (1½ hours, €17.10).

Mainland Ports to the North-Eastern Aegean

KAVALA Καβάλα
postcode 655 00 • pop 57,000

Modern Kavala, 163km east of Thessaloniki, serves as the main port for the island of Thasos. It's an attractive city, spilling gently down the foothills of Mt Symvolon to a large harbour. The old quarter of Panagia nestles under a massive Byzantine fortress.

Orientation & Information
Kavala's focal point is Plateia Eleftherias. The two main thoroughfares, Eleftheriou Venizelou and Erythrou Stavrou run west from here parallel with the waterfront.

The EOT (☎ 251 022 2425), on the western side of Plateia Eleftherias, has in-

formation on hotel prices and transport. It's open 8am to 2pm Monday to Friday.

The National Bank of Greece, on the corner of Megalou Alexandrou and Dragoumi, has an automatic exchange machine and an ATM. Midas Exchange, next to the EOT, is open 8.30am to 8pm Monday to Friday and 9am to 8pm Saturday.

Travellers can access email at Rebel Internet Cafe, Eleftheriou Venizelou 8.

Things to See
If you've got time to spare, spend it exploring the streets of **Panagia**, the old Turkish quarter occupying the promontory southeast of Plateia Eleftherias. Its most conspicuous building is the **Imaret**, a huge structure with 18 domes, which overlooks the harbour from Poulidou. In Turkish times the Imaret was a hostel for theology students. It has now been restored and includes a pleasant cafe and restaurant (see Places to Eat).

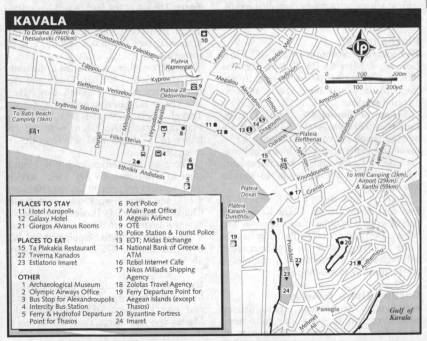

KAVALA

PLACES TO STAY
11 Hotel Acropolis
12 Galaxy Hotel
21 Giorgos Alvanos Rooms

PLACES TO EAT
15 Ta Plakakia Restaurant
22 Taverna Kanados
23 Estiatorio Imaret

OTHER
1 Archaeological Museum
2 Olympic Airways Office
3 Bus Stop for Alexandroupolis
4 Intercity Bus Station
5 Ferry & Hydrofoil Departure Point for Thasos
6 Port Police
7 Main Post Office
8 Aegean Airlines
9 OTE
10 Police Station & Tourist Police
13 EOT; Midas Exchange
14 National Bank of Greece & ATM
16 Rebel Internet Cafe
17 Nikos Miliadis Shipping Agency
18 Zolotas Travel Agency
19 Ferry Departure Point for Aegean Islands (except Thasos)
20 Byzantine Fortress
24 Imaret

To Drama (36km) & Thessaloniki (160km)
To Batis Beach Camping (3km)
To Irini Camping (2km), Airport (29km) & Xanthi (59km)
Gulf of Kavala

MAINLAND PORTS

The **archaeological museum** (☎ 251 022 2335, Erythrou Stavrou 17; admission €1.50, free Sun & public holidays; open 8.30am-3pm Tues-Sun) houses finds from ancient Amphipolis, between Thessaloniki and Kavala.

Places to Stay

Giorgos Alvanos Rooms (☎ 251 022 8412, Anthemiou 35) Singles/doubles €15/20.50. Giorgos Alvanos offers the cosiest environment in Kavala; the address is a beautiful 300-year-old house in Panagia.

Hotel Acropolis (☎ 251 022 3543, fax 251 083 2291, Eleftheriou Venizelou 29) Singles without bathroom €22, doubles with bathroom €50. The Acropolis is the closest thing to a budget hotel. Take the lift to reception as you enter the building.

Galaxy Hotel (☎ 251 022 4811, fax 251 022 6754, e galaxy@hol.gr, Eleftheriou Venizelou 27) Singles/doubles with bathroom €56/73. This is Kavala's best hotel, with spacious, attractively furnished rooms. All rooms have air-con and refrigerator.

Places to Eat

Ta Plakakia Restaurant (☎ 251 083 5761, Doïranis 4) Mezedes €3. Ta Plakakia, near Plateia Eleftherias, is a conveniently located place with a huge choice of low-priced mezedes.

Estiatorio Imaret (☎ 251 083 6286, Poulidou 32) Mains €4.50-7. Kavala's most atmospheric eating location is to be found inside the celebrated Imaret in Panagia. Ask for its speciality – Al Halili cheese, which is a tasty hot dip of cheese, tomato and onion.

Taverna Kanados (☎ 251 083 5172, Poulidou 27) Mains €5-7. The Kanados is one of several popular places opposite the Imaret. Don't be put off by the tacky murals – the food is good. It has a wide-ranging fish menu and other seafood specialities – try the mussels in tomato sauce.

Getting There & Away

Air Olympic Airways and Aegean Airlines both have two flights a day to Athens (€76.60). The airport is 29km east of

Kavala. Aegean runs buses to the airport (€3) for its passengers; Olympic passengers have to take a taxi – about €16.

The Olympic Airways office (☎ 251 022 5577) is at Ethnikis Andistasis 16, and Aegean (☎ 251 022 9000) is at Erythrou Stavrou 1.

Bus Buses to Athens (9½ hours, €36, three daily), Keramoti (one hour, €2.80, hourly) and Thessaloniki (two hours, €9.30, hourly) leave from the intercity bus station on Hrysostomou Kavalas.

Services to Alexandroupolis (2½ hours, €9.50), which originate in Thessaloniki, depart from the bus stop opposite – outside the 7-Eleven snack bar.

Getting to the Islands

Hydrofoil and ferry schedules are posted in the window of the port police near the hydrofoil departure point.

Ferry The quay for ferries and hydrofoils is at the eastern end of Ethnikis Antistasis. There are ferries every hour to Skala Prinou on Thasos (1¼ hours, €2.65, €13.50 for a car).

In summer there are ferries to Samothraki (four hours, €9.70). Times and frequency vary month by month. Buy tickets and check the latest schedule at Zolotas Travel Agency (☎ 251 083 5671), on Plateia Karaoli Dimitriou, near the entrance to the Aegean Islands ferry departure point.

There are four ferries weekly to Limnos (four to five hours, €9.70). Twice weekly these services continue to Lesvos (10 hours, €17), and once a week they continue to Chios (16 hours, €24). Ferries to Limnos call at Agios Efstratios (6¾ hours, €11.80) once a week. Nikos Miliadis Shipping (☎ 251 022 6147, fax 251 083 8767), Karaoli-Dimitriou 36, handles tickets.

Hydrofoil There are about nine hydrofoils daily to Limenas (30 minutes, €5) and two to Potos (€8) via Kallirahi, Maries and Limenaria. Purchase tickets at the port.

KERAMOTI

In summer, there are frequent ferries to Limenas on Thasos (40 minutes, €1.20, €8.50 for a car) from the small port of Keramoti, 46km south-east of Kavala. There are hourly buses to Keramoti (one hour, €2.80) from Kavala.

ALEXANDROUPOLIS

Αλεξανδρούπολη
postcode 681 00 • pop 37,000
Alexandroupolis, 328km east of Thessaloniki, is the main port for the island of Samothrace. It's a lively town with a sizeable student population, but with few attractions.

Orientation & Information

The town is laid out on a grid system stretching back from the waterfront, which is Karaoli Dimitriou at the eastern end and Megalou Alexandrou at the western end. The two main squares are Plateia Eleftherias and Plateia Polytehniou. Both are just one block north of Karaoli Dimitriou. The town's most prominent landmark is the large 19th-century lighthouse on the middle of the waterfront.

The main post office is on the waterfront on the corner of Nikiforou Foka and Megalou Alexandrou. The OTE is inland on the corner of Mitropolitou Kaviri and Eleftheriou Venizelou. Internet access is available at the Cafe Del Mar, Psarron 1.

The National Bank of Greece at Dimokratias 246 has an ATM.

Things to See

The **Ecclesiastical Art Museum of Alexandroupolis** (☎ 2551 26 359, Plateia Agiou Nikolaou; admission free; 9am-2pm Tue-Fri, 10am-1pm Sat) houses a priceless collection of icons and ecclesiastical ornaments brought to Greek Thrace by refugees from Asia Minor. The museum is in the grounds of the Agios Nikolaos Cathedral.

Places to Stay

Hotel Lido (☎ 2551 028 808, Paleologou 15) Singles/doubles without bathroom €16.20/ 22, with bathroom €22/27. This is an outstanding D-class hotel with comfortable rooms, one block north of the bus station.

Hotel Okeanis (☎ 2551 028 830, fax 2551 034 118, Paleologou 20) Singles/doubles €40/50. This C-class hotel, almost opposite the Lido, has very comfortable rooms.

MAINLAND PORTS

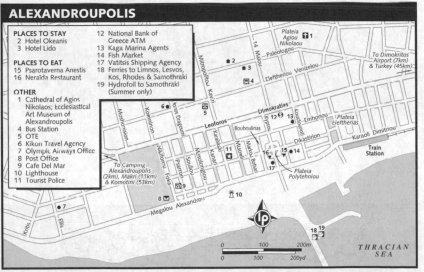

ALEXANDROUPOLIS

PLACES TO STAY
2 Hotel Okeanis
3 Hotel Lido

PLACES TO EAT
15 Psarotaverna Anestis
16 Neraïda Restaurant

OTHER
1 Cathedral of Agios Nikolaos; Ecclesiastical Art Museum of Alexandroupolis
4 Bus Station
5 OTE
6 Kikon Travel Agency
7 Olympic Airways Office
8 Post Office
9 Cafe Del Mar
10 Lighthouse
11 Tourist Police
12 National Bank of Greece ATM
13 Kaga Marina Agents
14 Fish Market
17 Vatitsis Shipping Agency
18 Ferries to Limnos, Lesvos, Kos, Rhodes & Samothraki
19 Hydrofoil to Samothraki (Summer only)

To Dimokritos Airport (7km) & Turkey (45km)

Plateia Agiou Nikolaou

Paleologou

Eleftheriou Venizelou

Dimokratias

Leoforos

Bouboulinas

Emhoriou

Plateia Eleftherias

Dikastirion

Karaoli Dimitriou

Train Station

Plateia Polytehniou

To Camping Alexandroupolis (2km), Makri (11km) & Komotini (53km)

Megalou Alexandrou

THRACIAN SEA

0   100   200m
0   100   200yd

Places to Eat

Neraïda Restaurant (☎ 2551 022 867, *Plateia Polytehniou*) Mains €4.70-6.50. This restaurant is a good choice and has a range of standard fare and some local specialities.

Psarotaverna Anestis (☎ 2551 027 037, *Athanasiou Diakou 5*) Mezedes €5. Opposite the fish market and one street east of Kyprou is this place where freshness is guaranteed. It looks very unassuming, but has a fine choice of mezedes, especially those with fish. *Mydia saganaki* (chilli mussels) are highly recommended.

Getting There & Away

Air Olympic Airways and Aegean Airlines both have two flights a day to Athens (€79.55 on Olympic). The airport is 7km east of town – about €4.50 by taxi. The Olympic Airlines office (☎ 2551 026 361) is at Ellis 6 while the Aegean Airlines office (☎ 2551 089 150) is at the airport.

Bus There are buses from the bus station on Eleftheriou Venizelou to Thessaloniki (six hours, €19, six daily) via Xanthi and Kavala.

Train There are five trains daily to Thessaloniki – two of which are intercity (5½ hours, €16.20). The train station is on Karaoli Dimitriou, just east of the port.

Getting to the Islands

Ferry There are up to three ferries daily to Samothraki in summer, dropping back to one daily in winter. Vatitsis Shipping Agency (☎ 2551 026 721, fax 2551 032 007, e saos@orfeasnet.gr), Kyprou 5 (opposite the port), handles tickets. Tickets cost €7.50, a car costs an exorbitant €33 and the trip takes two hours.

There is a weekly ferry to Rhodes (18 hours, €35) via Limnos (five hours, €12), Lesvos (11½ hours, €16.50), and a Friday ferry to Limnos, Agios Efstratios and Rafina (17¼ hours, €24). Kikon Travel (☎ 2551 025 455, fax 2551 034 755), Eleftheriou Venizelou 68, handles tickets.

Hydrofoil In summer there are hydrofoils to Samothraki (one hour, €14.70) and Limnos (three hours, €23.50). Kaga Marina (☎/fax 2551 081 700), Emboriou 70, handles tickets.

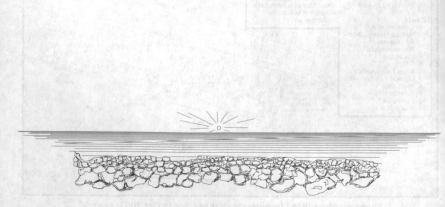

Saronic Gulf Islands
Νησιά του Σαρωνικού

The five Saronic Gulf Islands are the closest group to Athens. The closest, Salamis, is little more than a suburb of the sprawling capital. Aegina is also close enough to Athens for people to commute to work. Along with Poros, the next island south, it is a popular package-holiday destination. Hydra, once famous as the rendezvous of artists, writers and beautiful people, manages to retain an air of superiority and grandeur. Spetses, the most southerly island in the group, is a favourite with British holiday-makers.

Spetses has the best beaches, but these islands are not the place to be if you want long stretches of golden sand. And with the exception of the Temple of Aphaia, on Aegina, the islands have no significant archaeological remains.

Nevertheless, the islands are a popular escape for Athenians. Accommodation can be impossible to find between mid-June and mid-September, and weekends are busy all year round. If you plan to go at these times, it's a good idea to reserve a room in advance.

The islands have a reputation for high prices, which is a bit misleading. What is true is that there are very few places for budget travellers to stay – no camping grounds and only a couple of cheap hotels. There is plenty of good accommodation available if you are happy to pay €45 or more for a double. Midweek visitors can get some good deals. Food is no more expensive than anywhere else.

The Saronic Gulf is named after the mythical King Saron of Argos, a keen hunter who drowned while pursuing a deer that had swum into the gulf to escape.

SUGGESTED ITINERARIES
One Week
Starting from Athens, head to Aegina (two days), visiting the Temple of Aphaia and exploring the ruins of Paleohora; Poros warrants no more than a brief stopover on the way to tranquil Hydra (three days); continue to Spetses (two days). From Spetses, you can either return to Athens or continue by hydrofoil to one of the ports of the eastern Peloponnese.

Highlights

- The rambling ruins of the old town of Paleohora on Aegina
- Views over the Saronic Gulf from the Temple of Aphaia on Aegina
- Staying in Hydra's gracious old stone mansions
- Exploring the back roads of Spetses by motorcycle

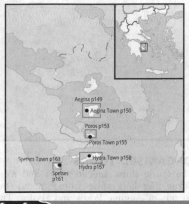

Aegina p149
● Aegina Town p150
Poros p153
● Poros Town p155
Spetses Town p163 ● Hydra Town p158
Spetses Hydra p157
p161

GETTING TO/FROM THE SARONIC GULF ISLANDS
Ferry
At least 10 ferries daily sail from Piraeus to Aegina Town (1½ hours, €4.40). Four continue to Poros (2½ hours, €6.45), two keep going to Hydra (3½ hours, €7.35) and one goes all the way to Spetses (4½ hours, €10).

Hydrofoil & Catamaran
Minoan Lines operates a busy schedule to the islands and nearby Peloponnesian ports with its Flying Dolphin hydrofoils. Services to Aegina leave from Piraeus' Great Harbour, while services to Hydra, Poros and Spetses leave from both the Great Harbour and Zea Marina.

SARONIC GULF ISLANDS

emerge as a commercial centre in about 1000 BC. By the 7th century BC, it was the premier maritime power in the region and amassed great wealth through its trade with Egypt and Phoenicia. The silver 'turtle' coins minted on the island at this time are thought to be the first coins produced in Europe. Aegina's fleet made a major contribution to the Greek victory over the Persian fleet at the Battle of Salamis in 480 BC.

Athens, uneasy about Aegina's maritime prowess, attacked the island in 459 BC. Defeated, Aegina was forced to pull down its city walls and surrender its fleet. It did not recover.

The island's other brief moment in the spotlight came during 1827–29, when it was declared the temporary capital of partly liberated Greece. The first coins of the modern Greek nation were minted here.

Aegina has since slipped into a more humble role as Greece's premier producer of pistachio nuts.

Aegina was named after the daughter of the river god, Asopus. According to mythology, Aegina was abducted by Zeus and taken to the island. Her son by Zeus, Aeacus, was the grandfather of Achilles of Trojan War fame.

ORGANISED TOURS

The cruise ships *Aegean Glory* and *King Saron* offer daily cruises from Piraeus to the islands of Aegina, Poros and Hydra. The cruises leave Piraeus at 9am, returning at about 7pm. Passengers get to spend about an hour on shore at each island – long enough to buy a souvenir and take the obligatory 'been there, done that' photo.

See the Organised Tours section of the Athens chapter for more information about these tours. The official price is €65, including buffet lunch, but tickets are often heavily discounted.

Aegina Αίγινα

postcode 180 10 • pop 11,000
Unassuming Aegina (**eh**-yee-nah) was once a major player in the Hellenic world, thanks largely to its strategic position at the mouth of the Saronic Gulf. It began to

Getting To/From Aegina

Ferry In summer there are at least 10 ferries daily from Aegina Town to Piraeus (1½ hours, €4.40) as well as services from Agia Marina (1½ hours, €3.25) and Souvala (1¼ hours, €3.10). There are at least three boats daily to Poros (one hour, €3.85) via Methana (40 minutes, €3.25), two daily to Hydra (two hours, €4.70), and one to Spetses (three hours, €7.35). The ferry companies have ticket offices at the quay, where you'll find a full list of the day's sailings.

Hydrofoil These operate almost hourly from 7am to 8pm between Aegina Town and the Great Harbour at Piraeus (35 minutes, €8.50), but there are no services south to Poros, Hydra or Spetses. Tickets are sold at the quay in Aegina Town.

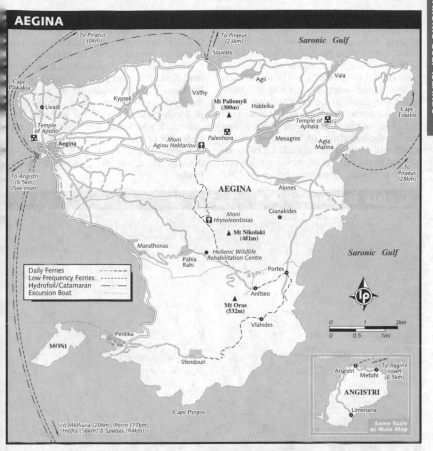

AEGINA

To Piraeus (30km)
To Piraeus (23km)
Saronic Gulf
Souvala
Cape Plakakia
Agii
Vaia
Livadi
Kypseli
Vathy
Mt Paliomyli (300m)
Haldeika
Temple of Apollo
Cape Tourlos
Aegina
Moni Agiou Nektariou
Paleohora
Temple of Aphaia
Mesagros
Agia Marina
To Piraeus (28km)
To Angistri (6.5km) (See Inset)
AEGINA
Alones
Moni Hrysoleontissas
Gianakides
Mt Nikolaki (431m)
Marathonas
Hellenic Wildlife Rehabilitation Centre
Saronic Gulf
Pahia Rahi
Portes
Anitseo
Mt Oros (532m)
Vlahides
Perdika
MONI
Sfendouri
Cape Pyrgos

Daily Ferries
Low Frequency Ferries
Hydrofoil/Catamaran
Excursion Boat

0   1   2km
0   0.5   1mi

To Angistri
Metohi
To Aegina Town (6.5km)
ANGISTRI
Limenaria
Same Scale as Main Map

To Methana (20km), Poros (77km), Hydra (56km) & Spetses (84km)

Services from Piraeus to Agia Marina (30 minutes) and Souvala (25 minutes) are operated by Sea Falcon Lines. Both trips cost €6.75 one way, €11.15 return.

Getting Around Aegina
There are frequent buses running from Aegina Town to Agia Marina (30 minutes, €1.40), via Paleohora and the Temple of Aphaia. Other buses go to Perdika (15 minutes, €0.80) and Souvala (20 minutes, €1.10). Departure times are displayed outside the ticket office which is on Plateia Ethnegersias.

There are numerous places in Aegina to hire motorcycles. Their advertised prices start from around €10.30 per day for a 50cc machine.

AEGINA TOWN
Aegina Town, which is located on the west coast, is the island's capital and main port. The town is a charming and bustling, if slightly ramshackle, place; its harbour is lined with colourful caiques. Several of the town's crumbling neoclassical buildings survive from its glory days as the Greek capital.

Phone numbers listed incorporate changes due in Oct 2002; see p55

Orientation & Information

The ferry dock and nearby small quay used by hydrofoils are on the western edge of town. A left turn at the end of the quay leads to Plateia Ethnegersias, where you'll find the bus terminal and post office. The town beach is 200m farther along. A right turn at the end of the quay leads to the main harbour.

Aegina doesn't have an official tourist office. The 'tourist offices' you'll see advertised on the waterfront are booking agencies, which will do no more than add a 25% commission to the price of whatever service you care to nominate. The tourist police (☎ 2297 027 777) are on Leonardou Lada, opposite the hydrofoil quay. The port police (☎ 2297 022 328) are next to the hydrofoil ticket office at the entrance to the hydrofoil quay.

The OTE is off Aiakou, which heads inland next to the port authority building. The National Bank of Greece is on the waterfront just past Aiakou, and the Credit Bank is 150m farther around the harbour. You can check your email at the Nesant Internet Cafe, Afeas 13, open 10am to 2am daily.

Kalezis Bookshop (☎ 2297 025 956), on the waterfront, has foreign newspapers and books.

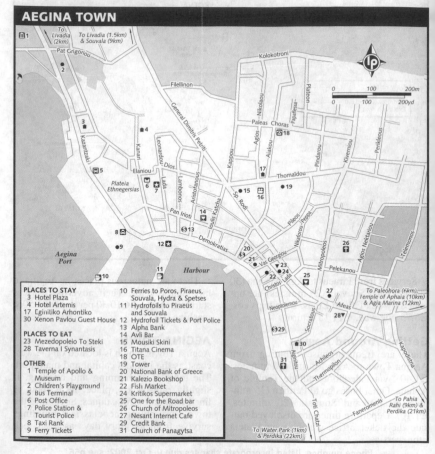

AEGINA TOWN

PLACES TO STAY
3 Hotel Plaza
4 Hotel Artemis
17 Eginitiko Arhontiko
30 Xenon Pavlou Guest House

PLACES TO EAT
23 Mezedopoleio To Steki
28 Taverna I Synantasis

OTHER
1 Temple of Apollo & Museum
2 Children's Playground
5 Bus Terminal
6 Post Office
7 Police Station & Tourist Police
8 Taxi Rank
9 Ferry Tickets
10 Ferries to Poros, Piraeus, Souvala, Hydra & Spetses
11 Hydrofoils to Piraeus and Souvala
12 Hydrofoil Tickets & Port Police
13 Alpha Bank
14 Avli Bar
15 Mousiki Skini
16 Titana Cinema
18 OTE
19 Tower
20 National Bank of Greece
21 Kalezio Bookshop
22 Fish Market
24 Kritikos Supermarket
25 One for the Road bar
26 Church of Mitropoleos
27 Nesant Internet Cafe
29 Credit Bank
31 Church of Panagytsa

Temple of Apollo

'Temple' is a bit of a misnomer for the one Doric column which stands at this site (☎ 2297 022 637; admission €1.50; open 8.30am-3pm Tues-Sun). The column is all that's left of the 5th-century Temple of Apollo, which once stood on the Hill of Koloni. The hill was the site of the ancient acropolis, and there are remains of a Helladic (early) settlement. The site, on the far side of the town beach, also has a **museum**.

Water Park

Aegina's Water Park (☎ 2297 022 540; adult/child €10.30/5.90; open 10am-8pm daily May-Oct), on the coast 1.5km south of Aegina Town, is a big hit with kids.

Places to Stay

Aegina Town doesn't have a huge choice of accommodation.

Hotel Plaza (☎ 2297 025 600, fax 2297 028 404, Kazantzaki 3) Singles/doubles with bathroom €20.55/23.50. The Plaza, on the waterfront 100m north of Plateia Ethnegersias, is a long-standing favourite with travellers. It has some good rooms overlooking the sea.

There are several *domatia* at the top of Leonardou Lada with singles/doubles for around €20.55/29.35.

Xenon Pavlou Guest House (☎ 2297 022 795, Aiginitou 21) Singles/doubles with bathroom €26.40/35.20. The Xenon Pavlou is a small family-run guesthouse tucked away behind the Church of Panagytsa on the south-eastern side of the harbour.

Hotel Artemis (☎ 2297 025 195, fax 2297 028 466, e pipinis@otenet.gr, Kanari 20) Singles/doubles with bathroom €29.35/47; air-con extra €5.90. This hotel, north of Plateia Ethnegersias, has a wide range of rooms and offers good discounts for midweek visitors.

Eginitiko Arhontiko (☎ 2297 024 968, fax 2297 024 156, e fotisvoulgarakis@aig .forthnet.gr, Cnr Thomaïdou & Agios Nikoloau) Singles/doubles/triples with bathroom €44/58.70/69, suite €88.05. This fine 19th-century sandstone *arhontiko* (mansion once belonging to an *arhon*, a leading town citi-

zen) has the most interesting rooms in town, particularly the ornate two-room suite.

Places to Eat

The harbour front is lined with countless cafes and restaurants – good for relaxing and soaking up the atmosphere, but not particularly good value.

Locals prefer to head for the cluster of *ouzeria* and restaurants around the fish markets at the eastern side of the harbour.

Mezedopoleio To Steki (☎ 2297 023 910, Pan Irioti 45) Seafood mezedes €3.55-7.35. This tiny place, tucked away behind the fish markets, must be the most popular restaurant in town. It's always packed with people tucking into the local speciality, barbecued octopus (€3.55), over a glass or two of ouzo.

Taverna I Synantasis (☎ 2297 024 309, Afeas 40) Mains €4.70-5.90. This place comes to life on Friday and Saturday night when there's live music from 10pm.

Kritikos Supermarket (☎ 2297 027 772, Pan Irioti 53) Self-caterers will find most things at this spot behind the fish markets.

Delicious local pistachio nuts are on sale everywhere, priced from €3.25 for 500g.

Entertainment

There are dozens of music bars dotted around the maze of small streets behind the waterfront.

One For the Road (☎ 2297 022 340, Afeas 3) This lively bar draws a young crowd with a mixture of modern Greek and rock music.

Avli (☎ 2297 026 438, Pan Irioti 17) Avli attracts an older audience with a mixture of '60s music and Latin.

Mousiki Skini (☎ 2298 022 922, Thomaïdou 4) Mousikini Skini is for serious night owls, with rembetika music on Wednesday, Friday, Saturday and Sunday night from midnight until 5am.

AROUND AEGINA
Temple of Aphaia

The splendid, well preserved Doric Temple of Aphaia (☎ 2297 032 398; admission €2.35; open 8.30am-7pm Mon-Fri, 8.30am-3pm Sat & Sun), a local deity of pre-Hellenic times, is the major ancient site of the Saronic

Gulf Islands. It was built in 480 BC when Aegina was at its most powerful.

The temple's pediments were decorated with outstanding Trojan War sculptures, most of which were spirited away in the 19th century and eventually fell into the hands of Ludwig I (father of King Otho). They now have pride of place in Munich's Glyptothek. The temple is impressive even without these sculptures. It stands on a pine-covered hill and commands imposing views over the Saronic Gulf as far as Cape Sounion.

Aphaia is 10km east of Aegina Town. Buses to Agia Marina (20 minutes, €1.20) stop at the site. A taxi from Aegina Town costs about €5.90.

Paleohora Παλαιοχώρα

The ruins of Paleohora, on a hillside 6.5km east of Aegina Town, are fascinating to explore. The town was the island's capital from the 9th century to 1826 when pirate attacks forced the islanders to flee the coast and settle inland. It didn't do them much good when the notorious pirate Barbarossa arrived in 1537, laid waste the town and carried the inhabitants off into slavery.

The ruins are far more extensive than they first appear. The only buildings left intact are the churches. There are more than two dozen of them, in various states of disrepair, dotted around the hillside. Remnants of frescoes can be seen in some.

In the valley below Paleohora is **Moni Agiou Nektariou**, an important place of pilgrimage. The monastery contains the relics of a hermit monk, Anastasios Kefalas, who died in 1920. When his body was exhumed in 1940 it was found to have mummified – a sure sign of sainthood in Greek Orthodoxy, especially after a lifetime of performing miracle cures. Kefalas was canonised in 1961 – the first Orthodox saint of the 20th century. The enormous new church that has been built to honour him is a spectacular sight beside the road to Agia Marina. A track leads south from here to the 16th-century **Moni Hrysoleontissas**, in a lovely mountain setting.

The bus from Aegina Town to Agia Marina stops at the turn-off to Paleohora.

Hellenic Wildlife Rehabilitation Centre

If you want to get an idea of the kind of toll that hunting takes on the nation's wildlife, pay a visit to the Hellenic Wildlife Rehabilitation Centre (☎ 2297 028 367, e hlcwfhos@ otenet.gr, w www.ekpaz.gr; admission free but donations appreciated; open 11am-1pm daily), known in Greek as the Elliniko Kentro Perithalifis Agrion Zoon.

At the time of research, the centre was preparing to move from the old jail in Aegina Town to new, custom-built premises about 10km to the south-west, near Pahia Rahi. The centre is on the left about 1km west of Pahia Rahi on the road to Mt Oros.

It is designed to handle the 4000-odd animals and birds that are brought here every year. They come from all over Greece; the majority have been shot.

Volunteers are welcome: the need is greatest in the winter months. The new centre has accommodation for volunteer workers. There is no public transport.

Perdika

The small fishing village of Perdika, 21km south of Aegina Town, is popular for its fish tavernas, with half-a-dozen places overlooking the harbour.

Beaches

Beaches are not Aegina's strong point. The east-coast town of **Agia Marina** is the island's premier tourist resort, but the beach is not great – if you can see it for package tourists. There are a couple of sandy patches that almost qualify as beaches between Aegina and Perdika, at the southern tip of the west coast.

MONI & ANGISTRI ISLETS
Ναμονα & Νααγκίστρι

The Moni and Angistri Islets lie off the west coast of Aegina, opposite Perdika. Moni, the smaller of the two, is a 10-minute boat ride from Perdika – frequent boats (10 minutes, €0.60) make the trip in summer.

Angistri is much bigger with around 500 inhabitants. There's a sandy beach at the port and other smaller beaches around the coast. Both package-holiday tourists and independent travellers find their way to Angistri, which is served by regular boats from Aegina Town and Piraeus.

Poros Πόρος

postcode 180 20 • pop 4000

The island of Poros is little more than a stone's throw from the mainland. The slender passage of water that separates it from the Peloponnesian town of Galatas is only 360m wide at its narrowest point.

Poros was once two islands, Kalavria and Sferia. These days they are connected by a narrow isthmus, cut by a canal for small boats and rejoined by a road bridge. The vast majority of the population lives on the small volcanic island of Sferia, which is more than half-covered by the town of Poros. Sferia hangs like an appendix from the southern coast of Kalavria, a large, well-

forested island that has all the package hotels. The town of Poros is not wildly exciting, but it can be used as a base for exploring the ancient sites of the adjacent Peloponnese.

Getting To/From Poros

Ferry There are at least eight ferries daily to Piraeus (2½ hours, €6.45), via Methana and Aegina (one hour, €3.85), two daily to Hydra (one hour, €3.25), and one to Spetses (two hours, €5). Ticket agencies are opposite the ferry dock.

Small boats shuttle constantly between Poros and Galatas (five minutes, €0.30) on the mainland. They leave from the quay opposite Plateia Iroön in Poros Town. Car ferries to Galatas leave from the dock on the road to Kalavria.

Hydrofoil There are six services daily from Piraeus (one hour, €12.95), one from Great Harbour and five from Zea Marina.

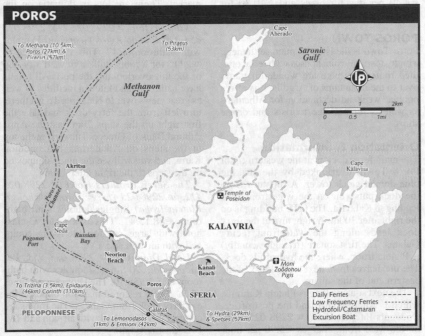

POROS

To Methana (10.5km),
Poros (27km) &
Piraeus (57km)

To Piraeus
(53km)

Cape
Aherado

*Saronic
Gulf*

*Methanon
Gulf*

0   1   2km
0   0.5   1mi

Akritsa

Poros Channel

Cape
Kalavria

Cape
Neda

*Russian
Bay*

⌘ *Temple of
Poseidon*

KALAVRIA

Pogonos
Port

Neorion
Beach

⌘ *Moni
Zoödohou
Pigis*

To Trizina (3.5km), Epidaurus
(46km) Corinth (110km)

Kanali
Beach

Poros

SFERIA

PELOPONNESE

Galatas

To Lemonodasos
(1km) & Ermioni (42km)

To Hydra (29km)
& Spetses (57km)

Daily Ferries ————
Low Frequency Ferries --------
Hydrofoil/Catamaran —·—·—
Excursion Boat ············

Phone numbers listed incorporate changes due in Oct 2002; see p55

There are also six hydrofoils south to Hydra (30 minutes, €6.15), two of which continue to Spetses (one hour, €10.60).

The Flying Dolphin agency is on Plateia Iroön, and has a timetable of departures posted outside.

Getting Around Poros

The Poros bus operates almost constantly along a route that starts near the hydrofoil dock on Plateia Iroön in Poros Town. It crosses to Kalavria and goes east along the south coast as far as Moni Zoödohou Pigis (10 minutes, €0.60), then turns around and heads west as far as Neorion Beach (15 minutes, €0.60).

Some of the caiques operating between Poros and Galatas switch to ferrying tourists to beaches in summer. Operators stand on the waterfront and call out their destinations.

There are several places on the road to Kalavria offering bikes for hire, both motorised and pedal-powered. Prices start at €4.40 per day for bikes and €10.30 for 50cc mopeds.

POROS TOWN

Poros Town is the island's main settlement, a pretty town of white houses with terracotta-tiled roofs, and there are wonderful views over to the mountains of Argolis. It is also a popular weekend destination for Athenians as well as for package tourists and cruise ships.

Orientation & Information

The main ferry dock is at the western tip of Poros Town, overlooked by the striking blue-domed clock tower. A left turn from the dock puts you on the waterfront road leading to Kalavria. The OTE building is on the right after 100m. A right turn at the ferry dock leads along the waterfront facing Galatas. The first square (triangle actually) is Plateia Iroön, where the hydrofoils dock. The bus leaves from next to the kiosk at the eastern end of the square.

The next square along is Plateia Karamis, which is where you'll find the post office. Coconuts Internet Café (☎ 2298 025 407), on the waterfront, charges €5.90 per hour

with a €1.50 minimum. It's open daily 10am to 2pm and 5pm to 11pm.

The National Bank of Greece is 500m farther along the waterfront. There are branches of the Alpha Bank and the Bank Emporiki on Plateia Iroön.

Poros does not have a tourist office. The tourist police (☎ 2298 022 462/256) are at Dimosthenous 10 – behind the Poros high school. Dimosthenous runs inland from the road to Kalavria, starting just beyond the small supermarket.

Suzi's Laundrette Service, next to the OTE, charges €8.80 to wash and dry a 5kg load.

Places to Stay

Poros has very little cheap accommodation.

If things are not too hectic, you may be offered a room by one of the *domatia* owners when you get off the ferry. Otherwise, head left along the waterfront and turn right after about 400m, beyond the small supermarket. There are lots of domatia on the streets around here.

Villa Tryfon (☎ 2298 022 215, 2298 025 854, Off Plateia Agios Georgiou) Doubles with bathroom €47. This is the place to head to for a room with a view. It's on top of the hill overlooking the port. All rooms have bathroom and kitchen facilities as well as great views over to Kalavria. To get there, turn left from the ferry dock and take the first right up the steps 20m past the Agricultural Bank of Greece. Turn left at the top of the steps on Aikaterinis Hatzopoulou Karra, and you will see the place signposted up the steps to the right after 150m.

The Seven Brothers Hotel (☎ 2298 023 412, fax 2298 023 413, ℮ 7brothrs@hol.gr, Plateia Iroön) Singles/doubles with bathroom €38.15/47. This is a smart C-class hotel with large, comfortable rooms equipped with air-con and TV.

Hotel Dionysos (☎ 2298 023 953, Papadopoulou 78) Singles/doubles with bathroom €35.20/58.70. The Dionysos occupies a beautifully restored mansion opposite the car ferry dock from Galatas. The rooms are comfortably furnished with air-con and TV. Breakfast is €4.40.

Places to Eat

Poros has some excellent restaurants.

Taverna Karavolos (☎ *2298 026 158*) Mains €3.25-5.90. Open from 7pm. Karavolos means 'big snail' in Greek and is the nickname of cheerful owner Theodoros. Sure enough, snails are a speciality of the house – served in a delicious thick tomato sauce. You'll find a range of imaginative mezedes like *taramokeftedes* (fish roe balls), and a daily selection of main courses like pork stuffed with garlic (€5). Bookings are advisable because Theodoros has only a dozen tables – and a strong local following.

The restaurant is signposted behind Cinema Diana on the road to Kalavria.

Taverna Platanos (☎ *2298 024 249, Plateia Agios Georgiou*) Mains €4.10-7.35. The Platanos is another popular spot, with seating beneath a large old plane tree in the small square at the top of Dimosthenous. Owner Tassos is a butcher by day and the restaurant specialises in spit-roast meats. You'll find specialities like *kokoretsi* (offal) and *gouronopoulo* (suckling pig).

The Flying Dutchman (☎ *2298 025 407, Off Plateia Karamis*) Mains €8.50-17.35. The Flying Dutchman has brought a touch of

POROS TOWN

PLACES TO STAY
2 Hotel Dionysos
3 Domatia
10 Villa Tryfon
22 Seven Brothers Hotel

PLACES TO EAT
6 Taverna Karavolos
8 Taverna Platanos
26 The Flying Dutchman

OTHER
1 Car ferries to Galatas
4 Supermarket
5 Cinema Diane
7 Tourist Police
9 Church of Agios Giorgios
11 OTE
12 Suzi's Laundrette
13 International Newspapers
14 Ferries to Aegina, Galatas, Hydra & Spetses
15 Clock Tower
16 Flying Dolphin Agency
17 Hydrofoils to Piraeus, Hydra & Spetses
18 Caïques to Galatas
19 Bus Stop
20 Bank Emporiki
21 Alpha Bank
23 Markets
24 Post Office
25 Coconuts
27 National Bank of Greece

Phone numbers listed incorporate changes due in Oct 2002; see p55

the exotic to the restaurant scene with a menu that includes Indonesian and Chinese dishes.

AROUND POROS
Poros has few places of interest and its beaches are no great shakes. **Kanali Beach**, on Kalavria 1km east of the bridge, is a mediocre pebble beach. **Neorion Beach**, 3km west of the bridge, is marginally better. The best beach is reputedly at **Russian Bay**, 1.5km past Neorion.

The 18th-century **Moni Zoödohou Pigis**, on Kalavria, has a beautiful gilded iconostasis from Asia Minor. The monastery is well signposted 4km east of Poros Town.

From the road below the monastery you can strike inland to the 6th-century **Temple of Poseidon**. The god of the sea and earthquakes was the principal deity worshipped on Poros. There's very little left of this temple, but the walk is worthwhile for the scenery on the way. From the site there are superb views of the Saronic Gulf and the Peloponnese. The orator Demosthenes, after failing to shake off the Macedonians who were after him for inciting the city-states to rebel, committed suicide here in 322 BC.

From the ruins you can continue along the road, which eventually winds back to the bridge. The road is drivable, but it's also a fine 6km walk that will take around two hours.

PELOPONNESIAN MAINLAND
The Peloponnesian mainland opposite Poros can easily be explored from the island.

The celebrated citrus groves of **Lemonodassos** (Lemon Forest) begin about 2km south-east of **Galatas**. There's no public transport, but it's an easy walk.

The ruins of ancient **Troizen**, legendary birthplace of Theseus, lie in the hills near the modern village of Trizina, 7.5km west of Galatas. There are buses to Trizina (15 minutes, €0.80) from Galatas, leaving a walk of about 1.5km to the site.

Getting There & Around
Small boats run between Galatas and Poros (five minutes, €0.30) every 10 minutes. A couple of buses daily depart for Nafplio

(two hours, €5.15) and can drop you off at the ancient site of Epidaurus (see the Peloponnese chapter for details on this site).

The district around Galatas is ideal for exploring by bicycle. These can be hired on the seafront in Galatas.

Hydra Υδρα

postcode 180 10 • pop 3000
Hydra (**ee**-drah) is the Saronic Gulf island with the most style. The gracious white and pastel stone mansions of Hydra Town are stacked up the rocky hillsides that surround the fine natural harbour. Film-makers were the first foreigners to be seduced by the beauty of Hydra. They began arriving in the 1950s when the island was used as a location for the film *Boy on a Dolphin*, among others. The artists and writers moved in next, followed by the celebrities, and nowadays it seems the whole world is welcomed ashore.

If you've been in Greece for some time you may fall in love with Hydra for one reason alone – the absence of kamikaze motorcyclists. Hydra has no motorised transport except for sanitation and construction vehicles. Donkeys (hundreds of them) are the only means of transport.

The name Hydra suggests the island once had plenty of water. Legend has it that the island was once covered with forests, which were destroyed by fire. Whatever the real story, these days the island is virtually barren and imports its water from the Peloponnese.

History
Like many of the Greek islands, Hydra was ignored by the Turks, so many Greeks from the Peloponnese settled on the island to escape Ottoman suppression and taxes. The population was further boosted by an influx of Albanians. Agriculture was impossible, so these new settlers began building boats. By the 19th century, the island had become a great maritime power. The canny Hydriots made a fortune by running the British blockade of French ports during the Napoleonic Wars. The wealthy shipping merchants built most of the town's

grand old arhontika from the considerable profits. It became a fashionable resort for Greek socialites, and lavish balls were a regular feature.

Hydra made a major contribution to the War of Independence. Without the 130 ships supplied by the island, the Greeks wouldn't have had much of a fleet with which to blockade the Turks. It also supplied leadership in the form of Georgios Koundouriotis, who was president of the emerging Greek nation's national assembly from 1822 to 1827, and Admiral Andreas Miaoulis, who commanded the Greek fleet. Streets and squares all over Greece are named after these two.

A mock battle is staged in Hydra harbour during the Miaoulia Festival held in honour of Admiral Miaoulis in late June.

Getting To/From Hydra

Ferry There are two ferries daily to Piraeus (3½ hours, €7.35), sailing via Poros (one hour, €3.25), Methana (1½ hours, €4.40) and Aegina (two hours, €4.70). There's also a daily boat to Spetses (one hour, €3.55). Departure times are listed on a board at the ferry dock.

You can buy tickets from Idreoniki Travel (☎ 2298 054 007), next to the Flying Dolphin office overlooking the port.

Hydrofoil Hydra is well served by the Flying Dolphin fleet with up to nine services daily to Piraeus (€13.50) – two to the Great Harbour, the rest to Zea Marina. Direct services take 1¼ hours, but most go via Poros (30 minutes, €5.90) and take 1½ hours. There are also frequent services to Spetses (30 minutes, €6.75), some of which call at Ermioni, adding 20 minutes to the trip. Many of the services to Spetses continue on to Porto Heli (50 minutes, €7.35). There is a daily service to Leonidio, Kyparissi, Gerakas and Monemvasia. This service also continues to Kythira four times weekly.

The Flying Dolphin office (☎ 2298 053 814) is on the waterfront opposite the ferry dock.

Getting Around Hydra

In summer, there are caiques from Hydra Town to the island's beaches. There are also water taxis (☎ 2298 053 690) which will take you anywhere you like. A water taxi to

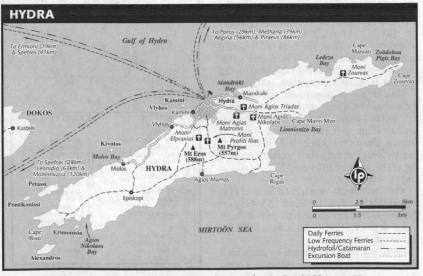

Phone numbers listed incorporate changes due in Oct 2002; see p55

Kamini costs €4.70, and €7.35 to Mandraki and Vlyhos.

The donkey owners clustered around the port charge around €7.35 to transport your bags to the hotel of your choice.

HYDRA TOWN

Most of the action in Hydra Town is concentrated around the waterfront cafes and shops, leaving the upper reaches of the narrow, stepped streets virtually deserted – and a joy to explore.

Orientation

Ferries and hydrofoils both dock on the eastern side of the harbour. The town's three main streets all head inland from the waterfront at the back of the harbour. Walking around from the ferry dock, the first street you come to is Tombazi, at the eastern corner. The next main street is Miaouli, on the left before the clock tower, which is the town's main thoroughfare. The third is Lignou, at the western extreme. It heads inland and links up with Kriezi, which runs west over the hills to Kamini. Lignou is best reached by heading up Votsi, on the left after the clock tower, and taking the first turn right.

Information

There is no tourist office, but Saitis Tours (☎ 2298 052 184, fax 2298 053 469), on the waterfront near Tombazi, puts out a useful free guide called *Holidays in Hydra*. You can find information about the island on the Internet at Ⓦ www.compulink.gr/hydranet.

Most things of importance are close to the waterfront. The post office is on a small side street between the Commercial (Emporiki) Bank and the National Bank of Greece. The tourist police (☎ 2298 052 205) can be found at the police station opposite the OTE on Votsi from mid-May until the end of September.

You can check your email at the Flamingo Internet Café (☎ 2298 053 485) on Tombazi. It's open noon to 11pm daily and charges €7.35 per hour with a €1.50 minimum.

There's a laundry service in the small market square near the post office. It's open

10am to 1.30pm and 5pm to 8.30pm daily and charges €10.30 to wash and dry a load.

Things to See

The **Historical Archives Museum of Hydra** (☎ 2298 052 355; admission €1.50; open 10am-4.30pm Tues-Sun) is close to the ferry dock on the eastern side of the Hydra harbour. The museum houses a collection of portraits and naval oddments, with an emphasis on the island's role in the War of Independence.

The **Byzantine Museum** (☎ 2298 054 071; admission €1.50; open 10am-5pm

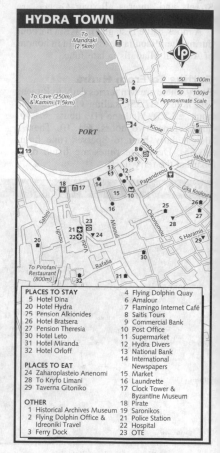

HYDRA TOWN

To Mandraki (2.5km)
To Cave (250m) & Kamini (1.5km)
PORT
Tombazi
Kiose
Sahtouri
Papandreou
Gika Kouloura
Oikonomou
S Haramis
Kriezi
Lignou
Votsi
Miaouli
Sahini
Rafalia
To Pirofani Restaurant (800m)

0 50 100m
0 50 100yd
Approximate Scale

PLACES TO STAY	
5	Hotel Dina
20	Hotel Hydra
25	Pension Alkionides
26	Hotel Bratsera
27	Pension Theresia
30	Hotel Leto
31	Hotel Miranda
32	Hotel Orloff

PLACES TO EAT	
24	Zaharoplasteio Anenomi
28	To Kryfo Limani
29	Taverna Gitoniko

OTHER	
1	Historical Archives Museum
2	Flying Dolphin Office & Idreoniki Travel
3	Ferry Dock
4	Flying Dolphin Quay
6	Amalour
7	Flamingo Internet Café
8	Saitis Tours
9	Commercial Bank
10	Post Office
11	Supermarket
12	Hydra Divers
13	National Bank
14	International Newspapers
15	Market
16	Laundrette
17	Clock Tower & Byzantine Museum
18	Pirate
19	Saronikos
21	Police Station
22	Hospital
23	OTE

Tues-Sun), upstairs at the Monastery of the Assumption of Virgin Mary, houses a collection of icons and assorted religious paraphernalia. The entrance is through the archway beneath the clock tower on the waterfront.

Places to Stay

Accommodation in Hydra is generally of a very high standard, and you pay accordingly. The prices listed here are for the high season, which in Hydra means every weekend as well as July and August.

Places to Stay – Budget

Hotel Dina (☎ 2298 052 248, *Stavrou Tsipi*) Singles/doubles with bathroom €29.35/35.20. The cheapest rooms are found at this small, cheery place. The high location means great views over the town and harbour.

Pension Theresia (☎ 2298 053 984, *fax 2298 053 983, Tombazi*) Singles/doubles with bathroom €29.35/44. This popular place is about 300m from the waterfront, and has clean, comfortable rooms with bathroom and a small communal kitchen.

Pension Alkionides (☎/fax 2298 054 055, *Off Oikonomou*) Singles/doubles with bathroom €35.20/44. The Alkionides is a good budget choice, tucked away about 250m from the port. All rooms have a fridge.

Hotel Hydra (☎/fax 2298 052 102, e *hydrahotel@aig.forthnet.gr, Sahini*) Singles/doubles with bathroom €35.20/49.90. This hotel has a great setting overlooking the town from the west. It has large, comfortable rooms. It's a fair haul to get there – more than 100 steps up Sahini from Lignou – but the views over the town and harbour are worth it.

Places to Stay – Mid-Range

Hotel Leto (☎ 2298 053 385, *fax 2298 053 806, Off Miaouli*) Doubles with bathroom €64.60-80.70. The Leto is a stylish place with beautiful polished timber floors. Prices include buffet breakfast. It's hidden away in the maze of streets behind the port, but signposted to the left off the first square on Miaouli.

Hotel Miranda (☎ 2298 052 230, *fax 2298 053 510*, e *mirhydra@hol.gr, Miaouli*) Doubles with bathroom €52.85-102.75, triples €117.40. Originally the mansion of a wealthy Hydriot sea captain, the Miranda has been beautifully renovated and converted into a very smart hotel. Breakfast is €7.35. The hotel is 300m from the port.

The Mansions of Hydra

The graceful mansions that line the hills around Hydra Town's perfect horseshoe harbour are a reminder of the days in the 18th and 19th centuries when Hydra ruled the waves in the Mediterranean.

The schooners built on the island were perfect for the time: light, fast and easily manoeuvred – essential qualities for outrunning the pirate ships that preyed on larger cargo vessels.

The canny Hydriots also had the ability to turn any war to their advantage. The Hydriots earned their spurs by carrying Russian wheat through the Bosphorus during the wars between Russia and the Turks in the 1780s, and then went on to hit it seriously rich by running the British blockade of French ports during the Napoleonic Wars.

The wealthy shipping captains opted to spend their profits building grand houses, known as *arhontiko*, which were built by masons brought in from the Peloponnese and Epiros. The architecture of these arhontiko is unusual: a local interpretation of the castle-style mansions seen in ports like Genoa and Venice. Outwardly plain, they were lavishly appointed within and furnished with the finest that money could buy.

The best examples are to be found on the western side of the harbour, where the massive Koundouriotis Mansion reigns supreme. It has been restored and is destined to be opened as a museum.

In the meantime, visitors will have to make do with visiting the homes of some of the less distinguished captains, whose homes have been converted into hotels like the Miranda and the Orloff (see Places to Stay under Hydra Town).

Places to Stay – Top End

Hotel Orloff (☎ 2298 052 564, fax 2298 053 532, ⓔ orloff@internet.gr, Rafalia) Singles/doubles with bathroom from €82.20/93.90. This is a beautiful old mansion with a cool, vine-covered courtyard at the back. The furnishings are elegant without being overstated, and each of the 10 rooms has a character of its own. Prices include buffet breakfast, served in the courtyard in summer. The hotel is about 250m from the port; head inland from the port and turn right onto Rafalia after the square.

Hotel Bratsera (☎ 2298 053 971, fax 2298 053 626, ⓔ tallos@hol.gr, Tombazi) Doubles with bathroom €102.70-161.40, 4-bed suites from €167.30. The Bratsera is another place with loads of character. It occupies a converted sponge factory about 300m from the port. It also has the town's only swimming pool. It's for guests only, but you'll qualify if you eat at its restaurant. Prices include breakfast.

Places to Eat

Hydra has dozens of tavernas and restaurants. Unlike the hotels, there are plenty of cheap places around – especially if you're prepared to head away from the waterfront.

Taverna Gitoniko (☎ 2298 053 615, Spilios Haramis) Mains €2.95-8.80. This taverna is better known by the names of its owners, Manolis and Christina. The menu is nothing special, but they have built up an enthusiastic local following through the simple formula of turning out consistently good traditional taverna food. Try the beetroot salad – a bowl of baby beets and boiled greens served with garlic mashed potato. The flavours complement each other perfectly. Get in early or you'll have a long wait.

To Kryfo Limani (The Secret Port; ☎ 2298 052 585) Meals €3.55-8.50. Tucked away on a small alleyway is this charming spot with seating beneath a large lemon tree, and delicious specials like hearty fish soup (€4.70).

Pirofani Restaurant (☎ 2298 053 175) Mains €5.90-8.80. For something special, head out to this excellent restaurant at Kamini. Owner Theo specialises in desserts

– so be sure to leave room for a slice o lemon meringue pie or chocolate and pea cake. The restaurant is at the base of the steps on the inland route between Kamin and Hydra Town; to get there, follow Kriez over the hill from Hydra Town.

Entertainment

Hydra boasts a busy nightlife. The action is centred on the bars on the south-western side of the harbour where places like **Pirate** (☎ 2298 052 711) and **Saronikos** (☎ 2298 052 589) keep going until almost dawn. Pirate plays Western rock while Saronikos plays Greek.

Amalour (mobile ☎ 69-7746 1357, Tombazi) This sophisticated cafe-bar, 100m from the port, sells a wide range of fresh juices as well as alcohol.

AROUND HYDRA

It's a strenuous but worthwhile one-hour walk up to **Moni Profiti Ilias**, starting from Miaouli. Monks still live in the monastery, which has fantastic views down to the town. It's a short walk from here to the convent of **Moni Efpraxias**.

The beaches on Hydra are a dead loss, but the walks to them are enjoyable. **Kamini**, about 20 minutes walk along the coastal path from town, has rocks and a very small pebble beach. **Vlyhos**, 20 minutes farther on, is an attractive village with a slightly larger pebble beach, two tavernas and a ruined 19th-century stone bridge.

From here, walkaholics can continue to the small bay at **Molos**, or take a left fork before the bay to the inland village of **Episkopi**. There are no facilities at Episkopi or Molos.

An even more ambitious walk is the three-hour stint from Hydra Town to **Moni Zourvas**, in the north-east of the island. Along the way you will pass **Moni Agias Triadas** and **Moni Agios Nikolaos**.

A path leads east from Hydra Town to the pebble beach at **Mandraki**.

Walking Tours

A range of guided walks around the island in spring and autumn is offered by **Lisa**

Bartsiokas (☎ 2298 053 836, fax 2298 053 842, e hydragr@otenet.gr; €14.70 per person). The walks take between five and eight hours, including breaks. There must be a minimum of four people.

Diving

Hydra Divers (☎ 2298 053 900, e diveinst@x-treme.gr, W www.divingteam.gr) is a new business offering dives at a range of locations around the nearby Peloponnese coast. It has introductory dives for €58.70, and packages for experienced divers such as four dives for €123.30. These prices include equipment.

Spetses Σπέτσες

postcode 180 50 • pop 3700
Pine-covered Spetses, the most distant of the group from Piraeus, has long been a favourite with British holiday-makers.

Spetses' history is similar to Hydra's. It became wealthy through shipbuilding, ran the British blockade during the Napoleonic Wars and refitted its ships to join the Greek fleet during the War of Independence. Spetsiot fighters achieved a certain notoriety through their pet tactic of attaching small boats laden with explosives to the enemy's ships, setting them alight and beating a hasty retreat.

The island was known in antiquity as Pityoussa (meaning 'pine-covered'), but the original forest cover disappeared long ago. The pine-covered hills that greet the visitor today are a legacy of the far-sighted and wealthy philanthropist Sotirios Anargyrios.

Anargyrios was born on Spetses in 1848 and emigrated to the USA, returning in 1914 an exceedingly rich man. He bought two-thirds of the then largely barren island and planted the Aleppo pines that stand today. He also financed the island's road system and commissioned many of the

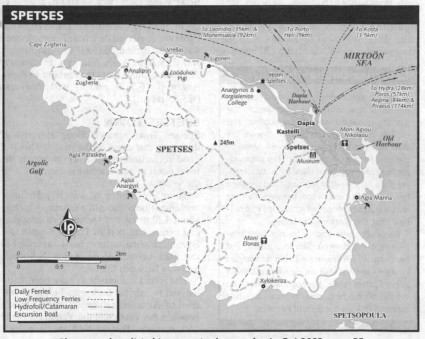

SPETSES

To Leonidio (35km) &
Monemvasia (92km)   To Porto
Heli (9km)   To Kosta
(3.5km)

Cape Zogheria

Vrellas

Ligoneri

MIRTOÖN
SEA

Analipsis   Zoödohos
Pigi

Zogheria   Hotel
Spetses

Anargyrios &
Korgialenios
College   Dapia
Harbour   To Hydra (28km),
Poros (57km),
Aegina (84km) &
Piraeus (114km)

Dapia

Kastelli   Moni Agiou
Nikolaou   Old
Harbour

▲ 245m   Spetses
Museum

SPETSES

Argolic
Gulf   Agia Paraskevi

Agioi
Anargyri   Agia Marina

Moni
Elonas

Xylokeriza

SPETSOPOULA

0   1   2km
0   0.5   1mi

Daily Ferries
Low Frequency Ferries
Hydrofoil/Catamaran
Excursion Boat

Phone numbers listed incorporate changes due in Oct 2002; see p55

town's grand buildings, including the Hotel Possidonion. He was a big fan of the British public (ie, private) school system, and established Anargyrios & Korgialenios College, a boarding school for boys from all over Greece. British author John Fowles taught English at the college in 1950–51, and used the island as a setting for his novel *The Magus*.

Getting To/From Spetses

Ferry There is one ferry daily to Piraeus (4½ hours, €10), via Hydra (one hour, €3.55), Poros (two hours, €5) and Aegina (three hours, €7.35). Two companies operate the service on alternate days. You'll find departure times on the waterfront outside Alasia Travel (☎ 2298 074 098), which sells tickets. The port police (☎ 2298 072 245) are opposite the quay.

There are also water taxis to Kosta (€10.30), just 15 minutes away on the Peloponnese mainland. There are three buses daily from Kosta to Nafplio (2¼ hours, €5).

Hydrofoil There are up to nine Flying Dolphins daily to Piraeus (2½ hours, €19.10). Most services travel via Hydra (30 minutes,

---

Lascarina Bouboulina

Spetses contributed one of the most colourful figures of the War of Independence, the dashing heroine Lascarina Bouboulina. Her exploits on and off the battlefield were the stuff of legend. She was widowed twice by the time the war began – both her shipowning husbands had been killed by pirates, leaving her a very wealthy woman – and she used her money to commission her own fighting ship, the *Agamemnon*, which she led into battle during the blockade of Nafplio.

Bouboulina was known for her fiery temperament and her countless love affairs, and her death was in keeping with her flamboyant lifestyle – she was shot during a family dispute in her Spetses home. Bouboulina featured on the old 50 drachma note, depicted directing cannon fire from the deck of her ship.

€7.05) and Poros (70 minutes, €10). There are also daily connections to Leonidio (one hour, €7.35) and Monemvasia (1½ hours, €12.65).

Getting Around Spetses

Spetses has two bus routes. There are three or four buses daily from Plateia Agias Mamas in Spetses Town to Agioi Anargyri (40 minutes, €1.40), via Agia Marina and Xylokeriza. Departure times are displayed on a board by the bus stop. There are hourly buses to Ligoneri (€0.60) departing from in front of the Hotel Possidonion.

No cars are permitted on the island. Unfortunately this ban has not been extended to motorbikes, resulting in there being more of the critters here than just about anywhere else. The colourful horse-drawn carriages are a pleasant but expensive way of getting around. Prices are displayed on a board where the carriages gather by the port.

Boat Water taxis (☎ 2298 072 072) go anywhere you care to nominate from opposite the Flying Dolphin office at Dapia Harbour. Fares are displayed on a board. Sample one-way fares include €17.60 to Agia Marina and €35.20 to Agioi Anargyri. In summer, there are caiques from the harbour to Agioi Anargyri (€5.30 return) and Zogheria (€3.55 return).

SPETSES TOWN

Spetses Town sprawls along almost half the north-east coast of the island. This is a good reflection of the way in which the focal point of settlement has changed over the years.

There's evidence of an early Helladic settlement near the old harbour, which is about 1.5km east of the modern commercial centre and port of Dapia. Roman and Byzantine remains have been unearthed in the area behind Moni Agios Nikolaos, halfway between the two.

The island is thought to have been uninhabited for almost 600 years before the arrival of Albanian refugees fleeing fighting between the Turks and the Venetians in the 16th century. They settled on the hillside just inland from Dapia, the area now known as Kastelli.

The Dapia district has a few impressive arhontika, but the prettiest part of town is around the old harbour.

Orientation & Information

The quay at Dapia Harbour serves both ferries and hydrofoils. A left turn at the end of the quay leads east along the waterfront on Sotirios Anargyris, skirting a small square where the horse-drawn carriages wait. The road is flanked by a string of uninspiring, concrete C-class hotels, and emerges after 200m on Plateia Agias Mamas, next to the town beach. The bus stop for Agioi Anargyri is next to the beach. The post office is on the street running behind the hotels; coming from the quay, turn right at Hotel Soleil and then left.

The waterfront to the right of the quay is also called Sotirios Anargyris. It skirts Dapia Harbour, passes the grand old Hotel Possidonion and continues west around the bay to Hotel Spetses and becomes the road to Ligoneri.

The main road inland from Dapia is N Spetson, which runs south-west off the small square where horse-drawn carriages wait. It soon becomes Botassi, which continues inland to Kastelli. These two streets are among the few on Spetses with street signs.

There is no tourist office on Spetses. The tourist police (☎ 2298 073 100) are based in the police station – on the well-signposted road to the museum – from mid-May to September.

The OTE is behind Dapia Harbour, opposite the National Bank of Greece. Internet access is available at Delfinia Net Café (☎ 2298 075 051) on Plateia Agias Mamas, open daily 9am to 2am.

Things to See

The **old harbour** is a delightful place to explore. It is ringed by old Venetian buildings,

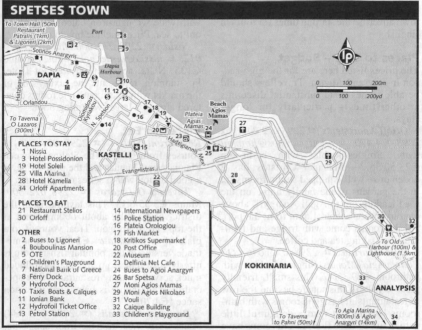

SPETSES TOWN

To Town Hall (50m)
Restaurant
Patralis (1km)
& Ligoneri (2km)

Port

Sotirios Anargyris

DAPIA

Dapia Harbour

Hatziyiannis

Orlandou

To Taverna
O Lazaros
(300m)

Domidous Kyriakou

N. Spetson

Plateia
Agias
Mamas

Beach
Agios
Mamas

Hadziyiannis Mexi

KASTELLI

Evangelistras

KOKKINARIA

To Taverna
to Pahni (50m)

ANALYPSIS

To Old
Harbour (100m) &
Lighthouse (1.5km)

To Agia Marina
(800m) & Agioi
Anargyri (14km)

0   100   200m
0   100   200yd

PLACES TO STAY
1 Nissia
3 Hotel Possidonion
19 Hotel Soleil
25 Villa Marina
28 Hotel Kamelia
34 Orloff Apartments

PLACES TO EAT
21 Restaurant Stelios
30 Orloff

OTHER
2 Buses to Ligoneri
4 Bouboulinas Mansion
5 OTE
6 Children's Playground
7 National Bank of Greece
8 Ferry Dock
9 Hydrofoil Dock
10 Taxis Boats & Caïques
11 Ionian Bank
12 Hydrofoil Ticket Office
13 Petrol Station

14 International Newspapers
15 Police Station
16 Plateia Orologiou
17 Fish Market
18 Kritikos Supermarket
20 Post Office
22 Museum
23 Delfinia Net Cafe
24 Buses to Agioi Anargyri
26 Bar Spetsa
27 Moni Agios Mamas
29 Moni Agios Nikolaos
31 Vouli
32 Caique Building
33 Children's Playground

Phone numbers listed incorporate changes due in Oct 2002; see p55

and filled with boats of every shape and size – from colourful little fishing boats to sleek luxury cruising yachts. The shipbuilders of Spetses still do things the traditional way and the shore is dotted with the hulls of emerging caiques. The walk from Dapia Harbour takes about 20 minutes. **Moni Agios Nikolaos** straddles a headland at the halfway mark.

The **museum** (☎ 2298 072 994; admission €1.50; open 8.30am-2.30pm Tues-Sun) is housed in the arhontiko of Hadzigiannis Mexis, a shipowner who became the island's first governor. While most of the collection is devoted to folklore items and portraits of the island's founding fathers, there is also a fine collection of ships' figureheads. The museum is hidden away in the back streets of Evangelistras, but is clearly signposted from Plateia Orologiou.

The mansion of Lascarina Bouboulina (see the boxed text), behind the OTE building, has now been converted into a **museum** (☎ 2298 072 416; adult/child €2.95/0.90; open 9am-5pm Tues-Sun). Billboards around town advertise the starting times for tours in English.

Places to Stay – Budget
The prices listed here are for the high season in July and August. Travellers should be able to negotiate substantial discounts at other times – particularly for longer stays.

Orloff Apartments (☎ 2298 072 246, fax 2298 074 470, e orloff_christos@hotmail .com) Singles/doubles with bathroom €23.50/35.20. Manager Christos has a dozen or so well-equipped studio rooms set in the gardens of the family home on the road leading out to Agioi Anargyri, above the old harbour about 1.5km from the port. All the rooms come with fridge and facilities for making tea and coffee.

Villa Marina (☎ 2298 072 646, Off Plateia Agias Mamas) Singles/doubles with bathroom €29.35/47. This small, friendly place is just off this square beyond the row of restaurants. It has good rooms with bathrooms looking out onto a delightful little garden full of fresh flowers. All rooms have

refrigerators and there is a well-equipped communal kitchen downstairs.

Hotel Kamelia (☎ 2298 072 415) Singles/ doubles with bathroom €35.20/41.10. This hotel is signposted to the right at the supermarket, 100m past Plateia Agias Mamas on the road that leads inland to Agioi Anargyri. It is almost hidden beneath a sprawling burgundy bougainvillea. Rooms have bathrooms and are spotless.

Otherwise, you might be forced to fall back on one of the uninspiring C- and D-class places that line the waterfront between the ferry dock and Plateia Agias Mamas, or seek help from one of the travel agents.

Places to Stay – Mid-Range & Top End
Hotel Possidonion (☎ 2298 072 308, fax 2298 072 208) Singles/doubles/triples with bathroom €49.90/64.60/73.40. The Possidonion is a wonderful old Edwardian-style hotel that overlooks the seafront just south of the Dapia harbour. It has seen better days, but it remains an imposing building with wide wrought-iron balconies looking out to sea. Prices include breakfast.

Nisia (☎ 2298 075 000, fax 2298 075 012, e nissia@otenet.gr) Doubles around €135. Nisia, about 200m west of Hotel Possidonion, represents the luxury end of the market with apartment-style rooms clustered around a large swimming pool.

Places to Eat
Restaurant Stelios (☎ 2298 073 748) 3 courses from €8.25. The Stelios, between Plateia Agias Mamas and the post office, is a good option with a series of set menus.

Taverna O Lazaros (☎ 2298 072 600) Mains €3.55-6.15. This taverna is in the district of Kastelli, about 600m inland at the top end of Spetson. Treat yourself to a plate of *taramasalata* (€2.35); its homemade version of this popular fish-roe dip is utterly different from the mass-produced muck served at many restaurants. The speciality of the house is baby goat in lemon sauce (€4.70).

Restaurant Patralis (☎ 2298 072 134) Mains €4.10-7.65, fresh fish from €32.30/kg.

Fish fans should head out to the Patralis, about 1.5km west of Dapia on the road to Ligoneri. It has a great setting, a good menu and the fish are supplied by the restaurant's own boat. The fish a la Spetses (€7.05), a large tuna or swordfish steak baked with veg-etables and lots of garlic, goes down perfectly with a cold beer.

Orloff (☎ *2298 075 255*) Mains €4.70-7.05. If character is what you want, you won't find a better place than this, 600m from Plateia Agios Mamas on the coast road to the old harbour. The early-19th cen-tury port-authority building has been con-verted into a stylish restaurant specialising in mezedes.

Kritikos Supermarket (☎ *2298 074 361, Kentriki Agora)* Self-caterers can head to this supermarket which is next to Hotel Soleil on the waterfront near Plateia Agias Mamas.

Entertainment

Bar Spetsa (☎ *2298 074 131)* For a quiet beer and a great selection of music from the '60s and '70s, try this bar, 50m beyond Plateia Agias Mamas on the road to Agioi Anargyri.

1 Vouli (☎ *2298 074 179)* Call into this classic old-fashioned wine bar at 10am and

you'll realise why nothing very much ever happens on Spetses. It's always busy with locals gossiping over a morning tumbler of wine (€0.90), poured from one of the giant barrels that line the walls. Come along equipped with a few snacks to share around. It overlooks the old harbour about 800m from Plateia Agias Mamas.

AROUND SPETSES

Spetses' coastline is speckled with numer-ous coves with small, pine-shaded beaches. A 24km road (part sealed, part dirt) skirts the entire coastline, so a motorcycle is the ideal way to explore the island.

The beach at **Ligoneri**, west of town, has the attraction of being easily accessible by bus. **Agia Marina**, to the south of the old harbour, is a small resort with a crowded beach. **Agla Paraskevi** and **Agioi Anargyri**, on the south-west coast, have good, albeit crowded, beaches; both have water sports of every description. A large mansion be-tween the two beaches was the inspiration for the Villa Bourani in John Fowles' *The Magus.*

The small island of **Spetsopoula** to the south of Spetses is owned by the family of the late shipping magnate Stavros Niarchos.

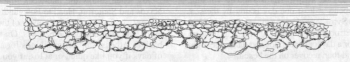

Cyclades Κυκλαδες

The Cyclades (kih-**klah**-dez) are the quint-essential Greek islands – rugged outcrops of rock dotted with brilliant-white buildings offset by vividly painted balconies and bright-blue church domes, all bathed in dazzling light and fringed with golden beaches lapped by aquamarine seas.

Goats and sheep are raised on the mountainous, barren islands, as well as some pigs and cattle. Naxos is the most fertile island, producing potatoes and other crops for export to Athens and neighbouring islands. Many islanders still fish, but tourism is becoming the dominant source of income.

Some islands, especially Mykonos, Santorini (Thira) and Ios, have eagerly embraced tourism – their shores are spread with sun lounges, umbrellas and water-sports equipment. Other islands, such as Andros, Syros, Kea, Serifos and Sifnos, are less visited by foreigners but, thanks to their proximity to the mainland, are popular weekend and summer retreats for Athenians.

To Greek people, Tinos is not a holiday island but the country's premier place of pilgrimage – a Greek Lourdes. Other islands, such as Anafi and the Little Cyclades east of Naxos, are little more than clumps of rock with tiny, depopulated villages.

The Cyclades are so named because they form a circle (*kyklos*) around the island of Delos, one of the country's most significant ancient sites.

SUGGESTED ITINERARIES
One Week
Spend two days on Naxos, exploring the hilltop Kastro and backcountry, lush Tragaea region and villages of Halki, Filoti and Apiranthos. Catch a ferry to Santorini and spend three or four days here, staying in Fira or Oia to view the spectacular sunsets, and visit Ancient Akrotiri and Fira's museums. Take a trip to Thirasia and the volcanic islets. Spend at least one day lazing by the sea. Head to Syros to explore the graceful neoclassical city of Ermoupolis and the hilltop village of Ano Syros for a day, or head to Ios and dance the night away and then recover on the beach.

Highlights

- Spectacular sunsets over Santorini's submerged volcano

- Walks through the verdant countryside of Naxos and Andros, and the drier landscape of Folegandros

- Unspoilt, whitewashed villages on Amorgos, Folegandros and Sifnos

- Ouzo and freshly grilled fish at beachside tavernas

- Uncrowded island beaches and bays with crystal-clear water

- The island-sized archaeological site of ancient Delos

- Hedonistic nightlife on Mykonos, Santorini and Ios

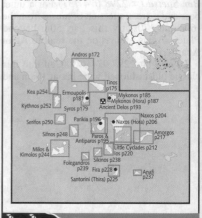

Two Weeks
Spend a day and night on Syros and explore Ermoupolis and Ano Syros. On Mykonos, sample the nightlife, and take an excursion to Ancient Delos. Then follow the one-week itinerary for Naxos and Santorini. Head to Folegandros for a day or two. Soak up the atmosphere of the lovely Hora, and visit one of the beaches. On the way back to Athens, stop off at Sikinos for a couple of days if you like quiet, or at Ios, if you feel the

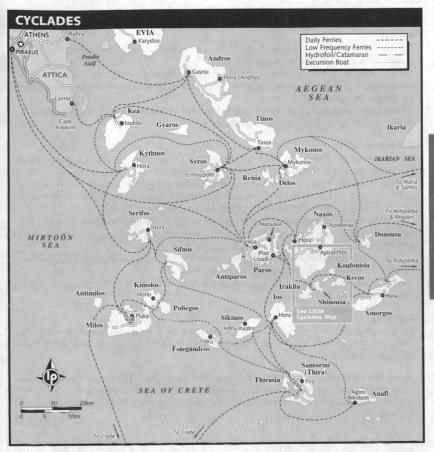

CYCLADES

AEGEAN SEA

Daily Ferries	-------
Low Frequency Ferries	- - - - -
Hydrofoil/Catamaran	-·-·-
Excursion Boat	·········

ATHENS
Rafina
EVIA
Karystos
PIRAEUS
Petalia Gulf
ATTICA
Andros
Gavrio
Hora (Andros)
Lavrio
Kea
Ioulida
Gyaros
Cape Sounion
Tinos
Ikaria
Kythnos
Hora
Syros
Ermoupolis
Tinos
Mykonos
Mykonos
IKARIAN SEA
Renia
Delos
To Ikaria & Samos
MIRTOÖN SEA
Serifos
Hora
Naoussa
Naxós
Apollonas
To Astypalea & Rhodes
Donousa
Parikia
Hora
Apiranthos
To Astypalea
Sifnos
Piso Livadi
Paros
Koufonisia
Keros
Antiparos
Iraklia
See Little Cyclades Map
Shinousa
Hora
Amorgos
Antimilos
Kimolos
Horio
Poliegos
Sikinos
Ios
Plaka
Hóra/Kastro
Hora
Milos
Hora
Folegandros
Santorini (Thira)
Thirasia
Fira
SEA OF CRETE
Agios Nikolaos
Anafi
To Crete
To Crete

0   10   20km
0   5   10mi

CYCLADES

need to party. Amorgos would make a good alternative to Folegandros. From Amorgos you can make a side trip to the cute little island of Koufonisia before heading back to Athens.

HISTORY

The Cyclades have been inhabited since at least 7000 BC, and there is evidence that the obsidian (hard, black volcanic glass used for manufacturing sharp blades) on Milos was exploited as early as 7500 BC. Around 3000 BC, the Cycladic civilisation, a culture famous for its seafarers, appeared. During the Early Cycladic period (3000–2000

BC) there were settlements on Keros, Syros, Naxos, Milos, Sifnos and Amorgos. It was during this time that the famous Cycladic marble figurines were sculpted.

In the Middle Cycladic period (2000–1500 BC), many of the islands were occupied by the Minoans – at Akrotiri, on Santorini, a Minoan town has been excavated. At the beginning of the Late Cycladic period (1500–1100 BC), the Cyclades passed to the Mycenaeans. The Dorians followed in the 8th century BC, bringing Archaic culture with them.

Most of the Cyclades joined the Delian League in 478 BC, and by the middle of the

CYCLADES

Getting it Straight – Things You Should Know Before You Go

Ferries
Outside high season (June to September), there is a major diminution of ferry services. The services quoted in this chapter are for high season.

If you're travelling outside these peak periods, contact the port police at your mainland departure point and at your destination island for an accurate list of ferry services. Telephone numbers are listed in the guide.

Ferry routes and services also change from day to day and month to month, not to mention year to year – on-the-ground information is invaluable.

Accommodation
Everyone in Europe, it seems, wants to go island hopping during the months of July and August. Accommodation in the Cyclades at this time is scarce – and also mighty expensive.

The prices quoted in this book are high season prices that will generally only be in operation from mid-July to August. For the rest of the season (May to early July and late August to late September), prices drop to around 40% to 50% of the quoted price.

For a standard room with bathroom in a pension, expect to pay from €14.50 to €23.30 a double outside high season. Don't let the prices quoted in this chapter scare you off – or cause you to pass up a trip (or a particular island) that you could, in fact, afford.

To complicate things further, from November to April, the Cyclades virtually close down, and most people involved with the tourist industry return to Athens.

Pensions are your best option for accommodation if you're travelling during this period, but call ahead to make sure they are open.

Camping
Most camping grounds in the Cyclades are unlikely to be the green oases you expect – with a few exceptions, they're often desolate, dry and dusty, and the ground is hard and rocky. Here's a useful tip from a reader:

Try and take a tent that is as free-standing as possible and requires few pegs – as most sites seem to consist of mainly crushed road stone. We met Greeks who, aware of this, had made their own pegs out of ankle iron. I ended up purchasing some nine-inch nails and a small hammer from a hardware store, which worked very well.

Ray West

Also, most, but not all, camping grounds will charge you extra if you bring a car (€2.10 to €3.50) or motorbike (€1.50 to €2.10) on site.

Car Hire
Car hire costs €20.30 to €49.30 depending on the island and the season. Expect to pay less from May to June.

Some destinations such as Ios, Santorini and Kea charge high prices throughout the tourist season, while others such as Tinos and Paros are far more reasonable.

The Meltemi
The Cyclades are more exposed to the north-westerly *meltemi* wind than other island groups, making for some literally hair-raising, exhausting wind-battered days. The winds can often play havoc with ferry schedules (especially on smaller vessels that ply the Little Cyclades routes). Take this into consideration if you're travelling on a tight schedule.

th century the islands were members of a fully fledged Athenian empire. In the Hellenistic era (323–146 BC) the islands fell under the control of Egypt's Ptolemies and, later, the Macedonians. In 146 BC, the islands became a Roman province and trade links were established with many parts of the Mediterranean, bringing prosperity.

After the division of the Roman Empire into western and eastern entities in AD 395, the Cyclades were ruled from Byzantium (Constantinople). Following the fall of Byzantium in 1204, the Franks gave the Cyclades to Venice, which parcelled the islands out to opportunistic aristocrats. The most powerful was Marco Sanudo (self-styled Duke of Naxos), who acquired Naxos, Paros, Ios, Santorini, Anafi, Sifnos, Milos, Amorgos and Folegandros.

The islands came under Turkish rule in 1537. Neglected by the Ottomans, they became backwaters prone to pirate raids, hence the labyrinthine, hilltop character of their towns – the mazes of narrow lanes were designed to disorientate invaders. Nevertheless, the impact of piracy led to massive depopulation; in 1563 only five out of 16 islands were still inhabited.

In 1771 the Cyclades were annexed by the Russians during the Russian-Turkish War, but were reclaimed by the Ottomans a few years later. The Cyclades' participation in the Greek War of Independence was minimal, but they became havens for people fleeing islands where insurrections against the Turks had led to massacres.

The fortunes of the Cycladics have been revived by the tourism boom that began in the 1970s. Until then, many islanders lived in abject poverty and many more gave up the battle and headed for the mainland in search of work.

GETTING TO/FROM & AROUND THE CYCLADES

For information on travel within the Cyclades, see the individual island entries.

Air

Olympic Airways links Athens with Naxos, Syros, Santorini, Mykonos, Paros and Milos. Santorini has direct flights to/from Mykonos, Thessaloniki, Iraklio (Crete) and Rhodes, and Mykonos has flights to/from Thessaloniki and Rhodes (see individual island sections for prices).

Ferry

Ferry routes tend to separate the Cyclades into western, northern, central and eastern subgroups. Most ferries serving the Cyclades connect one of these subgroups with Piraeus, Lavrio or Rafina on the mainland. The central Cyclades (Paros, Naxos, Ios and Santorini) are the most visited and have the best links with the mainland, usually Piraeus.

The northern Cyclades (Andros, Tinos, Syros and Mykonos) also have very good connections with the mainland. The jumping-off point for Andros is Rafina, but it's possible to access it from Piraeus by catching a ferry to Syros, Tinos or Mykonos and connecting from there.

The western Cyclades (Kea, Kythnos, Milos, Serifos, Sifnos, Folegandros and Sikinos) have less frequent connections with the mainland. Lavrio is the mainland port for ferries serving Kea.

The eastern Cyclades (Anafi, Amorgos, Iraklia, Shinousa, Koufonisia and Donousa) are the least visited and have the fewest links with the mainland. They are best visited from Naxos and Santorini.

There are usually relatively good connections within each of the subgroups, but infrequent connections between them. When you plan your island-hopping, it pays to bear this pattern of ferry routes in mind. However, Paros is the ferry hub of the Cyclades, and connections between different groups are usually possible via Paros if not direct.

The following table gives an overview of high-season ferry services to the Cyclades from the mainland and Crete.

Fast Boats & Catamaran

Large high-speed boats and cats are now major players on Cyclades routes. The travel time is usually half that of regular ferries. Seats fill fast in July and August, especially on weekends, so it's worth booking your ticket a day or so in advance.

CYCLADES

Ferry Connections to the Cyclades

origin	destination	duration (hours)	price (€)	frequency
Agios Nikolaos (Crete)	Milos	7	14.80	3 weekly
Iraklio (Crete)	Mykonos	9	18.80	3 weekly
Iraklio	Naxos	7½	16.15	2 weekly
Iraklio	Paros	7-8	16.15	2 weekly
Iraklio	Santorini	3¾	12.05	3 weekly
Iraklio	Syros	10	17.60	1 weekly
Iraklio	Tinos	10¼	20.00	2 weekly
Lavrio	Kea	1¼	5.30	2 daily
Lavrio	Kythnos	3½	7.00	4 weekly
Lavrio	Syros	3½	10.80	2 weekly
Piraeus	Amorgos	10	13.10	15 weekly
Piraeus	Anafi	11	20.10	4 weekly
Piraeus	Donousa	7	14.20	3 weekly
Piraeus	Folegandros	6-9	14.80	4 weekly
Piraeus	Ios	7	15.70	4 daily
Piraeus	Iraklia	6¾	14.00	4 weekly
Piraeus	Kimolos	6	13.40	2 weekly
Piraeus	Koufonisia	8	13.70	4 weekly
Piraeus	Kythnos	2½	9.10	3 daily
Piraeus	Milos	5-7	14.80	2 daily
Piraeus	Mykonos	6	15.40	3 daily
Piraeus	Naxos	6	14.80	6 daily
Piraeus	Paros	5	15.10	6 daily
Piraeus	Santorini	9	17.70	4 daily
Piraeus	Serifos	4½	11.60	1 daily
Piraeus	Sifnos	5	12.80	1 daily
Piraeus	Sikinos	10	17.40	9 weekly
Piraeus	Syros	4	13.10	3 daily
Piraeus	Tinos	5	14.00	2 daily
Rafina	Amorgos	10¾	14.70	2 weekly
Rafina	Andros	2	7.35	2 daily
Rafina	Mykonos	4½	12.65	2 daily
Rafina	Paros	7	21.20	3 daily
Rafina	Syros	5	11.00	1 daily
Rafina	Tinos	3¾	11.00	2 daily
Sitia (Crete)	Milos	9	16.00	3 weekly
Thessaloniki	Mykonos	14	29.05	3 weekly
Thessaloniki	Naxos	15	27.30	1 weekly
Thessaloniki	Paros	15-16	28.70	2 weekly
Thessaloniki	Santorini	17¾	29.05	3 weekly
Thessaloniki	Syros	12	26.40	1 weekly
Thessaloniki	Tinos	13	28.50	2 weekly

Andros Άνδρος

postcode 845 00 • pop 8781
Andros is the northernmost island of the Cyclades and the second largest after Naxos, with a coastline of 110km. It is also one of the most fertile, producing citrus fruit and olives, and is unusual in that it has retained its pine forests and mulberry woods. There is plentiful water – indeed, Andros is famous for its water, which is bottled at Sariza spring in the village of Apikia.

More distinctive features are its dovecotes (although Tinos has more of them) and elaborate stone walls. Many of the old water mills and oil mills are now being restored. If you have a sweet tooth, seek out the island's walnut and almond sweets: *kalsounia*, *amygdolota*, and *karidaki*, a deliciously sticky treat of whole, unripe walnuts in a syrup of cinnamon, cloves, nutmeg and honey.

Getting To/From Andros
Ferry At least two ferries daily leave Andros' main port of Gavrio for Rafina (two hours, €7.30). Daily ferries run to Tinos (1½ hours, €5.60) and Mykonos (2½ hours, €7.80); allowing daily connections to Syros and Paros in the high season. Services run direct to Syros three times a week (two hours, €5.80). There is a weekly service to Paros (3½ hours, €10.80), Naxos (4½ hours, €12.20), Kythnos (€11.70) and Kea (€13.20).

Catamaran One catamaran weekly goes to Rafina (one hour, €14.70), Tinos (35 minutes, €10.80), Mykonos (1¼ hours, €15.70), Paros (two hours, €16.80), Amorgos (three hours, €27.50) and Ios (4½ hours, €26).

Getting Around Andros
Around nine buses daily (fewer on weekends) link Gavrio and Hora (30 minutes, €2.50) via Batsi (15 minutes, €1); schedules are posted at the bus stop in Gavrio and Hora and outside Andros Travel in Batsi; otherwise, call ☎ 2282 022 316 for information. A taxi (☎ 2282 022 171) from Batsi to Hora costs €17.60. Caiques from Batsi go to some of the island's nicest beaches.

GAVRIO Γαύριο
Gavrio, on the west coast, is the main port of Andros. Nothing much happens in Gavrio, but there are lovely beaches nearby.

Orientation & Information
The ferry quay is in the middle of the waterfront and the bus stop is next to it. Turn left from the quay and walk along the waterfront for the post office. The tourist office opposite the quay is rarely open. The port police (☎ 2282 071 213) are on the waterfront.

Places to Stay & Eat
If you decide to stay in town, look for *domatia* signs along the waterfront.

Hotel Galaxy (☎/fax 2282 071 228) Doubles €34.80. This hotel with reasonable rooms is to the left of the quay.

Andros Holiday Hotel (☎ 2282 071 384, fax 2282 071 097) Singles/doubles with aircon €68.40/85.50. Overlooking the beach, this hotel has a restaurant, bar and tennis court. Breakfast is included in the price.

Veggera (☎ 2282 071 077) Dishes €2.30-8.80, plus seafood by the kilo. This is a nice eatery, serving excellent meat dishes, with tables on a large plateia one block back from the waterfront. Turn right from the quay and take the first right after the Batsi road.

To Konaki (☎ 2282 071 733) Dishes €1.50-7.40. On the waterfront, this relaxed ouzeria has local specialities such as *fourtalia* (omelette with savoury sausage and potato).

BATSI Μπατσί
postcode 845 03
Batsi, 8km south of Gavrio, is Andros' major resort. The attractive town encircles a bay with a fishing harbour at one end and a nice sandy beach at the other. There is no EOT, but Andros Travel (☎ 2282 041 252, fax 2282 041 608, [e] androstr@otenet.gr), near the car park, and Greek Sun Holidays (☎ 2282 041 198, fax 2282 041 239, [e] greeksun@travelling.gr) are helpful and can handle everything from accommodation to sightseeing and ferry tickets. Car hire is available at Auto Europe (☎ 2282 041 995, fax 2282 041 239) based at Greek

CYCLADES

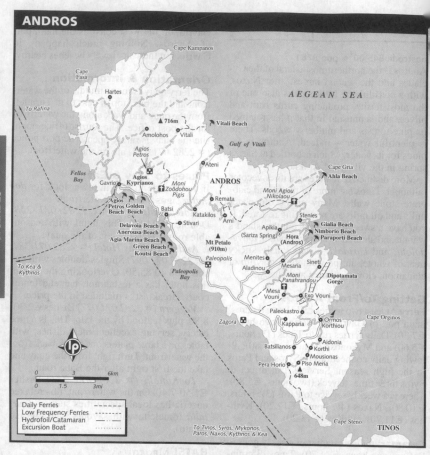

ANDROS

AEGEAN SEA

Gulf of Vitali

Cape Kampanos

Cape Fasa

Hartes

To Rafina

Cape Gria

Ahla Beach

▲ 716m

Amolohos   Vitali   ⊁ Vitali Beach

Agios Petros

Fellos Bay

Gavrio   **Agios Kyprianos**

Moni Zoödohou Pigis

ANDROS

Moni Agiou Nikolaou

Ateni

Remata

Agios Petros Golden Beach   Batsi

Katakilos

Stenies   ⊁ Gialia Beach
⊁ Nimborio Beach
Apikia   ⊁ Paraporti Beach
(Sariza Spring)   **Hora (Andros)**

Delavoia Beach
Anerousa Beach
Agia Marina Beach
Green Beach
Koutsi Beach

Stivari   Arni

▲ Mt Petalo (910m)

Paleopolis

Menites
Aladinou

Mesaria   Sineti

Moni Panahrandou   Dipotamata Gorge

Paleopolis Bay

Mesa Vouni   Exo Vouni

To Kea & Kythnos

Zagora

Paleokastro

Kapparia   Ormos Korthiou   Cape Orginos

Aidonia

Batsilianos   Korthi

Pera Horio   Mousionas
Piso Meria

▲ 648m

Cape Steno   **TINOS**

To Tinos, Syros, Mykonos,
Paros, Naxos, Kythnos & Kea

Daily Ferries
Low Frequency Ferries
Hydrofoil/Catamaran
Excursion Boat

0   3   6km
0   1.5   3mi

CYCLADES

Sun Holidays. Bike hire is available on the waterfront for €14.70.

The post office is near the large car park. The taxi rank, bus stop and National and Alpha banks (with ATMs) are all on the main square near the fishing boats. A stepped path leads up from behind the square through lush vegetation sprouting along a watercourse.

Organised Tours

Andros Travel organises island tours from May to October (€17.60 to €23.50) that take in Menites, Apikia, Moni Agiou Niko-

laou, Korthi and Paleopolis. Small-group guided half- and full-day walks following old paths through beautiful countryside range from €13.20 to €23.50.

Places to Stay & Eat

Scan the waterfront and the side streets behind Hotel Chryssi Akti for *domatia* signs.

Cavo d'Oro (☎ 2282 041 776, fax 2282 042 706) Doubles €40.80. At the beach end of the waterfront, above the taverna, all rooms here have telephone, TV and air-con.

Karanasos Hotel (☎ 2282 041 480) Singles/doubles €40.80/46.60. This hotel,

0m from the beach, has pleasant rooms with telephones.

Hotel Chryssi Akti (☎ 2282 041 237) Singles/doubles €43.70/52.50. Right on the beach, and towering over the domatia behind it, this hotel has a pool, and rooms have TV, phone and balcony.

Likio Studios (☎ 2282 041 050, fax 2282 042 000) Double/family studios €52.50/82.50. Open year-round. This relaxing place is set back from the beach amid masses of greenery and geraniums. The spacious studios, with kitchen, TV, phone and balcony, are spotless. Likio is about 250m past Dino's Rent a Bike.

There are a few decent tavernas along the waterfront. *Cavo d'Oro* does a fine clay-pot mousakas; *Kandouni*, next door, specialises in dishes baked in a wood-fired oven. There's also *Oti Kalo* and *Stamatis* by the main square.

Entertainment
There are several lively bars on the waterfront, including *Nameless* (☎ 2282 041 488) by the Avro Hotel, which attracts all the young things, and *Capricio Music Bar* (☎ 2282 041 770), which plays a Greek and international sound mix.

HORA (ANDROS) Χώρα (Ανδρος)
Hora is on the east coast, 35km east of Gavrio, and is strikingly set along a narrow peninsula. It's an enchanting place full of surprises, and there are some fine old neoclassical mansions.

Orientation & Information
The bus station is on Plateia Goulandri. To the left as you face the sea is a tourist information office (☎ 2282 025 162), which operates only in July and August, and the main pedestrian thoroughfare where the post office, OTE and National Bank of Greece (with ATM) are found. Walk along here towards the sea for Plateia Kaïri, the central square, beyond which is the headland. Steps descend from the square to Paraporti and Nimborio Beaches. The street leading along the promontory ends at Plateia Riva, where there is a bronze statue of an unknown

sailor. The ruins of a Venetian fortress stand on an island joined to the tip of the headland by an old, steeply arched bridge.

Museums
Hora has two outstanding museums; both were endowed by Vasilis Goulandris, a wealthy ship owner and Andriot. Contents at the **archaeological museum** (☎ 2282 023 644, Plateia Kaïri; adults/students €1.50/free; open 8.30am-3pm Tues-Sun) include the 2nd century BC Hermes of Andros and finds from the ancient cities of Zagora and Paleopolis.

The **museum of modern art** (☎ 2282 022 650; adult/student €5.90/3 June-Sept, €3/1.50 Oct-May; open 10am-2pm daily & 6pm-10pm Sat-Mon June-Sept, 10am-4pm daily Oct-May) has special international exhibitions held over June and September. It's down the stairs, to the left of the archaeological museum.

There is also a **nautical museum** (☎ 2282 022 275; open 10am-2pm & 6pm-9pm Mon-Sat, 10am-2pm Sun) near the end of the promontory.

Places to Stay & Eat
Karaoulanis Rooms (☎/fax 2282 024 412, **e** riva@otenet.gr) Doubles/self-contained apartments €30.20/72.50. Run by a young couple, the rooms are in an atmospheric spot in Plakoura, near Nonnas restaurant. Follow the steps down from the museum of modern art to reach it.

Alcioni Inn (☎ 2282 024 533, Nimborio) Doubles from €46.60. Located on the waterfront, most rooms in this place are self-contained, some come with balconies with ocean views. Cheaper rooms are also available.

Hotel Egli (☎ 2282 022 303) Doubles with shared/private bathroom €30.20/59. This recently renovated hotel is between the two squares, off the right side of the main road as you head towards the sea. Breakfast is included.

Parea Taverna (☎ 2282 023 721, Plateia Kaïri) Dishes €1.50-5. Parea has commanding water views and reasonable food.

Nonnas (☎ 2282 023 577) Dishes €3.50-10.30. This is a lovely *mezedes* place in the old port area known as Plakoura, on the way to Nimborio Beach; to get there continue past the museum of modern art.

Ta Delfinia (☎ 2282 024 179, Nimborio) Dishes €2-5.60. On the waterfront, Delfinia has excellent home-cooked fare.

Cabo del Mar (☎ 2282 025 001) Dishes €3-14.50. Del Mar, at the far end of Nimborio, has a lovely setting and a good reputation. There are also several good fish tavernas at Gialia, the next beach from Nimborio, including *Balas* and *Ta Gialia*.

AROUND ANDROS

About 2.5km from Gavrio, the **Agios Petros tower** is an imposing circular watchtower dating from Hellenistic times – possibly earlier. Look for the signpost for Agios Petros, also the name of a village.

Along the coast road from Gavrio to Batsi is a turn-off left leading 5km to the 12th-century **Moni Zoödohou Pigis**, where a few nuns still live (open to visitors before noon only). Between Gavrio and Paleopolis Bay are several nice beaches: **Agios Kyprianos** (where a former church is now a beachfront **taverna**), **Delavoia** (nudist), **Green Beach** and **Anerousa**.

An old path running between the villages of **Arni** and **Remata**, both east of Batsi, passes water mills. In Remata, a renovated 19th-century olive-oil mill now houses a **museum**. **Paleopolis**, 9km south of Batsi on the coast road, is the site of Ancient Andros, where the Hermes of Andros was found. There is little to see, but the mountain setting is lovely. **Menites**, south-west of Hora, has springs and a row of drinking fountains with spouts shaped like lions' heads.

From the pretty village of **Mesaria**, it's a strenuous two-hour walk to the 12th-century **Moni Panahrandou**, the island's largest and most important monastery. **Apikia**, north-west of Hora, is famous for its mineral springs. Near **Sineti**, the wild **Dipotamata Gorge** and its water mills are EU-protected. An old cobbled path, once the main route from Korthi to Hora, leads along the gorge.

The pretty blue-green bay and holiday hamlet at **Ormos Korthiou**, in the southeast, has a lot of faded charm and several good restaurants. The Korthi Nautical Club (📧 noka@andros.gr) holds swimming lessons (€14.70 per week) and group windsurfing courses (€23.50 per week) during July and August.

Places to Stay & Eat

Anerousa Beach Hotel (☎ 2282 041 044, fax 2282 041 444) Singles/doubles with breakfast €60.50/72.30. Just around the bay from Batsi, this plush hotel has its own private bay.

Hotel Korthion (☎ 2282 061 218, fax 2282 061 118) Singles/doubles €30.50/34.90 with bath. This hotel is on the shore at Ormos Korthiou.

Asimoleyka (☎ 2282 024 150, Ipsilou-Syrapouries) Meals €10.30. Five kilometres from Nimborio Beach, this taverna has views of the hora and makes excellent traditional dishes.

Tinos Τήνος

postcode 842 00 • pop 7747
Tinos is green and mountainous, like nearby Andros. The island is a Greek Orthodox place of pilgrimage, so it's hardly surprising that churches feature prominently among the attractions. The celebrated Church of Panagia Evangelistria dominates the uninteresting capital, while unspoilt hill villages and ornate white-washed dovecotes are rural attractions.

Tinos also has a large Roman Catholic population – the result of its long Venetian occupation. The Turks didn't succeed in wresting the island from the Venetians until 1715, long after the rest of the country had surrendered to Ottoman rule.

Getting To/From Tinos

Ferry At least six ferries daily go to Mykonos (30 minutes, €3.50), and one daily to Rafina (3½ hours, €11.15) and Andros (1½ hours, €5.30). There is at least two daily to Syros (50 minutes, €3.70) and Piraeus (six hours, €14).

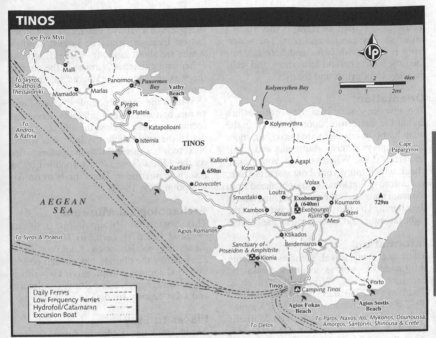

TINOS

Cape Fyra Myti
Malli
Panormos • Panormos Bay
Vathy Beach
Mamados · Marlas
To Skyros, Skiathos & Thessaloniki
Pyrgos
Plateia
Katapolioani
To Andros & Rafina
Isternia
TINOS
Kolymvythra Bay
Kolymvythra
Cape Papargyros
Kardiani
Kalloni
Komi
Agapi
▲650m
Dovecotes
Volax
AEGEAN SEA
Smardaki
Loutra
Exobourgo (640m)
Exobourgo Ruins
Koumaros
Kambos
Xinara
▲729m
Steni
Mesi
To Syros & Piraeus
Agios Romanos
Ktikados
Berdemiaros
Sanctuary of Poseidon & Amphitrite
Kionia
Tinos
Camping Tinos
Porto
Agios Fokas Beach
Agios Sostis Beach
To Paros, Naxos, Ios, Mykonos, Dounoussa, Amorgos, Santorini, Shinousa & Crete
To Delos

Daily Ferries
Low Frequency Ferries
Hydrofoil/Catamaran
Excursion Boat

0   2   4km
0   1   2mi

CYCLADES

Four weekly ferries go to Ikaria (3½ hours, €9.60).

Three ferries weekly go to Thessaloniki (14 hours, €28.50), and daily services to Paros (2½ hours, €5.30) and Santorini (five hours, €5.50).

Two weekly services run to Naxos (4¼ hours, €6) and Iraklio on Crete (10¼ hours, €20). There is one weekly ferry to Donousa (2½ hours, €10.30), Amorgos (3½ hours, €8.80), Ios (5½ hours, €9) and Skiathos (7½ hours, €17.60).

Fast Boat & Catamaran There are at least three services daily to Mykonos (15 minutes, €5.90) and Rafina (1½ hours, €22.30).

There are daily services to Paros (1¼ hours, €10.50), five weekly to Piraeus (three hours, €28.50), one weekly to Andros (35 minutes, €10.80), daily to Syros (two hours, €6.90) and two weekly to Ios (three hours, €18). There are also weekly services to Amorgos (2¾ hours, €18.60) and Shinousa (three hours, €14).

Excursion Boat Excursion boats run daily to Delos (€17.60) 10am Tuesday to Saturday and 9am Sunday June to September.

Getting Around Tinos

There are frequent buses from Tinos (Hora) to Kionia and several daily to Panormos via Pyrgos and Kambos, and to Porto. Buses leave from the station on the waterfront, opposite the National Bank of Greece. The travel agent next to the bank has a timetable in its front window.

However, by far the best way to explore the island is by motorcycle (prices start at €8.80 a day) or car (€20.50 a day); the roads are generally pretty good. Motorcycles and cars can be hired along the waterfront at Hora; try Koulis Rent-a-Car & Moto (☎ 2283 023 955), at the southern end of the waterfront.

Phone numbers listed incorporate changes due in Oct 2002; see p55

TINOS (HORA)

Tinos, also known as Hora, is the island's rather shabby capital and port. The waterfront is lined with cafes and hotels, while the little streets behind have shops and stalls catering to pilgrims and tourists.

Orientation

The new ferry quay is at the north-western end of the waterfront, about 300m from the main harbour, but there are two other, more central, quays where catamarans and smaller ferries dock. When you buy your ticket, check which quay your boat departs from.

Leoforos Megaloharis, straight ahead from the main harbour, is the route pilgrims take to the church. The narrow Evangelistria, to the right facing inland, also leads to the church.

Information

There are many travel agencies supplying information as well as accommodation and car hire services. Windmills Travel & Tourism (☎ 2283 023 398, fax 2283 023 398, e windmills@travelling.gr), at Kionion 2 above the new ferry quay, and Malliaris Travel (☎ 2283 024 241, fax 2283 024 243, e malliaris@thn.forthnet.gr), on the waterfront near Hotel Posidonion, are helpful.

The post office is located at the south-eastern end of the waterfront, just past the bus station and the Agricultural Bank of Greece (with ATM), next door to Hotel Tinion – turn right from the quay. The OTE is situated on Megaloharis, not far from the church. The pebbled town beach of Agios Fokas is a 10-minute walk south from the waterfront.

The port police (☎ 2283 022 348) are on the waterfront, near the Hotel Oceanis.

Church of Panagia Evangelistria

This surprisingly small church (open 8am-8pm daily) is a neoclassical marble confection of white and cream, with a high bell tower. The ornate facade has white, graceful upper and lower colonnades. The final approach is up carpeted steps, doubtless a relief to pious souls choosing to crawl. Inside, the miraculous icon is draped with gold, silver, jewels and pearls, and surrounded by gifts from the hopeful.

A lucrative trade in candles, icon copies, incense and evil-eye deterrents is carried out on Evangelistria. The largest candles, which are about 2m long, cost €3; after an ephemeral existence burning in the church, the wax remains are gathered, melted and resold.

Within the church complex, several **museums** house religious artefacts, icons and secular artworks. Below the church, a crypt marks the spot where the icon was found. Next to it is a memorial to the sailors killed on the *Elli*, a Greek ship torpedoed by an Italian submarine in Tinos' harbour on Assumption Day, 1940.

Archaeological Museum

This somewhat disappointing museum (☎ 2283 022 670, Leoforos Megaloharis; admission €1.50; open 8am-3pm Tues-Sun), below the church, has a small collection that includes impressive clay *pithoi* (large storage jars), a few Roman sculptures and a 1st-century sundial.

Places to Stay

Avoid Tinos on 25 March (Annunciation), 15 August (Feast of the Assumption) and 15 November (Advent), unless you want to join the huddled masses who sleep on the streets at these times.

Camping Tinos (☎ 2283 022 344, fax 2283 025 551) Adult/tent €4.40/2.70, bungalows with/without bathroom €17.40/13.30. This is a lovely site with good facilities south of the town, near Agios Fokas. It also has comfortable bungalow rooms shaded by bursts of bougainvillea. A minibus meets ferries. The camping ground is about a five-minute walk from the ferry quay and is clearly signposted from the waterfront; head towards the Oceanic Hotel.

Look for domatia signs along Evangelistria and other streets leading inland from the waterfront, especially behind Rooms to Rent Yiannis.

Rooms to Rent Yiannis (☎ 2283 022 575) Doubles with/without bathroom €34.90/23.50, apartments €43.50. On the waterfront next to Hotel Oceanis and five

Beware the Evil Eye

When travelling through Greece – particularly in rural areas – you may notice that some bus drivers keep a chain bearing one or two blue stones dangling over the dashboard. Or you may spot a small, plastic blue eye attached to the cross hanging around someone's neck.

Puzzle no longer. The Greeks are not sporting colours in support of their favourite soccer team or to show a particular political leaning. No – they are warding off the evil eye.

The evil eye is associated with envy, and can be cast – apparently unintentionally – upon someone or something that is praised or admired (even secretly). So those most vulnerable to the evil eye include people, creatures or objects of beauty, rarity and value. Babies are particularly vulnerable, and those who admire them will often spit gently on them to repel any ill effects. Adults and older children who are worried about being afflicted by the evil eye will wear blue.

Who then is responsible for casting the evil eye? Well, most culprits are those who are already considered quarrelsome or peculiar in some way by the local community. And folk with blue eyes are regarded with extreme suspicion – no doubt more than partly because being blue-eyed is a trait Greeks associate with Turks. All these quarrelsome, peculiar or blue-eyed folk have to do is be present when someone or something enviable appears on the scene – and then the trouble starts.

If, during your travels, someone casts the evil eye on you, you'll soon know about it. Symptoms include dizziness, headaches, a feeling of 'weight' on the head or tightening in the chest. Locals will point you in the direction of someone, usually an old woman, who can cure you.

The cure usually involves the curer making the sign of the cross over a glass of water, praying silently and, at the same time, dropping oil into the glass. If the oil disappears from the surface, it proves you have the evil eye – but also cures it, for the 'blessed' water will be dabbed on your forehead, stomach and at two points on your chest (at the points of the crucifix).

Apparently, the cure works. But you know the old adage about prevention being better than cure. If you're worried about the evil eye, don't take any chances – wear blue.

CYCLADES

minutes from the beach, is this clean, homey place. Its shared balcony is a perfect place to chill and watch the sun set.

Hotel Posidonion (☎ *2283 023 121, fax 2283 025 808*) Singles/doubles €49/67.90. This hotel on the waterfront opposite the bus station has bright rooms with balcony.

Hotel Tinion (☎ *2283 022 261, fax 2283 024 754*) Doubles €49. At the southern end of the waterfront near the roundabout, rooms at this grand old place have balconies, TV and air-con.

Places to Eat & Drink
The waterfront is lined with places serving the usual fare – none of them outstanding.

Pallada Taverna (☎ *2283 023 516*) Dishes €1.70-5.60, seafood by the kilo. Just off the waterfront, at the rear of the Hotel Lito, Pallada serves hearty, if somewhat oily, traditional dishes; the wine is poured from huge barrels overhead.

Mixhalis Taverna (☎ *2283 023 498*) Dishes €2-8.80, seafood by the kilo. In the narrow first lane to the right off Evangelistria, Mixhalis is noted for high-quality meat.

To Epilekto (☎*2283 025/024 619*) On the waterfront, Epilekto is one of the better choices for a generous breakfast. It also has rooms.

Koursaros (☎ *2283 023 963*) Near the Hotel Lito on the waterfront, this darkly-lit bar plays a mix of Greek and world music.

AROUND TINOS
Unless you've come solely to visit the church, you'll need to explore the countryside and its 42 villages to make the most of Tinos. Most of the island is still farmed in one way or another, and you should look out for livestock (including piglets, goats and donkeys) wandering onto roads.

Kionia, 3km north-west of Hora, has several small beaches, the nearest overlooked by Tinos Beach Hotel. The site of the **Sanctuary of Poseidon & Amphitrite**, before the hotel, dates from the 4th century BC. Poseidon was worshipped because hc banished the snakes that once infested the island.

At **Porto**, 6km east of Hora, there's a sandy, uncrowded beach. **Kolymvythra Bay**, beyond Komi, has two beautiful sandy beaches; a lovely road leads through reed beds and vegetable gardens to the bay.

Further along the coast there's a small beach at **Panormos** from where distinctive green marble quarried in nearby **Marlas** was once exported. **Pyrgos** is a picturesque village where marble is still carved. There's a marble sculpture school, **Dellatos Marble Sculpture Studio** (☎ 2283 023 164, fax 2283 023 460, W www.tinosmarble.com) open to both novice and experienced sculptors for two-week terms year-round. The village also has several little workshops with traditional items such as lintels and plaques (which both adorn houses around the village) and figurines for sale. About three buses per day run to Pyrgos; from there it's a pleasant 2km walk to Panormos.

The ruins of the Venetian fortress of **Exobourgo**, atop a 640m-high hill, stand sentinel over a cluster of unspoilt villages. At the fortress, built on an ancient acropolis, the Venetians made their last stand against the Turks in 1715. The ascent can be made from several villages; the shortest route is from Xinara. It's a steep climb, but the views are worth it.

The famous basket weavers of Tinos are based in the tiny, lime-washed traditional village of **Volax**, nestled on a spectacular rocky plain in the centre of the island. You can usually buy direct from the workshops, but if they're shut for siesta, a small souvenir shop sells baskets. There is a small **folkloric museum** (ask at the souvenir shop for someone to open it for you) and an attractive Catholic chapcl; follow the path beyond the amphitheatre, opposite O Rokos taverna. Buses to Volax are rare indeed, so hire a car or motorcycle to get there.

O Rokos (☎ 2283 041 989, Volax) Dishes €1.50-7.40. This is one of the best tavernas on the island, serving fresh produce. Everything is delicious, right down to the olives and capers in the Greek salad.

Syros Σύρος

postcode 841 00 • pop 19,870

Many tourists come to Syros merely to change ferries. This is a pity because the capital, Ermoupolis (named after Hermes, god of trade, messengers and thieves) is a beautiful city with inhabitants who have not become tourist-weary.

Syros' economy depends little on tourism, and though its ship-building industry (once the most vigorous in Greece) has declined, it has textile factories, dairy farms and a horticultural industry that supplies the rest of the Cyclades with plants and flowers.

If you have a sweet tooth, don't miss the famous *loukoumia* (Turkish delight) and *halvadopites* (nougat).

History

Excavations of an Early Cycladic fortified settlement and burial ground at Kastri in the island's north-east, dating from 2800–2300 BC, reveal that the inhabitants farmed, fished and had close connections with other communities.

In the Middle Ages, Syros was the only Greek island with an entirely Roman Catholic population, the result of conversions by the Franks who took over the island in 1207. This gave it the support and protection of the west (particularly the French) during Turkish rule.

Syros remained neutral during the War of Independence and thousands of refugees from islands ravaged by the Turks fled here, bringing the Orthodox religion. They built a new settlement (now called Vrodado), and the port town of Ermoupolis. After independence, Ermoupolis became the commercial, naval and cultural centre of Greece.

Today, Syros' population is 40% Catholic and 60% Orthodox. Ermoupolis' ornate churches and neoclassical mansions are testimonies to its former grandeur.

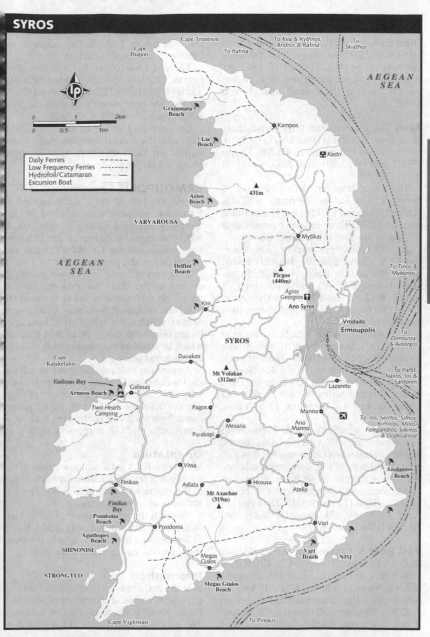

Getting To/From Syros

Air Olympic Airways operates at least one flight daily except Tuesday to/from Athens (€54.30/62.80 one way). The Olympic Airways office (☎ 2281 088 018, fax 2281 083 536) is on the waterfront, near the bus station, around the corner from Naxou street.

Ferry There are at least three ferries daily from Syros to Piraeus (four hours, €13.10), two to Tinos (50 minutes, €3.70), Lavrio (3½ hours €10.80) and Mykonos (1¼ hours, €5.10).

There is at least one daily to Paros (1½ hours, €5.10), Iraklio (7½ hours, €17.60), Rafina (5¾ hours, €10.50) and Naxos (three hours, €6.60). There are daily connections to Andros via Tinos (2¾ hours, €8.80).

At least four ferries weekly go to Amorgos (4½ hours, €10.50), Ios (2¾ hours, €11), Ikaria (2½ hours, €9.60), Samos (five hours, €15.40) and Santorini (5¼ hours, €12.50); and one weekly serves Crete (8½ hours, €17.20) and Rafina (five hours, €10.55).

At least twice weekly there are boats to Andros (1¾ hours, €5.80), Kea (three hours, €8.20), Kythnos (two hours, €5.90), Sifnos (5½ hours, €6.40), Serifos (three to five hours, €6.90), Kimolos (five hours, €9) and Milos (six hours, €9) and once weekly to Donousa (3½ hours, €8.20).

There are weekly ferries to Thessaloniki (12 hours, €26.40), Sikinos (six hours, €8.40), Folegandros (six hours, €8.80), Patmos (five hours, €14), Leros (seven hours, €15.40), Kalymnos (eight hours, €16), Kos (nine hours, €18.30), Nisyros (11 hours, €13.40), Tilos (12 hours, €17.20), Symi (13 hours, €19.50), Skiathos (€18.80) and Rhodes (15½ hours, €22).

Fast Boat & Catamaran Services depart daily for Piraeus (2½ hours, €26.40), Rafina (1¾ hours, €21.15), Paros (45 minutes, €9.50), Naxos (1½ hours, €12.40), Ios (2¼ hours, €21.40), Santorini (three hours, €25.90), Mykonos (30 minutes, €9.50) and Tinos (two hours, €6.90).

Getting Around Syros

Frequent buses do a southern loop around the island from Ermoupolis, calling at all beaches mentioned in the text.

There is a bus to Ano Syros every morning at 10.30am, except Sunday (€0.90). Taxis (☎ 2281 086 222) charge about €2.50 for the ride up to Ano Syros from the port; it's an easy 25-minute walk back.

Cars can be hired from about €23.50 a day, and there are numerous moped-hire outlets on the waterfront near Kimolou (from €8.80 per day).

ERMOUPOLIS Ερμούπολη

During the 19th century, a combination of fortuitous circumstances resulted in Ermoupolis becoming Greece's major port. It was superseded by Piraeus in the 20th century, but is still the Cyclades' capital and largest city, with a population of over 13,000.

It's a very affluent, lively town; its wealth evident in the many restored neoclassical mansions, the marble-paved streets, and the chic little backstreet boutiques. Unlike most of the Cyclades, the occupants of Ermoupolis are busy with things other than tourism, which in itself adds immeasurable real-life charm to the place.

As the boat sails into the port you will see the Catholic settlement of Ano Syros to the left, and the Orthodox settlement of Vrodado to the right, both set on hills. Spilling down from each and skirting the harbour is Ermoupolis – it's an impressive sight.

Orientation

Most boats dock at the south-western end of the bay, but ferries occasionally berth closer to the centre of town, near Hiou. The bus station is also by the quay.

To reach the central square, Plateia Miaouli, turn right from the quay, and left into El Venizelou. There are public toilets around the bay to the east, and off Antiparou.

Information

In summer there is an information booth on the waterfront, near the corner of Nikolaou Filini, about 100m north-east of the quay. The travel agents Enjoy Your Holidays

ERMOUPOLIS

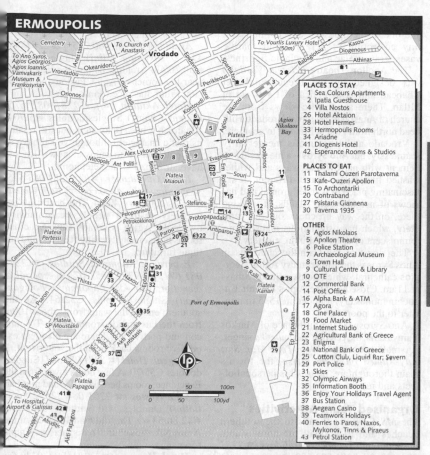

PLACES TO STAY
1 Sea Colours Apartments
2 Ipatia Guesthouse
4 Villa Nostos
26 Hotel Aktaion
28 Hotel Hermes
33 Hermopoulis Rooms
34 Ariadne
41 Diogenis Hotel
42 Esperance Rooms & Studios

PLACES TO EAT
11 Thalami Ouzeri Psarotaverna
13 Kafe-Ouzeri Apollon
15 To Archontariki
20 Contraband
27 Psistaria Giannena
30 Taverna 1935

OTHER
3 Agios Nikolaos
5 Apollon Theatre
6 Police Station
7 Archaeological Museum
8 Town Hall
9 Cultural Centre & Library
10 OTE
12 Commercial Bank
14 Post Office
16 Alpha Bank & ATM
17 Agora
18 Cine Palace
19 Food Market
21 Internet Studio
22 Agricultural Bank of Greece
23 Enigma
24 National Bank of Greece
25 Cotton Club; Liquid Bar; Severn
31 Skies
32 Olympic Airways
35 Information Booth
36 Enjoy Your Holidays Travel Agent
37 Bus Station
38 Aegean Casino
39 Teamwork Holidays
40 Ferries to Paros, Naxos, Mykonos, Tinos & Piraeus
43 Petrol Station

CYCLADES

(☎ 2281 087 070, fax 2281 082 739, Ⓦ enjoy-holidays.gr), opposite the bus station on the waterfront, can help with accommodation and ferry tickets.

The post office is on Protopapadaki and the OTE is on the eastern edge of Plateia Miaouli. Internet Studio (☎/fax 2281 081 653), on the waterfront, provides Internet access at reasonable rates.

There are ATMs at the Alpha Bank on El Venizelou, the Commercial Bank on Voko-topoulo, the National Bank of Greece on Protopapadaki and the Agricultural Bank of Greece on El Venizelou at the waterfront.

The police station (☎ 2281 082 610) is beside the Apollon Theatre, just north of the OTE. Syros' port police (☎ 2281 082 690, 2281 088 888) are on the eastern side of the waterfront.

Things to See

Plateia Miaouli is the hub of bustling Ermoupolis. It's flanked by palm trees and open-air cafes and dominated by the magnificent neoclassical **town hall**, designed by the German architect Ernst Ziller. The small **archaeological museum** at the rear (☎ 2281 088 487; admission €1.50; open

8.30am-3pm Tues-Sun), founded in 1834 and one of the oldest in Greece, houses a tiny collection of ceramic and marble vases, grave stelae and Cycladic figurines.

The **Apollon Theatre** (*Plateia Vardaki*) was designed by the French architect Chabeau and is a replica of La Scala in Milan. There are terrific views from the church of **Anastasis**, on top of Vrodado Hill; head north from Plateia Miaouli to get there.

Vrodado and Ermoupolis merge fairly seamlessly, but **Ano Syros** – a medieval settlement with narrow alleyways and white-washed houses – is quite different. It's a fascinating place to wander around and has views of neighbouring islands. If walking there, on the way up check out the **cemetery**, which has ostentatious mausoleums reminiscent of Athens' First Cemetery.

The finest of the Catholic churches in Anos Syros is the 13th-century **Agios Georgios** cathedral, which holds a Sunday mass at 11am. Close by is the **Agios Ioannis** Capuchin monastery, founded in 1535 to minister to the poor.

Ano Syros was the birthplace of Markos Vamvakaris, the celebrated *rembetika* singer. A small **museum** (*10am-1pm Mon-Sat; July-August only*) on Piatsa, the town's main thoroughfare, houses his personal effects and records.

Organised Tours & Activities

The *MS Esperors II* sails to the southern beaches and to a small offshore island. Book through ***Teamwork Holidays*** (☎ 2281 083 400, fax 2281 083 508, e teamwork@ otenet.gr) 3-hour cruises €11.75.

Cyclades Sailing (☎ 2281 082 501, fax 2281 082 536, e csail@otenet.gr) can organise yachting charters, as can ***Nomikos Sailing*** (☎ 2281 088 527); call direct or book through Enjoy Your Holidays.

Places to Stay

Domatia owners meet ferries. There is a high concentration of domatia in the streets behind the waterfront.

Hermopoulis Rooms (☎ 2281 087 475) Doubles €46.60. On Naxou, the bougainvillea-cloaked balconies of these compact, self-contained rooms offer snatched glimpses of the water.

Ariadne (☎ 2281 080 245, fax 2281 086 454, 9 Nikolaou Filini) Singles/doubles €30.20/49. Ariadne, behind the waterfront near the corner of Agios Proiou and Nikolaou Filini, has nice rooms.

Hotel Aktaion (☎/fax 2281 082 675, Plateia Kanari) Singles/doubles €52/64. Aktaion has been renovated, but still retains its rustic character (although you'll have to pay much more to enjoy it now). Rooms have air-con, TV and telephone.

Ipatia Guesthouse (☎/fax 2281 083 575, e ipatiaguest@yahoo.com, 3 Babagiotou) Singles/doubles €42/64. This beautiful, exquisitely restored neoclassical mansion overlooks Agios Nikolaos Bay. Spacious rooms have original ceiling frescoes and antique furniture.

Esperance Rooms & Studios (☎ 2281 081 671, fax 2281 085 707, e espernik@ otenet.gr; Cnr Akti Papagou & Folegandrou) Singles/doubles €52/64. At the southern end of the waterfront, about 100m from the bus station, rooms have TV, aircon and port views. There are also less expensive rooms back from the waterfront.

Diogenis Hotel (☎ 2281 086 301) Singles/ doubles €55/70. A few doors away from the Esperance, rooms here have TV and minibar.

Villa Nostos (☎ 2281 084 226, 2 Spartiaton) Doubles with/without bathroom €42.80/54.60. This old mansion west of the Agios Nikolaos church has spacious, simple rooms.

Hotel Hermes (☎ 2281 083 011, fax 2281 087 412, Plateia Kanari) Doubles from €82.50. This spiffy B-class hotel on the waterfront has comfortable rooms. Breakfast is included in the price.

Sea Colours Apartments (☎ 2281 083 400, fax 2281 083 508, e teamwork@ otenet.gr) Studios/apartments €56.50/110. Open year-round. North-east of the port, this modern mansion has nice apartments. To find it, descend the steps after Agios Nikolaos church; it's on the right, perched above lovely Agios Nikolaos Bay.

Vourlis Luxury Hotel (☎/fax 2281 088 440, Mavrokordatou 5) Doubles from €94.25.

Vourlis is a beautifully restored neoclassical mansion about 150m beyond Ipatia Guesthouse. Suites have antique furniture and many have spectacular sea views. Make sure you book well in advance.

Places to Eat
The waterfront and the southern edge of Plateia Miaouli are lined with restaurants and cafes.

Psistaria Giannena (☎ 2281 082 994, *Plateia Kanari*) Dishes €1.70-19.80, seafood by the kilo. This *psistaria* specialises in *kokoretsi* (spit-roasted lamb's entrails) and spiced rolled pork.

Contraband (☎ 2281 081 028) Dishes €1.70-8.80. In a narrow walkway behind the waterfront, this small cafe has delicious seafood and generous dishes.

Taverna 1935 Dishes €2-8.80. One of the better waterfront places, with moderately priced traditional fare, including fresh fish.

Kafe-Ouzeri Apollon (☎ 2281 088 461) Dishes €1.70-4.40. On Stefanou, this ouzeri is a great place to sample octopus and fish grilled over hot coals.

To Archontariki (☎ 2281 081 744, 8 Em Roidi) Dishes €1.50-8.80. One block south-east of Plateia Miaouli, off Vikela, Archontariki is deservedly popular. Its extensive menu features the regular fare plus delicious dishes such as parsley salad (€2.35) and fennel pie (€3.80). The wine list includes regional favourites from all over Greece.

Thalami Ouzeri Psarotaverna (☎ 2281 085 331) Dishes €2.35-18.60, seafood by the kilo. On Souri, Thalami overlooks Agios Nikolaos Bay. The food is pretty good and *kakavia*, a local fish soup, is available. To get there, follow Souri (which runs off the southern side of Plateia Miaouli) east to its end.

Frankosyriani (☎ 2281 084 888, Piatsa) Dishes €2.35-4. Up in Ano Syros near the Vamvakaris museum, Frankosyriani is a great place to stop for a drink and mezedes, although food is only served in the evening. The view from the terrace is superb and you can sing along with Vamvakaris as you sup.

There are several other good *cafes* in Ano Syros that take in the views and atmosphere.

The best place for fresh produce is the *food market* on Hiou.

Entertainment
There are plenty of bars around Plateia Miaouli and along the waterfront.

Agora (☎ 2281 088 329, Plateia Miaouli) Adjacent to Piramatiko Bakery, this restaurant-bar is very subdued and positively glows with Syros style.

The Cotton Club, next door to Hotel Aktaion, is the hub of waterfront nightlife. Androu, the narrow lane to The Cotton Club's left is door-to-door bars, including *Enigma*, a metal hang-out with an interesting, edgy atmosphere.

If you're looking for something a little more hip, head to *Liquid Bar* (☎ 2281 082 284), nearby, where the resident DJ plays a House and Greek mix. *Severn*, next door, is also a hot spot for a drink.

If bouzouki is your thing, there are quite a few places. Try *Skies*, on the waterfront near Taverna 1935.

Cine Palace (☎ 2281 082 313, Plateia Miaouli) Admission €5.60. Open 9.30pm June-Sept. This outdoor cinema screens mainstream new release English- and French-language films subtitled in Greek.

GALISSAS Γαλησσψς
The west coast resort of Galissas has one of the island's best beaches: a 900m crescent of dark sand, shaded by tamarisk trees. Armeos, a walk round the rocks to the left of the bay, is an official nudist beach. There are two travel agents, including Galissas Tours (☎ 2281 042 801, fax 2281 042 801, ⓔ galtours@syr.forthnet.gr).

Places to Stay
Two Hearts Camping (☎ 2281 042 052, fax 2281 043 290, ⓔ etta@otenet.gr) Adult/tent €5.30/2.70. Set in a pistachio orchard about a kilometre from the village, this camping ground has most facilities; turn right at Galissas Tours and follow the signs. A minibus meets ferries in high season.

There are plenty of domatia available, mostly much of a muchness in standard concrete box style.

Rooms P Sicala (☎ *2281 042 643*) Doubles €25.30. On the way to Two Hearts Camping, this is a cute little traditional place shaded by flowering vines; book early.

Karmelina Rooms (☎ *2281 042 320*) Doubles €26. On the right of the main road, not far from the branch road to the beach, Karmelina's has clean rooms and a communal kitchen.

Pension Blue Sky (☎ *2281 043 410, fax 2281 043 411*) Doubles/apartments €52/64. This popular pension is close to Karmelina Rooms.

Hotel Benois (☎/fax *2281 042 833,* e *h-benois@otenet.gr*) Singles/doubles with breakfast €46.50/67.90. This modern hotel is close to the beach. Rooms have TV and air-con.

Dolphin Bay Resort (☎ *2281 042 924, fax 2281 042 843,* e *dbh@otenet.gr*) Doubles with breakfast €107. This A-class property is a large, white cluster of buildings left of the beach as you face the sea. Rooms have satellite TV.

Places to Eat

Markos O Psilos (☎ *2281 043 924*) Dishes €1.50-7.10. Next to the minimarket, this place serves good-value meals, as do most of the other tavernas.

Argo Café Bar (☎ *2281 042 819*) Dishes €3-7.30. This colourful bar-cafe, around the corner from Hotel Benois is a nice relaxing place to hang out, with comfy cushions and deck chairs on the patio.

AROUND SYROS

The beaches south of Galissas all have domatia and some have hotels. The first is **Finikas**, with a nice, tree-lined beach and a shop selling interesting old things as well as local crafts. The next, **Posidonia**, has a sand-and-pebble beach shaded by tamarisk trees.

Further south, **Agathopes** has a nice, tree-bordered sandy beach. On the south coast, tranquil **Megas Gialos** has two sand beaches.

Vari, the next bay, has a sandy beach, but is more developed. **Azolimnos**, the next beach along, has a few **fish tavernas**. Kini is fast becoming popular – it has a long stretch of beach and many new hotels.

Places to Stay

Vari has a few places to stay.

Hotel Domenica (☎ *2281 061 216, fax 2281 061 289*) Doubles with/without sea view €59/49. Some rooms in this hotel by the sea have kitchen and TV.

Hotel Kamelo (☎ *2281 061 217, fax 2281 061 117, Vari*) Singles/doubles €34.90/59. This modern hotel has rooms with air-con and TV.

Mykonos Μκονος

postcode 846 00 • pop 6170

Mykonos is perhaps the most visited and expensive of all Greek islands (although these days Santorini runs a pretty close second) and it has the most sophisticated nightlife, as well as uninhibited beach raves. Despite its reputation as the gay capital of Greece, this shouldn't – and doesn't – deter others. The days when Mykonos was the favourite rendezvous for the world's rich and famous may be over, but the island probably still has more poseurs per square metre than any other Mediterranean resort.

Depending on your temperament, you'll either be captivated or take one look and stay on the ferry. Barren, low-lying Mykonos would never win a beauty contest, but it has some decent beaches and is the jumping-off point for the sacred island of Delos.

Getting To/From Mykonos

Air There are at least five flights daily to/from Athens (€70.15/78.65 one way), as well as flights to Santorini (€54 one way, daily except Friday), Thessaloniki (€91.30, three weekly) and Rhodes (two weekly, €78.10).

Ferry Mykonos has daily services to Rafina (4½ hours, €12.65) via Tinos (30 minutes, €3.50) and Andros (2½ hours, €7.80); to Piraeus (six hours, €16.50) via Tinos and Syros (1½ hours, €5), Paros (two hours, €6.10); connect at Paros for Naxos. Daily ferries also run to Ios (four hours, €9.60).

There are three ferries a week to Thessaloniki (14 hours, €29.05).

CYCLADES

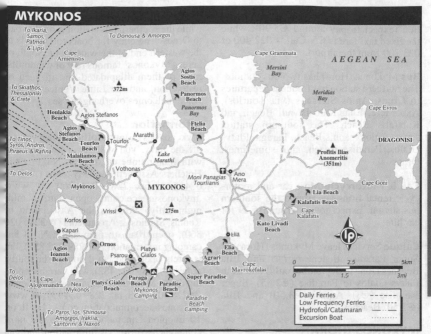

MYKONOS

There are two ferries weekly to Santorini (six hours, €10.50), and four weekly to Amorgos (2½ hours, €9.30), Iraklia (five to eight hours, €8.80), Shinousa (six hours, €8.80) and Crete (nine hours, €14.80).

One weekly runs to Donousa (two hours, €8.80), Patmos (nine hours, €15.70), Lipsi (ten hours, €15.40) and Skiathos (8½ hours, €80.80). One daily goes to Samos (five hours, €15.40) and Ikaria (2¾ hours, €9.60).

Fast Boat & Catamaran There are two daily services connecting Mykonos with Andros (1¼ hours, €15.70) and three daily to Tinos (15 minutes, €5.90). Five daily services go to Rafina (two hours, €25.25) and two daily go to Piraeus (three hours, €30.80) and Syros (30 minutes, €9.50). There are three daily services to Paros (45 minutes, €10.30), which connect with services to Naxos (1½ hours, €11.75), Santorini (three to four hours, €16.90) and Ios (2¾ hours,

€14.70). One service weekly goes directly to Ios (1¾ hours, €16) and Shinousa (2½ hours, €13). One weekly service goes to Amorgos (2¼ hours, €18.60).

Excursion Boat Boats for Delos (20 to 30 minutes, €5.60 return) leave at 9am, 9.30am, 10.15am, 11am, 11.40pm and 12.50pm, from the quay at the western end of the port, returning between 12.20pm and 3pm daily except Monday (when the site is closed).

Between May and September, guided tours are conducted in English, French and German; tours depart at 10.15am. Tickets are available from several travel agencies.

A boat also departs for Delos from Platys Gialos at 10.15am daily.

Getting Around Mykonos
To/From the Airport Buses do not serve Mykonos' airport, which is 3km south-east of the town centre; make sure you arrange

an airport transfer with your accommodation (expect to pay around €5.90); while the fixed taxi fare is €5. Call ☎ 022 400 or 023 700 from the airport.

Bus Mykonos (Hora) has two bus stations. The northern station has frequent departures to Ornos, Agios Stefanos (via Tourlos), Ano Mera, Elia, Kato Livadi Beach and Kalafatis Beach. The southern station serves Agios Ioannis Beach, Paraga, Platys Gialos, Paradise Beach, and, sometimes, Ornos.

Car & Motorcycle Most car and motorcycle rental firms are around the southern bus station. Expect to pay around €29 for car hire.

Caique Services leave Mykonos (Hora) for Super Paradise Beach, Agrari and Elia Beaches (June to September only) and from Platys Gialos to Paradise (€2.35), Super Paradise (€3), Agrari (€3.50) and Elia (€3.50) Beaches.

MYKONOS (HORA)

Mykonos, the island's port and capital, is a warren-like Cycladic village turned toy town. It can be very hard to find your bearings – just when you think you've got it worked out, you'll find yourself back at square one. Throngs of pushy people add to the frustration. Familiarise yourself with the three main streets that form a horseshoe behind the waterfront and you'll have a fighting chance of finding your way around.

Even the most disenchanted could not deny that Mykonos – a conglomeration of chic boutiques, houses with brightly painted balconies, and bougainvillea and geraniums growing against whiter-than-white walls – has a certain charm.

Orientation

The waterfront is to the right of the ferry quay (facing inland), beyond the tiny, somewhat grubby, town beach. The central square is Plateia Manto Mavrogenous (usually called Taxi Square), south along the waterfront.

The northern bus station is near the OTE while the southern bus station is on the road to Ornos. The quay for boats to Delos is at the western end of the waterfront. South of here is Mykonos' famous row of windmills, most of them dilapidated and in need of restoration, and the Little Venice quarter, where balconies overhang the sea.

Information

Mykonos has no tourist office. When you get off the ferry, you will see a low building with four numbered offices. No 1 is the Hoteliers Association of Mykonos (☎ 2289 024 540, fax 2289 024 760, W www .mykonosgreece.com), open 8am to midnight daily; No 2 is the Association of Rooms, Studios & Apartments (☎ 2289 026 860), open 10am to 6pm daily; No 3 has camping information (☎ 2289 022 852), but is rarely open; and No 4 houses the tourist police (☎ 2289 022 482), with variable opening times. Mykonos Accommodation Center (☎ 2289 023 408, fax 2289 024 137, W www .mykonos-accommodation.com), 1st floor, 10 Enoplon Dinameon, provides the most comprehensive tourist information and can find mid-range to top-end accommodation, as well as gay-friendly accommodation.

The Olympic Airways office is by the southern bus station (☎ 2289 022 490, fax 2289 023 366).

The National Bank of Greece (with ATM) is on the waterfront (and there are also several banks by the ferry quay). Two doors away, Delia Travel (☎ 2289 022 322, fax 2289 024 440) represents American Express.

The post office is in the southern part of town, with the police (☎ 2289 022 235) next door. The OTE is beside the northern bus station.

Angelo's Internet Cafe (☎ 2289 024 106), on the road between the southern bus station and the windmills, provides the best email access. Most Internet cafes are outrageously over-priced in Mykonos; if possible, wait until Paros or Syros to email.

The Public Medical Center of Mykonos (☎ 2289 023 994/996) is on the road to Ano Mera. The port police (☎ 2289 022 716) are on the waterfront, above the National Bank.

MYKONOS (HORA)

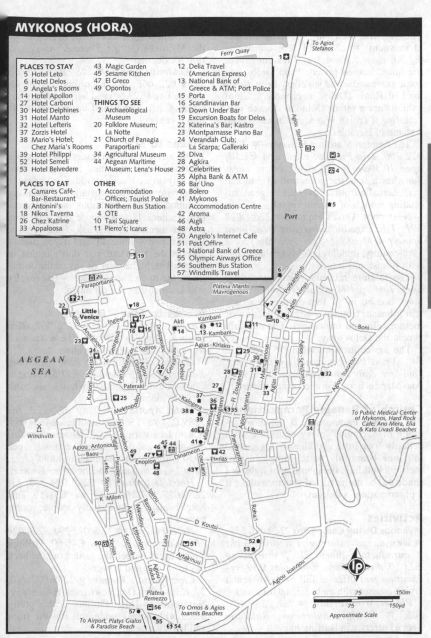

PLACES TO STAY
5 Hotel Leto
6 Hotel Delos
9 Angela's Rooms
14 Hotel Apollon
27 Hotel Carboni
30 Hotel Delphines
31 Hotel Manto
32 Hotel Lefteris
37 Zorzis Hotel
38 Mario's Hotel;
    Chez Maria's Rooms
39 Hotel Philippi
52 Hotel Semeli
53 Hotel Belvedere

PLACES TO EAT
7 Camares Café-
    Bar-Restaurant
8 Antonini's
18 Nikos Taverna
26 Chez Katrine
33 Appaloosa

43 Magic Garden
45 Sesame Kitchen
47 El Greco
49 Opontos

THINGS TO SEE
2 Archaeological
    Museum
20 Folklore Museum;
    La Notte
21 Church of Panagia
    Paraportiani
34 Agricultural Museum
44 Aegean Maritime
    Museum; Lena's House

OTHER
1 Accommodation
    Offices; Tourist Police
3 Northern Bus Station
4 OTE
10 Taxi Square
11 Pierro's; Icarus

12 Delia Travel
    (American Express)
13 National Bank of
    Greece & ATM; Port Police
15 Porta
16 Scandinavian Bar
17 Down Under Bar
19 Excursion Boats for Delos
22 Katerina's Bar; Kastro
23 Montparnasse Piano Bar
24 Verandah Club;
    La Scarpa; Galleraki
25 Diva
28 Agkira
29 Celebrities
35 Alpha Bank & ATM
36 Bar Uno
40 Bolero
41 Mykonos
    Accommodation Centre
42 Aroma
46 Aigli
48 Astra
50 Angelo's Internet Cafe
51 Post Office
54 National Bank of Greece
55 Olympic Airways Office
56 Southern Bus Station
57 Windmills Travel

CYCLADES

Museums

There are five museums. The **archaeological museum** (☎ 2289 022 325; admission €1.50; open 8.30am-3pm Tues-Sun), near the quay, houses pottery from Delos and some grave stelae and jewellery from the island of Renia (Delos' necropolis). Chief exhibits are a pithos (Minoan storage jar), featuring a Trojan War scene in relief, and a statue of Heracles.

The **Aegean Maritime Museum** (☎ 2289 022 700, Tria Pigadia; admission €1.50; open 10.30am-1pm & 6.30pm-9pm Tues-Sun) has a fantastic collection of nautical paraphernalia from all over the Aegean, including models of ancient vessels.

Next door, **Lena's House** (☎ 2289 022 591; Tria Pigadia; admission free; open 6pm-9pm Mon-Sat, 7pm-9pm Sun) is a 19th-century, middle class Mykonian house with furnishings intact.

The **folklore museum** (admission free; open 7pm-9pm Mon-Sat, 6.30pm-8.30pm Sun), housed in an 18th-century sea captain's house, features a large collection of memorabilia and furnishings. The museum is near the Delos quay.

The **agricultural museum** (☎ 2289 022 748, Agiou Ioannou; admission free; open 4pm-6pm daily Jun-Sept), near the road to Ano Mera, is housed in a renovated windmill.

Church of Panagia Paraportiani

The Panagia Paraportiani is the most famous of Mykonos' many churches. It is actually four little churches amalgamated into one beautiful, white, lumpy, asymmetrical building; the interplay of light and shade on the multifaceted structure make it a photographer's delight.

Activities

Mykonos Diving Club (☎/fax 2289 026 539; Ⓦ www.diveadventures.gr, Paradise Beach; 2 introductory dives €105, snorkelling €23.50, diving course €406, plus €59 certification fee) offers a full range of scuba diving courses with multi-lingual instructors.

Planet Windsurfing (☎/fax 2289 072 345, Ⓦ www.pezi-huber.com, Kalafatis Beach) offers windsurfing hire.

Organised Tours

Excursion boats run day trips to Delos. See the Mykonos Getting There & Away section for details.

Windmills Travel (☎ 2289 023 877, fax 2289 022 066) is the booking agent for snorkelling (€23.50) and horse-riding tours (from €29), and island cruises (€34.90, four weekly).

Places to Stay

If you arrive without a reservation between July and September and manage to find suitably priced accommodation, take it. Otherwise seek the assistance of local accommodation organisations (see Information earlier). If you choose domatia from owners meeting ferries, ask if they charge for transport – some do; and if you plan to stay in the hora and you don't intend to party all night, be wary of any of the domatia on the main thoroughfares – bar revelry will keep you awake till dawn.

Places to Stay – Budget

Angela's Rooms (☎ 2289 022 967, Taxi Square) Doubles €46.40. These are nice rooms in a very central location.

Mario's Hotel (☎/fax 2289 024 680, Kalogera) Singles/doubles €32/52. Next to Chez Maria's Rooms, this hotel has comfortable rooms.

Hotel Apollon (☎ 2289 022 223, fax 2289 024 237) Singles/doubles €46.50/64. For a place with a bit of character, try this old-world hotel. It's been around since 1930 and most of the furniture looks older, but it's very well kept and the owner is sweet.

Hotel Delphines (☎ 2289 024 505, fax 2289 027 307, Mavrogenous) €38/59. This hotel is also run by friendly people; rooms have TV.

Hotel Philippi (☎ 2289 022 294, 2289 024 680, Kalogera) Doubles €46.60. Philippi has an agrarian feel; the garden out the back has fruit trees and flowers.

Chez Maria's Rooms (☎ 2289 022 480, 27 Kalogera) Doubles/triples €43.50/59. Next door to Hotel Philippi is this pretty place with potted geraniums out the front and lovely rooms.

Hotel Lefteris (☎ 2289 027 117, 9 Apollonos) Singles/doubles €46.50/61. This hotel is in the residential backstreets away from the hubbub. Some of the rooms have a balcony. Signs point from Taxi Square.

Hotel Carboni (☎ 2289 022 217, fax 2289 023 264) Doubles/triples €49/61. This D-class hotel on Andronikou Matogianni has plain but clean rooms with TV.

Places to Stay – Mid-Range

Hotel Delos (☎ 2289 022 517, fax 2289 022 312) Doubles/triples €72.50/88. This C-class hotel is in a great location, right on the waterfront by the town beach.

Hotel Manto (☎ 2289 022 330, fax 2289 026 664) Singles/doubles €61/85.50. This hotel is just off Mavrogenous, and has simple rooms, some with balcony.

Zorzis Hotel (☎ 2289 022 167, fax 2289 024 169, e zorzis@otenet.gr, 30 Kalogera) Doubles €81. This rather smart hotel is in a central location, but is reasonably sheltered from bar noise.

Places to Stay – Top End

Hotel Leto (☎ 2289 022 207, fax 2289 023 985) Singles/doubles/studios with breakfast €197/255/290. Even with a recent facelift, the hotel's rooms are looking outdated, but it does have a chic poolside area and balcony views facing the town beach.

Hotel Belvedere (☎ 2289 025 122, fax 2289 025 126, e reservations@belvederehotel .com) Doubles from €218. Much better value can be found at the Belvedere, away from the town centre, in the Rohari area. The Belvedere has jacuzzis, a massage therapist, fitness studio, DVD and Internet corner. Rooms have balconies with town views, and the hotel has a pool, bar and lounge area.

Hotel Semeli (☎ 2289 027 466, fax 2289 027 467, e semeliht@otenet.gr, Rohari) Doubles with breakfast €160. Adjacent to the Belvedere, Semeli is run by the same family. The hotel is built around the old family house and old-world charm is combined with modern comforts.

For more top-end listings, see the Beaches and Ano Mera sections.

Places to Eat

The high prices charged in many eating establishments in the area are not always indicative of quality. The fish served in most of the tavernas is likely to be cheap frozen stuff imported from Asia, which often tastes like warmed up old boots. If you want good fish, you're best off trying another island.

Antonini's (☎ 2289 022 319, Taxi Square) Dishes €2.50-12.20. This is where the locals go for reliably good Greek food.

Nikos Taverna (☎ 2289 024 320, Porta) Dishes €2.70-13.20, seafood by the kilo. Up from the Delos quay, the food at Nikos is nothing great, but it's better than what's on offer in a lot of the other 'traditional' places.

Camares Cafe-Bar-Restaurant (☎ 2289 028 570). Dishes €2.35-13.20. On the waterfront by Taxi Square, expect to dine on what you'd likely find in a cafe at home – risotto, salads and seafood.

Magic Garden (☎ 2289 026 217) Dishes €7.30-13.20. Formerly Gatsby's, it has retained the same slightly refined atmosphere and still serves some interesting food, including shrimp with spinach and green apple in a hot black sauce (€13.20).

Appaloosa (☎ 2289 027 086) Dishes €2-13.40. This Mexican-inspired place on Mavrogeneous has guacamole and nachos, as well as more substantial burgers and pasta dishes.

El Greco (☎ 2289 022 074, Tria Pigadia) Dishes €4.20-18.90, seafood by the kilo. El Greco offers dishes such as, zucchini stuffed with Mykonos cheese and fennel (€5.70) and *sofrito* (Corfu-style veal with parsley, garlic and vinegar; €9.30). Some of their fish is local.

Sesame Kitchen (☎ 2289 024 710, Tria Pigadia) Dishes €5.30-20.10. A few doors up from El Greco, this restaurant serves innovative fare, much of it vegetarian, including Delos salad with *arugula*, Mykonos goat's cheese and sesame seeds (€11).

Chez Maria's Garden (☎ 2289 027 565) Set menu €17.40. There's a lovely outdoor candle-lit setting at Maria's, and the food is always good, if pricey.

CYCLADES

Chez Katrine (☎ 2289 022 169, Gerasimou at Nikou) Meal with wine from €52.50. Probably the classiest restaurant on Mykonos, Katrine serves Greek food with a French twist. It's been open since 1971 and has diligent service and a relaxed, unfussy atmosphere.

There's a cluster of cheap fast-food outlets and creperies in the centre of town; *Opontos* serves gyros for €1.50. There are also several *supermarkets* and *fruit stalls*, particularly around the southern bus station area.

Entertainment

The Little Venice quarter has dreamy sunset bars perched right on the water's edge, some with glowing candle-lit tables. The music leans towards smooth soul sounds and lounge easy-listening gems. Head to *Katerina's Bar* (☎ 2289 023 084), *Verandah Club* (☎ 2289 026 262), *Galleraki* (☎ 2289 027 188) and *La Scarpa* (☎ 2289 023 294).

Aroma (☎2289 027 148, Kalogera) is open for coffee and breakfast by day, and by night transforms into an exclusive bar, complete with face-and-fashion police on the door – watch out!

On Enaplon Dinameon there is a cluster of large bars playing a mix of dance and lounge music, depending on the crowd, including *Astra* (☎ 2289 024 767). Opposite El Greco, *Aigli* (☎ 2289 027 265) has a huge outdoor area. *Agkira* (☎ 2289 024 273) and the tragically named *Celebrities* (☎ 2289 022 333), both on Matogianni, are in a similar vein, but rather more chic.

Bar Uno (☎ 2289 022 689, Kalogera), near Alpha Bank, is less straightjacket chic and far more fun – raucous evenings are the go here. *Bolero* (☎ 2289 024 877, Malamatenias) plays world music.

The *Scandinavian Bar* (☎ 2289 022 669) and the *Down Under Bar* nearby, have less fashionista, less edge and the drinks are cheaper – so if that suits head on over.

Hard Rock Cafe (☎ 2289 072 162), about 4km along the Ano Mera road, has the usual Hard Rock gimmickry and a restaurant and nightclub. A shuttle bus runs from the 24-hour down-at-heel *Yacht Club* (☎ 2289 023

430), by the port, to the Hard Rock every half-hour between noon and 4am.

By the folk museum, *La Notte* is the place to go for an authentic Greek night of clubbing – bouzouki and contemporary Greek dance music is on the play list.

Gay Bars Mykonos is a gay travel destination in danger of being overrun by heterosexuals *(quelle horreur!)*, but bastions of gay nightlife survive year after year. *Kastro* (☎ 2289 023 072) in Little Venice is the place to kick start the night with cocktails as the sun sets. Around 11pm, things get a bit livelier at *Porta* (☎ 2289 027 807), which is reputably the best bar to cruise and gets full to overflowing late in the evening. Afterwards head to *Pierro's* (☎ 2289 022 177), a dance club, playing heavy-beat house, that also has raucous drag shows. Adjoining it, *Icarus* has several different spaces, a bar, rooftop terrace and 'darkrooms'. And then there's *Diva* (☎ 2289 027 271), which is where the gals like to hang, but it generally has a mixed crowd.

Cinemas *Cinemanto* (☎ 2289 027 190) Admission €5.90. Sessions 9pm & 11pm. If you're tired of partying, this outdoor cinema and taverna could provide some welcome respite; it screens new films every two days.

AROUND MYKONOS
Beaches

The nearest beaches to Hora are **Malaliamos** and the tiny, crowded **Tourlos**, 2km to the north. **Agios Stefanos**, 2km beyond, is larger, but just as crowded. To the south, beyond Ornos, is **Agios Ioannis**, where *Shirley Valentine* was filmed. **Psarou**, east of Ornos, is a pretty little cove. **Platys Gialos**, on the south-west coast, is bumper to bumper sun lounges backed by very ordinary package tour hotels – really not nice at all.

From Platys Gialos, caiques call at the island's best beaches further south: **Paradise**, **Super Paradise**, **Agrari** and **Elia**. Nudism is accepted on all these beaches. **Elia** is the last caique stop, so is the least crowded.

The next beach along, **Kato Livadi**, is relatively quiet. North-coast beaches are exposed to the meltemi, but **Panormos** and **Agios Sostis** are sheltered and uncrowded.

Places to Stay Mykonos has two camping grounds; minibuses from the camping grounds meet ferries.

Paradise Beach Camping (☎ *2289 022 852, fax 2289 024 350)* Camp sites €21.80, single/double bungalows €55/72.50. This site on Paradise Beach is close to the action but has overpriced facilities and readers have complained of lecherous staff, dirty toilets and overcrowding.

Mykonos Camping (☎/*fax 2289 024 578;* W *www.mycamp.gr)* Adult/tent €7/3.50; 2-person bungalows €23.50 per person. This cosy camping ground is on quieter Paraga Beach (a 10-minute walk from Platys Gialos) and has good facilities.

There are many top-end places around the coast.

Villa Katerina (☎ *2289 023 414, fax 2289 022 503)* Double studios €82.50. This quiet, romantic place, 300m up the hill above Agios Ioannis, has a garden and pool.

Princess of Mykonos (☎ *2289 023 806, fax 2289 023 031)* Doubles with/without sea view €177/142. At Agios Stefanos, this A-class place was once a Jane Fonda hangout. Breakfast is included.

Aphrodite Beach Hotel (☎ *2289 071 367, fax 2289 071 525)* Doubles/triples with breakfast €188.50/230. On Kalafatis Beach, this A-class hotel has masses of facilities including water sports.

Ornos Beach Hotel (☎ *2289 023 216, fax 2289 022 483,* W *www.ornosbeach.com.gr)* Doubles €130.50. This hotel has great sea views and a swimming pool.

Ano Mera Άνω Μέρα

The village of Ano Mera, 7km east of Hora, is the island's only inland settlement. On its central square is the 6th-century **Moni Panagias Tourlianis** (☎ *2289 071 249; visits by prior arrangement),* which has a fine carved marble bell tower, an ornate wooden iconostasis carved in Florence in the late 1700s, and 16th-century icons painted by members of the Cretan School. Speakers, turned way up to level 11, blast

Super Clubbing Paradise

Paradise Beach and Super Paradise have world reputations as fevered sun, dance and body worshipping sand strips.

Paradise is a long arc of pebbled beach, covered from headland to headland in sun lounges. Head there early if you're after a quiet swim because after 3pm the bars fire up. The beaches also have a reputation as gay beats, but the sheer numbers of young heterosexuals makes any gay presence virtually unnoticeable (no doubt much to the chagrin of the gay crowd).

The *Beach Bar* is a boozy low-clothes zone with twenty-somethings grooving the day away in front of giant speakers thumping out dance sounds. Unbelievably, less than 10m away at *Tropicana Bar* (☎*2289 027 271),* there's more of the same.

For big-name international DJs and all-night clubbing head to *Cavo Paradiso* (☎*2289 027 205, 2289 026 124; open at 3am July-Aug; entry from (17.60),* 300m above Paradise Beach. Paradiso is one of the top three summer dance clubs in the world – to whet your dancing appetite check out W www.cavoparadiso.gr for a line-up of upcoming DJs.

For news of clubbing events in the Cyclades (and elsewhere in Greece) – subscribe to the excellent up-to-date Web site City Vibe (W www.thecityvibe.com).

CYCLADES

out beautiful Orthodox hymns, which makes for a powerful experience.

Ano Mera Hotel (☎ *2289 071 215, fax 2289 071 276)* Singles/doubles/triples €78/88/117.50. This A-class hotel has a pool, restaurant and disco. Breakfast is included in the price.

The central square is edged with *tavernas*. Near the bus stop, *O Apostolis* has decent traditional food.

Delos Δύλος

Despite its diminutive size, the World Heritage-listed Delos (☎ *2289 022 259; site & museum €3.50; open 9am-3pm Tues-Sun)* is one of the most important archaeological sites in Greece, and certainly the most important in the Cyclades. Lying a few kilometres off the west coast of Mykonos, this sacred island is the mythical birthplace of the twins Apollo and Artemis.

History

Delos was first inhabited in the 3rd millennium BC. In the 8th century BC, a festival in honour of Apollo was established; the oldest temples and shrines on the island (many donated by Naxians) date from this era. For a long time, the Athenians coveted Delos, seeing its strategic position as one from where they could control the Aegean. By the 5th century BC, it had come under their jurisdiction.

Athens' power grew during the Persian Wars, and in 478 BC it established an alliance known as the Delian League that kept its treasury on Delos. Athens carried out a number of 'purifications', decreeing that no-one could be born or die on Delos, thus strengthening its control over the island by removing the native population.

Delos reached the height of its power in Hellenistic times, becoming one of the three most important religious centres in Greece and a flourishing centre of commerce. It traded throughout the Mediterranean and was populated with wealthy merchants, mariners and bankers from as far away as Egypt and Syria. These inhabitants built

temples to the various gods worshipped in their homelands, although Apollo remained the principal deity.

The Romans made Delos a free port in 167 BC, which brought even greater prosperity – due largely to a lucrative slave market that sold up to 10,000 people a day. Later, Delos was prey to pirates and to looters of antiquities.

Getting To/From Delos

See Excursion Boats in the Mykonos section for schedules and prices of services from Mykonos. Boats also operate to Delos from Tinos and Paros.

ANCIENT DELOS
Orientation & Information

The quay where excursion boats dock is south of the tranquil Sacred Harbour. Many of the most significant finds from Delos are in the National Archaeological Museum in Athens. The site museum has an interesting collection, and it now also houses the lions from the Terrace of the Lions (those on the terrace itself are plaster-cast replicas).

Overnight stays on Delos are forbidden, and boat schedules allow a maximum of six or seven hours there. Bring water and food, as the cafeteria's offerings are poor value for money. Wear a hat and sensible shoes. If you hire a guide once you get to Delos, you'll need to fork out more cash.

Exploring the Site

Following is an outline of some significant archaeological remains on the site. For further details, buy a guidebook at the ticket office, or – even better – take a guided tour.

If you have the energy, climb Mt Kythnos (113m), which is south-east of the harbour, to see the layout of Delos. There are terrific views of the surrounding islands on clear days. The path to Mt Kythnos is reached by walking through the **Theatre Quarter**.

It was in this quarter that Delos' wealthiest inhabitants built their houses. These houses surrounded peristyle courtyards, with mosaics (a status symbol) the most striking feature of each house. These colourful mosaics were exquisite art works, mostly

ANCIENT DELOS

1 Stadium
2 Gymnasium
3 Sanctuary of Archegetes
4 Lake House
5 House of Diadumenos
6 House of Comedians
7 Hill House
8 Institution of the
  Poseidoniasts
9 Palaestra
10 Roman Wall
11 Agora of the Italians
12 Terrace of the Lions
   (Replicas Only)
13 Stoa of Poseidon
14 Dodekatheon

15 Stoa of Antigonas
16 Sanctuary of Dionysos
17 Tourist Pavillion
18 Museum
19 Monument of the Bulls
20 Temple of Apollo
21 Temple of the Athenians
22 Poros Temple
23 Temple of Artemis
24 Keraton
25 Stoa of the Naxiots
26 House of the Naxiots
27 Ferries to Mykonos
28 Agora of the Competialists
29 Stoa of Philip V
30 South Stoa

31 Agora of the Delians
32 House of Dionysos
33 House of Cleopatra
34 Wall of the Triarus
35 House of the Trident
36 Cistern
37 Theatre
38 House of the Masks
39 House of the Dolphins
40 Shrine to the Samothracian
   Great Gods
41 House of Hermes
42 Sanctuary of the Syrian Gods
43 Shrine to the Egyptian Gods
44 Sacred Cave
45 Warehouses

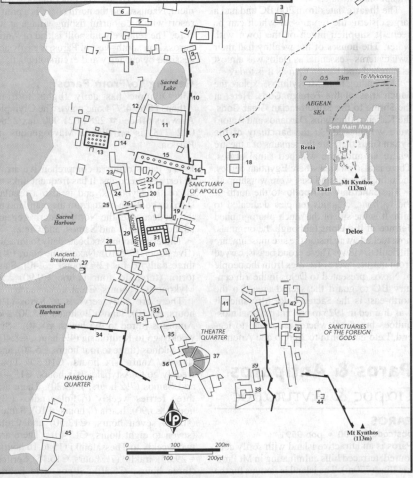

CYCLADES

AEGEAN
SEA

To Mykonos

Renia

Ekati

Mt Kynthos
(113m)

Delos

See Main Map

0   0.5   1km

Sacred
Lake

Sacred
Harbour

Ancient
Breakwater

Commercial
Harbour

SANCTUARY
OF APOLLO

Sacred
Way

THEATRE
QUARTER

HARBOUR
QUARTER

SANCTUARIES
OF THE FOREIGN
GODS

Mt Kynthos
(113m)

0   100   200m
0   100   200yd

representational and offset by intricate geometric borders. The most lavish dwellings were the **House of Dionysos** (named after the mosaic depicting the wine god riding a panther) and the **House of Cleopatra** (where headless statues of the owners were found). The **House of the Trident** was one of the grandest. The **House of the Masks**, probably an actors' hostelry, has another mosaic of Dionysos resplendently astride a panther, and the **House of the Dolphins** has another exceptional mosaic.

The **theatre** dates from 300 BC and had a large cistern, the remains of which can be seen. It supplied much of the town with water. The houses of the wealthy had their own cisterns – essential as Delos was almost as parched and barren then as it is today.

Descending from Mt Kythnos, explore the **Sanctuaries of the Foreign Gods**. Here, at the **Shrine to the Samothracian Great Gods**, the Kabeiroi (the twins Dardanos and Aeton) were worshipped. At the **Sanctuary of the Syrian Gods** there are the remains of a theatre where an audience watched ritual orgies. There is also an area where Egyptian deities, including Serapis and Isis, were worshipped.

The **Sanctuary of Apollo**, to the north of the harbour, contains temples dedicated to him. It is the site of the much-photographed **Terrace of the Lions** (although the originals, now tucked away inside the site museum, are difficult to view). These proud beasts, carved from marble, were offerings from the people of Naxos, presented to Delos in the 7th century BC to guard the sacred area. To the north-east is the **Sacred Lake** (dry since it was drained in 1925 to prevent malarial mosquitoes breeding) where, according to legend, Leto gave birth to Apollo and Artemis.

Paros & Antiparos
Πάρος & Αντίπαρος

PAROS
postcode 844 00 • pop 9591
Paros is an attractive island with softly contoured, terraced hills culminating in Mt Profitis Ilias (770m). The island is famous for the pure-white marble from which it prospered from the Early Cycladic period onwards – the *Venus de Milo* was carved from Parian marble, as was Napoleon's tomb.

Paros is now the main ferry hub for the Greek islands. The port town of Parikia is the busiest on the island, largely because of the volume of people waiting for ferry connections. The hubbub surrounding the ferry quay is countered by the charming and peaceful old hora that lies one block back from the waterfront. The other major settlement, Naoussa, on the north coast, is a pretty resort with a colourful fishing village at its core. The relatively unspoilt island of Antiparos, 1km south-west of Paros, is easily accessible by car ferry and excursion boat.

Getting To/From Paros
Air Olympic has daily flights to/from Athens (€65.45/74 one way). The Olympic Airways office (☎ 2284 021 900, fax 2284 022 778) is on Plateia Mavrogenous in Parikia.

Ferry Paros offers a comprehensive array of ferry connections. It has frequent links to all of the Cyclades, and is also a regular stop for boats en route from the mainland to the Dodecanese, the North-Eastern Aegean islands of Ikaria and Samos, and Crete.

There are around six boats daily to Piraeus (five hours, €15.10), Naxos (one hour, €4), three daily to Ios (2½ hours, €7.40), Santorini (three to four hours, €9.90) and Mykonos (1¾ hours, €5.30).

There are daily services to Syros (1½ hours, €5.10), Tinos (2½ hours, €5.30) and Amorgos (three to 4½ hours, €8.40). Six weekly go to Koufonisia (4½ hours, €8.40) and Sikinos (three to four hours, €5.40), and five to Anafi (six hours, €10.50). Four weekly go to Astypalea (six hours, €15.40) and Samos (7½ hours, €13.20). There are three ferries weekly to Folegandros (3½ hours, €5.90), Ikaria (4 hours, €10), Samos (six to seven hours, €13.50) and Crete (seven to eight hours, €15.40). There are two weekly to Thessaloniki (15 to 16 hours, €29.05), Iraklio (7½ hours, €16.15), Serifos (three hours, €6.30), Sifnos (two hours,

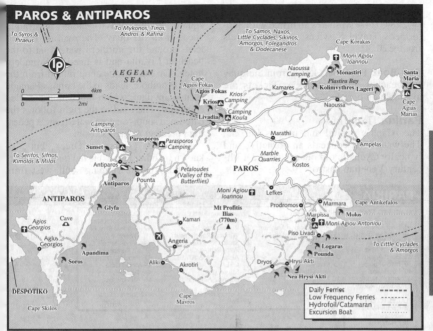

PAROS & ANTIPAROS

€5.70), Milos (4½ hours, €8.40), Kimolos (4½ hours, €6.90), Shinousa (four hours, €6.40) and Donousa (two to four hours, €7).

There is one boat weekly to Skiathos (10 hours, €18.70), Rhodes (12 to 15 hours, €20), Kos (six to eight hours, €13.20), Patmos (four hours, €12.20), Leros (5½ hours, €13.70), Megisti (20 hours, €25), Nissyros (9½ hours, €13.70), Tilos (10½ hours, €15.70), Andros (3½ hours, €10.80) and Symi (11 hours, €18.60).

There is also a half-hourly car ferry available which runs from Pounta on the west coast of Paros to Antiparos (10 minutes, €0.60 one way, €5.30 car); the first ferry departs for Antiparos at around 7am, and the last boat returning leaves Antiparos at 1.30am.

Fast Boat & Catamaran There are three daily catamarans to Rafina (2½ hours, €25.55), at least two daily catamarans to Naxos (30 minutes, €8.20), Tinos (1¼ hours, €10.50), Syros (45 minutes, €9.60), Mykonos (one hour, €10.30), Ios (1½ hours, €14.30) and Santorini (2¼ hours, €17.70). There are ten services weekly to Piraeus (2½ hours, €30.25) and two weekly to Andros (two hours, €16.80) and Amorgos (1½ to 2 hours, €16.90).

Excursion Boat In summer, frequent excursion boats depart for Antiparos from Parikia.

Getting Around Paros

Bus There are around seven buses daily from Parikia to Naoussa via Dryos, Hrysi Akti, Marpissa, Marmara, Prodromos, Kostos, Marathi and Lefkes, and frequent buses to Pounta (for Antiparos), Aliki (via Petaloudes and the airport). Around 12 buses daily link Parikia and Naoussa directly.

Car, Motorcycle & Bicycle There are numerous rental outlets along the waterfront and all around the island. Paros Rent-a-Car (☎ 2284 024 408) shares an office with Santorineos Travel Services and has models from €20.30.

Taxi Boat Taxi boats leave from the quay for beaches around Parikia. Tickets are available on board.

Parikia Παροικία

The island's capital and port is Parikia. The waterfront conceals an attractive and typically Cycladic old quarter with a 13th-century Venetian kastro.

Orientation & Information The main square, Plateia Mavrogenous, is straight ahead from the quay. The road on the left leads around the northern waterfront to the beach at Livadia and is lined with modern hotels. On the left, heading inland from the quay, Prombona leads to the famous Panagia Ekatontapyliani, which lies within a walled courtyard. The road to the right follows the cafe-lined south-western waterfront, a pedestrian precinct in high season.

Market St (Agora in Greek, but also known by other names) is the main commercial thoroughfare running south-west from

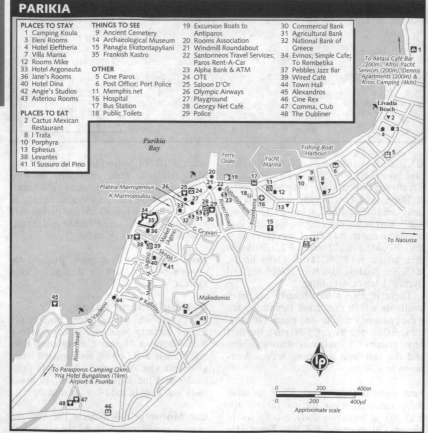

PARIKIA

PLACES TO STAY
1 Camping Koula
3 Eleni Rooms
4 Hotel Eleftheria
7 Villa Marisa
12 Rooms Mike
33 Hotel Argonauta
36 Jane's Rooms
40 Hotel Dina
42 Angie's Studios
43 Asteriou Rooms

PLACES TO EAT
2 Cactus Mexican Restaurant
8 I Trata
10 Porphyra
13 Ephesus
38 Levantes
41 Il Sussuro del Pino

THINGS TO SEE
9 Ancient Cemetery
14 Archaeological Museum
15 Panagia Ekatontapyliani
35 Frankish Kastro

OTHER
5 Cine Paros
6 Post Office; Port Police
11 Memphis.net
16 Hospital
17 Bus Station
18 Public Toilets

19 Excursion Boats to Antiparos
20 Rooms Association
21 Windmill Roundabout
22 Santorineos Travel Services; Paros Rent-A-Car
23 Alpha Bank & ATM
24 OTE
25 Saloon D'Or
26 Olympic Airways
27 Playground
28 Georgy Net Café
29 Police

30 Commercial Bank
31 Agricultural Bank
32 National Bank of Greece
34 Evinos; Simple Cafe; To Rembetika
37 Pebbles Jazz Bar
39 Wired Café
44 Town Hall
45 Alexandros
46 Cine Rex
47 Comma, Club
48 The Dubliner

To Aktaia Café Bar (200m), Afros Yacht Services (200m), Dennis Apartments (200m) & Krios Camping (4km)

Parikia Bay

Plateia Mavrogenous
A Marinopoulou

Ferry Quay

Yacht Marina

Fishing Boat Harbour

Livadia Beach

Ektontapiliani

Prombona

River/Road

Market St (Agora)

G Gravari

Skopa

Market St (Agora)

P Kallirou

Makedonias

D Vasikou

River/Road

To Naoussa

To Parasporos Camping (2km), Yria Hotel Bungalows (1km), Airport & Pounta

0   200   400m
0   200   400yd
Approximate scale

Plateia Mavrogenous through the old town, which is all narrow pedestrian streets.

Kiosks on the quay give out information on domatia and hotels (see Places to Stay). By the bay, Santorineos Travel Services (☎ 2284 024 245, fax 2284 023 922, e santorineos-travel@ticketcom.gr) can help with accommodation, ferry tickets and tours. Santorineos is also the representative for American Express and MasterCard.

The National Bank of Greece, the Commercial Bank of Greece and police (☎ 2284 023 333) are all on Plateia Mavrogenous. The bus station is 50m left of the quay (looking inland), and the post office is 300m further along. The OTE is on the waterfront, to the right of the ferry quay (facing inland). The cosy Wired Café (☎ 2284 022 003), on Market St, Memphis.net, near the bus station, and Georgy Net Café (☎ 2284 022 543), near the Commercial Bank, all provide Internet access, with Georgy Net offering the best rates and new machines.

The port police (☎ 2284 021 240) are back from the northern waterfront, near the post office.

Afros Yacht Services (☎ 2284 023 625), next door to Aktaia Cafe Bar at Livadia Beach, is a yacht chandlery and does sail and boat repairs.

Things to See The **Panagia Ekatontapyliani** (☎ 2284 021 243; open 8am-1pm & 4pm-9pm daily), which dates from AD 326, is one of the most splendid in the Cyclades. The building is actually three distinct churches: Agios Nikolaos, the largest, with lovely columns of Parian marble and a carved iconostasis, is in the east of the compound; the others are the Church of Our Lady and the Baptistery. The name translates as Our Lady of the Hundred Gates, although only 99 doors have been counted. It is said that when the 100th is found, İstanbul will return to Greek jurisdiction.

Next to a school behind the Panagia Ekatontapyliani, the **Archaeological Museum** (☎ 2284 021 231; admission €1.50; open 8.30am-3pm Tues-Sun) has some interesting reliefs and statues, including a Gorgon, but the most important exhibit is a fragment of the 4th-century Parian Chronicle, which lists the most outstanding artistic achievements of ancient Greece. It was discovered in the 17th century by the Duke of Arundel's cleric, and most of it ended up in the Ashmolean Museum, Oxford. Typically, some of the most exquisite pieces are only plaster casts – the originals having long since been displaced to museums in New York and Germany.

North along the waterfront there is a fenced **ancient cemetery** dating from the 7th century BC; it was excavated in 1983. Roman graves, burial pots and sarcophagi are floodlit at night. Photographs and other finds are exhibited in an attached building, but it's rarely open.

The **Frankish Kastro** was built on the remains of a temple to Athena by Marco Sanudo, Venetian Duke of Naxos, in AD 1260. Not much remains, save an impressively large wall with cross-sectional chunks of columns from the temple embedded in it. To find it, head west along Market St and take the first right.

Activities & Organised Tours *Eurodivers Club (☎/fax 2284 092 071,* W *www .eurodivers.gr)* PADI open-water certification course €377. Down the coast at Pounta, this club offers scuba diving courses and dives for all levels and interests.

Aegean Diving School (☎ 2284 041 778, fax 2284 041 978, mobile ☎ 69 7484 0084, W *www.ageandiving.gr)* PADI open-water certification €375. Based at New Golden Beach, this school also offers a range of scuba courses from beginners to advanced.

Marel Tours (☎ 2284 021 258, fax 2284 024 181) has a trip to Lefkes and the quarries at Marathi (from €18.90); book through travel agents.

Places to Stay All camping grounds have minibuses that meet the ferries.

Camping Koula (☎ 2284 022 081, fax 2284 022 740, e *koula@otenet.gr)* Adult/ tent €5.90/2.35. This site, 1km along the northern waterfront at Livadia, is the most central.

Parasporos Camping (☎/fax 2284 022 268) Adult/tent €5.90.50. This site is 2km

Phone numbers listed incorporate changes due in Oct 2002; see p55

CYCLADES

south of Parikia and 300m from the beach, and gets the thumbs up from readers. A minibus meets ferries.

Krios Camping (☎ *2284 021 705,)* Adult/tent €5.90.50. This site is on Krios Beach, beyond Livadia Beach. It runs a taxi boat across the bay to Parikia every 10 minutes for €1.50 per person (return). It also has a restaurant and minimarket.

The Rooms Association (☎*/fax 2284 024 528, after hours* ☎ *2284 022 220)* on the quay has information on domatia; otherwise domatia owners meet ferries. For hotel details, call ☎ 2284 024 555 (Parikia) or ☎ 2284 041 333 (around the island).

Rooms Mike (☎ *2284 022 856)* Doubles/triples €30.20/43.50, self-contained studios €43.50/46.60. Mike's place is deservedly popular; rooms have TV, shared kitchen and a roof terrace. To get there, walk 50m left from the quay – it's next to Memphis.net.

Jane's Rooms (☎ *2284 021 338)* Doubles €46.60. In the atmospheric old Kastro, rooms have sea views and balconies; apartments are also available nearby. To reach it, facing the town, follow the road right for 200m. It's up the next set of stairs beyond the signpost for the Frankish Kastro; or Jane will meet you at the port if you book ahead.

Villa Marisa (☎ *2284 022 629, fax 2284 023 286)* Doubles/triples €43.50/29. This friendly pension has nice rooms.

Elini Rooms (☎ *2284 022 714, fax 2284 024 170,* e *roomelen@otenet.gr)* Singles/doubles €49/52. Rooms don't have views, but there's a pretty bougainvillea-covered courtyard area. Turn right at Hotel Argo by Livadia Beach to reach Elini's; transfer to/from the port is available.

Hotel Eleftheria (☎ *2284 022 047)* Doubles €43.50. This welcoming hotel nearby Livadia Beach has a rooftop terrace, and breakfast is available. Turn right at Taverna Katerina on the waterfront.

Angie's Studios (☎ *2284 023 909, fax 2284 024 346)* Singles/doubles €61/69.60. These studios are out in the back blocks, but it's a nice walk there from the centre of town. They are dripping with bougainvillea and have a pleasant patio and lawn.

Hotel Dina (☎ *2284 023 325, Market St)* Singles/doubles €46.50/52.50. This hotel is in the old town and all rooms have balconies.

Hotel Argonauta (☎*/fax 2284 021 440)* Singles/doubles €52/64. This lovely, central C-class hotel, on the main square, has sparkling rooms with air-con and balcony.

Dennis Apartments (☎*/fax 2284 022 466)* Doubles €49. For something a bit more rural and quiet, head to these spacious apartments, near Livadia. Take the first major road on the right after Camping Koula to get there, or telephone in advance to be picked up from the boat.

There are also plenty of run-of-the-mill hotels to choose from along the waterfront at Livadia, near Camping Koula.

Yria Hotel Bungalows (☎ *2284 024 154, fax 2284 021 167,* e *yria1@otenet.gr)* Singles/doubles with breakfast €127/168. This fine A-class property, 2.5km south of Parikia, overlooks pretty Parasporos Beach. It has a restaurant, bar, pool and tennis courts.

Places to Eat *I Trata* Meals €2.35-11.75. Near the ancient cemetery, Trata has very good seafood, not least its shrimp *saganaki*, and a stimulating array of mezedes, fresh fish and salads.

Porphyra Dishes €2.35-11.75. On the opposite side of the cemetery, Porphyra (named after a shellfish famed for its purple dye and ability to drill a hole into its prey) specialises in unusual seafood delicacies, including raw shellfish. Tamer offerings include fresh fish, calamari and prawns cooked to perfection.

Ephesus Dishes €1.50-8.80. This Anatolian place behind the hospital has delicious, herb-laden home-made dips and appetisers, a large selection of kebabs, and stuffed pizzas cooked in a wood-fired oven.

Levantis (☎ *2284 023 613, Market St)* Dishes €3.20-7.70. This is an interesting place in a garden setting with creative international cuisine.

Il Sussuro del Pino Dishes €1.90-11.75, seafood by the kilo. This place earns a big zero for friendliness, but has fresh fish and unusual dishes such as artichokes with calamari. Follow the signs from Skopa, which runs off Market St.

Cactus Mexican Restaurant (☎ 2284 024 164) Dishes €2.10-9.30. By the beach at Livadia, this restaurant has Mexican as well as Greek and international fare.

Entertainment Most bars are along the south-western waterfront, including some busy rooftop bars, like *Evinos* and *Simple Cafe*. Below the Simple Cafe is *To Rembetika*, which has rembetika music most nights.

Perched above the waterfront, **Pebbles Jazz Bar** (☎ 2284 022 283) plays classical music by day and jazz in the evenings, and has occasional live music.

Alexandros (☎ 2284 023 133) Open 5pm. This restored windmill right on the water's edge is a dreamy spot for a quiet drink.

Aktaia Cafe Bar (☎ 2284 069 7039) Meals €2-8.80. At the northern end of Livadia Beach, this is *the* chilled place for a drink. It's popular with visiting yachties and serves cafe fare at lunch and in the evening, including laksa and risotto.

Saloon D'Or (☎ 2284 022 176) Most big nights out start with warm-up drinks on the waterfront here, and then carry on to the cluster of rowdy nightclubs, further south.

The Dubliner (☎ 2284 021 113) Admission €3. The Dubliner houses the Down Under Bar, the Scandinavian Bar and Paros Rock, all theme bars. If you want to drink, get drunk and dance on tables – get on down. The lamely named **Comma, Club** is nearby.

Avoid any bars offering very cheap cocktails (invariably made from the local *bombes* (moonshine). See the boxed text 'Bombes Beware!' later.

Cinemas Popular open-air cinemas are **Cine Paros**, in Livadia's backstreets, and **Cine Rex** nearby The Dubliner at the southern end of the waterfront. Admission is €5.90 for both places and screening times are 9pm and 11pm.

Around Paros *Punda Beach Club* (☎ 2284 041 717, **W** www.pundabeach.gr) This all-day clubbing venue at Punda is a huge complex with a swimming pool, bar, restaurant and, as a matter of necessity, an in-house tattooist and Cuban cigar maker.

Naoussa Ναουσσα

Naoussa, on the north coast, has metamorphosed in twenty years from a peaceful and pristine fishing village into a popular tourist resort. For many visitors, Naoussa *is* Paros; its popularity is due in part to its proximity to nice beaches and to its slightly upmarket, French Riviera feel. It's certainly a lot less hectic than Parikia. Despite an incursion by package tourists, Naoussa remains relaxed.

Naoussa is still a working harbour with piles of yellow fishing nets, bright caiques, and little ouzeria with rickety tables and raffia chairs, although smart music bars are making inroads here. Behind the central square (where the bus terminates) is a picturesque village, with narrow alleyways whitewashed with fish and flower motifs.

Naoussa Information (☎ 2284 052 158) is an exceptionally helpful information booth near the bus station. It can book accommodation and also has mud maps of the village. **Nissiotissa Tours** (☎ 2284 051 480), left off the main square, can book accommodation and tours, and also has a book exchange.

The post office is a tedious uphill walk from the central square. An Alpha Bank (with ATM) is by the bus station.

Things to See In July and August, **Naoussa Paros** (**e** parafolk@otenet.gr), a nationally known folk-dancing group based in Naoussa, performs every Sunday (€7.30); book at Naoussa Information.

Naoussa's **Byzantine museum** (admission €1.50; open 11am-1.30pm & 7pm-9pm Tues, Thur, Sat & Sun) is housed in the blue-domed church, about 200m uphill from the town centre. A small **folklore museum** (admission €1.50; open 7pm-9pm daily) and the **folklore collection of Naoussa** (☎ 2284 052 284), which focuses on regional costumes, are both signposted from the post office.

The best beaches are **Kolimvythres**, which has interesting rock formations; and **Monastiri**, which has a *clubbing venue* above water and some good snorkelling underwater. Low-key **Lageri** is also worth seeking out. **Santa Maria**, on the other side of the eastern headland, is good for windsurfing. From Naoussa, caiques go to Kolimvythres, Monastiri, Lageri and Santa Maria.

Activities & Organised Tours Scuba diving courses are offered by the *Santa Maria Diving Club* (☎/fax 2284 053 007, W www.isdc.gr/santamaria) Introductory dive €52.50, diploma courses €377. Limited English is spoken here; snorkelling gear is available for hire.

Naoussa Paros Sailing Center (☎ 2284 052 646, e sailing@par.forthnet.gr) Full day €43.50 per person. Departs 9.30am. This company offers sailing tours to Naxos, Delos or Iraklia; half-day tours and yacht charters are also available.

Kokou Riding Centre 1/2/3 hours €20.50/ 29/40.80. Morning and evening horse rides are operated by Kokou. Rides start from the central square; book with any of the travel agents.

Nissiotissa Tours can organise excursions to Naxos, Delos, Mykonos, Santorini and Amorgos.

Places to Stay There are two camping grounds. Minibuses from both meet ferries.

Naoussa Camping (☎ 2284 051 595) Adult/tent €5.30/3. This shady camping ground is at Kolimvythres. It has a small taverna and lovely bays nearby.

Surfing Beach (☎ 2284 052 491, fax 2284 051 937, e info@surfbeach.gr) Adult/ tent €5.30/3. This camping ground, at Santa Maria, has a windsurfing and water-ski school (windsurfing courses €14.70 per hour, water-skiing from €17.40 per hour). The staff are decidedly surly, though it has reasonable facilities.

Anna's Rooms (☎ 2284 051 538) Doubles €40.80. Anna's has simple, clean rooms with patio. To get there, turn right off the main road into town at Hotel Atlantis (just before the main square).

Hotel Gallini (☎/fax 2284 051 210) Doubles €40.80. Directly behind the blue dome of the church, this small hotel has nice rooms.

Hotel Madaky (☎ 2284 051 475, fax 2284 052 968) Singles/doubles €49/53.70. This decent E-class hotel is off the central square.

Hotel Stella (☎ 2284 051 317, fax 2284 053 617, e hotelstella@usa.net) Singles/ doubles €36.30/56.50. In the heart of town, this pension has a shady garden. To reach it, turn left from the central square at Café Naoussa, then take the first right; continue past a small church on the left.

You'll find there is no shortage of good self-contained accommodation.

Sunset Studios & Apartments (☎/fax 2284 052 060, e sunsetmm@otenet.gr) Doubles/apartments €53.70/69.60,. Nice rooms and 2-bedroom apartments with telephone and air-con are on offer. Face inland from the main square, follow the one-way street uphill, and turn right at the T-junction – it's on the left.

Katerina's (☎ 2284 051 642) 2-bedroom apartments €59. This is a stunning place with red shutters and a beautiful patio with views over town and beach. As you come into town, Katerina's is off the main road to the right, behind the OTE.

Spiros Apartments (☎/fax 2284 052 327, Kolimvythres) Doubles/triples €46.50/49. These attractive apartments are right on the beach.

Hotel Fotilia (☎ 2284 052 581, fax 2284 052 583) Doubles with breakfast €72.50. This elegant B-class hotel, near the big church 200m uphill from the town centre, has spacious, traditional rooms. There is an old windmill in its courtyard, as well as a jacuzzi and pool.

Places to Eat *Moshonas Ouzeri* (☎ 2284 051 623) Dishes €2.50-8.80, seafood by kilo. Pronounced 'Moskonas', this ouzeria at the harbour serves great fish, supplied by their own fishing boat.

Papadakis Dishes €2.50-8.80. Don't miss Papadakis, on the waterfront. The food is traditional, but inventive. The octopus and onion stew is luscious, and there are refreshing salads with fennel, soft local cheese and an assortment of olives and greens.

Perivolaria Dishes €5.30-16. Open from 7pm. This garden restaurant, on the left, along from the bus stop, is a fine, upmarket place. It serves Greek and Italian cuisine and has a take-away pizza bar.

Taverna Christos (☎ *2284 051 901*) Dishes €2.70-10.30. Open from 7pm. On the way to the post office, Christos is another good option; it's just behind Avra Tours.

Around Paros

Marathi Maraqi In antiquity Parian marble was considered the world's finest. The **marble quarries** have been abandoned, but it's exciting to explore the area. Take the Lefkes bus and get off at Marathi village, where you'll find a signpost to the quarries.

Lefkes (Λεκες) **to Moni Agiou Antoniou** (Μονή Αγίου Αντωνίου) Lefkes, 12km south-east of Parikia, is the island's highest and loveliest village, and was its capital during the Middle Ages. It boasts the magnificent **Agias Trias** cathedral, with it's shaded entrance of olive trees, as well as the **Museum of Popular Aegean Civilisation**, an amphitheatre and an interesting library.

From the central square, a signpost points to a well-preserved Byzantine paved path, which leads to the village of **Prodromos**. Just below the village the path takes a sharp left, which is easy to miss because there isn't a sign – don't take the wider route straight ahead. The walk through beautiful countryside takes about an hour.

From Prodromos, it's a short walk to either **Marmara** or **Marpissa**. From Marmara, it's a stroll to the sandy beach at **Molos**; from Marpissa you can puff your way up a steep, paved path to the 16th-century **Moni Agiou Antoniou** atop a 200m-high hill. On this fortified summit, the Turks defeated Paros' Venetian rulers in 1537. Although the monastery and its grounds are generally locked, there are breathtaking views.

After this exertion, you'll probably feel like having a swim at the nice little beach at **Piso Livadi**. This pretty fishing village is well on the way to becoming a resort.

Candaca Travel (☎ *2284 041 449, fax 041 449,* e *candaca@otenet.gr*) can arrange accommodation and car rental, and also has Internet access.

Places to Stay & Eat There are some *domatia* on the road into Lefkes, including *Studio Calypso* (☎ *2284 041 583*).

Hotel Pantheon (☎/fax *2284 041 700*) Doubles €42. The only mid-range hotel accommodation in Lefkes, it has comfortable rooms with balconies. This is a great place to base yourself for a walking holiday.

There are plenty of places to stay and eat overlooking the harbour in Piso Livadi and *Stavros Taverna* is recommended. There's a *camping ground* on the outskirts of town.

Petaloudes Πεταλοδες In July and August, butterflies almost enshroud the copious foliage at Petaloudes *(Valley of the Butterflies; admission €1.20; open 9am-7pm Mon-Sat, 9am-1pm & 4pm-8pm Sun July & Aug)*. It's 8km south of Parikia. The butterflies are actually tiger moths, but spectacular all the same. Travel agents organise tours from both Parikia and Naoussa; or take the Aliki bus and ask to be let off at the Petaloudes turn-off.

Beaches Apart from the beaches already mentioned, there is a good beach at **Krios**, accessible by taxi boat (€2 return) from Parikia. Paros' most talked about beach, **Hrysi Akti** (Golden Beach), on the southeast coast, is nothing spectacular, but it's popular with windsurfers. Equipment for various **water sports**, including catamaran sailing, water-skiing and windsurfing, is available from the **Fanatic Fun Centre** (☎ *69-3830 7671,* W *www.fanatic-paros .com; board hire from €11.75 per hour, one-week courses €160)*.

The coast between Piso Livadi and Hrysi Akti has some decent, empty beaches, although there are newish beach resorts springing up and swallowing up the coastline all the time, such as those at **Nea Hrysi Akti** (New Golden Beach).

ANTIPAROS

postcode 840 07 • pop 819

Antiparos was once regarded as the quiet alternative to Paros, but development is increasing. The permanent inhabitants live in an attractive village (also called Antiparos)

CYCLADES

that is rapidly becoming obscured by tourist accommodation. It's still a very pleasant place and is a popular holiday spot for families with young kids. No cars are allowed in the village, which makes it even nicer.

Getting To/From Antiparos

For details on boats from Paros, see Getting There & Away under Paros.

The only bus service on Antiparos runs to the cave in the centre of the island (€3). In summer, this bus continues to Soros and Agios Georgios.

Orientation & Information

To reach the village centre if you've come from Pounta, turn right from the quay, walk along the waterfront and turn left into the main street at Anarghyros restaurant. If you've come by excursion boat, walk straight ahead from the quay.

The post office is a fair way down on the left. The OTE, with currency exchange and ferry information, is just beyond. The central square is left at the top of the main street and then right, behind Smiles Cafe.

There are several travel agencies, including Antiparos Travel Agency (☎ 2284 061 300, fax 2284 061 465), by the waterfront, which can organise accommodation.

To reach the kastro, another Marco Sanudo creation, go under the stone arch that leads north off the central square.

Beach bums will direct you to the decent beaches. Nudism is only permitted at Camping Antiparos.

Cave of Antiparos

Despite previous looting of stalactites and stalagmites, this cave (admission €3; open 10am-3.30pm daily summer) is still awe-inspiring. In 1673, the French ambassador, Marquis de Nointel, organised a Christmas Mass (enhanced by a large orchestra) inside the cave for 500 Parians.

There are buses every hour from the village of Antiparos (€1.20 one way) or you can take an excursion boat (high season only) from Antiparos village (€3.50) or Parikia (€7.40); the price includes the 1.5km bus ride from the landing stage to the cave.

Activities & Organised Tours

Blue Island Divers (☎/fax 2284 061 493, **w** www.blueisland-divers.gr) 4-day PADI open-water course €290, advanced course €246, snorkelling day trip €17.40/8.80 adult/child. Based on the main pedestrian thoroughfare, Blue Island has a wide range of dive options and can organise accommodation.

The **MS Thiella** tours around the island daily, stopping at several beaches. The tour includes lunch; book at travel agents.

Places to Stay & Eat

Camping Antiparos (☎/fax 2284 061 221) Adult/tent €4.40/2.30. This well-equipped camping ground, planted with bamboo, is on a beach 1.5km north of the quay; signs point the way.

Domatia are prevalent, especially in the area behind Kouros Village, and there are several hotels.

Argo (☎ 2284 061 419, fax 2284 061 186) Singles/doubles €30.20/49, double studios €82.50. On the road to Camping Antiparos, this small friendly place is recommended by readers, and also has a very good **taverna**. Breakfast is included in the price.

Anarghyros (☎ 2284 061 204) Singles/doubles €34.9/43.50. Rooms have air-con and TV and overlook the fishing harbour.

Hotel Mantalena (☎ 2284 061 206, fax 2284 061 550, **e** mantalenahotel@par .forthnet.gr) Doubles/triples €59/64. This hotel is further along from Anarghyros, to the left. All rooms have air-con and a balcony overlooking the port and there's a nice terrace.

The main street has many cafes and tavernas, including the popular **Taverna Yorgis** on the right, which serves Greek family staples and specialises in fish. **Taverna Klimataria** on the path to Fanari is also worth seeking out.

Maki's (☎ 2284 061 616) Dishes €2-8.20. Maki's has two tavernas, one on the waterfront, and the better of the two opposite the OTE. Try the very generous prawn souvlaki with calamari (€8.20).

Stillwaters Restaurant (☎ 2284 024 537, **e** stillwatersap@aol.com, Apandima Beach)

Dishes €4.40-10.30. Only a step away from the water, Stillwaters is a British-run operation which serves modern international cuisine.

Agios Georgios, in the south, has several *tavernas*.

Entertainment
Signposted left off Market St, *Yam Bar Cafe* is an open-air chill-out bar, with views of the sea. It plays a mix of Latin and House music.

The casual *Time Marine Beach Club* (☎ *2284 061 575*), about five minutes' walk from the port at Fanari Beach, is a great spot for a game of backgammon and a beer after a swim.

Naxos Ναξος

postcode 843 00 • pop 18,000
According to legend, it was on Naxos that Theseus abandoned Ariadne after she helped him find his way out of the Cretan labyrinth. She didn't pine long – she was soon ensconced in the arms of Dionysos, the god of wine and ecstasy and the island's favourite deity. Ever since, Naxian wine has been considered a fine remedy for a broken heart.

The island is the Cyclades' largest and most fertile, producing olives, grapes, figs, citrus, corn and potatoes. Rugged mountains and lush green valleys also make it one of the most beautiful. Mt Zeus (1004m; also known as Mt Zas or Zefs) is the archipelago's highest peak.

Naxos was an important Byzantine centre and boasts about 500 churches and monasteries, many containing interesting frescoes. Some of the early Christian basilicas were originally ancient temples.

The island is a wonderful place to explore on foot and walking is now a major draw for many visitors, especially Germans. Many old paths linking villages, churches and other sights still survive. For detailed route information, consult Christian Ucke's excellent *Walking Tours on Naxos*, available from local bookshops.

Getting To/From Naxos
Air There is at least one flight daily to/from Athens (€66.90/75.45 one way). Olympic Airways is represented by Naxos Tours, who also sell ferry tickets.

Ferry Naxos has around six ferry connections daily with Piraeus (six hours, €14.80), Paros (one hour, €4), Ios (1¼ hours, €6.10) and Santorini (three hours, €9); and four daily with Mykonos (three hours, €6).

There is one daily boat to Tinos (4¼ hours, €6.60), Syros (three hours, €6.60), Iraklia (1¼ to 5¼ hours, €4.50), Shinousa (1¾ to five hours, €4.80), Koufonisia (2½ to 4¼ hours, €4.80), Amorgos (two to 5¾ hours, €7) and Donousa (one to four hours, €5).

There are four ferries weekly to Anafi (four hours, €10.30) and Samos (4¾ to 7½ hours, €15.40).

There are three ferries weekly to Fourni (four hours, €11.20), Samos (five to six hours, €15.50) and Ikaria (3½ hours, €9).

There are two boats weekly to Astypalea (5½ hours, €12.90), Rhodes (10 hours, €17.90), Sikinos (three hours, €5.10) and Folegandros (three hours, €7.40).

One goes weekly to Thessaloniki (15 hours, €27.30), Kos (15 hours, €13.50), Iraklio (seven hours, €16.15), Andros (4½ hours, €12.20) and, late in the season, to Skiathos (8½ hours, €21.80).

Fast Boat & Catamaran There are at least two catamarans daily to Paros (30 minutes, €8.20), Mykonos (1½ hours, €11.75) and Piraeus (3¼ hours, €30.20); four weekly to Syros (1½ hours, €12.40); two weekly to Santorini (1½ hours, €19.20); and one weekly to Ios (50 minutes, €12.20).

Excursion Boat There are daily excursions to Mykonos (€26) and frequent excursions to Delos; book through travel agents.

Getting Around Naxos
To/From the Airport There is no shuttle bus, but buses to Agios Prokopios Beach and Agia Anna pass close by. A taxi costs €7.40.

Phone numbers listed incorporate changes due in Oct 2002; see p55

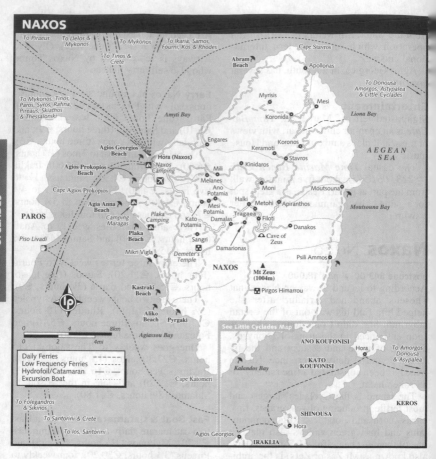

NAXOS

Bus Frequent buses run to Agia Anna (€0.90) from Hora. Five buses daily serve Filoti (€1.20) via Halki (€1), four serve Apiranthos (€1.70) via Filoti and Halki, at least three serve Apollonas (€3.20), Pyrgaki (€1.20) and Melanes (€0.90). There are less frequent departures to other villages.

Buses leave from the end of the wharf; timetables are posted outside the bus station and the Naxos Tourist Information Centre in Hora.

Car, Motorcycle & Bicycle You can hire cars and motorcycles as well as 21-speed all-

terrain bicycles from the waterfront outlets in Hora. Bicycle hire starts at €4.40. You'll need all the gears – the roads are steep, winding and not always in good condition. Remember that this is a relatively large island: It's 35km from Naxos to Apollonas.

HORA

Hora, on the west coast, is the island's port and capital. It's a large town, divided into two historic neighbourhoods – Bourgos, where the Greeks lived, and Kastro, on the hill above, where the Venetian Catholics lived.

A causeway to the north of the port leads to the Palatia Islet and the unfinished **Temple of Apollo**, Naxos' most famous landmark. Legend has it that when İstanbul is returned to Greece, the temple door will miraculously appear.

There are some good swimming areas along the waterfront promenade below the temple. The town's northern shore, called Grotta – nicknamed Grotty by some tourists – is not good for swimming as it's very exposed, rocky and riddled with sea urchins. South-west of the town is the sandy beach of Agios Georgios.

Orientation

The ferry quay is at the northern end of the waterfront, with the bus terminal in front. The busy waterfront is lined with cafes and restaurants and is the focus of most of the action. Behind the waterfront, a warren of little laneways and steps leads up to the Kastro.

Information

Information booths on the quay give out information about hotels and domatia. The privately owned Naxos Tourist Information Centre (NTIC; ☎ 2285 025 201, emergency ☎ 2285 024 525, fax 2285 025 200, e apollon-hotel@naxos-island.com), opposite the quay, provides in-depth advice on accommodation, excursions and rental cars; luggage storage is available (€1.50). Note that the NTIC does not sell ferry tickets.

Zas Travel (☎ 2285 023 330, fax 2285 023 419) and Naxos Tours (☎ 2285 022 095, 2285 023 043, e naxostours@naxos-island.com) are both helpful travel agencies that sell boat tickets and organise accommodation, tours and rental cars.

There are at least three ATMs on the waterfront. The OTE is 150m further south. For the post office, continue past the OTE, cross Papavasiliou and take the left branch where the road forks. Internet access is available from Matrix Cyber Café (☎/fax 25 627, e enquiries@matrixnaxos.com, W www.matrixnaxos.com) and Zoom (☎ 2285 023 675) on the waterfront.

The police are south-east of Plateia Protodikiou (☎ 2285 022 100). The port police (☎ 2285 023 300) are in the town hall, south of the quay.

The island is endowed with many springs; look for public taps and drinking fountains where you can refill your water bottle.

Things to See & Do

After leaving the waterfront, turn into the winding backstreets of Bourgos. The most alluring part of Hora is the residential **Kastro**, with winding alleyways and whitewashed houses. Marco Sanudo made the town the capital of his duchy in 1207, and there are some handsome Venetian dwellings, many with well-kept gardens and the insignia of their original residents. Take a stroll around the Kastro during siesta to experience its hushed, medieval atmosphere.

The **archaeological museum** (☎ 2285 022 725, admission €3; open 8.30am-3pm Tues-Sun) is in the Kastro, housed in a former school where Kate Nikos Kazantzakis was briefly a pupil. The contents include Hellenistic and Roman terracotta figurines. There are also, more interestingly, some early Cycladic figurines.

Close by, the crumbling **Della Rocca-Barozzi Venetian Museum** (☎ 2285 022 387; open 10am-3pm & 7pm-10pm daily; multilingual guided tours €4.40/1.50 adult/student, Kastro tours €10.30/5.90), is within the Kastro ramparts by the north-west gate. It was, until recently, still a residence; a visit is a brief, voyeuristic journey back in time. Sunset concerts are held here several times a week.

The Roman Catholic **cathedral** (open 6.30pm daily), also in the Kastro, is worth visiting (tours at 6pm) as well. The **Naxos Cultural Centre** nearby has exhibitions over summer.

Organised Tours

NTIC offers day tours of the island by bus (€17.60) or caique (€38, including barbecue). One-day walking tours (€43.50 for two people) are offered three times weekly.

Cruises run to different destinations daily run from Agia Anna. Cruises head either to Iraklia and Koufonisia, Shinousa and Koufonisia, or Antiparos; book at travel agents.

CYCLADES

CYCLADES

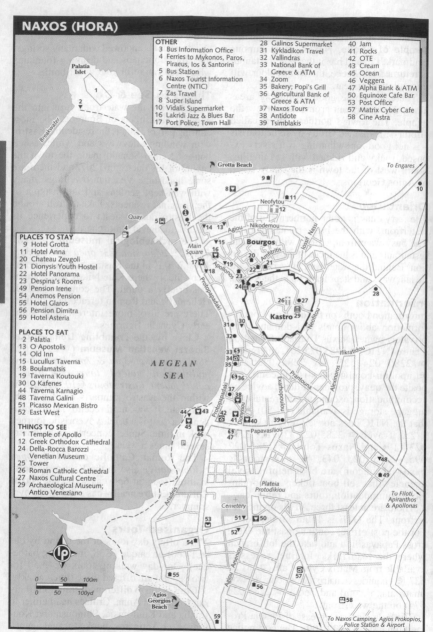

NAXOS (HORA)

OTHER
3 Bus Information Office
4 Ferries to Mykonos, Paros, Piraeus, Ios & Santorini
5 Bus Station
6 Naxos Tourist Information Centre (NTIC)
7 Zas Travel
8 Super Island
10 Vidalis Supermarket
16 Lakridi Jazz & Blues Bar
17 Port Police; Town Hall

28 Galinos Supermarket
31 Kykladikon Travel
32 Vallindras
33 National Bank of Greece & ATM
34 Zoom
35 Bakery; Popi's Grill
36 Agricultural Bank of Greece & ATM
37 Naxos Tours
38 Antidote
39 Tsimblakis

40 Jam
41 Rocks
42 OTE
43 Cream
45 Ocean
46 Veggera
47 Alpha Bank & ATM
50 Equinoxe Cafe Bar
53 Post Office
57 Matrix Cyber Cafe
58 Cine Astra

PLACES TO STAY
9 Hotel Grotta
11 Hotel Anna
20 Chateau Zevgoli
21 Dionysis Youth Hostel
22 Hotel Panorama
23 Despina's Rooms
49 Pension Irene
54 Anemos Pension
55 Hotel Glaros
56 Pension Dimitra
59 Hotel Asteria

PLACES TO EAT
2 Palatia
13 O Apostolis
14 Old Inn
15 Lucullus Taverna
18 Boulamatsis
19 Taverna Koutouki
30 O Kafenes
44 Taverna Karnagio
48 Taverna Galini
51 Picasso Mexican Bistro
52 East West

THINGS TO SEE
1 Temple of Apollo
12 Greek Orthodox Cathedral
24 Della-Rocca Barozzi Venetian Museum
25 Tower
26 Roman Catholic Cathedral
27 Naxos Cultural Centre
29 Archaeological Museum; Antico Veneziano

Palatia Islet

Breakwater

Grotta Beach

To Engares

Quay

Neofytou

Agiou Nikodemou

Bourgos

Iosif Nassi

Main Square

Amtritris

Apollonos

Protopapadaki

Kastro

Neofitou

Ifikratidou

AEGEAN SEA

Prantouna

Exathropoulou

Alexinoros

Protopapadaki

Dionysou

Papavasiliou

Aradus

Plateia Protodikiou

Cemetery

Agiou Argeniou

To Filoti, Apiranthos & Apollonas

Agios Georgios Beach

To Naxos Camping, Agios Prokopios, Police Station & Airport

0   50   100m
0   50   100yd

Small-group mountain-biking tours for €5.90 per person are also on offer; contact *Iain* (☎ 2285 024 641, **e** *eastwest@naxos island.com*), or drop into the East West restaurant.

Places to Stay – Budget
There are several camping grounds near Hora. All have good facilities and some offer walking tours. Minibuses meet the ferries.

Naxos Camping (☎ 2285 023 500) €4.65 per person. This place is 1km south of Agios Georgios Beach and has a swimming pool.

Camping Maragas (☎/fax 2285 024 552) €4.65 per person. This site is at Agia Anna Beach. *Plaka Camping* (☎ 2285 042 700, fax 2285 042 701) €4.65 per person. This site is 6km from town at Plaka Beach.

Dionysos Youth Hostel (☎ 2285 022 331) Dorm beds €5.90, singles/doubles €14.70/17.60. Open year-round. This is a good place to meet other travellers, and has dorm beds and simply furnished rooms. The hostel is signposted from Agiou Nikodemou, Bourgos' main street.

Many domatia owners meet ferries. *Despina's Rooms* (☎ 2285 022 356) Singles/doubles from €23.20/34.90. This 400-year-old family home is on the edge of the Kastro, nearby Chateau Zevgoli. The views here are impressive and rooms are comfortable.

Pension Dimitra (☎ 2285 024 922) Doubles/triples €30.20/49. This pension is right on Agios Georgios Beach; rooms have a balcony.

Pension Irene (☎ 2285 023 169, **e** *irenepension@hotmail.com*) Doubles around €29. This pension is south-east of the town centre and has cooking facilities. *Hotel Anna* (☎ 2285 025 213) Singles/ doubles €29/34.90, triples €43.50 with kitchenette. This is a nice place near the Orthodox cathedral.

Anemos Pension (☎ 2285 025 098) Doubles €40.60. This pension is near the post office.

Hotel Panorama (☎/fax 2285 024 404) Doubles €46.60. This hotel near the Kastro has a roof garden with superb views; rooms are lovely and quiet.

Places to Stay – Mid-Range
Hotel Grotta (☎ 2285 022 215, fax 2285 022 000, **e** *grotta@naxos-island.com*) Singles/doubles €49/61. This friendly hotel has splendid sea views from its dining room (though only a limited number of rooms have views).

Chateau Zevgoli (☎ 2285 026 123, fax 2285 025 200) Doubles €46.60-72.50. In Bourgos, Zevgoli has traditionally furnished rooms.

Hotel Argo (☎ 2285 025 330, fax 2285 024 910) Singles/doubles with air-con €38/52.50. This hotel is on Agios Georgios Beach and rooms all have balcony with either sea or mountain view, TV and kitchenette.

Hotel Glaros (☎ 2285 023 101, fax 2285 024 877) Singles/doubles with breakfast €43.50/56.50. Rooms here have a sea view.

Hotel Asteria (☎ 2285 023 002, fax 2285 022 334) Singles/doubles €46.40/75.40. Down by the beach at Agios Georgios and run by friendly staff, Asteria a good mid-range option.

Places to Eat
Naxos seems to be overflowing with good restaurants, popular local favourites include *Taverna Koutouki*, *Boulamatsis*, *Popi's Grill* (the best place for souvlaki), and *Taverna Galini*.

O Apostolis (☎ 2285 026 777) Dishes €0.90-20.50. Apostolis is a great place for mezedes, fresh fish and grilled octopus (a local speciality); Follow the path from the Old Inn, past Arali and turn right.

The Old Inn (☎ 2285 026 093) Dishes €3.50-11. The Old Inn has German fare with the occasional Greek influence. On offer are dishes, such as home-made sausages with beer sauce, potatoes and salad.

Lucullus Taverna (☎ 2285 022 569) Dishes €1.70-11.30. Lucullus is one of the oldest tavernas in Naxos, operating since 1905, and has a relaxed dining area cloaked in grape vines.

Taverna Karnagio (☎ 2285 023 057) Dishes €1.70-5.80, seafood by the kilo. Owned by an eccentric fisherman, Karnagio has limited, but excellent, choices on offer.

Phone numbers listed incorporate changes due in Oct 2002; see p55

CYCLADES

Palatia (☎ 2285 026 588) Dishes €1.50-8.80, seafood by the kilo. At the end of the promenade, Palatia is a lovely spot with tables right on the water's edge. It serves light meals and seafood.

Picasso Mexican Bistro (☎ 2285 025 408) Mains €3.50-9.30. Open 7pm-midnight. Arrive early and nab a table – Picasso and its *burritos*, *fajitas* and *quesadillas* are very popular.

East West (☎ 2285 024 641, off Arseniou) Mains €5.60-9.90. If you're hankering for Chinese, Indian or Thai favourites, head to East West. It's not as good as the real thing – but it's still good.

Immediately adjacent to Zoom bookshop is the town's best *bakery*. The cheapest *supermarkets* are Galinos and Vidalis, both a little way out of town.

Naxian specialities include *kefalotyri* (hard cheese), honey, *kitron* (a liqueur made from the leaves of the citron tree), *raki*, ouzo, and fine white wine. Head to *Tsimblakis* on Papavasiliou, a fascinating, cavernous old place selling local produce.

Entertainment

Sunset Concerts Evening concerts, featuring traditional instruments, are held several times weekly in the outdoor grounds of the *Venetian Museum* (☎ 2285 022 387).

Bars Arseniou St, nearby Picasso, is buzzing early in the evening. *Equinoxe Cafe Bar* (☎ 2285 025 839) is a fine place to take in all the energy and atmosphere of the street. It plays a mix of Spanish, Mojo, disco and Latino grooves.

One block back from the waterfront, *Rocks* is a popular late-night bar, while *Jam* is a small, dark low-key place that plays rock and assorted odd-bod sounds.

Antidote has at least 55 different types of beer from around the world, while *Lakridi Jazz & Blues Bar*, on the way to the Kastro, is a nice, laid-back little place.

Nightclubs For clubbing, head to *Cream*, *Ocean* and *Veggera Bar* (☎ 2285 023 567), all at the end of the waterfront near the OTE. Expect to hear a mix of House, techno

and electronica. On Saturday night, Veggera has a fun '70s- and '80s-inspired night.

Super Island, right on the waterfront, at Grotta Beach, is a huge dance space and *the* late-night venue.

Cinemas *Cine Astra* (☎ 2285 025 381) Admission €5.90. Sessions 9pm & 11pm. About a five-minute walk from Plateia Protodikiou, Cine Astra shows new release mainstream films and has a bar.

Shopping

At *Vallindras* (☎ 2285 022 227) on the waterfront, you can find kitron liqueur in beautiful French and Italian bottles, as well as ouzo.

In the streets heading up to the Kastro you can find beautiful embroidery and hand-made silver jewellery.

Antico Veneziano, an upmarket antique store and gallery, in a restored home in the Kastro, makes for a fascinating visit.

AROUND NAXOS
Beaches

Agios Georgios is just a typical town beach, but you can windsurf here and the water is so shallow that it seems you could wade to Paros, visible in the distance (the beach becomes so crowded that you may develop an uncontrollable desire to do so).

Flisvos Sport Club (☎/fax 2285 024 308, ✉ flisvos@otenet.gr) holds a free windsurfing trial lesson every Saturday at 4pm. The club also rents out catamarans and mountain bikes.

The next beach south is **Agios Prokopios**, a sheltered bay. This is followed by **Agia Anna**, a lovely long arc of sand. Sandy beaches continue down as far as **Pyrgaki**. There are *domatia* and *tavernas* aplenty along this stretch, and any of these beaches would make a good spot to stop for a few days. Other worthy beaches are **Plaka**, **Aliko**, **Mikri Vigla** and **Kastraki**. **Abram**, north of Hora, is also a nice spot.

Tragaea Τραγαία

The lovely Tragaea region is a vast plain of olive groves and unspoilt villages harbouring

Glory Days of the Citron

The citron *(Citrus medica)* looks like a very large, lumpy lemon. It has a thick rind and an interior yielding little juice. This seemingly useless fruit was introduced to the Mediterranean area in about 300 BC, probably by Alexander the Great, and up until the Christian era it was the only citrus fruit cultivated in Europe. In antiquity the citron was known for its medicinal qualities and was also a symbol of fertility and affluence. The ancient Greeks called it the 'median' apple (from Media, the ancient Greek name for Persia).

Citron trees are fussy about where they'll grow – they need abundant water and do not tolerate any wind or cold – but they have been happy on Naxos for centuries. Although the fruit is barely edible in its raw state, the Naxians discovered that the rind becomes quite exquisite when preserved in syrup. They also put the aromatic leaves to good use by creating *kitroraki*, a raki distilled from grape skins and citron leaves. By the late-19th century the preserved fruit and a sweet version of kitroraki, known as *kitron*, had cult followings outside Greece and were popular exports to Russia, Austria, France and the USA. Kitron was so much in demand that it became the mainstay of the island's economy and, by the early 20th century, Naxos was carpeted with citron orchards.

Alas, kitron went out of vogue after WWII; even the islanders abandoned it, seduced by the invasion of exotic alcohols from the outside world. In the 1960s most citron trees were uprooted to make way for more useful, more profitable crops.

This might seem like a sad story but fear not, the citron is on the rise. On Naxos, Vallindras distillery in Halki still distils citron the old-fashioned way, using leaves collected from the orchards in the autumn and winter. The harvesting of leaves is an arduous, time-consuming task, due to the trees' thorns, and if too many leaves are taken the tree can be destroyed. The leaves are laid out in a dry room, dampened with water and then placed with alcohol and water in a boiler fuelled by olive wood. The distillate is added to water and sugar, and citron is born.

These days approximately 13,000 to 15,000L of kitron are produced each year at Vallindras. Still, this is nowhere near enough to meet current demand, and nothing can be done about this until more citron trees are planted. It is nearly impossible to get hold of kitron outside Greece, so make sure you track some down while visiting its island home. It comes in three strengths and degrees of sweetness: The green is the traditional Naxian liqueur and has the most sugar and least alcohol; the yellow has little sugar, more aroma and more alcohol; the white falls somewhere in between and resembles Cointreau. Kitron is very good after dinner, especially after fish.

If you want to see citron trees in action, look for orchards around Hora and in Engares, Melanes, Halki and Apollonas.

numerous little Byzantine churches. **Filoti**, on the slopes of Mt Zeus, is the region's largest village. On the outskirts of the village (coming from Hora), an asphalt road leads off right into the heart of the Tragaea. This road brings you to the isolated hamlets of **Damarionas** and **Damalas**.

From Filoti, you can also reach the **Cave of Zeus**. From the end of the signposted road, a path leads past a small spring and a handful of goats. Follow the markers to the cave – a steep and strenuous half-hour walk. The cave is best explored with a torch. The path is also an excellent spot to view the

peak of Mt Zeus; a stark and strikingly barren rocky peak.

The picturesque village of **Halki** has several tower houses built by aristocratic families as refuges and lookouts in the days of pirate raids and feuds between the islanders and the Venetians and Turks. The best preserved is the **Gratsia Pyrgos**; to reach it turn right at **Panagia Protothronis**, which is itself worth checking out for its fine frescoes. It is on the main road near the bus stop.

The **Vallindras distillery** (☎ 2285 031 220), housed in a lovely old building in the centre of Halki, offers kitron tastings and impromptu tours. A few steps away is *L' Olivier* (☎ 2285 032 829), a ceramic studio and craft gallery that specialises in detailed crockery ceramics focused around that most sacred of plants, the olive tree. Olive products from candles to oil are also on sale.

Agii Apostoli (Holy Apostles) church in Metohi is famous for its odd triple-storey architecture, while **Agios Mamas**, near Potamia, is known for its early 'cross in a square' layout. The **Panagia Drosiani**, at **Moni** north of Halki, is one of the oldest and most important churches in the Balkans. Successive layers of frescoes have been uncovered, some dating back to the 7th century. If it's locked, seek out the priest's wife and ask for the key.

South-west of the Tragaea, near **Sangri**, an impressive **Temple to Demeter** (also known as Dimitra's Temple) has been restored. The small church next to the temple was originally built from remnants of the temple and was recently demolished and rebuilt so that the temple material could be salvaged. Signs point the way from Sangri.

Melanes Μέλανες

Near the hillside villages of Melanes and Mili, there is a 2m-high, unfinished 6th-century BC **kouros** (male statue), abandoned in a quarry that is now encircled by orchards. The Kondylis family, who own the land, are the official guardians.

Next to the site is a little *cafe* of sorts where an old lady serves Greek coffee, wine, omelettes and salads. Another, less famous, kouros was found nearby a few years ago; ask at the cafe for directions.

From Melanes you can walk down to **Kato Potamia**, **Mesi Potamia** and **Ano Potamia**, where there are more orchards and lovely tavernas. From there, it's not far to Halki, where you can catch the bus back to town.

Places to Eat *Taverna Xenakis* (☎ 2285 062 374) Dishes €1.50-5.50. In Melanes, Xenakis has delicious rabbit and free-range chicken; if you order an hour in advance, you will be served a feast.

Yanni's in Halki in the main square, serves perfect village salads (€4.40) with lashings of *myzithra*, the local cheese; one salad is enough for two.

Pirgos Himarrou Πύργος Χειμάρρου

South of Filoti, in the island's remote southeast, the Pirgos Himarrou is a well preserved cylindrical marble tower dating from Hellenistic times. It is three storeys high with an internal spiral staircase. One theory holds that it was a lookout post used to warn of approaching pirates, but the position of the tower in a place with limited views discounts this. It was more likely a fortified house on a prosperous farmstead – the marble base of a large olive or wine press lies nearby.

After checking out the tower, continue south for a swim at **Kalandos Bay**. Take food and water as there are no shops or tavernas.

Apiranthos Απείρανθος

Apiranthos is a handsome village of stone houses and marble-paved streets. Its inhabitants are descendants of refugees who fled Crete to escape Turkish repression. The village is known for its communist tendencies – its most famous son is Manolis Glezos, the resistance fighter who during WWII replaced the Nazi flag atop the Acropolis with the Greek one. He later became the parliamentary representative for the Cyclades.

Right of the village's main thoroughfare (coming from the Hora-Apollonas road) is a **museum of natural history** *(open 8.30am-3pm Tues-Sun)*. Just before the museum a path on your left leads to the centre of town, the **geology museum** *(open 8.30am-3pm Tues-Sun)* and the **archaeology museum** *(admission €3; open 8.30am-3pm Tues-Sun)*. The museums are sometimes open later in summer.

Just before the beautiful main square dominated by a huge plane tree is *Lefteris* where you can eat in the garden overlooking the valley. It has a selection of delicious home-made sweets and baklava. Apiranthos has no accommodation.

Moutsouna Μουτσούνα

The road from Apiranthos to Moutsouna winds through spectacular mountain scenery.

Formerly a busy port shipping the emery mined in the region, Moutsouna is now something of a ghost town. It feels peaceful rather than spooky and there are some nice beaches with superbly clear water. There are a few pensions and *tavernas* here.

Apollonas Απολλωνας

Apollonas, on the north coast, was once a tranquil fishing village, but is now a popular resort. It has a small sandy beach and a larger pebble one.

Hordes of day-trippers come to see the gargantuan 7th century BC **kouros**, which lies in an ancient quarry a short walk from the village. The largest of three on the island (the other two are in the Melanes region), it is signposted to the left as you approach Apollonas on the main inland road from Hora. This 10.5m statue was apparently abandoned unfinished because it cracked. Apollonas has several *domatia* and *tavernas*.

The inland route from Hora to Apollonas winds through spectacular mountains – a worthwhile trip. With your own transport you can return to Hora via the west-coast road, passing through wild and sparsely populated country with awe-inspiring sea views. Several tracks branch down to secluded beaches.

Little Cyclades
Μικρές Κυκλάδες

The chain of small islands between Naxos and Amorgos is variously called the Little Cyclades, Minor Islands, Back Islands and Lesser Islands. Only four – Donousa, Koufonisia (comprising Ano Koufonisia and Kato Koufonisia), Iraklia and Shinousa – have permanent populations.

All were densely populated in antiquity, as is evident from the large number of graves found. In the Middle Ages, the islands were uninhabited except by pirates and goats. After independence, intrepid souls from Naxos and Amorgos began to reinhabit them, and now each island has a small population. Until recently, their only visitors were Greeks returning to their roots. These days they receive a few tourists, mostly backpackers looking for splendid beaches and a laid-back lifestyle.

Donousa is the northernmost of the group and farthest from Naxos. The others are clustered near the south-east coast of Naxos. Each has a public telephone and post agency. Money can usually be changed at the general store or post agency, but rates are lousy – bring cash with you .

Getting To/From the Little Cyclades

Links with the Little Cyclades are regular but tenuous, so make sure you have plenty of time before embarking on a visit – these islands do not make a convenient last stop a few days before you're due to fly home!

At least a few times a week the Fast Boat *Express Skopelitis* provides a lifeline service between Naxos and Amorgos via the Little Cyclades (see the Naxos and Amorgos sections for details), but it's small, extremely slow, and susceptible to bad weather (make sure you're wearing warm, wet-weather gear on board – expect to get wet!). In high season it operates several routes, with regular runs from Amorgos to Koufonisia (one hour, €4.40), Shinousa (1½ hours, €5.90) Iraklia and Naxos, returning by the same route, and a run from Amorgos to Donousa. There is also one weekly ferry from Donousa to Syros (3½ hours, €8.20) and Tinos (2½ hours, €10.30); two weekly to Mykonos (two hours, €8.80) and Paros (two to four hours, €7); one weekly catamaran from Shinousa to Tinos (three hours, €14) and Mykonos (2½ hours, €13). Two weekly ferries go to Paros (four hours, €6.40). One daily ferry goes to Naxos (1¾ to five hours, €4.80), Iraklia and Naxos, returning by the same route; and Naxos to Paros (Piso Livadi) to Iraklia, Shinousa, Koufonisia, Donousa and Amorgos.

Once a week the Fast Boat *Express Apollon* sails from Piraeus to each of the Little Cyclades via Naxos, continuing to Amorgos. A few other large ferries call at the islands in high season, often at ungodly hours.

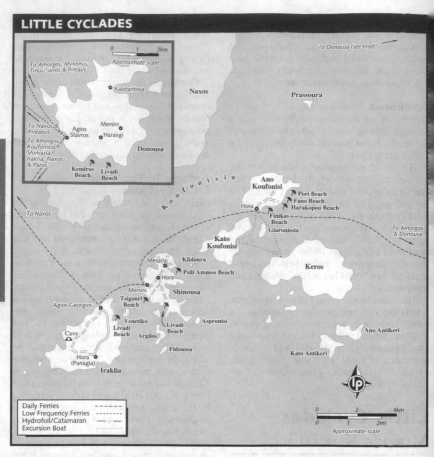

LITTLE CYCLADES

Map labels:

To Donousa (see inset)

0   1   2km
Approximate scale

To Amorgos, Mykonos, Tinos, Syros & Pireaus

Kalotaritissa

Naxos

Prassoura

To Naxos & Pireaeus

Agios Stavros   Mersini

Haravgi

Donousa

To Amorgos, Koufonisia, Shinousa, Iraklia, Naxos & Paros

Kendros Beach   Livadi Beach

K o u f o n i s i a

Ano Koufonisi

Pori Beach
Fano Beach
Harakopou Beach

Hora
Finikas Beach
Glaronissia

To Naxos

Kato Koufonisi

Keros

To Amorgos & Donousa

Mesaria   Klidoura
Hora   Psili Ammos Beach

Shinousa

Mersini   Tsigouri Beach

Agios Georgios

Venetiko   Livadi Beach
Cave   Argilos   Livadi Beach

Aspronisi

Ano Antikeri

Hora (Panagia)   Fidoussa

Iraklia

Kato Antikeri

Daily Ferries
Low Frequency Ferries
Hydrofoil/Catamaran
Excursion Boat

0   2   4km
0   2mi
Approximate scale

Because of its northerly position, it is sometimes easier to get to Donousa from Mykonos than from Naxos.

IRAKLIA Ηρακλεια
postcode 843 00 • pop 110

This rather barren island has a couple of tiny villages, a nice beach and not much else, save a small clique of Germans who return each year. The island's only sight as such is a **cave** with fine stalactites. Tourism is increasing, but amenities (including rooms) are few. The port and main village is **Agios Georgios**. It's very quiet and not

particularly scenic, although the deep cove-like harbour is rather pretty. The way into town is to the right, around the port beach, and then left up the hill. From here the town's two main roads fork around a cactus-filled ravine.

The right fork leads to Melissa, the general store that sells ferry tickets. Melissa also has a cardphone, serves as the island's post office and has domatia. The left fork leads past the second minimarket (which is also Perigiali restaurant) and more domatia. You can exchange money at Melissa and at Maistrali bar-cafe.

A new sealed road leads off to the left (as you face inland from the harbour). This runs to **Livadi** – the island's nicest beach, and the stomping ground of a picturesque herd of goats. Farther on is the tiny village of **Hora**, also known as Panagia.

Places to Stay & Eat
All domatia and tavernas are in Agios Georgios, although a few spring up on the beach at Livadi in high season. Domatia owners make the boats, but the shortage of rooms makes it a sellers' market – take whatever you can get and don't bother looking for bargains. In high season doubles go for around €29. If possible, call ahead.

The most central rooms are near the port and include: *Melissa* (☎ 2285 071 539, fax 2285 071 561) with doubles from €43.50; *Anthi & Angelo's* (☎ 2285 071 486) with doubles for €34.90; and *Manolis* (☎ 2285 071 569, fax 071 561) which has doubles for €34.90 (open high season only).

Alexandra (☎ 2285 071 482, fax 2285 071 545) Doubles €34.90. Up on the windy hill on the way to Livadi, rooms here have nice patios and are just a stone's throw from the beach.

Anna's Place (☎/fax 2285 071 145) Doubles €34.90. This swish place also has deluxe apartments with a view.

Marietta (☎ 2285 071 252) Doubles €29. Marietta has nice rooms right on the beach at Livadi.

There are three tavernas in Agios Georgios, all serving fresh fish and the usual fare. *Perigiali*, a popular place, has a large marble table encircling an old pine tree. *O Pevkos*, also known as Dimitri's, is more traditional and shaded by an even larger pine. You'll be led into the kitchen to choose your meal; for breakfast try the yogurt served with the local thyme honey.

Maistrali (☎ 2285 071 807), opposite Pevkos, is the local cafe-bar; it also sells ferry tickets and has *rooms*.

SHINOUSA Σχοινοσα
postcode 843 00 • pop 120
Shinousa (skih-**noo**-sah) is a little gem of an island with a lively **hora** and smiling residents. The hora (also known as Panagia) has sweeping views of the sea and neighbouring islands on all sides, and nestles inconspicuously into the rolling golden landscape. Although a recent spate of building on the outskirts of the hora and by the beaches has taken place, there's still a very pastoral feeling about the island, which has its share of happy cows, chickens, donkeys and goats.

Ferries pull in at the harbour in **Mersini**, home to the island's fishing boats. The hora is 1km uphill, so try to get a lift with one of the locals offering rooms. Dirt tracks lead from the hora to numerous beaches around the coast; take food and water, because, with the exception of **Tsigouri**, there are no shops or tavernas at the beaches.

There's a public telephone in the main square and a couple of general stores sell stamps. The first among these sells ferry tickets. Tickets are also sold at the port a few minutes before boats arrive. There is a travel agency at Grispos Tsigouri Beach Villas in Tsigouri, which has ferry information and tickets.

Places to Stay
There are a few rooms down at Mersini, but if you want to see the rest of the island you're much better off staying in the hora.

Kyra Pothiti (☎ 2285 071 184) Doubles €29. In the centre of the village on the main street, Pothiti has nice, cosy rooms with balcony.

Anna Domatia (☎ 2285 071 161, fax 2285 071 948) Singles/doubles €26.10/32. On the road to Mesaria, Anna's has good, clean rooms.

Hotel Sunset (☎ 2285 071 948, fax 2285 071 948) Singles/doubles €32/43.50. This is a brand new, comfortable but impersonal complex. It's run by the folk at Anna Domatia.

Grispos Tsigouri Beach Villas (☎ 2285 071 930, fax 2285 071 176, e grispos@ nax.forthnet.gr) Doubles with breakfast €55. This is a crazy family affair about 500m away from the hora, down by the beach at Tsigouri. It's close to the beach, but if you want to pop into the hora occasionally, you're faced with a long walk uphill.

Panorama (☎ *2285 071 160)* Doubles €38, with kitchen €43.50. By the beach at Livadi, Panorama is similarly isolated.

Places to Eat

You're unlikely to have any very uplifting culinary adventures on Shinousa, an island where you might want to do a bit of self-catering. Outside high season the only establishment open for lunch is *Kyra Pothiti*. All drinks and meals come with obligatory serves of home-made *myzithra*. Steer clear of the greasy-spoon *giouvetsi* (meat with macaroni) and stick to fish and baked vegetables. *Panorama* has good salads and charcoal-grilled fish, and *tavernas* at the port serve freshly caught fish and lobster. The *bakery* just past Anna Domatia on the road to Mesaria is a good place to have breakfast.

To Kentro Kafeneio is the most popular and nicest looking bar, but is pretty much a male-only domain; brave women may wish to transgress its boundaries.

Cafe-Pub Margarita, down the steps just around the corner, is the only other bar.

KOUFONISIA Κουφονήσια
postcode 843 00 • pop 284

Koufonisia is the only one of the Little Cyclades that's anywhere near the tourist trail, and it has a lot to offer. It's really two islands, Ano Koufonisi and Kato Koufonisi, but only the latter is permanently inhabited.

Despite being the smallest of the Little Cyclades, Koufonisia is the most densely populated, which adds quite a bit of life to its hora. Every family is involved with fishing – the island boasts the largest fishing fleet in Greece in proportion to its population. And because it's so attractive, it hasn't suffered from an exodus of young people to the mainland and the consequent ghost-town effect seen on many of the Cyclades; in fact, it's brimming with happy children and teenagers.

The beaches are picture-perfect swathes of golden sand lapped by crystal-clear turquoise waters; the locals are hospitable and friendly; and food and accommodation

options are far more plentiful and refined than on neighbouring islands.

A caique ride away, **Kato Koufonisi** has beautiful beaches and a lovely church. Archaeological digs on **Keros**, the large lump of rock that looms over Koufonisia to the south, have uncovered over 100 Early Cycladic figurines, including the famous harpist and flautist now on display in Athens' archaeological museum. There are no guides at the site.

Orientation & Information

Koufonisia's only settlement extends behind the ferry quay and around the pretty harbour filled with the island's fishing flotilla. The older part of town, the hora, is on the low hill behind the quay.

From the quay head right towards the town beach, and take the first road to the left. Continue to the crossroads, then turn left onto the village's main pedestrian thoroughfare, decorated with flower motifs.

Along here you'll find a small mini-market and an inconspicuous ticket agency (look for the dolphins painted above the door). Also here is the tiny OTE. The post office is on the first road to the left as you come from the ferry quay.

Koufonisia Tours (see Organised Tours later) sells ferry tickets and can organise accommodation on the island.

The town beach sees a few swimmers, but mostly serves as a football field (fishing nets are strung up on the goal posts) for the local kids. Cars and pedestrians heading to the south coast road also traverse it.

Beaches

Koufonisia is blessed with some outstanding beaches and a wild coastal landscape of low sand dunes punctuated by rocky coves and caves. The dunes are covered in wild flowers and hardy shrubs.

A walk along the south coast road is the nicest way to access the island's beaches. The road extends a couple of kilometres from the eastern end of the town beach to **Finikas**, **Harakopou** and **Fano** Beaches.

However, the best beaches and swimming places are farther along the path that follows the coast from Fano to the superb stretch of sand at **Pori**. A *cantina* operates in high season selling delicious cheese pies and cold drinks. Pori can also be reached by an inland road that heads east from the crossroads in the hora.

Organised Tours
Koufonisia Tours (☎ *2285 071 671, fax 2285 074 091, Villa Ostria*), can organise caique trips to Keros and Kato Koufonisi.

Places to Stay
Koufonisia Camping (☎/fax 2285 071 683) Camp sites €9.30 for 2. This site is by the beach at Harakopou; though there's not much shade, it's adequate.

Rooms Maria (☎ *2285 071 778*) Apartments €34.90. At the western end of the village, Maria's has cute two-person apartments overlooking the small fishing harbour. To get there, walk along the main pedestrian street and take the first left after Scholeio bar.

Rooms to Let Akrogiali (☎ *2285 071 685*) Doubles €35.70. Akrogiali has nice rooms with sea views at the eastern end of the beach.

Lefteris Rooms (☎/fax 2285 071 458) Doubles/triples/quads €30.20/34.90/46.60. These rooms are on the town beach.

Katerina's (☎ *2285 071 670*) Doubles €40.80. On the road leading from the port to the hora, Katerina's has nice clean doubles with balcony and shared kitchen.

Villa Ostria (☎/fax 2285 071 671) Doubles with/without breakfast €59/52.50. This is a cosy little hotel with very comfortable rooms with telephone and veranda. To get there, walk along the town beach and take the first left.

Keros Hotel (☎ *2285 071 600, fax 2285 071 601*) Doubles €59-69.60. This hotel, near the post office, has nice rooms.

Hotel Finikas (☎ *2285 071 368, fax 2285 071 744*) Doubles €23.20-43.50. On the beach at Finikas, this hotel has both simple and swish rooms; all rooms have a balcony.

Places to Eat
Giorgos At the eastern end of the waterfront on the road to the beaches, Giorgos has excellent fish and good wines from all over Greece.

Everything at *Captain Nikolas* is delicious, but the grilled fresh fish, is hard to beat. The restaurant looks out over the small harbour at the western end of the village; to get there, follow the main pedestrian street (past signage for another unrelated Captain Nikolas taverna) to the end and turn left. *Nikitouri*, past the Keros Hotel, also has good fish.

Below the rooms of the same name *Lefteris* has fine, reasonably priced Greek standards and is one of the few places open for lunch.

Next to the windmills above the quay, *Fanari* has good wood-fired pizzas, *pastitsio* and gyros. *Scholeio* is a cosy little bar and creperie occupying an old schoolhouse at the far end of the main pedestrian street.

Out of town, there's a *taverna* by the beach at Finikas and an excellent fish taverna, *Taverna Giannis* (☎ *2285 074 074*) on Kato Koufonisi.

DONOUSA Δονούσα
postcode 843 00 • pop 110
Donousa is the least accessible of the Little Cyclades because it's too far north to be a convenient stop for ferries en route to more popular islands. The main attraction here, as on Iraklia, is that there is nothing much to do except lie on the beach.

Agios Stavros is the main settlement and the island's port. It has a reasonably nice beach, which also serves as a thoroughfare for vehicles and foot traffic. Behind the beach there are lush vegetable gardens and vineyards.

Kendros, over the hill to the west, is a sandy and secluded beach. **Livadi**, the next beach along, sees even fewer visitors. As on many of the other small islands, a frenzy of road construction is currently under way on Donousa, making many of the walks, which used to be so pleasurable, a lot less attractive.

There is one public telephone, up the hill two streets back from the waterfront; look for the large satellite dish above the OTE shack. Stamps are sold at the minimarket on the street running behind the beach.

CYCLADES

There is a ticket agency, Roussos Travel (☎ 2285 051 648, fax 2285 051 649) on the waterfront.

Places to Stay & Eat
Camping is tolerated at Kendros, although there are no facilities and you'll need to hike into town for food and water.

Spiros Skopelitis Rooms (☎ 2285 051 586) Doubles €32. Halfway along the town beach, are these nice bungalows, decorated with oriental rugs, set in a shady garden.

Nikitas Markoulis Rooms Doubles around €32. These rooms can be found near the *kafeneio*.

To Ilio Vasilema (☎ 2285 051 570) Doubles €32. At the far end of the town beach, Ilio also has reasonable *rooms*; all have bathrooms and some have a kitchen.

Aposperitis, next to Spiros Skopelitis, serves the usual fare, as does *To Ilio Vasilema*.

The hub of village life is *Kafeneio To Kyma* by the quay. Everyone seems to pass through here at least once a day and in the evenings it gets rather lively.

Amorgos Αμοργος

postcode 840 08 • pop 1630
Elongated Amorgos (ah-mor-**goss**) is the most easterly Cycladic island. With rugged mountains and an extraordinary monastery clinging to a cliff, Amorgos is an enticing island for those wishing to venture off the well-worn Mykonos-Paros-Santorini route. It also offers excellent walking.

Amorgos has two ports, Katapola and Aegiali; boats from Naxos usually stop at Katapola first. The beautiful, unspoilt capital, Hora (also known as Amorgos), is up high, north-east of Katapola.

Getting To/From Amorgos
Ferry Most ferries stop at both Katapola and Aegiali, but check if this is the case with your ferry. There are daily boats to Naxos (two to 5¾ hours, €7), Koufonisia (one hour, €4.40), Shinousa (1½ hours, €5.90), Iraklia (two hours, €6.10) and

Paros (three hours, €8.40), but some of these go to the resort of Piso Livadi (three to 4½ hours, €8) rather than Parikia, and Piraeus (10 hours, €15.40).

Ferries also serve Mykonos (2½ hours, €9.30, four weekly), Donousa (30 minutes, €4.65, four weekly), Astypalea (2½ hours, €8.40, two weekly) and Syros (4½ to 9½ hours, €10.50, four weekly). There is a twice-weekly boat to Rafina (10¾ hours, €14.70) via Tinos and Andros.

Fast Boat & Catamaran Weekly services run from Katapola to Rafina (five hours, €29.05), Paros (1½ to 2½ hours, €16.90), Mykonos (2¼ to four hours, €18.60), Ios (1½ hours, €12.80), Tinos (2¾ hours, €18.60) and Andros (3½ to 6¼ hours, €27.50). Several services will also stop at Aegiali.

Getting Around Amorgos
Regular buses go from Katapola to Hora (15 minutes, €0.70), Moni Hozoviotissis (15 minutes, €0.70), Agia Anna Beach (20 minutes, €0.70) and less frequent services go to Aegiali (30 minutes, €1.30); however there are fewer services on weekends. There are also buses from Aegiali to the picturesque village of Langada. Schedules are posted on bus windscreens.

Cars and motorcycles are available for rent from Travel Agency N. Synodinos in Katapola and Aegialis Tours (☎ 2285 073 107, fax 2285 073 394, Ⓦ www .amorgos-aegialis.com) in Aegiali.

KATAPOLA Κατάπολα
Katapola, the principal port, is a pretty town occupying a large, dramatic bay in the most verdant part of the island. A smattering of remains from the ancient Cretan city of Minoa, as well as a Mycenaean cemetery, lie above the port. Amorgos has also yielded many Cycladic finds; the largest figurine in the National Archaeological Museum in Athens was found in the vicinity of Katapola.

Boats dock either in front of the central square or to the right (facing inland). The bus station is on the waterfront, near the square.

AMORGOS

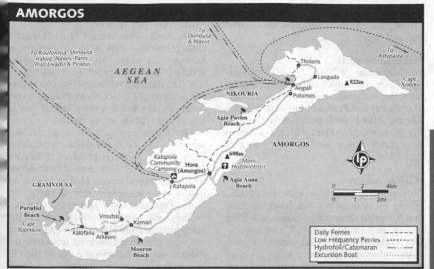

To Donousa & Naxos

To Koufonisia, Shinousa, Iraklia, Naxos, Paros (Piso Livadi) & Piraeus

AEGEAN SEA

To Astypalea

Tholaria

Langada

▲822m

Aegiali

Potamos

Cape Xodoto

NIKOURIA

Agia Pavlos Beach

AMORGOS

Katapola Community Camping

Hora (Amorgos)

▲698m

Moni Hozoviotissis

Katapola

Agia Anna Beach

GRAMVOUSA

Paradisi Beach

Cape Kalotasoi

Vroutsis

Kamari

Kalofana

Arkesini

Mouron Beach

Daily Ferries
Low Frequency Ferries
Hydrofoil/Catamaran
Excursion Boat

0   2   4km
0   1   2mi

CYCLADES

Travel Agency N. Synodinos (☎ 2285 071 201, fax 2285 071 278, ℮ synodinos@nax.forthnet.gr) is very helpful (and is open year-round). Ferry tickets, money exchange and car rental are available.

The port police (☎ 2285 071 259) and regular police (☎ 2285 071 210) are on the central square. There is a post office on the square, and limited Internet access is available at Hotel Minoa. A bank (with ATM) is on the waterfront nearby the travel agency. There is a bookshop opposite Idiston cafe.

Places to Stay & Eat

Katapola Community Camping (☎ 2285 071 802) Adult/tent €3.70/2.30. This shady site is back from the northern end of the waterfront. It doesn't pick up from the ferry wharf. Turn left from the quay (as you face inland) and continue past the turn-off for the Hora. Turn right at the next paved road and walk about 100m.

Domatia owners usually meet ferries.

Pension Amorgos (☎ 2285 071 013, fax 2285 071 214) Singles/doubles €30.20/34.90. Rooms at this pension, on the waterfront near the square, are spotless.

Diosmarini (☎ 2285 071 636, ℮ diosmarini @yahoo.com) Doubles/triples €30.20/52, apartments €88. This new pension is tucked away to the left, up the steps behind the northern end of the harbour. Rooms are pleasant and most have balconies.

Villa Katapoliani (☎/fax 2285 071 064) Doubles/studios €49/59. Just before Panagia Katapoliani, this renovated Cycladic building has nice rooms, all with balcony and a view of the garden.

Hotel Minoa (☎ 2285 071 480, fax 2285 071 003) Doubles with breakfast €67.90. This C-class hotel on the square has comfortable double rooms with air-conditioning and telephone. It also has a reasonable taverna *Mythos*.

Vitsenzos (☎ 2285 071 518) Dishes €2.10-7.80, seafood by the kilo. At the northern end of the waterfront beyond Pension Maroussa, this cafe has good, reasonably priced daily specials. Traditional *Psaropoula*, nearby, is the best taverna for seafood, and *Mouragio* on the waterfront near the square, is also a good traditional place.

Idiston (☎ 2285 074 165) Dishes €0.80-5.80. Idiston, a smart little cafe in the laneway around the corner from Hotel Minoa, has classic Greek sweets, herbal teas and liqueurs.

Entertainment
The Moon Bar (☎ *2285 071 598*) This laid-back place with tables under a large tree by the water is the nicest place to have a drink; it's just beyond Pension Maroussa. Nearby *The Big Blue Pub*, named after the film *The Big Blue*, which was partly filmed in Amorgos, glows a neon blue at night and gets very busy.

HORA Αμοργος
This amazingly well-preserved Cycladic village is 400m above sea level, so high that it's often shrouded in clouds when the rest of the island is sunny. It's an impressive sight, all white and capped with a 13th-century kastro atop a large lump of rock. The village has some surprisingly sophisticated bars and cafes.

The bus stop is on a square at the edge of town. The post office is on the main square, reached by a pedestrian laneway from the bus stop. The OTE is in a new building on the main road near the high school.

The **archaeology museum** (*open 9am-1pm & 6pm-8.30pm Tues-Sun*) is on the main pedestrian thoroughfare, near Cafe Bar Zygol.

Places to Stay & Eat
There are no hotels, but domatia are available.

Rooms to Rent (☎ *2285 071 216*) Singles/doubles €17.40/23. This nice little domatia on the main pedestrian thoroughfare has good value rooms. By the main bus square, *Pension Ilias* (☎ *2285 071 277*) and *Pension Panorama* (☎ *2285 071 606*), both with doubles for €43.50, have views over the valley.

Kastanis Dishes €1.90-5.30. On the main pedestrian thoroughfare, Kastanis is a staunchly traditional place; try the chicken with peppers (€4.40).

Cafe Bar Zygol (☎ *2285 071 359*) Open 8am-3am daily. Zygol's rooftop terrace is a fine spot to take in the Hora.

MONI HOZOVIOTISSIS
Μονή Χωζοβιοτίσσιζ
A visit to the 11th-century Moni Hozoviotissis (*Open 8am-1pm & 5pm-7pm daily*) is unreservedly worthwhile, as much for the spectacular scenery as for the monastery itself. The dazzling white building clings precariously to a cliff face above the east coast. A few monks still live there and, if you're lucky, one will show you around.

The monastery contains a miraculous icon found in the sea below the monastery, having allegedly arrived unaided from Asia Minor, Cyprus or Jerusalem, depending on which legend you're told. Modest dress is required – long trousers for men, and long skirt or dress and covered shoulders for women.

The walk to the monastery down the steep hillside from Hora is breathtaking; an old stepped path winds down from near the radio tower (at the opposite end of the village to the bus station). There's also a bus; the monastery bus stop is at the Agia Anna road junction, about 500m uphill from the monastery itself.

AEGIALI Αιγιαλη
Aegiali is Amorgos' other port. The atmosphere is much more laid-back than Katapola – a leftover hippy vibe from the free camping days of the 70s is discernible – and there is a good beach stretching left of the quay.

Internet access is available at Amorgos Net Cafe, next to Aegialis Tours. Nautilus Travel Agent (☎ 2285 073 032) opposite Aegialis Tours sells ferry tickets and provides general tourist information.

Organised Tours
Aegialis Tours (see Getting Around earlier) Island tours €17.60. Departs 10am-4pm. Aegialis organises a bus outing around the island with stops at Agia Pavlos, Moni Hozoviotissis, Hora and Mouron. Afternoon donkey-riding expeditions cost €14.70 per hour.

Places to Stay
As in Katapola, domatia owners meet the ferries.

Aegialia Camping, a pleasant and shaded site, is on the road behind Lakki Village; go left from the port and follow the signs.

Rooms in the Garden (☎ 2285 073 315) Definitely worth investigating, these small bungalows, with verandahs, have a rural setting. They're at the far end of the beach; a path leads from the beach to the studios.

Rooms Irini (☎ 2285 073 237) Doubles €45. This pretty place is at the top of the steps after the terrace restaurants.

Lakki Village (☎ 2285 073 253, fax 2285 072 344) Singles/doubles €43.50/49; 2-person/4-person apartments €78.30/110. Right on the beach, Lakki has immaculate rooms and apartments. There are also luxury two-person apartments with air-con, view and traditional furniture for €75.40. The pension has a delightful garden, a taverna and a bar. Breakfast is included.

Pension Poseidon (☎ 2285 073 453, fax 2285 073 007) Singles/doubles/studios €30.20/46.50/52. At the base of the hill behind the waterfront, Poseidon has nice rooms, some with views. The studios have kitchens.

Grispos Hotel (☎ 2285 073 502, fax 2285 073 557) 2-person/4-person studios €52/82.50. This hotel, up a witheringly steep hill behind the waterfront, has spacious studios.

Aegialis Hotel (☎ 2285 073 393, fax 2285 073 395, e aegialis@hotmail.com) Singles/doubles €68.20/101.50. This hotel sits above two sandy beaches and is the classiest place around. It has a seawater pool, two bars and a restaurant.

Places to Eat & Drink
To Limani (☎ 2285 073 269) Dishes €1.50-5.80, seafood by the kilo. Expect good traditional fare prepared with home-grown produce at Limani, behind Aegialis Tours. Its walls also double as an exhibition space for local artists.

To Koralli Dishes €1.60-7.30. Up a flight of stairs beyond the cluster of cafes by the windmill, this fish taverna has tasty seafood *meze* platters.

Restaurant Lakki (☎ 2285 073 253) Dishes €2.35-8.80. Home-grown ingredients make all the difference here – the food

is simple yet fragrant and delicious. Interesting wines are also available.

Disco The Que (☎ 2285 073 212) The hippy vibe is alive and well at this sandy beachside cafe run by an alternative clique. The play list is eclectic, and any opportunity to celebrate the wax and wane of the moon in the form of a party is embraced.

AROUND AMORGOS
Pebbled **Agia Anna Beach**, on the east coast south of Moni Hozoviotissis, is the nearest decent beach to both Katapola and Hora. The setting is stunning, with a vista of rocky granite islets just offshore. It gets very busy in the high season, and there's a small cantina on the cliff top selling food and drinks.

Langada and **Tholaria** are the most picturesque of the villages inland from Aegiali.

Ios Ιος

postcode 840 01 • pop 2000

Ios – the apogee of sun, sea and sex – is the *enfant terrible* of the Greek islands. There's no denying that most visitors come to party hard, but for those who are looking for a more relaxing stay, the island also offers plenty to explore: beautiful beaches, a pretty capital and an interesting rocky, Mars-like landscape. Ios also has a tenuous claim to being Homer's burial place; his tomb is in the island's north.

Getting To/From Ios
Ferry There are at least four daily connections with Piraeus (seven hours, €16.30), Paros (2½ hours, €7.40) and Naxos (1¼ hours, €6.40). There are daily boats to Mykonos (four hours, €9.60) and Santorini (1¼ hours, €5.60), five weekly to Sikinos (30 minutes, €3.20) and Folegandros (1½ hours, €4.65), four weekly to Anafi (three hours, €6.10) and Syros (2¾ hours, €11).

There are weekly boats to Crete (six hours, €13.20), Kimolos (2½ hours, €5.90), Milos (3½ hours, €8.80), Sifnos (five hours, €7.80), Serifos (six hours, €8.80), Tinos (5½ hours, €9) and Kythnos (seven hours, €10.50).

CYCLADES

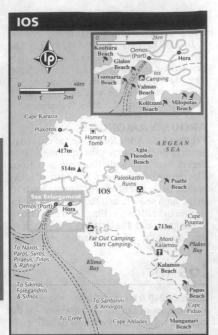

Fast Boat & Catamaran There are daily catamarans to Santorini (30 minutes, €9.60), Naxos (50 minutes, €12.20), Paros (1½ hours, €14.30), Syros (2¼ hours, €22.40) and Rafina (four hours, €25.55). Services travel twice a week to Tinos (three hours, €18); and also once a week to Amorgos (two hours, €16.60), Mykonos (1¾ hours, €14.70) and Andros (4½ hours, €26).

Getting Around Ios
In summer, crowded buses run between Ormos, Hora (€0.80) and Milopotas Beach (€0.80) about every 15 minutes. Private excursion buses go to Manganari Beach (€4.40, 10.30am and 12.30am) and Agia Theodoti Beach (€0.80).

Caiques travelling from Ormos to Manganari cost €7.34 per person for a return trip (departings 11am daily). Ormos and Hora both have car and motorcycle rental firms.

HORA, ORMOS & MILOPOTAS
Ios has three population centres, all very close together on the west coast: the port (Ormos); the capital, Hora (also known as the 'village'), 2km inland from the port; and Milopotas, the beach 1km downhill from Hora. Gialos Beach stretches west of the port.

Orientation
The bus terminal in Ormos is right of the ferry quay on Plateia Emirou. If you want to walk from the port to Hora, turn left from Plateia Emirou, then immediately right and you'll see the stepped path leading up to the right after about 100m. The walk takes about 15 minutes.

In Hora, the church is the main landmark. It's opposite the bus stop, across the car park. To reach the central square of Plateia Valeta from the church, head in to the village and turn left at the junction. There are public toilets up the hill behind the main square. The road straight ahead from the bus stop leads to Milopotas Beach.

Information
Amiridakis Travel (☎ 2286 091 252, fax 2286 091 067), in front of the ferry quay, is very helpful; Acteon Travel (☎ 2286 091 343, fax 2286 091 088, ⓔ acteon@otenet .gr), on the square near the quay, is the American Express representative, and has branches in Hora and Milopotas. There is a hospital (☎ 2286 091 227) 250m north-west of the quay, on the way to Gialos, and there are several doctors in Hora. The port police (☎ 2286 091 264) are at the southern end of the waterfront, just before Ios Camping.

In Hora, the National Bank of Greece, behind the church, and the Commercial Bank nearby both have ATMs. To get to the post office from the church, continue uphill along the edge of the village, past the bakery, and take the second left.

The OTE is in Hora, along the street that leads right (east) from the top of the port steps; a signpost points the way.

Things to See & Do
Hora itself is a very lovely Cycladic village with myriad laneways and cute houses and

shops. Its charm is most evident during day-light hours when the bars are shut and the locals come out of the woodwork.

The only real 'cultural' attraction is the **archaeological museum** (*admission free; open 8.30am-3pm Tues-Sun*) in Hora. The building is immaculately decked out, but the exhibits are a tad disappointing. It's in the yellow building by the bus stop.

The views from the top of the hill in Hora are worth the climb, especially at sunset. On the way, pause at **Panagia Gremiotissa**, the large church next to the palm tree.

Activities

Snorkel gear, windsurfers and canoes can be hired from **Mylopotas Water Sports Center** (☎ 2286 091 622, fax 2286 091 451, e iossport@otenet.gr; windsurfing rental €16/46.50 per hour/day). It's based at Milopotas. Waterskiing is also an option (€17.40/52 per hour/day).

Worthwhile sailing and snorkelling options around Ios or to Sikinos, with hands-on sailing involved, are available from **Frog's Sails** (*mobile* ☎ 69-4563 5590, e frogs@otenet.gr; cruises €43.50, book 2 days in advance). You should be able to find the captain down at the port or ask at Cafe Cyclades (also by the port); you can also book at travel agents.

Places to Stay

Ormos *Ios Camping* (☎ 2286 092 035, fax 2286 092 101) €5.90 per person. This camping ground is well set up, with a pool with sea vista and a restaurant. Sleeping bunks (slabs of concrete) are available for those without a tent. Turn right at Plateia Emirou and walk along the waterfront to find it.

Zorba's Rooms (☎ 2286 091 871) Singles/doubles €11.75/34.90, 3-4 person apartments €61. Straight ahead from the quay in Ormos, Zorba's has neat rooms.

Hotel Poseidon (☎ 2286 091 091, fax 2286 091 069) Singles/doubles/triples €47.90/59/72.50. There are stunning views from the swimming pool at this hotel, which is very good value outside July and August. From the waterfront, turn left at Enigma Bar and climb the steps on the left.

Sun Club (☎ 2286 092 140, fax 2286 092 140, e acteon@otenet.gr) Rooms €93.10. Sun Club, on the road to Hora, has immaculate rooms with bath, TV, phone and sea view. There's also a pool and bar.

Gialos Beach *Pension O Kampos* (☎ 2286 091 424) Doubles with/without bath €34.90/ 29. Set back a bit from the beach, this is a great, old-fashioned pension.

Galini Pension (☎/fax 2286 091 115) Doubles/triples €52/59. Next door to Pension O Kampos, this pension has a lovely shady garden.

Hotel Glaros (☎/fax 2286 091 876) Rooms with breakfast €59. This is a relaxed, family-run place on the beach.

Hotel Yialos Beach (☎ 2286 091 421, fax 2286 091 866) Rooms €64. This is a friendly place with nicely designed Cycladic-style units around a pool. Rooms have air-con, phone and balcony.

Hora to Milopotas *Fiesta Rooms* (☎ 2286 091 766) Doubles €38. On the Ormos-Hora road, run by the same family who run Fiesta

CYCLADES

taverna, these basic rooms are clean and comfortable.

Markos Village (☎ *2286 091 059, fax 2286 091 060,* e *markovlg@otenet.gr)* Dorm beds/doubles €11.75/43.50. Popular Markos Village is 50m from the bus stop. Nice double rooms have air-con, TV and balcony and there's a swimming pool.

Francesco's (☎/fax 2286 091 223, e *fragesco@otenet.gr)* Dorm beds €10.30; doubles with/without bathroom €34.90/26. Francesco's is a lively meeting place for backpackers, with a bar and terrace and a wonderful view of the bay.

Rooms Helena (☎ *2286 091 595)* Singles/doubles €23/29. This is an old-style place with a bit of character; it's on the left, halfway between Hora and the beach.

There are lots of domatia signs on the route towards Milopotas Beach from the Hora bus stop.

Hermes Rooms (☎ *2286 091471)* and ***Pelagos*** (☎ *2286 091 112)* and ***Petradi*** (☎ *2286 091 510, fax 2286 091 660)* all have doubles with terrace views for €59.

Katerina Rooms to Let (☎ *2286 091 614, fax 2286 092 049)* Doubles €46.60. Farther along from Hermes, Katerina's is set in a lovely garden and breakfast is served on its terrace.

Milopotas *Far Out Camping* (☎ *2286 091 468, fax 2286 092 303,* w *www.faroutclub .com)* Adult/tent €5.90/1.50, small/large bungalows €8.80/14.70. This site is a slick, over hyped but super-popular operation. It has a 24-hour bar, restaurant and two swimming pools (open to everyone on the beach). The basic 'bungalows' look like dog kennels; the larger ones are decent and have double and single beds. There's little tree cover and roofed areas provide most of the shade.

Stars Camping (☎ *2286 091 302, fax 2286 091 612,* e *purplepigios@hotmail .com)* Camp sites €5.90, dorm beds €14.70, bungalows €17.60 per person. Shaded by tall trees, Stars is a smaller and less hard-sell place than Far Out. It has a swimming pool and bar.

Nissos Ios Hotel (☎ *2286 091 610, fax 2286 091 306)* 3-bed dorms/singles/doubles €23/52/59. On the beach, Nissos has kooky '70s-style murals in all of its well-kep rooms.

Drakos Twins (☎/fax 2286 091 626, Singles/doubles €30.20/34.90 Also known as Elpis, this taverna has nice rooms right on the beach.

Hotel Ios Plage (☎/fax 2286 091 301 e *contact@iosplage.com)* Doubles/triples €59/76.90. This French-run hotel situated at the far end of Milopotas Beach has simply decorated rooms, with large mosquito nets draped over the beds. There is a lively bar here and an excellent *French restaurant*.

Ios Palace Hotel (☎ *2286 091 269, fax 2286 091 082,* e *ios@matrix.kapatel.gr)* Singles/doubles €93/107, suites €246. This plush place consists of a cluster of traditional Cycladic cubes rising up the hill at the Hora end of Milopotas Beach. The four-person suites have a private pool. Breakfast is included in the room rate.

Places to Eat
Ormos *Ciao Café* (☎ *2286 028 581)* Dishes from €1.90. Right by the ferry quay, this smart little cafe has filled baguettes and *ciabatta*; there's a small Internet cafe situated next door.

Gialos Beach *To Coralli* (☎ *2286 091 272, fax 2286 091 552)* Dishes €3.50-11. Coralli has the reputation (and there's a lot of competition in carbohydrate-hungry Ios) as the best place for wood-fired pizza.

Hora *Pithari Taverna* (☎ *2286 091 379)* Dishes €2.35-8.80. Behind the large church, Pithari serves cheap, traditional Greek dishes.

Lord Byron (☎ *2286 092 125)* Dishes €2.70-14. Close to Pithari Taverna this *mezedopolion* has a very cosy atmosphere augmented by rembetika music; different mezedes are served every day.

Pinocchio Ristorante (☎ *2286 091 470)* Dishes €4.10-12.80. This pizzeria has good pizza, *calzone* and pasta, and *panna cotta* for dessert. Look for the signs and Pinocchio standing outside.

La Buca (☎ 2286 091 447) Dishes €4.10-10.30. Next to the bus stop, La Buca has reasonably authentic Italian food, including wood-fired pizza, calzone, pasta and nice salads.

Fiesta (☎ 2286 091 766) Breakfast €1-4.65, dishes €1.70-8.80. Fiesta, on the Ormos-Hora road, has good Greek food as well as wood-fired pizzas – all made with fresh produce in generous portions (authentic English-style fish and chips is also an option!).

Saini's (☎ 2286 091 106) Dishes €2.35-5.70 Open year-round, until 5am July-August. Saini's serves fine Greek originals and wine by the barrel and bottle; expect occasional live music as well. To find it, go past Ali Baba's and turn left; it's down a dark alley.

There are also numerous *gyros stands* where you can get a cheap bite.

Koumbara In Koumbara head to *Taverna Polydoros* (☎ 2286 091 132), or to *Filippos* for spectacular seafood.

Milopotas *Drakos Taverna* (☎ 2286 091 281) Dishes €1.70-7.30, seafood by the kilo. This legendary taverna at the southern end of the beach is not to be missed.

Hotel Ios Plage (☎ 2286 091 301) Dishes €4.40-11.75. Ios Plage serves French cafe fare, such as *croque monsieur* and Roquefort salad, during the day and more elaborate meals after 8pm.

Harmony (☎ 2286 091 613) Dishes €4.40-12.80. At the village end of Milopotas beyond the Ios Palace, Harmony restaurant-bar has a lovely terrace dotted with deckchairs and hammocks. Tex-Mex food is the main attraction, although the pizza, pasta, grills and breakfasts are also pretty good.

Entertainment

Ios nightlife can be fairly well summarised by the advertising flyer for one of its bars, the Blue Note. It reads: 'You wanna have fun? Dance on the Bar? Get Drunk?' And, that in essence, is what Ios is all about.

At night Hora's tiny central square is transformed into a noisy, crowded open-air party so packed that frottage can become an inescapable option. The crowd is mostly made up of alcohol-swilling backpackers in their teens and early 20s – if you're older (say past 30...), you'll unfailingly feel somewhat past your use-by-date. In this case, the best approach can be to treat it all as a spectator sport (or head immediately to the escape-hatch options or to the Greek music-bars on Gliaros Beach).

Popular bars and clubs on the square include *Disco 69* (check out its logo – subtle indeed), which is generally full of crash-and-burn types, *Slammer Bar* (☎ 2286 092 119), infamous for its 'Tequila Slammer with the Hammer' where the drinker (or is that 'drunk'?) wears a helmet, slams the tequila, and then gets boinked on the head (sounds great, doesn't it?) and *Red Bull* (☎ 2286 091 019), which has a devoted following for inexplicable reasons. The neon-lit *Flames Bar* just off the square is also a popular dance spot.

A gauntlet of themed bars are scattered about the Hora, drawing on tenuous links between hard-drinking nations. 'Scandinavian' bars include the ever-crowded *Blue Note* (☎ 2286 092 271) and *Fusion*. For a touch of the Irish, there is *Sweet Irish Dream* (☎ 2286 091 141; admission €5.90, before 2am free). Its only Celtic connection is the Guinness on tap as well as the likelihood of some lively footwork – it has a nightclub upstairs with purposely built tables for dancing. *The Little Irish Bar* on the

path up from the Hora, is a popular, low-key spot for an early evening drink.

The Jungle Bar – Down Under Aussie & Kiwi Bar (☎ 2286 092 702), opposite the bus stop, revels in the sport of drinking – it hosts a weekly 100 Club, where participants sit around a table, fenced off from the crowd, and drink a shot of beer every minute – with the expected thunderous results.

Ios Club (☎ 2286 091 410) is one of the island's oldest bars, and provides sweeping views and a relaxed, quiet place for a drink. Head there for a cocktail to watch the sunset. To find it, walk right along the pathway by the Sweet Irish Dream.

Ali Baba's (☎ 2286 091 558) is a relaxed place to kick back and wait for the evening to begin, and plays movies between 8pm-10pm; Asian food is also available. From the bus stop, keep the church on your left, continue past the jewellery shops, then turn right.

Orange Bar, 150m beyond the central square, is a good, laid-back escape hatch, as

is *Cafe Click* (☎ 2286 092 477), which makes excellent top-shelf cocktails. *Cafe Astra* (2286 921 830), is a perfect, dark little bar that plays House and attracts an older, less desperate to drink crowd. It's above the Hora branch of Acteon Travel.

For Greek music, head to *Fantastico* (2286 091 539) by the Hora bus stop, or to the sleek dance bar *Di Porto* (☎ 2286 091 685) on Gliaros Beach, near Coralli. *Marina Bar* (☎ 2286 091 557) overlooking Gialos Beach, also plays good Greek music.

There are a couple of big dance clubs on the Milopotas road, but they don't open until July. *Mojo Club* (info ☎ mobile 69-7275 9318; admission €11.75) brings in international DJs from Moscow, UK Amsterdam. *Scorpion's* is another late-night dance venue.

If you still want to know more, head to W www.iospartyisland.com.

AROUND IOS
Apart from the nightlife, the beaches are what lure travellers to Ios. From Ormos, it's a 10-minute walk past the little church of Agia Irini for **Valmas Beach**. **Kolitzani Beach**, south of Hora, down the steps by Scorpion's, is also nice. **Koubara**, a 30-minute walk north-west of Ormos, is the official nudist beach. **Tsamaria**, nearby, is nice and sheltered when it's windy elsewhere.

Vying with Milopotas for best beach is **Manganari**, a long swathe of fine white sand on the south coast, reached by bus or by excursion boat in summer. There are several domatia; see Places to Stay & Eat.

Agia Theodoti, **Psathi** and **Kalamos** Beaches, all on the north-east coast, are more remote. **Moni Kalamou**, on the way to Manganari and Kalamos, stages a huge religious festival in late August and a festival of music and dance on 7 September.

Places to Stay & Eat
Dimitri's (☎ 2286 091 483, Manganari) Doubles €43.50. Dimitri's, behind Antonio's Restaurant, has lovely rooms.

Hotel Manganari (☎ 2286 091 200, fax 2286 091 204) Villas €113. This very private hotel is accessible only by boat and has

---

Bombes Beware!

Unfortunately, there's no such thing as a free cocktail – don't expect top-shelf (or even bottom-shelf) spirits. The cheap local moonshine used in mixed drinks and cocktails is bad news, as one reader pointed out:

There is a huge black market for alcohol distilled from rubbing alcohol – drinks made with this strange brew are called *bombes* and leave you with a nasty hangover (a lot of people say you can go blind from drinking too much of this). Most bars basically serve a mix of 'clean' and 'dirty' cocktails – but the really sketch bars serve all *bombes*. I've heard that on some islands some bars even advertise with billboards that say: BOMBES 1000dr – CLEAN DRINKS 2000dr

Cemile Kavountzis

Ios is notorious for this practice (but not alone) – so watch out. The safest (and usually cheaper) drinks are ouzo, bottled beer and the premixed bottled drinks like Gordon's Space and Rigo.

SANTORINI (THIRA)

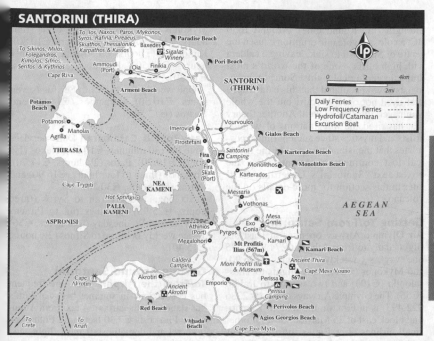

CYCLADES

villas for two people. Breakfast, dinner and port transfer are included.

Antonio's Restaurant (☎ *2286 091 483, Manganari*) Dishes €2.10-5.30. This restaurant has incredibly fresh fish and good grills; make sure you sample the different homemade cheeses.

Cristos Taverna (☎ *2286 092 286*) Dishes €1.70-10.30, doubles €29. Christos has excellent fresh fish at Manganari. ***Rooms*** are also available.

Santorini (Thira)
Σαντορίνη (Θα)

postcode 847 00 ● pop 9360

Santorini, officially known as Thira, is regarded by many as the most spectacular of all the Greek islands. Thousands visit annually to gaze in wonder at the submerged caldera, a vestige of what was probably the biggest volcanic eruption in recorded history. Although it gets crowded and is overly commercial, Santorini is unique and should not be missed. The caldera is a real spectacle – it's worth arriving by ferry rather than catamaran or hydrofoil if you want to experience the full dramatic impact. The main port is Athinios. Buses (and taxis) meet all ferries and cart passengers to Fira, the capital, which teeters on the lip of the caldera, high above the sea.

History

Greece is susceptible to eruptions and earthquakes – mostly minor – but on Santorini these have been so violent as to change the shape of the island several times.

Dorians, Venetians and Turks occupied Santorini, as they did all other Cycladic islands, but its most influential early inhabitants were the Minoans. They came from Crete some time between 2000 and 1600 BC, and the settlement at Akrotiri dates from the height of their great civilisation.

The island then was circular and called Strongili (the Round One). Around 1650 BC, a colossal volcanic eruption caused the centre of Strongili to sink, leaving a caldera with high cliffs – one of the world's most dramatic geological sights. Some archaeologists have speculated that this catastrophe destroyed not only Akrotiri but the whole Minoan civilisation as well. Another theory that has fired the imaginations of writers, artists and mystics since ancient times, postulates that the island was part of the mythical lost continent of Atlantis. See the boxed text 'Santorini's Unsettling Past' later in this section for more details on the volcano.

Getting To/From Santorini

Air Olympic Airway operates at least six flights daily to/from Athens (€74.85/83.35 one way), six weekly to Rhodes (€76.90) and Mykonos (€54), daily flights to Thessaloniki (€103) and two weekly to Iraklio (€56). The Olympic Airways office (☎ 2286 022 493) is in Fira, on the road to Kamari, one block east of 25 Martiou. Several other small airlines offer flights to/from Athens and Thessaloniki. Maria's Tours & Travel sell tickets for the small operators and for Olympic airlines.

Ferry Santorini is the southernmost island of the Cyclades, and as a major tourist destination it has good connections with Piraeus and Thessaloniki on the mainland, as well as with Crete. Santorini also has useful services to Anafi, Folegandros and Sikinos.

There are at least four boats daily to Naxos (three hours, €9.30), Paros (three to four hours, €9.90), Ios (1¼ hours, €5.60), Piraeus (nine hours, €18.60) and Tinos (five hours, €12.50), and two weekly for Kythnos (eight hours, €10.30) and Folegandros (1½ to 2½ hours, €5.30). Change at Naxos for Amorgos.

Three boats weekly go to Anafi (one hour, €5.90), Sifnos, (six hours, €9.30), Thessaloniki (18 to 19½ hours, €31.15), Sikinos (2½ hours, €5.60), Iraklion on Crete (3¾ hours, €12.05) and also Skiathos (13½ hours, €25).

There are two weekly ferries running to Mykonos (six hours, €10.50), Crete (four hours, €11.75), Milos (four hours, €10.80), Kimolos (3½ hours, €9.30) and Syros (5¼ hours, €12.50), Kythnos (eight hours, €10.30).

One weekly ferry goes to Serifos (seven hours, €10.50), Karpathos (€14.80) and Kassos (€12.50).

Fast Boat & Catamaran Daily services go to Ios (30 minutes, €10.30), Naxos (1½ hours, €19.20), Paros (2¼ hours, €17.70), Mykonos (three to four hours, €16.90) and Rafina (5¼ hours, €30.20).

Six boats weekly run to Syros (three hours, €25.90). Services run to Piraeus daily, except Wednesday (four hours, €36). Twice weekly boats go to Sifnos (2½ hours, €15.40).

Getting Around Santorini

To/From the Airport There are frequent bus connections in summer between Fira's bus station and the airport. A taxi from Athinios to Fira costs €7.30 (set fare). Enthusiastic hotel and domatia staff meet flights and some also return guests to the airport.

Bus In summer, buses leave Fira's bus station hourly for Akrotiri (€1.20) and every half-hour for Oia (€0.90), Monolithos (€0.80), Kamari (€0.80) and Perissa (€1.30). There are less frequent buses to Exo Gonia (€0.80), Perivolos (€1.30) and Vlihada (€1.50).

Buses leave Fira, Kamari and Perissa for the port of Athinios (€1.20) 1½ hours before most ferry departures. Buses for Fira meet all ferries, even late at night.

Boat From the seafront at Ancient Akrotiri, you can catch a caique to Red Beach, White Beach and Black Beach for around €4.40. Caiques also run regularly from Perissa to Red Beach.

Car, Motorcycle & Bicycle Fira has many car-, motorcycle- and bicycle-rental firms. Hired wheels are the best way to explore the island as the buses are intolerably over-

Santorini's Unsettling Past

Santorini's violent volcanic history is visible everywhere – in black sand beaches, raw lava-layered cliffs plunging into the sea, earthquake-damaged dwellings and in the soil's fertility, which supports coiled-up grape vines. The volcano may be dormant, but it's not dead. Santorini's caldera ('cauldron'), which often has a surface as calm and glassy as a backyard fish pond, could start to boil at any moment...

Santorini first appeared when the landmass known as Aegis, which joined the European and Asian continents, was gradually flooded around one million years ago, leaving only the highest peaks above water. Profitis Ilias and Monolithos are both ancient rocks dating back to this time. At some point a complex of submarine, overlapping shield volcanoes began to toil and trouble, eventually erupting and filling in the area between Santorini's mountains with lava. This process continued for thousands of years and over time the island took on a conical shape.

Eventually the volcanoes became dormant, and vegetation established itself in the fertile ash. Around 3000 BC the first human settlers arrived and, from evidence found at Akrotiri, it appears that they led very idyllic lives and fashioned a highly evolved culture.

But the peace and harmony didn't last, and around 1650 BC a chain of earthquakes and eruptions culminated in one of the largest explosions in the history of the planet. Thirty cubic kilometres of magma spewed forth and a column of ash 36km high jetted into the atmosphere. So much magma was ejected that the magma chambers of the volcano gave way and the centre of the island collapsed, producing a caldera that the sea quickly filled. It's hard to imagine the magnitude of the explosion, but it is often compared to thousands of atomic bombs detonating simultaneously. The event sent ash all over the Mediterranean, and it also generated huge tsunamis (tidal waves) that travelled with dangerous force all the way to Crete and Israel. Anafi was hit by a wave 250m high. The fallout from the explosion was more than just dust and pumice – it's widely believed that the catastrophe was responsible for the demise of Crete's Minoan culture, one of the most powerful civilisations in the Aegean at that time. After the Big One, Santorini once again settled down for a time and allowed plants, animals and humans to recolonise it. In 236 BC the rumbles from the deep resumed and volcanic activity separated Thirasia from the main island. Further changes to the landscape continued intermittently. In 197 BC the islet now known as Palia Kameni appeared in the caldera, and in AD 726 there was a major eruption that catapulted pumice all the way to Asia Minor. The south coast of Santorini collapsed in 1570, taking the ancient port of Eleusis with it. In 1650 earthquakes and explosions caused tsunamis and killed and blinded many people on the island. An eruption of lava in 1707 created Nea Kameni Islet next to Palia Kameni, and further eruptions in 1866–70, 1925–6, 1928, 1939-41 and 1950 augmented it. A major earthquake measuring 7.8 on the Richter scale savaged the island in 1956, killing scores of people and destroying most of the houses in Fira and Oia. If you walk around the laneways of Fira, you will see many abandoned mansions.

Volcanic activity has been pretty low-key since 1956, but minor tremors are quite common and the ground shakes, usually imperceptibly, almost every day. A major earthquake is due at any moment, but the locals don't seem worried – they seem to like living on the edge. For lovers of impermanence, precariousness and drama, no other place even comes close.

CYCLADES

crowded in summer and you'll usually be lucky to get on one at all; be very patient and cautious when driving – the narrow roads, especially in Fira, can be a nightmare.

Taxi There is a taxi stand in the main square. Call a taxi on ☎ 2286 023 951 or 2286 022 555.

Cable Car & Donkey Cable cars shunt cruise-ship and excursion-boat passengers up to Fira from the small port below, known as Fira Skala. Tickets cost €3 one way.

FIRA Φα
The commercialism of Fira has not diminished its all-pervasive, dramatic aura. Walk

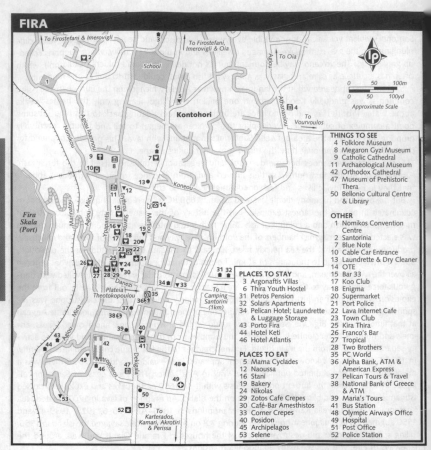

FIRA

To Firostefani & Imerovigli

School

Kontohori

To Oia

To Firostefani,
Imerovigli & Oia

To Vourvoulos

To
Camping
Santorini
(1km)

Fira
Skala
(Port)

Plateia
Theotokopoulou

Danezi

To
Karterados,
Kamari, Akrotiri
& Perissa

0   50   100m
0   50   100yd
Approximate Scale

THINGS TO SEE
4   Folklore Museum
8   Megaron Gyzi Museum
9   Catholic Cathedral
11 Archaeological Museum
42 Orthodox Cathedral
47 Museum of Prehistoric
    Thera
50 Bellonio Cultural Centre
    & Library

OTHER
1   Nomikos Convention
    Centre
2   Santorinia
7   Blue Note
10 Cable Car Entrance
13 Laundrette & Dry Cleaner
14 OTE
15 Bar 33
17 Koo Club
18 Enigma
20 Supermarket
21 Port Police
22 Lava Internet Cafe
23 Town Club
25 Kira Thira
26 Franco's Bar
27 Tropical
28 Two Brothers
35 PC World
36 Alpha Bank, ATM &
    American Express
37 Pelican Tours & Travel
38 National Bank of Greece
    & ATM
39 Maria's Tours
41 Bus Station
48 Olympic Airways Office
49 Hospital
51 Post Office
52 Police Station

PLACES TO STAY
3   Argonaftis Villas
6   Thira Youth Hostel
31 Petros Pension
32 Solaris Apartments
34 Pelican Hotel; Laundrette
    & Luggage Storage
43 Porto Fira
44 Hotel Keti
46 Hotel Atlantis

PLACES TO EAT
5   Mama Cyclades
12 Naoussa
16 Stani
19 Bakery
24 Nikolas
29 Zotos Cafe Crepes
30 Café-Bar Amesthistos
33 Corner Crepes
40 Posidon
45 Archipelagos
53 Selene

to the edge of the caldera for spectacular views of the cliffs and their multicoloured strata of lava and pumice.

Orientation

The central square is Plateia Theotokopoulou. The main road, 25 Martiou, runs north-south, intersecting the square and is lined with travel agencies. The bus station is on 25 Martiou, 50m south of Plateia Theotokopoulou. West of 25 Martiou the streets are old pedestrian laneways; Erythrou Stavrou, one block west of 25 Martiou, is the main commercial thoroughfare.

Another block west, Ypapantis runs along the crest of the caldera and provides some staggering panoramic views. Head north on Nomikou for the cable car station. If you keep walking along the caldera – and it's well worth it – you'll come to the Nomikos Convention Centre and, eventually, the cliff-top villages of Firostefani and Imerovigli. Keep going and you'll reach Oia.

Information

Fira doesn't have an EOT or tourist police. It's best to seek out the smaller travel agents in Fira, where you'll generally receive more helpful service. Readers have recommended Maria's Tours (☎ 2286 024 701, fax 2286 023 848) and Pelican Tours & Travel (☎ 2286 022 220, fax 2286 022 570), both can book accommodation and ferry tickets, and Maria's has reasonably priced car rental (from €29).

The National Bank of Greece is between the bus station and Plateia Theotokopoulou, on the caldera side of the road. American Express is represented by Alpha Bank on Plateia Theotokopoulou. Both banks have ATMs. The post office is about 150m south of the bus station.

PC World (☎ 2286 025 551), above Santo Volcano Tours & Travel on the main square, has the best value Internet (€3 for a one-hour card). Lava Internet Cafe (☎ 2286 025 551), up from the main square, has a better atmosphere, but a minimum of 20 minutes only is possible at more expensive rates.

There is a laundrette and dry cleaner 200m north of Plateia Theotokopoulou, underneath Pension Villa Maria, and another laundrette next to Pelican Hotel; locked luggage storage is also possible at this laundrette (€1.50).

The hospital (☎ 2286 022 237) is on the road to Karterados, near the Olympic Airways office. The police station (☎ 2286 022 649) is south of Plateia Theotokopoulou; the port police (☎ 2286 022 239) are north of the square.

Museums

The **Museum of Prehistoric Thera** (☎ 2286 022 217; admission free; 8.30am-3pm Tues-Sun) is a new museum near the bus station. It houses extraordinary finds which were excavated from Akrotiri (where to date only 5% of the area has been excavated). Most impressive is the glowing gold ibex figurine, measuring around 10cm in length and dating from the 17th century BC, which was discovered in mint condition in 1999.

Megaron Gyzi Museum (☎ 2286 022 244; admission €3; open 10.30am-1pm & 5pm-8pm Mon-Sat, 10.30am-4.30pm Sun), behind the Catholic cathedral, has local memorabilia, including fascinating photographs of Fira before and immediately after the 1956 earthquake.

The **archaeological museum** (☎ 2286 022 217; adult/students €2.35/1.20; open 8.30am-3pm Tues-Sun), opposite the cable-car station, houses finds from Akrotiri and Ancient Thira, some Cycladic figurines, and Hellenistic and Roman sculpture.

There is a small **folklore museum** (admission €3) on the road to Oia, notable for its canava (wine-making cellar).

For the past few years the **Nomikos Convention Centre** (☎ 2286 023 016; adult/student €3/1.50; open 10am-9pm daily), also known as the Thera Foundation, has displayed three-dimensional photographic reproductions of the Akrotiri frescoes. To get there, follow the old Byzantine path along the caldera, past the cable-car station.

The **Bellonio Cultural Centre & Library** (admission free; open 9am-2pm daily & 6pm-9pm Tues-Sun), next to the post office, has a large collection of books and occasional exhibitions about Santorini.

Organised Tours

Tour agencies operate trips to Thirasia, the volcanic island of Nea Kameni, Palia Kameni's hot springs and Oia; book at travel agencies.

Places to Stay – Budget

Camping Santorini (☎ 2286 022 944, fax 2286 025 065, e santocam@otenet.gr) Adult/tent €5.90/2.70, basic bungalows €26. This camping ground has some shade and modest facilities, but it's a long way from the nearest beach. There's a self-serve restaurant and a pool (though a reader's letter reported staff hassling people to buy drinks when lounging by the pool). It's 400m east of Plateia Theotokopoulou – look for the sign.

The fairly aggressive owners of accommodation who greet boats and buses are now confined to 'official' information booths. Some owners of rooms in Karterados (3km south-east of Fira) claim that their rooms are in town; ask to see a map showing the location. If you're looking for a caldera view, expect to pay at least double the prices elsewhere.

Thira Youth Hostel (☎ 2286 023 864) Dorm beds from €10.30, beds on roof €5.90, doubles with bathroom €34.90. This massive hostel, 300m north of Plateia Theotokopoulou, is a dilapidated, grubby old place that was formerly part of the Catholic monastery. Some of the double rooms have remnants of antique furniture.

Petros Pension (☎ 2286 022 573, fax 2286 022 615) Doubles €30.20. On the pension-filled road to Santorini Camping, this is a fine place close to the main square; pick up and drop off to the port and airport is possible.

Hotel Keti (☎ 2286 022 324, fax 2286 022 380) Doubles €52.50. This is a real gem with lovely traditional rooms dug into the cliffs.

Argonaftis Villas (☎ 2286 022 055) Doubles €59, 2-person/4-person apartments €61/85.50. Folksy paintings decorate many of the rooms, and one of the apartments is a traditional cave house.

Kafieris Hotel (☎ 2286 022 189) Doubles €49. This hotel, on the path up to Firostefani, not far from the convention centre, has lovely rooms on the caldera.

Apartments Gaby (☎/fax 2286 022 057) Doubles €52.50, 4-person apartments €117. This great place is near Kafieris Hotel.

Hotel Sofia Sigala (☎ 2286 022 802) Doubles €59. Farther up the hill, near Firostefani's main square, are these nice rooms.

Ioaniss Roussos Rooms (☎ 2286 022 611, fax 2286 028 186) Doubles €40.80. These rooms are near Hotel Sofia Sigala.

Places to Stay – Mid-Range & Top End

Pelican Hotel (☎ 2286 023 113) Singles/doubles/triples €67.90/80.40/96. Open year-round. This gloomy hotel, right in the centre of town, has comfortable rooms and breakfast is available.

Solaris Apartments (☎ 2286 022 631, fax 2286 028 581, e zefksi00@otenet.gr) Singles/doubles €69.60/99. Open year-round. Solaris is centrally located and has a pool, spa and gym, but no caldera views.

Porto Fira (☎ 2286 022 849, fax 2286 023 098) Singles/doubles €88.50/110. Hotels perched on the caldera's edge in Fira are naturally a bit more expensive, but this one's worth it.

Hotel Atlantis (☎ 2286 022 232, fax 2286 022 821, e atlantis@atlantishotel.gr) Singles/doubles with breakfast €122/183. This spacious, airy A-class hotel offers all comforts. Rooms have incredible views over the caldera.

Eterpi Villas (☎ 2286 022 541) 2-person studios €133, 3-person apartments €160. Up in Firostefani, Eterpi has traditional abodes dug into the caldera.

Spiliotica Apartments (☎ 2286 022 637, fax 2286 023 590, e spiliot@san.forthnet .gr) Doubles/triples €117/145. In Imerovigli, these are traditional abodes dug into the caldera. Spiliotica has a nice little cafe-bar and a small swimming pool.

Skaros Villas (☎ 2286 023 153) Doubles €88. Nearby Spiliotica, Skaros (also a traditional dwelling) is furnished in the traditional way, and has views, views, views.

Places to Eat

Fira has many terrible tourist-trap eateries, so it's worth being picky.

Nikolas (☎ 2286 024 550) Dishes €2.10-11.75. Opposite the Kira Thira bar, Nikolas has tasty traditional food and friendly service.

Naoussa (☎ 2286 024 869) Dishes €2.10-17.20. This upstairs eatery (not to be confused with the very average establishment at ground level), beyond Bar 33, serves excellent, reasonably priced Greek classics, with new specials daily.

Stani (☎ 2286 023 078) Dishes €2-9.60. Upstairs next to Koo Club, the roof-top restaurant Stani has good home-cooked food.

Posidon (☎ 2286 025 480) Dishes €2.35-12.80. Below the bus station, Poseidon has reasonable, inexpensive food and stays open late.

Archipelagos (☎ 2286 023 673) Dishes €3.80-22. This is a classy place with simple dishes like octopus cooked with eggplant and potatoes (€14).

Selene (☎ 2286 022 249, w www.selene .gr) Mains €17.20-18.30. This is one of the best restaurants in town and has a lovely, romantic atmosphere and creative dishes.

Among the best places for juices, coffee, cake and crepes are **Zotos Cafe Crepe** and **Café-Bar Amesthistos** (Erythrou Stavrou) where dishes are €2.35 to €5.90. Good breakfast places include **Mama Cyclades**, near Thira Youth Hostel, and **Corner Crepes** near the Museum of Prehistoric Thera.

There are several gyros stands up from the main square where you can grab a quick bite.

Firostefani & Imerovigli To Aktaion
(☎ 2286 022 336) Dishes €2.10-8.80. On the main square in Firostefani, this is a nice little taverna serving traditional food.

Skaros Fish Tavern (☎ 2286 023 616) Dishes €2.35-11.75. Farther up the caldera in Imerovigli, Skaros has excellent mezedes and fish as well as a spectacular view.

Entertainment
Kira Thira (☎ 2286 022 770) This is the oldest bar in Fira and a favourite haunt of both locals and travellers. It's a funky little candle-lit dive with an eclectic selection of sounds and occasional live music.

Tropical (☎ 2286 023 089) In an enviable position, Tropical is another long-established bar with a loyal clientele; it plays a mix of music from disco to rock.

Franco's Bar (☎ 2286 024 428) Franco's is the place to watch the sun set with cocktail in hand, although expect to pay for the privilege. There's also a sublime bar indoors, carved into the caldera.

After midnight Erythrou Stavrou is the place to head for a sweaty but sleek knees-up – unless you want to feel uncomfortably out of place, make sure you frock up in style. The five bars at **Koo Club** (☎ 2286 022 025) attract a Greek fashionista crowd and play the occasional Greek hit. The superkitsch **Town Club** (☎ 2286 022 820) is a smaller space playing a more even mix of Greek and international music. Shiny **Enigma** (☎ 2286 022 466) plays pure and unadulterated mainstream dance music.

Not far from the cable car station and the convention centre, **Santorinia** (☎ 2286 023 777) is popular with the young local crowd

and has traditional live music, including rembetika and laïko.

Bar 33 (☎ 2286 023 065), just past Koo Club, is a lively bouzouki place.

Two Brothers (☎ 2286 023 061) is an old rock bar that's worth stopping by for a drink, soaking up the Greek atmosphere, and then moving on.

Just by Thira Youth Hostel, **Blue Note** (☎ 2286 024 888) has an outdoor area and plays a mix of music – and there's no need to frock up – style is irrelevant here.

Shopping
Grapes thrive in Santorini's volcanic soil, and the island's wines are famous all over Greece and beyond. Local wines are widely available in Fira and elsewhere. Try the pricey 50-50 (so-called because 50% of the grapes are from the mainland and 50% are grown on Santorini) from Canava Nomikos, or the wines from Oia.

Cava Sigalas in Firostefani sells local fava beans, capers, caper leaves (a delicacy), wines and thyme honey.

AROUND SANTORINI
Ancient Akrotiri Παλαισ Ακρωτα
Ancient Akrotiri (☎ 2286 081 366; adult/student €5.30/1.7; open 8.30am-3pm Tues-Sun) was a Minoan outpost; excavations begun in 1967 have uncovered an ancient city beneath the volcanic ash. Buildings, some three storeys high, date to the late 16th century BC. The absence of skeletons and treasures indicates that inhabitants were forewarned of the eruption and escaped.

The actual site is a disappointment. At the time of writing it resembled a haphazard construction zone as a new roof was being built over the excavations. It's advisable to go with a guide to get the most out of the site.

The most outstanding finds are the stunning frescoes and ceramics, many of which are now on display at the Museum of Prehistoric Thera in Fira (there are none on display at the excavation site). Accurate fresco replicas are on display at the Nomikos Convention Centre also. On the way to Akrotiri, pause at the enchanting traditional settlement of **Megalohori**.

The winegrowers cooperative, **Santo Wines** (☎ *2286 022 596*, e *santowines@san.forth net.gr*), has a showcase selection here of regional produce taken from all over Greece.

Places to Stay & Eat *Caldera View Camping* (☎ *2286 082 010, fax 2286 081 889,* e *caldera@hol.gr*) Adult/tent €5.90/ 3.80; 2-person/4-person bungalows €93/ 125. This camping ground, near Akrotiri, doesn't have a view over the caldera, although it does have views across to the sea. It's a long way from any nightlife in a semi-rural area, but the facilities are very good and there's a swimming pool and free transfer to/from the port. Breakfast is included.

On the beach below the archaeological site there are some nice little fish *tavernas*, and *Hotel Akrotiri* (☎ *2286 081 375, fax 2286 081 377,* e *hotelakrotiri@yahoo .com*) which is a nice place to stay, with doubles including breakfast for €69.60.

Ancient Thira Αρχαία Θα
First settled by the Dorians in the 9th century BC, Ancient Thira (*Admission free; open 8.30am-3pm Tues-Sun*), consists of Hellenistic, Roman and Byzantine ruins. These include temples, houses with mosaics, an agora, a theatre and a gymnasium. The site has splendid views. It takes about 45 minutes to walk to the site along the path from Perissa on rocky, difficult ground. If you're driving, take the road from Kamari.

Moni Profiti Ilia Μοναπροφαηλία
This monastery crowns Santorini's highest peak, Mt Profitis Ilias (567m). Although it now shockingly shares the small peak with radio and TV pylons and a military radar station, it's worth the trek for the stupendous views. The monastery has an interesting **folk museum**. You can walk there from Pyrgos (1½ hours) or from Ancient Thira (one hour).

Oia Οία
The village of Oia (**ee**-ah) was devastated by the 1956 earthquake and has never fully recovered, but it is dramatic, striking and quieter than tourist-frenzied Fira, although its streets are also filled with expensive jewellery boutiques. Built on a steep slope of the caldera, many of its dwellings nestle in niches hewn into the volcanic rock. Oia is famous for its dramatic sunsets and its narrow passageways get crowded in the evenings. The most popular spot to watch the sunset is by the Kastro walls, and towards 7pm, everyone is jockeying for the best position.

From the bus turnaround, go left (following signs for the youth hostel), turn immediately right, take the first left, ascend the steps and walk across the central square to the main street, Nikolaou Nomikou, which skirts the caldera. There is an Alpha Bank (with ATM) on the main street.

You can get information, book hotels, cars and bikes, and use the Internet at Ecorama (☎/fax 2286 071 507, e ecorama@otenet.gr, W www.santorinitours.com), by the bus turnaround. Kargounas Tours (☎ *071 290*) on Nikolaou Nomikou is also helpful.

The last bus for Fira leaves Oia at 11.20pm in summer. After that, three to four people can bargain for a shared taxi for about €8.80. Six buses daily connect Oia with Baxedes beach.

The **maritime museum** (☎ *2286 071 156; adult/student* €*3/1.50; open 10am-2pm, 5pm-8pm Tues-Sun*) is housed in an old mansion and pays homage to Santorini's maritime history.

You can swim at breathtaking **Ammoudi**, the tiny port with excellent *fish tavernas* and colourful fishing boats that lies 300 steps below. If you turn left at the bottom of the stairs and go south around the headland, you'll find a lovely rocky swimming spot. In summer at least two boats and tours go from Ammoudi to Thirasia daily; check travel agents for departure times.

The traditional settlement of **Finikia**, just east of Oia, is a beautiful, quiet place to wander around.

Places to Stay *Oia Youth Hostel* (☎/fax *2286 071 465*) Dorm beds with breakfast €11.75. Open summer only. Oia's exceptional hostel has a whitewashed rooftop

Evening falls on Mykonos and the town prepares for the night ahead

Windmills at sunset, Mykonos

CHRIS CHRISTO

CHERYL CONLON

Folegandros is a small and rocky island of cultivated terraces that give way to precipitous cliffs.

ROSEMARY HALL

Domed church roof, Santorini

Whitewashed streetscape on Santorini

IZZET KERIBAR

IZZET KERIBAR

Water skiing is an increasingly popular activity on most of the Greek Islands

Looking for a quick getaway, Santorini

The black sands of Perissa beach, Santorini

Village lights illuminate the Santorini night

terrace and bar with great views; laundry facilities and family rooms are available. If it's a toss up between here and Fira's youth hostel – head here.

A little farther on there are several domatia with reasonable prices.

Irini Halari (☎ 2286 071 226) Singles/doubles/triples €23/29/38. On the main road near the pink church, Irini's has great views to the north-east. Next door, *Antonis* has similar rooms and prices.

Lauda Traditional Pension (☎ 2286 071 204, fax 2286 071 274) Singles/doubles €34.90/43.50, double/triple studios €52/69.60. This pension is on the main pedestrian thoroughfare overlooking the caldera.

Hotel Anemones (☎ 2286 071 342, fax 2286 071 220) Singles/doubles €29/43.50 On the main thoroughfare, near Thalami taverna, this hotel has nice rooms with balconies and caldera views.

Hotel Museum (☎ 2286 071 515, fax 2286 071 516) Studios/double apartments €105/119. This restored mansion is now a rather grand hotel with a pool by a landscaped garden.

Chelidonia (☎ 2286 071 287, fax 2286 071 649, **W** www.chelidonia.com) studios €130.50, 2-person/4-person apartments €113/157. If you can afford to splurge, Oia is the place to do it. For lovingly restored traditional cave dwellings, contact Chelidonia. The office is in the centre of town.

Zoe-Aegeas (☎/fax 2286 071 466) Studios with shared/private courtyard €101.50/130.50. Zoe-Aegeas has lovely two-person studios in traditional houses.

Katikies (☎ 2286 071 401, fax 2286 071 129, **e** katikies@otenet.gr) Doubles €203, suites from €267, honeymoon suite €435. This is one of the most beautiful hotels on the island and has a spectacular pool filled to the brim and balanced on the lip of the caldera.

Perivolas (☎ 2286 071 308, perivolas@san.forthnet.gr) Doubles €313.20. Perivolas is also a knockout.

Places to Eat & Drink *Thomas Grill*
(☎ 2286 071 769) Dishes €1.50-6.40. Thomas Grill is very popular with locals, due to its good, inexpensive food and ex-

cellent service. It's between the bus station and the church, down a small laneway.

Skala (☎ 2286 071 562) Dishes €2.70-13. There is no shortage of restaurants with a view; Skala, on the caldera, has excellent lamb, salads and hors d'oeuvres.

1800 (☎ 2286 071 485) Mains €13-23. Open from 7.30pm. In a restored sea captain's house complete with original furniture is this upmarket place serving contemporary Greek cuisine.

Strogili (☎ 2286 071 415) Dishes €2.70-29. This rooftop cafe-restaurant perched high above caldera is an excellent spot to watch the sun set.

Kastro (☎ 2286 071 045) Dishes €5.90-13. On the path down to Ammoudi, Kastro is another fine spot to marvel at the sunset. Dine on ravioli with spinach, fresh cream and shavings of roasted hazelnut (€9.30).

Karterados Καρτεραδος
There's not a lot to see here, and the old village with houses dug into a ravine is very neglected now that new apartments have been built on its periphery. However, accommodation is cheaper than in Fira and it makes a good base, providing you don't mind the 20-minute walk to town.

Pension George (☎/fax 2286 022 351, **e** pensiongeorge@san.forthnet.gr, **W** www.pensiongeorge.com) Singles €34.90, doubles €46.50-59. Run by a friendly Englishman, the pension has a swimming pool and views across to the sea. Rooms have balcony and some have air-con; call ahead to be picked up from Fira, the port or airport. Otherwise, walk or take a bus to the village turn-off. Follow the road and turn right after the church on your left. The pension is on the left.

Messaria Μεσσαρια
Situated at a shady junction between Karterados and Kamari, Messaria has a few tavernas and domatia. The main attraction is the **Arhontiko Argirou** (☎ 2286 031 669, fax 2286 033 064; open 9am-2pm & 4.30pm-7.30pm daily), a sumptuously restored neoclassical mansion that dates from 1888. You can also overnight here: Doubles

CYCLADES

CYCLADES

Fine Wine Ideas

The face of Santorini is the caldera and the crowds of people wanting a piece of it, but the interior of the island, the terraced rows of low, bunched vines that provide the only real greenery, represent its hardworking soul.

Seventy per cent of the island is covered in vines, most of it grown in small plots and picked by hand under backbreaking conditions. Harvest takes place in mid-August and this can be one of the most interesting, if frantic, times to visit Santorini's wineries.

The vines of Santorini, those bedraggled clumps of green, look that way for a reason. An ancient technique of vine-shaping is used. The vine is encouraged to grow in a basket shape and the grapes then safely grow in the centre, cocooned from Santorini's strong, sandy winds and fierce sun.

Santorini's trademark grape variety, Assyrtiko, is widely accepted as being an indigenous, ancient vine. The fine white cultivar, which delivers a crisp, clear wine with a citrus bouquet, has well-honed survival instincts – it's not only impervious to drought, but also to philoxia -a fungus that strikes cold fear in most vintners. Assyrtiko's survival is also helped along by Santorini's microclimate – it basks nightly in evaporation from sea mists.

The Assyrtiko dry whites and the amber-coloured, unfortified dessert wine *vinsanto*, made from grapes that are ripened in the sun for up to ten days, are Santorini's two lauded wines, but there's huge interest amongst local wine makers in crafting and experimenting with previously ignored indigenous ancient grape varieties, and in producing organic wine. In Santorini, so they say, it's impossible not to make good wine.

Most vineyards hold tastings and tours, and there are also wine museums.

Antoniou Winery (☎/fax 2286 023 557) Megolohori. Entry €1.50 includes tastings. Built early this century by Kyr-Giorgi Venetsanou, a chemist and winemaker with his eye on the export market, the present day Antoniou Winery is a masterpiece of free-form ingenuity. The canava is built into the cliffs directly above Athinos port, making prime use of gravity – a pipe 5550m in length flooded wine down the sheer cliff to waiting boats; wine is no longer made at this site, but it's a fascinating place to visit.

Boutari (☎ 2286 081 011, fax 2286 081 606, W www.boutari.gr) Megolohori. Open 10am-7pm Mon-Fri & 11am-7pm Sat-Sun. Tastings €0.70 a glass. Boutari is a slick operation – a multimedia show screens after 1pm, which is striking but ultimately uninformative.

---

are €52.50, while apartments with kitchen are €69.60.

Kamari

Kamari is a long strand covered by beach umbrellas and backed by package tour hotels, bars and nightclubs. Patches of tall pistachio orchards in the streets give some idea of how pretty Kamari once must have been.

Lios Tours (☎ 2286 033 765, fax 2286 033 661), on the main road into Kamari, is very helpful and can book accommodation.

Volcano Diving Centre (☎ 2286 033 177, W www.scubagreece.com) on the beach, offers dives and courses for beginners (from €59) and certified divers (from €88). Snorkel trips are also available (€18).

Lava Trails (☎ 2286 031 165, e simosvog@ yahoo.com; bike tour €23.20) full-day mountain-bike tour goes from Kamari to Exo Gonia, Vothonas, Messaria and Monolithos.

Cinema Kamari (☎ 2286 031 974, W www .cinekamari.gr; admission €5.90; sessions 9pm & 11.15pm daily), on the main road coming into Kamari, is a great open-air theatre set in a thicket of trees and showing recent releases. In July it hosts the three-day **Santorini Jazz Festival** (☎ 2286 033 452, W www.jazzfestival.gr), featuring lively performances by Greek and foreign musicians.

Just outside Kamari, make sure you visit **Art Space** (☎ 2286 032 774, Exo Gonia), at one of the oldest wineries on the island.

Fine Wine Ideas

Canava Roussos (☎/fax 2286 031 349) Open 10am-10pm daily Tastings €0.60 per glass. Established in 1836, at Episkopi-Mesa Gonia, just outside Kamari, Canava unfortunately doesn't run tours. However, tastings, including organic wines, are on offer in a relaxed bouganvillea-cloaked bar that is refreshingly down-to-earth compared to the Boutari or Santo set up. Try *nama*, the religious drop that Santorini exported to the Russians for centuries.

Hatzidakis Winery (☎ 2286 032 552, fax 2286 028 395, ⓔ hatzidakiswinery@san.forthnet.gr) Call before visiting this small organic winery based in the village of Pyrgos Kallistis Thera, near Moni Profiti Ilia.

Peter S. Nomikos Winery (☎ 2286 023 761, fax 2286 023 961) The makers of 50-50 (50% of the grapes are grown on the mainland, 50% are from Santorini), makes its wines in the heart of Fira, in a traditional canava that has been modernised. No tours are available.

Volcano Wines and Wine Museum (☎ 2286 031 322, fax 2286 022 300, ⓦ www.waterblue.gr) Entry €1.70 includes three tastings. On the way to Kamari, Volcano (also known as Lava) was established in 1880. The atmospheric Wine Museum, housed in a traditional canava, has some interesting displays including a 17th-century wooden wine press. One display rightfully urges drinkers to 'Give one thought to the toilsome hard work accumulated in one glass of Santorini wine'.

Santo Wines (☎ 2286 022 596, fax 2286 023 137, ⓔ santowines@san.forthnet.gr) Open 9am-sunset daily. Tour & tasting €4. Santo Wines, near Pyrgos, is the local vine growers' cooperative (grapes are sourced from over 900 growers) and is well worth supporting.

Sigalas (☎/fax 2286 071 644, mobile 69-7770 6930) Open 10am-7pm Mon-Fri & 11am-7pm Sat-Sun, June-Sept. With a young female oenologist, Sigalas is breaking boundaries. The boutique operation cultivates 10 acres and focuses on organic wines. Housed in an unobtrusive Cycladic building, the vineyard is the prettiest in Santorini and has views to the ocean. It's off the beach road between Oia and Vourvoulos (coming from Oia, turn right just after Paradisos taverna).

If you don't make it to the vineyards, options include **Kira Thira** bar, where you can try four different Santorini wines plus meze (€5), or if you're island hopping to Folegandros, seek out *the* bar for wine-lovers, tiny **Kellari** in the Hora, where good regional Greek wines are available by the glass in modern but rustic ambience. Perfect.

CYCLADES

Inside the cavernous rooms, there are some hauntingly beautiful pieces on display, including sculpture carved from lava rock. Wine making is in the owner's blood, so a tasting of his *vinsanto* adds to the whole experience.

Other Beaches

Santorini's black-sand beaches become so hot that a mat is essential. The nicest beaches are on the east coast.

The beach at the village of **Perissa** gets quite busy. Wreck and volcano dives are offered here by **Mediterranean Dive Club** (☎ 2286 083 080, ⓔ mdc@diveclub.gr; certified dive €43.50, PADI open-water certification €377, snorkelling cruise/hire €32/8.80).

Perivolos and **Agios Georgios**, farther south, are more relaxed.

Monolithos Beach, farther along again, near an abandoned tomato cannery, is less crowded and there are sometimes sizable waves to splash about in.

North of Monolithos, the beaches are almost deserted. **Red Beach**, near Ancient Akrotiri, is breathtaking – high red cliffs and hand-size pebbles submerged under clear water. **Vlihada**, also on the south coast, is much nicer. On the north coast near Oia, **Paradise** and **Pori** are both worth a stop.

At **Armeni** and **Ammoudi**, down the cliffs below Oia, you can plunge right into the caldera. If you're interested in exploring the depths, contact **Atlantis Diving** (☎ 2286 071

507, mobile 69 3222 3064, e *ecorama@ otenet.gr, Ammoudi).*

Places to Stay *Perissa Camping (☎ 2286 081 343, Perissa Beach)* Adult/tent €5.90/ 2.35. This camping ground is right on the foreshore, which is rare in the Cyclades. It has reasonable shade and stunning, rocky mountain views. There's a beach bar next door.

Plenty of *domatia* are available in Perissa and at Perivolos.

Hostel Anna (☎ 2286 082 182, fax 2286 081 943, e *annayh@otenet.gr)* Dorm beds €6.10; doubles/quads with pool €29/59. Also in Perissa, this hostel has kitchen facilities, Internet and a swimming pool; a minibus picks up guests from the port.

Stelio's Place (☎ 2286 081 860, fax 2286 081 707) Doubles €29. A minute from Perissa beach, is this popular place attracting a regular stream of backpackers; pick up (no drop off) to the port is possible.

Places to Eat *Leonidas (☎ 2286 082 170, Agios Georgios)* Dishes €2.35-11.75. Leonidas is a nice place to kick-back and have a relaxing ouzo or raki and a bite to eat.

There are several good tavernas near Perissa, including *The Nets (☎ 2286 082 818)*, which serves exquisite, delicate mezedes and seafood, and *Perivolos (☎ 2286 082 007)* nearby. On the beachfront in Perissa, *Taverna Lava (☎ 2286 081 776)* is a low-key place with excellent, unfussy traditional food.

There are a few *domatia* in the back-streets of Kamari, and one or two good tavernas away from the beach. Colourful *Ouzeria Pontios*, near the football ground, and *Taverna the Fat Man (☎ 2286 034 025)*, on the road into Kamari, are worth seeking out if you're in the area.

Mythos Mezedopoleio Dishes €2.35-11.75, fish by the kilo. In Monolithos, with tables on a stone wall overlooking the beach, this is a good stop for ouzo and a nibble.

Paradissos (☎ 2286 071 583) Dishes €2.10-7.30 On the Oia coast road near Sigalas winery, Paradissos is known for its home-style dishes.

THIRASIA (Θηρασιά) & VOLCANIC ISLETS

Unspoilt Thirasia was separated from Santorini by an eruption in 236 BC. The cliff-top hora, **Manolas**, has *tavernas* and *domatia*. It's a pretty place that gives some idea of what Santorini was like before tourism took over.

The *Nisos Thirasia* leaves Athinios port for Thirasia on Monday and Friday at the inconveniently early hour of 7am, returning at 2pm. On Wednesday it leaves Athinios at 7.45pm but does not return to Santorini. Tickets are available only at the port. There are also morning and afternoon boats to Thirasia from Oia's port of Ammoudi.

The islets of **Palia Kameni** and **Nea Kameni** are still volcanically active and can be visited on half-day excursions from Fira Skala and Athinios. Two-hour trips to Nea Kameni are also possible. A day's excursion taking in Nea Kameni, the hot springs at Palia Kameni, Thirasia and Oia is about €20.50. A tour around the caldera by glass-bottomed boat costs €20.50. Tours that include Ancient Akrotiri as well are available. Shop around Fira's travel agencies for the best deals and the nicest boats.

The very bella *Bella Aurora*, an exact copy of an 18th-century schooner, scoots around the caldera every afternoon on a sunset buffet dinner tour (€29), stopping for sight-seeing at Nea Kameni and for ouzo at Thirasia.

Anafi Αναφη

postcode 840 09 • pop 250

Unpretentious Anafi is a one-hour ferry ride east of Santorini. The main attractions are the beaches, the slow-paced, traditional lifestyle and the lack of commercialism – it's an ideal place to unwind. In mythology, Anafi emerged at Apollo's command when Jason and the Argonauts were in dire need of refuge during a storm. The island's name means 'no snakes'.

Its little port is **Agios Nikolaos**. The main town, the **hora**, is a 10-minute bus ride or steep 30-minute walk from the port.

To get to the hora's main pedestrian thoroughfare, head up the hill behind the ouzeria at the first bus stop. This street has most of the domatia, restaurants and minimarkets, and there is also a post office that opens occasionally. There are several lovely beaches near Agios Nikolaos; palm-lined **Klissidi**, a 10-minute walk east of the port, is the closest and most popular.

Anafi's main sight, **Moni Kalamiotissas**, is a three-hour walk from the hora in the extreme east of the island, near the meagre remains of a sanctuary to Apollo. **Monastery Rock** (584m) is the highest rock formation in the Mediterranean Sea. There is also a ruined Venetian kastro at **Kastelli**, east of Klissidi.

Jeyzed Travel (☎ 2286 061 253, fax 2286 061 352), down at the port, organises Monastery Rock climbs, sells ferry tickets, exchanges money and can help with accommodation.

Getting To/From Anafi

There are four ferries weekly to Ios (three hours, €6.10), Naxos (four hours, €10.30) and Paros (six hours, €10.50). Seven ferries weekly go to Santorini (one hour, €5.90) and four go to Piraeus (11 hours, €20.10), and one goes to Syros (eight hours, €12.80), two go to Folegandros (five hours, €7.60) and Sikinos (four hours, €5.90). Twice weekly there's a post boat to Santorini (3½ hours, €6.40).

Getting Around Anafi

An undersized bus carts passengers from the port up to the hora. Caiques serve various beaches and nearby islands.

Places to Stay & Eat

Camping is tolerated at Klissidi Beach, but the only facilities are at nearby tavernas.

Rooms in the hora are overpriced and pretty much of a muchness. Shop around if you can, but be careful not to miss out altogether. Domatia owners are looking for long stays – if you're only staying one night you should take whatever you can get. In high season, contact Jeyzed Travel in advance to be sure of a room; places at Klissidi fill fast, so book well in advance.

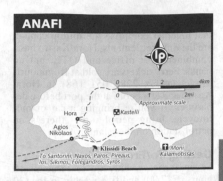

Rooms Rent Paradise (☎ 2286 061 243, fax 2286 061 253) Doubles €29. Paradise, on the main street, has clean rooms with a nice view.

Panorama (☎ 2286 061 292) Doubles €29. Next door to Rooms Rent Paradise, Panorama has similar rooms for the same price.

Anafi Rooms (☎ 2286 061 271) Doubles €38. These rooms are near Panorama.

Villa Apollon (☎ 2286 061 237, fax 2286 061 287, e vapollon@panafonet.gr) Doubles/studios €116/140.70. This villa at Klissidi Beach is the nicest and priciest. It has traditional rooms all with sea views.

Rooms to Let Artemis (☎ 2286 061 235) Rooms €38. Artemis is also at Klissidi.

Tavernas in the hora are all reasonably priced and have nice views. These include *Alexandra's* (☎ 2286 061 212), *Astrakan* (☎ 2286 061 249) and *To Steki* (☎ 2286 061 380). *Taverna Armenaki* (☎ 2286 061 234), below the main street, past To Steki, has a lively atmosphere and a menu that includes Cretan tacos, local greens and cheeses, and lamb. It also has raki with honey. Klissidi has a few *tavernas* as well.

Sikinos Σίκινος

postcode 840 10 • pop 287

If a quiet, unspoilt island is what you're looking for, Sikinos fits the bill. It has some nice beaches and a beautiful terraced landscape that drops dramatically down to the sea. The port of Alopronia, and the contiguous villages of Hora and Kastro that together comprise the hilltop capital, are the only settlements. Hora/Kastro has a combined post office and OTE, but no banks. Ferry tickets are sold at Koundouris Travel (☎/fax 2286 051 168) in Hora/Kastro and at a booth at the port before departures. If you're bringing a car or motorcycle, bring petrol too – there's no petrol station on the island.

Getting To/From Sikinos

Seven ferries weekly go to Piraeus (10 hours, €17.90) and five weekly to Ios (30 minutes, €3.20), two to Naxos (three hours, €5) and Syros (six hours, €8.40), six to Paros (four hours, €5.40), and four to Folegandros (45 minutes, €3.80). The ferries run to Santorini (2½ hours, €5.60), Kimolos (2½ hours, €5.30), Milos (three hours, €8.80) and Sifnos (five hours, €5.90). One weekly runs to Serifos (five hours, €5.90) and Thirasia (2½ hours, €5.60), and two run to Anafi (four hours, €5.90) and Kythnos (seven hours, €9.30).

Getting Around Sikinos

The local bus meets all ferries and runs between Alopronia and Hora/Kastro every half hour in August and less frequently at other times of the year. A timetable is sometimes posted near the minimarket.

Things to See & Do

The **Kastro** is a cute and compact place with some lovely old houses and friendly locals. In the centre there's a pretty square that was created in the '40s by the occupying Italians, who apparently planned to stay. The fortified **Moni Zoödohou Pigis** stands on a hill above the town.

Sikinos' main excursion is a one-hour scenic trek (or five-minute drive along a rather silly new road) south-west to **Episkopi**. When ruins there were investigated by 19th-century archaeologists, the Doric columns and inscriptions led them to believe it had originally been a shrine to Apollo, but the remains are now believed to be those of a 3rd century AD Roman mausoleum. In the 7th century the ruins were transformed into a

church, which was extended in the 17th century to become **Moni Episkopis** (*Open 6.30pm-8.30pm daily*). From here it's possible to climb up to a little church and ancient ruins perched on a precipice to the south, from where the views are spectacular.

Caiques run to nice beaches at **Agios Georgios**, **Malta** – with ancient ruins on the hill above – and **Karra**. **Katergo**, a swimming place with interesting rocks, and **Agios Nikolaos Beach** are both within easy walking distance of Alopronia.

Places to Stay & Eat

Alopronia has the bulk of accommodation.

Lucas Rooms to Let (☎ 2286 051 075) Doubles/apartments €32/43.50. Near the restaurant of the same name and recommended by readers, Lucas has doubles, and three- to four-person apartments.

Tasos Rooms (☎ 2286 051 005) Doubles €34.90. These bougainvillea-covered rooms are past the Rock Café.

Porto Sikinos (☎/fax 2286 051 220) Doubles with breakfast €69.60. This stylish B-class spot is on the port beach. A traditional Cycladic-style establishment, it has a bar and restaurant.

In Hora/Kastro, *To Steki tou Garbi* is a good grill house. There are also good *tavernas* at Agio Georgios. Down at the port, *Lucas* serves the best food. In high season a lovely *bar* opens over the water at the northern end of Alopronia's bay; at other times the *Rock Café*, above the quay, suffices.

Folegandros
Φολέγανδρος

The happiest man on earth is the man with fewest needs. And I also believe that if you have light, such as you have here, all ugliness is obliterated.
Henry Miller

postcode 840 11 • pop 650
Folegandros (fo-**leh**-gan-dross) is one of Greece's most enticing islands, bridging the gap between tourist traps and small, under-populated islands on the brink of total abandonment. The number of visitors is increasing, but most locals still make a living from fishing and farming.

Tourists come in search of unspoilt island life and, except for July and August, the island is uncrowded and blissful. The island has several good beaches – be prepared for strenuous walking to reach some of them – and a striking landscape of cultivated terraces that give way to precipitous cliffs.

The capital is the concealed cliff-top Hora, one of the prettiest capitals in the Cyclades. Boats dock at the small harbour of Karavostasis, on the east coast. The only other settlement is Ano Meria, 4km north-west of Hora.

Getting To/From Folegandros
Ferry There are four services weekly to Piraeus (six to nine hours, €15.40), Santorini (1½ to 2½ hours, €5.30), Ios (1½ hours, €4.65), Paros (four hours, €5.90), Naxos (three hours, €7.40) and Sikinos (40 minutes, €3.80).

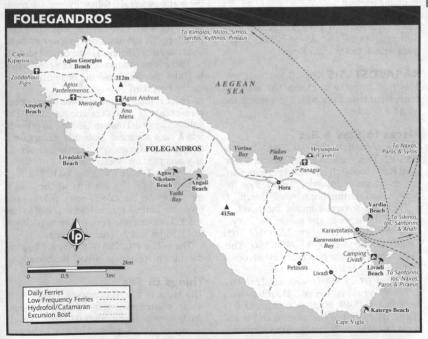

FOLEGANDROS

Three weekly services go to Syros (six hours, €8.80), Milos (2½ hours, €5.30), Sifnos (four hours, €5.30) and Serifos (five hours, €4.65).

Two weekly ferries go to Kimolos (1½ hours, €3.50) and Anafi (five hours, €7.60).

Once weekly there are ferries to Thirasia (1½ hours, €5.30) and Kythnos (six hours, €9).

Getting Around Folegandros

The local bus meets all boats and takes passengers to Hora (€0.80). From Hora there are buses to the port one hour before all ferry departures, even late at night. Buses from Hora run hourly to Ano Meria (€1), stopping at the road leading to Angali Beach. The bus stop for Ano Meria is on the western edge of town, next to the Sottovento Tourism Office. There is one overworked taxi (☎ 2286 041 048, mobile 69 4469 3957) on the island, and motorbikes, not cars, are the only form of transport available for hire.

In July and August, excursion boats make separate trips from Karavostasis to Kartergo, Angali and Agios Nikolaos and from Angali to Livadaki Beach.

KARAVOSTASIS Καραβοστασις

This port town lacks charm but makes a convenient base from which to explore the island's beaches.

Places to Stay & Eat

Camping Livadi (☎ 2286 041 204) Adult/tent €4.10/2. This site is at Livadi Beach, 1.2km from Karavostasis. It has a kitchen, minimart, bar, restaurant and laundry. Turn left on the cement road skirting Karavostasis Beach.

There are several domatia and hotels – look for the signs as you get off the ferry.

Aeolos Beach Hotel (☎ 2286 041 205) Singles/doubles/suites €32/49/67.90. This C-class hotel, on the beach, has clean rooms and a pretty garden.

Vrahos (☎ 2286 041 450, fax 2286 041 292, e vrahos@tee.gr) Doubles with breakfast €75.40. Built in traditional Cycladic style, Vrahos has an outdoor bar and breakfast area with views of the surround-

ing islands. It's at the far end of the beach beyond the Aeolos Beach Hotel.

Restaurant Kati Allo (☎ 2286 041 272) Dishes €1.70-4.65, seafood by the kilo. Part of the Poseidon Hotel, this restaurant has one of the best reputations for top-quality traditional food and fresh fish.

The cafe-bars *Evangelos* and *Sirma* (☎ 2286 041 527) are both on the beach, so you'll be face-to-face with fishermen working on their nets and kids playing; both serve snacks, sandwiches and meze. *Two Hearts* is also a nice place to eat, and Hotel Vrahos has a small, quiet bar with marvellous views.

HORA Χώρα

The captivating Hora, complete with a medieval kastro filled with little houses draped in bougainvillea, is perhaps the most beautiful capital in the Cyclades.

Orientation & Information

From the bus turnaround, facing away from the port, turn left and follow the curving road. An archway on the right leads to the kastro, where the walls have been incorporated into dwellings. A left turn leads to a row of three shady squares. The third is the central plateia.

There is no tourist police. The post office is 200m downhill from the bus turnaround, on the port road.

There is no bank, but all three travel agencies exchange travellers cheques, and Diaplous General Tourism Office can provide VISA cash advances. Note that, except for a couple of boutiques, credit cards are not usually accepted on Folegandros.

Maraki Travel (☎ 2286 041 273, fax 2286 041 149), by the first square, has a monopoly on the sale of ferry tickets, and provides limited Internet access; it also has a ticket booth at the port. It's open 10.30am to 12.15pm and 5.30am to 9.15pm.

The police (☎ 2286 041 249) are beyond the third plateia, past Nikos' Restaurant.

Things to See

The Hora is a well-preserved village with white churches, sugar-cube houses and shady squares. The medieval **Kastro**, a tangle of narrow streets spanned by low archways,

The Caper Caper

Capers are the unopened buds of the caper bush *Capparis spinosa*, which grows wild throughout the Mediterranean region. They have a radish-like, pungent taste and are usually pickled in vinegar. Capers were known to the ancient Greeks, and carbon dating of fossilised seeds and buds has shown that they were eaten as far back as 6000 BC in Iraq and Turkey.

Folegandros, Santorini and Anafi are all very proud of their capers, and Andros even has a town named after them – Kapparia. The bushes, which are small, fleshy and sprawling, often inhabit the stone walls that line old paths and divide fields. The harvesting of the buds and the leaves (a delicacy) from the low-lying plants is a laborious process that must be done by hand. Spring is caper-collecting season, although you can still find buds in abundance in early summer. Any buds not collected blossom into surprisingly showy pink and white flowers, which are, of course, also edible. The torpedo-shaped fruit is packed in salt or pickled in vinegar and eaten as well.

Capers have experienced a comeback in Greek cuisine, especially on the islands. Many tavernas, notably those that take pride in serving traditional local food, are spiking salads and mezedes with liberal sprinklings of these tasty buds. Delicious.

dates from when Marco Sanudo ruled the island in the 13th century. The houses' wooden balconies blaze with bougainvillea and hibiscus.

The newer village, outside the kastro, is just as pretty. From the first bus stop, a steep path leads up to the large church of the **Panagia** *(open 6pm-8pm)*, which is perched on a cliff top above the town.

Courses

The *Cycladic School* (☎ 2286 041 137, e a-f-pap@otenet.gr), founded on Folegandros in 1984, offers one and two-week courses in drawing, painting, Greek cookery, folk and modern dancing and Hatha yoga. Accommodation is included.

Organised Tours

Sottovento Tourism Office *(☎ 2286 041 444, fax 2286 041 430, e sottovento94@hotmail .com)* Adult/child €18.90/10.30, including lunch. Departs 10am Mon, Wed, Fri summer. Day trips by caique to hidden bays and beaches are offered by this company. It's by the bus stop for Ano Meria and Angali; if you have snorkelling gear, take it along. The office also organises accommodation.

Places to Stay

In July and August most domatia and hotels are booked solid; unless you're happy to join the homeless overspill down at

Camping Livadi, make sure you book well in advance. Diaplous General Tourism Office (☎ 2286 041 158, fax 2286 041 159, e diaplous@x-treme.gr), by the port-Hora bus stop books accommodation.

Spyridoula Rooms (☎ 2286 041 078, fax 2286 041 034) Doubles €43.50. This is one of numerous, reasonably priced domatia near the police station.

Artemis (☎ 2286 041 313) Doubles €49. Open year-round. Artemis is by the port-Hora bus station above its cosy cafe. Some rooms have sea views.

Hotel Polikandia (☎ 2286 041 322, fax 2286 041 323) Doubles €55. By the port-Hora bus stop, this new hotel has a lovely garden area to hang out in. Rooms have telephone, radio, fan and balcony.

Hotel Odysseus (☎ 2286 041 276, fax 2286 041 366) Doubles €59. This new hotel has a swimming pool and rooms have a balcony. It's next to Spyridoula Rooms.

Hotel Castro (☎/fax 2286 041 230) Doubles/triples with bathroom €55/78.30. Some of the cosy rooms at this atmospheric hotel have incredible views straight down the cliffs to the sea. Walk straight ahead from the kastro entrance and you'll find the hotel on the left. Breakfast is available.

Folegandros Apartments (☎ 2286 041 239, fax 2286 041 166, e foleaps@ath .forthnet.gr) Studios from €75.40. This C-class establishment can be found where the

CYCLADES

port bus terminates. It has well-equipped apartments and a swimming pool.

Anemomilos Apartments (☎ *2286 041 309)* Doubles from €90. Views don't come any better than from this top-of-the-range property by the bus station, although snooty reception staff don't come any worse either. Apartments are furnished with antiques, and there is one unit for the disabled.

Kallista (☎ *2286 041 555, fax 2286 041 554)* Singles/doubles €64/81. This A-class hotel has a swimming pool and views of the sea in the distance. The beds are a novelty – they have a traditional stone base. Kallista is on the street behind Sottovento Tourism Office.

Places to Eat

Punta (☎ *2286 041 063)* Dishes €2.35-6.40. Punta, at the port-Hora bus turn-around, has tables in a wild garden area. Excellent breakfast, spanakopitta, rabbit *stifado* (stew), lamb and vegetarian dishes are served at very reasonable prices in striking crockery made by one of the owners.

Apanemos Dishes €2-5. Next to the Sottovento Tourism Office, this friendly place is run by the same crew as Punta. It serves crepes, pasta and traditional dishes.

Melissa (☎ *2286 041 067)* Dishes €1.50-5.50. Melissa, on the main square under an umbrella of pepper trees, has good home-cooked food.

Piatsa Restaurant (☎ *2286 041 274)* Dishes €2.50-8.20. This is one of the best restaurants on the island and has interesting daily specials, as well as vegetarian dishes. It's on the second square past the kastro.

O Kritikos (☎ *2286 041 219)* Dishes €2-6.40. On the third square past the kastro (and with a rotisserie in front), O Kritikos serves succulent grilled meat.

Entertainment

On the main square, ***Astarti*** is a good place to go after dinner for Greek music. Opposite Punta, ***Kellari*** (☎ *2286 041 119)* is a moody little wine bar where regional Greek wines are available by the glass.

Arajo (☎ *2286 041 463)* is the place to go for a late-night drink and some Latin,

jazz and hip hop; it's on the road that lead west off the third square towards the Ano Meria bus stop and the Sottovento Tourism Office.

Next door to Sottovento, the vivid wall murals in ***Greco Café Bar*** (☎ *2286 041 456)* provide some promise for a colourful night out, while ***Laoumi***, left of Sottovento, is a tiny, atmospheric ouzeria.

In an idyllic setting a few minutes' walk from the Hora, ***Rakendia Sunset Bar*** has a fabulous view over the terraced dry-stone walls that lead down to the ocean. It's open early in the afternoon until late and is signposted off the road to Ano Meria.

AROUND FOLEGANDROS
Ano Meria Aνω Mερια

The settlement of Ano Meria stretches for several kilometres because small farms surround most of the dwellings. Agriculture is still very much alive at this end of the island and you'll see haystacks, market gardens, goats and donkeys.

The **folklore museum** *(admission €1.50; open 5pm-8pm daily)* is on the eastern outskirts of the village. Ask the bus driver to drop you off nearby.

There are several excellent tavernas in Ano Meria, including ***I Synantisi*** (☎ *2286 041 208)* and ***Mimi's*** (☎ *2286 041 377),* which specialise in *matsada* – a type of handmade pasta served with rabbit or rooster.

The very old and authentic kafeneio ***Barbakosta*** frequented by locals, is well worth a stop, as is the local ***bakery*** nearby, which makes excellent almond biscuits and the local sweet *karpouzenia*, a baked, soft melange of watermelon chunks, honey and sesame seeds.

Beaches

Karavostasis has a pretty white-pebbled beach. For **Livadi Beach**, follow the signs for Camping Livadi. The sandy and pebbled **Angali Beach** has a lovely aspect. There are several *domatia* here and two reasonable *tavernas*.

There are other good beaches at **Agios Nikolaos** and **Livadaki**, both west of Angali. The steep path to the beach at Agios

Nikolaos is exhausting, but it's worth it if you plan to have lunch here. Don't miss the octopus in wine sauce at *Taverna Papalagi*. **Agios Georgios** is north of Ano Meria. A path from Agios Andreas church in Ano Meria leads to Agios Georgios Beach. The walk takes about an hour.

Most of the beaches have no shops or tavernas, so make sure you take food and water.

Milos & Kimolos
Μήλος & Κίμωλος

MILOS
postcode 848 00 • pop 4390

Volcanic Milos (**mee**-loss), the most westerly island of the Cyclades, is overlooked by most foreign tourists. While not as visually dramatic as the volcanic islands of Santorini and Nisyros, it does have some mesmerising rock formations, hot springs and pleasant beaches. Flowers seem to grow in abundance on the island, and it appears wildly verdant and green when compared with its near neighbour Folegandros. A boat trip around the island allows you to visit most of Milos' stunning beaches (many inaccessible by road), coves and geologically interesting places.

Filakopi, an ancient Minoan city in the island's north-east, was one of the earliest settlements in the Cyclades. During the Peloponnesian Wars, Milos remained neutral, and was the only Cycladic island not to join the Athenian alliance. It paid dearly in 416 BC when avenging Athenians massacred the adult males and enslaved the women and children.

The island's most celebrated export, the beautiful *Venus de Milo* (a 4th-century-BC statue of Aphrodite) is far away in the Louvre (apparently having lost its arms on the way to Paris in the 19th century).

Since ancient times, the island has been quarried for minerals, resulting in huge gaps and fissures in the landscape. Obsidian was mined on the island and exported throughout the Mediterranean.

Getting To/From Milos

Air There is a daily flight to/from Athens (€52.85/61.30 one way). The Olympic Airways office (☎ 2287 022 380, fax 2287 021 884) is in Adamas, just past the main square, on the road to Plaka (and is worth going into just for the original '70s decor).

Ferry The *Nissos Kimolos* departs five times daily from Pollonia for Kimolos at 9am, 11am, 2.15pm, 6.30pm, 10.40pm (20 minutes, €1.70/1.30/7.80 per person/motorbike/car).

There are at least two ferries daily to Piraeus (five to seven hours, €16). There is at least one daily ferry to Sifnos (1¼ hours, €5.30), Serifos (two hours, €5.60) and Kythnos (3½ hours, €5.30). Six weekly ferries go to Kimolos (one hour, €4.65).

Five times weekly the *Vitsentsos Kornaros* sails to the Cretan ports of Agios Nikolaos (seven hours, €14.80) and Sitia (nine hours, €16), sometimes continuing on to Kassos (11 hours, €18.30), Karpathos (12 hours, €22) and Rhodes (13 hours, €25.90).

There are three weekly ferries to Folegandros (2½ hours, €5.30) and Sikinos (three hours, €8.80), and two weekly to Paros (4½ hours, €8.40). Services also run regularly to Milos.

There is one weekly ferry to Santorini (four hours, €9.60), Ios (5½ hours, €8.80) and Syros (six hours, €9).

Fast Boat & Catamarans One weekly service goes to Santorini (1¾, €19.20), and one daily to Sifnos (1¾, €7.70), Serifos (1¼, €8.80) and at least one daily to Piraeus (3¾ hours, €30).

Getting Around Milos

There are no buses to the airport, so you'll need to take a taxi (☎ 2287 022 219) for €3.80 from Adamas.

Buses leave Adamas for Plaka and Trypiti (both €1.10) every hour or so. Buses run daily to Pollonia (€0.80, nine daily), Paleohori (€1, eight daily), and Provatas (€1.10, eight daily), Milos Camping (eight daily) and Sarakiniko (two daily). Taxis can be ordered

CYCLADES

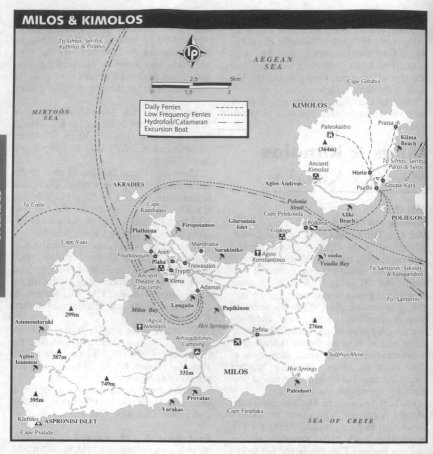

MILOS & KIMOLOS

on ☎ 2287 022 219. Cars, motorcycles and mopeds can be hired along the waterfront.

Adamas Αδαμας
postcode 848 01

Although Plaka is the capital, the rather plain port of Adamas has most of the accommodation.

To get to the town centre from the quay, turn right at the waterfront. The central square, with the bus stop, taxi rank and outdoor cafes, is at the end of this stretch of waterfront. Just past the square is a road to the right that skirts the town beach. Straight ahead is the town's main thoroughfare and the road to Plaka.

Milos' municipal tourist office (☎ 2287 022 445, W www.milostravel.com), opposite the quay, is one of the most helpful in the Cyclades, although it's open 10am-4pm in summer only. Terry's Travel (☎ 2287 022 640, fax 2287 022 261, e teristur@otenet.gr), is up the steps from the quay and organises tours and pricey windmill accommodation.

For the post office, turn right just after the square and take the third street on the left. There are ATMs on the main square. The police (☎ 2287 021 378) are on the main square, next to the bus stop; the port police (☎ 2287 022 100) are on the waterfront.

Mining Museum This museum (☎ 2287 022 481; admission free; open 9am-2pm & 6pm-9pm daily) has some interesting geological exhibits and traces the island's long mining history. To get there, take the first right after the central square and continue along the waterfront for about 500m.

Activities Dive courses are offered by **Milos Diving Center** (☎/fax 2287 041 296, W www.marras.gr/milosdiving). Based at Pollonia, Milos Diving is a member of the International Association for Handicapped Divers.

Milos Yachting (☎ 2287 022 079, fax 2287 023 723) has yachts and skippers for charter.

Organised Tours Milos Round 1 & 2 (☎ 2287 023 411) Tours €17.40. Departs 9am. These tour boats stop at beaches around the island and Kleftiko, pausing at Kimolos for lunch; tickets are available on the waterfront.

Andromeda Yachts (☎ 2287 023 680) Sailing trips €45 per person, sailing tours €240 per tour. Oct-Nov. Andromeda has sailing trips to the island's nicest beaches and coves; they feature a seafood lunch, ouzo and sweets. Sailing tours take place in the southwest Cyclades. Book through travel agencies or visit Andromeda on the waterfront.

Special Events The **Milos Festival**, a well-orchestrated event, is held in early July and features traditional dancing, cooking and jazz.

Places to Stay Arhivadolimni (Milos) Camping (☎ 2287 031 410, fax 2287 031 412, W www.miloscamping.com, Arhivadolimni) Adult/tent €4.80/3.50, bungalows €61. This camping ground has excellent facilities, including a restaurant, bar and bike rental. It's 6.5km east of Adamas; to get there, follow the signs along the waterfront from the central square.

In summer, lists of domatia are given out at the tourist office on the quay, but decent accommodation is quite thin on the ground – make sure you call ahead.

Ethelvina's Rooms (☎ 2287 022 169) Singles/doubles/triples €20.50/43.50/52.50. These excellent rooms are uphill from the bakery on the main square.

Langada Beach Hotel (☎ 2287 023 411, fax 2287 023 416) Singles/doubles/triples €30.20/49/61. Left of the ferry quay, behind Langada Beach, this is a huge complex with a pool.

Hotel Delfini (☎ 2287 022 001, fax 2287 023 409) Doubles €29/52.50 with shared/private bathroom. Behind Langada Beach Hotel, Delfini has friendly owners and nice simple rooms.

Hotel Dionysis (☎ 2287 022 117 fax 2287 022 118) Double/triple studios €61/78.30. Just up from the square near Olympic Airways, Dionysis has comfortable studios with TV and air-con.

Portiani Hotel (☎ 2287 022 940, fax 2287 022 766, e sirmalen@otenet.gr) Singles/ doubles from €67.90/88. On the waterfront at the square, the rooms have TV, air-con, phone, balcony and terrace. Rates include a buffet breakfast featuring fresh figs, comb honey, cheeses and homemade jams.

Villa Helios (☎ 2287 022 258, fax 2287 023 974, e heaton.theologitis@utanet.gr) Apartments €72.50. On the hill behind the quay, Helios has beautifully furnished two-person apartments with phone, TV and air-con.

Places to Eat Aragosta (☎ 2287 022 292) Mains €10.30-26. This upmarket Italian eatery, on the first staircase up from the port as you head into town, serves duck, lobster, turkey and pasta dishes.

O Kinigos (☎ 2287 022 349) Dishes €2.10-25.90, fish by the kilo. Superb Greek staples are on offer at this waterfront taverna, which is refreshingly crowded with locals.

Navagio (☎ 2287 023 392) beyond the Portiani Hotel is an excellent fish taverna.

Entertainment Akri (☎ 2287 022 064) is an overflowing, up-beat bar opposite Aragosta, up the first staircase by the port.

CYCLADES

CYCLADES

Vipera Lebetina, beyond Akri and named after the island's breed of poisonous snake, plays deafeningly loud rock and summer-loving hits, which is just what the young crowd of locals want.

Malion is a local bouzouki bar with live music, nearby Navagio.

Plaka & Trypiti Πλακα & Τρυπητα

Plaka, 5km uphill from Adamas, is a typical Cycladic town with white houses and labyrinthine laneways. It merges with the settlement of Trypiti to the south.

The **Milos Folk & Arts Museum** (☎ 2287 021 292; admission €1.50; open 10am-2pm, 6pm-8pm Tues-Sat, 10am-2pm Sun) is in a 19th-century house in Plaka. It's signposted at the bus turnaround in Plaka.

At the bus turnaround, turn right for the path to the **Frankish Kastro** built on the ancient acropolis. The 13th-century church, **Thalassitras**, is inside the walls. The final battle between ancient Melians and Athenians was fought on this hill. The kastro offers panoramic views of most of the island.

The **archaeology museum** (☎ 2287 021 629; admission €1.50; open 8.30am-3pm Tues-Sun) is in Plaka, near the junction with the road leading to the much signposted catacombs. Don't miss the perfectly preserved terracotta figurine of Athena (unlabelled) in the middle room. The room on the left has charming figurines from Filakopi.

Plaka is built on the site of Ancient Milos, which was destroyed by the Athenians and rebuilt by the Romans. There are some Roman ruins near Trypiti, including Greece's only Christian **catacombs** (☎ 2287 021 625; open 8am-3pm Tues-Sun). On the road to the catacombs, a sign points right to the well-preserved **ancient theatre**, which hosts the **Milos Festival** every July. On the track to the theatre, a sign points to where a farmer found the *Venus de Milo* in 1820. Opposite are remains of massive Doric walls. Fifty metres farther along on the cement road is a sign to the 1st-century catacombs. A passage leads to a large chamber flanked by tunnels that contained the tombs.

Places to Stay & Eat Both Plaka and Trypiti have *domatia*; ask at tavernas.

Arhontoula (☎ 2287 021 384) Dishes €2-8.20. Left from the bus turnaround in Plaka, Arhontoula has a large selection of meze, including cod with *skordalia* (garlic sauce) and interesting salads.

Alisahni (☎ 2287 023 485) Mains €5-11.30. Just around the corner from Arhontoula, this voguish place is also very good, with creative starters, such as tzatziki with pine nuts and almonds.

Utopia Cafe (☎ 2287 023 678) The view from this smart little cafe-bar is breathtaking. Utopia is open till late and signposted down a laneway opposite Arhontoula.

Erghina's (☎ 2287 022 524) Dishes €2.10-11.75. On the main 'road' through Trypiti to the left, local's describe Erghina's creations as 'dream food'. Try delicious dishes such as *pitaraki* (hard-cheese pie) and young wild goat with potatoes. *Methysmeni Politia* on the road to the catacombs, is also worth seeking out.

Around Milos

Klima, once the port of ancient Milos, is now a charming, unspoilt fishing village skirting a narrow beach below Trypiti and the catacombs. Whitewashed buildings, with bright blue, green and red doors and balconies, have boat houses on the ground floor and living quarters on the first floor.

Plathiena is a lovely sandy beach below Plaka. On the way to Plathiena you can detour to the fishing villages of **Areti** and **Fourkovouni**. The beaches of **Provatas** and **Paleohori**, on the south coast, are long and sandy, and there are hot springs at Paleohori. *Deep Blue* (☎ 2287 031 158) in Paleohori is an atmospheric terraced music cafe built into the surrounding rocks.

Pollonia, on the north coast, is a fishing village-cum-resort with a small beach and *domatia*. It serves as the jumping-off point for the boat to Kimolos. **Mandrakia** is a lovely fishing hamlet north-east of Plaka.

The Minoan settlement of **Filakopi** is 2km inland from Pollonia. Three levels of cities have been uncovered here – Early, Middle and Late Cycladic.

The islet of **Glaronisia**, off the north coast, is a rare geological phenomenon composed entirely of hexagonal volcanic stone bars.

Places to Stay & Eat *Hotel Panorama* (☎ *2287 021 623, fax 2287 022 112)* Doubles with breakfast €59. This is Klima's only hotel. It's 2km from the village. There's also a restaurant.

KIMOLOS

This small island lies just north-east of Milos. It receives few visitors, although there are *domatia*, *tavernas*, *bars* and decent beaches. Domatia owners meet ferries.

Those who do make the effort tend to be day-trippers arriving on the boat from Pollonia, on the north-eastern tip of Milos. The boat docks at the port of **Psathi**, from where it's 3km to the pretty capital of **Horio**. Seek out promising *To Kyma* (☎ *2287 051 001*) for a meal.

There's no petrol station on Kimolos – if you're bringing a car or moped from Milos, make sure you've got enough fuel. Donkeys are still the principal mode of transport, and there are tracks all around the island.

There are thermal springs at the settlement of **Prassa** on the north-east coast. **Beaches** can be reached by caique from Psathi. At the centre of the island is the 364m-high cliff on which sits the fortress of **Paleokastro**.

Day-trippers should try the local speciality, *ladenia*, a pizza-like pie with tomato, onion and olives.

Getting To/From Kimolos

Ferry Boats go daily to/from Pollonia on Milos, departing from Kimolos at 8am, 10am, 1.15pm, 5.30pm and 10pm (see the Milos Getting There & Away section for details).

There are three ferries weekly to Adamas (one hour, €3.80), Folegandros (1½ hours, €4.20) and Sikinos (2½ hours, €5.30).

There are four weekly to Sifnos (1½ hours, €4.40) and Serifos (two hours, €5.90).

Two weekly services go to Kythnos (three hours, €7.40), Syros (five hours,

€9), Paros (4½ hours, €6.90), Santorini (3½ hours, €9.30) and Piraeus (seven hours, €13.40).

Sifnos Σίφνος

postcode 840 03 • pop 2900

Sifnos coyly hides its assets from passing ferry passengers. At first glance it looks barren, but the port is in the island's most arid area. Explore and you'll find an abundantly attractive landscape of terraced olive groves and almond trees, with oleanders in the valleys and hillsides covered in wild juniper, which used to fuel potters' kilns. There are numerous dovecotes, white-washed houses and chapels. Plenty of old paths link the villages, which makes it an ideal island for walking.

During the Archaic period the island was very wealthy due to its gold and silver resources. To protect their loot the islanders constructed an elaborate communications network of watchtowers that used fire and smoke signals to warn of attack. The ruins of 55 towers have been located to date. By the 5th century BC the mines were exhausted and Sifnos' fortunes were reversed – the island became so poor that it was the butt of endless jokes in Athens and elsewhere.

The island has a long history of producing superior pottery because of the quality of its clay, and many shops sell local ceramics. Some potters' workshops are open to the public – it's quite mesmerising to watch them work.

Sifniot olive oil is highly prized throughout Greece, which might have something to do with the island's reputation for producing some of the country's best chefs. Local specialities include *revithia* (baked chickpeas), *revithokeftedes* (falafel-like vegetable balls), *xynomyzithra* (a sharpish fresh cheese) and almond sweets flavoured with orange flowers.

Getting To/From Sifnos

Ferry There are daily ferries to Milos (two hours, €4.65), Piraeus (five hours, €13.40) via Serifos (one hour, €4.40) and Kythnos

CYCLADES

(2½ hours, €5.90). There are three ferries weekly to Kimolos (1½ hours, €4.40), Folegandros (four hours, €5.30), Sikinos (five hours, €5.90) and Santorini (six hours, €9.30), and two weekly to Paros (two hours, €5.70) and Syros (5½ hours, €6.40).

Fast Boat & Catamaran There is a daily catamaran to Piraeus (2¾ hours, €26.40); four weekly to Kythnos (1¼ hours, €9.90); and one daily to Serifos (20 minutes, €7.30) and Milos (¾ hour, €7.70). There are five weekly catamarans to Santorini (2½ hours, €15.40).

Getting Around Sifnos

Frequent buses link Apollonia with: Kamares (€0.80), with some services continuing onto Artemonas; Kastro (€0.80), Vathi (€1.50), Faros (€0.80) and Platys Gialos (€1.50).

I Meropi Taverna runs a taxi-boat service to anywhere on the island. Taxis (☎ 2284 031 347) hover around the port and Apollonia's main square. Cars can be hired from Hotel Kamari (☎ 2284 033 383), in Kamares, and from Apollo Rent a Car (☎ 2284 032 237), in Apollonia from €29.

KAMARES Καμαρες

Unlike most villages on the island, the port of Kamares is a newish resort-style town. It has a nice enough 'holiday' feel about it, with lots of waterfront cafes and tavernas, and a reasonable sandy beach. The bus stop is the stand of tamarisk trees outside the municipal tourist office.

Opposite the quay, the very helpful municipal tourist office (☎ 2284 031 977) can find accommodation anywhere on the island (open until midnight). It also offers free luggage storage and has copies of the bus schedule.

Places to Stay & Eat

Camping Makis (☎/fax 2284 032 366) Adult/tent €4.20/2.35, rooms from €23.20. This site is just behind the beach, 600m north of the port. It's a nice place with an

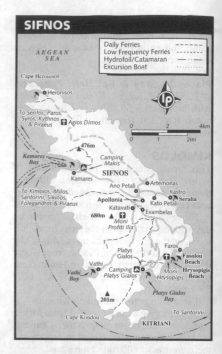

outdoor cafe area to hang out, a barbecue area, laundry and shaded sites.

Domatia owners rarely meet boats, and in high season it's best to book ahead.

Hotel Afroditi (☎ 2284 031 704, fax 2284 031 622, e hotel_afroditi@hotmail. com) Doubles with mountain/sea view €46.50/49. Beyond Hotel Boutaris, and opposite the beach, Hotel Afroditi is a popular place; breakfast is available.

Stavros Hotel (☎ 2284 031 641, fax 2284 031 709) Doubles €40.80. In the middle of the waterfront, Stavros has basic, clean rooms.

Hotel Kamari (☎ 2284 033 383, fax 2284 031 709) Doubles €49. This hotel, about 400m up the road to Apollonia, has attractive rooms.

There are several reasonably priced waterfront eateries serving good Greek staples, including *O-Simos*, *I Meropi*, *Ouzeri Kamares* and *Captain Andreas*, which is the best place for fish.

APOLLONIA Απολλώνια

The capital is situated on a plateau 5km up-hill from the port.

The bus stop for Kamares is on the lively central square where the post office and OTE are located; all other buses stop outside Hotel Anthousa. The main pedestrian thoroughfare – with jewellery and clothes shops, restaurants and bars – is to the right behind the museum. There is an Alpha Bank (with ATM) next to Hotel Sofia and the National Bank of Greece (with ATM), is about 50m out on the road to Artemonas; the police are another 50m beyond.

The interesting little **Museum of Popular Art** (☎ 2284 033 730; admission €0.90; open 10am-2pm & 6pm-10pm Tues-Sun), on the central square and just opposite the post office, contains old costumes, pots and textiles.

Places to Stay & Eat

Hotel Sofia (☎ 2284 031 238) Singles/doubles €23/38. This C-class hotel, north of the central square, has basic rooms and TV.

Hotel Sifnos (☎/fax 2284 031 624) Singles/doubles/triples €49/59/69.60. This C-class hotel, on the main pedestrian street that leads off to the right behind the museum, has immaculate rooms. It also has an excellent *taverna*.

Peristeronas Apartments (☎ 2284 071 288) Doubles/quads €72.50/90. This Sifnos-style house overlooking terraced fields is downhill from Hotel Anthousa.

Hotel Petali (☎/fax 2284 033 024) Doubles/triples €99/110. This newer, more upmarket hotel is about 100m along the footpath to Artemonas. It has spacious rooms with air-con, TV and telephone.

Apostoli tou Koutouki (☎ 2284 031 186) Dishes €2.20-10.30, fish by the kilo. Open 7pm. This eatery on the main street serves excellent meat dishes – try the veal cooked with oregano in a clay pot (€7.30).

Shopping

As well as fine ceramics and jewellery (there are a few workshops here), you can also find beautiful hand-woven textiles. On the main pedestrian thoroughfare, Margarita Baki has a tiny workshop.

AROUND SIFNOS

The pretty village of **Artemonas** is a short walk or bus ride north of Apollonia. Not to be missed is the walled cliff-top village of **Kastro**, 3km from Apollonia. The former capital, it is a magical place of buttressed alleys and whitewashed houses. It has a small **archaeological museum** (☎ 2284 031 022; admission free; open 8.30am-3pm Tues-Sun).

The pretty downhill walk along old paths from Apollonia to Kastro takes under an hour and you can return by bus. The path begins at the junction of the roads to Exambelas, Kastro and Kamares. The serene village of **Exambelas**, south of Apollonia, is said to be the birthplace of most of Sifnos' accomplished chefs.

The resort of **Platys Gialos**, 10km south of Apollonia, has a long sandy beach. The spectacularly situated **Moni Hrysopigis**, near Platys Gialos, was built to house a miraculous icon of the Virgin found in the sea by two fishermen. A path leads from the monastery to **Hrysopigis Beach**, although most people find a space in the rocks below the church and sunbathe and swim there. There is a taverna on the watch. **Vathi**, on the west coast, is a gorgeous sandy bay with several *tavernas*. **Faros** is a cosy little fishing hamlet with a couple of nice beaches nearby, such as the sweet little beach of **Fasolou**, up the stairs and over the headland from the bus stop.

Places to Stay & Eat

Platys Gialos has quite a few accommodation options, most of them oriented towards package tourists.

Camping Platys Gialos (☎ 2284 071 286) Adult/tent €3.50/2.20. This site is in an olive grove 700m from the beach.

Angeliki Rooms (☎/fax 2284 071 288) Doubles/triples €46.50/55. These rooms are right on the beach.

Platys Gialos Beach Hotel (☎ 2284 071 324, fax 2284 071 325) Doubles with breakfast €130.50. Rooms at this lodge-like hotel have air-con, TV, minibar and sea views.

There are quite a few rooms for rent in Faros right by the beach: Try *Margarita*

CYCLADES

(☎ 2284 071 438), *Aristi Pension* (☎ 2284 071 443) or *Villa Maria* (☎ 2284 071 421).

Fabrika (☎ 2284 071 427, *Faros*) Rooms €46.50. Fabrika has rooms in an atmospheric old flour mill.

In Artemonas, on the main square, *Liotrivi (Manganas;* ☎ 2284 031 246) serves robust traditional fare. *Margarita* (☎ 2284 031 058), nearby, is also worth seeking out.

Faros (☎ 2284 071 452) Dishes €1.50-11.75, fish by the kilo. This small taverna is the place to go for fish in Faros.

On the Rocks (☎ 2284 031 817, *Faros*) Dishes €3-5.50. Near Fasolou, this little cafe, serving crepes and pizzas, has a playful nautical theme.

Serifos Σέριφος

postcode 840 05 • pop 1020
Serifos is a barren, rocky island with a few pockets of greenery the result of tomato and vine cultivation. Livadi, the port, is on the south-east coast; the beautiful whitewashed capital, Hora, clings to a hillside 2km inland.

Getting To/From Serifos
Ferry & Catamaran There are daily ferries from Serifos to Piraeus (4½ hours, €11.90), Sifnos (one hour, €4.40), Milos (two hours, €5.30) and Kimolos (2½ hours, €5.90).

Four times weekly the Piraeus ferry stops at Kythnos (1½ hours, €5.60), and twice weekly boats go to Paros (two hours, €6.10), Syros (three to five hours, €5.90) and Folegandros (five hours, €5.30).

There are weekly boats to Santorini (seven hours, €10.50), Ios (six hours, €8.80) and Sikinos (five hours, €8.40).

One daily catamaran runs to Sifnos (20 minutes, €7.30), Milos (1¼ hours, €8.80) and Piraeus (2¼ hours, €23.20), and one weekly runs to Kythnos (45 minutes, €9).

Getting Around Serifos
There are frequent buses between Livadi and Hora (€0.80); a timetable is posted at the bus stop by the yacht marina. Motorcycles and cars can be hired from Krinas Travel (see the Livadi entry for contact details).

LIVADI Λιβάδι
This rather scrappy port is at the top end of an elongated bay. Continue around the bay for the ordinary town beach or climb over the headland that rises from the ferry quay for the pleasant, tamarisk-fringed beach at **Livadakia**. **Karavi Beach**, a walk farther south over the next headland, is the unofficial nudist beach. There is an Alpha Bank, with ATM, on the waterfront.

There is a useful tourist information office (☎ 2281 051 466) on the waterfront, which has a domatia list (in Greek). It's open 10am to 2pm and 6pm to 10pm daily.

Krinas Travel (☎ 2281 051 488, fax 2281 051 073, e sertrau@otenet.gr), upstairs next to Captain Hook Bar, 50m from the quay, offers a wide range of services, including car hire. The port police (☎ 2281 051 470) are up steps from the quay.

Places to Stay & Eat
Coralli Camping (☎ 2281 051 500, fax 2281 051 073, e coralli@mail.otenet.gr) Adult/ tent €4.40/2, double bungalows with mountain/sea view €52/64. This excellent site, shaded by tall eucalypts, is a step away from sandy Livadakia Beach.

The bungalows have phone, TV, fan. There's also a restaurant and minimarket, and a minibus meets all ferries. Part of the camping ground *Heaven Pool Bar*, fuelled by cocktail shakes, bare flesh and dance music, has a bit of a scene going on.

Anna Domatia (☎ 2281 051 263) Doubles €29. Anna's, about 500m along the waterfront next to Hotel Asteria, has airy rooms.

Eliza (☎/fax 2281 051 763) Doubles from €49, family rooms €75.40. Eliza's has a lovely garden. It's 100m from the beach on the turn-off road to the Hora.

Anastasia Rooms (☎ 2281 051 247, mobile ☎ 69 7225 1878) Doubles/Apartments €43.50/52. Next door to Meli on the waterfront, Anastasia has nice rooms.

Hotel Areti (☎ 2281 051 479, fax 2281 051 547) Singles/doubles €34.90/43.50. This light and bright hotel, on the hill above the ferry quay, has lovely rooms.

Rooms to Let Marianna (☎ 2281 051 338, fax 2281 052 057) Doubles/apartments €43.50/52.50. This is a nice, secluded, shady place which is set back a little from the waterfront.

Meli (☎ 2281 051 749) is a breezy little cafe with great sandwiches and crepes but mercilessly slow service – perhaps ask for a takeaway...

Perseus (☎ 2281 051 273) Dishes €2.35-13, seafood by the kilo. Farther along the waterfront, Perseus serves the best Greek standards.

Serifos Yacht Club (☎ 2281 051 888) Crowds spill out of this small bar onto the waterfront late in the evening. It's all very sedate during the daylight hours though, when it reverts to a bright little cafe.

Captain Hook Bar, above Krinas Travel, is another lively spot.

There are a couple of reasonable *tavernas* on the beach at Livadakia.

AROUND SERIFOS

The dazzling white **Hora**, clinging to a crag above Livadi, is one of the most striking Cycladic capitals. It can be reached either by bus or by walking up the steps from Livadi. The atmospheric town square is filled with tables from the eateries on its edge, watched over by the imposing neoclassical town hall. From here, more steps lead to a ruined 15th-century **Venetian Kastro** above the village. A peripheral path, hugging the cliff's edge, skirts the **Hora**.

The post office is by the first bus stop. A small **archaeological museum** (☎ 2281 031 022; admission free; 8.30am-3pm Tues-Sun), also off the central square, has pottery and sculpture uncovered from the fortress.

There are several small art workshops, including **Nikos Kourouniotis** (☎ 2281 033 668), a talented, but refreshingly humble, jeweller and illustrator; you'll find him on the main pedestrian thoroughfare.

A short walk downhill from the Hora leads to the tiny, pebbled beach of **Seralia**, which has several excellent fish tavernas. About an hour's walk north of Livadi (or a shorter drive) along a track (negotiable by motorbike) is **Psili Ammos Beach**. A path from Hora heads north to the pretty village of **Kendarhos** (also called Kallitsos), from where you can continue to the 17th-century fortified **Moni Taxiarhon**, which has impressive 18th-century frescoes. The walk from the town to the monastery takes about two hours, but you will need to take food and water as there are no facilities in Kendarhos.

Places to Stay & Eat

The Hora appears to remain relatively alive in the winter months and many places remain open.

Aegean Eye (☎ 2281 032 020/033 109) Double studios from €59, family rooms €72.50. On the edge of the cliff, Aegean Eye is a good down-to-earth option. All rooms have a kitchen (and a heater making it perfect for a winter break).

In the main square, the bar-cafe *Stou Stratou* (mobile ☎ 69-7233 7786) has a hint of Paris about it, while *Zorba's*, the taverna opposite the town hall, is worth investigating. Nearer the bus stop, *Leonidas* is recommended.

Kafe Bar Sunrise is a homey little alfresco bar perched on a mountain edge (accessible from the peripheral path), and

CYCLADES

somewhat surprisingly has a kids' playground – ideal for parents who want to imbibe in peace.

Remezzo (☎ *2281 031 930*), on the main pedestrian thoroughfare, is a chilled alfresco cafe. Snacks are available early in the day, and ambient music sets the scene in the evening.

Kythnos Κθνος

KYTHNOS

postcode 840 06 • pop 1632

Kythnos, the next island north of Serifos, is virtually barren. It is popular mainly with Athenian holiday-makers, as evidenced by the number of yachts moored at the marina, and there is little to enthuse about unless you're looking for a cure for rheumatism at the thermal baths.

The main settlements are the port of Merihas and the capital, Hora, also known as Kythnos. Merihas has an OTE, and there is an agency of the National Bank of Greece at Cava Kythnos travel agency and minimarket. Antonios Larentzakis Travel Agency (☎ 2281 032 104, 2281 032 291) sells ferry tickets, can arrange accommodation and rents cars and motorbikes. It's up the short flight of stairs near Ostria Taverna. Psaras Travel (☎ 2281 032 242, fax 2281 032 025), on the waterfront, also sells ferry tickets. Hora has the island's post office and police (☎ 2281 031 201). The port police (☎ 2281 032 290) are on the waterfront in Merihas.

Getting To/From Kythnos

Ferry There are at least three boats to Piraeus daily (2½ hours, €9.60). Most services coming from Piraeus continue to Serifos (1½ hours, €5.60), Sifnos (2½ hours, €5.90), Kimolos (three hours, €7.40) and Milos (3½ hours, €8.20).

There are three weekly ferries to Lavrio (3½ hours, €7), and Kea (1¼ hours, €4.65), and two to Folegandros (six hours, €9), Sikinos (seven hours, €9.30), Santorini (eight hours, €10.30) and Syros (two hours, €5.90).

A ferry runs once weekly to Andros (five hours, €11.70).

Fast Boat & Catamaran There are four services weekly to Piraeus (1½ hours, €18.20), and Sifnos (1¼ hours, €9.90) and regular services to Milos. One weekly service goes to Serifos (45 minutes, €9).

Getting Around Kythnos

There are regular buses from Merihas to Dryopida (€0.90), continuing to Kanala (€1.50) or Hora (€0.90). Less regular services run to Loutra (€1.50). The buses supposedly meet the ferries, but usually they leave from the turn-off to Hora in Merihas.

Taxis are a better bet, except at siesta time. There are only three taxis on the island; call ☎ 69 4474 3791, ☎ 69 4427 6656 or ☎ 69 4427 7609.

MERIHAS Μέριχας

Merihas does not have a lot going for it other than a small, dirty-brown beach. But it's a reasonable base and has most of the island's accommodation. There are better beaches within walking distance north of the quay (turn left facing inland).

Places to Stay & Eat

Domatia owners usually meet the boats, but if no-one is waiting, wander around the waterfront and backstreets and you'll see plenty of signs advertising rooms; alternatively head for Larentzakis Travel.

Kythnos Hotel (☎ *2281 032 092)* Doubles/triples €36.30/42. If you want to stay in this, the town's one hotel, you must book ahead. It's up the first set of steps on the way into town from the harbour and has decent rooms.

Ostria (☎ *2281 032 263)* Dishes €2.10-14.70, seafood by the kilo. On the waterfront near the ferry quay, Ostria has reasonable Greek fare. Try the black-eyed bean salad (€3). *Restaurant Kissos*, farther along the waterfront, also serves good standards.

Taverna to Kandouni (☎ *2281 032 220)* Dishes €2.10-11.75. Near the port police on the waterfront, Kandouni specialises in grilled meats; it also has *rooms* to let.

AROUND KYTHNOS

The capital, **Hora** (also known as Kythnos), lacks the charm of other Cycladic capitals. The main reason for visiting is the walk south to **Dryopida**, a picturesque town of red-tiled roofs and winding streets that was the island's capital in the Middle Ages. It takes about 1½ hours to cover the 6km. From Dryopida, you can either walk the 6km back to Merihas or catch a bus or taxi.

Loutra offers the only accommodation outside Merihas. The **thermal baths** at Loutra in the north-east are reputedly the most potent in the Cyclades. The best **beaches** are on the south-east coast, near the village of Kanala.

Places to Stay

There are several *domatia* at Loutra, while *Hotel Porto Klaras* (☎/fax *2281 031 276)* is reputed to be the best on the island, with doubles/self-contained studios available for €43.50/52.50.

Kea Κέα or Τζία

postcode 840 02 • pop 2400

Kea, to the north of Kythnos, is the closest of the Cyclades to the mainland. The island is a popular summer weekend escape for Athenians, but remains relatively untouched by tourism. While it appears largely barren from a distance, there is ample water and the bare hills hide fertile valleys filled with orchards, olive groves, and almond and oak trees (acorns, a raw material used by the tanneries, made the inhabitants rich in the 18th century). The main settlements are the port of Korissia, and the capital, Ioulida, 5km inland.

Getting To/From Kea

Services connect Kea with Lavrio (1¼ hours, €5.30) on the mainland at least twice daily and also with Kythnos (1¼ hours, €4.65) three times weekly. In addition, a direct service runs twice weekly to Kythnos and Syros (four hours, €8.20). One weekly service runs to Kea (€13.20).

Getting Around Kea

In July and August there are, in theory, regular buses from Korissia to Vourkari, Otzias, Ioulida and Pisses. In practice, however, the bus driver operates at his own whim; if there isn't a bus waiting for the boat, you're better off catching one of the taxis (☎ 2288 021 021 or 2288 021 228) that hang about near the port. There are two expensive motorcycle-rental outlets and a ridiculously expensive car-rental monopoly that is best avoided.

KORISSIA Κορησσία

The port of Korissia is an uninspiring place in spite of its setting on a large bay with a long, sandy beach.

The tourist police (☎ 2288 021 100) can be found one block back from the waterfront between June and September. The well-meaning but clueless tourist information office (☎ 2288 021 500), opposite the ferry quay, has lists of domatia in Greek. Stefanos Lepouras, next door at Stegali Bookshop (☎ 2288 021 435, fax 2288 021 012) is, in

fact, the unofficial tourist information officer and is an excellent source of information (including bus timetables), so make sure you repay the favour and buy all your postcards and books from him! He also changes money. Art Café (☎ 2288 021 181), on the waterfront, has Internet access (€2.10 per 20 minutes, €4.65 one hour). There is an ATM near the supermarket to the right of Hotel Karthea, and the Piraeus Bank (with ATM) is to the left of Hotel Karthea. There is a small ferry ticket office next to the car-rental agency on the waterfront.

Places to Stay & Eat
Domatia owners don't meet ferries, so if you're arriving late, make sure you have something booked.

Hotel Karthea (☎ *2288 021 204, fax 2288 021 417*) Singles/doubles €38/52.50. This glum C-class hotel with ordinary rooms and lots of stairs is the tall, concrete box at the corner of the bay.

There are better places along the road that runs behind the beach, including a couple of *domatia*.

Hotel Tzia (☎ *2288 021 305, fax 2288 021 140*) Doubles with breakfast €49. Tzia has lovely rooms that open right onto the beach.

Hotel Korissia (☎ *2288 021 484*) Singles/doubles €38/46.60, double/triple studios €59/67.90. Korissia has large, modern rooms. Turn right off the beach road at the canal; the hotel is on the right after about 150m.

Lagoudera, near the tourist office has good home-cooked local specialities, and *Taverna Akri* (☎ *2288 021 196*), near the Hotel Karthea, is popular with locals; however, the menu is only in Greek.

Head to Vourkari's hip cafes for any hope of cosmopolitan nightlife.

IOULIDA Ιουλίδα
Ioulida is a delightful higgledy-piggledy hillside town, full of alleyways and steps that beg to be explored. The architecture here is quite different from other Cycladic capitals – the houses have red-tiled roofs.

The bus turnaround is on a square just at the edge of town. An archway leads to Ioulida proper, and Ilia Malavazou, the main thoroughfare, leads uphill to the right. The post office is also along here on the right. The pathway continues uphill and crosses a small square, just beyond which, on the right, is an agency of the National Bank of Greece, signposted above a minimarket.

Things to See
The **archaeological museum** (☎ *2288 022 079; admission free; open 8.30am-3pm Tues-Sun*), on the main thoroughfare, houses local finds, mostly from Agia Irini. It was closed for renovations at the time of writing.

The celebrated **Kea Lion**, chiselled from a huge chunk of slate in the 6th century BC, lies on the hillside an easy, pleasant 10-minute walk north-east of town. The path to the lion leads off to the left (the main path goes sharp right). Keep walking past the cemetery and you'll find the gate that leads downhill to the watchful lion, which is surrounded by whitewashed rocks.

Places to Stay & Eat

There are a sprinkling of *domatia* in Ioulida, and several decent tavernas.

Estiatorio I Piatsa (☎ *2288 022 195*) Dishes €1.70-5.90. There are a couple of decent tavernas, including this one, just inside the archway, which serve generous plates of fresh fish.

Kalofagadon Dishes €1.70-8.20. Carnivores should not dilly-dally: go directly to Kalofagadon, on the main square, and order the lamb chops.

AROUND KEA

The beach road from Korissia leads past the lovely eucalyptus grove sheltering **Gialiskari Beach** to the ambient, tiny port of **Vourkari**, lined with yachts and cafes, 2.5km away. **Voukariani Art Gallery** (☎ *2288 021 458*), nestled in among all the smart cafes and restaurants, has changing exhibitions of world-class art works over the summer – it's well worth a visit.

Just north of Vourkari you will find the ancient site of **Agia Irini** (which is named after a nearby church). This is the site where a Minoan palace has since been excavated.

The road continues for another 3km to a sandy beach at **Otzias**. A dirt road continues beyond here for another 5km to the 18th-century **Moni Panagias Kastriani** (☎ *2288 024 348*), with a commanding position and terrific views; accommodation is a possibility here.

The island's best beach, 8km south-west of Ioulida, has the unfortunate name of **Pisses**. It is long and sandy and backed by a verdant valley of orchards and olive groves. **Flea**, also with an interesting name, occupies a lush valley and makes a nice walking destination from either Korissia or Ioulida.

Places to Stay & Eat

Kea Camping (☎ *2288 031 302, fax 2288 031 303, Pisses Beach*) Adult/tent €4.40/4.40, bungalows €43.50. Pines and eucalypts provide shade at this camping ground. It has a shop, bar and restaurant nearby. Self-contained bungalows are also available nearby.

Fanni & John's (☎ *2288 021 316*) Doubles €34.90. At Otzias, this friendly pension is set in a lush garden a short walk from the beach.

Gialiskari (☎ *2288 021 197*) Doubles €46.60. Overlooking the water just before Vourkari, this pretty pension has comfortable rooms.

Tastra is a dreamy little beach bar-cafe at Gialiskari Beach. All the eateries in Voukari are worthy establishments, but a new taverna, *Ennea Kores*, right around the end of the bay, is the one that is consistently recommended by the resident Athenian jet set for its service and food.

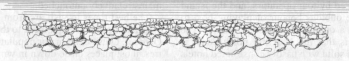

Crete Κρήτη

Crete is Greece's largest and most southerly island, and arguably the most beautiful. A spectacular mountain chain runs from east to west across the island, split into three ranges: the Mt Dikti Range in the east, the Mt Ida (or Mt Psiloritis) Range in the centre and the Lefka Ori (White Mountains) in the west. The mountains are dotted with agricultural plains and plateaus, and sliced by numerous dramatic gorges. Long, sandy beaches speckle the coastline, and the east coast boasts Europe's only palm-tree forest.

Administratively, the island is divided into four prefectures: Lasithi, Iraklio, Rethymno and Hania. Apart from Lasithi, with its capital of Agios Nikolaos, the prefectures are named after their major cities. The island's capital is Iraklio which is Greece's fifth-largest city. Nearly all Crete's major population centres are on the north coast. Most of the south coast is too precipitous to support large settlements.

Scenery and beaches aside, the island is also the birthplace of Europe's first advanced civilisation, the Minoan. If you intend to spend much time at the many Minoan sites, *Palaces of Minoan Crete* by Gerald Cadogan is an excellent guide.

Crete's size and its distance from the rest of Greece allowed an independent culture to evolve. Vibrant Cretan weavings are sold in many of the island's towns and villages. The traditional Cretan songs differ from those heard elsewhere in Greece. Called *mantinades*, these songs are highly emotive, expressing the age-old concerns of love, death and the yearning for freedom. You will still come across men wearing the traditional dress of breeches tucked into knee-high leather boots, and black-fringed kerchiefs tied tightly around their heads.

The attractions of Crete have not gone unnoticed by tour operators, and the island has the dubious honour of playing host to almost a quarter of Greece's tourists. The result is that much of the north coast is packed solid with hastily constructed hotels

Highlights

- Iraklio's Archaeological Museum and the Historical Museum of Crete
- The ancient Minoan site of Knossos
- The stunning expanse of the Lasithi Plateau
- Walking the gorge between Zakros and Kato Zakros, site of ancient Zakros
- Hania's beautiful old Venetian quarter
- Trekking the spectacular Samaria Gorge
- The lovely sand beaches and coves at Elafonisi
- Myrtos and Plakias – two south-coast villages that still welcome independent travellers

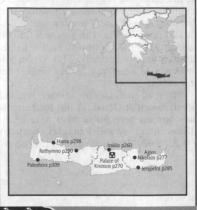

for package tourists, particularly between Iraklio and Agios Nikolaos and west of Hania. The tour operators have also taken over several of the southern coastal villages that were once backpacker favourites. The wild and rugged west coast, however, remains relatively untouched.

The best times to visit are from April to June and from mid-September to the end of October. Outside the major population centres, most places close down in winter.

For details on Crete see the Web sites: W www.interkriti.org, W www.infocrete .com and W www.explorecrete.com.

SUGGESTED ITINERARIES

One week

Spend two days in Iraklio; visit the Archaeological Museum, Historical Museum of Crete and Minoan site of Knossos. Have two days in Rethymno to visit the fortress and museums and explore the old quarter. If you have time take a day trip to the mountain town of Spili, or the resort of Plakias, if you prefer a beach. Spend three days in Hania to visit the museums, explore the old quarter and hike the Samaria Gorge. Recuperate the following day on the beach at Falasarna. Round off your trip with an evening of music and drinking at Café Kriti in Hania.

Two weeks

As above for the first two days. Overnight at one of the Lassithi Plateau villages and explore the Dikteon Cave and the plateau. Spend two nights in Sitia; visit the archaeological museum, walk the gorge to Kato Zakros, visit Ancient Zakros and have a swim. If you have time, visit Ancient Lato. Have two days in Rethymno to visit the fortress and museums and explore the old quarter. Overnight in Agia Galini to visit Phaestos and Agia Triada. Spend two nights in the mountain town of Spili, or the beach resort of Plakias, and visit Moni Preveli. Spend two nights in Hania to explore the old town and visit the museums. Head down to Paleohora for two nights and spend a day hiking the Samaria Gorge. If you have time, unwind on Elafonisi Beach the following day.

HISTORY

Although Crete has been inhabited since Neolithic times (7000–3000 BC), as far as most people are concerned its history begins with the Minoan civilisation. The glories of Crete's Minoan past remained hidden until British archaeologist Sir Arthur Evans made his dramatic discoveries at Knossos in the early 1900s. The term 'Minoan' was coined by Evans and derived from the King Minos of Greek mythology. Nobody knows what the Minoans called themselves.

Among the ruins unearthed by Evans were the famous Knossos frescoes. Artistically, the frescoes are superlative; the figures that grace them have a naturalism lacking in contemporary Cycladic figurines, ancient Egyptian artwork (which they resemble in certain respects), and the Archaic sculpture that came later. Compared with candle-smoke-blackened Byzantine frescoes, the Minoan frescoes, with their fresh, bright colours, look as if they were painted yesterday (see the boxed text 'The Mysterious Minoans').

But no matter how much speculation the frescoes inspire about the Minoans, all we really know is that early in the 3rd millennium BC an advanced people migrated to Crete and brought with them the art of metallurgy. Many elements of Neolithic culture lived on in the Early Minoan period (3000–2100 BC), but the Middle Minoan period (2100–1500 BC) saw the emergence of a society with unprecedented artistic, engineering and cultural achievements. It was during this time that the famous palace complexes were built at Knossos, Phaestos, Malia and Zakros.

Hot spots in Crete

When the sun is down and the full moon hangs high, grab your gladrags and head downtown. Greeks don't go out until after midnight and don't go home until the sun is up again.

Iraklio is not the prettiest town in Crete, but has the hippest nightlife. The bars and cafes around Plateia Venizelou are hyped-up as the non-stop crowds milling around the Morosini Fountain. The pedestrian area of Koraï and Perdikari is lined with stylish kafeneia that attract a before-disco crowd eager to see and be seen.

You may not want to buy real estate on Ikarou but this action-packed street serves up the wildest nightlife in town. The music is a contemporary mix of rock, techno and Greek.

Funky rock and roll joints play the dominant role in **Hania's** nightlife scene but there are also some cosy spots for jazz, light rock and Cretan music. When Haniotes want to party the night away in a disco, they're likely to head out to Platanias, a coastal resort about 11km west of Hania.

CRETE

CRETE

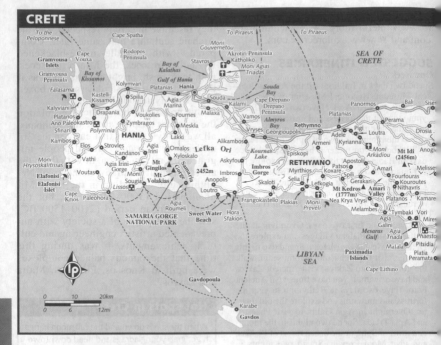

CRETE

To the Peloponnese · Cape Spatha · To Piraeus · Moni Gouvernetou · To Piraeus

Cape Vouxa · Rodopos Peninsula · Akrotiri Peninsula · Katholiko · **SEA OF CRETE**

Gramvousa Islets · Gramvousa Peninsula · Bay of Kissamos · Bay of Kalathas · Stavros · Moni Agias Triadas · Souda Bay

Fálasarna · Kolymvari · Platanias · Gulf of Hania · Hania · Souda · Cape Drepano · Panormos · Bali · Sise

Kastelli-Kissamos · Spilia · Agia Marina · Kalami · Drepano Peninsula · Perama · Drosia

Kalyviani · Platanos · Drapania · Voukolies · Fournes · Malaxa · Vamos · Vryses · Rethymno · Platanias · Pigi · Loutra

Ano Paleokastro · Sfinari · Polyrrinia · Zymbragos · Meskla · Lakki · Georgioupolis · Adele · Kyrianna · Moni Arkadiou · Mt Idi (2456m) · Anogia

Kambos · Elos · Strovles · Agia Irini · Omalos · **Lefka Ori** · Alikambos · Kournas Lake · Episkopi · Armeni · Apostoli · Amari · Melisse

Moni Hrysoskalitissas · Vathi · Kandanos · Mt Gingilos · Xyloskalo · Askyfou · 2452m · Imbros · **RETHYMNO** · Myrthios · Koxare · Spili · Gerakari · Fourfouras · Kourouтes

Elafonisi · Voutas · Agia Irini Gorge · Mt Volakias · Samaria Gorge · Imbros Gorge · Selia · Lefkogia · Mt Kedros (1777m) · Amari Valley · Nithavris

Elafonisi Islet · Sougia · Moni Lissos · Anopolis · Skaloti · Nea Krya Vrysi · Platanos · Kamare

Cape Krios · Paleohora · Loutro · Frangokastello · Plakias · Moni Preveli · Melambes · Tymbaki · Vori

Agia Roumeli · Sweet Water Beach · Hora Sfakion · **LIBYAN SEA** · Agia Galini · Agia Triada · Mires

SAMARIA GORGE NATIONAL PARK · Mesaras Gulf · Malala · Phaesto · Pitsidia · Platia Peramata

Paximadia Islands · Cape Lithino

0   10   20km
0   6   12mi

Gavdopoula · Karabe · Gavdos

Also during this time, the Minoans began producing their exquisite Kamares pottery (see Iraklio's Archaeological Museum section later in this chapter) and silverware, and became a maritime power trading with Egypt and Asia Minor. Around 1700 BC all four palace complexes were destroyed by an earthquake. Undeterred, the Minoans built bigger and better palaces on the sites of the originals, as well as new settlements in other parts of the island.

Around 1500 BC, when the Minoan civilisation was at its peak, the palaces were destroyed again, signalling the start of the Late Minoan period (1500–1100 BC). This destruction was probably caused by Mycenaean invasions, although the massive volcanic eruption on the island of Santorini (Thira) may also have had something to do with it. The Knossos palace was the only one to be salvaged. It was finally destroyed by fire around 1400 BC. The Minoan civilisation was a hard act to follow. The war-orientated Dorians, who arrived in 1100 BC, were pedestrian by comparison. The 5th century BC found Crete, like the rest of Greece, divided into city-states. The glorious classical age of mainland Greece had little impact on Crete, and the Persians bypassed the island. It was also ignored by Alexander the Great, so was never part of the Macedonian Empire.

By 67 BC, Crete had fallen to the Romans. The town of Gortyna in the south became the capital of Cyrenaica, a province that included large chunks of North Africa. Crete, along with the rest of Greece, became part of the Byzantine Empire in AD 395. In 1210 the island was occupied by the Venetians, whose legacy is one of mighty fortresses, ornate public buildings and monuments, and the handsome dwellings of nobles and merchants.

Despite the massive Venetian fortifications, which sprang up all over the island, by 1669 the whole of the Cretan mainland

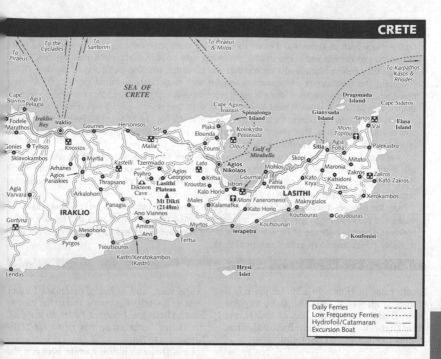

CRETE

was under Turkish rule. The first uprising against the Turks was led by Ioannis Daskalogiannis in 1770. This set the precedent for many more insurrections, and in 1898 the Great Powers intervened and made the island a British protectorate. It was not until the signing of the Treaty of Bucharest in 1913 that Crete officially became part of Greece, although the island's parliament had declared a de facto union in 1905.

The island saw heavy fighting during WWII. Germany wanted the island as an air base in the Mediterranean, and on 20 May 1941 German parachutists landed on Crete. It was the start of 10 days of fierce fighting that became known as the Battle of Crete. For two days the battle hung in the balance until Germany won a bridgehead for its air force at Maleme, near Hania. The Allied forces of Britain, Australia, New Zealand and Greece then fought a valiant rearguard action which enabled the British Navy to evacuate 18,000 of the 32,000 Allied troops

trapped on the island. The German occupation of Crete lasted until the end of WWII.

During the war a large active resistance movement drew heavy reprisals from the Germans. Many mountain villages were temporarily bombed 'off the map' and their occupants were shot. Among the bravest members of this resistance movement were the 'runners' who relayed messages on foot over the mountains. One of these runners, George Psyhoundakis, wrote a book based on his experiences entitled *The Cretan Runner*.

GETTING TO/FROM CRETE
The following section provides a brief overview of air and boat options to and from Crete. For more comprehensive information, see the relevant sections under specific town entries.

Air
Crete has two international airports. The principal one is at Iraklio and there is a

The Mysterious Minoans

Of the many finds at Knossos and other sites, it is the celebrated frescoes that have captured the imagination of experts and amateurs alike, shedding light on a civilisation hitherto a mystery. The message they communicate is of a society that was powerful, wealthy, joyful and optimistic.

Gracing the frescoes are white-skinned women with elaborately coiffured glossy black locks. Proud, graceful and uninhibited, these women were dressed in stylish gowns that revealed perfectly shaped breasts. The bronze-skinned men were tall, with tiny waists, narrow hips, broad shoulders and muscular thighs and biceps; the children were slim and lithe. The Minoans also seemed to know how to enjoy themselves. They played board games, boxed and wrestled, played leap-frog over bulls and over one another, and performed bold acrobatic feats.

As well as being literate, they were religious, as frescoes and models of people partaking in rituals testify. The Minoans' beliefs, like many other aspects of their society, remain an enigma, but there is sufficient evidence to confirm that they worshipped a nature goddess, often depicted with serpents and lions. Male deities were distinctly secondary.

From the frescoes it appears that women enjoyed a respected position in society, leading religious rituals and participating in games, sports and hunting. Minoan society may have had its dark side, however. There is evidence of human sacrifice being practised on at least one occasion, although probably in response to an extreme external threat.

smaller one at Hania. In addition there is a domestic airport at Sitia. All three airports have flights to Athens. Iraklio and Hania have flights to Thessaloniki; Iraklio also has flights to Rhodes and Santorini.

Ferry

Crete has ports at Iraklio, Hania, Rethymno, Agios Nikolaos, Sitia and Kastelli-Kissamos. The following are high-season schedules; services are reduced by about half during low season.

Direct daily ferries travel to Piraeus from Iraklio, Hania and Rethymno. There are three ferries weekly from Sitia via Agios Nikolaos to Piraeus, stopping at Milos. Three ferries weekly go from Iraklio to Thessaloniki via Santorini stopping twice a week at Paros and Tinos and once a week at Naxos, Skiathos, Syros and Volos. There are also three boats weekly to Rhodes from Agios Nikolaos via Sitia stopping at Kasos, Karpathos and Halki. Five ferries weekly sail from Kastelli-Kissamos to Antikythira, Kythira and Gythio with further stops at Kalamata and Piraeus.

GETTING AROUND CRETE

A fast national highway skirts the north coast from Hania in the west to Agios Nikolaos in the east, and is being extended farther west to Kastelli-Kissamos and to the east to Sitia. There are frequent buses linking all the major northern towns from Kastelli-Kissamos to Sitia.

Less frequent buses operate between the north-coast towns and resorts and places of interest on the south coast, via the mountain villages of the interior. These routes are Hania to Paleohora, Omalos (for the Samaria Gorge) and Hora Sfakion; Rethymno to Plakias, Agia Galini, Phaestos and Matala; Iraklio to Agia Galini, Phaestos, Matala and the Lasithi Plateau; Agios Nikolaos to Ierapetra; and Sitia to Ierapetra, Vaï, Palekastro and Kato Zakros.

There is nothing comparable to the national highway on the south coast and parts of this area have no roads at all. There is no road between Paleohora and Hora Sfakion, the most precipitous part of the south coast; a boat (daily from June through August) connects the two resorts via Sougia and Agia Roumeli.

As well as the bus schedules given in this chapter, clapped-out 'village buses' travel to just about every village which has a road to it. These usually leave in the early morning and return in the afternoon.

Central Crete

Central Crete is occupied by the Iraklio prefecture, named after the island's burgeoning major city and administrative capital. The area's major attractions are the Minoan sites of Knossos, Malia and Phaestos. The north coast east of Iraklio has been heavily exploited by the package tourism industry, particularly around Hersonisos.

IRAKLIO Ηράκλειο
postcode 710 01 • pop 115,124

The Cretan capital of Iraklio is a bustling modern city and the fifth largest in Greece. It has none of the charm of Hania or Rethymno, but it is a dynamic city boasting the highest average per capita income in Greece. That wealth stems largely from Iraklio's position as the island's trading capital, but also from the year-round flow of visitors who flock to nearby Knossos.

History

The Arabs who ruled Crete from AD 824 to 961 were the first people to govern from the site of modern Iraklio. It was known then as El Khandak, after the moat that surrounded the town, and was reputedly the slave-trade capital of the eastern Mediterranean.

El Khandak became Khandakos after Byzantine troops finally dislodged the Arabs, and then Candia under the Venetians who ruled the island for more than 400 years. While the Turks quickly overran the Venetian defences at Hania and Rethymno, Candia's fortifications proved as effective as they looked – an unusual combination. They withstood a siege of 21 years before the garrison finally surrendered in 1669.

Hania became the capital of independent Crete at the end of Turkish rule in 1898, and Candia was renamed Iraklio. Because of its central location, Iraklio became a commercial centre, and resumed its position as the island's administrative centre in 1971.

The city suffered badly in WWII, when most of the old Venetian and Turkish town was destroyed by bombing.

Orientation

Iraklio's two main squares are Plateia Venizelou and Plateia Eleftherias. Plateia Venizelou, instantly recognisable by its famous Morosini Fountain (better known as the Lion Fountain), is the heart of Iraklio and the best place from which to familiarise yourself with the layout of the city. The city's major intersection is a few steps south of the square. From here, 25 Avgoustou runs north-east to the harbour; Dikeosynis runs south-east to Plateia Eleftherias; Kalokerinou runs west to the Hania Gate; 1866 (the market street) runs south; and 1821 runs to the south-west. To reach Plateia Venizelou from the New Harbour, turn right, walk along the waterfront and turn left onto 25 Avgoustou.

Iraklio has three intercity bus stations. Station A, on the waterfront between the port and 25 Avgoustou, serves eastern Crete. A special bus station for Hania and Rethymno only is opposite Station A. Station B, just beyond the Hania Gate, serves Phaestos, Agia Galini and Matala. To reach the city centre from Station B walk through the Hania Gate and along Kalokerinou. For details on bus schedules, see the Iraklio Getting There & Away section.

Information

Tourist Offices EOT (☎ 281 022 8225, fax 281 022 6020) is just north of Plateia Eleftherias at Xanthoudidou 1. The staff at the information desk hand out maps and photocopied lists of ferry and bus schedules. Opening times are 8am to 2pm Monday to Friday. In high season it also opens on Saturday and Sunday.

The tourist police (☎ 281 028 3190) are found on Dikeosynis 10, are open 7am to 11pm.

Money Most of the city's banks are on 25 Avgoustou, including the National Bank of Greece at No 35. It has a 24-hour automatic exchange machine, as does the Alpha Bank at No 94. There is a handy Ergo Bank ATM at bus station A.

American Express is represented by Adamis Travel Bureau, (☎ 281 034 6202), 25 Avgoustou 23, open 8am to 2pm Monday

CRETE

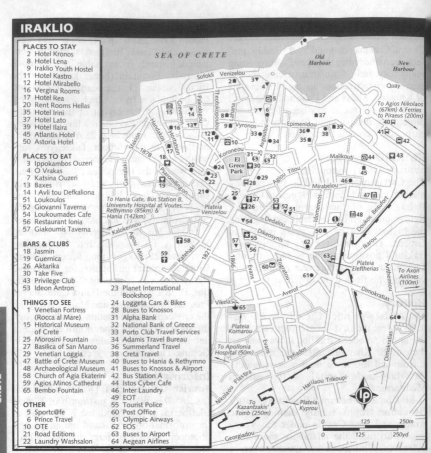

IRAKLIO

PLACES TO STAY
2 Hotel Kronos
8 Hotel Lena
9 Iraklio Youth Hostel
11 Hotel Kastro
12 Hotel Mirabello
16 Vergina Rooms
17 Hotel Rea
20 Rent Rooms Hellas
35 Hotel Irini
37 Hotel Lato
39 Hotel Ilaira
45 Atlantis Hotel
50 Astoria Hotel

PLACES TO EAT
3 Ippokambos Ouzeri
4 O Vrakas
7 Katsina Ouzeri
13 Baxes
14 I Avli tou Defkaliona
51 Loukoulos
52 Giovanni Taverna
54 Loukoumades Cafe
56 Restaurant Ionia
56 Giakoumis Taverna

BARS & CLUBS
18 Jasmin
19 Guernica
26 Aktarika
30 Take Five
43 Privilege Club
53 Ideon Antron

THINGS TO SEE
1 Venetian Fortress
(Rocca al Mare)
15 Historical Museum
of Crete
25 Morosini Fountain
27 Basilica of San Marco
29 Venetian Loggia
47 Battle of Crete Museum
48 Archaeological Museum
58 Church of Agia Ekaterini
59 Agios Minos Cathedral
65 Bembo Fountain

OTHER
5 Sportc@fe
6 Prince Travel
10 OTE
21 Road Editions
22 Laundry Washsalon
23 Planet International
Bookshop
24 Loggeta Cars & Bikes
28 Buses to Knossos
31 Alpha Bank
32 National Bank of Greece
33 Porto Club Travel Services
34 Adamis Travel Bureau
36 Summerland Travel
38 Creta Travel
40 Buses to Hania & Rethymno
41 Buses to Knossos & Airport
42 Bus Station A
44 Istos Cyber Cafe
46 Inter Laundry
49 EOT
55 Tourist Police
60 Post Office
61 Olympic Airways
62 EOS
63 Buses to Airport
64 Aegean Airlines

to Saturday. Thomas Cook (☎ 281 024 1108) is represented by Summerland Travel, Epimenidou 30.

Post & Communications The central post office is on Plateia Daskalogianni. Opening hours are 7.30am to 8pm Monday to Friday, and 7.30am to 2pm Saturday. From June through August there is a mobile post office at El Greco Park, just north of Plateia Venizelou, open 8am to 6pm Monday to Friday, and 8am to 1.30pm Saturday. The OTE, on Theotokopoulou just north of El Greco Park, opens 7.30am to 11pm daily.

Sportc@fe (☎ 281 028 8217), on the corner of 25 Avgoustou and Zotou, has fast modern machines and serves up coffee, beers and soft drinks while you surf. Istos Cyber Cafe (☎ 281 022 2120), Malikouti 2, charges €3.80 an hour to use its computers and also scans, prints, and faxes documents. There are a half-dozen computers with fast connections. It's open 9am to 1am daily.

Bookshops The huge Planet International Bookshop (☎ 281 028 1558) on the corner of Hortatson and Kydonias stocks most of the books recommended in this guide and has a large selection of Lonely Planet titles. Road Editions (☎/fax 281 034 4610, ✉ road@her.forthnet.gr) at Handakos 29 has the best selection of maps in Iraklio as well as a good range of Lonely Planet titles.

Laundry There are two self-service laundrettes: Laundry Washsalon at Handakos 18, and Inter Laundry at Mirabelou 25 near the Archaeological Museum. Both charge €5.90 for a wash and dry.

Luggage Storage The left-luggage office at Bus Station A charges €1 per day and is open 6.30am to 8pm daily. Other options are Prince Travel (☎ 281 028 2706), at 25 Avgoustou 30, which also charges €1.50, Washsalon (see Laundry) which charges €1.50 and the youth hostel at Vyronos 5 which charges €1.50.

Emergency The modern University Hospital (☎ 281 039 2111) at Voutes, 5km south of Iraklio, is the city's best-equipped medical facility. The Apollonia Hospital (☎ 281 022 9713), inside the old walls on Mousourou, is more convenient.

Archaeological Museum

Second in size and importance only to the National Archaeological Museum in Athens, this outstanding museum (☎ 281 022 6092, Xanthoudidou; admission €4.40; open 8am-7pm Tues-Sun, 12.30pm-7pm Mon) is just north of Plateia Eleftherias. If you are seriously interested in the Minoans you will want more than one visit, but even a fairly superficial perusal of the contents requires half a day. The museum closes at 5pm from late October to early April.

The exhibits, arranged in chronological order, include pottery, jewellery, figurines and sarcophagi as well as some famous frescoes, mostly from Knossos and Agia Triada. All testify to the remarkable imagination and advanced skills of the Minoans. Unfortunately, the exhibits are not very well explained. If they were, there would be no need to part with €6.50 for a copy of the glossy illustrated museum guide.

Room 1 is devoted to the Neolithic and Early Minoan periods. Room 2 has a collection from the Middle Minoan period. Among the most fascinating exhibits here are the tiny glazed reliefs of Minoan houses from Knossos.

Room 3 covers the same period with finds from Phaestos, including the famous **Phaestos disc**. The symbols inscribed on the disc have not been deciphered. Here also are the famous **Kamares pottery vases**, named after the sacred cave of Kamares where the pottery was first discovered. The four large vases in case 43 were part of a royal banquet set. They are of exceptional quality and are some of the finest examples of Kamares pottery.

Exhibits in Room 4 are also from the Middle Minoan period. Most striking is the 20cm black stone **Bull's Head**, which was a libation vessel. The bull has a fine head of curls, from which sprout horns of gold. The eyes of painted crystal are extremely lifelike. Also in this room are relics from a shrine at Knossos, including two fine figurines of **snake goddesses**. Snakes symbolised immortality for the Minoans.

Pottery, bronze figurines and seals are some of the exhibits displayed in Room 5. These include vases imported from Egypt and some Linear A and B tablets (see the boxed text 'Linear B Script'). The inscriptions on the tablets displayed here have been translated as household or business accounts from the palace at Knossos.

Room 6 is devoted to finds from Minoan cemeteries. Especially intriguing are two small clay models of grouped figures which were found in a *tholos* (Mycenaean tomb shaped like a beehive). One depicts four male dancers in a circle, their arms around each other's shoulders, possibly participating in a funeral ritual. The other model depicts two groups of three figures in a room flanked by two columns. Each group features two large seated figures being offered libations by a smaller figure. It is not known whether the large figures represent gods or departed mortals. On a more grisly level, there is a display of the bones of a horse sacrificed as part of Minoan worship.

CRETE

Linear B Script

MH

The methodical decipherment of the Linear B script by English architect and part-time linguist Michael Ventris was the first tangible evidence that the Greek language had a recorded history longer than any scholar had previously believed. The decipherment demonstrated that the language disguised by these mysterious scribblings was an archaic form of Greek 500 years older than the Ionic Greek used by Homer.

Linear B was written on clay tablets that lay undisturbed for centuries until they were unearthed at Knossos in Crete. Further clay tablets were unearthed later on the mainland at Mycenae, Tiryns and Pylos on the Peloponnese and at Thebes in Boeotia.

The clay tablets, found to be mainly inventories and records of commercial transactions, consist of about 90 different signs and date from the 14th to the 13th centuries BC. Little of the social and political life of these times can be deduced from the tablets, though there is enough to give a glimpse of a fairly complex and well-organised commercial structure.

For linguists, the script did not provide a detailed image of the actual language spoken, since the symbols were used primarily as syllabic clusters designed to give an approximation of the pronunciation of the underlying language. Typically, the syllabic cluster 'A-re-ka-sa-da-ra' is the woman's name Alexandra, but the exact pronunciation remains unknown.

Importantly, what is clear is that the language is undeniably Greek, thus giving the modern-day Greek language the second-longest recorded written history, after Chinese. The language of an earlier script, Linear A, remains to this day undeciphered. It is believed to be of either Anatolian or Semitic origin, though even this remains pure conjecture.

Finds in Room 7 include the beautiful **bee pendant** found at Malia. It's a remarkably fine piece of gold jewellery depicting two bees dropping honey into a comb. Also in this room are the three celebrated vases from Agia Triada. The **Harvester Vase**, of which only the top part remains, depicts a light-hearted scene of young farm workers returning from olive picking. The **Boxer Vase** depicts Minoans indulging in two of their favourite pastimes – wrestling and bull grappling. The **Chieftain Cup** depicts a more cryptic scene: a chief holding a staff and three men carrying animal skins.

Room 8 holds finds from the palace at Zakros. Don't miss the gorgeous little crystal vase found in over 300 pieces and was painstakingly reconstructed by museum staff.

Room 10 covers the postpalatial period (1350–1100 BC) when the Minoan civilisation was in decline and being overtaken by the warrior-like Mycenaeans. Nevertheless, there are still some fine exhibits, including a child (headless) on a swing.

Room 13 is devoted to Minoan sarcophagi. However, the most famous and spectacular of these, the **sarcophagus from Agia Triada**, is upstairs in Room 14 (the Hall of Frescoes). This stone coffin, painted with floral and abstract designs and ritual scenes, is regarded as one of the supreme examples of Minoan art.

The most famous of the Minoan frescoes are also displayed in Room 14. Frescoes from Knossos include the **Procession Fresco**, the **Griffin Fresco** (from the Throne Room), the **Dolphin Fresco** (from the Queen's Room) and the amazing **Bull-Leaping Fresco**, which depicts a seemingly double-jointed acrobat somersaulting on the back of a charging bull. Other frescoes here include the two lovely **Frescoes of the Lilies**

The wild and remote Cape Tigani with the rocky islet of Gramvousa offshore

Minoan watercarrier mural, Palace of Knossos, Crete

This wooden staircase – the *xyloskalo* – is the start point for the trek through the Samaria Gorge

Life's a struggle on Crete

The quiet beach and town of Plakias, Crete

Angelou – the heart of Hania's shopping district

from Amisos and fragments of frescoes from Agia Triada. More frescoes can be seen in Rooms 15 and 16. In Room 16 there is a large wooden model of Knossos.

Historical Museum of Crete

A fascinating range of bits and pieces from Crete's more recent past is housed in this museum (☎ 281 028 3219, Lysimahou Kalokerinou 7; admission €3; open 9am-5pm Mon-Fri, 9am-2pm Sat summer; 9am-3pm Mon-Sat winter), just back from the waterfront. The ground floor covers the period from Byzantine to Turkish rule, with plans, charts, photographs, ceramics and maps. On the 1st floor is the only El Greco painting on display in Crete. Other rooms contain fragments of 13th- and 14th-century frescoes, coins, jewellery, liturgical ornaments and vestments, and medieval pottery.

The 2nd floor has a reconstruction of the library of author Nikos Kazantzakis, with displays of his letters, manuscripts and books. Another room is devoted to Emmanouil Tsouderos, who was born in Rethymno and who was prime minister in 1941. There are some dramatic photographs of a ruined Iraklio in the Battle of Crete section. On the 3rd floor there is an outstanding folklore collection.

Other Attractions

Iraklio burst its city walls long ago but these massive fortifications, with seven bastions and four gates, are still very conspicuous, dwarfing the concrete structures of the 20th century. Venetians built the defences between 1462 and 1562. At the end of the Old Harbour's jetty is another Venetian fortress, the 16th-century Rocca al Mare (☎ 281 024 6211, Iraklio Harbour; admission €1.50; open 8am-6pm Mon-Sat, 10am-3pm Sun).

Several other notable vestiges from Venetian times survive in the city. Most famous is the Morosini Fountain on Plateia Venizelou. The fountain, built in 1628, was commissioned by Francesco Morosini, the governor of Crete. Opposite is the three-aisled 13th-century Basilica of San Marco. It has been reconstructed many times and is now an exhibition gallery. A little north of

here is the attractively reconstructed 17th-century Venetian loggia. It was a Venetian version of a gentleman's club where the male aristocracy came to drink and gossip.

The delightful Bembo Fountain, at the southern end of 1866, is shown on local maps as the Turkish Fountain, but it was actually built by the Venetians in the 16th century. It was constructed from a hotchpotch of building materials including an ancient statue. The ornate edifice next to the fountain was added by the Turks, and now functions as a snack bar.

The former Church of Agia Ekaterini, next to Agios Minos Cathedral, is now a museum (☎ 281 028 8825, Monis Odigitrias; admission €1.50; open 9am-1.30pm Mon-Sat, 5pm-8pm Tues, Thur & Fri). It houses an impressive collection of icons, most notably those painted by Mihail Damaskinos, the mentor of El Greco.

The Battle of Crete Museum (Cnr Doukos Beaufort & Hatzidaki; admission free; open 9am-1pm daily) chronicles this historic battle through photographs, letters, uniforms and weapons.

You can pay homage to Crete's most acclaimed contemporary writer, Nikos Kazantzakis (1883–1957), by visiting his tomb at the Martinenga Bastion (the best-preserved bastion) in the southern part of town. The epitaph on his grave, 'I hope for nothing, I fear nothing, I am free', is taken from one of his works.

Trekking

The Iraklio branch of the EOS (☎ 281 022 7609, Dikeosynis 53) operates the Prinos Refuge on Mt Ida, a 1½-hour walk from the village of Melisses, 25km south-west of Iraklio.

Organised Tours

Iraklio's travel agents run coach tours the length and breadth of Crete. Creta Travel (☎ 281 022 7002, Epimenidou 20–22) has a good range.

Places to Stay – Budget

The nearest camping grounds are 26km away at Hersonisos.

CRETE

Nikos Kazantzakis – Crete's prodigal son

Crete's most famous contemporary literary son is Nikos Kazantzakis. Born in 1883 in Iraklio, the then Turkish-dominated capital city of Crete, Kazantzakis spent his early childhood in the ferment of revolution and change that was creeping upon his homeland. In 1897 the revolution against Turkish rule that finally broke out forced him to leave Crete for studies in Naxos, Athens and later Paris. It wasn't until he was 31, in 1914, that he finally turned his hand to writing by translating philosophical books into Greek. For a number of years he travelled throughout Europe – Switzerland, Germany, Austria, Russia and Britain – thus laying the groundwork for a series of travelogues in his later literary career.

Nikos Kazantzakis was a complex writer and his early work was heavily influenced by the prevailing philosophical ideas of the time. The nihilistic philosophies of Nietzsche influenced his writings through which he is tormented by a tangible metaphysical and existentialist anguish. His relationship with religion was always troubling – his official stance being that of a non-believer, yet he seemed to always toy with the idea that perhaps God did exist. His self-professed greatest work is his *Odyssey*, a modern-day epic loosely based on the trials and travels of the ancient hero Odysseas (Ulysses). A weighty and complex opus of 33,333 seventeen syllable iambic verses, *Odyssey* never fully vindicated Kazantzakis' aspirations to be held in the same league as the Ancient's Greeks' Homer, the Romans' Virgil or the Renaissance Italians' Tasso.

Ironically it was much later in his career where Kazantzakis belatedly turned to novel writing that his star finally shone. It was through works like *Christ Recrucified* (1948), *Kapetan Mihalis* (1950) and *The Life and Manners of Alexis Zorbas* (1946) that he became internationally known. This last work gave rise the image of the ultimate, modern Greek male 'Zorba the Greek', immortalised in the Anthony Quinn and Melina Mercouri movie of the same name, and countless restaurants throughout Crete and Greece in general.

Kazantzakis died in Freiburg, Germany on 26 October 1957 while on yet one more of his many travels. Despite resistance from the orthodox church, he was given a religious funeral and buried in the southernmost bastion of the old walls of Iraklio. Among the writer's more optimistic quotes is: 'Happy is the man who before dying has the good fortune to travel the Aegean Seas. Nowhere else can one pass so easily from reality to the dream'. (Nikos Kazantzakis 1883–1957).

MH

Iraklio Youth Hostel (☎ *281 028 6281, fax 281 022 2947, Vyronos 5)* Dorm beds/doubles/triples €7.40/17.60/25. This GYHO establishment is a clean, well-run place, though a little on the quiet side. The dorms are single-sex and the rooms are basic. Luggage storage is available for €1.50 per piece and breakfast and dinner are served, if required.

Rent Rooms Hellas (☎ *281 028 8851, fax 281 028 4442, Handakos 24)* Dorm beds €6.80, doubles/triples/quads €22/26.50/31.70. Many travellers enjoy the lively atmosphere at this de facto youth hostel which has a roof garden and a bar. Luggage storage is free.

There are few *domatia* in Iraklio and not enough cheap hotels to cope with the number of travellers who arrive in high season.

Vergina Rooms (☎ *281 024 2739, Hortatson 32)* Doubles/triples €20.50/26.50. The pleasant Vergina Rooms is a characterful century-old house with a small courtyard and spacious, high-ceilinged rooms. Bathrooms are on the terrace and hot water is available upon request.

Hotel Rea (☎ 281 022 3638, fax 281 24 2189, Kalimeraki-Handakos) Singles/doubles €19/23.50, doubles/triples with bathroom €26.50/35.30. This handy place is clean, quiet and friendly.

Hotel Mirabello (☎ 281 028 5052, fax 281 022 5852, @ mirabhot@otenet.gr, Theotokopoulou 20) Singles/doubles €22/29.50, with bathroom €29.50/35.30. One of the nicest low-priced places in Iraklio would have to be the spiffy Mirabello on a quiet street in the centre of town. The rooms are immaculate.

Hotel Lena (☎ 281 022 3280, fax 281 024 2826, Lahana 10) Singles/doubles €23.50/32.50, doubles with bathroom €38.20. Hotel Lena has comfortable, airy rooms with phones and double-glazed windows; some have air-con, others have fans.

Places to Stay – Mid-Range

Hotel Kastro (☎ 281 0284 185, fax 281 022 3622, ⓦ www.kastro-hotel.gr, Theotokopoulou 22) Singles/doubles with breakfast €26.40/35.20. This is one of the cheapest B-class hotels. The rooms are large, contain telephones and have air-con.

Hotel Kronos (☎ 281 028 2240, fax 281 028 5853, @ kronosht@otenet.gr, Sofokli Venizelou 2) Singles/doubles €32.30/41. This place, which has large rooms in excellent condition, is the best-value C-class hotel. Try to get a room overlooking the sea.

Hotel Ilaira (☎ 281 022 7103, fax 281 024 2367, Ariadnis 1) Singles/doubles €41/52.80. These pleasant stucco and wood rooms have telephones and showers; some have TVs and others have small balconies with sea views.

Hotel Irini (☎ 281 022 6561, fax 281 022 6407, Idomeneos 4) Singles/doubles €47/61.60. This is a modern establishment with 59 large, airy rooms with TV (local stations only), radio, telephone and air-con.

Places to Stay – Top End

Hotel Lato (☎ 281 022 8103, fax 281 024 0350, @ info@lato.gr, Epimenidou 15) Singles/doubles with buffet breakfast €67/84. The Lato has rooms with spectacular sea views.

Atlantis Hotel (☎ 281 022 9103, fax 281 022 6265, @ atlantis@atl.grecotel.gr, Ygias 2) Singles/doubles with buffet breakfast €70.50/100. This A-class hotel offers comfortable rooms with air-conditioning. Facilities include a health studio, sauna and indoor swimming pool.

Astoria Hotel (☎ 281 034 3080, fax 281 022 9078, @ astoria@her.forthnet.gr, Plateia Eleftherias 11) Singles/doubles with buffet breakfast €83.70/106. This A-class hotel is the best place in town. Facilities include a glorious outdoor swimming pool.

Places to Eat – Budget

Iraklio has some excellent restaurants, and there's something to suit all tastes and budgets.

Giakoumis Taverna (Theodosaki 5-8) Mayirefta €2.30-4.40. Open noon-3pm & 7pm-10pm Mon-Sat. Theodosaki is lined with tavernas catering to the market on 1866 and this is one of the best. There's a full menu of Cretan specialities and turnover is heavy which means that the dishes are freshly cooked.

Restaurant Ionia (☎ 281 028 3213, Evans 3) Mayirefta €2.60-4.40. Open 7pm-midnight Mon-Sat. This is the place for good Cretan home cooking. Choose your meal from the pots and pans of pre-prepared food (mayirefta) on display.

O Vrakas (mobile ☎ 69-7789 3973, Plateia Anglon) Mains €2.90-3.50. Vrakas is a small street-side ouzeri that grills fresh fish al fresco in front of the diners. It's cheap and unassuming and the menu is limited, but still very popular with locals. Grilled octopus (€3.22) with ouzo is a good choice.

Ippokambos Ouzeri (☎ 281 028 0240, Mitsotaki 2) Mains €3.50-5.30. This place is as good as taverna-style eating gets. The interior is attractively decorated with cooking pots but most people prefer to squeeze onto one of the street-side tables.

Katsina Ouzeri (☎ 281 022 1027, Marineli 12) Mezedes €1.50-4.40. Open 7pm-1am Tues-Sun. This is an old neighbourhood favourite. Most people come for the lamb and pork roasted in a brick oven or the excellent stewed goat.

CRETE

Baxes (☎ 281 027 7057, Gianni Hronaki 14) Mains €3.22-5. Open 11am-2am daily. Now run by country folk, this simple restaurant offers Cretan special-occasion cooking. Lamb and goat are stewed for hours or roasted in a brick oven.

I Avli tou Defkaliona (☎ 281 024 4215, Kalokerinou 8) Mains €3.80-6.20. Open 8pm-4am Mon-Sat. In this charming taverna you'll soon forget you're in Crete's largest and least picturesque city. It offers a wide range of reasonably priced, imaginative mezedes and main dishes. It really gets rolling around 11pm when the tourists leave and the Cretans arrive.

Loukoumades Cafe (☎ 281 034 6005, Dikeosynis 8) Open 5am-midnight daily. If you haven't yet tried *loukoumades* (fritters with syrup; €1.50), then this is a good place to sample this gooey confection.

Whether you're self-catering or not, you'll enjoy a stroll up *1866* (the market street). This narrow street is always packed, and stalls spill over with produce of every description.

Places to Eat – Top End
Giovanni Taverna (☎ 281 034 6338, Koraï 12) Open noon-2.30pm & 7.30pm-midnight Mon-Sat. This is a splendid place with two floors of large, airy rooms and, in summer, outdoor eating on a quiet pedestrian street. The food is a winning Mediterranean combination of Greek and Italian specialities. The seafood platter for two costs €32.30.

Loukoulos (☎ 281 022 4435, Koraï 5) Grills €13-16. Open noon-3pm & 7pm-midnight Mon-Sat. Loukoulos offers luscious Mediterranean specialities. You can either choose the elegant interior or dine on the outdoor terrace under a lemon tree. All the vegetables are organically grown and vegetarians are well catered for.

Entertainment
Guernica (☎ 281 028 2988, Apokoronou Kritis 2) Open 10am-midnight. Guernica boasts traditional decor and contemporary rock which mix well to create one of Iraklio's hippest bar-cafes.

Take Five (☎ 281 022 6564, Akroleon dos 7) Open 10am-midnight. This is an old favourite on the edge of El Greco Park that doesn't get going until after sundown when the outside tables fill up with a diverse crowd of regulars. It's a gay-friendly place the music and ambience are low-key.

Jasmin (☎ 281 028 8880, Handakos 45) Open noon-midnight. This is a friendly bar/cafe with a back terrace that specialises in herbal tea but also serves alcoholic beverages. The nightly DJs play rock and world music as well as techno.

Aktarika (☎ 281 034 1225, Dedalou 2) Open 10am-1am. This is a large and airy upscale place next to the Morosini Fountain that bustles day and night. It has a great balcony and is a good place to come early in the evening for people-watching. The DJ plays jazz, rock and world music.

Ideon Antron (☎ 281 024 2041, Perdikari 1) Open 10am-1am. On trendy Koraï with its rows of post-modern kafeneia, this is a throwback to the past. The stone interior with its shiny wood bar creates a relaxed, inviting place.

Privilege Club (☎ 281 034 3500, Doukos Beaufort 7) Open 11pm to dawn. Iraklio's smart set packs this refurbished dancing club that can easily hold 1000 people. Like many of Crete's dancing clubs, there's international music (rock, techno etc) until about 2am when the Greek music takes over.

Getting There & Away
Air – Domestic Olympic Airways has at least six flights daily to Athens (€70.45) from Iraklio's Nikos Kazantzakis airport. It also has flights to Thessaloniki (€97, three weekly), Rhodes (€79.50, two weekly) and Santorini (€56, two weekly). The Olympic Airways office (☎ 281 022 9191) is at Plateia Eleftherias 42. The airport number is ☎ 281 024 5644.

Aegean Airlines has flights to Athens (€79.50, three daily) and Thessaloniki (€98.60, two daily). The Aegean Airlines office (☎ 281 034 4324, fax 281 034 4330) is at Leoforos Dimokratias 11. Its office is at the airport (☎ 281 033 0475).

Axon Airlines has flights to Athens (€70, two daily). The Axon Airlines office (☎ 281 033 1310) is located on Ethnikis Andistasis 134.

Air – International Olympic Airways flies to Larnaka, in Cyprus, from Iraklio (€148, two weekly).

Cronus Airlines offers direct connections to Paris and, in association with its partner Aegean Airlines, one-stop connections to Cologne/Bonn, Munich, Rome and Stuttgart.

Iraklio has lots of charter flights from all over Europe. Prince Travel (☎ 281 028 2706), 25 Avgoustou 30, advertises cheap last-minute tickets on these flights. Sample fares include London for €88 and Munich for €125.

Bus There are buses every half-hour (hourly in winter) to Rethymno (1½ hours, €5.60) and Hania (three hours, €10.90) from the Rethymno/Hania bus station opposite Bus Station A. Following is a list of other destinations from Bus Station A (☎ 281 024 5020, fax 281 034 6284, e ktelirla@otenet.gr):

destination	duration	fare	frequency
Agia Pelagia	45 min	€2.20	5 daily
Agios Nikolaos	1½ hr	€4.50	half-hourly
Arhanes	30 min	€1.20	15 daily
Hersonisos/Malia	1 hr	€2	half-hourly
Ierapetra	2½ hr	€6.80	7 daily
Lasithi Plateau	2 hr	€4.50	2 daily
Milatos	1½ hr	€3.50	1 daily
Sitia	3½ hr	€8.80	5 daily

Buses leave Bus Station B for:

destination	duration	fare	frequency
Agia Galini	2½ hr	€5	7 daily
Anogia	1 hr	€2.30	6 daily
Matala	2 hr	€5	9 daily
Phaestos	2 hr	€4.10	8 daily

Taxi There are long-distance taxis (☎ 281 021 0102 or 281 021 0168) from Plateia Eleftherias, opposite the Astoria Hotel and Bus Station B, to all parts of Crete. Sample fares include Agios Nikolaos (€33.80),

Rethymno (€42.50) and Hania (€69). A taxi to the airport costs around €5.90.

Ferry Minoan Lines and ANEK Lines operate ferries every evening each way between Iraklio and Piraeus (10 hours). They depart from both Piraeus and Iraklio between 7.45pm and 8pm. Fares are €21.70 deck class and €41.70 for cabins. The Minoan Lines' Highspeed boats, the F/B *Festos Palace* and F/B *Knossos Palace*, are much more modern and more comfortable than their ANEK rivals.

In summer and on weekends only, Minoan Lines runs six-hour day services on *Festos Palace* and *Knossos Palace*, departing Iraklio and Piraeus at 12.30pm and arriving at 6.30pm. This is by far the most convenient way to get to and from Crete.

Minoan also have three ferries weekly to Thessaloniki (23 hours, €38) via Santorini (3¾ hours, €12.05) and Mykonos (nine hours, €18.80). These services also stop at Paros (7½ hours, €16.15) and Tinos (10¼ hours, €20) twice weekly, and at Naxos (seven hours, €16.15), Syros (10 hours, €17.60) and Skiathos (17¾ hours, €30.80) once a week.

Iraklio's port police can be contacted on ☎ 281 024 4912.

Getting Around

To/From the Airport Bus No 1 goes to and from the airport every 15 minutes between 6am and 1am (€0.60). It leaves the city from near the Astoria Hotel on Plateia Eleftherias.

Bus Bus No 2 goes to Knossos every 10 minutes from Bus Station A (20 minutes, €0.80). It also stops on 25 Avgoustou and 1821.

Car, Motorcycle & Bicycle Most of the car- and motorcycle-rental outlets are on 25 Avgoustou. You'll get the best deal from local companies like Sun Rise (☎ 281 022 1609) at 25 Avgoustou 46, Loggeta Cars & Bikes (☎ 281 028 9462) at Plateia Kallergon 6, next to El Greco Park, or Ritz Rent-A-Car at Hotel Rea (see Places to Stay), which offers discounts for hotel guests.

CRETE

There are also many car rental outlets at the airport.

Mountain bicycles can be hired from Porto Club Travel Services (☎ 281 028 5264), 25 Avgoustou 20.

KNOSSOS Κνωσσός

Knossos *(k-nos-os)*, 5km from Iraklio, was the capital of Minoan Crete. Nowadays the site *(☎ 281 023 1940; admission €4.40; open 8am-7pm daily Apr-Oct, 8am-5pm daily winter)* is the island's major tourist attraction.

The ruins of Knossos were uncovered in 1900 by the British archaeologist Sir Arthur Evans. Heinrich Schliemann, who had earlier uncovered the ancient cities of Troy and Mycenae, had had his eye on the spot (a low, flat-topped mound), believing an ancient city was buried there, but was unable to strike a deal with the local landowner.

Evans was so enthralled by his discovery that he spent 35 years and £250,000 of his own money excavating and reconstructing sections of the palace. Some archaeologists have disparaged Evans' reconstruction, believing he sacrificed accuracy to his overly vivid imagination. However, most non-specialists agree that Sir Arthur did a good job and that Knossos is a knockout. Without these reconstructions it would be impossible to visualise what a Minoan palace looked like.

You will need to spend about four hours at Knossos to explore it thoroughly. There is absolutely no signage, so unless you have a travel guidebook, or hire a guide, you will have no idea what you are looking at. The cafe at the site is expensive – you'd do better to bring a picnic along.

History

The first palace at Knossos was built around 1900 BC. In 1700 BC it was destroyed by an earthquake and rebuilt to a grander and more sophisticated design. It is this palace

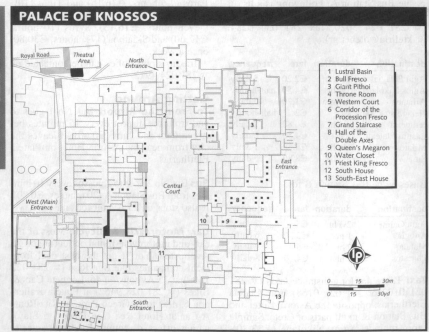

PALACE OF KNOSSOS

Royal Road
Theatral Area
North Entrance
West (Main) Entrance
Central Court
East Entrance
South Entrance

1 Lustral Basin
2 Bull Fresco
3 Giant Pithoi
4 Throne Room
5 Western Court
6 Corridor of the Procession Fresco
7 Grand Staircase
8 Hall of the Double Axes
9 Queen's Megaron
10 Water Closet
11 Priest King Fresco
12 South House
13 South-East House

0   15   30m
0   15   30yd

that Evans reconstructed. It was partially destroyed again sometime between 1500 and 1450 BC. It was inhabited for another 50 years before it was devastated once and for all by fire.

The city of Knossos consisted of an immense palace, residences of officials and priests, the homes of ordinary people, and burial grounds. The palace comprised royal domestic quarters, public reception rooms, shrines, workshops, treasuries and storerooms, all built around a central court. Like all Minoan palaces, it also doubled as a city hall, accommodating all the bureaucracy necessary for the smooth running of a complex society.

Until 1997 it was possible to enter the royal apartments, but the area was cordoned off before it disappeared altogether under the continual pounding of tourists' feet. Extensive repairs are under way but it is unlikely to open to the public again.

Exploring the Site

Numerous rooms, corridors, dogleg passages, nooks and crannies, and staircases prohibit a detailed walk-through description of the palace. However, Knossos is not a site where you'll be perplexed by heaps of rubble, trying to fathom whether you're looking at the throne room or a workshop. Thanks to Evans' reconstruction, the most significant parts of the complex are instantly recognisable (if not instantly found). On your wanders you will come across many of Evans' reconstructed columns, most painted deep brown-red with gold-trimmed black capitals. Like all Minoan columns, they taper at the bottom.

It is not only the vibrant frescoes and mighty columns which impress at Knossos; keep your eyes open for the little details which are evidence of a highly sophisticated society. Things to look out for include the drainage system, the placement of light wells, and the relationship of rooms to passages, porches, light wells and verandas, which kept rooms cool in summer and warm in winter.

The usual entrance to the palace complex is across the Western Court and along the **Corridor of the Procession Fresco**. The fresco depicted a long line of people carrying gifts to present to the king; only fragments remain. A copy of one of these fragments, called the **Priest King Fresco**, can be seen to the south of the Central Court.

If you leave the Corridor of the Procession Fresco and walk straight ahead to enter the site from the northern end, you will come to the **theatral area**, a series of steps, the function of which remains unknown. The area could have been a theatre where spectators watched acrobatic and dance performances, or the place where people gathered to welcome important visitors arriving by the Royal Road.

The **Royal Road** leads off to the west. The road, Europe's first (Knossos has lots of firsts), was flanked by workshops and the houses of ordinary people. The **lustral basin** is also in this area. Evans speculated that this was where the Minoans performed a ritual cleansing with water before religious ceremonies.

Entering the **Central Court** from the north, you pass the relief **Bull Fresco** which depicts a charging bull. Relief frescoes were made by moulding wet plaster, and then painting it while still wet.

Also worth seeking out in the northern section of the palace are the **giant pithoi**. Pithoi were ceramic jars used for storing olive oil, wine and grain. Evans found over 100 of these huge jars at Knossos, some 2m high. The ropes used to move them inspired the raised patterns decorating the jars.

Once you have reached the Central Court, which in Minoan times was surrounded by the high walls of the palace, you can begin exploring the most important rooms of the complex.

From the northern end of the west side of the Central Court, steps lead down to the **throne room**. This room is fenced off but you can still get a pretty good view of it. The centrepiece, the simple, beautifully proportioned throne, is flanked by the **Griffin Fresco**. (Griffins were mythical beasts regarded as sacred by the ancient Minoans.) The room is thought to have been a shrine, and the throne the seat of a high priestess, rather than a king. The Minoans did not worship their deities in

CRETE

great temples but in small shrines, and each palace had several.

On the 1st floor of the west side of the palace is the section Evans called the **Piano Nobile**, for he believed the reception and state rooms were here. A room at the northern end of this floor displays copies of some of the frescoes found at Knossos.

Returning to the Central Court, the impressive **grand staircase** leads from the middle of the eastern side of the palace to the royal apartments, which Evans called the Domestic Quarter. This section of the site is now cordoned off. Within the royal apartments is the **Hall of the Double Axes**. This was the king's *megaron*, a spacious double room in which the ruler both slept and carried out certain court duties. The room had a light well at one end and a balcony at the other to ensure air circulation.

The room takes its name from the double axe marks on its light well. These marks appear in many places at Knossos. The double axe was a sacred symbol to the Minoans. *Labrys* was Minoan for 'double axe' and the origin of our word 'labyrinth'.

A passage leads from the Hall of the Double Axes to the **queen's megaron**. Above the door is a copy of the **Dolphin Fresco**, one of the most exquisite Minoan artworks, and a blue floral design decorates the portal. Next to this room is the queen's bathroom, complete with terracotta bathtub and **water closet**, touted as the first ever to work on the flush principle; water was poured down by hand.

Getting There & Away

Regular buses operate from Iraklio. See Iraklio's Getting Around section for details.

GORTYNA Γόρτυνα

Conveniently, Crete's three other major archaeological sites lie close to each other forming a rough triangle some 50km south of Iraklio. They are best all visited together.

Lying 46km south-west of Iraklio, and 15km from Phaestos, on the plain of Mesara, is the archaeological site of Gortyna (*gor-tih-nah; ☎ 2892 031 144; admission €2.30; open 8am-7pm daily*), also called Gortys.

It's a vast and wonderfully intriguing site with bits and pieces from various ages strewn all over the place. The site was a settlement from Minoan to Christian times. In Roman times, Gortyna was the capital of the province of Cyrenaica.

The most significant find at the site was the massive stone tablets inscribed with the **Laws of Gortyna**, dating from the 5th century BC. The laws deal with just about every imaginable offence. The tablets are on display at the site.

The 6th-century **basilica** is dedicated to Agios Titos, a protege of St Paul and the first bishop of Crete. Other ruins at Gortyna include the 2nd-century AD **praetorium**, which was the residence of the governor of the province, a **nymphaeum**, and the **Temple of Pythian Apollo**. The ruins are on both sides of the main Iraklio-Phaestos road.

PHAESTOS Φαιστός

The Minoan site of Phaestos (*fes-tos; ☎ 2982 042 315; admission €3.50; open 8am-7pm daily, 8am-5pm daily Nov-Apr*), 63km from Iraklio, was the second most important palace city of Minoan Crete. Of all the Minoan sites, Phaestos has the most awe-inspiring location, with all-embracing views of the Mesara Plain and Mt Ida. The layout of the palace is identical to Knossos, with rooms arranged around a central court.

In contrast to Knossos, Phaestos has yielded very few frescoes. It seems the palace walls were mostly covered with a layer of white gypsum. Evans didn't get his hands on the ruins of Phaestos, so there has been no reconstruction. Like the other palatial period complexes, there was an old palace here which was destroyed at the end of the Middle Minoan period. Unlike the other sites, parts of this old palace have been excavated and its ruins are partially super-imposed upon the new palace.

The entrance to the new palace is by the 15m-wide **Grand Staircase**. The stairs lead to the west side of the **Central Court**. The best-preserved parts of the palace complex are the reception rooms and private apartments to the north of the Central Court; excavations continue here. This section was entered by an imposing portal with half columns at either side, the lower parts of which are still *in situ*. Unlike the Minoan freestanding columns, these do not taper at the base. The celebrated Phaestos disc was found in a building to the north of the palace. The disc is in Iraklio's Archaeological Museum.

Getting There & Away
There are buses to Phaestos from Iraklio's Bus Station B (1½ hours, €4.10, eight daily). There are also buses from Agia Galini (40 minutes, €1.50, six daily) and Matala (30 minutes, €1.20, five daily). Services are halved from December through February.

AGIA TRIADA Αγία Τριάδα
Agia Triada (*ah-yee-ah trih-ah-dha;* ☎ 2892 091 564; admission €2.90; open 8.30am-3pm daily) is a small Minoan site 3km west of Phaestos. Its principal building was smaller than the other royal palaces but built to a similar design. This, and the opulence of the objects found at the site, indicate that it was a royal residence, possibly a summer palace of Phaestos' rulers. To the north of the palace is a small town where remains of a *stoa* (long colonnaded building) have been unearthed.

Finds from the palace, now in Iraklio's Archaeological Museum, include a sarcophagus, two superlative frescoes and three vases: the Harvester Vase, Boxer Vase and Chieftain Cup.

The road to Agia Triada takes off to the right about 500m from Phaestos on the road to Matala. There is no public transport to the site.

MATALA Μάταλα
postcode 702 00 • pop 300
Matala (**mah**-tah-lah), on the coast 11km south-west of Phaestos, was once one of Crete's best-known hippie hang-outs. These days, Matala is a decidedly tacky tourist resort packed out in summer and bleak and deserted in winter. The sandy beach below the caves is, however, one of Crete's best, and the resort is a convenient base from which to visit Phaestos and Agia Triada.

It was the old Roman **caves** at the northern end of the beach that made Matala famous in the 1960s. There are dozens of them dotted over the cliff-face. They were originally tombs, cut out of the sandstone rock in the 1st century AD. In the 1960s, they were discovered by hippies, who turned the caves into a modern troglodyte city – moving ever higher up the cliff to avoid sporadic attempts by the local police to evict them.

Orientation & Information
Matala's layout is easy to fathom. The bus stop is on the central square, one block back from the waterfront. There is a mobile post office near the beach, on the right of the main road as you come into Matala. There is no bank or ATM; you can change money at Monza Travel (☎ 2892 045 757). The OTE is beyond here in the beach car park. Check your email at the Coffee Shop (☎ 2892 045 460), or at Zafiria Internet (☎ 2892 045 498); both charge around €4.40 per hour.

Places to Stay
Matala Community Camping (☎/fax 2892 045 340) Adult/tent €3.50/2.60. This is a reasonable site just back from the beach.

Komos Beach camp site (☎ 2892 042 332, Komos Pitsidion) Adult/tent €3.50/2.50. This site is at Komos Beach, about 4km before Matala on the road from Phaestos.

There are several pleasant options in Matala proper. Walk back along the main road from the bus station and turn right at Hotel Zafiria. This street is lined with budget accommodation.

Fantastic Rooms to Rent (☎ 2892 045 362, fax 2892 045 292) Doubles/triples €17.60/23.50. One of the cheapest accommodation options in Matala is this place, on the road leading inland. The comfortable rooms have a bathroom.

Pension Antonios (☎ 2892 045 123, fax 2892 045 690) Singles/doubles €11.70/17.60, double/triple apartments €23.50/26.40. Opposite Fantastic, this pension has attractively furnished rooms and apartments.

Hotel Zafiria (☎ 2892 045 366, fax 2892 045 725) Singles/doubles with breakfast €29.30/38.10. The sprawling Hotel Zafiria

CRETE

takes up a good portion of Matala's main road into town. At the hotel there is a spacious lobby-bar and rooms have balconies, sea views, and telephones.

Places to Eat
Eating in Matala is not an experience in haute cuisine, but you won't starve.

Taverna Manolis (☎ 2892 045 122) Grills €5.30-10.30. Split over two sides of the main street, this largish restaurant serves up standard fare at much the same prices as elsewhere.

Lions (☎ 2892 045 108) Daily specials €5.30-8.80. Overlooking the beach, Lions has been a popular place for quite a while. Its food is better than average.

Restaurant Zafiria (☎ 2892 045 455) Mains €5.30-8.80. A little more expensive than other places, this eatery has reasonably good food, though its location overlooking the car park is not the best.

Getting There & Away
There are buses between Iraklio and Matala (two hours, €5, nine daily), and between Matala and Phaestos (30 minutes, €1.20, five daily).

MALIA Μάλια
The Minoan site of Malia (☎ 2897 031 597; admission €2.30; open 8.30am-3pm daily), 3km east of the resort of Malia, is the only cultural diversion on the stretch of coast east of Iraklio, which otherwise has surrendered lock, stock and barrel to the package-tourist industry. Malia is smaller than Knossos and Phaestos, but like them consisted of a palace complex and a town. Unlike Knossos and Phaestos, the palace was built on a flat, fertile plain, not on a hill.

Entrance to the ruins is from the **West Court**. At the extreme southern end of this court there are eight circular pits which archaeologists think were used to store grain. To the east of the pits is the main entrance to the palace which leads to the southern end of the **Central Court**. At the south-west corner of this court you will find the **Kernos Stone**, a disc with 34 holes around its edge. Archaeologists still don't know what it was used for.

The **central staircase** is at the north end of the west side of the palace. The **loggia**, just north of the staircase, is where religious ceremonies took place.

Any bus going to or from Iraklio along the north coast can drop you at the site.

Eastern Crete

The eastern quarter of the island is occupied by the prefecture of Lasithi, named after the quaint plateau tucked high in the Mt Dikti Ranges rather than its uninspiring administrative capital of Agios Nikolaos, which is becoming something of a monument to package tourism. The main attractions, apart from the Lasithi Plateau, are the palm forest and beach at Vaï and the remote Minoan palace site of Zakros.

LASITHI PLATEAU
Οροπέδιο Λασιθίου
postcode 720 52

The first view of the mountain-fringed Lasithi Plateau, laid out like an immense patchwork quilt, is quite stunning. The plateau, 900m above sea level, is a vast expanse of pear and apple orchards, almond trees and fields of crops, dotted by some 7000 windmills. These are not conventional stone windmills, but slender metal constructions with white canvas sails. They were built in the 17th century to irrigate the rich farmland but few of the original windmills are now in service. Most have been replaced by less-attractive mechanical pumps. There are 20 villages dotted around the periphery of the plateau, the largest of which is **Tzermiado**, with 1300 inhabitants, a bank, post office and OTE. The other two major villages are **Psyhro** and **Agios Georgios**.

The plateau's rich soil has been cultivated since Minoan times. The inaccessibility of the region made it a hotbed of insurrection during Venetian and Turkish rule. Following an uprising in the 13th century, the Venetians drove out the inhabitants of Lasithi and destroyed their orchards. The plateau lay abandoned for 200 years.

Most people come to Lasithi on coach trips, but it deserves an overnight stay. Once the package tourists have departed clutching their plastic windmill souvenirs, the villages return to pastoral serenity.

Dikteon Cave Δίκταιον Αντρον

Lasithi's major sight is Dikteon Cave (☎ 2844 031 316, Psyhro; admission €2.40; open 8am-4pm daily), just outside the village of Psyhro. Here, according to mythology, Rhea hid the newborn Zeus from Cronos, his offspring-gobbling father. The cave, which has both stalactites and stalagmites, was excavated in 1900 by British archaeologist David Hogarth. He found numerous votive offerings, indicating the cave was a place of cult worship. These finds are housed in the Archaeological Museum in Iraklio.

It is a steep 15-minute walk up to the cave entrance along a fairly rough track, but you can opt to take a rather expensive donkey ride (€8.80) instead. There is a less obvious paved trail to the cave that starts from the left side of the carpark. It is not as well-shaded as the rougher track. Walk between the two restaurants and you will see people coming down from the paved track.

Places to Stay

Zeus Hotel (☎ 2844 031 284, Psyhro) Singles/doubles with bathroom €20.50/26.50. This is a modern D-class hotel on the west side of the village of Psyhro near the start of the Dikteon Cave road.

Hotel Dias (☎ 2844 031 207, Agios Georgios) Singles/doubles €12/14.50. On the main street in the village of Agios Georgios, Hotel Dias has pleasant rooms above the restaurant of the same name

Rent Rooms Maria (☎ 2844 031 209, Agios Georgios) Singles/doubles €18/20.50. On the north side of Agios Georgios, Maria has spacious stucco rooms decorated with weavings. The plant-filled enclosed garden is a pleasant place to relax.

Hotel Kourites (☎ 2844 022 194, Tzermiado) Singles/doubles with breakfast €29.50/35.50. On the left as you enter Tzermiado from the east side you'll see this hotel. There is free use of the hotel's bicycles.

Places to Eat

Stavros (☎ 2844 031 453, Psyhro) Mains €3-4.50. Stavros has a neat folksy interior and serves a good range of traditional Cretan dishes. Try goat in lemon and rice sauce (€4.40).

Platanos (☎ 2844 031 668, Psyhro) Ladera €2.70-3.80. Set under a large plane tree opposite Stavros is this alternative eatery. There's a good range of vegetable-based dishes, some of which are also cooked with snails (€3).

Taverna Rea (☎ 2844 031 209, Agios Georgios) Grills €4.50. Opposite the school on Agios Georgios' main street, Taverna Rea rustles up locally produced grilled meats and other staple Cretan fare.

Restaurant Kourites (☎ 2844 022 054, Tzermiado) Grills €4-5. Part of the hotel of the same name in Tzermiado, but 50m farther along the street, is this large restaurant that often has tour groups stopping by for lunch. Food is filling and wholesome.

Taverna Kri-Kri (☎ 2844 022 170, Tzermiado) Mayirefta €3.50-4. This little eatery on Tzermiado's main street serves simple, unfussy meals.

Getting There & Away

Public transport to the Dikteon Cave is problematic if you don't have your own wheels. From Agios Nikolaos there's an afternoon bus to Lasithi on Monday, Wednesday and Friday (2½ hrs, €5.60) and a morning bus from Lasithi to Agios Nikolaos also on Monday, Wednesday and Friday. From Iraklio there are two buses on weekdays to Lasithi (two hours, €4.50), and three on weekdays returning to Iraklio.

All buses go through Tzermiado and Agios Georgios before terminating at Psyhro at the foot of the road leading to Dikteon Cave.

AGIOS NIKOLAOS

Αγιος Νικόλαος
postcode 721 00 • pop 8093
Agios Nikolaos (ah-yee-os nih-ko-laos) is an undeniably pretty former fishing village. Today it is one of Crete's more attractive resort destinations. Boasting a fetching combination of port, lake, narrow streets and

CRETE

aquamarine seas, 'Agios' attracts a lot of people. By the early 1960s, it had become a chic hideaway for the likes of Jules Dassin and Walt Disney. By the end of the decade, package tourists were arriving in force. While there is superficially little to attract the independent traveller, there is reasonable accommodation, prices are not too horrendous and there is quite a bit of activity to keep all tastes catered for. A 40% drop in tourism in the summer of 2001 left the village reeling. The years to come may see Agios Nikolaos return to less frenetic levels of tourism and it may yet become a decent place once more.

Orientation

The town centre is Plateia Venizelou, 150m up Sofias Venizelou from the bus station (☎ 2841 022 234). The most interesting part of town is the picturesque Voulismeni Lake, which is ringed with tavernas. The lake is 200m from Plateia Venizelou. Walk northeast along Koundourou and turn left at the bottom and you will come to a bridge that separates the lake from the harbour. The tourist office is at the far side of the bridge.

Once over the bridge, if you turn right and follow the road as it veers left, you will come to the northern stretch of waterfront which is the road to Elounda. A number of large and expensive hotels are along here.

Alternatively, if you turn right at the bottom of Koundourou you will come to a stretch of waterfront with steps leading up to the right. These lead to the streets that have the highest concentration of small hotels and pensions.

Information

The municipal tourist office (☎ 2841 022 357, fax 2841 082 354, e detadan@agn .forthnet.gr), by the bridge, is open 8am to 9.30pm daily from the start of April to mid-November. The tourist police (☎ 2841 026 900), Kondogianni 34, open between 7.30am and 2.30pm daily.

The National Bank of Greece on Nikolaou Plastira has a 24-hour automatic exchange machine. The tourist office also changes money. The post office, 28 Oktovriou 9, is open 7.30am to 2pm Monday to Friday. The OTE is on the corner of 25 Martiou and K Sfakianaki. It is open 7am to 11pm daily.

Internet access is available at the pleasant Polyhoros (☎ 2841 024 876), 28 Oktovriou 13, open 9am to 2am daily. The well-stocked Anna Karteri Bookshop (☎ 2841 022 272) at Koundourou 5 next to the bank has maps, books in English and other languages and some Lonely Planet titles.

The general hospital (☎ 2841 025 221) is at Knossou 3.

Things to See

The **folk museum** (☎ 2841 025 093, Paleologou 4; admission €0.90; open 10am-3pm Sun-Fri), next to the tourist office, has a well-displayed collection of traditional handcrafts and costumes.

The **archaeological museum** (☎ 2841 022 943, Paleologou 74; admission €1.50; open 8.30am-3pm Tues-Sun), housed in a modern building, has a large, well-displayed collection from eastern Crete.

The **Local Aquarium of Agios Nikolaos** (☎ 2841 028 030, Akti Koundourou 30; admission €3.80; open 10am-9pm daily) has interesting displays of fish and information about diving (including PADI courses) and snorkelling throughout Crete.

Voulismeni Lake (Λίμνη Βουλισμένη) is the subject of many stories about its depth and origins. The locals have given it various names, including Xepatomeni (Bottomless), Voulismeni (Sunken) and Vromolimni (Dirty). The lake isn't bottomless – it is 64m deep. The 'dirty' tag came about because the lake used to be stagnant and gave off quite a pong in summer. This was rectified in 1867 when a canal was built linking it to the sea.

Beaches

The popularity of Agios Nikolaos has nothing to do with its beaches. The town beach, south of the bus station, and Kytroplatia Beach, have more people than pebbles. Ammoudi Beach, on the road to Elounda, is equally uninspiring.

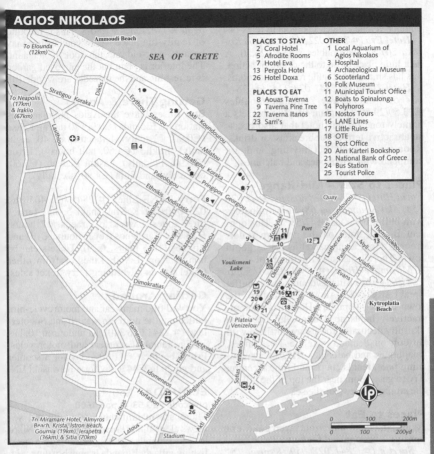

AGIOS NIKOLAOS

PLACES TO STAY
2 Coral Hotel
5 Afrodite Rooms
7 Hotel Eva
13 Pergola Hotel
26 Hotel Doxa

PLACES TO EAT
8 Aouas Taverna
9 Taverna Pine Tree
22 Taverna Itanos
23 Sarri's

OTHER
1 Local Aquarium of
   Agios Nikolaos
3 Hospital
4 Archaeological Museum
6 Scooterland
10 Folk Museum
11 Municipal Tourist Office
12 Boats to Spinalonga
14 Polyhoros
15 Nostos Tours
16 LANE Lines
17 Little Ruins
18 OTE
19 Post Office
20 Ann Karteri Bookshop
21 National Bank of Greece
24 Bus Station
25 Tourist Police

CRETE

The sandy beach at Almyros about 1km south of town is the best of the lot and tends to be less crowded than the others. There's little shade but you can rent umbrellas for €2 a day.

Organised Tours

Travel agencies in Agios Nikolaos offer coach outings to all Crete's top attractions.

Nostos Tours (☎ 2841 022 819, fax 2841 025 336, e *nostos@agn.forthnet.gr, Koundourou 30)* Nostos has boat trips to Spinalonga (€8.80) as well as guided tours of Phaestos and Matala (€30.80), the Samaria

Gorge (€36.70) and the Lasithi Plateau (€23.50).

Places to Stay – Budget

The nearest *camping ground* to Agios Nikolaos is near the Minoan site of Gournia (see Gournia later in this chapter).

Afrodite Rooms (☎ 2841 028 058, Korytsas 27) Singles/doubles with shared facilities €16.20/20.50. There's a tiny communal kitchen here.

Pergola Hotel (☎ 2841 028 152, fax 2841 025 568, Sarolidi 20) Singles/doubles with bathroom €17.60/23.50. Rooms here are comfortable and have fridges. There is an outdoor veranda under a pergola to relax on.

Hotel Eva (☎ 2841 022 587, Stratigou Koraka 20) Singles/doubles €23.50/26.50. A neat little place close to the centre of action, this has smallish but quite reasonable rooms.

Hotel Doxa (☎ 2841 024 214, fax 2841 024 614, Idomeneos 7) Singles/doubles €23.50/29.50 The plant-filled lobby sets a homely tone for this hotel that also boasts an attractive terrace for breakfast or drinks. Rooms are small but inviting and are equipped with telephones and balconies.

Places to Stay – Mid-Range

Coral Hotel (☎ 2841 028 363, fax 2841 028 754, Akti Koundourou 68) Singles/doubles with buffet breakfast €47/58.70. This opulent B-class hotel on the northern waterfront is about as upmarket as places get in town. There's also a swimming pool.

Miramare Hotel (☎ 2841 023 875, fax 2841 024 164) Singles/doubles with buffet breakfast €65/82. About 1km south of the town centre, Miramare Hotel has been attractively landscaped into a hillside. The skilfully decorated rooms are outfitted with air-con on demand, satellite TV, fridges, telephones and balconies. There's a swimming pool, tennis courts and fitness centre. Try to get a room near the top of the hill for the stunning views of the sea.

Places to Eat

Agios Nikolaos' waterfront tavernas are expensive – head inland for better value.

Sarri's (☎ 2841 028 059, Kyprou 15) Breakfast €3. Open 8am-midnight daily. This is the best breakfast spot in town and it stays open until the wee hours serving up mouth-watering food to locals.

Taverna Itanos (☎ 2841 025 340, Kyprou 1) Ladera €2.50-4. This is a vast place with beamed ceilings and stucco walls. It has a few tables on the sidewalk as well as comfortable banquettes. The food is traditional Cretan.

Taverna Pine Tree (☎ 2841 023 890 Paleologou 18) Mezedes €2.80-4.90. Dining alongside scenic Voulismeni Lake is one of the great pleasures of Agios Nikolaos and this is a good choice.

Aouas Taverna (☎ 2841 023 231, Paleologou 44) Mezedes €1.80-8. This is the kind of family-run place where your waiter may be a 10-year-old and the cook is her aunt. The interior is plain but the enclosed garden is refreshing and the mezedes are wonderful.

Getting There & Away

Bus Buses leave the Agios Nikolaos bus station for Elounda (€0.90, 20 daily), Kritsa (€0.90, 12 daily), Ierapetra (€2.40, eight daily), Iraklio (€4.60, half-hourly), Istron (€0.90, 11 daily), Lasithi Plateau (€5.60, one daily) and Sitia (€4.90, six daily).

Ferry LANE Lines (☎ 2841 026 465, fax 023 090), at K Sfakianaki 5, has ferries three times a week to Piraeus (12 hours, €23.20), Karpathos (seven hours, €13) and Rhodes (10½ hours, €19). Tickets can be bought from LANE Lines or from other travel agents advertising ferry ticket sales.

Getting Around

You will find many car and motorcycle-hire outlets on the northern waterfront. Scooterland (☎ 2841 026 340), Koundourou 10, has a huge range of scooters and motorcycles. Prices begin at €11.80 a day for a scooter and go up to €44 a day for a Kawasaki EN.

ELOUNDA Ελούντα
postcode 720 53 • pop 1600

There are magnificent mountain and sea views along the 11km road from Agios Nikolaos to Elounda. Although formerly a quiet fishing village, Elounda is now bristling with tourists and is only marginally calmer than Agios Nikolaos. But the harbour is attractive, and there's a sheltered lagoon-like stretch of water formed by the Kolokytha Peninsula.

Orientation & Information

Elounda's post office is opposite the bus stop. From there walk straight ahead to the clock tower and church which are on the central square. There is a OTE office next to the church. Elounda doesn't have tourist police, but there is a helpful tourist office (☎ 2841 042 464) opposite the church. Staff will help you find accommodation and change money.

Places to Stay & Eat

There's some good accommodation around, but nothing particularly cheap.

Corali Studios (*☎/fax 2841 041 712*) Double studios €35.30. On the north side of Elounda, about 800m from the clock-tower, are these handy self-catering studios, set in lush lawns with a shaded patio.

Hotel Aristea (*☎ 2841 041 300, fax 2841 041 302*) Singles/doubles €29.50/44. This hotel is in the town centre and most rooms have a sea view.

Nikos (*☎ 2841 041 439*) Grills €3.80-6.20. This is a decent choice for fish, which has outdoor tables under a canopy. Service can be erratic but food is reasonably cheap.

The Ferryman Taverna (*☎ 2841 041 230*) Greek specialities €7.40-9. The Ferryman is *the* place to eat in Elounda. It is expensive, but worth it. Dining is waterside and service is top class.

Getting There & Away

There are 20 buses daily from Agios Nikolaos to Elounda (20 minutes, €0.90).

KOLOKYTHA PENINSULA

Χερσόνησος Κολοκύθα

Just before Elounda (coming from Agios Nikolaos), a sign points right to ancient **Olous**, once the port of Lato. The city stood on and around the narrow isthmus (now a causeway) which joined the southern end of the Kolokytha Peninsula to the mainland. Most of the ruins lie beneath the water, and if you go snorkelling near the causeway you will see outlines of buildings and the tops of columns. The water around here appears to be paradise for sea urchins. The peninsula is a pleasant place to stroll and there is an early Christian mosaic near the causeway.

There is an excellent sandy beach 1km along a dirt road (just driveable) on the east side of the peninsula. The beach is sheltered, the water pristine and few visitors use it.

SPINALONGA ISLAND

Νήσος Σπιναλόγκα

Spinalonga Island lies just north of the Kolokytha Peninsula. The island's massive fortress (*admission €1.50; open 8am-7pm daily*) was built by the Venetians in 1579 to protect Elounda Bay and the Gulf of Mirabello. It withstood Turkish sieges for longer than any other Cretan stronghold, finally surrendering in 1715, some 30 years after the rest of Crete. The Turks used the island as a base for smuggling. Following the reunion of Crete with Greece, Spinalonga Island became a leper colony. The last leper died there in 1953 and the island has been uninhabited ever since. It is still known among locals as 'the island of the living dead'.

The island is a fascinating place to explore. It has an aura that is both macabre and poignant. The **cemetery**, with its open graves, is an especially strange place. Dead lepers came in three classes: those who saved up money from their government pension for a place in a concrete box; those whose funeral was paid for by relations and who therefore got a proper grave; and the destitute, whose remains were thrown into a charnel house.

Getting There & Away

There are regular excursion boats to Spinalonga Island from Agios Nikolaos and a boat every half-hour from the port in Elounda (€5.90). Alternatively, you can negotiate with the fishermen in Elounda and Plaka (a fishing village 5km farther north) to take you across. The boats from Agios Nikolaos pass Bird Island and Kri-Kri Island, one of the last habitats of the *kri-kri*, Crete's wild goat. Both these islands are uninhabited and designated wildlife sanctuaries.

KRITSA Κριτσά

The village of Kritsa (krit-**sah**), perched 600m up the mountainside 11km from Agios Nikolaos, is on every package itinerary. Tourists come in busloads to the village every day in summer. The villagers exploit these invasions to the full, and craft shops of every description line the main streets.

The tiny triple-aisled **Church of Panagia Kera** (*☎ 2841 051 525; admission €2.30; open 8.30am-3pm Mon-Fri, 8.30am-2pm Sat*) is on the right 1km before Kritsa on the Agios Nikolaos road. The frescoes that cover its interior walls are considered the most outstanding examples of Byzantine art on Crete. Unfortunately the church is usually packed with tourists.

Rooms Argyro (☎ *2841 051 174*) Singles/doubles €17.60/29.50. There's very little accommodation in Kritsa, but this is the best place to stay. Each room is immaculate and there is a little shaded restaurant downstairs for breakfast and light meals. The rooms are on the left as you enter the village.

O Kastellos (☎ *2841 051 254*) Mains €5.60-7.40. Grab a pizza or a hearty meal to eat under a plane tree here in the centre of town. Oven-cooked veal and pasta in a pot (€5.30) is recommended.

There are 12 buses daily from Agios Nikolaos to Kritsa (15 minutes, €0.70).

ANCIENT LATO Λατώ

The ancient city of Lato *(lah-***to***; admission €1.50; open 8.30am-3pm Tues-Sun)*, 4km north of Kritsa, is one of Crete's few non-Minoan ancient sites. Lato was founded in the 7th century BC by the Dorians and at its height was one of the most powerful cities on Crete. It sprawls over the slopes of two acropolises in a lonely mountain setting, commanding stunning views down to the Gulf of Mirabello.

The city's name derived from the goddess Leto whose union with Zeus produced Artemis and Apollo, both of whom were worshipped here. Lato is far less visited than Crete's Minoan sites.

In the centre of the site is a deep well, which is cordoned off. As you face the Gulf of Mirabello, to the left of the well are some steps which are the remains of a **theatre**.

Above the theatre was the **prytaneion**, where the city's governing body met. The circle of stones behind the well was a threshing floor. The columns next to it are the remains of a stoa which stood in the *agora* (commercial area). There are remains of a pebble mosaic nearby. A path to the right leads up to the **Temple of Apollo**.

There are no buses to Lato. The road to the site is signposted to the right on the approach to Kritsa. If you don't have your own transport, it's a pleasant walk through olive groves along this road.

GOURNIA Γουρνιά

The important Minoan site of Gournia *(goor-***nyah***; ☎ 2841 024 943; admission €1.50; open 8.30am-3pm Tues-Sun)* lies just off the coast road, 19km south-east of Agios Nikolaos. The ruins, which date from 1550 to 1450 BC, consist of a town overlooked by a small palace. The palace was far less ostentatious than the ones at Knossos and Phaestos because it was the residence of an overlord rather than a king. The town is a network of streets and stairways flanked by houses with walls up to 2m in height. Trade, domestic and agricultural implements found on the site indicate Gournia was a thriving little community.

Gournia is on the Sitia and Ierapetra bus routes from Agios Nikolaos and buses can drop you at the site.

Near the Minoan site is ***Gournia Moon Camping*** (☎/fax 2842 093 243, Gournia), the closest camping ground to Agios Nikolaos. It charges €3.50/2.60 per adult/tent. There's a swimming pool, restaurant, snack bar and minimarket. Buses to Sitia can drop you off outside.

MOHLOS Μόχλος
postcode 72 057 • pop 80

Mohlos (**moh**-los) is a pretty fishing village bedecked in hibiscus, bougainvillea and bitter laurel and reached by a 6km winding road from the main Sitia–Agios Nikolaos highway. It was once joined in antiquity to the homonymous island that now sits 200m offshore and was at one time a thriving Minoan community dating back to the Early Minoan period (3000–2000 BC).

Mohlos sees mainly French and German independent travellers seeking peace and quiet from the noise and hype farther west. There is a small pebble-and-grey-sand beach from which swimming is reasonable. Mohlos is an ideal travellers' rest stop with a high chill-out factor.

Orientation & Information

Mohlos is all contained within two or three blocks, all walkable within 10 minutes.

There is no bank, or post office in Mohlos and very few tourist facilities at all, other than a couple of gift shops. There are two minimarkets.

Places to Stay & Eat
There is quite a bit of accommodation for independent travellers.

Hotel Sofia (☎/*fax 2843 094 554*) Doubles/triples €29.50/32.30. These comfortable rooms are above the Sofia restaurant. The owner also has fully equipped two- to three-person studios 200m east of the harbour.

Spyros Rooms (☎/*fax 2843 094 204*) Doubles €29.50. These very pleasant and modern rooms all have a fridge and air-conditioning and a little way outside the village.

The restaurants abutting the harbour are all good. To start with, kick off with these two.

To Bogazi (☎ *2843 094 200*) Mezedes €1.50-4.50. With a sea view on two sides, To Bogazi is nearest the island and serves up over 30 inventive mezedes, many of which are vegetarian. The cuttlefish and pan-tossed greens is a suggested mains course (€5.30).

Sofia (☎ *2843 094 554*) Mayireftα €2.50-3.50. Mama's home cooking is the key ingredient on the menu at Sofia. Try artichokes with peas (€2.70), or cauliflower in wine sauce (€2.50). Vegetarians will love them.

Getting There & Away
There is no public transport travelling directly to Mohlos. Buses between Sitia and Agios Nikolaos will drop you off at the Mohlos turn-off. From there you'll need to hitch or walk the 6km to Mohlos village.

SITIA Σητεία
postcode 723 00 • pop 8000
Sitia (sih-**tee**-ah) is a good deal quieter than Agios Nikolaos. It is a pleasant traveller-friendly town and makes a good jumping-off point for the Dodecanese islands. A sandy beach skirts a wide bay to the east of town. The main part of the town is terraced up a hillside, overlooking the port. The buildings are a pleasing mixture of new and fading Venetian architecture.

Orientation & Information
The bus station is at the eastern end of Karamanli, which runs behind the bay. The town's main square, Plateia El Venizelou – recognisable by its palm trees and statue of a dying soldier – is at the western end of Karamanli.

There's no tourist office but Tzortzakis Travel (☎ 2843 025 080), Kornarou 150, is a good source of information. There are lots of ATMs and places to change money. The National Bank of Greece on the main square has a 24-hour exchange machine.

The harbour near the square is for small boats. Ferries use the large quay farther out, about 500m from Plateia Agnostou.

The post office is on Dimokritou. To get there from the main square, follow El Venizelou inland and take the first left. The OTE is on Kapetan Sifi, which runs uphill directly off Plateia El Venizelou.

Things to See & Do
Sitia's **archaeological museum** (☎ *2843 023 917, Pisokefalou; admission €1.50; open 8.30am-3pm Tues-Sun*) houses a well-displayed collection of local finds spanning from Neolithic to Roman times, with emphasis on the Minoan. The museum is on the left side of the road to Ierapetra.

Sitia produces superior sultanas, and a **sultana festival** is held in the town in the last week of August, during which wine flows freely and there are performances of Cretan dances.

Places to Stay
Sitia Youth Hostel (☎ *2843 028 062, Therisou 4*) Dorm beds/doubles €5/11.80. Sitia's youth hostel is on the road to Iraklio. It's a well-run place with hot showers and a communal kitchen and dining room.

Hotel Arhontiko (☎ *2843 028 172, Kondylaki 16*) Singles/doubles with shared facilities €17.70/20.50. This D-class hotel two streets uphill from the port is beautifully maintained and spotless. The owner enjoys sharing a bottle of raki with guests on the communal terrace.

Rooms to Let Apostolis (☎ *2843 028 172, Kazantzaki 27*) Doubles with fridge €23.50.

CRETE

This upmarket domatio is co-owned with Hotel Arhontiko. Kazantzaki runs uphill from the waterfront, one street north of the OTE.

Kazarma Rooms to Rent (☎ 2843 023 211, Ionias 10) Doubles with bathroom €26.50. This is an attractive place to stay, and is signposted from Patriarhou Metaxaki. There is a communal lounge and a well-equipped kitchen.

El Greco Hotel (☎ 2843 023 133, fax 2843 026 391, Arkadiou 13) Singles/doubles with bathroom €28/38. The well-signposted El Greco has more character than the town's other C-class places. Rooms are comfortable.

Itanos Hotel (☎ 2843 022 900, fax 2843 022 915, ✉ itanoshotel@yahoo.com, Karamanli 4) Singles/doubles €28/47. The B-class Itanos has a conspicuous location on the waterfront and a popular terrace restaurant. The comfortable rooms are outfitted with air-con, satellite TV, balconies and sound-proofing.

Places to Eat

There is a string of tavernas along the quay side on El Venizelou that offer an array of mezedes and fish dishes at comparable prices.

Mihos Taverna (Kornarou 117) Grills €4-5.50. This taverna on the waterfront has excellent charcoal-grilled souvlaki. This is one of the few decent waterfront eateries.

Kali Kardia Taverna (☎ 2843 022 249, Foundalidou 22) Mains €4-5.50. Open 10am-midnight daily. This place is excellent value and popular with locals. Walk up Kazantzaki from the waterfront, take the second right and the taverna is on the right.

Cafe Nato (mobile ☎ 69-7282 8503, Mastropavlou 43) Mezedes €1.50-2.50. Open noon-midnight daily. Cafe Nato, up from Hotel Nora, is a laid-back little taverna with outdoor tables that serves a variety of grilled meat, artisanal cheeses and good raki.

Symposio (☎ 2843 025 856, Karamanli 12) Mains €5.30-6.80. Symposio utilises all-Cretan natural products such as organic olive oil from the Toplou monastery. The food is top class. Rabbit in rosemary and wine sauce (€5.30) is recommended.

The Balcony (☎ 2843 025 084, Foundalidou 18) Mains €8.50-10.50. Open noon-3pm & 6.30pm-midnight. Providing the finest dining in Sitia, this has an extraordinarily creative menu that combines Greek, Italian and Mexican food.

Getting There & Away

Air The Olympic Airways office (☎ 2843 022 270) is at 4 Septemvriou 3. Sitia's tiny airport has flights to Athens twice a week for €75.40.

Bus There are six buses a day to Ierapetra (1½ hours, €3.80), five buses a day to Iraklio (3½ hours, €8.80) via Agios Nikolaos (1½ hours, €4.90), five to Vaï (one hour, €1.90), and two to Kato Zakros via Palekastro and Zakros (one hour, €3.40). The buses to Vaï and Kato Zakros run only between May and October; during the rest of the year, the Vaï service terminates at Palekastro and the Kato Zakros service at Zakros.

Ferry The F/B Vitsentzos Kornaros and F/B Ierapetra of LANE Lines link Sitia with Piraeus (14½ hours, €24), Kasos (four hours, €8.50), Karpathos (six hours, €11) and Rhodes (10 hours, €20) three times weekly. Departure times change annually, so check locally for latest information. Buy tickets at Tzortzakis Travel Agency (☎ 2843 022 631, 2843 28 900), Kornarou 150.

Getting Around

The airport (signposted) is 1km out of town. There is no airport bus; a taxi costs €3.80.

AROUND SITIA

Moni Toplou Μονή Τοπλού

The imposing Moni Toplou (☎ 2843 061 226, Lasithi; admission €2.40; open 9am-1pm & 2pm-6pm daily), 18km east of Sitia on the back road to Vaï, looks more like a fortress than a monastery. It was often treated as such, being ravaged by both the Knights of St John and the Turks. It holds an 18th-century icon by Ioannis Kornaros, one of Crete's most celebrated icon painters.

From the Sitia-Paleokastro road it is a 3km walk. Buses can drop you off at the junction.

Vaï Βάι

The beach at Vaï, on Crete's east coast 24km from Sitia, is famous for its palm forest.

There are many stories about the origin of these palms, including the theory that they sprouted from date pits spread by Roman legionaries relaxing on their way back from conquering Egypt. While these palms are closely related to the date, they are a separate species unique to Crete.

You'll need to arrive early to appreciate the setting, because the place gets packed in July and August. It's possible to escape the worst of the ballyhoo – jet skis and all – by clambering over a rocky outcrop (to the right, facing the sea) to a small secluded beach. Alternatively, you can go over the hill in the other direction to a quiet beach frequented by nudists.

There are two *tavernas* at Vaï but no accommodation. If you're after more secluded beaches, head north for another 3km to the ancient Minoan site of Itanos. Below the site are several good swimming spots.

There are buses to Vaï from Sitia (one hour, €1.80, five daily).

ZAKROS & KATO ZAKROS

Ζάκρος & Κάτω Ζάκρος
postcode 72 300 • pop 765

The village of Zakros (zah-kros), 37km south-east of Sitia, is the nearest permanent settlement to the Minoan site of Zakros, a further 7km away (see Ancient Zakros following).

Kato Zakros, next to the site, is a beautiful little seaside settlement that springs to life between March and October. If the weather is dry, there is a lovely two-hour walk from Zakros to Kato Zakros through a gorge known as the Valley of the Dead because of the cave tombs dotted along the cliffs. The gorge emerges close to the Minoan site.

Places to Stay

It's much better to stay at Kato Zakros, where there are four places to choose from, than at Zakros.

Poseidon Rooms (☎ 2843 026 893, fax 2843 026 894, e akrogiali@sit.forthnet.gr) Doubles with/without bathroom €26.50/

17.60. At the southern end of the waterfront, these rooms are small but very neat and clean and make for a good budget choice.

Athena Rooms (☎ 2843 026 893, fax 2843 026 894, e akrogiali@sit.forthnet.gr) Doubles with bathroom €26.50. A good-quality choice, these rooms are very pleasant with heavy stone walls and views of the beach from the balcony.

George's Villas (☎/fax 2843 026 833) Singles/doubles with bathroom €26.50/32.30. George's has spotless, beautifully furnished rooms with terraces. The villas are in a verdant, pine-fringed setting 800m along the old road to Zakros.

Rooms Coral (☎/fax 2843 027 064, e katozakrosgr@yahoo.com) Doubles €35.50. The excellent, smallish, spotlessly clean rooms here are equipped with Internet connectivity and all enjoy superb sea views from the communal balcony. There's a kitchen and fridge for guests' use.

Places to Eat

There are three decent restaurants in Kato Zakros, all next to each other.

Taverna Akrogiali (☎ 2843 026 893) Mains €4.40-7.40. There's soothing, seaside dining here with excellent service from owner Nikos Perakis. The speciality is grilled swordfish steak (€7.40).

Georgios Taverna Anesis (☎ 2843 026 890) Ladera €1.50 3.30. The owner specialises in home-cooked food and ladera dishes. Dining is under trees overlooking the beach.

Restaurant Nikos Platanakis (☎ 2843 026 887) Ladera €3-3.80. A wide range of Greek staples is available at this waterside spot as well as rarities such as rabbit, pheasant and partridge.

Getting There & Away

There are buses to Zakros via Palekastro from Sitia (one hour, €3, two daily). They leave Sitia at 11am and 2.30pm and return at 12.30pm and 4pm. From June through August, the buses continue to Kato Zakros.

CRETE

ANCIENT ZAKROS

The smallest of Crete's four palatial complexes, ancient Zakros (☎ 2843 026 987, Kato Zakros; admission €1.50; open 8am-7pm daily) was a major port in Minoan times, maintaining trade links with Egypt, Syria, Anatolia and Cyprus. The palace comprised royal apartments, storerooms and workshops flanking a central courtyard.

The town occupied a low plain close to the shore. Water levels have risen over the years so that some parts of the palace complex are submerged. The ruins are not well preserved, but a visit to the site is worthwhile for its wild and remote setting.

XEROKAMBOS Ξερόκαμπος
postcode 720 59 • pop 25

Xerokambos (kseh-**roh**-kam-bos) is a quiet, unassuming agricultural village on the far south-eastern flank of Crete. Its isolation has so far meant that tourism is pretty much low-key and most certainly of the unpackaged kind. It attraction lies in its isolation, a couple of splendid beaches, a few scattered tavernas and a scattering of studio accommodation that is ideal for people with peace and quiet in mind.

Ambelos Beach Studios *(☎/fax 2842 026 759)* Double/triple studios €29.50/32.50. These smallish, but cosy studios have kitchenettes and fridges. There is a BBQ and outdoor wood oven for guests, and a tree-shaded courtyard.

Akrogiali Taverna *(☎ 2842 026 777)* Mains €3. The only beachside taverna in Xerokambos, Akrogiali is 50m from Ambelos Beach. The food ranges from grills to fish, to home-cooked mayirefta. Look for it near Ambelos Beach Studios.

There are no buses to Xerokambos. To get there from Zakros take the Kato Zakros road, and on the outskirts of Zakros turn left at the signpost for Livyko View Restaurant. This 8km dirt road to Xerokambos is driveable in a conventional vehicle. Otherwise there is a good paved road from Ziros.

IERAPETRA Ιεράπετρα
postcode 722 00 • pop 9541

Ierapetra (yeh-**rah**-pet-rah) is Crete's most southerly major town. It was a major port of call for the Romans in their conquest of Egypt. After the tourist hype of Agios Nikolaos, the unpretentiousness of Ierapetra is refreshing, and the main business continues to be agriculture, not tourism.

Orientation & Information

The bus station (☎ 2842 028 237) is on the eastern side of town on Lasthenous, one street back from the beachfront. From the ticket office, turn right and after about 50m you'll come to a six-road intersection. There are signposts to the beach via Patriarhou Metaxaki, and to the city centre via the pedestrian mall section of Lasthenous.

The mall emerges after about 150m on to the central square of Plateia Eleftherias. To the north of the square is the National Bank of Greece and on the south side is Eurobank. Both banks have ATMs.

If you continue straight ahead from Plateia Eleftherias you will come to Plateia Georgiou Kounoupaki, where you'll find the post office at Vitsenzou Kornarou 7.

There is no tourist office, but South Crete Tours (☎ 2842 022 892), opposite the bus station, might have maps of Ierapetra. To reach it, turn right from Plateia Georgiou Kounoupaki.

You can check your email at the Polycafe Orpheas (☎ 2842 080 462), Koundouriotou 25, or The Net Internet Cafe (☎ 2842 025 900, e the_net_ier@yahoo.com), Koundourou 16.

Things to See

The one-room **archaeological museum** *(☎ 2842 028 721, Adrianou 2; admission €1.50; open 8.30am-3pm Tues-Sun)* is perfect for those with a short concentration span. Pride of place is given to an exquisite statue of Demeter.

If you walk south along the waterfront from the central square you will come to the **Venetian Fortress** *(Kato Meran; admission free; open 8.30am-3pm Tues-Sun)*, built in the early years of Venetian rule and strengthened by Francesco Morosini in 1626. It's in a pretty fragile state.

Inland from the fortress is the labyrinthine **old quarter**, a delightful place to lose yourself for a while. Look out for the Turkish mosque and Turkish fountain.

Beaches

Ierapetra has two beaches. The main town beach is near the harbour and the other beach stretches east from the bottom of Patriarhou Metaxaki. Both have coarse, grey sand.

The beaches to the east of Ierapetra tend to get crowded. For greater tranquillity, head for **Gaïdouronisi**, known also as **Hrysi**, where there are good, uncrowded sandy beaches, three tavernas and a stand of cedars of Lebanon, the only one in Europe. From June through August excursion boats (€16) leave for the islet every morning and return in the afternoon.

Places to Stay

Koutsounari Camping (☎ 2842 061 213, fax 2842 061 186, Koutsounari) Adult/tent €3.50/2.60. The nearest camping ground to Ierapetra is 7km east of Ierapetra at Koutsounari. It has a restaurant, snack bar and minimarket. Ierapetra-Sitia buses pass the site.

Hotel Coral (☎ 2842 022 846, Katzonovatsi 12) Singles/doubles €15/18, with bathroom €17.60/23.50. Rooms here are well kept and apartments are comfortable. The hotel is two blocks inland in the old town.

Katerina Rooms (☎ 2842 028 345, fax 2842 028 591, Markopoulou 95) Doubles with bathroom €32.50. On the seafront, Katerina has pleasant rooms. To reach the hotel from the bus station, follow Patriarhou Metaxaki to the waterfront.

Cretan Villa Hotel (☎/fax 2842 028 522, e cretan-villa@cretan-villa.com, w www.cretan-villa.com, Lakerda 16) Singles/doubles €26.50/35.50. This is a well-maintained

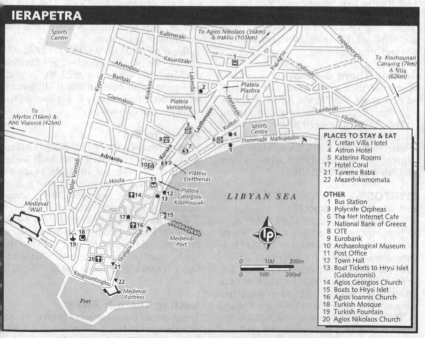

IERAPETRA

PLACES TO STAY & EAT
2 Cretan Villa Hotel
4 Astron Hotel
5 Katerina Rooms
17 Hotel Coral
21 Taverna Babis
22 Mezedokamomata

OTHER
1 Bus Station
3 Polycafe Orpheas
6 The Net Internet Cafe
7 National Bank of Greece
8 OTE
9 Eurobank
10 Archaeological Museum
11 Post Office
12 Town Hall
13 Boat Tickets to Hrysi Islet (Gaïdouronisi)
14 Agios Georgios Church
15 Boats to Hrysi Islet
16 Agios Ioannis Church
18 Turkish Mosque
19 Turkish Fountain
20 Agios Nikolaos Church

CRETE

18th-century house with traditionally furnished rooms and a peaceful courtyard. It is a five-minute walk from the bus station.

Astron Hotel (☎ 2842 025 114, fax 2842 025 91, Kothri 56) Singles/doubles with breakfast €41/73.50. The best hotel in town is the B-class Astron at the beach end of Patriarhou Metaxaki. The rooms here are comfortably furnished with satellite TV, telephone and air-conditioning.

Places to Eat
Most of the souvlaki outlets are on Kyrva and there is a swathe of restaurant along the promenade.

Taverna Babis (☎ 2842 024 048, Stratigou Samouil 68) Mains €3.50-5.50. Babis is one of the better tavernas along the waterfront. It has an enormous range of mezes dishes. Ask for *kakavia* (fish soup), or *steka* – a cream cheese made from curds.

Mezedokamomata (☎ 2842 028 286, Stratigou Samouil 74) Mezedes €1.70-3.80. Similar to Babis and only 50m farther along the street is this imaginative restaurant serving up a range of mezedes. If you like offal, ask for *splinandero*, or *omaties* rice and offal sausages.

Getting There & Away
In summer, there are six buses a day to Iraklio (2½ hours, €6.75) via Agios Nikolaos (one hour, €2.40), Gournia and Istron; eight to Makrygialos (30 minutes, €1.90); six to Sitia (1½ hours, €4.10) via Koutsounari (for camp sites); six to Myrtos (30 minutes, €1.20); and two a week to Ano Viannos (one hour, €2.50).

MYRTOS Μύρτος
postcode 722 00 • pop 433
Myrtos (**myr**-tos), on the coast 17km west of Ierapetra, is a sparkling village full of whitewashed houses with flower-filled balconies. It is a magnet for independent travellers, many of whom come only for a day or so, yet often stay on for a week or two. The village has a cosy, lived-in ambience where everyone seems to know each other.

You'll soon find your way around Myrtos which is built on a grid system. To get to the waterfront from the bus stop, facing south, take the road to the right passing Mertiza Studios on the right.

There is no post office, bank or OTE, but Aris Travel Agency (☎ 2842 051 017) on the main street has currency exchange. Internet access is available upstairs at Edem Cafe (☎ 2842 051 551), two blocks back from the waterfront.

Places to Stay
Hotel Myrtos (☎ 2842 051 227, fax 2842 051 215, W www.myrtoshotel.com) Singles/doubles with bathroom €17.50/23.50. This superior C-class place has large, well-kept rooms.

Cretan Rooms (☎ 2842 051 427) Doubles €26.50. These excellent traditional-styled rooms with balconies, fridges and shared kitchens are popular with independent travellers. They are prominently signposted from the village centre.

Nikos House (☎ 2842 051 116) 2-person/4-person apartments €35/40. Two blocks back from the waterfront, beneath the leaves of a large mulberry tree, are these large and comfortable apartments.

Big Blue (☎ 2842 051 094, fax 2842 051 121, e big-blue@ier.forthnet.gr) Singles/doubles with bathroom €23.50, 2-room apartments with 2 bathrooms & kitchenette €59. This nifty property is high up on the western edge of town.

Places to Eat
Myrtos Taverna (☎ 2842 051 227) Mains €3-6. Myrtos is popular with both locals and tourists both for its wide range of mezedes as well as for its vegetarian dishes. Rabbit in red wine sauce (€4.70) is recommended by the owner.

Taverna Akti (☎ 2842 051 584) Grills €4.40-6. Pleasant seafood dining and good food are Akti's attraction. Look for the 'daily specials' board to see what's on. Order octopus in red wine sauce (€6.50) if you see it.

Getting There & Away
There are six buses each day from the town of Ierapetra to Myrtos (30 minutes, €1.20).

The twice-weekly Ano Viannos–Ierapetra bus also passes through Myrtos.

MYRTOS TO ANO VIANNOS

Ano Viannos, 16km west of Myrtos, is a delightful village built on the southern flanks of Mt Dikti. The flower-decked **folklore museum** (☎ 2895 022 778, Ano Viannos; admission €1.50; open 10am-2pm daily) presents colourful costumes and traditional implements such as an olive press and key-making tools.

The village's 14th-century **Church of Agia Pelagia** (Ano Viannos; admission free; open 9am-8pm summer) is a tiny structure. The interior walls, covered with luscious frescoes by Nikoforos Fokas, are in need of restoration but can still be appreciated.

From Ano Viannos it's 13km south to the unspoilt and now contiguous villages of **Kastri** and **Keratokambos**, where there's a pleasant tree-lined beach.

The turn-off for **Arvi** (population 298) is 3km east of Ano Viannos. Arvi is bigger than Keratokambos, but only gets crowded during July and August. Hemmed in by cliffs, Arvi is a sun trap where bananas grow in abundance. The main street skirts a long sand-and-pebble beach. It's about a 15-minute walk inland to Moni Agiou Andoniou.

Places to Stay

Taverna & Rooms Lefkes (☎ 2895 022 719, Ano Viannos) Singles/doubles with bathroom €11.80/14.70. Ano Viannos' one domatia, this is 50m downhill from the large church. The rooms are over the taverna which has good Cretan specialities and a pleasant shady terrace.

Filoxenia Appartments (☎ 2895 051 371, Kastri) Double studios €35.30. The pickings in Kastri and Keratokambos are much better than Ano Viannos. These two-to three-person studios, wrapped in a flower shaded garden, are beautiful. Equipped with kitchenette and fridge, they make an ideal mid-range accommodation option.

Komis Studios (☎ 2895 051 390, fax 2895 051 593, ℮ pervass@otenet.gr, Keratokambos) Rooms €73.50. These stun-ningly decorated three-level apartments on the sea are built from stone, wood and stucco and outfitted with air-conditioning among other amenities. They are worth every cent.

Pension Gorgona (☎ 2895 071 353, Arvi) Doubles with bathroom €28. One of a few places to stay in Arvi, this pension on the main street has pleasant rooms.

Hotel Ariadne (☎ 2895 071 300, Arvi) Singles/doubles with bathroom €14.70/22. Farther west from Pension Gorgona, Hotel Ariadne has well-kept rooms.

Apartments Kyma (☎ 2895 071 344, Arvi) Apartments €23.50. At the eastern end of Arvi village you'll find these luxurious apartments.

Places to Eat

Morning Star Taverna (☎ 2895 051 209, Kastri) Mains €4.10-4.70. Grills and fish feature at this place in Kastri, with a mixed fish grill (€3.80) being a good bet. Tasty artichoke stew (€3) is a good choice for vegetarians.

Taverna Nikitas (☎ 2895 051 477, Keratokambos) Grills €4-5. By the sea in the centre of Keratokambos, this place offers delicious grills. Roast lamb and pork (€5) is recommended.

Restaurant Ariadne (☎ 2895 071 353, Arvi) Mains €3-4.50. Part of the hotel of the same name in Arvi, the restaurant here serves reasonable food with a mixture of grills and fish on offer.

Taverna Diktina (☎ 2895 071 249, Arvi) Mains around €4.50. This place features vegetarian food such as beans or stuffed tomatoes, both €3.

Getting There & Away

Public transport is poor. From Ano Viannos there are two buses weekly to Iraklio (2½ hours, €6.20) and Ierapetra (one hour, €2.80) via Myrtos. There is no bus service to Keratokambos or Arvi, but in term time it may be possible to use the school buses from Ano Viannos.

You can easily drive the 8km coastal dirt road between the towns of Kastri-Keratokambos and Arvi.

CRETE

Western Crete

The western part of Crete comprises the prefectures of Hania and Rethymno, which take their names from the old Venetian cities which are their capitals. The two towns rank as two of the region's main attractions, although the most famous is the spectacular Samaria Gorge. The south-coast towns of Paleohora and Plakias are popular resorts.

RETHYMNO Ρέθυμνο
postcode 741 00 • pop 23,355

Rethymno (reh-thim-no) is Crete's third-largest town. The main attraction is the old Venetian-Ottoman quarter that occupies the headland beneath the massive Venetian *fortezza* (fortress). The place is a maze of narrow streets, graceful wood-balconied houses and ornate Venetian monuments; several minarets add a touch of the Orient. The architectural similarities invite comparison with Hania, but Rethymno has a character of its own. An added attraction is a beach right in town.

The approaches to the town couldn't be less inviting. The modern town has sprawled out along the coast, dotted with big package hotels attracted by a reasonable beach.

History

The site of modern Rethymno has been occupied since Late Minoan times – the evidence can be found in the city's archaeo-logical museum. In the 3rd and 4th centuries BC, the town was known as Rithymna, an autonomous state of sufficient stature to issue its own coinage. A scarcity of references to the city in Roman and Byzantine periods suggest it was of minor importance at that time.

The town prospered once more under the Venetians, who ruled from 1210 until 1645, when the Turks took over. Turkish forces held the town until 1897, when it was taken by Russia as part of the occupation of Crete by the Great Powers.

Rethymno became an artistic and intellectual centre after the arrival of a large number of refugees from Constantinople in 1923. The city has a campus of the University of Crete, bringing a student population that keeps the town alive outside the tourist season.

Orientation

Rethymno is a fairly compact city with most of the major sights and places to stay and eat within a small central area. It is hard to get lost in the city though the maze of narrow and often winding streets may make you think the opposite.

Ethnikis Andistasis which leads into the Old Town via the Puerto Guora is the main drag in central Rethymno, while Eleftheriou Venizelou running south of the town beach is the main beachside drag.

To the east of Eleftheriou Venizelou stretches a long sandy beach and an uninterrupted stretch of hotels, cafes, bars and restaurants. The most atmospheric places to stay and eat are all close to the centre.

Boats arrive conveniently within a couple of hundred metres of the old port, while buses arrive on the western side of the city. You can walk from both the port and bus station to the centre within minutes. If you are driving or biking into town from the expressway, there are three possible entry points.

Information

Tourist Offices Rethymno's municipal tourist office (☎ 2831 029 148) is on the beach side of El Venizelou, opposite the junction with Kalergi. It's open 8.30am to 2.30pm Monday to Friday. The tourist police (☎ 2831 028 156) occupy the same building and are open from 7am to 10pm every day.

Money Banks are concentrated around the junction of Dimokratias and Pavlou Kountouriotou. The National Bank of Greece is on Dimokratias, on the far side of the square opposite the town hall. The Alpha Bank, at Pavlou Koundouriotou 29, and the National Mortgage Bank, next to the town hall, have 24-hour automatic exchange machines and ATMs.

Post & Communications The OTE is at Koundouriotou 28, and the post office is a block south at Moatsou 21. In summer there is a mobile post office about 200m south-east of the tourist office on El Venizelou. You can check your email at Galero (☎ 2831 054 345) on Plateia Rimini. It is open from very early to very late and charges €3.50 per hour.

Bookshops The International Press Bookshop (☎ 2831 024 111), Petihaki 15, stocks English novels, travel guides and history books. The Ilias Spondidakis bookshop (☎ 2831 054 307), Souliou 43, stocks novels in English, books about Greece, tapes of Greek music and has a small second-hand section.

Laundry The Laundry Mat self-service laundry (☎ 2831 056 196) at Tombazi 45, next door to the youth hostel, charges €7.50 for a wash and dry.

Things to See
Rethymno's 16th-century fortress (☎ 2831 028 101, Paleokastro Hill; admission €2.40; open 8am-8pm daily) is the site of the city's ancient acropolis. Within its massive walls once stood a great number of buildings, of which only a church and a mosque survive intact. The ramparts offer good views, while the site has lots of ruins to explore.

The **archaeological museum** (☎ 2831 029 975, Fortezza; admission €1.50; open 8.30am-3pm daily) is opposite the entrance to the fortress. The finds displayed here include an important coin collection. Rethymno has an excellent **Historical & Folk Art Museum** (☎ 2831 023 398, Vernardou 28–30; admission €3; open 9.30am-2.30pm Mon-Sat) which gives an excellent overview of the region's rural lifestyle with a collection of old clothes, baskets, weavings and farm tools.

Pride of place among the many vestiges of Venetian rule in the old quarter goes to the **Rimondi Fountain** with its spouting lion heads, and the 16th-century **loggia**.

At the southern end of Ethnikis Andistasis is the well-preserved **Porto Guora**, a remnant of the Venetian defensive wall. Turkish legacies in the old quarter include the **Kara Musa Pasa Mosque** near Plateia

Iroön and the **Neradjes Mosque**, which was converted from a Franciscan church.

Activities
The Happy Walker (☎/fax 2831 052 920, [e] info@happywalker.nl, [w] www.happy walker.nl, Tombazi 56) runs a varied program of mountain walks in the region. Most walks start in the early morning and finish with lunch and cost from about €20 onwards.

There is an **EOS** (☎ 2831 057 766, Dimokratias 12) in Rethymno.

The **Paradise Dive Centre** (☎ 2831 026 317, fax 2831 020 464, [e] pdcr@otenet.gr, El Venizelou 76) has activities and a PADI course for all grades of divers.

Special Events
Rethymno's main cultural event is the annual Renaissance Festival that runs during July and August. It features dance, drama and films as well as art exhibitions.

Some years there's a Wine Festival in mid-July held in the municipal park. Ask the tourist office for details.

Places to Stay – Budget
Elizabeth Camping (☎ 2831 028 694, fax 2831 050 401, Mysiria) Adult/tent €5/ 3.50. The nearest camping ground is near Mysiria Beach 3km east of Rethymno. The site has a taverna, snack bar and minimarket. There is a communal fridge, iced water 24 hours a day and free beach umbrellas and loungers. An Iraklio-bound bus can drop you at the site.

Rethymno Youth Hostel (☎ 2831 022 848, [e] manolis@yhrethymno.com, [w] www .yhrethymno.com, Tombazi 41) Beds €5.30. The hostel is friendly and well run with free hot showers. Breakfast is available and there's a bar in the evening. There is no curfew and the place is open all year.

Rent Rooms Sea Front (☎ 2831 051 981, fax 2831 051 062, [e] elotia@ret.forthnet.gr, El Venizelou 45) Singles/doubles with bathroom €20.50/26.50. This is a delightful pension which has only six very clean studio/apartments. The front rooms can be noisy at night, but you are close to the beach.

CRETE

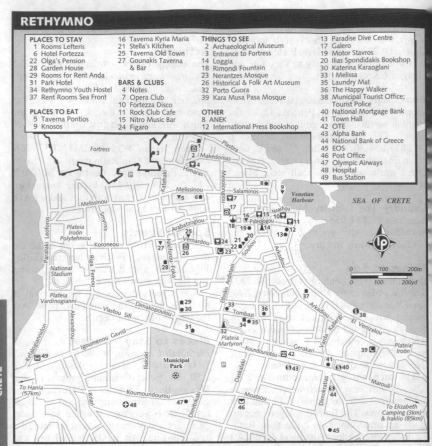

RETHYMNO

PLACES TO STAY
1 Rooms Lefteris
6 Hotel Fortezza
22 Olga's Pension
28 Garden House
29 Rooms for Rent Anda
31 Park Hotel
34 Rethymno Youth Hostel
37 Rent Rooms Sea Front

PLACES TO EAT
5 Taverna Pontios
9 Knosos
16 Taverna Kyria Maria
21 Stella's Kitchen
25 Taverna Old Town
27 Gounakis Taverna
   & Bar

BARS & CLUBS
4 Notes
7 Opera Club
10 Fortezza Disco
11 Rock Club Cafe
15 Nitro Music Bar
24 Figaro

THINGS TO SEE
2 Archaeological Museum
3 Entrance to Fortress
14 Loggia
18 Rimondi Fountain
23 Nerantzes Mosque
26 Historical & Folk Art Museum
32 Porto Guora
39 Kara Musa Pasa Mosque

OTHER
8 ANEK
12 International Press Bookshop

13 Paradise Dive Centre
17 Galero
19 Motor Stavros
20 Ilias Spondidakis Bookshop
30 Katerina Karaoglani
33 I Melissa
35 Laundry Mat
36 The Happy Walker
38 Municipal Tourist Office;
   Tourist Police
40 National Mortgage Bank
41 Town Hall
42 OTE
43 Alpha Bank
44 National Bank of Greece
45 EOS
46 Post Office
47 Olympic Airways
48 Hospital
49 Bus Station

Olga's Pension (☎ *2831 028 665,
Souliou 57*) Singles/studios €20.50/29.50.
The friendly Olga's is tucked away on the
touristy but colourful Souliou. A network of
terraces, all bursting with greenery, connects a wide range of rooms, some with
bath and sea views and others without.

Rooms Lefteris (☎ *2831 023 803, Kefalo-
gianni 25–26*) Singles/doubles with bathroom €23.50/29.50. All rooms are pleasant
but the front rooms have stunning sea views
although they can be noisy at night.

Rooms for Rent Anda (☎ *2831 023 479,
Nikiforou Foka 33*) Singles/doubles

€27/33. This is a great choice if you have
kids because it's just a short walk from
Rethymno's municipal park. The prettily
furnished rooms have private bathrooms
but no other amenities, although the owner
will gladly help you with anything you
need.

Garden House (☎ *2831 028 586, Nikiforou Foka 82*) Doubles/triples with bathroom €32.50/47. On a quiet street in
Rethymno's Old Town, this is an impeccably maintained 600-year-old Venetian
house retaining many of its original features
including impressive doors and a gorgeous

grape-arboured garden. The rooms are simple, comfortable and tasteful.

Places to Stay – Mid-Range
Park Hotel (☎ 2831 029 958, *Igoumenou Gavriil 9*) Singles/doubles with breakfast €32.50/41. The only missing ingredient here is an elevator to take you to rooms that are spread over two floors. The rooms are comfortable with air-con, TV, telephone, sound-proofing and balconies offering a view of the municipal park.

Hotel Fortezza (☎ 2831 055 551, fax 2831 054 073, e mliodak@ret.forthnet.gr, *Melissinou 16*) Singles/doubles with buffet breakfast €55.80/€70.50. Housed in a refurbished old building in the heart of the old town, these tastefully furnished rooms have TVs, telephones and air-con on demand.

Places to Eat
The waterfront along El Venizelou is lined with amazingly similar tourist restaurants staffed by fast-talking waiters desperately cajoling passers-by into eating at their establishments. The situation is much the same around the Venetian Harbour, except the setting is better and the prices higher.

To find cheaper food and a more authentic atmosphere, wander inland down the little side streets.

Stella's Kitchen (☎ 2831 028 665, *Souliou 55*) Breakfast €4.50-5.90. Open 8am-midnight daily. This tiny, homely spot on one of Rethymno's oldest streets serves up tasty snacks and a few meals. It's a good bet for breakfast as well.

Taverna Kyria Maria (☎ 2831 029 078, *Moshovitou 20*) Cretan dishes €2.40-6.50. Open 8am-1am daily. Wander down the little side streets to Kyria Maria, behind the Rimondi Fountain. This cosy, traditional taverna has outdoor seating under a leafy trellis with twittering birds.

Taverna Old Town (☎ 2831 026 436, *Vernardou 31*) 2-person set menus €12.30-15.30. Open noon-3pm & 7pm-midnight daily. The traditional Cretan food is well prepared and there are good-value set-price menus with wine.

Taverna Pontios (☎ 2831 057 624, *Melissinou 34*) Mains €2.70-4.50. Open noon-2.30pm & 6pm-midnight daily. This place proves once again that some of the best Cretan food comes from unassuming places. A convivial group of locals comes here for the delicious cheese-stuffed calamari, among other dishes.

Gounakis Taverna (☎ 2831 028 816, *Koroneou 6*) Mains €3.50-5.60. This place is worth visiting for its food as much as for its music (see Entertainment).

Knosos (☎ 2831 025 582, *Limani*) 2-person fish platter €35.30. Of all the harbourside restaurants, only at the diminutive Knosos can you guarantee fish freshness and honest service at a reasonable price. The most popular fish dish is *tsipoura* (bream, €29.50 per kilogram)

Entertainment
Gounakis Bar (☎ 2831 028 816, *Koroneou 6*) Open 8pm-1am. If you love drinking cheap wine and listening to live Cretan folk music, this is the place to go. There's music and impromptu dancing most nights.

Nitro Music Bar (☎ 2831 027 205, *Nearhou 26*) Open 10pm-dawn. In the heart of Rethymno's nightlife district, this is a crowded, friendly dance club with music programming that leans toward techno early in the evening and Greek music later on.

Fortezza Disco (*Nearhou 20*) Open 11pm-dawn. This is the town's showpiece disco. It's big and flashy with three bars, a laser show and a well-groomed international crowd that starts drifting in around midnight.

Opera Club (*Salaminos 30*) Open 11pm-dawn. Formerly a cinema, now a huge dance club, the OC has hired an attractive multilingual staff in an effort to capture the tourist market. The sounds are contemporary international.

Rock Club Cafe (☎ 2831 031 047, *Petihaki 8*) Open 9pm-dawn. RCC is Rethymno's trendiest hang-out. The crowd of young professionals fills the club nightly and for now this is where the action is.

Notes (☎ 2831 029 785, *Himaras 27*) Open 10am-midnight. Opened by a musician who has an excellent selection of

CRETE

Greek music, Notes is a quiet bar/cafe with a polished wood bar. It's a good place to escape the crowds along El Venizelou.

Figaro (☎ 2831 029 431, Vernardou 21) Open noon-midnight. Housed in an ingeniously restored old building, Figaro is an atmospheric bar which attracts a subdued crowd for drinks, snacks and rock music.

Shopping

Katerina Karaoglani (☎ 2831 024 301, Katehaki 4) Open 10am-11pm Mon-Sat. Friendly Katerina Karaoglani makes her pottery in the store. You'll find the standard blue-glazed Cretan ceramics of a better quality than the tourist shops deliver.

I Melissa (☎ 2831 029 601, Ethnikis Andistasis 23) Open 9am-8pm Mon-Sat. In addition to hand-made icons, Melissa sells candles, incense, oil lamps and other odorous objects.

Getting There & Away

Bus There are numerous services to both Hania (one hour, €5.30) and Iraklio (1½ hours, €5.60). There's a bus in each direction every half-hour in summer, every hour in winter. In summer there are also four buses a day to Plakias (one hour, €3.10), four to Agia Galini (1½ hours, €4.25), three to Moni Arkadiou (30 minutes, €1.80), one to Omalos (two hours, €8.50) and two to Preveli (€2.80). The morning bus to Plakias continues to Hora Sfakion (two hours, €4.70). Services to these destinations are greatly reduced in winter.

Ferry ANEK (☎ 2831 029 221, fax 2831 055 519, W www.anek.gr, Arkadiou 250) operates a daily ferry between Rethymno and Piraeus (10 hours, €22) leaving Rethymno and Piraeus at 7.30pm. Tickets are available from the company's office.

Getting Around

Most of the car-rental firms are near Plateia Iroön. Motor Stavros (☎ 2831 022 858), Paleologou 14, has a wide range of motorcycles and also rents bicycles.

AROUND RETHYMNO

Moni Arkadiou Μονή Αρκαδίου

Surrounded by attractive hill country, this 16th-century monastery *(Arkadi; monastery admission free, small museum €2; open 8am-1pm & 3.30pm-8pm daily)* is 23km south-east of Rethymno. The most impressive of the buildings is the Venetian baroque church. Its striking facade, which used to feature on the old 100 dr note, has eight slender Corinthian columns and an ornate triple-belled tower.

In November 1866 the Turks sent massive forces to quell insurrections which were gathering momentum throughout the island. Hundreds of men, women and children who had fled their villages used the monastery as a safe haven. When 2000 Turkish soldiers attacked the building, rather than surrender, the Cretans set light to a store of gunpowder. The explosion killed everyone, Turks included, except one small girl, who lived to a ripe old age in a village nearby. Busts of the woman, and the abbot who lit the gun powder, stand outside the monastery.

There are buses from Rethymno to the monastery (30 minutes, €1.80) at 6am, 10.30am and 2.30pm, returning at 7am, noon and 4pm.

Amari Valley Κοιλάδα Αμαρίου

If you have your own transport you can explore the enchanting Amari Valley, southeast of Rethymno, between Mts Ida and Kedros. The region harbours around 40 well-watered, unspoilt villages set amid olive groves and almond and cherry trees.

The valley begins at the picturesque village of **Apostoli**, 25km south-east of Rethymno. The turn-off for Apostoli is on the coast 3km east of Rethymno. The road forks at Apostoli and then joins up again 38km to the south, making it possible to do a circular drive around the valley. Alternatively, you can continue south to Agia Galini.

There is an EOS refuge on **Mt Ida**, a 10km walk from the small village of **Kouroutes**, 5km south of Fourfouras. For information contact the Rethymno EOS (see Activities in the Rethymno section).

RETHYMNO TO SPILI

Heading south from Rethymno, there is a turn-off to the right to the Late-Minoan cemetery of **Armeni** 2km before the modern village of Armeni. The main road south continues through woodland, which gradually gives way to a bare and dramatic landscape. After 18km there is a turn-off to the right for **Selia** and **Frangokastello** and, a little beyond, another turn-off for Plakias (this turn-off is referred to on timetables as the Koxare junction or Bale). The main road continues for 9km to Spili.

SPILI Σπήλι
postcode 740 53 • pop 710

Spili is a gorgeous mountain town with cobbled streets, rustic houses and plane trees. Its centrepiece is a unique Venetian fountain which spurts water from 19 lion heads. Tourist buses hurtle through but Spili deserves an overnight stay.

The post office and bank are on the main street. The huge building at the northern end of town is an ecclesiastic conference centre. The OTE is up a side street, north of the central square. The bus stop is just south of the square. Spili is on the Rethymno–Agia Galini bus route.

Places to Stay & Eat

Green Hotel (☎ 2832 022 225) Doubles with bathroom €19. Across from the police station on the main street, this is a homely place practically buried under plants and vines that also fill the interior. Rooms are attractive.

Heracles Rooms (☎ 2832 022 111, fax 2832 022 411) Singles/doubles with bathroom €23.50/29.50. Signposted from the main road are these excellent rooms which are sparkling and beautifully furnished.

Costas Inn (☎ 2832 022 040, fax 2832 022 043) Doubles/triples with bathroom €35.30/44. Farther along from Heracles, on the left, Costas Inn has well-kept, ornate rooms with satellite TV, radio and the use of a washing machine.

Taverna Costas (☎ 2832 022 040) Cretan dishes €2.50-4.50. Under the inn of the same name, this popular eatery is a very good choice. Food products including wine are organic. Try the traditional sweets for dessert.

Taverna Stratidakis (☎ 2832 022 006) Mayirefta €2.5-4.70. Opposite Costas Inn, this place serves excellent traditional Greek dishes. The specials of the day are in pots at the back of the room.

AROUND SPILI

Most people come to the alluring little village of **Patsos** to visit the nearby **Church of Agios Antonios** in a cave above a picturesque gorge. You can drive here from Rethymno, or you can walk from Spili along a scenic 10km dirt track.

To reach the track, walk along 28 Oktovriou, passing the lion fountain on your right. Turn right onto Thermopylon and ascend to the Spili-Gerakari road. Turn right here and eventually you will come to a sign for Gerakari. Take the dirt track to the left, and at the fork bear right. At the crossroads turn right, and continue on the main track for about one hour to a T-junction on the outskirts of Patsos. Turn left to get to the cave.

Heading west of Spili then south towards the coast at Plakias you will pass through the dramatic **Kourtaliotis Gorge** through which the river Megalopotamos rumbles on its way to the sea at **Preveli Beach**. About 8km before Plakias there is a turn-off to the left for Preveli Beach and **Moni Preveli** (see the Around Plakias section later in this chapter).

PLAKIAS Πλακιάς
postcode 740 60 • pop 139

The south-coast town of Plakias was once a tranquil fishing village before it became a retreat for adventurous backpackers. Plakias offers a good range of independent accommodation, some pretty decent eating options, a brace of good regional walks, a large sandy beach and enough nightlife to keep the nightbirds singing until dawn. All in all, Plakias is one of the better choices for independent travellers looking for a hang-out in Crete.

Orientation & Information

It's easy to find your way around Plakias. One street skirts the beach and another runs parallel to it one block back. The bus stop

CRETE

is at the middle of the waterfront. The 30-minute path to Myrthios begins just before the youth hostel.

Plakias doesn't have a bank, but Monza Travel Agency (☎ 2832 031 882, fax 2832 031 883), near the bus stop, offers currency exchange. From June to August a mobile post office is on the waterfront. Check your email at the one PC in the Ostraco Bar (☎ 2832 031 710) for €4.50 per hour.

Places to Stay

Camping Apollonia (☎ 2832 031 318) Adult/tent €3.80/2.20. On the right of the main approach road to Plakias, this place has a restaurant, minimarket, bar and swimming pool. While the site is at least shaded, it all looks rather scruffy and run-down.

Youth Hostel Plakias (☎ 2832 032 118, e info@yhplakias.com, w www.yhplakias .com) Dorm beds €6. Open 1 Apr-end Oct. For independent travellers this is *the* place to stay in Plakias. Manager Chris from the UK has created a very packie-friendly place with spotless dorms, green lawns, volleyball court, and Internet access. Partying is much in evidence here, helped along by Chris' eclectic music collection. Follow the signs from the waterfront. The hostel is tucked away in the olive trees behind the town, a 10-minute walk from the bus stop.

There is a wide range of independent domatia on offer. Most are signposted on a communal wooden sign board next to Monza Travel. Try these for starters.

Pension Kyriakos (☎ 2832 031 307, fax 2832 031 631) Doubles €20.50. 'If you don't like raki, stay away from here', says owner Kyriakos. His small, clean rooms have only coffee-making facilities, but that is made up for by ample raki, supplied by the gregarious owner.

Ippokambos (☎ 2832 031 525) Studios €23.50. The large, clean rooms here have flower-bedecked balconies, a fridge but no cooking facilities other than to make coffee or tea.

Morfeas Rent Rooms (☎/fax 2832 031 583) Singles/doubles with bathroom €20.50/ 29.50. Close to the bus stop and above a

supermarket, Morfeas has light, airy and attractively furnished rooms with fridge, phone and air-con.

Pension Thetis (☎ 2832 031 430, fax 2832 031 987) Double studios €29.50. Thetis is a very pleasant, family-oriented set of studios. Rooms have fridge and cooking facilities Relax in the cool and shady garden.

Castello (☎/fax 2832 031 112) Double studios €35.30. It is the relaxed owner Christos and his cool and shady garden that makes this place a happy haven. All rooms are cool, clean and fridge-equipped and have cooking facilities.

Places to Eat

Nikos Souvlaki (☎ 2832 031 921) All-in grill €4.70. Popular with packies and just inland from Monza Travel Agency, this is a good souvlaki place, where a monster mixed grill of gyros, souvlaki, sausage, hamburger and chips won't break the bank.

Taverna Sofia (☎ 2832 031 333) Cretan specials €3-5.90. In business since 1969, Sofia's is a solid choice. Check the meals on display from the trays in the window. The jovial gastronome owner recommends lamb in yogurt (€5.90).

Siroko (☎ 2832 032 055) Mains €3.50-7. On the far west side of the village, Siroko is a family-run place popular with travellers. Try the lamb in egg and lemon sauce (€5.60) or a mixed seafood grill (€7). Vegetarians are also catered for.

Getting There & Away

Plakias has good bus connections in summer, but virtually none in winter. A timetable is displayed at the bus stop. Summer services include four buses a day to Rethymno (one hour, €3.10) and one to Hora Sfakion. In winter there are three buses a day to Rethymno, two at weekends. It's possible to get to Agia Galini from Plakias by catching a Rethymno bus to the Koxare junction (referred to as Bale on timetables) and waiting for a bus to Agia Galini. This works best with the 11.30pm bus from Plakias, linking with the 12.45pm service from Rethymno to Agia Galini.

Getting Around

Cars Allianthos (☎ 2832 031 851) is a reliable car-rental outlet. Odyssia (☎ 2832 031 596), on the waterfront, has a large range of motorcycles and mountain bikes available for hire.

AROUND PLAKIAS

Myrthios Μύρθιος

This pleasant village is perched on a hillside overlooking Plakias and the surrounding coast. Apart from taking in the views, the main activity is walking, which you'll be doing a lot of unless you have your own transport.

Niki's Studios & Rooms (☎ 2832 031 593) Singles/doubles with bathroom €13.20/19, 2-person studios €26.50. There are a few domatia in the village, including this comfortable place just below Restaurant Panorama.

Restaurant Panorama (☎ 2832 032 077) Mains €4-5. This place lives up to its name; it has great views. It also does good food, including vegetarian dishes and delicious desserts.

Moni Preveli Μονή Πρέβελη

Standing in splendid isolation high above the Libyan Sea, 14km east of Plakias, is the well-maintained Moni Preveli (☎ 2832 031 246, Preveli; admission €2; open 8am-7pm daily mid-Mar–May, 8am-1.30pm & 3.30pm-7.30pm daily June-Oct). Like most of Crete's monasteries, it played a significant role in the islanders' rebellion against Turkish rule. It became a centre of resistance during 1866, causing the Turks to set fire to it and destroy surrounding crops. After the Battle of Crete in 1941, many Allied soldiers were sheltered here by Abbot Agathangelos before their evacuation to Egypt. In retaliation the Germans plundered the monastery. The monastery's **museum** contains a candelabra presented by grateful British soldiers after the war.

From the road to the monastery, a road leads downhill to a large car park from where a steep foot track leads down to Preveli Beach.

From June through August there are two buses daily from Rethymno to Moni Preveli.

Beaches

Preveli Beach – known officially as Paralia Finikodasous (Palm Beach) – at the mouth of the Kourtaliotis Gorge, is one of Crete's most photographed and popular beaches. The river Megalopotamos meets the back end of the beach before it conveniently loops around its assorted bathers and empties into the Libyan Sea. The beach is fringed with oleander bushes and palm trees and used to be popular with freelance campers before camping was officially outlawed.

A steep path leads down to it from a large car park below Moni Preveli, or you can bike to within several hundred metres of the beach by following a signposted 5km rough dirt road from a stone bridge to the left just off the Moni Preveli main road. You can also get to Preveli Beach from Plakias by boat from June through August for €8.80 return, or by taxi boat from Agia Galini for €17.50 return.

Between Plakias and Preveli Beach there are several secluded **coves** popular with freelance campers and nudists. Some are within walking distance of Plakias, via **Damnoni Beach**. To reach them ascend the path behind Plakias Bay Hotel. Just before the track starts to descend turn right into an olive grove. At the first T-junction turn left and at the second turn right. Where six tracks meet, take the one signposted to the beach. Walk to the end of Damnoni Beach and take the track to the right, which passes above the coves. Damnoni Beach itself is pleasant out of high season, despite being dominated by the giant Hapimag tourist complex.

AGIA GALINI Αγία Γαλήνη

postcode 740 56 • pop 1009

Agia Galini (ah-**yee**-ah ga-**lee**-nee) is another picturesque erstwhile fishing village which really has gone down the tubes due to an overdose of tourism. Hemmed in against the sea by large sandstone cliffs and phalanxes of hotels and domatia, Agia Galini is rather claustrophobic – an ambience which is not ameliorated by an ugly, cement-block-littered harbour. Still, it does boast 340 days of sunshine a year, and some places remain open out of season. It's a convenient base from which to visit

CRETE

Phaestos and Agia Triada, and although the town beach is mediocre, there are boats to better beaches.

Orientation & Information
The bus station is at the top of Eleftheriou Venizelou, which is a continuation of the approach road. The central square, overlooking the harbour, is downhill from the bus station. You'll walk past the post office on the way and the OTE is on the square. There is no bank but there are lots of travel agencies with currency exchange. Check your email at Cosmos Internet (☎ 2832 091 262, e damvax@ yahoo.com). It's open from 9am until late and charges €3.50 per hour.

Places to Stay
Agia Galini Camping (☎ 2832 091 386) Adult/tent €3.80/2.30. This camping ground is next to the beach, 2.5km east of the town. It is signposted from the Iraklio–Agia Galini road. The site is well shaded and has a restaurant, snack bar and mini-market.

Candia Rooms (☎ 2832 091 203) Singles/doubles with bathroom €14.70/17.60. This place has very basic rooms. To get there take the first left opposite the post office.

Areti (☎ 2832 091 240) Singles/doubles with bathroom & balcony €17.60/29.50. This place with pleasant rooms is on the road to town.

Hotel Selena (☎ 2832 091 273) Singles/doubles with bathroom €29.50/35.30. Open all year. The rooms here are D class. To reach the hotel, walk downhill from the bus station, turn left after the post office, take the second turning right and turn left at the steps.

Stohos Rooms (☎ 2832 091 433) 2-person/3-person studios €36/39. This is the only accommodation on the beach.

Places to Eat
Restaurant Megalonisos Mains €2.40-3.80. Open 9am-midnight daily. Near the bus stop, this is one of the town's cheapest restaurants, if not the friendliest.

Medousa Taverna (☎ 2832 091 487) Grills €4.50-5.50. Open noon-2am daily Apr-Oct. In the town centre, this taverna is

owned by a German/Greek couple and presents a menu of specialities from both countries.

Onar (☎ 2832 091 288) Mezedes €1.70-5.30. Open 8am-1am daily Mar-Nov. Onar (meaning 'dream' in Homeric Greek) overlooks the harbour and is a good place to come for breakfast, mezedes, or cocktails.

Madame Hortense (☎ 2832 091 215) Mains €6.20-11.80. Open 11am-midnight daily. The most elaborate restaurant-bar in town is on the top floor of the three-level Zorbas complex on the harbour. Cuisine is Greek Mediterranean, with a touch of the East. Try chicken in curry sauce (€6.50).

Getting There & Away
Bus The story is the same as at the other beach resorts: heaps of buses in summer, skeletal services in winter. In peak season there are seven buses a day to Iraklio (2½ hours, €4.90), four to Rethymno (1½ hours, €4.25), six to Matala (45 minutes, €2) and six to Phaestos (40 minutes, €1.40). You can get to Plakias by taking a Rethymno-bound bus and changing at Koxare (Bale).

Taxi Boat In summer there are daily taxi boats from the harbour to the beaches of Agios Giorgios, Agios Pavlos and Preveli (Palm Beach). These beaches, which are west of Agia Galini, are difficult to get to by land. Both are less crowded than, and far superior to, the Agia Galini beach. Departures are between 9.30am and 10.30am.

AROUND AGIA GALINI
The outstanding **Museum of Cretan Ethnology** (☎ 2892 091 112, *Vori; admission €3; open 9am-3pm Mon-Fri Nov-Mar, 10am-6pm Apr-Oct*) is in the pleasant, unspoilt village of Vori, 14km from Agia Galini, just north of the main Agia Galini– Iraklio road.

HANIA Χανιά
postcode 731 00 • pop 65,000
Hania (hahn-*yah*) is Crete's second city and former capital. The beautiful, crumbling Venetian quarter of Hania that surrounds the Old Harbour is one of Crete's

best attractions. A lot of money has been spent on restoring the old buildings. Some of them have been converted into very fine accommodation while others now house chic restaurants, bars and shops.

The Hania district gets a lot of package tourists, but most of them stick to the beach developments that stretch out endlessly to the west. Even in a town this size many hotels and restaurants are closed from November to April.

Hania is a main transit point for trekkers going to the Samaria Gorge.

History

Hania is the site of the Minoan settlement of Kydonia, which was centred on the hill to the east of the harbour. Little excavation work has been done, but the finding of clay tablets with Linear B script has led archaeologists to believe that Kydonia was both a palace site and an important town.

Kydonia met the same fiery fate as most other Minoan settlements in 1450 BC, but soon re-emerged as a force. It was a flourishing city-state during Hellenistic times and continued to prosper under Roman and Byzantine rule.

The city became Venetian at the beginning of the 13th century, and the name was changed to La Canea. The Venetians spent a lot of time constructing massive fortifications to protect the city from marauding pirates and invading Turks. This did not prove very effective against the latter, who took Hania in 1645 after a two-month siege.

The Great Powers made Hania the island capital in 1898 and it remained so until 1971, when the administration was transferred to Iraklio.

Hania was heavily bombed during WWII, but enough of the old town survives for it to be regarded as Crete's most beautiful city.

Orientation

The town's bus station is on Kydonias, two blocks south-west of Plateia 1866, one of the city's main squares. From Plateia 1866 to the Old Harbour is a short walk north down Halidon.

The main hotel area is to the left as you face the harbour, where Akti Koundourioti leads around to the old fortress on the headland. The headland separates the Venetian port from the crowded town beach in the quarter called Nea Hora.

Zambeliou, which dissects Halidon just before the harbour, was once the town's main thoroughfare. It's a narrow, winding street, lined with craft shops, hotels and tavernas.

Information

Tourist Offices Hania's EOT (☎ 2821 092 943, fax 2821 092 624) is at Kriari 40, close to Plateia 1866. It is well organised and considerably more helpful than most. Opening hours are 7.30am to 2.30pm weekdays. The tourist police (☎ 2821 073 333) are at Kudonias 29 and are open the same hours.

Money The National Bank of Greece on the corner of Tzanakaki and Giannari and the Alpha Bank at the junction of Halidon and Sakalidi have 24-hour automatic exchange machines. There are numerous places to change money outside banking hours. Most are willing to negotiate the amount of commission, so check around.

Post & Communications The central post office is at Tzanakaki 3, open 7.30am to 8pm Monday to Friday, and 7.30am to 2pm Saturday. The OTE is next door at Tzanakaki 5, open 7.30am to 10pm daily. Internet access is available at Vranas Studios (☎ 2821 058 618), on Agion Deka, open 9am to 2am, or at Internet C@fe (☎ 2821 073 300) on Theotokopoulou 53; open 8am-3am; €3.50 per hour.

Bookshops The George Haïkalis Bookshop (☎ 2821 042 197), situated on Plateia Venizelou, sells English-language newspapers, books and maps.

Laundry Both Laundry Fidias at Sarpaki 6 and the Afroditi Laundry at Agion Deka 18 charge €5.90 for a wash and dry.

Left Luggage Luggage can be stored at the bus station for €1.50 per day.

CRETE

CRETE

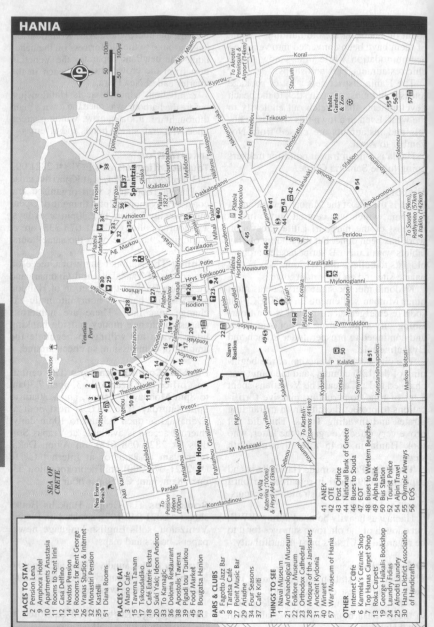

HANIA

Splantzia

Venetian Port

Lighthouse

SEA OF CRETE

Nea Hora Beach

Nea Hora

To Akrotiri Peninsula & Airport (14km)

Koraï

Stadium

Public Garden & Zoo

To Souda (9km), Rethymno (57km) & Iraklio (142km)

To Souda

To Kastelli-Kissamos (41km)

To Pension Ideon (100m)

To Villa Katerina (100m) & Hrysi Akti (3km)

To Pardali

To Konstandinou

PLACES TO STAY
2 Pension Lena
9 Amphora Hotel
10 Apartments Anastasia
11 Rooms to Rent Irini
12 Casa Delfino
14 Nostos Pension
16 Rooms for Rent George
26 Vranas Studios & Internet
32 Monastiri Pension
35 Kastelli
51 Diana Rooms

PLACES TO EAT
3 Mano Cafe
15 Taverna Tamam
17 Tsikoudadiko
18 Café Eaterie Ekstra
20 Suki Yaki; Ideon Andron
33 To Karnagic
36 Doloma Restaurant
38 Apostolis Taverna
39 Pigadi tou Tourkou
45 Food Market
53 Bougatsa Henion

BARS & CLUBS
5 Fagotto Jazz Bar
8 Taratsa Café
27 Point Music Bar
29 Ariadne
34 Four Seasons
37 Cafe Kriti

THINGS TO SEE
1 Naval Museum
21 Archaeological Museum
22 Folklore Museum
23 Orthodox Cathedral
28 Mosque of the Janissaries
31 Ancient Kydonia
40 Minaret
57 War Museum of Hania

OTHER
4 Internet C@fe
6 Karmela's Ceramic Shop
7 Top Hanas Carpet Shop
13 Roka Carpets
19 George Halkiadis Bookshop
24 Laundry Fidias
25 Afroditi Laundry
30 Hania District Association of Handicrafts
41 ANEK
42 OTE
43 Post Office
44 National Bank of Greece
46 Buses to Souda
47 EOT
48 Buses to Western Beaches
49 Alpha Bank
50 Bus Station
52 Tourist Office
54 Alpin Travel
55 Olympic Airways
56 EOS

Museums

Housed in the 16th-century Venetian Church of San Francisco is the **archaeological museum** (☎ 2821 090 334, Halidon 21; admission €1.50; open 8am-4.30pm Tues-Sun). The Turkish fountain in the grounds is a relic from the building's days as a mosque.

The museum houses a well-displayed collection of finds from western Crete dating from the Neolithic to the Roman era. Exhibits include statues, pottery, coins, jewellery, three splendid floor mosaics and some impressive painted sarcophagi from the Late-Minoan cemetery of Armeni.

The **naval museum** (☎ 2821 091 875; Akti Koundourioti; admission €1.80; open 10am-4pm daily) has an interesting collection of model ships, naval instruments, paintings and photographs. It is housed in the fortress on the headland overlooking the Venetian port.

Hania has an interesting **folklore museum** (☎ 2821 090 816, Halidon 46B; admission €1.50; open 9am-3pm & 6pm-9pm Mon-Fri). There is also the new **War Museum of Hania** (Tzanakaki; admission free; open 9am-1pm Tues-Sat).

Other Attractions

The area to the east of the Old Harbour, between Akti Tombazi and Karaoli Dimitriou, is the site of **ancient Kydonia**.

The search for Minoan remains began in the early 1960s and excavation work continues sporadically. The site can be seen at the junction of Kanevaro and Kandanoleu, and many of the finds are on display in the archaeological museum.

Kydonia has been remodelled by a succession of occupiers. After ejecting the Arabs, the Byzantines set about building their *kastelli* (castle) on the same site, on top of the old walls in some places and using the same materials. It was here, too, that the Venetians first settled. Modern Kanevaro was the Corso of their city. It was this part of town that bore the brunt of the bombing in WWII.

The massive **fortifications** built by the Venetians to protect their city remain impressive today. The best-preserved section is the western wall, running from the fortezza to the **Siavo Bastion**. It was part of a defensive system begun in 1538 by engineer Michele Sanmichele, who also designed Iraklio's defences.

The **lighthouse** at the entrance to the harbour is the most visible of the Venetian monuments. It looks in need of tender loving care these days, but the 30-minute walk around the sea wall to get there is worth it.

You can escape the crowds of the Venetian quarter by taking a stroll around the **Splantzia quarter** – a delightful tangle of narrow streets and little plateies.

Whether you are self-catering or not you should at least feast your eyes on Hania's magnificent covered **food market**. It makes all other food markets look like stalls at a church bazaar. Unfortunately, the central bastion of the city wall had to be demolished to make way for this fine cruciform creation, built in 1911.

Activities

Alpin Travel (☎ 2821 053 309, Boniali 11–19; open 9am-2pm Mon-Fri & sometimes after 7pm) offers many trekking programs. The owner, George Andonakakis, helps run the **EOS** (☎ 2821 044 647, Tzanakaki 90) and is the guy to talk to about serious climbing in the Lefka Ori. George can provide information on Greece's mountain refuges, the E4 trail, and climbing and trekking in Crete in general.

Trekking Plan (☎ 2821 060 861), in Agia Marina, on the main road next to Santa Marina Hotel, offers treks (around €23.50) to the Agia Irini Gorge and climbs of Mt Gingilos, among other destinations. It also offers a full program of mountain-bike tours (from €26.50) at varying levels of difficulty.

Children's Activities

If your child has lost interest in Venetian architecture by the end of the first street, head for the **public garden** between Tzanakaki and Dimokratias. There's plenty to occupy children here, including a playground, a small zoo with a resident kri-kri (the Cretan wild goat) and a children's resource centre that has a small selection of books in English.

CRETE

Organised Tours

Tony Fennymore (☎ *2821 087 139, mobile 69-7253 7055,* e *FennysCrete@hotmail .com,* w *www.fennyscrete.ws*) 2hr walks €10.30. This historian is a wealth of information about Hania's history and culture. From April to July and September to October his two-hour walking tours begin at the 'Hand' monument on Plateia Talo at the bottom of Theotokopoulou. He also runs various guided minibus tours around the region. His witty and indispensable walking guide *Fenny's Hania* (€7.40) is available at Roka Carpets (see Shopping).

Places to Stay – Budget

Hania Camping (☎ *2821 031 138, fax 2821 033 371, Hrysi Akti*) Adult/tent €4.40/3.20. This facility, 3km west of town on the beach, is the nearest camping ground to Hania. It is shaded and has a restaurant, bar and minimarket. Take a Kalamaki Beach bus (every 20 minutes) from the south-east corner of Plateia 1866 and ask to be let off there.

The most interesting accommodation in town is around the Venetian port, but bear in mind it's a noisy area with numerous music bars. If you get a room in the back you'll have a better shot at a good night's sleep but you may swelter in the summer heat without the harbour breeze.

Rooms for Rent George (☎ *2821 088 715, Zambeliou 30*) Singles/doubles €14.70/ 20.50. If it's character you're after, you can't do better than this 600-year-old house dotted with antique furniture.

Diana Rooms (☎ *2821 097 888, P Kalaïdi 33*) Singles/doubles with bathroom €14.70/20.50. If you want to hop straight out of bed and onto an early morning bus bound for the Samaria Gorge, the best rooms around the bus station are here. They are light, airy and clean.

Monastiri Pension (☎ *2821 054 776, Ag Markou 18*) Doubles €32.50. This pension has a great setting right next to the ruins of the Moni Santa Maria de Miracolioco in the heart of the old kastelli. Rooms are fair value; they're simple with shared bathrooms but some have a sea view. There's a convenient communal kitchen for preparing meals.

Pension Lena (☎ *2821 086 860,* e *lenachania@hotmail.com, Ritsou 3*) Singles/doubles €26.50/32.50. This friendly pension is in an old Turkish building. There is a common kitchen for guests and owner Lena from Hamburg makes guests feel very welcome.

Rooms to Rent Irini (☎ *2821 093 909, Theotokopoulou 9*) Doubles with bathroom €35.30. Irini has clean, simply furnished rooms.

Apartments Anastasia (☎ *2821 088 001, fax 2821 046 582, Theotokopoulou 21*) Studios €38.20. These are stylish, well-equipped studios.

Kastelli (☎ *2821 057 057, fax 2821 045 314, Kanevaro 39*) Singles/doubles €26.50/ 29.50, apartments €47-58.70 depending on size. At the quieter, eastern end of the harbour, Kastelli has renovated apartments with high ceilings, white walls and pine floors. There's no TV or telephone, but some rooms have attractive views.

Places to Stay – Mid-Range

Most places in this category are renovated Venetian houses, and there are some very stylish ones about.

Nostos Pension (☎ *2821 094 740, fax 2821 094 743, Zambeliou 42–46*) Singles/ doubles with bathroom €41/64.50. Mixing Venetian style and modern fixtures, this is a 600-year-old building which has been modelled into classy split-level rooms/ units, all with kitchens. Try to get a room in front for the harbour view.

Vranas Studios (☎/fax *2821 058 618, Agion Deka 10*) Studios €44 in Aug. This place (at which prices are discounted by at least 40% outside August) is on a lively pedestrian street and has spacious, immaculately maintained studios which come with kitchenettes. All the rooms have polished wooden floors, balconies, TV and telephones and they can provide air-conditioning for a supplement.

Places to Stay – Top End

Amphora Hotel (☎ *2821 093 224, fax 2821 093 226,* e *reception@amphora.gr,* w *www .amphora.gr, Parodos Theotoko-poulou 20*)

Singles/doubles with buffet breakfast €60/85. This is Hania's most historically evocative hotel. It is located in an immaculately restored Venetian mansion with rooms around a courtyard. There's no elevator and no air-con but the rooms are elegantly decorated and some have views of the harbour. Front rooms can be noisy in the summer.

Casa Delfino (☎ 2821 093 098, fax 2821 096 500, e casadel@cha.forthnet.gr, Theofanous 7) Doubles/apartments with buffet breakfast €117/205. This modernised 17th-century mansion features a splendid courtyard of traditionally patterned cobblestones and 19 individually decorated suites. All have air-con, satellite TV, telephones, hair dryers, minibars and safes.

Places to Eat – Budget

The two restaurants in the *food market* are good places to seek out traditional cuisine. Their prices are almost identical. You can get a solid chunk of swordfish with chips for €4.50. More adventurous eaters can tuck into a bowl of garlic-laden snail and potato casserole for €3.80.

Doloma Restaurant (☎ 2821 051 196, Kalergon 8) Mayirefta €3-4.70. Open 7.30pm-1am Mon-Sat. You'll find very similar fare to the market restaurants here. This place is a great favourite with students from the nearby university.

Bougatsa Hanion (☎ 2821 043 978, Apokoronou 37) For a treat try the excellent *bougatsa tyri* (filo pastry filled with local myzithra cheese; €1.80) which comes sprinkled with a little sugar.

Mano Cafe (☎ 2821 072 265, Theotokopoulou 62) Continental breakfasts €3.70. Open 8am-midnight daily. This is a tiny place and has very little seating, but offers good-value breakfasts and snacks.

Places to Eat – Mid-Range

The port is the place to go for seafood. The prices are not cheap especially considering most of the seafood is frozen, but the setting is great. There are some chic places in the streets behind the port.

Apostolis Taverna (☎ 2821 045 470, Enosis 6) 2-person seafood platter €23.40.

Open noon-midnight daily. This taverna is a favourite with locals.

Taverna Tamam (☎ 2821 058 639, Zambeliou 49) Vegetarian specials €3-5.50. Open 1pm-12.30am daily. An old Turkish *hammam* (bathhouse) here has been converted into this taverna, where you'll find tasty soups and a good range of well-prepared main dishes.

Cafe Eaterie Ekstra (☎ 2821 075 725, Zambeliou 8) Vegetarian dishes €3.50-4.20. This place offers a choice of Greek and international dishes. There are set menus and many vegetarian dishes.

Tsikoudadiko (☎ 2821 072 873, Zambeliou 31) Cretan specials €4-7.50. Tsikoudadiko offers a good mixed plate of mezedes in a splendid old plant-filled courtyard.

Pigadi tou Tourkou (☎ 2821 054 547, Sarpaki 1–3) Mains €5.80-8. Open 7pm-midnight Wed-Mon. This is in the heart of the old Turkish residential district of Splantzia and has a wide range of Middle Eastern dishes, as well as occasional live music.

Suki Yaki (☎ 2821 074 264, Halidon 28) 2-person set menu €25-35. Open noon-midnight daily. Entered through an archway, this is a Chinese restaurant run by a Thai family. The result is a large Chinese menu supported by a small selection of Thai favourites.

To Karnagio (☎ 2821 053 336, Plateia Katehaki 8) Cretan specialities €3.50-7.60. Open noon-1am. This is the best place in Hania for outstanding Cretan specialities, including the zucchini-cheese pies known as *bourekia*.

Entertainment

Café Kriti (☎ 2821 058 661, Kalergon 22) Open 6pm-1am. This is a rough-and-ready joint but it's the best place in Hania to hear live Cretan music. Music starts after 8.30pm.

Ideon Andron (☎ 2821 095 598, Halidon 26) Open noon-midnight. In the middle of busy, touristy Halidon, this place offers a more sophisticated atmosphere with discreet music and a garden seating.

Fagotto Jazz Bar (☎ 2821 071 887, Angelou 16) Open 7pm-2am. Black-and-white photographs of jazz greats line the walls.

CRETE

It's housed in a restored Venetian building and offers the smooth sounds of jazz and light rock.

Point Music Bar (☎ *2821 057 556, Sourmeli 2)* Open 9.30pm-2am. This is a good rock bar for those allergic to techno. When the interior gets steamy you can cool off on the balcony overlooking the harbour.

Taratsa Café (☎ *2821 074 960, Akti Koundourioti 54)* Open 8am-1am. On the waterfront, this place plays rock music at a volume that renders conversation possible only for lip readers, but you can escape to the outdoor terrace.

Ariadne (☎ *2821 050 987, Akti Tombazi 2)* Open 10am-1am. Formerly a disco, Ariadne has taken on a sleek new look and now uses its excellent sound system to play a variety of music. There's jazz early in the evening followed by rock.

Four Seasons (☎ *2821 055 583, Akti Tombazi 29)* Open 10am-1am. Drinks around €5.90. This rock bar on the harbour attracts a fashionable group of young Haniotes. The harbourside terrace is always full.

Shopping

Good-quality hand-made leather goods are available from shoemakers on Skrydlof, off Halidon, where shoes cost from €30. The old town has many craft shops.

Roka Carpets (☎ *2821 074 736, Zambeliou 61)* You can watch Mihalis Manousakis weave his wondrous rugs on a 400-year-old loom using methods that have remained essentially unchanged since Minoan times. This is one of the few places in Greece where you can buy the genuine item. Prices begin at €23.50 for a small rug.

Top Hanas Carpet Shop (☎ *2821 058 571, Angelou 3)* This place specialises in old Cretan *kilims* (flat-woven rugs) that were traditional dowry gifts; prices start at €88.

Karmela's Ceramic Shop (☎ *2821 040 487, Angelou 7)* Karmela's produces ceramics using ancient techniques and also displays unusual jewellery handcrafted by young Greek artisans.

Hania District Association of Handicrafts (☎ *2821 056 386, Akti Tombazi 15)* The embroidery, weaving and ceramics are

well executed but the sculptures of Greek mythological figures are unusually fine.

Getting There & Away

Air Olympic Airways has at least four flights a day to Athens which range in price from €53-76.60. There are also two flights a week to Thessaloniki (€103.30). The Olympic Airways office (☎ 2821 057 701) is at Tzanakaki 88.

Aegean Airlines has up to six daily flights to Athens (€55) and two to Thessaloniki (€90). Their office (☎ 2821 063 366, fax 2821 063 669) is at the airport. The airport is on the Akrotiri Peninsula, 14km from Hania.

Axon Airlines has flights to Athens (€70, two daily). The Axon Airlines office (☎ 2821 020 928) is at Hania airport.

Bus Buses depart from Hania's bus station for the following destinations:

destination	duration	fare	frequency
Elafonisi	2 hr	€7.40	1 daily
Falasarna	1½ hr	€4.90	2 daily
Hora Sfakion	2 hr	€4.90	3 daily
Iraklio	2½ hr	€10	half-hourly
Kastelli-Kissamos	1 hour	€3.10	14 daily
Kolymbari	45 min	€2	half-hourly
Lakki	1 hr	€2	4 daily
Moni Agias Triadas	30 mins	€1.30	3 daily
Omalos	1 hr	€4.50	4 daily (for Samaria Gorge)
Paleohora	2 hr	€4.90	4 daily
Rethymno	1 hr	€5.30	half-hourly
Sougia	2 hr	€4.50	1 daily
Stavros	30 min	€1.20	6 daily

Ferry Ferries for Hania dock at Souda, about 7km east of town. There is at least one ferry a day for the 10-hour trip to/from Piraeus. ANEK has a boat nightly at 8.30pm for €20.50. The ANEK office (☎ 2821 027 500) is opposite the food market. Souda's port police can be contacted on ☎ 2821 089 240.

Getting Around

There is no airport bus. A taxi to the airport costs about €11.80.

Local buses (blue) for the port of Souda leave from outside the food market. Buses for the western beaches leave from Plateia 1866.

Car rental outlets include Avis (☎ 2821 050 510), Tzanakaki 58; Budget (☎ 2821 092 778), Karaïskaki 39; and Europrent (☎ 2821 040 810, 2821 27 810), Halidon 87. Most motorcycle-rental outlets are on Halidon.

AKROTIRI PENINSULA
Χερσόνησος Ακρωτήρι

The Akrotiri (ahk-ro-**tee**-rih) Peninsula, to the east of Hania, has a few places of fairly minor interest, as well as being the site of Hania's airport, port and a military base. There is an immaculate **military cemetery** at Souda, where about 1500 British, Australian and New Zealand soldiers who lost their lives in the Battle of Crete are buried. The buses to Souda port from outside the Hania food market can drop you at the cemetery.

If you haven't yet had your fill of Cretan monasteries, there are three on the Akrotiri Peninsula. The impressive 17th-century **Moni Agias Triadas** (*Akrotiri; admission €1.20; open 6am-2pm & 5pm-7pm daily*) was founded by the Venetian monks Jeremiah and Laurentio Giancarolo. The brothers were converts to the Orthodox faith.

The 16th-century **Moni Gouvernetou** (*Our Lady of the Angels; Akrotiri; open 8am-12.30pm & 4.30pm-7.30pm daily*) is 4km north of Moni Agias Triada. The church inside the monastery has an ornate sculptured Venetian facade. Both Moni Agias Triadas and Moni Gouvernetou are still in use.

From Moni Gouvernetou, it's a 15-minute walk on the path leading down to the coast to the ruins of **Moni Ioannou Erimiti**, known also as **Moni Katholikou**. The monastery is dedicated to St John the Hermit who lived in the cave behind the ruins. It takes another 30 minutes to reach the sea.

There are three buses daily (except Sunday) to Moni Agias Triadas from Hania's bus station (€1.30).

HANIA TO XYLOSKALO

The road from Hania to the beginning of the Samaria Gorge is one of the most spectacular routes on Crete. It heads through orange groves to the village of **Fournes** where a left fork leads to **Meskla**. The main road continues to the village of **Lakki**, 24km from Hania. This unspoilt village in the Lefka Ori Mountains affords stunning views wherever you look. The village was a centre of resistance during the uprising against the Turks, and during WWII.

From Lakki, the road continues to **Omalos** and **Xyloskalo**, start of the Samaria Gorge.

Places to Stay & Eat

Hotel Gigilos (☎ *2825 067 181, Omalos*) Singles/doubles €11.80/17.60. This is the friendliest hotel in Omalos. Rooms are rather barely furnished but are large and clean.

Hotel Exari (☎ *2825 067 180, fax 2825 067 124, Omalos*) Rooms €20.50. Exari was renovated in 2000 and has pleasant, well-furnished rooms as well as an attached restaurant. The owners give lifts to walkers to the start of the Samaria Gorge.

Kallergi Hut (☎ *2825 033 199, Omalos*) Bunk beds €4.50. The EOS (Greek Mountaineering Club) maintains this hut located in the hills between Omalos and the Samaria Gorge. It has 45 beds, electricity (no hot water) and makes a good base for exploring Mt Gingilos and surrounding peaks.

SAMARIA GORGE
Φαράγγι της Σαμαριάς

It's a wonder the stones and rocks underfoot haven't worn away completely, given the number of people who tramp through the Samaria (sah-mah-rih-**ah**) Gorge (☎ *2825 067 179; admission €3.50; open 6am-3pm daily 1 May–mid-Oct*). Despite the crowds, a trek through this stupendous gorge is still an experience to remember.

At 18km, the gorge is supposedly the longest in Europe. It begins just below the Omalos Plateau, carved out by the river that flows between Mt Psiristra (1766m) and Mt Volakias (2115m). Its width varies from 150m to 3m and its vertical walls reach 500m at their highest points. The gorge has an incredible number of wildflowers, which are at their best in April and May.

It is also home to a large number of endangered species. They include the Cretan

CRETE

The Good Oil

The olive has been part of life in the eastern Mediterranean since the beginnings of civilisation. Olive cultivation can be traced back about 6000 years. It was the farmers of the Levant (modern Syria and Lebanon) who first spotted the potential of the wild European olive *(Olea europaea)* – a sparse, thorny tree that was common in the region. These farmers began the process of selection that led to the more compact, thornless, oil-rich varieties that now dominate the Mediterranean.

Whereas most Westerners think of olive oil as being just a cooking oil, to the people of the ancient Mediterranean civilisations it was very much more. As well as being an important foodstuff, it was burned in lamps to provide light, it could be used as a lubricant and it was blended with essences to produce fragrant oils.

The Minoans were among the first to grow wealthy on the olive, and western Crete remains an important olive-growing area, specialising in high-quality salad oils. The region's showpiece Kolymvari Cooperative markets its extra-virgin oil in both the USA (Athena brand) and Britain (Kydonia brand).

Locals will tell you that the finest oil is produced from trees grown on the rocky soils of the Akrotiri Peninsula, west of Hania. The oil that is prized above all others, however, is *agourelaio*, meaning unripe, which is pressed from green olives.

Few trees outlive the olive. Some of the fantastically gnarled and twisted olive trees that dot the countryside of western Crete are more than 1000 years old. The tree known as *dekaoktoura*, in the mountain village of Anisaraki – near Kandanos on the road from Hania to Paleohora – is claimed to be more than 1500 years old.

Many of these older trees are being cut down to make way for improved varieties. The wood is burnt in potters' kilns and provides woodturners with the raw material to produce the ultimate salad bowl for connoisseurs. The dense yellow-brown timber has a beautiful swirling grain.

wild goat, the kri-kri, which survives in the wild only here and on the islet of Kri-Kri, off the coast of Agios Nikolaos. The gorge was made a national park in 1962 to save the kri-kri from extinction. You are unlikely to see too many of these shy animals, which show a marked aversion to trekkers.

An early start helps to avoid the worst of the crowds, but during July and August even the early bus from Hania to the top of the gorge can be packed.

The trek from Xyloskalo, the name of the steep wooden staircase that gives access to the gorge, to Agia Roumeli takes around six hours. Early in the season it's sometimes necessary to wade through the stream. Later, as the flow drops, it's possible to use rocks as stepping stones.

The gorge is wide and open for the first 6km, until you reach the abandoned village of Samaria. The inhabitants were relocated when the gorge became a national park. Just south of the village is a small church dedicated to Saint Maria of Egypt, after whom the gorge is named.

The gorge then narrows and becomes more dramatic until, at the 12km mark, the walls are only 3.5m apart – the famous **Iron Gates**.

The gorge ends just north of the almost abandoned village of Old Agia Roumeli. From here the path continues to the small, messy and crowded resort of Agia Roumeli, with a much-appreciated pebble beach and sparkling sea.

Spending the night in the gorge is not permitted.

What to Bring

Rugged footwear is essential for walking on the uneven ground covered by sharp stones. Don't attempt the walk in unsuitable footwear – you will regret it. You'll also need a hat and sunscreen. There's no need to take water. While it's inadvisable to drink water from the main stream, there are plenty of springs along the way spurting delicious cool water straight from the rock. There is nowhere to buy food, so bring something to snack on.

Getting There & Away

There are excursions to the Samaria Gorge from every sizable town and resort on Crete. Most travel agents have two excursions: 'Samaria Gorge Long Way' and 'Samaria Gorge Easy Way'. The first comprises the regular trek from the Omalos Plateau to Agia Roumeli; the second starts at Agia Roumeli and takes you as far as the Iron Gates.

Obviously it's cheaper to trek the Samaria Gorge under your own steam. Hania is the most convenient base. There are buses to Xyloskalo (Omalos; one hour, €4.50) at 6.15am, 7.30am, 8.30am and 1.45pm. There's also a direct bus to Xyloskalo from Paleohora (1½ hours, €4.55) at 6am.

AGIA ROUMELI TO HORA SFAKION

Agia Roumeli (Αγία Ρούμελη) has little going for it, but if you have just trekked through the Samaria Gorge and are too exhausted to face a further journey, there is a hotel here – see Places to Stay & Eat.

The small but rapidly expanding fishing village of **Loutro** (Λουτρό) lies between Agia Roumeli and Hora Sfakion. Loutro doesn't have a beach but there are rocks from which you can swim.

An extremely steep path leads up from Loutro to the village of **Anopolis**. Alternatively, you can save yourself the walk by taking the Hania-Skaloti bus – see Getting There & Away.

From Loutro it's a moderate 2½ hour walk along a coastal path to **Hora Sfakion**. On the way you will pass the celebrated **Sweet Water Beach**, named after freshwater springs which seep from the rocks. Freelance campers spend months at a time here. Even if you don't feel inclined to join them, you won't be able to resist a swim in the translucent sea.

Places to Stay & Eat

Hotel Agia Roumeli (☎ 2825 091 232, fax 2825 091 232, Agia Roumeli) Singles/doubles with bathroom €20.50/26.40 This D-class property is the only hotel in Agia Roumeli.

Porto Loutro (☎ 2825 091 433, Loutro) Doubles with bathroom €26.40. This place is in, as the name suggests, Porto Loutro.

There are also a number of *domatia* and *tavernas* in Agia Roumeli, Loutro and Anopolis, where you'll pay around €23.50 for a double.

Getting There & Away

There are three boats daily from Agia Roumeli to Hora Sfakion (1¼ hours, €4.50) via Loutro (45 minutes, €2.70). They connect with the bus back to Hania, leaving you in Hora Sfakion just long enough to spend a few euros. There's also a boat from Agia Roumeli to Paleohora (€6.50) at 4.45pm, calling at Sougia (€3.20).

The Hania-Skaloti bus runs via Anopolis. It leaves Hania at 2pm and returns the following morning, calling in at Anopolis at 7am.

HORA SFAKION Χώρα Σφακίων

postcode 730 01 • pop 340

Hora Sfakion (ho-rah sfah-kee-on) is a small coastal port where hordes of walkers from the Samaria Gorge spill off the boat and onto the bus. As such, in high season it can seem like Piccadilly Circus at rush hour. Most people pause only long enough to catch the next bus out.

Hora Sfakion played a prominent role during WWII when thousands of Allied troops were evacuated by sea from the town after the Battle of Crete.

Orientation & Information

The ferry quay is at the eastern side of the harbour. Buses leave from the square on the eastern side. The post office and OTE are on the square, and the police station overlooks it. There is no tourist office or tourist police.

Places to Stay & Eat

Accommodation in the village is of a reasonable quality and value. Some of the better accommodation is on the waterfront.

Rooms Stavris (☎ 2825 091 220, fax 2825 091 152, e info@sfakia-crete.com) Singles/doubles €17.60/19. Up the steps at

CRETE

the western end of the port, Hotel Stavros has clean rooms with bathrooms.

Hotel Samaria (☎ *2825 091 261, fax 2825 091 161)* Singles/doubles with bathroom €14.70/20.50. This decent hotel is on the waterfront.

Livikon (☎ *2825 091 211, fax 2825 091 222)* Singles/doubles in high season €35.30/38.20. Livikon has large, brightly decorated rooms with stone floors and sea views.

The adjoining Samaria and Livikon hotels have a *taverna* (☎ *2825 091 320)* downstairs that has a good selection of mayirefta and vegetarian dishes. Main dishes cost €2.70-4.20.

Getting There & Away

Bus There are three buses a day from Hora Sfakion to Hania (two hours, €4.50). In summer only there are two daily buses to Plakias (1¼ hours, €3.50) via Frangokastello, leaving at 10.30am and 5.30pm, and two to Rethymno (two hours, €5.30), at 10.30am and 7.30pm.

Boat From June through August there are daily boats from Hora Sfakion to Paleohora (three hours, €8) via Loutro, Agia Roumeli and Sougia. The boat leaves at 10.30am and 12.30pm. There are also three or four boats a day to Agia Roumeli (one hour, €4.50) via Loutro (15 minutes, €1.50). From 1 June there are boats to Gavdos Island (€8) on Thursday, Friday, Saturday and Sunday leaving at 10.30am and returning at 2.45pm.

AROUND HORA SFAKION

The road from Vryses to Hora Sfakion cuts through the heart of the Sfakia region in the eastern Lefka Ori. The inhabitants of this region have long had a reputation for fearlessness and independence – characteristics they retain to this day. Cretans are regarded by other Greeks as being immensely proud and there is none more so than the Sfakiot.

One of Crete's most celebrated heroes, Ioannis Daskalogiannis, was from Sfakia. In 1770, Daskalogiannis led the first Cretan insurrection against Ottoman rule. When help promised by Russia failed to materialise, he gave himself up to the Turks to save his followers. As punishment the Turks skinned him alive in Iraklio. Witnesses related that Daskalogiannis suffered this excruciating death in dignified silence.

The Turks never succeeded in controlling the Sfakiots, and this rugged mountainous region was the scene of fierce fighting. The story of their resistance lives on in the form of folk tales and *rizitika* (local folk songs).

The village of **Imbros**, 23km from Vryses, is at the head of the beautiful 10km Imbros Gorge, which is far less visited than the Samaria Gorge. To get there, take any bus bound for Hora Sfakion from the north coast and get off at Imbros. Walk out of the village towards Hora Sfakion and a path to the left leads down to the gorge. The gorge path ends at the village of **Komitades**, from where it is an easy walk by road to Hora Sfakion. You can of course do the trek in reverse, beginning at Komitades. The Happy Walker organises treks through this gorge (see Activities in the Rethymno section).

Frangokastello Φραγγοκάστελλο

Frangokastello is a magnificent fortress on the coast 15km east of Hora Sfakion. It was built by the Venetians in 1371 as a defence against pirates and rebel Sfakiots, who resented the Venetian occupation as much as they did the Turkish.

It was here in 1770 that Ioannis Daskalogiannis surrendered to the Turks. On 17 May 1828 many Cretan rebels, led by Hadzi Mihalis Dalanis, were killed here by the Turks. Legend has it that at dawn each anniversary their ghosts can be seen marching along the beach (see the boxed text 'Restless Spirits').

The castle overlooks a gently sloping, sandy beach. Domatia and tavernas are springing up rapidly here, but it's still relatively unspoilt.

Buses between Hora Sfakion and Plakias go via Frangokastello.

SOUGIA Σούγια
postcode 730 01 • pop 50

It's surprising that Sougia (**soo**-yiah) hasn't yet been commandeered by the package-tour crowd. With a wide curve of sand-and-pebble beach and a shady, tree-lined coastal road, Sougia's tranquillity has been preserved only because it lies at the foot of a narrow, twisting road that would deter most tour buses.

If you arrive by boat, walk about 150m along the coast to the town centre. If you arrive by bus, the bus will drop you on the coastal road in front of Santa Irene Hotel. The only other road intersects the coastal road by Santa Irene Hotel and runs north to the Agia Irini Gorge and Hania.

Sougia doesn't have a post office, OTE or bank, but you can change money at several places, including Polifimos Travel (☎ 2823 051 022) and Roxana's Office (☎ 2823 051 362). Both are just off the coastal road on the road to Hania. Check your email at Internet Lotos (☎ 2823 051 191) for €3 per hour at one of its six computers.

Places to Stay

There's no camping ground, but the eastern end of the long, pebbled beach is popular with freelance campers.

Pension Galini (☎/fax 2823 051 488) Singles/doubles with bathroom €20.50/€23.50, single/double studios €26.50/32.50. Next door to Aretousa, this pension has beautiful rooms.

Rooms Maria (☎ 2823 051 337) Doubles/triples with bathroom €29.50/35.30. This place is a block farther east on the coast from Santa Irene and has clean, white rooms.

Rooms Ririka (☎ 2823 051 167) Doubles €29.50. Next door to Rooms Maria is the equally attractive Rooms Ririka, also with rooms overlooking the sea.

Aretousa Rooms to Rent (☎ 2823 051 178, fax 2823 051 178) Singles/doubles €23.50/29.50. Inland, on the road to Hania, Aretousa has lovely rooms with wood-panelled ceilings and balconies.

Santa Irene Hotel (☎ 2823 051 342, fax 2823 051 182, e nanadakis@cha.forthnet.gr) Single/double studios €23.50/35.30.

The smartest accommodation is here. Air-conditioning costs €5.90 extra.

Places to Eat

Restaurants line the waterfront and there are more on the main street.

Kyma (☎ 2823 051 670) Fish dishes €17.60-23.50. Just on the seafront as you enter town, Kyma has a good selection of ready-made food as well as fresh fish dishes.

Taverna Rembetiko (☎ 2823 051 510) Ladera €2.70-3.50. Located on the road to Hania, this taverna has an extensive menu including various Cretan specialities such as boureki and stuffed zucchini flowers.

Getting There & Away

There's a daily bus travelling from Hania to Sougia (2½ hours, €4.70) at 1.30pm. Buses

---

Restless Spirits

The Frangokastello bloodshed of 17 May 1828 gave rise to the legend of the *Drosoulites*. The name comes from the Greek word *drosia* meaning 'moisture', which could refer to the dawn moisture that is around when the ghosts are said to appear, or the watery content of the spirits themselves. On the anniversary of the decisive battle (or in late May around dawn) it's said that a procession of ghostly figures – the ghosts of Hadzi Mihalis Dalanis and his followers – materialises around the fort and marches to the sea. The phenomenon has been verified by a number of independent observers. Although locals believe the figures are the ghosts of the slaughtered rebels, others theorise that it may be an optical illusion created by certain atmospheric conditions and that the figures may be a reflection of camels or soldiers in the Libyan Desert. When questioned about the ghostly phenomenon, locals are understandably a little reticent, but remain convinced that something does in fact happen. Most claim that the older residents of Frangokastello have seen the apparitions. Whether you will depends on your luck – or belief in ghosts.

---

going from Sougia to Hania leave at 7am. Sougia is on the Paleohora–Hora Sfakion boat route. Boats leave at 10.15am for Agia Roumeli (one hour, €3), Loutro (1½ hours, €5.50) and Hora Sfakion (two hours, €5.90). For Paleohora (one hour, €3.80) to the west there is a departure at 5.30pm.

PALEOHORA Παλαιοχώρα
postcode 730 01 • pop 1826

Paleohora was discovered by hippies back in the 60s and from then on its days as a tranquil fishing village were numbered. However, the resort operators have not gone way over the top – yet. The place retains a laid-back feel. It is also the only beach resort on Crete that does not close down in winter.

The little town is set on a narrow peninsula with a long, curving sandy beach exposed to the wind on one side and a sheltered pebbly beach on the other. On summer evenings the main street is closed to traffic and the tavernas move onto the road.

It's worth clambering up the ruins of the 13th-century **Venetian castle** for the splendid view of the sea and mountains. The most picturesque part of Paleohora is the narrow streets huddled around the castle.

From Paleohora, a six-hour walk along a scenic coastal path leads to Sougia, passing the ancient site of Lissos.

Orientation & Information

Paleohora's main street, El Venizelou, runs north to south, with several streets leading off east to the pebble beach. Boats leave from the old harbour at the southern end of this beach. At the southern end of El Venizelou, a west turn onto Kondekaki leads to the tamarisk-shaded sandy beach.

The municipal tourist office (☎ 2823 041 507) is next to the town hall on El Venizelou. It is open 10am to 1pm and 6pm to 9pm Wednesday to Monday between May and October.

The post office is on the road that skirts the sandy beach. On El Venizelou are the National Bank of Greece, with ATM, and the OTE (on the west side, just north of Kondekaki). Internet access is provided at Notos Internet (☎ 2823 042 110, e notos@

grecian.net) and at Erato Internet (☎ 2823 083 010, e erato@chania-cci.gr). Both charge €4.50 per hour.

Organised Tours

Various travel agents around town offer excursions to ancient Lissos (€22) and dolphin-watching trips (€13.20).

Places to Stay

Camping Paleohora (☎ 2823 041 225) Adult/tent €3.20/2. This ground is 1.5km north-east of the town, near the pebble beach. The site has a taverna but no minimarket.

Homestay Anonymous (☎ 2823 041 509) Singles/doubles €11.80/17.60. This is a great place for backpackers, with clean, simply furnished rooms set around a small, beautiful garden. There is a communal kitchen. The owner, Manolis speaks good English and is full of useful information for travellers.

Kostas Rooms (☎/fax 2823 041 248) Singles/doubles with bathroom €14.70/19. Near Homestay Anonymous, Kostas offers simple attractive rooms with ceiling fans, fridge and sea views.

Spamandos Rooms (☎ 2823 041 197) Doubles/triples with bathroom €23.50/26.50. In the old quarter, Spamandos has spotless, nicely furnished rooms.

Poseidon Hotel (☎ 2823 041 374/115, fax 2823 041 115) Singles/double studios €20.50/26.50. The studios here come equipped with fridges, air-con and kitchenettes and all have a little balcony.

Oriental Bay Rooms (☎ 2823 041 076) Singles/doubles with bathroom & ceiling fans €26.50/29.50. This place occupies the large modern building at the northern end of the pebble beach. The owner, Thalia, keeps the rooms immaculate. There's also a shaded terrace-restaurant overlooking the sea that serves decent meals.

Places to Eat

The eating choices are reasonably good.

O Baxes Grills €3.80-5.60. Open noon-midnight daily. In the street behind the OTE, this is a fine little taverna which does a good job on old favourites like fried aubergine (€2.40), or *dakos* (€2.40).

Dionysos Taverna (☎ 2823 041 243) Cretan dishes €3-5.30. Open 7pm-1am daily Mar-Oct. The very popular Dionysos is a bit more expensive than Baxes but also serves tasty food and a good range of vegetarian dishes from €1.80 to €4.50. It has a roomy interior and tables outside under the trees.

Pizzeria Niki (☎ 2823 041 534) Pizzas €3.80-4.70. Open 6.30pm-midnight daily Apr-Oct. Just off Kondekaki, this place has superior pizzas cooked in a wood-fired oven and served on a spacious outdoor terrace.

Third Eye (☎ 2823 041 234) Meals under €5.90. Open 8am-3pm & 6pm-midnight daily Mar-Nov. Vegetarians have a treat in store near the sandy beach. The menu includes curries and a range of Asian dishes. Unfortunately the place is closed in winter.

Caravella (☎ 2823 041 131) Open 11am-midnight daily Apr-Nov. Caravella has a prime position overlooking the old harbour and offers an array of fresh and competitively priced seafood. Fish is €22 a kilogram.

Entertainment

Outdoor Cinema Most visitors to Paleohora spend at least one evening at this well-signposted cinema. Entry is €4.50 and showings start at 9.45pm.

Paleohora Club (☎ 2823 042 230) This is another option for a night out. It is next to Camping Paleohora 1.5km north-east of the village. It kicks in after 11pm.

Nostos Night Club (☎ 2823 042 145) Open 6pm-2am. If you've seen the movie and don't fancy the trek to the disco, try this place right in town, between El Venizelou and the Old Harbour.

Getting There & Away

Bus In summer there are three buses a day to Hania (two hours, €4.70); in winter there are two. In summer, this service goes via Omalos at 6.30 am (1½ hours, €4.30) to cash in on the Samaria Gorge trade. For information call the bus station on ☎ 2823 041 914.

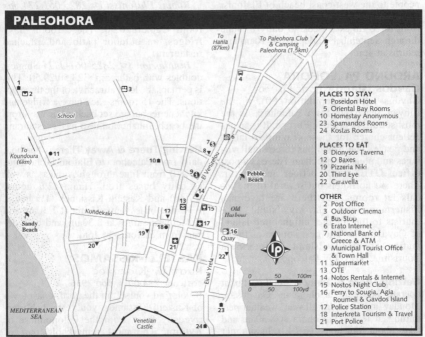

PALEOHORA

To Hania (87km)

To Paleohora Club & Camping Paleohora (1.5km)

School

To Koundoura (6km)

Pebble Beach

Sandy Beach

Kondekaki

Old Harbour

Quay

Entari Yriea

El Venizelou

MEDITERRANEAN SEA

Venetian Castle

0   50   100m
0   50   100yd

PLACES TO STAY
1   Poseidon Hotel
5   Oriental Bay Rooms
10 Homestay Anonymous
23 Spamandos Rooms
24 Kostas Rooms

PLACES TO EAT
8   Dionysos Taverna
12 O Baxes
19 Pizzeria Niki
20 Third Eye
22 Caravella

OTHER
2   Post Office
3   Outdoor Cinema
4   Bus Stop
6   Erato Internet
7   National Bank of Greece & ATM
9   Municipal Tourist Office & Town Hall
11 Supermarket
13 OTE
14 Notos Rentals & Internet
15 Nostos Night Club
16 Ferry to Sougia, Agia Roumeli & Gavdos Island
17 Police Station
18 Interkreta Tourism & Travel
21 Port Police

CRETE

Boat In summer there are daily ferries from Paleohora to Hora Sfakion (three hours, €8) via Sougia (one hour, €3.80), Agia Roumeli (two hours, €6.50) and Loutro (2½ hours, €7.90). The ferry leaves Paleohora at 9.30am, and returns from Hora Sfakion at 12.30pm. There's also a boat three/two times a week in summer/winter to Gavdos (four hours, €9.40) that leaves Paleohora at 8.30am. Tickets for all of these boats can be bought at Interkreta Tourism & Travel (☎ 2823 041 393, fax 2823 041 050), Kondekaki 4.

Getting Around
Car, Motorcycle & Bicycle All three can be hired from Notos Rentals (☎ 2823 042 110, ⓔ notos@grecian.net) on El Venizelou. Cars rent for around €23.50, a motorbike for €14.70 and bicycle for €3.

Excursion Boat The M/B *Elafonisos* gets cranked into action in mid-April ferrying people to the west-coast beach of Elafonisi (one hour, €3.80). The service builds up from three times a week to daily in June through September. It departs at 10am and returns at 4pm.

AROUND PALEOHORA
Gavdos Island Νήσος Γαύδος
Gavdos Island (population 50), in the Libyan Sea 65km from Paleohora, is the most southerly place in Europe. It is an excellent choice for those craving isolation and peace. The island has three small villages and pleasant beaches. There is a post office, OTE, police officer and doctor. There are no hotels but several of the locals let rooms, and there are tavernas. Fishermen from Gavdos Island take tourists to the remote, uninhabited island of Gavdopoula. The best source of information about the island is Interkreta Tourism & Travel in Paleohora.

Getting There & Away A small post boat operates between Paleohora and Gavdos on Monday and Thursday all year, weather permitting. It leaves Paleohora at 8.30am and takes about four hours (€9.40). In summer

there's also a Tuesday boat. The boats turn around from Gavdos almost immediately.

There are also four boats a week from Hora Sfakion to Gavdos (€8) and a weekly boat from Sougia (€7).

Elafonisi Ελαφονήσι
As one of the loveliest sand beaches in Crete it's easy to understand why people enthuse so much about Elafonisi, at the southern extremity of Crete's west coast. The beach is long and wide and is separated from Elafonisi Islet by about 50m of knee-deep water on its northern side. The islet is marked by low dunes and a string of semi-secluded coves that attract a sprinkling of naturists.

Places to Stay *Rooms Elafonissos* (☎ 2825 061 548) Double/triple studios €23.50/29.50. This place has a taverna overlooking the sea from its commanding position on a bluff.

Rooms Elafonissi (☎ 2825 061 274, fax 2825 097 907) Singles/doubles with bathroom €20.50/26.50. These rooms have fridges, an outdoor patio and attached restaurant.

Innahorion (☎ 2825 061 111) Singles/doubles with bathroom €23.50/29.50. This is perhaps the least attractive of the three options. The 15 rooms each have a fridge and kitchenette, but are set back a fair way from the beach. Innahorion also has a restaurant.

Getting There & Away There is one boat daily from Paleohora to Elafonisi (one hour, €3.80) from June through August, as well as daily buses from Hania (2½ hours, €7.40) and Kastelli-Kissamos (1½ hours, €3). The buses leave Hania at 7.30am and Kastelli-Kissamos at 8.30am, and both depart from Elafonisi at 4pm.

KASTELLI-KISSAMOS
Καστέλλι-Κίσσαμος
postcode 734 00 • pop 2936
If you find yourself in the north-coast town of Kastelli-Kissamos, you've probably arrived by ferry from the Peloponnese or Kythira. The most remarkable part of

Kastelli-Kissamos is its unremarkableness. It's simply a quiet town that neither expects nor attracts much tourism.

In antiquity, its name was Kissamos; it was the main town of the province of the same name. When the Venetians came along and built a castle here, the place became known as Kastelli. The name persisted until 1966 when authorities decided that too many people were confusing this Kastelli with Crete's other Kastelli, 40km south-east of Iraklio. The official name reverted to Kissamos, and that's what appears on bus and shipping schedules. Local people still prefer Kastelli, and many books and maps agree with them. An alternative that is emerging is to combine the two into Kastelli-Kissamos, which leaves no room for misunderstanding.

Orientation & Information

The port is 3km west of town. From June through August a bus meets the boats; otherwise a taxi costs around €3. The bus station is just below the square, Plateia Kissamou, and the main street, Skalidi, runs east from Plateia Kissamou.

Kastelli-Kissamos has no tourist office. The post office is on the main road. Signs from the bus station direct you through an alley on the right of Skalidi which takes you to the post office. Turn right at the post office and you'll come to the National Bank of Greece on the central square. Turn left at the post office and the OTE office is opposite you about 50m along the main road. There is also a string of pensions and tavernas along the sea below the bus station.

Places to Stay

There are three camping grounds to choose from.

Camping Kissamos (☎ 2822 023 444, fax 2822 023 464) Adult/tent €4.10/2.40. Close to the city centre, this place is convenient for the huge supermarket next door and for the bus station, but not much else. It's got great views of the olive-processing plant next door. Signs direct you there from the city centre.

Camping Mithymna (☎ 2822 031 444, fax 2822 031 000, Paralia Drapania)

Adult/tent €4.50/2.40. This is a much better choice than Camping Kissamos. It's 6km east of town, on an excellent shady site near the best stretch of beach. Facilities include a restaurant, bar and shop. Getting there involves a bus trip to the village of Drapanias – from where it's a pleasant 15-minute walk through olive groves to the site.

Camping Nopigia (☎ 2822 031 111, fax 2822 031 700, ℮ info@campingnopigia.gr, Nopigia) Adult/tent €3.90/2.50. This is a good site, 2km west of Camping Mithymna. While the beach is no good for swimming, the swimming pool here makes up for that.

Koutsounakis Rooms (☎ 2822 023 753) Singles/doubles with bathroom €13/19. One of the best deals in town, this is adjacent to the bus station. The rooms are spotless.

Hotel Kissamos (☎ 2822 022 086) Singles/doubles with bathroom & breakfast €19/25. This C-class hotel, west of the bus station on the north side of the main road, is in an uninspiring location but has good-value rooms.

Argo Rooms for Rent (☎/fax 2822 023 563, Plateia Teloniou) Singles/doubles with bathroom €20.50/29.50. The C-class Argo has spacious rooms. From the central square, walk down to the seafront, turn left, and you will come to the rooms on the left.

Thalassa (☎ 2822 031 231, ℮ skoulakis@otenet.gr, Ⓦ www.thalassa-apts.gr, Paralia Drapania) Double studios €35.30. If you have your own transport, this is an ideal spot to retreat to. All studios (sleeping two to five persons) are immaculate and are 50m from the beach. Thalassa is 6km east of Kissamos near Camping Mythimna.

Places to Eat

Restaurant Makedonas (☎ 2822 022 844) Ladera €2-2.70. For local colour go to this no-frills place just west of Plateia Kissamou, where you can dine on oil-based, home-cooked food. The beef patties in tomato sauce (bifteki stifado; €3.50) is recommended by the owner.

Papadakis Taverna (☎ 2822 022 340, Paralia Kissamou) Open 11am-midnight daily. Opposite Argo Rooms for Rent, this taverna has a good setting overlooking the beach and serves well-prepared fish dishes such as oven-baked fish (€5), or fish soup (€5). Fish is €29.50 per kilogram.

Getting There & Away

Bus There are 14 buses a day to Hania (one hour, €3), where you can change for Rethymno and Iraklio; and two buses a day for Falasarna (€1.90) at 10am and 5.30pm.

Ferry ANEN Ferries operates the F/B *Myrtidiotissa* on a route that takes in Antikythira (two hours, €6.50), Kythira (four hours, €12.90), Gythio (seven hours, €15.60), Kalamata (10 hours, €17.60) and Piraeus (19 hours, €17.60). It leaves Kastelli-Kissamos five times a week between 8am and 11am. You can buy tickets from Horeftakis Tours (☎ 2822 023 250) and the ANEN Office (☎ 2822 022 009 or 2822 024 030), both of which are on the right side of Skalidi, east of Plateia Kissamou.

Getting Around

Cars can be hired from Hermes (☎ 2822 022 980) on Skalidi, and motorcycles from Motor Fun (☎ 2822 023 400) on Plateia Kissamos.

AROUND KASTELLI-KISSAMOS
Falasarna Φαλάσαρνα

Falasarna, 16km west of Kastelli-Kissamos, was a Cretan city-state in the 4th century BC. There's not much to see, and most people are here for the superb beach, which is long, sandy and interspersed with boulders. There are several *domatia* at the beach.

From June through August there are three buses daily from Kastelli-Kissamos to Falasarna (€1.90) as well as buses from Hania (€4.90).

Gramvousa Peninsula
Χερσόνησος Γραμβούσα

North of Falasarna is the wild and remote Gramvousa Peninsula. There is a wide track, which eventually degenerates into a path, along the east-coast side to the sandy beach of **Tigani**, on the west side of the peninsula's narrow tip. The beach is overlooked by the two islets of Agria (wild) and Imeri (tame) Gramvousa. To reach the track, take a west-

bound bus from Kastelli-Kissamos and ask to be let off at the turn-off for the village of **Kalyviani** (5km from Kastelli-Kissamos). Walk the 2km to Kalyviani, then take the path that begins at the far end of the main street. The shadeless walk takes around three hours – wear a hat and take plenty of water. You don't have to inflict this punishment upon yourself to see the beautiful peninsula. From June through August there are daily cruises around the peninsula in the *Gramvousa Express* (€14.70). The boat leaves Kastelli-Kissamos at 9am and returns at 6pm.

Ennia Horia Εννιά Χωριά

Ennia Horia (Nine Villages) is the name given to the highly scenic mountainous region south of Kastelli-Kissamos, renowned for its chestnut trees. If you have your own transport you can drive through the region en route to Moni Hrysoskalitissas and Elafonisi or, with a little backtracking, to Paleohora. Alternatively, you can take a circular route, returning via the coast road. The village of **Elos** stages a chestnut festival on the third Sunday of October when sweets made from chestnuts are eaten. The road to the region heads inland 5km east of Kastelli-Kissamos.

Polyrrinia Πολυρρηνία

The ruins of the ancient city of Polyrrinia (po-lih-reh-**nee**-ah) lie 7km south of Kastelli-Kissamos, above the village of Ano Paleokastro (which is sometimes called Polyrrinia). It's a steep climb to reach the ruins but the views are stunning.

The city was founded by the Dorians and was continuously inhabited until Venetian times. There are remains of city walls, and an aqueduct built by Hadrian. It's a scenic walk from Kastelli-Kissamos to Polyrrinia, otherwise there is a very infrequent bus service – ask at the Kastelli-Kissamos bus station.

To reach the Polyrrinia road, walk east along Kastelli-Kissamos' main road, and turn right after the OTE.

Ano Paleokastro has only one taverna, *Taverna Odysseos*, which has mains at €3.50 to €5. Unfortunately there's no accommodation.

Dodecanese Δωδεκάνησα

Strung along the coast of western Turkey like jewels upon an aquamarine sea, the Dodecanese archipelago is closer to Asia Minor than mainland Greece. Because of their strategic and vulnerable position, they have encountered a greater catalogue of invasions and occupations than the rest of Greece.

The name Dodecanese ('dodecka' means 12 in Greek) derives from the time of the Ottoman Empire when 12 of the 18 islands were granted special privileges for having willingly submitted to the new Ottoman overlords, a rule which began in earnest in 1478. Intriguingly, the original Dodecanese did not include the largest and richest islands of Rhodes and Kos, as they had unwillingly been subjugated to the Ottomans; they consisted only of Patmos, Lipsi, Leros, Kalymnos, Astypalea, Nisyros, Tilos, Symi, Halki, Karpathos, Kasos and Kastellorizo.

The islands' vicissitudinous history has endowed them with a wealth of diverse archaeological remains, but these are not the islands' only attractions. The highly developed resorts of Rhodes and Kos have beaches and bars galore, while Lipsi and Tilos have appealing beaches, but without the crowds. The far-flung islands of Agathonisi, Arki, Kasos and Kastellorizo await Greek-island aficionados in pursuit of traditional island life, while everyone gapes at the extraordinary landscape that geological turbulence has created on Nisyros.

SUGGESTED ITINERARIES

One week

Spend two days on Rhodes, and explore the capital's medieval city. Visit either Lindos or the ancient city of Kamiros, or both if you hire a car and cross Rhodes' unspoilt mountainous interior. Spend the next two days chilling out on the beaches of tranquil Tilos or walking around the island. You may fit in a couple of days on Nisyros, with its extraordinary volcanic landscape, the picturesque villages of Emboreios and Nikea and an impressive ruined kastro on its ancient acropolis. Otherwise, make for Kos, birthplace of Hippocrates, to see its extensive ruins and enjoy its wild nightlife.

Highlights

- Sense Patmos, the stunning island of St John with an inimitable spirit of place. Here, it is said, God delivered the Book of Revelations

- Lie back and relax in Lipsi, an island where time stands still and which most people pass by. The annual feast of Panagia tou Harou draws pilgrims from all over the Dodecanese

- See the Asklipion in Kos, religious sanctuary to Asklepios, the god of healing, and home to a healing centre and a school of medicine where trainees followed the teachings of Hippocrates

- Walk around the Old Town of Rhodes, the splendid fortress city built by the Knights of St John and the largest inhabited medieval town in Europe

- Smell the sulphur from the rim of the volcano on the extraordinary island of Nisyros

- Head for Kastellorizo – a tiny rock in the sun, Greece's furthest outpost and location for the cult film *Mediterraneo*

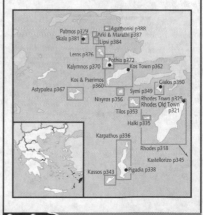

Agathonisi p388
Patmos p374
Skala p381
Arki & Marathi p397
Lipsi p384
Leros p376
Pothia p372
Kalymnos p370
Kos Town p362
Kos & Pserimos p360
Astypalea p367
Gialos p350
Symi p349
Nisyros p356
Rhodes Town p325
Rhodes Old Town p321
Tilos p353
Halki p335
Karpathos p336
Rhodes p318
Kastellorizo p345
Kassos p343
Pigadia p338

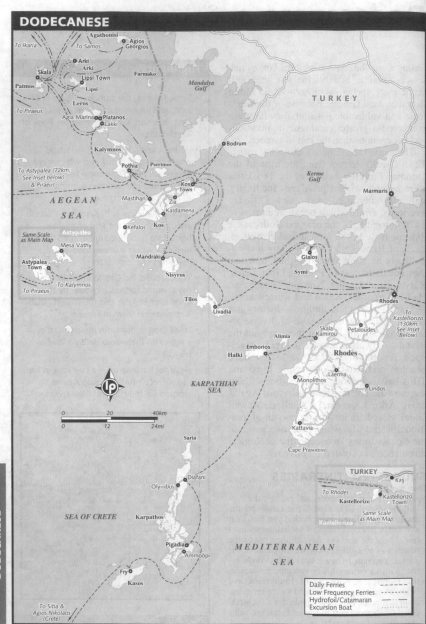

DODECANESE

To Ikaria
Agathonisi
To Samos
Agios Georgios
Arki
Arki
Skala
Lipsi Town
Patmos
Farmako
Lipsi
Mandalya Gulf
TURKEY
To Piraeus
Leros
Agia Marina
Platanos
Lakki
Bodrum
Kalymnos
Pothia
Pserimos
Kerme Gulf
To Astypalea (72km; See Inset below) & Piraeus
AEGEAN SEA
Mastihari
Kos Town
Zia
Kardamena
Marmaris
Same Scale as Main Map
Astypalea
Mesa Vathy
Kefalos
Kos
Astypalea Town
Mandraki
Gialos
Symi
To Piraeus
To Kalymnos
Nisyros
Tilos
Livadia
Rhodes
To Kastellorizo (130km; See Inset Below)
Alimia
Skala Kamirou
Petaloudes
KARPATHIAN SEA
Emborios
Halki
Rhodes
Laerma
Monolithos
Lindos
Saria
Kattavia
Cape Prasonisi
Diafani
TURKEY
Olympos
Kaş
To Rhodes
Kastellorizo
Kastellorizo Town
Karpathos
SEA OF CRETE
Same Scale as Main Map
Kastellorizo
Pigadia
MEDITERRANEAN SEA
Ammoopi
Fry
Kasos
To Sitia & Agios Nikolaos (Crete)

Daily Ferries	- - - - - -
Low Frequency Ferries	— · — · —
Hydrofoil/Catamaran	— — —
Excursion Boat	· · · · · ·

0   20   40km
0   12   24mi

Two weeks
Follow the one week itinerary, but spend three days on Rhodes to see more of the interior. Spend the night on Nisyros and enjoy a drink and dinner on Mandraki's delightful central square – the town undergoes a metamorphosis when the day-trippers leave. To recuperate from the liveliness of Kos, spend three days relaxing on Lipsi's uncrowded beaches, do more walking and take a day trip to remote and traditional Arki. Or, if even Lipsi sounds too touristy for you, go to quieter Agathonisi. Finally, en route to Piraeus, spend a day on Patmos to explore its monasteries.

HISTORY

The Dodecanese islands have been inhabited since pre-Minoan times; by the archaic period Rhodes and Kos had emerged as the dominant islands of the group. Distance from Athens gave the Dodecanese considerable autonomy and they were, for the most part, free to prosper unencumbered by subjugation to imperial Athens. Following Alexander the Great's death, Ptolemy I of Egypt ruled the Dodecanese.

The Dodecanese islanders were the first Greeks to become Christians. This was through the tireless efforts of St Paul, who made two journeys to the archipelago, and through St John, who was banished to Patmos, where he had his revelation.

The early Byzantine era saw the islands prosper, but by the 7th century AD they were plundered by a string of invaders. By the early 14th century it was the turn of the crusaders – the Knights of St John of Jerusalem, or Knights Hospitallers. The knights eventually became rulers of almost all the Dodecanese, building mighty fortifications, but not mighty enough to keep out the Turks in 1522.

The Turks were ousted by the Italians in 1912 during a tussle over possession of Libya. The Greeks, inspired by Mussolini's vision of a vast Mediterranean empire, made Italian the official language and prohibited the practice of Orthodoxy. The Italians constructed grandiose public buildings in the Fascist style, which was the antithesis of archetypal Greek architecture. More beneficially, they excavated and restored many archaeological monuments.

After the Italian surrender of 1943, the islands became battleground for British and German forces, with much suffering inflicted upon the population. The Dodecanese were formally returned to Greece in 1947.

GETTING TO/FROM THE DODECANESE

Air

Astypalea, Karpathos, Kasos, Kos, Leros and Rhodes have flights going to Athens. In addition, Rhodes has flights to Iraklio on Crete, Thessaloniki, and in summer to Mykonos and Santorini (Thira) in the Cyclades.

Ferry – Domestic

Ferry schedules to the Dodecanese are fairly complex, but they do follow a predictable and rarely varying pattern. Departure times in both directions tend to be geared to an early morning arrival at both Piraeus and Rhodes. This means that island-hopping southwards can often involve some antisocial hours.

The following table gives an overall view of ferry connections to the Dodecanese from the mainland and Crete in high season. The services from Alexandroupolis are subject to seasonal demand so check before committing yourself to the trip.

Connecting from the Dodecanese to the Cyclades can sometimes be difficult. It is possible to reach Astypalea from the Dodecanese and connect with ferries serving the Cyclades from there, but this is more by luck than by design.

Hydrofoil – Domestic

Kyriacoulis Hydrofoils operates daily services from the North-East Aegean island of Samos to the northern Dodecanese, and occasional services from Ikaria.

Ferry & Hydrofoil – International

There are ferries and hydrofoils to the Turkish ports of Marmaris and Bodrum from Rhodes and Kos respectively, and day trips to Turkey from Kastellorizo and Symi. Boats en route from Piraeus to Cyprus and Israel call at Rhodes.

DODECANESE

Ferry Connections to the Dodecanese

origin	destination	duration (hours)	price (€)	frequency
Alexandroupolis	Kos	26	33.50	1 weekly
Alexandroupolis	Rhodes	30	35.50	1 weekly
Piraeus	Astypalea	12	21.40	3 weekly
Piraeus	Halki	22	29.50	2 weekly
Piraeus	Kalymnos	10–13	21.80	1 daily
Piraeus	Karpathos	18½	24.40	4 weekly
Piraeus	Kasos	17	24.00	4 weekly
Piraeus	Kos	12–15	23.20	2 daily
Piraeus	Leros	11	19.70	1 daily
Piraeus	Lipsi	16	28.00	1 weekly
Piraeus	Nisyros	13–15	23.20	2 weekly
Piraeus	Patmos	9½	21.00	1 daily
Piraeus	Rhodes	15–18	26.70	2 daily
Piraeus	Symi	15–17	21.20	2 weekly
Piraeus	Tilos	15	21.80	2 weekly
Sitia	Halki	5½	11.90	2 weekly
Sitia	Karpathos	4	10.60	4 weekly
Sitia	Kasos	2½	7.70	4 weekly
Sitia	Rhodes	11	19.00	3 weekly
Thessaloniki	Kos	18	39.00	1 weekly
Thessaloniki	Rhodes	21	45.00	1 weekly

Rhodes Ρόδος

Rhodes (**ro**-dos in Greek), the largest island in the Dodecanese, with a population of over 98,000, is the number one package tour destination of the group. With 300 days of sunshine a year, and an east coast of virtually uninterrupted sandy beaches, it fulfils the two prerequisites of the sun-starved British, Scandinavians and Germans who flock there.

But beaches and sunshine are not its only attributes. Rhodes is a beautiful island with unspoilt villages nestling in the foothills of its mountains. The landscape varies from arid and rocky around the coast to lush and forested in the interior.

The World Heritage-listed Old Town of Rhodes stands as the largest inhabited medieval town in Europe, and its mighty fortifications are the finest surviving example of defensive architecture of the time.

History & Mythology

As is the case elsewhere in Greece, the early history of Rhodes is interwoven with mythology. The sun god Helios chose Rhodes as his bride and bestowed upon her light, warmth and vegetation. Their son, Cercafos, had three sons, Camiros, Ialysos and Lindos, who each founded the cities that were named after them.

The Minoans and Mycenaeans had outposts on the islands, but it was not until the Dorians arrived in 1100 BC that Rhodes began to exert power and influence. The Dorians settled in the cities of Kamiros, Ialysos and Lindos and made each an autonomous state. They utilised trade routes to the east which had been established during Minoan and Mycenaean times, and the island flourished as an important centre of commerce.

Rhodes continued to prosper until Roman times. It was allied to Athens in the Battle of Marathon (490 BC), in which the Persians were defeated, but had shifted to the Persian side by the time of the Battle of Salamis (480 BC). After the unexpected Athenian victory at Salamis, Rhodes hastily became an ally of Athens again, joining the Delian League in 478 BC. After the disastrous Sicilian Expedition (416–412 BC), Rhodes revolted against Athens and formed an alliance with Sparta, which it aided in the Peloponnesian Wars.

In 408 BC, the cities of Kamiros, Ialysos and Lindos consolidated their powers for mutual protection and expansion by co-founding the city of Rhodes. The architect Hippodamos, who came to be regarded as the father of town planning, planned the city. The result was one of the most harmonious cities of antiquity, with wide, straight streets connecting its four distinct parts: the acropolis, agora, harbour and residential quarter.

Rhodes became Athens' ally again, and together they defeated Sparta at the Battle of Knidos, in 394 BC. Rhodes then joined forces with Persia in a battle against Alexander the Great, but when Alexander proved invincible, hastily allied itself with him. In the skirmishes following Alexander's death, Rhodes sided with Ptolemy I.

In 305 BC, Antigonus, one of Ptolemy's rivals, sent his son, the formidable Demetrius Poliorketes (the Besieger of Cities), to conquer the city. Rhodes managed to repel Demetrius after a long siege. To celebrate this victory, the 32m-high bronze statue of Helios Apollo (Colossus of Rhodes), one of the Seven Wonders of the Ancient World, was built (see the boxed text).

After the defeat of Demetrius, Rhodes knew no bounds. It built the biggest navy in the Aegean and its port became a principal Mediterranean trading centre. The arts also flourished, and the Rhodian school of sculpture supplanted that of Athens as the foremost in Greece. Its most esteemed sculptor was Pythocrates, whose works included the *Victory of Samothrace*, and the relief of the *trireme* (warship) at Lindos.

When Greece became the battleground upon which Roman generals fought for leadership of the empire, Rhodes allied itself with Julius Caesar. After Caesar's assassination in 44 BC, Cassius besieged Rhodes, destroying its ships and stripping the city of its artworks, which were then taken to Rome. This marked the beginning of Rhodes' decline. In AD 70, Rhodes became part of the Roman Empire.

In AD 155, Rhodes Town was badly damaged by an earthquake, and in 269 the Goths invaded, rendering further damage. When the Roman Empire split, Rhodes became part of the Byzantine province of the Dodecanese. Raid upon raid followed: the Persians in 620, the Saracens in 653, then the Turks.

The Colossus of Rhodes

Whether the famous Colossus of Rhodes ever actually existed can never be proven, since there are no remains and no tangible evidence other than the reports of ancient travellers. The statue was apparently commissioned by Demetrius Poliorketes in 305 BC after he finally capitulated to Rhodian defiance following his long and ultimately failed siege of Rhodes in that same year.

The bronze statue was built over 12 years (294–282 BC) and when completed stood 32m high. What is not clear is where this gargantuan statue stood. Popular medieval belief has it astride the harbour at Mandraki (as depicted on today's T-shirts and tourist trinkets), but it is highly unlikely that this is the case and it's also technically unfeasible.

An earthquake in either AD 225 or 226 toppled the statue, most likely on land, where the remains lay undisturbed for 880 years. In AD 654 invading Saracens had the remains broken up and sold for scrap to a Jewish merchant in Edessa (in modern-day Turkey). The story goes that after being shipped to Syria, it took almost 1000 camels to convey it to its final destination.

DODECANESE

RHODES

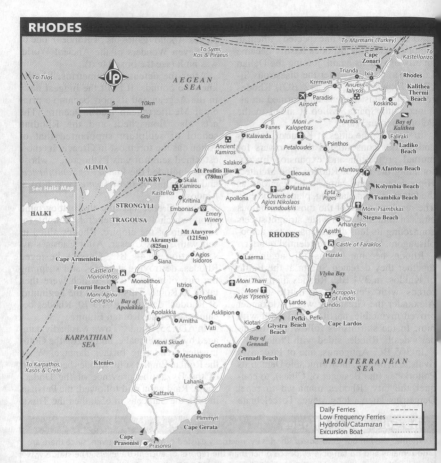

When the crusaders seized Constantinople, Rhodes was given independence. Later the Genoese gained control. The Knights of St John arrived in Rhodes in 1309 and ruled for 213 years until they were ousted by the Ottomans. Rhodes suffered several earthquakes during the 19th century, but greater damage was rendered to the city in 1856 by an explosion of gunpowder which had been stored and forgotten – almost 1000 people were killed and many buildings were wrecked. In 1947, after 35 years of Italian occupation, Rhodes became part of Greece along with the other Dodecanese islands.

Getting To/From Rhodes

All the addresses listed in this section are in Rhodes Town.

Air Olympic Airways has at least five flights daily travelling to Athens (€84), two daily to Karpathos (€44.30), one daily to Kastellorizo (€35.80), six weekly to Santorini (€76.90), four weekly to Iraklio (€79.50), three weekly to Kasos (€44.30) and two weekly to Thessaloniki (€105.40) and Mykonos (€78). The Olympic Airways office (☎ 2241 024 571) is located at Ierou Lohou 9.

Aegean Airlines and Axon Airlines offer cheaper options. Aegean Airlines has flights to Athens (€75, four daily), Thessaloniki (€107.50, one daily) and Iraklio (€75, one daily). Through its partner Cronus Airlines, Aegean Airlines offers one stop connections to a number of European destinations. Aegean Airlines (☎ 2241 024 166, fax 2241 024 431) is at Ethelondon Dodekanision 20 while Cronus (☎ 2241 025 444, fax 2241 028 468, ⓔ info@cronus.gr) is at 25 Martiou 5. Axon Airlines has flights to Athens (€73.40, two daily). The Axon Airlines office (☎ 2241 032 224) is at Ethelondon Dodekanision 20.

Castellania Travel Service (☎ 2241 075 860, fax 2241 075 861, ⓔ castell@otenet .gr), on Plateia Ippokratous, specialises in youth and student fares, and is one of the best places for low-cost air tickets.

Ferry – Domestic Rhodes is the main port of the Dodecanese and offers a complex array of departures.

The following table lists scheduled domestic ferries from Rhodes to other islands in the Dodecanese in high season.

The EOT and the municipal tourist office located in Rhodes Town can provide you with schedules.

destination	duration (hours)	price (€)	frequency
Astypalea	10	15.00	2 weekly
Halki	1½	5.90	9 weekly
Kalymnos	5½	13.20	1 daily
Karpathos	3½	13.50	3 weekly
Kasos	5	16.00	2 weekly
Kastellorizo	3½	12.00	2 weekly
Kos	3½	10.30	1 daily
Leros	7½	14.00	1 daily
Lipsi	9½	15.30	1 weekly
Nisyros	3¾	8.80	3 weekly
Patmos	8½	17.00	1 daily
Piraeus	15–18	26.70	2 daily
Symi	2	5.40	1 daily
Tilos	2½	8.50	4 weekly

The weekly ferry from Rhodes to Alexandroupolis also stops at Samos (nine hours, (21) in the North-East Aegean.

Ferry – International Poseidon Lines and Salamis Lines both stop at Rhodes en route from Piraeus to Cyprus (Lemesos/Limassol) and Israel (Haifa). From Rhodes to Cyprus takes 15 hours (€70.50), with a further 11 hours to Haifa (€117.40). There is an additional €17.60 port tax on top of these fares. The boats leave Rhodes on Tuesday and Friday. You can buy tickets from Kydon Tours (☎ 2241 023 000, fax 2241 032 741) at Ethelondon Dodekanision 14, in the New Town, or Kouros Travel (☎ 2241 024 377, 2241 022 400), Karpathou 34.

There are no scheduled car ferry services between Marmaris in Turkey and Rhodes. Travellers with a vehicle may have to wait up to four days for an unscheduled crossing to be arranged. A ferry will be dispatched from Marmaris to pick up passengers with a vehicle only if there is also a vehicle to be transported from Marmaris. The crossing takes 2½ hours.

Fares for crossings to Marmaris were as follows at the time of research: passenger €47, motorbike €88, car €176. Greek port taxes are an extra €8.80. Turkish port taxes are US$10 per person and US$3 per vehicle.

If you do plan to cross to Turkey, be prepared to wait. Contact Triton Holidays (☎ 2241 021 690, fax 2241 031 625, ⓔ info@ tritondmc.gr), Plastira 9, Mandraki, upon arrival to arrange a crossing.

Immigration and customs are on the quay.

Hydrofoil – Domestic Kyriacoulis Hydrofoils (☎ 2241 024 000, fax 2241 020 272), on the quay at Plateia Neoriou 6, operates the following services from Rhodes in high season:

destination	duration (hours)	price (€)	frequency
Astypalea	5½	30.50	1 weekly
Kalymnos	3½	26.00	1 weekly
Os	2	20.60	2 daily
Leros	3½	28.00	3 weekly
Nysiros	2¼	17.20	1 weekly
Patmos	3½	32.20	3 weekly
Symi	1	9.80	2 weekly
Tilos	1¼	17.10	2 weekly

DODECANESE

Phone numbers listed incorporate changes due in Oct 2002; see p55

Tickets are available from Triton Holidays (see Ferry – International). There is an additional daily hydrofoil, the *Aegli*, run and owned by the island Symi, with a daily service (€9.40/18.50 one way/return) to and from Gialos on Symi.

Hydrofoil – International There are two or three daily hydrofoils to Marmaris (one hour, weather permitting) April to October. Fares are currently cheaper than ferries at €32.30/ 39.70 one way/return (plus US$10 Turkish port tax, payable in Turkey). You buy tickets from Triton Holidays, but you must submit your passport a day before your journey. This is currently the only scheduled transport option to and from Turkey.

Catamaran The *Dodekanisos Express* starts its daily run up the Dodecanese at around 8.30am each day stopping at Kos, Kalymnos and Leros daily with stops at other times in Symi, Halki, Tilos, Nisyros, Lipsi and Patmos. Kastellorizo was on the schedule when we were there; check to see if it is included when you travel.

Tickets may be bought at Skevos Travel (☎ 2241 022 461, fax 2241 022 354, ℮ skeyos@rho.forthnet.gr) at Amerikis 11, or from the offices of Dodekanisos Naftiliaki (☎ 2241 070 590, fax 2241 070 591, ℮ info@12ne.gr) at Afstralias 3.

The Tilos-owned *Sea Star* departs Rhodes each morning at 9am for Tilos (55 minutes, €16.20) and Nisyros (€16.50). See Triton Holidays for tickets.

Caique See the Getting There & Away section for Halki for information about caiques between Rhodes and Halki.

Excursion Boat There are excursion boats to Symi (€12 return) every day in summer, leaving Mandraki Harbour at 9am and returning at 6pm. You can buy tickets at most travel agencies, but it is better to buy them at the harbour, where you can check out the boats and haggle. Look for shade and the size and condition of the boat, as these vary greatly. You can buy an open return if you want to stay on Symi.

Getting Around Rhodes

To/From the Airport The airport is 16km south-west of Rhodes Town, near Paradisi. There are 21 buses daily between the airport and Rhodes Town's west side bus station (for routes down the west side of Rhodes; €1.50). The first leaves Rhodes Town at 5am and the last at 11pm; from the airport, the first leaves at 5.55am and the last at 11.45pm.

Bus Rhodes Town has two bus stations. From the east side bus station on Plateia Rimini there are 18 buses daily to Faliraki (€1.50), 14 to Lindos (€3.10), three to Kolymbia (€1.50), nine to Gennadi (€3.70) via Lardos, and four to Psinthos (€1.60).

From the west side station next to the New Market there are buses every half hour to Kalithea Thermi (€1.50), 10 to Koskinou (€1.50), five to Salakos (€2.70), two to ancient Kamiros (€3.40), one to Monolithos (€4.40) via Skala Kamirou, and Embonas (€3.90). The EOT and municipal tourist office give out schedules.

Car & Motorcycle There are numerous car and motorcycle rental outlets in Rhodes Town's New Town. Shop around and bargain because the competition is fierce.

Taxi Rhodes Town's main taxi rank is east of Plateia Rimini. There are two zones on the island for taxi meters: zone one is Rhodes Town and zone two (slightly higher) is everywhere else.

Rates are a little higher between midnight and 6am. Sample fares are: airport €10.30, Filerimos €8, Petaloudes €14.70, ancient Kamiros €20.60, Lindos €25 and Monolithos €32.30. Taxi company contact phone numbers include ☎ 2241 064 712, ☎ 2241 064 734 and ☎ 2241 064 778.

Disabled travellers may call Savvas Kafkakis who runs a special taxi on mobile ☎ 697 413 1882.

Bicycle The Bicycle Centre (☎ 2241 028 315), Griva 39, Rhodes Town, has three-speed bikes for €2.70 and mountain bikes for €3.80.

Excursion Boat There are excursion boats to Lindos (€15 return) every day in summer, leaving Mandraki Harbour at 9am and returning at 6pm.

RHODES TOWN
postcode 851 00 • pop 42,400

The heart of Rhodes Town is the Old Town, enclosed within massive walls. Avoid the worst of the tourist hordes by beginning your exploration early in the morning. But at any time, away from the main thoroughfares and squares, you will find deserted labyrinthine alleyways. Much of the New Town to the

north is dominated by package tourism, but it does have a few places of interest to visitors.

Orientation

The Old Town is nominally divided into three sectors: the Kollakio or Knights' Quarter, the Hora and the Jewish quarter. The Kollakio comprises the northern sector and is roughly bordered by Agisandrou and Theofiliskou which run east to west. The Kollakio contains most of the medieval historical sights of the Old Town. The Hora, often known as the Turkish Quarter, is primarily the commercial sector and contains most of the shops and

RHODES OLD TOWN

PLACES TO STAY		
26	Maria's Rooms	
27	Mike and Mama's Pension	
30	Pension Olympos	
31	Marco Polo Mansion	
38	Hotel Cava d'Oro	
39	Hotel Spot	
41	Hotel Via Via	
48	Mango Rooms & Cafe Bar	
51	Pension Minos	
52	Apollo Tourist House	
53	Pension Andreas	
54	Pink Elephant	

PLACES TO EAT	
22	Myrovolos
28	Diafani Garden Restaurant
32	Cleo's Italian Restaurant
37	Mystagogia
43	Taverna Kostas
45	Araliki
46	Nisyros
50	L'Auberge Bistrot

THINGS TO SEE	
1	Temple of Aphrodite
3	Palace of the Grand Masters
4	Entrance to Moat #2
6	Inn of Spain
7	Inn of Provence
8	Chapelle Française
9	Inn of France
10	Museum of Decorative Arts
11	Inn of Auvergne
12	Old Knights' Hospital
13	Inn of the Order of the Tongue of Italy
14	Palace of Villiers de l'Île Adam
21	Archaeological Museum
23	Clock Tower
24	Mosque of Süleyman
25	Turkish Library
29	Mustafa Pasha Baths (Hammam)
33	Agios Spyridon Church (Kavakli Mosque)
35	Castellania Fountain
40	Kahal Shalom Synagogue
42	Ibrahim Pasha Mosque
49	Recep Pasha Mosque
55	Entrance to Moat

OTHER	
2	Commercial Bank of Greece
5	Old Town Post Office Branch
15	National Bank of Greece
16	Departure Point for F/B Nisos Kalymnos & Dodekanisos Express Catamaran
17	Departure Point for Boats to Turkey
18	Customs Office
19	Commercial Bank ATM
20	Port Police
34	Castellenia Travel Service
36	Resalto Club
44	Kafe Besara
47	Folk Dance Theatre

DODECANESE

Phone numbers listed incorporate changes due in Oct 2002; see p55

restaurants. Sokratous and its northerly extension Orfeos are the Hora's main thoroughfares. The sector is bordered to the east by Perikleous, beyond which is the quieter, mainly residential Jewish Quarter. The Old Town is accessed by nine main gates *(pyles)* and two rampart-access portals. The whole town is a mesh of Byzantine, Turkish and Latin architecture with quiet, twisting alleyways punctuated by lively squares. While you will inevitably get lost at some point, it will never be for long.

The commercial centre of the New Town lies north of the Old Town and is easily explored on foot. Most commercial activity is centred on two blocks surrounding Plateia Kyprou. The hotel district is centred on a large sector bordered by 28 Oktovriou and G Papanikolaou. The main square of the New Town is Plateia Rimini, just north of the Old Town. The tourist offices, bus stations and main taxi rank are on or near this square.

The commercial harbour, for international ferries and large inter-island ferries, is east of the Old Town. Excursion boats, small ferries, hydrofoils and private yachts use Mandraki Harbour, farther north.

Information

Tourist Offices The EOT (☎ 2241 023 255, fax 2241 026 955, ⓔ eot-rodos@otenet.gr), on the corner of Makariou and Papagou, supplies brochures and maps of the city, and will helps find accommodation. It's open 7.30am to 3pm Monday to Friday. In summer the same service is provided by Rhodes' municipal tourist office (☎ 2241 035 945), Plateia Rimini. Opening times are 8am to 8pm Monday to Saturday and 8am to noon on Sunday; it's closed in winter.

From either of these you can pick up the *Rodos News*, a free English-language newspaper.

The tourist police (☎ 2241 027 423) are next door to the EOT and open 24 hours daily. The port police may be contacted on ☎ 2241 022 220.

Money The main National Bank of Greece and the Alpha Credit Bank are on Plateia Kyprou. In the Old Town there is a National

Bank of Greece on Plateia Mousiou, and a Commercial Bank of Greece nearby. All have ATMs. Opening times are 8am to 2pm Monday to Thursday, 8am to 1.30pm Friday.

American Express (☎ 2241 021 010) is represented by Rhodos Tours, Ammohostou 18.

Post & Communications The main post office is on Mandraki Harbour. Opening times are 7.30am to 8pm Monday to Friday. The Old Town post office branch is open seven days. The OTE at Amerikis 91 is open 7am to 11pm daily.

For Internet access try Rock Style Internet Cafe (☎ 2241 027 502, ⓔ info@rockstyle .gr), Dimokratias 7, just south of the Old Town, or Mango Cafe Bar (☎ 2241 024 877, ⓔ karelas@hotmail.com), Plateia Dorieos 3, in the Old Town.

Bookshops Second Story Books (mobile ☎ 697 759 4320), Amarantou 24, in the New Town has a broad selection of second-hand foreign-language books.

Laundry Wash your clothes at Lavomatique, 28 Oktovriou 32, or Express Servis, Dilberaki 97 (off Orfanidou). Both charge around €3 a load. Express Laundry, Kosta Palama 5, does service washes for €3.50.

Luggage Storage You can store luggage at Planet Holidays (☎ 2241 035 722), Gallias 6, for €2.60 for two hours and €3.50 for up to two days. You can negotiate a price for a longer period.

Emergency Rhodes' general hospital (☎ 2241 080 000) is at Papalouka, just north-west of the Old Town. For emergency first aid and the ambulance service, call ☎ 2241 025 555 or ☎ 2241 022 222.

Old Town

In medieval times, the Knights of St John lived in the Knights' Quarter and other inhabitants lived in the Hora. The 12m-thick city walls are closed to the public, but you can do **guided walks** *(☎ 2241 023 359; €3.50; 2.45pm Tues & Sat)*, starting at the courtyard of the Palace of the Grand Masters.

Knights' Quarter An appropriate place to begin an exploration of the Old Town is the imposing cobblestone **Avenue of the Knights** (Ippoton), where the knights lived. The knights were divided into seven 'tongues' or languages, according to their place of origin – England, France, Germany, Italy, Aragon, Auvergne and Provence – each responsible for protecting a section of the bastion. The Grand Master, who was in charge, lived in the palace, and each tongue was under the auspices of a bailiff. The knights were divided into soldiers, chaplains and ministers to the sick.

To this day the street exudes a noble and forbidding aura, despite modern offices now occupying most of the inns. Its lofty buildings stretch in a 600m-long unbroken wall of honey-coloured stone blocks, and its flat facade is punctuated by huge doorways and arched windows. The inns reflect the Gothic styles of architecture of the knights' countries of origin. They form a harmonious whole in their bastion-like structure, but on closer inspection each possesses its own graceful and individual embellishments.

First on the right, if you begin at the eastern end of the Avenue of the Knights, is the **Inn of the Order of the Tongue of Italy** (1519); next to it is the **Palace of Villiers de l'Île Adam**. After Sultan Süleyman had taken the city, it was Villiers de l'Île who had the humiliating task of arranging the knights' departure from the island. Next along is the **Inn of France**, the most ornate and distinctive of all the inns. On the opposite side of the street is a wrought-iron gate in front of a Turkish garden.

Back on the right side is the **Chapelle Française** (Chapel of the Tongue of France), embellished with a statue of the Virgin and Child. Next door is the residence of the Chaplain of the Tongue of France. Across the alleyway is the **Inn of Provence**, with four coats of arms forming the shape of a cross, and opposite is the **Inn of Spain**.

On the right is the magnificent 14th-century **Palace of the Grand Masters** (☎ 2241 023 359, Ippoton; admission €3.50; open 8.30am-3pm Tues-Sunday). It was destroyed

in the gunpowder explosion of 1856 and the Italians rebuilt it in a grandiose manner, with a lavish interior, intending it as a holiday home for Mussolini and King Emmanuel III. It is now a museum, containing sculpture, mosaics taken from Kos by the Italians, and antique furniture.

In the 15th-century knights' hospital is the **archaeological museum** (☎ 2241 027 657, Plateia Mousiou; admission €2.40; open 8.30am-3pm Tues-Sat; 8.30am-3pm Sun). Its most famous exhibit is the exquisite Parian marble statuette, the *Aphrodite of Rhodes*, a 1st-century BC adaptation of a Hellenistic statue. Less charming to most people is the 4th-century BC *Afroditi Thalassia* in the next room. However, writer Lawrence Durrell was so enamoured of this statue that he named his book *Reflections on a Marine Venus* after it. Also in this room is the 2nd-century BC marble *Head of Helios*, found near the Palace of the Grand Masters where a Temple of Helios once stood.

MH

Aphrodite of Rhodes, found in Rhodes Old Town's archaeological museum

DODECANESE

The **Museum of the Decorative Arts** (☎ *2241 072 674, Plateia Argyrokastrou; admission €1.50; open 8.30am-3pm Tues-Sun*), farther north, houses a collection of artefacts from around the Dodecanese.

On Plateia Symis, there are the remains of a 3rd-century BC **Temple of Aphrodite**, one of the few ancient ruins in the Old Town.

Hora The Hora has many Ottoman legacies. During Turkish times, churches were converted to mosques, and many more were built from scratch. Most are now dilapidated. The most important one is the newly renovated, pink-domed **Mosque of Süleyman**, at the top of Sokratous. It was built in 1522 to commemorate the Ottoman victory against the knights, then rebuilt in 1808.

Opposite is the 18th-century **Turkish library** (*Plateia Arionos; admission free; open 9.30am-4pm Mon-Sat*). It was founded in 1794 by Turkish Rhodian Ahmed Hasuf and houses a small collection of Persian and Arabic manuscripts and a collection of Korans written by hand on parchment.

The Jewish Quarter The Jewish Quarter of the Old Town is an almost forgotten sector of Rhodes Town, where life continues at an unhurried pace and where local residents live almost oblivious to the hubbub of the Hora, no more than a few blocks away. This area of quiet streets and sometimes dilapidated houses was once home to a thriving Jewish community. Descendants of Sephardic Jews from Spain, the Jewish community here spoke Ladino (a dialect based on Spanish) and numbered over 2000 souls at the height of its prosperity.

The **Kahal Shalom synagogue** on Dosiadou has a commemorative plaque to the many members of Hora's large Jewish population who were sent to Auschwitz during the Nazi occupation. Jews still worship here and it is usually open in the morning. Close by is Plateia Martyron Evreon (Square of the Jewish Martyrs).

New Town

The **Acropolis of Rhodes**, south-west of the Old Town on Monte Smith, was the site of the ancient Hellenistic city of Rhodes. The hill is named after the English admiral Sir Sydney Smith, who watched for Napoleon's fleet from here in 1802. It has superb views.

The site's restored 2nd-century **stadium** once staged competitions in preparation for the Olympic Games. The adjacent **theatre** is a reconstruction of one used for lectures by the Rhodes School of Rhetoric. Steps above here lead to the **Temple of Pythian Apollo**, with four re-erected columns. The unenclosed site can be reached on city bus No 5.

North of Mandraki, at the eastern end of G Papanikolaou, is the graceful **Mosque of Murad Reis**. In its grounds are a Turkish cemetery and the Villa Cleobolus, where Lawrence Durrell lived in the 1940s, writing *Reflections on a Marine Venus*.

The town **beach** begins north of Mandraki and continues around the island's northernmost point and down the west side of the New Town. The best spot is on the northernmost point, where it's not quite as crowded.

Activities

Scuba Diving Three diving schools operate out of Mandraki: **Waterhoppers Diving Centre** (☎/fax *2241 038 146, mobile* ☎ *69 3296 3173,* ℮ *water-hoppers@rodos.com, Perikleous 29*), **Diving Centres** (☎ *2241 061 115, fax 2241 066 584, Lissavonas 33*) and **Scuba Diving Trident School** (☎/fax *2241 029 160, S. Zervou 2*). All offer a range of courses including a 'One Day Try Dive' for €40 to €50. You can get information from their boats at Mandraki. Kalithea Thermi is the only site around Rhodes where diving is permitted.

Greek Dancing Lessons The **Nelly Dimoglou Dance Company** (☎ *2241 020 157, Folk Dance Theatre, Andronikou; admission €10.30 per person, group €7.40 per person; performances 9.30pm Mon, Wed, Fri*), gives lessons and stages performances.

Organised Tours

Triton Holidays (☎ *2241 021 690, fax 2241 031 625,* ℮ *info@tritondmc.gr, Plastira 9, Mandraki*) This place offers a wide range of

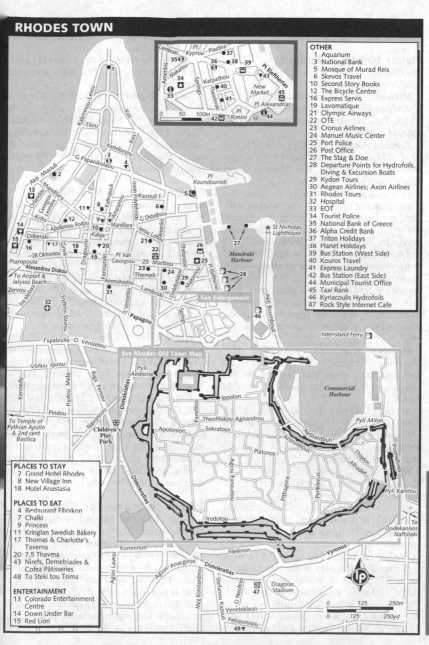

RHODES TOWN

OTHER
1 Aquarium
3 National Bank
5 Mosque of Murad Reis
6 Skevos Travel
10 Second Story Books
12 The Bicycle Centre
16 Express Servis
19 Lavomatique
21 Olympic Airways
22 OTE
23 Cronus Airlines
24 Manuel Music Center
25 Port Police
26 Post Office
27 The Stag & Doe
28 Departure Points for Hydrofoils,
   Diving & Excursion Boats
29 Kydon Tours
30 Aegean Airlines; Axon Airlines
31 Rhodos Tours
32 Hospital
33 EOT
34 Tourist Police
35 National Bank of Greece
36 Alpha Credit Bank
37 Triton Holidays
38 Planet Holidays
39 Bus Station (West Side)
40 Kouros Travel
41 Express Laundry
42 Bus Station (East Side)
44 Municipal Tourist Office
45 Taxi Rank
46 Kyriacoulis Hydrofoils
47 Rock Style Internet Cafe

PLACES TO STAY
2 Grand Hotel Rhodes
8 New Village Inn
18 Hotel Anastasia

PLACES TO EAT
4 Restaurant Ellinikon
7 Chalki
9 Princess
11 Kringlan Swedish Bakery
17 Thomas & Charlotte's
   Taverna
20 7,5 Thavma
43 Nirefs, Demetriades &
   Cofea Pâtisseries
48 To Steki tou Tsima

ENTERTAINMENT
13 Colorado Entertainment
   Centre
14 Down Under Bar
15 Red Lion

DODECANESE

tours, and provides specialist advice on any of the islands and Turkey.

Places to Stay – Budget

The Old Town has a reasonable selection of budget accommodation.

Mike and Mama's Pension (☎ 2241 025 359, Menekleous 28) Singles/doubles €20.50/ 23.50. This pension is a reasonably comfortable option.

Pension Andreas (☎ 2241 034 156, fax 2241 074 285, e andreasch@otenet.gr, w www.hotelandreas.com, Omirou 28D) Singles/doubles with bathroom €32.50. This exceptionally friendly pension has clean, pleasant rooms and a terrace bar with terrific views and does great breakfasts. There is a private garden, library and Internet centre for guests across the street.

Apollo Tourist House (☎ 2241 032 003, e hotelapollo@email.com, w www.apollo -touristhouse.com, Omirou 28C) Singles/ doubles €20/41. This is a small cosy pension, with shared bathrooms and kitchen, a small courtyard and friendly Spanish-Chilean owner. Renovations are planned for 2002.

Pension Minos (☎ 2241 031 813, Omirou 5) Singles/doubles €26.50/32.30. This pension has spotless, spacious rooms and a roof garden with views of the Old Town.

Maria's Rooms (☎ 2241 022 169, Menekleous 147) Doubles without/with bathroom €29.50/35.20. This establishment, just off Sokratous, has pleasant, clean-smelling rooms.

Hotel Spot (☎/fax 2241 034 737, e spothot@otenet.gr, Perikleous 21) Singles/ doubles with bathroom €32.30/ 35.20. The Spot has exceptionally clean, pleasant rooms. There is also a small book exchange, left luggage facilities and Internet access for guests.

Pink Elephant (☎/fax 2241 022 469, Irodotou 42) Doubles without/with bathroom €26.50/29.50, triples with bathroom €35.20. Despite the name, this hotel's attractive decor is blue and white.

Pension Olympos (☎/fax 2241 033 567, Agiou Fanouriou) Singles/doubles €29.30/

41. This pension has pleasant rooms with bathroom and television, and an attractive little courtyard.

Most of the New Town's hotels are modern and characterless, but there are some exceptions.

New Village Inn (☎/fax 2241 034 937, e newvillageinn@rho.forthnet.gr, Konstantopedos 10) Singles/doubles €23.50/ 35.20. This New Town inn has tastefully furnished rooms with refrigerator and fan, and a traditional stone-walled courtyard, festooned with plants.

Places to Stay – Mid-Range

Mango Rooms (☎/fax 2241 024 877, e karelas@hotmail.com, Plateia Dorieos 3) Doubles/triples €44/45. This place has clean, nicely furnished rooms with bathroom, TV, ceiling fan, safety box and refrigerator.

Hotel Via Via (☎/fax 2241 077 027, e vi avia@rho.forthnet.gr, Lisipou 2) Doubles/ triples with bathroom €47/58.70. Just off Pythagora, this pristine hotel has tastefully furnished rooms and is open in winter.

Hotel Cava D'Oro (☎ 2241 036 980, Kistiniou 15) Doubles triples €40/61. Michael Palin stayed in one of the very tasteful old stone rooms during the series *Pole to Pole*. Rooms have air-con, TV and telephone.

Hotel Anastasia (☎ 2241 028 007, fax 021 815, e finikas2@otenet.gr, 28 Oktovriou 46). Doubles/triples €42.50/52.80. This New Town hotel, in a former Italian mansion, is set back from the road, and is reasonably quiet. The high-ceilinged rooms, with tiled floors, are spotless, and the rates include breakfast.

Places to Stay – Top End

Rhodes is full of top-end resort-style accommodation. Try these two for starters.

Marco Polo Mansion (☎/fax 2241 025 562, e marcopolo@rho.forthnet.gr, Agiou Fanouriou 40-42). Doubles €80-130; min 1 week. Featured in glossy European magazines is this old-fashioned Anatolian inn decorated in rich Ottoman-era colours. This cool and shady lodging, right in the heart of the Old Town, is run by the ebullient Effie Dede.

Grand Hotel Rhodes (☎ 2241 0026 284, ax 2241 035 589, Akti Miaouli) Singles/ doubles €80/120. Next to the beach is the pretty but pricey Grand Hotel with bars, restaurant and swimming pools. It is open all year and has rooms with either a pleasant garden or sea view; the price includes breakfast.

Places to Eat – Budget

Old Town Avoid the touts and tack along Sokratous and around Plateia Ippokratous. Hit the back streets to find less touristy places to eat.

Taverna Kostas (☎ 2241 026 217, Pythagora 62) Mains €5-7. Popular Kostas' is good value and has stood the test of time with its repeat clientele and good grills and fish dishes.

Diafani Garden Restaurant (☎ 2241 026 053, Plateia Arionos) Mayirefta €4-5. Back in the Old Town, this restaurant on a quiet square serves home-style, reasonably priced dishes. Try the excellent mousakas (€5) or stifado (€7.40).

Araliki (☎ 2241 073 708, Aristofanous 45) Mezedes €2.50 3.50. This atmospheric kafeneio serves creative mezedes including several vegetarian versions.

Myrovolos (☎ 2241 038 693, Lahitos 13) Mains €4.50-6. Minuscule Myrovolos is a welcome antidote to Rhodes' tacky tourist restaurants. Excellent, imaginative food is served up and there is live music from 6pm to 8pm. Sample the seafood with ouzo special (€11.80).

New Town The New Town has some surprisingly good places to eat, as long as you are prepared to look.

Kringlan Swedish Bakery (☎ 2241 039 090, I Dragoumi 14) Breakfast €5.50. This bakery in the New Town serves sandwiches and pastries that are out of this world; great for breakfast.

Chalki (☎ 2241 033 198, Kathopouli 30) Mezedes €2.50-5. Chalki is a down-to-earth and thoroughly idiosyncratic eatery. Choose from an enticing display of mezedes, and down them with excellent draught wine.

7,5 Thavma (☎ 2241 039 805, Dilberaki 15) Mains €5.50-7.50. 7,5 Thavma is a Swedish-influenced diner with Greek and Swedish dishes alternating on an inventive fusion menu. Recommended dishes are tiger prawns (€7.60) and salmon (€7).

Thomas & Charlotte's Taverna (☎ 2241 073 557, Georgiou Leondos 8) Mains €5-6.50. This taverna serves a wide selection of standard Greek dishes. Try the tasty *kleftiko* (€6.50), a slow-cooked mixture of meat and vegetables served wrapped in greaseproof paper.

Places to Eat – Mid-Range & Top End

Old Town *Nisyros* (☎ 2241 031 741, Agiou Fanouriou 45-47) Mains €7.30-13. A beautiful and tastefully decorated restaurant with impeccable service and a wide range of Greek dishes. Dining is in a leafy, secluded courtyard.

Cleo's Italian Restaurant (☎ 2241 028 415, Agiou Fanouriou 17) Pasta dishes €5.40-10. This is a sophisticated place with a cool, elegant interior and a quiet courtyard.

Mystagogia (☎ 2241 032 981, Themistokleous 5) Mezedes €2-7. Opened in late 1999, Mystagogia draws its charm as much from the open fireplace for winter meals as from its carefully cooked dishes. *Bekri mezes* or 'drunkard's mezes' (spicy pork or beef cubes in tomato sauce; €11.50) is recommended for the curious and hungry.

L'Auberge Bistrot (☎ 2241 034 292, Praxitelous 21) Mains €6.50-8. If you crave something other than Greek food, this bistro serves terrific French dishes. Enjoy a fine Côte du Rhône Rouge (€11.80) to wash it all down.

New Town *Restaurant Ellinikon* (☎ 2241 028 111, G Papanikolaou 6) Mains €5-6.50. This restaurant excels in traditional Greek fare. The stifado is highly recommended, but leave room for the luscious iced caramel, which often features as dessert of the day.

Princess (☎ 2241 020 068, Mandilara 26) Mains €6-8. This is a classy place offering Mediterranean dishes from Greece, Spain, Italy and the Middle East. Great for that

DODECANESE

special, romantic night out; the chef's recommendation: gorgonzola chicken (€9.40).

To Steki tou Tsima (☎ 2241 074 390, *Peloponisou 22*) Seafood mezedes €4.50-5.50. To Steki is an unpretentious and totally untouristy fish restaurant on the south side of New Town. Sample from an imaginative and occasionally unusual array of fish (such as *yermanos*, €7.50) and shellfish-based mezedes (try *fouskes*, €3.50).

Cafes

Feverish touting reaches its acme at the patisseries for people-watching, with names like *Nirefs*, *Demetriades* and *Cofea* bordering the New Market. Nevertheless, they're convivial meeting places. Coffee and cake costs around €5.50.

There's a lively cafe strip on S. Venizelou.

Entertainment

Old Town *Son et Lumière* (☎ 2241 021 922, *entrance Plateia Rimini*) Admission €3.50. This sound-and-light show, staged in the grounds of the Palace of the Grand Masters, depicts the Turkish siege of Rhodes and is superior to most such efforts. A noticeboard outside gives the times for performances.

Kafe Besara (☎ 2241 030 363, *Sofokleous 11-12*) This Aussie-owned place is one of the Old Town's liveliest bars, and a great place to hang about.

Mango Cafe Bar (☎ 2241 024 877, *Dorieos 3*) This bar claims to have the cheapest drinks in the Old Town as well as Internet access and is the preferred haunt of local expats, scuba divers and diehard travellers.

Resalto Club (☎ 2241 020 520, *Plateia Damagitou*) Admission free, beer €6, cocktails €9. Open 11pm until late. This Greek music centre features live music on weekends. The repertoire ranges from *entehno* (artistic compositional) to *laïko* (popular) to *rembetiko* (blues).

New Town There is a plethora of discos and bars in New Town – over 600 at last count and rising. The two main areas are called Top Street and the Street of Bars. Top Street is Alexandrou Diakou and the Street of Bars is Orfanidou, where a

cacophony of Western music blares from every establishment.

Down Under Bar (☎ 2241 032 982, *Orfanidou 37*) Shots €3. For a wild night of dancing on the bar, make for this place.

Red Lion (*Orfanidou 9*) Pints €2.30. For something more subdued, this bar has the relaxed atmosphere of a British pub. Ron and Vasilis will gladly answer questions about Rhodes for the price of a drink.

Colorado Entertainment Centre (☎ 2241 075 120, *Akti Miaouli & Orfanidou 57*) This is a popular place. The Colorado consists of three venues in one – the Dancing Club, the Heaven Night Club and a live band venue. There is more than enough fun for a week in this enormous palace of hype.

Shopping

Good buys in Rhodes' Old Town are gold and silver jewellery, leather goods and ceramics (although leather goods are cheaper in Turkey). Look around and be discriminating – it's quite acceptable to haggle.

Manuel Music Center (☎ 2241 028 266, 25 Martiou 10-13) For good-quality Greek music, ie, not 'Zorba the Greek does Syrtaki' tourist music, all the latest and more Greek CDs are on sale here.

Getting Around Rhodes Town

Local buses leave from Mandraki. Bus No 2 goes to Analipsi, No 3 to Rodini, No 4 to Agios Dimitrios and No 5 to Monte Smith. You can buy tickets at the kiosk on Mandraki.

EASTERN RHODES

Rhodes' best beaches are on the east coast. There are frequent buses to Lindos, but some beaches are a bit of a trek from the road. It's possible to find uncrowded stretches of coast even in high season.

Kalithea Thermi, 10km from Rhodes Town, is a derelict Italian-built spa. Within the complex are crumbling colonnades, domed ceilings and mosaic floors. Buses from Rhodes Town stop opposite the turn-off to the spa. The beach is used by Rhodes' diving schools (see Activities in the Rhodes Town section). To the right there's a small sandy beach (with a snack bar); take the track which veers right from the turn-off to the spa. Kalithea is currently being restored.

Faliraki Beach, 5km farther south, is the island's premier resort and comes complete with high-rise hotels, fast-food joints and bars. Although the main stretch of beach is crowded, the bay at the extreme southern end is uncrowded and popular with nude bathers. The bus stop is close to the beach.

Ladiko Beach is next along. Touted locally as 'Anthony Quinn Beach', this is in fact two back-to-back coves with a pebbly beach on the north side and volcanic rock platforms on the south. The swimming is good and development is relatively low-key.

At Kolymbia, further down the coast, a right turn leads in over 4km of pine-fringed road to the **Epta Piges** (Seven Springs), a beautiful spot where a lake fed by springs can be reached either along a path or through a tunnel. There are no buses around here, so take a Lindos bus and get off at the turn-off.

Back on the coast, **Kolymbia** and **Tsambika** are good but crowded beaches. A steep road (signposted) leads in 1.5km to reach **Moni Tsambikas**, from where there are terrific views. The monastery is a place of pilgrimage for childless women. On 18 September, the monastery's festival day, women climb up to it on their knees and then pray to conceive.

Arhangelos, 4km farther on and inland, is a large agricultural village with a tradition of carpet weaving and handmade goatskin boots production. Just before Arhangelos there is a turn-off to **Stegna Beach**, and just after to the lovely sandy cove of **Agathi**; both are reasonably quiet. The **Castle of Faraklos** above Agathi was a prison for recalcitrant knights and the island's last stronghold to fall to the Turks. The fishing port of **Haraki**, just south of the castle, has a pebbled beach. There are more beaches between here and Vlyha Bay, 2km from Lindos.

Places to Stay & Eat Accommodation at Faliraki Beach is monopolised by package tour companies, so you are advised to move on, or camp if you have the gear.

Faliraki Camping (☎ 2241 085 358, Faliraki) Adult/tent €3.50/2.70. This once pleasant ground with restaurant, bar and minimarket is now marred by ugly construction work for new studios.

Dining in Faliraki is basically hit-and-miss. If you are serious about eating here, you might as well have a curry or a pizza.

Faliraki Raj (☎ 2241 086 986, Lindou) Curry €6-7. Opposite the church, Faliraki Raj won't be same as home, but will make a spicy change from mousakas.

La Strada Ristorante (☎ 2241 085 878, Lindou) Pizzas €4-5. Apart from crispy, wood-oven pizzas, La Strada offers up over 100 variations of pasta, fish and meat.

Lindos Λίνδος
postcode 851 07 • pop 724
Lindos village, 47km from Rhodes, lies below the Acropolis and is a showpiece of dazzling-white 17th-century houses, many

with courtyards with black-and-white *hohlakia* (pebble mosaic) floors. Once the dwellings of wealthy admirals, many have been bought and restored by foreign celebrities. The main thoroughfares are lined with tourist shops and cafes, so you need to explore the labyrinthine alleyways to fully appreciate the place.

Lindos is the most famous of the Dodecanese's ancient cities, receiving 500,000 visitors a year. It was an important Doric settlement because of its excellent vantage point and good harbour. It was first established around 2000 BC and is overlaid with a conglomeration of Byzantine, Frankish and Turkish remains.

After the founding of the city of Rhodes, Lindos declined in commercial importance, but remained an important place of worship. The ubiquitous St Paul landed here en route to Rome. The Byzantine fortress was strengthened by the knights, and also used by the Turks.

The 15th-century **Church of Agia Panagia** on Acropolis is festooned with 18th-century frescoes.

Orientation & Information The town is pedestrianised. All vehicular traffic terminates on the central square of Plateia Eleftherias, from where the main drag, Acropolis, begins. The donkey terminus is a little way along here.

The municipal tourist information office (☎ 2244 031 900) is on Plateia Eleftherias, open 7.30am to 9pm daily. Pallas Travel (☎ 2244 031 494, fax 2244 031 595) and Lindos Sun Tours (☎ 2244 031 333), both on Acropolis, have room-letting services. The latter also rents cars and motorcycles.

The Commercial Bank of Greece, with ATM, is by the donkey terminus. The National Bank of Greece is on the street opposite the Church of Agia Panagia. Turn right at the donkey terminus for the post office. There is no OTE, but there are cardphones on Plateia Eleftherias and the Acropolis. Lindos' two Internet cafes are near the post office.

The privately owned Lindos Lending Library, on Acropolis, is well stocked with English books. It also has a laundrette (€7.30 per load).

The Acropolis of Lindos The Acropolis (*☎ 2244 031 258; admission €3.50; open 8am-6.30pm Tues-Sun, 12.30pm-6.30pm Mon*) is spectacularly perched atop a 116m-high rock. It's about a 10-minute climb to the well-signposted entrance gate. Once inside, a flight of steps leads to a large square.

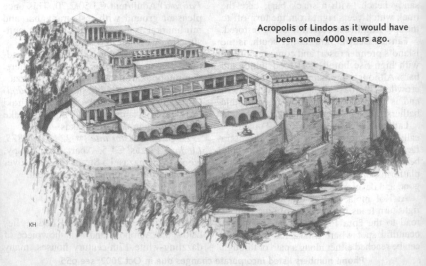

Acropolis of Lindos as it would have been some 4000 years ago.

KH

On the left (facing the next flight of steps) is a trireme (warship) hewn out of the rock by the sculptor Pythocretes. A statue of Hagesandros, priest of Poseidon, originally stood on the deck of the ship. At the top of the steps ahead, you enter the Acropolis by a vaulted corridor. At the other end, turn sharp left through an enclosed room to reach a row of storerooms on the right.

The stairway on the right leads to the remains of a 20-columned **Hellenistic stoa** (200 BC). The Byzantine **Church of Agios Ioannis** is to the right of this stairway. The wide stairway behind the stoa leads to a 5th-century BC propylaeum, beyond which is the 4th-century **Temple to Athena**, the site's most important ancient ruin. Athena was worshipped on Lindos as early as the 10th century BC, so this temple has replaced earlier ones on the site. From its far side there are splendid views of Lindos village and its beach.

Donkey rides to the Acropolis cost €3.50 one way.

Places to Stay & Eat Accommodation is expensive and reservations are essential in summer. The following two places are near each other on the north side of the village. Follow the donkeys heading to the Acropolis for about 150m to find them. *Lindos Pension* (☎ 2244 031 369) Doubles €35.20. This is the cheapest option. Rooms are small and plain, but clean and pleasant.

Pension Electra (☎ 2244 031 266, Lindos) Doubles with bathroom €50. Electra has a roof terrace with superb views and a beautiful shady garden. Rooms have air-con.

Kalypso (☎ 2244 031 669) Mains €5.50-7. Set in one of Lindos' historic buildings, Kalypso is open for lunch and dinner. Try either sausages in mustard, chicken in coconut sauce or rabbit stew in red wine.

WESTERN RHODES
Western Rhodes is more green and forested than the east coast, but it's more exposed to winds so the sea tends to be rough, and the beaches are mostly of pebbles or stones. Nevertheless, tourist development is rampant, and consists of the suburb resorts of Ixia, Trianda and Kremasti. Paradisi, despite being next to the airport, has retained some of the feel of a traditional village.

Ialysos Ιαλυσός
Like Lindos, Ialysos, 10km from Rhodes, is a hotchpotch of Doric, Byzantine and medieval remains. The Doric city was built on Filerimos Hill, which was an excellent vantage point, attracting successive invaders. The only ancient remains are the foundations of a 3rd-century BC temple and a restored 4th-century BC fountain. Also at the site are the restored **Monastery of Our Lady** and the **Chapel of Agios Georgios**.

The ruined **fortress** *(admission €2.40; open 8am-5pm Tues-Sun)* was used by Süleyman the Magnificent during his siege of Rhodes Town. No buses go to ancient Ialysos. The airport bus stops at Trianda, on the coast. Ialysos is 5km inland from here.

Ancient Kamiros
Αρχαία Κάμειρος
The extensive **ruins** *(admission €2.40; open 8am-5pm Tues-Sun)* of the Doric city of Kamiros stand on a hillside above the west coast, 34km from Rhodes Town. The ancient city, known for its figs, oil and wine, reached the height of its powers in the 6th century BC. By the 4th century BC, it had been superseded by Rhodes. Most of the city was destroyed by earthquakes in 226 and 142 BC, but the layout is easily discernible.

From the entrance, walk straight ahead and down the steps. The semicircular rostrum on the right is where officials made speeches to the public. Opposite are the remains of a **Doric temple** with one standing column. The area next to it, with a row of intact columns, was probably where the public watched priests performing rites in the temple. Ascend the wide stairway to the ancient city's main street. Opposite the top of the stairs is one of the best preserved of the **Hellenistic houses** that lined the street. Walk along the street, ascend three flights of steps, and continue ahead to the ruins of the 3rd-century **great stoa**, which had a 206m portico supported by two rows of Doric columns. It was built on top of a huge

DODECANESE

6th-century cistern which supplied the houses with rainwater through an advanced drainage system. Behind the stoa, at the city's highest point, stood the **Temple to Athena**, with terrific views inland.

Buses from Rhodes Town to Kamiros stop on the coast road, 1km from the site.

Kamiros to Monolithos

Skala Kamirou, 13.5km south of Ancient Kamiros, is a fairly unremarkable place sporting a few market gardens, a scattering of tavernas and a petrol station. More importantly, it serves as the access port for travellers heading to and from the island of Halki (see the Halki section later). The road south from here to Monolithos has some of the island's most impressive scenery. From Skala Kamirou the road winds uphill with great views across to Halki. This is just a taste of what's to come at the ruined 16th-century **Castle of Kastellos**, reached along a rough road from the main road, 2km beyond Skala Kamirou. There is a left fork to Embonas (see The Interior, later in this section) 8km farther along. The main road continues for another 9km to **Siana**, a picturesque village below Mt Akramytis (825m), famed for its honey and *souma*, a local firewater.

The village of Monolithos, 5km beyond Siana, has the spectacularly sited **Castle of Monolithos** perched on a sheer 240m high rock and reached along a dirt track. Continuing along this track, at the fork bear right for **Moni Georgiou** and left for the very pleasant shingled **Fourni Beach**.

Places to Stay & Eat There is little accommodation along this stretch of coast.

Hotel Thomas (☎ 2246 061 291, *Monolithos*) Doubles €29.50. You could try this hotel in Monolithos village.

Althemeni Restaurant (☎ 2246 031 303, *Skala Kamirou*) Fish €40 per kg. This place is right on the harbourfront and offers a wide range of fish, as well as grills and mayirefta.

SOUTHERN RHODES

South of Lindos, Rhodes becomes progressively less developed. Although **Pefki**, 2km south of Lindos, does get package tourists,

it's still possible to get out of earshot of other tourists, away from the main beach.

Lardos is a pleasant village 6km west of Lindos and 2km inland from Lardos Beach. From the far side of Lardos a right turn leads in 4km to **Moni Agias Ypsenis** (Monastery of Our Lady) through hilly, green countryside.

Heading south from Lardos, don't miss the almost hidden **Glystra Beach**, 4km south along the coast road. This diminutive bay is one of the best swimming spots along the whole eastern coastline.

The well-watered village of **Laerma** is 12km north-west of Lardos. From here it's another 5km to the beautifully sited 9th-century **Moni Tharri**, which was the island's first monastery and has been re-established as a monastic community. It contains some fine 13th-century frescoes.

Asklipion, 8km north of Gennadi, is an unspoilt village with the ruins of yet another castle and the 11th-century **Church of Kimisis Theotokou**, which has fine Byzantine wall paintings.

Gennadi Γεννάδι
postcode 851 09 • pop 542

Gennadi, (ye-**nah**-dhi) 13km south of Lardos is an attractive, largely untouched agricultural village masquerading as a holiday centre. For independent travellers it is probably the best base for a protracted stay in the south. The village itself, a patchwork of narrow streets and whitewashed houses, is set several hundred metres back from the beach.

Places to Stay & Eat *Effie's Dreams Apartments* (☎ 2244 043 410, fax 2244 043 437, e *dreams@srh.forthnet.gr*, w *www .rodosnet.gr*) Doubles/triples €35.50/44. This place, right by an enormous 800-year-old mulberry tree, has modern, spotlessly clean studios with lovely rural and sea vistas from the communal balcony. The friendly Greek-Australian owners will meet you if you call ahead. Internet access is also available.

Effie's Dream Cafe Bar (☎ 2244 043 410) Snacks €2.50-4. Below the apartments of the same name, Effie's serves drinks and tasty snacks such as village sausage with onions and peppers (€2.40).

I Kouzina tis Mamas (☎ 2244 043 547) Pasta dishes €3.50. You will find this pizza and pasta restaurant along the main street, dishing up a wide range of Greek grills as well.

Gennadi to Prasonisi

From Gennadi an almost uninterrupted beach of pebbles, shingle and sand dunes extends down to **Plimmyri**, 11km south. It's easy to find deserted stretches.

From Plimmyri the main road continues to **Kattavia**, Rhodes' most southerly village. The 11km dirt road north to Messanagros winds through terrific scenery. From Kattavia a 10km road leads south to the remote **Prasonisi**, the island's southernmost point, once joined to Rhodes by a narrow sandy isthmus now split by encroaching seas. It's a popular spot for windsurfing.

Places to Stay & Eat *Studios Platanos* (☎ 2244 046 027, Lahania) Studios €26.50-30. Owned by the proprietors of Taverna Platanos, each air-conditioned studio has a kitchenette and fridge. Lahania is signposted 2km off the main highway.

Taverna Platanos (☎ 2244 046 027, Plateia Iroön Polytehniou, Lahania) Mains €3-5. Platanos makes for a popular Sunday outing, dining on the tiny village square amid running water. The food served is wholesome and filling village fare; try chickpeas (€2.60) or locally produced pork chops (€5).

The Faros Taverna (☎ 2244 091 030, Prasonisi) Doubles €30; meals €7-8. One of two tavernas on the beach, Faros has comfortable rooms that attract windsurfers. The attached restaurant serves up tasty, filling fare.

South of Monolithos

Rhodes' south-west coast doesn't see as many visitors as other parts of the island. It is lonely and exposed and has only recently acquired a sealed road, completing the network around this southern quadrant of the island. Forest fires in recent years have devastated many of the west-facing hillsides and there is a general end-of-the-world feeling about the whole region.

The beaches south of Monolithos are prone to strong winds. From the important crossroads village of **Apolakkia**, 10km south of Monolithos, a road crosses the island to Gennadi, passing through the unspoilt villages of **Arnitha** and **Vati** with an optional detour to **Istrios** and **Profilia**. A turn-off to the left 7km south of Apolakkia leads to the 18th-century **Moni Skiadi**. It's a serene place with terrific views down to the coast, and there is free basic accommodation for visitors.

THE INTERIOR

The east-west roads that cross the island have great scenery and very little traffic. If you have transport they're well worth exploring. It's also good cycling territory if you have a suitably geared bicycle.

Petaloudes Πεταλούδες

Petaloudes (*Valley of the Butterflies; admission €2.20; open 8.30am-sunset 1 May-30 Sept*), one of the more popular 'sights' on the package tour itinerary, is reached along a 6km turn-off from the west coast road, 2.5km south of Paradisi.

The so-called 'butterflies' (*Callimorpha quadripunctarea*) are in fact strikingly coloured moths that are lured to this gorge of rustic footbridges, streams and pools by the scent of the resin exuded by the styrax trees. Regardless of what you may see other tourists doing, do not make any noises to disturb the butterflies; their numbers are declining rapidly, largely due to noise disturbance. Better still, don't visit and leave them alone. If you must, there are buses to Petaloudes from Rhodes Town.

Around Petaloudes

From Petaloudes a winding cross-island road leads to the 18th-century **Moni Kalopetras** built by Alexander Ypsilandis, the grandfather of the Greek freedom fighter. This same road leads across the central mountain spine of roads through a rather dry landscape full of olive trees to the pretty village of **Psinthos** which makes for a very pleasant lunch break.

From Psinthos you can choose to loop back to Rhodes Town (22km) via a fast but undistinguished direct route passing through **Kalythies**, or head further south and pick up the very pretty cross island route from **Kolymbia** to **Salakos**.

Places to Stay & Eat *Artemidis Restaurant & Rooms* (☎ 2241 051 735, *Psinthos*) Doubles €30. This restaurant serves tasty traditional Greek fare and has a swimming pool. The rooms are above the restaurant.

Pigi Fasouli Estiatorio (☎ 2241 050 071, *Psinthos*). Mains €4.50-6. Dine on succulent steaks or mezedes under cool plane trees next to running water. Look for signs from the main square in Psinthos to find it.

Salakos & Mt Profitis Ilias
Σάλακος & Ορος Προφήτης Ηλίας
This route to Mt Profitis Ilias (pro-**fee**-tis ee-**lee**-as) and Salakos (**sah**-la-kos) across the north central highlands of Rhodes is perhaps the most scenic of all the day-trip drives or rides. It can be tackled from either the west or the east coast of Rhodes, though the most attractive way is from east to west.

Start at the signposted turn-off near **Kolymbia**. Shortly beyond you may wish to stop briefly to visit **Epta Piges** (Seven Springs), a cool, shady valley with running water and, you guessed it, seven springs. This is a popular tourist attraction in its own right. Heading up and inland you will next come to the villages of **Arhipoli** and **Eleousa**, once used by the Italians as hill stations. The road now climbs through a landscape that becomes more and more forested. Two kilometres from Eleousa you will pass the small Byzantine church of **Agios Nikolaos Foundouklis** with its faded frescoes. This is a good picnic spot – there are tables, chairs and spring water.

It is a further 6km along a winding, pine-shrouded road to the summit of **Mt Profitis Ilias** (780m). The surrounding forest is lush and cool and a pleasant relief for cyclists.

It is downhill from here and a further 12km of winding and cruising will bring you to the village of **Salakos**. If you are on foot you can walk down on an established track that begins near the easy-to-find **Moni Profiti Ilia**. It will take you about 45 minutes to walk down to Salakos. The village is a cheery place, with a small square and fountain and several cafes for coffee or cold beers.

From Salakos it is only 9.5km downhill to the west coast village of **Kalavarda**.

Wine Country
From Salakos you may detour to **Embonas** on the slopes of Mt Attavyros (1215m), the island's highest mountain. Embonas is the wine capital of Rhodes and produces some of the island's best tipples. The red Cava Emery, or Zacosta and white Villare from Emery wines in Embonas in Rhodes are good choices. You can taste and buy them in the **Emery Winery** (☎ 2246 029 111, *Embonas; free wine tasting to 3pm Mon-Fri*).

Embonas village is no great shakes, despite being touted by EOT as a 'traditional village'. You may wish to detour around Mt Attavyros to **Agios Isidoros**, 14km south of Embona, a prettier and still unspoilt wine-producing village that you can visit en route to Siana.

Halki Χάλκη

postcode 851 10 • pop 280
Halki is a small rocky island just 16km off the west coast of Rhodes. Like many small islands in the Dodecanese it has suffered the depredations of a failed economy (sponge diving), a chronic lack of water and subsequent population depletion due to migration. Many Halkiots now live in Tarpon Springs, Florida, where they have established a buoyant sponge-fishing community. Still, Halki has undergone a rejuvenation in recent years thanks to rather select visitors who come to Halki with discreet villa and studio rental.

Getting To/From Halki
Ferry L.A.N.E. Lines of Crete includes Halki on its long, twice weekly 'milk run' from Rhodes to Piraeus via Crete and Milos.

Such destinations include Rhodes (two hours, €6), Karpathos-Pigadia (three hours, €6.30), Crete-Sitia (7½ hours, €11.90) and Piraeus (22 hours, €29.50).

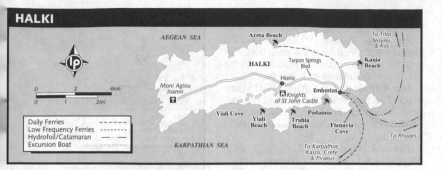

HALKI

AEGEAN SEA

Areta Beach

To Tilos
Nisyros
& Kos

HALKI

Tarpon Springs
Blvd

Kania
Beach

Horio

Moni Agiou
Ioanni

Knights
of St John Castle

Emborios

Yiali Cove

Yiali
Beach

Podamos

Trahia
Beach

Ftenayia
Cove

To Rhodes

KARPATHIAN SEA

To Karpathos,
Kasos, Crete
& Piraeus

Daily Ferries
Low Frequency Ferries
Hydrofoil/Catamaran
Excursion Boat

0   2   4km
0   1   2mi

Hydrofoil One hydrofoil a week connects Halki with Rhodes (1¼ hours, €11.50), Tilos (3¼ hours, €18) and Kalymnos (4½ hours, €24.50). Check for current departure days.

Catamaran The *Dodekanisos Express* catamaran calls in twice a week at Halki on its run up the Dodecanese to Patmos. From Halki the departure north is at around 9.55am and back to Rhodes at around 7.40pm.

Caique Halki is linked to Skala Kamirou on Rhodes. Departures (1½ hours, €5.50) from Halki are at 6am (Monday to Saturday) and 9am (Sunday). From Skala Kamirou departures are 2.30pm (Monday to Saturday) and 4pm (Sunday).

To get to Skala Kamirou from Rhodes Town, take the 1.30pm Monolithos bus from the west side bus station (€3.50). There are no connecting buses on Sunday morning.

Getting Around Halki

There are no buses or taxis on the island, or rental cars or motorbikes, but there are water taxis to the main beaches and the island of Alimnia. Better bring a stout pair of walking shoes.

EMBORIOS Εμπορειός

The attractive port town of Emborios resembles Gialos on Symi, but on a smaller scale. The port is draped around a horseshoe bay and former sea captains' mansions – some renovated, others still in a state of disrepair – rise up around the bay in a colourful architectural display. Cars

are all but banned from the harbour, so the Emborios waterside enjoys a tranquil, motor-free setting.

Orientation & Information

The quay is in the middle of the harbour. There is one road out of Emborios, grandly named Tarpon Springs Boulevard for the ex-Halkiots in Florida, who financed most of its construction. It passes Podamos, the island's only sandy beach, and goes as far as Moni Agiou Ioanni.

There is no official tourist office on Halki. The two travel agents on the harbour may help out with queries. There is no bank or ATM on Halki – the nearest is on Rhodes. The travel agents will exchange money.

Things to See

The impressive stone **clock tower** at the southern side of the harbour is a gift from the Halkiots of Florida. While the clock tower may look good, don't rely on it for the time. Each of the four faces is stuck on a different hour of the day.

The **Church of Agios Nikolaos** has the tallest belfry in the Dodecanese and boasts a particularly well-made and impressive hohlaki courtyard on the east side.

Places to Stay & Eat

Accommodation is in short supply. Book beforehand wherever possible. *Captain's House* (☎ 2246 045 201) Doubles with bathroom €29.50. This beautiful 19th-century mansion with period furniture and a tranquil, tree-shaded garden is the most pleasant

DODECANESE

place to stay. It is owned by a retired Greek sea captain and his British wife.

Argyrenia Rooms (☎ *2246 045 205*) Doubles €20.50. Rooms are small but clean and this place is open all year. It is at the junction with the road to Kania beach.

Mavri Thalassa (☎ *2246 045 021*) Mains €4-5. This restaurant at the end of the harbour is well regarded by locals and does good fish dishes. The shrimp with rice (€5) is recommended.

Taverna Maria (☎ *2246 045 089*) Mayirefta €3. This is a friendly family restaurant with good mayirefta dishes. The owners' special is lamb fricassee (€5.30).

AROUND HALKI

Podamos beach is the closest and the best beach. It is a 15-minute walk from Emborios in the direction of Horio. There is one cantina and one restaurant.

Horio, a 30-minute walk along Tarpon Springs Boulevard from Emborios, was the 'pirate-proof' inland town. Once a thriving community of 3000 people, it's now derelict and uninhabited. A path leads from Horio's churchyard to a Knights of St John castle.

Moni Agiou Ioanni is a two-hour, 8km, unshaded walk along a concrete road from Horio. The church and courtyard, protected by the shade of an enormous cypress tree, is a quiet, tranquil place, but it comes alive each year from 28–29 August during the feast of the church's patron, St John. During this time there is music and dancing and free food and wine. Beds are available all year for a small donation to the church.

Karpathos
Κάρπαθος

postcode 857 00 ● pop 5323

If ever there was a Greek island that combined the right proportions of size, attractiveness, remoteness, water activities and general good feel, that island might just be the elongated island of Karpathos (*kar*-pah-thos), midway between Crete and Rhodes. Karpathos has rugged mountains, numerous

beaches – among the best in the Aegean – and unspoilt villages. So far, it has not succumbed to the worst excesses of mass tourism.

The island is traversed by a north-south mountain range. For hundreds of years the north and south parts of the island were isolated from one another and so they developed independently. It is even thought that the northerners and southerners have different ethnic origins. The northern village of Olymbos is of endless fascination to ethnologists for the age-old customs of its inhabitants.

Karpathos has a relatively uneventful history. Unlike almost all other Dodecanese islands, it was never under the auspices of the Knights of St John. It is a wealthy island, receiving more money from emigrants living abroad (mostly in the USA) than any other Greek island.

Getting To/From Karpathos

Air There are four flights weekly to and from Athens (€88.40), up to two daily to Rhodes (€44.30) and three weekly to Kasos (€23.50). The Olympic Airways office (☎ 2245 022 150) is on the central square in Pigadia. The airport is 18km south-west of Pigadia.

Ferry Karpathos shares the same essentially limited ferry services as its neighbours Halki and Kasos. Windy weather can sometimes delay arrivals and departures.

L.A.N.E. Lines of Crete provides three services weekly to Rhodes (four hours, €13.50) via Halki (three hours, €8.20) as well as to Piraeus (18½ hours, €24.40) via Milos (13 hours, €22). Kasos (1½ hours, €5.60) is served by three weekly services.

Note that these ferries also serve the ports of Sitia (4¼ hours, €10.60) and Agios Nikolaos (seven hours, €12.90) in Crete.

Getting Around Karpathos

To/From the Airport There is no airport bus. Travellers must take a taxi (€8.80) or seek independent transport.

Bus Pigadia is the transport hub of the island; a schedule is posted at the bus terminal.

Buses serve most of the settlements in southern Karpathos. The fare is between €1 and €1.30. There is no bus between Pigadia and Olymbos or Diafani, but a bus meets the excursion boats from Pigadia at Diafani and transports people up to Olymbos.

Car, Motorcycle & Bicycle Gatoulis Car Hire (☎ 2245 022 747, fax 2245 022 814), on the east side of Pigadia on the road to Aperi, rents cars, motorcycles and bicycles. Possi Travel (☎ 2245 022 235) also arranges car and motorcycle hire.

The 19.5km stretch of road from Spoa to Olymbos is unsurfaced, but you can drive it, with care. Do not tackle this road by motorcycle or scooter. If you rent a vehicle, make it a small jeep and fill up your tank before you leave.

Taxi Pigadia's taxi rank (☎ 2245 022 705) is on Dimokratias, near the bus station. A price list is displayed. Sample taxi fares from Pigadia are as follows: Ammoöpi (€4.40), Arkasa (€8.80), Pyles (€8.80), Kyra Panagia (€14.70) and Diafani (€61.60).

Excursion Boat In summer there are daily excursion boats from Pigadia to Diafani for €14.70 return. There are also frequent boats to the beaches of Kyra Panagia and Apella for €9. Tickets can be bought at the quay.

From Diafani, excursion boats go to nearby beaches and occasionally to the uninhabited islet of Saria where there are some Byzantine remains.

PIGADIA Πηγάδια
pop 1692

Pigadia (pi-**gha**-dhi-ya) is the island's capital and main port. It's a modern town, pleasant enough, but without any eminent buildings or sites. The town is built on the edge of Vrondi Bay, a 4km-long sandy beach where you can rent water sports equipment. On the beach are the remains of the early Christian basilica of Agia Fotini.

Orientation & Information
From the quay, turn right and take the left fork onto Apodimon Karpathion, Pigadia's

DODECANESE

main thoroughfare, which leads to the central square of Plateia 5 Oktovriou.

Pigadia doesn't have an EOT but there is a local tourist information office (☎ 2245 023 835, fax 2245 023 836) in a kiosk in the middle of the harbourfront. The police (☎ 2245 022 224) are near the hospital. Nearby are the post office and OTE. Possi Travel (☎ 2245 022 148, fax 2245 022 252) is the main travel agency for ferry and air tickets.

The National Bank of Greece, which has an ATM, is situated on Apodimon Karpathion. The bus station is one block up from the waterfront on Dimokratias. There's a laundrette, Laundro Express, on Mitropolitou Apostolou. Caffe Galileo Internet 2000 (☎ 2245 023 606, ⓔ caffegal@otenet.gr), on Apodimon Karpathion, has Internet access.

Places to Stay

There's plenty of accommodation and owners usually meet the boats.

Harry's Rooms (☎ 2245 022 188, *Kyprou 2*) Singles/doubles €17.60/20.50. These rooms, just off 28 Oktovriou, are spotless.

Elias Rooms (☎ 2245 022 446, ⓔ *elias rooms@hotmail.com*) Singles/doubles with bathroom €20.50/23.50. These cosy rooms are in a quiet part of town with great views. The owner is friendly and helpful.

Rose's Studios (☎/fax 2245 022 284) Double studios €23.50 with kitchen. Fairly high up behind Pigadia are these well-kept studios with bathroom and kitchen.

Hotel Karpathos (☎ 2245 022 347) Singles/doubles with bathroom €23.50/25. This C-class hotel has light, airy rooms.

Hotel Avra (☎ 2245 022 388, 2245 023 486, *28 Oktovriou 50*) Doubles €29.50. This E-class hotel has small but comfortable rooms with ceiling fan, fridge and a small common kitchen.

Hotel Titania (☎ 2245 022 144, fax 2245 023 307) Singles/doubles €38/45. This C-class hotel, opposite the Karpathos, has

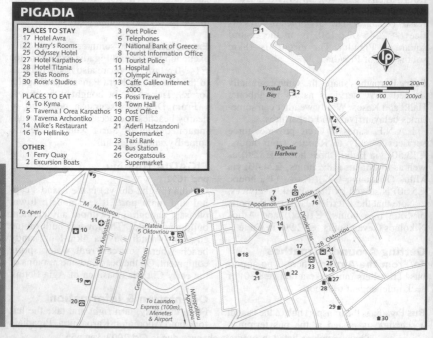

PIGADIA

PLACES TO STAY
17 Hotel Avra
22 Harry's Rooms
25 Odyssey Hotel
27 Hotel Karpathos
28 Hotel Titania
29 Elias Rooms
30 Rose's Studios

PLACES TO EAT
4 To Kyma
5 Taverna I Orea Karpathos
9 Taverna Archontiko
14 Mike's Restaurant
16 To Helliniko

OTHER
1 Ferry Quay
2 Excursion Boats

3 Port Police
6 Telephones
7 National Bank of Greece
8 Tourist Information Office
10 Tourist Police
11 Hospital
12 Olympic Airways
13 Caffe Galileo Internet 2000
15 Possi Travel
18 Town Hall
19 Post Office
20 OTE
21 Aderfi Hatzandoni Supermarket
23 Taxi Rank
24 Bus Station
26 Georgatsoulis Supermarket

Vrondi Bay

Pigadia Harbour

To Aperi

M. Mattheou

Ethnikis Andristasis

Plateia 5 Oktovriou

Georgiou Lozou

Apodimon

Karpathion

Dimokratias

28 Oktovriou

To Laundro Express (100m), Menetes & Airport

Mitropolitou Apostolou

DODECANESE

spacious, pleasant rooms and is open all year.

Odyssey Hotel (☎ *2245 023 240, fax 2245 023 762)* Double/triple studios €35.20/41. Each studio has a kitchenette, phone, music, TV, fridge, room safe and balcony, and fans are available on demand.

Places to Eat

Mike's Restaurant (☎ *2245 022 727, Apodimon Karpathion)* Grills €4.20-10.80. One of the longer-standing and more popular eateries, Mike's serves up consistently good, solid fare at reasonable prices.

Taverna I Orea Karpathos (☎ *2245 022 501, Limani)* Mains €3.50-5. Near the quay, I Orea Karpathos serves a wide range of traditional Karpathian dishes and reputedly the best *makarounes* (€4.40) in Pigadia.

To Helliniko (☎ *2245 023 932, Apodimon Karpathion)* Daily specials €3.80-8.80. Boasting a pleasant outdoor terrace and a tasteful interior, the Helliniko's Karpathian goat stifado (€5) is particularly commendable.

To Kyma (☎ *2245 022 496, Limani)* Fish €28/kg. To Kyma is known for its top-class fish dishes and offers fine harbourside dining.

Taverna Archontiko (☎ *2245 022 531)* Mains €5-9.50. Open evenings only. Rooftop dining is at its best at this popular restaurant. Try the green pepper chicken (€6.50).

Karpathos has several **supermarkets** (try Georgatsoulis or Aderfi Hatzandoni) and **bakeries**.

SOUTHERN KARPATHOS
Ammoöpi Αμμοοπή
If you are seeking sun and sand and some of the best and clearest water in the whole of the Aegean head for Ammoöpi (Amm-oh-oh-**pee**), 8km south of Pigadia. This is *the* place on the island to enjoy eating, sleeping, drinking, swimming and snorkelling to the max. There are four buses daily from Pigadia. Ammoöpi is a scattered beach resort without any centre or easily identifiable landmarks, so ask the bus or taxi driver to drop you off at whichever establishment you decide to check.

Places to Stay & Eat *Ammoöpi Beach Rooms* (☎ *2245 081 123, Mikri Ammoöpi)* Doubles €12. With spotless, simply furnished rooms, this is the cheapest place to stay. The rooms are at the northern end of Ammoöpi.

Hotel Sophia (☎/fax *2245 081 078)* Doubles/triples €36/44. This hotel is farther back along the main road, behind the Blue Sea Hotel.

Blue Sea Hotel (☎ *2245 081 036, fax 2245 081 095,* @ *huguette@hellasnet.gr)* Doubles €44. Each of the 27 comfortable double rooms has a fridge and ceiling fan and the owners host a 'Karpathos Night' (playing Karpathos music) every Wednesday evening.

Vardes (☎ *2245 081 111, fax 2245 081 112)* Double studios €44. For seekers of total quiet relaxation consider Vardes – a small block of very tasteful, spacious and airy studios set back against the hillside. All have phone and kitchenette.

Taverna Ilios (☎ *2245 081 148)* Mains €4.70-6. Offering Greek and international cuisine, Ilios serves up large portions and is just back from the beach. The chef recommends the Ilios fillet (€9.50) for diners.

Ammoopi Taverna (☎ *2245 081 138)* At the far northern end of Ammoöpi and right on the beach is this mid-range eatery. Food is good but service is brusque. There is a Greek music night once a week.

Menetes Μενετές
Menetes (Me-ne-**tes**) is perched on top of a sheer cliff which is 8km above Pigadia. It's a picturesque, unspoilt village with pastel-coloured neoclassical houses lining its main street. Behind the main street are narrow, stepped alleyways that wind between more modest whitewashed dwellings. The village has a little **museum** on the right as you come from Pigadia. The owner of Taverna Manolis will open it up for you.

Places to Stay & Eat *Mike Rigas domatia* (☎ *2245 081 269)* Doubles/triples with bathroom €16.20/20.50. These domatia are in a traditional Karpathian house on the north side of Menetes down a side road. The garden brims with trees and flowers.

Best Beach Guide

The Dodecanese is blessed with an abundance of beautiful beaches. The question is: where are they?

Ammoöpi Beach on Karpathos is probably the best overall beach in the Dodecanese for accessibility, beauty and water clarity. **Apella** and **Kyra Panagia** beaches also on Karpathos are less easily accessible, but offer great skin diving.

Lipsi in the far north of the Dodecanese has a collection of very presentable and quiet swimming choices such as **Katsadia** and **Makrys Gialos** beaches, while sandy **Podamos Beach** on Halki is one of the island's best features.

For windsurfing, head to the north coast of Kos – **Tingaki** and **Kamari** are popular spots, while **Afiarti Bay** on Karpathos and **Prasonisi** on Rhodes are only for the pros. Scuba divers are limited to **Therma Kallithea** in Rhodes and Kalymnos, while naturists will usually find at least one nudist beach on each of the islands.

Where there are people and crowds you'll find the dreaded – for some – jet skis and water skiing. Rhodes' Ixia beach is one such action spot.

The soft underbelly of Kos has the longest stretch of beach in the islands. There are more sandy beaches than days in the week; some are quiet, others are action-packed.

There's a beach for every taste in the Dodecanese; just pack your gear and find it!

Taverna Manolis (☎ 2245 081 103) Mains €4.50-7. This taverna dishes up generous helpings of grilled meat.

Fiesta Dionysos (☎ 2245 081 269) Mains €4-6. This place specialises in local dishes, including omelette made with artichokes and Karpathian sausages.

Arkasa & Finiki Αρκάσα & Φοινίκι

Arkasa (ar-**ka**-sa), 9km farther on, straddles a ravine. It is changing from a traditional village to holiday resort. Turn right at the T-junction to reach the authentic village square.

A turn-off left, just before the ravine, leads after 500m to the remains of the 5th-century Basilica of Agia Sophia. Two chapels stand amid mosaic fragments and columns. Agios Nikolaos beach is just south across the headland from here.

The serene fishing village of Finiki (fi-**ni**-ki) lies 2km north of Arkasa. There is no decent swimming here as in Arkasa, but it is a pretty diversion while on your way north. The little sculpture at the harbour commemorates the heroism of seven local fishers during WWII – locals will tell you the story.

Places to Stay & Eat *Glaros Studios* (☎ 2245 061 015, 2245 061 016, Agios Nikolaos) Double studios €44-50. Done out in Karpathiot style and right on Agios Nikolaos beach, these studios have raised sofa-style beds and large terraces with sun beds, and enjoy a cool sea breeze.

Eleni Studios (☎/fax 2245 061 248, Arkasa) Double apartments €44. These fully-equipped apartments are on the left along the road to Finiki. The tidy complex boasts a swimming pool.

Pine Tree Studios (mobile ☎ 69 7736 9948, Adia) Doubles €35. Above the restaurant of the same name, these comfortable fridge- and kitchenette-equipped studios make for a quiet rural retreat.

Dimitrios Fisherman's Taverna (☎ 2245 061 294, Finiki) Fish platter for 2 €14.70. Locals come from all over the island to eat the fresh fish at this cosy taverna just off Finiki harbour.

Pine Tree Restaurant (mobile ☎ 69 7736 9948, Adia) Ladera €3-4.50. About 9km north of Finiki you will find this peaceful oasis under pine trees overlooking the sea. Try the homemade bread, makarounes and stifado.

Lefkos Λεύκος

Lefkos (**lef**-kos), 13km north of Finiki, and 2km from the coast road, is a burgeoning resort centred around a little fishing quay. It is a beach-lover's paradise with five superb sandy beaches. In summer Lefkos gets crowded, but at other times it still has a rugged, off-the-beaten-track feel about it.

Local boat owners sometimes take visitors to the islet of Sokastro where there is a ruined castle. Another diversion from the beaches is the ancient catacombs, reached by walking inland and looking for the brown and yellow signpost to the catacombs.

Places to Stay & Eat Accommodation tends to be block-booked by tour companies in Lefkos. Call either of the following before turning up.

Sunset Studios (☎ 2245 071 171, fax 2245 071 407) Double studios €38. Sunset Studios are high up, overlooking Golden Beach. Rooms all have sea views and are immaculate.

Golden Sands Studios (☎ 2245 071 175, fax 2245 071 219) Double studios €35. These conveniently located, breezy studios, abutting Golden Beach, have well-equipped kitchens.

Small Paradise Taverna (☎ 2245 071 184) Ladera €2.40-3. This taverna serves tasty local dishes and fresh seafood on a vine-shaded terrace.

Tou Kalymniou to Steki (☎ 2245 071 449, Lefkos) Mains €4.40-6. Also known as 'O Kalymnios' and located right by the little fishing harbour, this restaurant dishes up fish (€26.50 per kg) as well as many traditional Greek dishes. Try the crayfish salad (€3.30).

Getting There & Around There are two buses weekly to Lefkos and a taxi costs €20.50. Hitching is dicey as there is not much traffic.

Lefkos Rent A Car (☎/fax 2245 071 057) is a reliable outlet with competitive prices. The owner will deliver vehicles free of charge to anywhere in southern Karpathos.

CENTRAL KARPATHOS

Aperi, Volada, Othos and Pyles, the well-watered mountain villages to the north of Pigadia, are largely unaffected by tourism. None has any accommodation, but all have tavernas and kafeneia. **Aperi** was the island's capital from 1700 until 1892. Its ostentatious houses were built by wealthy emigrants returning from the USA. Like Aperi, **Volada** has an air of prosperity.

Othos (altitude 510m) is the island's highest village. It has a small ethnographic museum. From Othos the road winds downhill to **Pyles**, a gorgeous village of twisting streets, pastel houses and citrus groves. It clings to the slopes of Mt Kali Limni (1215m), the Dodecanese's second-highest peak.

The fine beaches of **Ahata**, **Kyra Panagia** and **Apella** can be reached along mostly dirt roads off the east coast road, but are most easily reached by excursion boat from Pigadia. Kyra Panagia and Apella both offer accommodation and tavernas. These are the best places on Karpathos for snorkelling and skin diving.

Mesohori, 4km beyond the turn-off for Lefkos, is a pretty village of whitewashed houses and stepped streets. **Spoa** village is 5km farther on at the beginning of the 19.5km dirt road to Olymbos. It overlooks the east coast and has a track down to **Agios Nikolaos Beach**.

NORTHERN KARPATHOS
Diafani & Olymbos
Διαφάνι & Ολυμπος
Diafani is Karpathos' small northern port, where scheduled ferries stop six times weekly. There's no post office or bank, but Orfanos Travel Holidays (☎ 2245 051 410), has currency exchange. There's no OTE but there are cardphones.

Clinging to the ridge of barren Mt Profitis Ilias, 4km above Diafani, Olymbos is a living museum (population 330). Women wear bright, embroidered skirts, waistcoats and headscarves, and goatskin boots. The interiors of the houses are decorated with embroidered cloth and their facades feature brightly painted, ornate plaster reliefs. The inhabitants speak in a vernacular which contains some Doric words, and some of the houses have wooden locks of a kind described by Homer. Olymbos is a matrilineal society – a family's property passes down from the mother to the first-born daughter. The women still grind corn in windmills and bake bread in outdoor communal ovens.

Olymbos, alas, is no longer a pristine backwater caught in a time warp. Tourism has taken hold in a big way and is the village's

DODECANESE

main money spinner. The 'traditional' village is finding it ever harder to remain traditional and is in danger of becoming a kind of kitsch eco-Disney for day-trippers from Pigadia. Olymbos is still fascinating, but sadly rather overrated for what it ultimately has to offer.

Places to Stay & Eat – Olymbos Pension *Olymbos* (☎ 2245 051 252) Singles/doubles €14.70/17.60. These clean, simply furnished rooms are just off the main street.

Mike's Rooms (☎ 2245 051 304) Doubles €20.50. These rooms are just beyond the bus turnaround.

Hotel Aphrodite (☎ 2245 051 307) Doubles with bathroom €30. This hotel, near the central square, has immaculate rooms.

Makarounes are served at all the restaurants in Olymbos. *Olymbos Taverna* (☎ 2245 051 252) Mains €2.90-4. You'll eat solidly here; go for the makarounes (€2.90). The service, however, can be very slow.

Mike's Taverna (☎ 2245 051 304) Mains €2-4.50. This place, directly below Mike's Rooms, is also a good option, but can get busy with the day trippers.

Samiotiko '1769' (☎ 2245 051 272) Makarounes €3.50. For a good view and top-rate loukoumades and makarounes seek out this little cafe-restaurant on the main street.

Diafani Vananda Camping (☎ 2245 051 288) Adult/tent €3.20/2.30. If you walk 30 minutes (2km) north you will reach this well-watered camping ground and hippy-style kafeneio, 50m from pebbly Vananda Beach.

Nikos Hotel (☎ 2245 051 289) Singles/doubles €20.50/25. This hotel, with comfortable rooms and breakfast included, is on the left as you enter Diafani.

Hrysi Akti (☎ 2245 051 315, fax 2245 051 215) Doubles with bathroom €29.50. This hotel is opposite the caique quay in Diafani. The first floor rooms are better and have TV and fridge.

Balaskas Hotel (☎/fax 2245 051 320, e balaskashotel@yahoo.com) Doubles €29.50. This modern property, 100m inland from the harbour, has good rooms and breakfast is included.

Chrysi Akti Taverna (☎ 2245 051 215) Mains €3.80-5.30. This taverna is popular and the service is friendly.

Mayflower (☎ 2245 051 302) Mains €5.90. Next door to Hrysi Akti, Mayflower is about your only other convenient harbourside choice.

Kasos Κάσος

postcode 858 00 • pop 1088

Kasos, 11km south of Karpathos, is really the end of the line. It's the last Dodecanese island before Crete and looking south, it is the last Greek island before Egypt. It is neither particularly easy to get to, nor to get away from if the weather in these parts is inclement. Kasos is a rocky little island with prickly pear trees, sparse olive and fig trees, drystone walls, sheep and goats.

History

Despite being diminutive and remote, Kasos has an eventful history. During Turkish rule it flourished, and by 1820 it had 11,000 inhabitants and a large mercantile fleet. Mohammad Ali, the Turkish governor of Egypt, regarded this fleet as an impediment to his plan to establish a base on Crete from which to attack the Peloponnese and quell the uprising. So, on 7 June 1824, Ali's men landed on Kasos and killed around 7000 inhabitants. This massacre is commemorated annually on the anniversary of the slaughter and Kasiots return from around the world to participate.

During the late 19th century, many Kasiots emigrated to Egypt and around 5000 of them helped build the Suez Canal. Last century many emigrated to the USA.

Getting To/From Kasos

Air There are five flights weekly to Rhodes (€44.30), and two to Karpathos (€23.50). The Olympic Airways office (☎ 041 555) is on Kritis.

Ferry L.A.N.E. Lines of Crete includes Kasos on its long run to/from Rhodes and Piraeus via Karpathos, Crete and Milos. Sample fares are: Piraeus €24 (17 hours),

Rhodes €16.20 (6½ hours) and Sitia €7.70 (2½ hours).

Excursion Boat In summer the *Athina* excursion boat (☎ 2245 041 047) travels from Fry to the uninhabited Armathia Islet (€5.90 return) where there are sandy beaches.

Getting Around Kasos
There is no bus on Kasos. The airport is only 800m along the coast road from Fry.

There are just two taxis (☎ 2245 041 158, 2245 041 278) on Kasos. Motorbikes can be rented from Frangiskos Moto Rentals (☎ 2245 041 746) for €10.30 per day.

FRY Φρυ
Fry **(free)** is the island's capital and port. It can be thoroughly explored in under an hour. It's a pleasant, ramshackle kind of place with little tourism. Its narrow whitewashed streets are usually busy with locals in animated discussion. The town's focal point is the picturesque old fishing harbour of Bouka. The suburb of Emborios is 1km east of Fry.

Orientation & Information
Turn left at the quay to reach Bouka. Veer left, and then right, and continue along the waterfront to the central square of Plateia Iroön Kasou. Turn right here to reach Kritis, Fry's main street. To reach Emborios, continue along the waterfront passing the turn-off (signposted 'Ai Mammas') for Panagia, Poli and Moni Agiou Mamma.

Kasos does not have an EOT or tourist police, but Emmanuel Manousos, at Kasos Maritime and Travel Agency (☎ 2245 041 495, e kassos@kassos-island.gr), Plateia Iroön Kasou, is helpful.

The National Bank of Greece is represented by the supermarket on Kritis. There is a Commercial Bank ATM on the south side of Fry. Kasos Maritime and Travel Agency will exchange money. The post office is near the ATM. The OTE is behind Plateia

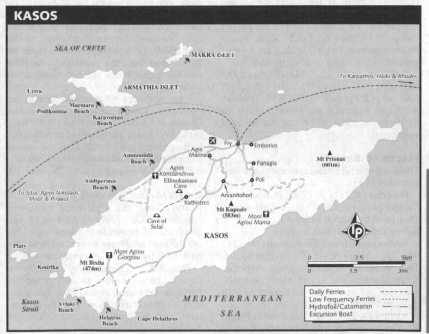

Dimokratias. Check your email at Kasosnet (☎ 2245 041 705, e kasos@kasosnet.gr) near Bouka for €4.40 per hour.

The port police (☎ 2245 041 288) are behind the Church of Agios Spyridon. The police (☎ 2245 041 222) are just beyond the post office.

Places to Stay

All of the island's accommodation is in Fry, except for one place in Emborios.

Ilias Koutlakis Rooms (☎ 2245 041 284, 2245 041 230, Hohlakoulia) Doubles with bathroom €29.50. These tidy, seafront rooms are on the left 300m along the road to Emborios.

Anesis Hotel (☎ 2245 041 234, Kritis 20) Singles/doubles with bathroom €20.50/25. This hotel is above a supermarket. Ask in the supermarket for the owner.

Anagennisis Hotel (☎ 2245 041 495, fax 041 036, e kassos@kassos-island.gr, Plateia Iroön Kasou) Singles/doubles €22/28, with bathroom €28/36.70. This hotel has clean and comfortable rooms.

Blue Sky (☎ 2245 041 047) 2/3 person studios €54.30/64.60. Some 400m metres inland these comfortable studios are another good choice for two or three persons.

Borianoula (☎ 2245 041 495, fax 2245 041 036, e kassos@kassos-island.gr, Emborios) 2/3 person studios €54.30/64.60. See Kasos Maritime and Travel Agency for the keys for these three reasonable-sized apartments.

Places to Eat

There are several restaurants and snack bars available in Fry.

O Mylos (☎ 2245 041 825, Plateia Iroön Kasou) Mains €3.50-4. Open year-round. This good restaurant offers tasty casserole dishes and grilled meat and fish.

Restaurant Mihail Karagiannis (☎ 2245 041 390) Mains €4-5. Open year-round. This dependable eating place opposite Kasos Maritime and Travel Agency is rough and ready but without a sign. Expect no frills grills and solid staple fare.

Astravi (☎ 2245 041 880, Bouka) Pizzas €5. Open evenings only. Above the Zantana

Cafe is this pizzeria and snack bar with great harbour views.

I Orea Bouka (☎ 2245 041 460, Bouka) Mains €4.50-5.50. This neat taverna has perhaps the most interesting food. I Orea Bouka, overlooking Bouka harbour, serves Greek fish and meat dishes and, occasionally, Egyptian specialities.

Entertainment

Cafe Zantana (☎ 2245 041 880, Bouka) Open 9am-late. Kasiots congregate at this trendy cafe which overlooks Bouka harbour. Mihalis, the owner, makes excellent cappuccino and cocktails.

Perigiali Bar (☎ 2245 041 767, Bouka) This diminutive bar between Bouka and Plateia Iroön Kasou is Kasos' night club. The music played is predominantly Greek.

AROUND KASOS

Kasos' best beach is the isolated, pebbled cove of **Helatros**, near Moni Agiou Georgiou. The beach has no facilities and little shade. You can get there along an 11km paved road and then a dirt road which bears left (downhill) from the road to the monastery, or along a slightly longer unpaved road from the monastery. **Avlaki** is another decent beach reached along a path from the monastery.

The mediocre **Ammounda beach**, beyond the airport near the blue-domed church of Agios Konstandinos, is the nearest to Fry. There are slightly better beaches farther along this stretch of coast, one of them the fine-pebble **Andiperatos beach** at the end of the road system. Neither has shade.

Agia Marina, 1km south-west of Fry, is a pretty village with a gleaming white-and-blue church. On 17 July the Festival of Agia Marina is celebrated here. From Agia Marina the road continues to verdant **Arvanitohori**, with fig and pomegranate trees.

Poli, 3km south-east of Fry, is the former capital, built on the ancient acropolis. **Panagia**, between Fry and Poli, has fewer than 50 inhabitants. Its once-grand sea captains' and ship owners' mansions are now derelict.

Monasteries

The island has two monasteries: **Moni Agiou Mamma** and **Moni Agiou Georgiou**. The uninhabited Moni Agiou Mamma on the south coast is a 1½ hour walk from Fry. Take the Poli road and turn left just before the village (signposted 'Ai Mammas'). The road winds uphill through a dramatic, eroded landscape of rock-strewn mountains, crumbling terraces and soaring cliffs. Eventually you will come to a sharp turn right (signposted again). From here the track descends to the blue-and-white monastery.

An 11km asphalt road leads from Fry to Moni Agiou Georgiou. There are no monks, but there is a resident caretaker for most of the year. Free accommodation *may* be available for visitors, but don't bank on it.

Kastellorizo (Megisti)
Καστελλόριζο (Μεγίστη)

postcode 851 11 ● pop 275

It takes a certain amount of decisiveness and a sense of adventure to come to tiny, rocky Kastellorizo (kah-stel-**o**-rih-zo), a mere speck on the map 118km east of Rhodes, its nearest Greek neighbour, yet only 2.5km from the southern coast of Turkey and its nearest neighbouring town, Kaş. Kastellorizo is so-named for the 'red castle' that once dominated the main port, but is also known as 'Megisti' (the largest), for it is the largest of a group of 14 islets that surround this isolated Hellenic outpost. Tourism is low-key, yet there are more Australian-Greek Kastellorizians here in summer than there are locals. There are no stunning beaches, but there are rocky inlets from where you can swim and snorkel.

The island featured in the Oscar-winning Italian film *Mediterraneo* (1991) which was based on a book by an Italian army sergeant.

KASTELLORIZO (MEGISTI)

1 Moni Agiou Stefanou
2 Paleokastro
3 Moni Agias Triadas
4 Knights of St John Castle
5 Moni Agiou Georgiou
6 Blue Cave

To Ro, Agios Georgios & Rhodes
To Kas (Turkey)
To Strongyli
Kastellorizo Town
Mandraki
▲ Vikla (273m)
Horafia
KASTELLORIZO (MEGISTI)
MEDITERRANEAN SEA

0   500   1000m
0   500   1000yd

Daily Ferries
Low Frequency Ferries
Hydrofoil/Catamaran
Excursion Boat

History

Kastellorizo has suffered a tragic history. Once a thriving trade port serving Dorians, Romans, Crusaders, Egyptians, Turks and Venetians, Kastellorizo came under Ottoman control in 1552. The island was allowed to preserve its language, religion and traditions, and its cargo fleet became the largest in the Dodecanese, allowing the islanders to achieve a high degree of culture and education.

Kastellorizo lost all strategic and economic importance after the 1923 Greece-Turkey population exchange. In 1928 it was ceded to the Italians, who severely oppressed the islanders. Many islanders chose to emigrate Australia, where today a disproportionate number still live.

During WWII, Kastellorizo suffered bombardment, and English commanders ordered the few remaining inhabitants to abandon the island. Most fled to Cyprus, Palestine and Egypt. When they returned they found their houses in ruins and re-emigrated. Subsequently, the island has never fully recovered from its population loss. In recent years, returnees have been slowly restoring buildings and the island

DODECANESE

Mediterraneo – the Movie

If you have not seen the movie before you come to Kastellorizo, do so when you go home. You will enjoy it immensely. If you cannot recognise a lot of the places depicted in the film, don't be surprised. Many of the scenes depicting a 1940s Kastellorizo were shot away from today's busy waterfront and centred instead on Mandraki Bay and the square abutting the church of Agiou Konstantinou & Elenis and the nearby school in the area known as Horafia. The famous soccer scene was shot at a then unpaved airport, while other scenes were shot at locations along the coastline.

The legacy of the movie still lingers, and many Italians now come in search of the locations, or simply to satisfy their curiosity about an island that had so obviously enchanted the protagonists of this 1991 classic. One of the main characters of the movie, the unassuming Antonio (Claudio Bigagli), who marries the prostitute Vasilissa (Vanna Barba), was spotted arriving, pack on back, at Kastellorizo airport one summer recently. Some old habits die hard.

now enjoys a tenuous, but pleasant resurgence of resettlement.

Getting To/From Kastellorizo

Air In July and August there are daily flights to and from Rhodes (€35.80), dropping to three weekly at other times. You can buy tickets from Dizi Tours & Travel (☎ 2246 049 241, fax 2246 049 240, e dizivas@otenet.gr) in Kastellorizo Town. A ramshackle bus ferries passengers between the airport and the port (€1.50).

Ferry & Catamaran Kastellorizo is the least well-connected island in the whole of the Dodecanese archipelago. Ferry links are subject to seasonal changes and the only direct domestic destination is Rhodes (four hours, €10.90). Check locally with Dizi Travel or Papoutsis Travel (☎ 2246 070 830, fax 2246 049 286, e paptrv@rho.forthnet .gr) for the latest details.

At the time of research the *Dodekanisos Express* catamaran was running to Kastellorizo twice a week. Contact Dodekanisos Naftiliaki (☎ 2241 070 590, e info@12ne .gr) in Rhodes for the current schedules.

Excursion Boat to Turkey Islanders go on frequent shopping trips to Kaş in Turkey and day trips (€14.70) are also offered to tourists. Look for the signs along the waterfront.

Note that one-way travellers may theoretically enter and exit Greece legally via this route. Report to the police if arriving from Kaş.

Getting Around Kastellorizo

Excursion boats go to the islets of **Ro, Agios Georgios** and **Strongyli** and the spectacular **Blue Cave** (Parasta), named for its brilliant blue water, due to refracted sunlight. All of these trips cost around €14.70 and leave at around 8.30am daily.

KASTELLORIZO TOWN

Along with Mandraki, its satellite neighbourhood over the hill and to the west, Kastellorizo Town is the only settlement on the island. Built around a U-shaped bay, its waterfront is skirted with imposing, sprucedup, three-storey mansions with wooden balconies and red-tiled roofs. It is undoubtedly pretty nowadays, but the alluring facade of today's waterfront contrasts starkly with backstreets of abandoned houses overgrown with ivy, crumbling stairways and stony pathways winding between them.

Orientation & Information

The quay is at the eastern side of the bay. The central square, Plateia Ethelondon Kastellorizou, abuts the waterfront almost halfway round the bay, next to the yachting jetty. The suburbs of Horafia and Mandraki are reached by ascending the wide steps at the east side of the bay.

On the bay's western side are the post office and police station (☎ 2246 049 333). There's no OTE but there are cardphones. The National Bank of Greece (with ATM) is near the waterfront. The port police (☎ 2246 049 333) are at the eastern tip of the bay.

Things to See

The **Knights of St John Castle** stands above the quay. A metal staircase leads to the top from where there are splendid views of Turkey. Within the castle, a well-displayed collection is held at the **museum** (☎ 2246 049 283; admission free; open 7am-2.30pm Tues-Sun). Beyond the museum, steps lead down to a coastal pathway, from where more steps go up the cliff to a **Lycian tomb** with a Doric facade. There are several along the Anatolian coast in Turkey, but this is the only known one in Greece.

Moni Agiou Georgiou is the largest of the monasteries that dot the island. Within its church is the subterranean Chapel of Agios Haralambos reached by steep stone steps. Here Greek children were given religious instruction during Turkish times. The church is kept locked; ask around the waterfront for the whereabouts of the caretaker. To reach the monastery ascend the conspicuous zigzag white stone steps behind the town and at the top take the path straight ahead.

Moni Agiou Stefanou, on the north coast, is the setting for one of the island's most important celebrations, Agios Stefanos Day on 1 August. The path to the little white monastery begins behind the post office. From the monastery, a path leads to a bay where you can swim.

Paleokastro was the island's ancient capital. Within its Hellenistic walls are an ancient tower, a water cistern and three churches. Concrete steps, just beyond a soldier's sentry box on the airport road, are the beginning of the steep path to Paleokastro.

Places to Stay – Budget

Accommodation is generally of a high standard. Most domatia do not display signs but it's not hard to find the owners – that is, if they don't find you first when you disembark.

Villa Kaserma (☎ 2246 049 370, fax 2246 049 365) Doubles/triples with bathroom €28/34. This red-and-white building standing above the western waterfront has very pleasant rooms.

Pension Palameria (☎ 2246 049 282, fax 2246 049 071) Doubles with bathroom €29.50. This converted building on the small square at the north-west corner of the waterfront has spotless rooms with kitchen/dining area. Inquire about them at To Mikro Parisi restaurant.

I Anaviosi (☎ 2246 049 302) Singles/doubles €17.60/23.50, doubles with bathroom €29.50. These rooms are above the Sydney Restaurant.

Panorama Studios (☎/fax 2246 049 098, mobile ☎ 697 247 7186, Mandraki) Doubles with bathroom €35.50. These are roomy, fridge-equipped studios. Some have balconies and views across to Kaş in Turkey.

Places to Stay – Mid-Range

Karnagio Apartments (☎/fax 2246 049 266) 2-3/5 person apartments €53/73.50. These traditionally furnished apartments are housed in a beautifully restored red and ochre mansion near the top of the harbour's west side.

Kastellorizo Hotel Appartments (☎ 2246 049 044, fax 2246 049 279, @ kastel@otenet .gr, W www.kastellorizohotel.gr) Singles/doubles €44. These are beautiful, fully equipped rooms.

Pension Mediterraneo (☎ 2246 049 368) Singles/doubles €59. Farther along the same side of the bay are these equally well-appointed rooms.

Places to Eat

Most restaurants are clustered along the busy waterfront.

Restaurant Orea Megisti (☎ 2246 049 282, Plateia Ethelondon Kastellorizou) This restaurant serves a range of well prepared casserole dishes (goat casserole €5.80) and also spit-roast goat and lamb, both of which are accompanied with rice cooked with herbs.

To Mikro Parisi (☎ 2246 049 282) Mains €4.50-5. To Mikro Parisi has been going strong for over 30 years. It serves generous helpings of grilled fish and meat. Fish soup (€6) is the speciality, but the stifado (€4.40) is also good.

Sydney Restaurant (☎ 2246 049 302) Mayirefta €3.50-4. This restaurant, a little farther around from To Mikro Parisi, serves up mayirefta and fish dishes and is also highly recommended.

DODECANESE

Tis Ypomonis (☎ 2246 049 224) This corner restaurant does a nightly roaring trade in souvlaki (€4.70), sausage and steaks.

Akrothalassa (☎ 2246 049 052) Grills €4.10. Dine under the vines at this relaxed taverna on the south side of the harbour, where good grills and fish are served up.

Restaurant Platania (☎ 2246 049 206, *Plateia Mihail & Patricias Kaïli*) Breakfast €6. This is an out-of-the-way, unpretentious place that appeared in the film *Mediterraneo*. Come here for good breakfasts and their *revithokeftedes* (chickpea rissoles, €2.60).

There are several easy-going cafeterias on the waterfront. *Kaz Bar* is a good place to kick off, since you can check your email first. Next, *Meltemi* (☎ 2246 049 214) has tempting waterside chairs and cold beers. You can hardly miss *Mythos Bar*, the brightly painted watering hole on the east side of the harbour.

Symi Σύμη

postcode 856 00 • pop 2300

Symi is a rocky, dry island 24km north of Rhodes. It lies within the geographical embrace of Turkey, 10km from the Turkish peninsula of Datça. The island has scenic rocky interior, with pine and cypress woods. It has a deeply indented coast with precipitous cliffs and numerous small bays with pebbled beaches, and is enormously popular with day trippers from Rhodes. Symi has good accommodation and eating choices and enjoys excellent transport links to the outside world. However, the island suffers from a severe water shortage and the day-tripper crowds can get a bit overwhelming at times.

History

Symi has a long tradition of both sponge-diving and shipbuilding. During Ottoman times it was granted the right to fish for sponges in Turkish waters. In return, Symi supplied the sultan with first-class boat builders and top-quality sponges.

These factors, and a lucrative shipbuilding industry, brought prosperity to the island. Gracious mansions were built and culture and education flourished. By the beginning of the 20th century the population was 22,500 and the island was launching some 500 ships a year. But the Italian occupation, the introduction of the steamship and Kalymnos' rise as the Aegean's principal sponge producer put an end to Symi's prosperity.

The treaty surrendering the Dodecanese islands to the Allies was signed on Symi on 8 May 1945.

Getting To/From Symi

Ferry, Catamaran & Hydrofoil Symi has up to four mainline ferries a week heading north to other Dodecanese islands and Piraeus. Additional links are provided by the F/B *Nisos Kalymnos*, or F/B *Hioni*. Services to Rhodes are much more frequent.

The *Dodekanisos Express* catamaran services the island at least twice a week.

Symi is connected by hydrofoil to Kos (one hour, €15.40), Kalymnos (1½ hours, €21.30), Astypalea (four hours, €26.70) and Rhodes (50 minutes, €9.80). Services tend to be weekend-oriented. The Symi-owned *Aigli* hydrofoil leaves Symi for Rhodes at 7.15am and returns to Symi at 5pm or 6pm.

Excursion Boat There are daily excursion boats running between Symi and Rhodes' Mandraki Harbour. The Symi-based *Symi I* and *Symi II* are the cheapest. They are owned cooperatively by the people of Symi, and operate as excursion boats as well as regular passenger boats. Tickets cost €10.30 return and can be bought on board.

Symi Tours has excursion trips to Datça in Turkey. The cost is a rather steep €59 return (including Turkish port taxes).

Getting Around Symi

Bus & Taxi A minibus makes frequent runs between Gialos and Pedi Beach (via Horio). Check the current schedule with Symi Tours. The flat fare is €0.65. The bus stop and taxi rank are on the east side of the harbour. Sample taxi tariffs arc Horio €2.40, Pedi €2.70 and Nimborios €4.20.

Excursion Boat Several excursion boats do trips to Moni Taxiarhou Mihail and Sesklia Islet where there's a shady beach. Check the

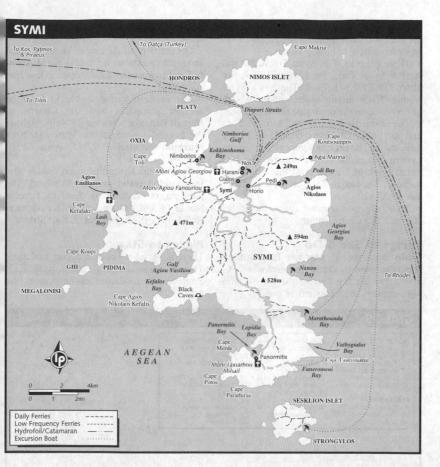

SYMI

To Kos, Patmos & Piraeus

To Datça (Turkey)

Cape Makria

To Tilos

HONDROS

NIMOS ISLET

PLATY

Diapori Straits

OXIA

Nimborios Gulf

Cape Toli

Nimborios

Kokkinohoma Bay

Agios Emilianos

Moni Agiou Georgiou

Harani

Nos

Cape Koutsoumpos

Agia Marina

▲ 249m

Pedi Bay

Moni Agiou Fanouriou

Gialos

Symi

Horio

Pedi

Agios Nikolaos

Cape Kefalaki

Ladi Bay

▲ 471m

Agios Georgios Bay

Cape Koupi

GHI

PIDIMA

Gulf Agiou Vasiliou

▲ 594m

SYMI

To Rhodes

MEGALONISI

Kefalos Bay

Black Caves

Nanou Bay

▲ 528m

Cape Agios Nikolaos Kefalis

Panormitis Bay

Lopidia Bay

Marathounda Bay

AEGEAN SEA

Cape Merde

Panormitis

Vathygialos Bay

Cape Faneromeni

Moni Taxiarhou Mihail

Faneromeni Bay

Cape Potos

Cape Parathiras

SESKLION ISLET

STRONGYLOS

Daily Ferries	– – – – –
Low Frequency Ferries	----------
Hydrofoil/Catamaran	— · — · —
Excursion Boat	············

0   2   4km
0   1   2mi

---

boards for the best value tickets. Symi Tours also has trips to the monastery (€30).

Excursion boats also go to some of the island's more remote beaches.

Taxi boats These small boats do trips to many of the island's beaches. The cost on average is about €8.

GIALOS Γιαλός

Gialos, Symi's port town, is a Greek treasure. Neoclassical mansions in a harmonious medley of colours are heaped up the steep hills flanking its U-shaped harbour. Behind their strikingly beautiful facades, however, many of the buildings are derelict. The town is divided into two parts: Gialos, the harbour, and Horio, above, crowned by the kastro (castle).

Gialos' beach is the crowded, minuscule Nos Beach. Turn left at the Italian-era clock tower at the north-eastern end of the harbour.

Orientation & Information

Arriving ferries, hydrofoils and the catamaran dock just to the left of the quay's clock tower. Excursion boats dock a little further along. The centre of activity in Gialos is

Phone numbers listed incorporate changes due in Oct 2002; see p55

DODECANESE

focused upon the promenade at the centre of the harbour. Kali Strata, a broad stairway, leads from here to hilltop Horio.

There is no EOT in Symi Town, but the staff at Symi Tours (☎ 2246 071 307, fax 2246 072 292) is helpful. There is a Symi Visitor Office sharing space with the ANES ticket office on the north side of the harbour.

The post office, police (☎ 2246 071 111) and port police (☎ 2246 071 205) are by the ferry quay. The OTE is signposted from the eastern side of the central square. The National Bank of Greece is at the top of the harbour. The Ionian Bank on the waterfront has an ATM.

There are two Internet cafes: the Roloï Bar and The Club Upstairs.

Things to See & Do

Horio consists of narrow, labyrinthine streets crossed by crumbling archways. As you approach the kastro, the once-grand 19th-century neoclassical mansions give way to modest stone dwellings of the 18th century.

On the way to the castle, archaeological and folklore exhibits are held in the **Museum of Symi** (admission €1.45; open 10am-2pm Tues-Sun).

The castle incorporates blocks from the ancient acropolis, and the **Church of Megali Panagia** is within its walls. Behind the central square is the **Symi Maritime Museum** (admission €1.45; open 12.30-2.30pm Tues-Sun).

Symi Tours has multilingual guides who lead **guided walks** around the island. The publication Walking on Symi by Francis Noble (€5.90) is on sale at Kalodoukas Holidays at the beginning of Kali Strata.

Places to Stay

There is very little budget accommodation. The cheapest doubles cost around €35. Some accommodation owners meet the boats.

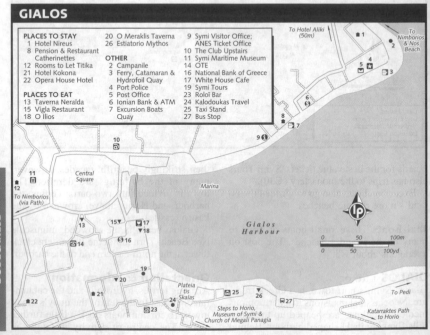

GIALOS

PLACES TO STAY
1 Hotel Nireus
8 Pension & Restaurant Catherinettes
12 Rooms to Let Titika
21 Hotel Kokona
22 Opera House Hotel

PLACES TO EAT
13 Taverna Neraïda
15 Vigla Restaurant
18 O Ilios
20 O Meraklis Taverna
26 Estiatorio Mythos

OTHER
2 Campanile
3 Ferry, Catamaran & Hydrofoil Quay
4 Port Police
5 Post Office
6 Ionian Bank & ATM
7 Excursion Boats Quay
9 Symi Visitor Office; ANES Ticket Office
10 The Club Upstairs
11 Symi Maritime Museum
14 OTE
16 National Bank of Greece
17 White House Cafe
19 Symi Tours
23 Roloï Bar
24 Kalodoukas Travel
25 Taxi Stand
27 Bus Stop

To Hotel Aliki (50m)
To Nimborios & Nos Beach
Central Square
To Nimborios (via Path)
Marina
Gialos Harbour
To Pedi
Plateia tis Skalas
Steps to Horio, Museum of Symi & Church of Megali Panagia
Katarraktes Path to Horio

0   50   100m
0   50   100yd

DODECANESE

Hotel Kokona (☎ *2246 071 549, fax 2246 072 620*) Singles/doubles with bathroom €35/41. This hotel has comfortable rooms. It's on the street to the left of the large church.

Pension Catherinettes (☎/fax *2246 072 698*, e *marina-epe@rho.forthnet.gr*) Doubles with/without sea view €44/28. Some of this pension's rooms have magnificent painted ceilings.

Hotel Fiona (☎ *2246 072 755, fax 2246 072 088*) Doubles/triples with bathroom €44/53. This hotel in Horio has lovely rooms with wood-panelled ceilings and great views. To reach it turn left immediately after To Klima Restaurant.

Hotel Nireus (☎ *2246 072 400, fax 2246 072 404*, e *nireus@altavista.com, Akti Georgiou Genista*) Singles/doubles €47/59. This hotel has elegant, traditional rooms and suites.

Opera House Hotel (☎ *2246 072 034, fax 2246 072 035*) Double/triple studios €65/80. These spacious studios in a peaceful garden are well signposted from the harbour.

Hotel Aliki (☎/fax *2246 071 665, Akti Georgiou Gennimata*) Singles/doubles €82/105. This pricey, A-class, traditional-style hotel is farther along from Hotel Nireus.

Places to Eat

Gialos Many of Gialos' restaurants are mediocre, catering for day-trippers. The following are exceptions.

Vigla Restaurant (☎ *2246 072 056*) Fish €9-11. This restaurant is at the top of the harbour and features fresh fish.

O Meraklis Taverna (☎ *2246 071 003*) Grills €4.70. This taverna is quietly popular and does good grills and mayirefta.

Taverna Neraïda (☎ *2246 071 841*) Mains €4-5. This excellent, low-priced option is beyond Hotel Glafkos. Fish souvlaki (€7.40) makes an interesting change.

O Ilios (☎ *2246 072 172*) Snacks €2-3. This English-run vegetarian restaurant is at the top of the harbour. It serves snacks and homemade cakes during the day and three-course meals in the evening. Service can be very slow at busy times.

Restaurant Les Catherinettes (☎ *2246 072 698*) Mixed mezedes €7.40. This restaurant, below the pension of the same name, offers an extensive range of well-prepared dishes.

Estiatorio Mythos (☎ *2246 071 488*) Mezedes €3-4.50. This is an unpretentious little place with top-class food. At lunchtime Mythos serves mainly pasta dishes, while mezedes feature in the evening.

Horio There are a couple of good restaurants at the top of the long staircase from Gialos.

To Klima (☎ *2246 072 693, Kali Strata*) Mains €6-7. To Klima serves well prepared Greek dishes and offers an enticing vegetarian menu.

Restaurant Syllogos (☎ *2246 072 148, Kali Strata*) Mains €5-7. This restaurant offers imaginative fare such as chicken with prunes and pork with leek (€5.90).

Entertainment

There are several lively bars in the streets behind the south side of the harbour.

White House Cafe (☎ *2246 071 372*) Drop by here in the evenings and enjoy occasional live music.

Jean & Tonic (☎ *2246 071 819*) Open 8pm-6am. Haul yourself up Kali Strata, work up a thirst and enjoy this expat-owned watering hole.

AROUND SYMI

Pedi is a little fishing village and burgeoning holiday resort in a fertile valley 2km downhill from Horio. It has some sandy stretches on its narrow beach. There are domatia, hotels and tavernas.

Nos Beach is the closest beach to Gialos. It's a five-minute walk north of the campanile. There is a taverna, bar and sun beds.

Nimborios is a long, pebbled beach 2km west of Gialos. It has some natural shade as well as sun beds and umbrellas. Water quality can be dicey and the one taverna here serves good but expensive food delivered with a rather sulky attitude. You can walk there from Gialos along a scenic path. Take the road by the east side of the central square, and continue straight ahead; the

Top Activities

If reading a long-neglected bestseller on a golden beach or eating your way from fish taverna to fish taverna is not enough for you, there's more to do in the Dodecanese than you imagine.

Hike off some of those kilos on quiet Tilos, where there are some of the best and most compact walking trails in the islands, none of which will take you more than two to three hours to complete. Because of the northern summer wind called the *meltemi*, the northern coast of large islands like Kos and Rhodes are magnets to **windsurfers**. Tingaki, Kamari and Mastihari on Kos draw many wind worshippers, as does the coastline just south of Rhodes Town at Ixia and Trianda. Afiarti Bay on Karpathos is for pros only – one missed wind and you'll end up in Libya!

Skin **diving** is available to anyone with a mask, snorkel and fins: the water is crystal clear more or less everywhere. Scuba divers are a bit more restricted, but diving outfits on the Kos and Rhodes waterfronts organise beginners and advanced dives on Rhodes and Kalymnos. **Sailing** is ideal around the islands, but you might want to contact a yacht charter company through your travel agent for the lowdown.

way is fairly obvious. Just bear left after the church and follow the stone trail.

Taxi boats go to **Agios Georgios Bay** and the more developed **Nanou Beach**, which has sun beds, umbrellas and a taverna, and **Agia Marina**, which also has a taverna. These are all shingle beaches. Symi's only sandy beach is the tamarisk-shaded **Agios Nikolaos**.

The remote **Marathounda** and **Agios Emilianos** beaches are reached by excursion boat.

Moni Taxiarhou Mihail
Μονή Ταξιάρχου Μιχαήλ
Symi's principal sight is the large Moni Taxiarhou Mihail (Monastery of Michael of Panormitis) in Panormitis Bay, and it's the stopping-off point for many of the day trippers from Rhodes. A monastery was first built here in the 5th or 6th century, but the

present building dates from the 18th century. The katholikon contains an intricately carved wooden iconostasis, frescoes, and an icon of St Michael which supposedly appeared miraculously where the monastery now stands. St Michael is the patron saint of Symi, and protector of sailors.

The monastery complex comprises a museum, restaurant and basic guest rooms, where beds cost around €12; reservations are necessary in July and August.

Tilos Τήλος

postcode 850 02 • pop 280
Tilos is one of the few islands left in the Dodecanese that still retains something of its traditional character and where tourism has not widely impacted on the slow and carefree lifestyle of the islanders. Tilos lies 65km west of Rhodes, has good, uncrowded beaches, two abandoned, evocative villages, a well-kept monastery at the end of a spectacularly scenic road, and keeps its authentic Greek-island image intact. It's a terrific island for walkers, with vistas of high cliffs, rocky inlets and sea, valleys of cypress, walnut and almond trees, and bucolic meadows.

Tilos' agricultural potential is not utilised, since, rather than work the land for a pittance, young Tiliots prefer to leave for the mainland or emigrate to Australia or the USA.

There are two settlements: the port of Livadia, and Megalo Horio, 8km north.

History
Mastodon bones – midget elephants that became extinct around 4600 BC – were found in a cave on the island in 1974. The cave, **Harkadio**, is signposted from the Livadia-Megalo Horio road, but is kept locked. Erinna, one of the least-known of ancient Greece's female poets, lived on Tilos in the 4th century BC.

Elephants and poetry aside, Tilos' history shares the same catalogue of invasions and occupations as the rest of the archipelago.

Getting To/From Tilos
Ferry Tilos is served by G&A Ferries, D.A.N.E. Sea Lines, the Kalymnos-based

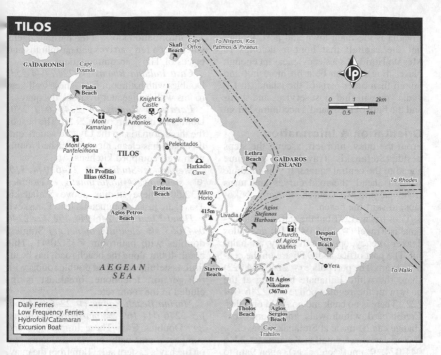

TILOS

Legend:
- Daily Ferries
- Low Frequency Ferries
- Hydrofoil/Catamaran
- Excursion Boat

F/B *Nisos Kalymnos* and Chios-based F/B *Hioni* with up to four services a week in high season. Tickets can be bought at Stefanakis Travel Agency (☎ 2246 044 360) in Livadia.

Hydrofoil Tilos sees only one or two hydrofoils a week. Check locally for departure/arrival days. Destinations include Rhodes (one hour, €17.10), Nisyros (40 minutes, €9.50) and Kos (1½ hours, €12.15), with connections further afield.

Catamaran The Tilos-owned *Sea Star* (☎ 2246 077 048) connects Tilos daily with Nisyros and Rhodes. *Sea Star* departs Tilos for Nisyros mid-morning daily (35 minutes, €9.50) and for Rhodes in late afternoon (55 minutes, €16.20).

The *Dodekanisos Express* calls in at Tilos two to three times a week in summer as an intermediate stop on its daily run up the Dodecanese from Rhodes and back. Tickets can be bought at Stefanakis Travel Agency.

Excursion Boat There are a number of excursions advertised around Livadia. They range from €14.70 to €20.60. A high-speed inflatable boat goes to small beaches around the island, but it's a pricey €22 per person; ask at Tilos Travel Agency (☎ 2246 044 294, e office@tilostravel.co.uk).

Getting Around Tilos

Tilos' public transport consists of two buses: a minibus and a full-sized bus. There are seven services daily from Livadia to Megalo Horio, Agios Antonios and Eristos. Fares are about €1.20. On Sunday there is a special excursion bus to Moni Agiou Panteleimona (€2.95 return) which leaves Livadia at 11am and gives you one hour at the monastery.

Tilos has two taxis: Taxi Mike (mobile ☎ 69 4520 0436) and Nikos Logothetis (mobile ☎ 69 4498 1727). Both are available at any time.

DODECANESE

Phone numbers listed incorporate changes due in Oct 2002; see p55

LIVADIA Λιβάδεια

Livadia is the main town and port, though not the capital: that honour belongs to Megalo Horio. It's a sleepy, pleasant enough place, though it can be a bit more hot and humid than other parts of the island. In Livadia you will find most services and shops and the bulk of the island's accommodation.

Orientation & Information

From the quay, turn left, ascend the steps beside Stefanakis Travel, and continue ahead to the central square. If you continue straight ahead, the road curves and turns right, passing the Church of Agios Nikolaos, to skirt the beach.

Tilos has no EOT but the staff at both Stefanakis Travel (☎ 2246 044 310) and Tilos Travel Agency, opposite the quay, are helpful. The post office and OTE are on the central square. The port police (☎ 2246 044 322) share the white Italianate building at the quay with the regular police (☎ 2246 044 222). There is no bank and no ATM on Tilos. Credit card withdrawals and money exchange can be made at Stefanakis Travel.

You can check email at Kosmos (☎ 2246 044 074, e pnut@otenet.gr), open 9am to 1.30pm and 7.30pm to 11.30pm. Access costs €2.95 for 30 minutes.

Walks

There are a number of popular walks that can easily be made from Livadia. One is a return hike to **Stavros beach**, an hour's steady walk along a well-marked trail that starts from near the Tilos Mare Hotel in Livadia. This is the easiest and perhaps most accessible of the walks, and the lure of a dip at the fine-pebble beach is enough to attract a steady line of walkers.

A second walk is a longer return track to the small abandoned settlement of **Yera** and its accompanying beach access at **Despoti Nero**. From Livadia follow the road past Agios Stefanos on the east side of the bay and keep walking. Allow half a day for this hike.

Another walk, mostly bypassing the main road system, leads from Livadia to the abandoned ghost-village of **Mikro Horio**. This will take about 45 minutes.

Places to Stay

The information kiosk at the harbour opens whenever a ferry arrives and has photos and prices of Tilos' accommodation.

Casa Italiana Rooms (☎ 2246 044 253) Doubles with bathroom €24. These well-kept rooms with refrigerator overlook the quay.

Paraskevi Rooms (☎ 2246 044 280) Doubles with bathroom €29.50. The best of the three domatia on the Livadia waterfront, this place has clean, nicely furnished rooms with well-equipped kitchens.

Stefanakis Studios (☎ 2246 044 310, e stefanakis@rho.forthnet.gr) Doubles €32.50. These studios above Stefanakis Travel are just as commendable as Paraskevi.

Hotel Eleni (☎ 2246 044 062, fax 2246 044 063, e elenihtl@otenet.gr) Singles/ doubles with bathroom €35.20/41. This hotel, 400m along the beach road, has beautiful, tastefully furnished double rooms with refrigerator, telephone; breakfast is included in the room rate.

Marina Beach Rooms (☎ 2246 044 066, fax 2246 044 169, e marinaroom@otenet .gr) Doubles €41. These immaculate and compact rooms with sea-view balconies are on the bay's eastern side, 1km from the quay.

Faros Rooms (☎ 2246 044 068, fax 2246 044 029, e dimkouk@otenet.gr) Doubles/ triples €41/48.50. A little farther along from Marina Beach, rooms here are spotless and tastefully furnished.

Places to Eat

Sofia's Taverna (☎ 2246 044 340) Mayirefta €3. This taverna, 100m along the beach road, serves delicious, home-cooked food.

Taverna Blue Sky (☎ 2246 044 259) Mezedes €1.80-3.20. Blue Sky, on the harbour, is good for grilled fish and vegetarian mezedes.

Taverna Michalis (☎ 2246 044 359) Grills €5.30. Head to this popular tourist taverna, beyond the central square, for tasty grilled meat.

Restaurant Irina (☎ 2246 044 206) Mayirefta €4-5. With its relaxing waterside location, Irina does great home-made food, including excellent mousakas and aubergine slippers (*papoutsakia*).

Joanna's Cafe Bar (☎ *2246 044 145*) Pizza €4.50-6. This cafe bar is a popular breakfast and brunch hang-out, serving excellent coffee, yogurt and muesli, pizza and delicious home-made cakes.

Entertainment
There are one or two bars on Livadia's waterfront, but serious ravers head for the spooky abandoned village of Mikro Horio 3km from Livadia.

Mikro Horio Music Bar (☎ *2246 044 081, Mikro Horio*) Take the minibus provided and enjoy this place where the music belts out until 4am in summer.

MEGALO HORIO Μεγάλο Χωριό
Megalo Horio, the island's capital, is a serene whitewashed village. Its alleyways are fun to explore and the village makes a great alternative base if you are looking for a taste of rural life in Tilos. There are domatia, a couple of restaurants and two lively, atmospheric bars to keep visitors bedded, fed and suitably watered. From here you can visit the **Knight's Castle**, a taxing 40-minute walk along a track starting at the north end of the village.

The little **museum** on the main street houses finds from the Harkadio Cave. It's locked, but if you ask at the town hall on the first floor someone will show you around.

Places to Stay & Eat
Miliou Rooms & Apartments (☎ *2246 044 204*) Doubles €19. This reasonable place is on the main street.

Elefantakia Studios (☎ *2246 044 242*) Doubles €29. These kitchenette- and fridge-equipped studios are next to Miliou Rooms & Apartments.

To Kastro (☎ *2246 044 232*) Grills €4.50. This is the best place to eat. It is on the village's south side, overlooking the Eristos plain below. Great barbecue-grilled meats and home cooking are the highlights here.

Entertainment
Megalo Horio has two atmospheric bars. *Ilakati*, on the steep road signposted Kastro,

plays rock and blues, and *Anemona* (☎ *2246 044 090*), at the top of the steps that start by the To Kastro restaurant, plays mainly Greek music.

AROUND MEGALO HORIO
Just before Megalo Horio, a turn-off to the left leads after 2.5km to the pleasant, tamarisk-shaded **Eristos Beach**, a mixture of gritty sand and shingle. A signposted turn-off to the right from this road leads to the quiet settlement of **Agios Antonios**. **Plaka Beach**, 3km farther west, is dotted with trees and affords some free camping.

The 18th-century **Moni Agiou Panteleimona** is 5km beyond here along a scenic road. It is uninhabited but well maintained, with fine 18th-century frescoes. The island's minibus driver takes groups of visitors here on Sunday. A three-day festival takes place at the monastery, beginning on 25 July.

Places to Stay & Eat
The Megalo Horio municipality is finally getting around to formalising a *camping ground* on Eristos Beach, but no details were available at time of research. Expect to pay around €5 for one person and a tent.

Tropicana Taverna & Rooms (☎ *2246 044 020, Eristos*) Doubles/triples €17.50/22. Tropicana is on the Eristos road and its restaurant serves up good mayirefta dishes (€2.60-3.20).

Eristos Beach Hotel (☎/fax *2246 044 024, Eristos*) Doubles €32. This hotel, right on the beach, has excellent, airy studios for up to four persons with fridge and kitchenette.

Nisyros Νίσυρος

☎ 2242 • postcode 853 03 • pop 1000

Nisyros (**nee**-sih-ros) is one of those quirky Greek islands that is not on the usual island-hopping circuit. It has no stunning sandy beaches and supports a rather low-key tourist infrastructure that favours individuals, yachties and lost souls.

Nisyros is an almost round, rocky island and has something that no other Greek island

DODECANESE

has – its own volcano. The landscape is at the same time rocky, lush and green, yet it has no natural water.

The lunar landscape of the interior is offset by craggy peaks and rolling hillsides leading down to brown pebbly beaches that see relatively few visitors. The island's settlements are the capital of Mandraki, the fishing village of Pali and the crater-top villages of Emborios and Nikea.

Getting To/From Nisyros

Nisyros is linked to the Dodecanese by almost daily ferries. There is an extra service four times a week sailing to Kardamena on Kos with the caique *Chrysoula* (two hours, €3).

The island is serviced by two hydrofoils a week heading both north and south and catamarans three to five times a week.

In summer there are daily excursion boats from Kardamena, Kefalos and Kos Town on Kos (€13-18).

Getting Around Nisyros

Bus There are two companies running up to 10 excursion buses every day to the volcano (€6 return) with 40 minutes waiting time between 9.30am and 3pm. There are in addition three daily buses to Nikea (€1.60) via Pali. The bus stop is at the quay.

Motorcycle There are also three motorcycle-rental outlets available on Mandraki's main street.

Taxi There are two taxis on Nisyros: Babis Taxi (☎ 2242 031 460) and Irene's Taxi (☎ 2242 031 474). Sample fares are: the volcano €17.60 return, Nikea €10.30 and Pali €4.70.

Excursion Boat From June to September there are excursion boats (€8 return) to the pumice-stone islet of Giali where there is a good sandy beach.

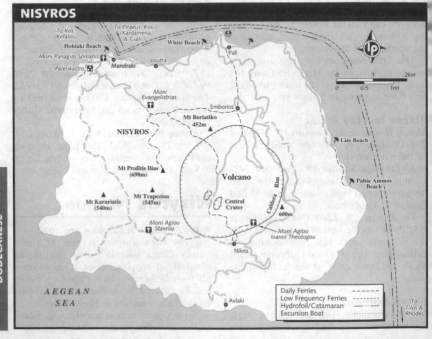

NISYROS

AEGEAN SEA

To Kos (Kefalos)
To Piraeus, Kos (Kardamena) & Giali
Hohlaki Beach
Moni Panagias Spilianis
Paleokastro
Mandraki
White Beach
Pali
Loutra
Moni Evangelistrias
Emborios
Mt Boriatiko 452m
NISYROS
Lies Beach
Mt Profitis Ilias (698m)
Volcano
Caldera Rim
Pahia Ammos Beach
Mt Trapezina (545m)
Mt Karariatis (540m)
Central Crater
600m
Moni Agiou Stavrou
Moni Agiou Ioanni Theologou
Nikea
Avlaki
To Tilos & Rhodes

Daily Ferries	– – –
Low Frequency Ferries	········
Hydrofoil/Catamaran	— · —
Excursion Boat	— — —

MANDRAKI Μανδράκι

Mandraki is the attractive port and capital of Nisyros. Its two-storey houses have brightly painted wooden balconies. Some are whitewashed but many are painted in bright colours, predominantly ochre and turquoise. The web of streets huddled below the monastery and the central square are especially charming.

Orientation & Information

To reach Mandraki's centre, walk straight ahead from the quay. At the fork bear right; the left fork leads to Hotel Porfyris. Beyond here a large square adjoins the main street, which proceeds to Plateia Aristotelous Fotiadou, then continues diagonally opposite, passing the town hall. Turn left at the T-junction for the central square of Plateia Ilikiomeni.

Tourist information is willingly dispensed by Nisyrian Travel (☎ 2242 031 204) at the quay, open 10am to 1pm and 6pm to 8pm daily. The staff here, and at Enetikon Travel on the main street, is helpful.

The post office, port police (☎ 2242 031 222) and the regular police (☎ 2242 031 201) share premises opposite the quay. The Co-operative Bank of the Dodecanese offers currency exchange and credit card withdrawals, but has no ATM. Travel agents will usually exchange money with no hassles.

Things to See

Mandraki's greatest tourist attraction is the clifftop 14th-century **Moni Panagias Spilianis** (*Virgin of the Cave;* ☎ 2242 031 125; *admission free; open 10.30am-3pm*), crammed with ecclesiastical paraphernalia. Turn right at the end of the main street to reach the steps up to the monastery.

The impressive Mycenaean era acropolis, **Paleokastro** (Old Kastro), above Mandraki, has well-preserved Cyclopean walls built of massive blocks of volcanic rock. Follow the route signposted 'kastro', near the monastery steps. This eventually becomes a path. At the road turn right and the kastro is on the left.

Hohlaki is a black-stone beach and can usually be relied upon for swimming unless the wind is up and then the water can get rough. To get there, walk to the end of the waterfront, go up the steps and turn right onto a stone-laid path. It's a five-minute walk away.

Places to Stay

Mandraki has a fair amount of accommodation, but owners do not usually meet incoming ferries. There is no camping ground here.

Hotel Romantzo (☎/fax 2242 031 340) Singles/doubles with bathroom €23.50/30. If you turn left from the quay, you will come to this hotel with clean, well-kept rooms. The rooms are above a snack bar and there is a large communal terrace with a refrigerator, tables and chairs.

Three Brothers Hotel (☎ 2242 031 344, fax 2242 031 640) Singles/doubles with bathroom €20.50/30. This hotel, opposite Hotel Romantzo, is another pleasant option.

Iliovasilema Rooms (☎ 2242 031 159) Doubles €24. This place is in an excellent location, but right in the middle of the tourist traffic on the waterfront.

Haritos Hotel (☎ 2242 031 322, fax 2242 031 122) Doubles/triples €44/53. Open year-round. These are well-appointed rooms all with fridge, TV and telephone. Look for them on the Pali road.

Hotel Porfyris (☎/fax 2242 031 376) Singles/doubles €30/53. This C-class hotel, Mandraki's best, has a swimming pool.

Places to Eat

On Nisyros, be sure to try the non-alcoholic local beverage called *soumada*, made from almond extract. Another speciality of the island is *pitties* (chickpea and onion patties).

Taverna Nisyros (☎ 2242 031 460) Grills €4-5. This taverna, just off the main street, is a cheap and cheerful little place and is open all day. Good charcoal grills and souvlakia.

Tony's Tavern (☎ 2242 031 460) Breakfast €3.50. Tony's, on the waterfront, does great breakfasts and superb meat dishes, and has a wide range of vegetarian choices. Try the excellent gyros – the best on the island according to Tony.

DODECANESE

Kleanthes Taverna (☎ *2242 031 484*) Mezedes €3. This taverna beyond Tony's has good mezedes.

Restaurant Irini (☎ *2242 031 365*, *Plateia Ilikiomeni*) Mayirefta €2.60. This restaurant on the central square is recommended for its low-priced home cooking.

Taverna Panorama (☎ *2242 031 185*) Grills €3.80. Near Hotel Porfyris, this is another commendable option. Try suckling pig or goat.

Shopping

Artin Caracasian Studio (*mobile* ☎ *69 4566 8413*) This art photographer is now based in Nisyros. See and buy his excellent photographs of Nisyros (€2.90-7.30). You can also hear and buy the *Visions of Nisyros* CD (€14.60) – a dreamy musical work by two German musicians and on sale in Artin's studio on the waterfront.

AROUND NISYROS
The Volcano

Nisyros is on a volcanic line which passes through the islands of Aegina, Paros, Milos, Santorini, Nisyros, Giali and Kos. The island originally culminated in a mountain of 850m, but the centre collapsed 30,000–40,000 years ago after three violent eruptions. Their legacy is the white and orange pumice stones that can still be seen on the northern, eastern and southern flanks of the island, and the large lava flow that covers the whole southwest of the island around Nikea village. The first eruption partially blew off the top of the ancestral cone, but the majority of the sinking of the central part of the island came about as a result of the removal of magma from within the reservoir underground.

Another violent eruption occurred in 1422 on the western side of the caldera depression (called Lakki), but this, like all others since, emitted steam, gases and mud, but no lava. The islanders call the volcano Polyvotis, because during the Great War between the gods and the Titans, the Titan Polyvotis annoyed Poseidon so much that Poseidon tore off a chunk of Kos and threw it at Polyvotis. This rock pinned Polyvotis under it and the rock became the island of Nisyros. The hapless Polyvotis from that day has been groaning and sighing while trying to escape – hence the volcano's name.

There are five craters in the **caldera** (*admission €1*). A path descends into the largest one, Stefanos, where you can examine the multicoloured fumaroles, listen to their hissing and smell their sulphurous vapours. The surface is soft and hot, making sturdy footwear essential.

The easiest way to visit the volcano is by tourist bus, but you will share your experience with the hoards of mid-morning daytrippers. Better still, walk in from Nikea, or even Mandraki, or take a cab before 10.30am.

Emborios & Nikea
Εμπορειός & Νίκαια

Emborios and Nikea perch on the volcano's rim. From each, there are stunning views down into the caldera. Only a handful of inhabitants linger on in Emborios. You may encounter a few elderly women sitting on their doorsteps crocheting, and their husbands at the kafeneio. But generally, the winding, stepped streets are empty, the silence broken only by the occasional braying of a donkey or the grunting of pigs.

In contrast to Emborios, picturesque Nikea, with 50 inhabitants, buzzes with life. It has dazzling white houses with vibrant gardens and a central square with a lovely pebble mosaic. The bus terminates on Plateia Nikolaou Hartofyli. Nikea's main street links the two squares.

The steep path down to the volcano begins from Plateia Nikolaou Hartofili. It takes about 40 minutes to walk it one way. Near the beginning you can detour to the signposted **Moni Agiou Ioanni Theologou**.

Places to Stay & Eat Emborios has no accommodation for tourists and no tavernas, but there is at least one place to eat.

To Balkoni (☎ *2242 031 607*) Meals €5-6. Enjoy the view of the crater over lunch.

Community Hostel (☎ *2242 031 401*, *Plateia Nikolaou Hartofili*) Doubles €19. This simple community-run hostel is Nikea's only accommodation.

Pali Πάλοι

Pali is a small yachtie port with some simple accommodation and plenty of places to eat. The island's best beaches are here and at **Lies**, 5.5km farther on. **Pahia Ammos** beach is a further 15 minutes' walk from Lies along a coastal track.

Places to Stay & Eat *Hotel Ellinis*
(☎ 2242 031 453) Doubles €30. Rooms here are small and fairly basic but are OK for a night or two's stay.

Afroditi Restaurant (☎ 2242 031 242) Grills €5-6. This is the best of the bunch of Pali's five eateries. Dining is waterside, though motorbikes and cars weave between tables. The owners of the restaurant rent a *house* in Pali for €44, which accommodates up to five people.

Kos Κως

postcode 853 00 (Psalidi 852 00)
● pop 30,000

Kos is the third-largest island of the Dodecanese and one of its most fertile and well watered. It lies only 5km from the Turkish peninsula of Bodrum. It is second only to Rhodes in its wealth of archaeological remains and its tourist development, with most of its beautiful beaches wall-to-wall with sun beds and parasols. It's a long, narrow island with a mountainous spine.

Pserimos is a small island between Kos and Kalymnos. It has a good sandy beach, but unfortunately becomes overrun with daytrippers from both of its larger neighbours.

History

Kos' fertile land attracted settlers from the earliest times. So many people lived here by Mycenaean times that it sent 30 ships to the Trojan War. During the 7th and 6th centuries BC, Kos flourished as an ally of the powerful Rhodian cities of Ialysos, Kamiros and Lindos. In 477 BC, after suffering an earthquake and subjugation to the Persians, it joined the Delian League and flourished. Hippocrates (460–377 BC), the father of medicine, was born and lived on the island. After Hippocrates' death, the Sanctuary of Asclepius and a medical school were built, which perpetuated his teachings and made Kos famous throughout the Greek world.

Ptolemy II of Egypt was born on Kos, thus securing it the protection of Egypt, under which it became a prosperous trading centre. In 130 BC, Kos came under Roman domination, and in the 1st century AD it

---

Hippocrates – the First GP

Hippocrates is often called the father of medicine yet little is known for certain about his life. He is believed to have lived between 460 and 377 BC, but 'facts' about his birth and medical practices owe more to mythology and legends than to hardcore evidence. The earliest known biography of him is *Life of Hippocrates*, by Soranus, a Roman physician. This work was published about AD 100, more than 400 years after Hippocrates' death.

Hippocrates' fame probably resulted from about 80 anonymously written medical works that became part of the collection of the Library of Alexandria after about 200 BC. Those writings became linked with Hippocrates and are known by scholars as the *Hippocratic corpus*. However, it cannot be proved that Hippocrates actually wrote any of these works.

Hippocrates' medicine challenged the methods of many physicians who used magic and witchcraft to treat disease. It taught that diseases had natural causes and could therefore be studied and possibly cured according to the workings of nature. Under Hippocratic medicine, a well-trained physician could cure illness with knowledge gained from medical writings or from experience. Modern medicine is based on this assumption.

MH

DODECANESE

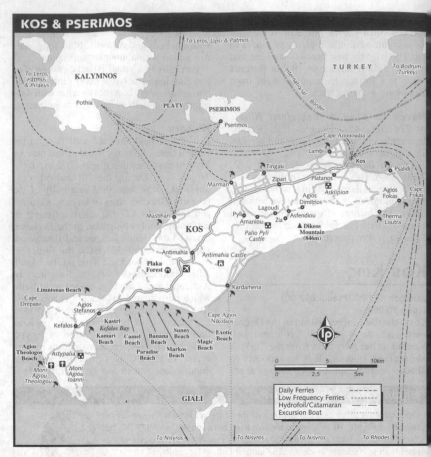

KOS & PSERIMOS

was administered by Rhodes, with which it came to share the same vicissitudes, right up to the tourist deluge of the present day.

Getting To/From Kos

Air There are three flights daily to Athens (€76.60). The Olympic Airways office (☎ 2242 028 330) is at Vasileos Pavlou 22, in Kos Town. The airport (☎ 2242 051 229) is 27.5km from Kos Town near the village of Andimahia.

Ferry – Domestic Kos is well connected with all the islands in the Dodecanese and

Piraeus. In summer there is a weekly ferry service to Samos and Thessaloniki. Services are offered by three major companies: D.A.N.E. Sealines (☎ 2242 027 311), G&A Ferries (☎ 2242 028 545), the F/B *Nisos Kalymnos* and sometimes the F/B *Hioni*. Sample fares are: Rhodes (3½ hours) €10.30, Piraeus (12 to 15 hours) €23.20, Patmos (4 hours) €8.50.

Ferry – International There are daily ferries in summer travelling from Kos Town to Bodrum (otherwise known as ancient Halicarnassus) in Turkey (one hour,

The distinctive profile of a Greek Orthodox priest on Rhodes

GEORGE TSAFOS

Umbrellas and sun-lovers, Pigadia, Dodecanese

GEORGE TSAFOS

GEORGE TSAFOS

Plateia Ippokratous, Old Town, Rhodes City

Old Town fortifications, Rhodes City

Relaxing on the alluring waterfront of Kastellorizo's town harbour, Dodecanese

Sulphur crystals around Nisyros' volcano

Looking towards Kefalos and Kefalos Bay, Kos

Walking along tranquil beaches with vistas of high cliffs, rocky inlets and sea, Tilos, Dodecanse

€30 to €38 return, including Turkish port tax). Boats leave at 8.30am and return at 4pm. Many travel agents around Kos Town sell tickets; Exas Travel (☎ 2242 028 545) is a good bet.

Hydrofoil & Catamaran Kos is served by Kyriacoulis Hydrofoils and the *Dodekanisos Express* catamaran. In high season there are daily shuttles, morning and evening, to and from Rhodes (two hours, €20.60), with good connections to all the major islands in the group, as well as Samos (four hours, 24.50), Ikaria (3½ hours, €19.50), Ikaria (2¾ hours, €23) and Fourni (3½ hours, €22) in the North-Eastern Aegean. From Samos you can easily connect with the Cyclades.

Information and tickets are readily available from the many travel agents.

Excursion Boat From Kos Town there are many boat excursions, around the island and to other islands. Examples of return fares are: Kalymnos €9; Pserimos, Kalymnos and Platy €18; and Nisyros and Giali €19. There is also a daily excursion boat from Kardamena to Nisyros (€12 return) and from Mastihari to Pserimos and Kalymnos.

Getting Around Kos
To/From the Airport An Olympic Airways bus (€3) leaves the airline's office two hours before each flight. The airport is 26km south-west of Kos Town, near the village of Antimahia, and is poorly served by public transport, though buses to and from Kardamena and Kefalos stop at the roundabout nearby.

Many travellers choose to share a taxi into town (€13 to €14).

Bus The bus station (☎ 2242 022 292, fax 2242 020 263) is at Kleopatras 7, just west of the Olympic Airways office. There are 10 buses daily to Tingaki (€1.20), three to Zia (€1.20), five to Pyli (€1.20), five to Mastihari (€1.70), six to Kardamena (€1.90) and six to Kefalos (€2.50) via Paradise, Agios Stefanos and Kamari beaches.

There are frequent local buses to the Asklipion, Lambi and Agios Fokas from the bus stop on Akti Koundourioti in Kos Town.

Car, Motorcycle & Bicycle There are numerous car, motorcycle and moped rental outlets.

You'll be tripping over bikes to rent. Prices range from €3.50 for an old boneshaker to €10 for a top-notch mountain bike.

Tourist Train You can take a guided tour of Kos in the city's (vehicular) Tourist Train (20 minutes, €1.50), which runs 10am to 2pm and 6pm to 10pm starting from the Municipality Building. Or take a train to the Asklipion and back (€2.05 return), departing on the hour 9am to 6pm Tuesday to Sunday.

Excursion Boat These boats line the southern side of Akti Koundourioti in Kos Town and make trips around the island.

KOS TOWN
Kos Town, on the north-east coast, is the island's capital and main port. The Old Town was destroyed by an earthquake in 1933. The New Town, although modern, is picturesque and lush, with an abundance of palms, pines, oleander and hibiscus. The Castle of the Knights dominates the port, and Hellenistic and Roman ruins are strewn everywhere. It's a pleasant enough place and can easily be covered on foot in half a day.

Orientation
The ferry quay is north of the castle. Excursion boats dock on Akti Koundourioti to the south-west of the castle. The central square of Plateia Eleftherias is south of Akti Koundourioti along Vasileos Pavlou. Kos' so-called Old Town is on Ifestou; its souvenir shops, jewellers and boutiques denude it of any old-world charm, though.

South-east of the castle, the waterfront is called Akti Miaouli. It continues as Vasileos Georgiou and then G Papandreou, which leads to the beaches of Psalidi, Agios Fokas and Therma Loutra.

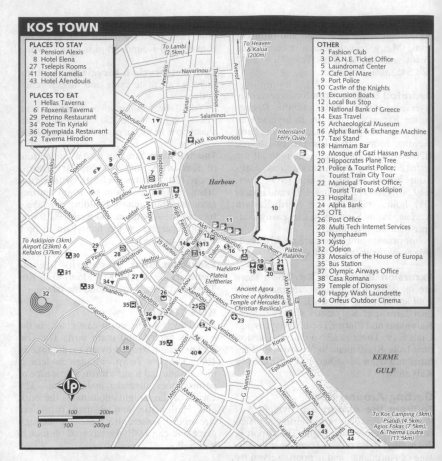

KOS TOWN

PLACES TO STAY
4 Pension Alexis
8 Hotel Elena
27 Tselepis Rooms
41 Hotel Kamelia
43 Hotel Afendoulis

PLACES TO EAT
1 Hellas Taverna
6 Filoxenia Taverna
29 Petrino Restaurant
34 Pote Tin Kyriaki
36 Olympiada Restaurant
42 Taverna Hirodion

OTHER
2 Fashion Club
3 D.A.N.E. Ticket Office
5 Laundromat Center
7 Cafe Del Mare
9 Port Police
10 Castle of the Knights
11 Excursion Boats
12 Local Bus Stop
13 National Bank of Greece
14 Exas Travel
15 Archaeological Museum
16 Alpha Bank & Exchange Machine
17 Taxi Stand
18 Hammam Bar
19 Mosque of Gazi Hassan Pasha
20 Hippocrates Plane Tree
21 Police & Tourist Police;
   Tourist Train City Tour
22 Municipal Tourist Office;
   Tourist Train to Asklipion
23 Hospital
24 Alpha Bank
25 OTE
26 Post Office
28 Multi Tech Internet Services
30 Nymphaeum
31 Xysto
32 Odeion
33 Mosaics of the House of Europa
35 Bus Station
37 Olympic Airways Office
38 Casa Romana
39 Temple of Dionysos
40 Happy Wash Laundrette
44 Orfeus Outdoor Cinema

Information

Kos Town's municipal tourist office (☎ 2242 024 460, fax 2242 021 111, ✉ dotkos@hol.gr) is at Vasileos Georgiou 1. The staff is efficient and helpful, and the office is open 8am to 8pm Monday to Friday and 8am to 3pm Saturday May to October.

The tourist police (☎ 2242 022 444) and regular police (☎ 2242 022 222) share the yellow Municipality Building opposite the quay. The port police (☎ 2242 028 507) are at the corner of Akti Koundourioti and Megalou Alexandrou.

The post office is on Vasileos Pavlou and the OTE is at Vyronos 6. Kos Town has two good Internet cafes; Cafe Del Mare (☎ 2242 024 244, ✉ sotiris@cybercafe.gr) at Megalou Alexandrou 4 and Multi Tech Internet Services (☎ 2242 023 584, ✉ info @multitech.gr) at El Venizelou 55.

Both the National Bank of Greece on Antinavarhou Ioannidi and the Alpha Bank on El Venizelou have ATMs. The Alpha Bank on Akti Koundourioti has a 24-hour automatic exchange machine.

The hospital (☎ 2242 022 300) is at Ippokratous 32. The Happy Wash laundrette is at Mitropolis 20 and the Laundromat Center is at Alikarnassou 124.

Archaeological Museum

There are many statues from various periods and a fine 3rd-century AD mosaic in the vestibule of the archaeological museum (☎ 2242 028 326, Plateia Eleftherias; admission €2.40; open 8am-2.30pm Tues-Sun). The most renowned statue is that of Hippocrates.

Archaeological Sites

The ancient agora (admission free) is an open site south of the castle. A massive 3rd-century BC stoa, with some reconstructed columns, stands on its western side. On the north side are the ruins of a Shrine of Aphrodite, Temple of Hercules and a 5th-century Christian basilica.

North of the agora is the lovely cobblestone Plateia Platanou where you can pay your respects to the Hippocrates Plane Tree, under which Hippocrates is said to have taught his pupils. Plane trees don't usually live for more than 200 years – so much for the power of the Hippocratic oath – though in all fairness it is certainly one of Europe's oldest. This once-magnificent tree is held up with scaffolding, and looks to be in its death throes. Beneath it is an old sarcophagus converted by the Turks into a fountain. Opposite the tree is the well-preserved 18th-century Mosque of Gazi Hassan Pasha, its ground floor now converted into souvenir shops.

From Plateia Platanou a bridge leads across Finikon (called the Avenue of Palms) to the Castle of the Knights (☎ 2242 027 927, Leoforos Finikon; admission €2.40; open 8am-2.30pm Tues-Sun). Along with the castles of Rhodes Town and Bodrum, this impregnable fortress was the knights' most stalwart defence against the encroaching Ottomans. The castle, which had massive outer walls and an inner keep, was built in the 14th century. Damaged by an earthquake in 1495, it was restored by the Grand Masters d'Aubuisson and d'Amboise (each a master of a 'tongue' of knights) in the 16th century. The keep was originally separated from the town by a moat (now Finikon).

The other ruins are mostly in the southern part of the town. Walk along Vasileos Pavlou to Grigoriou and cross over to the restored Casa Romana (☎ 2242 023 234, Grigoriou 5; admission €1.40; open 8am-2.30pm Tues-Sun), an opulent 3rd-century Roman villa which was built on the site of a larger 1st-century Hellenistic house. Opposite here are the scant ruins of the 3rd-century Temple of Dionysos.

Facing Grigoriou, turn right to reach the western excavation site. Two wooden shelters at the back of the site protect the 3rd-century mosaics of the House of Europa. The best-preserved mosaic depicts Europa's abduction by Zeus in the guise of a bull. In front of here an exposed section of the Decumanus Maximus (the Roman city's main thoroughfare) runs parallel to the modern road, then turns right towards the nymphaeum, which consisted of once-lavish latrines, and the xysto, a large Hellenistic gymnasium, with restored columns. On the opposite side of Grigoriou is the restored 3rd-century odeion.

Places to Stay

Kos Camping (☎ 2242 023 910, Psalidi) Adult/tent €4.40/2.30. This facility, 3km along the eastern waterfront, is Kos' one camping ground. It's a well-kept, shaded site with a taverna, snack bar, minimarket, kitchen and laundry.

Pension Alexis (☎ 2242 028 798, fax 2242 025 797, Irodotou 9) Singles/doubles €17.60/25. This convivial pension with clean rooms is highly recommended. The friendly, English-speaking Alexis promises never to turn anyone away, and he's a mine of information.

Hotel Afendoulis (☎ 2242 025 321, fax 2242 025 797, Evripilou 1) Singles/doubles with bathroom €29.50/35.50. On the other side of town, and also owned by Alexis, is this tastefully furnished hotel. Laundry for guests costs €5.80 a load.

Hotel Kamelia (☎ 2242 028 983, fax 027 391, e kamelia_hotel@hotmail.com) Open year-round. Singles/doubles €16.50/41. On a quiet tree-lined street, this is a pleasant C-class hotel.

DODECANESE

Hotel Elena (☎ *2242 022 740, Megalou Alexandrou 7)* Doubles/triples with bathroom €23.50/31. This D-class hotel is a commendable budget option. Another recommended place is *Tselepis Rooms* (☎ *2242 028 896, Metsovou 8)*, where singles/doubles with bathroom cost €30.80/36.50.

Places to Eat
The restaurants lining the central waterfront are generally expensive and poor value; avoid them and head for the back streets.

Taverna Hirodion (☎ *2242 026 634, Artemisias 27)* Mains €5-6. This taverna serves good and inexpensive food, though it's a little out of the way. The pork fillet in brandy sauce (€10.30) is considered the house speciality.

Olympiada Restaurant (☎ *2242 023 031, Kleopatras 2)* Pasta €3.50. This unpretentious place behind the Olympic Airways office serves reasonably priced, tasty food.

Filoxenia Taverna (☎ *2242 024 967, Cnr Pindou & Alikarnassou)* Mixed platters €7-8.50. This taverna has a good reputation for traditional home-cooked food. Try the filling gyros platter.

Hellas Taverna (☎ *2242 022 609, Psaron 7)* Mains €4.50-6. This restaurant is highly recommended with good *bekri mezes* and pastitsio among the dishes on offer.

Pote tin Kyriaki (☎ *2242 027 872, Pisandrou 9)* Pittes €3.50. Open evenings only, closed Sunday. This is another fine choice, with a good line in home-made pittes.

Petrino Restaurant (☎ *2242 027 251, Plateia Ioannou Theologou)* Mains €8-9. Open evenings only. This is a stylish place in a stone mansion, with outdoor eating in a romantic garden setting. Try chicken stuffed with spinach, cheese and mint sauce.

Entertainment
Kos Town has two streets of bars, Diakon and Nafklirou, that positively pulsate in high season. Most bars belt out techno, but *Hammam Bar* *(Akti Koundourioti 1)* plays Greek music.

Kos Town has five discos among which are the following.

Fashion Club (☎ *2242 022 592, Kanari 2)* This indoor venue has three air-con bars.

Heaven (☎ *2242 023 874, Akti Zouroudi 5)* This outdoor venue plays mostly house and has a swimming pool.

Kalua (☎ *2242 024 938, Akti Zouroudi 3)* Next door to Heaven, the music here is more mixed and includes R&B. It's an outdoor venue and also has a swimming pool.

There is also an outdoor cinema, *Orfeus* (☎ *2242 025 036, Fenaretis 3)*, open summer only; entry costs €5.90.

AROUND KOS TOWN
Asklipion Ασκληπιείον
The island's most important ancient site is the Asklipion (☎ *2242 028 763, Platani; admission €2.40; open 8.30am-6pm Tues-Sun)*, built on a pine-covered hill 4km south-west of Kos Town. From the top there is a wonderful view of Kos Town and Turkey. The Asklipion consisted of a religious sanctuary to Asclepius, the god of healing, a healing centre, and a school of

The Asklipion
as it may have looked
2000 years ago

medicine, where the training followed the teachings of Hippocrates.

Hippocrates was the first doctor to have a rational approach to diagnosing and treating illnesses. Until AD 554 people came from far and wide to be treated here, as well as for medical training.

The ruins occupy three levels. The **propylaea**, Roman-era public **baths** and remains of guest rooms are on the first level. On the next level is a 4th-century BC **altar of Kyparissios Apollo**. West of this is the **first Temple of Asclepius**, built in the 4th century BC. To the east is the 1st-century BC **Temple to Apollo**; seven of its graceful columns have been re-erected. On the third level are the remains of the once-magnificent 2nd-century BC **Temple of Asclepius**.

Frequent buses go to the site, but it is pleasant to cycle or walk there.

AROUND KOS

Kos' main road runs south-west from Kos Town with turn-offs for the mountain villages and the resorts of Tingaki and Marmari. Between the main road and the coast, a quiet road, ideal for cycling, winds through flat agricultural land as far as Marmari.

The nearest decent beach to Kos Town is the crowded **Lambi Beach**, 4km to the north. Farther round the coast, **Tingaki**, 9km from Kos Town, has an excellent, long, pale sand beach. **Marmari Beach**, 4km west of Tingaki, is slightly less crowded. Windsurfing is popular at all three beaches.

Vasileos Georgiou (later G Papandreou) in Kos Town leads to the three crowded beaches of **Psalidi**, 3km from Kos Town; **Agios Fokas**, 7km away; and **Therma Loutra**, 11km away. The latter has hot mineral springs which warm the sea.

Antimahia (near the airport) is a major island crossroads. A worthwhile detour is to the **Castle of Antimahia** on a turn-off to the left, 1km before Antimahia. There's a ruined settlement within its well-preserved walls.

Kardamena, 27km from Kos Town and 5km south-east of Antimahia, is an over-developed, tacky resort best avoided, unless you want to take an excursion boat to Nisyros (see the Getting To/From Kos section).

Mastihari Μαστιχάρι

Mastihari, (mas-ti-**ha**-ri) north of Andimahia and 30km from Kos Town, is an important village in its own right. It's a resort destination, but also an arrival/departure point for ferries to Pothia on Kalymnos. It is better equipped to cater for independent travellers, with a good selection of domatia. Mastihari is just that little bit more 'Greek' than its resort neighbours further east, Marmari and Tingaki. From here there are excursion boats to Kalymnos and the island of **Pserimos**.

Places to Stay & Eat There's loads of accommodation in Mastihari.

Rooms to Rent Anna (☎ 2242 059 041) Doubles €20.50. Walk 200m inland along the main road to these rooms, on the left.

To Kyma (☎ 2242 059 045) Singles/doubles €17.60/23.50. This is a pleasant, small, family-run hotel with smallish but presentable rooms which enjoy a good sea breeze. There is a clean and homely communal kitchen for guests' use.

Rooms Panorama (☎/fax 2242 059 145) Double studios €29.50. Most of these tidy studios with kitchenette overlook the west beach.

Kali Kardia Restaurant (☎ 2242 059 289) Fish dishes €6.50-7.50. Right on the central square, this busy eatery is commendable and the fish is particularly good.

Mountain Villages

Several attractive villages are scattered on the northern slopes of the green and wooded, alpine-like Dikeos mountain range. At **Zipari**, 10km from the capital, a road to the south-east leads to **Asfendiou**. From Asfendiou, a turn-off to the left leads to the pristine hamlets of **Agios Georgios** and **Agios Dimitrios**. The road straight ahead leads to the village of **Zia**, which is touristy but worth a visit for the surrounding countryside and some great sunsets.

Lagoudi is a small, unspoilt village to the west of Zia. From here you can continue to **Amaniou** (just before modern Pyli) where there is a left turn to the ruins of the medieval village of **Pyli**, overlooked by a ruined castle.

Phone numbers listed incorporate changes due in Oct 2002; see p55

DODECANESE

Places to Eat *Palia Pygi* (☎ *2242 041 510, Pyli)* Grills €5. Just off the central square at modern Pyli, this little taverna overlooking a lion-headed fountain serves tasty grills and mayirefta.

Taverna Olympia (☎ *2242 069 121, Zia)* Mains €4.50-5. Open year-round. This establishment cashes in not on its view (which is nonexistent), but its solid, reliable local cuisine and repeat clientele.

Taverna Panorama (☎ *2242 069 367, Bagiati-Asfendiou)* Open evenings only. Mezedes €3-3.50. With nary a tourist in sight, good mezedes and excellent service, Panorama enjoys a great night-time view. It's 3km from Zipari on the Asfendiou road.

Kamari & Kefalos
Καμάρι & Κέφαλος
From Antimahia the main road continues south-west to the huge Kefalos Bay, fringed by a 5km stretch of sandy beaches which are divided into roughly six 'name' beaches, each signposted from the main road. The most popular is **Paradise Beach**, while the most undeveloped is **Exotic Beach**. **Banana Beach** (also known as **Langada Beach**) is a good compromise.

Agios Stefanos Beach at the far western end is taken up by a vast Club Med complex. The beach, reached along a short turn-off from the main road, is still worth a visit to see the island of Agios Stefanos (named after its church), which is within swimming distance, and the ruins of two 5th-century basilicas to the left of the beach as you face the sea. The beach continues to Kamari.

Kefalos, 43km south-west of Kos Town, is the sprawling village perched high above Kamari beach. It's a pleasant place with few concessions to tourism. The central square, where the bus terminates, is at the top of the 2km road from the coast. There is a post office and bank with an ATM here.

The southern peninsula has the island's most wild and rugged scenery. **Agios Theologos beach** is on the east coast, 7km from Kefalos at the end of a good sealed road. Body surfing is popular here and boards can be rented. Sunsets are stunning.

Limnionas, 10km north of Kefalos, is a little fishing harbour. Its two small sandy beaches rarely get crowded.

Places to Stay & Eat Much of the accommodation in Kefalos Bay is monopolised by tour groups. Try these two independent operators for starters. Both are on the Kamari seafront about 200m on the right from Sebastian Tours.

Anthoula Studios (☎ *2242 071 904, mobile* ☎ *694 633 5950, Kamari)* Double appartments €41. This is spotless ground floor accommodation with kitchen, fridge and balcony with lounger. Bookings are essential.

Rooms to Let Katerina (☎ *2242 071 397, Kamari)* Double studios €38.50. These are nearby and also a good choice, although they are a bit smaller.

Kamari is full of picture menu restaurants catering to package-tourist diners from the UK. Be adventurous; seek further afield.

Psarotaverna (mobile ☎ *69 4456 0770, Limnionas)* Catering mainly to a Greek clientele, Miltos delivers the freshest fish – guaranteed (sea bream costs €7.50 to €8.50).

Restaurant Agios Theologos (mobile ☎ *69 7450 3556, Agios Theologos)* This restaurant abutting Agios Theologos beach serves good fish dishes (white snapper is €9 to €10), home-made goat cheese and scrumptious home-baked bread. It's the best place on Kos to watch the sunset over dinner.

Astypalea
Αστυπάλαια

postcode 859 00 • pop 1000
Astypalea (ah-stih-**pah**-lia), the most westerly island of the archipelago, is an island in search of a sense of belonging. Geographically and architecturally it is more akin to the Cyclades islands, but administratively it is a Dodecanese island. Sited more or less equidistant between its nearest Cycladic neighbour, Amorgos, to the west and its fellow Dodecanese island, Kos, to the east, Astypalea effectively has a foot in both camps.

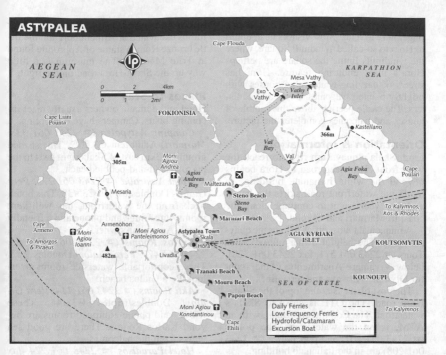

ASTYPALEA

AEGEAN SEA

KARPATHION SEA

Cape Flouda

Mesa Vathy

Exo Vathy

Vathy Inlet

Cape Liani Pounta

FOKIONISIA

Vaï Bay

366m

Kastellano

Cape Poulari

Moni Agiou Andrea

305m

Agios Andreas Bay

Maltezana

Vaï

Agia Foka Bay

Mesaria

Steno Beach

Steno Bay

Marmari Beach

To Kalymnos, Kos & Rhodes

Cape Armeno

Moni Agiou Ioanni

Armenohon

Moni Agiou Panteleimonos

Astypalea Town

Skala

Hora

AGIA KYRIAKI ISLET

KOUTSOMYTIS

To Amorgos & Piraeus

482m

Livadia

Tzanaki Beach

Moura Beach

Papou Beach

SEA OF CRETE

KOUNOUPI

To Kalymnos

Moni Agiou Konstantinou

Cape Ehili

Daily Ferries
Low Frequency Ferries
Hydrofoil/Catamaran
Excursion Boat

0 2 4km
0 1 2mi

With a wonderfully picturesque hilltop hora and bare, gently contoured hills, high mountains, green valleys and sheltered coves, it's surprising Astypalea does not get more foreign tourists. It is, however, very popular with Athenians.

Getting To/From Astypalea

Air There are five flights weekly from Astypalea to Athens (€66). Astypalea Tours (☎ 2243 061 571), in Astypalea Town, is the agent for Olympic Airways.

Ferry Lying between the Cyclades and the Dodecanese, Astypalea is the most easterly destination of some Cyclades services, and the most westerly of the Dodecanese services. Departure times are more favourable when heading west and north.

The F/B *Nisos Kalymnos* or F/B *Hioni* do round trips to Astypalea from Kalymnos twice a week. Other services are provided by D.A.N.E. Sealines and G&A Ferries. Tickets

are available from the Paradisos Ferries Agency (☎ 2243 061 224, fax 2243 061 450).

Hydrofoil Between June and September there is one hydrofoil a week plying a round trip from Rhodes (5½ hours, €30.50) to Astypalea via Symi, Kos and Kalymnos.

Getting Around Astypalea

Bus From Skala a bus travels fairly frequently to Hora and Livadia (€0.60), and from Hora and Skala to Maltezana (€0.90) via Marmari.

Excursion Boat In summer there are daily excursion boats to the island's less accessible beaches and to Agia Kyriaki Islet (€6). Tickets can be bought from the stalls by the boats.

ASTYPALEA TOWN

Astypalea Town, the capital, consists of the port of Skala and hilltop district of Hora, crowned by a fortress. Skala can be a noisy,

DODECANESE

busy place despite its small size, and few linger here to relax. Most visitors head uphill to Hora to so-called Windmill Square, where the windmills lining the square are perhaps Hora's most enduring feature. Hora has streets of dazzling-white cubic houses with brightly painted balconies, doors and banisters. The castle peering above this jumble of houses and balconies completes the picture.

Orientation & Information

From Skala's quay, turn right to reach the waterfront. The steep road to Hora begins beyond the white Italianate building. In Skala the waterfront road skirts the beach and then veers right to continue along the coast to Marmari and beyond.

A municipal tourist office adjoins the quayside cafe. The helpful owner of Astypalea Tours (☎ 2243 061 571, fax 2243 061 328), below Vivamare Apartments, is the agent for Olympic Airways and ferry lines.

The post office is at the top of the Skala-Hora road. The OTE is close to Skala's waterfront. The Commercial Bank, with an ATM, is on the waterfront. The police (☎ 2243 061 207) and port police (☎ 2243 061 208) are in the Italianate building.

Castle

During the time of the Knights of St John, Astypalea was occupied by the Venetian Quirini family, who built the imposing castle. In the Middle Ages the population lived within its walls, but gradually the settlement outgrew them. The last inhabitants left in 1948 and the stone houses are now in ruins. Above the tunnel-like entrance is the Church of Our Lady of the Castle and within the walls is the Church of Agios Giorgios.

Archaeological Museum

Skala sports a small but well-presented archaeological museum (☎ 2243 061 206; admission €1.50; open 8am-2.30pm Tues-Sun). The whole island of Astypalea is in fact a rich trove of archaeological treasure and many of the finds are on display here. The collection runs from the prehistoric-Mycenaean period through to the Middle Ages. Look out for a fine selection of grave offerings from two Mycenaean chamber tombs excavated at Armenohori and the little bronze Roman statue of Aphrodite found at Trito Marmari. The museum is a little way up the Skala-Hora road on the right.

Places to Stay

Hotel and domatia owners usually meet incoming boats. Campers have one option.

Camping Astypalea (☎ 2243 061 338, *Marmari*) Adult/tent €3.50/2. This shaded ground is 3km east of Skala right next to the narrow sand-and-pebble beach.

Hotel Australia (☎ 2243 061 275, *Pera Gialos*) Doubles/triples €35/38. This hotel, back from the waterfront, has well-kept rooms with fridge and phone and a friendly Greek-Australian owner.

Karlos Rooms (☎ 2243 061 330, fax 2243 061 477, *Pera Gialos*) Doubles €35. These comfortable waterside rooms overlook Pera Gialos beach.

Akti Rooms (☎ 2243 061 114, *Pera Gialos*) Doubles/triples €38/44. These fridge- and phone-equipped rooms are beyond Karlos Rooms. There are good sea views from the balconies.

Hotel Paradisos (☎ 2243 061 224, fax 2243 061 450, *Skala*) Singles/doubles with bathroom €29.50/40. This ageing but well-maintained hotel has comfortable rooms.

Aphrodite Studios (☎ 2243 061 478, fax 2243 061 087, *Skala*) Double/triple studios €38/44. These beautiful, well-equipped studios are between Skala and Hora. Take the Hora road, turn left after the shoe shop and it's on the left.

Places to Eat

There' a decent selection of good restaurants both in Skala and up in Hora.

Karavos (☎ 2243 061 072, *Pera Gialos*) Vegetarian dishes €3-4. Excellent home-cooked food is served up at this homey and diminutive eatery right on the Pera Gialos waterfront. Try stuffed zucchini flowers, or *poungia* (cheese foldovers).

Restaurant Australia (☎ 2243 061 067, *Skala*) This old-style restaurant, below Hotel Australia, serves delicious fish; the speciality is lobster and macaroni (€8.80).

Restaurant Astropalia (☎ *2243 061 387, Skala*) Grills €6. Enjoy wonderful views down to Skala from the terrace at this place.

Ouzeri Meltemi (☎ *2243 061 479, Hora*) Mezedes €3.20. Opposite the windmills in Hora, this is a great place to hang out to watch the sunset.

Egeon Mezedopolio (☎ *2243 061 730, Hora*) Snacks €3.50. Just a couple of doors along from Meltemi, this mezes cafe serves up excellent snacks and mezedes.

LIVADIA Λιβάδια

The little resort of Livadia lies in the heart of a fertile valley 2km from Hora. Its beach is the best on the island, but also the most crowded.

Quieter beaches can be found farther south at **Tzanaki**, the island's unofficial nudist beach, and at **Agios Konstantinos** below the monastery of the same name. You can drive to Agios Konstantinos beach along a reasonably-surfaced dirt road, or walk the 3km in about 40 minutes.

Places to Stay & Eat

There are a few comfortable places to stay in Livadi and a sprinkling of restaurants.

Gerani Rooms (☎ *2243 061 484*) Doubles/triples with bathroom €29.50/32. This place is a pleasant budget option; the rooms come with refrigerator.

Kaloudis Domatia (☎ *2243 061 318*) Doubles €32.50. These domatia with a communal kitchen are another good option.

Jim Venetos Studios & Apartments (☎ *2243 061 490, fax 2243 061 423*) Double studios €38, 4-person apartments €59. A sign at the western end of the waterfront points to this place, which has attractive studios and apartments.

Trapezakia Exo (☎ *2243 061 083*) Mains €3.50-4.50. A neat little snack bar-cum-restaurant, Trapezakia Exo is right on the beach at the western end of the waterfront. Snack on sandwiches or enjoy the cuttlefish speciality (€3.50).

OTHER BEACHES

Marmari, 2km north-east of Skala, has three bays with pebble-and-sand beaches. **Steno** Beach, 2km further along, is one of the better but least frequented beaches on the island. It's sandy, has shade and is well-protected. **Maltezana** (also known as **Analipsi**) is 7km beyond Marmari in a fertile valley on the isthmus. A former Maltese pirates' lair, it's a scattered, pleasantly laid-back settlement, but its two beaches are somewhat grubby. There are some remains of Roman baths with mosaics on the settlement's outskirts.

The road from Maltezana is reasonable as far as **Vaï**, and is gradually improving beyond. **Mesa Vathy** is a fishing hamlet with a beach at the end of a narrow inlet. It takes about 1½ hours to walk here from Vaï. From Mesa Vathy a dirt road leads to **Exo Vathy**, another hamlet with a beach.

Places to Stay & Eat

There are quite a few accommodation options in Maltezana, but many only operate during the summer.

Maltezana Rooms (☎ *2243 061 446, Maltezana*) Doubles €25. These fairly standard rooms are 50m east of the quay, just back from the beach.

Villa Varvura (☎ *2243 061 443, Maltezana*) Double/triple studios €44/50. Varvara has fourteen blue-and-white painted studios over-look a vegetable garden 100m from the beach. All have TVs and fridges.

Ovelix Taverna (☎ *2243 061 260, Maltezana*) Fish dishes €7-8. This recommended taverna 100m inland from the quay does good fish meals.

Almyra Restaurant (☎ *2243 061 451, Maltezana*) Fish dishes €7.50-8.50. Next to the quay, this is another recommended spot for seafood. Both this and Ovelix operate 1 June to 30 September.

Kalymnos Κάλυμνος

postcode 852 00 • pop 18,200

Kalymnos (**kah**-lim-nos), only 2.5km south of Leros, is a mountainous, arid island, speckled with fertile valleys. Kalymnos is renowned as the 'sponge-fishing island', but with the demise of this industry it is now exploiting its tourist potential. It faces a tough

DODECANESE

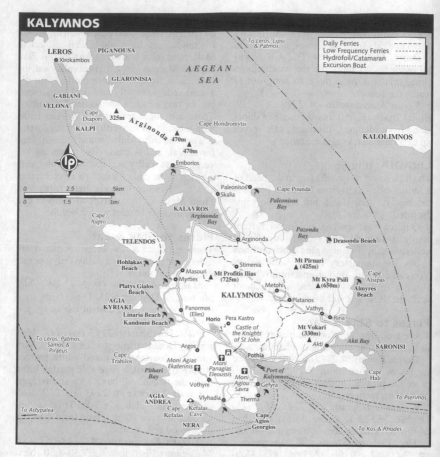

KALYMNOS

Daily Ferries	– – – – –
Low Frequency Ferries	- - - - -
Hydrofoil/Catamaran	— · — · —
Excursion Boat	· · · · · · · ·

To Leros, Lipsi & Patmos

LEROS
○ Xirokambos

PIGANOUSA

GLARONISIA

GABIANI
VELONA

KALPI
Cape Diapori
▲ 325m *Arginonda*

AEGEAN SEA

Cape Hondromytis

KALOLIMNOS

▲ 470m
▲ 470m

○ Emborios

Paleonisos ○
Skalia

Cape Pounda

Paleonisos Bay

KALAVROS
Arginonda Bay

Pazonda Bay

🏖 Drasonda Beach

Cape Aspro

TELENDOS

○ Arginonda

Hohlakas Beach

Masouri
Myrties

★ Stimenia

Mt Profitis Ilias (725m)

Mt Pirnari ▲ (425m)

Cape Atsipas

Metohi

Mt Kyra Psili ▲(650m)

Almyres Beach

Platys Gialos Beach

AGIA KYRIAKI

Panormos (Elies)

KALYMNOS

Platanos ○

Linaria Beach
Kandouni Beach

Horio

Pera Kastro
Castle of the Knights of St John

Vathys

Rina ○

To Leros, Patmos, Samos & Piraeus

Argos ○

Mt Vokari ▲ (330m)

Akti

Akti Bay

SARONISI

Cape Trahilos

Pithari Bay

Moni Agias Ekaterinis

Moni Panagias Eleousis

Pothia

Port of Kalymnos

Cape Hali

To Astypalea

Vothyni

AGIA ANDREA

Vlyhadia

Moni Agiou Savra

Gefyra

Therma

To Pserimos

Cape Kefalas
Kefalas Cave

NERA

Cape Agios Georgios

To Kos & Rhodes

0   2.5   5km
0   1.5   3mi

---

job. While there is plenty on offer to entice travellers – good food, accommodation and rugged scenery – the pull of Kos on the package tourism industry is just too strong and the majority of people flying into the region stay on Kos. The modest numbers that do make it across to Kalymnos find an island that is still in touch with its traditions and where the euro goes that little bit further.

Getting To/From Kalymnos

Air Most people going to Kalymnos fly to Kos and transfer to the Mastihari-Pothia local ferry.

Olympic Airways is represented by Kapellas Travel (☎ 2243 029 265) in Pothia.

Ferry Kalymnos is on the main north-south route for ferries to and from Rhodes and Piraeus and is reasonably well serviced with one or more daily departures. Services are provided by D.A.N.E. Lines, G&A Ferries, Miniotis Lines and the local F/B *Nisos Kalymnos*. Sample destinations are: Piraeus (10 to 13 hours) €21.80, Rhodes (five hours) €13.20, Astypalea (three hours) €7.40, Kos (1½ hours) €4.40 and, Patmos (2½ hours) €7.70 and Samos (four hours) €10.

The car and passenger ferries F/B *Olympios Apollon* and F/B *Atromitos* leave between three and six times daily between 7am and 8pm from Pothia to Mastihari on Kos (50 minutes, €2.80).

Hydrofoil & Catamaran Kalymnos is currently served by Kyriacoulis Hydrofoils linking Kalymnos with most islands in the north and south Dodecanese group. Sample destinations are: Rhodes (3½ hours, €26), Patmos (1½ hours, €15), Astypalea (two hours, €14.80) and Samos (3½ hours, €19.50). Tickets can be bought from Mikes Magos Travel Agency (☎ 2243 028 777, fax 2243 022 608).

The *Dodekanisos Express* catamaran calls in once daily during Ssummer on its run up and down the Dodecanese chain. Fares are similar to those of the hydrofoil.

Excursion Boat In summer there are three excursion boats daily from Pothia to Mastihari on Kos, and one to Pserimos (€6). Other excursions run by the caique *Irini* include Nera, Vlyhadia, Platys Island, Akti and Vathys and Kefala cave. There are also daily excursions from Myrties to Xirokambos on Leros (€4,40 one way).

Getting Around Kalymnos
Bus In summer there is a bus on the hour from Pothia to Masouri (€0.80) via Myrties, to Emborios (€0.90) three times weekly and to Vathys (€0.90) four times daily. Buy tickets from Themis Minimarket in Pothia as they are not available on the bus.

Motorcycle There are several motorcycle rental outlets along Pothia's waterfront.

Taxi Shared taxis are a feature of Kalymnos. They cost a little more than buses and run from the Pothia taxi stand (☎ 2243 050 300) on Plateia Kyprou to Masouri. They can also be flagged down en route. A regular taxi to Emborios costs €12.50 and to Vathys €9.

Excursion Boat From Myrties there are daily excursion boats to Emborios (€15). Day trips to the Kefalas Cave (€18), impressive for its stalactites and stalagmites, run from both Pothia and Myrties.

POTHIA Πόθια
Pothia (**poth**-ya), the port and capital of Kalymnos, is a fairly large town by Dodecanese standards. It is built amphitheatrically around the slopes of the surrounding hills and valley, and its visually arresting melange of colourful mansions and houses draped over the hills make for a photogenic sight when you first arrive. While Pothia can be brash and busy and its narrow vehicle- and motorbike-plagued streets can be a challenge to pedestrians, the island capital is not without its charm.

Orientation & Information
Pothia's quay is at the southern side of the bay. Most activity is centred on the main square, Plateia Eleftherias, abutting the busy waterfront. The main commercial centre is on Venizelou along which are most of the shops. The National, Commercial and Ionian Banks (with ATMs) are close to the waterfront.

In the middle of the central promenade is a seasonal tourist information kiosk (☎ 2243 050 879), open 7.30am to 10pm in summer. There are two Internet cafes in Pothia: Neon Internet Cafe 3 (☎ 2243 028 343, Agios Nikolaos) and Neon Internet Cafe 1 (☎ 2243 048 318, Hristos). Rates are €1.50 for 30 minutes and they are open 8.30am to midnight. The post office is a 10 minute walk north-west of Plateia Eleftherias.

The police (☎ 2243 029 301) are on Patriarhou Maximimou before the post office while the port police (☎ 2243 029 304) are at the start of the quay.

Things to See & Do
East of Plateia Kyprou, housed in a neoclassical mansion which once belonged to a wealthy sponge merchant, is the **Archaeological Museum** (☎ 2243 023 113, Agios Mammas; admission €1.50; open 10am-2pm Tues-Sun). In one room there are some Neolithic and Bronze Age objects. Other rooms are reconstructed as they were when the Vouvalis family lived here.

DODECANESE

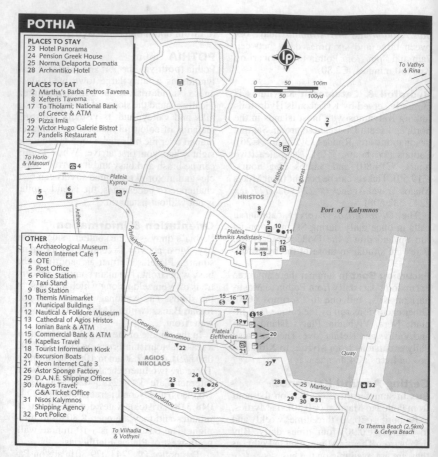

POTHIA

PLACES TO STAY
23 Hotel Panorama
24 Pension Greek House
25 Norma Delaporta Domatia
28 Archontiko Hotel

PLACES TO EAT
2 Martha's Barba Petros Taverna
8 Xefteris Taverna
17 To Tholami; National Bank of Greece & ATM
19 Pizza Imia
22 Victor Hugo Galerie Bistrot
27 Pandelis Restaurant

OTHER
1 Archaeological Museum
3 Neon Internet Cafe 1
4 OTE
5 Post Office
6 Police Station
7 Taxi Stand
9 Bus Station
10 Themis Minimarket
11 Municipal Buildings
12 Nautical & Folklore Museum
13 Cathedral of Agios Hristos
14 Ionian Bank & ATM
15 Commercial Bank & ATM
16 Kapellas Travel
18 Tourist Information Kiosk
20 Excursion Boats
21 Neon Internet Cafe 3
26 Astor Sponge Factory
29 D.A.N.E. Shipping Offices
30 Magos Travel; G&A Ticket Office
31 Nisos Kalymnos Shipping Agency
32 Port Police

To Vathys & Rina
To Horio & Masouri
Plateia Kyprou
HRISTOS
Port of Kalymnos
Plateia Ethnikis Andistasis
AGIOS NIKOLAOS
Plateia Eleftherias
Quay
Martiou
To Vlihadia & Vothyni
To Therma Beach (2.5km) & Gefyra Beach
Antheon
Patriarhou
Maximmou
Georgiou Ikonomou
Irodotou
Patitiri
Agoras

In the centre of the waterfront is the **Nautical & Folklore Museum** (☎ *2243 051 361, Hristos; admission €1.50; open 8am-1.30pm Mon-Fri, 10am-12.30pm Sat*). Its collection is of traditional regional dress as well as a section on the history of sponge diving.

Places to Stay

Domatia owners often meet the ferries, but there are enough options around town to make finding a place to stay an easy task.

Pension Greek House (☎ *2243 023 752, Agios Nikolaos*) Singles/doubles with bathroom €16.20/23.50. This pension, inland from the port, is a pleasant budget option with cosy wood-panelled rooms with kitchen facilities.

Norma Delaporta Domatia (☎ *2243 048 145, Agios Nikolaos*) Doubles €20. Norma Delaporta rents these rooms with kitchen and verandah behind the Astor Sponge Factory.

Hotel Panorama (☎ *2243 022 138, Agios Nikolaos*) Doubles €31. This hotel is situated high up and enjoys one of the best views in Pothia. The place is clean and breezy and it has a pleasant breakfast area; breakfast is included in the room rates.

DODECANESE

Archontiko Hotel (☎/fax 2243 024 149, *Agios Nikolaos*) Singles/doubles €28/38. Open year-round. At the south of the quay, is a cool and pleasant hotel in a renovated century-old mansion. Rooms all have fridges, TV and phone and breakfast is included.

Places to Eat

Xefteris Taverna (☎ 2243 028 642, *Hristos*) Stifado €4.40. Open lunch & dinner daily. This century-old and pretty basic taverna serves delicious, inexpensive food. The meal-sized dolmades and the stifado are recommended.

Pizza Imia (☎ 2243 050 809, *Hristos*) Pizza for 2 €6.50. Devour scrumptious wood-oven pizza in all permutations and flavours at this place.

To Tholami (☎ 2243 051 900, *Hristos*) This well-established eatery is popular with locals. Suggested dishes are octopus balls (*ohtapodokeftedes*) and grilled tuna steaks (€5.90).

Martha's Barba Petros Taverna (☎ 2243 029 678, *Hristos*) Of the fish tavernas on the eastern waterfront, this is the best; the crab salad (€4.50) is a delicious and filling starter.

Pandelis Restaurant (☎ 2243 051 508, *Agios Nikolaos*) Open all day year-round. Meat dishes €4.50. The specialities at this homely eatery are goat in red wine sauce and the home-made dolmades.

AROUND POTHIA

The ruined **Castle of the Knights of St John** (or Kastro Hrysoherias) looms to the left of the Pothia-Horio road. There is a small **church** inside the battlements.

Pera Kastro was a pirate-proof village inhabited until the 18th century. Within the crumbling walls are the ruins of stone houses and six tiny, well-kept churches. Steps lead up to Pera Kastro from Horio. It's a strenuous climb but the splendid views make it worthwhile.

A tree-lined road continues from Horio to **Panormos** (also called Elies), a pretty village 5km from Pothia. Its pre-war name of Elies (olives) derived from its abundant olive groves, which were destroyed in WWII. An

enterprising post-war mayor planted many trees and flowers to create beautiful panoramas wherever one looked – hence its present name, meaning 'panorama'. The sandy beaches of **Kandouni**, **Linaria** and **Platys Gialos** are all within walking distance.

The monastery **Moni Agiou Savra** is reached along a turn-off left from the Vothyni and Vlihadia road. You can enter the monastery but a strict dress code is enforced, so wear long sleeves and long trousers or skirts.

MYRTIES & MASOURI

Μυρτιές & Μασούρι

From Panormos the road continues to the west coast with stunning views of Telendos Islet until the road winds down into **Myrties** (myr-**tyez**) and **Masouri** (mah-**soo**-ri). These contiguous and busy twin resorts host the lion's share of Kalymnos' package holiday industry. The two centres are essentially one long street packed head to tail with restaurants, bars, souvenir shops and minimarkets. On the land side apartments and studios fill the hillside while on the seaside a dark, volcanic sand beach provides reasonable swimming opportunities.

Come here if you like an active holiday. There are exchange bureaus, car and motorbike rental outlets and even an Internet cafe. From Myrties there's a daily caique to Xirokambos on Leros (€4.40 one way).

Places to Stay & Eat

Most accommodation in Masouri and Myrties is block-booked by tour groups. There are a couple of places that deal with walk-ins.

Rita Studios (☎ 2243 024 021, *Masouri*) Doubles €30. Rita's has largish, airy rooms with kitchenette and big balconies for outdoor dining.

Studios Sevasti (☎ 2243 047 854, *Masouri*) Doubles €30. Next door to Rita Studios this similar establishment has quiet, decent rooms.

To Iliovasilema (☎ 2243 047 683, *Masouri*) Mains €4-5. Service here is truly excellent and the food equally so. The *kontosouvli* (Cypriot-style, spit roasted meat) is tops. It's on the central road through Masouri.

DODECANESE

Taverna I Galazia Limni (☎ 2243 047 016, Myrties) Mains €4.50. Octopus balls, squid and saganaki mussels are all recommended dishes. Pitched mainly at a Greek clientele, this cosy taverna is off the main road near Myrties beach.

TELENDOS ISLET Νήσος Τέλενδος

The lovely, tranquil and traffic-free islet of Telendos, with a little quayside hamlet, was part of Kalymnos until separated by an earthquake in AD 554. Nowadays it's a great escape from busy Myrties and Masouri. Frequent caiques for Telendos depart from the Myrties quay between 8am and 11pm (€2 return).

If you turn right from the Telendos quay you will pass the ruins of a Roman basilica. Farther on, there are several pebble-and-sand beaches. To reach the far superior 100m long and fine-pebbly **Hohlakas Beach**, turn left from the quay and then right at the sign to the beach. Follow the paved path up and over the hill for 10 minutes.

Places to Stay

Telendos has several domatia. All have pleasant, clean rooms with bathroom. Opposite the quay is *Pension & Restaurant Uncle George* (☎ 2243 047 502, 2243 23 855, ℮ unclegeorgeingreece@hotmail.com), with studios for €24. *Nicky Rooms* (☎ 2243 047 584), with pleasant doubles for €19.50, is to the right of the quay. Adjoining the cafe of the same name is *On the Rocks Cafe Rooms* (☎ 2243 048 260, fax 2243 048 261, ℮ otr@telendos.com), with two- or three-person apartments for €32.50.

Hotel Porto Potha (☎ 2243 047 321, fax 2243 048 108, ℮ portopotha@klm .forthnet.gr) Doubles/triples €28/37. This hotel, beyond On the Rocks Cafe, has well-kept rooms and a swimming pool.

Places to Eat

On the Rocks Cafe (☎ 2243 048 260) Souvlaki €5. The Greek-Australian owner serves well-prepared meat and fish dishes as well as vegetarian mousakas and souvlaki. It becomes a lively music bar at night and on Friday and Monday evenings it's 'Greek Night'.

Barba Stathis (☎ 2243 047 953) Mains €5-6. Barba Stathis does a great spin on octopus in red sauce (ohtapodi stifado), as well as octopus balls. Look for it in a little lane behind the waterfront.

EMBORIOS Εμπορειός

The scenic west-coast road continues 11.5km farther to Emborios, where there's a pleasant, shaded sand-and-pebble beach. One of the nicest places to stay is *Harry's Apartments* (☎ 2243 040 062), where double/ triple apartments cost €26.50/32.50.

Paradise Restaurant (☎ 2243 040 062) Harry's Apartments also runs the adjoining restaurant. There's a good line in vegetarian dishes (€6) such as chickpea croquettes (revithokeftedes) and pies (pittes) with fillings such as aubergine, vegetables and onion.

VATHYS & RINA Βαψύς & Ρίνα

Vathys, 13km north-east of Pothia, is one of the most beautiful and peaceful parts of the island. Vathys means 'deep' in Greek and refers to the slender fjord that cuts through high cliffs into a fertile valley, where narrow roads wind between citrus orchards. There is no beach at Vathys' harbour, Rina, but you can swim off the jetty at the south side of the harbour. Water taxis (☎ 2243 031 316) take tourists to quiet coves nearby.

Places to Stay & Eat

Vathys has two places to stay, both at Rina.
Hotel Galini (☎ 2243 031 241, fax 2243 031 100) Doubles with bathroom €24. This C-class hotel has well-kept rooms with balcony and breakfast included.

Pension Manolis (☎ 2243 031 300, Rina) Singles/doubles with bathroom €19/ 22. This pension, above the right side of the harbour, has beautiful rooms. There is a communal kitchen and terraces surrounded by an attractive garden.

Restaurant Galini (☎ 2243 031 241, Rina) Mains €4-5. Part of Hotel Galini, this is a friendly place to eat. Roast local pork (€4.40) and grilled octopus (€4) are two recommended dishes.

Taverna tou Limaniou (☎ 2243 031 206) Mains €4.50-5.50. In a stone-clad building is this cosy family taverna. Ask for the pork and chicken special (€5.80), or the garlic prawn saganaki (€7.40).

Leros Λέρος

postcode 854 00 • pop 8059
Travellers looking for an island that is unmistakably Greek and still relatively untouched by mass commercial tourism will find it on Leros, a destination surprisingly little known by foreign travellers, though well known for years by the discerning Greek public. Leros is a medium-sized island in the northern Dodecanese offering an attractive mix of sun, sea, rest and recreation, a stunning medieval castle and some excellent dining opportunities.

The island offers gentle, hilly countryside dotted with small holdings and huge, impressive, almost landlocked bays, which look more like lakes than open sea. The immense natural harbour at Lakki was the principal naval base of the Italians in the eastern Mediterranean, and is now a curious living architectural museum of Italian fascist Art Deco buildings.

Getting To/From Leros
Air There is a flight daily to Athens (€69). The Olympic Airways office (☎ 2247 022 844) is in Platanos, before the turn-off for Pandeli. The airport (☎ 2247 022 777) is in at Partheni in the north. There is no airport bus.

Ferry Leros is on the main north-south route for ferries between Rhodes and Piraeus. There are daily departures from Lakki to Piraeus (11 hours, €19.70), Kos (3¼ hours, €6.20) and Rhodes (7¼ hours, €14), as well as two weekly to Samos (3½ hours, €5.50).

Hydrofoil & Catamaran In summer there are hydrofoils and a catamaran every day to Patmos (45 minutes, €9.50), Lipsi (20 minutes, €7.20), Samos (two hours, €15), Kos (one hour, €12.30) and Rhodes (3¼ hours, €28). Hydrofoils and the catamaran leave from Agia Marina.

Excursion Boat The caique leaves Xirokambos 7.30am daily for Myrties on Kalymnos (€4.70 one way). In summer Lipsi-based caiques make daily trips between Agia Marina and Lipsi. The trip costs €14.70 return.

Getting Around Leros
The hub for Leros' buses is Platanos. There are four buses daily to Partheni via Alinda and six buses to Xirokambos via Lakki (€0.60 flat fare).

There is no shortage of car, motorcycle and bicycle rental outlets around the island.

LAKKI Λακκί
Arriving at Lakki (lah-**kee**) by boat is like stepping into an abandoned Fellini film set. The grandiose buildings and wide tree-lined boulevards dotted around the Dodecanese are best (or worst) shown here, for Lakki was built as a Fascist showpiece during the Italian occupation. Few people linger in Lakki, though it has decent accommodation and restaurants and there are some secluded swimming opportunities on the road past the port. Check your email at Barrage Internet Café (☎ 2247 024 813) in Lakki, open 8am to 1am, with rates of €3 per hour.

XIROKAMBOS Ξηρόκαμπος
Xirokambos Bay, on the south of the island, is a low-key resort with a gravel-and-sand beach and some good spots for snorkelling. Just before the camping ground, on the opposite side, a signposted path leads up to the ruined fortress of **Paleokastro**.

Diving courses are offered by the **Panos Diving Club** (☎ *2247 023 372, mobile* ☎ *694 763 3146; 10-day course around* €*366 all-inclusive*).

Places to Stay & Eat
Camping Leros (☎ *2247 023 372*) Adult/tent €4.50/2.30. The island's only camping ground, this is on the right coming from Lakki. It's pleasant and shaded though the ground is a little hard. There is a small restaurant and bar.

Villa Alexandros (☎ *2247 022 202*) Doubles €44. About 100m from the beach, this is a better but more expensive choice.

DODECANESE

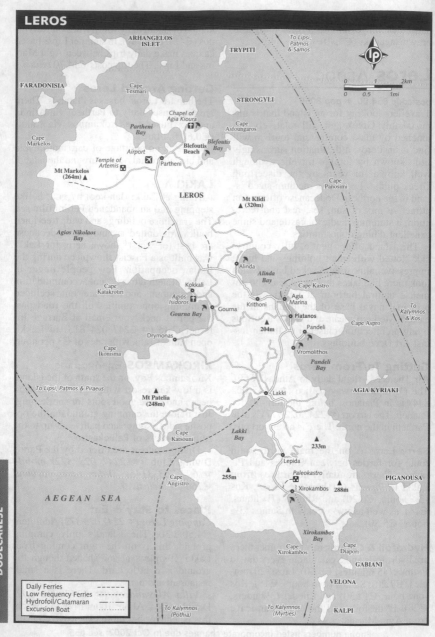

LEROS

ARHANGELOS ISLET

TRYPITI

To Lipsi,
Patmos
& Samos

FARADONISIA

Cape
Tesmari

STRONGYLI

Chapel of
Agia Kioura

Cape
Asfoungaros

*Partheni
Bay*

Cape
Markelos

*Blefoutis
Bay*

Blefoutis
Beach

Airport

Cape
Panosimi

Temple of
Artemis

Partheni

Mt Markelos
(264m) ▲

LEROS

Mt Klidi
(320m) ▲

*Agios Nikolaos
Bay*

Alinda

*Alinda
Bay*

Cape
Katakrotiri

Kokkali

Cape Kastro

To
Kalymnos
& Kos

Agios
Isidoros

Krithoni

Agia
Marina

Gourna Bay

Gourna

Platanos

Cape Aspro

Pandeli

204m ▲

Drymonas

Vromolithos

Cape
Ikonisma

*Pandeli
Bay*

To Lipsi, Patmos & Piraeus

Lakki

AGIA KYRIAKI

Mt Patelia
(248m) ▲

*Lakki
Bay*

233m ▲

Cape
Katsouni

Lepida

255m ▲

Cape
Angistro

Paleokastro

Xirokambos

288m ▲

PIGANOUSA

AEGEAN SEA

*Xirokambos
Bay*

Cape
Xirokambos

Cape
Diapori

GABIANI

VELONA

To Kalymnos
(Pothia)

To Kalymnos
(Myrties)

KALPI

Daily Ferries
Low Frequency Ferries
Hydrofoil/Catamaran
Excursion Boat

0   1   2km
0   0.5   1mi

DODECANESE

To Kyma (☎ 2247 025 248) Mayirefta
€3.50-4. Straddling the road at the eastern
side of the bay and under the shade of
tamarisk trees is this relaxing restaurant.
Try fried calamari, or a dish from the daily
mayirefta selection.

PLATANOS & AGIA MARINA
ΠλάτανοVω & Αγία Μαρίνα
Platanos (plah-ta-nos), the capital of Leros,
is 3km north of Lakki. It's a picturesque
place spilling over a narrow hill pouring
down to the port of Agia Marina to the north,
and Pandeli to the south, both within walking distance. The port of **Agia Marina** (ay-i-
a ma-ri-na) has a more authentic ambience
than Alinda resort to the north. Platanos is
the main shopping area for the island, and
while it doesn't offer much in the way of eating or accommodation options, it's a very
pleasant place to spend a leisurely hour or so
browsing. It is also the starting point for path
up to the **Castle of Pandeli** *(admission €0.88
castle, €1.50 castle & museum; open 8am-
1pm & 5pm-8.30pm daily)*.

Orientation & Information
The focal point of Platanos is the lively central square, Plateia N Roussou. Harami
links this square with Agia Marina.

There is a tourist information kiosk at the
quay. Laskarina Tours (☎ 2247 024 550, fax
2247 024 551), at the Eleftheria Hotel, and
Kastis Travel & Tourist Agency (☎ 2247
022 140), near the quay in Agia Marina, are
very helpful. Laskarina Tours organises
trips around the island (€11 to €18).

The post office and OTE share premises
on the right side of Harami. You can access
the Internet at Enallaktiko Cafe (☎ 2247
025 746) in Agia Marina.

The National Bank of Greece is on the
central square. There is a Commercial Bank
ATM in Agia Marina. The police station
(☎ 2247 022 222) is in Agia Marina. The bus
station and taxi rank are both on the Lakki-
Platanos road, just before the central square.

Places to Stay & Eat
Eleftheria Hotel (☎ 2247 023 550) Doubles with bathroom €32.50. This C-class

hotel, near the taxi rank, has pleasant, well-
kept rooms.

You are probably better off heading down
to Agia Marina to eat, as the only real option
in Platanos is the *cafe* on the central square.

Ouzeri-Taverna Neromylos (☎ 2247 024
894, Agia Marina) Mains €4-5.50. There
are several tavernas at Agia Marina, the
most atmospheric of which is this one next
to a former watermill. Night-time dining is
best when lights illuminate the watermill.

Entertainment
Agia Marina is the heart of the island's
nightlife, with several late-night music bars.

Enallaktiko Cafe (Agia Marina) Beer
€1.50. This popular hang-out has pool,
video games and Internet access.

PANDELI
Walking south from Platanos, you'll arrive
at **Pandeli**, a little fishing village-cum-resort
with a sand-and-shingle beach. Just outside
of Platanos, beyond the turn-off for Pandeli,
a road winds steeply down to **Vromolithos**
where there's a good shingle beach.

Places to Stay
At *Pension Roza* (☎ 2247 022 798) on the
waterfront doubles/triples cost €17.50/23.50.

Rooms to Rent Kavos (☎ 2247 023 247)
has reasonable doubles for €32.50, a bit
farther along from Pension Roza.

Pension Happiness (☎ 2247 023 498)
Singles/doubles with bathroom €29.50/
32.50. Pension Happiness, on the left down
from Platanos, has modern, sunny rooms.

Pension Rodon (☎ 2247 022 075) Doubles
€26.50-32.50. Open year-round. This place is
up near the main road halfway between Pandeli and Vromolithos, next to Dimitris Taverna. It is an excellent and popular choice.

Places to Eat
Dimitris Taverna (☎ 2247 025 626)
Mezedes €3-4.50. This is one of Leros'
best tavernas. Its delicious mezedes include
cheese courgettes, stuffed calamari, and
onion and cheese pies; main courses include
chicken in retsina and pork in red sauce. It's
high up near the main road.

Psaropoula (☎ 2247 025 200) Mains €5. Right on the beach, Psaropoula has a wide-ranging menu featuring fish; prawn souvlaki with bacon is a good choice.

Entertainment
Savana Bar Open mid-afternoon-late. In Pandeli, head for this bar, run by two English guys. It has a great music policy: you can choose what you want.

KRITHONI & ALINDA
Κριθώνι & Αλίντα
Krithoni and Alinda are contiguous resorts on the wide Alinda Bay, 3km north-west of Agia Marina. On Krithoni's waterfront there is a poignant, well-kept **war cemetery**. After the Italian surrender in WWII, Leros saw fierce fighting between German and British forces. The cemetery contains the graves of 179 British, two Canadian and two South African soldiers.

Alinda, the island's biggest resort, has a long, tree-shaded sand-and-gravel beach. If you walk beyond the development you'll find some quiet coves.

Places to Stay & Eat
Hotel Gianna (☎/fax 2247 024 135, Alinda) Singles/doubles €26.50/38. Just beyond the war cemetery, a road veers left to this place, which has nicely furnished rooms.

Studios & Apartments Diamantis (☎ 2247 022 378, Alinda) Doubles/triples €35.50/44. This sparkling, pine-furnished place is behind the cemetery.

Tassos Studios I (☎ 2247 022 769, fax 023 769, Krithoni) 2-4 person studios €47. Beautiful fully-equipped mini-apartments close to Krithoni beach, with the same owners as Tassos II in Agia Marina.

Finikas Taverna (☎ 2247 022 695, Alinda) Mezedes €2.50-4.20. This waterfront taverna in Alinda offers up 15 types of salad and 16 different mezedes and has an equally extensive menu of well-prepared Greek specialities.

GOURNA Γούρνα
The wide bay of Gourna, on the west coast, has a similar beach to Alinda but is

less developed. At the northern side, the chapel of **Agios Isidoros** is on a tranquil islet reached by a causeway.

NORTHERN LEROS
Partheni is a scattered settlement north of the airport. Despite having a large army camp, it's an attractive area of hills, olive groves, fields of beehives and two large bays.

Artemis, the goddess of the hunt, was worshipped on Leros in ancient times. Just south of the airport there's a signposted turn to the left that leads to the **Temple of Artemis**. A dirt track turns right 300m along it. Where the track peters out, clamber up to the left. You will see the little derelict **Chapel of Agia Irini**. There's little in the way of ancient ruins but it's a strangely evocative, slightly eerie place.

Farther along the main road there is a turn-off to the right to **Blefoutis Bay**, which has a shaded sand-and-pebble beach and a good taverna. Beyond this turn-off, the main road skirts **Partheni Bay** and its poor beach. But if you continue straight ahead, turn right at the T-junction, go through a gate to pass the **Chapel of Agia Kioura**, then through another gate and bear right, you'll come to a lovely secluded pebbled cove.

Patmos Πάτμος

postcode 855 00 • pop 2663
Patmos could well be *the* ideal Greek island destination. It has a beguiling mix of qualities that make it a seductively pleasant holiday destination. It appeals in equal doses to the culturally inclined, the religiously motivated, gastronomes and sun-worshippers, shoppers, yachties, bookaholics and travellers simply seeking to unwind. Patmos is a place of pilgrimage for both Orthodox and Western Christians, for it was here that St John wrote his divinely inspired revelation (the Apocalypse). Patmos is instantly palatable and entices the visitor to linger and to almost certainly return another time.

History
In AD 95, St John the Divine was banished to Patmos from Ephesus by the pagan

Roman Emperor Domitian. While residing in a cave on the island, St John wrote the *Book of Revelations*. In 1088 the Blessed Christodoulos, an abbot who came from Asia Minor to Patmos, obtained permission from the Byzantine Emperor Alexis I Komninos to build a monastery to commemorate St John. Pirate raids necessitated powerful fortifications, so the monastery looks like a mighty castle.

Under the Duke of Naxos, Patmos became a semi-autonomous monastic state, and achieved such wealth and influence that it was able to resist Turkish oppression. In

the early 18th century, a school of theology and philosophy was founded by Makarios and it flourished until the 19th century.

Gradually the island's wealth polarised into secular and monastic entities. The secular wealth was acquired through shipbuilding, an industry that diminished with the arrival of the steam ship.

Getting To/From Patmos
Ferry Patmos is on the main north-south route for ferries to and from Rhodes and Piraeus and is reasonably well serviced with at least one and sometimes more daily

PATMOS

Daily Ferries	- - - - -	
Low Frequency Ferries	··········	
Hydrofoil/Catamaran	———	
Excursion Boat	— — —	

DODECANESE

Phone numbers listed incorporate changes due in Oct 2002; see p55

departures from Skala. Services are provided by D.A.N.E. Lines and G&A Ferries, while the F/B *Nisos Kalymnos* or F/B *Hioni* provide additional links to Agathonisi and Samos.

Hydrofoil & Catamaran There are daily hydrofoils to Rhodes (five hours, €32.20), via Kalymnos (1½ hours, €15) and Kos (2¼ hours, €16.75), and to Fourni (40 minutes, €10.50), Ikaria (1¼ hours, €10.90) and Samos (one hour, €10.801). Twice a week, a hydrofoil runs to and from Agathonisi (40 minutes, €10).

The *Dodekanisos Express* catamaran calls in at Patmos six times a week during summer. Tickets can be bought at the Dodekanisos Shipping Agency (☎ 2247 029 303, ⓔ liapi@klm.forthnet.gr) in Skala. Prices are similar to hydrofoil ticket prices.

Excursion Boat The local *Patmos Express* leaves Patmos daily for Lipsi at 10am (€6 return) and returns from Lipsi at 4pm.

The Patmos-based *Delfini* (☎ 2247 031 995) goes to Marathi every day in high season – Monday and Thursday at other times. Twice a week it also calls in at Arki. From Marathi a local caique will take you across to Arki.

Getting Around Patmos

Bus From Skala there are 11 buses daily in July and August to Hora (€0.65), eight to Grikos (€0.70) and four to Kambos (€0.70). The frequency drops off during the rest of the year. There is no bus service to Lambi.

Motorcycle There are lots of motorcycle and car rental outlets in Skala. Competition is fierce, so shop around. Australis Motor Rentals (☎ 2247 032 284) rents scooters for between €8.80 and €18 per day.

Taxi Taxis congregate at Skala's taxi rank. Sample fares are: Meloï Beach €2.40, Lambi €4.40, Grikos €3.50 and Hora €3.

Excursion Boat Boats go to all the island's beaches from Skala, leaving about 11am and returning about 4pm.

SKALA Σκάλα
Patmos' port town is Skala (**ska**-la), a bright and glitzy town draped around a curving bay and only visible from arriving ships once the protective headland has been rounded. It's a busy port and large cruise ships are often anchored offshore and smaller ones at Skala's harbour. Once the cruise ships and daily ferries depart, Skala reverts to being a fairly normal, livable port town. It has a wide range of good accommodation and restaurants, and all the island's major facilities are here.

Orientation & Information

Facing inland from the quay, turn right to reach the main stretch of waterfront where excursion boats and yachts dock. The right side of the large, white Italianate building opposite the quay overlooks the central square. For the road to Hora, turn left from the quay and right at Taverna Grigoris.

The generally useless municipal tourist office (☎ 2247 031 666), open summer only, shares the Italianate building with the post office and police station. Astoria Travel (☎ 2247 031 205, fax 2247 031 975), on the waterfront near the quay, and Travel Point (☎ 2247 032 801, fax 2247 032 802, ⓔ info@travelpoint.gr), just inland from the central square, are helpful. The latter has a room-finding service.

The National Bank of Greece on the central square has an ATM. Inland from the central square is another smaller square; the OTE is on the left side of the road heading inland from here. The hospital (☎ 2247 031 211) is 2km along the road to Hora.

Patmos' port police (☎ 2247 031 231) are behind the large quay's passenger-transit building. The bus terminal and taxi rank (☎ 2247 031 225) are at the large quay.

Places to Stay – Budget

Domatia owners meet the boat. If you are not scooped up by one, there are a couple of budget places along the Hora road.

Pension Sofia (☎ 2247 031 876) Doubles/triples with bathroom €23.50/26.50. Head up along the Hora road and look for this comfortable pension 250m on the left. The rooms have balconies.

Pension Maria Pascalidis (☎ 2247 032 152), farther up the Hora road, is similar to Sofia and has singles/doubles for €14.50/ 23.50.

Hotel Rex (☎ 2247 031 242) Singles/ doubles with bathroom €20.50/26.50. This fairly basic D-class hotel is on a narrow street opposite the cafeteria/passenger-transit building.

About 500m north of the main harbour is Netia, a quieter district with a number of accommodation options.

Pension Avgerinos (☎/fax 2247 032 118, *Netia*) Doubles with bathroom €44. Pen-sion Avgerinos is run by a welcoming Greek-Australian couple. The rooms' views are very good.

Villa Knossos (☎ 2247 032 189, fax 22 47 032 284, *Netia*) Doubles/triples with bathroom €41/44. This villa, set in a lovely garden, has immaculate rooms with balcony.

Australis Apartments (☎ 2247 032 562, fax 2247 032 284, *Netia*) Doubles €47. Nearby and easy to find is Australia Apartments where rooms have TV and fully equipped kitchenette.

Australis Hotel (☎ 2247 032 189, 2247 032 284, *Netia*) Singles/doubles €38/44.

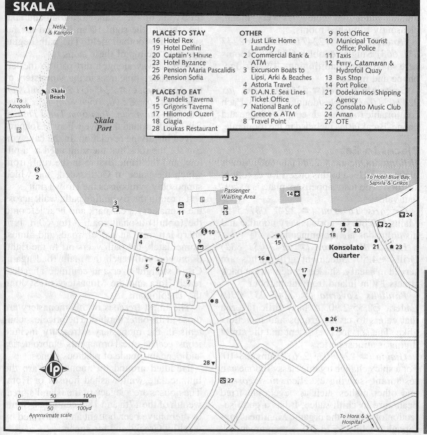

SKALA

PLACES TO STAY
16 Hotel Rex
19 Hotel Delfini
20 Captain's House
23 Hotel Byzance
25 Pension Maria Pascalidis
26 Pension Sofia

PLACES TO EAT
5 Pandelis Taverna
15 Grigoris Taverna
17 Hiliomodi Ouzeri
18 Giagia
28 Loukas Restaurant

OTHER
1 Just Like Home Laundry
2 Commercial Bank & ATM
3 Excursion Boats to Lipsi, Arki & Beaches
4 Astoria Travel
6 D.A.N.E. Sea Lines Ticket Office
7 National Bank of Greece & ATM
8 Travel Point

9 Post Office
10 Municipal Tourist Office; Police
11 Taxis
12 Ferry, Catamaran & Hydrofoil Quay
13 Bus Stop
14 Port Police
21 Dodekanisos Shipping Agency
22 Consolato Music Club
24 Aman
27 OTE

To Acropolis

Netia, & Kampos

Skala Beach

Skala Port

To Hotel Blue Bay, Sapsila & Grikos

Passenger Waiting Area

Konsolato Quarter

To Hora & Hospital

0   50   100m
0   50   100yd
Approximate scale

DODECANESE

Set amidst a leafy garden, the Australis also has larger rooms for up to six persons.

Places to Stay – Mid-Range
On the south side of the harbour are other pricier options.

Hotel Delfini (☎ 2247 032 060, fax 2247 032 061) Singles/doubles €35.50/54.30. This C-class hotel has well-kept rooms. The front rooms have individual balconies with blue-and-white tables and cane chairs overlooking the street.

Hotel Blue Bay (☎ 2247 031 165, fax 2247 032 303, ℮ bluebayhotel@yahoo .com, ⓦ www.bluebay.50g.com) Singles/doubles €44/59. This Australian-Greek owned waterfront hotel has very clean, pleasantly furnished rooms.

Hotel Byzance (☎ 2247 031 052 fax 2247 031 663) Singles/doubles €53/62. Rooms here have air-conditioning, TV, fridge, phone and music.

Captain's House (☎ 2247 031 793, fax 2247 034 077) Singles/doubles €53/73. Each comfortable room has air-con, TV, fridge and phone. Breakfast is included in the room rate.

Places to Eat
Hiliomodi Ouzeri (☎ 2247 034 080) Mezes platter €6. Head to this ouzeri for excellent seafood. The tasty appetisers plate is excellent value.

Grigoris Taverna (☎ 2247 031 515) Mains €.3.80. Grigoris is very popular and his dolmades are recommended.

Loukas Restaurant (☎ 2247 031 832) Grills €4.50. Succulent grill dishes are served in a leafy, shaded garden, in the back streets 150m inland from the harbour.

Pandelis Taverna (☎ 2247 031 230) Ladera €2.35-2.90. A busy little taverna that caters to cruise groups and travellers alike. The service is efficient and the street dining is atmospheric.

Giagia (☎ 2247 033 226) Mains €8-10. For a spicy change try this classy Indonesian restaurant, serving excellent *nasi goreng* and other dishes such as vegetarian fried bean curd in chilli sauce. It has a good selection of wines; the organic Mantinea Spyropoulou white (€13.20) is recommended.

Entertainment
Skala's music nightlife revolves around a scattering of bars and the odd club or two. *Consolato Music Club* (☎ 2247 031 194) is a popular bar that is open year-round.

Aman (☎ 2247 032 323) Nearby is another popular spot. This is more a place to sit outside on its tree-shaded patio and relax to music while nursing a cold beer or cocktail.

MONASTERIES & HORA
The immense **Monastery of St John the Theologian**, with its buttressed grey walls, crowns the island of Patmos. A 4km asphalt road leads in from Skala, but many people prefer to walk up the Byzantine path. To do this, walk up the Skala-Hora road and take the steps to the right 100m beyond the far side of the football field. The path begins opposite the top of these steps.

A little way along, a dirt path to the left leads through pine trees to the **Monastery of the Apocalypse** (☎ 2247 031 234; admission free, treasury €2.90; open 8am-1pm Mon-Sat, 8am-noon Sun, 4pm-6pm Tues, Thur & Sun), built around the cave where St John received his divine revelation. In the cave you can see the rock that the saint used as a pillow, and the triple fissure in the roof, from which the voice of God issued, and which supposedly symbolises the Holy Trinity.

To rejoin the Byzantine path, walk across the monastery's car park and bear left onto the (uphill) asphalt road. After 60m, turn sharp left onto an asphalt road, and almost immediately the path veers off to the right. Soon you will reach the main road again. Cross straight over and continue ahead to reach Hora and the Monastery of St John the Theologian.

The finest frescoes of this monastery are those in the outer narthex. The priceless contents in the monastery's **treasury** include icons, ecclesiastical ornaments, embroideries and pendants made of precious stones.

Huddled around the monastery are the immaculate whitewashed houses of **Hora**. The houses are a legacy of the island's great wealth of the 17th and 18th centuries. Some of them have been bought and renovated by wealthy Greeks and foreigners.

Places to Stay & Eat

There are no hotel or domatia signs in Hora. There is accommodation but it is expensive and the best places are pre-booked months in advance. Try Travel Point in Skala, who have at least 10 traditional houses for rent.

Vangelis Taverna (☎ 2247 031 967) Mains €4.50. This taverna on the central square is deservedly popular. Good bets are bekri mezes (pork cubes in a spicy sauce with vegetables) and the similar spetsofaï.

To Balkoni (☎ 2247 032 115) Mains €5-6.50. The best dining views from Hora are afforded by 'The Balcony' which affords stunning views at night down to Skala. The food is excellent; beef and liver with onions is one of the specials.

NORTH OF SKALA

The pleasant, tree-shaded **Meloï Beach** is just 2km north-east of Skala, along a turn-off from the main road.

Two kilometres farther along the main road there's a turn-off right to the relatively quiet **Agriolivado Beach**. The main road continues to the inland village of **Kambos** and then descends to the shingle beach from where you can walk to the secluded pebbled **Vagia Beach**. The main road ends at **Lambi**, 9km from Skala, where there is a beautiful beach of multicoloured pebbles.

Places to Stay & Eat

Stefanos Camping (☎ 2247 031 821, Meloï) Adult/tent €3.80/2. This good camping ground, with bamboo-shaded sites, a mini-market, cafe bar and motorcycle rental facilities, is at Meloï. The rainbow-coloured minibus meets most boats.

Rooms to Rent (☎ 2247 031 213, Meloï) Doubles €22. These basic domatia are 50m back from the beach. The family also owns some newer rooms nearby, where doubles with bathroom are €24.

Ta Kavourakia (☎ 2247 031 745, Kambos) Meals €8-9. Ta Kavourakia is popular with Italians and serves up good fish dishes.

George's Place (☎ 2247 031 881, Kambos) Snacks €3-5. George's is on the beach and serves light snacks and drinks. You can play backgammon to laid-back music.

Psistaria Leonidas (☎ 2247 031 490, Lambi) Mayirefta €2.50-3.50. Leonidas on Lambi beach rustles up a wide range of homemade mayirefta dishes, various fish of the day plates and highly recommended saganaki (€3.80).

SOUTH OF SKALA

Sapsila is a quiet little corner 3km south of Skala, ideal for book lovers who want space and quiet and an underused beach to read on. **Grikos**, 1km further along over the hill, is a relaxed low-key resort with a narrow sandy beach. Farther south, the long, sandy, tree-shaded **Psili Ammos** can be reached by excursion boat or walking track.

Places to Stay & Eat

Matheos Studios (☎ 2247 032 119, Sapsila) Double/triple studios €29/41. This relaxed getaway is a neat place to stay for a week or so. The seven self-contained studios are set in a quiet, leafy garden 200m from Sapsila beach.

Stamatis Rooms (☎ 2247 031 302, Grikos) Doubles with bathroom €35. The rooms at this, the cheapest place to stay in Grikos, are comfortable enough.

Flisvos Restaurant (☎ 2247 031 764, Grikos) Full meals €8-9. Flisvos is a well-shaded, modern taverna. Accompany your meal with their fruity, slightly spritzig draft wine. There is also a seasonal *taverna* on Psili Ammos.

Lipsi Λειψοί

postcode 850 01 • pop 606

Lipsi (lip-**see**), 12km east of Patmos and 11km north of Leros, is the kind of place that few people know about, and once they have discovered it feel disinclined to share their discovery with others. It's a friendly, cheery place with just about the right balance of remoteness and 'civilisation'. There is comfortable accommodation, a pleasing choice of quality restaurants and a good selection of underpopulated beaches. Apart from two or three days a year when pilgrims and revellers descend upon Lipsi for its major festival, you can have most of it to yourself.

DODECANESE

Getting To/From Lipsi

Ferry Lipsi is not well served by ferries. The F/B *Nisos Kalymnos* or F/B *Hioni* make up for the deficit somewhat with at least four visits a week providing links both north and south. Hellas Ferries occasionally call in.

Hydrofoil & Catamaran In summer, hydrofoils call at Lipsi at least twice daily on their routes north and south between Samos, in the North-Eastern Aegean, and Rhodes. The *Dodekanisos Express* catamaran calls in three times a week. Sample fares are Rhodes (4½ hours) €29.70 and Patmos (20 minutes) €7.

Excursion Boat The *Captain Makis* and *Anna Express* do daily trips in summer to Agia Marina on Leros and to Skala on Patmos (both €14.70 return). *Black Beauty* and *Margarita* do 'Five Island' trips for around the same price. All four excursion boats can be found at the small quay and all depart at around 10am each day.

Getting Around Lipsi

Lipsi has three minibuses going to Platys Gialos (€0.90), Katsadia and Hohlakoura (both €0.80). Two taxis also operate on the island. There are several motorcycle rental outlets.

LIPSI TOWN
Orientation & Information

All boats dock at Lipsi Town, where there are two quays. The ferries, hydrofoils and catamaran all dock at the larger, outer jetty, while excursion boats dock at a smaller jetty nearer the centre of Lipsi town.

From the large quay, facing inland, turn right. Continue along the waterfront to the large Plateia Nikiforios, which is just beyond Hotel Calypso. Ascend the wide steps at the far side of Plateia Nikiforios and bear right to reach the central square. The left fork leads to a second, smaller square.

The municipal tourist office (☎ 2247 041 288) is on the central square, but you may find Laid Back Holidays (☎ 2247 041 141,

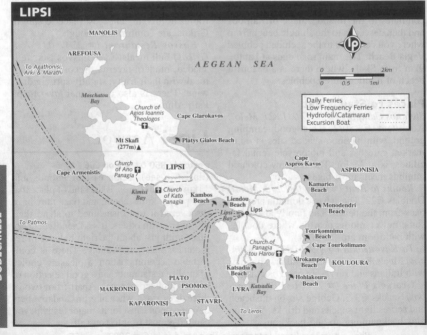

LIPSI

AEGEAN SEA

MANOLIS

AREFOUSA

To Agathonisi,
Arki & Marathi

Moschatou
Bay

Church of
Agios Ioannis
Theologos

Cape Glarokavos

Mt Skafi
(277m) ▲

Platys Gialos Beach

Church
of Ano
Panagia

LIPSI

Cape
Aspros Kavos

ASPRONISIA

Cape Armenistis

Kimisi
Bay

Church
of Kato
Panagia

Kambos
Beach

Liendou
Beach

Kamaries
Beach

Monodendri
Beach

To Patmos

Lipsi
Bay

Lipsi

Tourkomnima
Beach

Cape Tourkolimano

Church of
Panagia
tou Harou

Xirokampos
Beach

KOULOURA

Katsadia
Beach

Hohlakoura
Beach

PLATO
PSOMOS

MAKRONISI

KAPARONISI

STAVRI

PILAVI

LYRA

Katsadia
Bay

To Leros

Daily Ferries
Low Frequency Ferries
Hydrofoil/Catamaran
Excursion Boat

0   0.5   1mi
0   1   2km

fax 2247 041 343) or Lipsos Travel (☎/fax 2247 041 215) more helpful. The post office and OTE are on the central square, and there is a freestanding Commercial Bank ATM near the wide steps. Paradisis Travel changes money and cashes Eurocheques. The police (☎ 2247 041 222) are in the large white building opposite Paradisis Travel. The port police (☎ 2247 041 133) are in the long white building to the right of the wide steps.

Things to See & Do

Lipsi's **museum** *(Plateia, admission free; open 11am-1pm)* is on the central square. Its small display of exhibits include pebbles and plastic bottles of holy water from around the world.

The town beach of **Liendou** is a short walk from the waterfront. More strenuous entertainment can be enjoyed by walking to each of the island's beaches (see Beaches later).

Places to Stay

Studios Kalymnos (☎ *2247 041 141, fax 2247 041 343,* e *lbh@otenet.gr)* Doubles €32. One of the more appealing and certainly the most friendly place to stay is at these neat and airy studios, a 10-minute walk from the quay. Studios Kalymnos are set in a cool garden with a barbecue for guests, with soothing chill-out music played during the day. Owner Nick can usually be found at the Laid Back Holidays booth on the ferry quay.

O Glaros (☎ *2247 041 360)* Doubles €23.50. Set back on the hill about 100m from Plateia Nikiforios is this choice. There are a few smallish but airy and comfortable rooms with a wide communal balcony and a well-equipped communal kitchen.

Flisvos Pension (☎ *2247 041 261)* Doubles/triples €29.50/35.20. This simple pension is just beyond the police station.

Hotel Calypso (☎/fax *2247 041 420)* Doubles/ triples with bathroom €29.50/35.20. Opposite the excursion boat quay you'll find this D-class hotel with comfortable rooms.

Rooms Galini (☎ *2247 041 212, 2247 041 012)* Doubles with bathroom €35.20. High up overlooking the harbour, Galini has pleasant, light rooms with refrigerator, cooking ring and balcony.

Rizos Studios (☎/fax *2247 041 215)* Doubles/triples €44/50. These exceptionally well-equipped and well-located studios are brand new. Each unit is equipped with every kitchen utensil imaginable and enjoys a view over Liendou Bay. Contact Lipsos Travel for location details.

Places to Eat & Drink

There's a string of restaurants and cafes on the waterfront between the two quays as well as one or two places up near the main square.

Yiannis Restaurant (☎ *2247 045 395)* Grills €4.70. This place near the main ferry quay is popular and highly recommended.

Psarotaverna Theologos (☎ *2247 041 248)* Fish €20.50/kg. Further along the quay, Theologos only opens when the owner has fish to cook and that is not every day. However, the fish is guaranteed to be very fresh.

The Rock (☎ *2247 041 180)* Mezedes €1-2. This coffee bar and ouzeri offers some unusual mezedes such as sea urchins with ouzo (€1.50). The tasty grilled octopus is a standard mezes.

Kalipso Restaurant (☎ *2247 041 060)* Grills €4-5. Adjoining the hotel of the same name, Kalipso serves very tasty, low-priced food.

Cafe du Moulin (☎ *2247 041 416)* Snacks €3-4. Up on the main square is this French- and Greek-speaking establishment. It's good for light lunches – omelettes, mousakas and the like.

Meltemi Night Club Night owls head here for music and drinks. Greek music usually kicks in later on and it stays open until late – or early, depending on how you view your day.

AROUND THE ISLAND
Beaches

Lipsi has quite a few beaches and all are within walking distance. Some are shaded, some are not. Some are sandy, others gravelly. At least one is for nudism. Getting there makes for pleasant walks passing through countryside dotted with smallholdings, olive groves and cypresses, but buses also go to most of them.

DODECANESE

The Miracle of Lipsi

Every year a small miracle happens on the small island of Lipsi. An icon of the Virgin Mary in the blue-domed church of Agios Ioannis in Lipsi Town has small sprig of dried lilies encased within the glass protecting the icon. Every year on August 24 the dried lily sprig comes to life and a cluster of white buds appears thereon and blossoms. Amid much pomp and ceremony, the icon is taken in procession from the church of Agios Ioannis to the small chapel of the Panagia tou Harou – the curiously-named Virgin of Charon, so-named because this is the only icon in the Orthodox world that shows the Virgin holding a dead Jesus. Here a ceremony, attended by nearly all the islanders and hundreds of visiting pilgrims, takes place. The religious ceremony is followed by a night-long feast (paneyiri).

The story goes that a young woman once prayed for assistance for her son from the Virgin. Her prayer was duly answered and, in gratitude, she left a small bouquet of lilies near the icon of the Virgin. The lilies withered in due course, but on 24 August, the day of the Virgin's Assumption into Heaven, the lilies sprang to life once more and have done so ever since. This once sceptical writer took part in the procession and did indeed espy the revitalised lily buds popping up under the protective glass. Sleight-of-hand, or a true miracle? Decide for yourselves next 24 August.

Liendou Beach is the most accessible and naturally most popular beach. The water is very shallow and calm; this is the best beach for children.

Next along is sandy **Kambos Beach** a 1km, 15-minute walk along the same road that leads to Platys Gialos. Take the dirt road off to the left. There is some shade available.

Beyond Kambos Beach the road takes you, after about 40 minutes, to **Platys Gialos**, a lovely but narrow sandy beach with a decent taverna. The water is turquoise-coloured, shallow and ideal for children. The minibus runs here.

South 2km from Lipsi town is the sand-and-pebble **Katsadia Beach**, shaded with

tamarisk trees and easily reached on foot, or by the hourly minibus. There are two restaurants here and the water is clean and protected.

The pebble **Hohlakoura Beach**, to the east of Katsadia, is near the **Church of Panagia tou Harou** but offers neither shade nor facilities. Farther north, **Monodendri** is the island's unofficial nudist beach. It stands on a rocky peninsula, and there are no facilities. It is a 3km, 50-minute walk to get there, though it is reachable by motor bike.

Places to Eat

Gambieris Taverna (☎ 2247 041 087, Katsadia) Ladera €2.50-3.50. This small, rustic taverna, above the beach at Katsadia, is owned by an elderly couple who serve simple meat and fish dishes.

Dilaila Cafe Restaurant (☎ 2247 041 041, Katsadia) Mains €3-5. Nearer the beach, this modern spot is owned by English-speaking Christodoulos. Recommended dishes include vegetarian mousakas (€4.40) and chickpea patties (€3).

Kostas Restaurant (mobile ☎ 69 4496 3303, Platys Gialos). Grills €4-5; fish €5-7. Open 8am-6pm Jul-Aug, later on Wed & Sat. Owner Kostas Makris dishes up excellent fish and grill dishes as well as suckling pig (€6) in his restaurant overlooking the beach at Platys Gialos.

Arki & Marathi

Getting To/From Arki & Marathi

The F/B *Nisos Kalymnos* or *F/B Hioni* call in once a week, but this depends on the weather. In summer the Lipsi-based excursion boats visit Arki and Marathi, and the Patmos-based caique *Delfini* (☎ 2247 031 995) does frequent trips (€11.80 return).

ARKI Αρκοί

postcode 850 01 • pop 50

Tiny Arki, 5km north of Lipsi, is hilly, with shrubs but few trees. Its only settlement, the little west coast port, is also called Arki. Islanders make a meagre living from fishing.

There is no post office, OTE or police on the island, but there is a cardphone. Away from its little settlement, the island seems almost mystical in its peace and stillness.

Things to See & Do

The **Church of Metamorfosis** stands on a hill behind the settlement. From its terrace are superb views of Arki and its surrounding islets. The cement road between Taverna Trypas and Taverna Nikolaos leads to the path up to the church. The church is locked but ask a local if it's possible to look inside.

Several secluded sandy coves can be reached along a path skirting the right side of the bay. To reach the path, walk around the last house at the far right of the bay, go through a little wooden gate in the stone wall, near the sea, and continue ahead.

Tiganakia Bay on the south-east coast has a good sandy beach. To walk there from Arki village, take the cement road which skirts the north side of the bay. The bay is reached by a network of goat tracks and lies at the far side of the headland. You will recognise it by the incredibly bright turquoise water and the offshore islets.

Places to Stay & Eat

Arki has three tavernas, two of which have double rooms.

O Trypas Taverna & Rooms (☎ 2247 032 507) Doubles with bathroom €23.50; meals €5-6. This restaurant and hostelry is to the right of the quay, as you face inland. Suggested dishes are black-eyed beans (*fasolia mavromatika*) and *pastos tou Trypa*, a kind of salted fish dish.

Taverna Nikolaos Rooms (☎ 2247 032 477), open all year, has doubles for €24 and meals for around €6; try the potatoes *au gratin*. *Taverna Manolas*, opposite the quay with meals from €5 to €6, is also highly commendable.

MARATHI Μαράθι

Marathi is the largest of Arki's satellite islets. Before WWII it had a dozen or so inhabitants, but now has only one family. The old settlement, with an immaculate little church, stands on a hill above the harbour. The island has a superb sandy beach.

ARKI & MARATHI

Places to Stay & Eat

Marathi has two tavernas, both of which rent rooms and are owned by the island's only permanent inhabitants, who speak English.

Taverna Mihalis (☎ 2247 031 580) Doubles €23.50; meals €4-6. This taverna, the friendlier and cheaper of the two places to eat and sleep at, has comfortable doubles.

Taverna Pandelis (☎ 2247 032 609) has comfortable doubles for €30 and meals for €4 to €6.

Agathonisi
Αγαθονήσι

postcode 850 01 • pop 112

Agathonisi is a sun-bleached, often ignored speck of rock an hour's sail south of Samos. The island attracts yachties, serious island hoppers and the curious as well as latter-day Robinson Crusoes all seeking what Agathonisi has to offer – plain peace and quiet. Bring a stack of novels to this island and relax. There are only three settlements of any stature in the island: the port of Agios Georgios, the uphill and inland village of Megalo

DODECANESE

Horio and the smaller settlement of Mikro Horio all of which are less than 1km apart.

Getting To/From Agathonisi

Agathonisi is linked to Samos and Patmos about four times a week by the F/B *Nisos Kalymnos* and the F/B *Hioni*. A hydrofoil also links the island with Samos and destinations further south Monday to Saturday.

Getting Around Agathonisi

There is no public transport, but it takes less than 15 minutes to walk from Mikro Horio to Megalo Horio or to Agios Giorgios.

AGIOS GIORGIOS Αγιος Γεώργιος

The village of Agios Giorgios (**agh**-ios ye-or-yi-os) is a delightful little place with just enough waterfront activity to stop you sinking into a state of inertia. It has a pebbled beach and **Spilia Beach**, also pebbled, is close by, reached along the track around the far side of the bay.

Orientation & Information

Boats dock at Agios Giorgios from where cement roads ascend right (facing inland) to Megalo Horio and left to Mikro Horio. There is no tourist information, post office, bank or OTE, but there are cardphones.

The one police officer, who is also the port police and customs officer, has an office in the white building at the beginning of the Megalo Horio road.

Places to Stay & Eat

Domatia Giannis (☎ 2247 029 062) Doubles/triples €24/26. The newest establishment on the scene comprises comfortable rooms each of which takes between two and three persons, with four at a pinch. Inquire at the Glaros Restaurant.

Pension Maria Kamitsi (☎/fax 2247 029 003) Doubles with bathroom €22. This pleasant and friendly establishment is easy to find.

Theologias Rooms (☎ 2247 029 005) Doubles with bathroom €22. This place is next door to Pension Maria Kamitsi.

Glaros Restaurant (☎ 2247 029 062) Grills €4.50-5. This is perhaps the best place to eat. Try *markakia* – feta cheese fin-

AGATHONISI

Daily Ferries
Low Frequency Ferries
Hydrofoil/Catamaran
Excursion Boat

AEGEAN SEA

PSATHONISI

Katholika

AGATHONISI

Agios Georgios

Hohlia Bay

Mikro Horio

Megalo Horio

Church of Agios Nikolaos

Spilia Beach

Tholos Beach

To Samos

To Lipsi & Patmos

KOUNELONISI

gers in vine leaves with a special sauce. Owners Voula and Yiannis speak English.

George's Taverna (☎ 2247 029 007) Fish €7-8. This excellent taverna is the closest to the quay. George and his German wife speak English.

AROUND AGATHONISI

Megalo Horio is Agathonisi's biggest village. It doesn't have accommodation for tourists. **Tholos Beach** and **Katholika**, an abandoned fishing hamlet, are reached by the cement road from Megalo Horio. At the T-junction turn left to reach Tholos Beach, near a fish farm. You can visit the **Church of Agios Nikolaos**; ask a local if it's possible to look inside. **Katholika** is reached by turning left at the T-junction. There's not much to see but the walk is worth it for the views.

Places to Eat

Restaurant I Irini (☎ 2247 029 054, *Megalo Horio*) Meals €5-6. This restaurant on the central square has good solid meals.

Kafeneio/Pantopoleio Ta 13 Adelfia (*Megalo Horio*) Meals €4.50-6. Also on the central square, this kafeneio is a good budget place to eat.

North-Eastern Aegean Islands
Τα Νησιά του Βορειοανατολικού Αιγαίου

The North-Eastern Aegean Islands are grouped together more for convenience than for any historical, geographical or administrative reason. Apart from Thasos and Samothraki, they are, like the Dodecanese, much closer to Turkey than to the Greek mainland but, unlike the Dodecanese, they are not close to one another. This means island-hopping is not the easy matter it is within the Dodecanese and Cyclades, although, with the exception of Thasos and Samothraki, it is possible.

These islands are less visited than either the Dodecanese or the Cyclades. Scenically, they also differ from these groups. Mountainous, green and mantled with forests, they are ideal for hiking but most are also blessed with long stretches of delightful beaches.

Although historically diverse, a list of the islands' inhabitants from classical times reads like a who's who of the ancient world. Some of the North-Eastern Aegean Islands also boast important ancient sites. All of them became part of the Ottoman Empire and were then reunited with Greece after the Balkan Wars in 1912.

There are seven major islands in the group: Chios, Ikaria, Lesvos (Mytilini), Limnos, Samos, Samothraki and Thasos. Fourni situated near Ikaria, Psara and Inousses near Chios, and Agios Efstratios near Limnos are small, little-visited islands in the group.

Accommodation throughout the North-Eastern Aegean island chain tends to be a little more expensive than on some of Greece's more touristed islands, but bear in mind that the high-season (July to August) prices quoted in this chapter are 30% to 50% cheaper out of season.

SUGGESTED ITINERARIES

One week

With only seven days, you will be a bit pushed, so plan your ferry trips carefully, or just spend the whole week on one island. Fly out to Lesvos (Mytilini) or take a fast boat. Make sure you visit Mithymna (Molyvos) and the capital,

Highlights

- Lush, subtropical Samos – a paradise for lovers of nature
- The olive trails in Lesvos' Plomari region – great for long, magical walks
- The mystical Sanctuary of the Great Gods on remote Samothraki
- Thasos' dense forests, traditional villages and multitude of superb beaches
- Ikaria's Caribbean-like beaches and quirky, laid-back inland villages
- Village festivals on Lesvos and Ikaria
- Medieval Mesta, the most atmospheric of Chios' mastic villages

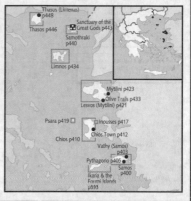

Thasos (Limenas) p448
Thasos p446
Sanctuary of the Great Gods p443
Samothraki p440
Limnos p434
Mytilini p423
Olive Trails p433
Lesvos (Mytilini) p421
Psara p419
Inousses p417
Chios Town p412
Chios p410
Vathy (Samos) p403
Pythagorio p405
Samos p400
Ikaria & the Fourni Islands p393

Mytilini. If you're interested in hiking, head for hills near Plomari, where there are nice trails through olive groves. Those interested in beaches, should spend a couple of days at Skala Eresou. You could easily spend a week on Lesvos, but if you fancy a change take a ferry to Chios and spend a night in one of the atmospheric and intriguing Mastihohoria (mastic villages). Fly or sail back to the mainland.

If you're interested in spending the whole week on one island, Thasos makes a good alternative to Lesvos. To get there, fly to Kavala and take the ferry from Keramoti.

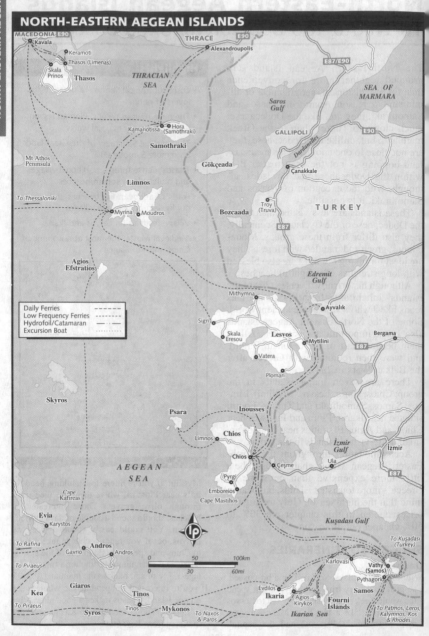

NORTH-EASTERN AEGEAN ISLANDS

Daily Ferries
Low Frequency Ferries
Hydrofoil/Catamaran
Excursion Boat

MACEDONIA E90
Kavala
Keramoti
Skala Thasos (Limenas)
Prinos
Thasos
THRACE E90
Alexandroupolis
E87/E90
THRACIAN SEA
Saros Gulf
SEA OF MARMARA
Kamariotissa
Hora (Samothraki)
Samothraki
Gökçeada
GALLIPOLI E90
Dardanelles
Çanakkale
Mt Athos Peninsula
Limnos
To Thessaloniki
Myrina Moudros
Bozcaada
Troy (Truva)
TURKEY
Agios Efstratios
Edremit Gulf
Mithymna
Ayvalık
Sigri
Skala Eresou
Lesvos
Bergama
Vatera
Mytilini
E87
Skyros
Plomari
Psara
Inousses
Limnos
Chios
Izmir Gulf
Izmir
Chios
AEGEAN SEA
(Pyrgi)
Emboreios
Cape Mastihos
Çeşme
Ula
E87
Cape Kafireas
Evia
Karystos
Kuşadası Gulf
To Rafina
Andros
Gavrio Andros
To Kuşadası (Turkey)
To Piraeus
Karlovasi
Vathy (Samos)
Pythagorio
Kea
Giaros
Tinos
Evdilos
Ikaria
Agios Kirykos
Samos
To Patmos, Leros, Kalymnos, Kos & Rhodes
To Piraeus
Syros
Tinos
Mykonos
To Naxos & Paros
Ikarian Sea
Fourni Islands

0   50   100km
0   30   60mi

Ferry Connections to the North-Eastern Aegean Islands

origin	destination	duration	price (€)	frequency
Alexandroupolis	Agios Efstratios	7 hours	13.50	1 weekly
Alexandroupolis	Chios	16 hours	26.00	2 weekly
Alexandroupolis	Limnos	5 hours	12.00	2 weekly
Alexandroupolis	Samos	20 hours	25.00	1 weekly
Alexandroupolis	Samothraki	2 hours	7.00	1 daily
Kavala	Agios Efstratios	6 hours	6.50	1 weekly
Kavala	Chios	16 hours	24.00	1 weekly
Kavala	Lesvos (Mytilini)	10 hours	20.00	2 weekly
Kavala	Limnos	5 hours	11.50	4 weekly
Kavala	Samothraki	4 hours	9.00	2 weekly
Kavala	Thasos (Skala Prinos)	1½ hours	3.00	1 hourly
Kavala	Thasos (Limenas)	1¾ hours	3.00	1 daily
Keramoti	Thasos (Limenas)	35 mins	1.50	1 hourly
Piraeus	Chios	8 hours	17.00	1 daily
Piraeus	Ikaria	9 hours	17.00	1 daily
Piraeus	Lesvos (Mytilini)	12 hours	22.50	1 daily
Piraeus	Limnos	13 hours	21.00	4 weekly
Piraeus	Samos	13 hours	20.50	2 daily
Rafina	Agios Efstratios	8½ hours	15.00	2 weekly
Rafina	Limnos	10 hours	17.00	4 weekly
Thessaloniki	Chios	18 hours	32.00	2 weekly
Thessaloniki	Lesvos	13 hours	25.00	2 weekly
Thessaloniki	Limnos	7 hours	16.50	2 weekly

Two weeks

Fly or take a ferry to Lesvos and follow the one-week itinerary to Chios. Continue on to Samos, which has interesting ruins, lovely scenery, and a reasonably busy nightlife, then on to Ikaria, if you want a laid-back and idiosyncratic few days. Spend a night or two on Fourni en route to Ikaria if quiet beaches are more your thing. Take the overnight boat back to Piraeus or fly to Athens from Samos or Ikaria to finish your trip.

GETTING TO/FROM THE NORTH-EASTERN AEGEAN ISLANDS
Air
Samos, Chios, Lesvos, Limnos and Ikaria have air links with Athens. In addition, Samos, Chios, Lesvos and Limnos have flights to Thessaloniki. Lesvos is connected to both Limnos and Chios by local flights.

Ferry – Domestic
The above table gives an overview of the scheduled domestic ferries to this island group travelling from mainland ports during the high season. Further details and information on inter-island links can be found under individual island entries.

Ferry – International
In summer there are daily ferries from Samos to Kuşadası (for Ephesus) and from Chios to Çesme. Ferries from Lesvos to Ayvalık run four times weekly.

Hydrofoil
In summer there are regular hydrofoil links running between Kavala and Thasos and there are also some hydrofoils travelling between Alexandroupolis and Samothraki. Hydrofoils also operate out of Samos where they head west towards Ikaria, south towards the Dodecanese as well as north towards Chios and Lesvos.

Ikaria & the Fourni Islands

pop 9000

Ikaria (Ικαρία; ih-kah-**ree**-ah) is a rocky and mountainous island which is fertile, with an abundance of cypress trees, pine forests, olive and fruit trees – Ikarian apricots are especially luscious. At present the island's tourism is low-key, but Ikaria is slowly being 'discovered' by Germans and Austrians seeking a quiet alternative. Ikaria's beaches at Livadia and Mesahti, near Armenistis on the north coast, have to be rated as among the best in Greece.

Ailing Greeks have visited Ikaria since ancient times because of its therapeutic radioactive springs which they believe to be the most efficacious in Europe. One spring is so highly radioactive that it was deemed unsafe and forced to close.

The name Ikaria originates from the mythical Icarus. Another myth ascribes the island as the birthplace of Dionysos, the Greek god of wine, fruitfulness and vegetation.

Ikaria has two ports, Agios Kirykos on the south coast, and Evdilos on the north coast. The island's best beaches are on the north coast, west of Evdilos.

Ikaria is a bit of an oddity as a tourist destination. Long neglected by mainland Greece and used as a dumping ground for left-wing political dissidents by various right-wing governments, Ikaria and Ikarians have a rather devil-may-care approach to things, including tourism. The islanders, while welcoming tourists, are taking a slow approach to cultivating the tourist dollar. The result is that Ikaria is an island that may take a bit of getting used to at first, but will surely remain long in your memory.

Getting To/From Ikaria

Air In summer there are six flights weekly to Athens (€66), usually departing in the early afternoon. The Olympic Airways office (☎ 2275 022 214) is in Agios Kirykos, though tickets can also be bought from Blue Nice Agency (☎ 2275 031 990, fax 2775 031 752) in Evdilos. There is no bus to the airport and a taxi will cost around €10.

Ferry Nearly all ferries that call at Ikaria's ports of Evdilos and Agios Kirykos are on the Piraeus-Samos route. Generally there are departures daily from Agios Kirykos and three to four weekly from Evdilos. There are five ferries a week to Mykonos (2½ hours, €9.60) and Samos (five hours, €15.40); four to Tinos (3½ hours) and Syros (2½ hours), and three to Paros (four hours, €10) and Naxos (3½ hours, €9). Buy tickets at Roustas Travel (☎ 2275 022 441, fax 2275 031 428) and the GA Ferries agency (☎ 2275 022 426) in Agios Kirykos or from Roustas Travel and Blue Nice Agency in Evdilos.

Chios-based Miniotis Lines also runs a couple of small boats twice weekly to Chios (8½ hours, €15) from Agios Kirykos via Fourni and Samos.

Hydrofoil Agios Kirykos handles the majority of Ikaria's hydrofoil services. In summer there are five connections weekly to the Fourni Islands (20 minutes, €6), four to Pythagorio on Samos (1¼ hours, €13.50), three to Patmos (1¼ hours, €11) and Kos (2¾ hours, €23), and weekly services to Chios, Kalymnos and Leros.

Hydrofoils to/from Evdilos are not as frequent, but they do exist. Check with Dolihi Tours (☎ 2275 023 230, fax 2275 022 346) for the latest information.

Caique A caique leaves Agios Kirykos at 1pm on Monday, Wednesday and Friday for Fourni, the largest island in the miniature Fourni archipelago. The caique calls at the main settlement and usually at Hrysomilia or Thymena, where there are domatia and tavernas. Tickets cost €3 one way. Day excursion boats to Fourni from Agios Kirykos cost around €9, a bit more from Evdilos on the north coast.

Getting Around Ikaria

Bus Ikaria's bus services are almost as mythical as Icarus, but they do occasionally exist. In summer a bus is supposed leave Evdilos for Agios Kirykos at 8am daily and return to

The annual Panagia tou Harou feast draws pilgrims to Lipsi

Looking over Skala, Patmos

Da dum, da dum, da dum dum dum – swimming in Rina Bay, Kalymnos, Dodecanese

The religious Panagia tou Harou procession is followed by a night-long feast in Lipsi, Dodecanese

The dome of the Church of Agios Therapon is a feature of Mytilini's charming waterfront, Lesvos

Bed of hydrangeas, Manolates

Koumaradei – one of Samos' many mountain villages

IKARIA & THE FOURNI ISLANDS

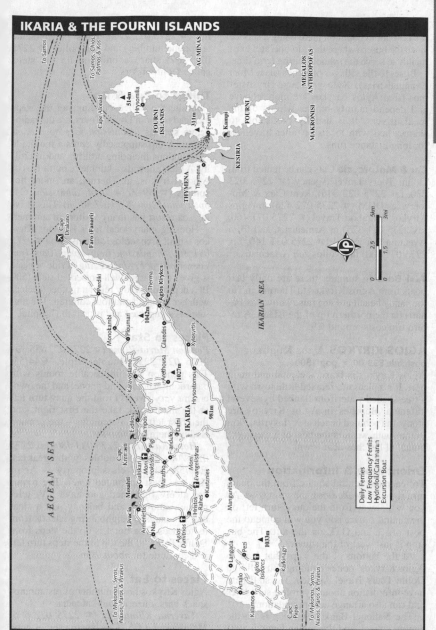

Daily Ferries
Low Frequency Ferries
Hydrofoil/Catamaran
Excursion Boat

Evdilos at noon, or thereabouts. However, it's best not to count on there being a service since the buses (where they do operate) exist mainly to serve the schools during term time.

Buses to the villages of Rahes (near Moni Evangelistrias), Xylosyrtis and Hrysosto-mos from Agios Kirykos are more elusive and depend mainly on the whims of the local drivers. It is usually preferable to share a taxi with locals or other travellers for long-distance runs.

Car & Motorcycle Cars can be rented from Dolihi Tours Travel Agency (☎ 2275 023 230, fax 2275 022 346), Rent Cars & Motorcycles DHM (☎ 2275 022 426) in Agios Kirykos, Marabou Travel (☎ 2275 071 460, fax 2275 071 325) in Armenistis, and from Aventura Car Rental (☎ 2275 031 140, fax 2275 071 400) in Evdilos and Armenistis.

Taxi Boat In summer there are daily taxi boats from Agios Kirykos to Therma and to the sandy beach at Faro (also known as Fanari) on the northern tip of the island. A return trip costs around €9.

AGIOS KIRYKOS Αγιος Κήρυκος
postcode 833 00 • pop 1800
Agios Kirykos is Ikaria's capital and main port. It's a pleasant, relaxed little town with a tree-shaded waterfront flanked by several kafeneia. Beaches in Agios Kirykos are stony; the pebbled beach at Xylosyrtis, 7km to the south-west, is the best of a mediocre bunch of beaches near town.

Orientation & Information
To reach the central square from the quay, turn right and walk along the main road. As you walk away from the quay, turn left on the central square and you will come to the post office and OTE on the left. The bus stop is just west of the square.

At the bottom of the steps that lead to Agios Kirykos' police building you will find Dolihi Tours Travel Agency. The staff here have information about hydrofoil schedules and can also arrange accommodation.

The National Bank of Greece is on the central square, and the Ionian Bank is next

to Dolihi Tours; both have ATMs. The police (☎ 2275 022 222), tourist police (same telephone number) and port police (☎ 2275 022 207) share a building up the steps above Dolihi Tours.

Things to See & Do
Opposite the police building, up the steps that lead up from Dolihi Tours, are the **radio-active springs** *(Admission €2; open 8am-11am)*. A dip supposedly cures a multitude of afflictions including arthritis and infertility. A pleasant walk a kilometre north-east of Agios Kirykos, at Therma, are more **hot springs** *(☎ 69 7714 7014, admission €3; open 8am-12pm & 6pm-7.30pm)*. This thriving spa resort has many visitors in summer.

Housing many local finds is Agios Kirykos' small **archaeological museum** *(☎ 2275 031 300; admission free; open 10am-1pm Tues, Thurs & Fri July & Aug)*. Pride of place is given to a large, well-preserved stele (500 BC) depicting in low relief a mother (seated) with her husband and four children. The museum is signposted and is near the hospital.

Places to Stay
Pension Maria-Elena (☎ 2275 022 835, fax 2275 022 223) Doubles/triples €44/53. This pension has impeccable rooms with bathroom, balcony and phone, and the owners are very sweet. From the quay turn left at the main road, take the first right, and then first left into Artemidos – the pension is along here on the right.

Hotel Kastro (☎ 2275 023 480, fax 2275 023 700) Singles/doubles with breakfast €49/58. This C-class property is Agios Kirykos' best-appointed hotel. The rooms are nicely furnished and have TV, telephone, bathroom and balcony. On a clear day you can see neighbouring islands from its terraces. The hotel is up the steps from Dolihi Tours; at the top of the steps turn left and continue for about 20m.

Places to Eat
Agios Kirykos has a number of restaurants, snack bars, ouzeria and kafeneia.
Taverna Klimataria (☎ 2275 022 686) Mains around €5. This taverna serves good

grilled meats in a neat little courtyard hidden away in the backstreets and is open all year.

Restaurant Dedalos (☎ 2275 022 473) Mains around €4.50. On the main square, this restaurant offers delicious fresh fish including a good fish soup. Its draught wine is highly recommended.

Filoti Pizzeria Restaurant (☎ 2275 023 088) Small/large pizza €4.50/10.50. This is one of the town's best regarded restaurants. Apart from the smokily delectable wood-fired pizza, there are good pasta, souvlaki and chicken dishes. The restaurant is at the top of the cobbled street that leads from the butcher's shop.

To Tzaki (☎ 2275 022 113) Mains around €4. If you feel like a brisk walk and fancy a change of scenery, try this nifty little taverna in the village of Glaredes, about 4km west of Agios Kirykos.

Entertainment
At the top of the steps leading south from the central square, is *Ftero,* looking out over the port towards Fourni – it's a very pleasant spot for a tipple.

AGIOS KIRYKOS TO THE NORTH COAST
The island's main north-south asphalt road begins west of Agios Kirykos and links the capital with the north coast. As the road climbs up to the island's mountainous spine there are dramatic mountain, coastal and sea vistas. The road winds through several villages, some with traditional stone houses topped with rough-hewn slate roofs. It then descends to the island's second port of Evdilos, 41km by road from Agios Kirykos.

This journey is worth taking for the views, but if you are based in Agios Kirykos and want to travel by bus you will more than likely have to stay overnight in Evdilos or Armenistis. A taxi back to Agios Kirykos will cost around €24. Hitching is usually OK, but there's not much traffic.

EVDILOS Εύδηλος
postcode 833 00 • pop 440
Evdilos, the island's second port, is a small fishing village. Like Agios Kirykos it's a

pleasant and relaxing place, though its charms only reveal themselves in the evening, when the waterfront gets quite lively. To see some lovely old houses and a cute little church, walk up Kalliopis Katsouli, the cobbled street leading uphill from the waterfront square.

You may prefer to head further west to the island's best beaches. There is, nonetheless, a reasonable beach to the east of Evdilos. Walk 100m up the hill from the square and take the path down past the last house on the left. If you are heading to Ikaria by boat and intend to base yourself on the north coast, take a boat direct to Evdilos rather than Agios Kirykos.

Information
There is an ATM (the only one on this side of the island) at the western end of the waterfront, where you'll also find the ticket agencies for NEL (☎ 2275 031 572) and Hellas Ferries (☎ 2275 031 990). Aventura (☎ 2275 031 140), in a side street leading from the centre of the waterfront, rents cars and bikes, sells tickets and gives general information.

Courses
Hellenic Cultural Centre (☎ 2275 031 982, 2275 031 978, W www.hcc.gr/courses/english/index.htm) May-Oct. This centre offers courses in Greek language, culture, literature, dancing and cooking. All levels of language proficiency are catered for; many professional translators undertake the three-month intensive course.

Places to Stay
Spyros Rossos Domatia (☎ 2275 031 518) Doubles with bathroom €29.50. Facing the sea from the middle of the waterfront is this plush-looking building on the far right with black wrought-iron balconies and orange life buoys.

Korali Rooms (☎ 2275 031 924) Doubles with bathroom €35. These clean and simple rooms (some with balcony overlooking the waterfront) are above the restaurant of the same name, at the western end of the harbour. Look for the blue and white facade.

Ikarian Panigyria

Throughout the summer there are *panigyria*, night-long festivals held on saints' days. The festas offer the islanders a chance to get to know one another and also serve as important fundraisers for the local community – which is why the food and wine can be a little more expensive than you might expect. Make sure you get in the spirit of things though – don't just order a salad!

Festivals held in villages in the western end of the island take place on the following dates:

14 May – Agios Isidoros
40 days after Orthodox Easter – Armenistis
29 June – Pezi
6 August – Hristos Rahes
15 August – Langada

Evdilos has two good-quality hotels.

Hotel Atheras (☎ *2275 031 434, fax 2275 031 926*) Singles/doubles €47/53. This B-class hotel is a breezy, friendly place with modern rooms with balconies. There's also a small pool and bar. It's in the backstreets, about 200m from the port. The hotel has cheaper studios and rooms in nearby Kerame.

Hotel Evdoxia (☎ *2275 031 502, fax 2275 031 571*) Doubles €60. Open year-round. At the top of the hill is this small B-class hotel, worth considering if you don't mind the petty house rules and the climb home from the centre of town. There is a minimarket with basic provisions, a laundry service, money exchange and a restaurant (see Places to Eat).

For a quiet stay upon arrival in Evdilos you might consider making the 3km (40-minute) walk to Kampos (see West of Evdilos), where there are *domatia*, a couple of excellent beaches and restaurants. Take a taxi if you have a lot of luggage.

Places to Eat

To Keïmali (☎ *2275 031 923, Plateia Evdilou*) Mains around €4.50. Open from 7pm. In summer, there are a number of eateries to choose from, including this nice little place on the waterfront square. Try the grilled meat dishes or the souvlaki in pita €1.

Cuckoo's Nest (☎ *2275 031 540, Plateia Evdilou*) Mezedes around €2, mains from €4. Open from 7pm. This ouzeri, also on the harbour, serves tasty mezedes and mains and has a comprehensive selection of bottled Ikarian wine. All the meat is local.

Hotel Evdoxia Restaurant (☎ *2275 031 502*) Mains €3.50-6. With home-cooked food and a view, this is a good meeting place for travellers. You can even order your favourite dish if you are staying at the hotel.

WEST OF EVDILOS
Kampos Κάμπος
postcode 833 01 • pop 127

Kampos, 3km west of Evdilos, is an unspoilt little village with few concessions to tourism. Although it takes some believing, sleepy little Kampos was the island's ancient capital of Oinoe (etymologically derived from the Greek word for wine). The name comes from the myth that the Ikarians were the first people to make wine. In ancient times Ikarian wine was considered the best in Greece, but a phylloxera outbreak in the mid-1960s put paid to many of the vines. Production is now low-key and mainly for local consumption. Ancient coins found in the vicinity of Kampos have a picture of Dionysos, the wine god, on them. Kampos' sandy beach is excellent and easily accessible.

Information The irrepressible Vasilis Dionysos, who speaks English, is a fount of information on Ikarian history and walking in the mountains. You will often find him in his gloomy but well-stocked village store – on the right as you come from Evdilos. The village's post box is outside this shop and inside there is a metered telephone. There is also a cardphone nearby.

Things to See & Do As you enter Kampos from Evdilos, the ruins of a **Byzantine palace** can be seen up on the right. In the centre of the village there is a small **museum** (☎ *2275 031 300; admission free; open 8am-2pm*). It houses Neolithic tools,

Q-RAY

Dionysos – God Of Wine

geometric vases, fragments of classical sculpture, figurines and a fine 'horse head' knife sheath carved from ivory.

Next to the museum is the 12th-century **Agia Irini**, the island's oldest church. It is built on the site of a 4th-century basilica, and columns standing in the grounds are from this original church. Agia Irini's frescoes are currently covered with whitewash because of insufficient funds to pay for its removal. Vasilis Dionysos has the keys to the museum and church.

The village is also a good base for mountain walking. A one-day circular walk along dirt roads can be made, taking in the village of **Dafni**, the remains of the 10th-century Byzantine **Castle of Koskinas** and the villages of **Frandato** and **Maratho**. The trek up to the little Byzantine **Chapel of Theoskepasti**, jammed in beneath an overhanging lump of granite, is worth the effort. Inside you will be shown the skulls of a couple of macabre internees. To get to the chapel and the neighbouring **Moni Theoktistis**, where there are beautiful 300-year-old frescoes, look for the signs at the village of Pigi on the road to Frandato. A lovely woman named Evangelia runs a kafeneio at the monastery.

Places to Stay & Eat *Vasilis & Yiannis Dionysos Domatia* (☎ 2275 031 300, ☎/fax 2275 031 688) Doubles with bathroom

€26.50. These two brothers create a wonderful family atmosphere for their guests, and the rooms are very pleasant. The optional enormous breakfasts are something to be experienced and are accompanied by good Greek music. From Evdilos, take the dirt road to the right from near the cardphone and follow it round to the blue and white building on your left. Alternatively, make your presence known at the village store. Call in advance and Vasilis will organise a taxi from the port.

Vasilis cooks delicious fish for his guests and his original pita recipe is exquisite.

Klimataria (☎ 2275 030 470) Mains around €4. This moderately priced taverna is in the village.

Pashalia (☎ 2275 031 346) Mains around €4.50. This taverna is nearby and is probably the better of the two.

Armenistis Αρμενιστής
postcode 833 01 • pop 70

Armenistis, 15km west of Evdilos, is the island's largest resort. It has two beautiful long beaches of pale golden sand, separated by a narrow headland. Places to stay are springing up quickly here, but it's still visited predominantly by independent travellers. Marabou Travel (☎ 2275 071 460, fax 2275 071 325), on the road which skirts the sea, organises walking tours and jeep safaris on the island. Aventura (☎ 2275 071 117), by the zaharoplasteio before the bridge, rents cars and sells tickets. Just east of Armenistis a road leads inland to **Moni Evangelistrias** and the thriving community of **Rahes**, which offers excellent opportunities for hiking (see the boxed text 'Strange Rahes').

From Armenistis a road continues 3.5km west to the small and secluded pebbled beach of **Nas** at the mouth of a stream. This is Ikaria's unofficial nudist beach. Behind the beach are some scant remains of a **temple of Artemis**. Nas has in recent times begun to witness a mini-boom and there are now quite a few domatia and tavernas.

Places to Stay – Budget *Rooms Ikaros* (☎ 2275 071 238) Most doubles €15, single/double rooftop 'penthouse' €18/23.50 (less

Strange Rahes

The hillside town of Hristos Rahes, and its neighbouring villages (which are collectively known as Rahes), is famous for the strange hours it keeps. No-one is quite sure why, but the villages in these parts like to stay up late – shops are open 9pm till 3am!

Another oddity of this region is the design of the older houses. Many of them were built out of the local stone and have a sloping, one-sided roof. There are no windows or chimneys, just a low door that's obscured by a high wall in front. This unique design served to camouflage the villages in the days when the threat of pirate raids was very real.

If you have the time and energy, it's best to explore the region on foot. The local community has published a walking map with excellent notes called *The Round of Rahes on Foot*; it's available at most tourist shops and supermarkets.

for longer stays). This is one of Armenistis' cheapest places to stay. It has a cool shady garden nestled in among the village's oldest houses. The elderly owner, Dimitris Hroussis, speaks a little English and is friendly. The place is signposted as you enter the village.

Kirki (☎ 2275 071 254, fax 2275 071 083) Double rooms/studios with bathroom €29/41. These rooms are on the right as you approach town. Each room has a private terrace overlooking the sea.

Pashalia Restaurant Domatia (☎/fax 2275 071 226) Doubles with bathroom €35. These domatia, above the restaurant of the same name, have a superb location at the eastern end of Armenistis beach, right on the water. Rooms are clean and nicely furnished, some have kitchens and most have sea-view balconies.

Rooms Fotinos (☎ 2275 071 235) Doubles with/without bathroom €29/18. At the approach to the village, before the road forks, you will see these rooms on the left. They are light, airy and nicely furnished.

Pension Thea (☎ 2275 071 491) Doubles €29. This new pension is at Nas, but the

rooms are quite exposed to the sun. Still, they have a fridge and sea view.

Places to Stay – Mid-Range *Hotel Daidalos* (☎ 2275 071 390, fax 2275 071 393) Singles/doubles with breakfast €53/67.50. This C-class property, around to the west of the village, is one of Armenistis' best hotels. It has a cool and inviting interior and nicely furnished rooms. The hotel has a sea-water swimming pool.

Villa Dimitri (☎/fax 2275 071 310, ⓦ www .villa-dimitri.de) 2-person studios & apartments with private patios €38-61. The most exquisite accommodation on the island is this Cycladic-inspired pension belonging to Dimitris Ioannidopoulos. The individual studios and apartments, 800m west of Armenistis, spill down a cliff that overlooks the sea amid a riotous profusion of flowers and plants. Bookings are essential and should be for a minimum of one week.

Places to Eat Wherever you eat, see if you can try some of the locally made light but potent wine.

Pashalia Taverna (☎ 2275 071 302) Mains around €5. The first place along the harbour road, this taverna offers prompt service and a variety of excellent ready-made dishes. Try the filling pasta and veal in a clay pot or the *katsikaki* (kid goat).

Delfini (☎ 2275 071 254) Mains around €5. Directly opposite and below the Pashalia Taverna is this folksy restaurant offering great grilled souvlaki (and good fish) to complement the view over the water. The meat here is local.

Kafestiatorio O Ilios (☎ 2275 071 045) Mains around €4.50. This simple place at the end of the harbour road has some of the best seafood – the owner is a fisherman.

To Mouragio Mains around €5. This harbourside option is known for its large souvlakia.

To Symposio (☎ 2275 071 222) Mains around €7. This place on the Armenistis harbourside offers unusual though overly complicated fare, some of it with a German twist.

Astra (☎ 2275 071 255) Mains around €5. Nas now has six tavernas, of which this one is probably the best. Some dishes are wood-oven cooked. Try the potato salad – almost a meal in itself – or ask to sample the oven-cooked kid and wash it down with the mean draught red wine.

FOURNI ISLANDS Οι Φούρνοι
postcode 834 00 • pop 1030
The Fourni Islands are a miniature archipelago lying between Ikaria and Samos. Two of the islands are inhabited: Fourni and Thymena. The capital of the group is **Fourni** (also called Kampos), which is the port of Fourni Island. Fourni has one other village, tiny Hrysomilia, 10km north of the port; the island's only road connects the two. The islands are mountainous and a good number of beaches are dotted around the coast.

The telephone number of Fourni's port police is ☎ 2275 051 207. Fourni has local police (☎ 2275 051 222) and a doctor (☎ 2275 051 202).

Fourni is the only island with accommodation for tourists and is ideal for those seeking a quiet retreat. Other than the settlement of Fourni itself and a beach south over the headland at **Kampi**, the island offers little else besides eating, sleeping and swimming. Most of the islanders make a living from fishing, sending their catch to the Athens fish market.

Places to Stay & Eat
Manolis & Patra Markaki Rooms (☎ 2275 051 268, ☎/fax 2275 051 355) Doubles €23.50, 4-person apartments €41. These gorgeous rooms and apartments are decorated with heirlooms, pretty curtains and old furniture. The rooms are opposite the ferry pier, above the Markakis Cafe-Bar. Ask also about the rooms and apartments they have elsewhere on the island.

Maria & Kostas Markakis Pension (☎ 2275 051 148) Doubles €33. This tidy pension is at the south end of the waterfront.

Taverna Nikos (☎ 2275 051 253) Mains around €4.50. This taverna on the waterfront will keep you amply supplied with fresh fish and other grilled dishes.

Miltos (☎ 2275 051 407) Mains around €4.50. Also on the waterfront, Miltos serves similar fare to Taverna Nikos.

Getting To/From Fourni
Ferry Fourni lies on the ferry route between Piraeus and Samos. As well as daily boats to Ikaria (40 minutes, €3), there are five ferries weekly to Samos (two hours, €6), and three weekly to Piraeus via Paros (3¼ hours, €9) and Naxos (four hours, €8). These ferries stop at Mykonos (4½ hours, €9) and Syros (5½ hours, €13) once a week. Tickets are available from an office on the corner of the waterfront and the main shopping street.

Hydrofoil Hydrofoils call at Fourni on the route from Ikaria to Samos and the Dodecanese. See the Getting To/From Ikaria section for details of services.

Getting Around Fourni
There are three boats a week from Fourni to Hrysomilia and Thymena.

Samos Σάμος

pop 32,000
Samos is the closest of all the Greek islands to Turkey, from which it is separated by the 3km-wide Mykale Straits. The island is the most visited of the North-Eastern Aegean group. Charter flights of tourists descend on the island from many northern European countries. Samos is a popular transit point for travellers heading from the Cyclades to Turkey and vice versa. Most barely pause in Samos, which is a pity because the island has a lot to offer.

Despite the package tourists, Samos is still a destination worth visiting. Forays into its hinterland are rewarded with unspoilt villages and mountain vistas. In summer the humid air is permeated with heavy floral scents, especially jasmine. This, and the prolific greenery of the landscape, lends Samos an exotic and tropical air. Orchids are grown here for export and an excellent table wine is made from the local muscat grapes.

Samos has three ports: Vathy (Samos) and Karlovasi on the north coast, and Pythagorio on the south coast.

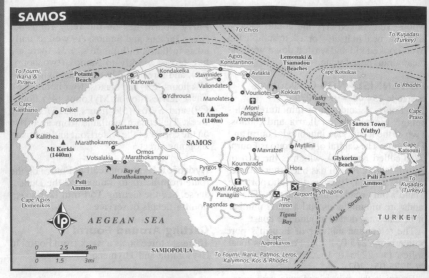

History

The first inhabitants of Samos, the Pelasgian tribes, worshipped Hera, whose birthplace was Samos. Pythagoras was born on Samos in the 6th century BC. Unfortunately, his life coincided with that of the tyrant Polycrates, who in 550 BC deposed the Samian oligarchy. As the two did not see eye to eye, Pythagoras spent much of his time in exile in Italy. Despite this, Samos became a mighty naval power under Polycrates, and the arts and sciences also flourished. 'Big is beautiful' seems to have been Polycrates' maxim – almost every construction and artwork he commissioned appears to have been ancient Greece's biggest. The historian Herodotus wrote glowingly of the tyrant's achievements, stating that the Samians had accomplished the three greatest projects in Greece at that time: the Sanctuary of Hera (one of the Seven Wonders of the Ancient World), the Evpalinos Tunnel and a huge jetty.

After the decisive Battle of Plataea (479 BC), in which Athens had been aided by the Samians, Samos allied itself to Athens and returned to democracy. In the Battle of Mykale, which took place on the same day as the Battle of Plataea, the Greek navy (with many Samian sailors) defeated the Persian fleet. However, during the Peloponnesian Wars, Samos was taken by Sparta.

Under Roman rule Samos enjoyed many privileges, but after successive occupations by the Venetians and Genoese it was conquered by the Turks in 1453. Samos played a major role in the uprising against the Turks in the early 19th century, much to the detriment of its neighbour, Chios (see the Chios section later in this chapter).

Trekking

Samos is a popular place for rambling, or more demanding mountain treks. Its natural fecundity and appealing combination of mountains and sea make it a popular destination for walkers from all over Europe. Should you be planning a hike on Samos, Brian and Eileen Anderson's *Landscapes of Samos*, a pocket guide to walks on the island, contains descriptions of over 20 walks.

Getting To/From Samos

Air There are at least four flights daily from Samos to Athens (€63) and three flights weekly to Thessaloniki (€88). The Olympic Airways office (☎ 2273 027 237) is on the corner of Kanari and Smyrnis in Vathy (Samos). There is also an Olympic Airways office (☎ 2273 061 213) on Lykourgou Logotheti in Pythagorio. The airport is 4km west of Pythagorio.

Ferry – Domestic Samos is the transport hub of the North-Eastern Aegean, with ferries to the Dodecanese and Cyclades as well as to the other North-Eastern Aegean Islands. Schedules are subject to seasonal changes, so consult any of the ticket offices for the latest versions. ITSA Travel (☎ 2273 023 605, fax 2273 027 955, e itsa@gemini .diavlos.gr) is the closest agency to the ferry terminal in Vathy (Samos). Your luggage can also be stored for free whether you buy a ticket or not. Ferries depart from both Vathy (Samos) and Pythagorio.

To Piraeus there are at least two ferries daily (13 hours, €20.50). Two to three ferries daily go to Ikaria (2½ hours, €6) and four boats a week to Fourni (two hours, €6); three weekly to Chios (four hours, €9); one weekly to Lesvos (seven hours, €12.50), Limnos (11 hours, €20), Alexandroupolis (20 hours, €25) and sometimes Kavala (20 hours, €25). Three to four ferries per week to Naxos (6 hours, €15.50) and Paros (6½ hours, €13.50), with connections to Mykonos, Ios, Santorini and Syros. There are about three ferries a week to Patmos (2½ hours, €6.50), two to Leros (3½ hours, €5.50) and Kalymnos (four hours, €10), and one to Kos (5½ hours, €11.50) and Rhodes (nine hours, €21).

Ferry – International In summer two ferries go daily from Vathy (Samos) to Kuşadası (for Ephesus) in Turkey. From Pythagorio there is one boat a week. From November to March there are one to two ferries weekly. Tickets cost around €41 (plus €21 port taxes). Daily excursions are also available from 1 April to 31 October and for an additional €25 you can visit Ephesus. Tickets are available from many outlets but the main agent is ITSA Travel.

Bear in mind that the ticket office will require your passport in advance for port formalities. Turkish visas, where required, are issued upon arrival in Turkey for US$45.

Check with the Turkish diplomatic mission in your home country for the requirements since these change frequently.

Hydrofoil In summer hydrofoils link Pythagorio twice daily with Patmos (one hour, €11), Leros (two hours, €15), Kos (3½ hours, €19.50) and Kalymnos (2½ hours, €19.50). Also from Pythagorio there are dolphins four times per week to Fourni (50 mins, €11.50) and Ikaria (1½ hours, €13.50), daily to Lipsi (1½ hours, €11.50) and twice a week to Agathonisi (35 minutes, €9).

There are also two services weekly from Vathy (Samos) to Fourni (1¾ hours, €11.50) and Ikaria (2¼ hours, €13.50). Also from Vathy (Samos) there are three dolphins a week to Chios (1½ hours, €18), two a week to Lesvos (four hours, €25), at least three times a week to Patmos (€17), Kos (€24.50), Leros (€21) and Kalymnos (€23.50). Schedules are subject to frequent changes, so contact the tourist office in Pythagorio or the port police (☎ 2273 061 225) for up-to-date information. Tickets are available from By Ship Travel in Pythagorio (☎ 2273 062 285, fax 2273 061 914) and Vathy (☎ 2273 022 116) or ITSA Travel in Vathy.

Excursion Boat In summer there are excursion boats four times weekly between Pythagorio and Patmos (€29.50 return) leaving at 8am. For an additional €18.50 you can visit the monastery. Daily excursion boats also go to the little island of Samiopoula for €18/9 with/without lunch. There is also a boat tour of Samos once or twice a week, leaving from Pythagorio; it costs €32.50 and does not include lunch.

Getting Around Samos
To/From the Airport There are no Olympic Airways buses to the airport. A taxi from Vathy (Samos) should cost about €9. Alternatively, you can take a local bus to Pythagorio and a taxi to the airport from there for about €3.50.

Bus Samos has an adequate bus service that continues till about 8pm in summer. On weekdays, there are 14 buses daily from

Vathy (Samos) bus station (☎ 2273 027 262) to both Kokkari (20 minutes, €1.50) and Pythagorio (25 minutes, €1), seven to Agios Konstantinos (40 minutes, €1.50) and Karlovasi (via the north coast, one hour, €2.50), five to the Ireon (25 minutes, €2), five to Mytilinii (20 minutes, €1), and two to Ormos and Votsalakia (two hours, €4.50).

In addition to frequent buses to/from Vathy (Samos) there are five buses from Pythagorio to the Ireon and four to Mytilinii. Pay for your tickets on the bus. Services are greatly reduced on weekends, with virtually no buses running on Sundays.

Car & Motorcycle Samos has many car-rental outlets, including Hertz (☎ 2273 061 730), Lykourgou Logotheti 77, and Europcar (☎ 2273 061 522), Lykourgou Logotheti 65, both in Pythagorio.

There are also many motorcycle-rental outlets on Lykourgou Logotheti. Many of the larger hotels can arrange motorcycle or car rental for you.

Taxi From the taxi rank (☎ 2273 028 404) on Plateia Pythagorou in Vathy (Samos), approximate tariffs are as follows: Kokkari €9, Pythagorio €8, Psili Ammos €7.50, Avlakia €8.50, the airport €9, and the Ireon €9.

VATHY (SAMOS) Βαθύ (Σάμος)
postcode 831 00 • pop 5790
The island's capital is the large and bustling Vathy, also called Samos, on the north-east coast. The waterfront is crowded with tourists who rarely venture to the older and extremely attractive upper town of Ano Vathy where 19th-century, red-tiled houses perch on a hillside. The lower and newer town is strung out along Vathy Bay and it is quite a walk from one end to the other.

Orientation
From the ferry terminal (facing inland) turn right to reach the central square of Plateia Pythagorou on the waterfront. It's recognisable by its four palm trees and statue of a lion. A little farther along and a block inland are the shady municipal gardens. The waterfront road is called Themistokleous Sofouli.

Information
The municipal tourist office (☎ 2273 028 530) is just north of Plateia Pythagorou in a little side street, but it only operates during the summer season. The staff will assist in finding accommodation.

The tourist police (☎ 2273 027 980) and the regular police are at Themistokleous Sofouli 129 on the south side of the waterfront.

The National Bank of Greece is on the waterfront just south of Plateia Pythagorou and the Commercial Bank is on the east side of the square. Both sport ATMs.

The post office is on Smyrnis, four blocks from the waterfront. The OTE is on Plateia Iroön, behind the municipal gardens.

The Diavlos NetCafe (☎ 2273 022 469) is at Themistoklous Sofouli 160, near the police station. Access is fast and costs €3 per hour. It's open 8am to 11.30pm, year-round.

The island's bus station (KTEL) is on Ioannou Lekati. The taxi rank (☎ 2273 028 404) is on Plateia Pythagorou. Samos' hospital (☎ 2273 027 407) is on the waterfront, north of the ferry quay.

The port police (☎ 2273 027 318) are just north of the quay, one block back from the waterfront.

Things to See
Apart from the charming old quarter of Ano Vathy, which is a peaceful place to stroll, and the municipal gardens, which are a pleasant place to sit, the main attraction of Vathy (Samos) is the **archaeological museum** (☎ 2273 027 469, adult/student €2.50/1.50; open 8.30am-3pm Tues-Sun).

Many of the fine exhibits in this well laid out museum are a legacy of Polycrates' time. They include a gargantuan (4.5m) *kouros* statue found in the Ireon (Sanctuary of Hera). In true Polycrates fashion, it was the largest standing kouros ever produced. The collection includes many statues, mostly from the Ireon, bronze sculptures, stelae and pottery.

Places to Stay – Budget
Vathy does not have a camping ground. Be wary of touts who may approach you as you disembark and tell you that places listed in this guide are closed – it's usually not true.

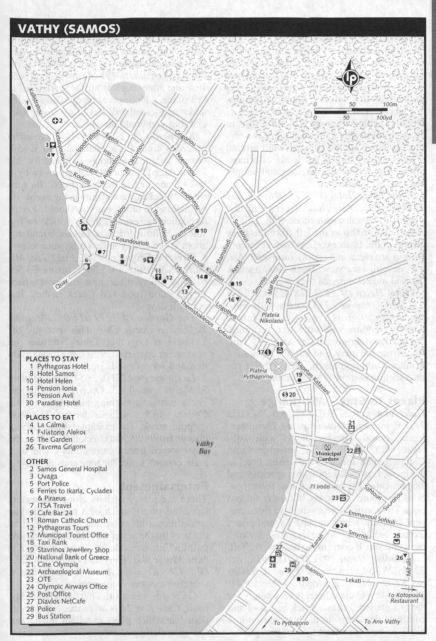

VATHY (SAMOS)

PLACES TO STAY
1 Pythagoras Hotel
8 Hotel Samos
10 Hotel Helen
14 Pension Ionia
15 Pension Avli
30 Paradise Hotel

PLACES TO EAT
4 La Calma
13 Psiltario Alekos
16 The Garden
26 Taverna Grigoris

OTHER
2 Samos General Hospital
3 Ovaga
5 Port Police
6 Ferries to Ikaria, Cyclades
  & Piraeus
7 ITSA Travel
9 Cafe Bar 24
11 Roman Catholic Church
12 Pythagoras Tours
17 Municipal Tourist Office
18 Taxi Rank
19 Stavrinos Jewellery Shop
20 National Bank of Greece
21 Cine Olympia
22 Archaeological Museum
23 OTE
24 Olympic Airways Office
25 Post Office
27 Diavlos NetCafe
28 Police
29 Bus Station

Vathy
Bay

Plateia
Pythagornu

Plateia
Nikolaou

Municipal
Gardens

To Pythagorio

To Ano Vathy

To Kotopoula
Restaurant

Pension Ionia (☎ *2273 028 782, Manoli Kalomiri 5*) Singles/doubles €15/18. The cheapest and perhaps homeliest places to stay are the domatia here – the rooms are clean and pretty. To get there from the quay, turn right onto the waterfront, left at Stamatiadi, then left into Manoli Kalomiri.

Pension Avli (☎ *2273 022 939, Areos 2*) Doubles with bathroom €23.50. Close to Pension Ionia, this traditional place is a former Roman Catholic convent, built around a lovely courtyard. It has loads of atmosphere. The rooms are spacious and simply but tastefully furnished.

Pythagoras Hotel (☎ *2273 028 422, fax 2273 028 893,* e *smicha@otenet.gr, Kallistratou 12*) Doubles with phone €28. This C-class hotel, 800m to the left from the ferry arrival point, is an excellent budget option. Rooms are clean and simply furnished. Ask for one with a sea view. There's also a snack bar and nice communal terrace.

Hotel Helen (☎ *2273 028 215, fax 2273 022 866, Grammou 2*) Doubles with bathroom €29.50. This C-class establishment has cosy rooms with attractive furniture. Rooms have air-con, fridge and TV. Turn right from the quay, and left just before the Roman Catholic church, veer right at the intersection and the hotel is on the right.

Places to Stay – Mid-Range
Hotel Samos (☎ *2273 028 377, fax 2273 023 771,* e *hotsamos@otenet.gr, 11 Themistokleous Sofouli*) Singles/doubles with bathroom €32/40.50. This grand-looking, C-class establishment is the nearest hotel to the quay. It is well kept with a spacious and elegant cafeteria, bar, snack bar, restaurant, breakfast room, TV room, billiard room and pool. The comfortable rooms have fitted carpets, balcony, telephone and TV and prices include breakfast. On leaving the quay turn right and you'll come to the hotel on the left.

Paradise Hotel (☎ *2273 023 911, fax 2273 028 754,* e *paradise@gemini.diavlos .gr, Kanari 21*) Singles/doubles €26.50/ 41. This modern C-class hotel is very handy for the bus station. It has a snack bar, pool and comfortable rooms. In the high season it is likely to be booked out by tour groups.

Places to Eat
When dining out on Samos don't forget to sample the Samian wine, extolled by Byron.

Estiatorio Alekos (☎ *2273 092 629, Lykourgou Logotheti 49*) Mains around €5. Just one street back from the waterfront is this place, which serves ready-made staples and made-to-order dishes. It's nothing special, but you could do worse.

Kotopoula (☎ *2273 028 415, Vlamaris*) Mezedes around €3, mains around €4.50. Greeks escape the tourists and head for this vine-cloaked restaurant, hidden away by a leafy plane tree in the backstreets. Its spit-roasted chicken (served only in the evenings) is the thing to order, but you should also try the delicious *revithokeftedes* (chickpea rissoles). Follow Ioannou Lekati inland for about 800m until you find it on your left.

Taverna Grigoris (☎ *2273 022 718, Mihalis 5*) Appetisers €1.50-3, mains €3.50-6. This folksy place near the post office serves good food and Greek dishes. It's open all day.

The Garden (☎ *2273 024 033, Manolis Kalomiris*) Mains €3-8. This spot, just off Lykourgou Logotheti (entry is from the next street up to the north) has a garden setting and serves good Greek standards.

La Calma (☎ *2273 022 654, Kefalopoulou 7*) Mains around €5. Open 7pm-midnight. For a romantic evening ambience, try La Calma, which overlooks the sea. The food (pepper steak, for example) makes for a change from standard Greek fare, though the microwaved frozen carrots that come with main courses lower the tone considerably.

Entertainment
There are plenty of bars along the waterfront, all pretty much of a muchness. For something a bit more interesting, head to the bars by the water on Kefalopoulou, just past La Calma restaurant. These include *Escape Music Bar*, *Cosy* and *Ovaga* (☎ *2273 025 476, Kefalopoulou 13*), which has a stunning terrace by the water.

On a side street off Themistokleous Sofouli, *Cafe Bar 24* is an intimate little outdoor bar which plays excellent music and has an underhyped candle-lit ambience.

Cine Olympia (☎ *2273 025 011, Gymnasiarhou Kateraini 27*) Admission €6. Sessions at 9.30pm. This cinema shows recent Hollywood releases, in English with Greek subtitles.

Shopping

Vathy has some interesting little shops tucked in behind the waterfront Plateia Pythagora. If you're interested in jewellery and old things, stop by *Stavrinos jewellery shop* (☎ *2273 027 273, Cnr Kontaxi & Cyrillou*). The shop has been around since 1870 and so has some of the stock. Mihali Stavrinos is quite a character and will help you choose something special.

PYTHAGORIO Πυθαγόρειο
postcode 831 03 • pop 1400
Pythagorio, on the south east coast of the island, is 14km from Vathy (Samos). Today, it's a busy yet pretty tourist resort with streets lined with red hibiscus and pink oleander. It has a somewhat upmarket feel and is a convenient base from which to visit the ancient sites of Samos.

Pythagorio stands on the site of the now World Heritage listed ancient city of Samos. Although the settlement dates from the Neolithic era, most of the remains are from Polycrates' time (around 550 BC). The mighty jetty of Samos projected almost 450m into the sea, protecting the city and its powerful fleet from the vagaries of the Aegean. Remains of this jetty lie below and beyond the smaller modern jetty, which is on the opposite side of the harbour to the quay. The town beach begins just beyond the jetty. All boats coming from Patmos, and other points south of Samos, dock at Pythagorio.

Orientation

From the ferry quay, turn right and follow the waterfront to the main thoroughfare of Lykourgou Logotheti, a turn-off to the left. Here there are supermarkets, greengrocers,

PYTHAGORIO

To Evpalinos Tunnel & Moni Panagias Spilianis
To Evpalinos Tunnel
To Vathy (Samos) & Psili Ammos Beach
To Airport & Ireon

Polykratous
 Anstarhou
Odyssea Onopoa
Polykratous
A Embolou
Damos
Esopou
Evpalinou
Egeou Pelagous
Egeou
Lykourgou Logotheti
Melissou
Nikolaou
Heras
Plateia Irinis
Roikou
Despoti Kyrillou
S Stirou
Metamorfosis
Kapetan A
Pythagora S Georgiadi
Despoti Kyrillou
Vathikoti
Konstantinou Kanari
A Lykourgou
Kontaxi
Pythagora
D Rafaila
Themistokli Sofouli
Plateia Tarsana

Harbour

AEGEAN SEA

Plateia Irinis

PLACES TO STAY
18 Polixeni Hotel
19 Hotel Elpis
20 Pension Arokaria
22 Hotel Evripoli
23 Hotel Damo

PLACES TO EAT
12 Symposium
13 Taverna ta Platania
16 Poseidonas
17 Restaurant Remataki

0   40   80m
0   40   80yd

Quay

OTHER
1 Olympic Airways
2 Police
3 Post Office
4 Bus Stop
5 National Bank of Greece
6 Parking
7 Temple of Aphrodite
8 Commercial Bank ATM
9 By Ship Travel
10 Tourist Office
11 Taxi Rank
14 Pythagorio Museum
15 Port Police
21 Castle of Lykourgos Logothetis
24 OTE
25 Ferries to Patmos, Lipsi, Agathonisi, Leros, Kalymnos, Kos, Fourni & Ikaria

Phone numbers listed incorporate changes due in Oct 2002; see p55

bakers, travel agents and numerous car, motorcycle and bicycle rental outlets. The central square of Plateia Irinis is farther along the waterfront.

Information

The tourist office (☎ 2273 062 274, fax 2273 061 022) is on the south side of Lykourgou Logetheti. The English-speaking staff is particularly friendly and helpful and give out a town map, bus timetable and information about ferry schedules. It's also a currency exchange, and is open 8am to 10pm daily.

The tourist police (☎ 2273 061 100) are also on Lykourgou Logetheti, to the left of the tourist office.

The post office and the National Bank of Greece are both on Lykourgou Logetheti. The OTE is on the waterfront near the quay.

The bus station (actually a bus stop) is on the south side of Lykourgou Logotheti. There is a taxi rank (☎ 2273 061 450) on the corner of the waterfront and Lykourgou Logotheti.

Things to See

Walking north-east on Polykratous from the town centre, a path left passes traces of an ancient theatre. The **Evpalinos Tunnel** can also be reached along this path: take the left fork after the theatre. The right fork leads up to **Moni Panagias Spilianis** (Monastery of the Virgin of the Grotto). The city walls extend from here to the Evpalinos Tunnel.

Back in town, the remains of the **Castle of Lykourgos Logothetis** are at the southern end of Metamorfosis. The castle was built in 1824 and became a stronghold of Greek resistance during the War of Independence.

In the town hall at the back of Plateia Irinis, is the **Pythagorio Museum** (☎ 2273 061 400, Plateia Irinis; admission free; open 8.45am-2pm Tues-Sat). It has some finds from the Ireon.

Between Lokourgou and the car park are the **ruins of Aphrodite.**

Evpalinos Tunnel The 1034m-long Evpalinos Tunnel (☎ 2273 061 400; adult/student/senior €1.50/1/1, EU students free; open 8.45am-2.45pm Tues-Sun) completed

in 524 BC, is named after its architect. It penetrated through a mountainside to channel gushing mountain water to the city. The tunnel is, in effect, two tunnels: a service tunnel and a lower water tunnel seen at various points along the narrow walkway. The diggers began at each end and met in the middle, an achievement of precision engineering that is still considered remarkable.

In the Middle Ages the inhabitants of Pythagorio used the tunnel as a hide-out during pirate raids. The tunnel is fun to explore, though access to it is via a very constricted stairway. If you are tall, portly, or suffer from claustrophobia, give it a miss!

The tunnel is most easily reached from the western end of Lykourgou Logotheti, from where it is signposted. If you arrive by road, a sign points you to the tunnel's southern mouth as you enter Pythagorio from Samos.

Places to Stay

Many of Pythagorio's places to stay are block-booked by tour companies.

Hotel Elpis (☎ 2273 061 144, Metamorfosis Sotiros) Singles/doubles with fridge €21/23.50. This is a neat and clean D-class hotel.

Pension Arokaria (☎ 2273 061 287, Metamorfosis Sotiros) Doubles €35.50. This is a pleasant and quiet place for independent travellers. It has a cool and leafy garden, and a lovely owner.

Hotel Evripili (☎ 2273 061 096, fax 2273 061 897) Single/doubles €35.50/44. This is a friendly place occupying a stone building not far from the waterfront. The rooms are cosy and nicely furnished.

Polixeni Hotel (☎ 2273 061 590, fax 2273 061 359) Doubles with balcony and air-con around €59. This homely place on the waterfront has nicely furnished, clean and comfortable rooms.

Hotel Damo (☎ 2273 061 303, fax 2273 061 745) 2-3 person studios €60. This C-class place is near the OTE and has agreeable self-contained studios.

Places to Eat

The waterfront is packed with restaurants all offering much the same fare.

Restaurant Remataki (☎ 2273 061 104)
Mezedes €2-6, mains €4-7. This restaurant
is at the beginning of the town beach. It has
an imaginative menu of carefully prepared,
delicious food – it's a miracle that a place
this good has survived in a tourist enclave.
Try a meal of various mezedes for a change:
revithokeftedes, *piperies Florinis* (Florina
peppers) and *gigantes* (lima beans) make a
good combination. The artichoke soup and
dolmadakia are also excellent.

Poseidonas (☎ 2273 062 530) Mains €5-
12. Next door to Remataki, this popular
restaurant serves some interesting dishes,
including Chinese-inspired seafood.

Taverna ta Platania (☎ 2273 061 817,
Plateia Irinis) Mains €4-6. This taverna is
a block inland from Restaurant Remataki,
opposite the museum, and away from the
more expensive waterfront eateries.

Symposium (☎ 2273 061 938) Mains
€5-11. This upmarket restaurant is known
for its steaks and Greek classics.

AROUND PYTHAGORIO
Ireon Ηραίον
The Sacred Way, once flanked by thousands of statues, led from the city to the
Ireon (☎ 2273 095 277; *adult/student
€2.50/1.50, free for EU students; open
8.30am-3pm Tues-Sun*). The Ireon was a
sanctuary to Hera, built at the legendary
place of her birth, on swampy land where
the River Imbrasos enters the sea.

There had been a temple on the site since
Mycenaean times, but the one built in the
time of Polycrates was the most extraordinary: it was four times the size of the
Parthenon. As a result of plunderings and
earthquakes only one column remains
standing, although the extent of the temple
can be gleaned from the foundations. Other
remains on the site include a stoa, more
temples and a 5th-century basilica.

The Ireon is now listed as a World Heritage Site. It is on the coast 8km west of
Pythagorio.

Mytilinii Μυτιληνιοί
The fascinating **palaeontology museum**
(☎ 2273 052 055; *admission €1.50, free Sun;*

*open 9am-2pm, 5pm-7pm Mon-Sat, 10.30am-
2.30pm Sun*), on the main thoroughfare of the
inland village of Mytilinii, between Pythagorio and Vathy (Samos), houses skeletons of
prehistoric animals. Included in the collection
are remains of animals that were the an-
tecedents of the giraffe and elephant. From
the museum it's a nice walk to Agia Triada
monastery, where there's an ossuary.

Beaches
Sandy **Psili Ammos** (not to be confused with
a beach of the same name near Votsalakia) is
the finest beach near Pythagorio. This gently
sloping beach is ideal for families and is
popular, so be there early to grab your spot.
The beach can be reached by car or scooter
from the Vathy-Pythagorio road (signposted), or by excursion boat (€9) from
Pythagorio, leaving each morning at 9am
and returning at 4pm. There are also buses
from Vathy (Samos). **Glykoriza Beach,**
nearer Pythagorio, is dominated by a few hotels nearby, but is a clean, public beach of
pebbles and sand and is a good alternative to
the sometimes very busy Psili Ammos.

Places to Stay & Eat The following
places are all at Psili Ammos.

Elena Apartments (☎ 2273 023 645, fax
2273 028 959) Double apartments €41.
This place, right on the beach, has rather
cramped self-contained double apartments.

Apartments Psili Ammos (☎ 2273 025
140, mobile ☎ 69 7482 9025, fax 2273 025
140) 2-person studios €41. Near Elena
Apartments is this place, which has self
contained rooms.

Restaurant Psili Ammos (☎ 2273 028
301) Prices €3-5.50. This taverna is
favourably located overlooking the beach;
the food is good.

Sunrise Mains around €4. This is a more
intimate eatery, also with a good beach out-
look.

SOUTH-WEST SAMOS
The south-west coast of Samos remained
unspoilt for longer than the north coast, but
in recent years a series of resorts has sprung
up alongside the best beaches. The area east

of Marathkampos was ravaged by fires in 2000, and it will be some years before the forests recover.

Ormos, 50km from Vathy, has a pebble beach. From here a road leads 6km to the inland village of **Marathokampos**, which is worth a visit for the stunning view down to the immense Bay of Marathokampos. **Votsalakia**, 4km west of Ormos and known officially as Kampos, and the much nicer **Psili Ammos** (not to be confused with the Psili Ammos near Pythagorio), 2km beyond, have long, sandy beaches. There are many domatia and tavernas on this stretch of coast though it has a rather scrappy feel to it and lacks the intimacy of smaller coastal resorts.

With your own transport you may like to continue from Psili Ammos along a stunning route that skirts mighty Mt Kerkis, high above the totally undeveloped and isolated west coast. The road passes through the village of **Kallithea**, and continues to **Drakeï**, where it terminates.

WEST OF VATHY (SAMOS)
The road which skirts the north coast passes many beaches and resorts. The fishing village of **Kokkari**, 10km from Vathy (Samos), is also a holiday resort with a pebble beach. The place is very popular with tourists, but it is exposed to the frequent summer winds and for that reason is a favourite of windsurfers. Rooms, studios and tavernas abound, all offering much the same quality.

Beaches extend from here to **Avlakia**, with **Lemonaki** and **Tsamadou** beaches being the most accessible for walkers staying in Kokkari. Clothing is optional at these two secluded beaches. Continuing west, beyond Avlakia, the road is flanked by trees, a foretaste of the scenery encountered on the roads leading inland from the coast. A turn-off south along this stretch leads to the delightful mountain village of **Vourliotes**, from where you can walk another 3km to **Moni Panagias Vrondianis**. Built in the 1550s, it is the island's oldest extant monastery; a sign in the village points the way.

Continuing along the coast, a 5km road winds its way up the lower slopes of Mt Ampelos through thick, well-watered

woodlands of pine and deciduous trees, to the gorgeous village of **Manolates**. The area is rich in bird life, with a proliferation of nightingales, warblers and thrushes. There are no buses to Manolates, so you'll have to find your own way (Agios Konstantinos is the nearest bus stop). The Samians say that if you have not visited either Vourliotes or Manolates, then you have not seen Samos.

Back on the coast, the road continues to the pretty flower-filled village of **Agios Konstantinos**. Beyond here it winds through rugged coastal scenery to the town of **Karlovasi**, Samos' third port. The town consists of three contiguous settlements: Paleo (old), Meson (middle) and Neo (new). It once boasted a thriving tanning industry, but now it's a lacklustre town with little of interest for visitors. The nearest beach is the sand and pebble **Potami**, 2km west of town.

Places to Stay
Despite the onset of package tourism, Kokkari still has many accommodation options for independent travellers.

In the high season the EOT (☎ 2273 092 217) operates in the village and will assist in finding accommodation. The bus stops on the main road at a large stone church, and the EOT is a little way down the street opposite the church.

Pension Eleni (☎ 2273 092 317, fax 2273 092 620) Doubles €29.50. This pension has immaculate, tastefully furnished rooms with bathroom. From the large stone church in Kokkari, continue along the main road; at the T-junction veer left and, 50m along on the left, next to the Dionyssos Garden restaurant, there's a sign pointing to the pension. There are many more domatia, apartments and small hotels along this stretch of road, which is just one block back from the waterfront.

Kalypso Rooms to Rent (☎ 2273 094 124) Doubles €23.50. Farther west along the coast road, close to a beach, are these rooms, named after their friendly and kind owner. They are well kept and surrounded by a gorgeous garden. Doubles have bathrooms and use of a communal kitchen. Coming from Kokkari, turn right opposite the turn-off for Manolates (signposted) and after 50m you will come to a sign pointing to the rooms. The bus stop is just before the Manolates turn-off.

Studios Sandy (☎ *2273 094 415*) Double & triple studios €29.50. Next door to Kalypso, these pleasant and cosy studios are a good option.

Studio Angella (☎ *2273 094 478, Athens 2105 059 708, mobile* ☎ *69 7297 5722*) Doubles €26.50. In Manolates try this studio.

Traditional Greek House (☎ *2273 094 331*) Doubles €20.50. Phone to inquire about rooms in this nice little unnamed house in Manolates.

If you get stuck in Karlovasi there are several budget *hotels* and *domatia*, some signposted from the central square where the bus terminates.

Places to Eat

There are many reasonably priced restaurants to be found in Kokkari, all offering 'English menus' and the usual range of bland tourist fare.

Paradisos Restaurant (☎ *2273 094 208*) Mains around €6, with wine or beer around €10.50. This restaurant, at the turn-off to Manolates, serves delectable dishes.

Loukas Taverna (☎ *2273 094 541*) Mains €3-4. In Manolates, head for this taverna for the best and cheapest food around as well as great views. Try the stuffed courgette flowers and the special home-made *moshato* wines. Follow the prominent signs to the back end of the village.

Chios Χίος

pop 54,000

Chios (**hee**-os) does not feature prominently on the travel circuit. Situated rather awkwardly on the ferry routes and without a tangible international profile, the island attracts curious travellers and expat Greeks rather than hordes of package tourists, though those that do come find the island subtly rewarding in its own distinct way. Like its neighbours Samos and Lesvos, Chios is a large island covering 859 sq km. It is separated from the Turkish Karaburun Peninsula by the 8km-wide Chios Straits.

A large number of highly successful ship owners come from Chios and its dependencies, Inousses and Psara. This, and its mastic production, have meant that Chios has not needed to develop a large tourist industry. In recent years, however, package tourism has begun to make inroads, though it's limited to a fairly small coastal stretch south of Chios. The mastic villages of the south and its role as a stepping stone to Turkey is what primarily brings travellers to Chios.

History

In ancient times, Chios, like Samos, excelled in the arts, which reached their peak in the 7th century BC when the Chios school of sculpture produced some of Greece's most eminent sculptors of the time. The technique of soldering iron was invented in this school. During the Persian Wars, Chios was allied to Athens, but after the Battle of Plataea it became independent, and prospered because it didn't have to pay the annual tribute to Athens.

In Roman times Chios was invaded by Constantine, who helped himself to its fine sculptures. After the fall of Byzantium, the island fell prey to attacks by pirates, Venetians, Catalans and Turks. It revived somewhat under the Genoese, who took control in the 14th century. However, it was recaptured by the Turks in 1566 and became part of the Ottoman Empire.

In the 19th century, Chios suffered two devastations. In 1822 the Samians cajoled the people of Chios into assisting them in an uprising against Ottoman rule. The Turks retaliated by sacking Chios, killing 25,000 of its inhabitants and taking almost twice that number into slavery. The massacre was the subject of Victor Hugo's poem *L'Enfant de Chios* and Eugène Delacroix's painting *Le Massacre de Chios* (in the Louvre). In 1881 the island suffered a violent earthquake which killed almost 6000 people and destroyed many of the buildings in the capital.

Getting To/From Chios

Air Chios has on average five flights daily to Athens (€59), three weekly to Thessaloniki (€76.30) and one weekly to Lesvos

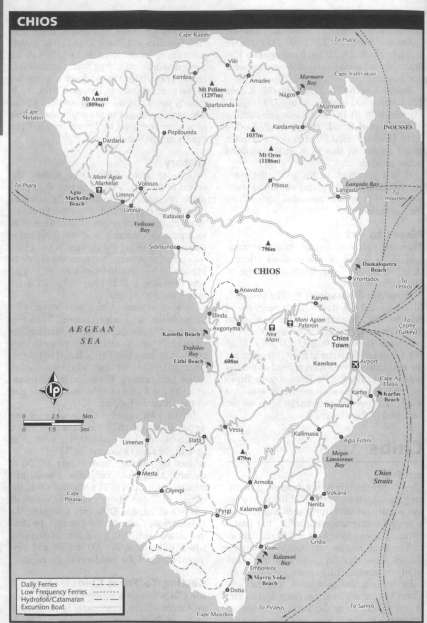

CHIOS

To Psara

Cape Kambi

Viki

Kambia

Mt Amani
(809m)

Mt Pelineo
(1297m)

Amades

*Marmaro
Bay*

Cape Vamvakias

Nagos

Spartounda

Marmaro

Cape
Melanio

1037m

Kardamyla

INOUSSES

Pispilounda

Dardaria

Mt Oros
(1186m)

Moni Agias
Markelas

Volissos

Pitious

Langada Bay

Langada

To Psara

Agia
Markella
Beach

Limnos

To
Inousses

Limnia

Katavasi

*Volissos
Bay*

Sidirounda

CHIOS

796m

*Daskalopetra
Beach*

Vrontados

To
Lesvos

Anavatos

Karyes

*AEGEAN
SEA*

Elinda

Avgonyma

Moni Agion
Pateron

Nea
Moni

To
Çeşme
(Turkey)

Kastella Beach

*Trahilos
Bay*
Lithi Beach

608m

**Chios
Town**

Airport

0   2.5   5km
0   1.5   3mi

Kambos

Cape Ag
Elenis

Karfas

Karfas
Beach

Thymiana

Vessa

Kallimasia

Agia Fotini

Limenas

Elata

479m

*Megas
Limnionas
Bay*

*Chios
Straits*

Mesta

Olympi

Armolia

Vokaria

Cape
Petasas

Pyrgi

Kalamoti

Nenita

Gridia

Komi

*Kalamoti
Bay*

Emboreios

*Mavra Volia
Beach*

Dotia

To Piraeus

To Samos

Cape Mastihos

Daily Ferries
Low Frequency Ferries
Hydrofoil/Catamaran
Excursion Boat

(€41.50). The Olympic Airways office (☎ 2271 020 359) is on Leoforos Aigaiou in Chios. The airport is 4km from Chios. There is no Olympic Airways bus, but a taxi to/from the airport should cost about €4.

Ferry – Domestic In summer at least one ferry goes daily to Piraeus (eight hours, €17) and Lesvos (three hours, €10.50). There's one per week to Kavala (16 hours, €24) and two to Thessaloniki (18 hours, €32), via Limnos (11 hours, €16), and Alexandroupolis (16 hours, €26), via Limnos and Samothraki (14 hours, €23). There are three boats weekly to Samos (four hours, €9) and one per week to Kos (nine hours, €15.30) and Rhodes (15 hours, €21.50). Tickets for these routes can be bought from the NEL office (☎ 2271 023 971, fax 2271 041 319) at Leoforos Aigaiou 16 in Chios.

Miniotis Lines (☎ 2271 024 670, fax 2271 025 371, [e] miniotis@compulink.gr, [w] www.miniotis.gr) at Neorion 23 in Chios is smaller, and runs small boats to Karlovasi (four hours, €8), Vathy (4½ hours, €9.50) and Pythagorio (five hours, €9.50) on Samos twice a week. Three times a week these boats continue on to Fourni (7½ hours, €15) and Ikaria (8½ hours, €18). It also has three boats weekly to Psara (3½ hours, €8). Miniotis boats occasionally dock at the eastern end of the harbour, at the corner of Aigaiou and Kokali.

The *Oinoussai II,* another small local boat, runs to and from Oinousses (1¼ hours, €3, purchase tickets on board) every day except Thursday and Sunday. It leaves Chios at 2pm and Inousses at 9am, so you must stay overnight. There are also daily water taxis between Langada and Inousses (€30, shared between the passengers).

Ferry – International Boats to Turkey run all year from Chios. During April and October there are usually three ferries weekly to Çeşme, leaving Chios at 8.30am and returning at 6.30pm. During May there is an additional sailing and from July to September there are daily sailings. The fare is €38.50/50 one-way/return (not including the €9 port tax). Further information and tickets can be obtained from Miniotis Lines. There are special daily excursion rates that often work out cheaper. Check with local agencies offering such trips.

Travellers requiring visas for Turkey can obtain them upon arrival in Çeşme for around US$45.

Hydrofoil In summer there are about three hydrofoils a week to Samos (3½ hours, €23) and Lesvos (1½ hours, €20).

Getting Around Chios

Bus From the long-distance bus station in Chios there are, in summer, eight buses daily to Pyrgi (€2), five to Mesta (€2.50) and six to Kardamyla (€2) via Langada. There are four buses a week to Volissos (€2.50). Only one or two buses weekly do the journey to Anavatos (€1.50) via Nea Moni and Avgonyma. There are fairly regular buses to the main beaches of Emborios, Komi, Nagos and Lithi. Buses to Karfas Beach are serviced by the blue (city) bus company. Schedules are posted at both bus stations.

Car & Motorcycle The numerous car-rental outlets in the town of Chios include Aegean Travel (☎ 2271 041 277, [e] aegeantr@otenet.gr, Aigaiou 114), at the northern end of the waterfront. In summer it's a good idea to book in advance for weekends.

Taxi Call ☎ 2271 041 111 for a taxi.

CHIOS TOWN
postcode 821 00 • pop 22,900

The town of Chios, on the east coast, is the island's port and capital. It's a large settlement, home to almost half of the island's inhabitants. Its waterfront, flanked by concrete buildings and trendy bars, is noisy in the extreme, with an inordinate number of cars and motorcycles careering up and down. The atmospheric old quarter, with many Turkish houses built around a Genoese castle, and the lively market area, are both worth a stroll. Chios doesn't have a beach; the nearest is the sandy beach at Karfas, 6km south.

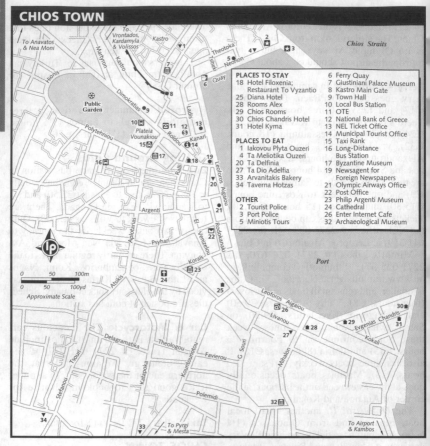

CHIOS TOWN

PLACES TO STAY
18 Hotel Filoxenia;
   Restaurant To Vyzantio
25 Diana Hotel
28 Rooms Alex
29 Chios Rooms
30 Chios Chandris Hotel
31 Hotel Kyma

PLACES TO EAT
1 Iakovou Plyta Ouzeri
4 Ta Meliotika Ouzeri
20 Ta Delfinia
27 Ta Dio Adelfia
33 Arvanitakis Bakery
34 Taverna Hotzas

OTHER
2 Tourist Police
3 Port Police
5 Miniotis Tours

6 Ferry Quay
7 Giustiniani Palace Museum
8 Kastro Main Gate
9 Town Hall
10 Local Bus Station
11 OTE
12 National Bank of Greece
13 NEL Ticket Office
14 Municipal Tourist Office
15 Taxi Rank
16 Long-Distance
   Bus Station
17 Byzantine Museum
19 Newsagent for
   Foreign Newspapers
21 Olympic Airways Office
22 Post Office
23 Philip Argenti Museum
24 Cathedral
26 Enter Internet Cafe
32 Archaeological Museum

Orientation

Most ferries dock at the northern end of the
waterfront at the western end of Neorion.
Bear in mind that some ferries from Piraeus
arrive at the very inconvenient time of 4am –
worth remembering if you are planning to
find a room. The old Turkish quarter (called
Kastro) is to the north of the ferry quay. To
reach the town centre from here, follow the
waterfront round to the left and walk along
Leoforos Aigaiou. Turn right onto Kanari to
reach the central square of Plateia Vounakiou. To the north-west of the square are the
public gardens, and to the south-east is the

market area. The main shopping streets are
south of the square. As you face inland, the
bus station for local buses (blue; ☎ 2271 022
079) is on the right side of the public gardens,
and the station for long-distance buses
(green; ☎ 2271 027 507) is on the left.

Information

The municipal tourist office (☎ 2271 044
389, fax 2271 044 343, ⓔ infochio@otenet
.gr) is at Kanari 18. The extremely helpful
and friendly staff can provide information
on accommodation, car rental, bus and boat
schedules, and more. The book *Hiking*

Routes on Chios is available here for €4.50. The office is open 7am to 10pm daily.

The post office and OTE are both one block back from the waterfront while most banks are between Kanari and Plateia Vounakiou. There is an ATM halfway along Aplotarias.

The Enter Internet Cafe (☎ 2271 041 058) is at Aigaiou 48 (upstairs), on the southern waterfront, and charges €4 an hour.

The tourist police (☎ 2271 044 427) and the port police (☎ 2271 044 432) are at the eastern end of Neorion.

Museums

The most interesting museum is the **Philip Argenti Museum** (*☎ 2271 023 463, Koraïs; admission €1.50; museum & library open 8am-2pm Mon-Thur, 5pm-7.30pm Fri, 8am-12.30pm Sat*). Situated in the same building as the **Koraïs Library**, one of the country's largest libraries. The museum, which is near the cathedral, contains embroideries, traditional costumes and portraits of the wealthy Argenti family.

The town's other museums are not so compelling. The **archaeological museum** (*☎ 2271 044 239, Mihalon 10; admission €1.50; open 8am-7pm Tues-Sun*) contains sculptures, pottery and coins. It sometimes has interesting temporary exhibits. The **Byzantine Museum** (*☎ 2271 026 866, Plateia Vounakiou; admission free; open 10am-1pm Tues-Sun*) is housed in a former mosque, the Medjitie Djami.

Just inside the Kastro's main gate, is the tiny **Giustiniani Palace Museum** (*☎ 22/1 022 819; €1.50 Mon-Sat, admission €1 Sun; open 8am-7pm Mon-Sat, 8am-3pm Sun*). It holds a few restored wall paintings of prophets, and other Byzantine bits and pieces.

Places to Stay – Budget

With over 30 *domatia* to choose from, budget accommodation is fairly plentiful in Chios. Call into the municipal tourist office for a full listing. Be aware, though, that accommodation in central Chios can be very noisy – choose carefully.

Chios Rooms (*☎ 2271 020 198, mobile ☎ 69 7283 3841, Aigaiou 110*) Singles/

doubles/triples €18/24/35.50, some with private bathroom. This beautifully decked-out neoclassical place is a real find. It's clean, comfortable and full of interesting artworks and old pieces of furniture. It's upstairs, above Aegean Travel, at the east end of the waterfront.

Rooms Alex (*☎ 2271 026 054, Livanou 29*) Doubles with bathroom €29.50. This is another domatia option. Alex has six doubles and there is a relaxing roof garden festooned with flags. Alex will pick you up at your boat if you call him. He will also help with car or bike rentals and give general information on Chios.

Places to Stay – Mid-Range & Top End

Diana Hotel (*☎ 2271 044 180, fax 2271 026 748, El Venizelou 92*) Singles/doubles with breakfast €43/53. This D-class place is a good hotel aimed primarily at the Greek business market.

Hotel Filoxenia (*☎ 2271 026 559, fax 2271 028 447, Voupalou 8*) Doubles with bathroom, fridge, air-con & balcony €59. This is signposted from the waterfront and is above Restaurant To Vyzantio. The foyer has a lovely faded decadence about it, but the rooms are lacking such charm and are somewhat overpriced.

Hotel Kyma (*☎ 2271 044 500, fax 2271 044 600, ⓔ kyma@chi.forthnet.gr, Evgenias Chandris 1*) Singles/doubles with TV, air-con & phone €44/64.56. The C-class Kyma occupies a century-old mansion and has lots of character. Try to get one of the rooms overlooking the sea. The breakfast is magnificent (and included in the room rate). The helpful owners can organise driving itineraries that include accommodation in Mesta and Volissos.

Chios Chandris Hotel (*☎ 2271 025 768, Evgenias Chandris 2, ⓔ chios@chandris .gr, ⓦ www.chandris.gr*) Singles/doubles with breakfast €79.50/106, 3-person studios & 2-person suites €176. This classy international-style hotel is the best on the island. All rooms have a balcony with sea view. There's a pool, restaurant and bar, full room service and many other facilities.

Places to Eat

Arvanitakis Bakery (Cnr Katapoka & Kountouriotou) The bread baked here is some of the best you'll find in Greece. Try the whole wheat.

Restaurant To Vyzantio (☎ 2271 041 035, Cnr Ralli & Roïdou) Mains around €3.50. This bright, cheerful and unpretentious place serves good traditional Greek fare at low prices.

Iakovou Plyta Ouzeri (☎ 2271 023 858, Agiou Georgiou Frouriou 20) Mezedes from around €3. Tucked away in the old town is this ouzeri specialising in tasty fish mezedes.

Ta Meliotiko Ouzeri (☎ 2271 040 407) Salads and vegetable dishes around €2.50, seafood around €6. This basic place on the waterfront near the police station dishes out huge helpings of delicious Greek salads, seafood and vegetable appetisers. Be hungry.

Ta Delfinia (☎ 2271 022 607, Aigaiou 36) Mains from around €3.50. This waterfront taverna is a bit touristy (with photo menus), but the food and service are good and it's the best place to watch street life.

Ta Dio Adelfia (☎ 2271 021 313, Livanou 38) Mains around €4.50. This taverna with a pleasant walled garden is opposite Rooms Alex.

Taverna Hotzas (☎ 2271 042 787, Kondyli 3) Most dishes around €3.50. Open evenings Mon-Sat year round. This taverna at the southern end of town is an institution, with lots of ugly cats and a lovely garden littered with lemon trees. Try the fava, the *mastelo* (grilled cheese) and the grilled fish. To get there, walk up Aplotarias and turn right at the fork along Stefanou Tsouri; follow it until you come across the restaurant.

CENTRAL CHIOS

North of the town of Chios is an elongated beachside suburb leading to **Vrontados** where you can sit on the supposed stone chair of Homer, the Daskalopetra, though it is quietly accepted that it's unlikely to have been used by Homer himself. It's a serene spot though, and it would not be hard to imagine Homer and his acolytes reciting epic verses to their admiring followers.

Immediately south of Chios is a warren of walled mansions, some restored, others crumbling, called the **Kampos**. This was the preferred place of abode of wealthy Genoese and Greek merchant families from the 14th century onwards. It's easy to get lost here so keep your wits about you. It's best to tour the area by bicycle, moped or car, since it is fairly extensive. Chios' main beach resort, **Karfas**, is here too, 7km south of Chios. The beach is sandy though comparatively small with some moderate development and some A-class hotels; if you like your beaches quiet, look elsewhere.

In the centre of the island is the 11th-century **Nea Moni** *(admission free; open 8am-1pm, 4pm-8pm)*. This large monastery, now World Heritage-listed, stands in a beautiful mountain setting, 14km from Chios. Like many monasteries in Greece it was built to house an icon of the Virgin Mary who appeared before the eyes of three shepherds. In its heyday the monastery was one of the richest in Greece with the most preeminent artists of Byzantium commissioned to create the mosaics in its katholikon.

During the 1822 atrocities the buildings were set on fire and all the resident monks were massacred. There is a macabre display of their skulls in the ossuary at the monastery's little chapel. In the earthquake of 1881 the katholikon's dome caved in, causing damage to the mosaics. Nonetheless, the mosaics, esteemed for the striking contrasts of their vivid colours and the fluidity and juxtapositions of the figures, still rank among the most outstanding examples of Byzantine art in Greece. A few nuns live at the monastery. The bus service to the monastery is poor, but travel agents in Chios have excursions here and to the village of Anavatos.

Ten kilometres from Nea Moni, at the end of a road that leads to nowhere, stands the forlorn ghost village of **Anavatos**. Its abandoned grey-stone houses stand as lonely sentinels to one of Chios' great tragedies. Nearly all the inhabitants of the village perished in 1822 and today only a small number of elderly people live there, mostly in houses at the base of the village. Anavatos is a striking village, built on a precipitous cliff which the villagers chose to hurl themselves over, rather than be taken captive by the Turks. Narrow, stepped pathways wind between the houses to the summit of the village.

The beaches on the mid-west coast are not spectacular, but they are quiet and generally undeveloped. **Lithi Beach**, the southernmost, is popular with weekenders and can get busy.

SOUTHERN CHIOS

Southern Chios is dominated by medieval villages that look as though they were transplanted from the Levant rather than built by Genoese colonisers in the 14th century. The rolling, scrubby hills are covered in low mastic trees that for many years were the main source of income for these scattered settlements (see the boxed text 'Gum Mastic').

There are some 20 *Mastihohoria* (mastic villages); the two best preserved are Pyrgi and Mesta. As mastic was a lucrative commodity in the Middle Ages, many an invader cast an acquisitive eye upon the villages, necessitating sturdy fortifications. The archways spanning the streets were to prevent the houses from collapsing during earthquakes. Because of the sultan's fondness for mastic chewing gum, the inhabitants of the Mastihohoria were spared in the 1822 massacre.

Pyrgi Πυργί
pop 1300

The largest of the Mastihohoria, and one of the most extraordinary villages in the whole of Greece, is the fortified village of Pyrgi, 24km south-west of Chios. The vaulted streets of the fortified village are narrow and labyrinthine, but what makes Pyrgi unique are the building facades, decorated with intricate grey and white designs. Some of the patterns are geometric and others are based on flowers, leaves and animals. The technique used, called *xysta*, is achieved by coating the walls with a mixture of cement and black volcanic sand, painting over this with white lime, and then scraping off parts of the lime with the bent prong of a fork, to reveal the matt grey beneath.

From the main road, a fork heading to the right (coming from Chios) leads to the

Gum Mastic

Gum mastic comes from the lentisk bush, and conditions in southern Chios are ideal for its growth. Many ancient Greeks, including Hippocrates, proclaimed the pharmaceutical benefits of mastic. Ailments it was claimed to cure included stomach upsets, chronic coughs and diseases of the liver, intestines and bladder. It was also used as an antidote for snake bites. During Turkish rule Chios received preferential treatment from the sultans who, along with the ladies of the harem, were hooked on chewing gum made from mastic.

Until recently, mastic was widely used in the pharmaceutical industry, as well as in the manufacture of chewing gum and certain alcoholic drinks, particularly arak, a Middle Eastern liqueur. In most cases mastic has now been replaced by *raki*, a Greek firewater. But mastic production may yet have a future. Some adherents of alternative medicine claim that it stimulates the immune system and reduces blood pressure and cholesterol levels. Chewing gum made from mastic can be bought on Chios, under the brand name Elma.

heart of the village and the central square. The little 12th-century **Church of Agios Apostolos**, just off the square, is profusely decorated with well-preserved 17th-century frescoes. Ask at the taverna or kafeneio for the church's caretaker, who will open it up for you. The facade of the larger church, on the opposite side of the square, has the most impressive xysta of all the buildings here.

Places to Stay & Eat *Giannaki Rooms* (☎ 2271 025 888, mobile ☎ 69 4595 9889, fax 2271 022 846) Doubles €44. This old house has been fully renovated and offers rooms with TV and air-con. Book ahead.

Taverna Kanios (☎ 2271 072 150) Most dishes around €2.50. This little taverna on the central square (on the right as you face the large church) is the main eating option.

There's an upstairs *pizzeria* on the square but it's not always open.

Emboreios Εμπορειός

Six kilometres to the south of Pyrgi, Emboreios was the port of Pyrgi in the days when mastic production was big business. These days Emboreios is a quiet place, perfect for people who like to relax. As you come from Chios, a signpost points left to Emboreios, just before you arrive at Pyrgi.

Mavra Volia Beach is at the end of the road and has unusual black volcanic pebbles as its main attraction. There is another more secluded beach, just over the headland along a paved track.

Places to Stay & Eat *Studio Apartments Vasiliki (☎ 2271 071 422)* Doubles €35.50. These studios in Emboreios are often full, but the same people also have rooms in Mavra Volia.

Neptune (☎ 2271 070 020) Seafood around €4.50. This taverna has the most prominent position in Emboreios.

Porto Emborios (☎ 2271 070 025) Mains around €4.50, appetisers €3. On the main square this shady place is very pleasant, with an old stone facade decorated with hanging strings of chillies and garlic and fishing nets. It has good home-cooked food, including roast lamb.

Mesta Μεστά

Continuing on the main road from Pyrgi, after 5km you will reach the mastic village of **Olympi**. It's less immediately attractive than its two neighbours but still worth a brief stop.

Mesta, 5km on, has a very different atmosphere from that created by the striking visuals of Pyrgi and should be on any visitor's itinerary. Nested among low hills, the village is exquisite and completely enclosed within massive fortified walls. Entrance to the maze of streets is via one of four gates. This method of limiting entry to the settlement and its disorienting maze of streets and tunnels is a prime example of 14th-century defence architecture, as protection against pirates and marauders. The labyrinthine cobbled streets of bare stone houses and arches have a melancholy aura, though it's a cheerful place, with women chatting on their front steps as

they shell almonds and fresh *revithia* (chickpeas) or tie bundles of sweet-smelling herbs.

The village has two churches of the Taxiarhes (archangels). The older one dates from Byzantine times and has a magnificent 17th-century iconostasis. The second one, built in the 19th century, has very fine frescoes.

Orientation Buses stop on Plateia Nikolaou Poumpaki, on the main road outside Mesta. To reach the central square of Plateia Taxiarhon, with your back to the bus shelter, turn right, and then immediately left, and you will see a sign pointing to the centre of the village.

Places to Stay & Eat *Despina Floris Rooms (☎ 2271 076 050, fax 2271 076 529)* Double studios around €32.50. This clearing house for renovated rooms is perhaps the best place to start if you're looking for somewhere to stay. Despina, who also runs Mesaonas restaurant on the square, speaks good English.

Anna Floradis Rooms (☎ 2271 028 891, 2271 076 455/176) Doubles €38. These five, very comfortable rooms are next to the church.

Karambelas Apartments (☎ 2271 022 068, 10 Ilia Mandalaka) Doubles €59. These exquisite, spotless studios in a renovated medieval house belong to the family that run the O Morias Sta Mesta taverna. Rooms contain beautiful handmade textiles and stone wall niches. You can negotiate a much better rate outside high season. Ask at the taverna if no-one answers the phone.

O Morias Sta Mesta (☎ 2271 076 400, Plateia Taxiarhon) Mains around €4.50. Dionyssis Karambelas, the affable owner of this restaurant – one of the two on Plateia Taxiarhon in romantic courtyard settings – is originally from the Peloponnese (hence the name of the restaurant: Morias is the old name for the Peloponnese). Dionyssis will provide you with superb country cooking. Ask to try the *hortokeftedes* (vegetable patties) and an unusual wild green, *kritamos* (rock samphire), that grows by the sea. The bread is homemade and the unusually sweet olives taste like mastic. You may be given a glass of *souma*, an ouzo made from figs, or a mastic firewater.

Mesaonas *(☎ 2271 076 050, Plateia Taxiarhon)* Mains around €4.50. This restaurant on the square is also very good. It specialises in traditional recipes made with local ingredients. The wine, oil, cheese and, of course, the souma, are all from Mesta.

NORTHERN CHIOS
Northern Chios is characterised by its craggy peaks (Mt Pelineo, Mt Oros and Mt Amani), deserted villages and scrawny hillsides once blanketed in rich pine forests. The area is mainly for the adventurous and those not fazed by tortuous roads.

Volissos is the main focus for the villages of the north-western quarter. Reputedly Homer's place of birth, it is today a quiet settlement, capped with an impressive Genoese fort. Volissos' port is **Limnia**, a workaday fishing harbour. It's not especially appealing, but has a welcoming *taverna*. You can continue to **Limnos**, a kilometre away, where caiques sometimes leave for Psara. The road onwards round the north end is very winding and passes some isolated villages.

On the eastern side a picturesque road leads out of Vrontados through a landscape that is somewhat more visitor-friendly than the western side. **Langada** is the first village, wedged at the end of a bay looking out towards Inousses. Next are **Kardamyla** and **Marmaro**, the two main settlements. If you fancy a dip, head a few kilometres farther to the lush little fishing hamlet of **Nagos**. It has a nice beach with coloured pebbles.

Beyond Nagos, the road winds upwards, skirting the craggy Mt Pelineo. The scenery is green enough, but settlements are fewer and more remote. **Amades** and **Viki** are two villages you will traverse before hitting the last village, **Kambia**, perched high up on a ridge overlooking bare hillsides and the sea far below. From here a mostly sealed road leads you round Mt Pelineo, past a futuristic phalanx of 10 huge wind-driven generators on the opposite side of the valley, and back to the trans-island route near Volissos.

Places to Stay
Hotel Kardamyla *(☎ 2272 023 353, fax 2271 044 600)* Doubles €65. If you choose to stay up in Marmaro, try this comfortable hotel run by the same management as Hotel Kyma in Chios.

Volissos Restored Houses *(☎ 2274 021 413/421, fax 2274 021 521)* Studios from €44. These beautifully renovated village houses, some with patios, look out over the gently sloping landscape towards the sea. It's a nice spot if you're looking for peace and quiet.

Inousses Οινούσσες

Off the north-eastern coast of Chios lie nine tiny islets, collectively called Inousses. Only one of these, also called Inousses, is inhabited. Those who live here permanently make their living from fishing and sheep farming. The island has three fish farms and exports small amounts of fish to Italy and France. Inousses is hilly and covered in scrub and has good beaches.

However, these facts apart, this is no ordinary Greek island. Inousses may be small, but it is the ancestral home of around 30% of Greece's ship owners. Most of these wealthy maritime barons conduct their business from Athens, London and New York, but in summer return with their families to Inousses, where they own luxurious mansions.

There is a rumour that these ship owners offer financial incentives to discourage people from opening tavernas or domatia on

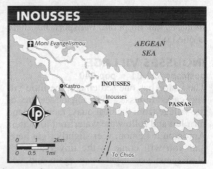

the island, because they don't want to attract foreign tourists. It may not be possible to vouch for the truth of this but certainly tourism is not encouraged on the island: no domatia owners come to meet the boat, there are no domatia signs and wandering around the streets fails to bring offers of accommodation. The place has a curiously barren and sterile air since there are few tourist facilities and even fewer visitors. Several islanders have stated that Inousses has a few domatia, but they are vague as to their whereabouts.

On a more positive note – and if these quirks have not discouraged you from going to Inousses – the island's town has some nice neoclassical mansions and abandoned houses; good beaches (**Kastro Beach** is the usual swimming stop for day-trippers); and no tourists. In the town of Inousses there is a large naval boarding school. If you visit during term time you may well encounter the pupils parading around town to bellowed marching orders.

Getting To/From Inousses
The island is served only by the local ferry boat *Oinoussai II*, which plies everyday (except Thursday and Sunday) between the island and the town of Chios. It leaves Chios at 2pm and Inousses at 9am, so is of no use for day trips. Purchase tickets on board for €3 (one way). The trip takes about one hour. There are also daily water taxis (☎ 69 4416 8104) to/from Langada. The one-way fare is €30, which is split between the passengers. In summer there are sometimes excursion boats from Chios to the island.

Getting Around Inousses
Inousses has no public transport, but there is one taxi.

INOUSSES VILLAGE
postcode 821 01 • pop 640
The island has one settlement, the little village called Inousses. To reach the 'centre' of the village from the boat quay, facing inland turn left and follow the waterfront to Plateia Antoniou P Lemou; veer slightly right here, and you will come to the tiny Plateia tis Naftisynis; veer right once again and you

will see ahead Restaurant & Kafeneio Pateroniso, near the highly decorated cream and brick-red building. Facing this establishment turn right and ascend the steps. There's not a lot to see in the centre, apart from the church, but it is near the island's only hotel.

If you turn left at Restaurant Pateroniso and then take the first right into Konstantinou Antonopoulou you will come to the National Bank of Greece which, one can surmise, is kept very busy. Next door to the bank is a combined post office and OTE.

The police (☎ 2271 055 222) are at the top of the steps that lead to the town centre.

Maritime Museum
This museum (☎ 2271 055 182; admission €1.50; open 10am-1.30pm) is between the Restaurant Pateroniso and the National Bank of Greece. It opened in 1990 and the benefactors were wealthy ship owners from the island. Many island families donated nautical memorabilia, which includes *objets d'art*, photographs, models of early ships, cannons and nautical instruments.

Places to Stay & Eat
There is no camping ground on the island and camping freelance would definitely be frowned upon.

Hotel Thalassoporos (☎ 2271 055 475) Singles/doubles with bathroom €23.50/ 35.50. Inousses' one hotel is this bland C-class property at the top of the steps that lead to the village centre. It's unlikely ever to be full, but just in case, phone ahead in July and August.

Restaurant Pateroniso (☎ 2271 055 586) Mains around €4.50. This is Inousses' only restaurant outside the summer months. The food is reasonably priced and well prepared, but you will not be made to feel welcome – if it's busy with locals, you'll be ignored altogether.

The little fish taverna *Zepagas* – open only in summer – is at the far western end of the harbour.

There are a couple of bars. *Remezzo* is a small bar on the waterfront, while *Trigono* is up in the village and mainly patronised by the few local young people left on the island.

The town has four *grocery stores*. One of the two on the waterfront thankfully serves as a bit of a snack bar (though your options are limited to cheese pies, canned dolmades and whatever else you can glean from its shelves) and has tables out the front. The other two are in the centre of the village, on the road that leads up to the prominent Agios Nikolaos church.

ISLAND WALK

Although most of this three-hour circular walk is along a narrow cement road, you are unlikely to meet much traffic. Take plenty of water and a snack with you as there are no refreshments available along the way. Also take your swimming gear as you will pass many of the island's beaches and coves.

Just beyond the maritime museum you will see a signpost to **Moni Evangelismou**. This will take you along the cement road that skirts the west coast. Along the way you will pass several inviting beaches and coves. Only **Apiganos Beach** is signposted, but there are others which are easily accessible from the road. After about one hour the road loops inland, and a little farther along is the entrance to the palatial Moni Evangelismou, surrounded by extensive grounds.

Within the convent is the mummified body of Irini Pateras, daughter of the late Panagos Pateras, a multimillionaire ship owner. Irini became a nun in her late teens and died in the early 1960s when she was 20. Her distraught mother decided built the convent in memory of her daughter. In the Greek Orthodox religion, three years after burial the body is exhumed and the bones cleaned and reburied in a casket. When Irini's body was exhumed it was found to have mummified rather than decomposed; this phenomenon is regarded in Greece as evidence of sainthood. Irini's mother is now abbess of the convent, which houses around 20 nuns. Only women may visit the convent and of course they must be appropriately (modestly) dressed.

Continuing along the cement road, beyond the entrance to the convent, you will come to two stone pillars on the left. The wide path between the pillars leads in 10 minutes to an enormous white cross which is a **memorial** to St Irini. This is the highest point of the island and commands stunning views over to northern Chios and the Karaburun Peninsula in Turkey. About 20 minutes farther along, the cement road gives way to a dirt track. Continue straight ahead to reach the town of Inousses.

Psara Ψαρά

postcode 821 04 • pop 500

Psara (psah-**rah**) lies off the north-west coast of Chios. The island is 9km long and 5km wide and is rocky with little vegetation. During Ottoman times Greeks settled on the remote island to escape Turkish oppression. By the 19th century, many of these inhabitants, like those of Chios and Inousses, had become successful ship owners. When the rallying cry for self-determination reverberated through the country, the Psariots zealously took up arms and contributed a large number of ships to the Greek cause. In retaliation the Turks stormed the island and killed all but 3000 of the 20,000 inhabitants. The island never regained its former glory and today all of the inhabitants live in the island's one settlement, also called Psara.

Like Inousses, Psara sees few tourists.

Places to Stay

EOT Guesthouse (☎ 2274 061 293) Single/double rooms €53/59, single/double studios €41/47. The old parliament building has been converted into an EOT guesthouse. Breakfast is included in the price of

all rooms. Information may be obtained by either telephoning the guesthouse or ringing ☎ 2251 027 908 in Lesvos.

There are also *domatia* in Psara and a small number of *tavernas*.

Getting To/From Psara
Ferries leave Chios for Psara (3½ hours, €8) at 7am three times weekly, returning at noon. Call Miniotis Lines (☎ 2271 024 670) in Chios or check with a local agent for current departure days since these change from year to year. Local caiques also run from Limnos (three hours, €4.50) on the west coast of Chios about once a week, but departure times are unpredictable and often depend on the prevailing weather conditions.

Lesvos (Mytilini)
Λέσβος (Μυτιλήνη)

pop 88,800
Lesvos is the third-largest island in Greece, after Crete and Evia. It's north of Chios and south-east of Limnos. Most Greeks call the island Mytilini, also the name of the capital. The island is mountainous with two bottleneck gulfs penetrating its south coast. The south and east of the island are fertile, with numerous olive groves. In contrast to the south and east, the west has rocky and barren mountains, creating a dramatic moonscape.

Lesvos produces the best olive oil in Greece and has many olive oil refineries. Many abandoned olive oil and soap factories are now being renovated and revived as cultural centres. Aside from olive oil, Lesvos is famous for its ouzo, its sardines from the Gulf of Kalloni (eaten raw, like sashimi marinated in salt, and very good with ouzo) and its *ladotyri*, a sheep's milk cheese that is kept in oil for one to two years. If you go in search of ladotyri, make sure you ask for the real thing – the commercial stuff is coated with paraffin.

Lesvos is becoming a popular package-holiday destination, but is large enough to absorb tourists without seeming to be overrun. Still, it's best to visit outside the peak tourist months of July and August. Early spring and late autumn are ideal for trekking. There's a lot to see here; you could easily spend two weeks taking in the sights and still feel you've run out of time to see everything.

History
In the 6th century BC, Lesvos was unified under the rule of the tyrant Pittakos, one of ancient Greece's Seven Sages. Pittakos succeeded in resolving the long-standing animosity between the island's two cities of Mytilini and Mithymna. This new-found peace generated an atmosphere conducive to creativity, and Lesvos became a centre of artistic and philosophical achievement.

Terpander, the musical composer, and Arion, the poet, were both born on Lesvos in the 7th century BC. Arion's works influenced the tragedians of the 5th century BC such as Sophocles and Euripides. In the 4th century BC, Aristotle and Epicurus taught at an exceptional school of philosophy which flourished on Lesvos.

Sappho, one of the greatest poets of ancient Greece, was born on Lesvos around 630 BC. Unfortunately little of her poetry is extant, but what remains reveals a genius for combining passion with simplicity and detachment, in verses ofx beauty and power.

On a more prosaic level, Lesvos suffered at the hands of invaders and occupiers to the same extent as all other Greek islands. In 527 BC the Persians conquered the island, but in 479 BC it was captured by Athens and became a member of the Delian League. In the following centuries the island suffered numerous invasions, and in 88 BC it was conquered by Julius Caesar. Byzantines, Venetians, Genoese and Turks followed.

However, through all these vicissitudes the arts retained a high degree of importance. The primitive painter Theophilos (1866–1934) and the Nobel Prize-winning poet Odysseus Elytis (1911–96) were born on Lesvos. The island is to this day a spawning ground for innovative ideas in the arts and politics, and is the headquarters of the University of the Aegean. The Lesvos campus of the university is the home of the environmental studies and social anthropology departments.

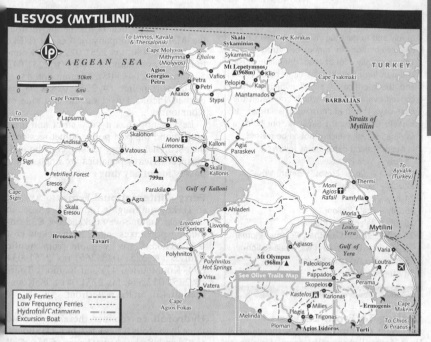

LESVOS (MYTILINI)

Trekking

Lesvos has some nice trekking trails in the north and south. Some of these were marked with colour-coded signs, but these days only a few signs are left; nonetheless, the trails are easy to follow. These walks can be taken in sections, or over a few days, stopping off along the way where appropriate. They are a mixture of dirt vehicle tracks and pedestrian trails. The main trails are **Vatera to Yera**, **Petra to Lapsarna**, **Kapi to Sykaminia** and **Sigri to Eresos**. There are many other walking trails on the island, including those in the olive-growing region around Plomari (see the boxed text 'Olive Trails' in this chapter). Of these, the **Skopelos-Karionas-Kastelos-Trigonas/Plagia** day trek is the most popular.

Bird-Watching

Bird-watching – or 'birding', as experts call it – is big business in Lesvos. The island is the transit point and home to over 279 species of birds ranging from raptors to waders. As a result, Lesvos is attracting an ever-increasing number of visitors – human and feathered – particularly in spring. There are four main observation areas centred on Eresos, Petra, Skala Kallonis and Agiasos. The major aim of birders seems to be spotting the elusive Cinereous bunting and Kruper's nuthatch.

A folksy and detailed handbook to the hobby is Richard Brooks' *Birding in Lesbos*, which is available on Lesvos.

Special Events

Throughout summer, villages hold festivals on the name day of their church. These two-day festas with very ancient origins usually involve the racing of beautifully decorated horses and the sacrifice of a bull. For a list of dates and villages, see the boxed text 'Festival Time'.

If you're visiting the island in February, don't miss carnival in the town of Agiasos – among other things, the locals perform hilariously vulgar comedies.

NORTH-EASTERN AEGEAN

Festival Time

In July and August the villages of Lesvos hold wild celebrations in honour of patron saints. There's usually a lot of food, drink, live music and dancing all night, as well as horse races and the sacrifice of a bull, which is then cooked overnight with wheat and eaten the next day. This traditional dish is known as *keskek*. On 6 August Skala Kalloni holds a sardine festival, which is not to be missed.

Major festival dates are as follows:

1 July – Agia Paraskevi
20 July – Agiasos, Eresos, Plomari, Vrisa
22 July – Skopelos
24 July – Eresos
25 July – Skala Kalloni
26 July – Paleokipos, Plomari
27 July – Eresos, Gavathas, Perama, Plomari
6 August – Eresos, Andissa, Skala Kalloni
15 August – Agiasos, Kerami
30 August – Vafios

Getting To/From Lesvos

Air With Olympic Airways there are at least four flights daily from Lesvos to Athens (€71.60) and around one daily to Thessaloniki (€76.30), as well as one flight weekly to Chios (€41.50) and four flights a week to Limnos (€48.50). Aegean (☎ 2251 061 120, fax 2251 061 801) flies between Lesvos and Athens three times a day and Thessaloniki once a day. Note that Lesvos is always referred to as Mytilini on air schedules. The Olympic Airways office (☎ 2251 028 659) in Mytilini is at Kavetsou 44 (Kavetsou is a southerly continuation of Ermou). The airport is 8km south of Mytilini. A taxi to/from the airport will cost about €6.

Ferry – Domestic In summer there is at least one ferry daily to Piraeus (12 hours, €22.50) via Chios (three hours, €10.50) and two weekly highspeed services (six hours, €40). There are two ferries weekly to Kavala (10 hours, €20) via Limnos (six hours, €15.50), two weekly to Thessaloniki (13 hours, €25) via Limnos and one to Alexandroupolis (11½ hours, €16.50). Ferry ticket

offices line the eastern side of Kountourioti, in Mytilini. Get tickets for the above from the Maritime Company of Lesvos (NEL; ☎ 2251 028 480, fax 2251 028 601), Kountourioti 67, or Samiotis Tours (☎ 2251 042 574, fax 2251 041 808), Kountourioti 43.

The port police (☎ 2251 028 827) are next to Picolo Travel on the east side of Kountourioti.

Lesvos now has a very strict anti-drug policy, and the port police sometimes conduct searches of ferry passengers who look 'suspect'. Heavy penalties are imposed for possession of any drugs.

Ferry – International Ferries to Ayvalık in Turkey run roughly four times a week in high season. One-way tickets cost €38 (including port taxes) and return tickets cost €47. Tickets are available from Aeolic Cruises (☎ 2251 023 266, fax 2251 034 694, Kountourioti 47) and Samiotis Tours (☎ 2251 042 574, fax 2251 041 808, Kountourioti 43), on the waterfront.

Hydrofoil In summer there are around three hydrofoils a week to Chios (1½ hours, €20) and Samos (five hours, €25). Call Kyriacoulis (☎ 2251 020 716), Kountourioti 73, for the latest schedule.

Getting Around Lesvos

Bus Lesvos' transport hub is the capital, Mytilini. In summer, from the long-distance bus station (☎ 2251 028 873) there are three buses daily to Skala Eresou (2½ hours, €6.50) via Eresos, five buses daily to Mithymna (1¾ hours, €4.50) via Petra, and two buses to Sigri (2½ hours, €6.50). There are no direct buses between Eresos, Sigri and Mithymna. If you wish to travel from one of these villages to another, change buses in the town of Kalloni, which is 48km from Eresos and 22km from Mithymna. There are five buses daily to the south-coast resort of Plomari (1¼ hours, €3). A timetable is posted in the window at the bus station.

Car & Motorcycle The many car-hire outlets in Mytilini include Hertz (☎ 2251 042 576, mobile ☎ 69 3605 7676), which is based at Samiotis Tours (☎ 2251 042 574, fax 2251 041 808), Kountourioti 43, on the waterfront, and Troho Kinisi (☎ 2251 046 611, mobile ☎ 69 3223 7900), which operates from the Erato Hotel just south of the Olympic Airways office.

Many motorcycle-rental firms are located along the same stretch of waterfront. You will, however, be better off hiring a motorcycle or scooter in Mithymna or Skala Eresou, since Lesvos is a large island and an underpowered two-wheeler is not really a practical mode of transport for getting around.

Ferry In summer there are hourly ferries (five minutes, €1) between Perama and Koundouroudia, near Loutra. Buses to Mytilini meet all ferries.

MYTILINI TOWN Μυτιλήνη
postcode 811 00 • pop 23,970

Mytilini, the capital and port of Lesvos, is a large workaday town. If you are enthralled by pretty towns like Mykonos you won't necessarily find the same ambience in Mytilini. However, this town has its own attractions, including a lively harbour and nightlife, once-grand 19th-century mansions

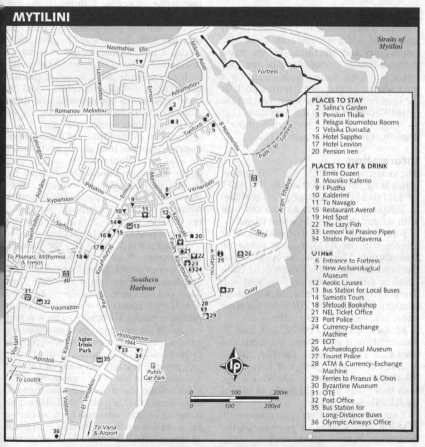

MYTILINI

PLACES TO STAY
2 Salina's Garden
3 Pension Thalia
4 Pelagia Koumiotou Rooms
5 Vetsika Domatia
16 Hotel Sappho
17 Hotel Lesvion
20 Pension Iren

PLACES TO EAT & DRINK
1 Ermis Ouzeri
8 Mousiko Kafenio
9 I Psatha
10 Kalderimi
11 To Navagio
15 Restaurant Averof
19 Hot Spot
22 The Lazy Fish
33 Lemoni kai Prasino Piperi
34 Stratos Psarotaverna

OTHER
6 Entrance to Fortress
7 New Archaeological Museum
12 Aeolic Cruises
13 Bus Station for Local Buses
14 Samiotis Tours
18 Sfetoudi Bookshop
21 NEL Ticket Office
23 Port Police
24 Currency-Exchange Machine
25 EOT
26 Archaeological Museum
27 Tourist Police
28 ATM & Currency-Exchange Machine
29 Ferries to Piraeus & Chios
30 Byzantine Museum
31 OTE
32 Post Office
35 Bus Station for Long-Distance Buses
36 Olympic Airways Office

(which are gradually being renovated), and jumbled streets. You will love Mytilini if you enjoy seeking out traditional kafeneia and little backstreet ouzeria, or if you take pleasure in wandering through unfamiliar towns. With a large university campus and a year-round population, Mytilini – unlike most island towns – is also lively in winter.

The northern end of Ermou, the town's main commercial thoroughfare, is a wonderful ramshackle street full of character. It has old-fashioned zaharoplasteia, grocers, fruit and vegetable stores, bakers, and antique, embroidery, ceramic and jewellery shops.

Orientation

Mytilini is built around two harbours (north and south) which occupy both sides of a promontory and are linked by the main thoroughfare of Ermou. East of the harbours is a large fortress surrounded by a pine forest. All passenger ferries dock at the southern harbour. The waterfront here is called Kountourioti and the ferry quay is at its southern end. The northern harbour's waterfront is called Navmahias Ellis.

Information

The tourist police (☎ 2251 022 776) have an office at the entrance to the quay. The EOT (☎ 2251 042 511), 6 Aristarhou, is open 8am to 2.30pm Sunday to Friday and can help with information about the entire island.

Banks, including the National Bank of Greece with an ATM, can be found on Kountourioti. There is also an ATM and an exchange machine at the Commercial Bank booth on this street, near the ferry terminal. The post office is on Vournazon, west of the southern harbour. The OTE is on the same street just west of the post office.

Sfetoudi Bookshop (☎ 2251 022 287), Ermou 51, sells good maps, postcards and books on Lesvos. Look for *The Sacred Water: the Mineral Springs of Lesvos* and *39 Coffee Houses and a Barber's Shop*, both beautifully produced books of photos by Jelly Hadjidimitriou.

You can find more information on Mytilini, and Lesvos in general, on the Internet at Ⓦ www.greeknet.com.

Things to See & Do

Mytilini's imposing **castle** *(adult/student €1.50/1; open 8.30am-3pm)* was built in early Byzantine times, renovated in the 14th century by Fragistco Gatelouzo, and subsequently enlarged by the Turks. The surrounding pine forest is a pleasant place for a picnic.

One block north of the quay and housed in a neoclassical mansion is the **archaeological museum** *(☎ 2251 022 087; admission €1.50 both museums; open 8.30am-3pm Tues-Sun)*. It has a large array of impressive finds from Neolithic to Roman times. It's a fascinating collection, with interesting ceramic figurines, including some somersaulting women, and gold jewellery. There are excellent notes in Greek and English. There is also a **new archaeological museum** *(8 Noemvriou; open 8am-7pm)*, 400m away, with impressive displays, including spectacular mosaics – whole housefuls – laid out under glass so that you can walk over them. Admission is included in the ticket for the other archaeological museum.

The dome of the **Church of Agios Therapon** can be spotted from almost anywhere on the southern waterfront. The church has a highly ornate interior with a huge chandelier, an intricately carved iconostasis and priest's throne, and a frescoed dome. The **Byzantine Museum** *(☎ 2251 028 916; admission €1; open 10am-1pm Mon-Sat)* in the church's courtyard houses some fine icons.

Whatever you do, don't miss the **Theophilos Museum** *(☎ 2251 041 644; admission €1.50; open 9am-2.30pm & 6pm-8pm Tues-Sun May-Sept, 9am-1pm & 4pm-6pm Tues-Sun Oct & Apr, 9am-2pm Tues-Sun Nov-Mar)*. It houses the works of the prolific primitive painter Theophilos, who was born on Lesvos. Several prestigious museums and galleries around the country now proudly display his works. However, he lived in abject poverty, painting the walls of kafeneia and tavernas in return for sustenance.

Next door, commemorating the artist and critic Stratis Eleftheriadis (he Gallicised his name to Teriade) who was born on Lesvos but lived and worked in Paris, is the **Teriade Museum** *(☎ 2251 023 372; admission*

€1.50; open 9am-8pm Tues-Sun). It was largely due to Teriade's efforts that Theophilos' work gained international renown. On display are reproductions of Teriade's own illustrations and his collection of works by 20th-century artists, including such greats as Picasso, Chagall and Matisse.

These museums are 4km from Mytilini in the village of **Varia**, where Theophilos was born. Take a local bus from the bus station at the northernmost section of Kountourioti.

Loutra Yera (*Admission €1.50; open 7am-8pm daily*), 5km west of Mytilini on the Gulf of Yera, is worth a visit if you're interested in hot springs. The cool white marble interior is steamy and dreamy.

Places to Stay – Budget

Most of these domatia are in little side streets off Ermou, near the northern harbour.

Pension Iren (☎ 2251 022 787, *Komninaki 41*) Doubles/triples with breakfast €25/30. This place has the nearest domatia to the quay. It has clean and simply furnished rooms. Komninaki is one block behind the eastern section of Kountourioti.

Salina's Garden (☎ 2251 042 073, *Fokeas 7 & Kinikiou 1*) Singles/doubles €21/22. These cosy and clean rooms are in a delightful garden, and guests can use the lovely kitchen to prepare their own meals. The rooms are signposted from the corner of Ermou and Adramytiou.

Pension Thalia (☎ 2251 024 640, *Kinikiou 1*) Doubles/triples with bathroom €23.50/26.50. Coming from Ermou, if you turn right opposite Salina's rooms you will reach these clean, bright rooms in a large family house.

Vetsika Domatia (☎ 2251 024 968, *Tsertseti 1*) Singles/doubles €18/23.50. These rooms in an old neoclassical house near the castle are nothing fancy but they are clean and quiet.

Pelagia Koumiotou Rooms (☎ 2251 020 643, *Tsertseti 6*) Doubles/triples €21/26.50. These rooms near the castle are quite nice and the owner is very friendly. Walk along Mikras Asias and turn left into Tsertseti; the rooms are on the right.

Places to Stay – Mid-Range

There are several hotels on the southern waterfront.

Hotel Lesvion (☎ 2251 022 037, *fax 2251 042 493, Kountourioti 27a*) Singles/doubles with TV & phone €29.50/51.50. This hotel is on the west side of the harbour. The rooms are a bit scruffy but they're passable. Better rates can usually be negotiated.

Hotel Sappho (☎ 2251 022 888, *fax 2251 024 522, Kountourioti 31*) Singles/doubles €32.50/53. This place is just two doors away from Hotel Lesvion.

Places to Eat

You will eat well on Lesvos whether you enjoy fish dishes, traditional Greek food, international cuisine or vegetarian meals. You might wish to avoid the restaurants on the western section of the southern waterfront where the waiters tout for customers. These restaurants are atypical of Mytilini as they pander to tourists and serve bland, overpriced food.

Restaurant Averof (☎ 2251 022 180, *Ermou 52 & Prokymaia*) Mains around €3.50. This place, in the middle of the southern waterfront, is a no-nonsense traditional restaurant serving hearty Greek staples like *patsas* (tripe soup). Despite its earthy cuisine it has a classy romantic ambience and excellent service.

Kalderimi (☎ 2251 046 577, *Thasou 3*) Appetisers €1.50-3, mains around €6. Closer to the main harbour, locals congregate at this little ouzeri with tables that spill out into the street. The food is very good – in contrast to the service, which is indifferent.

Ermis Ouzeri (☎ 2251 026 232, *Kornarou 2*) Mezedes-style meal with beer around €9. This small, mildly ramshackle, but delightfully atmospheric ouzeri has yet to be discovered by the mass tourist crowd. It is at the north end of Ermou on the corner with Kornarou. Its interior is decorated with scattered antiques, old watercolour paintings and old black and white photos of previous clients.

I Psatha (☎ 2251 045 922, *on Hrysostomou*) Open evenings only. Mains €4.50. If you want some good-value meat dishes such as souvlaki, check out this place off Ermou. There is an old jukebox that actually works.

Stratos Psarotaverna (☎ *2251 021 739, Hristougennon 1944*) Mains around €7.50. Head to this place at the bottom end of the main harbour for top-quality fish dishes. Tables from all the surrounding restaurants take over the road in summer.

Lemoni kai Prasino Piperi (☎ *2251 024 014, Cnr Koundouroti & Hristougennon*) Mains €6-12. If you're looking for a change, check out this classy Italian-Mediterranean place overlooking the harbour. It's upstairs, above a souvlaki joint.

Aspros Gatos (☎ *2251 061 670*) Mains €5.50-13.50. In Neapolis Mytilinis, towards the airport, is this great steak house with a Greek-Mediterranean menu. Most of the recipes are traditional Greek, but some Asian ingredients are also used. It's in a big garden and there's a kids' playground on site.

Entertainment

Mousiko Kafenio (*Cnr Mitropoleos & Vernardaki*) Open 7.30am-2am. This is a hip place – arty without being pretentious. Drinks are mid-price range rather than cheap, but worth it for the terrific atmosphere.

The Lazy Fish (☎ *2251 044 831, Imvrou 5*) Open Sept-July. For good beer and a nibble try this establishment, which is especially cosy and popular in the winter. It's set back from the southern end of Komninaki and is a bit difficult to find – look for a stone building with black wrought-iron wall lamps at the entrance.

Hot Spot On the east side of the harbour, this joint is known for its good music, and you can borrow board games here. It's a nice place to be at sunset.

To Navagio (☎ *2251 021 310, Arhipelagos 23*) This upmarket yet casual place in the centre of the waterfront serves a good variety of alcoholic beverages as well as fresh juices, hearty breakfasts and great coffee.

Getting To/From Mytilini

Mytilini has two bus stations: the one for long-distance buses is just beyond the south-western end of Kountourioti; the bus station for buses to local villages is on the northernmost section of Kountourioti. For motorists, there is a large free parking area just south of the main harbour.

NORTHERN LESVOS

Northern Lesvos is dominated economically and physically by the exquisitely preserved traditional town of Mithymna, a town of historical, and modern, importance in Lesvos' commercial life. The neighbouring beach resort of Petra, 6km south, receives low-key package tourism, and the villages surrounding Mt Lepetymnos are authentic, picturesque and worth a day or two of exploration. Sykaminia, Mantamados and Agia Paraskevi in particular, are very pretty. Moni Taxiarhon, near Mantamados, is also worth a visit. Skala Sykaminias is a nice beach.

Mithymna Μήθυμνα
postcode 811 08 • pop 1333

Although this town has officially reverted to its ancient name of Mithymna (Methymna), most locals still refer to it as **Molyvos**. It is 62km from Mytilini and is the principal town of northern Lesvos. The one-time rival to Mytilini, picturesque Mithymna is nowadays the antithesis of the island capital. Its impeccable stone houses with brightly coloured shutters reach down to the harbour from a castle-crowned hill. Its two main thoroughfares of Kastrou and 17 Noemvriou are winding, cobbled and shaded by vines. In contrast to Mytilini, Mithymna's pretty streets are lined with souvenir shops.

Orientation & Information From the bus stop, walk straight ahead towards the town. Where the road forks, take the right fork into 17 Noemvriou. At the top of the hill, the road forks again; the right fork is Kastrou and the post office is along here on the left. The left fork is a continuation of 17 Noemvriou.

There is a small municipal tourist office (☎ 2253 071 347), on the left, between the bus stop and the fork in the road. The National Bank of Greece is on the left, next to the tourist office and has an ATM. There is also a Commercial Bank booth with an ATM directly opposite.

A Balm for the Soul

Lesvos has many mineral springs, most dating back to ancient times. The baths are usually housed in old whitewashed buildings that look like sunken church domes. Small holes in the roof let in rays of sunlight, creating a magical dappled effect on the water. The pools are usually made of marble.

In times past, before houses had their own bathrooms, these communal baths were the place people came to bathe and talk.

With the exception of the ramshackle abandoned hot springs at Thermi (which are worth a visit, if you like faded grandeur), it's possible to take a dip at all of the baths. There are springs at Loutra Yera (near Mytilini) and Eftalou (near Mithymna) and two in the vicinity of Polyhnitos. The properties of the waters are outlined in the following text.

Loutra Yera

These springs are west of Mytilini, on the Gulf of Yera. It's thought that there was once a temple to Hera at this site, where ancient beauty pageants took place. The springs contain radium and are 39.7°C. They are recommended for infertility, rheumatism, arthritis, diabetes, bronchitis, gall stones, dropsy and more.

Polyhnitos

South-east of Polyhnitos, these springs are in a pretty, renovated Byzantine building. These are some of the hottest springs in all of Continental Europe, with a temperature of 87.6°C, and are recommended for rheumatism, arthritis, skin diseases and gynaecological problems.

Lisvorio

About 5km north of the Polyhnitos springs, these are just outside the little village of Lisvorio. There are two quaint little baths here, situated on either side of a stream, with pretty vegetation all around. At the time of writing these buildings were in disrepair, but it is thought that they will be renovated soon. One of the baths is in reasonable condition and it's possible to have a soak. The temperature and the properties of the waters are similar to those at Polyhnitos.

Eftalou

These baths on the beach not far from Mithymna are idyllic. The bathhouse is an old whitewashed vault with a pebbled floor. The water is perfectly clear and is 46.5°C. These springs are recommended for rheumatism, arthritis, neuralgia, hypertension, gall stones and gynaecological and skin problems.

Things to See & Do One of the most pleasant things to do in Mithymna is to stroll along its gorgeous streets. If you have the energy, the ruined 14th-century **Genoese castle** (☎ 2253 071 803; admission €1.50; open Tues-Sun 8am-7pm) is worth clambering up to for fine views of the coastline and over the sea to Turkey. From this castle in the 15th century, Onetta d'Oria, wife of the Genoese governor, repulsed an onslaught by the Turks by putting on her husband's armour and leading the people of Mithymna into battle. In summer the castle is the venue for a drama festival; ask for details at the tourist office.

The beach at Mithymna is pebbled and crowded, but in summer **excursion boats** leave at 10.30am daily for the superior beaches of Eftalou, Skala Sykaminias and Petra. Trips cost around €16 and up, depending on the itinerary; sunset cruises and boat 'safaris' are also available. Contact Faonas Travel (☎ 2253 071 630, e tekes@otenet.gr), down at the port, for more information.

Eftalou's **hot spring** (☎ 2253 071 245; admission €2.50; open 8am-1pm & 3pm-8pm) is an entrancing place right on the beach – don't miss it.

Phone numbers listed incorporate changes due in Oct 2002; see p55

Places to Stay – Budget *Camping Mithymna* (☎ *2253 071 169*) Adult/tent €3/2. Open early June. This excellent and refreshingly shady camping ground is 1.5km from town and signposted from near the tourist office. Although it opens in early June, you can usually camp if you arrive a bit earlier than that.

There are over 50 official domatia in Mithymna; most consist of only one or two rooms. All display domatia signs and most are of a high standard. The municipal tourist office will help you if you can't be bothered looking; otherwise, the best street to start at is 17 Noemvriou.

Nassos Guest House (☎ *2253 071 022, Arionos*) Rooms about €23.50. Among the first signposted rooms you will come to are those in this old Turkish house by the lovely Betty Katsaris. Arionos leads off 17 Noemvriou to the right. The rooms are simply furnished and most have a panoramic view. Stop by Betty's restaurant (see Places to Eat) if there's no-one at the rooms.

Myrsina Baliaka Domatia (☎ *2253 071 414, Myrasillou*) Doubles around €26.50. A beautifully restored stone building houses these domatia. From the bus stop walk towards the town and take the second right by the cardphone. The domatia are 50m on your right. Look out for the prominent green shutters.

Molyvos Hotel I (☎ *2253 071 556, fax 2253 071 640*) Doubles with bath & phone €32.50. This pleasant hotel has spacious clean rooms and friendly staff. There's a lovely terrace overlooking the water, and they serve a good breakfast. It's down there near the beach.

Places to Stay – Mid-Range *Amfitriti Hotel* (☎ *2253 071 741, fax 2253 071 744*) Singles/doubles with breakfast €38.50/62. This very lux-looking place is down near the water and the old olive press, not far from the town beach and its cluster of bars. There's a lovely swimming pool and the hotel itself is quite classy.

Hotel Olive Press (☎ *2253 071 205, fax 2253 071 647*) Singles/doubles with bath, phone, fridge & air-con €54.50/79.50. This converted olive-oil factory on the beach is often full, but call ahead and you might be in luck.

Hotel Sea Horse (☎ *2253 071 630, fax 2253 071 374,* e *tekes@otenet.gr*) Doubles €73.50. Down at the fishing harbour, this hotel has bright breezy rooms with balcony and all mod-cons.

Hotel Eftalou (☎ *2253 071 584, fax 2253 071 669,* e *parmakel@otenet.gr*) Doubles €59. This pleasant C-class hotel with comfortable rooms is among the cluster of small, low-key resort hotels on the road out to Eftalou. There's a swimming pool and a restaurant.

Hotel Delfinia (☎ *2253 071 315, fax 2253 071 524,* e *delfinia@otenet.gr*) Singles/doubles with sea view & breakfast €55.50/73.50. This older but superior hotel caters mainly to packages, but is very accommodating to independent travellers. It's a kilometre out of Mithymna on the road to Petra.

Places to Eat The streets 17 Noemvriou and Kastrou have a wide range of restaurants serving typical Greek fare.

Betty's (☎ *2253 071 421, 17 Noemvriou*) Mains around €5. If you're looking for a lovely atmosphere try this place which occupies an old bordello. Good grills and home-cooked meals such as pastitsio and mousakas are the specialities. The elegant rooms upstairs provide a view of the water from on high. To get there, take the downhill fork after passing uphill through the tunnel.

O Gatos (☎ *2253 071 661, 17 Noemvriou*) Mains around €5. With a sleeping cat on its doorstep, this little place has a classy feel and a great view from its giant balcony. Heading uphill, it's on the left as you come out of the tunnel.

Captain's Table (☎ *2253 071 241*) Appetisers €2-6, mains €5-10. For more of a fishing-village ambience, head down to the far end of the little harbour where there is a clutch of restaurants, the best of which is this Australian-Greek place. The mezedes are exquisite: try *adjuka* – a Ukrainian-inspired spicy aubergine dish – or the unique spinach salad. There is live bouzouki music once a week.

Taverna tou Ilia (☎ 2253 071 536) Mains around €4.50. For a change of scenery and a meal with a view, head up to this taverna at Vafios, 8km inland from Mithymna. The food is top-notch. *Pikilia* (a plate of mixed appetisers) costs around €4 per person, while lamb dishes are around €5. All of the meat is local and the food is very traditional.

Petra Πέτρα

postcode 811 09 • pop 1150

Petra, 5km south of Mithymna, is a popular coastal resort with a long sandy beach shaded by tamarisk trees. Despite tourist development it remains an attractive village retaining some traditional houses. Petra means 'rock', and looming over the village is an enormous, almost perpendicular rock which looks as if it's been lifted from Meteora in Thessaly. The rock is crowned by the 18th-century **Panagia Glykophilousa** (Church of the Sweet Kissing Virgin). You can reach it by climbing the 114 rock-hewn steps – worth it for the view. Petra, like many settlements on Lesvos, is a 'preserved' village. It has not and will not make any concessions to the concrete monstrosities that characterise tourist development elsewhere in Greece. The nearby village of Petri, to the east, has some nice old kafeneia and provides an excellent vantage point from which you can survey Petra and its surrounding landscape.

Petra has a post office, OTE, bank, medical facilities and bus connections. There's also an interesting refurbished Turkish mansion known as **Vareltzidaina's House** (*admission free; open 8am-7pm Tues-Sun*) Between the rock and the waterfront, it can be difficult to find, but the locals can point you in the right direction.

Places to Stay *Women's Agricultural Tourism Collective* (☎ 2253 041 238, fax 2253 041 309) Singles/doubles around €15/21. There are about 120 private rooms available in Petra, but your best bet for accommodation is to head straight for this women's collective, Greece's first. The women can arrange for you to stay with a family in the village. The office is on the central square, upstairs in the restaurant above Cantina; enter from the street behind the waterfront.

Studio Niki (☎ 2253 041 601) Doubles with kitchenette around €29.50. Of the cluster of small pensions at the western end of Petra's waterfront, this place with tidy rooms is a good bet. Book well in advance for peak season.

Places to Eat *Syneterismos* (☎ 2253 041 238, fax 2253 041 309) Mains €4. This very popular and friendly place, belonging to the Women's Agricultural Tourism Collective, has mouth-watering mousakas and Greek salad. It's upstairs on the waterfront square, above Cantina; enter from the street running one block behind the waterfront.

To Tyhero Petalo (☎ 2253 041 755) Mains around €5. This taverna, towards the eastern end of the waterfront, has attractive decor and sells ready-made food.

O Rigas (☎ 2253 041 405) Mains around €4.50. Open 7pm. For something very authentic, head up to the old village to this wisteria-swathed taverna, which is the oldest in Petra. It has a very laid-back feel and the music is excellent. To get there walk uphill around the rock and keep going straight ahead for about 500m.

WESTERN LESVOS

Western Lesvos is different from the rest of the island and this becomes apparent almost immediately as you wind westward out of Kalloni. The landscape becomes drier and barer and there are fewer settlements, though they look very tidy and their red-tiled roofs add vital colour to an otherwise mottled green-brown landscape. The far western end is almost devoid of trees other than the petrified kind. Here you will find Lesvos' 'petrified forest' on a windswept and barren hillside. One resort, a remote fishing village, and the birthplace of Sappho are what attract people to western Lesvos.

Eresos & Skala Eresou

Ερεσός & Σκάλα Ερεσού

postcode 881 05 • pop 1560

Eresos, 90km from Mytilini, is a traditional inland village. It is reached via the road

Sappho

Sappho is renowned chiefly for her poems that speak out in favour of lesbian relationships, though her range of lyric poetry extends beyond works of an erotic nature. She was born around 630 BC in the town of Eresos on the western side of Lesvos. Little is known about her private life other than that she was married, had a daughter and was exiled to Sicily in about 600 BC. Only fragments remain of her nine books of poems, the most famous of which are the marriage songs. Among her works were hymns, mythological poems and personal love songs. Most of these seem to have been addressed to a close inner-circle of female companions. Sappho uses sensuous images of nature to create her own special brand of erotic lyric poetry. It is a simple yet melodious style, later copied by the Roman poet Catullus.

Lesvos, and Eresos in particular, is today visited by many lesbians paying homage to Sappho.

MH

junction just after the hillside village of Andissa. The road leading down to Eresos, through what looks like a moonscape, belies what is ahead. Beyond the village of Eresos a riotously fertile agricultural plain leads to Eresos' beach annexe, Skala Eresou, which is 4km beyond on the west coast. It is a popular resort linked to Eresos by an attractive, very straight tree-lined road. A new sealed road links Eresos with Kalloni via Parakila and Agra.

Skala Eresou is built over ancient Eresos, where Sappho (c630–568 BC) was born. Although it gets crowded in summer it has a good, laid-back atmosphere. It is also a popular destination for lesbians who come on a kind of pilgrimage in honour of the poet. If you're a beach-lover you should certainly visit – there is almost 2km of coarse silvery-brown sand.

Orientation & Information From the bus turnaround at Skala Eresou, walk towards the sea to reach the central square of Plateia Anthis & Evristhenous abutting the waterfront. The beach stretches to the left and right of this square. Turn right at the square onto Gyrinnis and just under 50m along you will come to a sign pointing left to the post office; the OTE is next door.

Krinellos Travel (☎ 2253 053 246, 2253 053 982, e krinellos@otenet.gr), close to the

main square, is helpful. They arrange accommodation, car, motorcycle and bicycle hire, and treks on foot or on horses and donkeys. Neither Skala Eresou nor Eresos has a bank.

Things to See Eresos' archaeological museum (admission free; open 8.30am-3pm Tues-Sun) houses archaic, classical Greek and Roman finds including statues, coins and grave stelae. The museum, in the centre of Skala Eresou, stands near the remains of the early Christian Basilica of Agios Andreas.

The **Petrified Forest** (☎ 2253 054 434, admission €1.50, open 8am-4pm daily), as the EOT hyperbolically refers to this scattering of ancient tree stumps, is near the village of Sigri, on the west coast north of Skala Eresou. Experts reckon the petrified wood is at least 500,000, but possibly 20 million, years old. If you're intrigued, the forest is easiest reached as an excursion from Skala Eresou; inquire at travel agencies. If you're making your own way, the turn-off to the forest is signposted 7km before the village of Sigri.

Sigri itself is a beautiful, peaceful fishing port with a delicious edge-of-the-world feeling. In Sigri, the **Natural History Museum of the Lesvos Petrified Forest** (☎ 2253 054 434, admission €1.50, open 8am-9pm daily) is a very swish place with background information on the forest, and, of course, a few tree stumps.

Places to Stay There are a few domatia in Eresos but most people head for Skala Eresou, where there are a number of domatia, pensions and hotels.

Pete Metaxas Studios (☎ 2253 053 506) Singles/doubles €21/23.50. These small studios are at the north-west end of the waterfront, one block back from the beach.

Sappho Hotel (☎ 2253 053 233, fax 2253 053 174) Singles/doubles with breakfast & sea view €26.50/48.50; doubles without view €41. This C-class property is a small women-only hotel on the waterfront. It can be noisy here, though.

Hotel Galini (☎ 2253 053 137/174, fax 2253 053 155) Doubles with bathroom €48. This C-class property has small but airy rooms with private balcony. It is clearly signposted.

Places to Eat The shady promenade offers many eating options, most with beach and sea views across to Chios and Psara.

Gorgona (☎ 2253 053 320) Appetisers €2-4, mains €4.50-6. Gorgona, with its stone-clad facade, is as good a place to start as any. It's at the south-eastern end of the promenade.

Soulatso (☎ 2253 052 078) Appetisers & salads around €2, mains around €4.50. Fresh fish (from €4.50) and a nice array of appetisers (including a decent ladotyri) are served at this place in the middle of the waterfront.

Margaritatari (☎ 2253 053 042) For a good breakfast or afternoon tea, head to this waterfront cafe to sample scrumptious Austrian pastries, including apple strudel (€5.50).

Popular watering holes include *Tenth Muse*, on the square, which is a favourite lesbian bar; *Parasol*, on the waterfront, with a funky tropical feel and exotic cocktails; and *Notorious*, at the far south-eastern end of the promenade, in an isolated, romantic spot overlooking the water.

SOUTHERN LESVOS
Southern Lesvos is dominated by Mt Olympus (968m). Pine forests and olive groves decorate its flanks.

Fascinating Fossil Find

Lesvos is hardly the kind of place that you would associate with great excitement in the musty and dusty world of palaeontology. Nonetheless, the island has been thrust onto centre stage recently with the extraordinary discovery of fossils of animals, fish and plants at Vatera, a sleepy beach resort located on the south coast of Lesvos, hitherto more associated with sun and sand than fossilised fish.

Among the fossils found in the Vatera region are elephants, mastodons, giraffes, bones of rhinoceros and hippopotamus, deer, tortoises, snails, fish, and pieces of a gigantic prehistoric horse. Dated up to 5.5 million years old, the fossils are being temporarily displayed at the Museum of Natural History in the neighbouring village of Vrisa, just 2km from the excavation sites.

The large village of **Agiasos** on the northern flank of Mt Olympus features prominently in local tourist publications and is a popular day-trip destination. Agiasos is picturesque but not tacky, with artisan workshops making everything from handcrafted furniture to pottery. Its winding, cobbled streets lead you to the church of the Panagia Vrefokratousa with its Byzantine Museum and Popular Museum in the courtyard.

Plomari on the south coast is a pleasant, crumbling resort town. A large, traditional village, it also has a laid-back beach settlement. Most people stay at **Agios Isidoros**, 3km to the east where there is a narrow, overcrowded beach. **Tarti**, east of Agios Isidoros, is a much nicer beach. On the other side of Plomari, **Melinda** is a very pretty, serene fishing village with a beach. There are three tavernas in Melinda, all offering rooms and cheap hearty food.

About one hour's walk from Melinda, west along the coast, the **Panagia Krifti** is a little church built in a cave near a hot spring.

Low-key, though slightly desolate, family resort of **Vatera** is over to the east and reached via the inland town of **Polyhnitos**.

Olive Trails

In the vicinity of Plomari, the old paths that link the hill villages are being restored and it's now possible to spend anywhere from an afternoon to a few days exploring this pretty region on foot. Local clubs have been clearing the paths since 1997 and a government program has been sponsoring their efforts since 2000. The preservation of the paths is an ongoing project, and volunteers are welcome.

All walks traverse olive groves with old *setia* (dry-walled terraces) and *damia* (small one-storey stone houses). You'll also pass through lush dells filled with old oaks, wild pears and pistachios, plane trees, pink hollyhocks and other wildflowers, and herbs, as well as higher, drier forests of pine and juniper. There are startling views down to the sea. Along the way there are many springs, rivers and streams as well as old mills and olive presses. In general, it's best to walk these paths in spring or autumn. The trails are clearly signposted, and there are maps in villages and at the airport.

The major routes are as follows:

Melinda-Paleohori
Distance: 1.2km. Duration: 30 minutes. This trail starts at the fishing village of Melinda and follows the Selandas river for 200m. It ascends to the living village of Paleohori, passing a spring with potable water along the way. The trail ends at one of the village's two olive presses, where there is now a museum.

Paleohori-Rahidi
Distance: 1km. Duration: 30 minutes. The path here is 2m to 4m wide and paved with white stone. It ascends to Rahidi, which used to be the summer residence of the villagers from Paleohori. There are two springs along the way, and vineyards. There are about 40 nice old houses in Rahidi and a kafeneio that opens in summer. Rahidi, which now has a population of about five, first received electricity in 2001. There are stunning views from here. If you like, you can continue to Agios Ioannis along the same path.

Melinda-Kournela
Distance: 1.8km. Duration: 40 minutes. An old stone path climbs from the beach at Melinda to Kournela, a village of about 50 houses, with a current population of three to four people. There are big shady plane trees, a triple-spouted fountain where people used to wash clothes, and an old steam-driven olive mill. There are good views across to Paleiohori and Rahidi.

Kournela-Milos
Distance: 800m. Duration: 20 minutes. This trail descends to Milos, where there's an old flour mill. The village is at a crossroads, with paths leading to Paleohori, Melinda, Kournela and Megalohori.

Melinda-Milos
Distance: 2km. Duration: one hour. This level trail follows the Selandas River and passes a few houses, some ruined olive mills, one spring and two bridges. There is some unusual vegetation, including orange and mandarin trees. It's a shady trail, good for summer.

Milos-Amaxo
Distance: 1.75km. Duration: one hour. This very level trail follows the Melinda River, through vineyards and plane, poplar and pine forests. There are springs and fountains with good drinking water

In Polyhnitos there are **hot springs** (see Activities) and a **folk museum** (☎ 2253 041 007; open 10am-1pm Tues-Sun). There is a small **museum of natural history** (admission €1; open 9am-3pm) at Vrisa, between Polyhnitos and Vatera.

Activities
There are many opportunities for **walking** on old olive trails in the hills above Plomari (see the boxed text 'Olive Trails'). You can go **horse-riding** (€15/hr) on the trails; contact Kostas Moukas (mobile ☎ 69 3244 7517)

Olive Trails

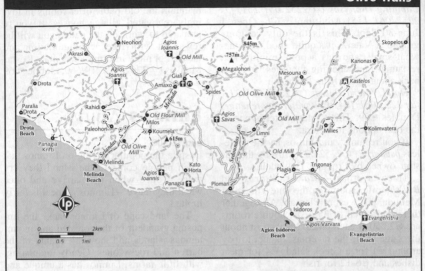

along the way. Nice wooden bridges made of chestnut cross the river. It's possible to start this walk from Amaxo, after driving from Plomari. If you're a good rider, you can mountain bike all the way from Amaxo down to Melinda.

Amaxo-Giali-Spides
Distance: 1.5km. Duration: 45 minutes. This trail follows a dirt road for about 500m to Giali, then ascends to Spides on a path. Halfway between Amaxo and Giali there's a little church with a picnic table that makes a nice spot for lunch.

Skopelos-Karionas-Kastelos-Trigonas/Plagia
Distance: 8km. Duration: 3 hours. This route follows a dirt road from Skopelos to Karionas, but there are cobbled paths the rest of the way. At the ruined castle known as Kastelos, there's now a small church. It's possible to take a detour to the village of Milies, where there is a fountain and some nice old houses. A path from Milies continues to Kolimvatera.

Plomari-Mesouna
Distance: 6km. Duration: 3 hours. The trail follows the Sedoundas River past many old houses. There's an olive processing plant in the village of Limni and about 4km upriver there's an old watermill that used to crush olives.

for details. Good-quality **mountain bikes** can be rented from Kostas for €23.50 a day.

A visit to the Polyhnitos **hot springs** (☎ 2252 041 449, fax 2252 042 678; open 7am-10am & 4pm-6pm daily), where there's a renovated bathhouse that dates from the Byzantine period, is worthwhile. There are also hot springs at Lisvorio, clearly signposted from the village. The facilities near the spring are currently undergoing repair, but the old caretaker will let you have a soak if he's there.

Phone numbers listed incorporate changes due in Oct 2002; see p55

Places to Stay & Eat
Camping Dionysos (☎ 2252 061 151, fax 2252 061 155) Adult/tent €6/6. Open 1 June-30 Sept. This is the only camping ground at Vatera. It's quite good, if somewhat small, and has a pool, minimarket, restaurant and cooking facilities. It is set back about 100m from the beach.

Hotel Vatera Beach (☎ 2252 061 212, fax 2252 061 164, ℮ hovatera@otenet.gr) Doubles €59. This C-class hotel is one of the best options in Vatera.

If you're hungry in Agiasos, try the name-less *psistaria (☎ 2252 022 236)*, by the bus stop, owned by Prokopis Douladellis.

Three tavernas – *Maries*, *Psaros* and *Bill's* – offer rooms in the cute village of Melinda, just west of Plomari. All together there are a total of 35 beds; double rooms are €23.50 at each place. Meals cost about the same at all the tavernas; expect to pay around €1 for a Greek salad, €4 for meat dishes and €6-12 for fish.

In Milies, near Plomari, the people who maintain the old paths offer rooms in lovingly renovated village houses. If you're prepared to work on the paths, you will be rewarded with free accommodation and meals. For more information contact Kostas Moukas (☎ 2252 032 719/660, mobile ☎ 69 3244 7517).

Limnos Λήμνος

pop 16,000
Despite the popular saying on Limnos that when people come to the island they cry twice – once when they arrive and once when they leave – Limnos' appeal is fairly limited.

The landscape of Limnos lacks the imposing grandeur of the forested and mountainous islands and the stark beauty of the barren and rocky ones. Gently undulating, with little farms, Limnos has a unique and

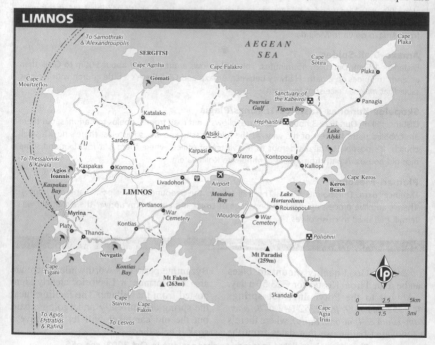

understated appeal. In spring vibrant wild flowers dot the landscape, and in autumn purple crocuses sprout forth in profusion. Large numbers of flamingoes grace the lakes of eastern Limnos and the coastline boasts some fine beaches. The island is sufficiently off the beaten track to have escaped the adverse effects of mass tourism.

History

Limnos' position near the Straits of the Dardanelles, midway between the Mt Athos Peninsula and Turkey, has given it a traumatic history. To this day it maintains a large garrison, and jets from the huge air base loudly punctuate the daily routine.

Limnos had advanced Neolithic and Bronze Age civilisations, and during these times had contact with peoples in western Anatolia, including the Trojans. In classical times the twin sea gods, the Kabeiroi, were worshipped at a sanctuary on the island, but later the Sanctuary of the Great Gods on Samothraki became the centre of this cult.

During the Peloponnesian Wars, Limnos sided with Athens and suffered many Persian attacks. After the split of the Roman Empire in AD 395 it became an important outpost of Byzantium. In 1462 it came under the domination of the Genoese who ruled Lesvos. The Turks succeeded in conquering the island in 1478 and Limnos remained under Turkish rule until 1912. Moudros Bay was the Allies' base for the disastrous Gallipoli campaign in WWI.

Getting To/From Limnos

Air In summer there are two to three flights daily to Limnos from Athens (€55.50), six weekly from Thessaloniki (€56) and four flights weekly to Lesvos (€48.50). The Olympic Airways office (☎ 2254 022 214) is on Nikolaou Garoufallidou, opposite Hotel Paris, in Myrina.

The airport is 22km east of Myrina. An Olympic Airways bus from Myrina to the airport (€3) connects with all flights. Alternatively, a taxi will cost you about €12.

Ferry In summer four ferries weekly go from Limnos to Kavala (four to five hours,

€9.70) and to Rafina (10 hours, €17) via Agios Efstratios (1½ hours, €5). In high season there is usually one boat per week to Sigri in Lesvos (six hours, €13.50). There are also three boats weekly to Chios (11 hours, €16) and Piraeus (13 hours, €21) via Lesvos, and one or two to Piraeus directly. There are two boats weekly to Thessaloniki (seven hours, €16.50) and one to two to Alexandroupolis (five hours, €12) via Samothraki (three hours, €7.50).

In addition, *Aiolis*, a small local ferry, does the run to Agios Efstratios (2½ hours, €5) three times weekly. Tickets can be bought at Myrina Tourist & Travel Agency (☎ 2254 022 460, fax 2254 023 560, e root@mirina.lim.forthnet.gr) on the harbourfront in Myrina.

Hydrofoil In July and August there are around two hydrofoils weekly to and from Alexandroupolis (three hours, €23.50) via Samothraki (1½ hours, €15). The hydrofoil schedule is notoriously unreliable, so check with Myrina Tourist & Travel Agency (☎ 2254 022 460, fax 2254 023 560, e root@mirina.lim.forthnet.gr) for the latest version.

Excursion Boat Every Sunday in July and August *Aiolis* does a roundtrip to the small island of Agios Efstratios (see Agios Efstratios, later in the chapter). The boat usually leaves at about 8am and returns from Agios Efstratios at 5pm.

Getting Around Limnos

Bus Bus services on Limnos are poor. In summer there are two buses daily from Myrina to most of the villages. Check the schedule (scribbled on a blackboard in Greek) at the bus station (☎ 2254 022 464) on Plateia Eleftheriou Venizelou.

Car & Motorcycle In Myrina, cars and jeeps can be rented from Myrina Rent a Car (☎ 2254 024 476, fax 2254 022 484) on Kyda near the waterfront. Prices range from €30 to €45 for a small car or jeep, depending on the season. There are several motorcycle-hire outlets on Kyda.

MYRINA Μύρινα
postcode 814 00 • pop 4340

Myrina is the capital and port of Limnos. Surrounded by massive hunks of volcanic rock, it is not immediately perceived as a picturesque town, but it is animated, full of character and unfettered by establishments pandering to tourism.

The main thoroughfare of Kyda is a charming paved street with clothing stores, traditional shops selling nuts and honey, old-fashioned kafeneia and barber shops – the latter are testimony to the island's military presence. Down the side streets you'll see (interspersed with modern buildings) little whitewashed stone dwellings, decaying neoclassical mansions and 19th-century wattle-and-daub houses with overhanging wooden balconies. A Genoese castle looms dramatically over the town.

Orientation & Information
From the end of the quay turn right onto Plateia Ilia Iliou. Continue along the waterfront passing the Hotel Lemnos and the town hall. A little farther along you will see the Hotel Aktaion, set back from the waterfront. Turn left here, then immediately veer half-left onto Kyda. Proceeding up here you will reach the central square where the National Bank of Greece and the OTE are located. The taxi rank (☎ 2254 023 033) is also on this square. Continue up Kyda and take the next turn right onto Nikolaou Garoufallidou. The post office is here on the right. Back on Kyda, continue for another 100m and you will come to Plateia Eleftheriou Venizelou where you will see the bus station.

There is a small tourist information kiosk on the quay. A laundrette (☎ 2254 024 392) is on Nikolaou Garoufallidou, opposite the Olympic Airways office. The police station (☎ 2254 022 201) is at the far end of Nikolaou Garoufallidou – on the right coming from Kyda. The port police (☎ 2254 022 225) are on the waterfront near the quay.

Things to See & Do
As with any Greek island **castle**, the one towering over Myrina is worth climbing up to. From its vantage point there are magnificent views over the sea to Mt Athos. As you walk from the harbour, take the first side street to the left by an old Turkish fountain. An inconspicuous sign here points you to the castle.

Myrina has two decent sandy **beaches** right in town. The first, known as Romeïkos Gialos, stretches north from the castle and can be reached by walking along Kyda from the harbour, and taking any of the streets off to the left. The next one, separated by a small headland, is known as Riha Nera (shallow water), so named because of its gently shelving beach which is ideal for children.

In Myrina, and housed in a neoclassical mansion, is the **archaeological museum** *(admission €1.50; open 8am-2.30pm Mon-Sat, 9am-2.30pm Sun & public holidays)*. Worth a visit, it contains finds from all the three sites on Limnos. The museum overlooks the beach, next to the Hotel Castor.

Organised Tours
Theodoros Petridis Travel Agency (☎ 2254 022 039, fax 2254 022 129) Tours €35.50. June-Sept. This travel agency organises round-the-island boat trips. They include stops for swimming and lunch.

Places to Stay – Budget
There is an information board with a map of the island and the names and telephone numbers of all domatia and hotels in Limnos on the harbourfront square. Budget accommodation is thin on the ground in Myrina.

Apollo Pavillion (☎/fax 2254 023 712, e apollo47@otenet.gr) Dorm beds €9 per person, double studios with/without air-con €50/44. This neoclassical place, with friendly English-speaking owners, has spacious and clean rooms with a variety of accommodation options. Book ahead in summer. Walk along Nikolaou Garoufallidou from Kyda and you will see the sign 150m along on the right.

Hotel Lemnos (☎ 2254 022 153, fax 2254 023 329) Doubles €50. This place on the harbourfront is about the cheapest hotel accommodation you will find. Most rooms have TV, phone, bath and balcony.

Places to Stay – Mid-Range & Top End

Blue Waters Hotel (☎ 2254 024 403, fax 2254 025 004, e bwkon@otenet.gr) Doubles €68. This clean and comfortable place on the beachfront at Romeïkos Gialos, north of the Kastro, has spacious rooms with air-con, phone, TV and fridge. It's the most centrally located of the mid-range options.

Hotel Filoktitis (☎/fax 2254 023 344, Ethnikis Antistaseos 14) Singles/doubles with balcony, TV & fridge €44/50. Above the restaurant of the same name, this pleasant hotel inland from Riha Nera has very friendly owners. The rooms are nice and big. To get there follow Maroulas (the continuation of Kyma) and take Ethnikis Antistaseos at the fork in the road, or head inland for a few blocks from the beach.

Arion Beach Apartments (☎ 2254 022 144, fax 2254 022 147) Doubles/triples €47/57.50. Thirty metres from the Riha Nera beach is this lovely homely place with friendly English-speaking owners. The rooms are huge with fridge, air-con and stove and have big balconies. To get there, take Seferi, the first street on your right as you walk over the hill to Riha Nera from Romeïkos Gialos. Look for the Arion's sign just a few doors up.

Diamantidis Hotel (☎ 2254 022 397, fax 2254 023 187) Singles/doubles with breakfast €59/94. This A-class property is one of the island's best hotels. Rooms are spacious and airy. The hotel is located inland from Myrina town on the main road.

Places to Eat

Restaurants are of a high standard on Limnos. Several fish restaurants line the waterfront.

Taverna Glaropoula (☎ 2254 024 069) Meal of small fish, salad & wine €12. Locals give top marks to this cosy little taverna with a nice harbourside location.

O Platanos Taverna (☎ 2254 022 070) Main course, salad & local wine around €10.50. Halfway along Kyda is this small, unassuming but very pleasant taverna, on the left as you walk from the waterfront. It is on a small square under a couple of huge

plane trees and makes an attractive alternative to the waterfront establishments.

Filoktitis (☎ 2254 023 344, Ethnikis Antistaseos 14) Mains around €4. Open lunch & dinner. This exceedingly popular and jolly restaurant is 200m inland from Riha Nera beach. The food is excellent and less expensive than the harbourside joints. It offers a range of ready-made dishes, including a good pastitsio. To find it follow Maroulas (the continuation of Kyma) and take Ethnikis Antistaseos at the fork in the road, or head inland for a few blocks from the beach.

WESTERN LIMNOS

North of Myrina, turn left just past the little village of **Kaspakas** and a narrow road will lead you down to the beach at **Agios Ioannis**. The beach is pleasant enough, but Agios Ioannis consists of a few desultory fishing shacks, scattered beach houses and a couple of tavernas, one of which has its tables set out in the embrace of a large volcanic rock.

Inland from Kaspakas, the barren hilly landscape dotted with sheep and rocks (particularly on the road to Katalako via Sardes and Dafni) reminds you more of the English Peak District than an Aegean island. The villages themselves have little to cause you to pause and you will certainly be an object of curiosity if you do. There is a remote and completely undeveloped beach at Gomati on the north coast and it can be reached by a good dirt road from Katalako.

Heading 3km south from Myrina you will reach **Platy**. It's a fairly scrappy little resort, but the beach is okay.

Back on the beach road, if you continue past the Lemnos Village Resort Hotel, you will come to a sheltered sandy cove with an islet in the bay. The beach here is usually less crowded than Platy. **Thanos Beach** is the next bay around from Platy; it is also less crowded, and long and sandy. To get there, continue on the main road from Platy to the cute little village of Thanos, where a sign points to the beach. **Nevgatis**, the next bay along, is deserted but a trifle windy. Continuing along the coast road you'll come to the almost picturesque village of **Kontias**, marked by a row of old windmills.

CENTRAL LIMNOS

Central Limnos is flat and agricultural with wheat fields, small vineyards, and cattle and sheep farms. The island's huge air-force base is ominously surrounded by endless barbed-wire fences. The muddy and bleak Moudros Bay cuts deep into the interior, with **Moudros**, the second-largest town, positioned on the eastern side of the bay. Moudros does not offer much for the tourist other than a couple of small hotels with tavernas on the waterfront. The harbour has none of Myrina's picturesque qualities.

One kilometre out of Moudros on the road to Roussopouli, you will come across the **East Moudros Military Cemetery**, where Commonwealth soldiers from the Gallipoli campaign are buried. Limnos, with its large protected anchorage, was occupied by a force of Royal Marines on 23 February 1915 and was the principal base for this ill-fated campaign. A metal plaque, inside the gates, gives a short history of the Gallipoli campaign. A second Commonwealth cemetery, **Portianos War Cemetery**, is at Portianos, about 6km south of Livadohori on the trans-island highway. The cemetery is not as obvious as the Australian-style blue and white street sign with the name Anzac St. Follow Anzac St to the church and you will find the cemetery off a little lane behind the church.

EASTERN LIMNOS

Eastern Limnos has three archaeological sites (*admission free; all open 8am-7pm*). The Italian School of Archaeologists has uncovered four ancient settlements at **Poliohni**, on the island's east coast. The most interesting was a sophisticated pre-Mycenaean city, which predated Troy VI (1800–1275 BC). The site is well laid-out and there are good descriptions in Greek, Italian and English. However, there is nothing too exciting to be seen; the site is probably of greater interest to archaeological buffs than casual visitors.

The second site is that of the **Sanctuary of the Kabeiroi** (Ta Kaviria) in north-eastern Limnos on the shores of remote Tigani Bay. This was originally a site for the worship of Kabeiroi gods predating those of Samothraki

(see Sanctuary of the Great Gods, under Samothraki, later in this chapter). There is little of the Sanctuary of Samothraki's splendour, but the layout of the site is obvious and excavations are still being carried out.

The major site, which has 11 columns, is that of a Hellenistic sanctuary. The older site is farther back and is still being excavated. Of additional interest is the cave of Philoctetes, the hero of the Trojan War, who was abandoned here while a gangrenous leg (a result of snakebite) healed. The sea cave can be reached by a path that leads down from the site. The cave can actually be entered by a hidden, narrow entrance (unmarked) to the left of the main entrance.

You can reach the sanctuary easily, if you have your own transport, via a fast road that was built for the expensive (and now white elephant) tourist enclave, Kaviria Palace. The turn-off is 5km to the left, after the village of **Kontopouli**. From Kontopouli you can make a detour to the third site, along a rough dirt track to **Hephaistia** (Ta Ifestia), once the most important city on the island. Hephaestus was the god of fire and metallurgy and, according to mythology, was thrown here from Mt Olympus by Zeus. The site is widely scattered over a scrub-covered, but otherwise desolate, small peninsula. There is not much to see of the ancient city other than low walls and a partially excavated theatre. Excavations are still under way.

The road to the northern tip of the island is worth exploring. There are some typical Limnian villages in the area and the often deserted beach at **Keros** is popular with windsurfers. Flocks of flamingos can sometimes be seen on shallow **Lake Alyki**. From the cape at the north eastern tip of Limnos you can see the islands of Samothraki and Imvros (Gökçeada) in Turkey.

Agios Efstratios
Άγιος Ευστράτιος

postcode 815 00 • pop 290

The little-known island of Agios Efstratios, called locally Aï-Stratis, merits the title of perhaps the most isolated island in the Aegean. Stuck more or less plumb centre in the North Aegean some distance from its nearest neighbour Limnos, it has few cars and fewer roads, but a steady trickle of curious foreign island-hoppers seeking to find some peace and quiet.

Large numbers of political exiles were sent here for enforced peace and quiet before and after WWII. Among the exiled guests were such luminaries as composer Mikis Theodorakis and poets Kostas Varnalis and Giannis Ritsos.

The little village of Aï-Stratis was once picturesque, but in the early hours of the morning of 21 February 1968 a violent earthquake, with its epicentre in the seas between Limnos and Aï-Stratis, virtually destroyed the vibrant village in one fell swoop. Many people emigrated as a result and there are now large numbers of islanders living in Australia and elsewhere.

Ham-fisted intervention by the then ruling junta saw the demolition of most of the remaining traditional homes and in their place, cheaply built concrete boxes were erected to house the islanders. Needless to say, the islanders are still pretty miffed over 30 years after the event, and the remaining hillside ruins stand silent sentinel over a rather lacklustre village today.

Still, if you yearn for serenity and traffic-free bliss, and enjoy walking, Aï-Stratis is a great place to visit. It has some fine beaches – though most are only accessible by caique – ample accommodation, simple island food and a surprisingly busy nightlife.

There is a post office, one cardphone and one metered phone for the public.

Getting To/From Agios Efstratios

Agios Efstratios is on the Kavala-Rafina ferry route, which includes Limnos. There are two services weekly to Rafina (8½ hours, €15), six to Limnos (1½ hours, €5) and one per week to Alexandroupolis (6¾ hours, €13.50).

In addition, the small local ferry *Aiolis* putters to and from Limnos three times a week on Monday, Wednesday and Friday. On the off-days, during summer, *Aiolis*

does a more or less daily excursion run from Limnos. But the harbour is exposed to the west winds, causing ferry services to often be cancelled or delayed.

Beaches

Apart from the reasonable village beach of dark volcanic sand, the nearest beach worth making the effort to visit is **Alonitsi** on the north-east side of the island. It is a long, totally undeveloped, pristine strand and it can be all yours if you are prepared to walk the 90 minutes to reach it. To get there take the little track from the north-east side of the village, starting by a small bridge, and follow it up towards the power pylons. Halfway along the track splits; take the right track for Alonitsi, or the left track for the **military lookout** for great views. **Lidario**, a beach on the west side can be reached – with difficulty – on foot, but is better approached by sea, if you can get someone to take you there.

Places to Stay & Eat

Accommodation options in Agios Efstratios are now pretty good. There is no hotel on the island but there are currently about 100 beds available and you will always find somewhere to stay unless you turn up at the height of the summer season without a reservation.

Xenonas Aï-Strati (☎ 2254 093 329) Doubles €35.50. This spotless and airy place is run by Julia and Odysseas Galanakis. The rooms are in one of the few buildings that survived the earthquake on the north-eastern side of the village.

Malama Panera Domatia (☎ 2254 093 209) Doubles €35.50. These domatia, on the south side of the village, are as equally well appointed as Xenonas Aï-Strati.

There are also other unofficial *domatia* available. Ask at the little convenience store, if you get stuck. You can fax the community fax machine (fax 2254 093 210) if you want to make a booking.

Places to eat are fairly inexpensive, though fish still tends to be a bit on the steep side.

Thanasis Taverna (☎ 2254 093 269) Mains around €4.50. This fairly obvious community-run taverna stands overlooking the harbour.

Tasos Ouzeri Mains around €4.50. Open only in summer. This place is diagonally opposite Thanasis Taverna and offers similar fare.

Samothraki
Σαμοθράκη

pop 2800

The egg-shaped island of Samothraki is 32km south-west of Alexandroupolis. Scenically it is one of the most awe-inspiring of all Greek islands. It is a small island, but a great deal of diverse landscape is packed into its 176 sq km. Its natural attributes are dramatic, big and untamed, culminating in the mighty peak of Mt Fengari (1611m), the highest mountain in the Aegean. Homer related that Poseidon watched the Trojan War from Mt Fengari's summit.

The jagged, boulder-strewn Mt Fengari looms over valleys of massive gnarled oak and plane trees, thick forests of olive and pine, dense shrubbery and damp, dark

glades where waterfalls plunge into deep, icy pools. On the gentler, western slopes of the island there are corn fields studded with poppies and other wild flowers in spring. Samothraki is also rich in fauna. Its springs are the habitat of a large number of frogs, toads and turtles; in its meadows you will see swarms of butterflies and may come across the occasional lumbering tortoise. On the mountain slopes there are an inordinate number of bell-clanking goats. The island's beaches, with one exception, are pebbly.

Samothraki's ancient site, the Sanctuary of the Great Gods, at Paleopolis, is one of Greece's most evocative ancient sites. Historians are unable to ascertain the nature of the rites performed here, and its aura of potent mysticism prevails over the whole island.

The island's culinary speciality is *katsikaki* (kid goat), prepared in a multitude of ways; restaurants usually serve it roasted.

History

Samothraki was first settled around 1000 BC by Thracians who worshipped the Great Gods, a cult of Anatolian origin. In 700 BC the island was colonised by people from

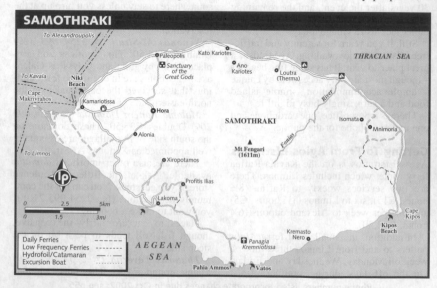

SAMOTHRAKI

To Alexandroupolis
To Kavala
To Limnos
Cape Makrivrahos
Niki Beach
Kamariotissa
Paleopolis
Sanctuary of the Great Gods
Kato Kariotes
Ano Kariotes
Loutra (Therma)
Hora
Alonia
Xiropotamos
Profitis Ilias
Lakoma
SAMOTHRAKI
Mt Fengari (1611m)
Fonias River
Isomata
Mnimoria
THRACIAN SEA
Panagia Kremniotissa
Pahia Ammos
Vatos
Kremasto Nero
Kipos Beach
Cape Kipos
AEGEAN SEA

0   2.5   5km
0   1.5   3mi

Daily Ferries
Low Frequency Ferries
Hydrofoil/Catamaran
Excursion Boat

Lesvos, who absorbed the Thracian cult into the worship of the Olympian gods.

This marriage of two cults was highly successful and by the 5th century BC Samothraki had become one of Greece's major religious centres, attracting prospective initiates from far and wide to its Sanctuary of the Great Gods. Among the luminaries initiated into the cult were King Lysander of Sparta, Philip II of Macedon and Cornelius Piso, Julius Caesar's father-in-law. One famous visitor who did not come to be initiated was St Paul, who dropped in en route to Philippi.

The cult survived until paganism was outlawed in the 4th century AD. After this the island became insignificant. Falling to the Turks in 1457, it was united with Greece, along with the other North-Eastern Aegean Islands, in 1912. During WWII Samothraki was occupied by the Bulgarians.

Getting To/From Samothraki

Ferry In summer, Samothraki has daily ferry connections with Alexandroupolis (two hours, €7.50), at least two per week to Kavala (four hours, €9.70), and one per week to Limnos (three hours, €8). There are also a couple of boats a week to Sigri (Lesvos) in peak season. Outside high season, boats to/from Kavala are nonexistent. Schedules are listed on the window of a kiosk (☎ 2551 041 505) opposite the pier. Ferry tickets can be bought at Niki Tours (☎ 2551 041 465, fax 2551 041 304), in Kamariotissa, and from the kiosk.

Hydrofoil In summer there are two to three hydrofoils daily between Samothraki and Alexandroupolis (one hour, €14.70). For departure details contact Niki Tours or the ticket kiosk (☎ 2551 041 505) in Kamariotissa.

Getting Around Samothraki

Bus In summer there are at least four buses daily from Kamariotissa to Hora (€0.75) and Loutra (Therma), via Paleopolis. Some of the Loutra buses continue to the nearby camping grounds. There are four buses daily to Profitis Ilias (via Lakoma).

Car & Motorcycle Cars and small jeeps can be rented from Niki Tours (☎ 2551 041 465, fax 2551 041 304) and Kyrkos Rent a Car (☎ 2551 041 620, mobile ☎ 69 7283 9231). A small car is about €45. Motorcycles can be rented from Rent A Motor Bike (☎ 2551 041 057), opposite the ferry quay.

Taxi For a taxi, call ☎ 2551 041 733, 2551 041 341 or 2551 041 077.

Excursion Boat Depending on demand, caiques do trips from the Kamariotissa jetty to Pahia Ammos and Kipos beaches, and the *Samothraki* excursion boat does trips around the island.

KAMARIOTISSA Καμαριώτισσα
postcode 680 02 • pop 826

Kamariotissa, on the north-west coast, is Samothraki's port. Hora (also called Samothraki), the island's capital, is 5km inland from here. Kamariotissa is the transport hub of the island, so you may wish to use it as a base. It's a cheerful flower-filled place with vaguely lively nightlife.

Orientation & Information

The bus station is on the waterfront just east of the quay (turn left when you disembark). There is no EOT or tourist police, and the regular police are in Hora. Opposite the bus station you will find Niki Tours, which is marginally helpful. There are two ATMs on the waterfront, but no post office or OTE – those are in Hora. Cafe Parapente, just back from the waterfront on the left side of the road leading up to Hora, offers Internet access for €3 an hour. The port police (☎ 2551 041 305) are east along the waterfront.

General information about the island, including boat schedules, can be found at **Ⓦ** www.samothraki.com.

Places to Stay

Domatia owners often meet ferries in Kamariotissa, and *domatia* are easy to find in the compact port.

Hotel Kyma (☎ 2551 041 263) Singles with shared bath €30, doubles/triples with bathroom, fridge & air-con €40/48. This little hotel, along the tree-lined waterfront road, has comfortable, homely rooms and friendly owners.

Niki Beach Hotel (*☎ 2551 041 545, fax 2551 041 461*) Singles/doubles with bathroom & TV €40/47. This spacious C-class hotel, just past the Hotel Kyma, has a lovely garden and is fronted by poplar trees.

Aeolos Hotel (*☎ 2551 041 595, fax 2551 041 810*) Singles/doubles with breakfast €50/60. Behind the Niki Beach, this B-class property has a swimming pool and a commanding position on a hill overlooking the sea. The rooms, which come with bathroom, fridge, TV, telephone and air-con, are comfortable enough but nothing special.

Places to Eat

Despite an abundance of cafe-bars, breakfast joints and ouzeria, Kamariotissa's eating establishments are all pretty run of the mill.

If you are just looking for a quick bite, try one of the **gyros stands** on the waterfront. A souvlaki or gyros costs about €4.50.

Klimataria Restaurant (*☎ 2551 041 535*) Mains from €4.50. At the eastern end of the waterfront road, this pleasant restaurant serves an unusual speciality called *giani-otiko*, an oven-baked dish of diced pork, potatoes, egg and other goodies (€5.50). It also serves a good pastitsio (€4.50).

I Synantisi (*☎ 2551 041 308*) Fish from €5. For simple fresh fish, try this ouzeria on the waterfront between the ferry dock and the bus stop. The food is straightforward but excellent.

Psistaria Pizzeria Skorpios (*☎ 2551 041 920*) Pizzas €6-9, grilled meat dishes from €4.50. A few doors up from Klimitaria, Skorpios serves decent home-made pizzas (take-away available) and grilled meat in no-frills surroundings.

HORA Χώρα

Hora, concealed in a fold of the mountains above Kamariotissa, occupies a striking site. The crumbling red-tiled houses – some of grey stone, others whitewashed – are stacked up two steep rocky mountainsides cloaked with pine trees. The twisting cobbled streets resound with cockerels crowing, dogs barking and donkeys braying, rather than the ubiquitous roar of motorcycles. The village is totally authentic with no concessions to tourism. The ruined castle at the top of the main thoroughfare offers sweeping vistas down to Kamariotissa. It is an open site with free entrance.

Orientation & Information

To get to Hora's narrow winding main street, follow the signs for the kastro from the central square where the bus turns around. Here on the main street, which is nameless (as are all of Hora's streets; houses are distinguished by numbers), are the OTE, the Agricultural Bank and the post office.

The police (*☎ 2551 041 203*) station is in the ruined castle at the top of Hora's main street. Further up on the main street, on the right, a fountain gushes refreshing mountain water.

Places to Stay & Eat

There are no hotels in Hora. There are two reasonably priced **pensions** just off the central square, but the best places to stay in Hora are **domatia** in private houses. Almost all of these are unofficial and do not display signs. If you ask in one of the kafeneia you will be put in touch with a room owner.

Taverna-Ouzeri I Plateia Mains from €3. This taverna on the central square offers grilled meat and a couple of vegetarian options. The tomato-and-feta saganaki is not bad.

SANCTUARY OF THE GREAT GODS

Το Ιερό των Μεγάλων Θεών

Next to the little village of Paleopolis, 6km north-east of Kamariotissa, is the Sanctuary of the Great Gods (*admission free; open 8.30am-8.30pm Tues-Sun*). The extensive site, lying in a valley of luxuriant vegetation between Mt Fengari and the sea, is one of the most magical in the whole of Greece. The Great Gods were of greater antiquity than the Olympian gods worshipped in the official religion of ancient Greece. The principal deity, the Great Mother (Alceros Cybele), was worshipped as a fertility goddess.

SANCTUARY OF THE GREAT GODS

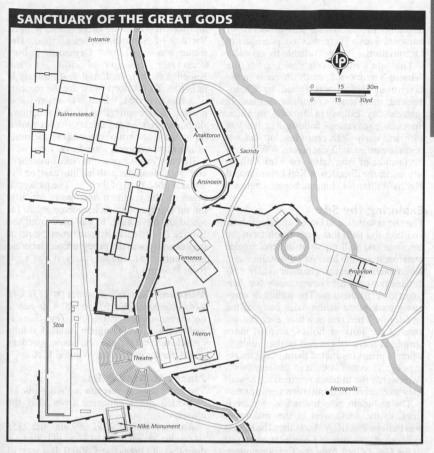

Entrance

Ruinenviereck

Anaktoron

Sacristy

Arsinoein

Temenos

Propylon

Stoa

Hieron

Theatre

Necropolis

Nike Monument

0   15   30m
0   15   30yd

When the original Thracian religion became integrated with the state religion, the Great Mother was merged with the Olympian female deities Demeter, Aphrodite and Hecate. The last of these was a mysterious goddess, associated with darkness, the underworld and witchcraft. Other deities worshipped here were the Great Mother's consort, the virile young Kadmilos (god of the phallus), who was later integrated with the Olympian god Hermes; as well as the demonic Kabeiroi twins, Dardanos and Aeton, who were integrated with Castor and Pollux (the Dioscuri), the twin sons of Zeus and

Leda. These twins were invoked by mariners to protect them against the perils of the sea. The formidable deities of Samothraki were venerated for their immense power. In comparison, the Olympian gods were a frivolous and fickle lot.

Initiates were sworn on punishment of death not to reveal what went on at the sanctuary; so there is only very flimsy knowledge of what these initiations involved. All that the archaeological evidence reveals is that there were two initiations, a lower and a higher. In the first initiation, gods were invoked to bring about a spiritual rebirth within the candidate. In the second initiation the candidate was absolved of transgressions. There was no prerequisite for initiation – it was available to anyone.

The site's most celebrated relic, the Winged Victory of Samothrace (now in the Louvre in Paris), was found by Champoiseau, the French consul, at Adrianople (present-day Edirne in Turkey) in 1863. Sporadic excavations followed in the late 19th and early 20th centuries, but did not begin in earnest until just before WWII when the Institute of Fine Arts, New York University, under the direction of Karl Lehmann and Phyllis Williams Lehmann, began digging.

Exploring the Site

The site is labelled in Greek and English. If you take the path that leads south from the entrance you will arrive at the rectangular **anaktoron**, on the left. At the southern end was a **sacristy**, an antechamber where candidates put on white gowns ready for their first (lower) initiation. The initiation ceremony took place in the main body of the anaktoron. Then one at a time each initiate entered the holy of holies, a small inner temple at the northern end of the building, where a priest instructed them in the meanings of the symbols used in the ceremony. Afterwards the initiates returned to the sacristy to receive their initiation certificate.

The **arsinoein**, which was used for sacrifices, to the south-west of the anaktoron, was built in 289 BC and was then the largest cylindrical structure in Greece. It was a gift to the Great Gods from the Egyptian queen Arsinou. To the south-east of here you will see the **sacred rock**, the site's earliest altar, which was used by the Thracians.

The initiations were followed by a celebratory feast which probably took place in the **temenos**, to the south of the arsinoein. This building was a gift from Philip II. The next building is the prominent Doric **hieron**, which is the most photographed ruin on the site; five of its columns have been reassembled. It was in this temple that candidates received the second initiation.

On the west side of the main path (opposite the hieron) are a few remnants of a theatre. Nearby, a path ascends to the **Nike monument** where the magnificent Winged Victory of Samothrace once stood. The statue was a gift from Demetrius Poliorketes (the 'besieger of cities') to the Kabeiroi for helping him defeat Ptolemy II in battle. To the north-west are the remains of a massive **stoa**, which was a two-aisled portico where pilgrims to the sanctuary sheltered. Names of initiates were recorded on its walls. North of the stoa are the ruins of the **ruinenviereck**, a medieval fortress.

Retrace your steps to the Nike monument and walk along the path leading east; on the left is a good plan of the site. The path continues to the southern **necropolis** which is the most important ancient cemetery so far found on the island. It was used from the Bronze Age to early Roman times. North of the cemetery was the **propylon**, an elaborate Ionic entrance to the sanctuary; it was a gift from Ptolemy II.

Museum The site's museum (☎ 2551 041 474; admission €1.50, free Sun & public holidays; open 8.30am-3pm Tues-Sun) is well laid out, with English labels. Exhibits include terracotta figurines, vases, jewellery and a plaster cast of the Winged Victory.

Places to Stay & Eat

There are several *domatia* at Paleopolis, all of which are signposted from near the museum.

Kastro Hotel (☎ 2551 089 400, fax 2551 041 000, W www.kastrohotel.gr) Singles/doubles with breakfast €50/80. Just west of Paleopolis, above the coast road, this C-class property offers simple but comfortable rooms with a sea view. The hotel has a swimming pool.

I Asprovalta (☎ 2551 098 250) Fish from around €5. Overlooking the sea, this serene little taverna in Kato Kariotes, just past Paleopolis, serves delicious fresh seafood.

AROUND SAMOTHRAKI

Loutra (Therma) Λουτρά (Θερμά)

Loutra, also called Therma, is 14km east of Kamariotissa and a short walk inland from the coast. It's in an attractive setting with a profusion of plane and horse-chestnut trees, dense greenery and gurgling creeks. While not an authentic village, it is the nearest Samothraki comes to having a holiday resort. Many of its buildings are purpose-built domatia, and most visitors to the island seem to stay here. If you visit before mid-May, be prepared to find most places closed.

The village takes both its names from its therapeutic, sulphurous, mineral springs. Whether or not you are arthritic you may enjoy a **thermal bath** (☎ 2551 098 229; admission €1.50; open 6am-11am & 5pm-7pm). The baths are in the large white building by the bus stop.

Places to Stay Samothraki's two official camping grounds are both near Loutra, on the beach, and both are signposted 'Multilary Campings'. Rest assured, the authorities mean municipal, not military, camping grounds.

Multilary Camping (Camping Plateia; ☎ 2551 041 784, 2551 098 291) Adult/tent €3/3. Open June-Aug. This site is to the left of the main road, 2km beyond the turn-off for Loutra, coming from Kamariotissa. It is shady, with toilets and cold showers but no other amenities.

Multilary Camping (☎ 2551 041 491, 2551 098 244) Adult/tent €3/3. Open June-Aug. This second site is 2km farther along the road. It has a minimarket, restaurant and hot showers, but is a rather dry camping ground.

Domatia owners meet the buses at Loutra.

Mariva Bungalows (☎ 2551 098 230, fax 2551 098 374) Doubles with bathroom & breakfast €48. These spacious C-class bungalows, set on a hillside in a secluded part of the island, near a waterfall, are perhaps the loveliest place to stay on Samothraki. To reach the hotel take the first turn left along the road which leads from the coast up to Loutra. Follow the signs to the hotel, which is 600m along this road.

Kaviros Hotel (☎ 2551 098 277, fax 2551 098 278) Singles/doubles €38/41. This B-class hotel is bang in the middle of Loutra, just beyond the central square. It looks like a concrete bunker but is a pleasant family-run place surrounded by greenery.

Places to Eat In Loutra there are a number of restaurants and tavernas scattered throughout the upper and lower village.

Paradisos Restaurant (☎ 2551 095 267) Mains from €4. In the upper village try this restaurant, which plies its trade under a huge plane tree and its welcome shade. Take the road to the right from the bus stop to find it.

Fengari Restaurant (☎ 2551 098 321) Mains from €4. This restaurant, signposted from near the bus stop, cooks its food in traditional Samothraki ovens. It is hidden away on a backstreet – follow the signs from Kaviros Hotel.

Kafeneio Ta Therma (☎ 2551 098 325), next to the bus stop and baths, serves excellent coffee, drinks and mezedes, as well as superb homemade sweets. Try the figs in syrup.

Fonias River

Visitors to the north coast should not miss the walk along the Fonias River to the **Vathres** rock pools. The walk starts at the bridge over the river 4.7km east of Loutra – the track being over-optimistically signposted as a vehicular road. After an easy 40-minute walk along a fairly well-marked track you will come to a large rock pool fed by a dramatic 12m-high waterfall. The water is pretty cold but very welcome on a hot day. Locals call the river the 'Murderer' – winter rains can transform the waters into a raging torrent.

Beaches

The gods did not over-endow Samothraki with good beaches. However, its one sandy beach, **Pahia Ammos**, on the south coast, is superb. You can reach this 800m stretch of sand along an 8km winding road from Lakoma. In summer there are caiques from Kamariotissa to the beach. Around the headland is the equally superb **Vatos Beach**, used mainly by nudists.

Opposite Pahia Ammos, on a good day, you can see the mass of the former Greek island of Imvros (Gökçeada), ceded to the Turks under the Treaty of Lausanne in 1923.

Samothraki's other decent beach is the pebbled **Kipos Beach** on the south-east coast. It can be reached via the road skirting the north coast. However, there are no facilities here other than a shower and a freshwater fountain, and there is no shade. It pales in comparison to Pahia Ammos. Kipos Beach can also be reached by caique from Kamariotissa.

Places to Stay & Eat *Yiannis Kapelas Rooms* (☎ *2551 095 119, 2551 095 139*) Doubles with breakfast €35. These domatia at Pahia Ammos are on the beach, above the *Taverna Pahia Ammos*, which serves fresh fish and other dishes on it's beautiful terrace. Book ahead if you want to stay here.

Other Villages

The small villages of **Profitis Ilias**, **Lakoma** and **Xiropotamos** in the south-west, and **Alonia** near Hora, are serene unspoilt villages all worth a visit. The hillside Profitis Ilias, with many trees and springs, is particularly delightful and has several tavernas, of which *Vrahos* (☎ *2551 095 264*) is famous for its delicious roast kid. Asphalt roads lead to all of these villages.

Thasos Θάσος

pop 13,530

Thasos lies 10km south-east of Kavala. It is almost circular in shape and although its scenery is not quite as awesome as Samothraki's it has some pleasing mountain vistas. The EOT brochures tout it as the 'emerald isle', and despite bad fires in recent years it is indeed a marvel of lushness and greenery. Villages are shaded by huge oaks and plane trees watered by streams and springs. The main attractions of Thasos, aside from its villages and forests, are its many excellent white-sand beaches and the archaeological remains in and around the capital, Thasos (Limenas). A good asphalt road goes around the island, so all the beaches are easily accessible.

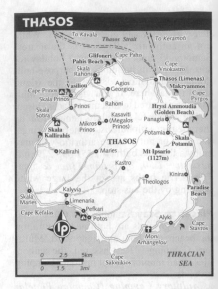

Although Thasos can get quite crowded with tourists, including many on package tours, there are enough rooms for everyone even in the high season and Thasos has no less than five camping grounds dotted around its coast. A notice opposite the bus station in Limenas lists the town's hotels, and also, very helpfully, indicates which hotels remain open in the winter.

It's worth seeking out the local olive oil, salted olives, figs and green walnuts in syrup, and honey.

History

Thasos has been continuously inhabited since the Stone Age. Its ancient city was founded in 700 BC by Parians, led there by a message from the Delphic oracle. The oracle told them to 'find a city in the Isle of Mists'. From Thasos, the Parians established settlements in Macedonia and Thrace, where they mined for gold at Mt Pangaion.

Gold was also mined on Thasos, and the islanders were able to develop a lucrative export trade based on ore, marble, timber and wine, as well as gold. As a result Thasos built a powerful navy, and culture flourished. Famous ancient Thassiots included the painters Polygnotos, Aglafon Aristofon and the sculptors Polyclitos and Sosicles. The merchants of Thasos traded with Asia Minor, Egypt and Italy.

After the Battle of Plataea, Thasos became an ally of Athens, but war broke out between the two cities when Athens attempted to curtail Thasos' trade with Egypt and Asia Minor. The islanders were defeated and forced into joining the Delian League; the heavy tax imposed crippled its economy. Thasos' decline continued through Macedonian and Roman times. Heavy taxes were imposed by the Turks, and many inhabitants left the island; during the 18th century the population dropped from 8000 to 2500.

Thasos was revived in the 19th century when Mohammed Ali Pasha of Egypt became governor of Kavala and Thasos. Ali allowed the islanders to govern themselves and exempted them from paying taxes. The revival was, however, short-lived. The Egyptian governors who superseded Ali Pasha plundered the island's natural resources and imposed heavy taxes. In 1912, along with the other islands of the group, Thasos was united with Greece. Thasos was occupied by Bulgarians and Germans in WWII.

In recent years Thasos has once again struck 'gold'. This time it's 'black gold', in the form of oil which has been found in the sea around the island. Oil derricks can now be spotted at sea at various locations around Thasos. It's also a major provider of very white marble – the quarries are fast creating huge holes in the island's mountainsides.

Getting To/From Thasos

Ferry There are ferries every two hours between Kavala, on the mainland, and Skala Prinos (1¼ hours, €2.65). There is one ferry daily between Limenas and Kavala, departing at 6am and returning at 2pm. Ferries direct to Limenas leave every hour or so in summer from Keramoti (40 minutes, €1.20), 46km south-east of Kavala. If you are coming from Kavala airport, catch a taxi (15 minutes, €9) to the ferry at Keramoti instead of Kavala – it's much closer, the ferries go direct to Thasos (Limenas), and the ferry ride

itself is much quicker. Ferry schedules are posted at the ticket sales booths (☎ 2593 022 318) and port police (☎ 2593 022 106) in Limenas and Skala Prinos.

Hydrofoil There are six hydrofoils every day between Limenas and Kavala (45 minutes, €6).

Getting Around Thasos

Bus Thasos (Limenas) is the transport hub of the island. There are at least seven buses daily to Limenaria (via the west coast villages, €3) and many to Skala Potamia at the south end of Hrysi Ammoudia (Golden Beach) via Panagia and Potamia. There are five buses a day to Theologos and three to Alyki (€2.50). Three buses daily journey in a clockwise direction all the way around the island (3½ hours, €7) and another three go anticlockwise. Timetables are available from the bus station (☎ 2593 022 162).

Car & Motorcycle Cars can be hired from Avis Rent a Car (☎ 2593 022 535, fax 2593 023 124) on the central square in Limenas or in Skala Prinos (☎ 2593 072 075) and Potamia (☎ 2593 061 735). There are many other agencies, so you may want to shop around. In Limenas you can hire motorcycles and mopeds from Billy's Bikes (☎ 2593 022 490), opposite the foreign-language newspaper agency, and 2 Wheels (☎ 2593 023 267), on the road from Prinos.

The coast road is about 100km all in all, but due to winding mountain roads a full circuit with stops takes about a day.

Bicycle Bicycles can be hired from Babis Bikes (☎ 2593 022 129), on a side street between 18 Oktovriou and the central square in Limenas.

Excursion Boat The *Eros 2* excursion boat (☎ 2593 022 704) makes trips around the island three to four times a week, with stops for swimming and a barbecue. The boat leaves from the old harbour at 9.45am (but you should be there at 9.30am) and returns at 5.30pm. The price is €23.50, including barbecue. There are also a couple of water taxis running regularly to Hrysi Ammoudia (Golden Beach) and Makryammos beaches.

THASOS (LIMENAS)
Θάσος (Λιμένας)
postcode 640 04 • pop 2610
Thasos, on the north-east coast, is the main port and capital of the island. Confusingly, it is also called Limenas and Limin. The island's other port is Skala Prinos, on the west coast. Thasos is built on top of the ancient city, so ruins are scattered all over the place. It is also the island's transport hub, with a reasonable bus service to the coastal resorts and villages.

Orientation & Information
The quay for ferries and hydrofoils is at the centre of the waterfront. The port police (☎ 2593 022 106) and ferry ticket booths (☎ 2593 022 318) are here, opposite the Hotel Timoleon. The central square is straight ahead from the waterfront. The town's main

thoroughfare is 18 Oktovriou, which is parallel to the waterfront, before the central square. Turn left into 18 Oktovriou from the quay to reach the OTE on the right. Take the next turn right into Theogenous and the second turn right for the post office, which is on the left. Millennium Internet Cafe (☎ 2593 058 089), on the waterfront, is open 8am-1am and has Web access for €3 an hour.

Laundry Express (☎ 2593 022 235), just off the central square, provides laundry and dry-cleaning services.

The helpful tourist police (☎ 2593 023 111) are on the waterfront near the bus station. They will assist in finding accommodation if necessary.

The National Bank of Greece is on the waterfront opposite the quay and has an exchange machine and ATM. The newsagent on Theogenous sells English-language newspapers.

The bus station is on the waterfront; to reach it turn left from the quay. To reach the

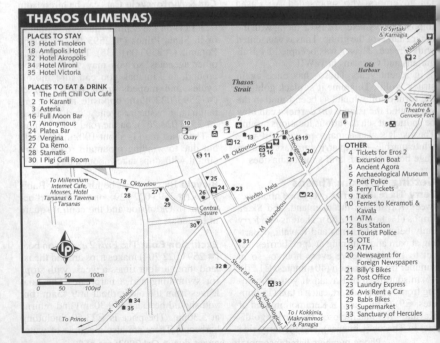

THASOS (LIMENAS)

PLACES TO STAY
13 Hotel Timoleon
18 Amfipolis Hotel
32 Hotel Akropolis
34 Hotel Mironi
35 Hotel Victoria

PLACES TO EAT & DRINK
1 The Drift Chill Out Cafe
2 To Karanti
3 Asteria
16 Full Moon Bar
17 Anonymous
24 Platea Bar
25 Vergina
27 Da Remo
28 Stamatis
30 I Pigi Grill Room

OTHER
4 Tickets for Eros 2 Excursion Boat
5 Ancient Agora
6 Archaeological Museum
7 Port Police
8 Ferry Tickets
9 Taxis
10 Ferries to Keramoti & Kavala
11 ATM
12 Bus Station
14 Tourist Police
15 OTE
19 ATM
20 Newsagent for Foreign Newspapers
21 Billy's Bikes
22 Post Office
23 Laundry Express
26 Avis Rent a Car
29 Babis Bikes
31 Supermarket
33 Sanctuary of Hercules

town's picturesque small harbour, turn left from the quay and walk along the waterfront. There are town beaches both east and west of the waterfront.

Things to See

Thasos' **archaeological museum** (☎ 2593 022 180), next to the ancient agora at the small harbour, has been closed for years but is expected to reopen in 2002. The most striking exhibit is a very elongated 6th-century-BC **kouros** statue that stands in the foyer. It was found on the acropolis of the ancient city of Thasos. Other exhibits include pottery and terracotta figurines and a large well-preserved head of a rather effeminate Dionysos. The ancient city of Thasos was excavated by the French School of Archaeology, so the museum's labelling is in French and Greek.

The **ancient agora** (admission free) next to the museum was the bustling marketplace of ancient and Roman Thasos – the centre of its civic, social and business life. It's a pleasant, verdant site with the foundations of stoas, shops and dwellings.

The **ancient theatre**, nearby, has also been closed for almost a decade but is expected to reopen early 2002. When the theatre reopens, performances of ancient dramas and comedies will be staged annually. The theatre is signposted from the small harbour.

From the theatre a path leads up to the **acropolis** of ancient Thasos where there are substantial remains of a medieval fortress built on the foundations of the ancient walls that encompassed the entire city. From the topmost point of the acropolis there are magnificent views. From the far side of the acropolis, steps carved into the rock lead down to the foundations of the ancient wall. From here it's a short walk to the Limenas-Panagia road at the southern edge of town.

Special Events

In July and August, pending the reopening of the ancient theatre, performances of ancient plays are held as part of the Kavala Festival of Drama. Information and tickets can be obtained from the EOT in Kavala or the tourist police on Thasos.

Courses

Holiday workshops in a variety of disciplines are held each summer at Markyammos, a couple of kilometres from Thasos (Limenas). Courses include traditional Greek dance, Greek cooking, ceramics, painting, Pilates body control, hatha yoga, aromatherapy, reflexology, shiatsu massage, and trekking and climbing. Prices vary; seven yoga classes costs around €73.50, while a 6-hour trek on Mt Ipsario is €37 including lunch. Call ☎ 2593 022 101 for more information.

Places to Stay – Budget

Limenas has many reasonably priced **domatia**. If you are not offered anything when you arrive, look for signs around the small harbour and the road to Prinos.

Hotel Victoria (☎ 2593 022 556, fax 2593 022 132) Doubles €38.50. This comfortable place is next door to Hotel Mironi and is run by the same owner.

Hotel Tarsanas (☎ 2593 023 933) Doubles €41. This little hotel is a kilometre west of town on a quiet beach. Rooms have bathroom and kitchen. It has a very good restaurant and bar.

Hotel Mironi (☎ 2593 023 256, fax 2593 022 132) Singles/doubles with bathroom, air-con & fridge €29.50/47. This is a modern and spacious hotel with lots of cool marble. From the ferry quay walk to 18 Oktovriou and turn right and then left on the road signposted to Prinos. The hotel is along here on the left.

Hotel Akropolis (☎/fax 2593 022 488, e fivos3@otenet.gr) Singles/doubles with bathroom, TV, fridge & air-con €41/53. This well-maintained, century-old mansion on the Street of the French Archaeological School one block south of the central square, has a lovely garden out front and a foyer filled with wondrous family heirlooms. The rooms are somewhat pokey and cramped but comfortable enough.

Places to Stay – Mid-Range & Top End

Hotel Timoleon (☎ 2593 022 177, fax 2593 023 277) Singles/doubles with breakfast €44/53. This B-class property has clean spacious rooms with balcony, air-con, TV and phone. It is on the waterfront, just beyond the bus station, and provides a free minibus to/from Nysteri Beach.

Amfipolis Hotel (☎ 2593 023 101, fax 2593 022 110, cnr 18 Oktovriou & Theogenous) Singles/doubles/suites with buffet breakfast €45.50/73.50/103. This A-class hotel occupies a grand old tobacco factory. Rooms are elegantly furnished and have interesting wood-panelled ceilings. The hotel has two bars, a restaurant and a pool.

Makryammos Bungalows (☎ 2593 022 101, fax 2593 022 761, e makryamo@mail .otenet.gr) Singles/doubles with breakfast €75/91. This attractive, slightly hippie-ish resort was the first on the island and is situated on an idyllic beach a couple of kilometres south-east of Thasos (Limenas). There are around 200 bungalows hidden in the forest behind the beach, all very private and furnished in an elegant traditional style with marble floors. Incorporated into the complex is a restaurant, taverna, tennis court, swimming pools, water-sports equipment, etc. Excellent child-minding facilities are provided free of charge. The hotel also serves as the venue for 'alternative holiday workshops' (see Courses) that have a new-age bent.

Places to Eat
Limenas has a great selection of restaurants serving well-prepared food.

I Kokkinia (☎ 2593 023 729) Appetisers €2.50, mains €4-6. This little taverna is on the Street of the French Archaeology School, on the outskirts of Limenas, on the way to Panagia and Makryammos. Fish is the speciality (the owner's father is a fisherman), but chargrilled meat and other traditional dishes are also offered.

I Pigi Grill Room (☎ 2593 022 941) Mains €3-5. This restaurant, on the central square, is an inviting, unpretentious place next to a spring. The food is good and the service friendly and attentive. Try *stifado* (stew in tomato sauce) or mussel saganaki.

Vergina (☎ 2593 023 807) Mains around €4.50. On one of the streets leading from the main square to 18 Oktovriou, this place

with tables outside has good grills, including souvlaki.

Mouses (☎ 2593 023 697) Mains €3-8. Named in honour of the seven muses (not mices), this beachside place west of the port specialises in fish but also serves other things. Try the *taramokeftedes* (fish roe rissoles). There's live music several nights a week.

Asteria (☎ 2593 022 403) Mains €4-7.50. On the old harbour, this restaurant serves classic Greek cuisine such as mousakas, pastitsio, *kleftiko* (lamb stuffed with feta and tomato, and baked in a white sauce) and *fasolakia*.

Syrtaki (☎ 2593 023 353) Mains around €5. Just beyond the old harbour, along the beach, this place serves good traditional Greek fare. Try the lamb kleftiko or the *stamnato* (pork and vegetables in a clay pot).

Da Remo (☎ 2593 022 890, 18 Oktovriou) Pizzas €4-12. This pizza place is a cut above usual Greek pizzerias; home delivery is an option.

Taverna Tarsanas (☎ 2593 023 933) Mezedes €2.50, mains €3-20. This lovely place, a kilometre west of Thasos on the site of a former boatbuilders, serves the most exquisite seafood on the island. There are lots of interesting seafood mezedes that you won't find anywhere else. Fresh lobster (€44/kg) – difficult to find on Thasos – is always available. Traditional meat dishes are also served.

Stamatis (☎ 2593 022 131, 18 Oktovriou) This zaharoplasteio has been going since 1958. It's the best place for coffee and sweets.

Entertainment
Platea Bar (☎ 2593 022 144) This earthy, quirky little bar with shaman-style handcrafted decor is a local favourite. It's known for its reliably good music and casual, welcoming atmosphere. Look for it on the central square.

To Karanti (☎ 2593 024 014) This outdoor ouzeri next to the fishing boats on the old harbour, has one of the most beautiful settings in Thasos. Its relaxed atmosphere is enhanced by excellent Greek music. Aside from a full bar, breakfast and mezedes are available.

The Drift Chill Out Cafe With a nice laid-back outdoor setting by the water north-east of the old harbour, this bar is a refreshing option.

Beyond the old harbour, *Karnagia* is a lovely place to have a drink at sunset. Sited where wooden boats are still built, it has a dramatic locale at the end of the promontory.

Anonymous (☎ 2593 022 847, 18 Oktovriou) this bar serves English-style snacks and Guinness in a can, as well as many other beers.

Full Moon (☎ 2593 023 230) Next door to Anonymous Cafe, this watering hole has an Australian owner and is also very popular.

EAST COAST

The hillside villages of **Panagia** and **Potamia** are a bit touristy but very picturesque. Both are 4km west of Golden Beach. The Greek-American artist Polygnotos Vagis was born in Potamia in 1894 and some of his work can be seen in the **Polygnotos Vagis Museum** (☎ 2593 061 400; open 9.30am-12.30pm & 6pm-9pm Tues-Sat, 10am-1pm Sun & holidays) in the village next to the main church. (The municipal museum in Kavala also has a collection of Vagis' work.)

The long and sandy **Hrysi Ammoudia** (Golden Beach) is one of the island's best beaches, though it can get a trifle crowded. Roads from both Panagia and Potamia lead down to it, and the bus from Limenas calls at both villages before continuing to the southern end of the beach, which is known as Skala Potamia.

The next beach south is at the village of **Kinira**, and just south of here is the very pleasant **Paradise Beach**. The little islet just off the coast here is also called Kinira. **Alyki**, on the south-east coast, is a magical, spectacular place consisting of two quiet beaches back to back on a headland and some quaint old houses. The southernmost beach is the better of the two. There is a small archaeological site near the beach and an ancient, submerged marble quarry. Here marble was cut and loaded on ships from the 6th century BC to the 6th century AD.

The road linking the east side with the west side runs high across the cliffs, providing some great views of the bays at the bottom of the island. Along here you will come to **Moni Arhangelou**, an old monastery built on top of cliffs directly opposite Mt Athos on the mainland. It's possible to visit, and the nuns sell some handpainted icons, crosses and other paraphernalia.

Places to Stay & Eat

Golden Beach Camping (☎ 2593 061 472, fax 2593 061 473) Adult/tent €4/2.50. This place, smack in the middle of Hrysi Ammoudia, is the only camping ground on this side of the island; it's only a stone's throw from the inviting water. Facilities are good and include a minimarket.

Hotel Emerald (☎ 2593 061 979, fax 2593 061 451) Self-contained double/quad studios with kitchen €59/73.50. This hotel up the hill at the northern end of Hrysi Ammoudia has a pool and other facilities and very nice rooms; it's often prebooked by package tours.

Apartments Kavouri (☎ 2593 062 031). 2-3 person apartments €47. These spacious studios have balconies and fully equipped kitchens. They are at the far southern end of Skala Potamia, near the bus turnaround.

Hotel Elvetia (☎ 2593 061 231, fax 2593 061 451) Doubles with fridge €35. This hotel in Panagia has pleasant doubles. With your back to the fountain in the central square of Panagia (where the bus stops), turn left and take the first main road to the left; the hotel is on the left.

Hotel Hrysafis (☎/fax 2593 061 451) Doubles with bathroom €35.50. This vine-covered hotel is just beyond Hotel Elvetia, on the right, and has the same owners as the Elvetia.

Thassos Inn (☎ 2593 061 612, fax 2593 061 027) Doubles with TV, bathroom, phone, heating & balcony €47. Open summer & winter. This lovely hotel in Panagia is up the hill, in the cool of the forest. Built in traditional style, it has views over the slate rooftops of the village. From the bus stop, follow the small street leading from the fountain. Turn right at the sign to the hotel about 20m up the street, just past the honey shop, and follow the babbling brook.

There are *domatia* at both Kinira and Alyki.

Drosia/Platanos (☎ 2593 062 172, 2593 061 340) Salads €2-4, mains €4-5. This popular taverna is on Panagia's central square.

Phedra Mains €4-10. In the middle of Hrysi Ammoudia (Golden Beach), this was one of the first restaurants on Thasos and is deservedly popular.

Avalon (☎ 2593 062 060) Mains €4-10. In an imposing old monastery at the southern end of Hrysi Ammoudia in Skala Potamia, this establishment serves traditional fare as well as pizza and fish.

Taverna Captain (☎ 2593 061 160). Fish €5.50-9. In Skala Potamia, this somewhat touristy place offers up decent fish.

Psarotaverna O Glaros Fish meals €5-10. This is perhaps the best of the tavernas at Alyki, and it offers a nice view over the bay.

I Oraia Alyki (☎ 2593 053 074) Mains €4-6. On the beach at Alyki is this simple taverna with good fish, and sometimes, homemade cheese.

WEST COAST

The west coast consists of a series of beaches and seaside villages, most with Skala (literally 'step' or 'ladder', but also meaning a little pier) before their names. Roads lead from each of these to inland villages with the same name (minus the 'skala'). Travelling from north to south the first beach is **Glifoneri**, closely followed by **Pahia Ammos** (Pahis Beach). The first village of any size is **Skala Rahoni**. This is Thasos' latest development, having recently been discovered by the package-tour companies. It has an excellent camping ground and the inland village of **Rahoni** remains unspoilt. A wide range of water-sports equipment can be hired from Skala Rachoni Watersports (☎ 2593 081 056).

Skala Prinos, the next coastal village, and Thasos' second port, is nothing special. There is an ATM here. **Vasiliou**, about 1km south of the port, is a very nice beach backed by trees. The hillside villages of Mikros Prinos and Megalos Prinos, collectively known as **Kasaviti**, are gorgeous and lush, with excellent tavernas (see Places to Eat).

Skala Sotira and **Skala Kallirahis** are pleasant and both have small beaches. Kallirahi, 2km inland from Skala Kallirahis, is a peaceful village with steep narrow streets and old stone houses. It has a large population of skinny, anxious-looking cats and word has it that the locals are scared of dogs. Judging by the graffiti and posters, there are also a lot of communists (though not as many as in Skala Potamia).

Skala Maries is a delightful fishing village and one of the least touristy places around the coast. It was from here, early in the 20th century, that the German Speidel Metal Company exported iron ore from Thasos to Europe. There are beaches at both sides of the village, and between here and Limenaria there are stretches of uncrowded beach. **Maries**, Skala Marie's inland sister village, is very pretty and has a lovely square.

Limenaria is Thasos' second-largest town. It's a crowded though pleasant resort with a narrow sandy beach. The town was built in 1903 by the Speidel Metal Company. There are slightly less crowded beaches around the coast at **Pefkari** and **Potos**.

From Potos a scenic 10km road leads inland to **Theologos**, which was the capital of the island in medieval and Turkish times. This one of the island's most beautiful villages and the only mountain settlement served by public transport. The village houses are of whitewashed stone with slate roofs. It's a serene place, still unblemished by mass tourism.

Places to Stay

Camping Perseus (☎/fax 2593 081 242) Adult/tent €3/2. This facility, at Skala Rahoni, is a pleasant, grassy camping ground among olive trees. The cook at the site's taverna will prepare any Greek dish you wish if you place your order a day in advance.

Camping Prinos (☎ 2593 071 171) Adult/tent around €3.50/2.50. This EOT-owned site, at Skala Prinos, is well maintained with lots of greenery and shade and is about a kilometre or so south of the ferry quay, in Vasiliou.

Camping Daedalos (☎/fax 2593 058 251) Adult/tent around €3.50/2. This camping ground is just north of Skala Sotira right on the beach. It has a minimarket, restaurant and bar. Sailing, windsurfing and water-skiing lessons are also on offer.

Camping Pefkari (☎ 2593 051 190) Adult/tent around €3/3. This nifty camping ground is at Pefkari Beach, south of Limenaria. It requires a minimum three-night stay. Look carefully for the sign; it is not so obvious.

All of the seaside villages have *hotels* and *domatia* and the inland villages have rooms in private houses. For information about these inquire at kafeneia or look for signs.

Alexandra Beach Hotel (☎ 2593 052 391, fax 2593 051 185, e alexandra@ tha.forthnet.gr) Singles/doubles with all mod-cons €84/116.50. Rates considerably less outside high season. This resort-like complex is near Potos and is one of the island's best hotels. Aside from the very nice beach there's a restaurant, pool, bar, tennis court and more. Breakfast and dinner are included in the room rate.

Places to Eat

Psisteria Glifoneri Mains around €4. At Glifoneri Beach, on the way from Thasos (Limenas) to Skala Rahoni, this place is on a small beach with a freshwater spring. Try the excellent homemade mussel saganaki with feta.

Pefkospilia (☎ 2593 081 051) Appetisers €1.50-3, mains €3.50-18. This cute traditional family-run taverna by the water at Pahis, just off the road between Thasos (Limenas) and Skala Rahoni, is in a beautiful spot under a large pine tree. It serves delectable local specialities, including the sought-after fish known as *mourmoures* (€23.50/kg),

kravourosalata (crab salad, €3) and *htapodokeftedes* (octopus rissoles, €2.50).

Taverna Drosia (☎ 2593 081 270) Most mains €3-5. This taverna in a grove of plane and oak trees on the outskirts of Rahoni features live bouzouki on Friday, Saturday and Sunday evenings. Chargrilled meat is the speciality of the house, though they also have fresh seafood and precooked dishes.

Taverna O Andreas (☎ 2593 071 760) Mains from €3. This homespun taverna on Kasaviti's serene central square shaded by ancient plane trees, serves excellent soup, vegetable dishes, meat and oven-cooked foods. The whole family participates in cooking, and, judging by the food, they're passionate about it. Chirping birds, and cute cats chasing each other around the plane tree will entertain you as you quietly savour your meal.

Vasilis (☎ 2593 072 016). Mains around €4. This beautiful, traditional wooden place on the road into Kasaviti has very good local food but is worth visiting for its stunning old-world architecture alone.

Taverna Orizontes (☎ 2593 031 389) Mains around €4. This taverna, the first on the left as you enter Theologos, features *rembetika* nights.

Augustus Mains €4-7.50. Specialising in grilled meat, including goat and lamb, this bouzouki joint is also in Theologos. The bouzouki action takes place on Friday, Saturday and Sunday nights. Strangely passive ducks swim around in a floodlit pond – just one of the kitschy highlights that await you.

Ciao Tropical Beach Bar (☎ 2593 081 136) Open day & night. More Hawaiian than Hawaii, this beach bar in Pahis is quite a work of art. The owner has meticulously created everything by hand, from the umbrellas to the wood-carved lamps and furniture. You have to see it to believe it.

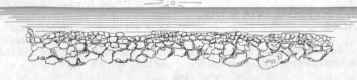

Evia & the Sporades
Εύβοια & Οι Σποράδες

Evia, Greece's second-largest island, is so close to the mainland historically, physically and topographically that one tends not to regard it as an island at all. Athenians regard Evia as a convenient destination for a weekend break, so consequently it gets packed. Except for the resort of Eretria, however, it is not frequently visited by foreign tourists.

The Sporades lie to the north and east of Evia and to the east and south-east of the Pelion Peninsula, to which they were joined in prehistoric times. With their dense vegetation and mountainous terrain, they seem like a continuation of this peninsula. There are 11 islands in the archipelago, four of which are inhabited: Skiathos, Skopelos, Alonnisos and Skyros. The first two have a highly developed tourist industry, whereas Alonnisos and Skyros, although by no means remote, are far less visited and retain more local character.

SUGGESTED ITINERARIES
One week
Starting in Athens, take the bus to Kymi in Evia and then the ferry to Linaria in Skyros. Give delectable Skyros at least two days of your time. Take a hydrofoil to Alonnisos and work your way towards Volos on the mainland, visiting the islands of Skopelos and Skiathos en route.
Two weeks
Try this adventurous route if you have time. From Athens head to Rafina in Attica and take the ferry to Karystos in Evia. Work your way up to Kymi in Evia, perhaps taking in Eretria on Evia's west side and some walking up Mt Dirfys from the inland village of Steni. From Kymi in Evia follow the one-week itinerary, allowing two to three days on each island of the Sporades. Finally exit from Skiathos to Thessaloniki (ferry or hydrofoil) and return to Athens by train.

GETTING TO/FROM EVIA & THE SPORADES
Air
Skiathos airport receives charter flights from northern Europe and there are also do-

- The changing tides of the Evripous Channel that so puzzled Aristotle
- Skiathos' golden beaches – among the best in Greece
- Getting delightfully lost in the labyrinthine streets of picturesque Skopelos Town
- Quirky Skyros and pretty Skyrian houses – Greece's hidden island treasure
- Relaxing on Alonnisos, one of the area's greenest and most underrated islands

mestic flights to Athens. Skyros airport has domestic flights to Athens and occasional charter flights from airports in the Netherlands.

Bus
From Athens' Terminal B bus station there are buses every half-hour to Halkida from 5.45am to 9.45pm (one hour, €4.30), two daily to Paralia Kymis (3¼ hours, €9.70) and three daily to Loutra Edipsou (3½ hours, €8.50). From the Mavromateon terminal Athens, there are buses every 45 minutes to Rafina (for Karystos and Marmari; one hour, €1.30).

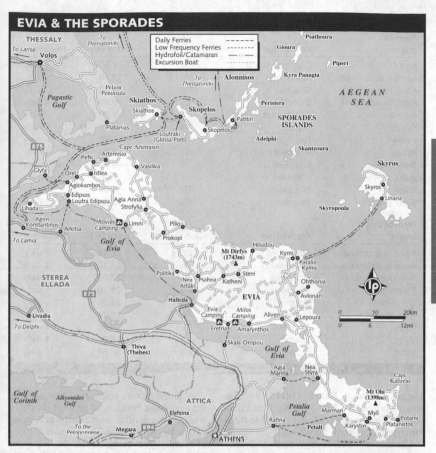

Train

There are hourly trains from Athens' Larisis station to Halkida (1½ hours, €3.55).

Ferry

There is no ferry from Thessaloniki to the Sporades, but from 29 June to 16 September there is a daily catamaran to Alonnisos (3¾ hours, €21), Skopelos (three hours, €26), Skiathos (four hours, €32.30) and Agios Konstantinos (6½ hours, €44).

The table following gives an overall view of the available ferries to this island group from mainland ports in high season. Further

details and inter-island links can be found under each island entry.

Hydrofoil

Hydrofoil links by and large follow similar routes as the ferries, except for the Evia (Kymi) to Skyros (Linaria) link. The table following gives an overall view of the hydrofoil connections in high season. Further details and inter-island links can be found under each island entry. The summer hydrofoil timetable is usually available in late April from Minoan Flying Dolphin (☎ 21 0428 0001, fax 21 0428 3526), Akti

Ferry & Hydrofoil Connections to Evia & the Sporades

Ferries

origin	destination	duration (hours)	price (€)	frequency
Agia Marina	Evia (Nea Styra)	¾	1.90	5 daily
Agios Konstantinos	Alonnisos	5½	13.30	1 daily
Agios Konstantinos	Skiathos	3½	9.40	2 daily
Agios Konstantinos	Skopelos	4½	9.40	4 daily
Arkitsa	Evia (Loutra Edipsou)	1	1.60	12 daily
Kymi	Skyros	2¼	7.10	2 daily
Rafina	Evia (Karystos)	1¾	5.60	2 daily
Rafina	Evia (Marmari)	1¼	3.80	4 daily
Skala Oropou	Evia (Eretria)	½	0.90	half-hourly
Volos	Alonnisos	5	11.50	3 daily
Volos	Skiathos	3½	8.00	4 daily
Volos	Skopelos	4½	10.00	4 daily

Hydrofoils

origin	destination	duration (hours)	price (€)	frequency
Agios Konstantinos	Alonnisos	2½	26.40	3 daily
Agios Konstantinos	Skiathos	1½	17.10	3 daily
Agios Konstantinos	Skopelos	2¼	23.60	3 daily
Thessaloniki	Alonnisos	4½	25.50	1 daily
Thessaloniki	Skiathos	3½	23.50	6 weekly
Thessaloniki	Skopelos	4¾	26.40	1 daily
Volos	Alonnisos	2½	22.60	4 daily
Volos	Skiathos	1¼	16.80	4 daily
Volos	Skopelos	2¼	20.60	5 daily

Themistokleous 8, Piraeus GR-185 36. The Athens office (☎ 21 0324 4600) is at Filellinon 3. The timetable is also available from local hydrofoil booking offices.

Cheaper return fares apply on most hydrofoil services.

Evia Εύβοια

The island of Evia (**eh**-vih-ah) will probably never be a prime destination for foreign tourists, but if you're based in Athens with a few days to spare, and (preferably) your own transport, a foray into Evia is well worthwhile for its scenic mountain roads, pristine inland villages, and a look at some resorts which cater for Greeks (including one for ailing Greeks), rather than for foreign tourists.

A mountainous spine runs north-south; the east coast consists of precipitous cliffs, whereas the gentler west coast has a string of beaches and resorts. The island is reached overland by a bridge over the Evripous Channel to the island's capital, Halkida. At the mention of Evia, most Greeks will eagerly tell you that the current in this narrow channel changes direction around seven times daily, which it does, if you are prepared to hang around to watch it. The next bit of the story, that Aristotle became so perplexed at not finding an explanation for this mystifying occurrence that he threw himself into the channel and drowned, can almost certainly be taken with a grain of salt.

Getting Around Evia

Halkida is the transport hub of Evia. There are buses to Kymi Town (2½ hours, €5.30, nine daily) via Eretria, two of which continue to Paralia Kymis to link up with the ferry arrivals/departures. There are also buses to Steni (one hour, €1.90, six daily), Limni (2½ hours, €4.70, four daily), Loutra Edipsou (3½ hours, €6.70, two daily) and Karystos (3½ hours, €6.70, three daily) via Eretria. Timetables are outside the ticket office.

HALKIDA Χαλκίδα
postcode 341 00 • pop 45,000
Halkida was an important city-state in ancient times, with several colonies dotted around the Mediterranean. The name derives from the bronze manufactured here in antiquity (*halkos* means 'bronze' in Greek). Today it's a lively industrial and agricultural town, but with nothing of sufficient note to warrant an overnight stay.

However, if you have an hour or two to spare between buses then have a look at the archaeological museum (*☎ 2221 025 131, Leoforos Venizelou 13; admission €1.50; open 8.30am-3pm Tues-Sun*); it's worth a mosey around. It houses finds from Evia's three ancient cities of Halkida, Eretria and Karystos, including a chunk from the pediment of the Temple of Dafniforos Apollo at Eretria.

The Halkida train station is on the mainland side of the bridge. To reach central Halkida, turn right outside the train station, walk over the bridge, turn left and you will find Leoforos Venizelou, Halkida's main drag, off to the right.

The phone number of the Halkida tourist police is ☎ 2221 087 000.

Diving
Sport Apollon Scuba Diving Centre (*☎ 2221 086 369*) in Halkida offers a range of diving activities for all grades. The dives take place off the Alikes coast, north of Evia.

CENTRAL EVIA
Steni Στενή
postcode 340 03 • pop 1300
From Halkida, it's 31km to the lovely mountain village of Steni, with gurgling springs and plane trees.

Steni is the starting point for the climb up Mt Dirfys (1743m), Evia's highest mountain. The EOS-owned *Dirfys Refuge (☎ 2228 051 285)*, at 1120m, can be reached along a 9km dirt road, or after a three-hour walk along a forest footpath. From the refuge it's two hours to the summit. You should not attempt this walk unless you are an experienced trekker and take a reliable trekking guidebook with you. For further information contact the EOS (☎ 2228 025 230), Angeli Gyviou 22, Halkida. A road continues from Steni to Hiliadou, on the north coast, where there is a fine pebble-and-sand beach.

Places to Stay & Eat *Hotel Dirfys (☎ 2228 051 217)* Singles/doubles €23.50/ 35.30. This is the best value of Steni's two hotels, and is located 50m uphill from the bus terminal. It has comfortable, carpeted rooms with great views from the balconies.

Mouria Ouzeri (☎ 2228 051 234) Mains €2.90-5.90. This ouzeri on the central square serves generous portions of tender chargrilled chicken (€4.10) and lamb chops (€5.90) and very palatable local bulk wine.

Ouzeri Vrachos (☎ 2228 051 546) Mains €2.90-5.90. A huge helping of fried gavros and Greek salad is €5.90 at this little eatery on the central square.

Taverna Platanos (☎ 2228 051 225) Mains €3.50-7.30 It's worth the short walk from Steni, 500m along the Steni-Hiliadou road, to this taverna in a verdant setting by a brook. Char-grilled lamb, chicken or goat is €5.30.

Kymi Κύμη
postcode 340 03 • pop 3850
The town of Kymi is built on a cliff 250m above the sea. The port of Kymi (called Paralia Kymis), 4km downhill, is the only natural harbour on the precipitous east coast, and the departure point for ferries to Skyros.

Kymi is really quite attractive in a rather ramshackle way. If you like untouristy, lively workaday towns, you may enjoy an overnight stay. However, Paralia Kymis, squeezed between cliff and sea, is a drab place and there's little reason to linger.

EVIA & THE SPORADES

The **folklore museum** (☎ 2222 022 011; admission free; open 5pm-7.30pm Wed & Sat, 10am-1pm Sun), on the road to Paralia Kymis, has an impressive collection of local costumes and memorabilia, including a display commemorating Kymi-born Dr George Papanikolaou, inventor of the Pap smear test.

Places to Stay & Eat *Hotel Beis* (☎ 2222 022 604, fax 2222 029 113, ℮ hotelbeis@ yahoo.gr) Singles/doubles €26.40/38.20. This hotel on the waterfront has comfortable, well-maintained rooms and is the better of Paralia Kymis' two hotels.

Chalkidou Domatia (☎ 2222 023 896, Athinon 14) Singles/doubles €23.50/29.40. These well-kept domatia, 100m south of the central square, have great views down to Paralia Kymis from the balconies.

To Kouzouli Mezedopeio (☎ 2222 023 786, Galani 34) Mains €2.90-5.90. This little blue-and-white eatery 100m north of the central square has tasty offerings such as saganaki, stuffed green peppers and meatballs.

In Paralia Kymis a string of *restaurants* lines the waterfront.

NORTHERN EVIA

From Halkida a road heads north to **Psahna**, the gateway to the highly scenic mountainous interior of northern Evia. The road climbs through pine forests to the beautiful agricultural village of **Prokopi**, 52km from Halkida. The inhabitants are descendants of refugees who, in 1923, came from Prokopion (present-day Ürgüp) in Turkey, bringing with them the relics of St John the Russian. On 27 May (St John's festival), hordes of pilgrims come to worship his relics in the Church of Agios Ioannis Rosses.

At Strofylia, 14km beyond Prokopi, a road heads south-west to **Limni**, a pretty (but crowded) fishing village with whitewashed houses and a beach. With your own transport or a penchant for walking, you can visit the 16th-century **Convent of Galataki**, 8km south-east of Limni. Its *katholikon* (main church) has fine frescoes. Limni has several *hotels* and *domatia*. There's one camping

ground, *Rovies Camping* (☎ 2227 071 120), on the coast, 13km north-west of Limni.

The road continues to the sedate spa resort of **Loutra Edipsou** (119km from Halkida) whose therapeutic sulphur waters have been celebrated since antiquity. Many luminaries, including Aristotle, Plutarch, Strabo and Plinius, sang the praises of these waters. The waters are reputed to cure many ills, mostly of a rheumatic, arthritic or gynaecological nature. Today the town has Greece's most up-to-date hydrotherapy-physiotherapy centre. If you're interested, contact any EOT or the EOT Hydrotherapy-Physiotherapy Centre (☎ 2226 023 501), Loutra Edipsou. Even if you don't rank among the infirm you may enjoy a visit to this resort with its attractive setting, a beach, many domatia and hotels.

SOUTHERN EVIA
Eretria Ερέτρια
postcode 340 08 • pop 5000

As you head east from Halkida, Eretria is the first major place of interest. Ancient Eretria was a major maritime power and also had an eminent school of philosophy. The city was destroyed in AD 87 during the Mithridatic War, fought between Mithridates (king of Pontos) and the Roman commander Sulla. The modern town was founded in the 1820s by islanders from Psara fleeing the Turkish. Once Evia's major archaeological site, it has metamorphosed into a tacky package-tourist resort.

Things to See From the top of the **ancient acropolis**, at the northern end of town, there are splendid views over to the mainland. West of the acropolis are the remains of a palace, temple, and a theatre with a subterranean passage once used by actors. Close by, the **Museum of Eretria** (☎ 2211 062 206; admission €1.50; open 8am-3pm Tues-Sun) contains well-displayed finds from ancient Eretria. In the centre of town are the remains of the **Temple of Dafniforos Apollo** and a mosaic from an ancient bath.

Places to Stay Eretria has loads of *hotels* and *domatia*. The two camping grounds nearby are used more by visitors with motor campers than with tents.

Eva Camping (☎ *2211 068 081, fax 2211 068 083*) Adult/tent €3.50/4.40. This is a well-organised site at Malakonda, 5km west of Eretria, with a restaurant, bar and clean facilities.

Milos Camping (☎ *2211 060 460, fax 2211 060 360*) Adult/tent €2.90/4.40 This camping ground on the coast 1km west of Eretria has good shade and all the amenities expected of a well-run site.

Karystos Κάρυστος
postcode 340 01 • pop 4500

Continuing east from Eretria, the road branches at Lepoura: the left fork leads to Kymi, the right to Karystos (**kah**-ris-tos). Set on the wide Karystian Bay, below Mt Ohi (1398m), Karystos is the most attractive of southern Evia's resorts and is flanked by two long sandy beaches. The town was designed on a grid system by the Bavarian architect Bierbach, who was commissioned by King Otho. If you turn right from the quay you will come to the central square of Platcia Amalias which abuts the waterfront. Further along the waterfront is the remains of a 14th-century Venetian castle, the **Bourtzi**, which has marble from a temple dedicated to Apollo incorporated into its walls.

Organised Tours *South Evia Tours Travel Agency* (☎ *2224 025 700, fax 2224 029 011,* ✉ *root@set.hlk.forthnet.gr,* 🖳 *www.setours .tripod.com, Plateia Amallas 7*) With helpful English speaking staff, this company offers a range of services including car hire, accommodation and excursions. The latter include walks in the foothills of Mt Ohi and a cruise around the Petali Islands.

Places to Stay & Eat Karystos has three easy-to-find hotels on the waterfront.

Hotel Als (☎ *2224 022 202, Opposite ferry quay*) Singles/doubles €23.50/38. Although somewhat lacklustre, the rooms are comfortable and clean here.

Hotel Galaxy (☎ *2224 022 600, fax 2224 022 463, Cnr Kriezotou & Odysseos*) Singles/

doubles with breakfast €29.40/44.80. This hotel has air-con rooms with TV, music channels and balconies.

Hotel Karystion (☎ *2224 022 391, fax 2224 022 727, Kriezotou 2*) Singles/doubles/triples with breakfast €41/52.80/ 64.50. The modern, carpeted rooms at this hotel 100m east of the Bourtzi have air-con, satellite TV, and balconies with sea views.

Cavo d'Oro (☎ *2224 022 326*) Mains €2.90-5.90. Join the locals in this cheery little alleyway restaurant one block west of the main square, where tasty oil-based dishes *(ladera)* cost from €2.90 and meat dishes are €4.40.

Marinos Restaurant (☎ *2224 024 126, Opposite ferry quay*) Mains €2.90-7.60. The pick of the bunch from the restaurants lining the waterfront, the Marinos has ladera and fresh fish. Whitebait is €3.80 a portion and most other fish is €38 a kilogram.

Around Karystos

The ruins of **Castello Rossa** (Red Castle), a 13th-century Frankish fortress, are a short walk from **Myli**, a delightful, well-watered village 4km inland from Karystos. The aqueduct behind the castle once carried water from the mountain springs and a tunnel led from this castle to the Bourtzi in Karystos. A little beyond Myli there is an **ancient quarry** scattered with fragments of the once-prized Karystian marble.

With your own transport you can explore the sleepy villages nestling in the southern foothills of Mt Ohi. From the charming village of **Platanistos** a 5km dirt road (driveable) leads to the coastal village of **Potami** with its sand-and-pebble beach.

Skiathos Σκιάθος

postcode 370 02 • pop 4100

The good news is that much of the pine-covered coast of Skiathos is blessed with exquisite beaches of golden sand. The bad news is that in July and August the island is overrun with package tourists and is expensive. Despite the large presence of

EVIA & THE SPORADES

sun-starved northern Europeans, and the ensuing tourist excess, Skiathos is still a pretty island and not surprisingly one of Greece's premier resorts.

The island has only one settlement, the port and capital of Skiathos Town, on the south-east coast. The rest of the south coast is one long chain of holiday villas and hotels. The north coast is precipitous and less accessible. Most people come to the island for the beaches and nightlife, but the truly curious will discover some picturesque walks, hidden valleys and even quiet beaches.

Getting To/From Skiathos

Air As well as the numerous charter flights from northern Europe to Skiathos, during summer there are up to five flights daily to Athens (€56.95). The Olympic Airways office (☎ 2427 022 200) is in Skiathos Town on the right side of Papadiamanti, the main thoroughfare, as you walk inland.

Ferry In summer, there are ferries from Skiathos to Volos (3½ hours, €8, three to four daily), Agios Konstantinos (3½ hours, €9.40, two daily) and Alonnisos (two hours, €5.30, four to six daily) via Glossa

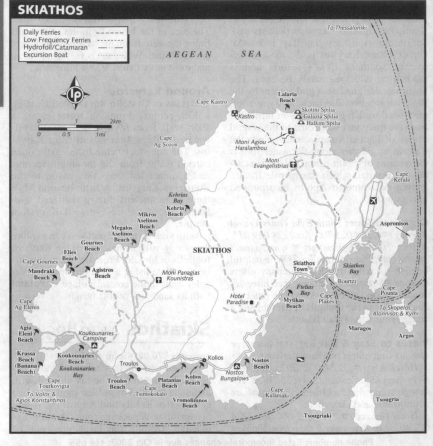

SKIATHOS

Daily Ferries
Low Frequency Ferries
Hydrofoil/Catamaran
Excursion Boat

AEGEAN SEA

To Thessaloniki

Cape Kastro

Kastro

Lalaria Beach

Skotini Spilia
Galazia Spilia
Halkini Spilia

Cape Ag Sozon

Moni Agiou Haralambou

Moni Evangelistrias

Cape Kefala

Kehrias Bay

Kehria Beach

Mikros Aselinos Beach

Megalos Aselinos Beach

Gournes Beach

Elies Beach

Cape Gournes

Mandraki Beach

Agistros Beach

SKIATHOS

Moni Panagias Kounistras

Aspronisos

Skiathos Town

Skiathos Bay

Ftelias Bay

Mytikas Beach

Cape Plakes

Bourtzi

Cape Pounta

Cape Ag Elenis

Hotel Paradise

To Skopelos, Alonnisos & Kymi

Agia Eleni Beach

Koukounaries Camping

Maragos

Argos

Krassa Beach (Banana Beach)

Koukounaries Beach

Koukounaries Bay

Troulos

Kolios

Nostos Beach

Cape Tourkovigia

Troulos Beach

Platanias Beach

Kolios Beach

Nostos Bungalows

To Volos & Agios Konstantinos

Cape Tsimokokalo

Vromolimnos Beach

Cape Kalamaki

Tsougria

Tsougriaki

(Skopelos) and Skopelos Town (1½ hours, €4.10).

From mid June to late September, Minoan Lines has a weekly service north to Thessaloniki (5¾ hours, €13.30), and south to Tinos (7½ hours, €17.60), Mykonos (8½ hours, €18.80), Paros (10 hours, €20), Santorini (13½ hours, €25) and Iraklio (17¾ hours, €30.80). Tickets can be bought from Alkyon Tourist Office (☎ 2427 022 029) at the bottom of Papadiamanti in Skiathos Town. The port police can be contacted on ☎ 2427 022 017.

Hydrofoil In summer, there is a bewildering array of hydrofoils from Skiathos and around the Sporades in general. Among the main services, there are hydrofoils from Skiathos to Volos (1¼ hours, €16.80, three or four daily), and Alonnisos (one hour, €11.20, eight to 10 daily) via Glossa (Skopelos) and Skopelos Town (35 minutes, €8.50). There are also hydrofoils to Agios Konstantinos (1½ hours, €17.10, two or three daily) and Thessaloniki (4½ hours, €26, one daily). There are also services to the Pelion Peninsula and various ports in northern Evia. Hydrofoil tickets may be purchased from Alkyon Tourist Office.

Getting Around Skiathos
Bus Crowded buses leave Skiathos Town for Koukounaries Beach (30 minutes, €0.90) every half-hour between 7.30am and 10.30pm. The buses stop at all the access points to the beaches along the south coast.

Car & Motorcycle Car-hire outlets in Skiathos Town including Alamo (☎ 2427 023 025) and Euronet (☎ 2427 024 410), as well as heaps of motorcycle-hire outlets, are along the town's waterfront.

Excursion Boat Excursion boats travel to most of the south-coast beaches from the old harbour. Trips around the island cost about €13.20 and include a visit to Kastro, Lalaria Beach and the three caves of Halkini Spilia, Skotini Spilia and Galazia Spilia, which are only accessible by boat.

SKIATHOS TOWN
Skiathos Town, with its red-roofed, white-washed houses, is built on two low hills. It is picturesque enough, although it doesn't have the picture-postcard attractiveness of Skopelos or Skyros Towns. The islet of Bourtzi (reached by a causeway) between the two harbours is covered with pine forest. The town is a major tourist centre, with hotels, souvenir shops, travel agents and bars dominating the waterfront and main thoroughfares.

Orientation
The quay is in the middle of the waterfront, just north of Bourtzi Islet. To the right (as you face inland) is the straight, new harbour; to the left, and with more character, is the curving old harbour used by local fishing and excursion boats. The main thoroughfare of Papadiamanti strikes inland from opposite the quay. The central square of Plateia Trion Ierarhon is just back from the middle of the old harbour and has a large church in the middle.

Information
The tourist police office (☎ 2427 023 172), opposite the regular police about halfway along Papadiamanti, next to the high school, operates 8am to 9pm daily during the summer season.

The post office, OTE and National Bank of Greece are all located on Papadiamanti. The bus terminus is at the northern end of the new harbour. There are several ATMs and a couple of automatic exchange machines around town. The Skiathos Internet Centre (☎ 2427 022 021) is at Miaouli 12.

Museum
Skiathos was the birthplace of the well-known Greek short-story writer and poet Alexandros Papadiamantis, as well as the novelist Alexandros Moraïtidis. Papadiamantis' house is now a museum (☎ 2427 023 843, Plateia Papadiamantis; admission €0.90; open 9am-1pm & 5pm-8pm Tues-Sun). It holds a small collection documenting his life.

EVIA & THE SPORADES

Organised Tours

Various local operators run excursion-boat trips around the island. See Getting Around Skiathos.

Places to Stay

Most accommodation is booked solid by package-tour operators from July to the end of August, when prices are often double those of low season. Prices quoted here are for high season. There is a kiosk on the harbourfront with information on room availability. If you're brave enough to arrive during the summer rush, then just about any travel agent will endeavour to fix you up with accommodation. Worth trying is Alkyon Tourist Office (☎ 2427 022 029).

Hotel Karafelas (☎ 2427 021 235, *Papadiamanti 59*) Singles/doubles €29.40/52.80. The pleasant rooms at this hotel have verandas overlooking a small garden and there's a communal kitchen.

Hotel Marlton (☎ 2427 022 552, *Evagelistrias 10*) Singles/doubles/triples €41/50/60. This hotel has well-kept modern rooms with air-con and refrigerators. Some rooms have balconies overlooking a garden.

Hotel Akti (☎ 2427 022 024, fax 2427 022 430) Singles/doubles €41/53, 4-person apartments €88. For a central location with a waterfront views, try this hotel on the new harbour waterfront with pleasant airy rooms.

Places to Eat

Most eateries in Skiathos are geared to the tourist trade and are expensive. Finding some decent cuisine can be a matter of trial and error.

Avra (☎ 2427 021 008) Mains €4.10-5.60. The Avra, one of the swathe of restaurants just down from Plateia Trion Ierarhon, above the old harbour, is one of the bargains of Skiathos. It serves huge helpings of succulent chicken (€4.40), pork (€5) and lamb (€5.60) with french fries and salad.

O Kavouras (☎ 2427 021 094, *Opposite hydrofoil terminal*) Mains €4.70-6. The food here is consistently tasty and reasonably priced. Popular starters are baked potato with butter (€0.60) and crab salad (€3.30); mains include octopus casserole (€5.20) and chicken with okra (€4.70).

Taverna Ouzeri Kabourelia (☎ 2427 021 112) Mains €4.70-7.40. If you're partial to hummus you'll enjoy this delicious version

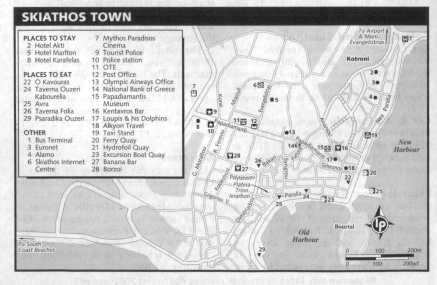

SKIATHOS TOWN

PLACES TO STAY
2 Hotel Akti
5 Hotel Marlton
8 Hotel Karafelas

PLACES TO EAT
22 O Kavouras
24 Taverna Ouzeri Kabourelia
25 Avra
26 Taverna Folia
29 Psaradika Ouzeri

OTHER
1 Bus Terminal
3 Euronet
4 Alamo
6 Skiathos Internet Centre

7 Mythos Paradisos Cinema
9 Tourist Police
10 Police station
11 OTE
12 Post Office
13 Olympic Airways Office
14 National Bank of Greece
15 Papadiamantis Museum
16 Kentavros Bar
17 Loupis & his Dolphins
18 Alkyon Travel
19 Taxi Stand
20 Ferry Quay
21 Hydrofoil Quay
23 Excursion Boat Quay
27 Banana Bar
28 Borzoi

Beaches

Which island has the region's best beaches? It depends a little on what you're after.

If all you want is to spread yourself on the sand then Skiathos is ideal. Its **Koukounaries** beach is probably the nearest you'll get in Greece to the archetypal beach of your south-sea-island dreams. Touted as Greece's best beach, and as the third best in the world by some biased locals, – in August, like most beaches on the south coast, it can seem like a third of the world is actually there. **Agia Eleni** and **Mandraki** are quieter and not as gusty as the meltemi-prone north-coast beaches. Agia Eleni is reputedly ideal for windsurfing. Most south-coast beaches have water sports and **Nostos** has the only diving school in the Sporades. Photographers and snorkellers should head for pebbled Lalaria, which has extraordinary rock formations.

Skopelos' beaches are less picture-postcard-perfect. Many suffer from an identity crisis, not knowing whether to be sand, shingle or pebble, so have patches of all three. **Milia** is a lovely long pebbled beach. Nearby, pebbled **Panormos**, is the only beach with organised water sports. There are quiet coves a short walk to the west. **Limnonari** beach is one of Skopelos' few sandy beaches. Between it and Cape Myti there are secluded coves only accessible on foot. **Velanio** is recommended for snorkelling – and that's not because it's a skinny dippers' beach!

If you don't like the annoying way sand gets into your body's orifices and stubbornly clings there, then **Alonnisos'** beaches are mostly pebbled. The island is recommended for snorkelling; there are no spectacular coral reefs or psychedelic marine life, but thanks to fishing restrictions you will see an abundance of our little finned friends.

Skyros has the splendid **Molos-Magazia** stretch of golden, gently shelving sand, which out of high season is uncrowded. Just north of here there are secluded sandy coves. **Palamari** is another superb, uncrowded sandy beach, and **Atsitsa** is a good spot for snorkelling.

('pea puree' on the menu) costing €2.65 at the Kabourelia, on the old harbour waterfront. The beef stifado (€5.60) and lamb giouvetsi (€5.60) are also highly commendable.

Psaradika Ouzeri (☎ 2427 023 412) Mains €4.10-10. Not surprisingly, as it's next to the fish market, this place at the far end of the old harbour waterfront specialises in fresh fish. If you're on a limited budget then plump for gavros at €4.10 a portion.

Taverna Folia (☎ 2427 023 196) Mains €2.90-5.90. Tables at this taverna are set out in a peaceful tree-shaded alley. Well-prepared hot and cold mezedes are offered and grilled fish, meat and ready-made food. From Plateia Trion Ierarhon, walk along Athan Diakou and follow the signs.

Entertainment

Scan Papadiamanti and Polytehniou (better known as Bar Street) to see which disco or bar takes your fancy.

Banana Bar (☎ 2427 021 232, Polytehniou) In high season this wild bar seethes with UK and Scandinavian tourists indulging in marathon boozing sessions. Give it a miss if you don't like punishingly loud music.

Borzoï (☎ mobile 69-4496 4351, Polytehniou) The Borzoï has an atmospheric stone-walled interior as well as a pretty garden set around an old olive press. Greek, Latin American, jazz, blues and rock is played.

Kentavros Bar (☎ 2427 022 980, Off Plateia Papadiamantis) The long-established Kentavros promises rock, soul, jazz and blues, and gets the thumbs up from locals and expats.

Mythos Paradiso Cinema (☎ 2427 023 975) Entry €5.90. You can catch an English-language movie at this outdoor cinema, signposted from the ring road.

Shopping

Loupos & his Dolphins (☎ 2427 023 777, Plateia Padiamantis) This high-class place sells original icons and very fine ceramics and jewellery.

EVIA & THE SPORADES

AROUND SKIATHOS
Beaches
With some 65 beaches to choose from, beach-hopping on Skiathos can become a full-time occupation. Many are only accessible by caique and the ones that are more easily accessible tend to get crowded.

Buses ply the south coast stopping at the beach access points. The ones nearest town are extremely crowded; the first one worth getting off the bus for is the pine-fringed, long and sandy **Vromolimnos Beach**, which has been awarded an EU blue flag for cleanliness. Farther along, **Platanias** and **Troulos Beaches** are also good but both, alas, are very popular. The bus continues to **Koukounaries Beach**, backed by pine trees and a lagoon and touted as the best beach in Greece. Nowadays it's best viewed at a distance, from where the 1200m long sweep of pale gold sand does indeed look beautiful.

Krassa Beach, at the other side of a narrow headland, is more commonly known as **Banana Beach**, because of its curving shape and soft yellow sand. It is nominally a nudist beach, though the skinny-dippers tend to abscond to **Little Banana Beach** around the corner if things get too crowded.

Agia Eleni Beach, a short walk west of Koukounaries, is reputedly the best beach for windsurfing. All the south-coast beaches have water-skiing and windsurfing outlets, and motorboats are available for hire at Koukounaries Beach.

The north coast's beaches are less crowded but are exposed to the strong summer *meltemi* winds. From Troulos a road heads north to sandy **Megalos Aselinos Beach**. Turn left onto a dirt road to reach this beach. A right fork leads to **Mikros Aselinos Beach** and farther on to **Kehria Beach**, also reachable by a dirt road from nearer Skiathos Town.

Lalaria, on the northern coast, is a striking beach of pale grey, egg-shaped pebbles, much featured in tourist brochures. It is most easily reached by excursion boat from Skiathos Town.

Diving
Dolphin Diving (☎ 2427 021 599, 2427 022 525) Located on Nostos Beach, this is the only diving school in the Sporades. Both the Beginners and Advanced Dives cost €35.30. The Discovery Dive, which explores locations 30m deep, is €44.80.

Kastro Κάστρο
Kastro, perched dramatically on a rocky headland above the north coast, was the fortified pirate-proof capital of the island from 1540 to 1829. It consisted of some 300 houses and 20 churches and the only access was by a drawbridge. Except for two churches, it is now in ruins. Access is by steps, and the views from it are tremendous. Excursion boats come to the beach below Kastro, from where it's an easy clamber up to the ruins.

Moni Evangelistrias
Μονή Ευαγγελίστριας
The 18th-century Moni Evangelistrias is the most appealing of the island's monasteries. It is in a delightful setting, poised above a gorge, 450m above sea level, and surrounded by pine and cypress trees. The monastery, like many in Greece, was a refuge for freedom fighters during the War of Independence, and the islanders claim the first Greek flag was raised here in 1807.

The monastery is an hour's walk from town or you can drive here. It's signposted off the Skiathos Town ring road, close to the turn-off to the airport.

Places to Stay & Eat
Koukounaries Camping (☎/fax 2427 049 250) Adult/tent €5.85/2.95. This excellent site at the eastern end of Koukounaries Beach is the only officially recognised camping ground in the Sporades. It has clean toilets and showers, a minimarket and taverna.

Nostos Bungalows (☎ 2427 022 420, fax 2427 022 525) 2/4-person bungalows €97/181. These gorgeous, stylishly furnished bungalows overlooking Nostos Beach, 5km from Skiathos Town, are in a well-designed complex, with bars, a restaurant, pool and tennis court.

Hotel Paradise (☎ 2427 021 939, fax 2427 023 346) Doubles €100. This smallish hotel is in a tranquil setting surrounded by a pine forest high above the coast, 4km west of Skiathos Town. It has tastefully furnished air-con rooms and a restaurant and bar. If you're driving, look for the hotel sign along the coast road. Otherwise book ahead to arrange a lift from town in the hotel's bus.

Skopelos Σκόπελος

postcode 370 03 • pop 5000

Skopelos is less commercialised than Skiathos, but until recently seemed to be following hot on its trail. However, in recent years locals seem to have become determined to keep the island's traditions and character intact and not succumb to the worst accesses of mass tourism. Skopelos is a beautiful island. It is heavily pine-forested and has vineyards, olive groves and fruit orchards. It is noted for its plums and almonds, which are used in many local dishes.

Like Skiathos, the north-west coast is exposed, with high cliffs. The sheltered southeast coast harbours many beaches but, unlike Skiathos, most are pebbled. There are two large settlements: the capital and main port of Skopelos Town on the east

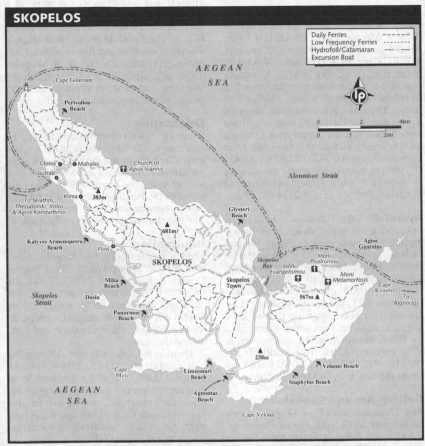

SKOPELOS

Daily Ferries	– – – – –
Low Frequency Ferries	· · · · · · ·
Hydrofoil/Catamaran	– · – · –
Excursion Boat	· · · · · · · ·

AEGEAN SEA

Cape Gourouni

Perivoliou Beach

Glossa • ○ Mahalas

Loutraki •

Church of Agios Ioannis

Klima ▲ 383m

Alonnisos Strait

To Skiathos, Thessaloniki, Volos & Agios Konstantinos

▲ 681m

Glysteri Beach

Kalyves Armenopetra Beach

Flins

SKOPELOS

Agios Georgios

Milia Beach

Skopelos Strait

Dasia

Skopelos Bay

Moni Evangelismou

Moni Prodromou

Moni Metamorfosis

Cape Kiourto

To Alonnisos

Skopelos Town

567m ▲

Panormos Beach

258m ▲

Cape Myti

Limnonari Beach

Velanio Beach

Staphylos Beach

Agnontas Beach

AEGEAN SEA

Cape Velona

EVIA & THE SPORADES

coast; and the lovely, unspoilt hill village of Glossa, the island's second port, 3km north of Loutraki on the west coast.

Skopelos has yielded an exciting archaeological find. In ancient times the island was an important Minoan outpost ruled by Staphylos, who, according to mythology, was the son of Ariadne and Dionysos. *Staphylos* means grape in Greek and the Minoan ruler is said to have introduced wine making to the island. In the 1930s a tomb containing gold treasures, and believed to be that of Staphylos, was unearthed at Staphylos, now a resort.

Getting To/From Skopelos

Ferry In summer there are three ferries daily to Alonnisos from Glossa (1¼ hours, €3.20) and Skopelos Town (30 minutes, €3.20). There are also ferries to Volos (4½ hours, €10, four daily), to Agios Konstantinos (4½ hours, €9.40, two daily) and to Skiathos (1½ hours, €4.40, four or five daily). The times given are from Skopelos Town; from Glossa it's one hour less. Boats from Glossa actually depart from Loutraki, on the coast. Tickets are available from Lemonis Agents (☎ 2424 023 055, fax 2424 023 095) on the waterfront near the old quay in Skopelos Town. The telephone number of Skopelos' port police is ☎ 2424 022 180.

Hydrofoil Like Skiathos, Skopelos is linked to a number of destinations by hydrofoil. The main services during summer include: to Alonnisos (20 minutes, €6.50, eight or nine daily), to Skiathos (one hour, €8.50, 10 to 12 daily), to Volos (2¼ hours, €20.60, five daily), to Agios Konstantinos (2¼ hours, €23.60, three daily) and to Thessaloniki (4½ hours, €26.40, five or six a week). In addition, there are also services to the Pelion Peninsula and to various ports in Evia. Purchase tickets from Kosifis Travel (☎ 2424 022 767, fax 2424 023 608) opposite the new quay in Skopelos Town.

Getting Around Skopelos

Bus There are buses from Skopelos Town all the way to Glossa/Loutraki (one hour, €2.35, eight daily), a further three that go

only as far as Milia (35 minutes, €1.80) and another two that go only as far as Agnontas (15 minutes, €0.80).

Car & Motorcycle There are a fair number of car- and motorcycle-rental outlets in Skopelos Town, mostly at the eastern end of the waterfront. Among them is Motor Tours (☎ 2424 022 986, fax 2424 022 602) next to Hotel Eleni.

SKOPELOS TOWN

Skopelos Town is one of the most captivating towns in the Sporades. It skirts a semicircular bay and clambers in tiers up a hillside, culminating in a ruined fortress. Dozens of churches are interspersed among tall, dazzlingly white houses with brightly shuttered windows and flower-adorned balconies. Traditionally, roofs in Skopelos Town were tiled with beautiful rough-hewn bluestone, but these are gradually being replaced with mass-produced red tiles.

Orientation

Skopelos Town's waterfront is flanked by two quays. The old quay is at the western end of the harbour and the new quay is at the eastern end. All ferries and hydrofoils now use the new quay. From the ferry, turn right to reach the bustling waterfront lined with cafes, souvenir shops and travel agencies. The bus station is to the left of the quay.

Information

There is no tourist office on Skopelos. However, the staff at the privately owned Thalpos Leisure & Services (☎ 2424 022 947, fax 2424 023 057, e thalpos@otenet.gr, w www .holidayislands.com), on the waterfront, are helpful offering a wide range of services, including booking accommodation and tours around the island.

There is no tourist police. The regular police station (☎ 2424 022 235) is above the National Bank. The post office lurks in an obscure alleyway: walk up the road opposite the bus station, take the first left, the first right and the first left and it's on the right. A sign in the middle of the waterfront points inland to the OTE.

The National Bank of Greece is on the waterfront near the old quay; it has an ATM. To reach Skopelos' self-service laundrette go up the street opposite the bus station, turn right at Platanos Taverna and it's on the left.

You can check your email at the Click & Surf Café (☎ 2424 023 093), one block back from the waterfront.

Things to See & Do

Strolling around town and sitting at the waterside cafes will probably be your chief occupations in Skopelos Town, but there is also a small **folk art museum** (☎ 2424 023 494, Hatzistamati; admission free; open 7am-10pm daily). At the time of writing, it was closed but should re-open in 2002.

Places to Stay

Skopelos Town is still a place where you have a good chance of renting a room in a family house, and people with rooms to offer meet the ferries and hydrofoils. There are no camping grounds on the island.

The Rooms & Apartments Association of Skopelos (☎ 2424 024 567), on the waterfront near the old quay, might be a good starting point.

EVIA & THE SPORADES

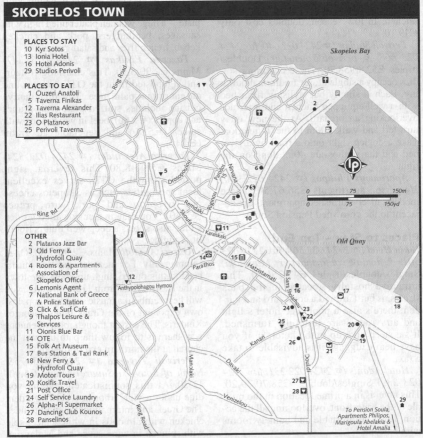

SKOPELOS TOWN

PLACES TO STAY
10 Kyr Sotos
13 Ionia Hotel
16 Hotel Adonis
29 Studios Perivoli

PLACES TO EAT
1 Ouzeri Anatoli
5 Taverna Finikas
12 Taverna Alexander
22 Ilias Restaurant
23 O Platanos
25 Perivoli Taverna

OTHER
2 Platanos Jazz Bar
3 Old Ferry & Hydrofoil Quay
4 Rooms & Apartments Association of Skopelos Office
6 Lemonis Agent
7 National Bank of Greece & Police Station
8 Click & Surf Café
9 Thalpos Leisure & Services
11 Oionis Blue Bar
14 OTE
15 Folk Art Museum
17 Bus Station & Taxi Rank
18 New Ferry & Hydrofoil Quay
19 Motor Tours
20 Kosifis Travel
21 Post Office
24 Self Service Laundry
26 Alpha-Pi Supermarket
27 Dancing Club Kounos
28 Panselinos

Skopelos Bay

Ring Road

Drosopoulou

Nirvana

Pandora

Reginou

Remdaki

Stoufa

Karaiskaki

Ring Rd

Parathos

Anthypolohagou Hymou

Old Quay

Ilia Sara Sheldihou

Hatzistamati

Manjaki

Ring Road

Kanari

Dakai

Gouldi

Venizelou

To Pension Soula, Apartments Philipos, Marigoula Abelakia & Hotel Amalia

0   75   150m
0   75   150yd

Places to Stay – Budget

Pension Soula (☎ *2424 022 930)* Doubles/
triples with bath €38.20/50. This welcoming place, in a large garden in a quiet part
of town, has attractive, modern rooms.
Turn left at the new quay and at Hotel
Amalia turn left again and after 200m bear
right.

Places to Stay – Mid-Range

Kyr Sotos (☎ *2424 022 549, fax 2424 023
668)* Doubles/triples €52.80/63.40. The delightful and popular rooms at this characterful pension in the middle of the waterfront
have wooden floors and ceilings. There's a
little courtyard and well-equipped communal
kitchen. In low season, doubles cost only
€19.10.

Perivoli Studios (☎ *2424 022 640, fax 2424
023 668,* e *perivoli@otenet.gr)* Doubles/
triples €52.80/58.70. These charming studios occupy a single-storey traditional building. Each is simply but stylishly furnished
with a well-equipped kitchen and a terrace
overlooking an orchard. At the new quay
turn left and walk 300m to the T-junction.
Take a dogleg right onto a road by a river
bed and the studios are 40m along on the
right.

Apartments Philipos (☎ *2424 022 930)*
2/4-person apartments €56/67.50. These
modern, nicely furnished apartments are adjacent to the co-owned Pension Soula.

Places to Stay – Top End

Ionia Hotel (☎ *2424 022 568, fax 2424 023
301,* e *ionia@vol.forthnet.gr, Manolaki)*
Singles/doubles/triples €47/76/ 90. This
attractive hostelry, located in the back
streets, is built around a courtyard and garden; there's also a pool. The hotel's light
and airy rooms are tastefully furnished.
It's a steep hike up to the hotel, so if you
have heavy luggage it is advisable to take
a taxi.

Hotel Adonis (☎ *2424 022 231, fax 2424
023 239)* Singles/doubles €58.70/79.20.
This hotel is in a prime location in the middle of the waterfront, overlooking all the action. It has comfortable and homely rooms
with balconies.

Places to Eat

At the restaurants on Skopelos the quality is
somewhat better than that on Skiathos. Several are on or near Tria Platania, known locally as Souvlaki Square.

O Platanos (☎ *2424 023 067, Souvlaki
Square)* Mains €5.60-10.30. Just back from
the bus station this popular place has tables
beneath a large plane tree. A mixed
mezedes for two is €21.15 and mixed souvlaki special is €10.30.

Ilias Restaurant (☎ *2424 023 971, Souvlaki Square)* Mains €5.90-14.70. The Ilias
offers a wide variety of mezedes; grills, however, are its speciality. If you're feeling glut-
tonous then plump for the 'variety of meat
plate' – a huge wooden platter piled high with
sausages, beefburgers, pork and chicken
kebab, french fries and salad garnish.

Taverna Finikas (☎ *2424 023 247)*
Mains €2.90-5.90. This charming restaurant, signposted from the OTE, is set round
an enormous palm tree. The imaginative
cuisine includes stuffed pork with prunes
and apples (€5.60), beef in wine sauce with
spices (€5.90) and vegetable au gratin
(€4.40).

Taverna Alexander (☎ *2424 022 324)*
Mains €5.90-8.80 This taverna, signposted from the OTE, serves excellent
local specialities such as Skopelos cheese
pie, *tyropitta* and pork with prunes
(€7.30). You dine in a cosy walled garden
which also sports a deep well that is floodlit at night.

Ouzeri Anatoli Mains €2.90-7.30. Open
summer only. For mezedes and live music,
head to this ouzeri, high up above the town
in the Kastro. Here from 11pm onwards, you
will hear rembetika music sung by Skopelos'
own exponent of the Greek blues, Georgos
Xindaris. The easiest though most strenuous
way there is to follow the path up past the
church at the northern end of the quay.

Perivoli Taverna (☎ *2424 023 758,
North of Souvlaki Square)* Mains €5.90-
11.20. At this sophisticated taverna you
dine under a vine arbor in a pretty garden.
The Greek and international menu includes
chicken with almonds in white sauce, sole
with spinach in wine sauce and Malaysian

chicken with soya sauce (all €7.35). The menu also includes vegetarian dishes and there's a good selection of Greek wines.

Alpha-Pi supermarket (Doulidi) This is a well-stocked supermarket, just inland from the bus station.

Entertainment

Oionos Blue Bar (☎ 2424 023 731, Near OTE) This cool little bar offers jazz, blues, soul and ethnic music. It serves 17 beers, 25 malt whiskies and a wide range of cocktails.

Platanos Jazz Bar (☎ 2424 023 661, Opposite old quay) You can hear jazz, blues and Latin American music at this long-established atmospheric place. It's open all day and serves breakfast on its shady terrace – an ideal place to recover from a hangover.

For more lively entertainment there is a strip of clubs along Doulidi, just off Souvlaki Square. Each attracts its own age group; poke your nose in to see if you fit in.

Panselinos (☎ 2424 024 488, Doulidi) If you would like to hear some live rembetika then this is the place to head for.

Dancing Club Kounos (☎ 2424 023 623, Doulidi) The DJ spins house, acid, and hard rock at this hot spot. Some Greek music is also played.

GLOSSA Γλώσσα

Glossa, Skopelos' other major settlement, is another whitewashed delight and is also considerably quieter than the capital. It has managed to retain the feel of a pristine Greek village.

The bus stops in front of a large church at a T-junction. As you face the church, the left road winds down to Loutraki and the right to the main thoroughfare of Agiou Riginou. Along here you'll find a bank and a few small stores.

Skopelos' beaches are just as accessible by bus from Glossa as they are from Skopelos Town; Milia, the island's best beach, is actually closer to Glossa. There are also places to stay and tavernas at Loutraki, but there's not a lot to do other than hang around, eat, sleep and drink since the narrow pebble beach is not so inviting.

Places to Stay & Eat

Hotel Atlantes (☎ 2424 033 223, Opposite bus stop) Singles/doubles €29.40/50. This pleasant hotel was closed for renovation at the time of writing, but is scheduled to re-open in 2002.

Rooms Kerasia (☎ 2424 033 373) Doubles €41. This modern place, in a tranquil setting, has clean, well-maintained rooms with balconies. Just before you enter Glossa from Skopelos Town turn left down a narrow road to reach the rooms.

Glossa also has a few other rooms in private houses – inquire at *kafeneia*.

Agnanti Taverna & Bar (☎ 2424 033 076, Agiou Riginou) Mains €4.50-8.20. It's worth a trip to Glossa just to eat at this taverna, where local produce is used to create imaginative and delectable food. Herb fritters (€3.50) are just one of the many delicious starters. The mains also offer plenty of choice with such offerings as goat with artichokes (€7.90) and chicken with okra (€5.30). There are superb views over to Evia from the taverna's roof terrace.

AROUND SKOPELOS
Monasteries

Skopelos has many monasteries, several of which can be visited on a scenic, although quite strenuous, one-day trek from Skopelos Town. Facing inland from the waterfront, turn left and follow the road which skirts the bay and then climbs inland (signposted 'Hotel Aegeon'). Continue beyond the hotel and you will come to a fork. Take the left fork for the 18th-century **Moni Evangelismou** (now a convent). From here there are breathtaking views of Skopelos Town, 4km away. The monastery's prize piece is a beautiful and ornately carved and gilded iconostasis in which there is an 11th-century icon of the Virgin Mary.

The right fork leads to the uninhabited 16th-century **Moni Metamorfosis**, the island's oldest monastery. From here the track continues to the 18th-century **Moni Prodromou** (now a nunnery), 8km from Skopelos Town.

EVIA & THE SPORADES

Walking Tours

There is a useful English-language walking guide to Skopelos called *Skopelos Trails* by Heather Parsons (☎ 2424 024 022, W www.skopelos.net/walks). It costs €11.15 and is available in waterfront stores.

Heather also leads guided walks. Her evening walk to Panormos Beach (€10) is very popular as you finish off the four-hour hike with a swim and a meal.

Beaches

Skopelos' beaches are mostly pebbled, and almost all are on the sheltered south-west and west coasts. All the buses stop at the beginning of paths which lead down to them. The first beach along is the crowded sand-and-pebble **Staphylos Beach**, 4km south-east from Skopelos Town. From the eastern end of the beach a path leads over a small headland to the quieter **Velanio Beach**, the island's official nudist beach. **Agnontas**, 3km west of Staphylos, has a small pebble beach and from here caiques sail to the superior and sandy **Limnonari Beach**, in a sheltered bay flanked by rocky outcrops.

From Agnontas the road cuts inland through pine forests before re-emerging at the sheltered and steeply shelving **Panormos Beach**. This is the only beach which has organised water sports. The next beach along, **Milia**, is considered the island's best – a long swathe of tiny pebbles.

Places to Stay & Eat

There are hotels and domatia at Staphylos, Limnonari, Panormos and Milia.

Limnonari Rooms (☎ 2424 023 046, e lemonisk@otenet.gr, Behind Limnonari Beach) Doubles €55.70. This domatia, in a peaceful setting, has airy, nicely furnished rooms. There is a well-equipped communal kitchen and a large terrace.

Taverna Pefkos (☎ 2424 022 080, Overlooking Staphylos Beach) Mains €2.90-7.30. This welcoming taverna serves tasty traditional Greek dishes and pastas. There are romantic views from its terrace when there is a full moon.

Taverna Pavlos (☎ 2424 022 409) Mains €2.90-5.90. Reputedly the best of the three

waterside tavernas at Agnontas, the Pavlos specialises in fish. Sardines are €14.70 and red mullet is €38.10 a kilogram.

Alonnisos
Αλόννησος

postcode 370 05 • pop 3000

Alonnisos is still a serene island despite having been ferreted out by 'high-quality' package-tour companies. Package tourism would no doubt have taken off in a bigger way had the airport (erroneously and optimistically shown on island maps) materialised. This project was begun in the mid-1980s, but the rocks of Alonnisos proved unyielding and the politics Byzantine, making the construction of a runway impossible.

Alonnisos once had a flourishing wine industry, but in 1950 the vines were struck with the disease phylloxera and, robbed of their livelihood, many islanders moved away. Fate struck another cruel blow in 1965 when a violent earthquake destroyed the hill-top capital of Alonnisos Town (now called Old Alonnisos, Hora or Palio Horio). The inhabitants abandoned their hill-top homes and were subsequently re-housed in hastily assembled concrete dwellings at Patitiri. In recent years many of the derelict houses in the capital have been bought for a song from the government and renovated by British and German settlers. There is now a flourishing expat artist community, several of whom reside here year-round.

Alonnisos is a green island with pine and oak trees, mastic and arbutus bushes, and fruit trees. The west coast is mostly precipitous cliffs but the east coast is speckled with pebbled beaches. The water around Alonnisos has been declared a marine park, and is the cleanest in the Aegean. Every house has a cesspit, so no sewage enters the sea.

Getting To/From Alonnisos

Ferry There are ferries to Volos (five hours, €11.50, two or three daily), four to five daily to both Skopelos Town (30 minutes, €3.20) and Skiathos (two hours, €5.60), and one daily to Agios Konstantinos (5½ hours, €13.30). Tickets can be purchased from Alonnisos Travel (☎ 2424 065 198, fax 2424 065 511) in Patitiri. The port police (☎ 2424 065 595) are on the quayside at Patitiri.

Hydrofoil As with Skiathos and Skopelos, there are a lot of connections in summer. The more important ones include up to five daily to Volos (2½ hours, €22.60), eight or nine daily to both Skopelos Town (20 minutes, €6.50) and Skiathos (40 minutes, €11.20), two or three daily to Agios Konstantinos (2½ hours, €26.40), and one daily to Thessaloniki (4½ hours, €25.50).

In addition, there are also services to the Pelion Peninsula and various ports in Evia. Tickets may be purchased from Ikos Travel (☎ 2424 065 320, fax 2424 065 321), opposite the quay in Patitiri.

Getting Around Alonnisos
Bus In summer, Alonnisos' one bus plies more or less hourly between Patitiri (from opposite the quay) and Old Alonnisos

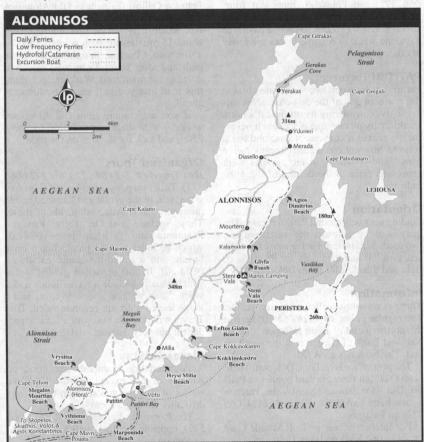

ALONNISOS

Daily Ferries	– – – – –
Low Frequency Ferries	· · · · · ·
Hydrofoil/Catamaran	––––––
Excursion Boat	· · · · · · · ·

0   2   4km
0   1   2mi

AEGEAN SEA

Cape Gerakas

Pelagonisos Strait

Gerakas Cove

Yerakas

Cape Gregali

▲ 316m

Ydoneri

Merada

Diasello

Cape Paliofanaro

Cape Kalami

ALONNISOS

LEHOUSA

▲ Agios Dimitrios Beach

▲ 180m

Mourtero

Cape Maistra

Kalamakia

Glyfa Mouth

Steni Vala ☐ Ikaros Camping

▲ 348m

Steni Vala Beach

Vasilikos Bay

PERISTERA

▲ 260m

Megali Ammos Bay

Alonnisos Strait

Leftos Gialos Beach

Milia

Cape Kokkinokastro

Kokkinokastro Beach

Vrysitsa Beach

Hrysi Milia Beach

Cape Telion
Megalos Mourtias Beach

Old Alonnisos (Hora)

Patitiri

Votsi

Patitiri Bay

To Skopelos, Skiathos, Volos & Agios Konstantinos

Vythisma Beach

Cape Mavri Pounta

Marpounda Beach

AEGEAN SEA

EVIA & THE SPORADES

Phone numbers listed incorporate changes due in Oct 2002; see p55

(€0.90). There is also a service to Steni Vala from Old Alonnisos via Patitiri (€1).

Motorcycle There are several motorcycle-hire outlets on Pelasgon, in Patitiri. Be wary when taking the tracks off the main trans-island road down to the island's beaches since some of these tracks are steep and slippery.

Boat The easiest way to get to the east coast beaches is by the taxi boats that leave from the quay in Patitiri every morning.

Patitiri Travel (☎ 2424 065 154, fax 2424 066 277), on Pelasgon, rents out four-person 15-horsepower motor boats. The cost is €52.85/132/293.50 for one day/three days/one week in August. Prices are lower at other times.

PATITIRI Πατητήρι

Patitiri sits between two sandstone cliffs at the southern end of the east coast. Not surprisingly, considering its origins, it's not a traditionally picturesque place, but it nevertheless makes a convenient base and has a relaxed atmosphere. Patitiri means 'wine press' and is where, in fact, grapes were processed prior to the demise of the wine industry.

Orientation
Finding your way around Patitiri is easy. The quay is in the centre of the waterfront and two roads lead inland. Facing away from the sea, turn left and then right for Pelasgon or right and then left for Ikion Dolopon.

Information
There is no tourist office or tourist police. The regular police (☎ 2424 065 205) are at the northern end of Ikion Dolopon and the National Bank of Greece is at the southern end. The bank has an ATM.

The post office is on Ikion Dolopon. There is no OTE but there are card phones in Patitiri, Old Alonnisos and Steni Vala. There is a laundrette called Gardenia (☎ 2424 065 831) on Pelasgon.

For Internet access go to Il Monde Café (☎ 2424 065 834) on Ikion Dolopon.

Walks
There are many walking opportunities on Alonnisos and the best walks are gradually being waymarked. At the bus terminal in Old Alonnisos a notice board details some of the walks.

The English-language *Alonnisos on Foot: A Walking & Swimming Guide* by Bente Keller & Elias Tsoukanas (€8.20) describes a number of interesting walks. It can be bought at Ikos Travel and local bookshops.

From Patitiri to Old Alonnisos a delightful path winds through shrubbery and orchards. Walk up Pelasgon and, 80m beyond Pension Galini, the path to Old Alonnisos starts. After 10 minutes turn right at a water tap, which may not be functioning. After about 15 minutes the path is intersected by a dirt road. Continue straight ahead on the path and after about 25 minutes you will come to the main road. Walk straight along this road and you will see Old Alonnisos ahead.

If you are coming from Old Alonnisos walk down the main road to Patitiri for about 350m and look for the sign on the right.

Organised Tours
Ikos Travel (☎ 2424 065 320, fax 2424 065 321) This company offers several excursions; talk to the genial and knowledgeable manager, Pakis Athanasiou, about these. They include one to Kyra Panagia, Psathoura and Peristera islets (€41.0) which includes a good picnic lunch on a beach, and a round-the-island excursion (€35.20). It also organises guided walks which usually include a picnic lunch and a swim. Stout walking shoes, trousers and a long-sleeved shirt are recommended. Ikos Travel will provide you with a locally produced, but very detailed, walking map.

Places to Stay
Accommodation standards are good on Alonnisos and, except for the first two weeks of August, you shouldn't have any difficulty finding a room.

The Rooms to Let service (☎ 2424 065 577), opposite the quay, will help you find a room on any part of the island.

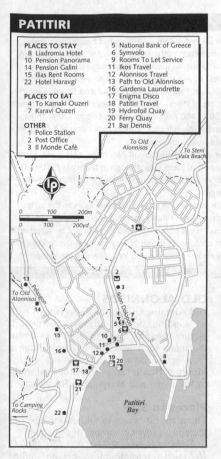

PATITIRI

PLACES TO STAY
8   Liadromia Hotel
10 Pension Panorama
14 Pension Galini
15 Ilias Rent Rooms
22 Hotel Haravgi

PLACES TO EAT
4   To Kamaki Ouzeri
7   Karavi Ouzeri

OTHER
1   Police Station
2   Post Office
3   Il Monde Cafè

5   National Bank of Greece
6   Symvolo
9   Rooms To Let Service
11 Ikos Travel
12 Alonnisos Travel
13 Path to Old Alonnisos
16 Gardenia Laundrette
17 Enigma Disco
18 Patitiri Travel
19 Hydrofoil Quay
20 Ferry Quay
21 Bar Dennis

To Old
Alonnisos

To Steni
Vala Beach

0   100   200m
0   100   200yd

To Old
Alonnisos

To Camping
Rocks

Patitiri
Bay

EVIA & THE SPORADES

The pleasant rooms and studios here are very clean. The rooms have a communal kitchen with kettle and sink, and the studios have a well-equipped kitchen area.

Pension Galini (☎ 2424 065 573, fax 2424 065 094, Pelasgon) Singles/doubles/5-person/6-person apartments €35.30/41/52.80/64.50. This pension, on the left 400m up Pelasgon, has beautifully furnished blue, white and yellow rooms and a fine flower-festooned terrace.

Places to Stay – Mid-Range

Liadromia Hotel (☎ 2424 065 521, fax 2424 065 096, e liadromia@alonnisos.com) Doubles €50, triple studios €70.40. This impeccably maintained hotel was the first to open in Patitiri. The attractive rooms are full of character with stucco walls, hand-embroidered curtains, stone floors and traditional carved-wood furniture. Walk inland up Ikion Dolopon and take the first turn right up the steps, follow the path around and the hotel is on the left.

Hotel Haravgi (☎ 2424 065 090, fax 2424 065 189) Singles/doubles/triples with breakfast €41/52.80/64.50, double/triple studios €52.80/64.50. This hotel has modern rooms and there is a peaceful communal terrace overlooking the sea. To reach the hotel, turn left at the port and beyond the waterfront tavernas take the steps up to the right. At the top turn right to reach the hotel.

Places to Eat

Greek-island-hopping gourmets should definitely include Alonnisos on their 'must visit' lists as it has some top-notch eateries. Weight-watchers should, however, scrutinise menus carefully as many dishes contain liberal amounts of cream.

To Kamaki Ouzeri (☎ 2424 065 245, Ikion Dolopon) Mains €4.40-5.90. Mezedes are the speciality of this little ouzeri although the mains are also commendable. Among the delicious offerings are chickpea puree (€2.90) and cuttlefish in green sauce (€4.40).

Karavi Ouzeri (☎ 2424 066 100, Opposite National Bank) Mains €4.40-7.30. This superlative ouzeri has a delectable choice of

Places to Stay – Budget

Pension Panorama (☎ 2424 065 240, fax 2424 065 598) 3 person studios/family apartments €41/70.40. The highly commendable Panorama has well-equipped studios and apartments in a sparkling white, blue-shuttered building high above the harbour. The owner, Eleni Athanasiou, often meets the incoming boats. Take the first left off Ikion Dolopon and follow the path upwards until you see the rooms on your right.

Ilias Rent Rooms (☎ 2424 065 451, fax 2424 065 972, Pelasgon 27) Doubles/2-person/3-person studios €29.40/41/44.80.

Alonnisos Marine Park

The National Marine Park of Alonnisos – Northern Sporades is an ambitious but belatedly conceived project begun in May 1992. Its prime aim was the protection of the endangered Mediterranean monk seal, but also the preservation of other rare plant and animal species threatened with extinction.

The park is divided into two zones. Zone B, west of Alonnisos, is the less accessible of the two areas and comprises the islets of Kyra Panagia, Gioura, Psathoura, Skantzoura and Piperi. Restrictions on activities apply on all islands and in the case of Piperi, visitors are banned, since the island is home to around 33 species of bird, including 350 to 400 pairs of Eleanora's falcon. Other threatened sea birds found on Piperi include the shag and Audouin's gull. Visitors may approach other islands with private vessels or on day trips organised from Alonnisos.

Zone A comprises Alonnisos Island itself and the island of Peristera off Alonnisos' east coast. Most nautical visitors base themselves here at the yacht port of Steni Vala, though in theory the little harbour of Yerakas in the north of the island could serve as a base, though there are no facilities whatsoever. Restrictions on activities here are less stringent.

For the casual visitor the Alonnisos Marine Park is somewhat inaccessible since tours to the various islands are fairly limited and run during summer only. Bear in mind also that the park exists for the protection of marine animals and not for the entertainment of human visitors, so do not be surprised if you see very few animals at all. In a country not noted in its recent history for long-sightedness in the protection of its fauna, the Alonnisos Marine Park is a welcome and long-overdue innovation.

---

mezedes and mains. There is cheese pie (€0.90), mussel pilaf (€5.90), chicken filled with bacon, chilli peppers, cream and cheese (€5.90) and many other delectable dishes to choose from.

The waterfront restaurants are all much of a muchness – take your pick and hope for the best.

Entertainment

Symvolo Bar (☎ 2424 066 156) You can enjoy jazz, blues, funk and rock at the Symvolo, two doors down from the National Bank. The atmospheric interior is a medley of traditional north African and Greek furniture and decorations. Cocktails include the lethal Rusty Nail (whisky and Drambuie) and the gentler Alexander (cognac, milk and cinnamon).

Bar Dennis (☎ 2424 065 569) This long-established bar on the southern waterfront is open all day and plays jazz, blues and Greek music. As well as alcoholic beverages and coffees it serves luscious ice cream.

Enigma Disco (☎ 2424 065 333, Pelasgon) Enigma rocks to teenybopper tunes when the tourist season kicks in.

OLD ALONNISOS

Old Alonnisos (Hora or Palio Horio) with its winding stepped alleys is a tranquil, picturesque place with lovely views. From the main road just outside the village a path leads down to pebbled Megalos Mourtias Beach and other paths lead south to Vythisma and Marpounda Beaches.

Places to Stay

There are no hotels in Old Alonnisos, but there is a growing number of domatia.

Fadasia House (☎ 2424 065 186, Plateia Hristou) Singles/doubles/2-person studios €23.50/35.30/44.80. This good-value place, near the central square, has attractive modern rooms and most have wood-raftered ceilings. The studios have a sink, refrigerator and hot plates.

Rooms & Studios Hiliadromia (☎/fax 2424 065 814, Plateia Hristou) Doubles/2-person studios €35.30/44.80. The attractive rooms at the Hiliadromia have white stucco walls and stone floors. The studios have well-equipped kitchens and some have good sea views.

Konstantina Studios (☎ 2424 065 900, fax 2424 066 165, postal address: Alonnisos,

North Sporades, Greece 370 05) This accommodation is the most luxurious in Old Alonnisos. It comprises spacious, traditionally furnished 2-/3-person studios with well-equipped kitchens and marble bathrooms; all with balconies with sea views. There is a garden with a barbecue for guests' use. Prices depend on the time of year and length of stay. For more information contact the proprietor, Konstantina Vlakou.

Places to Eat

Taverna Aloni (☎ 2424 065 550, Near bus terminal) Mains €4.10-5.30. At the Aloni you can tuck into good traditional taverna food while enjoying the superb sea views from its terrace.

Nappo (☎ 2424 065 579) Mains €5-6.20. The Italian owner, Paolo, serves up top-rate pizzas at this restaurant, signposted from the main street.

Astrofengia (☎ 2424 065 182) Mains €5.30-11.70. This sophisticated restaurant, signposted from the bus terminal, offers exquisite mezedes such as hummus (€0.60) and rosti made with baked potato, bacon and cream (€3.50). The equally stimulating mains include vegetarian cannelloni (€5.90), beef and beer casserole (€7.30) and ostrich stroganoff (€11.70). Tempting desserts are on offer too (all €2.34).

Paraport Taverna (☎ 2424 065 608, main street) Mains €5-8.80. This taverna features some unusual and delicious items on its menu. Paraport pie (made from bacon, cheese and peppers) is €4.40 and seafood risotto is €4.70.

AROUND ALONNISOS

Most of Alonnisos' beaches are on the east coast which also means they avoid the strong summer meltemi winds and the flotsam that gets dumped on the west coast beaches. Apart from the road from Patitiri to Old Alonnisos, the only road is one which goes north to the tip of the island. It is driveable and sealed all the way though the last settlement, Yerakas (19km), is a bit of a let-down when you get there. Dirt tracks lead off to the beaches. Another sealed road leads to the yacht port of Steni Vala and a little farther as far as Kalamakia.

The first beach is the gently shelving **Hrysi Milia Beach**, which is the best beach for children. The next one up is **Kokkinokastro**, a beach of red pebbles. This is the site of the ancient city of Ikos (once the capital); there are remains of city walls and a necropolis under the sea.

Steni Vala is a small fishing village with a permanent population of 30 and good beach nearby. There are three tavernas and 30-odd rooms in *domatia*, as well as *Ikaros Camping* (☎ 2424 065 258). This is a small camping ground, but it is right on the beach and has reasonable shade from olive trees. Try *Taverna Steni Vala* (☎ 2424 065 590) for both food and lodgings. Mind you don't trip over the posing yachties; they're thick on the ground.

Kalamakia, 3km farther north, has a good beach, rooms and tavernas. **Agios Dimitrios Beach**, farther up still, is an unofficial nudist beach. There are no organised water sports on Alonnisos.

ISLETS AROUND ALONNISOS

Alonnisos is surrounded by eight uninhabited islets, all of which have rich flora and fauna. The largest remaining population of the monk seal *(Monachus monachus)*, a Mediterranean sea mammal faced with extinction, lives in the waters around the Sporades. These factors were the incentive behind the formation of the **marine park** in 1983, which encompasses the sea and islets around Alonnisos. Its research station is on Alonnisos, near Gerakas Cove. See the boxed text 'Alonnisos Marine Park'.

Piperi, to the north-east of Alonnisos, is a refuge for the monk seal and it is forbidden to set foot there without a licence to carry out research.

Also north-east of Alonnisos, **Gioura** has many rare plants and a rare species of wild goat. **Kyra Panagia** has good beaches and two abandoned monasteries. **Psathoura** has the submerged remains of an ancient city and the brightest lighthouse in the Aegean.

Peristera, just off Alonnisos' east coast, has several sandy beaches and the remains

EVIA & THE SPORADES

of a castle. **Lehousa** sits immediately north-west of here.

Skantzoura, to the south-east of Alonnisos, is the habitat of falcons and the rare Aegean seagull. The eighth islet is tiny **Adelphi**, between Peristera and Skantzoura.

Skyros Σκύρος

postcode 340 07 • pop 2800

Skyros is some distance from the rest of the group and differs topographically. Almost bisected, its northern half has rolling, culti-vated hills and pine forests, but the largely uninhabited south is barren and rocky. It is less visited by tourists than other islands of the Sporades, and with the demise in 2000 of the hydrofoil link with the other Sporades and Volos this trend will probably continue. A number of expats, particularly English and Dutch, have made Skyros their home.

There are only two settlements of any worth on the island: the small port of Linaria, and Skyros Town, the capital, 10km away on the east coast. Skyros is visited by poseurs rather than package tourists – and as

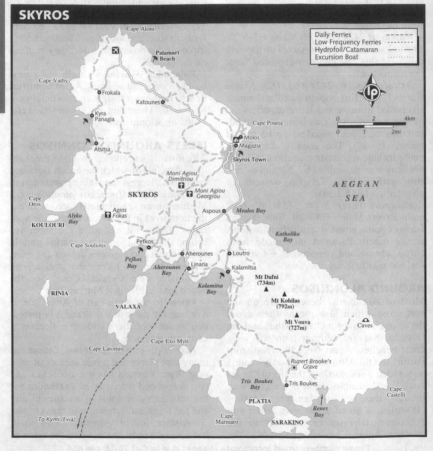

SKYROS

Daily Ferries
Low Frequency Ferries
Hydrofoil/Catamaran
Excursion Boat

Cape Aloni
Palamari Beach
Cape Vathy
Frokala
Katounes
Kyra Panagia
Atsitsa
Cape Pouria
Molos
Magazia
Skyros Town
Moni Agiou Dimitriou
Cape Oros
SKYROS
Moni Agiou Georgiou
Agios Fokas
Alyko Bay
KOULOURI
Aspous
Mealos Bay
AEGEAN SEA
Cape Souliotis
Pefkos
Katholiko Bay
Pefkos Bay
Aherounes
Loutro
Aherounes Bay
Linaria
Kalamitsa
RINIA
Kalamitsa Bay
Mt Dafni (734m)
VALAXA
Mt Kohilas (792m)
Mt Vouva (727m)
Caves
Cape Latomio
Cape Exo Myti
Rupert Brooke's Grave
Tris Boukes Bay
Tris Boukes
To Kymi (Evia)
PLATIA
Cape Marmaro
Renes Bay
SARAKINO
Cape Castelli

many of these are wealthy young Athenians as foreigners. Skyros also has quite a different atmosphere from other islands in this region, reminding you more of the Cyclades than the Sporades, especially the stark, cubist architecture of Skyros Town.

Some visitors come to Skyros to attend courses at the Skyros Centre, a centre for holistic health and fitness. See the Skyros Town section for details. Solo women travellers are increasingly drawn to Skyros because of its reputation as a safe, hassle-free island.

Skyros' factual history was mundane in comparison to its mythological origins until Byzantine times, when rogues and criminals from the mainland were exiled on Skyros. Rather than driving away invading pirates, these opportunistic exiles entered into a mutually lucrative collaboration with them.

The exiles became the elite of Skyrian society, furnishing and decorating their houses with elaborately hand-carved furniture, plates and copper ornaments from Europe, the Middle East and East Asia. Some of these items were brought by seafarers and some were looted by pirates from merchant ships.

Those people on the island before the mainland exiles arrived soon began to emulate the elite in their choice of decor, so local artisans cashed in by making copies of the furniture and plates, a tradition which continues to this day. Almost every Skyrian house is festooned with plates, copperware and hand-carved furniture.

Other traditions also endure. Many elderly Skyrian males still dress in the traditional baggy pantaloons and *trohadia* (multi-thonged footwear unique to the island). The Skyros Lenten Carnival is Greece's weirdest and most wonderful festival, and is the subject of Joy Koulentianou's book *The Goat Dance of Skyros*. See the 'Skyros Carnival' boxed text.

Another special feature of Skyros which shouldn't go unmentioned, although it will probably go unseen, is the wild Skyrian pony, a breed unique to Skyros. The ponies used to roam freely but are now almost extinct. The only ones you are likely to see are tame ones kept as domestic pets.

Skyros Carnival

In this pre-Lenten festival, which takes place on the last two Sundays before *Kathara Deftera* (Clean Monday – the first Monday in Lent), young men don goat masks, hairy jackets and dozens of copper goat bells. They then proceed to clank and dance around town, each with a partner (another man), dressed up as a Skyrian bride but also wearing a goat mask. Women and children also wear fancy dress. During these revelries there is singing and dancing, performances of plays, recitations of satirical poems and drinking and feasting. These riotous goings-on are overtly pagan, with elements of Dionysian festivals, goat worship (in ancient times Skyros was renowned for its excellent goat meat and milk), and the cult of Achilles, the principal deity worshipped here. The transvestism evident in the carnival may derive from the fact that Achilles hid on Skyros dressed as a girl to escape the oracle's prophecy that he would die in battle at Troy.

Finally, Skyros was the last port of call for the English poet Rupert Brooke (1887–1915), who died of septicaemia at the age of 28 on a ship off the coast of Skyros in 1915, en route to Gallipoli.

Getting To/From Skyros

Air In summer there are only two flights weekly (Wednesday and Sunday) between Athens and Skyros (50 minutes, €47). It is rumoured that a private air service will eventually supplement Olympic's severely reduced schedule. For tickets see Skyros Travel Agency, in Skyros Town.

Ferry There are ferry services at least twice daily in summer, provided by F/B *Lykomidis*, between the port of Kymi (Evia) and Skyros (two hours, €7.10). You can buy ferry tickets from Lykomidis Ticket Office (☎ 2222 091 789, fax 2222 091 791), on Agoras in Skyros Town. There is also a ferry ticket office at Linaria.

Skyros Travel Agency also sells tickets for the Kymi-Athens bus (3¼ hours, €8.60) which meets the ferry on arrival at Kymi.

EVIA & THE SPORADES

Getting Around Skyros

In addition to the options listed here, it is also possible to join a boat trip to sites around the island. See Organised Tours under the Skyros Town entry.

Bus In high season there are five buses daily from Skyros Town to Linaria (€0.70) and Molos (via Magazia). Buses for both Skyros Town and Molos meet the boats at Linaria. However, outside of high season there are only two buses to Linaria (to coincide with the ferry arrivals) and none to Molos. Bus services to Kalamitsa, Pefkos and Atsitsa are organised on an ad hoc basis during summer. Contact Skyros Travel for full details.

Car & Motorcycle Cars and 4WD vehicles can be rented from Skyros Travel Agency. A car goes for between €38.20 and €41 and a 4WD from €44.80 to €55.80. Motorcycles can be rented from Motorbikes (☎ 2222 092 022). To find it, walk north and take the first turn right past Skyros Travel.

SKYROS TOWN

Skyros' capital is a striking, dazzlingly white town of flat-roofed Cycladic-style houses draped over a high rocky bluff, topped by a 13th-century fortress and the monastery of Agios Georgios. It is a gem of a place and a wander around its labyrinthine, whitewashed streets will probably produce an invitation to admire a traditional Skyrian house by its proud and hospitable owner.

Orientation

The bus terminal is at the southern end of town on the main thoroughfare of Agoras, an animated street lined with tavernas, snack bars and grocery shops, and flanked by narrow winding alleyways. To reach the central square of Plateia Iroön walk straight ahead up the hill.

Beyond Plateia Iroön, Agoras forks, with the right fork leading up to the fortress and Moni Agiou Georgiou (with fine frescoes), from where there are breathtaking views. The left fork leads to Plateia Rupert Brooke, dominated by a disconcerting bronze statue of a nude Rupert Brooke. The frankness of

the statue caused an outcry among the islanders when it was first installed in the 1930s. From this square a cobbled, stepped path leads in 15 minutes to Magazia Beach.

Information

Skyros does not have an EOT or tourist police, but you can find most information from Skyros Travel Agency (☎ 2222 091 600, fax 2222 092 123, e skyrostravel@hol.gr) on Agoras, including room bookings. To get to the regular police (☎ 2222 091 274) take the first right after Skyros Travel Agency, and turn right at the T-junction.

The National Bank of Greece is on Agoras next to the central square. It sports an ATM. Foreign-language newspapers and magazines can be bought at an agency opposite the bank.

The post office is on the west side of the central square. The OTE is opposite the police station. Internet access is available from 9am to 11pm at Mepoh Café Bar on Agoras.

Things to See & Do

Skyros Town has two museums. The **archaeological museum** (☎ 2222 091 327, Near Plateia Rupert Brooke; admission €1.50; open 8.30am-3pm Tues-Sun) features an impressive collection of artefacts from Mycenaean to Roman times, as well as a traditional Skyrian house interior, transported in its entirety from the home of the benefactor.

The **Faltaïts Museum** (☎ 2222 091 232, Near Plateia Rupert Brooke; admission €1.50; open 10am-1pm & 5.30pm-8pm daily) is a private museum housing the outstanding collection of a Skyrian ethnologist, Manos Faltaïts. The collection includes costumes, furniture, books, ceramics and photographs.

The English co-owner of Mepoh Café Bar (see Information), Janet Smith, is a Reiki Master and, at the time of writing, planned to open a **Reiki Centre** (☎ 2222 029 039, e janetinskyros@hotmail.com) opposite the cafe.

The versatile Niko Sikkes (☎ 2222 092 707 or 2222 092 158) leads **walking tours** around Skyros. He also gives **talks** on the traditions and culture of Skyros (in Dutch and English) at the Faltaïts Museum. For more information phone him or call at his shop, the Argos.

Courses

Skyros Centre (*☎ 020-7267 4424, fax 7284 3063, e skyros@easynet.co.uk, 92 Prince of Wales Rd, London NW5 3NE, UK*) This centre runs courses on a whole range of subjects, from yoga and dancing, to massage and windsurfing. The emphasis is on developing a holistic approach to life. There is a branch in Skyros Town, but the main 'outdoor' complex is at Atsitsa Beach, on the west coast. For detailed information on its fortnightly programs contact the Skyros Centre.

Kristina's Cooking School Course A$600 (€319.90) In the off season, Australian and long-term Skyros resident Kristina Brooks-Tsalapatani of Kristina's at Pegasus (see Places to Eat) runs this cooking school. Her Greek cookery course runs over five mornings, teaching a maximum of eight nascent gastronomes all about cooking Greek-style. Bookings are essential.

Organised Tours

Skyros Travel Agency (*☎ 2222 091 600, fax 2222 092 123*) This agency runs a boat excursion (€16.15) to Sarakino Islet and the Pendckali and Gerania sea caves.

Places to Stay

Accommodation in Skyros Town is usually in the form of rooms, often decorated with traditional plates, in family houses. Since these can be hard to find yourself, you will often be met at the bus stop with offers of domatia from the women who run them. It's not a bad idea to take up one of these offers, at least for starters. Prices should be in the €22.40 to €34 range for a double, though as elsewhere there are seasonal fluctuations.

Failing that, head for Skyros Travel Agency (see Information) for references to suitable rooms.

Hotel Elena (*☎ 2222 091 738, 091 070*) Singles/doubles €11.70/23.50, singles/doubles/triples with bath €15/30/35.20. This aged hotel has clean rooms and most have a refrigerator and a balcony. From the bus terminal walk north and take the first right.

SKYROS TOWN

PLACES TO STAY		8	Kalypso
32	Hotel Elena	9	Neoptolemos
34	Hotel Nefeli	10	Pharmacy
35	Styriana Spitia	14	Skyros Travel Agency
		16	Motorbikes
PLACES TO EAT		17	Moni Agiou Georgiou
4	Anemos Cafè & Ouzeri	18	Fortress
		19	Police Station
11	O Pappous kai Ego	20	OTE
12	Margetis	21	Lykomidis Ticket Office
13	Kristina's at Pegasus	22	Reiki Centre
15	Liakos Cafè & Restaurant	23	Mepoh Cafè Bar
		24	National Bank of Greece
OTHER		25	Foreign Language Agency
1	Faltaïts Museum	26	Iroön
2	Plateia Rupert Brooke	27	Kata Lathos
		28	Taxi Rank
3	Archaeological Museum	29	Plateia Iroön
5	Skyros Centre	30	Apokalypsis
6	Argo Shop	31	Post Office
7	Skyros Shop	33	Bus Stop

0   50   100m
0   50   100yd

To Magazia Beach

Vardali   Melagoni

Kamara

Sirivli   Kohilia

Path to Magazia Beach

Krokos

Lalares   17

Korentis   18

Maheras

See Enlargement

Kondili   32

To Kristina's Restaurant & Pension Nikolas

23 21
22
30
31 24 25
29 26
28 27

0   25   50m
0   25   50yd

35
34
To Linaria & Stone Club

EVIA & THE SPORADES

Pension Nikolas (☎ *2222 091 778, fax 2222 093 400)* Rooms €44.80-58.70. This pension has attractive, well-maintained rooms and is a good option for visitors wanting a quiet place to stay. From the bus terminal walk back towards Linaria for 50m and where the main road veers left, continue straight ahead and uphill following the signs.

Hotel Nefeli & Skyriana Spitia Studios (☎ *2222 091 964, fax 2222 092 061)* Singles/doubles/3-person studios €50/62/79. The Nefeli has lovely rooms with old photographs depicting traditional Skyrian life. It sports a large swimming pool. The hotel is on the left just before you enter Skyros Town. The adjoining studios are well equipped and furnished in traditional Skyrian style.

Places to Eat

In recent times good restaurants in Skyros have proliferated like mushrooms in a dark cellar.

O Pappous kai Ego (☎ *2222 093 200, Agoras)* Mains €4.70-7.30. This popular place with a stylish interior serves unusual mezedes such as mushrooms with cream (€3.20) and squid with aniseed; tasty mains include chicken in wine (€4.70) and pork in soya sauce (€7.30).

Margetis (☎ *2222 091 311, Agoras)* Mains €8.80-17.60. This is the place to go for fresh fish. Other restaurants sell fish but Margetis specialises in it. Red mullet and sea bream are €30.10 a kilogram.

Kristina's at Pegasus (☎ *2222 091 897)* Mains €4.70-6.50. Open Mon-Sat. This long-established place, signposted from the central square, was something of a gastronomic trail blazer on Skyros. Kristina conjures up delectable Greek and international dishes using local produce. The *kaseri* and *sac* cheeses (local specialities), chicken fricassee and cheesecake are highly recommended. Mains include a vegetarian mixed plate (€4.70). Dining is on a relaxing little terrace.

Liakos Café & Restaurant (☎ *2222 093 509)* Mains €5.60-8.20. During the day you can have a drink or meal in the Liakos' serene interior where botanical prints grace the walls. In the evening most people prefer to sit out on the roof terrace. The imaginative menu includes fava (€2.60), aubergines stuffed with feta (€2.90), rice with mussels and tomato sauce (€5.90) and chicken with yoghurt (€5.40). Turn right after Skyros Travel Agency.

Anemos Cafe & Ouzeri (☎ *2222 092 822, Near Plateia Rupert Brooke)* Mains €4.10-7.30. At Anemos you can enjoy a relaxing drink, snack or main meal on a romantic terrace overlooking Magazia. Among the interesting mezedes offered are cuttlefish with spinach (€4.70) and the intriguing-sounding vegetarian aphrodisiac (€3.80). There's an equally creative range of main dishes and desserts, and the wines include regional favourites from all over Greece.

Entertainment

Nightlife centres around the bars on Athinos, all of which are tastefully decorated. One gets the impression neither the locals or expats would tolerate tackiness. There's always some place open all year due to the large transient population of young soldiers.

Kata Lathos (☎ *2222 091 671, Opposite central square)* Popular with a young crowd, this bar which has a roof garden plays rock, jazz and blues.

Apokalypsis (*mobile 69-7238 7599, Next to post office)* This place gets top marks for its stylish interior. The evening kicks in with soul, followed by hits from the 60s and 70s, and finishes off in the wee hours with Greek music.

Iröon (☎ *2222 093 122, Opposite central square)* This bar is another favourite with the young crowd; it belts out rock, soul and funk.

Kalypso (☎ *2222 092 160)* The farther north you go along Agoras the more mellow the sounds. At the classy little Kalypso, where Agoras forks, mostly jazz and blues is played.

Neoptolemos (☎ *2222 092 484, Next to Kalypso)* Like its neighbour, this pleasant bar is one of the quieter ones. As well as breakfasts, coffees and juices, it offers 70 different cocktails.

Mepoh Café Bar (☎ *2222 091 016, Agoras)* When the computers shut down at the

Mepoh everyone gets down to the serious business of drinking and listening to an eclectic range of music.

Stone *(☎ 2222 092 355)* Skyros has three discos. Stone, just south of Skyros Town, was the 'in' disco at the time of writing.

Kavos Bar *(☎ 2222 093 213)* Kavos, at Linaria, is a popular spot for drinks and evening gossip. Try to be here when the Lykomidis ferry comes in and witness the impressive sound when Richard Strauss' *Also Sprach Zarathustra* is blasted out over the bay from huge speakers. Better still, listen out for it while on the ferry – the sound is better.

MAGAZIA & MOLOS
Μαγαζιά & Μώλος

The resort of Magazia is at the southern end of a splendid, long sandy beach, a short distance north of Skyros Town; quieter Molos is at the northern end of the beach. Although the two are contiguous, Magazia is a compact and attractive place of winding alleys, whereas, with the exception of its windmill and the adjacent rock-hewn Church of Agios Nikolaos, the town of Molos is a characterless, spread-out development.

Places to Stay – Budget & Mid-Range

Skyros Camping *(☎ 2222 092 458)* Adult/tent €4.40/4.40. In Magazia, opposite the steps up to Skyros Town, is this camping ground, Skyros' only one. It's unofficial and rather run-down, with thirsty-looking olive trees offering shade.

Ferogia Domatia *(☎ 2222 091 828, Magazia)* Singles/doubles/triples/4-person apartment €23.50/35.30/41/58.70. These spotless rooms, on the beach, have pleasant modern furniture, refrigerators and balconies. The apartment is beautifully furnished and contains lovely antique Skyrian ceramics displayed on carved-wood shelves.

To Perigiali *(☎ 2222 091 889, fax 2222 092 770, ⓔ perigiali@skyrosnet.gr)* Singles/doubles/2/4-person studios €44.80/50/52.80/64.50. These well-equipped and attractive studios near the southern end of Magazia Beach are surrounded by a beautiful garden.

Diadameia Domatia *(☎ 2222 092 008, fax 2222 092 009, Near Skyros Camping)* Doubles/triples €55.70/64.70. These spacious and beautifully furnished rooms above the family ceramics shop in Magazia have air-con and a refrigerator.

Hotel Paradise *(☎ 2222 091 220/560, fax 2222 091 443, next to bus terminal)* Doubles/triples €58.70/73.50. This pleasant Molos hotel has rooms with cream marble floors and white walls. Each room has air-con, refrigerator and TV.

Places to Stay – Top End

Skyros Palace *(☎ 2222 091 994, fax 2222 092 070)* Doubles/triples €60/74.80. This is the island's most luxurious hotel. It's a complex of tasteful apartments, north of Molos. Each apartment has air-con, verandas and music channels. The complex has a cafe, bar, restaurant, TV lounge and swimming pool, and is 50m from a good beach. Mosquitoes can be a problem: ask for a mosquito zapper.

Places to Eat

Stefanos *(☎ 2222 091 272)* Mains €3.50-7.30. This restaurant has a great location overlooking Magazia Beach, at the southern end. A range of ready-made food and grilled meat and fish is offered.

Tou Thoma to Magazi *(☎ 2222 091 903)* At this taverna on the beach at Molos the freshness of the fish is guaranteed as it's caught by the owner's father, a local fisherman. A portion of the restaurant's lobster and spaghetti is €14.70 and red mullet is €20.50 a kilogram.

Anemomilos Ouzeri & Bar *(☎ 2222 093 373)* Mains €3.80-7.30. In a splendid setting at Molos' 19th-century windmill near the little rock-hewn Church of Agios Nikalaos, the Anemomilos serves well-prepared food during the day, and in the evening metamorphoses into a lively bar. Mezedes include fava (€2.60), squid (€2.60) and calamari (€3.50); chicken souvlaki (€5.30) and shrimps in tomato sauce (€7.30) feature in the mains.

Shopping

Diadameia Ceramic Shop (☎ 2222 92 008) A good selection of Skyrian ceramics is on sale at this shop in Magazi below the domatia of the same name.

Skyros Shop It's hard to imagine any non-Skyrian wanting to wear the multi-thonged *trohadia*, except maybe a foot fetishist who is into bondage. They can be bought at this shop on the street leading to Plateia Rupert Brooke.

Argo Shop (☎ 2222 92 158, Opposite Skyros Shop) This shop, owned by expat Dutchman, Niko Sikkes, sells high-quality copies of ceramics from the Faltaïts Museum.

Woodcarvings are a classy buy, though they can be expensive. There are several *workshops* scattered round town.

AROUND SKYROS
Beaches

At **Atsitsa**, on the west coast, there's a tranquil pebble beach shaded by pines. The beach attracts freelance campers, and there's the main outdoor centre of the Skyros Centre and a *taverna* with domatia here. Just to the north is the even less crowded beach of **Kyra Panagia** (also with freelance campers).

At **Pefkos**, 10km south-east of Atsitsa, there is another good but small beach and a taverna. If you don't have transport take a Skyros Town-Linaria bus and ask to be let off at the turn-off. It's a 3km walk from there to the beach. Farther east, the pebble-

and-sand beach at **Kalamitsa** is reasonable but not really worth the extra effort to get there and there is not much shade. There are no organised water sports on Skyros.

Palamari, near the airport, is a long stretch of sandy beach which does not get crowded.

Rupert Brooke's Grave

Rupert Brooke's well-tended grave is in a quiet olive grove just inland from Tris Boukes Bay in the south of the island. The actual grave is poorly marked with a rough wooden sign in Greek on the roadside, but you can hardly miss it. The gravestone is inscribed with some verses of Brooke's among which is the following apt epitaph:

> If I should die think only this of me:
> That there's some corner of a foreign field
> That is forever England.

No buses go to this corner of the island. However, you can take an excursion boat to Sarakino Islet, or drive or walk along a good, graded scenic road from Kalamitsa, built for the Greek navy, which now has a naval station on Tris Boukes Bay.

If you walk it will take about 1½ hours; take food and water. If you have come this far with the aim of getting to the sea, you will have to turn back since the area farther down the hill is restricted by the Greek navy and the road onwards is closed.

Ionian Islands Τα Επτάνησα

The Ionian group, known in Greek as the Heptanisa or 'the Seven Islands', consists of seven main islands anchored in the Ionian Sea: Corfu, Paxi, Kefallonia, Zakynthos, Ithaki, Lefkada and Kythira (the last is more accessible from the Peloponnese). The islands differ from other island groups – they're more reminiscent of Corfu's neighbour Italy, not least in light, and their colours are mellow and green compared with the stark, dazzling brightness of the Aegean.

These islands receive a lot of rain (Corfu has the nation's highest rainfall) and, consequently, the vegetation, with the exception of the more exposed Kythira, is more luxuriant. Overall, vegetation combines elements of the tropical with forests that could be northern European: Exotic orchids as well as wildflowers emerge below spring snowlines, and eucalypts and acacias share soil with plane, oak and maple trees. The islands do not experience the *meltemi*, and as a result they can be extremely hot in summer.

The culture and cuisine of each Ionian island is unique and differs from the Aegean islands and Crete. Influences from Mediterranean Europe and Britain have also been stronger, yet have developed with special individuality on each island.

For information on this region on the Internet, see |W| www.ionianislands.gr.

SUGGESTED ITINERARIES
One week
Northern Ionians Spend two days in Corfu Town; explore the narrow streets of the old town and visit the museums. Visit Durrell territory in the pretty north-east coast. Spend one night in Paleokastritsa or Lakones; see the sights of the area, and have a meal at one of the restaurants on the Lakones-Makrades road. Spend a day at a west-coast resort and catch a sunset at Pelekas, or head to the unspoilt Diapondia Islands. Spend one or two nights on Paxi, and be sure to visit Antipaxi.

Southern Ionians Spend a couple of days on Lefkada, explore the capital and relax on a west-coast beach, plus visit Meganisi on a day trip or overnight there. Spend two days on Ithaki, visiting

Highlights

- Wandering the narrow streets of Corfu's old town and admiring the fine Venetian buildings
- Walking the ancient olive groves of Paxi and swimming in the crystal-clear water of Antipaxi
- Travelling the dramatic west coast of Lefkada, with its incredible beaches and exquisite blue water
- Exploring the traditional, unspoilt villages and fine pebble beaches of Meganisi
- Unwinding on the beautiful white-sand beach of Myrtos in Kefallonia with a bottle of the island's unique Robola white wine
- Relaxing in the picturesque fishing villages of Frikes and Kioni on Ithaki, Odysseus' homeland
- Visiting the tranquil inland villages of Kythira, and swimming at the island's lovely undeveloped beaches

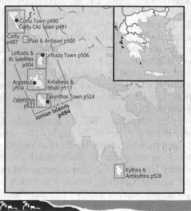

IONIAN ISLANDS

Vathy and the villages of Anogi, Frikes and Kioni. Have two days in Fiskardo on Kefallonia (in the high season stay elsewhere and visit on a day trip), to see Assos village and Myrtos Beach. Spend one day in Sami to visit the nearby caves and Antisamos Beach, or a day in Argostoli.

Two weeks
Combine the above itineraries, but allow an extra
day for travel between the two island groups.

HISTORY & MYTHOLOGY

The origin of the name Ionian is obscure but
is thought to derive from the goddess Io.
Yet another of Zeus' paramours, Io, while
fleeing the wrath of a jealous Hera (in the
shape of a heifer), happened to pass through
the waters now known as the Ionian Sea.

If we are to believe Homer, the islands
were important during Mycenaean times;
however, no magnificent palaces or even
modest villages from that period have been
revealed, although Mycenaean tombs have
been unearthed. Ancient history lies buried
beneath tonnes of earthquake rubble –
seismic activity has been constant on all
Ionian islands, including Kythira.

According to Homer, Odysseus' kingdom consisted not only of Ithaca (Ithaki)
but also encompassed Kefallonia, Zakynthos and Lefkada. Ithaca has long been controversial. Classicists and archaeologists in
the 19th century concluded that Homer's
Ithaca was modern Ithaki, his Sami was
Sami on Kefallonia, and his Zakynthos was
today's Zakynthos, which sounded credi-
ble. But in the early 20th century German
archaeologist Wilhelm Dorpfeld put a span-
ner in the works by claiming that Lefkada
was ancient Ithaca, modern Ithaki was ancient Sami and Kefallonia was ancient
Doulichion. His theories have now fallen
from favour with everyone except the
people of Lefkada.

By the 8th century BC, the Ionian islands
were in the clutches of the mighty city-state
of Corinth, which regarded them as stepping
stones on the route to Sicily and Italy. A
century later, Corfu staged a successful revolt against Corinth, which was allied to
Sparta, and became an ally of Sparta's arch-
enemy, Athens. This alliance provoked
Sparta into challenging Athens, thus precip-
itating the Peloponnesian Wars (431–404
BC). The wars left Corfu depleted, as they
did all participants, and Corfu became little
more than a staging post for whoever happened to be holding sway in Greece. By the

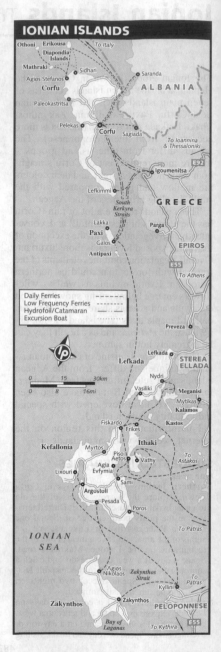

IONIAN ISLANDS

Daily Ferries
Low Frequency Ferries
Hydrofoil/Catamaran
Excursion Boat

0   15   30km
0   8   16mi

end of the 3rd century BC, Corfu, along with the other Ionian islands, had become Roman. Following the decline of the Roman Empire, the islands saw the usual waves of invaders that Greece suffered. After the fall of Constantinople, the islands became Venetian.

Corfu was never part of the Ottoman Empire. Paxi, Kefallonia, Zakynthos, Ithaki and Kythira were variously occupied by the Turks, but the Venetians held them longest. The exception was Lefkada, which was Turkish for 200 years. The Ionian islands fared better under the Venetians than their counterparts in the Cyclades.

Venice fell to Napoleon in 1797. Two years later, under the Treaty of Campo Formio, the Ionian islands were allotted to France. In 1799 Russian forces wrested the islands from Napoleon, but by 1807 they were his again. By then, the all-powerful British couldn't resist meddling. As a result, in 1815, after Napoleon's downfall, the islands became a British protectorate under the jurisdiction of a series of Lord High Commissioners.

British rule was oppressive but, on a more positive note, the British constructed roads, bridges, schools and hospitals, established trade links and developed agriculture and industry. However, the nationalistic fervour in the rest of Greece soon reached the Ionian islands. A call for *enosis* (political union with Greece) was realised in 1864 when Britain relinquished the islands to Greece. In WWII the Italians invaded Corfu as part of Mussolini's plan to resurrect the mighty Roman Empire. Italy surrendered to the Allies in September 1943 and, in revenge, the Germans massacred thousands of Italians who had occupied the island. The Germans also sent some 5000 Corfiot Jews to Auschwitz.

A severe earthquake shook the Ionian islands in 1953. It did considerable damage, particularly on Zakynthos, Kefallonia and Ithaki.

GETTING TO/FROM THE IONIANS
Air
Corfu, Kefallonia, Zakynthos and Kythira have airports; Lefkada has no airport but Aktion airport, near Preveza on the mainland, is a 30-minute bus journey away. All these airports have frequent flights to/from Athens. See W www.olympic-airways.gr for information.

Many charter flights come from northern Europe and the UK to Corfu, and Kefallonia, Zakynthos and Aktion also receive such tourist flights.

Bus
Buses run between Corfu and both Athens and Thessaloniki, and between Athens and Paxi, Kefallonia and Zakynthos. Lefkada is joined to the mainland by a causeway and can be reached by bus from Athens as well as Patras. Buses from Athens to Corfu, Lefkada, Kefallonia and Zakynthos depart from the intercity bus terminal at Kifissou 100, 7km north-west of Omonia.

See W www.ktel.org for limited schedule details.

Ferry – Domestic
The Peloponnese has several departure ports for the Ionian islands: Patras for ferries to Kefallonia, Ithaki, Paxi and Corfu; Kyllini for ferries to Kefallonia and Zakynthos; and Piraeus, Kalamata, Neapoli and Gythio for Kythira, which is also connected with Crete (Kastelli-Kissamos) by ferry. Epiros has one port, Igoumenitsa, for Corfu and Paxi; and Sterea Ellada has one, Astakos, for Ithaki and Kefallonia (although this service is limited to the high season). There are numerous Internet sites offering information on ferry timetables; among the best is W www.ferries.gr.

The following table gives an overall view of the available scheduled domestic ferries to this island group from mainland ports in high season. Further details and inter-island links can be found under each island entry.

Ferry – International
From Corfu, ferries depart for Brindisi, Bari, Ancona, Trieste and Venice in Italy. At least three times weekly in summer, a ferry goes from Kefallonia to Brindisi via Igoumenitsa and Corfu. In July and August this ferry also calls at Zakynthos and Paxi.

From Corfu it's also possible to catch a ferry to Albania.

Ferry Connections to the Ionian Islands

origin	destination	duration (hours)	price (€)	frequency
Astakos	Piso Aetos (Ithaki)	2¾	5.00	1 daily
Gythio	Diakofti (Kythira)	2½	7.05	3 weekly
Igoumenitsa	Corfu Town	1¾	4.10	up to 14 daily
Igoumenitsa	Lefkimmi (Corfu)	1	2.50	6 daily
Igoumenitsa	Gaïos (Paxi)	1¾	5.00	1 daily
Kyllini	Zakynthos Town	1¼	4.40	up to 7 daily
Kyllini	Argostoli (Kefallonia)	2¾	8.80	2 daily
Kyllini	Poros (Kefallonia)	1½	6.20	2 daily
Neapoli	Agia Pelagia (Kythira)	1	5.90	2-3 daily
Patras	Corfu Town	7	17.90	1 daily
Patras	Sami (Kefallonia)	2½	10.00	2 daily
Patras	Vathy (Ithaki)	3½	10.90	2 daily
Piraeus	Diakofti	6½	16.50	2 weekly
Sagiada	Corfu Town	¾	3.80	1 weekly

Hydrofoil

There are a few useful hydrofoil services between the mainland and the Ionians. Between May and September there is a triangular service linking Igoumenitsa, Corfu and Paxi. From June to August a fast service links Kythira with Piraeus (usually via a few ports in the eastern Peloponnese).

Corfu & the Diapondia Islands

postcode 491 00 • pop 111,040
Corfu is the second-largest and greenest Ionian island, and also the best known. In Greek, the island's name is Kerkyra. It was Homer's 'beautiful and rich land', and Odysseus' last stop on his journey home. Shakespeare reputedly used it as a background for *The Tempest*. In the 20th century, the Durrells, among others, extolled its virtues.

With its beguiling landscape of vibrant wildflowers and slender cypress trees rising out of shimmering olive groves, Corfu is considered by many as Greece's most beautiful island. With the highest rainfall, it's also the nation's major vegetable garden and produces scores of herbs, and the mountain air is heavily scented.

There's a lot of information about Corfu on the Internet, but surprisingly we've yet to find the definitive site offering all the information you'll need, as exists for the other Ionian islands.

Getting To/From Corfu

Air Corfu has at least three Olympic Airways flights to/from Athens daily (€84), and three flights a week to/from Thessaloniki (€73.40). The Olympic Airways office (☎ 2661 038 694) is at Polyla 11, Corfu Town.

Aegean Air (☎ 2661 027 100) has two or three flights daily between Athens and Corfu for a similar price. Aegean Air's office is at the airport.

Bus KTEL buses run two or three times daily between Corfu Town and Athens (11 hours, €26.70) – some services go via Lefkimmi in the island's south. There is also a service once or twice daily to/from Thessaloniki (nine hours, €25.70); for both destinations budget an additional €3 for the ferry between Corfu and the mainland. Tickets must be bought in advance; Corfu's KTEL long-distance bus station and ticket office is on Avramiou, inland from the new port.

Ferry – Domestic Hourly ferries run between Corfu and Igoumenitsa (1¾ hours,

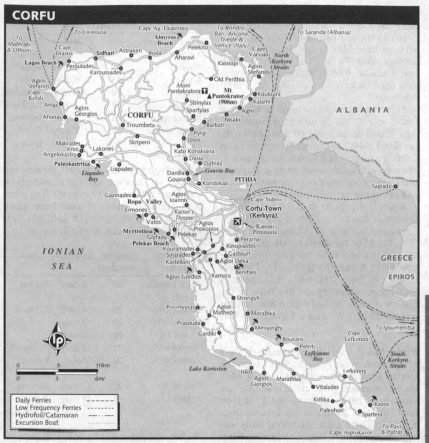

CORFU

€4.10). Every Friday a ferry goes to Sagiada on the mainland (45 minutes, €3.80). Car ferries go to Paxi (3½ hours, €8.80) four times weekly, via Igoumenitsa (but the hydrofoil is more frequent, faster and not much more expensive). You can travel to Patras on one of the frequent international ferries that call at Corfu in summer. Corfu's port police can be contacted on ☎ 2661 032 655.

There are also half a dozen ferries daily between Lefkimmi in the island's south and Igoumenitsa (one hour, €2.50). Lefkimmi's port police are on ☎ 2662 023 277.

Ferry – International Corfu is on the Patras-Igoumenitsa ferry route to Italy (Brindisi, Bari, Ancona, Trieste, Venice), though some ferries originate in Igoumenitsa. Ferries go a few times daily to Brindisi (seven hours, €42 to €48 depending on the company), and in summer usually once daily to Bari (10 hours, €45), Ancona (14 hours, €64.60), Trieste (21 hours, €70.50) and Venice (30 hours, €64.60). See also the Igoumenitsa Getting There & Away section in the Northern Greece chapter and the Patras Getting There & Away section in the Peloponnese chapter.

Phone numbers listed incorporate changes due in Oct 2002; see p55

Italian Ferries and Ventouris Ferries operate high-speed catamaran services between Corfu and Brindisi. There are daily services from May to mid-September. The journey takes 3¼ hours and fares are €56 in low season, €65 in high season (passengers aged under 26 are eligible for a 20% discount).

Shipping agencies selling tickets are found mostly on Xenofondos Stratigou. Alsi Travel & Shipping (☎ 2661 080 030, fax 2661 044 148), directly across from Corfu's new port at Ethnikis Antistaseos 1, can help with information on most shipping lines – the assortment of companies, routes and prices can get confusing!

Much less popular than the Italy-bound ferries is the twice-daily ferry between Corfu and Saranda in Albania (one hour, €11.80). Most travellers to Albania need a visa, so it's best to investigate this before you leave home. Alternatively, Petrakis Lines (☎ 2661 031 649), Eleftherious Venizelou, offers regular day trips to the historical areas around Agiou Saranda for around €52.80. No visa is required for this trip.

Hydrofoil Petrakis Lines operates a fleet of passenger-only hydrofoils between Corfu, Igoumenitsa and Paxi from May until September. There are at least two services daily between Corfu and Paxi (one hour direct or 1¾ hours via Igoumenitsa, €11.20). There's one hydrofoil daily except Monday from Corfu to Igoumenitsa, and four weekly from Igoumenitsa to Corfu.

Getting Around Corfu

To/From the Airport There is no bus service between Corfu Town and the airport. Bus Nos 6 and 10 from Plateia San Rocco in Corfu Town stop on the main road 500m from the airport (en route to Benitses and Ahillion).

Bus Destinations of KTEL buses (green-and-cream) from Corfu Town's long-distance bus station (☎ 2661 030 627), on Avramiou, are as follows:

destination	duration (minutes)	frequency	via
Agios Gordios	40	5 daily	Sinarades
Agios Stefanos	90	3 daily	Sidhari
Aharavi	90	4 daily	Roda
Glyfada	45	6 daily	Vatos
Kavos	90	10 daily	Lefkimmi
Loutses	75	2 daily	Kassiopi
Messonghi	45	3 daily	Benitses
Paleokastritsa	45	7 daily	Gouvia
Pyrgi	30	7 daily	Ipsos

Fares range from €1 to €2.80. Sunday and holiday services are reduced considerably, and some routes don't run at all. The numbers and destinations of local buses (dark blue) from the bus station (☎ 2661 031 595) at Plateia San Rocco, Corfu Town, are:

destination (bus no)	duration (minutes)	frequency	via
Agios Ioannis (11)	30	7 daily	Pelekas
Ahillion (10)	20	6 daily	Gastouri
Aqualand (8)	20	12 daily	
Kanoni (2)	20	half-hourly	
Kastellani (5)	25	13 daily	Kourmades
Kontokali (7)	30	half-hourly	Gouvia & Dasia
Perama (6)	30	13 daily	Benitses
Potamos (4)	45	11 daily	Evroupoli & Tembloni

Tickets are either €0.50 or €0.70 depending on the length of journey, and can be bought on board or from the booth on Plateia San Rocco.

Car & Motorcycle Car and motorbike rental places are plentiful in Corfu Town and in most of the resort towns on the island. There are numerous agencies opposite the old and new ports in Corfu Town, plus most travel agencies will be able to organise a vehicle for you. It's worth shopping around to get a good deal.

Car-hire companies in Corfu Town include Sunrise (☎ 2661 026 511), Ethnikis Antistasis 16, and Sixt (☎ 2661 044 017),

A village clings to the side of a hill on Lesvos, North-Eastern Aegean Islands.

Attack of the wild white pelican, Skala Kallonis, Lesvos

Wildflowers, Lesvos

Beaches all to yourself, Ikaria

Taking in the views from near Angelokastro, Corfu

Century old olive groves, Paxi

Tower of St Spyridon, Corfu

Lively waterfront of Vasiliki village on Lefkada island

Eleftheriou Venizelou 22. Budget (☎ 2661 028 590) and Europcar (☎ 2661 046 931) share an office at Eleftheriou Venizelou 32.

Easy Rider (☎ 2661 043 026), Eleftheriou Venizelou 50 (at the new port), rents scooters and motorbikes.

CORFU TOWN
pop 36,000

The island's capital, Corfu Town (Kerkyra), is built on a promontory. It's a gracious medley of many occupying influences, which never included the Turks. The Spianada (Esplanade) is green, gardened and boasts Greece's only cricket ground, a legacy of the British. The Liston, a row of arcaded buildings flanking the north-western side of the Spianada, was built during the French occupation and modelled on Paris' Rue de Rivoli. The buildings function as upmarket cafes, lamplit by night. Georgian mansions and Byzantine churches complete the picture. The Venetian influence prevails, particularly in the old town, wedged between two fortresses. Narrow alleyways of 18th-century shuttered tenements in muted ochres and pinks are more reminiscent of Venice or Naples than Greece.

Orientation

The town is separated into northern and southern sections. The old town is in the northern section between the Spianada and the New Fortress to the west. The Old Fortress is east of here and projects out to sea, cut off from the town by a moat. The southern section is the new town.

The old port is north of the old town, and the new port is west. Between them is the hulking New Fortress. The long-distance bus station is off Avramiou, inland from the new port. The local bus station is on Plateia San Rocco. Local buses serve the town and nearby villages.

Information

Tourist Offices Corfu's EOT office (☎ 2661 037 520, fax 2661 030 298) is well hidden on the 1st floor of a building on the corner of Rizospaston Voulefton and Polyla; it's open 8am to 2pm weekdays.

The tourist police (☎ 2661 030 265) are on the 3rd floor of Samartzi 4, just off Plateia San Rocco.

Money Banks can be found around Plateia San Rocco and by both ports. The National Bank of Greece is where Voulgareos becomes Theotoki. Alpha Bank has a large branch on Kapodistria behind the Liston. There is a handy bureau de change booth on the southern corner of the cricket ground.

Post & Communications The post office is on Leoforos Alexandras, and the OTE phone office is nearby at Mantzarou 9.

There are now a handful of Internet cafes in Corfu: Netoikos at Kaloxairetou 14, between Agios Spyridon church and the Liston; On Line Internet Cafe at Kapodistria 28, opposite the Spianada; Hobby.Net at Solomou 32, by the steps leading to the New Fortress; and Cyber Café Corfu, about 200m west of the new port at Gardikioti 3 (turn left at the Yamaha store). The going rate is €4.40 to €5.90 per hour.

Medical Services The Corfu General Hospital (☎ 2661 088 200, 2661 045 811) is on I Andreadi. Readers have recommended Dr Yannopapas (☎ 2661 049 350), a British-trained doctor with rooms at Mantzarou 1, by the OTE.

Things to See & Do

The star exhibit of the **Archaeological Museum** (☎ 2661 030 680, Vraïla 5; admission €2.40; open 8.30am-3pm Tues-Sun) is the *Gorgon Medusa* sculpture, one of the best-preserved pieces of Archaic sculpture found in Greece. It was part of the west pediment of the 6th-century-BC Temple of Artemis at Corcyra (the ancient capital), a Doric temple that stood on the Kanoni Peninsula south of the town. The petrifying Medusa is depicted in the instant before she was beheaded by Perseus. This precipitated the birth of her sons, Chrysaor and Pegasus (the winged horse), who emerged from her headless body. Note the disturbing snakes that emerge from Medusa's hair.

Phone numbers listed incorporate changes due in Oct 2002; see p55

CORFU TOWN

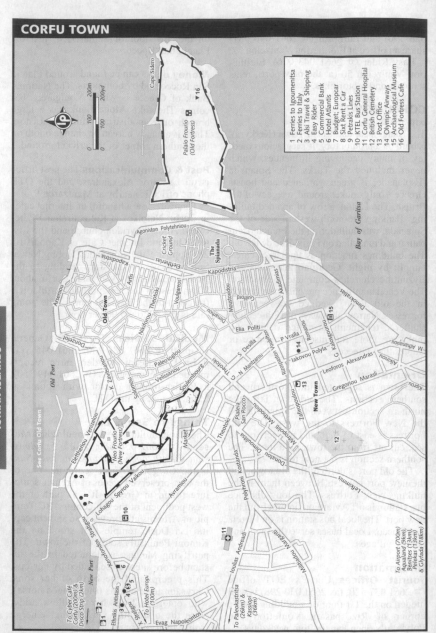

Cape Sidero

Palaio Frourio
(Old Fortress)

Bay of Garitsa

Agoniston Polytehniou

Cricket
Ground

The
Spianada

Kapodistria

Kapodistria

Eleftherias

Artis

Voulgareos

Nikiforou Theotoki

Guilford

Old Town

Arseniou

Mostokdou

Akadimias

Dimstiou

Elia Politi

Donzelot

Paleologou

S. Desilla

Theotoki

N. Mantzarou

P Vraila

Romanou

Iakovou Polyla

Dinokratis

15

Velissariou

Soulembourg

G. Kalogeouniou

Leoforos Alexandras

M Athanasiou

Solomou

K. Zavitsanou

Eleftheriou Venizelou

New Town

G.

Gregoriou Marasli

13

Aktinon

Kipou

Sea Corfu Old Town

Old Port

New Frourio
(New Fortress)

Mitropolii Methodou

Zafiropouilou

Rodostoki Voulgareos

Lefkimmis

9

8
7

Lohagou Spyrou Vaikou

Piateia
San Rocco

Market

I Theotoki

Donatou Dimoulitsa

Donatou Dimoulitsa

Dimoulitsa

12

Avramiou

Polyhroni Kostanda

Xenokopouios Stralia

10

New Port

11

Ethnikis Antistasis

6

5
4
3

To Cyber Café
Corfu (200m) &
Disco Strip (2km)

2
1

Stralias

To Hotel Europi.
(100m)

Evag Napoleontos

Ioulias Andreadi

Militadou Marseni

To Paleokastritsa
(26km) &
Kassiopi
(36km)

To Airport (700m)
Aqualand (9km),
Benitses (13km),
Pelekas (13km)
& Glyfada (18km)

200m
200yd
0　　100
0　　100

IONIAN ISLANDS

1　Ferries to Igoumenitsa
2　Ferries to Italy
3　Aksi Travel & Shipping
4　Easy Rider
5　Commercial Bank
6　Hotel Atlantis
7　Budget; Europcar
8　Sixt Rent a Car
9　Petrakis Lines
10　KTEL Bus Station
11　Corfu General Hospital
12　British Cemetery
13　Post Office
14　Olympic Airways
15　Archaeological Museum
16　Old Fortress Cafe

16

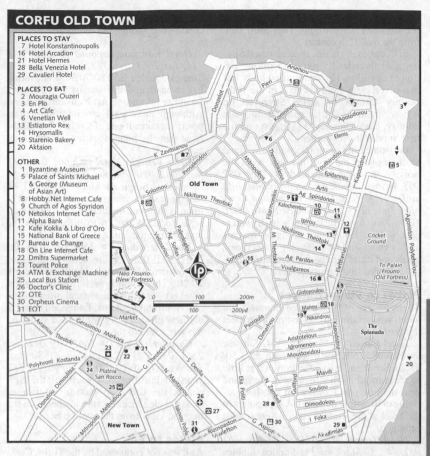

CORFU OLD TOWN

PLACES TO STAY
7   Hotel Konstantinoupolis
16 Hotel Arcadion
21 Hotel Hermes
28 Bella Venezia Hotel
29 Cavalieri Hotel

PLACES TO EAT
2   Mouragia Ouzeri
3   En Plo
4   Art Cafe
6   Venetian Well
13 Estiatorio Rex
14 Hrysomallis
19 Starenio Bakery
20 Aktaion

OTHER
1   Byzantine Museum
5   Palace of Saints Michael
    & George (Museum
    of Asian Art)
8   Hobby.Net Internet Cafe
9   Church of Agios Spyridon
10 Netoikos Internet Cafe
11 Alpha Bank
12 Kafe Koklia & Libro d'Oro
15 National Bank of Greece
17 Bureau de Change
18 On Line Internet Cafe
22 Dmitra Supermarket
23 Tourist Police
24 ATM & Exchange Machine
25 Local Bus Station
26 Doctor's Clinic
27 OTE
30 Orpheus Cinema
31 EOT

IONIAN ISLANDS

Just north of the cricket ground is the **Museum of Asian Art** (☎ 2661 030 433; admission free; open 8.30am-3pm Tues-Sun). It houses an impressive collection that includes Chinese and Japanese porcelain, bronzes, screens, sculptures, theatrical masks, armour, books and prints, as well as artworks from Thailand, Korea and Tibet. The museum is housed in the Palace of Saints Michael & George, built in 1819 as the British Lord High Commissioner's residence.

Inside the Church of Our Lady of Antivouniotissa, is the **Byzantine Museum** (☎ 2661 038 313, off Arseniou; admission €1.50; open 8.30am-3pm Tues-Sun). It has an outstanding collection of Byzantine and post-Byzantine icons dating from the 13th to the 17th centuries.

Apart from the pleasure of wandering the narrow streets of the old town and the gardens of the Spianada, you can explore the two fortresses, Corfu Town's most dominant landmarks. The promontory on which the **Neo Frourio** (New Fortress; admission €1.50; open 9am-9pm daily May-Oct, closed off season) stands was first fortified in the 12th century. The existing remains date from 1588. The ruins of the **Palaio Frourio**

(Old Fortress; ☎ 2661 048 310; admission €2.40; open 8.30am-7pm Tues-Sun) date from the mid-12th century.

In Corfu, many males are christened Spyros after the island's miracle-working patron St Spyridon. His mummified body lies in a silver, glass-fronted coffin in the 16th-century **Church of Agios Spyridon** on Agiou Spyridonos. It is paraded on Palm Sunday, Easter Sunday, 11 August and the first Sunday in November.

For something completely different and to contrast the old with the new, visit the heavily promoted **Aqualand** *(☎ 2661 052 963, W www.aqualand.com.gr; adult/ child under 12 €16.20/10.30, discounted entry after 3pm; open 10am-6pm daily May-Oct, 10am-7pm July-Aug)*. This garish waterpark is 9km from town in Agios Ioannis and is chock-full of countless waterslides, pools and other family-oriented attractions (all included in the entry price).

Places to Stay – Budget

There are no EOT-approved *domatia* but locals who unofficially let rooms often meet the boats.

Hotel Europi (☎ 2661 039 304) Singles/doubles €17.60/29.40, with bath €23.50/ 35.20. Small and basic, the Europi has little to recommend it other than being cheap and near the new port (convenient for those arriving or departing by ferry). A sign points to the hotel at the western end of Xenofondos Stratigou.

Hotel Hermes (☎ 2661 039 268, fax 2661 031 747, G Markora 14) Singles/doubles €26.40/30.80, with bath €30.80/38.15. The Hermes is in an atmospheric if noisy location, directly opposite one end of the bustling daily fruit and vegetable market. It has basic, timeworn rooms and is popular with backpackers.

Places to Stay – Mid-Range & Top End

Hotel Atlantis (☎ 2661 035 560, fax 2661 046 480, e atlanker@mail.otenet.gr, Xenofondos Stratigou 48) Singles/doubles €61.60/76.30. Directly opposite the new port, Atlantis is handy if you are arriving

late or leaving early. It has pleasant air-conditioned rooms, but the location can be noisy.

Hotel Konstantinopoulis (☎ 2661 048 716, fax 2661 048 718, Zavitsianou 11) Singles/doubles €52.80/70.50. Renovation has reincarnated this shabby backpacker's favourite into a fine Art Nouveau hostelry. Although there's no air-conditioning, its position makes it one of Corfu's best deals. Note that the hotel does not accept credit cards.

Bella Venezia Hotel (☎ 2661 046 500, fax 2661 020 708, e belvenht@hol.gr, Zambeli 4) Singles/doubles €61.60/73.40. In a quietish location in the southern part of town is this well-maintained, neoclassical-style hotel. Wake up to breakfast in the lovely large garden.

Hotel Arcadion (☎ 2661 037 670, fax 2661 045 087, e arcadion@otenet.gr, Kapodistria 44) Singles/doubles €61.60/ 79.20. This smartly refurbished central hotel is right by the Liston and offers pleasant, comfortable rooms. Entrance is not via the new ground-floor McDonald's, but on the side street to the right.

Cavalieri Hotel (☎ 2661 039 041, fax 2661 039 283, Kapodistria 4) Singles/doubles €73.40/102.70. Occupying a 300-year-old building just south of the Spianada, the Cavalieri has an interior of classical elegance. Be sure to check out the magical view from the rooftop bar.

Places to Eat

As it was not conquered by the Turks, Corfu maintains a distinctive cuisine influenced by other parts of Europe.

Starenio Bakery (☎ 2661 047 370, Guildford 59) Pies €1.80. This lovely little food store offers a great assortment of home-made vegetable pies (the usual – cheese and spinach – plus more unusual fare like zucchini, leek or eggplant, and a very tasty wild herb). It also sells a tempting array of cakes and pastries and divinely gooey baklava.

Hrysomallis (☎ 2661 030 342, Nikiforou Theotoki 6) Mains average €5. Just behind the expensive Liston cafe strip is one of

Is it Cricket?

Newcomers to Corfu's Liston promenade cafe scene may be puzzled by the sight of men dressed in white surrounding another man dressed in white attempting to hit a hard leather ball out of the rather scruffy park with a long willow bat. This is cricket – Greek-style. Travellers from the former British Empire will recognise and delight at this eccentric and quintessentially British game replete with its sixes, fours, LBWs and owzats!

The game was imported to Corfu by the British during their 49-year hegemony of the island from 1815 to 1864. It has remained firmly entrenched in Corfu ever since. The few teams around the island gather to battle it out on sunny Sundays. While the pitch has seen better days and the distance from the batting crease to the tables of the Liston cafes can seem alarmingly close, the game is played with unusual verve and enthusiasm. This is also the only place in Greece where cricket is played.

The basic aim, for those unfamiliar with the game, is to score 'runs' by hitting the ball as far as possible and then running to and fro between the wooden wickets before the ball is returned by the fielders. Batters are considered 'out' when the ball hits their wickets, when a fielder catches the ball before it bounces, when the ball hits the leg when it could have hit the wicket, or when the fielder hits the wickets before the batter has returned to the crease after running.

It's a complex game and spectators enjoy its subtleties as well as its seemingly slow pace as much as the players do. Good cricket-watching is almost always accompanied by copious amounts of beer, the occasional shouts of encouragement from the sidelines and the odd comment on the weather. It wouldn't be cricket any other way – even in Greece.

Corfu's oldest restaurants, a no-frills place where you can dine on staples such as *mousakas* (layers of eggplant and zucchini, minced meat and potatoes topped with cheese sauce and baked), *yemista* (stuffed tomatoes or green peppers), *pastitsio* (baked cheese-topped macaroni) and local dishes like *sofrito* (lamb or veal with garlic, vinegar and parsley) and *pastitsada* (beef with macaroni, cloves, garlic, tomatoes and cheese). Prices are extremely reasonable and the quality high, which must be why the locals flock here.

Indulge in a little people-watching on the Liston. You will pay around €4.10 to €4.70 for coffee and croissant at any of the cafes, and can sit either under the loggia or across the road in the open-air terraces that border the cricket ground. The place comes alive with locals in the late evening.

Venetian Well (☎ 2661 044 761, Plateia Kremasti) Mains €13.50-19. Just inland from the old port is this delightful, well-hidden eatery (turn left past the cathedral and look for the signs). The romantic setting includes plenty of outdoor tables in the square, which features (funnily enough) a decorative Venetian well. Meals are not

cheap, but the food is excellent and includes creative dishes such as duck served with cumquats and lamb with sun-dried tomatoes and goat's milk cheese.

Mouragia Ouzeri (Arseniou 15) Appetisers around €2.05. Despite not being absolute waterfront like its neighbouring eateries, Mouragia is the pick of the trio of restaurants here due to its great range of *mezedes*.

Estiatorio Rex (☎ 2661 039 649, Kapodistria 66) Mains to €11. This well-established restaurant has operated behind the Liston since 1932. It's now a popular upmarket eatery offering well-prepared dishes, including quality seafood and traditional Greek favourites.

Cafes There are a number of cafes in Corfu Town that are not really 'places to eat' so much as places to linger over a *nes frappé* (and a light snack perhaps) and rest weary sightseeing bones. Their real attraction is usually a lovely setting and invariably a stupendous view. Among the best of these cafes are the peaceful and shady *Art Cafe*, in gardens behind the Palace of Saints Michael and George; the *Old*

Fortress Cafe, inside the (surprise!) Old Fortress complex; *En Plo*, meaning 'by the sea' and it is, literally, inches from the water at the corner of Arseniou and Kapodistria (you need to go down a sloping road to the Faliraki area – this is a popular spot for sunbathing and swimming); and *Aktaion*, on the waterfront opposite the Spianada.

Self-Catering Head to the colourful stalls of the bustling *produce market*, open from morning to early afternoon daily except Sunday, for fresh fruit, vegetables and fish. It's north of Plateia San Rocco, by the southern wall of the New Fortress. *Dimitra supermarket*, next to Hotel Hermes on G Markora, will supply you with the groceries you can't pick up at the nearby produce market.

Entertainment

Having fun in Corfu is comprised mainly of strolling around, sitting at the cafes on the Liston or being cool at the multitude of little cafes and bars that dot the old and new town. Popular Liston bars include *Kafe Koklia* and *Libro d'Oro*.

Corfu's disco strip is 2km north-west of the new port. Here, high-tech palaces cater mainly to locals and to holidaying Greeks and Italians in high season. The holidaying northern Europeans tend to stay and party in their resort areas – the most popular are Dasia, Ipsos, Kassiopi, Sidhari and Agios Gordios (ie, the Pink Palace). Don't expect an evening at any of the 'disco strip' clubs to be a cheap night out. Drinks cost around €4.40 each and you usually pay a sizable cover charge to get in. The big and flashy *Hippodrome* and *Apokalipsis!* are very popular

Corfu Nightlife

Corfu Town's bars, cafes and clubs are good places to get a feel for the island and hang out among the locals. The brash and often pricey 'Disco Strip' to the north-west of town is positively heaving with holidaying Greeks and Italians in July and August.

If you're happy to acknowledge your tourist status, you can't miss Tripa taverna in the tiny inland village of **Kinopiastes**. For a great, albeit slightly cliched, night out, visit Tripa for excellent local food, friendly service and an entertaining floorshow of Greek dancing.

Holiday-makers tend to party in their resort areas – ie, a short stumble away from their accommodation. After all, who wants to be navigating unfamiliar roads after sampling the local liquor? That said, taxis are usually pretty regular and prices are reasonable. If nightlife is what you're after you'll find it in abundance in the resorts along the east and north coasts. Pubs, bars and clubs of varying degrees of tackiness feature in all the larger towns – especially Dasia, Ipsos and Pyrgi, Kassiopi, Roda (one of the island's largest nightclubs, Millennium, is here), Sidhari, Agios Stefanos, Benitses and Moraitika.

The infamous **Pink Palace** at Agios Gordios is the place for backpackers looking for action (sun, sea and sex feature pretty highly on guests' agenda, as does getting sozzled). You get a free shot of ouzo upon check-in and it's all downhill from there... You may prefer to enjoy the great sunsets at one of the bars scattered around the small hilltop village of **Pelekas**, a more laid-back location without the youthful feeding frenzy of Agios Gordios.

Virtually at the southern tip of the island is notorious **Kavos**, a latter-day ladsville best avoided. It is to here most of the British lager louts seem to have been banished and where the inevitable mayhem they cause can be isolated from the rest of the island. It's chock-full of cheap package tourists – many tour reps organise nights out entitled 'Kaos in Kavos', and let's just say that good wholesome fun is the last thing on anyone's mind...

Don't fret that Corfu Town has the only cinema on the island – numerous pubs, bars and cafes in most large resort towns show the latest DVD movies (when they're not broadcasting English football, rugby or cricket matches, that is).

IONIAN ISLANDS

with holidaying Italians. If you ask the locals, *Coca* is the place to go to late, with good DJs and mostly foreign music. *Sodoma*, next to Coca, also has its fans and offers a mixture of overseas and Greek music.

If it's visual entertainment you want, Corfu Town has the *Orpheus* cinema (☎ 2661 039 768, *Aspioti*), which shows English-language films with Greek subtitles for about €5.30.

NORTH OF CORFU TOWN

Most of the coast of northern Corfu is package-tourist saturated, and thoroughly de-Greeked, though once you venture beyond the main package resorts ending at Pyrgi you enter some of Corfu's most privileged scenery. Writers Lawrence and Gerald Durrell spent much of their creative years along this coastline which, in parts, is little more than a short boat hop to the Albanian coastline opposite.

Dasia and **Ipsos** are brash tourist strips full of bars, restaurants and cafes. The beach is narrow and a busy road separates the sea from the fun and entertainment. More or less extending out of Ipsos is **Pyrgi**, 16km north of Corfu Town, where a road continues east around the base of **Mt Pantokrator** (906m), the island's highest peak. From Pyrgi, another road snakes north and inland over the western flank of the mountain to the north coast. A detour can be made to the picturesque village of **Strinylas** from where a road leads through stark terrain to the summit, Moni Pantokratora and stupendous views.

Heading west around the winding coastal road you will first hit **Nisaki**, little more than a small cove with a pebble beach, a couple of tavernas and some domatia. The tiny cove of **Agni** offers three excellent tavernas (and nothing else). The next village of interest is **Kalami**, where the White House was the home of the Durrell brothers. The building is perched right on the water's edge and must have been idyllic during the writers' sojourn here.

Just round the next headland is the pretty little harbour of **Kouloura**, home to a pleasant restaurant. From both Kalami and Kouloura

the houses and buildings of Butrint in neighbouring Albania can be seen quite clearly.

Kassiopi is the next major port of call. It is a sizable resort village around a circular harbour. There is a reasonable beach just west of Kassiopi round the headland. The coast road continues past the lovely long (and surprisingly undeveloped) beach of **Almyros** to the resort of **Roda**, a rather uninspiring place after the arresting scenery of the north-eastern coast and the beach scene is not all that brilliant. **Sidhari**, also a rather tacky tourist resort, is not much better.

Pleasant **Agios Stefanos**, farther around the coast (and not to be confused with the small village of Agios Stefanos on the north-eastern coast), has a long sandy beach extending under the lee of high sand cliffs. Regular boats to the Diaponia islands (see the Diapondia Islands section) leave from the little harbour 1.5km from the village centre.

Places to Stay & Eat

There are a number of good camping grounds along the north-eastern coast.

Dionysus Camping Village (☎/fax 2661 091 760, ℮ *laskari7@otenet.gr*). Adult/tent €4.10/2.40, bungalows €7.40 per person. Large, shady Dionysus is well signposted on the right between Dafnila and Dasia. It boasts good facilities, including a pool, shop and restaurant. Bungalows are little more than simple huts with two or four beds and no facilities.

Karda Beach Camping (☎/fax 2661 093 595, ℮ *campco@otenet.gr*) Adult/tent €4.70/3.50, bungalows €32.30 plus €4.70 per person. Continuing along the road from Dasia to Ipsos is this quite luxurious camping ground, close to the beach and with excellent facilities including a pool and restaurant. Bungalows are a good option – they're small but fully equipped and have their own bathroom.

Manessis Apartments (☎ 2661 081 474, ℮ *diana@otenet.gr*) Apartments €73.40 sleeping up to 4. By Aleka's lace shop at the end of Kassiopi's harbour are these appealing two-bedroom apartments, with bougainvillea cascading down the balconies. The owner, an Irish woman with great

IONIAN ISLANDS

information about the area, only rents to independent travellers.

San Stefanos Golden Beach Hotel (☎ *2663 051 053*) Double rooms €32.30, double studios €41.10, 4-person apartments €73.40. This pleasant hotel, with comfortable rooms and a small apartment complex nearby, is on the way to the port and has a great view over the bay.

White House (☎ *2661 091 251*) Mains €5-10.60. If you're a Durrell fan, you can have a nostalgic meal at Kalami's White House and ponder the view as you search for your own literary inspiration. The restaurant slightly trades off its name and position, but a decent fish meal is reasonable value at around €9.40.

SOUTH OF CORFU TOWN

The Kanoni Peninsula, 4km from Corfu Town, was the site of the ancient capital but little has been excavated. **Mon Repos Villa**, at its north-eastern tip, was Prince Philip's birthplace. The beautiful wooded grounds *(admission free; open 8am-7pm daily)* can be explored, and the residence has finally been restored to its former glory and is open to the public as a museum. Opposite the entrance are two excavation sites; one is the ruins of the 5th-century **Basilica of Agia Kerkyra**, built on the site of a 5th-century-BC temple.

The coast road continues south with a turn-off to **Ahillion Palace** (☎ *2661 056 245; admission €3; open 9am-6pm daily)*, near the village of Gastouri and well signposted. In the 1890s it was the summer palace of Austria's Empress Elizabeth (King Otho of Greece was her uncle), and she dedicated the villa to Achilles. The beautifully landscaped garden is guarded by kitsch statues of the empress' other mythological heroes.

The Brothers Durrell

The name Durrell is synonymous with Corfu, though it is perhaps surprising that of the two brothers – Lawrence (1912–90) and Gerald (1925–95) – it is the naturalist Gerald rather than the poet and novelist Lawrence who has so inextricably linked the name of this famous duo with the island of Corfu and the little village of Kalami on Corfu's north-eastern coast.

Gerald Durrell was born in India and gained considerable repute among conservationists for his role in breeding endangered animal species for eventual release in the wild. He was also a prolific author, producing more than 35 informative yet amusing books about animals. Durrell's love of animals started when living in Corfu in the 1930s. His best-known books were *The Overloaded Ark* (1953), *Three Singles to Adventure* (1953), *My Family and other Animals* (1956), *A Zoo in My Luggage* (1960) and *Birds, Beasts and Relatives* (1969).

MH

Brother Lawrence, also born in India, was the dedicated writer in the family. He was at once a novelist, poet, writer of topographical books, verse plays and farcical short stories. He is best known for the Alexandria Quartet, a series of four interconnected novels. His Greek trilogy included *Prospero's Cell* (1945), in which he describes his life in Corfu during 1937 and 1938, *Reflections on a Marine Venus* (1953), for which he spent two years in Rhodes in 1945–46 as press officer for the Allied government, and *Bitter Lemons of Cyprus* (1957), where he spent 1952 to 1956 as a teacher and government official – latterly during the Cypriot insurgency.

Both brothers were well known around Corfu and some of the older restaurant owners near Corfu Town's Liston still remember their illustrious literary patrons. Their former house overlooking the sea at the village of Kalami is now a fish restaurant.

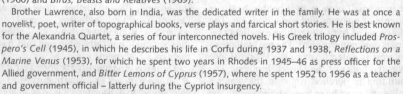

The resort of **Benitses** used to be the playground of holiday hooligans, but in recent times has made strenuous efforts to get its act together. Still, the excesses of too much package tourism in the past have taken the sheen off the little fishing village, but the narrow winding streets of the old village still maintain an air of authenticity.

Heading farther south you will next hit **Moraïtika** and **Messonghi**, two resorts that have merged into one. They're similar to Benitses but quieter. The beach scene, while not ideal, is certainly better than its neighbour farther north. The winding coastal road between Messonghi and **Boukaris** is decidedly more appealing and is dotted with a few tavernas and small pebbly beaches.

Places to Stay & Eat

There is accommodation aplenty around Benitses and farther south along the coast, but as there's not much here to hold the independent traveller for long, you're better off staying elsewhere.

Tripa (☎ *2661 056 333*) Set banquet €29.40. This friendly, well-known taverna is touristy and a bit over the top, but it's very popular. It's been around a long time and the food is surprisingly good – and plentiful (come hungry!). It's in the little inland village of Kinopiastes (8km from Corfu Town), and has hosted its fair share of illustrious patrons. The sumptuous set banquet has a wide range of original Corfiot dishes, and the price includes drinks (beer, wine and soft drink) and a floor show of Greek dancing.

THE WEST COAST

Corfu's best beaches are on the west coast. **Paleokastritsa**, 26km from Corfu, is the coast's largest resort. Built around sandy and pebbled coves with a green mountain backdrop, it's incredibly beautiful. Once paradisal, it's been the victim of development. While the water here looks enticing, it is generally considerably colder than at other parts of the island – but then this area is Corfu's prime diving location and snorkelling is also a popular activity. **Corkyra Dive Club** (☎/fax *2663 041 206,*

@ *cfudiveclub@ker.forthnet.gr,* W *www .corfuxenos.gr/sports/cdiveclub.htm*) is based in Paleokastritsa and offers dives and diving courses for beginners and experienced divers. Dives, with equipment supplied, start from €41.10.

Moni Theotokou (*admission free, donation expected; open 7am-1pm & 3pm-8pm daily*) perches on the rocky promontory at Paleokastritsa. The monastery was founded in the 13th century but the present building dates from the 18th century. A small adjacent museum contains icons.

From Paleokastritsa a path ascends to the unspoilt village of **Lakones**, 5km inland. Walk back along the approach road and you'll see a signposted footpath on the left. There are superb views along the 6km road west to **Makrades** and **Krini**. The restaurants along the way extol the views from their terraces.

Farther south, the beach at **Ermones** is near **Corfu Golf Club** (☎/fax *2661 094 220,* @ *cfugolf@hol.gr,* W *www.corfugolfclub .com*), among the largest in Europe. Hill-top **Pelekas**, 4km away, is renowned for its spectacular sunsets. It can be as busy as the coast, but with young independent travellers rather than package tourists (see the excellent Web site at W www.pelekas .com). Pelekas is close to three lovely sandy beaches, **Glyfada**, **Pelekas** and **Myrtiotissa**, the last an unofficial nudist beach. Don't miss the superb panoramic views over Corfu from **Kaiser's Throne**, a lookout high up above Pelekas village.

Agios Gordios, home to the infamous Pink Palace, is a popular backpacker hang-out 8km south of Glyfada. It's a laid-back kind of place and will appeal to travellers interested primarily in the booze-and-beach scene.

Places to Stay & Eat

Paleokastritsa Camping (☎ *2663 041 204, fax 2663 041 104*) Adult/tent €3.80/3.30. You'll find this camping ground right of the main approach road to town. It's a shady and well-organised place, with a restaurant on site and lots of conveniences very close by (ie, minimarket, swimming pool), but is a fair way back from the beaches.

IONIAN ISLANDS

Paleokastritsa also has many hotels, studios and domatia. A good starting point is the family-run *Astakos Taverna* (☎ 2663 041 068, ⒺＥ *alex_ziniatis@hotmail.com*), in the centre of town between the main beach and the most northerly beach. The owners offer rooms for €17.60 to €26.40 – they have rooms above the taverna and also in the quieter side street.

Golden Fox (☎ 2663 049 101/2, fax 049 319, Ⓔ *goldfox@otenet.gr*, Ⓦ *www.gold enfox.gr*) High up overlooking Paleokastritsa and just beyond the village of Lakones is this scenic spot with magnificent views over the coast. The Golden Fox has terraces on three levels and includes a restaurant, a snack bar and a pool bar. The swimming pool here (open to the public and free of charge) must have the best view in the whole of Greece. This complex also has a few well-maintained studios to rent (from €44 to €64.60 depending on season).

Pension Tellis & Brigitte (☎ 2661 094 326, Ⓔ *martini@pelekas.com*) Rooms €17.60-23.50. A good-value option in Pelekas and close to the central square is the bougainvillea-smothered Tellis & Brigitte. The rooms are simple and the service friendly. Prices vary depending on season and length of stay.

Levant Hotel (☎ 2661 094 230, fax 2661 094 115, Ⓔ *levant@otenet.gr*, Ⓦ *www.levant -hotel.com*) Doubles €93.90. Open year-round. This stylish, neoclassical building, once a private house, is one of the most elegant hotels on the island. It's near Kaiser's Throne lookout and has charming, helpful staff, magnificent rooms and a restaurant terrace with awesome views.

Pink Palace (☎ 2661 053 103/4, fax 2661 053 025, Ⓔ *pink-palace@ker.forthnet .gr*, Ⓦ *www.thepinkpalace.com*) A/B-class rooms €26.40/22 per person with breakfast & dinner. Open year-round. You'll either love or hate this huge, garish complex. It's definitely not everyone's cup of tea, but it's pretty much considered a 'must do' on the Europe backpacker circuit, and it's designed for under-25s who want fun and sun without the hassles of having to look for it. There are two categories of accommodation

and, somewhat surprisingly, the new A-class rooms are extremely pleasant; B class is hostel-style rooms that can sleep up to four. The drawcard is the debauchery for which this place is (in)famous. There's a nightly disco until late, a 24-hour bar, theme parties and lots of watersports opportunities. A big pink bus will pick you up from the port.

Sunrock (☎ 2661 094 637, fax 2661 094 056, Ⓔ *sunrock@nettaxi.com*, Ⓦ *www .geocities.com/sunrock_corfu*) 4-person rooms €16.20 per person, with bathroom €19.10 per person. Open year-round. Prices include breakfast and dinner. Behind Pelekas Beach is family-run Sunrock (formerly known as Vrachos), which is becoming another backpacker favourite. The market is quite clearly hostel-going young backpackers, and meals (home-cooked) are included in the price. You can be picked up from the port. The bar and taverna are open to the public.

Jimmy's Restaurant & Rooms (☎ 2661 094 284, Ⓔ *jimmyspelekas@hotmail.com*) Doubles €23.50-29.40, triples €38.20-44. At the intersection of the roads to Pelekas Beach, Kaiser's Throne and Corfu Town is Jimmy's, a popular hang-out with friendly multilingual staff. Its specialities are Corfiot dishes such as sofrito, pastitsada and *burdeto* (fish with paprika and cayenne), and it has excellent choices for vegetarians, including vegetarian mousakas. Jimmy's also has pleasant rooms for rent above the restaurant.

Mirtiotisa (☎ 2661 094 113, Ⓔ *sks_mirtia@ hotmail.com*) Five minutes uphill from Myrtiotissa beach is this busy restaurant, in an idyllic setting and serving the usual taverna fare. It also has simple, agreeable rooms (singles/doubles €17.60/29.40 year-round) and the garden doubles as an unofficial beach car park.

THE DIAPONDIA ISLANDS
Τα Διαπόντια Νησιά

Scattered like forgotten stepping stones to Puglia in Italy lie a cluster of little-known and even less-visited satellite islands belonging administratively to Corfu. Of the five islands only three are inhabited, though many of their original residents have long since departed for the lure of New York City and only return in the summer months to renew their ties.

Ereikousa (Ερείκουσα; population 702) is the closest Diapondia island to Corfu and therefore perhaps the most visited. Wild and wooded **Mathraki** (Μαθράκι; population 297) is the least developed of the trio but offers solitude and some fine walking. **Othoni** (Οθονοί; population 648) is largest of the group and also the farthest out; it's popular with Italian yachties.

Often isolated by tricky seas, the islands are worth the extra effort to visit them and serious island collectors should place them high on their agenda. Development is proceeding slowly and cautiously and all offer one or two places to stay and eat. Most people visit on day trips from Sidhari or Agios Stefanos, though regular ferries do link the islands with both Agios Stefanos, on the north-western tip of Corfu, and Corfu Town.

If you're keen on visiting the Diapondia islands, your best bet is to contact San Stefano Travel (☎/fax 2663 051 910, ⓔ steftrav@ otenet.gr) located in Agios Stefanos. Friendly Noula and her super-helpful staff will give you the lowdown on all the ferry options from Agios Stefanos and know of the various accommodation possibilities on each island.

Getting To/From the Diapondia

The most reliable link is the thrice-weekly service from Corfu Town with the *Alexandros II*, which leaves at around 6.30am Tuesday, Thursday and Saturday for the long haul round Corfu to bring supplies and the odd vehicle. It leaves from opposite the BP petrol station between the new and old ports, and a one-way journey will cost €5 to €5.60.

From Agios Stefanos a small passenger boat, the *Nearchos* (information on ☎ 69 4499 9771), services Mathraki and Othoni twice a week (€3 to €3.50 one way, Monday and Wednesday, weather permitting), and a different boat (information on ☎ 2633 071 586) services Erikousa and Othoni, also twice weekly (Tuesday and Thursday; similar

prices). Schedules vary without warning so check beforehand.

The easiest solution may be to jump on a day excursion out of Sidhari or Agios Stefanos. Excursions are advertised widely around hotels and travel agencies in the area.

Paxi & Antipaxi

PAXI Παξοί

postcode 490 82 • pop 2440

Paxi (pahx-ee), 10km long and 4km wide, is the smallest main Ionian island. It has a captivating landscape of dense, centuries-old olive groves, snaking drystone walls, derelict farmhouses and abandoned stone olive presses. The olive trees have amazingly twisted, gnarled and hollowed trunks, which gives them the look of sinister, ancient monsters.

Paxi has escaped the mass tourism of Corfu and caters for small, discriminating tour companies. People come here because they have fallen in love with Paxi's inimitable cosy feel, or have heard about its friendly islanders and its captivating scenery.

There are only three coastal settlements – Gaïos, Longos and Lakka – and a few inland villages. The whole island is walkable, though good roads do cover its length. Paxi is an absolute must for any serious island-hopper and is worth the extra effort needed to get here.

For information on the Internet, see Ⓦ www.paxos-greece.com.

Getting To/From Paxi

Bus There is a direct bus service to Athens (7½ hours, €27.20 plus €10.30 hydrofoil ticket between Paxi and Igoumenitsa) twice weekly. Tickets are available from Bouas Travel (☎ 2662 032 401) on the Gaïos waterfront. Buses from Athens to Paxi depart from Hotel Vienni (☎ 21 0524 9143/4/5), Pireos 20 in Athens (near Plateia Omonias) twice weekly.

Ferry – Domestic A daily car ferry, the *Theologos*, sails between Paxi and Igoumenitsa on the mainland, and twice a week it sails on to Corfu (otherwise you need to change ferries in Igoumenitsa). The Paxi-Igoumenitsa trip takes 1¾ hours and costs €5; Paxi-Corfu (via Igoumenitsa) takes 3½ hours and costs €5.60. A second car ferry, the *Agia Theodora*, also runs the Paxi-Igoumenitsa route twice weekly. Ferries dock at Gaïos' new port 1km east of the central square, though excursion boats dock by the central square and along the quay towards the new port.

Tickets for Corfu and Igoumenitsa can be obtained from most of the travel agencies on the island. Staff at Paxos Magic Holidays are very helpful, and its Web site (W www .paxosmagic.com) has up-to-date links with the ferry timetables. Paxi's port police can be contacted on ☎ 2662 031 222.

Ferry – International Italian Ferries and Ventouris Ferries both operate high-speed catamaran services between Brindisi and Paxi (4¾ hours, €82.20). Both run three times weekly from 27 July to 2 September. Tickets and information can be obtained from Paxos Magic Holidays in Gaïos.

Hydrofoil Petrakis Lines operates popular passenger-only hydrofoils between Corfu, Igoumenitsa and Paxi from May until September. There are at least two services daily between Corfu and Paxi – these often stop in Igoumenitsa en route. Prices from Paxi are €10.30 to Igoumenitsa (one hour) and €11.20 to Corfu (one hour direct or 1¾ hours via Igoumenitsa).

For detailed information in Paxi contact Bouas Travel (☎ 2662 032 401), or Petrakis Lines (☎ 2661 031 649) in Corfu.

Getting Around Paxi

The island's bus links Gaïos and Lakka via Longos up to five times daily (€1.20). A taxi from Gaïos to Lakka or Longos costs around €8.80; the taxi rank in Gaïos is on the waterfront by the main square.

Alfa Hire (☎ 2662 032 505, fax 2662 032 688) in Gaïos rents cars, and Rent a Scooter Vassilis (☎ 2662 032 598) opposite the bus stop in Gaïos has the biggest range of scooters and mopeds on the island.

Gaïos Γάιος

Gaïos, on a wide, east-coast bay, is the island's capital. It's a delightfully attractive place with crumbling, 19th-century red-tiled pink, cream and whitewashed buildings. The fortified Agios Nikolaos Islet almost fills its harbour. Panagia Islet, named after its monastery, lies at the northern entrance to the bay.

Orientation & Information The main square abuts the central waterfront. The main street of Panagioti Kanga runs inland from here to another square where you'll find the bus stop. The post office is just beyond here and the OTE is next door. (The only Internet cafe on the island at the time of research was Akis Bar in the town of Lakka.)

There is no tourist office, but staff at Paxos Magic Holidays (☎ 2662 032 269, fax 2662 032 122, e info@paxosmagic .com, W www.paxosmagic.com), on Panagioti Kanga, are very helpful.

Things to See & Do The excellent **Cultural Museum of Paxi** *(☎ 2662 032 556; admission €1.50; open 11am-1.30pm & 7.30pm-11pm daily)*, in an old school on the

PAXI & ANTIPAXI

To Corfu & Brindisi
To Igoumenitsa
To Parga

PAXI

South Kerkyra Straits

Lakka
Kastanitha Cave
Longos
Fontana
Magazia

Panagia Islet

Ortholithos Stack
Bogdanatika
Agrilas Bay
Agrilas
Vellianitatika

Gaïos
Agios Nikolaos Islet

Ozias
MONGONISI

Trypitos

ANTIPAXI

Vrika Beach
Voutoumi Beach

Vigla
Agrapidia

IONIAN SEA

Daily Ferries
Low Frequency Ferries
Hydrofoil/Catamaran
Excursion Boat

0   2   4km
0   1   2mi

IONIAN ISLANDS

waterfront, has a well-displayed eclectic collection. Don't miss the mind-boggling stirrups hanging from a four-poster bed – a 19th-century sex aid.

The best way to get to know Paxi is to walk the island along its many pathways lined with drystone walls through the countless olive groves that blanket the island. Pick up a copy of the excellent *Bleasdale Walking Map of Paxos* (€8.80), available at most of the travel agencies around town, which comes with an explanatory booklet.

Places to Stay Accommodation tends to mostly consist of prebooked studios and apartments, though you can usually find somewhere private to stay. All the island's agencies can help, and all produce glossy brochures detailing the villas and apartments on their books.

San Giorgio Rooms to Rent (☎ 2662 032 223) Double rooms €44, double studios €52.80. This is the first accommodation option you'll encounter if you're walking from the new port. The large pension, with well-kept, airy rooms, is signposted above the waterfront, 200m north of the central square.

Up the hill opposite the bus stop are a few reasonably priced domatia, including *Magda's Domatia* (☎ 2662 032 573), with cheap, basic rooms, and, next door, *Spiro's Domatia* (☎ 2662 031 172), with rooms in better nick than his neighbour's.

Thekli Zenebisis (☎/fax 2662 032 313) 2-person studios €64.60. Possibly the best-value studios in Gaïos are run by the delightful Thekli. Her immaculate and well-equipped rooms all have balconies and good views. They're tricky to find (up two sets of steps behind the museum) – call ahead and Thekli will meet you at the port. Prices drop to as low as €29.40 in low season.

Paxos Beach Hotel (☎ 2662 032 211, fax 2662 032 695, e zerbas1@otenet.gr, w www.paxosbeachhotel.gr) Doubles/triples with half-board €102.70/133.50. This bungalow complex, 1.5km south of Gaïos and overlooking the sea, is tastefully furnished rooms in a pretty setting. The complex has a tennis court, beach, bar and restaurant.

Places to Eat Gaïos has a glut of generally good eating places.

Restaurant Mambo (☎ 2662 032 670) Mains €5-11.75. Countless locals and return visitors alike agree that this waterfront restaurant is the best place for an evening meal, and the always-full tables attest to its popularity. There's the added attraction of perhaps the best baked feta in all of Greece.

Taverna Dodos (☎ 2662 032 265) Mains to €8.80. In a pretty, colourful garden in the southern part of town (back from the waterfront – follow the signs) is this relaxed family taverna. All the taverna favourites are featured on the menu, and there are good choices for vegetarians.

Authentiko (☎ 2662 032 647) Mains €4.40-8.80. Great eating can be had at friendly Authentiko, with a vine-covered canopy area close to the bus stop. This place does home-cooked dishes, and the specials change regularly. Enticing offerings include char-grill tuna steak, oven-baked lamb with yogurt and stewed duck in red-pepper sauce.

George's Corner Mains to €7, sandwiches & pittas €0.90-5.30. Cheap and cheerful, plus popular and quick, George's is on the main square and offers great pittas and burgers and an array of other snacks.

Self-catering supplies can be picked up at the *Paxos Market & Delicatessen* (☎ 2662 031 160) on the central square. There's a good *bakery* next door to *Cafe Kalimera Espresso Bar* (the latter serves up excellent coffee), just west of the central square.

Around Paxi

Paxi's gentle east coast has small pebble beaches, while the west coast has awesome vistas of precipitous cliffs, punctuated by several grottoes only accessible by boat. You can walk to **Trypitos**, a high cliff from where there are stunning views of Antipaxi. From Gaïos, walk south-west along the Makratika road and turn right uphill at Villa Billy's, marked with a small sign on the wall. Stay on the main track and just before it ends turn left onto a narrow path which leads to Trypitos.

The small fishing village-cum-resort of **Longos** is 5km north of Gaïos, and has a

IONIAN ISLANDS

few beaches nearby. It's much smaller than Gaïos and has a more intimate feel. The village consists of little more than a cramped square and a winding waterfront. It's a great base if you want a quieter stay.

The pretty harbour of **Lakka** lies at the end of a deep, narrow bay on the north coast and is a popular yachtie call. There are a couple of decent beaches around either side of the bay's headland (including Harami Beach, with water sports on offer), and there are some great walks from here.

Places to Stay & Eat *Babis Dendias*
(☎/fax 2662 031 597) 4-person studios €102.70, one-week stay preferred. Most of the accommodation in Longos is monopolised by tour companies, and your best independent bet is Babis Dendias – inquire at his *pantopoleio* (general store), 20m beyond the bus stop. Babis has fully equipped accommodation for up to four people – he has properties both in town and just outside, plus knows of locals with rooms to rent. Prices fall to a bargain €52.80 in low season.

Routtsis Holidays (☎ 2662 031 807, fax 2662 031 161, e routsis-holidays@ker .forthnet.gr, w www.forthnet.gr/routsishol idays/) This waterfront agency in Lakka is the agent for many rooms and villas in and around town. Properties on the books include two hotels – the *Lefkothea* has good-value rooms with shared bathroom and communal kitchen and feels a little like a hostel. The *Ilios* is similar but all rooms have private bathrooms.

There are good eating options in Longos and Lakka, mostly scattered around their waterfronts.

Vassilis (☎ 2662 031 587) Mains €5.30-12. Smart, waterfront Vassilis in Longos has been widely praised, and indeed it's tough to get an outside table without pre-booking. The food is very good – bordering on 'gourmet Greek' – but portions are disappointingly small.

I Gonia (☎ 2662 031 060) Mains average €7.40. Longos locals insist that 'the Corner' is the most authentic place on the waterfront, offering tasty, good-value grilled meats as well as standard taverna fare.

Taxidi (☎ 2662 031 325) Right at the end of the Longos harbour, in a whitewashed building with two seafront terraces, is this inviting cocktail bar run by friendly Spiros. Even if you don't fancy one of his intoxicating fresh melon and vodka mega-cocktails, it's worth calling in for some local advice. He usually knows of several individuals who have private rooms to rent.

La Rosa di Paxos (☎ 2662 031 471) Mains to €13.20. On the eastern side of the Lakka waterfront is this upmarket place, one of the prettiest restaurants in the Ionians. Tables spill over two terraces and are surrounded by flowering plants. The international menu gives a nod to Greek cuisine but there's also a heavy Italian influence (including tiramisu for dessert), plus lots of grilled vegetables in local olive oil and fresh fish displayed in a fridge on the waterside.

Klimataria (☎ 2662 030 075) Mains to €10.30. Under a vineyard-covered canopy on the main square of Lakka is this English-run place, offering a few well-done Greek dishes but also some real variety, including chicken balti, lemon stir-fry chicken and a vegie bake. There's a good selection of home-made cakes, plus you can pre-order sandwiches for a picnic.

In the evening, there are a number of central waterside bars good for a drink or three. *Akis* (☎ 2662 031 665) has the distinction of being the only place on Paxi where you can access the Internet.

ANTIPAXI Αντίπαξοι
Diminutive Antipaxi, 2km south of Paxi, is covered with grape vines from which excellent wine is produced. Caiques and tourist boats run daily out of Gaïos and usually pull in at a couple of beaches offering good swimming in exquisitely clear water. Vrika Beach at the north-eastern tip is sandy and gently sloping. Two restaurants, *Spiro's Taverna* and *Vrika Taverna*, serve the often-busy tourist trade, plus provide beach umbrellas for hire. Spiros (☎ 2662 031 172 during the day in season; ☎ 2662 032 417 at night and in winter) from Spiro's Taverna offers accommodation on the island for those who like isolation. Fully

equipped houses go for €88 for two people, €146.80 for four people.

A path links Vrika Beach with Voutoumi Beach, farther south around a couple of headlands. Voutoumi Beach is very pretty, but is made up of large pebbles. A *taverna* high up on the bluff serves hungry bathers, and a new beachside restaurant was under construction at the time of research.

If you don't fancy just beach bumming, take a walk up to the scattered settlement of **Vigla**, stopping to admire the many little vineyards along the way and dotted throughout the village.

Getting To/From Antipaxi

The cheapest way to get to Antipaxi is via the boat run by Antipaxos Lines (known as 'Nicos Boat') from Gaïos that leaves at 10am and returns from Vrika Beach at 5pm. The cost is €3.50 return.

In high season there are half a dozen high-speed express boats that leave the Gaïos waterfront between 10am and 1pm. The return boats leave Vrika Beach at 2.30pm and 5pm (and will pick up from Voutoumi Beach if requested). Tickets cost €4.40 return and can be bought from the kiosk on the quay. Most round-the-island excursions stop in at Antipaxos.

Lefkada & Meganisi

LEFKADA Λευκάδα
postcode 311 00 • pop 22,500
Lefkada is the fourth-largest island in the Ionians. Joined to the mainland by a narrow isthmus until the occupying Corinthians dug a canal in the 8th century BC, its 25m strait is spanned from the mainland by a causeway.

Lefkada has 10 satellite islets: Meganisi, Kalamos, Kastos, Madouri, Skorpidi, Skorpios, Sparti, Thilia, Petalou and Kythros.

Lefkada is mountainous with several peaks over 1000m. It is also fertile, well watered by underground streams, with cotton fields, acres of dense olive groves, vineyards, fir and pine forests.

Once a very poor island, Lefkada's beauty is also in its people who display in-

tense pride in their island. Many of the older women wear traditional costume. A festival of 'speech and art' takes place every summer and includes a well-established international folklore festival in late August.

For information on the Internet, see Ⓦ www.lefkas.net.

Getting To/From Lefkada
Air Lefkada has no airport but Aktion airport, near Preveza on the mainland, is a 30-minute bus journey away. It has daily flights in summer between Athens and Preveza (€52.25). Lefkada's Olympic Airways office (☎ 2645 022 881) is at Dorpfeld 1; Preveza's (☎ 2682 028 343) is at Irinis 37.

Bus From Lefkada Town's KTEL bus station (☎ 2645 022 364) there are buses to Athens (5½ to six hours, €20.55, four or five daily), Patras (three hours, €9.10, two weekly), Thessaloniki (eight hours, €25, at least two weekly) and Aktion airport (20 to 30 minutes, €1.50, four or five daily).

Ferry The F/B *Agia Marina* runs between Vasiliki and Fiskardo (one hour, €3.30) on Kefallonia, Piso Aetos (two hours, €4.30) on Ithaki and then to Sami back on Kefallonia (2½ hours, €5.90). In summer it runs once or twice daily. Also in high season a ferry leaves daily from Nydri for Frikes on Ithaki and then Fiskardo.

You can contact Lefkada Town's port police on ☎ 2645 022 322, Vasiliki's on ☎ 2645 031 323.

Getting Around Lefkada
From Lefkada Town, frequent buses go to Nydri and Vlyho (up to 18 daily in high season), Poros (two daily) and Vasiliki (five daily). There are regular buses to Karya (seven daily), Agios Nikitas (up to six daily), Kalamitsi (two daily) and Athani (two daily). Other villages are served by one or two buses daily. Sunday services are reduced.

Cars can be hired in Lefkada Town from Europcar (☎ 2645 023 581), Panagou 6, by the harbour, and Budget (☎ 2645 024 643), its neighbour. Rent a motorbike from Motorcycle Rental Santas (☎ 2645 025 250), next

IONIAN ISLANDS

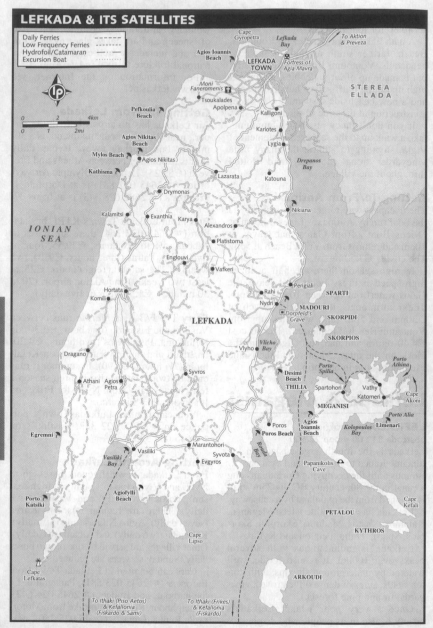

LEFKADA & ITS SATELLITES

Daily Ferries
Low Frequency Ferries
Hydrofoil/Catamaran
Excursion Boat

Cape Gyropetra
Lefkada Bay
To Aktion & Preveza

Agios Ioannis Beach

LEFKADA TOWN
Fortress of Agia Mavra

Moni Faneromenis
Tsoukalades
Apolpena
Kalligoni

STEREA ELLADA

Pefkoulia Beach

Kariotes

Lygia

Agios Nikitas Beach

Drepanos Bay

Mylos Beach
Agios Nikitas
Kathisma

Lazarata
Katouna

Drymonas

Kalamitsi
Exanthia
Karya
Nikiana

IONIAN SEA

Alexandros

Platistoma

Englouvi

Vafkeri

Hortata
Komili

Rahi
Perigiali

SPARTI

Nydri
MADOURI

LEFKADA

Dorpfeld's Grave

SKORPIDI
SKORPIOS

Vlyho
Vlicho Bay

Porto Athina

Dragano

Porto Spilia

Cape Akoni

Syvros

Desimi Beach
THILIA
Spartohori
Vathy
Katomeri

MEGANISI

Athani
Agios Petra

Porto Alia
Limenari

Egremni

Poros
Poros Beach

Agios Ioannis Beach

Kolopoulos Bay

Marantohori

Vasiliki
Syvota
Evgyros

Rouda Bay

Vasiliki Bay

Papanikolis Cave

Agiofylli Beach

Porto Katsiki

PETALOU

Cape Kefali

KYTHROS

Cape Lipso

Cape Lefkatas

ARKOUDI

To Ithaki (Piso Aetos) & Kefallonia (Fiskardo & Sami)

To Ithaki (Frikes) & Kefallonia (Fiskardo)

to the new Ionian Star Hotel, near the docks. Many of the large car-rental companies are also represented in Nydri.

Lefkada Town
pop 6800

Lefkada Town, the island's capital and primarily a yachting port, is built on a promontory at the south-eastern corner of a salty lagoon, which is used as a fish hatchery.

The town was devastated by earthquakes in 1867 and 1948. After 1948, many houses were rebuilt in a unique style, with upper floors of painted sheet metal or corrugated iron that is strangely attractive, constructed in the hope they would withstand future earthquakes. The belfries of churches are made of metal girders – another earthquake precaution. Damage from the 1953 earthquake was minimal.

Orientation The bus station is on the eastern waterfront. The town's animated main thoroughfare, Dorpfeld, starts just south of the causeway at Hotel Nirikos. This street is named after 19th-century archaeologist Wilhelm Dorpfeld, who is held in high esteem for postulating that Lefkada, not Ithaki, was the home of Odysseus. Dorpfeld leads to Plateia Agiou Spyridonos, the main square. After the square the thoroughfare's name changes to Ioannou Mela. It is lined with interesting shops and several *kafeneia*.

Information There is no tourist office on Lefkada. The tourist police (☎ 2645 026 450) are in the same building as the regular police on Dimitriou Golemi, but they are not particularly helpful.

The National Bank of Greece and the Ionian Bank (both with ATMs) and the post office are on the eastern side of Ioannou Mela. The OTE is on Plateia Zambelou. You can get onto the Net at the large Internet Cafe (☎ 2645 021 507) on Koutroubi, just off 8th Merarchias (next to the Commercial Bank of Greece). It's a few minutes' walk south-west of the bus station.

Things to See Housed in a new building at the corner of Sikelianou and Svoronou

(part of the cultural centre) is the **Archaeological Museum** (☎ 2645 021 635; admission free; open 8.30am-3pm Tues-Sun). It has a small, well displayed and labelled collection of artefacts found on the island. One of the earliest objects, dating from the late 6th century BC, is a delicate terracotta figurine of nymphs dancing around a flute player. Other figurines date from the Archaic and Hellenistic periods.

Works by icon painters from the Ionian school are displayed in a **collection of post-Byzantine icons** (☎ 2645 078 062; admission free; open 8.30am-1.30pm Tues-Sat, 5pm-7.30pm Tues & Thurs). It's housed in a late-19th-century building off Ioannou Mela (if it appears to be closed, ask at the Public Library of Lefkada upstairs).

The 14th-century Venetian **Fortress of Agia Mavra** is on the mainland. It was first established by the crusaders but the remains mainly date from the Venetian and Turkish occupations of the island. **Moni Faneromenis**, 3km west of town, was founded in 1634, destroyed by fire in 1886 and rebuilt. It's now inhabited by a few monks and nuns, and the monastery's church can be visited. The views of the lagoon and town are worth the ascent.

West of the lagoon, past windmills, is **Agios Ioannis Beach**, a great place to view the sunset. The nearest beaches to town are at the northern side of the lagoon, about a 2km walk away.

Places to Stay *Karlotes Beach Camping* (☎ 2645 071 103) Adult/tent €5/4.40. This is the nearest camping ground to Lefkada Town – it's 5km south of the capital on the east coast. It's a pleasant if overgrown ground offering plenty of shade plus a pool to cool off in.

Hotel Byzantio (☎/fax 2645 022 629, ☎ 2645 021 315, Dorpfeld 4) Doubles €35.20. This slightly scruffy, hostel-style place has good-value rooms in a very central location.

Hotel Santa Maura (☎ 2645 021 308, fax 2645 026 253) Singles/doubles €41.10/49.90. The nicest place to stay in Lefkada Town is this bright and breezy

IONIAN ISLANDS

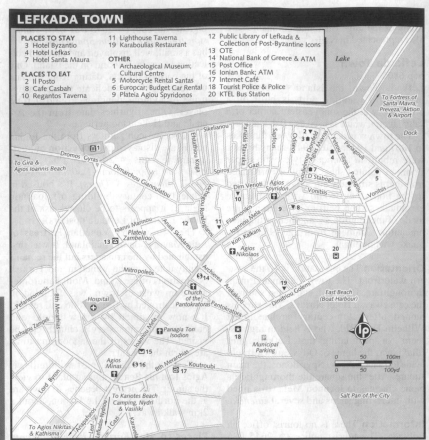

LEFKADA TOWN

PLACES TO STAY
3 Hotel Byzantio
4 Hotel Lefkas
7 Hotel Santa Maura

PLACES TO EAT
2 Il Posto
8 Cafe Casbah
10 Regantos Taverna

11 Lighthouse Taverna
19 Karaboulias Restaurant

OTHER
1 Archaeological Museum;
   Cultural Centre
5 Motorcycle Rental Santas
6 Europcar; Budget Car Rental
9 Plateia Agiou Spyridonos

12 Public Library of Lefkada &
    Collection of Post-Byzantine Icons
13 OTE
14 National Bank of Greece & ATM
15 Post Office
16 Ionian Bank; ATM
17 Internet Café
18 Tourist Police & Police
20 KTEL Bus Station

place off Dorpfeld, halfway between the main square and the waterfront. The immaculate rooms are large and airy, and each has a balcony, TV, fridge and air-con.

Hotel Lefkas (☎ 2645 023 916, fax 2645 024 579, Panagou 2) Singles/doubles €55.80/88. The Lefkas, with its palatial lobby, faces the port. Rooms are not nearly as grand as the hotel's exterior and lobby would have you expect, but they certainly offer all you'll need for a comfortable stay.

Places to Eat *Karaboulias Restaurant* (☎ 2645 021 367) Mains to €10.30. Kara-

boulias fish taverna, on the eastern waterfront, offers traditional fare with flair. As well as its pavement tables, it has seating across the road on the quayfront, but sadly the view is of construction of the new marina, due for completion in 2004.

Regantos Taverna (☎ 2645 022 855, Vergioti 17) Mains to €8.80. Tucked away west of the main thoroughfare is this atmospheric little place, painted an eye-catching and appealing combination of blue and yellow. The menu features all the grilled and baked Greek standards, plus well-prepared seafood dishes.

Lighthouse Taverna (☎ 2645 025 117, *Filarmonikis 14*) Mains to €8.80. We must admit to some cynicism when we saw all the guidebook recommendations photocopied and pasted in this taverna's window, but we came to the conclusion that all were genuine. Sotiris and his family have a good time running this friendly eatery and they offer tasty, good-value Greek favourites in their delightful, vine-covered garden.

The western side of the waterfront is lined with hip bars and cafes frequented by fashionable Lefkadians. *Il Posto*, at the end of Dorpfeld, is a cool place to hang out. *Cafe Casbah* on Plateia Agiou Spyridonos offers excellent people-watching and is a great venue for chilling out.

Around Lefkada

Nydri A sleepy fishing village not so long ago, Nydri, 16km south of Lefkada Town, fell hook, line and sinker to the lure of the tourist trade. Now it's a busy, commercialised but fun town from where you can cruise around the islets of **Madouri**, **Sparti**, **Skorpidi** and **Skorpios**, plus visit **Meganisi**. Shop around for the full range of excursions – a day trip taking in Meganisi and Skorpios costs from €8.80 to €14.70 (the higher price will usually include an extra such as a beach barbecue lunch).

The privately owned Madouri islet, where the Greek poet Aristotelis Valaoritis (1824–79) spent his last 10 years, is off limits. It's not officially possible to land on Skorpios, where Aristotle, sister Artemis and children Alexander and Christina Onassis are buried in a cemetery visible from the sea, but you can swim off a sandy beach on the northern side of the island.

If you would rather explore the islets independently, boats can be hired from Trident Travel Agency (☎ 2645 092 978, fax 2645 092 037, [e] trident@otenet.gr) on the main street.

The quiet village of **Vlyho** is 3km south of Nydri. Beyond here, a road leads to a peninsula where Wilhelm Dorpfeld is buried. Just west of the Nydri-Vlyho road are the Bronze Age ruins that he excavated, leading him to believe Lefkada was Homer's Ithaca.

Places to Stay & Eat There are a large number of rooms and studios in Nydri though a fair few get block-booked by tour companies. Try Samba Tours (☎ 2645 092 658, fax 2645 092 659) for assistance with accommodation and most other tourist services.

Dessimi Beach Camping (☎ 2645 095 225, fax 2645 095 190) Adult/tent €5/3.80. This basic but pleasant camping ground is south of Nydri, signposted after the village of Vlyho. It's right on the beach, but the waterfront sites are tough to come by. There's boat rental directly in front.

Gorgona Hotel (☎/fax 2645 092 268) Double rooms €29.40, double studios €58.70. In a side street off the main road opposite the Avis car-rental office, you'll find this friendly, family-run place. Set in a shady, flower-filled garden that's home to a few ducks, the Gorgon offers simple, spotlessly clean rooms and studios.

Ta Kalamia (☎ 2645 092 983) Mains €5.30-11.80. One of the most interesting eateries in town is this stylish place, on the main drag and with a large garden area out back. The English version of the menu is a delightful read – fancy some 'mashroom's ala Hellinic', 'baby goad', 'scared rabbit in beer' or 'saute shrimps with in poef garlic'? No matter – the food is excellent.

Poros Beach This little village overlooks Rouda Bay and makes a great alternative base to the often-raucous Nydri, although your own transport is an asset. The beach is good and there are boats for hire.

Poros Beach Camping & Bungalows (☎ 2645 095 452, fax 2645 095 152) Adult/tent €5.90/5.30, doubles €41.10, 2-bedroom bungalows (sleeping 4) €82.20. This large, popular complex on the way into the village has something for everyone, and facilities are excellent – there's a restaurant, mini-market, bar and swimming pool.

Rouda Bay Hotel (☎ 2645 095 600, fax 2645 095 631, [e] roudabay@corfu-island .com) Double studios €58.70. This 'hotel' is a very attractive complex of studios and maisonettes set around a courtyard smack in the middle of the beachfront. The spacious

IONIAN ISLANDS

rooms are beautifully furnished and are a cut above those you normally encounter.

Vasiliki Purported to be *the* best windsurfing location in Europe, Vasiliki is a pretty fishing village with a below-average beach (but that's OK as most visitors are here to engage in more active pursuits than sunbathing and paddling). It attracts a sizable, largely youthful, crowd each season and you can hop over to Kefallonia and Ithaki from here if you are heading south.

If they're not already booked solid, you can rent windsurfing equipment from **Club Vass** (*Greece* ☎ *2645 031 588, UK* ☎ *01920-484121,* W *www.clubvass.com*) on the beach, and possibly get some lessons too. Priority is, understandably, given to people who have come on one of their all-inclusive package holidays from the UK, but it's worth asking if you're keen to give it a go.

Next door to Club Vass, **Wildwind** (*Greece* ☎/fax *2645 031 610, UK* ☎ *01920-484516,* W *www.wildwind.co.uk*) rents out catamarans and offers instruction on a similar basis (ie, if equipment is not being used by their guests).

Caiques take visitors from Vasiliki to swim at the best beaches on the west coast, and a boat will also take you to the unspoilt **Agiofylli Beach**, to the town's south.

Places to Stay & Eat The best bet for accommodation is to drop in to Samba Tours (☎ 2645 031 520, fax 2645 031 522) on the main road into town.

Camping Vassiliki Beach (☎ *2645 031 308, fax 2645 031 458*) Adult/tent €5.60/

Ionians' Best Beaches

As you travel around the Ionians you'll find water so exquisitely blue you'll swear it's been retouched by a photographer. The best locations for taking in this awesome sight include the beaches of Antipaxi, the entire west coast of Lefkada, gorgeous Myrtos Beach on Kefallonia, and photogenic Shipwreck Beach on Zakynthos. The water is chilly for swimming in spring, but heats up considerably through the summer and stays pleasantly warm until late October.

Corfu has some great beaches but few are undeveloped. Head for the lovely sandy stretches of the west coast including: **Glyfada**, **Pelekas Beach** and **Myrtiotissa** (the latter is the island's unofficial nudist beach); the picturesque coves in and around **Paleokastritsa** (you can take a taxi boat to nearby grottos and beaches inaccessible by road); and the island's north-east. Paxi has numerous pretty coves but no beaches of note – take a boat to Antipaxi instead.

Lefkada's west coast offers some of the best beaches in the Ionians. **Kathisma**, **Egremeni** and **Porto Katsiki** are remarkably underdeveloped, perhaps due to their relative inaccessibility and the lack of major resort towns on this side of the island. Alternatively, get off the beaten track at lovely **Agios Ioannis** beach on the satellite island of Meganisi.

On Kefallonia, **Skala Beach** is long and sandy and offers good water sports, but it's outshone by **Myrtos** on the west coast near Assos (spectacularly set between limestone cliffs) and **Antisamos**, just east of the town of Sami in a stunning, verdant setting.

Ithaki is similar to Paxi in that it features a number of pretty coves rather than long stretches of beach, and these are great to explore by private motorboat. Your best option may be the regular taxi boat from Vathy to lovely **Gidaki Beach**.

Zakynthos' **Shipwreck Beach** is indeed stunning (but definitely *not* when half-a-dozen large cruise boats pull in) – take a small boat there in the morning or afternoon. The long, sandy stretch at **Gerakas**, in the island's south-east, is popular with both loggerhead turtles and humans, so development is kept in check and there are no water sports to upset the underwater residents.

Kythira's beaches are low-key affairs in contrast to the busy shores of the larger, more touristed Ionians, and accessibility sometimes presents a problem. Still, it's worth the effort. Popular picturesque stretches include **Fyri Ammos** and **Kaladi**.

5.30. This happening camping ground is a very popular place for windsurfers – that much is clear by the amount of equipment scattered around. This well-shaded place is well run and has good facilities.

Pension Holidays (☎/fax 2645 031 426) Doubles €44. Friendly Spiros offers simply furnished rooms with air-con, TV, fridge and balcony at reasonable prices. Head down the main street to the waterfront, turn left and you'll come across the pension.

Alexander Restaurant (☎ 2645 031 858) Mains to €9.70. Busy Alexander, on the waterfront, offers an excellent range of well-prepared Italian and Greek dishes, and judging by the crowds the punters are happy.

West Coast Beach lovers should skip Lefkada's east coast and head straight for the west. The sea here is possibly the best in the Ionian – an incredible pale turquoise blue that is almost iridescent – and most beaches feature pale golden or white sand. The best beaches include **Porto Katsiki**, **Egremni** and **Kathisma**. All are signposted off the road leading to the island's southwestern promontory (a sanctuary of Apollo once stood at **Cape Lefkatas**).

The town of **Agios Nikitas** is hardly Lefkada's best-kept secret, but it is the island's most picturesque and tasteful resort. There's not much of a beach to speak of here, so most people head to beautiful **Mylos Beach** just around the headland, which is inaccessible by road – you have to take a taxi boat from the tiny Agios Nikitas beach.

Olive Tree Hotel (☎ 2645 097 453, fax 2645 097 153, e olivetreehotel@hotmail .com) Doubles/triples €52.80/58.70. Set, as its name suggests, among olive trees (signposted down a small path off the main road just north of Agios Nikitas), this friendly place has simple but pleasant rooms, all with balcony and with some kitchen facilities.

MEGANISI Μεγανήσι
postcode 310 83 • pop 1250
Meganisi has the largest population of Lefkada's three inhabited satellite islets and is the easiest to visit, but like many small Greek

islands it has suffered population depletion. It's easily visited on a day trip, independently or on one of the excursion boats from Nydri that visit a few of the satellite islands.

Meganisi's a tranquil islet with a lovely, verdant landscape and deep bays of turquoise water, fringed by pebbled beaches. It's visited primarily by yachties and is untouched by package-tour operators. It has three settlements: the capital of Spartohori (above the small port of Spilia), the port of Vathy and the village of Katomeri.

Getting To/From Meganisi
The *Meganisi* ferry boat runs about six times daily between Nydri (the southern end of the quay) and Meganisi (35 to 45 minutes, €1.40). It usually calls in first at Porto Spilia and then into Vathy before heading back to Nydri.

Whether you're visiting for a day on the ferry or plan to stay longer, you may want to bring over a car or moped from Nydri, as there is nowhere to rent transport on the island.

Spartohori & Porto Spilia
Quiet Spartohori, with narrow, winding lanes and pretty, flower-bedecked houses, perches on a plateau above Porto Spilia, where the ferry docks. No-one lives at Spilia, but there are several popular tavernas. A road ascends steeply to Spartohori or you can walk the 1km there up steps. To reach Spartohori's main street and central square turn right at Tropicana Pizzeria. Alternatively, take the road out of Porto Spilia and instead of veering right to Spartohori, veer left to reach a pleasant pebble beach.

One of the island's best beaches is **Agios Ioannis**, a long stretch of small pebbles 3km south-west of Spartohori.

Places to Stay & Eat There's no official camping ground, but wild camping is tolerated at Porto Spilia, in the area behind the restaurant Locanta Salitzo (☎ 2645 051 646). Inquire here before setting up, and expect to pay about €4.40 per person.

Tropicana Pizzeria (☎ 2645 051 846) Pizzas to €5.60. Friendly Giorgios is the man to see if you want good home-made pizzas, or

Ionian Activities

It hardly needs to be said that the best activities in this part of the world are centred on, under or around water. Don't be disheartened if you're not fortunate enough to be **sailing** around the Ionians in a private yacht – there are countless opportunities here to rent a small motorboat, cruise the coast, and find your own small coves and deserted beaches. Among the best places for this are the north-east coast of Corfu, the east coast of Paxi, and the east coast of Lefkada, out of Nydri (taking in some of the satellite islands).

There are also opportunities for **diving** in the crystal-clear waters off the larger Ionian islands. Dive centres on Corfu, Lefkada, Kefallonia and Zakynthos offer dives and instruction for all levels, including beginners (Paxi has a centre for experienced divers only). One of the most popular diving areas is Paleokastritsa on Corfu's west coast – and not far from Paleokastritsa in Ermones you can play golf at one of the few courses in Greece.

Anyone interested in **windsurfing** and/or **catamaran sailing** should head straight for Vasiliki on Lefkada. Vasiliki Bay is one of Europe's best windsurfing locations (light onshore winds in the morning are perfect for beginners, brisk cross-shore winds in the afternoon suit the experts). A number of UK-based companies can be found on the beach here but it can be difficult to rent their equipment if you haven't signed up for one of their all-inclusive deals (ie, flights, accommodation, tuition and kit rental). In the low and mid-season rental is possible, subject to availability, so it's worth asking.

Of course, there's the appealing option of **beach-bumming** (hell, you're on holiday), or there are countless opportunities to parasail, waterski, rent pedaloes or kayaks or take rides on 'bananas' and 'ringos' behind speedboats. On the larger islands you won't have to look too far to find these activities – there's usually an operator on the main resort beaches.

For those not so keen on getting wet, **walking** is an extremely popular pastime. Heading off the main roads allows you to see much more of the countryside and enjoy the unspoilt traditional villages, pretty wildflowers and often spectacular views. There are a number of books and booklets devoted to the subject (there's usually one covering each island), including *The Second Book of Corfu Walks* by Hilary Whitton Paipeti, which also contains mountain-bike tour details. A new development of great interest to walkers is the 250km Corfu Trail, which traverses the island and should take between eight and 12 days to complete (see W www.travelling.gr/corfutrail for information).

Given the Ionians' hilly terrain, it's not surprising that mountain-biking is becoming more popular in this region (see W www.mountainbikecorfu.gr).

---

if you're after a place to stay in Spartohori. Giorgios can contact a room-owner for you, who will meet you at the pizzeria and guide you to your lodgings. *Nikos* (☎ 2645 051 050), *Yiannis* (☎ 2645 051 695) and *Giorgios* (☎ 2645 051 409) all have rooms in the €23.50 to €29.40 range, and it's wise to book ahead for July and August.

Taverna Porto Spilia, down in the ferry-docking area below Spartohori, is a sprawling, bustling waterside eatery offering all the local favourites. *Taverna Lakis*, on Spartohori's square, offers tasty Greek fare and features Greek evenings, which tourists from Nydri often attend (brought over by excursion boat). When things really get

going, Mamma Lakis, who is no spring chicken, has been known to dance with a table on her head.

Vathy & Katomeri

Vathy is the island's second port. The post office is on the waterfront near the quay. Farther round there's a children's playground in an area resembling a town square. Beyond here, the road climbs to Katomeri, 700m away. From Katomeri you can visit a number of good beaches, including Fanari and Limonari.

Hotel Meganisi (☎ 2645 051 240, fax 2645 051 639) Doubles €64.60. The island's only hotel is the cosy Meganisi, well signposted in Katomeri. It offers spotless, modern rooms with air-con, a lovely swimming pool and outdoor area, plus a restaurant serving tasty traditional dishes.

To find private accommodation in Vathy and surrounds, the best contact is helpful, English-speaking Kiki at *Cafe Risko* (☎ *2645 051 134,* e *vathi_blues@hotmail.com*), on the square in Vathy. Kiki can help find you one of the 20-odd rooms in town priced (very roughly) from €23.50 in low season, €44 in high. Risko is an excellent place to stop by anyway – it offers pizza, pasta and gelati in a pleasant garden, there's a computer set up for Internet access, plus you can change money or browse the book exchange.

Another good dining option is *Taverna Porto Vathy*, a charming fish taverna right next to the ferry quay.

Kefallonia & Ithaki

KEFALLONIA Κεφαλλονιά
pop 39,579
Kefallonia, the largest of the Ionian islands, has rugged, towering mountains. The highest, Mt Enos (1627m), is the Mediterranean's only mountain with a unique fir forest species, *Abies Cephalonica*. While not as tropical as Corfu, Kefallonia has many species of heavily scented herbs and wildflowers.

Kefallonia's capital is Argostoli but the main port is Sami, on the south-eastern coast. As the island is so big and mountainous, travelling between towns is time consuming.

A good Web site to gather information on the island and its many towns is w www.kefaloniathewaytogo.com.

Getting To/From Kefallonia
Air There is at least one flight daily between Kefallonia and Athens (€65.50). The Olympic Airways office (☎ 2671 028 808) in Argostoli is at Rokou Vergoti 1.

Bus There are a few options for the bus journey to Athens from Kefallonia. There is a daily bus plying the Argostoli-Poros-Kyllini-Patras-Athens route (€24.50 to Athens), a

bus taking the Argostoli-Kyllini-Athens route (€25) and another on the Argostoli-Sami-Patras-Athens route (€23.90). Prices include ferry tickets, and all journeys take around eight hours. For information contact the KTEL bus station (☎ 2671 022 276) on the southern waterfront in Argostoli.

Ferry – Domestic Kefallonia has six ports: Sami (port police ☎ 2674 022 031), Argostoli (☎ 2671 022 224), Poros (☎ 2674 072 460), Lixouri (☎ 2671 094 100), Pesada and Fiskardo (☎ 2674 041 400).

At least two ferries daily connect Sami with Patras (2½ hours, €10) and Vathy on Ithaki (one hour, €3.80). From Poros (1¼ hours, €6.15) and Argostoli (2¼ hours, €8.80), at least two ferries ply daily to Kyllini in the Peloponnese.

In summer, boats leave Sami to go Piso Aetos in Ithaki (40 minutes, €1.80), then Fiskardo (1½ hours, €3.30). From Fiskardo they continue to Vasiliki in Lefkada (three hours, €5.90) and return to Kefallonia later in the day. Daily ferries also run in high season on a route between Fiskardo, Frikes (Ithaki) and Nydri (Lefkada).

From Pesada in the south there are two high-season services daily (1¼ hours, €3.80) travelling to Agios Nikolaos on Zakynthos (travel agents in Kefallonia sell tickets to 'Skinari', but the port town is actually called Agios Nikolaos). There is inexplicably no bus to the remote port of Pesada, and virtually no buses from Agios Nikolaos to anywhere in Zakynthos, making crossing without your own transport quite difficult – not to mention costly if you rely on taxis. Both these ports are quite a distance from the major towns in the respective islands.

Ferry – International In high season there is a regular ferry plying the route between Patras, Sami, Igoumenitsa and Brindisi in Italy. To get to other ports in Italy, you need to take the ferry first from Sami to Patras.

Tickets can be obtained from Vassilatos Shipping (☎ 2671 022 618, fax 2671 024 992) on Metaxa 54, opposite the port authority in Argostoli. In Sami, inquire at

IONIAN ISLANDS

IONIAN ISLANDS

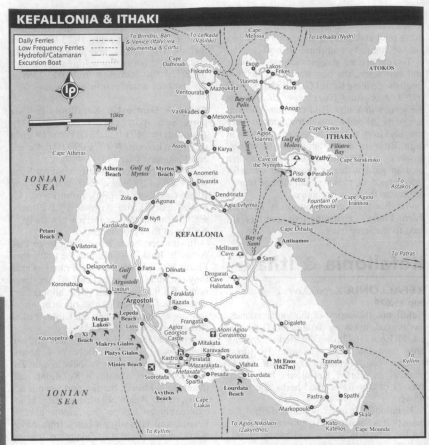

KEFALLONIA & ITHAKI

Daily Ferries
Low Frequency Ferries
Hydrofoil/Catamaran
Excursion Boat

0   5   10km
0   3   6mi

Blue Sea Travel (☎ 2674 023 007, e blue-mare@otenet.gr).

Getting Around Kefallonia

To/From the Airport The airport is 9km south of Argostoli. There is no airport bus. A taxi costs €7.40.

Ferry Car ferries run hourly between Lixouri and Argostoli. The journey takes 30 minutes, and tickets (€0.90 per person) are sold on board.

In summer, you can catch a morning ferry from Sami to Fiskardo (via Piso Aetos

on Ithaki), or sometimes an afternoon ferry, which runs direct.

Bus From Argostoli's bus station there are seven buses daily to the Lassi Peninsula (€0.90), four buses to Sami (€2), two to Poros (€3), two to Skala (€2.70) and two to Fiskardo (€3.30). There is a daily east-coast service linking Katelios with Skala, Poros, Sami, Agia Efimia and Fiskardo. No buses operate on Sunday.

Car & Motorcycle In Argostoli, cars can be hired from Reliable Rent a Car (☎ 2671

023 613), next to the Olympic Airways office at R Vergoti 3, and motorcycles from Sunbird Motor Rent (☎ 2671 023 723), on the waterfront. The Avis representative is CBR Travel (☎ 2671 022 770) at the southern end of the central square.

Argostoli Αργοστόλι
postcode 281 00 • pop 7300

Argostoli, unlike Zakynthos Town, was not restored to its former Venetian splendour after the 1953 earthquake. It's a modern, lively port set on a peninsula. Its harbour is divided from Koutavos lagoon by a British-built causeway connecting it with the rest of Kefallonia.

Orientation & Information The modern and (for once) user-friendly KTEL bus station is on the southern waterfront near the causeway; the main ferry quay is at the waterfront's northern end. The EOT (☎ 2671 022 248), on the northern waterfront beside the port police, is open 8am to 2.30pm weekdays (in July and August it also opens 5pm to 9.30pm weekdays, and in August it often opens on weekends).

The centre of Argostoli's activity is Plateia Vallianou, the huge palm-treed central square up from the waterfront off 21 Maïou, and its surrounding streets. Other hubs are the waterfront (Antoni Tristi, which becomes Ioannou Metaxa to the south), and pedestrianised Lithostrotou, two blocks inland, lined with smart shops and cafes.

There are banks with ATMs along the northern waterfront and on Lithostrotou. The post office is on Lithostrotou and the OTE is on G Vergoti. Excelixis (☎ 2671 025 530), signposted off Lithostrotou (behind the Greek Orthodox Church), offers Internet access.

Things to See Argostoli's archaeological museum (☎ 2671 028 300, R Vergoti; admission €1.50; open 8.30am-3pm Tues-Sun) has a well-displayed collection of island relics including Mycenaean finds from tombs.

The **Korgialenio History and Folklore Museum** (☎ 2671 028 835, R Vergoti; ad-

mission €3; open 9am-2pm Mon-Sat) has a busy but good collection of traditional costumes, furniture and tools, items which belonged to British occupiers, and photographs of pre- and post-earthquake Argostoli.

KTEL organises day tours of the island (taking in Drogarati Cave, Melissani Lake and Fiskardo) for €17.60, and day trips to Ithaki for €29.40. Inquire at the bus station.

The town's closest sandy beaches are **Makrys Gialos** and **Platys Gialos**, 5km south in the package-resort area of the Lassi Peninsula. Regular buses serve the area.

Places to Stay The EOT should be able to give you a list of locals offering inexpensive domatia.

Argostoli Beach Camping (☎ 2671 023 487, fax 2671 024 525) Adult/tent €4.70/4.40. This OK camping ground – one of only two on the island – is on the coast, 2km north of town. It has decent enough facilities but is not a patch on the camping ground at Sami.

Vivian Villa (☎ 2671 023 396, fax 2671 028 670, ⓔ villaviv@otenet.gr, Deladetsima 9) Doubles €49.90, double studios €58.70 (for triples add 20%); 4-person apartments €88. Easily the nicest place in town is this small complex, run by superfriendly, English-speaking Vivian and Nick. They offer spacious, spotless accommodation and if they're full, they'll always attempt to find you somewhere else to stay.

Kyknos Studios (☎ 2671 023 398, fax 2671 025 943, M Geroulanou 4) Double studios €35.20. Another good option is these pleasant, simple studios set behind a garden not far from the square.

There's a string of hotels along the waterfront, and a number around the bustling main square.

Hotel Tourist (☎/fax 2671 022 510, Antoni Tristi 109) Singles/doubles €35.20/52.80. The refurbished Tourist, on the waterfront, offers pleasant rooms and good facilities.

Hotel Ionian Plaza (☎ 2671 025 581, fax 2671 025 585, Plateia Vallianou) Singles/doubles €40.50/62.50. Argostoli's smartest hotel is the marble-decorated Ionian Plaza, right on the main square. The lobby and public areas are impressively stylish; the

IONIAN ISLANDS

ARGOSTOLI

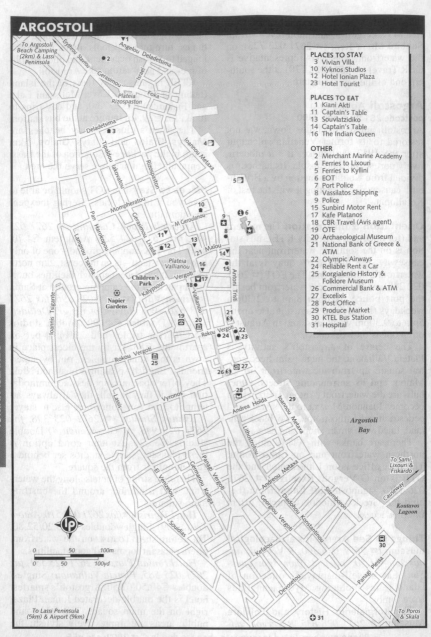

PLACES TO STAY
3 Vivian Villa
10 Kyknos Studios
12 Hotel Ionian Plaza
23 Hotel Tourist

PLACES TO EAT
1 Kiani Akti
11 Captain's Table
13 Souvlatzidiko
14 Captain's Table
16 The Indian Queen

OTHER
2 Merchant Marine Academy
4 Ferries to Lixouri
5 Ferries to Kyllini
6 EOT
7 Port Police
8 Vassilatos Shipping
9 Police
15 Sunbird Motor Rent
17 Kafe Platanos
18 CBR Travel (Avis agent)
19 OTE
20 Archaeological Museum
21 National Bank of Greece & ATM
22 Olympic Airways
24 Reliable Rent a Car
25 Korgialenio History & Folklore Museum
26 Commercial Bank & ATM
27 Excelixis
28 Post Office
29 Produce Market
30 KTEL Bus Station
31 Hospital

Argostoli Bay

To Sami,
Lixouri &
Fiskardo

Causeway

Koutavos Lagoon

To Poros
& Skala

To Argostoli
Beach Camping
(2km) & Lassi
Peninsula

Plateia
Rizospaston

Plateia
Vallianou

Children's
Park

Napier
Gardens

To Lassi Peninsula
(5km) & Airport (9km)

IONIAN ISLANDS

rooms – all with balconies overlooking the square – are very pleasant.

Places to Eat Among the pricey cafes on the main square is the very popular *Souvlatzidiko*, next to Hotel Aeon, offering tasty gyros for about €1.50.

Captain's Table (☎ 2671 023 896, Rizospaston 3) Mains €4.40-14.50. Just off the central square (behind Hotel Ionian Plaza), upmarket Captain's is one of Argostoli's top restaurants and the place to go for a splurge. Despite the fact that the place prides itself on its fish and seafood, choosing either can inflate the bill considerably. You'll do well with any of the meat dishes, and there are gourmet offerings such as duck in orange sauce and even ostrich fillet. There's a sister restaurant, also called the *Captain's Table* (☎ 2671 027 170), on the corner of the waterfront and 21 Maïou. This place also has high-quality food but a more casual feel, and more casual prices.

The Indian Queen (☎ 2671 022 632, Lavraga 2) Mains €5.20-10.30. Give your tastebuds a rest from fish, feta and mousakas and head to this place just off the main square (opposite Hotel Mirabel). A good selection of curries and tandoori and balti dishes is on offer, and vegetarians should fare well.

Kiani Akti (☎ 2671 026 680) Mains €5-13.20. The fish and the mezes here are excellent, but it's the setting that's the main attraction. Located on a jetty opposite the Merchant Marine Academy at the northern end of the waterfront, you can dine while the water laps under your feet.

Pick up self-catering supplies from the huge waterfront *produce market*. Opposite are good bakeries and grocery stores.

No surprises that the main hub for nightlife are the cafe-bars on the main square, with tables spilling out onto the road and music pumping out of the speakers until late. *Kafe Platanos* (☎ 2671 028 282, Plateia Vallianou) is the classiest of the bunch, with chandeliers inside and tables and wicker chairs scattered around a lovely large plane tree outside.

Sami Σάμη
postcode 280 82 • pop 1000

Sami, 25km north-east of Argostoli and the main port of Kefallonia, was also devastated by the 1953 earthquake. It now has undistinguished buildings, but its setting is pretty, nestled in a bay and flanked by steep hills. It's worth an overnight stay to visit the

IONIAN ISLANDS

The Cult of Captain Corelli

Kefallonia receives its fair share of package tourists but not on the same scale as Corfu and Zakynthos, although that may soon change due to some heavy Hollywood exposure.

The island has received unprecedented publicity in recent years thanks to Louis de Bernières' novel *Captain Corelli's Mandolin* (released in the USA as *Corelli's Mandolin*). It was on a package holiday to Kefallonia that the author, a former soldier, received his inspiration for the story. Instead of relaxing on the beach he spent his holiday learning about the island's history, and the resulting book tells the emotional story of a young Italian army officer sent to Kefallonia during WWII and his relationships with the locals, his fellow soldiers and German commanders. Most beach bums will have a dog-eared copy of the novel, and copies are available in almost every minimarket and bookstore on the island.

Publicity for the island reached fever pitch in the summer of 2001 with the release of the movie based on the book, starring Nicholas Cage as Corelli and co-starring Penelope Cruz and John Hurt (plus hundreds of Kefallonian extras, as photos in shops, hotels and restaurants all over the island will attest). The movie was filmed entirely on location in Kefallonia in 2000, largely in and around the town of Sami. You'll be disappointed if you see the film then visit Sami hoping to marvel at its pretty Venetian architecture. Sami was largely reduced to rubble in the 1953 earthquake that devastated most of the island, and the town you see in the movie was all a cleverly constructed set.

nearby caves and beach. A post office, OTE and bank are in town. Buses for Argostoli usually meet ferries.

Places to Stay & Eat *Karavomylos Beach Camping* (☎ 2674 022 480, fax 2674 022 932, [e] valettas@hol.gr) Adult/tent €4.70/4.40. This well-kept beachfront ground is 800m west of Sami – turn right from the quay and follow the coast. It's a large, shady place and offers all manner of facilities: minimarket, laundry, restaurant, playground and Internet access.

Hotel Melissani (☎/fax 2674 022 464) Singles/doubles €38.20/49.90. This pleasant older-style hotel is signposted from the eastern end of the waterfront. Rooms are comfortable and offer comforts such as TV and fridge.

Delfinia (☎ 2674 022 008) Mains €3.80-10.30. All the places to eat in Sami are clustered along the harbour, and the tavernas are much of a muchness. One of the better places – and popular with the locals – is Delfinia, which does fish and meat on the grill, has a wider than normal choice of vegetarian Greek dishes and often features a musician serenading diners (not with a mandolin – at least not yet).

Riviera (☎ 2674 023 233) Mains €3-6.50. Riviera is a pleasant waterfront place where you can while away some time over good coffee, breakfast or a light meal (omelette, pizza, pasta, etc). Simple, inexpensive domatia are offered above the cafe.

Around Sami

Be sure to visit gorgeous **Antisamos Beach**, 4km north-east of Sami. The long, stony beach is in a lovely green setting backed by verdant hills. The drive here is also a highlight, offering dramatic views.

Mellisani Cave (*admission €4.70, including boat trip*) is a subterranean seawater lake. When the sun is overhead its rays shine through an opening in the cave ceiling, lighting the water's many shades of blue. The cave is 2.5km from Sami, well signposted beyond the seaside village of Karavomylos. The large **Drogarati Cave** (*admission €3*) has impressive stalactites.

It's signposted from the Argostoli road, 4km from Sami. Both caves are open all day.

The fishing village of **Agia Evfymia** with its pebbled beach is 10km north of Sami. It is another popular yachting stop, and there are a few hotels and some studios and domatia here.

Fiskardo Φισκάρδο

postcode 280 84 • pop 300

Fiskardo, 50km north of Argostoli, was the only village not devastated by the 1953 earthquake. Framed by cypress-mantled hills, and with fine Venetian buildings, it's a delightful place, even if it is a little dolled up for the tourists. It's especially popular with yachties.

The bus will drop you off on the road that bypasses Fiskardo. Walk across the car park, descend the steps to the left of the church and continue ahead to Fiskardo's central square and waterfront.

You can get to Fiskardo by ferry from Lefkada and Ithaki or by bus from Argostoli.

Places to Stay & Eat It will be tough to find accommodation in high season if you haven't prebooked. At other times it's OK, but prices are high.

Regina's Rooms (☎ 2674 041 125) Doubles with/without bath €44/35.20. Behind the town, by the car park area, is this reasonably priced place run by friendly Regina. Rooms are simple and among the cheapest in town, and there's a good-value cafe here too.

Stella Apartments (☎ 2674 041 211, fax 2674 041 262, [e] stella@kef.forthnet.gr) Double studios €67.50. This yellow-and-green complex around from the harbour offers comfortable studios in a very pleasant setting. Across the road from the apartments is a set of steps leading down to a cove for swimming.

Nicholas Taverna (☎/fax 2674 041 307) Mains €4.70-11.20. To the right as you disembark the ferry is this excellent taverna with a great view over Fiskardo, run by exuberant Nicholas and sons. Food is very good, and the studio accommodation offered here is first class (studios priced from €93.90).

The Captain's Cabin (☎ 2674 041 007) Mains to €8.80. You can't miss Captain's on the seafront, a popular watering hole for visiting yachties. Food on offer here is from a limited version of the standard Greek/international menu.

Lagoudera (☎ 2674 041 275) Gyros €1.50, mains €3.30-8.20. In a pretty setting just back from the harbourfront is Lagoudera, known for its grilled meat and serving up tasty gyros, souvlaki, steaks and lamb chops.

Around Fiskardo

Assos is a gem of whitewashed and pastel houses, straddling the isthmus of a peninsula on which stands a Venetian fortress. Assos was damaged in the 1953 earthquake but sensitively restored with the help of a donation from the city of Paris. There's some accommodation on the road into town. Try *Linardos Studios* (☎/fax 2674 051 563), with immaculate double studios for €55.80.

There's an outstanding white sandy beach at **Myrtos**, 3km south of Assos. If you explore by boat, you'll find nearby hidden coves between tall limestone cliffs.

Southern Kefallonia

Kastro, above the village of **Peratata**, 9km south-east of Argostoli, was the island's capital in the Middle Ages. Ruined houses stand beneath the 13th-century castle of **Agios Georgios**, which affords magnificent views.

The villages of **Vlahata** on the principal Argostoli-Poros road and Lourdata (or Lourdas) down the hillside on the coast have merged into one. **Lourdata Beach** is long and sandy. **Kato Katelios** is a charming little place, not quite a thriving resort but no longer the small farming and fishing community that it once was.

Poros is overdeveloped and has a rather scruffy, pebbled beach. **Skala**, on the southern tip, is a preferable resort with a long, fine, sand beach backed by a pine wood, but at the time of research it was extremely tough to find accommodation in Skala that was not block-booked by tour operators. Poros has better accommodation options for the independent traveller.

Odyssia (☎ 2671 081 615, fax 2671 081 614) 4-person apartments €73.40. In Kato Katelios, just back from the waterfront, these apartments are incredibly spacious and fully equipped for a pleasant longer stay.

If you wish to stay in Skala, contact Vangelis at Skalina Tours (☎ 2671 083 275, fax 2671 083 475) for assistance with independent accommodation.

Makis Studios & Apartments (☎/fax 2674 072 501) Double studios €52.80, 4-person apartments €73.40. These immaculate studios in Poros are run by friendly, helpful folk.

ITHAKI Ιθάκη
postcode 283 00 • pop 3100

Ithaki (ancient Ithaca) was Odysseus' long-lost home, the island where the stoical Penelope sat patiently, weaving a shroud. She told her suitors, who believed Odysseus was dead, that she would choose one of them once she had completed the shroud. Cunningly, she unravelled it every night in order to keep her suitors at bay, as she awaited Odysseus' return.

Ithaki is separated from Kefallonia by a strait only 2km to 4km wide. The unspoilt island has a harsh, precipitous east coast and a soft, green west coast. The interior is mountainous and rocky with pockets of pine forest, stands of cypresses, olive groves and vineyards. Because of its general lack of good beaches, Ithaki doesn't attract large crowds, but it's a great place to spend a relaxing, quiet holiday.

A decent Web site to find more information is Ⓦ www.ithaki.org.

Getting To/From Ithaki

There are two ferries daily connecting Vathy with Patras (3¾ hours, €10.90) via Sami (one hour, €3.80) on Kefallonia. There's also a ferry doing a circular route between Piso Aetos on the west coast and Vasiliki on Lefkada via Fiskardo and on to Sami on Kefallonia. (Piso Aetos has no settlement and consists of a dock, a small ticket booth and a canteen. Taxis usually meet boats.)

In high season, a daily ferry sails between Frikes (northern Ithaki), Fiskardo

IONIAN ISLANDS

and Nydri on Lefkada, and a daily ferry also runs between Piso Aetos and Astakos on the mainland (2¾ hours, €5). Ithaki's port police can be contacted on ☎ 2674 032 909.

Getting Around Ithaki

The island's one bus runs twice daily to Kioni (via Stavros and Frikes) from Vathy (€1.50). It's primarily a bus for getting children to school so its limited schedule is not well suited to travellers on day trips. Taxis are quite expensive (eg, €17.60 for the Vathy-Frikes trip). In Vathy, Spiros & Nikos Rent a Bike (☎ 2674 033 243) is behind the nautical & folklore museum, and AGS Rent a Car (☎ 2674 032 702, fax 2674 033 551) is on the waterfront beside the town hall.

Vathy Βαθύ

pop 1800

Vathy (also known as Ithaki Town) is small with a few twisting streets, a central square, nice cafes and restaurants, and a few tourist shops, grocers and the like. Old mansions rise up from the seafront.

Orientation & Information The ferry quay is on the western side of the bay. To reach the central square of Plateia Efstathiou Drakouli, turn left and follow the waterfront. The main thoroughfare, Kallinikou, is parallel to, and one block inland from, the waterfront.

Ithaki has no tourist office, but there are agencies on the main square that can help with information. The tourist police (☎ 2674 032 205) are on Evmeou, which runs south from the middle of the waterfront.

The National Bank of Greece (with ATM) is just south-west of the central square. The post office is on the central square and the OTE is farther east along the waterfront. Ogygia Net-Café, a few metres inland from the harbour (turn up the alley by Café Lo Spuntino, signposted 'Flowers'), offers Internet access for €3 per hour.

Things to See & Do Behind Hotel Mentor, is a small **archaeological museum** (☎ 2674 032 200; admission free; open 8.30am-3pm Tues-Sun). The charming **nautical & folklore**

museum (admission €0.70; open 9.30am-3.30pm Mon-Fri) is housed in an old generating station just back from the waterfront (signposted) and displays clothing (including traditional dress), household items and furniture as well as shipping paraphernalia.

Boat excursions leave from Vathy harbour in the summer months and include a round-Ithaki trip and a day trip to Lefkada. There is also a taxi boat to lovely **Gidaki Beach**, north-east of Vathy.

Places to Stay *Vasiliki Vlassopoulou Domatia* (☎ 2674 032 119) Doubles €23.50. Turn left from the quay and right at the town hall, take the steps ahead, and you will see the sign for these pleasant, older-style domatia, set around a pretty garden terrace. The owners speak very little English.

Dimitrios Maroudas Rooms & Apartments (☎/fax 2674 032 751) Double rooms with shared bath €23.50, 2-/4-person apartments with kitchen & bathroom €52.80. Just off the eastern waterfront, this place is signposted 180m beyond the OTE (two blocks behind Century Music Club). It's a family-run place providing clean, simple rooms and apartments.

Captain Yiannis Hotel (☎ 2674 033 311, fax 2674 032 849) Double rooms €58.70, studios & apartments from €73.40. This hotel complex is on the opposite side of the harbour to the ferry dock and is not well signposted. It's about 1km from town and you'll know you've reached it by the smart swimming pool and bar area (there's also a tennis court). There's a feeling of space, as the clean, comfortable rooms and apartments are well spread out over the property.

Perantzada 1811 (☎ 2674 023 914, fax 2674 033 493, ⓔ arthotel@otenet.gr) Double rooms with/without sea view €200/170.20. With rooms straight out of a magazine, this gorgeous boutique hotel oozes style (and prices to match). Funky furniture, interesting artwork, colourful rooms, gourmet breakfast and lovely outdoor areas (including beanbags to relax in) combine to make this hotel quite unique in all the Ionians. The pretty, pale-blue building is one block back from the waterfront on the eastern side of town.

Odysseus & Ithaki

Ithaki (Ithaca) has long been the symbolic image for the end of a long journey. For mythical hero Odysseus (Ulysses), Ithaki was the home he left to fight in the Trojan Wars. According to the often wild tales recounted in Homer's *Iliad*, though more specifically in the *Odyssey*, it took the wily hero Odysseus 10 long years to return home to Ithaki from Troy on the Asia Minor coast.

Tossed by tempestuous seas, attacked by sea monsters, delayed by a cunning siren yet helped on his way by friendly Phaeacians, Odysseus finally made landfall on Ithaki. Here, disguised as a beggar, he teamed up with his son Telemachus and his old swineherd Eumaeus, and slayed a castleful of conniving suitors who had been eating him out of home and fortune while trying unsuccessfully to woo the ever-patient and faithful Penelope, Odysseus' long-suffering wife who had waited 20 years for him to return.

Despite Ithaki owing its fame to such illustrious classical connections, no mention of the island appears in writings of the Middle Ages. As late as AD 1504 Ithaki was almost uninhabited following repeated depredations by pirates. The Venetians were obliged to induce settlers from neighbouring islands to repopulate Ithaki. Yet the island is described in considerable detail in the *Odyssey*, which matches in many respects the physical nature of the island today. 'The Fountain of Arethousa' has been identified with a spring rising at the foot of a sea cliff in the south of the island and the 'Cave of the Nymphs' with a fairly nondescript cave up from the Bay of Phorkys. However, many Homerists have been hard-pressed to ascribe other locales described in the *Odyssey* – particularly Odysseus' castle – to actual places on the islands since scant archaeological remains assist the researcher. Other Homerists conclude that Ithaki may well have been Lefkada, a theory espoused by German archaeologist Willem Dorpfeld, though this idea seems to have fallen on rocky ground in more recent times.

Odysseus as a mythical man is everyone's hero, a pre-classical Robin Hood or John Wayne, both villain and king bundled into one well-marketed package. Classical Greek writers presented him sometimes as an unscrupulous politician, and sometimes as a wise and honourable statesman. Philosophers usually admired his intelligence and wisdom. To listeners of yore he was the hero underdog that everyone wanted to see win. Whether he actually existed or not is almost irrelevant since the universal human qualities that he embodied are those that most of us, whether we want to or not, admire and aspire to.

Places to Eat Try the sweet, gooey *rovani*, the local speciality made with rice, honey and cloves, at one of the *zaharoplasteia* on or near the main square.

Sirens Yacht Club Restaurant & Bar (☎ 2674 033 001) Mains €4.10-8.50. This classy place is tucked away well back from the waterfront, not far from the bank. It's run by locals who have returned to Ithaki after migrating to New York and their imaginative menu offers lots of great small dishes you can really make a meal from. Try the mini cheese pies and the baked feta with tomato and peppers.

Kantouni (☎ 2674 032 918) Mains to €10.30. Make your selection from a kitchen full of freshly prepared home-style fare at this restaurant on the waterfront. There's a great selection of pies with fillings such as spinach, cheese, onion, leek and chicken, and tasty oven-baked casserole dishes like lamb with potatoes and beef in red sauce.

Gregory's Taverna (☎ 2674 032 573) Mains €4.40-9.10. On the eastern side of the harbour, a 15-minute walk from town, is this friendly place serving up a great selection of starters, plus well-prepared meats (lamb chops, fillet steak) and seafood (this is a great place to splurge on lobster).

Drakouli Café (☎ 2674 033 435) Young locals meet at this stylish cafe in a waterfront mansion, which was the home of George Drakoulis, a wealthy Ithakan shipowner. It's a good spot for a drink but the snack menu is limited. Other popular cafebars line the eastern harbourfront, and this is where the nightlife is centred.

Around Ithaki

Ithaki has a few sites associated with Homer's *Odyssey*. Though none is impressive, you may enjoy (or endure) the scenic walks to them. The most renowned is the **Fountain of Arethousa**, where Odysseus' swineherd, Eumaeus, brought his pigs to drink and where Odysseus, on his return to Ithaca, went to meet him disguised as a beggar after receiving directions from the goddess Athena. Lesser mortals have to deal with inadequate signposting. The walk takes 1½ to two hours. Take plenty of water as the spring shrinks in summer.

A shorter trek is to the **Cave of the Nymphs**, where Odysseus concealed the splendid gifts of gold, copper and fine fabrics that the Phaeacians had given him. The cave is signposted from the town. Below the cave is the **Bay of Dexa** (where there is decent swimming and usually some watersports), thought to be ancient Phorkys where the Phaeacians disembarked and laid the sleeping Odysseus on the sand.

The location of Odysseus' palace has been much disputed and archaeologists have been unable to find conclusive evidence. Schliemann erroneously believed it was near Vathy, whereas present-day archaeologists speculate it was on a hill near Stavros.

Anogi Fourteen kilometres north of Vathy is Anogi, the old capital. The restored 12th-century church of **Agia Panagia** has beautiful Byzantine frescoes. Ask in the kafeneio on the square for Gerasimos who has the key.

Frikes There's really not much to this charming fishing village in among windswept cliffs – a few waterfront restaurants and stores and that's it. Kiki Travel Agency (☎/fax 2674 031 387, ⓔ kikitrav@otenet.gr), owned by helpful Angeliki Digaletou, has a range of services including accommodation help, moped hire and sailing trips.

Kiki Domatia (☎/fax 2674 031 387, ⓔ kikitrav@otenet.gr) Doubles €41.10. These spotless domatia are in a lovely blue-and-yellow harbourfront building and the simple rooms include basics such as kettle, toaster and fridge.

Aristotelis Apartments (☎ 2674 031 079, fax 031 179, ⓔ arisvill@otenet.gr) Double studios €47, 4-person maisonette €58.70. This smart new development of eight apartments is near Hotel Nostos as you come into Frikes and offers excellent value. Rooms are well sized and attractively furnished; all have fully equipped kitchens, plus there's a nice outdoor barbecue area.

Restaurant Ulysses (☎ 2674 031 733) Mains to €7.40, fish and lobster priced by the kilogram. This casual waterfront restaurant offers fresh fish and lobster (which you choose from a large tank), plus good grilled meats and favourite pasta dishes.

Kioni Four kilometres south-east of Frikes, Kioni is perhaps one of Ithaki's better-kept secrets. It is a small village draped around a verdant hillside spilling down to a picturesque little harbour where yachties congregate. There are tavernas and a couple of bars, though it's not the best place to swim. Instead, seek out the little bays between Kioni and Frikes.

Maroudas Apartments (☎ 2674 031 691, fax 2674 031 753) Double studios €41.10. This place, opposite the doctor's surgery on the narrow road into town, is probably Kioni's cheapest accommodation. It has

Ready for the day ahead, Kathisma, Ionian Islands

White-washed house, Hora

The superb clear water and white sand of Levrehio beach, near Longos, Paxi

Quayside, Longos, Paxi

Lunch with a view, looking down to Paleokastritsa from Lakones

View of Skyros' distinct cubist architecture

Say cheese: camera friendly mule, Skyros

The pebble beach south of Limni near the Convent of Galataki on Northern Evia

well-maintained, well-equipped studios. Inquire in person at the nearby souvenir store across from the small supermarket.

Captain's Apartments (☎ 2674 031 481, fax 2674 031 090) Double studios/4-person apartments €47/64.60. Signposted as you enter Kioni are these tastefully furnished and spacious apartments run by the very friendly Dellaporta family. Each of the units has a phone, TV and outdoor verandah area.

Kalipso (☎ 2674 031 066) Mains to €10.30. Sit right by the colourful small boats lining this tiny harbour and enjoy Kalipso's house speciality, its famous onion pie. There's also a good selection of seafood and traditional dishes on offer at this popular yachtie restaurant.

Zakynthos
Ζάκυνθος

postcode 291 00 • pop 32,560

Zakynthos (**zahk**-in-thos) has inspired many superlatives. The Venetians called it Fior' di Levante (flower of the orient). The poet Dionysios Solomos wrote that 'Zakynthos could make one forget the Elysian Fields'. Indeed, it is an island of exceptional natural beauty and outstanding beaches.

Unfortunately, Zakynthos' coastline has been the victim of the most unacceptable manifestations of package tourism. The lack of general budget accommodation and a rapacious attitude to tourism on the part of islanders make Zakynthos the least attractive of the Ionian islands as a destination for independent travellers. Even worse, tourism is endangering the loggerhead turtle, *Caretta caretta* (see the boxed text later in this section), and the Mediterranean monk seal, *Monachus monachus*.

There is more information available on the Internet, see W www.zakynthos-net.gr or W www.zanteweb.gr.

Getting To/From Zakynthos
Air There is at least one daily flight between Zakynthos and Athens (€63.40). The Olympic Airways office (☎ 2695 028 611) in Zakynthos Town is at Alexandrou Roma 16.

Bus There are five buses daily from Zakynthos Town to Patras (3½ hours, €9.10). The same buses continue on to Athens (seven hours, €20.85). There is also a twice-weekly service to Thessaloniki (€34.50). Ticket prices include the ferry fare between Zakynthos and Kyllini.

Ferry Depending on the season, between three and seven ferries daily operate from Zakynthos Town to Kyllini in the Peloponnese (1½ hours, €4.40). Tickets can be obtained from the Zakynthos Shipping Cooperative (☎ 2695 041 500, fax 2695 048 301) at Lombardou 40 in Zakynthos Town.

From the northern port of Agios Nikolaos a car ferry shuttles across to Pesada on Kefallonia from May to October (1¼ hours, €3.80). There is inexplicably no bus from Pesada to anywhere else on Kefallonia, and virtually no buses from Agios Nikolaos to anywhere in Zakynthos, making crossing without your own transport quite difficult – not to mention costly if you rely on taxis. Both these ports are quite a distance from the major towns on the respective islands (although Agios Nikolaos has a few tavernas and rooms for rent). Check with the port police (☎ 2695 042 417) for the times of the ferry; there are usually two services daily, in the morning and evening.

Getting Around Zakynthos
To/From the Airport There is no shuttle service between Zakynthos Town and the airport, 6km to the south-west. A taxi costs between €4.40 and €5.90.

Bus Frequent buses go from Zakynthos Town's modern bus station (☎ 2695 022 255) on Filita, one block back from the waterfront, to Alikes (€1), Tsilivi (€0.80), Argasi (€0.80) and Laganas (€0.80). Bus services to other villages are poor (one or two daily). Check the current schedule at the bus station.

IONIAN ISLANDS

ZAKYNTHOS

IONIAN ISLANDS

Car & Motorcycle Avis (☎ 2695 027 512, fax 2695 026 330) has an office just by Plateia Agiou Markou. Ionian Rentals (☎ 2695 048 946) rents cars and bikes. Its office in Zakynthos Town is on Makri, and it has branches in a number of resort towns on the island.

ZAKYNTHOS TOWN
pop 10,250
Zakynthos Town is the capital and port of the island. The town was devastated by the 1953 earthquake but was reconstructed with its former layout preserved in wide

arcaded streets, imposing squares and gracious neoclassical public buildings. It is hardly cosy, given its strung-out feel, but it is a reasonable place for an overnight stop and in comparison to many of the overtouristed parts of the island there is at least a semblance of Greekness left in the town.

Orientation & Information
The central Plateia Solomou is on the waterfront of Lombardou, opposite the ferry quay. Another large square, Plateia Agiou Markou, is behind it. The bus station

is on Filita, one block back from the waterfront and south of the quay. The main thoroughfare is Alexandrou Roma, parallel to the waterfront and several blocks inland.

Zakynthos Town has no tourist office. The tourist police (☎ 2695 027 367) are at Lombardou 62.

The National Bank of Greece is just west of Plateia Solomou, and directly next door is a Commercial Bank. Both have ATMs. The post office is at Tertseti 27, one block west of Alexandrou Roma. The OTE is just off Plateia Solomou. Top's (☎ 2695 026 650) at Filita 34, near the bus station, offers Internet access. Zakynthos' hospital (☎ 2695 042 514) is west of town.

Things to See

The **Byzantine museum** (☎ 2695 042 714, *Plateia Solomou; admission €2.40; open 8am-2.30pm Tues-Sun*) houses an impressive collection of ecclesiastical art which was rescued from churches razed in the earthquake.

The **Museum of Solomos** (☎ 2695 028 982, *Plateia Agiou Markou; admission €2.40; open 9am-2pm daily*) is dedicated to Dionysios Solomos (1798–1857), who was born on Zakynthos and is regarded as the father of modern Greek poetry. His work *Hymn to Liberty* became the stirring Greek national anthem. The museum houses memorabilia associated with his life, but the focus is really for Greek visitors.

Places to Stay

There are plenty of mid-range hotels in Zakynthos Town, but the problem is quality rather than quantity. The hotels are all generally dated, and rooms are usually small and quite dreary.

Zante Camping (☎ 2695 061 710, fax 2695 063 030) Adult/tent €4.40/3.50. This site at Tragaki in the Tsilivi area, is the nearest camping ground to Zakynthos Town (about 5km away). It's a pleasant shaded ground with a minimarket and its own path down to the beach.

Saint Loukas Rooms for Rent (☎ 2695 026 809, *Plateia Agiou Louka 2*) Double studios €41.10. Just back from the waterfront,

behind the Europcar car-rental office, is a building of well-kept rooms and studios run by friendly owners who lived in Canada for 12 years. The front rooms have balconies overlooking the harbour but you may suffer with traffic noise.

Phoenix (☎ 2695 023 514, fax 2695 045 083, *Plateia Solomou*) Singles/doubles €35.20/47. This unremarkable hotel, conveniently located on the main square and close to the ferry quay, has clean, standard rooms.

Hotel Alba (☎ 2695 026 641, fax 2695 026 642, *L Ziva 38*) Singles/doubles €44.90/57.20. Just off Plateia Agiou Markou is this pleasant, good-value hotel with small but adequate rooms.

Hotel Palatino (☎/fax 2695 045 400, ⓔ *palatzak@otenet.gr, Kolkotroni 10*) Doubles €73.40. This newly refurbished hotel, five minutes' walk north of the main square, offers the most spacious and modern rooms in town. It's popular with businesspeople mid-week so it's worth booking ahead.

Places to Eat

Cafes featuring *mandolato*, a local nougat sweet, are found along Alexandrou Roma, as are good souvlaki and gyros places. Street vendors on Plateia Solomou sell cheap, barbecued corn on the cob. There's a *fresh-produce market* on Filioti, and a well-stocked *supermarket* on the corner of Filioti and the waterfront.

Arekia (☎ 2695 026 346) There is no menu at this popular, non-touristy place, a 10-minute walk north of the main square along the waterfront. The owner tells you what's been made that day and you choose, and although the food is good hearty Greek fare and very reasonably priced, it's not really what you come for. There is live music – kantades and the *arekia* of the restaurant's name – most nights from about 10pm. You'll probably have as much fun as the singers, even if you don't understand a word of the songs.

To Spiti tou Lata (*House of Latas;* ☎ 2695 041 585) Mains to €11.20. The setting here is wonderful, with tables spread out under a bougainvillea-covered pergola

Phone numbers listed incorporate changes due in Oct 2002; see p55

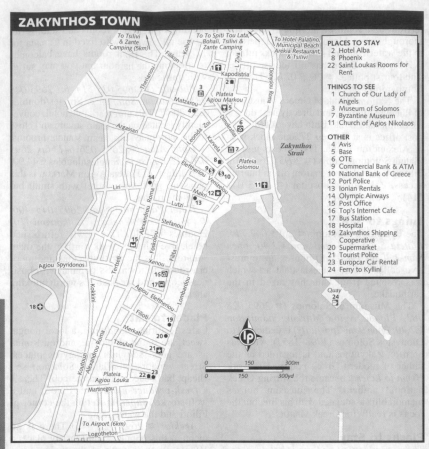

ZAKYNTHOS TOWN

PLACES TO STAY
2 Hotel Alba
8 Phoenix
22 Saint Loukas Rooms for Rent

THINGS TO SEE
1 Church of Our Lady of Angels
3 Museum of Solomos
7 Byzantine Museum
11 Church of Agios Nikolaos

OTHER
4 Avis
5 Base
6 OTE
9 Commercial Bank & ATM
10 National Bank of Greece
12 Port Police
13 Ionian Rentals
14 Olympic Airways
15 Post Office
16 Top's Internet Cafe
17 Bus Station
18 Hospital
19 Zakynthos Shipping Cooperative
20 Supermarket
21 Tourist Police
23 Europcar Car Rental
24 Ferry to Kyllini

and fabulous views over Zakynthos Town to Mt Skopos. Head out of town, up to Bochali near the Venetian *kastro* (walled town). Take Dionysiou Roma north, turn left at Plaza Hotel following signs to Bochali and then first left after the Maritime Museum. The menu includes a good selection of mezedes and Greek cooked dishes but the to-order grilled meats and fish are the speciality. There's also traditional music.

Base (☎ 2695 042 409, *Plateia Agiou Markou*) This hip bar is a good place for a daytime coffee or evening drink. It's particularly popular with young Zantiots as a night-time hangout, and there is often a DJ playing music.

AROUND ZAKYNTHOS

Loggerhead turtles come ashore to lay their eggs on the golden-sand beaches of the huge Bay of Laganas, on Zakynthos' south coast. Laganas is a highly developed, tacky resort and is a truly dreadful place to spend a holiday unless you like lager and loud discos and would rather be in the UK than Greece. Avoid it like the plague, or at least drop by to see how Mammon and mass

At Loggerheads

The loggerhead turtle *(Caretta caretta)* is one of Europe's most beautiful yet most endangered marine species. In Greece the loggerhead turtle nests on two of the Ionian islands, on the Peloponnese coast and in Crete. It prefers large tracts of clean, flat and uninhabited sand. So too do basking tourists from northern Europe and it is this fateful convergence of interests that has led to the turtle being placed under the threat of extinction.

KN

The female turtle lays about 120 eggs the size of ping-pong balls in the sand in preferred sites. After laying her eggs she returns to the sea and the eggs must lie undisturbed for up to 60 days before the hatchlings emerge. For at least 150 million years the turtle has survived geological and climatic changes but the changes to its environment caused by modern mass tourism has rung alarm bells within the conservation world.

Zakynthos hosts the largest congregation of nests. There is an average of 1300 nests per year along the 5km stretch of the Bay of Laganas on the island's south coast alone. In recent years this popular resort has come under repeated fire with conservation lobbies clashing with local authorities and businesses involved in the lucrative tourist trade. Operators who make handsome profits from renting out beach umbrellas and sunbeds have attracted particular criticism. Umbrella poles indiscriminately destroy eggs and nests and the very existence of humans anywhere near the nesting sites is totally counterproductive to the turtles' survival.

In 1999 the Greek government declared the Bay of Laganas area a National Marine Park (W www.nmp-zak.org) and strict regulations are now in force regarding boating, mooring, fishing and watersports in designated maritime zones. At the resort of Laganas itself much of the damage has already been done, but other beaches in the area, such as Gerakas, are now completely off-limits between dusk and dawn during the breeding season (nesting occurs from late May to late August, hatching from late July to late October). There are other regulations in effect (ie, cars, bikes and horses are not allowed on nesting beaches, umbrellas are only allowed in designated areas, lights cannot be shone directly onto nesting beaches), but unfortunately these laws are not particularly well enforced.

The Zakynthos branch of Archelon (W www.archelon.gr), the Sea Turtle Protection Society of Greece, has an excellent public information centre at Gerakas and regularly hosts informative slide shows at hotels in the area. The organisation accepts volunteers (minimum one-month commitment) for all its monitoring and research programs.

IONIAN ISLANDS

tourism have met in the most abominable set of circumstances.

Kalamaki is not much quieter than Laganas and it's tough to find accommodation that hasn't been block-booked by tour operators. Beachside **Keri** (follow the sign off the main road indicating Limni Keriou) is a better choice, although its narrow, stony beach is not much to write home about.

The Vasilikos Peninsula, south-east of Zakynthos Town beyond the busy resort of Argasi, offers a number of small, beachfront settlements off the main road, and there are tavernas and accommodation options at all these places. The first decent place to stop is **Kaminia**, followed by the sandy cove of **Porto Zoro**. Virtually at the tip of the east coast, **Banana Beach** is a more pleasant place to hang out with a long (albeit narrow) strip of golden sand. There are plenty of watersports, umbrellas and sun lounges. **Agios Nikolaos** at the

Phone numbers listed incorporate changes due in Oct 2002; see p55

Shipwreck Beach

The famous Shipwreck Beach (Navagio), whose photos grace virtually every tourist brochure about Zakynthos, is at the north-western tip of the island. It truly is a splendid beach with crystalline, aquamarine waters, but when some seven large excursion boats on round-the-island cruises pull up here at around midday every day and offload their passengers by the hundreds, the place really loses its appeal. Don't go on one of these cruises unless you fancy nine hours on a crowded boat offering overpriced snack food and generally travelling too far from the coastline to allow you to see much of interest.

You're better off taking a small boat trip to Shipwreck Beach or the Blue Caves (in the island's north-east), and these are best done from the lighthouse at Cape Skinari at the far northern tip of the island (3km after Agios Nikolaos). From here, the Potamitis brothers (☎ 2695 031 132) take small boats (many with glass bottoms) at frequent intervals to either venue for €5.90 (they will also act as a taxi boat to Shipwreck Beach, taking you there and picking you up a pre-arranged time). You can also visit Shipwreck Beach on a small excursion boat from the little harbour of Vromi Bay on the west coast, which in turn is reached from Anafonitria.

Avoid the crowds by visiting in the morning or from mid-afternoon, and take food, drink and a beach umbrella as there are no facilities.

And be sure to visit the precariously perched lookout platform over Shipwreck Beach, on the west coast, signposted between Anafonitria and Volimes. Be warned that this is not a place for those afraid of heights, but the view is definitely worth it.

very end of the peninsula also has great (turtle-free) watersports facilities.

Beyond ghastly Mavratzis (dominated by the mock fortress of the Zante Palace Hotel) is the more pleasant beach of **Porto Roma**, although this narrow strip of sand can get crowded. On the other side of the peninsula, facing Laganas Bay, is Zakynthos' best beach, the long and sandy **Gerakas**. This is one of the main turtle-nesting beaches (see boxed text 'At Loggerheads') and access to the beach is strictly forbidden between dusk and dawn during the breeding season.

You can semi-escape from the tourist hype by visiting the accessible west-coast coves such as lovely **Limnionas** or **Kambi** (the latter has great tavernas for sunset-watching). Get even more off the beaten path by touring the inland farming villages, and make an effort to visit tiny **Gyri** in the centre of the island, where there is a cosy taverna with live arekia music on weekends.

Places to Stay & Eat
Tartaruga Camping (☎ 2695 051 967, fax 2695 053 023) Adult/tent €4.40/3. If you're travelling on the road from Laganas to Keri, you'll pass the well-signposted turn-off to this lovely camping ground, with a wonderful setting amid terraced olive groves and vineyards and a trail down to the beach. There are also some rooms for rent here but these usually need to be booked in advance.

Seaside Apartments to Let (☎ 2695 043 297) Double studios €44, 4-bed apartments €73.40. These delightful rooms are above the beachfront Keri Tourist Center (a glorified minimarket and gift shop). Their bright, modern decor is fabulously enhanced by artwork done by the friendly owner.

Sea View Village (☎ 2695 035 178, fax 2695 035 152, ℮ seaview@zakynthos-net .gr) Doubles/triples/quads €73.40/88/102.70. Easily one of the nicest new complexes we've seen is this smart, 26-room resort just south of the turn-off to Kaminia Beach, well positioned for exploration of the area's beaches. Modern, spacious studios and apartments are a cut above many others on offer, and the central pool and bar area is lovely.

Gerakas Taverna & Bar (☎ 2695 035 248) Mains €4.40-9.40. This pleasant family-run place is on the road heading to the Gerakas beach. It offers an extensive menu featuring many Greek favourites – grilled meats, oven-baked dishes, lots of fish etc. There's also a cocktail bar, plus sales of local organic produce (oil, honey, olives, wine and cheese), and the owners have a few reasonably priced studios to rent.

Kythira & Antikythira

KYTHIRA Κύθηρα
postcode 80 100 • pop 3100

The island of Kythira (**kee**-thih-rah) is to many Greeks the Holy Grail of island-hopping. The *Road to Kythira*, a well-known 1973 song by Dimitris Mitropanos, epitomises what for most people is the end of a line that is never reached. Indeed, given its location, you have to make a special effort get here.

Some 30km long and 18km wide, Kythira dangles off the Laconian Peninsula of the Peloponnese between the often turbulent Ionian and Aegean Seas. It is a curiously barren island in parts, with misty moors, hidden valleys and winding lanes. More than 40 villages are scattered evenly across the island, and ghosts are said to roam the inland villages. Kythira was part of the British Ionian protectorate for many years, evidenced by the sprinkling of arched stone bridges around the island.

Kythira is the least 'Ionian' of the Ionian island group. Physically separated from its nearest neighbour Zakynthos by a long stretch of sea, it is administered from Piraeus and mostly resembles the Cyclades in appearance and architecture.

Mythology suggests that Aphrodite was born in Kythira. She is supposed to have risen from the foam where Zeus had thrown Cronos' sex organ after castrating him. The goddess of love then re-emerged near Pafos in Cyprus, so both islands haggle over her birthplace.

The EOT has begun encouraging tourists to visit Kythira but it's still unspoilt. Its attractions are its relatively undeveloped beaches, its enduring feel as a special island and the fact that it is 'the end of the line'.

Kythira's main port is Agia Pelagia, though hydrofoils depart from and arrive at the custom-built port of Diakofti (as do ferries when the weather is bad). Public transport on Kythira ranges from abysmal to nonexistent, so bringing your own wheels or renting them locally is advisable.

For information on the Internet, see the Web sites **W** www.kythira.com and **W** www .kytheranet.com.

Getting To/From Kythira

Air There are daily flights between Kythira and Athens (€52.80). The airport is 10km east of Potamos, and the Olympic Airways office (☎ 2736 033 362) is on the central square in Potamos. Book also at Kythira Travel (☎ 2736 031 390) in Hora.

Ferry ANEN Lines operates the *Myrtidiotissa* on a weekly schedule between Piraeus, Kythira, Antikythira, Kastelli-Kissamos (Crete), Kalamata and Gythio (both in the Peloponnese). Twice a week the ferry runs directly between Piraeus and Kythira (6½ hours, €16.50). The ferry arrives at and departs from Diakofti. From mid-June to mid-September there are three weekly connections between Kythira and Gythio (2½ hours, €7.10). Four times a week the ferry runs between Kythira and Kastelli-Kisamos (four hours, €12.90). Information and tickets are available from Porfyra Travel (☎/fax 2736 031 888, **e** porfyra@otenet.gr) in Livadi.

The *Nisos Kythira* shuttles two or three times daily between Agia Pelagia and Neapoli (one hour, €4.40). Tickets are sold at the quay before departure, or by Sirenes Travel Club (☎ 2736 034 371) in Potamos. In case of bad weather, the boat arrives at and departs from Diakofti, not Agia Pelagia.

The port police (☎ 2736 033 280) are at Agia Pelagia on the waterfront. Diakofti's port police are on ☎ 2736 034 222.

Hydrofoil From June to mid-September, there are daily hydrofoils from Diakofti to Zea in Piraeus (€30.80). It takes 3½ hours direct

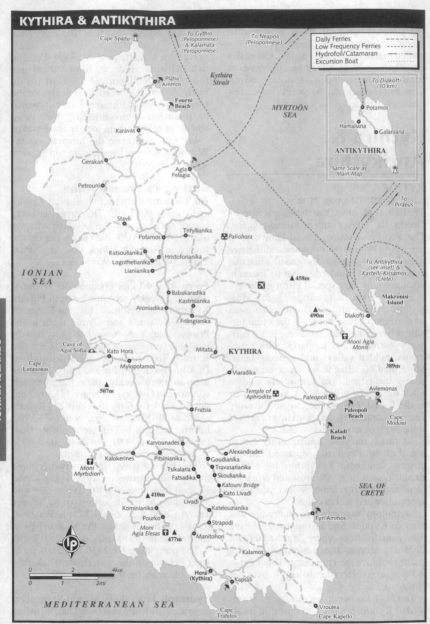

KYTHIRA & ANTIKYTHIRA

Cape Spathi

To Gythio
(Peloponnese)
& Kalamata
(Peloponnese)

To Neapoli
(Peloponnese)

Platia
Ammos

Kythira
Strait

Fourni
Beach

MYRTOÖN
SEA

Daily Ferries	– – – –
Low Frequency Ferries	– – – –
Hydrofoil/Catamaran	— — —
Excursion Boat	· · · · ·

Karavas

To Diakofti
(30 km)

Potamos

Gerakari

Agia
Pelagia

Harhaliana

Galaniana

Petrouni

ANTIKYTHIRA

Same Scale as
Main Map

To
Piraeus

Stavli

Potamos

Trifyllianika

Paliohora

Katsoulianika

Hristoforianika

Logothetianika

Lianianika

To Antikythira
(see inset) &
Kastelli-Kissamos
(Crete)

I O N I A N
S E A

▲ 458m

Babakaradika

Kastrisianika

Makronisi
Island

Aroniadika

Frilingianika

▲ 490m

Diakofti

Moni Agia
Monis

Cape
Limnionas

Cave of
Agia Sofia

Kato Hora

Mylopotamos

Mitata

KYTHIRA

Viaradika

▲ 389m

Avlemonas

▲ 507m

Temple of
Aphrodite

Paleopoli

Fratsia

Paleopoli
Beach

Cape
Modoni

Kaladi
Beach

Karvounades

Alexandrades

Kalokerines

Pitsinianika

Goudianika

Travasarianika

Moni
Myrtidion

Tsikalaria

Fatsadika

Skoulianika

SEA OF
CRETE

Katouni Bridge

Kato Livadi

▲ 410m

Livadi

Kominianika

Katelouzianika

Pourko

Strapodi

Fyri Ammos

Moni
Agia Elesas

▲ 477m

Manitohori

Kalamos

0   2   4km
0   1   2mi

Hora
(Kythira)

Kapsali

MEDITERRANEAN SEA

Cape
Trahilos

Vroulea

Cape Kapello

(three times a week), or five hours via Neapoli, Monemvassia, Kiparissi and Leonidio, in the eastern Peloponnese (four times a week). Tickets are available at Kythira Travel (☎ 2736 031 490) on the main square in Hora.

Getting Around Kythira

There is no regular public transport on the island. Not surprisingly, there are many taxis, but the best way to see the island and explore the small villages and difficult-to-access beaches is with your own transport. Helpful Panayotis at Moto Rent (☎ 2736 031 600, fax 2736 031 789) on Kapsali's waterfront rents cars and mopeds.

Hora Χώρα
pop 550

Hora (or Kythira), the pretty capital, with white, blue-shuttered houses, perches on a long, slender ridge 2km uphill from Kapsali. The central square, planted with hibiscus, bougainvillea and palms, is Plateia Dimitriou Staï. The main street runs south of it.

The post office is on the square, as are the National Bank of Greece and Agricultural Bank, both with ATMs. Just south of the square is Anonymo (also called Cafe No-Name), a cafe-bar offering Internet access (€5.90 per hour). The police station (☎ 2736 031 206) is near the kastro.

Hora has no tourist office but English-speaking Panayotis offers information to tourists at his Moto Rent office (☎ 2736 031 600) on Kapsali's waterfront.

Things to See

Hora's Venetian **kastro**, built in the 13th century, is at the southern end of town. If you walk to its southern extremity, passing the Church of Panagia, you will come to a sheer cliff – from here there's a stunning view of Kapsali and on a good day of Antikythira.

North of the central square, near the turn-off to Kapsali, is the **archaeological museum** *(☎ 2736 031 789; admission free; open 8.45am-3pm Tues-Sat, 9.30am-2.30pm Sun)*. It features gravestones of British soldiers and their infants who died on the island in the 19th century. A large marble lion from around 550 BC is also exhibited.

Call in to **Stavros** *(☎ 2736 031 857)*, a store north of the square (opposite the turn-off to Kapsali) and pick up some of the local produce, including some of Greece's best honey.

Places to Stay *Castello Rooms (☎ 2736 031 069, fax 2736 031 869, e jfatseas@ otenet.gr)* Doubles €35.20, studios sleeping up to three €44. There's a sign at the southern end of the main street to these spacious rooms and studios.

Papadonicos Rooms (☎ 2736 031 126) Double studios €35.20, 4-person apartments €52.80. These pleasant studios are a bit farther south from Castello Rooms, in an old converted house with a pleasant terrace garden area. This is one of few places in this part of the island open year-round.

Hotel Margarita (☎ 2736 031 711, fax 2736 031 325, e fatseasp@otenet.gr) Singles/doubles €70.50/82.20 high season. This charming hotel, off the main street between the central square and kastro, offers very pleasant rooms (all with TV and telephone) in a renovated 19th-century mansion featuring a lovely old staircase. Breakfast is served on a pretty whitewashed terrace.

Places to Eat There are not a lot of restaurant choices in Hora, but there's a decent selection of cafes offering snacks, largely clustered around the central square and with a few along the main street.

Fournos (☎ 2736 034 289) Snacks €2.10-11.80. Run by Lili, a Greek-Australian, this place offers a good selection of snacks a cut above the usual fare – eg, tasty antipasto plates, homemade quiche and pies and a very decent burger. There are tables and chairs on the square, although the cafe itself is tucked away slightly off a side street.

Zorba's (☎ 2736 031 655) There's no menu as such here at this *psistaria* south of the square, and vegetarians will struggle. Customers choose from a display of freshly prepared meat and the owners grill it for you, and will whip up a salad to accompany it. Prices vary according to what's on offer, but costs are very reasonable.

Kapsali Καψάλι
postcode 801 00 • pop 70

Kapsali is a picturesque village down a winding road from Hora. It looks particularly captivating from Hora's castle, with its twin sandy bays and curving waterfront. Restaurants and cafes line the beach, and safe sheltered swimming is Kapsali's trademark. Not surprisingly, this is a very popular place so accommodation can be scarce unless you book well ahead. It can also get pretty crowded in high season, so if you like your beach in solitude look elsewhere.

Offshore you can see the stark rock island known as the **Avgo** (Egg) rearing above the water. It is here that Kytherians claim Aphrodite sprang from the sea.

As well as cars and mopeds, bicycles, canoes and pedal boats can be hired from Panayotis at Moto Rent (☎ 2736 031 600), on the waterfront. He also offers waterskiing opportunities.

Places to Stay & Eat *Camping Kapsali*
(☎ 2736 031 580) Adult/tent €3.30/3. Open June-mid Sept. This small pine-shaded ground (well signposted off the road from Hora) is 400m from Kapsali's quay, behind the village. It's a quiet spot with minimal facilities and is better suited to small tents rather than large campervan setups.

Vassilis Studios (☎ 2736 031 125, fax 2736 031 553) Double studios €73.40. On the road between Hora and Kapsali is this attractive green-and-white complex of studios, not far from the beach. Olga, the friendly owner, offers spacious studios with lovely wooden floors and good bay views.

Raikos Hotel (☎ 2736 031 629, fax 2736 031 801, ℮ raikoshotel@techlink.gr) Doubles/ triples €85.10/102.70. Signposted off the Hora-Kapsali road is this very smart, friendly hotel, offering spacious, pleasantly decorated rooms with terraces overlooking Kapsali and Hora's kastro. There's a lovely pool and bar area too.

Hydragogio (☎ 2736 031 065) Mains to €12.30, lobster and fish priced by the kilogram. This lively eatery at the far end by the rocks specialises in fresh fish and mezedes.

It's a good place to splurge on lobster, if your budget stretches that far. The wine list is comprehensive and excellent.

There are numerous restaurants and cafes lining Kapsali's waterfront, plus a good assortment of bars – this is probably the liveliest town on the island as far as nightlife goes. *Shaker* and *Barbarossa* are popular.

Potamos Ποταμός
pop 680

Potamos, 10km from Agia Pelagia, is the island's commercial hub. On Sunday morning it attracts almost every islander to market. The National Bank of Greece (with ATM) is on the central square. The post office is just north of the central square.

Hotel Porfyra (☎ 2736 033 329, 2736 033 924) Double/triple studios €47/52.80, 4-person apartments €61.60. At Potamos' one hotel, spotless self-contained units surround a pleasant internal courtyard. The sign is in Greek only – look for it almost opposite the post office north of the main square.

Taverna Panaretos (☎ 2736 034 290) Mains to €8.80. This bustling taverna on the central square serves well-prepared international and Greek dishes, including tempting seafood risotto and pasta.

Ta Katsigouro (☎ 2736 033 880) Snacks to €4.40. This place is also known as the Greek-Aussie snack bar and has a logo incorporating a kangaroo's body and a goat's head. It's just south of the square and serves up great souvlaki, gyros and burgers.

Mylopotamos Μυλοπόταμος
pop 90

Mylopotamos is an alluring, verdant village. Its central square is flanked by a much-photographed church and kafeneio, *O Platanos*, which offers simple, excellent fare in a gorgeous setting. It's worth a stroll to the **Neraïda** (water nymph) waterfall, with luxuriant greenery and mature, shady trees. As you reach the church, take the right fork and follow the signs to an unpaved road leading down to the falls.

To reach the abandoned **kastro** of Mylopotamos, take the left fork after the kafeneio and follow the sign for Kato Hora (lower village). The road leads to the centre of Kato Hora, from where a portal leads into the spooky kastro, with derelict houses and well-preserved little churches (usually locked).

Farther along the same road is the **Cave of Agia Sofia**, reached by a precipitous, unpaved 2km road. Irregular opening times are usually pinned on the side of the church in Mylopotamos.

Agia Pelagia Αγία Πελαγία
pop 280
Kythira's northern port of Agia Pelagia is a simple, friendly waterfront village ideal for relaxing and swimming. Mixed sand-and-pebble beaches are either side of the quay.

Places to Stay & Eat Prebooking in high season is almost essential in Agia Pelagia.

Georgos Kambouris Domatia (☎ 2736 033 480) Doubles €49.90. This is one of the friendliest and most pleasant places to stay. Georgos' wife, Maria, maintains spotless, airy rooms. The building is just in front of Hotel Romantica.

Hotel Kytheria (☎ 2736 033 321, fax 2736 033 825) Doubles €64.60. This welcoming hotel, on the beach and owned by helpful Angelo from Australia, has very comfortable, tidy rooms.

Venardos Hotel (☎ 2736 034 205, fax 2736 033 850, ℮ venardos@otenet.gr) Singles/doubles/triples €64.60/76.30/88. Open year-round. This large hotel has sizable, airy rooms and a lovely terrace area. Australians get a special welcome.

Faros Taverna (☎ 2736 033 343) Mains to €7.40. This blue-and-white taverna close to the quay serves good, economical Greek staples.

Moustakias (☎ 2736 033 519) Mains to €8.80. This ouzeri, next to the minimarket, offers food ranging from mezedes to grilled meats to seafood, including all the traditional Greek favourites.

Sempreviva Patisserie (☎ 2736 033 390) Cakes & pastries to €3. For breakfast, Sempreviva serves wickedly delicious Greek cakes and freshly brewed coffee.

Around Kythira
If you have transport, a tour round the island is rewarding. The monasteries of **Agia Moni** and **Agia Elesa** are mountain refuges with superb views. **Moni Myrtidion** is a beautiful monastery surrounded by trees. From Hora, drive north-east to the picturesque village of **Avlemonas** via **Paleopoli** with its wide, pebbled beach. Here, archaeologists spent years searching for evidence of a temple at Aphrodite's birthplace. Be sure to also visit the spectacularly situated ruins of the Byzantine capital of **Paleohora**, in the island's north-east.

Just north of the village of Kato Livadi make a detour to see the remarkable, and seemingly out-of-place, British-made **Katouni Bridge**, a legacy of Kythira's time as part of the British protectorate in the 19th century. In the far north of the island the village of **Karavas** is verdant and very attractive and close to both Agia Pelagia and the reasonable beach at **Platia Ammos**. Beachcombers should seek out **Kaladi Beach**, near Paleopoli. Another good beach is **Fyri Ammos**, closer to Hora.

Places to Eat *Filio* (☎ 2736 031 549) Mains to €8.80. It's well worth going out of your way to visit this great restaurant in Kalamos, one of the nicest on the island. In a lovely garden setting you'll be offered countless traditional Kytherian dishes by friendly, helpful staff.

Estiatorion Pierros (☎ 2736 031 014). While heading out across the island, stop in at great little roadside establishment in Livadi, where you'll find no-nonsense traditional Greek staples. There's no menu – visit the kitchen to see what's been freshly cooked.

Sotiris (☎ 2736 033 722) Seasonal fish and lobster priced by the kilogram. This popular fish taverna in pretty Avlemonas offers well-prepared fresh catch and is known for its lobster and excellent fish soup.

ANTIKYTHIRA Αντικύθηρα
pop 70
The tiny island of Antikythira, 38km south-east of Kythira, is the most remote island in the Ionian group. It has only one

IONIAN ISLANDS

settlement, **Potamos**, one doctor, one police officer, one teacher (with a only handful of pupils), one telephone and a monastery. It doesn't have a post office or bank. The only accommodation for tourists is 10 basic rooms in two purpose-built blocks, open in summer only. Potamos has a kafeneio and taverna.

Getting To/From Antikythira Surprisingly, there's only bare-bones ferry connections between Kythira and Antikythira, even in high season. ANEN Lines' *Mirtidiotissa* calls in twice weekly – on Saturday

in the wee small hours on the way from Kythira to Crete, and Sunday going the opposite way, so technically a brief stay is possible, if you don't mind arriving on the island at 2.45am! Outside of high season, schedules are even less conducive to a visit. The journey from Kythira to Antikythira costs €6.20 and takes two hours. This is not an island for tourists on a tight schedule, and will probably only appeal to those who really like their isolation. For information and tickets, contact Porfyra Travel (☎/fax 2736 031 888, @ porfyra@otenet.gr) in Livadi on Kythira.

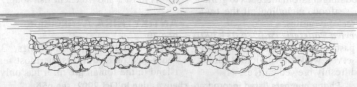

Language

The Greek language is probably the oldest European language, with an oral tradition of 4000 years and a written tradition of approximately 3000 years. Its evolution over the four millennia was characterised by its strength during the golden age of Athens and the Democracy (mid-5th century BC); its use as a lingua franca throughout the Middle Eastern world, spread by Alexander the Great and his successors as far as India during the Hellenistic period (330 BC to AD 100); its adaptation as the language of the new religion, Christianity; its use as the official language of the Eastern Roman Empire; and its eventual proclamation as the language of the Byzantine Empire (380–1453).

Greek maintained its status and prestige during the rise of the European Renaissance and was employed as the linguistic perspective for all contemporary sciences and terminologies during the period of Enlightenment. Today, Greek constitutes a large part of the vocabulary of any Indo-European language, and much of the lexicon of any scientific repertoire.

The modern Greek language is a southern Greek dialect which is now used by most Greek speakers both in Greece and abroad. It is the result of an intralinguistic influence and synthesis of the ancient vocabulary combined with words from Greek regional dialects, namely Cretan, Cypriot and Macedonian.

Greek is spoken throughout Greece by a population of around 10 million, and by some five million Greeks who live abroad.

Pronunciation

All Greek words of two or more syllables have an acute accent which indicates where the stress falls. For instance, άγαλμα (statue) is pronounced *aghalma*, and αγάπη (love) is pronounced *aghapi*. In the following transliterations, bold lettering indicates where stress falls. Note also that **dh** is pronounced as 'th' in 'then'; **gh** is a softer, slightly guttural version of 'g'.

Greetings & Civilities

Hello.
  *ya*sas   Γειά σας.
  *ya*su (informal)   Γειά σου.
Goodbye.
  *an*dio   Αντίο.
Good morning.
  kali*me*ra   Καλημέρα.
Good afternoon.
  *he*rete   Χαίρετε.
Good evening.
  kalis*pe*ra   Καλησπέρα.
Good night.
  kali*ni*hta   Καληνύχτα.
Please.
  paraka*lo   Παρακαλώ.
Thank you.
  efharis*to   Ευχαριστώ.
Yes.
  *ne   Ναι.
No.
  *ohi   Οχι.
Sorry. (excuse me, forgive me)
  sigh*no*mi   Συγγνώμη.
How are you?
  ti *ka*nete?   Τι κάνετε;
  ti *ka*nis?   Τι κάνεις;
  (informal)
I'm well, thanks.
  ka*la efharis*to   Καλά ευχαριστώ.

Essentials

Do you speak English?
  mi*la*te anglika?   Μιλάτε Αγγλικά;
I understand.
  katala*ve*no   Καταλαβαίνω.
I don't understand.
  dhen katala*ve*no   Δεν καταλαβαίνω.
Where is ...?
  pou *i*ne ...?   Πού είναι ...;
How much?
  *po*so *ka*ni?   Πόσο κάνει;
When?
  *po*te?   Πότε;

The Greek Alphabet & Pronunciation

Greek	Pronunciation Guide		Example		
Α α	a	as in 'father'	αγάπη	*agha*pi	love
Β β	v	as in 'vine'	βήμα	*vi*ma	step
Γ γ	gh	like a rough 'g'	γάτα	*gha*ta	cat
	y	as in 'yes'	για	*ya*	for
Δ δ	dh	as in 'there'	δέμα	*dhe*ma	parcel
Ε ε	e	as in 'egg'	ένας	*e*nas	one (m)
Ζ ζ	z	as in 'zoo'	ζώο	*zoo*	animal
Η η	i	as in 'feet'	ήταν	*i*tan	was
Θ θ	th	as in 'throw'	θέμα	*the*ma	theme
Ι ι	i	as in 'feet'	ίδιος	*i*dhyos	same
Κ κ	k	as in 'kite'	καλά	ka*la*	well
Λ λ	l	as in 'leg'	λάθος	*la*thos	mistake
Μ μ	m	as in 'man'	μαμά	ma*ma*	mother
Ν ν	n	as in 'net'	νερό	ne*ro*	water
Ξ ξ	x	as in 'ox'	ξύδι	*ksi*dhi	vinegar
Ο ο	o	as in 'hot'	όλα	*o*la	all
Π π	p	as in 'pup'	πάω	*pao*	I go
Ρ ρ	r	as in 'road', a slightly trilled r	ρέμα	*re*ma	stream
			ρόδα	*ro*dha	tyre
Σ σ, ς	s	as in 'sand'	σημάδι	si*ma*dhi	mark
Τ τ	t	as in 'tap'	τόπι	*to*pi	ball
Υ υ	i	as in 'feet'	ύστερα	*i*stera	after
Φ φ	f	as in 'find'	φύλλο	*fi*lo	leaf
Χ χ	h	as the *ch* in Scottish *loch*, or like a rough *h*	χάνω	*ha*no	I lose
			χέρι	*he*ri	hand
Ψ ψ	ps	as in 'lapse'	ψωμί	pso*mi*	bread
Ω ω	o	as in 'hot'	ώρα	*o*ra	time

Combinations of Letters

The combinations of letters shown here are pronounced as follows:

Greek	Pronunciation Guide		Example		
ει	i	as in 'feet'	είδα	*i*dha	I saw
οι	i	as in 'feet'	οικόπεδο	i*ko*pedho	land
αι	e	as in 'bet'	αίμα	*e*ma	blood
ου	u	as in 'mood'	πού	*pou*	who/what
μπ	b	as in 'beer'	μπάλα	*ba*la	ball
	mb	as in 'amber'	κάμπος	*kam*bos	forest
ντ	d	as in 'dot'	ντουλάπα	dou*la*pa	wardrobe
	nd	as in 'bend'	πέντε	*pen*de	five
γκ	g	as in 'God'	γκάζι	*ga*zi	gas
γγ	ng	as in 'angle'	αγγελία	ange*li*a	classified
γξ	ks	as in 'minks'	σφιγξ	*sfinks*	sphynx
τζ	dz	as in 'hands'	τζάκι	*dza*ki	fireplace

The pairs of vowels shown above are pronounced separately if the first has an acute accent, or the second a dieresis, as in the examples below:

γαϊδουράκι	gaidhou*ra*ki	little donkey
Κάιρο	*ka*iro	Cairo

Some Greek consonant sounds have no English equivalent. The υ of the groups αυ, ευ and ηυ is generally pronounced 'v'. The Greek question mark is represented with the English equivalent of a semicolon ';'.

Small Talk

What's your name?
pos sas lene? Πώς σας λένε;
My name is ...
me lene ... Με λένε ...
Where are you from?
apo pou iste? Από πού είστε;

I'm from ...
ime apo ... Είμαι από ...
America
tin ameriki την Αμερική
Australia
tin afstralia την Αυστραλία
England
tin anglia την Αγγλία
Ireland
tin irlandhia την Ιρλανδία
New Zealand
ti nea zilandhia τη Νέα Ζηλανδία
Scotland
ti skotia τη Σκωτία

How old are you?
poson hronon iste? Πόσων χρονών είστε;
I'm ... years old.
ime ... hronon Είμαι ... χρονών.

Getting Around

What time does the ... leave/arrive?
ti ora fevyi/ ftani to ...? Τι ώρα φεύγει/ φτάνει το ...;

plane	*aeroplano*	αεροπλάνο
boat	*karavi*	καράβι
bus (city)	*astiko*	αστικό
bus (intercity)	*leoforio*	λεωφορείο
train	*treno*	τραίνο

I'd like ...
tha ithela ... Θα ήθελα ...
a return ticket
isitirio me epistrofi εισιτήριο με επιστροφή
two tickets
dhio isitiria δυο εισιτήρια
a student's fare
fititiko isitirio φοιτητικό εισιτήριο

Signs

ΕΙΣΟΔΟΣ	Entry
ΕΞΟΔΟΣ	Exit
ΩΘΗΣΑΤΕ	Push
ΣΥΡΑΤΕ	Pull
ΓΥΝΑΙΚΩΝ	Women (toilets)
ΑΝΔΡΩΝ	Men (toilets)
ΝΟΣΟΚΟΜΕΙΟ	Hospital
ΑΣΤΥΝΟΜΙΑ	Police
ΑΠΑΓΟΡΕΥΕΤΑΙ	Prohibited
ΕΙΣΙΤΗΡΙΑ	Tickets

first class
proti thesi πρώτη θέση
economy
touristiki thesi τουριστική θέση
train station
sidhirodhro- mikos stathmos σιδηροδρομικός σταθμός
timetable
dhromologio δρομολόγιο
taxi
taxi ταξί

Where can I hire a car?
pou boro na nikyaso ena aftokinito? Πού μπορώ να νοικιάσω ένα αυτοκίνητο;

Directions

How do I get to ...?
pos tha pao sto/ sti ...? Πώς θα πάω στο/ στη ...;
Where is ...?
pou ine ...? Πού είναι...;
Is it near?
ine konda? Είναι κοντά;
Is it far?
ine makria? Είναι μακριά;

straight ahead	*efthia*	ευθεία
left	*aristera*	αριστερά
right	*dexia*	δεξιά
behind	*piso*	πίσω
far	*makria*	μακριά
near	*konda*	κοντά
opposite	*apenandi*	απέναντι

Can you show me on the map?
*borite na mou to **dhi**xete sto **har**ti?*
Μπορείτε να μου το δείξετε
στο χάρτη;

Around Town

I'm looking for (the) ...
psahno ya ...
Ψάχνω για ...

bank	*tra**pe**za*	τράπεζα
beach	*para**li**a*	παραλία
castle	*ka**stro***	κάστρο
church	*ek**kli**sia*	εκκλησία
... embassy	*tin ... pres**vi**a*	την ...
		πρεσβεία
market	*agho**ra***	αγορά
museum	*mu**si**o*	μουσείο
police	*astyno**mi**a*	αστυνομία
post office	*tahydhro**mi**o*	ταχυδρομείο
ruins	*ar**he**a*	αρχαία

I want to exchange some money.
the**lo na exaryi**ro**so lef**ta
Θέλω να εξαργυρώσω λεφτά.

Accommodation

Where is ...?
*pou **i**ne ...?* Πού είναι ...;
I'd like ...
***the**lo **e**na ...* Θέλω ένα ...

a cheap hotel
*fti**no** xenodo**hi**o* φτηνό ξενοδοχείο
a clean room
*katha**ro** dho-* καθαρό δωμάτιο
matio
a good hotel
*ka**lo** xenodo**hi**o* καλό ξενοδοχείο
a camp site
***kam**ping* κάμπιγκ

single	*mo**no***	μονό
double	*dhi**plo***	διπλό
room	*dho**ma**tio*	δωμάτιο
with bathroom	*me **ba**nio*	με μπάνιο
key	*kli**dhi***	κλειδί

How much is it ...?
*po**so** **ka**ni ...?* Πόσο κάνει ...;
per night
*ti vradh**ya*** τη βραδυά

Emergencies

Help!
*voith**ya!*** Βοήθεια!
Police!
*astyno**mia!*** Αστυνομία!
There's been an accident.
*e**yi**ne a**ti**hima* Εγινε ατύχημα.
Call a doctor!
*fo**nax**te **e**na* Φωνάξτε ένα
*ya**tro!*** ιατρό!
Call an ambulance!
*tilefo**ni**ste ya* Τηλεφωνήστε για
*astheno**fo**ro!* ασθενοφόρο!
I'm ill.
*ime a**ro**stos* (m) Είμαι άρρωστος
*ime a**ro**sti* (f) Είμαι άρρωστη
I'm lost.
*eho ha**thi*** Εχω χαθεί
Thief!
***klef**ti!* Κλέφτη!
Go away!
***fi**ye!* Φύγε!
I've been raped.
*me **vi**ase **ka**pyos* Με βίασε
κάποιος.
I've been robbed.
*me**klep**se **ka**pyos* Μ'έκλεψε
κάποιος.
Where are the toilets?
*pou **i**ne i* Πού είναι οι
*toua**le**tez?* τουαλέτες;

for ... nights
*ya ... vradh**yez*** για ... βραδυές
Is breakfast included?
*symberilam**va**ni* Συμπεριλαμβάνει
*ke pro-**i**no?* και πρωϊνό;
May I see it?
*bo**ro** na to dho?* Μπορώ να το δω;
Where is the bathroom?
*pou **i**ne to**ba**nio?* Πού είναι το
μπάνιο;
It's expensive.
*ine akri**vo*** Είναι ακριβό.
I'm leaving today.
***fev**gho **si**mera* Φεύγω σήμερα.

Food

breakfast	*pro-ino*	πρωϊνό
lunch	*mesimvrino*	μεσημβρινό
dinner	*vradhyno*	βραδυνό
beef	*vodhino*	βοδινό
bread	*psomi*	ψωμί
beer	*byra*	μπύρα
cheese	*tyri*	τυρί
chicken	*kotopoulo*	κοτόπουλο
Greek coffee	*ellinikos kafes*	ελληνικός
		καφές
iced coffee	*frappe*	φραππέ
lamb	*arni*	αρνί
milk	*ghala*	γάλα
mineral	*metalliko*	μεταλλικό
water	*nero*	νερό
tea	*tsai*	τσάι
wine	*krasi*	κρασί

I'm a vegetarian.
  ime hortofaghos   Είμαι χορτοφάγος.

Shopping

How much is it?
  poso kani?
  Πόσο κάνει;
I'm just looking.
  aplos kitazo
  Απλώς κοιτάζω.
I'd like to buy ...
  thelo n'aghoraso ...
  Θέλω ν΄αγοράσω ...
Do you accept credit cards?
  pernete pistotikez kartez?
  Παίρνετε πιστωτικές κάρτες;
Could you lower the price?
  borite na mou kanete mya kaliteri timi?
  Μπορείτε να μου κάνετε μια
  καλύτερη τιμή;

Time & Dates

What time is it?
  ti ora ine?   Τι ώρα είναι;

It's ...	*ine* ...	είναι ...
1 o'clock	*mia i ora*	μία η ώρα
2 o'clock	*dhio i ora*	δύο η ώρα
7.30	*efta ke misi*	εφτά και μισή
am	*to pro-i*	το πρωί
pm	*to apoyevma*	το απόγευμα
today	*simera*	σήμερα
tonight	*apopse*	απόψε
now	*tora*	τώρα
yesterday	*hthes*	χθες
tomorrow	*avrio*	αύριο

Sunday	*kyriaki*	Κυριακή
Monday	*dheftera*	Δευτέρα
Tuesday	*triti*	Τρίτη
Wednesday	*tetarti*	Τετάρτη
Thursday	*pempti*	Πέμπτη
Friday	*paraskevi*	Παρασκευή
Saturday	*savato*	Σάββατο

January	*ianouarios*	Ιανουάριος
February	*fevrouarios*	Φεβρουάριος
March	*martios*	Μάρτιος
April	*aprilios*	Απρίλιος
May	*maïos*	Μάιος
June	*iounios*	Ιούνιος
July	*ioulios*	Ιούλιος
August	*avghoustos*	Αύγουστος
September	*septemvrios*	Σεπτέμβριος
October	*oktovrios*	Οκτώβριος
November	*noemvrios*	Νοέμβριος
December	*dhekemvrios*	Δεκέμβριος

Health

I need a doctor.
  hriazome yatro   Χρειάζομαι ιατρό.
Can you take me
to hospital?
  borite na me pate   Μπορείτε να με πάτε
  sto nosokomio?   στο νοσοκομείο;
I want something for ...
  thelo kati ya ...   Θέλω κάτι για ...
diarrhoea
  dhiaria   διάρροια
insect bites
  tsimbimata apo   τσιμπήματα από
  endoma   έντομα
travel sickness
  naftia taxidhiou   ναυτία ταξιδιού

aspirin
  aspirini   ασπιρίνη
condoms
  profylaktika   προφυλακτικά
  (kapotez)   (καπότες)
contact lenses
  faki epafis   φακοί επαφής
medical insurance
  yatriki asfalya   ιατρική ασφάλεια

Numbers

0	*midhen*	μηδέν	20	*ikosi*	είκοσι
1	*enas*	ένας (m)	30	*trianda*	τριάντα
	mia	μία (f)	40	*saranda*	σαράντα
	ena	ένα (n)	50	*peninda*	πενήντα
2	*dhio*	δύο	60	*exinda*	εξήντα
3	*tris*	τρεις (m & f)	70	*evdhominda*	εβδομήντα
	tria	τρία (n)	80	*oghdhonda*	ογδόντα
4	*teseris*	τέσσερεις (m & f)	90	*eneninda*	ενενήντα
	tesera	τέσσερα (n)	100	*ekato*	εκατό
5	*pende*	πέντε	1000	*hilii*	χίλιοι (m)
6	*exi*	έξη		*hiliez*	χίλιες (f)
7	*epta*	επτά		*hilia*	χίλια (n)
8	*ohto*	οχτώ			
9	*enea*	εννέα	one million		
10	*dheka*	δέκα		*ena ekatomyrio*	ένα εκατομμύριο

Glossary

Achaean civilisation – see *Mycenaean civilisation*

acropolis – citadel; highest point of an ancient city

AEK – Athens football club

agia (f), agios (m) – saint

agora – commercial area of an ancient city; shopping precinct in modern Greece

amphora – large two-handled vase in which wine or oil was kept

ANEK – Anonymi Naftiliaki Eteria Kritis; main shipping line to Crete

Archaic period (800–480 BC) – also known as the Middle Age; period in which the city-states emerged from the 'dark age' and traded their way to wealth and power; the city-states were unified by a Greek alphabet and common cultural pursuits, engendering a sense of national identity

architrave – part of the *entablature* which rests on the columns of a temple

arhontika – 17th- and 18th-century AD mansions which belonged to arhons, the leading citizens of a town

Arvanites – Albanian-speakers of northwestern Greece

Asia Minor – the Aegean littoral of Turkey centred around İzmir but also including İstanbul; formerly populated by Greeks

askitiria – mini-chapels; places of solitary worship

baglamas – miniature *bouzouki* with a tinny sound

basilica – early Christian church

bouleuterion – council house

bouzouki – stringed lute-like instrument associated with *rembetika* music

bouzoukia – 'bouzoukis'; used to mean any nightclub where the *bouzouki* is played and low-grade blues songs are sung; see *skyladika*

buttress – support built against the outside of a wall

Byzantine Empire – characterised by the merging of Hellenistic culture and Christianity and named after Byzantium, the city on the Bosphorus which became the capital of the Roman Empire in AD 324; when the Roman Empire was formally divided in AD 395, Rome went into decline and the eastern capital, renamed Constantinople after Emperor Constantine I, flourished; the Byzantine Empire dissolved after the fall of Constantinople to the Turks in 1453

caique – small, sturdy fishing boat often used to carry passengers

capital – top of a column

cella – room in a temple where the cult statue stood

choregos – wealthy citizen who financed choral and dramatic performances

city-states – states comprising a sovereign city and its dependencies; the city-states of Athens and Sparta were famous rivals

classical Greece – period in which the city-states reached the height of their wealth and power after the defeat of the Persians in the 5th century BC; ended with the decline of the city-states as a result of the Peloponnesian Wars, and the expansionist aspirations of Philip II, King of Macedon (ruled 359–336 BC), and his son, Alexander the Great (ruled 336–323 BC)

Corinthian – order of Greek architecture recognisable by columns with bell-shaped capitals with sculpted elaborate ornaments based on acanthus leaves

cornice – the upper part of the *entablature*, extending beyond the *frieze*

crypt – lowest part of a church, often a burial chamber

Cycladic civilisation (3000–1100 BC) – civilisation which emerged following the settlement of Phoenician colonists on the Cycladic islands

cyclopes – mythical one-eyed giants

dark age (1200–800 BC) – period in which Greece was under Dorian rule

delfini – dolphin; a common name for a hydrofoil

diglossy – the existence of two forms of one language within a country; has existed in Greece for most of its modern history

dimarhio – town hall

Dimotiki – Demotic Greek language; the official spoken language of Greece

domatio (s), domatia (pl) – room; a cheap accommodation option available in most tourist areas

Dorians – Hellenic warriors who invaded Greece around 1200 BC, demolishing the city-states and destroying the Mycenaean civilisation; heralded Greece's 'dark age', when the artistic and cultural advancements of the Mycenaeans and Minoans were abandoned; the Dorians later developed into land-holding aristocrats which encouraged the resurgence of independent city-states led by wealthy aristocrats

Doric – order of Greek architecture characterised by a column which has no base, a fluted shaft and a relatively plain capital, when compared with the flourishes evident on Ionic and Corinthian capitals

ELPA – Elliniki Leshi Periigiseon & Aftokinitou; Greek motoring and touring club

ELTA – Ellinika Tahydromia; Greek post office

entablature – part of a temple between the tops of the columns and the roof

EOS – Ellinikos Orivatikos Syllogos; Greek alpine club

EOT – Ellinikos Organismos Tourismou; national tourism organisation which has offices in most major towns

Epitaphios – picture on cloth of Christ on his bier

estiatorio – restaurant serving ready-made food as well as a la carte dishes

ET – Elliniki Tileorasi; state television company

evzones – famous border guards from the northern Greek village of Evzoni; they also guard the Parliament building

Filiki Eteria – friendly society; a group of Greeks in exile; formed during Ottoman rule to organise an uprising against the Turks

flokati – shaggy woollen rug produced in central and northern Greece

fluted – (of a column) having vertical indentations on the shaft

frappé – iced coffee

frieze – part of the *entablature* which is above the *architrave*

galaktopoleio (s), galaktopoleia (pl) – a shop which sells dairy products

Geometric period (1200–800 BC) – period characterised by pottery decorated with geometric designs; sometimes referred to as Greece's 'dark age'

GESEE – Greek trade union association

giouvetsi – casserole of meat and pasta

Hellas, Ellas or Ellada – the Greek name for Greece

Hellenistic period – prosperous, influential period of Greek civilisation ushered in by Alexander the Great's empire-building and lasting until the Roman sacking of Corinth in 146 BC

Helots – original inhabitants of Lakonia whom the Spartans used as slaves

hora – main town (usually on an island)

iconostasis – altar screen embellished with icons

Ionic – order of Greek architecture characterised by a column with truncated flutes and capitals with ornaments resembling scrolls

kafeneio (s), kafeneia (pl) – traditionally a male-only coffee house where cards and backgammon are played

kafeteria – upmarket *kafeneio*, mainly for younger people

kalderimi – cobbled footpath

kasseri – mild, slightly rubbery sheep's-milk cheese

kastro – walled-in town

Katharevousa – purist Greek language; very rarely used these days

katholikon – principal church of a monastic complex

kefi – an undefinable feeling of good spirit, without which no Greek can have a good time

KKE – Kommounistiko Komma Elladas; Greek communist party

Koine – Greek language used in pre-Byzantine times; the language of the church liturgy

kore – female statue of the Archaic period; see *kouros*

kouros – male statue of the Archaic period, characterised by a stiff body posture and enigmatic smile

KTEL – Kino Tamio Ispraxeon Leoforion; national bus cooperative; runs all long-distance bus services

Kypriako – the 'Cyprus issue'; politically sensitive and never forgotten by Greeks and Greek Cypriots

ladera – oil-based dishes

libation – in ancient Greece, wine or food which was offered to the gods

Linear A – Minoan script; so far undeciphered

Linear B – Mycenaean script; has been deciphered

lyra – small violin-like instrument, played on the knee; common in Cretan and Pontian music

makarounes – pasta dish stirfried in butter and onions and sprinkled with cheese

malakas – literally 'wanker'; used as a familiar term of address, or as an insult, depending on context

mangas – 'wide boy' or 'dude'; originally a person of the underworld, now any streetwise person

mayirefta – pre-cooked food usually served in cheaper restaurants

mayiria – cook houses

megaron – central room of a Mycenaean palace

meltemi – north-easterly wind which blows throughout much of Greece during the summer

metope – sculpted section of a Doric *frieze*

meze (s), mezedes (pl) – appetiser

Middle Age – see *Archaic period*

Minoan civilisation (3000–1100 BC) – Bronze Age culture of Crete named after the mythical king Minos and characterised by pottery and metalwork of great beauty and artisanship

moni – monastery or convent

Mycenaean civilisation (1900–1100 BC) – first great civilisation of the Greek mainland, characterised by powerful independent city-states ruled by kings; also known as the Achaean civilisation

myzithra – soft sheep's-milk cheese

narthex – porch of a church

nave – aisle of a church

Nea Dimokratia – New Democracy; conservative political party

necropolis – literally 'city of the dead'; ancient cemetery

nefos – cloud; usually used to refer to pollution in Athens

NEL – Naftiliaki Eteria Lesvou; Lesvos shipping company

neo kyma – 'new wave'; left-wing music of the boites and clubs of 1960s Athens

nomarhia – prefecture building

nomos – prefectures into which the regions and island groups of Greece are divided

nymphaeum – in ancient Greece, building containing a fountain and often dedicated to nymphs

OA – Olympiaki Aeroporia or Olympic Airways; Greece's national airline and major domestic air carrier

odeion – ancient Greek indoor theatre

odos – street

ohi – 'no'; what the Greeks said to Mussolini's ultimatum when he said surrender or be invaded; the Italians were subsequently repelled and the event is celebrated on 28 October

omphalos – sacred stone at Delphi which the ancient Greeks believed marked the centre of the world

OSE – Organismos Sidirodromon Ellados; Greek railways organisation

OTE – Organismos Tilepikinonion Ellados; Greece's major telecommunications carrier

oud – a bulbous, stringed instrument with a sharply raked-back head

ouzeri (s), ouzeria (pl) – place which serves *ouzo* and light snacks

ouzo – a distilled spirit made from grapes and flavoured with aniseed

Panagia – Mother of God; name frequently used for churches

panigyria – night-long festivals held on saints' days

Pantokrator – painting or mosaic of Christ in the centre of the dome of a Byzantine church

pantopoleio – general store

PAO – Panathinaïkos football club

PAOK – main Thessaloniki football club

paralia – waterfront

PASOK – Panellinio Sosialistiko Komma; Greek socialist party

pediment – triangular section (often filled with sculpture) above columns, found at the front and back of a classical Greek temple

periptero (s), periptera (pl) – street kiosk

peristyle – columns surrounding a building (usually a temple) or courtyard

pinakotheke – picture gallery

pithos (s), pithoi (pl) – large Minoan storage jar

pittes – pies; usually filled with cheese, vegetables or meat

plateia – square

Politiki Anixi – Political Spring; centrist political party

Pomaks – minority, non-Turkic Muslim people from northern Greece

Pontians – Greeks whose ancestral home was on the Black Sea coast of Turkey

PRO-PO – Prognostiko Podosferou; Greek football pools

propylon (s), propylaia (pl) – elaborately built main entrance to an ancient city or sanctuary; a propylon had one gateway and a propylaia more than one

psarotaverna – taverna specialising in seafood

psistaria – restaurant serving grilled food

rembetika – blues songs commonly associated with the underworld of the 1920s

retsina – resinated white wine

rhyton – another name for a libation vessel

rizitika – traditional, patriotic songs of Crete

sacristy – room attached to a church where sacred vessels etc are kept

sandouri – hammered dulcimer from Asia Minor

Sarakatsani – Greek-speaking nomadic shepherd community from northern Greece

SEO – Syllogos Ellinon Orivaton; Greek mountaineers' association

skites (s), skiti (pl) – hermit's dwelling

Skopia – what the Greeks call the Former Yugoslav Republic of Macedonia (FYROM)

skyladika – literally 'dog songs'; popular, but not lyrically challenging, blues songs often sung in *bouzoukia* nightclubs

spilia – cave

stele (s), stelae (pl) – grave stone which stands upright

stoa – long colonnaded building, usually in an *agora*; used as a meeting place and shelter in ancient Greece

taverna – traditional restaurant which serves food and wine

temblon – votive screen

tholos – Mycenaean tomb shaped like a beehive

toumberleki – small lap drum played with the fingers

triglyph – sections of a Doric *frieze* between the *metopes*

trireme – ancient Greek galley with three rows of oars on each side

tsikoudia – Cretan version of *tsipouro*

Tsingani – Gypsies or Roma

tsipouro – distilled spirit made from grapes

vaulted – having an arched roof, normally of brick or stone

velentza – *flokati* rug

Vlach – traditional, semi-nomadic shepherds from northern Greece who speak a Latin-based dialect

volta – promenade; evening stroll

volute – spiral decoration on Ionic capitals

xythomyzithra – soft sheep's-milk cheese

zaharoplasteio (s), zaharoplasteia (pl) – patisserie; shop which sells cakes, chocolates, sweets and, sometimes, alcoholic drinks

Thanks

Many thanks to the travellers who used the last edition and wrote to us with helpful hints, useful advice and interesting anecdotes:

Theo Baak, Niki Bales, CB Belcher, Adam Bell, Karen Bernat, Geoff Binns, Lars Björk, Martin Bjornstrom, Sarah Boniface, Tim Bower, Joanna & Don Box, Domi Branger, Jan Bullerdieck, David & Jane Campbell, Peter Causton, Clair Chatel, Daniele Clavenzani, Helen Conway, Ruth Cookson, Diane Cotter, Harry Crawford, Stephen Cross, Madi Dale, Maxime de Caritat, Jonathan Del Mar, Marius den Hartog, Kostis Diamantopoulos, Marianna Dioxini, Michelle Dodd, Hans Doettling, John Dynan, Robin Eley Jones, Zeynep Erginoglu, Gillian Farley, James Fawcett, Christian Ferrari, Charlie Ferrero, Debra Filippin, Karin Fiscner, Tom Flaherty, Hayley Fletcher, Gemma French, Simona Frigerio, WA Fuller, Adam Galbraith, Reshma Ganpat, Paul W Gioffi, Athina Gorezis, Anne Grainger, Nancy Grant, Frank Greenhill, Katja & Christoph Grimm, Thomas Haunstein, Bruce Hawker, Phil Heinecke, Katia Hiliopoulos, Katie Hill, John & Rosemary Hillard, David Hitch, Sara-Jane Hodge, Gerald Holt, Sandra L Huard, Joanne Hutchinson, Will Hynds, Jennifer Jansma, Eivind Jorgensen, Nancy Kartsonas, Kostas Katavoutas, Charlie Kiss, Andrea Kutzer, Svein Kvaloy jr, Wan Kwong Young, Stephen Lamb, Denise Lee, George Liangas, Aina Magnusson, Nicki Miquel, Dominique Moollan, Simon Munt, Vicky Nicholas, Judith Nielsen, Stelios Nikolaou, Mette Nygerd, Tove and Kjell Nygren, Peter Oberholzer, Jacquie Olsen, Kurt Osbourne, Ros Osbourne, Christopher Packham, Matt Paradise, Thea Parkin, Sophie Percival, Niki Pilidou, David John Pitts, Sean Plamondon, Emiko Priest, Chris Rees, Tony Richmond, Dawn Roberts, Matthew Rothschild, John Rowe, Tuan Samahon, Alejandro Sanfeliu, Gerard Sayers, Jeremias Schmidt, Nicolas Schmidt, Philippa H Scriven, David Shade, Nidhi Sharma, Vern & Cindy Simpson, Andy Sparrow, John Spilos, John Steedman, Timothy Sullivan, Matthias Sunkler, Hiroyuki Tanaka, Metaxia Tsoukatos, Anna Vardakastanis, Bettina Vine, Sonny von Herck, George S Vrontos, J Wagner, James Walker, Karen Walsh, Jeremy Watts, Kenny Wheeler, Maciej Wieczorek, Veryan Wilkie-Jones, Peta Woodland, Andy Young, Heidi Yu

LONELY PLANET

You already know that Lonely Planet produces more than this one guidebook, but you might not be aware of the other products we have on this region. Here is a selection of titles that you may want to check out as well:

Greece
ISBN 1 86450 334 3
US$19.99 • UK£12.99

Greek phrasebook
ISBN 0 86442 683 6
US$7.99 • UK£4.50

Mediterranean Europe
ISBN 1 86450 154 5
US$27.99 • UK£15.99

Europe phrasebook
ISBN 1 86450 224 X
US$8.99 • UK£4.99

Rhodes & the Dodecanese
ISBN 1 86450 117 0
US$15.99 • UK£9.99

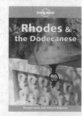

Crete
ISBN 1 74059 049 X
US$15.99 • UK£9.99

World Food Greece
ISBN 1 86450 113 8
US$13.99 • UK£8.99

Europe on a shoestring
ISBN 1 86450 150 2
US$24.99 • UK£14.99

Read This First: Europe
ISBN 1 86450 136 7
US$14.99 • UK£8.99

Corfu & the Ionians
ISBN 1 74059 070 8
US$14.99 • UK£8.99

Available wherever books are sold

Index

Abbreviations

Ath – Athens
Cre – Crete
Cyc – Cyclades
Dod – Dodecanese

Evi – Evia & the
Sporades
Ion – Ionian Islands
MP – Mainland Ports

NEA – North-Eastern Aegean
Islands
SG – Saronic Gulf Islands
Spo – Sporades

Text

A

accommodation 71-3
Acropolis (Ath) 116-17, **117**
activities 81-5, *see also*
individual activities
Adamas (Cyc) 244-6
Aegiali (Cyc) 218-19
Aegina (SG) 148-53, **149**
Aegina Town (SG) 149-51, **150**
Agathonisi (Dod) 387-8, **388**
Agia Galini (Cre) 295-6
Agia Marina (Dod) 377
Agia Pelagia (Ion) 531
Agia Roumeli (Cre) 305
Agia Triada (Cre) 273
Aglos Efstratlos (NEA) 438-40
Agios Georgios 517
Agios Giorgios (Dod) 388
Agios Gordios (Ion) 497
Agios Ioannis (Ion) 508
Agios Kirykos (NEA) 394-5
Agios Konstantinos (MP) 142-3
Agios Nikolaos (Cre) 275-8, **277**
Agios Stefanos (Ion) 495
Agni (Ion) 495
air travel
airlines 87, 99
airports 87
to/from Greece 90-93
within Greece 99-101
Akri (Dod) 386-7
Akrotiri Peninsula (Cre) 303
Alexandroupolis (MP) 145-6,
145
Alinda (Dod) 378
Almyros (Ion) 495
Alonnisos (Spo) 470-6, **471**
Alonnisos Marine Park (Spo) 474

Bold indicates maps.

Amari Valley (Cre) 292-3
Ammoöpi (Dod) 339
Amorgos (Cyc) 216-19, **217**
Anafi (Cyc) 236-7, **237**
Anavatos (NEA) 414-15
Ancient Agora (Ath) 117
Ancient Akrotiri (Cyc) 231-6
ancient sites
Acropolis (Ath) 116-17, **117**
Acropolis of Lindos (Dod) 331
Acropolis of Rhodes (Dod)
324
Agia Triada (Cre) 273
Ancient Agora (Ath) 117
Ancient Akrotiri (Cyc) 231-6
Ancient Thira (Cyc) 232
Asklipion (Dod) 364-5
Byzantine Palace (NEA) 396
Delos (Cyc) 192-4, **193**
Exobourgo (Cyc) 178
Gournia (Cre) 280
Kamiros (Dod) 331-2
Knossos (Cre) 270-2, **270**
Kydonia (Cre) 299
Lato (Cre) 280
Paleohora (SG) 152
Phaestos (Cre) 272-3
Pirgos Himarrou (Cyc) 210
Poliohni (NEA) 438
Sanctuary of Poseidon &
Amphitrite (Cyc) 178
Sanctuary of the Great Gods
(NEA) 442-4
Sanctuary of the Kabeiroi
(NEA) 438
Temple of Aphaia (SG) 151-2
Temple of Aphrodite (Dod)
324
Temple of Apollo (SG) 151
Temple of Dafniforos (Evi)
458

Temple of Dionysos (Dod)
363
Temple of Poseidon (SG)
156
Temple of Pythian Apollo
(Dod) 324
Temple to Athena (Dod) 331
Troizen (SG) 156
Zakros (Cre) 284
Andros (Cyc) 171-4, **172**
Andros Hora (Cyc) 173-4
animals, treatment of 42-4
Ano Mera (Cyc) 191-2
Ano Meria (Cyc) 242
Ano Viannos (Cre) 287-8
Anogi (Cyc) 520
Antikythira (Ion) 531-2, **528**
Antiparos (Cyc) 201-4, **195**
Antipaxi (Ion) 502-3
Antisamos (Ion) 508
Antisamos Beach (Ion) 516
Apiranthos (Cyc) 210
Apollonas (Cyc) 211
Apollonia (Cyc) 249
Aqualand (Ion) 492
Archaeological Museums
Crete 263-5, 289, 299
Cyclades 173, 176, 197,
205, 229, 254
Dodecanese 323, 363, 368
Evia & Sporades 457, 478
Ionian Islands 489, 505,
518, 529
National Archaeological
Museum (Ath) 118
North-Eastern Aegean 394,
402, 413, 424, 430, 449
architecture 27-8
Argostoli (Ion) 513-15, **514**
Arkasa (Dod) 340
Armenistis (NEA) 397-9

545

Boxed Text

MAP LEGEND

CITY ROUTES

Freeway — Freeway	═ ═ ═ ═ Unsealed Road
Highway — Primary Road	One Way Street
Road — Secondary Road	Pedestrian Street
Street — Street	Stepped Street
Lane — Lane	)═ ═ ═ Tunnel
On/Off Ramp	Footbridge

AREA FEATURES

Building	Beach
Park, Gardens	+ + + Cemetery
Market	Plaza

WATER TRANSPORT

Daily Ferry	Hydrofoil
Low Frequency Ferry	Excursion Boat

REGIONAL ROUTES

Tollway, Freeway	
Primary Road	
Secondary Road	
Minor Road	

TRANSPORT ROUTES & STATIONS

Train	Walking Trail
Underground Train	Walking Tour
Metro	Path
Cable Car, Funicular	Pier or Jetty

HYDROGRAPHY

River, Creek	Dry Lake, Salt Lake
Canal	Spring, Rapids
Lake	Waterfalls

BOUNDARIES

International	
State	
Disputed	
Fortified Wall	

POPULATION SYMBOLS

❂ CAPITAL — National Capital	◉ CITY — City	● Village — Village
◉ CAPITAL — Regional Capital	● Town — Town	Urban Area

MAP SYMBOLS

▪ Place to Stay	▼ Place to Eat	● Point of Interest

✈ Airport	Church, Cathedral	Monument	Taxi Rank
Archaeological Site	Cinema	▲ Mountain	Telephone
Bank	Dive Site	Museum, Theatre	Tomb
Bar, Music Venue	Embassy, Consulate	Parking, Petrol	Tourist Information
Bus Stop, Terminal	Hospital, Clinic	Police Station	Transport (General)
Castle, Fortress	Internet Cafe	Post Office	Winery
Cave	Lighthouse, Lookout	Shopping Centre	Windmill

Note: not all symbols displayed above appear in this book

LONELY PLANET OFFICES

Australia
Locked Bag 1, Footscray, Victoria 3011
☎ 03 8379 8000 fax 03 8379 8111
email: talk2us@lonelyplanet.com.au

USA
150 Linden St, Oakland, CA 94607
☎ 510 893 8555 TOLL FREE: 800 275 8555
fax 510 893 8572
email: info@lonelyplanet.com

UK
10a Spring Place, London NW5 3BH
☎ 020 7428 4800 fax 020 7428 4828
email: go@lonelyplanet.co.uk

France
1 rue du Dahomey, 75011 Paris
☎ 01 55 25 33 00 fax 01 55 25 33 01
email: bip@lonelyplanet.fr
www.lonelyplanet.fr

World Wide Web: www.lonelyplanet.com *or* AOL keyword: lp
Lonely Planet Images: lpi@lonelyplanet.com.au